R. Gupta's®

Popular Master Guide

SSC-CHSL

Combined Higher Secondary Level (10+2)

Data Entry Operator (DEO)

Lower Division Clerk (LDC)

Junior Secretarial Assistant (JSA)

TIER-I

Recruitment Exam

2027
EDITION

RAMESH PUBLISHING HOUSE, NEW DELHI

Published by: O.P. Gupta *for* Ramesh Publishing House

Admin. Office

12-H, New Daryaganj Road, Opp. Officers' Mess,
New Delhi-110002 ✆ 23275224, 23245124

E-mail: info@rameshpublishinghouse.com

For Online Shopping: www.rameshpublishinghouse.com

Showroom

- Balaji Market, Nai Sarak, Delhi-110006 ✆ 23282525 📱 9354373464
- 4457, Nai Sarak, Delhi-110006

Book Code: R-1331

ISBN: 978-93-5012-022-4

Price: ₹ 540

Printed by : Repro India Ltd.

CONTENTS

Previous Years' Paper, 2025 1-20

Previous Years' Paper, 2024 1-20

Previous Years' Paper, 2023 .... A1-A24

Previous Years' Paper, 2022 .... A25-A40

Previous Years' Paper, 2021 .... A41-A56

Previous Years' Paper, 2020 1-16

Previous Years' Paper, 2019 17-32

- **QUANTITATIVE APTITUDE 1-104**

  Simplification; L.C.M. & H.C.F.; Surds & Indices; Ratio & Proportion; Average; Percentage; Profit and Loss; Simple & Compound Interest; Alligation or Mixture; Time, Speed & Distance; Time, Work & Wages; Partnership; Problem Based on Age; Mensuration; Data Interpretation (Table); Data Interpretation (Bar Graphs and Pie Chart); Permutation & Combination; Probability; Logarithms; Linear and Quadratic Equation; Trigonometry.

- **GENERAL INTELLIGENCE 1-112**

  Letter Series; Wrong Letter Series; Repeat Series; Number Series; Wrong Number Series; Word Analogy; Number Analogy; Odd One Out; Coding and Decoding; Statement Analysis; Place Arrangement; Direction Sense; Blood Relationships; Arranging in Order; Calendar, Clock & Time; Rows and Ranks; Common Property; Permutations & Combinations; Symbol Substitution; Missing Numbers; Matrices; Alphabet Problems; Logical Diagram; Syllogism; Drawing Conclusions; Drawing Assumptions; Course of Action; Venn Diagrams; Diagrammatic Puzzle; Completing an Incomplete Pattern; Spotting Hidden Pattern; Components of Figures; Lateral Inversion; Folded or Unfolded Pattern.

- **ENGLISH LANGUAGE 1-96**

  Spelling Errors; Spotting Errors; Articles; Prepositions; Synonyms & Antonyms; One Word Substitutions; Idioms and Phrases; Narration; Voice; Sentence Completion; Sentence Improvement; Reordering Words & Sentences; Comprehension Passages; Cloze Test.

- **GENERAL AWARENESS 1-120**

  Indian History; Geography; Indian Polity; General Science; General Knowledge; Multiple Choice Questions.

Scheme of Examination

The Computer Based Examination will be conducted in two tiers as Tier-I & Tier-II.

TIER-I

Part	Subject	No. of Questions	Maximum Marks	Total Duration/Timing
I	English Language (Basic Knowledge)	25	50	60 Minutes
II	General Intelligence	25	50	
III	Quantitative Aptitude (Basic Arithmetic Skill)	25	50	
IV	General Awareness	25	50	

- The Tier-I Examination will consists of Objective Type Multiple Choice Questions only. The questions will be set in English, Hindi and any language opted by the candidate in the application form, for Part-II, III & IV of Tier-I examination.
- There will be negative marking of 0.50 marks for each wrong answer.

TIER-II

Session	Subject	Number of Questions	Maximum Marks	Time allowed
Session-I	**Section I:**			1 hour (for each section)
	Module-I: Mathematical Abilities	30	60 × 3 = 180	
	Module-II: Reasoning and General Intelligence	30		
	Section-II:			
	Module-I: English Language and Comprehension	40	60 × 3 = 180	
	Module-II: General Awareness	20		
	Section-III:			15 Minutes
	Module-I: Computer Knowledge Module	15	15 × 3 = 45	
Session-II	**Section-III**			
	Module-II: Skill Test/Typing Test Module			
	Part A: Skill Test for DEOs			15 Minutes
	Part B: Typing Test for LDC/JSA			10 Minutes

Note—• It will be mandatory for the candidate to qualify all the sections of Tier-II. Tier-II will consist of Objective Type, Multiple Choice Questions, except for Module-II of Section-III. The questions will be set in English and Hindi except for Module-II (*i.e.*, English Language and Comprehension module) in Section-II. • There will be negative marking of 1 mark for each wrong answer in Section-I, Section-II and Module-I of Section-III. • Module-I of Section-III i.e., Computer Knowledge Test is mandatory but qualifying in nature. • Skill Test/Typing Test will be of qualifying nature. • Errors in the Skill Test will be calculated up to 2 decimal places.

Previous Years' Paper

SSC—Combined Higher Secondary Level (CHSL : 10 + 2)

Data Entry Operator (DEO)/ Lower Division Clerk (LDC)/ Junior Secretarial Assistant (JSA)

Tier-I, Recruitment Exam-2025

(Exam held on 13-11-2025)

English Language

1. Identify the part of the sentence that contains a grammatical error.

The new manager / is responsible of / the entire marketing / campaign.

A. The new manager
B. is responsible of
C. the entire marketing
D. campaign

2. Fill in the blank with the most appropriate phrase :

As the deadline approached, the team was working _______ to finalize the report.

A. under wraps B. around the corner
C. against the clock D. in high spirits

3. Select the most appropriate synonym of the word :

Hapless

A. Fortunate B. Lucky
C. Unlucky D. Successful

4. Fill in the blank with the most appropriate idiom :

She took the criticism _______ and used it to improve her performance.

A. at face value
B. with a grain of salt
C. in stride
D. out of context

5. Which of the following sentences uses the word "saw" with the **same meaning** as in the following sentence?

"He saw the car coming too late"

A. She used a hand saw to cut the plank in half.
B. We needed a power saw to cut through the thick branch.
C. I saw a beautiful sunset last night.
D. The lumberjack's saw was very loud.

Directions (Qs.No. 6-10): *Read the following passage and answer the questions based on it :*

Online purchasing, which combines unmatched ease with a distinct set of disadvantages, has completely changed how consumers behave. Accessibility is its main benefit; customers may explore and buy things from almost anywhere at any time, and there is frequently a greater selection than in physical stores. Important lures include competitive pricing, made possible by internet retailer' reduced overhead, and the

1. B	2. C	3. C	4. C	5. C

simplicity of comparing prices from several providers. However, there are significant drawbacks to online shopping's virtual nature. Delivery-related discontent may result from the inability to personally inspect things before purchase. Concerns over shipping delays, unstated expenses, and the effects of packaging and transportation on the environment are becoming more widespread. Additionally, the individualised customer service experience may be weakened by a lack of human interaction.

6. What is the primary advantage of online purchasing according to the text?
A. It allows for in-person inspection of products
B. It provides easy access to a wider selection of items from anywhere at any time
C. It offers higher prices than physical stores
D. It eliminates the need for shipping

7. What is one of the key benefits of online shopping in terms of pricing?
A. Higher prices due to store overhead costs
B. competitive pricing due to lower overhead costs for online retailers
C. Fixed prices with no possibility of comparison
D. Prices that remain constant across all platforms

8. What is a significant drawback of online shopping mentioned in the text?
A. Lack of variety in products
B. The inability to inspect products before purchasing
C. Higher prices for shipping
D. Limited access to the internet

9. What are some growing concerns related to the environmental impact of online shopping?
A. Increased store visits
B. Concerns over shipping delays
C. Higher fuel consumption from physical stores
D. Limited product availability

10. What aspect of the customer experience may be weakened by online shopping?
A. The ability to compare prices easily
B. Personalized customer service due to lack of human interaction
C. The variety of products available
D. Convenience of purchasing from anywhere

11. Choose the correctly spelt word :
A. Beaurocrat B. Burocrat
C. Bureaucrat D. Buroucrat

12. Choose the correctly spelt word:
A. Iresistible B. Irresistable
C. Irresistible D. Irresistble

13. Choose the correct meaning of the idiom :
As thick as thieves
A. Very close and loyal
B. Very secretive
C. Very sneaky
D. Very quiet

14. Choose the correct one-word substitute for :
A person who studies birds
A. Biologist B. Ornithologist
C. Ecologist D. Zoologist

15. Select the most appropriate antonym of the word :
Felicity
A. Misery
B. Despair
C. Sorrow
D. Anger

6. B	7. B	8. B	9. B	10. B	11. C	12. C	13. A	14. B	15. A

16. Select the most appropriate antonym of the word :

Repudiate

A. Reject
B. Disown
C. Deny
D. Accept

17. Choose the correct one-word substitute for :

A place where records and documents are stored

A. Archive
B. Library
C. Storage
D. Depository

18. Change the following sentence into the Active form.

Let the emergency meeting be convened at 10 AM without delay.

A. Convene the emergency meeting at 10 AM without delay.
B. The emergency meeting should be convened at 10 AM without delay.
C. They will convene the emergency meeting at 10 AM without delay.
D. An emergency meeting is convened at 10 AM without delay.

19. Select the option that expresses the given sentence in indirect voice.

The company CEO announced, "We will not be able to meet the deadline for this quarter, which is a great disappointment for all of us, but we will have to work harder next time."

A. The company CEO announced that they will not be able to meet the deadline for this quarter, which is a great disappointment for all of us, but that they will have to work harder next time.
B. The company CEO announced that they would not be able to meet the deadline for this quarter, which was a great disappointment for all of them, but that they would have to work harder the next time.
C. The company CEO announced that they would not be able to meet the deadline for that quarter, which was a great disappointment for all of them, but that they would have to work harder next time.
D. The company CEO announced that they would not be able to meet the deadline for that quarter, which was a great disappointment for all of them, but that they would have to work harder the next time.

20. Choose the most suitable option to replace the highlighted part of the sentence :

I am not one of these people who believes in rumours.

A. believer
B. believe
C. believing
D. to believe

21. Choose the most suitable option to replace the highlighted part of the sentence :

The organized sellers with the ability to control their price-lines, or pass on any increase in cost to customers, should be able to maintain or improve profit margin.

A. should be able to maintain or improve profit margins
B. will be able to maintains or improve profit margin
C. will be able to maintain or improves profit margin
D. will be abled to maintain or improve profit margin

16. D	**17.** A	**18.** A	**19.** D	**20.** B	**21.** A

22. Choose the correct passive voice transformation of the sentence:

The students are completing their assignments.

A. The assignments are being completed by the students.

B. The assignments are completed by the students.

C. The assignments were completed by the students.

D. The assignments have been completed by the students.

23. Select the option that expresses the given sentence in direct voice.

The captain explained that the ship had been sailing for three weeks and they had faced a severe storm the previous night.

A. The captain explained, "The ship was sailing for three weeks, and we faced as severe storm last night."

B. The captain explained, "The ship has been sailing for three weeks, and we had faced a severe storm last night."

C. The captain explained, "The ship has been sailing for three weeks, and we faced a severe storm last night."

D. The captain explained, "The ship had been sailing for three weeks, and we faced a severe storm last night."

24. Rearrange the following sentence parts to form a meaningful and grammatically correct paragraph :

P. But the fleet was caught off guard as a sudden, strong storm blew in from the sea.

Q. Confident in their strategy to blockade the enemy port, the admiral gave the order for the ships to proceed.

R. The conflict became a desperate struggle for survival due to the unanticipated weather.

S. Without firing a shot, they were to cut off supplies and compel a surrender.

A. P, S, Q, R B. S, R, P, Q

C. Q, S, P, R D. R, S, P, Q

25. Rearrange the following sentence parts to form a meaningful and grammatically correct paragraph :

P. However, as the Empire grew, a series of internal and external pressures began to mount.

Q. The Roman Empire was the most powerful civilisation in history at its height.

R. Its gradual decline was caused by a confluence of political corruption, military overstretch, and economic instability.

S. Its vast network of roads, laws, and military outposts brought a period of peace and prosperity.

A. R, S, P, Q B. P, S, Q, R

C. R, P, S, Q D. Q, S, P, R

General Intelligence

26. If HARMONY is coded as KDUPRQB, then what would BALANCE be?

A. EDODQFH B. EDLDQFH

C. EDLDQGI D. EDFDRFH

27. In a particular code language, if ARCHAEOLOGICAL is coded as BSDIBFPMPHJDBM and ANTHROPOLOGICAL is coded as BOUISPQPMPHJDBM, then what is the code for PSYCHOLOGICAL?

A. QTZDIPMPHJDBM

B. QSZDIPMPHJDBM

C. QTZDIPMPHJCBM

D. QTZDIPMPGJDBM

22. A	23. C	24. C	25. D	26. A	27. A

28. In a specific coding system, if MATHEMATICS is coded as NBUIFNBUJDT and GEOGRAPHY is coded as HFPHSBQUIZ, then what is the code for CHEMISTRY?

A. DIFNJTUSZ B. DIFNJTVRZ
C. DIFNJTRSZ D. DIFNJTTRZ

29. Here some problem or solution of the problem is given in the statement you have to choose the appropriate logical deduction for given statement.

Statement :

Advancements in surveillance technology have improved national security and crime prevention. However, concerns about mass surveillance and privacy violations have sparked debates on ethical boundaries and government overreach. Critics demand transparent policies and public oversight.

Conclusions :

I. Surveillance technology has both benefits and risks.
II. Public oversight and clear policies are needed to balance privacy and security.
III. Surveillance should be completely banned to protect individual freedom.

Which conclusion necessarily follows?

A. Only I follows
B. I and II follow
C. Only III follows
D. All follow

30. Each item describes a situation and is followed by four possible responses. Indicate the response you find most appropriate. Choose only one response for each item. The responses will be evaluated based on the level of appropriateness for the given situation.

A student has only 3 days left before an exam. She hasn't completed half the syllabus. What's the best strategy?

A. Watch motivational videos to calm nerves
B. Sleep less and cover all topics
C. Focus on high-weightage and familiar topics
D. Give up and skip the exam

31. In this type of questions, question is provided with substitutes for various mathematical symbols, followed by a question involving calculation of an expression or choosing the correct/incorrect equation. You have to put the real signs in the given equation and then solve the questions as required.

If '^' stands for '×', '%' stands for '–', '&' stands for '÷', '*' stands for '+', then find the value of : 13%9*12%14 = ?

A. 5 B. 2
C. 3 D. 1

32. In this type of questions, question is provided with substitutes for various mathematical symbols, followed by a question involving calculation of an expression or choosing the correct/incorrect equation. You have to put the real signs in the given equation and then solve the questions as required.

If '–' stands for '÷', '?' stands for '+', '%' stands for '–', '$' stands for '×', then find the value of : 4%13?9$14 = ?

A. 117 B. 114
C. 118 D. 116

33. Your colleague shares personal problems affecting their work. You are not their manager. Best social intelligence response?

A. Spread their issues as office gossip to get sympathy
B. Offer to help them prioritize tasks and suggest they talk to HR or supervisor
C. Tell them to leave work at home
D. Ignore since it's not your concern

28. A	**29.** B	**30.** C	**31.** B	**32.** A	**33.** B

34. In a line of 40 children, Sita is 15th from the beginning and Rita is 18th from the end. How many children are there between. Sita and Rita?

A. 6 B. 7
C. 8 D. 9

35. In a temple, 25 oil lamps are lit in a row. What is the position of the 9th lamp from left when counted from the right?

A. 16th B. 17th
C. 18th D. 15th

36. In each question below is given a statement followed by two courses of action numbered I and II. You have to assume everything in the statement to be true and on the basis of the information given in the statement, decide which of the suggested courses of action logically follow(s) for pursuing.

Statement:

A high number of accidents are occurring at a railway crossing due to lack of proper signalling systems.

Course of action:

I. Install automated signalling systems at the crossing immediately.
II. Ban train services on that route permanently.

A. Only I follows
B. Only II follows
C. Both follow
D. Either I or II follows

37. Each question given below consists of a statement, followed by two arguments numbered I and II. You have to decide which of the arguments is a 'strong' argument and which is a 'weak' argument.

Statement:

Should voting be made compulsory?

Argument:

I. Yes, it ensures better representation.
II. No, people should have freedom of choice.

A. Only I is strong
B. Only II is strong
C. Both I and II are strong
D. Neither I nor II is strong

38. Few of the letters are given followed by a question mark (?) these letters are following a specific pattern you have to give the correct option which can replace question mark.

What comes next: C, G, L, R, ?

A. Y B. Z
C. A D. B

39. Few of the letters are given followed by a question mark (?) these letters are following a specific pattern you have to give the correct option which can replace question mark.

In the sequence U, Q, M, I, ?

A. D B. E
C. F D. G

40. In this question some conditions or circumstances is provided to you, you have to make logical judgement according to mentioned circumstances and mark the correct judgement for question.

A municipal council must allocate a limited budget for infrastructure. The council has the choice to repair an old bridge, build a new park, improve water supply, or enhance local transportation. What action is most justified if the town has recently faced water shortages?

A. Repair the old bridge
B. Build a new park
C. Improve the water supply
D. Enhance local transportation

34. B	**35.** B	**36.** A	**37.** C	**38.** A	**39.** B	**40.** C

41. Four meaningful words are given in the options you have to check that which of the following words cannot be formed from the letters.

'MANAGEMENT'

A. AGENT B. MEANT
C. MANGE D. MANTLE

42. In this type of questions, question is provided with some issues/disputes/problem, followed by few methods to resolve the problem in statement choosing the appropriate problem solving method that can be implemented.

An employee claims a colleague took credit for his idea. HR must resolve. Best step?

A. Investigatate by collecting evidence from both sides
B. Ignore to avoid conflict
C. Promote the claimant to appease
D. Fire the colleague immediately

43. In each of the following questions, there is a certain relationship between two given letter pairs on one side of (::) and pair is given on another side of (::) where another pair is to be found from the given alternatives, having the same relationship with this pair as the pairs of the given pair bear. Choose the best alternative.

UV : ST :: QR : ?

A. OO B. OP
C. ON D. PP

44. In each of the following questions, there is a certain relationship between two given letters pairs on one side of (::) and pair is given on another side of (::) where another pair is to be found from the given alternatives, having the same relationship with this pair as the pairs of the given pair bear. Choose the best alternative.

AE : EI :: IO : ?

A. OS B. OU
C. IU D. OA

45. Find the next element that replace the ? Logically

56, 71, 88, 107, ?

A. 136 B. 123
C. 128 D. 143

46. Find the next element that replace the ? Logically

0, 7, 26, 63, ?

A. 131 B. 123
C. 124 D. 140

47. Find the next element that replace the ? Logically

2, 14, 38, 86, ?

A. 182 B. 191
C. 194 D. 175

48. In three of the following pairs are same by same pattern except one pair. Which pair does not follow this pattern?

A. 18 : 27 B. 36 : 45
C. 54 : 63 D. 72 : 80

49. Select the option that represents the correct order of the given words as they would appear in an English dictionary.

1. Circulation 2. Circumference
3. Circumscribed 4. Circumstance
5. Circumstantial

A. 1, 2, 3, 4, 5 B. 2, 3, 1, 4, 5
C. 1, 2, 4, 3, 5 D. 2, 1, 3, 4, 5

50. Select the option that represents the correct order of the given words as they would appear in an English dictionary.

1. Memory 2. Method
3. Middle 4. Modern
5. Moment 6. Monday

A. 1, 2, 3, 4, 5, 6
B. 1, 3, 2, 4, 5, 6
C. 1, 2, 3, 4, 6, 5
D. 1, 3, 2, 4, 6, 5

41. D **42.** A **43.** B **44.** B **45.** C **46.** C **47.** A **48.** D **49.** A **50.** A

Quantitative Aptitude

51. A, B and C enter into a partnership. A invests ₹ 80,000, B invests ₹ 60,000, and C invests ₹ 40,000. After 6 month's B increases his capital by 25%, while C decreases his capital by 10%. At the end of 1 year, the total profit is ₹ 1,20,000. What is C's share in the profit?

A. ₹ 20,000 B. ₹ 24,582
C. ₹ 30,000 D. ₹ 35,789

52. If $\sin A = \frac{7}{25}$ and $\cos B = \frac{24}{25}$, find $\sin A \cos B + \cos A \sin B$:

A. $\frac{168}{625}$ B. $\frac{13}{25}$
C. $\frac{336}{625}$ D. $\frac{24}{25}$

53. A trader buys 50 kg of rice at ₹ 50 per kg and 30 kg of a different variety at ₹ 60 per kg. He mixes the two varieties and sells the entire mixture at ₹ 55 per kg. What is his total profit or loss?

A. ₹ 100 profit B. ₹ 100 loss
C. ₹ 200 profit D. ₹ 200 loss

54. Two numbers are respectively 20% less and 30% more than a third number. What is the ratio of the two numbers?

A. 8 : 13 B. 2 : 3
C. 4 : 5 D. 7 : 9

55. The average of 8 numbers is 45. If each of the first 4 numbers is increased by 5 and each of the last 4 numbers is decreased by 3, what will be the new average?

A. 45 B. 47
C. 46 D. 48

56. The HCF of $24 \times 3^2 \times 5^3 \times 7$ and $23 \times 5 \times 7 \times 11$ is:

A. 23 B. 5
C. 7 D. 35

57. The population of a town increases by 20% in the first year, decreases by 10% in the second year, and again increases by 25% in the third year. If the population at the beginning was 40,000, what will it be after 3 years?

A. 24,000 B. 43,200
C. 48,000 D. 54,000

58. A thief escapes from a bank at 10:00 AM at a speed of 20 km/h. A police car starts chasing him at 10:30 AM at a speed of 30 km/h. At what time will the police car catch the thief?

A. 11:00 AM B. 11:30 AM
C. 12:00 PM D. 12:30 PM

59. A can do a work in 15 days, B in 30 days. They start together but A leaves after 5 days. In how many more days will B complete the remaining work?

A. 15 days B. 6 days
C. 7 days D. 8 days

60. A jeweler marks a necklace at 30% above its cost price. She gives a cash discount of ₹ 150 on the marked price. If the necklace is sold for ₹ 1800 and she earns a profit of 20%, what is the cost price of the necklace?

A. ₹ 1500 B. ₹ 1200
C. ₹ 1450 D. ₹ 1600

61. A sum of money doubles itself in 8 years at a certain rate of simple interest. In how many years will it become five times itself at the same rate?

A. 16 years B. 24 years
C. 32 years D. 40 years

51. B **52.** C **53.** A **54.** A **55.** C **56.** D **57.** D **58.** B **59.** A **60.** A **61.** C

62. Rohan invests a portion of a total sum of ₹ P in Scheme A for 4 years and the remaining amount in Scheme B for 5 years. Scheme A offers a simple interest rate of r% per annum, while Scheme B offers a simple interest rate of $(r+2)\%$ per annum. The amount invested in Scheme A is 50% more than the amount invested in Scheme B. If the total interest earned from both schemes is ₹ 1,920 and the amount invested in Scheme A is ₹ 2,400, what is the simple interest rate r?

A. 10% B. 15%
C. 5% D. 12%

63. What is the value of $a^2 + b^2 + c^2$ if $a + b + c = 12$ and $ab + bc + ca = 40$?

A. 84 B. 64
C. 44 D. 144

64. Which of the following numbers can possibly be a perfect square?

A. 245982 B. 496838
C. 178343 D. 571536

65. A shopkeeper mixes 4 litres of a milk solution containing 25% fat with 6 liters of another milk solution containing 40% fat. What is the fat percentage in the final mixture?

A. 30% B. 32%
C. 34% D. 35%

66. If the radius of a sphere is increased by 20 per cent, by what percentage will its volume increase?

A. 76.6 B. 60.5
C. 72.8 D. 78.4

67. The total surface area of a solid hemisphere is 300π cm^2. Find its volume.

A. 500π cm^3
B. 125π cm^3
C. $\frac{333}{2}\pi$ cm^3
D. $\frac{2000}{3}\pi$ cm^3

68. Which of the following is in ascending order?

A. 1/2, 0.55, 3/5, 0.625
B. 1/2, 3/5, 0.55, 0.625
C. 0.55, 1/2, 0.625, 3/5
D. 1/2, 0.55, 0.625, 3/5

69. The area of a circle is 144π cm^2. What is the length of the circumference of the circle?

A. 82.5 cm B. 19.8 cm
C. 22.5 cm D. 75.4 cm

70. If $27^3 \div 3^5 = 3^n$, find n.

A. 3 B. 6
C. 5 D. 4

71. If $x - y = 8$ and $xy = 5$, what is the value of $x^3 - y^3 + 8(x + y)^2$.

A. 1256 B. 1304
C. 3456 D. 3245

72. Simplify : $\frac{(\sin(x)+\cos(x))^2}{1+\sin(x)\cos(x)}$

A. $\frac{6+5\sin(x)\cos(x)}{1+\sin(x)\cos(x)}$

B. $\frac{7+8\sin(x)\cos(x)}{3+\sin(x)\cos(x)}$

C. $\frac{9+2\sin(x)\cos(x)}{7+\sin(x)\cos(x)}$

D. $\frac{1+2\sin(x)\cos(x)}{1+\sin(x)\cos(x)}$

62. A **63.** B **64.** D **65.** C **66.** C **67.** D **68.** A **69.** D **70.** D **71.** B **72.** D

73. If $\sin A = \frac{5}{13}$, find tanA.

A. $\frac{7}{13}$ B. $\frac{5}{12}$

C. $\frac{8}{15}$ D. $\frac{9}{13}$

74. In a right triangle ABC, right-angled at B, if $\tan A = \frac{1}{\sqrt{3}}$, what is the value of $2\sin A\cos A$?

A. $\frac{\sqrt{3}}{2}$ B. $\frac{\sqrt{3}}{5}$

C. $\frac{\sqrt{3}}{7}$ D. $\frac{\sqrt{3}}{8}$

75. The equation of a line is $5x - 2y = 10$. What is the slope of a line perpendicular to this line?

A. -8 B. $\frac{-2}{5}$

C. $\frac{6}{7}$ D. 7

General Awareness

76. Who was the first woman Director-General of the Archaeological Survey of India?

A. Kamala Das B. Debala Mitra

C. Anna Chandy D. Chitra Ramkrishna

77. Who took oath as the Chief Minister of Andhra Pradesh in June 2024?

A. Revanth Reddy

B. N. Chandrababu Naidu

C. Mohan Yadav

D. Vishnu Deo Sai

78. In February 2025, who launched a policy report titled 'Expanding Quality Higher Education through States and State Public Universities'?

A. NITI Aayog

B. Ministry of Education

C. NGO Pratham

D. Azad Foundation

79. Which ministry launched the Swavalambini initiative in March 2025 to promote women entrepreneurship in India?

A. Ministry of Women and Child Development

B. Ministry of Rural Development

C. Ministry of Commerce and industry

D. Ministry of Skill Development and Entrepreneurship

80. In India, which of the following is a report published under MoSPI?

I. Periodic Labour Force Survey

II. Monthly infrastructure Performance Review Report

A. Only I B. Only II

C. Both I and II D. Neither I nor II

81. The Sudasari Great Indian Bustard Breeding centre is in which of the following state?

A. Rajasthan B. Tamil Nadu

C. Kerala D. Karnataka

82. Who is the author of a travel book 'From Heaven Lake: Travels Through Sinkiang and Tibet', which won the Thomas Cook Travel Book Award?

A. Sarah Joseph

B. Rohit Lal

C. Kanchana Banerjee

D. Vikram Seth

73. B **74.** A **75.** B **76.** B **77.** B **78.** A **79.** D **80.** C **81.** A **82.** D

83. The 'Vamsi', a traditional instrument of Tamil Nadu, is a ______.

A. Flute B. Drum
C. Sarod D. Manjira

84. 'Swang' dance is performed in which of the following Indian state of India?

A. Goa B. Kerala
C. Karnataka D. Uttar Pradesh

85. In the context of Indian satellite, the INSAT is used for which of the following purpose?

I. Television broadcasting

II. Weather Forecasting

A. Only I
B. Only II
C. Both I and II
D. Neither I nor II

86. Newton's third law of motion states that ______.

A. For every action, there is an equal and opposite reaction
B. For every action, the reaction is opposite but greater in magnitude
C. The rate of change of momentum of an object is proportional to the applied unbalanced force in the direction of force
D. An object in motion remains in motion unless acted upon by a force

87. What is the formula for pressure?

A. Pressure = force/area
B. Pressure = force × area
C. Pressure = area/force
D. Pressure = (force × force)/area

88. The uncrewed Gaganyaan-G1 mission, scheduled for December 2025, will carry a female-looking half-humanoid robot to test human functions and onboard systems. What is the name of this robot?

A. Manavi B. Vyommitra
C. Bumika D. Rokshak

89. In August 2025, which organisation received an order worth ₹ 62000 crores for 97 LCA Mk1A fighter jets from the Indian government?

A. HAL B. AWE Indi
C. DRDO D. AVANI

90. In 1722, Sawai Raja Jai Singh was given the governorship of which of the following regions?

A. Bengal B. Awadh
C. Agra D. Odisha

91. Which of the following tax are imposed on goods imported into and exported out of India?

A. Excise duty
B. Customs duty
C. Wealth tax
D. Estate duty

92. The target of National Logistics Policy is to improve India's Logistics performance index ranking to among top 25 countries by ______.

A. 2027 B. 2030
C. 2040 D. 2047

93. In which year was the Special Economic Zones (SEZs) policy was launched in India?

A. 1998 B. 2002
C. 1999 D. 2000

94. An Indian state can be divided or its boundary altered by which of the following?

A. The State Legislature
B. Parliament
C. President
D. Supreme Court

83. A	**84.** D	**85.** C	**86.** A	**87.** A	**88.** B
89. A	**90.** C	**91.** B	**92.** B	**93.** D	**94.** B

95. Which of the following is NOT constitute the hinterland of Marmagao port?

A. Karnataka
B. Goa
C. Southern Maharashtra
D. Himachal Pradesh

96. What is a capital goods industry?

A. Industry that deals in external commercial borrowings.
B. Industry that exports food products.
C. Industry that process raw agricultural product.
D. Industry producing machines and tools.

97. In the context of trade policy tools, which of the following is considered as tariff measure?

I. Export taxes

II. Import taxes

A. Only I
B. Only II
C. Both I and II
D. Neither I nor II

98. As of February 2025, Scheduled Tribe (ST) individuals comprising ______ of the total population in India.

A. 8.6% B. 5.5%
C. 9.8% D. 12.2%

99. What is the process called when organisms acquire oxygen from outside the body to break down food sources?

A. Respiration B. Digestion
C. Photosynthesis D. Fermentation

100. The 'Charaksamhita' is a treatise on which of the following subjects?

A. Medicine B. Astronomy
C. Architecture D. Mathematics

EXPLANATORY ANSWERS

1. The error is the preposition used after "responsible." Standard usage is "responsible for" something, not "responsible of." So it should read: "The new manager is responsible for the entire marketing campaign."

2. The phrase "against the clock" means working with great urgency because time is limited. Since the sentence mentions that the deadline was approaching, it implies that the team was working quickly to finish before time ran out. The other options do not express urgency related to time pressure, so "against the clock" is the most appropriate choice.

3. "Hapless" means unfortunate, unlucky, or ill-fated. Among the options, Unlucky matches the meaning most accurately.

4. The idiom "take something in stride" means to accept criticism or difficulty calmly and handle it well. The sentence means she accepted the criticism positively and used it to improve.

5. In "He saw the car coming too late," "saw" means noticed/observed with the eyes. The matching usage is "I saw a beautiful sunset last night," where "saw" also means observed visually.

6. The passage clearly states that the main benefit of online purchasing is its accessibility, allowing customers to explore and buy products from almost anywhere at any time, often with a wider selection than physical stores.

95. D	**96.** D	**97.** C	**98.** A	**99.** A	**100.** A

7. The text explains that online retailers often have reduced overhead costs compared to physical stores, which enables them to offer competitive pricing, making this a key pricing-related advantage.

8. A major drawback highlighted in the passage is that customers cannot personally inspect products before buying them, which can lead to dissatisfaction related to delivery and product quality.

9. The passage mentions growing concerns linked to online shopping such as shipping delays, unstated expenses, and environmental effects of packaging and transportation, making shipping delays a valid concern mentioned in the text.

10. The passage notes that the absence of direct human interaction in online shopping can weaken the individualized customer service experience, making this the correct choice.

11. Among the given options, "Bureaucrat" is the only word spelled correctly. The others contain incorrect letter arrangements that do not conform to standard English spelling.

12. The correct spelling requires double *r* and double *s*, followed by -ible. All other options miss or misplace essential letters, making them incorrect.

13. The idiom "as thick as thieves" means that people share a very close bond, trust each other deeply, and are strongly loyal to one another. It does not primarily refer to secrecy, sneakiness, or silence.

14. An ornithologist is a specialist who studies birds. The other options refer to broader or different fields of biological study and therefore do not precisely match the definition.

15. Felicity means happiness or great joy. The most direct and accurate opposite among the given options is misery, which denotes extreme unhappiness.

16. The verb repudiate means to reject, deny, or refuse to accept something. Therefore, its most appropriate antonym is accept, which conveys the opposite sense of agreeing to or approving something.

17. An archive is specifically a place where historical records, documents, and official files are systematically stored and preserved. The other options are either broader or not precise one-word substitutes in this context.

18. The given sentence is in passive form using "Let ... be convened." Converting it into active voice requires a direct imperative form, which is correctly achieved by "Convene the emergency meeting at 10 AM without delay."

19. In indirect speech, future tense "will" changes to "would," "this quarter" changes to "that quarter," and present tense "is" changes to "was." Pronoun "us" changes to "them," and "next time" appropriately becomes "the next time." Option D correctly applies all these necessary changes.

20. The relative clause "who believes in rumours" refers to people, which is plural. Therefore, the verb must also be plural. Replacing the highlighted part with "believe" maintains grammatical agreement and correctness.

21. The noun "profit margin" in this context refers to the margins of organized sellers in general, so it should be in the plural form "profit margins." Option A corrects this by using the proper plural noun and keeps the verb structure grammatically correct. The other options contain verb form errors ("maintains," "improves") or incorrect usage ("abled"), making them grammatically unsuitable.

22. The active sentence is in the present continuous tense ("are completing"), so the correct passive transformation must also be in the present continuous form, which is accurately expressed by "are being completed."

23. In converting indirect to direct speech, past perfect continuous ("had been sailing") becomes present perfect continuous ("has been sailing"), and "the previous night" correctly changes to "last night." This option maintains correct tense and meaning.

24. The logical flow begins with the admiral's decision (Q), followed by the planned strategy (S). Then comes the unexpected storm (P), and finally the resulting struggle for survival (R), making this the most coherent sequence.

25. The paragraph logically starts with the Roman Empire at its height (Q), followed by its achievements and prosperity (S). Then the shift introduced by "However" signals rising pressures (P), concluding with the causes of its decline (R).

26. The pattern in HARMONY → KDUPRQB shows that each letter is shifted +3 positions forward in the English alphabet (H→K, A→D, R→U, M→P, O→R, N→Q, Y→B). Applying the same +3 shift to BALANCE: B→E, A→D, L→O, A→D, N→Q, C→F, E→H. Hence, the coded form is EDODQFH.

27. In ARCHAEOLOGICAL → BSDIBFPMPHJDBM, every letter is shifted +1 (A→B, R→S, C→D, ..., L→M). The same +1 rule also matches ANTHROPOLOGICAL → BOUISPQPMPHJDBM. Therefore, PSYCHOLOGICAL coded with +1 becomes: P→Q, S→T, Y→Z, C→D, H→I, O→P, L→M, O→P, G→H, I→J, C→D, A→B, L→M = QTZDIPMPHJDBM.

28. MATHEMATICS → NBUIFNBUJDT shows a consistent +1 shift for each letter (M→N, A→B, T→U, ..., S→T). GEOGRAPHY → HFPHSBQUIZ confirms the same +1 pattern (G→H, E→F, ..., Y→Z). So CHEMISTRY becomes C→D, H→I, E→F, M→N, I→J, S→T, T→U, R→S, Y→Z = DIFNJTUSZ.

29. The statement clearly says surveillance improves security/crime prevention but also raises privacy/ethical concerns, so I necessarily follows (both benefits and risks exist). It also states critics demand transparent policies and public oversight, so II necessarily follows (need oversight and clear rules to balance). III does not follow because the passage discusses regulation and debate, not a complete ban.

30. With only 3 days left and half the syllabus pending, the most appropriate approach is smart prioritization rather than trying to do everything. High-weightage and familiar areas give the best score-return per hour and reduce panic. This also leaves some time for quick revision and practice, which is crucial near an exam.

31. Replace the symbols as given: %→–, *→+.

So, 13%9*12%14 = 13 – 9 + 12 – 14.
= 25 – 23 = 2

32. Replace the symbols as given:

%→–, ?→+, $→×.

So, 4%13?9$14 = 4 – 13 + 9 × 14.
= 4 – 13 + 126
= 130 – 13 = 117

33. This response shows empathy without gossiping, gives practical support to manage work impact, and guides them to the right formal support channel (HR/supervisor) since you are not their manager.

34. Sita is 15th from the beginning. Rita is 18th from the end, so from the beginning Rita's position is:

40 – 18 + 1 = 23.

Children between them:

23 – 15 – 1 = 7.

35. Total lamps = 25.

The 9th lamp from the left will be from the right:

25 – 9 + 1 = 17.

36. The problem stated is accidents due to lack of proper signalling. Installing automated signalling directly addresses the cause and is a practical preventive measure, so Course I logically follows. Permanently banning train services is an extreme step, not required by the statement, and it does not logically follow as the necessary action when the issue can be solved through safety upgrades.

37. Argument I is strong because compulsory voting can increase participation and lead to better representation of the population in election outcomes. Argument II is also strong because voting involves individual liberty, and forcing it can be seen as violating freedom of choice. Both arguments are relevant, logical, and directly address the question.

38. Convert letters to positions:

C = 3, G = 7, L = 12, R = 18.

The gaps are +4, +5, +6.

Next gap should be +7.

So 18 + 7 = 25, which is Y.

39. The pattern is −4 each time. Next is 9 − 4 = 5, which corresponds to E.

40. Since the town has recently faced water shortages, the most justified budget allocation is the one that addresses the immediate essential need affecting health and daily life. Improving water supply directly solves the pressing shortage problem, making it the most logical and justified choice among the options.

41. From "MANAGEMENT", letter counts are: M(2), A(2), N(2), G(1), E(2), T(1). There is no L available. So MANTLE cannot be formed because it requires the letter L, which is absent. The other words (AGENT, MEANT, MANGE) can be formed using available letters within the counts.

42. This is a workplace dispute involving credit/ownership of an idea, so HR should follow a fair process: hear both parties, check emails/meeting notes/witnesses, and then decide appropriately. Ignoring, promoting to appease, or firing immediately are unjustified and can worsen conflict or create unfairness.

43. UV → ST means each letter is shifted back by 2 (U→S, V→T). Apply the same to QR: Q→O, R→P. So the required pair is OP.

44. AE → EI shows a forward shift of +4 for each letter (A→E, E→I). Apply the same to IO: I→M and O→S, giving MS. Since MS is not present, check the vowel-sequence relationship instead: AE are consecutive vowels (A, E) and become the next two consecutive vowels (E, I). Similarly IO are consecutive vowels (I, O) and should become the next two consecutive vowels (O, U). Hence OU fits the intended pattern.

45. The given sequence is 56, 71, 88, 107.

Find the differences between consecutive terms:

71 − 56 = 15

88 − 71 = 17

107 − 88 = 19

The differences are increasing by 2 each time (15, 17, 19).

So, the next difference will be 21.

Next term = 107 + 21 = 128

Hence, the correct next element in the series is 128.

46. The pattern is $n^3 - 1$.

$1^3 - 1 = 0$, $2^3 - 1 = 7$,

$3^3 - 1 = 26$, $4^3 - 1 = 63$.

Next is $5^3 - 1 = 125 - 1 = 124$.

47. The pattern is $n^3 + 1$.

$1^3 + 1 = 2$, $2^3 + 1 = 9$ (not given), so check another consistent pattern: each term is 2 × previous +10, +? (doesn't fit).

Use differences:

14 - 2 = 12, 38 - 14 = 24, 86 - 38 = 48.

Differences double: 12, 24, 48.
Next difference = 96.
So next term = 86 + 96 = 182.

48. In A, B, C the second number is the first number +9:
18→27 (+9), 36→45 (+9), 54→63 (+9).
But 72→80 is +8, so it does not follow the same pattern.

49. All begin with "Circu...". After "Circu", compare next letters:
Circulation (1) comes before Circum... (*m*), so 1 first.
Among "Circum...": Circumference (*f*) comes before Circums... (*s*), so 2 next.
Then among Circums...: Circumscribed (*c*) comes before Circumst... (*t*), so 3 next.
Between Circumstance and Circumstantial: the shorter base word comes first, so 4 then 5.

50. Arrange the words in strict alphabetical (dictionary) order by comparing letters from left to right.

- All words start with M.
- Next letter comparison: Memory (Me...), Method (Me...), Middle (Mi...), Modern (Mo...),
- Moment (Mo...), Monday (Mo...).
- Among Memory and Method: compare memo vs meth → *m* comes before *t*, so Memory comes first, followed by Method.
- Middle (Mi...) comes after Me... words.
- Among Modern (Mod...), Moment (Mom...), Monday (Mon...): $d < m < n$, so the order is Modern, then Moment, then Monday.

Thus, the correct dictionary order is:
Memory, Method, Middle, Modern, Moment, Monday = 1, 2, 3, 4, 5, 6.

51. A's investment for 12 months
= 80,000 × 12
= 9,60,000

B's investment
First 6 months:
60,000 × 6 = 3,60,000
Next 6 months (25% increase):
60,000 + 25% of 60,000
= 75,000
75,000 × 6 = 4,50,000
Total for B = 3,60,000+4,50,000
= 8,10,000

C's investment
First 6 months:
40,000 × 6 = 2,40,000
Next 6 months (10% decrease):
40,000 – 10% of 40,000
= 36,000
36,000 × 6 = 2,16,000
Total for C = 2,40,000 + 2,16,000
= 4,56,000

Capital ratio
9,60,000 : 8,10,000 : 4,56,000
= 160 : 135 : 76
Total ratio = 160+135+76 = 371
C's share = 1,20,000 × 76/371
= 24,582 (approx.)

52. $\sin A = \frac{7}{25} \Rightarrow \cos A = \frac{24}{25}$

$\cos B = \frac{24}{25} \Rightarrow \sin B = \frac{7}{25}$

$\sin A \cos B + \cos A \sin B = \frac{7}{25}\cdot\frac{24}{25} + \frac{24}{25}\cdot\frac{7}{25}$

$= 2\times\frac{168}{625} = \frac{336}{625}$

53. Cost price
50 × 50 = 2,500
30 × 60 = 1,800
Total CP = 2,500 + 1,800
= 4,300

Total quantity
50 + 30 = 80 kg

Selling price

$80 \times 55 = 4{,}400$

Profit

$4{,}400 - 4{,}300 = 100$

54. Let the third number $= x$

First number $= 80\%$ of $x = 0.8x$

Second number $= 130\%$ of $x = 1.3x$

Ratio $0.8x : 1.3x = 0.8 : 1.3$

$= 8/10 : 13/10$

$= 8 : 13$

55. Original sum

$8 \times 45 = 360$

Increase in first 4 numbers

$4 \times 5 = 20$

Decrease in last 4 numbers

$4 \times 3 = 12$

New sum

$360 + 20 - 12 = 368$

New average

$368/8 = 46$

56. **Step 1:** Prime factorisation

$24 = 2^3 \times 3$

So first number:

$24 \times 3^2 \times 5^3 \times 7 = (2^3 \times 3) \times 3^2 \times 5^3 \times 7$

$= 2^3 \times 3^3 \times 5^3 \times 7$

Second number: $23 \times 5 \times 7 \times 11$

(23 and 11 are prime numbers.)

Step 2: Common prime factors

Compare: $2^3 \times 3^3 \times 5^3 \times 7$

$23 \times 5 \times 7 \times 11$

Common primes are: 5 and 7

Step 3: Take lowest powers

$5^{\min(3,1)} = 5$

$7^{\min(1,1)} = 7$

HCF $= 5 \times 7 = 35$

57. $40{,}000 \times 1.20 = 48{,}000$

$48{,}000 \times 0.90 = 43{,}200$

$43{,}200 \times 1.25 = 54{,}000$

58. Head start time

$10{:}30 - 10{:}00 = 0.5$ h

Head start distance

$20 \times 0.5 = 10$ km

Relative speed

$30 - 20 = 10$ km/h

Catch time after 10:30

$$\frac{10}{10} = 1 \text{ h}$$

$10{:}30 + 1 \text{ h} = 11{:}30$ AM

59. Rate of A $= \frac{1}{15}$

Rate of B $= \frac{1}{30}$

Work done in 5 days together

$$5\left(\frac{1}{15}+\frac{1}{30}\right) = 5\left(\frac{2}{30}+\frac{1}{30}\right) = 5\left(\frac{3}{30}\right)$$

$$= 5\left(\frac{1}{10}\right) = \frac{1}{2}$$

Remaining work

$$1-\frac{1}{2} = \frac{1}{2}$$

Time for B:

$$\frac{1/2}{1/30} = 15$$

60. $1800 = \text{CP} \times 1.20$

$$\text{CP} = \frac{1800}{1.20} = 1500$$

61. SI in 8 years = P(because P + SI = 2P)

For 5P, SI = 5P − P = 4P

SI in 8 years ⇒ 4P

When SI is P, time = 8 years

So, when SI is 4P,

time $= 8 \times 4 = 32$ years

62. A = 2400, A = 1.5B

⇒ B = 2400/1.5=1600

$$SI_A = \frac{2400 \times r \times 4}{100} = 96r$$

$$SI_B = \frac{1600 \times (r+2) \times 5}{100}$$

$= 80(r + 2) = 80r + 160$

$$96r + (80r + 160) = 1920$$
$$176r + 160 = 1920$$
$$176r = 1760$$
$$r = 10$$

63. $(a + b + c)^2$
$$= a^2 + b^2 + c^2 + 2(ab + bc + ca)$$
$$12^2 = a^2 + b^2 + c^2 + 2(40)$$
$$144 = a^2 + b^2 + c^2 + 80$$
$$a^2 + b^2 + c^2 = 144 - 80 = 64$$

64. $756^2 = 756 \times 756$
$$= 756(700 + 50 + 6)$$
$$= 756 \cdot 700 + 756 \cdot 50 + 756 \cdot 6$$
$$= 529200 + 37800 + 4536$$
$$= 571536$$

65. Fat $= 4 \times 25\% + 6 \times 40\%$
$$= 4 \times 0.25 + 6 \times 0.40$$
$$= 1 + 2.4 = 3.4$$
Total volume $= 4 + 6 = 10$
$$\text{Fat } \% = \frac{3.4}{10} \times 100 = 34\%$$

66. $V = \frac{4}{3}\pi r^3$

$r' = r + 0.20r = 1.2r$
$$\frac{V'}{V} = \frac{\frac{4}{3}\pi(1.2r)^3}{\frac{4}{3}\pi r^3} = (1.2)^3 = 1.728$$
% increase $= (1.728 - 1) \times 100 = 72.8\%$

67. The total surface area of a solid hemisphere is
$$3\pi r^2 = 300\pi$$
$$r^2 = 100$$
$$\Rightarrow \quad r = 10 \text{ cm}$$
The volume of a hemisphere is
$$V = \frac{2}{3}\pi r^3$$
$$= \frac{2}{3}\pi(10^3) = \frac{2000}{3}\pi \text{ cm}^3$$
Thus, the required volume is $\frac{2000}{3}\pi \text{ cm}^3$

68. Convert all numbers into decimal form for proper comparison:
$$\frac{1}{2} = 0.50$$
$$0.55 = 0.55$$
$$\frac{3}{5} = 0.60$$
$$0.625 = 0.625$$
Arrange in ascending order:
$0.50 < 0.55 < 0.60 < 0.625$
Thus, the correct ascending sequence is 1/2, 0.55, 3/5, 0.625.

69. Given area of circle:
$$\pi r^2 = 144\pi$$
$$r^2 = 144$$
$$r = 12 \text{ cm}$$
Circumference formula:
$$C = 2\pi r$$
$$= 2\pi(12) = 24\pi$$
Using $\pi \approx 3.1416$:
$$C = 24 \times 3.1416$$
$$= 75.3984 \approx 75.4 \text{ cm}$$
Hence, the circumference is 75.4 cm.

70. $27^3 \div 3^5 = 3^n$
$$27 = 3^3$$
$$(3^3)^3 \div 3^5 = 3^n$$
$$3^9 \div 3^5 = 3^n$$
$$3^{9-5} = 3^n$$
$$3^4 = 3^n$$
$$n = 4$$

71. Given, $x - y = 8$ and $xy = 5$.
$$(x + y)^2 = (x - y)^2 + 4xy$$
$$= 8^2 + 4(5)$$
$$= 64 + 20 = 84$$
$$x^2 + y^2 = (x + y)^2 - 2xy$$
$$= 84 - 10 = 74$$
$$x^2 + xy + y^2 = 74 + 5 = 79$$
$$x^3 - y^3 = (x-y)(x^2 + xy + y^2)$$
$$= 8 \times 79 = 632$$
$$8(x + y)^2 = 8 \times 84 = 672$$
$$x^3 - y^3 + 8(x + y)^2$$
$$= 632 + 672 = 1304.$$

72. $\dfrac{(\sin x + \cos x)^2}{1 + \sin x \cos x}$

$$= \frac{\sin^2 x + \cos^2 x + 2\sin x \cos x}{1 + \sin x \cos x}$$

$$= \frac{1 + 2\sin x \cos x}{1 + \sin x \cos x}$$

73. $\sin A = \dfrac{5}{13}$

$$\cos A = \sqrt{1 - \sin^2 A} = \sqrt{1 - \left(\frac{5}{13}\right)^2}$$

$$= \sqrt{\frac{169 - 25}{169}} = \frac{12}{13}$$

$$\tan A = \frac{\sin A}{\cos A} = \frac{\frac{5}{13}}{\frac{12}{13}} = \frac{5}{12}$$

74. $\tan A = \dfrac{1}{\sqrt{3}} \Rightarrow A = 30°$

$$\sin A = \frac{1}{2}, \ \cos A = \frac{\sqrt{3}}{2}$$

$$2\sin A \cos A = 2\left(\frac{1}{2}\right)\left(\frac{\sqrt{3}}{2}\right) = \frac{\sqrt{3}}{2}$$

75. $5x - 2y = 10$

$-2y = -5x + 10$

$$y = \frac{5}{2}x - 5 \Rightarrow m = \frac{5}{2}$$

$$m_{\perp} = -\frac{1}{m} = -\frac{1}{\frac{5}{2}} = -\frac{2}{5}$$

76. Debala Mitra was the first woman to serve as the Director-General of the Archaeological Survey of India. She held the position in the 1980s and is noted for her contributions to Indian archaeology and heritage conservation.

77. N. Chandrababu Naidu took oath as the Chief Minister of Andhra Pradesh in June 2024 after the Telugu Desam Party's victory in the state assembly elections.

78. The policy report titled "Expanding Quality Higher Education through States and State Public Universities" was launched in February 2025 by NITI Aayog, focusing on strengthening state-level higher education systems and public universities.

79. The Swavalambini initiative, launched in March 2025, was introduced by the Ministry of Skill Development and Entrepreneurship to promote women entrepreneurship through skill training, mentoring, and enterprise support.

80. The Periodic Labour Force Survey (PLFS) is a flagship statistical report published by the Ministry of Statistics and Programme Implementation (MoSPI), providing regular estimates on employment and unemployment indicators in India.

The Monthly Infrastructure Performance Review Report (also referred to as the Review of Infrastructure Industries) is also released under MoSPI and tracks the performance and growth trends of core infrastructure sectors such as coal, power, steel, cement, and refinery products.

Hence, both statements I and II are correct.

81. The Sudasari Great Indian Bustard Breeding Centre is located in Rajasthan, near the Desert National Park in Jaisalmer district, which is a key habitat for the critically endangered Great Indian Bustard.

82. *Travels Through Sinkiang and Tibet* is a well-known travel book authored by Vikram Seth, and it won the prestigious Thomas Cook Travel Book Award.

83. The Vamsi is a traditional flute, commonly associated with the musical traditions of Tamil Nadu and other parts of South India.

84. Swang is a traditional folk dance–drama form mainly associated with Haryana and western Uttar Pradesh. Among the given options, Uttar Pradesh is the correct answer.

85. The INSAT (Indian National Satellite System) is used for multiple purposes, including television broadcasting and weather forecasting, making both statements correct.

86. Newton's third law of motion states that forces in nature occur in pairs. When one object exerts a force on another, the second object simultaneously exerts a force of equal magnitude but in the opposite direction on the first object.

87. Pressure is defined as the force applied per unit area. Mathematically, it is expressed as P = F/A, meaning that for the same force, pressure increases when the area of contact decreases.

88. The half-humanoid robot Vyommitra, developed by ISRO, is designed to simulate human functions and test life-support systems during the uncrewed Gaganyaan missions, including the Gaganyaan-G1 mission scheduled for December 2025.

89. The order worth ₹ 62,000 crores for 97 LCA Mk1A fighter jets was awarded to Hindustan Aeronautics Limited (HAL), which is India's premier aerospace and defence manufacturing company responsible for producing the Tejas aircraft.

90. In 1722, Sawai Raja Jai Singh II, the ruler of Jaipur and a noted astronomer-administrator, was appointed the governor of Agra by the Mughal emperor. This position significantly increased his influence within the Mughal administration.

91. Customs duty is the tax imposed on goods when they are imported into or exported out of India. Excise duty applies to goods manufactured within the country, while wealth tax and estate duty relate to assets and inheritance, not trade.

92. The National Logistics Policy (NLP) aims to improve India's Logistics Performance Index (LPI) ranking to be among the top 25 countries by the year 2030, along with reducing logistics costs and improving efficiency.

93. India's Special Economic Zones (SEZs) policy was launched in 2000 as part of the Export–Import (EXIM) Policy 2000–2001, with the objective of promoting exports, investment, and employment.

94. Under Article 3 of the Indian Constitution, the Parliament has the power to form new states, alter the boundaries or names of existing states, or divide a state, subject to certain procedural requirements.

95. The hinterland of Marmagao Port includes Goa, Karnataka, and southern Maharashtra. Himachal Pradesh is geographically distant and not connected to the port's trade influence, so it is not part of its hinterland.

96. A capital goods industry produces goods such as machines, tools, equipment, and plants that are used in the production of other goods. These industries form the backbone of industrial and economic development.

97. Tariff measures are taxes imposed on cross-border trade. Both export taxes and import taxes involve duties levied on goods when they are exported or imported, so both are considered tariff measures.

98. As per Census-based demographic data used officially (and referenced up to 2023–25), Scheduled Tribes constitute about 8.6% of India's total population.

99. Respiration is the biological process in which organisms take in oxygen from the external environment and use it to break down food substances to release energy.

100. The Charaka Samhita is a foundational ancient Indian text of Ayurveda, dealing primarily with medicine, including diagnosis, treatment, pharmacology, and principles of health and disease.

Previous Years' Paper

SSC—Combined Higher Secondary Level (CHSL : 10 + 2)

Data Entry Operator (DEO)/ Lower Division Clerk (LDC)/ Junior Secretarial Assistant (JSA)

Tier-I, Recruitment Exam-2024

(Exam held on 11-07-2024)

English Language

1. Parts of the following sentence have been given as options. Select the option that contains an error.

Geeta was working now but she can be seen swimming in the river every evening.

A. swimming in the
B. river every evening.
C. but she can be seen
D. Geeta was working now

2. The following sentence has been split into four segments. Identify the segment that contains a grammatical error.

The manager asked / the cooking team, "Who / among you is to baked the / Christmas cake this year?"

A. Christmas cake this year?"
B. The manager asked
C. among you is to baked the
D. the cooking team, "Who

3. Select the grammatically INCORRECT sentence.

A. They often meet each other.
B. They always meet each other.
C. They quite meet each other.
D. They hardly meet each other.

4. The following sentence has been divided into four segments. Identify the segment that contains a grammatical error.

The new / secretary / does not likes / me.

A. me. B. secretary
C. The new D. does not likes

Directions (Q.No. 5-9): *In the following passage, some words have been deleted. Read the passage carefully and select the most appropriate option to fill in each blank.*

Teachers __(1)__ given continuous opportunities for self-improvement and to learn the latest innovations and advances in their professions. Each teacher ___(2)____expected to participate in at least 50 hours of CPD opportunities every year for their own professional development, driven ___(3)____ their own interests. CPD opportunities will, in particular, ____(4)_____cover the latest pedagogies regarding foundational literacy and numeracy, formative and adaptive assessment of learning outcomes, competency-based learning and related pedagogies, ____(5)_____experiential learning, arts-integrated, sports-integrated and storytelling-based approaches, etc.

1. D	2. C	3. C	4. D

5. Select the most appropriate option to fill in blank number (1).
A. shall be B. will be
C. can be C. would be

6. Select the most appropriate option to fill in blank number (2).
A. shall be B. would be
C. can be D. will be

7. Select the most appropriate option to fill in blank number (3).
A. by B. from
C. at D. for

8. Select the most appropriate option to fill in blank number (4).
A. carelessly B. systematically
C. roughly D. partially

9. Select the most appropriate option to fill in blank number (5).
A. same as B. such as
C. from as D. for as

10. Select the most appropriate ANTONYM of the underlined word.

The waters of Germany are <u>abundant</u> in fish, but there are few genera and species in them.
A. deficient B. flourish
C. allay D. discord

11. Select the most appropriate synonym of the given word.

Revolution
A. Stagnation B. Gyration
C. Harmony D. Order

12. Select the most appropriate ANTONYM for the given word.

Ghastly
A. Agitated B. Bitter
C. Relaxing D. Pleasant

13. Select the most appropriate option that can substitute the underlined segment in the given sentence. If there is no need to substitute it, select 'No substitution required'.

I opened the box beneath the table and <u>took of</u> a book, the Materia Medica.
A. took out
B. take off
C. took in
D. No substitution required

14. Parts of the following sentence have been given as options. Select the option that contains a spelling error.

I was alarmed lest we should be wreked.
A. I was B. be wreked.
C. we should D. alarmed lest

15. Based on the situation in the sentence, select the most appropriate idiom.

After many years of rivalry, the two schools decided to _______ and participate in a National Event together.
A. bell the cat
B. bury the hatchet
C. go cold turkey
D. be in the doldrums

16. Choose the option that best describes the meaning of the idioms and phrases underlined in the given sentence.

A <u>jack of all trades</u> cannot survive in the world of specialisation.
A. A good communicator
B. A person who can do many things but is not an expert in any
C. An expert of many jobs
D. A businessman

5. B	**6.** D	**7.** A	**8.** B	**9.** B	**10.** A
11. B	**12.** D	**13.** A	**14.** B	**15.** B	**16.** B

17. Select the most appropriate option that can substitute the underlined segment in the given sentence.

Do not <u>later about</u> the street.

A. loiter around
B. litre about
C. litter about
D. latter about

18. Select the most appropriate ANTONYM of the given word.

Compulsory

A. Optional
B. Reliable
C. Factional
D. Full-fledged

19. Select the most appropriate option that can substitute the underlined segment in the given sentence.

Well, I prefer eating at home <u>from eating out</u>.

A. and eating out
B. than eating out
C. while eating out
D. to eating out

20. Rectify the sentence by selecting the correct spelling from the options.

The advertisement of vacencies in education sector has received huge response.

A. Vecencies
B. Vacansies
C. Vecancies
D. Vacancies

21. Select the most appropriate ANTONYM of the underlined word in the given sentence.

The athlete looked <u>unsettled</u> before the race.

A. Confident
B. Reticent
C. Triumphant
D. Tangent

22. Select the most appropriate synonym of the given word.

Candid

A. Cruel B. Bright
C. Top D. Honest

23. Select the most appropriate option to fill in the blank.

The artist received a __________ from the audience.

A. handful of applause
B. round of applause
C. bunch of applause
D. plenty of applause

24. Select the most appropriate option that can substitute the underlined word in the given sentence.

The <u>experienced</u> surgeon handled the delicate procedure with care and precision.

A. seasoned
B. amateur
C. untrained
D. unskilled

25. Select the most appropriate ANTONYM of the underlined word in the following sentence.

I have left it to his <u>discretion</u> to accept or decline my offer.

A. Wisdom
B. Calculation
C. Inattention
D. Judgement

17. A	**18.** A	**19.** D	**20.** D	**21.** A	**22.** D	**23.** B	**24.** A	**25.** C

General Intelligence

26. Select the option figure in which the given figure (X) is embedded as its part (rotation is NOT allowed).

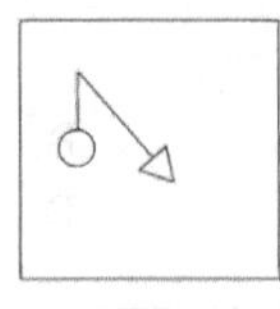

(X)

A. 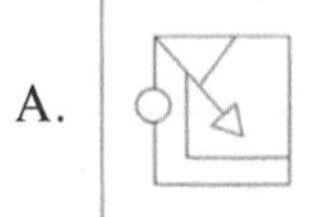 B. 

C. 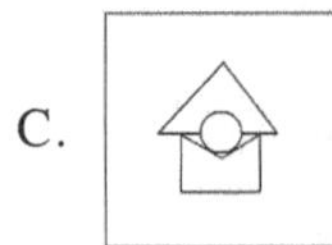 D. 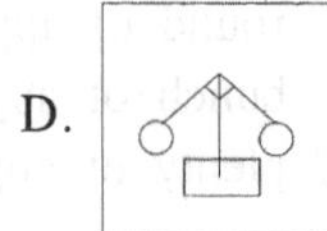

27. Each of the letters in the word FRANCHISE are arranged from left to right in alphabetical order to form a new word. How many letters are there in the English alphabetical series between the alphabet which is fifth from the left and the one which is third from the right in the newly formed word?

A. Seven B. Five
C. Four D. Six

28. CYRF is related to NJCQ in a certain way based on the English alphabetical order. In the same way, GBUM is related to RMFX. To which of the following is CZKP related, following the same logic?

A. NKVA B. NAKV
C. NKAV D. NAVK

29. If 'A' stands for '÷', 'B' stands for '×', 'C' stands for '+' and 'D' stands for '–', then the resultant of which of the following will be 421?

A. 63 B 7 A 125 D 5 C 5
B. 63 A 7 D 125 B 5 C 5
C. 63 B 7 D 125 A 5 C 5
D. 63 C 7 D 125 A 5 B 5

30. In this question, three statements are given, followed by three conclusions numbered I, II and III. Assuming the statements to be true, even if they seem to be at variance with commonly known facts, decide which of the conclusion(s) logically follows/follow from the statements.

Statements:
No rose is an orchid.
All roses are lilies.
All lilies are lotuses.

Conclusions:
I. Some lilies are orchids.
II. Some lotuses are orchids.
III. All lilies are orchids.

A. Both conclusions I and III follow
B. Neither conclusions I, II nor III follows
C. Both conclusions I and II follow
D. Both conclusions II and III follow

31. What would be the Roman numeral on the opposite side of 'V' if the given sheet is folded to form a cube?

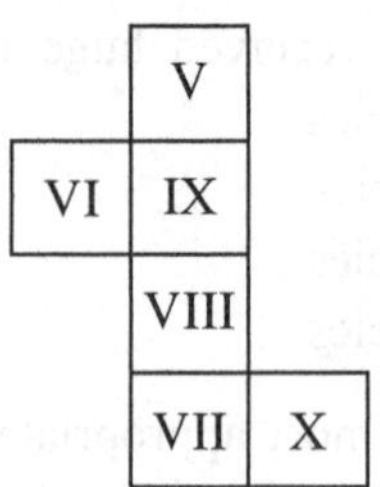

A. VII B. X
C. VIII D. VI

26. A	**27.** B	**28.** A	**29.** C	**30.** B	**31.** C

32. Select the correct mirror image of the given figure when the mirror is placed at AB as shown below.

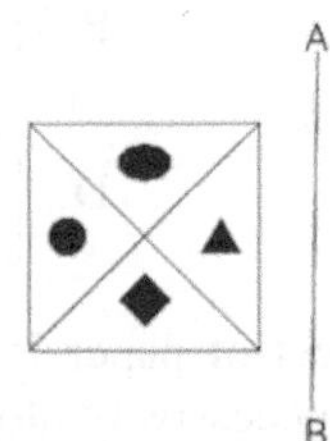

A. 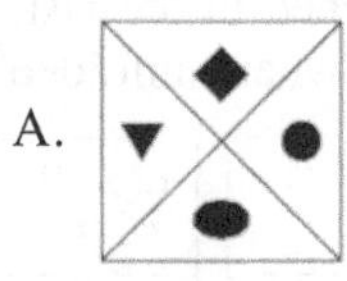

B. 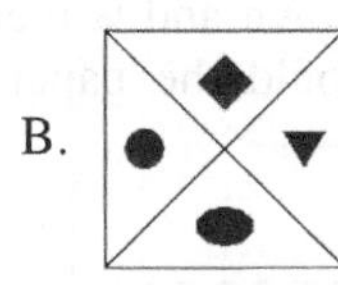

C. 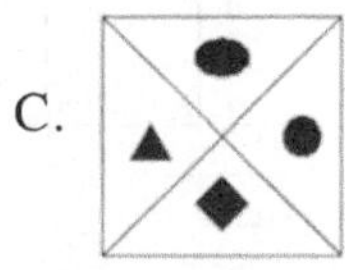

D. 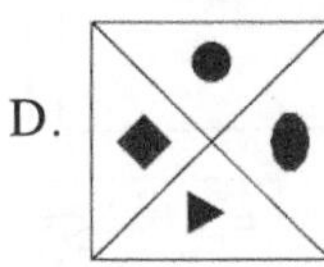

33. What should come in place of ? in the given series based on the English alphabetical order?

QRS MXB IDK EJT ?

A. PCA B. CPA
C. APC D. AAC

34. In a certain code language, 'mix jaggery well' is written as 'rb co ot' and 'well done boss' is written as 'cx rb op'. How is 'well' written in the given language?

A. co B. cx
C. ot D. rb

35. Find the number of triangles in the given figure:

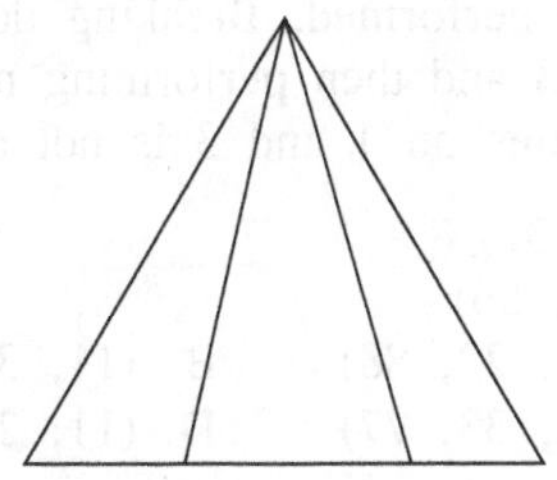

A. 8 B. 6
C. 4 D. 5

36. Which of the following letter-clusters can replace the question mark (?) in the given series to make it logically complete?

JMD, OHJ, ? , YXV, DSB

A. RST B. AOZ
C. TCP D. VCP

37. What should come in place of the question mark (?) in the given series?

86, 88, 90, 92, 94, ?

A. 99 B. 96
C. 97 D. 98

38. 78 is related to 30 following a certain logic. Following the same logic, 67 is related to 26.

To which of the following is 54 related, following the same logic?

A. 18 B. 20
C. 16 D. 28

39. What will come in the place of the question mark (?) in the following equation, if '+' and '−' are interchanged and '×' and '÷' are interchanged?

$125 \div 5 + 19 - 190 \times 19 = ?$

A. 606 B. 636
C. 616 D. 626

40. In a certain language, 'protect your health' is written as 'Df Bk Tu' and 'health is wealth' is written as 'Po Tu Le'. How is 'health' written in the given language?

A. Df B. Po
C. Bk D. Tu

41. IJLO is related to GHJM in a certain way based on the English alphabetical order. In the same way, HIKN is related to FGIL. To which of the following is EFHK related, following the same logic?

A. CEDI B. CDFI
C. CDEF D. CEFI

32. C	33. C	34. D	35. B	36. C	37. B	38. A	39. C	40. D	41. B

42. Three of the following four are alike in a certain way and thus form a group. Which is the one that does NOT belong to that group?

(Note: The odd one out is not based on the number of consonants/vowels or their position in the letter cluster.)

A. UXY B. JMN
C. DGH D. ORT

43. What will come in the place of the question mark (?) in the following equation, if '+' and '–' are interchanged and '×' and '÷' are interchanged?

$87 \div 3 + 35 - 88 \times 11 = ?$

A. 231 B. 233
C. 234 D. 232

44. If 25 August 2006 was Friday, then what was the day of the week on 25 August 2018?

A. Saturday B. Sunday
C. Thursday D. Wednesday

45. Identify the figure given in the options that when put in place of the question mark (?) will logically complete the series.

O	T	L	B	
B L T	4 B L	C 4 B	↑ C 4	?
4	C	↑	D	

A. 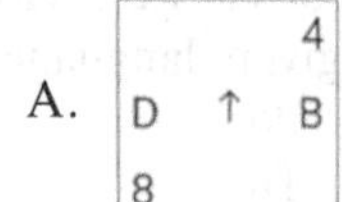
B. 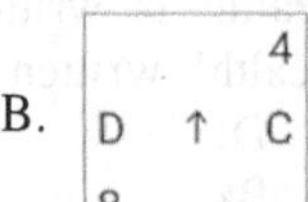
C. 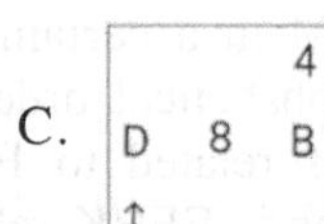
D. 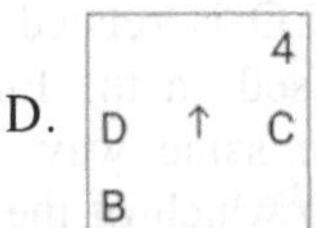

46. Which of the following numbers will replace the question mark (?) in the given series?

$\left[\frac{5}{9}\right], \left[\frac{14}{9}\right], \left[\frac{23}{9}\right], \left[\frac{32}{9}\right], \left[\frac{41}{9}\right], ?$

A. $\left[\frac{44}{9}\right]$ B. $\left[\frac{51}{9}\right]$
C. $\left[\frac{47}{9}\right]$ D. $\left[\frac{50}{9}\right]$

47. A square sheet of paper is folded along the dotted line successively along the directions shown and is then punched in the last. How would the paper look when unfolded?

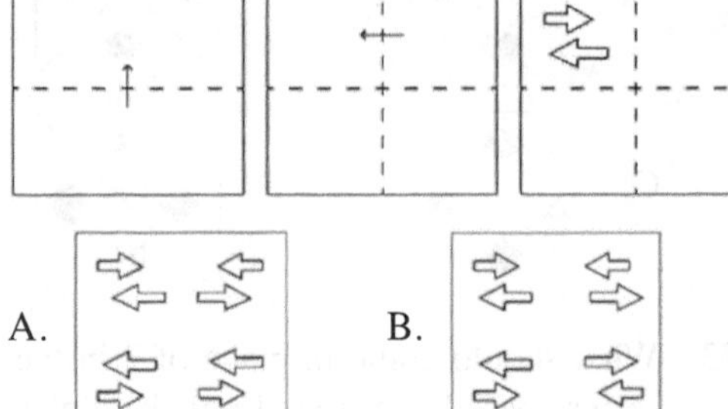

A. B.

C. 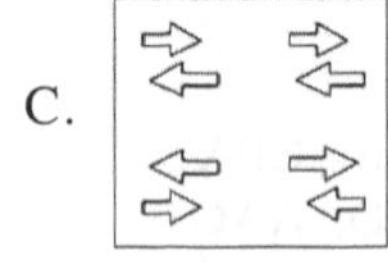
D. 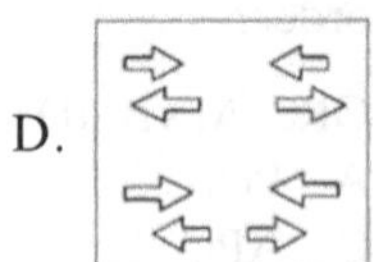

48. Select the set in which the numbers are related in the same way as are the numbers of the following sets.

(NOTE: Operations should be performed on the whole numbers, without breaking down the numbers into their constituent digits. E.g. 13 – Operations on 13 such as adding/subtracting/multiplying etc. to 13 can be performed. Breaking down 13 into 1 and 3 and then performing mathematical operations on 1 and 3 is not allowed.)

(4, 8, 32)
(7, 14, 56)

A. (11, 22, 88) B. (11, 33, 88)
C. (11, 33, 77) D. (11, 22, 77)

42. D	43. C	44. A	45. B	46. D	47. B	48. A

49. In a certain code language,

A % B means 'A is the mother of B'

A # B means 'A is the brother of B'

A @ B means 'A is the wife of B'

A & B means 'A is the father of B'

Based on the above, how is P related to T if 'P & Q % R # S @ T'?

A. Wife's father
B. Wife's mother's father
C. Wife's mother's brother
D. Wife's brother

50. What would be the letter on the opposite side of 'P' if the given sheet is folded to form a cube?

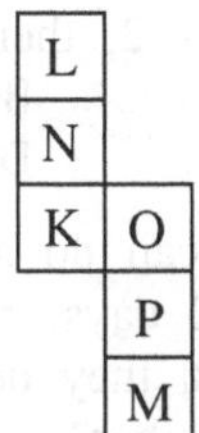

A. L B. N
C. M D. K

Quantitative Aptitude

51. The following bar graph represents the total number of students enrolled and the number of students who got campus placement in six different engineering colleges A, B, C, D, E, and F. Study the graph carefully and answer the question given below:

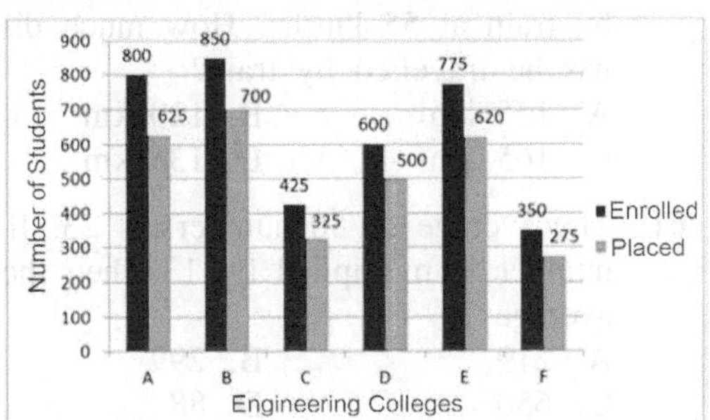

What per cent (correct up to two decimal places) of total enrolled students have got campus placements in colleges A, C, and F?

A. 86.67% B. 77.78%
C. 82.78% D. 79.67%

52. The following table gives the percentage of marks obtained by seven students in six different subjects in an examination.

The numbers in the brackets give the maximum marks in each subject.

Student	Subject (Max. Marks)					
	Maths	Chemistry	Physics	Geography	History	Computer Science
	(150)	(130)	(120)	(100)	(60)	(40)
Ayush	90	50	90	60	70	80
Aman	100	80	80	40	80	70
Sajal	90	60	70	70	90	70
Rohit	80	65	80	80	60	60
Muskan	80	65	85	95	50	90
Tanvi	70	75	65	85	40	60
Tarun	65	35	50	77	80	80

How many students secured a raw score of 135 in Maths?

A. 0 B. 2
C. 1 D. 3

53. If L is the mid-point of side BC of Δ ABC and the area of Δ ABL is 15 cm^2, then the area (in sq cm) of Δ ABC is:

A. 32 B. 30
C. 27 D. 25

49. B	**50.** B	**51.** B	**52.** B	**53.** B

54. In ΔABC, D and E are points on sides AB and AC, such that DE || BC. If AD = x, DB = $x - 3$, AE = $x + 3$ and EC = $x - 2$, then the value of x is:

A. 5.2 B. 4.0
C. 4.5 D. 4.2

55. X, Y and Z can do a work in 24 days, 5 days and 12 days, respectively. In how many days can they do the same work if they work together?

A. 4 days B. $3\frac{1}{13}$ days
C. $\frac{1}{24}$ days D. $\frac{7}{24}$ days

56. If $\frac{15}{8}+\left[\left\{\frac{4}{5}\text{ of }\frac{5}{12}\div\left(1\frac{1}{15}\right)\right\}\times 1\frac{7}{12}\right]$ is expressed in the form of $\frac{a}{b}$ where a and b are integers and relatively prime to each other, the value $4b - a$ is:

A. 313 B. 225
C. 164 D. 189

57. If the price of a commodity is increased by 36%, by what percentage (rounded off to 1 decimal place) should its consumption be decreased so that the expenditure of the commodity stays the same?

A. 26.5% B. 36%
C. 29.5% D. 32%

58. In an obtuse-angled triangle ABC, the length of its longest side AB is 50 cm and one of the other two sides is 42 cm. If the area of the triangle is 294 cm^2, what is the length (in cm) of its third side?

A. $8\sqrt{35}$ B. $15\sqrt{21}$
C. $2\sqrt{58}$ D. $12\sqrt{43}$

59. The given chart represents the sales of automobiles in India (by type, in million units) from the year 2011 to 2014.

Study the chart and answer the question that follows.

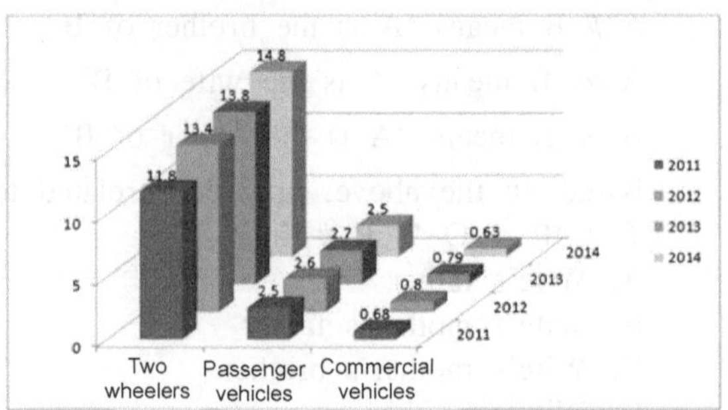

The percentage increase in the sales in 2013 over the previous year was the maximum for which of the categories of vehicles?

A. Two wheelers
B. Commercial vehicles
C. Passenger vehicles
D. Two wheelers and Passenger vehicles

60. Tom travelled 285 km in 6 hours. In his total travelling, he travelled the first part by bus at 40 km/hr and the remaining part by train at 55 km/hr. How much distance has he travelled by train?

A. 155 km B. 120 km
C. 165 km D. 135 km

61. The average of 50 numbers is 23. If each number is multiplied by 13, then the new average is:

A. 219 B. 299
C. 650 D. 88

62. What should be added to each term of the ratio 5 : 11 so that the ratio becomes 3 : 5?

A. 6 B. 4
C. 2 D. 5

63. A cylindrical candle, 14 cm in diameter and length 2 cm is melted to form a cuboid candle dimensions 7 cm × 11 cm × 2 cm. How many cuboidal candles can be obtained?

A. 4 B. 5
C. 2 D. 3

54. C	**55.** B	**56.** A	**57.** A	**58.** C	**59.** C	**60.** C	**61.** B	**62.** B	**63.** C

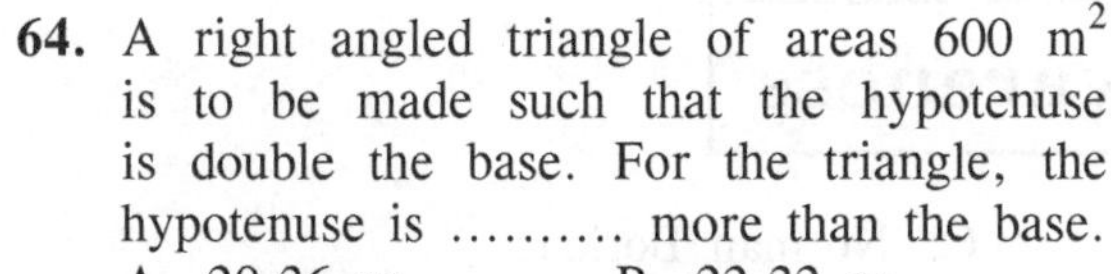

64. A right angled triangle of areas 600 m^2 is to be made such that the hypotenuse is double the base. For the triangle, the hypotenuse is .... more than the base.
A. 20.36 m B. 22.32 m
C. 24.36 m D. 26.32 m

65. How much simple interest will ₹ 5,000 earn in 14 months at a 12% interest rate per annum?
A. ₹ 600 B. ₹ 800
C. ₹ 700 D. ₹ 500

66. Refer to the bar graph below and answer the question that follows.

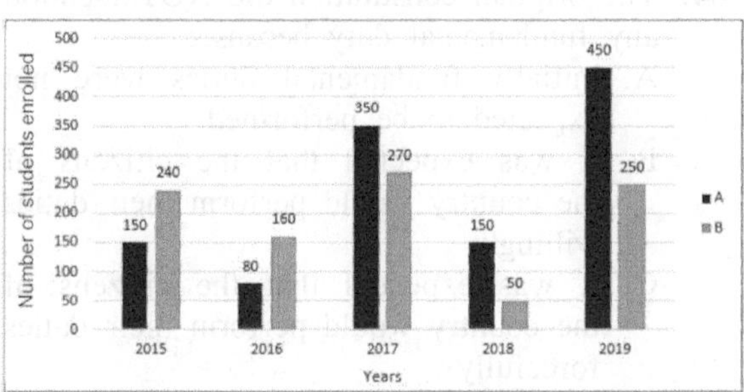

What is the difference between the number of students enrolled in Institute A in 2015 and 2017 and that in Institute B in 2016, 2018 and 2019?
A. 40 B. 150
C. 75 D. 100

67. If 10% of 24% of x is 240, then x = ?
A. 100 B. 1000
C. 10000 D. 100000

68. If tan A + sin A = x, tan A – sin A = y, what is the value of $x^2 - y^2$?
A. $\sqrt[2]{\frac{x}{y}}$ B. $\sqrt[4]{\frac{x}{y}}$
C. $\sqrt{xy}$ D. $\sqrt[4]{xy}$

69. The number 611611611611 is:
(*a*) divisible by both 6 and 11
(*b*) neither divisible by 6 nor by 11
(*c*) divisible by 6 only
(*d*) divisible by 11 only
A. (*d*) B. (*c*)
C. (*b*) D. (*a*)

70. My father is presently 25 years older than me. The sum of our ages 5 years ago was 39 years. Find my present age.
A. 13 years B. 12 years
C. 15 years D. 20 years

71. An election was held between two candidates. The winning candidate scored 54% of the valid votes and won by 88 votes. If 58 votes were declared invalid, then find the total number of votes polled in the election.
A. 1850 B. 1158
C. 1156 D. 2000

72. The salary of employees in a factory was reduced by 20% due to economic crisis. In order to have their salary back to original amount, it must be raised by:
A. 20% B. 12.5%
C. 40% D. 25%

73. What is the area (in square units) of the sector if the radius of the circle is given to be 24 units and the arc length is 7.5 units?
A. 135 B. 180
C. 45 D. 90

74. The volume of rectangular block is 12288 m^3. Its dimension are in the ratio of 4 : 3 : 2. If the entire surface is polished at the rate 2 paise per m^2, then find the total cost of polishing.
A. ₹ 33.28 B. ₹ 44.42
C. ₹ 66.56 D. ₹ 11.14

75. The marked price of a table lamp is ₹ 2,165. During the festive season, it is sold for ₹ 1,710.35. Find the percentage discount offered.
A. 21% B. 20.5%
C. 18% D. 22.5%

64. D	**65.** C	**66.** A	**67.** C	**68.** D	**69.** A
70. B	**71.** B	**72.** D	**73.** D	**74.** C	**75.** A

General Awareness

76. Which of the following is the fastest way to open the Help window in Microsoft Word?
A. Type 'help' in the search bar and then, press Enter
B. Click the Microsoft Office button and then, click Help
C. Press F1
D. Click the Help button on the ribbon

77. Which star is also known as the 'Pole Star'?
A. The West star B. The South star
C. The North star D. The East star

78. According to Census 2011, which union territory recorded the highest female literacy rate in India?
A. Delhi B. Lakshadweep
C. Chandigarh D. Puducherry

79. In Equestrian sports, ______ occurs when a horse or rider lowers an element of a jump that establishes the height of an obstacle.
A. canter B. curb
C. clean round D. knockdown

80. Which group of states was concentrated in the cotton production in the early years to develop textile industry?
A. West Bengal and Odisha
B. Bihar and West Bengal
C. Maharashtra and Gujarat
D. Punjab and Haryana

81. Which of the following hills is located in the Eastern-most part of India?
A. Patkai Bum Hills B. Jaintia Hills
C. Khasi Hills D. Garo Hills

82. Who among the following is NOT associated with the Green Revolution?
A. M.S. Swaminathan
B. P. Chidambaram
C. Norman Borlaug
D. Chidambaram Subramaniam

83. Who among the following is related to Hindustani classical singing?
A. Mallikarjun Mansur
B. Srinavasa Iyer
C. Aruna Sairam
D. Ramanuj Iyengar

84. The original constitution did NOT mention any fundamental duty because:
A. initially fundamental duties were not expected to be performed
B. it was expected that the citizens of the country would perform their duties willingly
C. it was expected that the citizens of the country would perform their duties forcefully
D. initially fundamental duties were punishable as per the constitution

85. Which of the following measures can be adopted by the government to reduce revenue deficit?
A. Offering freebies
B. Increasing subsidies
C. Increasing money supply
D. Tax reforms

86. Every year in the month of February, this camel festival is organised by Rajasthan Tourism Development Corporation in _____.
A. Barmer B. Bikaner
C. Jaisalmer D. Jodhpur

87. MLAs in which of the following states/UTs received an increase of about 66% in salaries and allowances w.e.f. 14 February 2023?
A. Tamil Nadu B. Lakshadweep
C. Delhi D. Bihar

76. C	**77.** C	**78.** B	**79.** D	**80.** C	**81.** A
82. B	**83.** A	**84.** B	**85.** D	**86.** B	**87.** C

88. From which book is the national song of India compiled?
A. Anandmath
B. Mandukya Upanishad
C. Katha Upanishad
D. Bharat Bharti

89. With reference to 'Saila dance' consider the following statements and select the correct option.
(*a*) A group comprising of male performers.
(*b*) The dance is performed with bamboo sticks.
(*c*) It is performed after the cutting of crops.
A. (*a*), (*b*), (*c*) B. Both (*b*) and (*c*)
C. Both (*a*) and (*c*) D. Both (*a*) and (*b*)

90. Who was the first person to conduct a systematic study of chromosomes during division and called this process mitosis?
A. Friedrich Miescher
B. Thomas Hunt Morgan
C. Antonie van Leeuwenhoek
D. Walther Flemming

91. In cricket, a fast, head-high delivery of the ball is referred to as ______.
A. grubber B. leg-bye
C. duck D. bouncer

92. According to the Census of India 2011, which of the following states has the largest Buddhist population?
A. Uttar Pradesh B. Maharashtra
C. Madhya Pradesh D. West Bengal

93. Who captained India to victory in the 2011 Cricket World Cup final win over Sri Lanka?
A. Sourav Ganguly
B. Mahendra Singh Dhoni
C. Sachin Tendulkar
D. Rahul Dravid

94. Which function is used to calculate the maximum value in a selected column in MS Excel?
A. Auto max B. High
C. Max D. Auto high

95. Which British colonel is remembered as the Butcher of Amritsar for his role in the Jallianwala Bagh massacre in 1919?
A. Reginald Dyer
B. Robert Clive
C. William Birdwood
D. William Slim

96. Thee 42nd Constitutional Amendment Act of Indian Constitution was passed in the year:
A. 1976 B. 1977
C. 1978 D. 1979

97. In which of the following liquids would anthracene dissolve easily?
A. Benzene B. Sodium chloride
C. Methane D. Water

98. In March 2023, the Uttarakhand government had approved how much horizontal reservation for statehood activists in state government jobs?
A. 10% B. 15%
C. 8% D. 5%

99. The Press and Registration of Books (PRB) Act was enacted in which year?
A. 1887 B. 1877
C. 1867 D. 1857

100. Who amongst the following Delhi Sultanate rulers sent his army under Malik Kafur's command to conquer South India?
A. Ghiyas-ud-din Balban
B. Iltutmish
C. Alauddin Khilji
D. Qutub-al-din Aibak

88. A	**89.** A	**90.** D	**91.** D	**92.** B	**93.** B	**94.** C
95. A	**96.** A	**97.** A	**98.** A	**99.** C	**100.** C	

Explanatory Answers

1. **(D):** The error in option D, "Geeta was working now," is due to the incorrect use of the present progressive tense "was working" in conjunction with "now," which typically requires the simple present or present continuous tense without a past form. A more appropriate construction would be "Geeta is working now," aligning the tense with the immediacy implied by "now."

2. **(C):** The segment "among you is to baked the" contains a grammatical error in the form of the verb "baked," which is incorrectly used in its past participle form. The correct form should be the infinitive "bake," following the construction "is to + base form of the verb," making the correct phrase "among you is to bake the."

3. **(C):** "They quite meet each other" is grammatically incorrect because the adverb "quite" does not properly modify the verb "meet" in this context. "Quite" is typically used to modify adjectives or other adverbs and is not used in standard English to directly modify verbs in this way. The sentence would be correct if transformed into "They meet each other quite often" or using another modifier appropriate for the verb.

4. **(D):** The error in "does not likes" is due to the incorrect verb form. With the auxiliary "does," the main verb should be in the base form; hence, the correct form is "like," making the correct phrase "does not like."

5. **(B):** "Will be" is the most appropriate modal verb for this blank, indicating a future certainty or planned action regarding the teachers being given opportunities. This aligns with the typical use of "will" to express decisions and promises about the future.

6. **(D):** "Will be" correctly suggests a future certainty or expectation that each teacher is expected to participate in professional development activities. It is used here to denote a definitive obligation or policy.

7. **(A):** The preposition "by" is correctly used to indicate the agent or cause in passive constructions. Here, it fits to show that the teachers' participation in CPD opportunities is driven by their own interests.

8. **(B):** "Systematically" fits properly to describe the manner in which CPD opportunities will cover the various pedagogies. It implies a thorough, methodical approach to the inclusion of new teaching methods in the program.

9. **(B):** "Such as" is the correct conjunction to introduce examples. It is used to specify instances like "experiential learning, arts-integrated, sports-integrated and storytelling-based approaches," following the introduction of the general category of CPD opportunities.

10. **(A):** The antonym of "abundant," which means plentiful or in large quantities, is "deficient," indicating a lack or shortage. This contrasts directly with the idea of abundance, making it the appropriate antonym.

11. **(B):** "Revolution" typically refers to a drastic and significant change or the movement in a circular path. "Gyration," which means the act of rotating or whirling, closely aligns with the second meaning, making it a synonym in the context of movement.

12. (D): "Ghastly" means causing great horror or fear; something that is unpleasant or shocking. The antonym "pleasant" directly opposes this, as it refers to something enjoyable and agreeable.

13. (A): "Took of" is incorrect and likely a typographical error for "took off," but in the context of removing something like a book from a box, the correct phrase is "took out," which means to remove or extract from a place.

14. (B): The spelling error is in "be wreked," where "wreked" should be spelled as "wrecked." The correction is necessary to conform to standard spelling conventions.

15. (B): "Bury the hatchet" is an idiom meaning to make peace with someone or settle differences, fitting the situation where two schools decide to end their rivalry and collaborate.

16. (B): "Jack of all trades" refers to a person who is competent in many skills but not necessarily outstanding in any particular one, which is perfectly described by Option B.

17. (A): "Later about" does not make sense contextually or grammatically. The correct phrase, "loiter around," means to hang around a place idly or without any serious intent, fitting the sentence's warning against such behaviour.

18. (A): The antonym of "compulsory," which means required or mandatory, is "optional," indicating something that is not obligatory but rather left to personal choice or discretion.

19. (D): The correct phrase to use when expressing preference between two options is "prefer [first option] to [second option]." Thus, "to eating out" is the appropriate substitution for "from eating out," making the sentence grammatically correct as "Well, I prefer eating at home to eating out."

20. (D): The correct spelling of the word referring to open positions or opportunities is "Vacancies." This conforms to standard English spelling rules, differentiating it from the incorrect alternatives presented.

21. (A): "Unsettled," which implies being nervous or not calm, has an antonym in "confident," which describes a state of being self-assured and stable. This directly contrasts with the sense of insecurity or nervousness implied by "unsettled."

22. (D): "Candid" means being truthful and straightforward, often in a refreshingly honest way. The synonym "honest" directly aligns with this definition, reflecting a similar meaning of openness and sincerity.

23. (B): A "round of applause" is a common phrase used to describe a form of applause that is given by an entire audience, typically in a circular or unanimous manner, indicating approval or praise. This phrase fits contextually and is widely recognized as the standard expression.

24. (A): "Experienced" refers to someone who has a lot of knowledge or skill in a particular area due to having done something frequently over a period of time. "Seasoned" is a synonym, indicating a person who has gained proficiency through long experience, which applies well to the surgeon described.

25. (C): "Discretion" means the freedom to decide what should be done in a particular situation. Its antonym would be "inattention," which implies a lack of consideration or disregard, contrasting directly with the thoughtful and deliberate nature of discretion.

27. (B): Given Word : FRANCHISE

Now, arranging the word in alphabetical order:

Word	F	R	A	N	C	H	I	S	E
Alphabetical order	A	C	E	F	H	I	N	R	S

Now, after arranged in alphabetical order the letter which is fifth from the left is: 'H', and the one which is third from the right is: 'N'.

In the English alphabetical series there are five letter between 'H' and 'N' i.e., 'I', 'J', 'K', 'L', 'M'.

Hence, correct option is (B).

28. (A): Given,

C Y R F
+11↓ +11↓ +11↓ +11↓
N J C Q

and

G B U M
+11↓ +11↓ +11↓ +11↓
R M F X

Similarly,

C Z K P
+11↓ +11↓ +11↓ +11↓
N K V A

Hence, CZKP related to NKVA as same logic.

29. (C): 63 B 7 D 125 A 5 C 5

After substituting the given symbols, the new expression will be:

$63 \times 7 - 125 \div 5 + 5$

$= 441 - 25 + 5 = 441 - 20 = 421.$

33. (C):

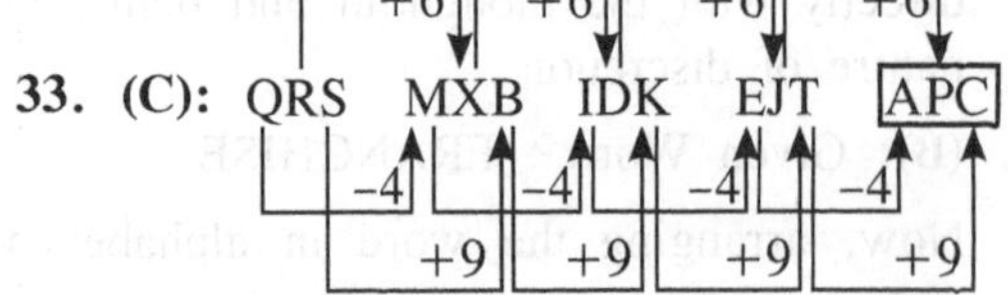

Hence, APC will come at the place of question mark.

36. (C):

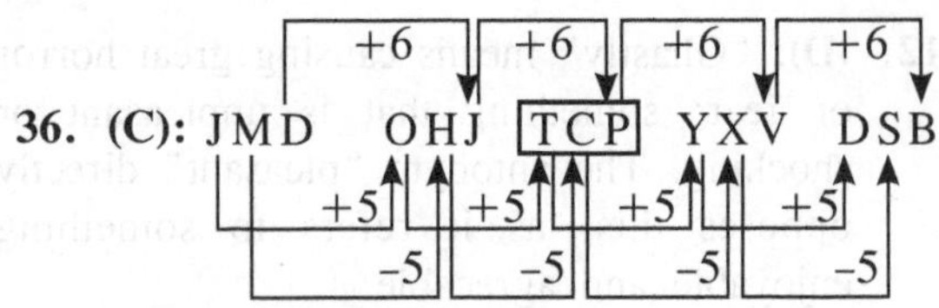

Hence, TCP will come at the place of question mark.

37. (B): 86 88 90 92 94 96
+2 +2 +2 +2 +2

Hence, 96 will come at the place of question mark.

38. (A): Given,

$78 \Rightarrow 7 + 8 = 15 \times 2 = 30$

and

$67 \Rightarrow 6 + 7 = 13 \times 2 = 26$

Similarly,

$54 \Rightarrow 5+4 = 9 \times 2 = 18$

Hence, 54 is related to 18.

39. (C): Given,

$125 \div 5 + 19 - 190 \times 19 = ?$

After interchanging,

$125 \times 5 - 19 + 190 \div 19 = ?$

$\Rightarrow 625 - 19 + 10 = ?$

$\Rightarrow 625 - 9 = ?$

$\Rightarrow ? = 616$

Hence, 616 will come at the place of question mark.

41. (B): Given,

I J L O
−2↓ −2↓ −2↓ −2↓
G H J M

and

H I K N
−2↓ −2↓ −2↓ −2↓
F G I L

Similarly,

E F H K

–2 ↓ –2 ↓ –2 ↓ –2 ↓

C D F I

Hence, EFHK is related to CDFI following the same logic.

42. (D): Checking options:

(A) U X Y

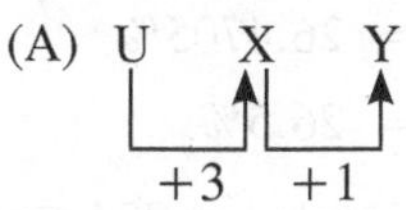

+3 +1

(B) J M N

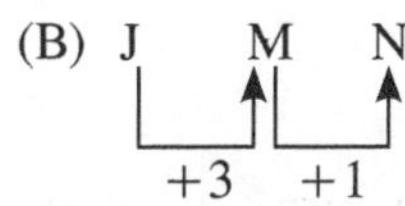

+3 +1

(C) D G H

+3 +1

(D) O R T

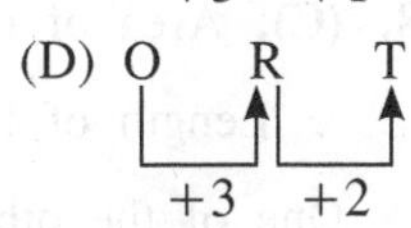

+3 +2

Hence, option (D), ORT is odd.

43. (C): Given,

87 ÷ 3 + 35 – 88 × 11 = ?

After interchanging,

87 × 3 – 35 + 88 ÷ 11 = ?

⇒ 261 – 35 + 8 = ?

⇒ 269 – 35 = ?

⇒ ? = 234

Hence, 234 will come at the place of question mark.

44. (A): Total number of days = 4383

365 × 12 + 3 days = 4383

$$4383 \div 7 = 626\frac{1}{7}$$

No. of odd days = 1

Hence, the day on 25 August 2018 was Saturday.

46. (D): $\left[\frac{5}{9}\right], \left[\frac{14}{9}\right], \left[\frac{23}{9}\right], \left[\frac{32}{9}\right], \left[\frac{41}{9}\right], \left[\frac{50}{9}\right]$

+1 +1 +1 +1 +1

Hence, $\left[\frac{50}{9}\right]$ will come at the place of question mark.

48. (A): Given, 4 8 32

×2 ×4

and 7 14 56

×2 ×4

Similarly, 11 22 88

×2 ×4

51. (B): Required %

$$= \frac{1225}{1575} \times 100 = 77.777 = 77.78\%$$

52. (B): Ayush = 90% of 150 = $\frac{90}{100} \times 150 = 135$

Sajal = 90% of 150 = $\frac{90}{100} \times 150 = 135$

Hence, required no. of students = 2.

53. (B):

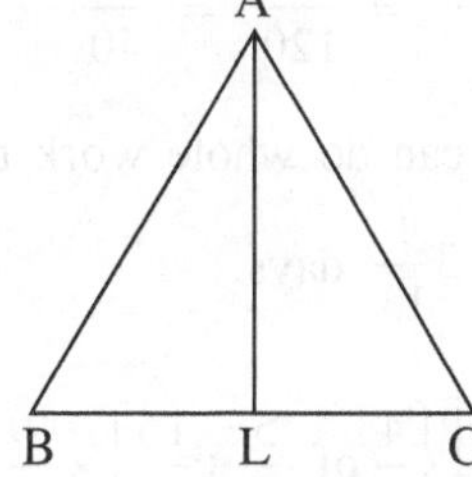

∵ AL is median of Δ ABC

∴ ar Δ ABL = ar Δ ACL

ar Δ ABL = 15 cm^2

∴ area of Δ ABC = 15 × 2 = 30 cm^2.

54. (C):

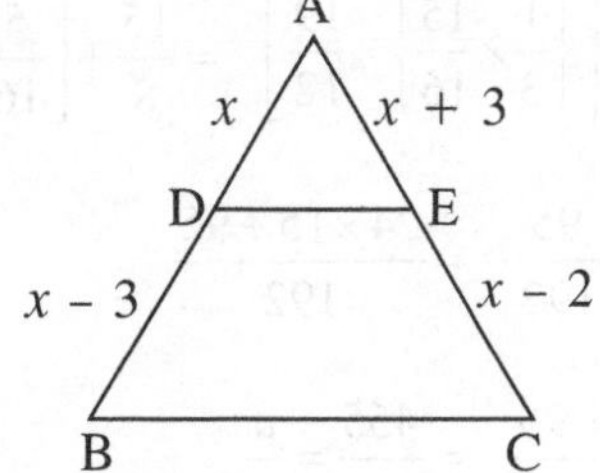

∵ DE || BC

$$\therefore \frac{AD}{DB} = \frac{AE}{EC}$$

$$\Rightarrow \frac{x}{x-3} = \frac{x+3}{x-2}$$

$$\Rightarrow x^2 - 2x = x^2 - 9$$

$$\Rightarrow 2x = 9$$

$$\Rightarrow x = \frac{9}{2} = 4.5.$$

55. (B): X's 1 day work $= \frac{1}{24}$

Y's 1 day work $= \frac{1}{5}$

Z's 1 day work $= \frac{1}{12}$

(X + Y + Z)'s 1 day work $= \frac{1}{24}+\frac{1}{5}+\frac{1}{12}$

$$= \frac{5+24+10}{120} = \frac{39}{120} = \frac{13}{40}$$

Hence, they can do whole work together in $\frac{40}{13}$ days $= 3\frac{1}{13}$ days.

56. (A): $\because \frac{15}{8}+\left[\left\{\frac{4}{5} \text{ of } \frac{5}{12} \div \frac{16}{15}\right\} \times \frac{19}{12}\right]$

$$= \frac{15}{8}+\left[\left\{\frac{4}{5}\times\frac{5}{12}\div\frac{16}{15}\right\}\times\frac{19}{12}\right]$$

$$= \frac{15}{8}+\left[\left\{\frac{1}{3}\times\frac{15}{16}\right\}\times\frac{19}{12}\right] = \frac{15}{8}+\left[\frac{5}{16}\times\frac{19}{12}\right]$$

$$= \frac{15}{8}+\frac{95}{192} = \frac{24\times15+95}{192}$$

$$= \frac{360+95}{192} = \frac{455}{192} = \frac{a}{b}$$

$\therefore$ Value of $4b - a = 4 \times 192 - 455$

$= 768 - 455 = 313.$

57. (A): Price increase % = 36%

To stay remain in expenditure of the commodity, consumption should be decreased by

$$= \left(\frac{100\times36}{100+36}\right)$$

$$= \frac{100\times36}{136}$$

$= 26.4705\%$

$= 26.5\%.$

58. (C): Area of the triangle $= 294 \text{ cm}^2$

$\because$ Length of longest side = 50 cm

One of the other two sides = 42 cm

Let third side $= 2\sqrt{58}$ cm $= \sqrt{4\times58}$

$= \sqrt{232} = 15.23$ cm

Now, $S = \frac{a+b+c}{2}$

$$= \frac{50+42+15.23}{2} = \frac{107.23}{2}$$

$= 53.62$ cm

Area of triangle $= \sqrt{s(s-a)(s-b)(s-c)}$

$$= \sqrt{53.62(53.62-50)(53.62-42)(53.62-15.23)}$$

$$= \sqrt{53.62\times3.62\times11.62\times38.39}$$

$$= \sqrt{86588.38}$$

$= 294.25 \text{ cm}^2$

Hence, third side of triangle $= 2\sqrt{58}$ cm.

60. (C): Let Tom travelled by bus for t_1 hrs. and by train for t_2 hrs.

$\because$ $t_1 = \frac{x}{40}$

and $t_2 = \frac{285-x}{55}$

$\therefore$ $t_1 + t_2 = 6$ hrs.

$\therefore \frac{x}{40}+\frac{285-x}{55}=6$

$\Rightarrow \frac{11x+8(285-x)}{440}=6$

$\Rightarrow 11x + 2280 - 8x = 440 \times 6 = 2640$

$\Rightarrow 3x = 2640 - 2280 = 360$

$\Rightarrow x = 120$ km

Hence, distance travelled by train

$= 285 - 120 = 165$ km.

61. (B): Total number $= 50 \times 23 = 1150$

Required new average $= \frac{1150\times13}{50}$

$= 23 \times 13 = 299.$

62. (B): Let x should be added to each term

$$\frac{5+x}{11+x}=\frac{3}{5}$$

$\Rightarrow 25 + 5x = 33 + 3x$

$\Rightarrow 2x = 33 - 25$

$\Rightarrow 2x = 8$

$\therefore x = 4.$

63. (C): $r = 7$ cm

Required no. of cuboidal candles

$= \frac{\text{Volume of cylinder}}{\text{Volume of each cuboid}} = \frac{\frac{22}{7}\times7\times7\times2}{7\times11\times2}$

$= 2.$

64. (D): A

(Right triangle ABC, right angle at B; AB = y, BC = x, AC = h)

$\because h^2 = x^2 + y^2$

Now, $h = 2x$

$\therefore (2x)^2 = x^2 + y^2$

$\Rightarrow 4x^2 - x^2 = y^2$

$\Rightarrow 3x^2 = y^2$

$\Rightarrow \sqrt{3}x = y$

Area of triangle $= \frac{1}{2}xy = 600$

$\Rightarrow \frac{1}{2}(x)\left(\sqrt{3}x\right)=600$

$\Rightarrow \sqrt{3}x^2 = 1200$

$\Rightarrow x^2 = \frac{1200}{\sqrt{3}}\times\frac{\sqrt{3}}{\sqrt{3}}=\frac{1200\sqrt{3}}{3}$

$\Rightarrow x^2 = 400\sqrt{3}$

$= 400 \times 1.732$

$= 400\times\frac{1732}{1000}$

$\Rightarrow x^2 = 692.8$

$\Rightarrow x = \sqrt{692.8} = 26.32$

$\therefore 2x = 52.64$

Hence, for the triangle, the hypotenuse is 26.32 m more than the base.

65. (C): S.I. $= \frac{5000\times12\times14}{12\times100} = ₹ 700$

66. (A): Required difference $= 500 - 460 = 40.$

67. (C): $\frac{10}{100}\times\frac{24}{100}x = 240$

$\Rightarrow x = \frac{240\times100\times100}{10\times24} = 10000.$

68. (D): $\because \tan A + \sin A = x$

$\Rightarrow \tan^2 A + \sin^2 A + 2\tan A.\sin A = x^2$ ...(*i*) and, tan A – sin A = y

$\Rightarrow \tan^2 A + \sin^2 A - 2 \tan A.\sin A = y^2$ ...(ii)

(i)-(ii) gives $x^2 - y^2 = 4 \tan A.\sin A$

$$xy = \tan^2 A - \sin^2 A$$

$$= \frac{\sin^2 A}{\cos^2 A} - \sin^2 A$$

$$= \frac{\sin^2 A(1-\cos^2 A)}{\cos^2 A}$$

$$= \frac{\sin^2 A}{\cos^2 A} \times \sin^2 A$$

$$= \tan^2 A.\sin^2 A$$

$\therefore \quad \sqrt{xy} = \tan A.\ \sin A$

Hence, value of $x^2 - y^2 = 4\sqrt{xy}$.

69. (A): Given number = 611611611611

6 + 1 + 1 + 6 + 1 + 1 = 16

1 + 6 + 1 + 1 + 6 + 1 = 16

Difference = 16 – 16 = 0

Then, the given number is divisible by 11.

∵ Last digit is not even

∴ Given number is not divisible by 6

Hence, the given number is divisible by 11 only.

70. (B): Let, my present age = x years

∴ Father's present age = $(x + 25)$ years

5 years ago,

$x - 5 + x + 25 - 5 = 39$

$\Rightarrow 2x + 15 = 39$

$\Rightarrow 2x = 39 - 15 = 24$

$\Rightarrow x = 12$

Hence, my present age = 12 years.

71. (B): 54% of x – 46% of x = 88

$\Rightarrow \frac{8}{100}x = 88$

$\Rightarrow x = 1100$

∵ Number of invalid votes = 58

Hence, total votes polled = 1100 + 58

= 1158

72. (D): Original amount must be raised

$$= \frac{20}{100-20} \times 100 = \frac{20}{80} \times 100 = 25\%.$$

73. (D): $\theta = \frac{l}{r} = \frac{7.5}{24} = \frac{5}{16}$ radian

$$\pi r = 180°$$

$$\frac{5}{16}r = \frac{180}{\pi} \times \frac{5}{16} = \frac{225°}{4\pi}$$

$$\text{Area of sector} = \frac{225}{4\pi \times 360} \times \pi \times 24 \times 24$$

$$= 6 \times 3 \times 5$$

= 90 square units.

74. (C): $4x \times 3x \times 2x = 12288$

$\Rightarrow x^3 = 512$

$\Rightarrow x = 8$

l = 32 m, b = 24 m and h = 16 m

Total surface area = 2(768 + 384 + 512)

$= 2 \times 1664 = 3328 \text{ m}^2$

∵ Cost of 1 m^2 = 2 paise

∴ Cost of 3328 m^2 = ₹ $\frac{2 \times 3328}{100}$ = ₹ $\frac{6656}{100}$

= ₹ 66.56.

75. (A): Discount = 2165 – 1710.35

= ₹ 454.65

$$\text{Discount } \% = \frac{454.65}{2165} \times 100$$

= 21%.

76. (C): Pressing F1 is a universally recognized shortcut for opening the Help window in many software applications, including Microsoft Word. This method provides immediate access to help resources without navigating through menus or typing in search bars.

77. (C): The North Star, also known as Polaris, is widely recognized as the Pole Star. It is very close to the North Celestial Pole, making it an essential celestial marker for navigation in the Northern Hemisphere.

78. (B): According to the 2011 Census of India, Lakshadweep recorded the highest female literacy rate among the Union Territories. This statistic highlights the educational achievements in Lakshadweep compared to other Union Territories.

79. (D): In equestrian sports, a "knockdown" occurs when a horse or rider causes a jump's rail (or another element that establishes the height of an obstacle) to fall. This term accurately describes this specific fault in jumping disciplines.

80. (C): Maharashtra and Gujarat have been key states in the development of India's textile industry, primarily due to their significant cotton production. These states' conducive climate and investment in cotton agriculture have historically supported their leading roles in the textile sector.

81. (A): The Patkai Bum Hills are located in the easternmost part of India, extending along the India-Myanmar border. These hills are part of the larger Patkai range, which forms the boundary between the two countries.

82. (B): P. Chidambaram is not associated with the Green Revolution, which was primarily an agricultural advancement initiative. The Green Revolution in India was significantly influenced by M.S. Swaminathan and others who worked on agricultural improvements, but not P. Chidambaram, who is known for his roles in finance and politics.

83. (A): Mallikarjun Mansur is a renowned figure in Hindustani classical music, specifically known for his exceptional contributions to the Jaipur-Atrauli gharana. His work and performances have left a significant mark on the Hindustani classical music tradition.

84. (B): The original Indian Constitution did not mention any fundamental duties because it was expected that the citizens would perform their duties willingly without the need for specific enumeration in the constitution. This reflects the initial trust in the civic responsibility and moral obligations of the citizens.

85. (D): Tax reforms are a practical measure that can be adopted by the government to reduce revenue deficit. Effective tax reforms can increase government revenue by broadening the tax base, improving tax compliance, and ensuring more efficient tax collection mechanisms, thereby helping to offset the revenue deficit.

86. (B): The camel festival referred to is the Bikaner Camel Festival, organised annually in the city of Bikaner, Rajasthan. This festival is a significant cultural event that showcases the rich traditions of the region, including camel races, camel parades, and various folk performances, attracting tourists and locals alike.

87. (C): The MLAs of Delhi received an increase of about 66% in salaries and allowances effective from 14 February 2023. This adjustment was made to align their compensation with the cost of living and responsibilities held by the MLAs in the capital territory.

88. (A): The national song of India, "Vande Mataram," is compiled from "Anandmath," a novel written by Bankim Chandra Chattopadhyay. This song plays a crucial role in India's national identity and was a source of inspiration during the Indian independence movement.

89. (A): Saila dance includes all three characteristics mentioned: (a) it is performed by a group of male performers, (b) involves dancing with bamboo sticks, and (c) typically occurs after the harvest of crops. This dance form is traditional to certain tribal communities and reflects their cultural practices linked to agricultural cycles.

90. (D): Walther Flemming was the first person to conduct a systematic study of chromosomes during cell division, and he coined the term "mitosis" to describe this process. His work laid the foundations for modern cellular genetics and significantly advanced the understanding of cell biology.

91. (D): In cricket, a "bouncer" is a type of delivery where the ball is bowled fast and reaches the batsman at around head height. This term describes the tactic used by fast bowlers to intimidate batsmen and disrupt their concentration and timing.

92. (B): According to the Census of India 2011, Maharashtra has the largest Buddhist population among Indian states. This significant Buddhist demographic is due in part to the historical influence and modern-day followers of Dr. B.R. Ambedkar, who led a mass conversion to Buddhism in the mid-20th century.

93. (B): Mahendra Singh Dhoni captained the Indian cricket team during the 2011 Cricket World Cup. Under his leadership, India won the final against Sri Lanka, securing their second World Cup victory. Dhoni's decisive six in the closing moments of the game remains one of the most iconic moments in cricket history.

94. (C): In MS Excel, the function used to calculate the maximum value from a range of cells is "MAX". This function can be applied to any group of numbers, and it returns the highest value among them, making it essential for data analysis tasks where determining the greatest numeric value is necessary.

95. (A): Colonel Reginald Dyer is historically remembered as the Butcher of Amritsar due to his role in the Jallianwala Bagh massacre in 1919. He ordered troops to fire on a gathering of unarmed civilians, resulting in a tragic loss of life and marking a significant and brutal event in the history of British India.

96. (A): The 42nd Constitutional Amendment Act, often referred to as the "Mini-Constitution," was passed in 1976. This act brought about extensive changes to the Indian Constitution, including amendments to the preamble and the alteration of numerous constitutional provisions. It was during the Emergency period under Indira Gandhi's government.

97. (A): Anthracene, an organic compound, dissolves easily in non-polar solvents due to its non-polar nature. Benzene, a non-polar solvent, is ideal for dissolving substances like anthracene, which are composed of large polycyclic aromatic hydrocarbons.

98. (A): In March 2023, the Uttarakhand government approved a 10% horizontal reservation for statehood activists in state government jobs. This reservation was intended to acknowledge and reward those who actively participated in movements advocating for the establishment of Uttarakhand as a separate state.

99. (C): The Press and Registration of Books (PRB) Act was enacted in the year 1867. This legislation was designed to regulate the printing and publication of books in India, mandating the registration of all printing presses and books published in the country.

100. (C): Alauddin Khilji, a ruler of the Delhi Sultanate, sent his general Malik Kafur to the southern part of India to extend his empire's territory. This military expedition led to several successful conquests in the region, significantly expanding the reach of the Delhi Sultanate into South India during Khilji's reign.

Previous Years' Paper

SSC—Combined Higher Secondary Level (CHSL : 10 + 2)

Data Entry Operator (DEO)/ Lower Division Clerk (LDC)/ Junior Secretarial Assistant (JSA)

Tier-I, Recruitment Exam-2023

(Exam held on 17-08-2023)

English Language

1. Select the most appropriate synonym of the given word.

Dynamic

A. Famous
B. Halt
C. Innate
D. Energetic

2. Choose the correct meaning of the underlined word in the given sentence.

The museum's archive is a great place to find valuable artifacts such as ancient manuscripts.

A. A collection of essays
B. A room to store lots of books
C. A room to store important official documents
D. A collection of historical documents or records

3. Select the most appropriate ANTONYM of the given word.

Guile

A. Deceit
B. Treachery
C. Honesty
D. Terseness

4. Select the most appropriate homophone to fill in the blank.

Ants ________ food during the summer and save it for winter.

A. horde   B. hoard
C. heard   D. herd

5. The following sentence has been divided into parts. One of them may contain an error. Select the part that contains the error from the given options. If you don't find any error, mark 'No error' as your answer.

A owl was / hooting throughout / the night.

A. A owl was
B. the night
C. No error
D. hooting throughout

6. Select the option that can be used as a one-word substitute for the given group of words.

One who studies the evolution of mankind

A. Anarchist
B. Amateur
C. Anthropologist
D. Antagonist

1. D	2. D	3. C	4. B	5. A	6. C

7. Select the most appropriate ANTONYM for 'redeem' in the given sentence.

Shantanu violated the rules of the college when he started screaming and shouting in the premises.

A. Screaming B. Violated
C. Premises D. Shouting

8. Select the option that can be used as a one-word substitute for the given group of words.

Something to be easily carried or moved

A. Robust B. Stagnant
C. Portable D. Fragile

9. Select the option that can be used as a one-word substitute for the given group of words.

An imagined place or state of things in which everything is perfect

A. Dwarf
B. Utopia
C. Chronology
D. Octogenarian

10. Select the option that can be used as a one-word substitute for the given group of words.

Poor physical or mental condition.

A. Ill nature B. Illicit
C. Ill-fated D. Ill health

11. The following sentence has been split into four segments. Identify the segment that contains a grammatical error.

They were laid / in the sun / the entire morning / till Sudharshan came.

A. till Sudharshan came
B. They were laid
C. the entire morning
D. in the sun

12. Select the correct spelling of the underlined word in the given sentence.

The feeling of weightlessness while skydiving is known to <u>exilarete</u> many people.

A. exilairate B. exhilarete
C. exilarate D. exhilarate

13. Select the option that expresses the given sentence in active voice.

I was never supported by my family.

A. My family have never supported me.
B. My family had never supported me.
C. My family never supported me.
D. My family never supports me.

14. The following sentence has been split into four segments. Identify the segment that contains a spelling error.

The famous author / clearly mentioned / all the names of his friends / in the acknolledgments of the book.

A. in the acknolledgments of the book
B. The famous author
C. clearly mentioned
D. all the names of his friends

15. Select the most appropriate ANTONYM of the given word.

Mean

A. Minute
B. Noble
C. Notorious
D. Novel

16. Select the most appropriate idiom for the underlined segment in the following sentence.

Nitish's promotion is <u>due</u>.

A. On the cards
B. Not worth his salt
C. With due respect
D. Done to death

7. B	8. C	9. B	10. D	11. B	12. D	13. C	14. A	15. B	16. A

17. Parts of a sentence are given below in jumbled order. Select the option that arranges the parts in the correct order to form a meaningful sentence.

(*a*) in social evolution by imitation
(*b*) by reason of its higher standard of living
(*c*) the royal style is the agent
(*d*) and cultural patterns are similarly transmitted by the dominant caste

A. (*c*), (*d*), (*a*), (*b*)
B. (*c*), (*a*), (*d*), (*b*)
C. (*b*), (*c*), (*d*), (*a*)
D. (*b*), (*a*), (*c*), (*d*)

18. Select the option that expresses the following sentence in passive voice.

An agitated gathering of workers in the company disturbed the meeting.

A. Meeting of the company was disturbed.
B. An agitated meeting of workers in the company disturbed the gathering.
C. The meeting was disturbed by an agitated gathering of workers in the company.
D. The gathering agitated the meeting of the company.

19. Select the most appropriate meaning of the given idiom.

Costs an arm and a leg

A. To be affordable
B. To be moderately priced
C. To be free of charge
D. To be very expensive

20. Select the most appropriate option to fill in the blank.

The ________ of the company's CEO was widely praised for her innovative leadership.

A. rein
B. rayne
C. rain
D. reign

Directions (Qs. No. 21-25): *In the following passage, some words have been deleted. Read the passage carefully and select the most appropriate option to fill in each blank.*

Globalisation is not a new _____1_____. Traders travelled vast distances in ancient times to buy commodities that were _____2_____ and expensive for sale in their homelands. The Industrial Revolution brought _____3_____ in transportation and communication in the 19th century that eased trade across borders. The think tank, Peterson Institute for International Economics (PIIE), states globalisation _____4_____ after World War I and nations moved toward _____5_____ as they launched import taxes to more closely guard their industries in the aftermath of the conflict.

21. Select the most appropriate option to fill in blank number 1.

A. power | B. variation
C. design | D. concept

22. Select the most appropriate option to fill in blank number 2.

A. plentiful | B. common
C. preserved | D. rare

23. Select the most appropriate option to fill in blank number 3.

A. chaos | B. advances
C. issues | D. a decline

24. Select the most appropriate option to fill in blank number 4.

A. trooped | B. soared
C. de-escalated | D. stalled

25. Select the most appropriate option to fill in blank number 5.

A. protectionism
B. integration
C. liberalisation
D. diversification

17. B **18.** C **19.** D **20.** D **21.** D **22.** D **23.** B **24.** D **25.** A

General Intelligence

26. A square sheet of paper is folded along the dotted line successively along the directions shown and is then punched in the end. How would the paper look when unfolded?

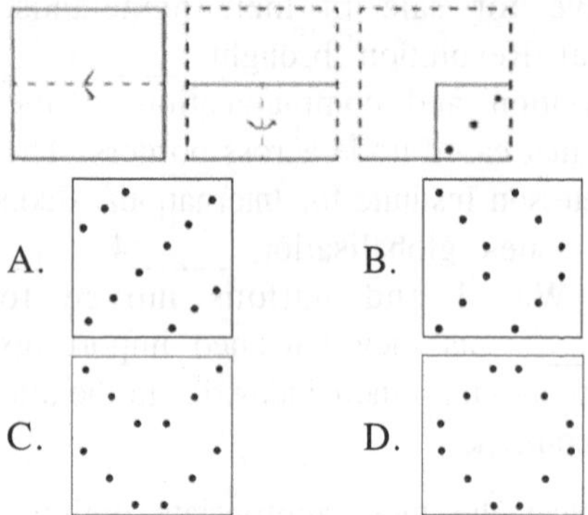

27. Read the given statements and conclusions carefully. Assuming that the information given in the statements is true, even if it appears to be at variance with commonly known facts, decide which of the given conclusions logically follow[s] from the statements.

Statements:
Some houses are trees.
All flowers are houses.
No vegetable is a flower.

Conclusions:
I. Some vegetables are houses is a possibility.
II. Some flowers are trees is a possibility.
III. No vegetable is a house.
A. Both conclusions II and III follow
B. Only conclusion II follows
C. Both conclusions I and II follow
D. Only conclusion III follows

28. If 'A' stands for '÷', 'B' stands for '×', 'C' stands for '+' and 'D' stands for '–', what will come in place of the question mark '?' in the following equation?

4 B 18 D 5 C 9 A 9 = ?

A. 88 B. 58
C. 78 D. 68

29. What will come in the place of '?' in the following equation, if '+' and '–' are interchanged with '÷' and '×' respectively?

88 + 8 – 17 × 16 ÷ 40 = ?

A. 203 B. 197
C. 200 D. 211

30. In a certain code language, 'BALD' is coded as '7680' and 'DRAB' is coded as '8097'. What is the code for 'L' in the given code language?

A. 8 B. 6
C. 0 D. 7

31. Select the combination of letters that when sequentially placed in the blanks of the given series will complete the series.

A_DE FGI_ _LNO PQ_T UV_Y

A. CJKSX B. CJKRW
C. BJKRW D. BJKSX

32. Select the wood-pair that best represents a similar relationship to the one expressed in the pair of words given below. (The words must be considered as meaningful English words and must not be related to each other based on the number of letters/consonant/vowels in the word.)

Heat : Cold

A. Encourage : Motivate
B. Compete : Success
C. Sustain : Persist
D. Demolish : Build

26. D	27. C	28. D	29. D	30. B	31. D	32. D

33. RSPT is related to VWTX in a certain way based on the English alphabetical order. In the same way, MNKO is related to QROS. Which of the following is GHEI related to, following the same logic?

A. KLHI B. KLJM
C. KLIM D. JKHL

34. Three of the following four are alike in a certain way and thus form a group. Which is the one that does NOT belong to that group?

(NOTE: Operations should be performed on the whole numbers, without breaking down the numbers into its constituent digits. E.g. 13- Operations on 13 such as adding/subtracting/multiplying etc. to 13 can be performed. Breaking down 13 into 1 and 3 and then performing mathematical operations on 1 and 3 is not allowed)

A. 2 - 6 B. 4 - 20
C. 5 - 30 D. 8 - 75

35. In a certain code language, 'QUEZAL' is coded as '82' and 'LUCKY' is coded as '72'. What is the code for 'ADVERSE' in the given code language?

A. 68 B. 78
C. 74 D. 62

36. GIEK is related to OQMS in a certain way based on the English alphabetical order. In the same way, KMIO is related to SUQW. To which of the following is EGCI related to following the same logic?

A. MQOK B. MOKQ
C. PRNT D. UWSY

37. The second number in the given number pairs is obtained by performing certain mathematical operations(s) on the first number. The same operation(s) are followed in all the number pairs except one. Find that odd number pair.

A. 5 : 20 B. 4 : 12
C. 7 : 42 D. 6 : 36

38. Based on the alphabetical order, three of the following four letter-clusters are alike in a certain way and thus form a group. Which of the following does NOT belong to that group?

A. WZB B. UWX
C. ORT D. GJL

39. In a certain code language,

A + B means 'A is the sister of B'

A – B means 'A is the husband of B'

A × B means 'A is the son of B'

A ÷ B means 'A is the mother of B'

Based on the above, how is F related to J if 'F × G – H ÷ I + J'?

A. Brother B. Mother's brother
C. Father D. Father's brother

40. If 9 July, 1978 is Sunday, then what will be the day of the week on 19 September 1983?

A. Monday B. Friday
C. Tuesday D. Sunday

41. How many triangles are there in the given figure?

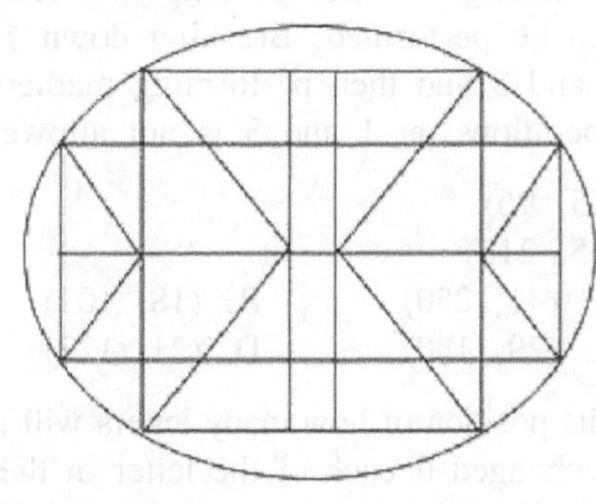

A. 24 B. 28
C. 22 D. 30

33. C	**34.** D	**35.** C	**36.** B	**37.** D	**38.** B	**39.** A	**40.** A	**41.** B

42. N is the brother of X, X is the wife of M, S is the daughter of M, K is the brother of S, P is the mother of N. How is K related to P?

A. Son's son B. Daughter's son
C. Mother's brother D. Sister's son

43. What should come in place of X in the given series?

23 31 47 71 103 X

A. 153 B. 147
C. 150 D. 143

44. Select the number from among the given options that can replace the question mark (?) in the following series.

136, 135, 137, 136, 138, 137, ?

A. 136 B. 140
C. 138 D. 139

45. In the following number-pairs, the second number is obtained by applying certain mathematical operations to the first number. Select the set in which the numbers are related in the same way as are the numbers of the following sets.

(NOTE: Operations should be performed on the whole numbers, without breaking down the numbers into its constituent digits. E.g. 13 - Operations on 13 such as adding/subtracting/multiplying etc. to 13 can be performed. Breaking down 13 into 1 and 3 and then performing mathematical operations on 1 and 3 is not allowed.)

(15, 96)
(35, 216)

A. (41, 250) B. (18, 102)
C. (29, 180) D. (21, 122)

46. The position of how many letters will remain unchanged if each of the letter in the word 'ACQUIRE' is arranged in alphabetical order?

A. Three B. Four
C. Two D. One

47. Select the correct mirror image of the given figure when the mirror is placed at MN as shown.

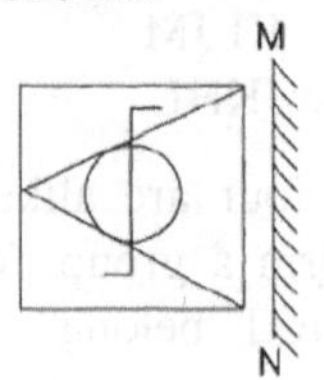

A. 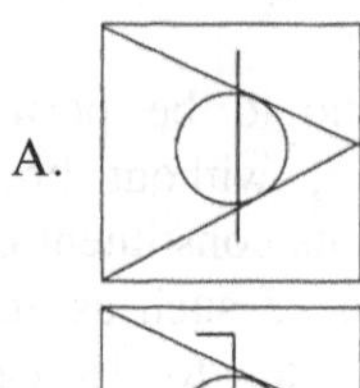
B. 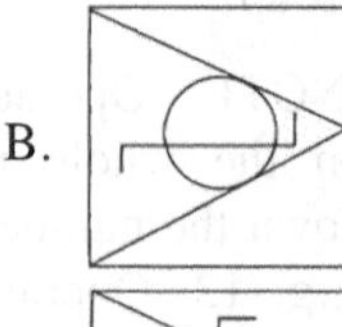
C. 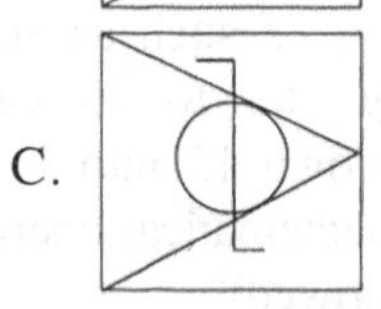
D. 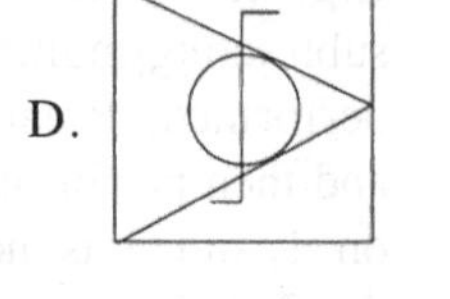

48. Select the combination of letters that when sequentially placed in the blanks of the given series will complete the series.

A_CD_CDAC_AB_ABC

A. AACD B. AABB
C. BBDD D. BDBD

49. Identify the figure given in the options which when put in place of the question mark (?) will logically complete the series.

A. 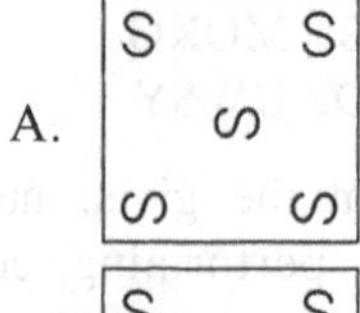
B. 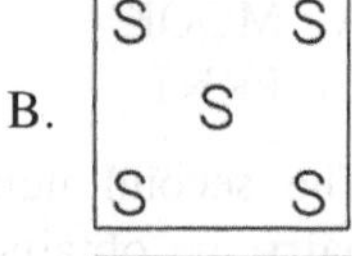
C.
D.

42. B	43. D	44. D	45. C	46. A	47. C	48. C	49. D

50. Select the set in which the numbers are related in the same way as are the numbers of the given sets.

(NOTE: Operations should be performed on the whole numbers, without breaking down the numbers into their constituent digits. E.g. 13—Operations on 13 such as adding/deleting/multiplying etc. to 13 can be performed. Breaking down 13 into 1 and 3 and then performing mathematical operations on 1 and 3 is not allowed.)

11 : 87 : 34

6 : 28 : 8

A. 9 : 25 : 54
B. 7 : 35 : 12
C. 8 : 19 : 47
D. 12 : 81 : 63

Quantitative Aptitude

51. The table below shows the laptop sold on different days by different wholesalers. Study the table and answer the questions that follow.

	Mon	Tues	Wed	Thurs	Fri
Wholesaler 1	22	20	14	24	10
Wholesaler 2	46	45	06	14	8
Wholesaler 3	18	40	07	15	19
Wholesaler 4	23	30	32	06	26

Laptop sold by wholesaler 1 and wholesaler 2 together on Thursday is what per cent of laptop sold by wholesalers 3 on Friday?

A. 200% B. 150%
C. 100% D. 50%

52. Find the area of a right-angled triangle whose base is 12 cm and hypotenuse is 13 cm.

A. 30 cm^2 B. 55 cm^2
C. 65 cm^2 D. 22 cm^2

53. Find the value of tan (50 + θ) – cot (40 – θ).

A. $\frac{1}{2}$ B. –1
C. 0 D. 1

54. In 2021, Sam received an annual increment in his salary by 40% but due to recession in 2022, the company started taking cost-cutting measures and his salary was reduced by 15%. What was the net change in his salary?

A. 17% increase
B. 19% increase
C. 9% decrease
D. 11% increase

55. A rod of 5 cm radius and 52 cm length is converted into a wire of 100 cm length of uniform thickness. The radius of the wire (in cm) is:

A. $\sqrt{13}$ B. $\sqrt{15}$
C. $\sqrt{23}$ D. $\sqrt{17}$

56. If $\left(y^2 + \frac{1}{y^2}\right) = 74$ and $y > 1$, find the value of $\left(y - \frac{1}{y}\right)$.

A. $6\sqrt{2}$
B. $-2\sqrt{19}$
C. $2\sqrt{19}$
D. $-6\sqrt{2}$

50. D **51.** A **52.** A **53.** C **54.** B **55.** A **56.** A

57. If a sum of money at simple interest becomes 45 times in 110 years, then in how many years will that sum become 23 times?

A. 48 B. 60
C. 55 D. 50

58. Two trains 320 m and 205 m in length are running towards each other on parallel lines. One train runs at the rate of 70 kmph and the other train runs at the rate of 56 kmph. Find the time they will take to cross each other (in seconds).

A. 10 B. 20
C. 12 D. 15

59. A can complete a task in the same time in which B and C work together. If A and B could complete it jointly in 10 days and C alone in 50 days, then B could complete it independently in:

A. 26 days
B. 27 days
C. 25 days
D. 23 days

60. What is the value of $(1 - \sin^2 A) \operatorname{cosec}^2 A$? Given A is an acute angle.

A. $\cot^2 A$ B. $\cos^2 A$
C. $\tan^2 A$ D. $\sin^2 A$

61. If $3x - 2y = 3$ and $xy = 9$, then find the value of $3x + 2y$.

A. 16 B. 13
C. 14 D. 15

62. Study the table given below and answer the question that follows.

The table below shows the total number of students studying different subjects in a college and the percentage of boys and girls.

Subject	Number of Students	Percentage of Girls	Percentage of Boys
Hindi	110	60	40
English	70	50	50
Physics	50	30	70
Chemistry	40	80	20
Mathematics	80	20	80
Computers	90	40	60

What is the ratio of the total number of girls in all the subjects to that of boys in all the subjects?

A. 5 : 6 B. 7 : 9
C. 6 : 7 D. 2 : 3

63. Simplify the following:

$18 \times [24 \div 70 \times \{25 \times 49 \div \{5 \times 7\}\}]$

A. 218 B. 216
C. 215 D. 220

64. A 40-litre mixture of milk and water contains milk and water in the ratio of 7 : 3. How many litres of water should be added to the mixture so that the resulting mixture has 60% of water in it?

A. 30 B. 35
C. 20 D. 25

65. ΔABC inscribe in a circle with center O. If AB = 9 cm, BC = 40 cm and AC = 41 cm, then what is the circum-radius of a triangle?

A. $20\frac{1}{2}$ cm B. $12\frac{1}{2}$ cm

C. $18\frac{1}{2}$ cm D. $16\frac{1}{2}$ cm

57. C **58.** D **59.** C **60.** A **61.** D **62.** A **63.** B **64.** A **65.** A

66. The compound interest accrued on a sum of ₹ 20,000 at the end of 2 years compounded annually is ₹ 2,050. Find the compound interest at the end of the 3rd year.

A. ₹ 3,153.50 B. ₹ 2,852.50
C. ₹ 3,152.50 D. ₹ 3,154.50

67. If $\tan 15° = 2-\sqrt{3}$, then the value of $\tan 15° \cot 75° + \tan 75° \cot 15°$ is:

A. 6 B. 10
C. 8 D. 14

68. A certain sum was to be divided between A and B in the ratio 8 : 5. However by mistake, it was divided in the ratio 5 : 8. Thus, A gets ₹ 300 less than his original share. Find the sum.

A. ₹ 2,600 B. ₹ 1,500
C. ₹ 1,300 D. ₹ 600

69. Akash sold a motorcycle to Navin at a profit of 10%. Navin sold it to Vinay at a profit of 20%. Vinay sold it to Vishal at a loss of 5%. If Vishal paid ₹ 62,700 for the motorcycle, then what was the cost of the motorcycle (in ₹) for Akash?

A. 48,000 B. 48,500
C. 52,500 D. 50,000

70. The perimeters of two similar triangles XYZ and PQR are respectively 62 cm and 42 cm. If PQ = 21 cm, find XY:

A. 27 cm B. 28 cm
C. 29 cm D. 31 cm

71. If $px + qy = 1$ and $qx + py = \frac{2pq}{p^2+q^2}$, then $(x^2 + y^2)(p^2 + q^2)$ is equal to:

A. 2 B. 3
C. 0 D. 1

72. The radii of two circles are 9 cm and 4 cm, the distance between their centres is 13 cm, then the length of the direct common tangent is:

A. 8 cm B. 14 cm
C. 12 cm D. 16 cm

73. If an electricity bill is paid before the due date, one gets a reduction of 13% on the amount of the bill. By paying the bill before the due date, Ravi got a reduction of ₹ 260.39. The amount of his electricity bill (in ₹) was:

A. 2,003 B. 2,580
C. 2,230 D. 2,064

74. A salesman marks his goods 30% above the cost and gives a discount of 10% on them. Find his gain or loss percentage.

A. Loss 7% B. Gain 7%
C. Loss 17% D. Gain 17%

75. Study the given pie-chart and answer the question that follows.

Percentage-wise distribution of teachers in six different subjects in a school is given in the pie-chart. The total number of teachers is 600. The ratio of male and female teachers is 3 : 1.

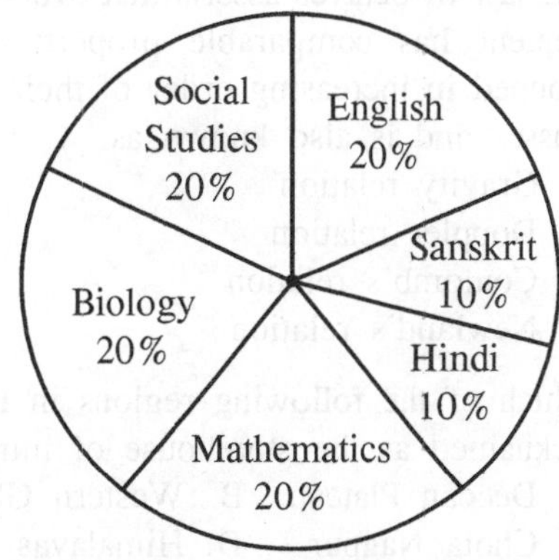

Find the ratio of teachers in English, Sanskrit and Hindi to teachers in Mathematics, Biology and Social Studies.

A. 2 : 5 B. 1 : 2
C. 2 : 3 D. 1 : 5

66. C	67. D	68. C	69. D	70. D	71. D	72. C	73. A	74. D	75. C

General Awareness

76. Which is the most powerful river in the world in terms of its volume and extensive drainage into the Atlantic Ocean?
A. Congo
B. Amazon
C. Amur
D. Nile

77. Which of the following statements about Akshdeep Singh is NOT true?
A. Akshdeep Singh won the National Race Walking Championship.
B. Akshdeep Singh qualified for the Paris 2024 Olympics and World Athletics Championships 2023.
C. Akshdeep Singh won a medal at Nomi in 2023.
D. In the men's 20 km race walk event, Akshdeep Singh clocked 1 hour 19 minutes 55 seconds, a new national record, to win the Silver medal.

78. The law of octaves asserts that every eighth element has comparable properties when grouped in increasing order of their atomic masses and is also known as:
A. Gravity relation
B. Doppler relation
C. Coulomb's relation
D. Newland's relation

79. Which of the following regions in India is nicknamed as the storehouse of minerals?
A. Deccan Plateau B. Western Ghats
C. Chota Nagpur D. Himalayas

80. Which of the following is consistent with import substitution policy?
A. Capital account convertibility
B. Flexible exchange rate policy
C. Tariffs and quotas
D. Current account convertibility

81. Which of the following will be considered as normal residents of India?
(*a*) Indians working in foreign embassies in India
(*b*) Ambassador for India in rest of the world
A. Only (*a*)
B. Only (*b*)
C. Both (*a*) and (*b*)
D. Neither (*a*) nor (*b*)

82. Which of the following is the most problematic and primary difficulty of barter exchanges as against money-based exchanges?
A. Bartered exchanges involve difficulty in preserving value.
B. Barter exchanges may result in an incorrect valuation of the goods transacted.
C. Barter exchanges may be imperfectly divisible.
D. Barter exchanges require a double coincidence of wants.

83. Who among the following personalities is a professional Kuchipudi Dancer?
A. Radha Sridhar
B. Surupa Sen
C. Anupama Hoskere
D. Kaushalya Reddy

84. Which region has the maximum concentration of Iron and Steel industries?
A. Shillong Plateau
B. Deccan Plateau
C. Chota Nagpur Plateau
D. Malwa Plateau

76. B	**77.** D	**78.** D	**79.** C	**80.** C	**81.** C	**82.** D	**83.** D	**84.** C

85. Who among the following has been accused of committing the judicial murder of Raja Nand Kumar?

A. Lord Wellesly
B. Lord Dalhousie
C. Lord Cornwallis
D. Warren Hastings

86. In which year did Swami Dayanand Saraswati establish Arya Samaj?

A. 1875 B. 1867
C. 1828 D. 1887

87. Which of the following is a transfer payment?

(*a*) Unemployment allowances
(*b*) Scholarships
(*c*) Retirement pension

A. Only (*a*)
B. All of (*a*), (*b*) and (*c*)
C. Only (*a*) and (*b*)
D. Only (*c*)

88. Which equation was verified by American scientists Nichols and Hull in 1903 by measuring the radiation pressure of visible light?

A. Pr = C/N B. P = L/M
C. P = F/A D. P = U/C

89. Match the items in List-I with those in List-II.

Measure of Money Supply	Formula
(*i*) M_1	(*a*) $M_1 + T_d$
(*ii*) M_2	(*b*) $C_p + D_d + O_d$
(*iii*) M_3	(*c*) $M_3 + TPO_d$
(*iv*) M_4	(*d*) $M_1 + POSB_d$

	(*i*)	(*ii*)	(*iii*)	(*iv*)
A.	(*d*)	(*a*)	(*c*)	(*b*)
B.	(*b*)	(*d*)	(*a*)	(*c*)
C.	(*a*)	(*d*)	(*b*)	(*c*)
D.	(*c*)	(*b*)	(*a*)	(*d*)

90. Sheorinarayan fair is held in which of the following states?

A. West Bengal
B. Jharkhand
C. Chhattisgarh
D. Madhya Pradesh

91. Where is Bhimrao Ambedkar Multipurpose Stadium situated?

A. Faizabad B. Ghaziabad
C. Kanpur D. Patna

92. Which of the following Articles of the Indian Constitution has the idea that 'No child below the age of fourteen years shall be employed to work in any factory or mine or engaged in any other hazardous employment'?

A. Article 22 B. Article 24
C. Article 19 D. Article 20

93. Totaram Sharma is associated with which of the following instruments?

A. Tanpura B. Panchavadyam
C. Pakhawaj D. Sarangi

94. The founders of Vijayanagara Empire were the feudatories of which of the following dynasties?

A. Hoysala B. Pandya
C. Kakatiya D. Chola

95. The Pakhawaj syllables are primarily used to conclude which of the following Indian classical dances?

A. Manipuri B. Kathak
C. Odissi D. Kathakali

96. Who among the following was a member of the Drafting Committee of the Constituent Assembly?

A. Dr. K.M. Munshi
B. B.N. Rao
C. T.T. Krisknamachari
D. N. Madhav Rau

85. D **86.** A **87.** B **88.** D **89.** B **90.** C **91.** A **92.** B **93.** C **94.** C **95.** C **96.** A

97. In the 2023 Women's World Boxing Championship gold medal match, Lovlina Borgohain defeated Australia's Caitlin Parker in the ________ kg weight category.
A. 70 B. 75
C. 80 D. 85

98. In March 2023, the Pension Fund Regulatory and Development Authority (PFRDA) amended the 2015 PFRDA Regulation to increase the age limit for the Ombudsman from 65 to ______ years.
A. 77 B. 80
C. 70 D. 90

99. The literacy rate of Andhra Pradesh state as per the Census of 2011 is ______ .
A. 66.48%
B. 67.02%
C. 66%
D. 68.5%

100. In which year did Rudolf Ludwig Karl Virchow formulate his famous aphorism 'Omnis cellula-e cellula' which became a part of the foundation of cell theory?
A. 1855 B. 1869
C. 1840 D. 1835

Explanatory Answers

1. (D): Dynamic refers to something characterized by constant change, activity, or progress. Energetic is the most appropriate synonym because it conveys a similar sense of vigor, activity, and movement. Both words suggest a high level of activity and motion, making energetic a suitable choice as a synonym for dynamic.

2. (D): In the context of the sentence, the term "archive" refers to a collection of historical documents or records that are preserved for research, reference, or historical purposes. Archives typically contain a wide range of materials such as manuscripts, letters, photographs, maps, and other documents that provide insight into the past.

3. (C): Guile refers to cunning, slyness, or craftiness, often used to deceive or manipulate others.

The most appropriate antonym for "guile" would be an attribute or quality that suggests honesty, straightforwardness, or sincerity.

4. (B): "Hoard" is a verb that means to accumulate or store something in a large quantity, especially for future use. In this context, it refers to ants collecting and storing food during the summer to use during the winter months.

5. (A): The error is in part A. "A owl was" should be corrected to "An owl was" because "owl" begins with a vowel sound, so it requires the article "an" instead of "a."

6. (C): An anthropologist is a social scientist who specializes in the study of humanity, particularly the study of human societies and cultures throughout history. This includes the study of human evolution, behaviour, and culture. Therefore, an anthropologist is someone who studies the evolution of mankind.

7. (B): When someone violates rules, they fail to uphold or follow them. So, the opposite of "violated" in this context would be to uphold or follow the rules. "Redeem" can

97. B **98.** C **99.** B **100.** A

mean to make up for a fault or mistake, to restore someone's reputation or honor, or to fulfill a promise or obligation. Therefore, the most appropriate antonym for "redeem" in this context would be the word that signifies the opposite of violating rules.

8. (C): "Portable" refers to something that is easy to carry or move from one place to another. It implies that the object is lightweight, compact, and designed for easy transportation. Portable items are often convenient for travel, commuting, or temporary use in different locations.

9. (B): It describes an imagined or idealized place or state where everything is perfect, often in terms of politics, society, laws, and customs. In a utopian society, there is typically equality, peace, harmony, and happiness among its inhabitants. The concept of utopia is often used in literature, philosophy, and political discourse to explore ideas about the ideal society and human aspirations.

10. (D): "Ill health" succinctly encapsulates the state of being in poor physical or mental condition. It encompasses a range of ailments, diseases, and conditions that impair one's well-being. Whether it's a physical illness or a mental health issue, "ill health" describes the condition of being unwell or suffering from discomfort or impairment.

11. (B): The error lies in segment B, "They were laid." The verb "were laid" is in the past tense and passive voice, suggesting that someone else laid them down.

However, the context of the sentence implies that the subjects ("they") laid themselves down in the sun, which requires the active voice.

12. (D): Exhilarate is the correct spelling for the word that means to make someone feel happy and excited.

13. (C): "My family never supported me," accomplishes this by placing the subject ("my family") at the beginning of the sentence and the verb "supported" indicates the action performed by the subject. This construction presents the sentence in active voice, making it clear that the family is the one not providing support.

14. (A): in the acknolledgments of the book

The correct spelling should be "acknowledgments." Therefore, the corrected segment is: in the acknowledgments of the book.

15. (B): The antonym "noble" suggests qualities such as honorable, generous, or possessing high moral principles. It stands in contrast to "mean," as it implies characteristics that are virtuous and commendable. Therefore noble is the most appropriate antonym for mean in this context.

16. (A): The idiom "on the cards" means that something is likely to happen or is expected to occur in the future. In the context of the sentence "Nitish's promotion is due," it suggests that Nitish's promotion is expected to happen soon or is very likely to occur.

17. (B): The sentence talks about the transmission of cultural patterns.

(*c*) "the royal style is the agent" introduces the concept of something influencing social evolution.

(*a*) "in social evolution by imitation" explains how the royal style acts as an agent (through imitation).

(*d*) "and cultural patterns are similarly transmitted by the dominant caste" adds another layer, suggesting dominant castes also influence cultural patterns.

(*b*) "by reason of its higher standard of living" provides a potential reason why the royal style might be imitated (because of a perceived better lifestyle).

18. (C): In the given sentence, the action of disturbing the meeting is performed by the subject "an agitated gathering of workers in the company." To transform this active sentence into passive voice, the object of the active sentence ("the meeting") becomes the subject of the passive sentence, and the subject of the active sentence ("an agitated gathering of workers in the company") becomes the agent, introduced by the preposition "by."

19. (D): The idiom "costs an arm and a leg" is used to emphasize that something is very expensive. It implies that the price of the item or service is so high that it feels as though one would have to pay a significant, perhaps exaggerated, amount—equivalent to the loss of a limb—to obtain it.

20. (D): In the given sentence, the word that best fits in the blank is reign. Reign refers to the period during which someone, particularly a monarch or ruler, holds power or authority. In this context, it suggests the period of leadership or authority of the company's CEO.

21. (D): Concept is the most fitting because it refers to a general idea, which aligns with the idea of globalization being a broad phenomenon.

22. (D): Rare makes sense because the passage talks about commodities that were not readily available and therefore valuable for trade.

23. (B): Advances is the most suitable choice because it signifies progress and improvement, which is what the Industrial Revolution brought to transportation and communication.

24. (D): Stalled indicates a halt or pause in progress, which aligns with the information that globalization slowed down after World War I.

25. (A): Protectionism refers to government policies that aim to shield domestic industries from foreign competition. This aligns with the passage mentioning nations raising import taxes to protect their industries.

27. (C): From given statements:

Conclusions:

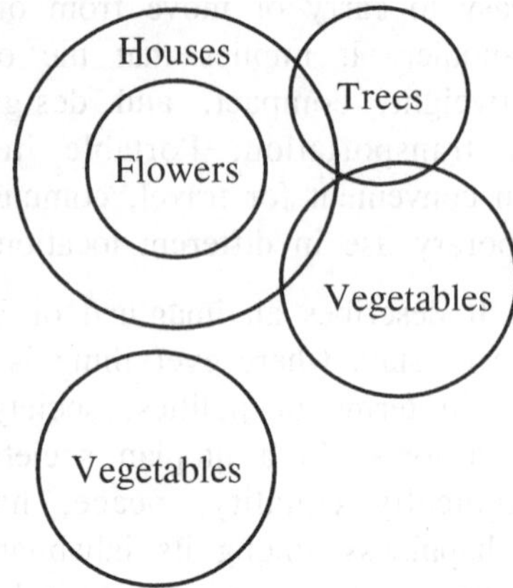

I. Some vegetables are houses is a possibility. (True)

II. Some flowers are trees is a possibility. (True)

III. No Vegetable is a house. (False)

Here, Both conclusions I and II follow.

28. (D): Given, A = ÷, B = ×, C = +, D = –

∴ 4B18D5C9A9

$= 4 \times 18 - 5 + 9 \div 9$

$= 4 \times 18 - 5 + 1$

$= 72 + 1 - 5$

$= 73 - 5 = 68.$

29. (D): Given, + and – are interchanged with ÷ and × respectively

∴ $88 + 8 - 17 \times 16 \div 40$

$= 88 \div 8 \times 17 - 16 + 40$

$= 11 \times 17 - 16 + 40$

$= 187 - 16 + 40$

$= 227 - 16 = 211.$

30. **(B):** Given, BALD = 7680 ...(i)

and DRAB = 8097 ...(ii)

From (i) and (ii), we get,

AD = 80

BL = 67

and BR = 79

Here, B = 7,

L = 6

and R = 9

Hence, 6 is code for 'L' in the given code language.

31. **(D):** BJKSX

+2 +2 +2 +2 +2

AB, DEFG, I J KL, NOPQ, STUV, XY

Here, Option (D) will complete the series.

33. **(C):** Given, R S P T

+4 +4 +4 +4

V W T X

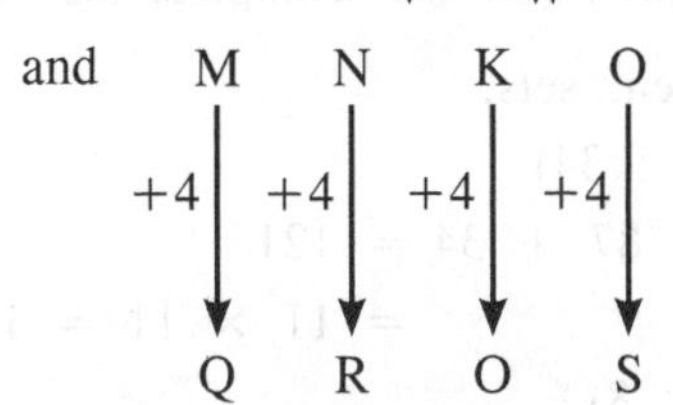

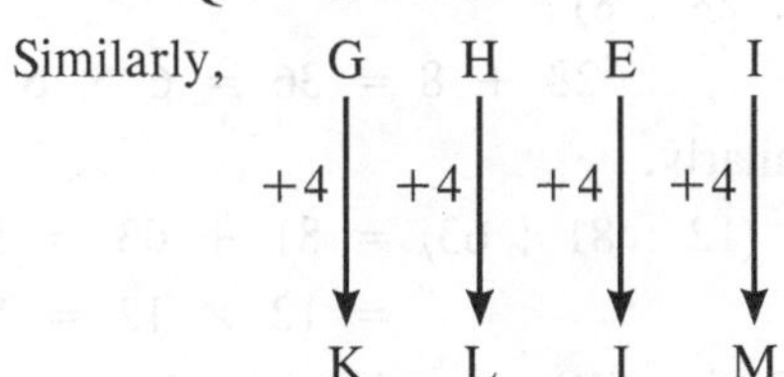

∴ GHEI is related to KLIM.

34. **(D):** (A) 2 – 6

$\Rightarrow$ $2 \times 2 + 2 = 4 + 2 = 6$

(B) 4 – 20

$\Rightarrow$ $4 \times 4 + 4 = 16 + 4 = 20$

(C) 5 – 30

$\Rightarrow$ $5 \times 5 + 5 = 25 + 5 = 30$

(D) 8 – 75

$\Rightarrow$ $8 \times 8 + 8 = 64 + 8 = 72$

Here, option (D) does not belong to that group.

35. **(C):** Given, QUEZAL = 82

$\Rightarrow 17 + 21 + 5 + 26 + 1 + 12 = 82$

LUCKY = 72

$\Rightarrow 12 + 21 + 3 + 11 + 25 = 72$

Similarly,

ADVERSE = ?

$\Rightarrow 1 + 4 + 22 + 5 + 18 + 19 + 5 = 74$

∴ 74 is the code for 'ADVERSE' in the given code language.

36. **(B):** Given, G I E K

+8 +8 +8 +8

O Q M S

and K M I O

+8 +8 +8 +8

S U Q W

Similarly, E G C I

+8 +8 +8 +8

M O K Q

∴ EGCI is related to MOKQ.

37. **(D):** (A) 5 : 20 $\Rightarrow$ 5 : 5 × 4

(B) 4 : 12 $\Rightarrow$ 4 : 4 × 3

(C) 7 : 42 $\Rightarrow$ 7 : 7 × 6

(D) 6 : 36 $\Rightarrow$ 6 : 6 × 6

Here, option (D) is the odd number-pair.

38. **(A):** (A) W Z B (+3, +2) (B) U W X (+2, +1)

(C) O R T (+3, +2) (D) G J L (+3, +2)

Here, option (B) does not belong to that group.

39. (A): 

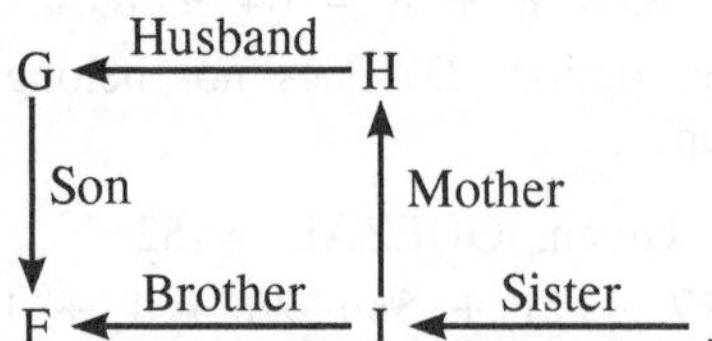

Here, F is the brother of J.

40. (A): Given, 9 July 1978 = Sunday

Number of odd day from 9 July, 1978 to 9 July, 1983

= (1 + 2 + 1 + 1 + 1) = 6

On 9 July 1983, it was Saturday

Now, Number of day from 10 July to 19 September, 1983

= 22 + 31 + 19

= 72 days

= 10 weeks + 2 days = 2 odd days

Hence, 19 September, 1983

= Saturday + 2 days = Monday

Hence, it was Monday.

42. (B): From given question,

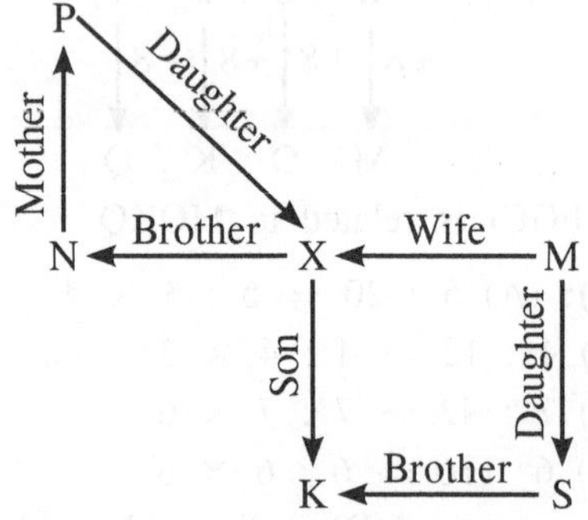

Here, K is the daughter's son of P.

43. (D): 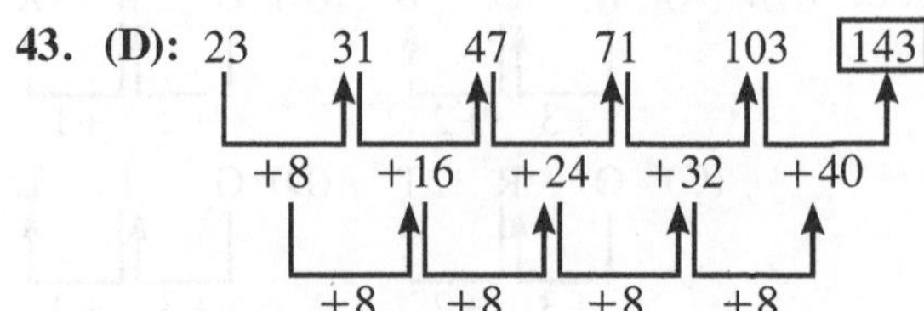

Here, 143 should come in place of X in the given series.

44. (D):

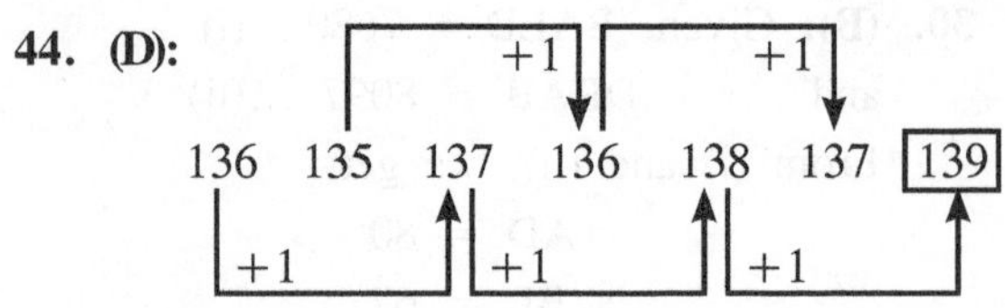

Here, ? = the next number = 139.

45. (C): Given, number of pairs

(15, 96)

$\Rightarrow \quad 15 \times 6 + 6 = 90 + 6$

$= 96$

(35, 216)

$\Rightarrow \quad 35 \times 6 + 6 = 210 + 6$

$= 216$

Similarly, (C) (29, 180)

$\Rightarrow \quad 29 \times 6 + 6 = 174 + 6$

$= 180$

∴ Option (C) are related in the same way as are the numbers of the given sets.

48. (C): BBDD

∴ A<u>B</u>CD, <u>B</u>CDA, C<u>D</u>AB, <u>D</u>ABC

Here, option (C) will complete the series.

50. (D): Given, sets,

(11 : 87 : 34)

$\Rightarrow \quad 87 + 34 = 121$

$= 11 \times 11 = 11^2$

(6 : 28 : 8)

$\Rightarrow \quad 28 + 8 = 36 = 6 \times 6 = 6^2$

Similarly,

(D) (12 : 81 : 63) = $81 + 63 = 144$

$= 12 \times 12 = 12^2$

∴ Option (D) are related in the same way as are the numbers of the given sets.

51. (A): From given table,

Laptop sold by wholesaler 1 and wholesaler 2 together on Thursday

$= 24 + 14 = 38$

and laptop sold by wholesalar 3 on Friday = 19

$\therefore \quad 19 \times \frac{x}{100} = 38$

$\Rightarrow \quad x = \frac{38 \times 100}{19} = 200\%$

Here, required per cent = 200%.

52. (A): Given, a right-angled-triangle
Base = 12 cm
and hypotenuse = 13 cm

$\therefore \quad p = \sqrt{h^2 - b^2}$

$= \sqrt{13^2 - 12^2}$

$= \sqrt{169 - 144} = \sqrt{25}$

$= 5$ cm

$\Rightarrow \quad p$ = Perpendicular

$= 5$ cm

$\therefore$ The area of a right-angled-triangle

$= \frac{1}{2} \times$ base $\times$ perpendicular

$= \frac{1}{2} \times 12 \times 5$

$= 30 \text{ cm}^2$.

53. (C): $\tan(50 + \theta) - \cot(40 - \theta)$

$= \tan(50 + \theta) - \cot[90 - (50 + \theta)]$

$= \tan(50 + \theta) - \tan(50 + \theta)$

$= 0$.

54. (B): Let original Salary = ₹ 100

Then, New salary $= 100 \times \frac{140}{100} \times \frac{100 - 15}{100}$

$= 100 \times \frac{140}{100} \times \frac{85}{100}$

$= 100 \times \frac{140}{100} \times \frac{85}{100} = 7 \times \frac{85}{5}$

$= 7 \times 17$

= ₹ 119

Hence, the net change in his salary = 19% increase.

55. (A): Let the radius of the wire be r cm
Then, Volume of a rod = Volume of the wire

$\Rightarrow \quad \pi(5)^2 \times 52 = \pi r^2 \times 100$

$\Rightarrow \quad 25 \times 52 = 100r^2$

$\Rightarrow \quad r^2 = \frac{25 \times 52}{100} = 13$

$\Rightarrow \quad r = \sqrt{13}$ cm

Hence, the radius of the wire = $\sqrt{13}$ cm.

56. (A): Given, $y^2 + \frac{1}{y^2} = 74$ and $y > 1$

$\because \quad \left(y - \frac{1}{y}\right)^2 = y^2 + \frac{1}{y^2} - 2y.\frac{1}{y}$

$= y^2 + \frac{1}{y^2} - 2$

$= 74 - 2 = 72$

$\Rightarrow \quad \left(y - \frac{1}{y}\right) = \sqrt{72} = \sqrt{36 \times 2}$

$\Rightarrow \quad \left(y - \frac{1}{y}\right) = 6\sqrt{2}$.

57. (C): $r = \frac{(n-1) \times 100}{t}$

and $t = \frac{(n-1) \times 100}{r}$

$\therefore \quad r = \frac{(45-1) \times 100}{110}$

$= \frac{44 \times 100}{110} = 40\%$

and $t = \frac{(23-1) \times 100}{40}$

$= \frac{22 \times 5}{2}$

$= 55$ years

$\therefore$ Required years = 55 years.

58. (D): Relative speed of train

$= (70 + 56)$ km/h

$= 126 \times \frac{5}{18}$

$= 21 \times \frac{5}{3}$

$= 7 \times 5$

$= 35$ m/s

and the length of two trains

$= (320 + 205)$ m

$= 525$ m

$\therefore$ Time taken by train to cross each-other

$= \frac{525}{35}$

$= 15$ seconds.

59. (C): Let A can complete a task in x day's $=$ (B + C) can complete it in x days

Then, A's 1 day's work

$=$ (B + C)'s 1 day's work $= \frac{1}{x}$

and given, (A + B)'s 1 day's work $= \frac{1}{10}$

and C's 1 day's work $= \frac{1}{50}$

$\therefore$ (A + B + C)'s 1 day's work

$= \frac{1}{10} + \frac{1}{50}$

$\Rightarrow \quad \frac{1}{x} + \frac{1}{x} = \frac{5+1}{50}$

$\Rightarrow \quad \frac{2}{x} = \frac{6}{50}$

$\Rightarrow \quad \frac{1}{x} = \frac{3}{50}$

A's 1 day's work $=$ (B + C)'s 1 day work

$= \frac{3}{25}$

B's 1 day's work $=$ (A + B)'s 1 day work $-$ A's 1 day work

$= \frac{1}{10} - \frac{3}{50}$

$= \frac{5-3}{50} = \frac{2}{50} = \frac{1}{25}$

Hence, B could complete it independently in 25 days.

60. (A): $(1 - \sin^2 A) \operatorname{cosec}^2 A$

$= \cos^2 A . \frac{1}{\sin^2 A} = \cot^2 A.$

61. (D): Given, $3x - 2y = 3$ and $xy = 9$

$\Rightarrow \quad (3x - 2y)^2 = 3^2$

$\Rightarrow 9x^2 + 4y^2 - 2 \times 3x \times 2y = 9$

$\Rightarrow 9x^2 + 4y^2 - 12xy = 9$

$\Rightarrow 9x^2 + 4y^2 - 12xy + 24xy$

$= 9 + 24xy$

$\Rightarrow 9x^2 + 4y^2 + 12xy = 9 + 24 \times 9$

$\Rightarrow \quad (3x + 2y)^2 = 9(1 + 24)$

$= 9 \times 25$

$\Rightarrow \quad (3x + 2y)^2 = 225 = (15)^2$

$\Rightarrow \quad 3x + 2y = 15.$

62. (A): From given table:

The total number of girls in all subjects

$= 110 \times \frac{60}{100} + 70 \times \frac{50}{100} + 50 \times \frac{30}{100} + 40 \times \frac{80}{100}$

$+ 80 \times \frac{20}{100} + 90 \times \frac{40}{100}$

$= 66 + 35 + 15 + 32 + 16 + 36$

$= 200$

and the total number of boys in all subjects

$= 110 \times \frac{40}{100} + 70 \times \frac{50}{100} + 50 \times \frac{70}{100} + 40 \times \frac{20}{100}$

$+ 80 \times \frac{80}{100} + 90 \times \frac{60}{100}$

$= 44 + 35 + 35 + 8 + 64 + 54$
$= 240$

Hence, required ratio $= 200 : 240$
$= 5 : 6.$

63. (B): $18 \times [24 \div 70 \times \{25 \times 49 \div (5 \times 7)\}]$

$$= 18\times\left[24 \div 70\times\left\{25\times49\times\frac{1}{5\times7}\right\}\right]$$

$= 18 \times [24 \div 70 \times \{5 \times 7\}]$
$= 18 \times [24 \div 70 \times 35]$

$$= 18\times\left[24\times\frac{1}{70}\times35\right]$$

$$= 18\times\left[24\times\frac{1}{2}\right]$$

$= 18 \times 12 = 216.$

64. (A): $\because$ Quantity of milk in mixture

$$= 40\times\frac{7}{7+3}$$

$$= 40\times\frac{7}{10}$$

$= 28$ litres

and quantity of water in mixture

$$= 40\times\frac{3}{10}$$

$= 12$ litres

Let x litres of water should be added

Then, $$12 + x = (40+x)\times\frac{60}{100}$$

$$\Rightarrow \quad 12 + x = (40+x)\times\frac{3}{5}$$

$\Rightarrow \quad 5(12 + x) = 3(40 + x)$
$\Rightarrow \quad 60 + 5x = 120 + 3x$
$\Rightarrow \quad 2x = 60$
$\Rightarrow \quad x = 30$ litres

Hence, required water $= 30$ litres.

66. (C): Compound interest $= P\left(1+\frac{r}{100}\right)^n - P$

$$\Rightarrow ₹\ 2050 = ₹\ 20{,}000\left[\left(1+\frac{r}{100}\right)^2 - 1\right]$$

$$\Rightarrow \left(1+\frac{r}{100}\right)^2 - 1 = \frac{2050}{20{,}000}$$

$$\Rightarrow \left(1+\frac{r}{100}\right)^2 = 1+\frac{41}{400} = \frac{441}{400}$$

$$\Rightarrow \left(1+\frac{r}{100}\right)^2 = \left(\frac{21}{20}\right)^2$$

$$\Rightarrow 1+\frac{r}{100} = \frac{21}{20}$$

$$\Rightarrow \frac{r}{100} = \frac{21}{20}-1 = \frac{1}{20}$$

$\therefore \quad r = 5\%$

Now, compound interest at the end of 3rd year

$$= P\left(1+\frac{r}{100}\right)^n - P$$

$$= P\left[\left(1+\frac{r}{100}\right)^n - 1\right]$$

$$= 20{,}000\left[\left(1+\frac{5}{100}\right)^3 - 1\right]$$

$$= 20{,}000\left[\left(\frac{21}{20}\right)^3 - 1\right]$$

$$= 20{,}000\left[\frac{9261}{8000} - 1\right]$$

$$= 20{,}000\left[\frac{1261}{8000}\right]$$

$$= 20\times\frac{1261}{8} = \frac{5\times1261}{2} = \frac{6305}{2}$$

$= ₹\ 3152.50.$

67. (D): Given,

$\tan 15° = 2 - \sqrt{3}$

$\therefore \tan 15° \cot 75° + \tan 75° \cot 15°$

$= \tan 15° \cot (90 - 15°)$

$\quad + \tan (90 - 15) \cot 15°$

$= \tan 15° \tan 15° + \cot 15° \cot 15°$

$= \tan^2 15° + \cot^2 15°$

$= \tan^2 15° + \dfrac{1}{\tan^2 15°}$

$= \left(2 - \sqrt{3}\right)^2 + \dfrac{1}{\left(2 - \sqrt{3}\right)^2}$

$= 4 + 3 - 4\sqrt{3} + \dfrac{1}{4 + 3 - 4\sqrt{3}}$

$= \left(7 - 4\sqrt{3}\right) + \dfrac{1}{\left(7 - 4\sqrt{3}\right)}$

$= \dfrac{(7 - 4\sqrt{3})^2 + 1}{7 - 4\sqrt{3}}$

$= \dfrac{49 + 48 - 56\sqrt{3} + 1}{7 - 4\sqrt{3}}$

$= \dfrac{98 - 56\sqrt{3}}{7 - 4\sqrt{3}}$

$= \dfrac{14\left(7 - 4\sqrt{3}\right)}{\left(7 - 4\sqrt{3}\right)} = 14.$

68. (C): Let a certain sum = ₹ x

Then, A's share $= \dfrac{8x}{13}$

B's share $= \dfrac{5x}{13}$

By Mistake,

A's share $= \dfrac{5x}{13}$

and B's share $= \dfrac{8x}{13}$

According to question,

$\dfrac{5x}{13} = \dfrac{8x}{13} - 300$

$\Rightarrow \dfrac{8x}{13} - \dfrac{5x}{13} = 300$

$\Rightarrow \dfrac{3x}{13} = 300$

$\Rightarrow x =$ ₹ 1300

Hence, The sum $= x$

= ₹ 1300.

69. (D): Let the C.P. of motorcycle for Akash be ₹ x

Then, C.P. of Motorcycle for Vishal

$= x \times \dfrac{110}{100} \times \dfrac{120}{100} \times \dfrac{95}{100}$

$\Rightarrow$ ₹ 67,800 $= x \times \dfrac{11}{10} \times \dfrac{6}{5} \times \dfrac{19}{20}$

$\Rightarrow x = \dfrac{62700 \times 10 \times 5 \times 20}{11 \times 6 \times 19}$

$= \dfrac{62700 \times 1000}{66 \times 19}$

$= \dfrac{3300 \times 1000}{66}$

$= 50 \times 1000$

$= 50{,}000$

Hence, the cost of the motorcycle for Akash = ₹ 50,000.

70. (D): Given, $\Delta XYZ \sim \Delta PQR$

$\therefore \dfrac{\text{Perimeter of } \Delta XYZ}{\text{Perimeter of } \Delta PQR} = \dfrac{XY}{PQ}$

$\Rightarrow \dfrac{64}{42} = \dfrac{XY}{21}$

$\Rightarrow XY = \dfrac{62 \times 21}{42}$

$\Rightarrow XY = 31$ cm.

73. (A): Let the amount of electric bill was ₹ x

Then, $x \times \frac{13}{100} = 260.39$

$\Rightarrow \quad x = \frac{26039}{13}$

$\Rightarrow \quad x =$ ₹ 2,003.

74. (D): Let C.P. of goods = ₹ 100

Then, M.P. = ₹ 130

$\therefore$ S.P. = $130 \times \frac{90}{100} = 117$

$\therefore$ Gain = S.P. – C.P.

= 117 – 100

= ₹ 17

and gain % = 17%.

75. (C): From given pie-chart:

The total number of teachers = 600

The total number of teachers in English, Sanskrit and Hindi

$= 600 \times \frac{20+10+10}{100}$

$= 6 \times 40$

$= 240$

and the total number of teachers in Mathematics, Biology and Social Studies

$= 600 \times \frac{(20+20+20)}{100}$

$= 6 \times 60$

$= 360$

$\therefore$ Required ratio = 240 : 360

= 2 : 3.

76. (B): The Amazon River is widely considered the most powerful river in the world based on its volume of water discharge and extensive drainage basin. It carries more water than any other river, accounting for approximately 20% of the total freshwater discharge into the oceans globally. The Amazon River originates in the Andes Mountains of South America and flows across the continent, draining into the Atlantic Ocean.

77. (D): This statement is not correct as Akshdeep Singh actually set a new national record while winning the gold medal (not silver) at the National Open Race Walking competition, clocking 1 hour 19 minutes and 38 seconds, not 1 hour 19 minutes and 55 seconds.

78. (D): The law of octaves, proposed by English chemist John Newlands in 1864, is also known as Newland's relation. It observed a recurring pattern in the properties of elements when arranged by their atomic masses. Newlands found that elements with similar chemical properties tended to appear every eight elements. Newlands' work is recognized as an important step in the history of chemistry.

79. (C): The Chota Nagpur Plateau, located in the eastern part of India, is often referred to as the "storehouse of minerals." This region is rich in mineral resources such as coal, iron ore, copper, mica, bauxite, manganese, and limestone, among others. The presence of these minerals has led to significant industrial development in the area, particularly in sectors such as mining, steel production, and manufacturing.

80. (C): Tariffs and quotas are consistent with import substitution policy because they impose barriers to imports, making foreign goods more expensive or restricting their quantity. By implementing tariffs (taxes on imports) and quotas (limits on the quantity of imports), countries can protect domestic industries from foreign competition, encourage domestic production, and stimulate economic growth.

81. (C):

(*a*) Indians working in foreign embassies in India are considered normal residents of India because they reside in India, even though they may be working for a foreign embassy.

(*b*) Ambassadors for India in the rest of the world are considered normal residents of India because they are representing India in other countries and are likely residing in those countries rather than India.

82. (D): Barter exchanges require a double coincidence of wants, which means that for a transaction to occur, both parties involved must have a desired good or service that the other party wants. This can be highly problematic and is considered the primary difficulty of barter exchanges compared to money-based exchanges. It often leads to inefficiencies and difficulties in finding suitable trading partners.

83. (D): Kaushalya Reddy is a well-known Kuchipudi dancer. Kuchipudi is a classical Indian dance form that originated in the state of Andhra Pradesh. Kaushalya Reddy has dedicated her career to practicing and promoting this traditional dance form. As a professional Kuchipudi dancer, she has likely undergone extensive training in Kuchipudi dance techniques, repertoire, and performance styles.

84. (C): The region in India with the maximum concentration of Iron and Steel industries is Chota Nagpur Plateau. This eastern Indian plateau spreads across the states of Jharkhand, Chhattisgarh, Odisha, and West Bengal.

It's known for its rich mineral resources, including coal, iron ore, copper, bauxite, mica, and manganese. These minerals provide the raw materials necessary for the iron and steel industry, making Chota Nagpur Plateau a hub for steel production in India.

85. (D): Warren Hastings, who served as the Governor-General of India from 1773 to 1785, faced accusations of committing the judicial murder of Raja Nand Kumar. Raja Nand Kumar was a prominent Indian nobleman and diwan (chief minister) of Bihar during the time of the British East India Company's rule in India.

He was arrested by Hastings on charges of corruption and forgery in 1775. Nand Kumar was tried in Calcutta (now Kolkata) and ultimately sentenced to death, despite many believing that the charges against him were politically motivated.

86. (A): Swami Dayanand Saraswati founded Arya Samaj in 1875 in Bombay, India. Arya Samaj is a Hindu reform movement that aimed to promote the values of Vedas (ancient Indian scriptures) and to counteract what Dayanand perceived as the corruptions that had crept into Hindu society over time.

Arya Samaj emphasized the principles of monotheism, social equality, and the rejection of idol worship, caste system, and rituals that were not in line with Vedic teachings.

87. (B): Transfer payments are payments made by the government to individuals or entities that are not in exchange for goods or services currently provided. They are a form of redistribution of wealth.

(*a*) Unemployment allowances are provided to people who are unemployed to help them financially during their job search.

(*b*) Scholarships are financial aid awarded to students to help cover the cost of education.

(*c*) Retirement pensions are regular payments made to individuals after they retire, typically from a fund to which they contributed during their working life.

88. (D): For the equation related to radiation pressure measured by Nichols and Hull, P = U/C. This equation expresses the relationship between the pressure exerted by electromagnetic radiation (light) and the energy density of that radiation. It essentially states that the pressure exerted by light is directly proportional to the energy density of the light and inversely proportional to the speed of light.

90. (C): The Sheorinarayan fair is held in the state of Chhattisgarh, India. It takes place in the town of Sheorinarayan, which is located in the Janjgir-Champa district of Chhattisgarh.

This fair is significant as it celebrates the cultural and religious heritage of the region. It usually occurs during the Hindu festival of Maghi Purnima, which falls in the month of January or February.

91. (A): Bhimrao Ambedkar Multipurpose Stadium, also known as Faizabad Stadium, is located in Faizabad, Uttar Pradesh, India. It is named after Bhimrao Ambedkar, an Indian jurist, economist, politician, and social reformer who is known as the chief architect of the Indian Constitution and a champion of social justice. The stadium serves as a multipurpose sports complex, hosting various sporting events, including cricket matches, football matches, athletic competitions, and cultural events.

92. (B): Article 24 of the Indian Constitution prohibits the employment of children in hazardous occupations. This provision reflects the commitment of the Indian Constitution to protect the rights and welfare of children and ensure their safety and well-being. By prohibiting the employment of children in hazardous occupations, Article 24 aims to prevent child exploitation, protect their health and development, and promote their right to education and a safe childhood.

93. (C): Totaram Sharma is a renowned master of the pakhawaj, which is a traditional Indian percussion instrument. It is commonly used in classical Indian music, particularly in the accompaniment of vocal and instrumental performances. Totaram Sharma is celebrated for his mastery of this instrument, known for his skillful playing technique, intricate rhythms, and deep understanding of classical music traditions.

94. (C): The founders of the Vijayanagara Empire, Harihara I and Bukka Raya I, were initially feudatories of the Kakatiya dynasty. The Kakatiyas ruled parts of present-day Telangana and Andhra Pradesh in South India. Harihara I and Bukka Raya I served as governors under the Kakatiya dynasty until its decline. Taking advantage of the weakening Kakatiya rule, they established their own kingdom in the region, eventually founding the Vijayanagara Empire around 1336 AD.

95. (C): Odissi is a classical dance form originating from Odisha, India. Traditionally, the Pakhawaj was the preferred percussion instrument for Odissi performances. While other instruments are now used as well, the Pakhawaj's rhythmic syllables ("bols") are still incorporated into Odissi dance to create a distinct musical and rhythmic vocabulary for the dance.

96. (A): Dr. K.M. Munshi, was a prominent Indian independence activist, politician, and scholar. He was a key figure in the drafting and framing of the Constitution of India. Dr. Munshi was appointed as a member of the Drafting Committee of the Constituent Assembly, which was tasked with the monumental responsibility of preparing the draft of the Indian Constitution. The committee was appointed on August 29, 1947, and was chaired by B. R. Ambedkar.

97. (B): The 2023 Women's World Boxing Championship gold medal match in the 75 kg weight category saw Lovlina Borgohain from India competing against Caitlin Parker from Australia. Lovlina Borgohain emerged victorious in this match, securing the gold medal. This achievement highlights Lovlina Borgohain's skill, determination, and prowess in the sport of boxing.

98. (C): In March 2023, the Pension Fund Regulatory and Development Authority (PFRDA) made amendments to the 2015 PFRDA Regulation regarding the age limit for the Ombudsman. Previously, the age limit for the Ombudsman was set at 65 years. However, with the amendment, the age limit was increased to 70 years, allowing individuals up to the age of 70 to serve as Ombudsman.

99. (B): The literacy rate of Andhra Pradesh state as per the Census of 2011 is 67.02%. This indicates the percentage of the population aged 7 and above who can read and write in any language. It reflects the level of education and literacy attainment within the state.

100. (A): Rudolf Virchow formulated his famous aphorism "Omnis cellula-e cellula" in 1855. This phrase, which translates to "every cell from a cell," became a pivotal part of the foundation of the cell theory. The cell theory states that all living organisms are composed of cells, and that cells arise from pre-existing cells.

Previous Paper (Solved)

SSC—Combined Higher Secondary Level–CHSL (10+2) TIER–1, Online Recruitment Exam–2022

(Exam held on 21-03-2023)

ENGLISH LANGUAGE

1. Choose the sentence with no spelling error.
A. I was rently at a literary festival
B. I was recently at a litrary festival
C. I was recently at a literary festival
D. I was recently at a literery fstival

2. Improve the underlined part of the sentence. Choose 'No improvement' as an answer if the sentence is grammatically correct.

There has been a noticeable fall in the number of children dying from malnutrition.
A. noticeable falling
B. No improvement
C. noticeably falling
D. noticeably falls

3. Rearrange the parts of the sentence in correct order.
P. application, which can also be used to log complaints about
Q. littering or caused by the animals, according to officials
R. registered with the local authority through a mobile phone
S. the residents of Noida can now get their pets like dogs or cats
A. QRPS B. SRPQ
C. PRQS D. RQPS

4. Find the part of the given sentence that has an error in it. If there is no error, choose 'No error'.

Near 800 million people worldwide lack updated sanitation.
A. updated sanitation.
B. people worldwide lack
C. No error
D. Near 800 million

5. Improve the underlined part of the sentence. Choose 'No improvement' as an answer if the sentence is grammatically correct.

Scientists have predicted that the cultivation of rice will be affected severe.
A. affect severe
B. No improvement
C. effecting severely
D. affected severely

6. The given sentence is in active voice. Change the voice of the sentence. Select the correct option from the sentences given in options.
She used the aerobic ball during workout.
A. During workout the aerobic ball were to be used by her.
B. During workout the aerobic ball will be used by her.
C. During workout the aerobic ball had been used by her.
D. During workout the aerobic ball was used by her

7. Choose the word that can substitute the given group of words.

A child born after the death of his father
A. Orphan B. Pseudonym
C. Posthumous D. Bigot

8. Select the option that will improve the bracketed part of the sentence. In case no improvement is needed, select 'No improvement'.

Dad said that, "She would have been a great sister if she was just a bit more careful".

A. No improvement
B. that, "She would have been a great sister if she were just a bit more careful"
C. "She would have been a great sister if she were just a bit more careful"
D. "She would have been a greatest sister if she was just a bit more careful"

9. Choose the word that means the same as the given word.

Fad

A. Sensation B. Standard
C. Classic D. Deviant

10. Select the most appropriate option to fill in the blank.

In space it is possible to identify and .... some unique characteristics of human physiology and biology.

A. isolate B. excess
C. replete D. partition

11. Choose the word that is opposite in meaning to the given word.

Devious

A. Outspoken B. Circuitous
C. Clandestine D. Serpentine

12. Choose the word that means the same as the given word.

Nacreous

A. Monochromatic B. Pale
C. Gloom D. Iridescent

13. Improve the underlined part of the sentence. Choose 'No improvement' as an answer if the sentence is grammatically correct.

Mary doesn't like cartoons because they are loud, so she <u>doesn't watched them</u>.

A. do not watched this
B. doesn't watch them
C. No improvement
D. does watching them

14. In the following question, out of the given four alternatives, select the alternative which best expresses the meaning of the Idiom/ Phrase.

To play with fire

A. Feel sick
B. To take foolish risk
C. To abuse
D. Show disappointment

15. Choose the incorrectly spelt word.

A. Flufy B. Gifted
C. Juggler D. Struggler

16. Parts of the following sentence are given as options. Identify the part that contains a grammatical error. If there is no error, select 'No error'.

That was a good/conversation, I look forward/ to meet you.

A. That was a good
B. to meet you.
C. conversation, I look forward
D. No error

17. Select the correct indirect form of the given sentence.

Nandini said, "I bought a pen yesterday."

A. Nandini said she did bought a pen the previous day.
B. Nandini said that she had bought a pen the previous day.
C. Nandini said that she had bought a pen yesterday.
D. Nandini says that she had bought a pen the previous day

18. Select the most appropriate meaning of the given idiom.

Backseat driver

A. A person who offers unsolicited advice.
B. To miss an appointed meeting
C. Attempt to get control over someone
D. To conclude proceedings

19. Choose the word that means the same as the given word.

Corrective

A. Commuting
B. Restorative
C. Compensatory
D. Sluggish

20. Rearrange the parts of the sentence in correct order.

Research shows

P. that medium-skilled employees who work
Q. in front of a computer and work beyond
R. 4.6 effective hours a day produce smaller
S. quantities of output per hour due to fatigue

A. RQSP B. PQSR
C. SQRP D. PQRS

Directions (Qs. No. 21-25): *In the following passage, some words have been deleted. Read the passage carefully and select the correct answer for the given blank out of the four alternatives.*

Rock candy is actually a collection of large sugar crystals that are "grown" from a sugar-water (1) .... Crystals form when the smallest particles of a substance, the molecules, arrange themselves in a/an (2) .... and repetitive pattern. Molecules are too small for us to see moving around and (3) .... themselves, but you can get a rough idea of what this would look like by taking a small shallow tray and filling it with marbles, ball bearings, or other spheres. As you (4) .... more spheres, the bottom of the tray becomes covered, then the spheres must form layers on top of (5) ...., and a structure or pattern emerges.

21. Select the most appropriate option to fill in blank number 1.

A. convergence
B. ramification
C. disposition
D. solution

22. Select the most appropriate option to fill in blank number 2.

A. orderly B. vastly
C. wholly D. adeptly

23. Select the most appropriate option to fill in blank number 3.

A. summarizing B. shielding
C. arranging D. dividing

24. Select the most appropriate option to fill in blank number 4.

A. add B. curse
C. please D. toil

25. Select the most appropriate option to fill in blank number 5.

A. others B. one
C. one another D. every other

GENERAL INTELLIGENCE

26. In the following question below are given some statements followed by some conclusions based on those statements. Taking the given statements to be true even if they seem to be at variance from commonly known facts. Read all the conclusions and then decide which of the given conclusion logically follows the given statements.

Statements:

I. Some A are T.
II. Some T are H.

Conclusions:

I. No T is A.
II. No H is T.
III. No A is H

A. Only conclusion I follows
B. All conclusion follow
C. Only conclusion II follows
D. Neither conclusion follows

27. In the following question, four number pairs are given. In each pair the number on left side of (–) is related to the number of the right side of (–) with some Logic/Rule/ Relation. Three pairs are similar on basis of same Logic/Rule/Relation. Select the odd one out from the given alternatives. (NOTE: Operations should be performed on the whole numbers, without breaking down the numbers into its constituent digits. E.g.13 – Operations on 13 such as adding/subtracting/multiplying etc. to 13 can be performed. Breaking down 13 into 1 and 3 and then performing mathematical operations on 1 and 3 is not allowed)

A. 56885 – 11377
B. 38515 – 7701
C. 74235 – 14847
D. 82695 – 16539

28. A series is given with one term missing. Select the correct alternative from the given ones that will complete the series.

TRAP, MMRE, FHIT, YCZI, ?

A. RYQY B. RXQX
C. RYQX D. RXQY

29. In the following question, select the missing number from the given series.

34, 71, 108, 145, ?, 219

A. 160 B. 182
C. 180 D. 172

30. Words given on the left side of (::) are related with each other by some Logic/Rule/Relation. Select the missing word/word pair on the right side of (::) from the given alternatives based on the same Logic/Rule/Relation.

Six : Hexagon :: ?

A. Four : Rectangle
B. Four : Pentagon
C. Three : Square
D. Seven : Octagon

31. Pointing towards a lady in a photo, Rinku said, "She is my son's sister's mother". How that lady is related to Rinku?

A. Daughter B. Daughter in law
C. Sister D. Wife

32. In the following question, select the odd letter/ letters from the given alternatives.

A. KLIO
B. RSPT
C. VWTX
D. HIFJ

33. Select the option figure in which the given figure is embedded. (Rotation is NOT allowed)

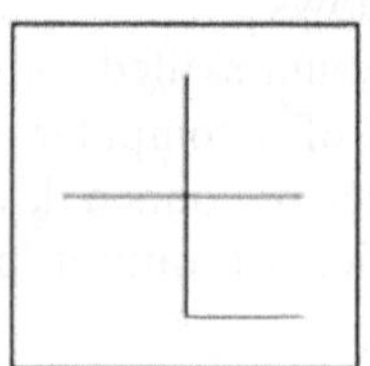

A. 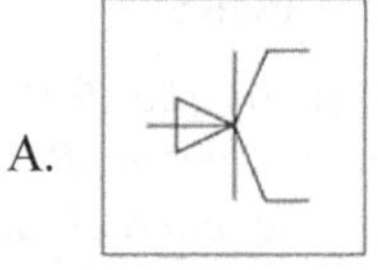 B. 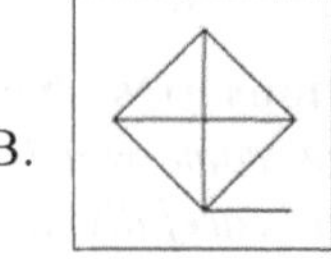

C. 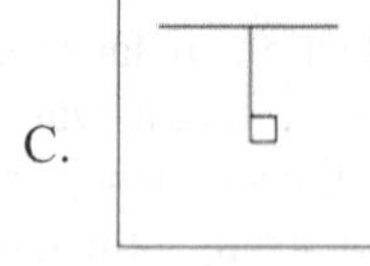 D. 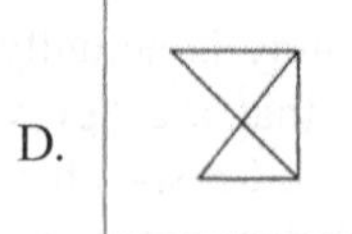

34. Select the option figure in which the given figure is embedded. (Rotation is NOT allowed)

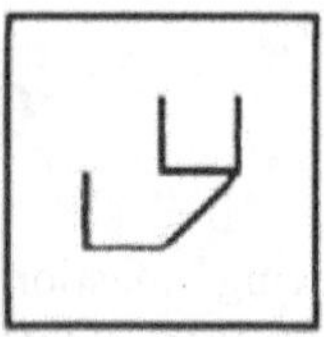

A. 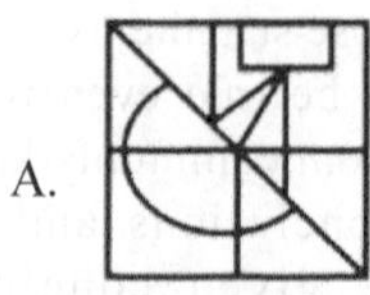 B. 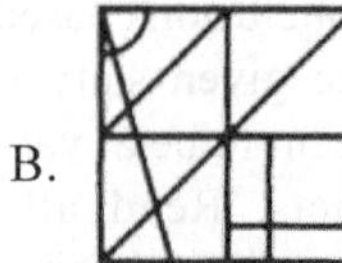

C. 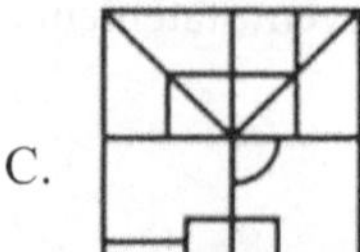 D. 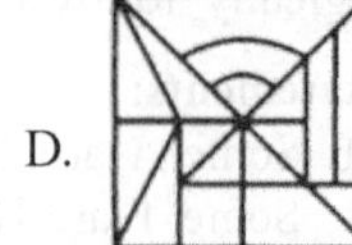

35. In the following question, select the related letters from the given alternatives.

PM : RO :: BC : ?

A. DE B. ZA
C. JK D. XY

36. After interchanging which two signs and two numbers (Not digits), the value of the given expression will be '45'?

$10 \times 8 \div 6 - 2 + 4$

A. + and –, 8 and 6
B. + and ×, 10 and 4
C. ÷ and –, 10 and 8
D. ÷ and –, 4 and 8

37. In a certain code language, 'ONLINE + THEIR' is coded as '11', 'FREE + NEW' is coded as '7'. What is the code for 'HELP + STUDENTS' in that code language?

A. 10 B. 12
C. 8 D. 6

38. Select the option in which the numbers shares the same relationship in set as that shared by the numbers in the given set. (NOTE: Operations should be performed on the whole numbers, without breaking down the numbers into its constituent digits. E.g.13 – Operations on 13 such as adding /subtracting /multiplying etc. to 13 can be performed. Breaking down 13 into 1 and 3 and then performing mathematical operations on 1 and 3 is not allowed)

(182, 79, 378)
(345, 16, 604)

A. (79, 18, 178) B. (53, 72, 82)
C. (68, 79, 193) D. (84, 64, 84)

39. How many cycles are not pedals?

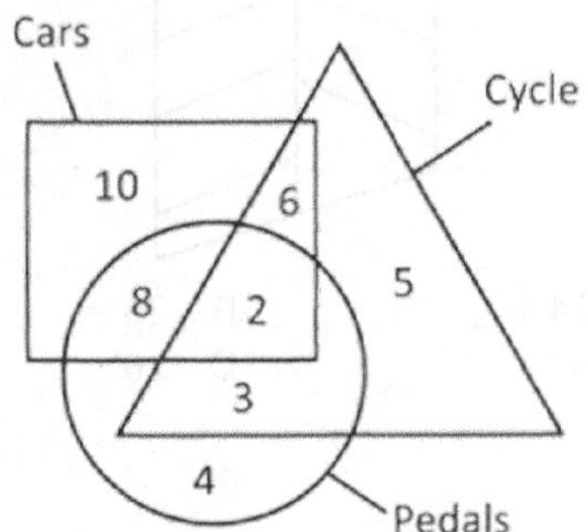

A. 8 B. 11
C. 7 D. 5

40. In a certain code language, 'PRINTS' is coded as 'QRLHQO'. What is the code for 'STRICT' in that code language?

A. RAGSQR B. RAGQSR
C. RAQGSR D. RGAQSR

41. In the following question, four number pairs are given. In each pair the number on left side of (–) is related to the number of the right side of (–) with some Logic/Rule/Relation. Three pairs are similar on basis of same Logic/Rule/Relation. Select the odd one out from the given alternatives. (NOTE: Operations should be performed on the whole numbers, without breaking down the numbers into its constituent digits. E.g.13 – Operations on 13 such as adding/subtracting/multiplying etc. to 13 can be performed. Breaking down 13 into 1 and 3 and then performing mathematical operations on 1 and 3 is not allowed)

A. 9 – 810
B. 11 – 1452
C. 7 – 392
D. 13 – 2368

42. If 13 @ 2 # 5 = 10 and 43 # 9 @ 16 = 50, then 8 @ 6 # 3 = ?

A. 7 B. 11
C. 10 D. 8

43. Select the option figure in which the given figure is embedded. (Rotation is NOT allowed)

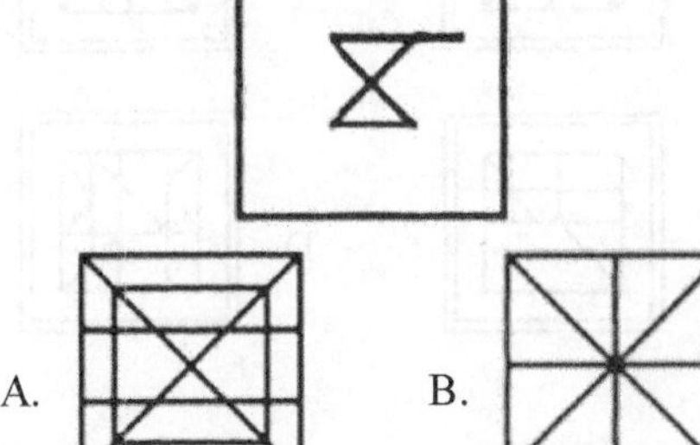

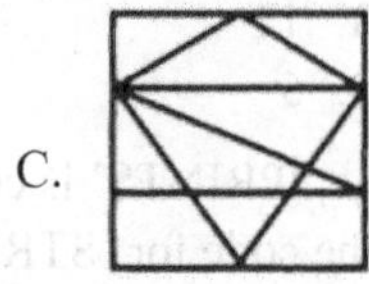

C. D.

44. Words given on the left side of (::) are related with each other by some Logic/Rule/Relation. Select the missing word/word pair on the right side of (::) from the given alternatives based on the same Logic/Rule/Relation.

Uttar Pradesh : Lucknow :: ?

A. Sikkim : Trivandrum
B. Rajasthan : Sikar
C. West Bengal : Kolkata
D. Chennai : Tamil Nadu

45. In the following question, select the odd word pair from the given alternatives.

A. Ottawa – Canada
B. Karachi – Pakistan
C. Rome – Italy
D. Canberra – Australia

46. Select the option figure in which the given figure is embedded. (Rotation is NOT allowed)

A. 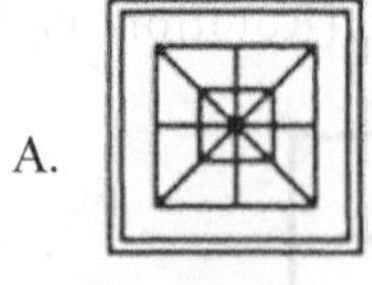 B. 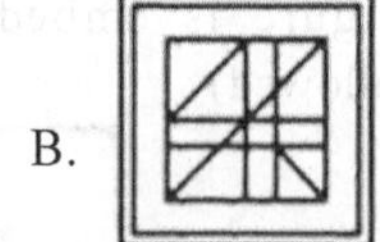

C. 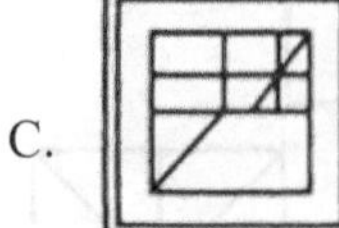 D. 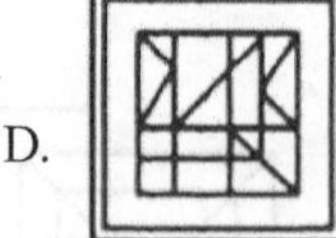

47. Select the correct option that indicates the arrangement of the given words in the order in which they appear in an English dictionary

1. Lean
2. League
3. Lecture
4. Layout
5. Leftist

A. 4, 2, 3, 1, 5 B. 2, 1, 5, 3, 4
C. 4, 2, 1, 3, 5 D. 4, 2, 1, 5, 3

48. Select the option that is related to the sixth number in the same way as the first number is related to the second number and third number is related to fourth number.

319 : 552 :: 146 : 379 :: ? : 774

A. 535 B. 639
C. 541 D. 479

49. Select the figure from the given options that can replace the question mark (?) in the following series:

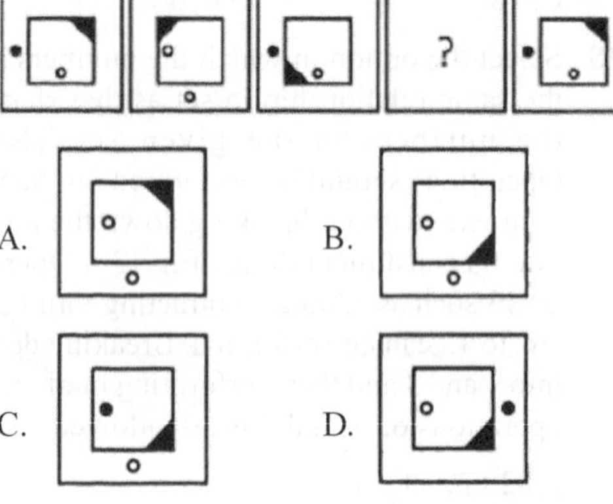

50. How many quadrilaterals are there in the given figure?

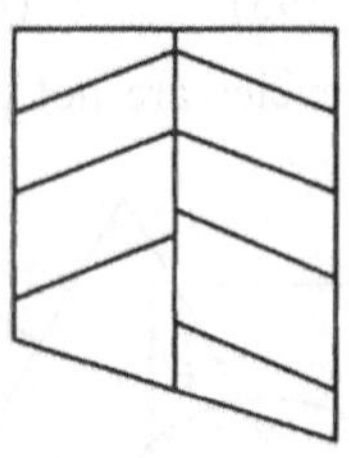

A. 24 B. 26
C. 22 D. 20

QUANTITATIVE APTITUDE

51. If tan $\tan A = \frac{3}{7}$, then what is the value of cosec A?

A. $\frac{2\sqrt{10}}{3}$ B. $\frac{7\sqrt{10}}{20}$

C. $\frac{\sqrt{58}}{3}$ D. $\frac{3}{\sqrt{58}}$

52. A 1800 metres long train crosses a man walking in opposite direction in 10 seconds. If the speed of train is 8 times to the speed of man, then what is the speed of train?

A. 576 km/hr B. 640 km/hr

C. 596 km/hr D. 570 km/hr

53. Distance of a chord RS from the centre is 20 cm. If the length of the this chord is 30 cm, then what will be the diameter of this circle?

A. 45 cm B. 55 cm

C. 60 cm D. 50 cm

54. The bar graph given below shows the sales of books (in thousand number) from six branches—B1, B2, B3, B4, B5 and B6 of a publishing company during two consecutive years 2000 and 2001.

Find the percentage (approximate) of the average sales of branches B2, B4 and B6 in the year 2001 to the average sales of branches B1, B3 and B5 in the year 2001.

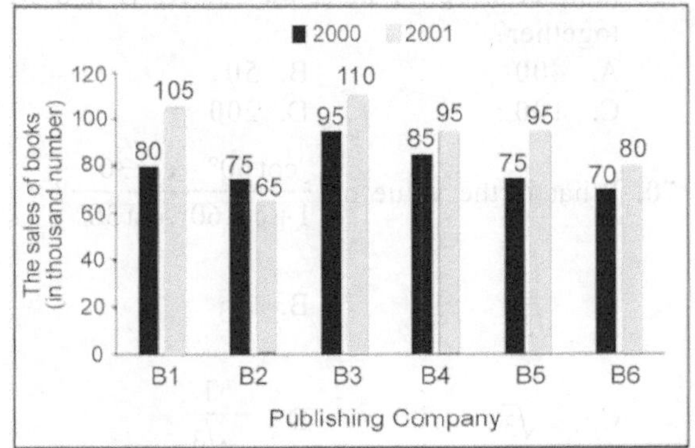

A. 97.95% B. 82.26%

C. 77.42% D. 92%

55. If $\frac{(17)^3 - (7)^3}{(17^2 + 7^2 + k)} = 10$, then what is the value of k?

A. 102 B. 119

C. 136 D. 85

56. What is the value of $4^2 - 3^2 + 6^2 - 5^2 + 8^2 - 7^2 + ... 92^2 - 91^2$?

A. 4272 B. 4280

C. 4278 D. 4275

57. ₹ 43,120 is divided among P, Q and R such that P's share is $\frac{4}{7}$ of total share of Q and R together and Q's share is $\frac{2}{5}$ of total share of P and R together. What is the share of R?

A. ₹ 15120 B. ₹ 14220

C. ₹ 16400 D. ₹ 18050

58. The bar graph given below shows the number of girls in 7 schools.

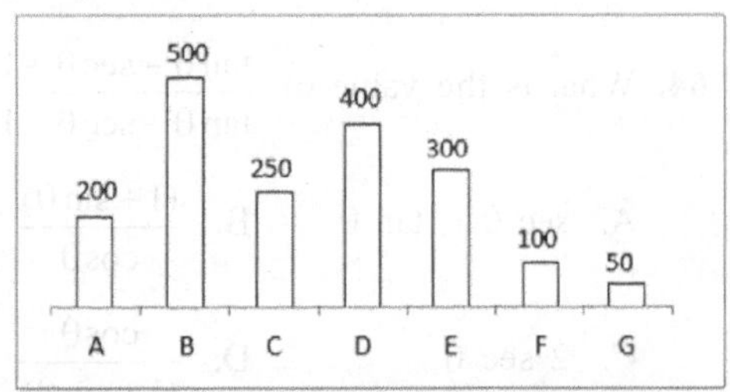

The number of girls in A is what per cent of the number of girls in F?

A. 100 per cent B. 200 per cent

C. 150 per cent D. 50 per cent

59. A merchant marks the price of his article 20 per cent above the cost price. If he allows 10 per cent discount, then what is the profit or loss percentage?

A. 8 per cent profit

B. 3.33 per cent loss

C. 6 per cent loss

D. 5 per cent profit

60. Three metallic cubes whose sides are 6 cm, 8 cm and 10 cm respectively are melted and converted into a single cube. If there is no loss of metal in this process, then what is the length of the side of the new cube?

A. 16 cm B. 14 cm
C. 12 cm D. 20 cm

61. The average of marks obtained by X and Y is 35 less than the average marks obtained by Y and Z. If the marks obtained by Z is 85, what is the marks obtained by X?

A. 155 B. 15
C. 35 D. 25

62. P sells a bottle to Q at a profit of 30 percent and Q sells it to R at a profit of 20 per cent. What is the ratio of cost prices of P and R?

A. 24 : 35 B. 25 : 39
C. 12 : 17 D. 13 : 19

63. A man borrows a sum of ₹ 12,000 which amounts to ₹ 13,200 in 2 years on simple interest. What would have been the amount if the rate of interest was doubled?

A. ₹ 13,400 B. ₹ 14,400
C. ₹ 12,400 D. ₹ 14,000

64. What is the value of $\frac{\tan\theta - \sec\theta + 1}{\tan\theta + \sec\theta - 1}$?

A. $\sec\theta + \tan\theta$ B. $\frac{(1+\sin\theta)}{\cos\theta}$

C. $2\sec\theta$ D. $\frac{\cos\theta}{(1+\sin\theta)}$

65. If $A = \frac{18 \div 9 \times 4}{15 \div 3 \times 5}$ and $B = \frac{18 \div 36 \times 3 + 5 \times 1 - 6}{18 \div 6 \times 20 - 3 \times 4 + 12}$, then what is the value of (A + B)?

A. $\frac{137}{600}$ B. $\frac{23}{100}$

C. $\frac{187}{600}$ D. $\frac{197}{600}$

66. Raman spends 50 per cent of his income. If his income increases by 10 per cent and the expenditure also increases by 10 per cent, then what will be the percentage increase in his savings?

A. 20 per cent B. 16.66 per cent
C. 10 per cent D. 8.33 per cent

67. Two identical circles intersect each other such that each passes through the centre of the other. Length of common chord is $16\sqrt{3}$ cm. What is the radius of each circle?

A. 16 cm B. $16\sqrt{3}$ cm

C. $16\sqrt{2}$ cm D. $8\sqrt{3}$ cm

68. A alone can complete the project in 10 days; B alone can complete it in 20 days while C alone can complete it in 30 days. They together earn ₹ 1,100 for the project. By how much do the total earnings of A and C exceed the earnings of B?

A. ₹ 600 B. ₹ 900
C. ₹ 700 D. ₹ 500

69. The line chart given below shows the number of girls in 7 schools.

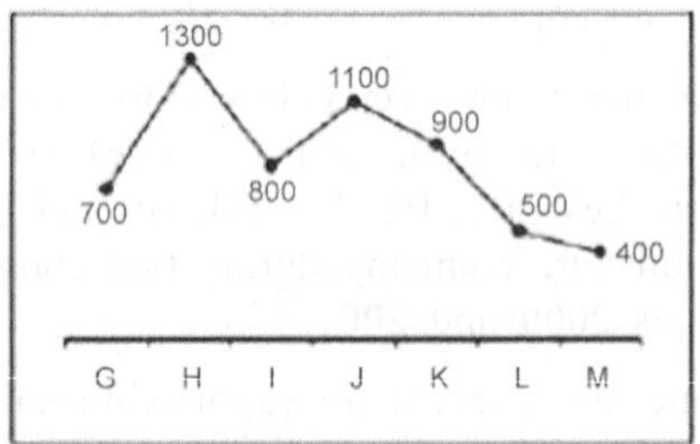

What is the difference between number of girls in school G, H and I together and the number of girls in school J, K, L and M together?

A. 400 B. 50
C. 100 D. 200

70. What is the value of $\frac{\cot 60° - \cot 30°}{1 + \cot 60°.\cot 30°}$?

A. $\frac{1}{\sqrt{3}}$ B. $\sqrt{3}$

C. $-\sqrt{3}$ D. $-\frac{1}{\sqrt{3}}$

71. The pie chart given below shows the number of girls in six schools. The total number of girls in all these six schools are 4000. Number of girls in a particular school is shown as a percentage of total number of girls in all these six schools.

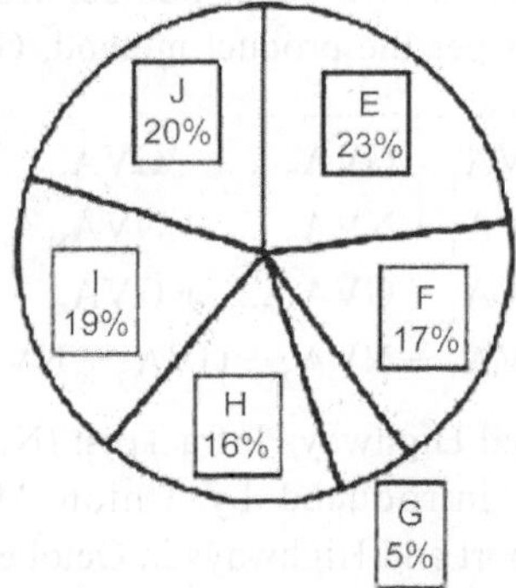

What is the value of central angle formed by sector F?

A. 48.4 degree B. 72.3 degree
C. 31.4 degree D. 61.2 degree

72. Angle subtended by a chord AB on the circumference is 90 degree. If radius of this circle is 8 cm, then what is the length of AB?

A. 16 cm B. 18 cm
C. 14 cm D. 12 cm

73. In ΔSTU, SE and TF are medians intersect each other at O. If UT = 34 cm, TF = 22.5 cm and SE = 24 cm, then what is the value of $\angle TOE$?

A. 75 degree B. 60 degree
C. 45 degree D. 90 degree

74. Which of the following is largest among $(125)^{\frac{1}{6}}, (11)^{\frac{1}{3}}, (12)^{\frac{1}{6}}, (5)^{\frac{1}{4}}$?

A. $(12)^{\frac{1}{6}}$ B. $(11)^{\frac{1}{3}}$
C. $(125)^{\frac{1}{6}}$ D. $(5)^{\frac{1}{4}}$

75. If $a+\frac{1}{a}=4$, then what is the value of $a^4+\frac{1}{a^4}$?

A. 206 B. 194
C. 204 D. 198

GENERAL AWARENESS

76. As per Global Hunger Index (GHI) 2022, India ranks at .... position.

A. 57th B. 77th
C. 97th D. 107th

77. What is the full form of EPROM?

A. Erasable Permanent Read Only Memory
B. Entire Programmable Read Only Memory
C. Erasable Programmable Read Only Memory
D. Entire Permanent Read Only Memory

78. Which of the following is monoatomic?

A. Nitrogen B. Oxygen
C. Chlorine D. Helium

79. Which of the following persons has been awarded the Nobel Peace Prize?

A. C. V. Raman
B. Kailash Satyarthi
C. Amartya Sen
D. Rabindranath Tagore

80. Gandhiji, aged ...., arrived in India in 1915 from South Africa.

A. 52 B. 46
C. 28 D. 34

81. Which among the following is a viral disease?

A. Chicken pox
B. Tuberculosis
C. Whooping Cough
D. Malaria

82. Which of the following is NOT a valid file format in MS-PowerPoint 365?

A. .pptm
B. .pwpt
C. .ppt
D. .pptx

83. The First Amendment Act, 1951 of the Indian constitution added which of the following schedules?
A. Tenth schedule
B. Ninth schedule
C. Eleventh schedule
D. Seventh schedule

84. The asteroid belt lies between which two planets?
A. Jupiter and Saturn
B. Mars and Jupiter
C. Saturn and Uranus
D. Mercury and Venus

85. Which among the following is not an All India Financial Institution?
A. ICICI Bank
B. National Bank for Agriculture and Rural Development
C. National Housing Bank
D. Export-Import Bank of India

86. Qawwali was brought in India from ....
A. Turkey B. Mongolia
C. Saudi Arabia D. Persia

87. Which country won the FIFA U-20 World Cup 2019?
A. Poland B. Norway
C. Ukraine D. South Korea

88. The approximate length of the Great Himalayan range, also known as the central axial range, is .... km from east to west.
A. 2800 B. 2500
C. 3000 D. 2100

89. What is the name of the mascot for 36th National Games, 2022?
A. Chanakya B. Kojima
C. Manikarnika D. Savaj

90. Identify the person from the given statements.

He founded e-commerce giant Amazon in 1994 out of his garage in Seattle. He stepped down as CEO to become executive chairman in July 2021.
A. Jack Ma B. Steve Jobs
C. Jeff Bezos D. Elon Musk

91. Western ghats are locally known as .... in Maharashtra.
A. Sahyadri B. Vindhya
C. Khadar D. Gondwana

92. If there are N firms in the economy, each assigned with a serial number from 1 to N, then as per the product method, GDP can be written as ....
A. $GVA_1 - GVA_2 \ldots\ldots - GVA_N$
B. $NVA_1 + NVA_2 \ldots\ldots + NVA_N$
C. $GVA_1 + GVA_2 \ldots\ldots + GVA_N$
D. $GVA_1 + NVA_2 + GVA_3 + NVA_4 \ldots\ldots$

93. National Highways Infra Trust (NHAI InvIT) bonds introduced by Union Minister of Transport and Highways in October 2022 will provide a effective yield of .... percent each year.
A. 6.05 B. 9.05
C. 7.05 D. 8.05

94. India won the only bronze medal in which team sports at Tokyo Olympics 2020 held in 2021?
A. Table Tennis B. Basketball
C. Field hockey D. Badminton

95. What is the average height of inner Himalayas?
A. 6000 metres B. 4500 metres
C. 5200 metres D. 7100 metres

96. Article 350A of the Indian constitution is related with ....
A. Special officers for linguistic minorities
B. Facilities for instruction in mother-tongue at primary stage
C. Direction for development of the Hindi language
D. Language to be used in Supreme Court and High Courts of India

97. What is the percentage of carbon dioxide in the air exhaled by human lungs?
A. 3.2 per cent B. 5.9 per cent
C. 2.3 per cent D. 4.4 per cent

98. Which Indian cricketer is also known as Little Master?
A. Umesh Yadav
B. Virat Kohli
C. Sunil Gavasker
D. Kapil Dev

99. When was Alluri Sitarama Raju arrested ending a two-year armed tribal struggle?
A. May 1924
B. January 1921
C. April 1919
D. December 1929

100. Which Indian festival celebrates the birth anniversary of spiritual leader Padmasambhava, founder of Tibet Tantric Buddhism?
A. Bakrid
B. Losar
C. Gurpurab
D. Hemis

ANSWERS

1. (C)	**2. (B)**	**3. (B)**
4. (D)	**5. (D)**	**6. (D)**
7. (C)	**8. (C)**	**9. (A)**
10. (A)	**11. (A)**	**12. (D)**
13. (B)	**14. (B)**	**15. (A)**
16. (B)	**17. (B)**	**18. (A)**
19. (B)	**20. (D)**	**21. (D)**
22. (A)	**23. (C)**	**24. (A)**
25. (C)		

26. (D): According to given statement

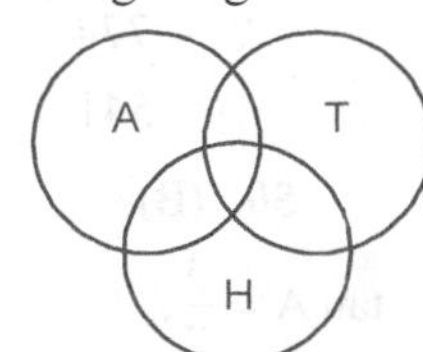

Conclusions: I. No T is A (false)
II. No H is T (false)
III. No A is H (false)

Hence, neither conclusion follows.

27. (B)

28. (B):

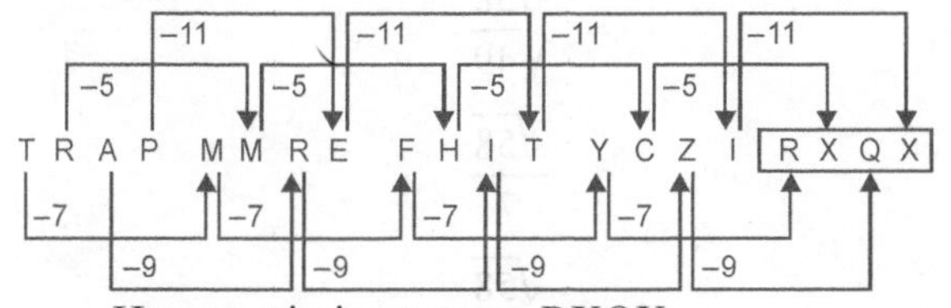

Hence, missing term = RXQX.

29. (B):

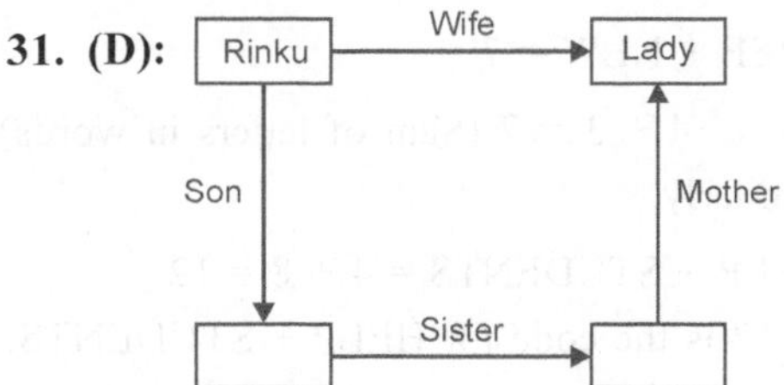

Hence, missing term = 182.

30. (A)

31. (D):

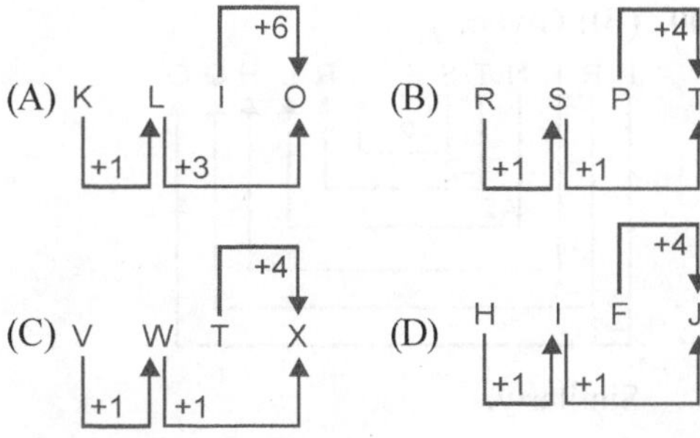

Here, lady is the wife of Rinku.

32. (A):

(A) K L I O — +1, +3, +6

(B) R S P T — +1, +1, +4

(C) V W T X — +1, +1, +4

(D) H I F J — +1, +1, +4

Here, option (A) is the odd letters from the given alternatives.

33. (B)

34. (C)

35. (A):

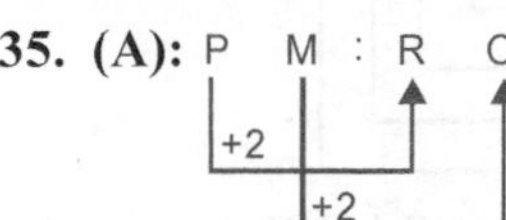

Similarly,

B C : D E

+2

+2

$\therefore$ PM : RO :: BC : **DE**

36. (D): ÷ and –, 4 and 8

$\therefore$ $10 \times 8 \div 6 - 2 + 4$

$= 10 \times 4 - 6 \div 2 + 8$

$= 10 \times 4 - 3 + 8$

$= 40 - 3 + 8$

$= 48 - 3$

$= 45$

Here, option (D) is correct.

37. (B): Given, ONLINE + THEIR = 11

$\Rightarrow$ 6 + 5 = 11 (Sum of letters in words)

FREE + NEW = 7

$\Rightarrow$ 4 + 3 = 7 (Sum of letters in words)

Similarly,

HELP + STUDENTS = 4 + 8 = 12

$\therefore$ 12 is the code for HELP + STUDENTS.

38. (A)

39. (B)

40. (B): Given,

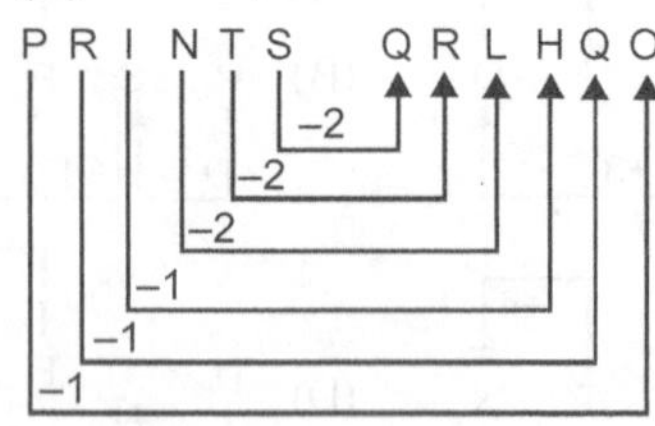

Similarly,

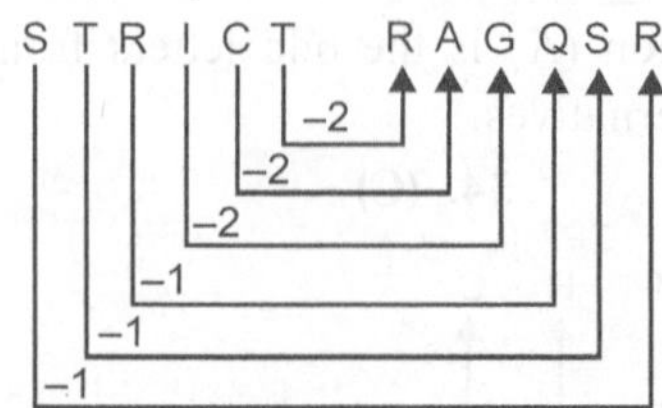

$\therefore$ STRICT is coded as RAGQSR.

41. (D): (A) 9 – 810 $\Rightarrow 9 \times 9 \times 10 = 810$

(B) 11 – 1452 $\Rightarrow 11 \times 11 \times 12 = 1452$

(C) 7 – 392 $\Rightarrow 7 \times 7 \times 8 = 392$

(D) 13 – 2368 $\Rightarrow 13 \times 13 \times 14 = 2366$

Here, in option (D) 2366 is not equal to 2368.

$\therefore$ Option (D) is the odd pair.

42. (B): Given, 13 @ 2 # 5 = 10

$\Rightarrow 13 + 2 - 5 = 10$

and 43 # 9 @ 16 = 50

$\Rightarrow 43 - 9 + 16 = 50$

Then, 8 @ 6 # 3

$= 8 + 6 - 3$

$= 14 - 3$

$= 11$

$\therefore$ 8 @ 6 # 3 = 11

43. (A) **44. (C)** **45. (B)**

46. (D) **47. (C)**

48. (C): 319 : 552 :: 146 : 379 :: ? : 774

Here, $552 - 319 = 233$

$379 - 146 = 233$

$\therefore$ $? = 774 - 233$

$= 541.$

49. (B) **50. (B)**

51. (C): Given, $\tan A = \frac{3}{7}$,

$$\therefore \quad \sec A = \sqrt{1+\tan^2 A} = \sqrt{1+\left(\frac{3}{7}\right)^2}$$

$$= \sqrt{1+\frac{9}{49}}$$

$$= \sqrt{\frac{58}{49}}$$

$$= \frac{\sqrt{58}}{7}$$

$$\Rightarrow \quad \sec A = \frac{\sqrt{58}}{7}$$

$\Rightarrow \quad \cos A = \dfrac{7}{\sqrt{58}}$

$\therefore \quad \sin A = \sqrt{1-\cos^2 A} = \sqrt{1-\dfrac{49}{58}}$

$= \sqrt{\dfrac{9}{58}} = \dfrac{3}{\sqrt{58}}$

$\Rightarrow \quad \sin A = \dfrac{3}{\sqrt{58}}$

$\therefore \quad \text{cosec } A = \dfrac{\sqrt{58}}{3}$

52. (A): Let the speed of man is x m/s

Then, the speed of train is $8x$ m/s

$\because$ Man walking in opposite direction

$\therefore$ Relative speed $= x + 8x = 9x$ m/s

Now, $\dfrac{\text{distance}}{\text{speed}} = \text{time}$

$\Rightarrow \dfrac{1800}{9x} = 10$

$\Rightarrow \dfrac{200}{x} = 10$

$\Rightarrow x = 20$ m/s

$\therefore$ The speed of train $= 8x = 8 \times 20$

$= 160 \text{ m/s} = 160 \times \dfrac{18}{5}$ km/h

$= 32 \times 18$ km/h $= 576$ km/h.

53. (D): Given, chord RS = 30 cm

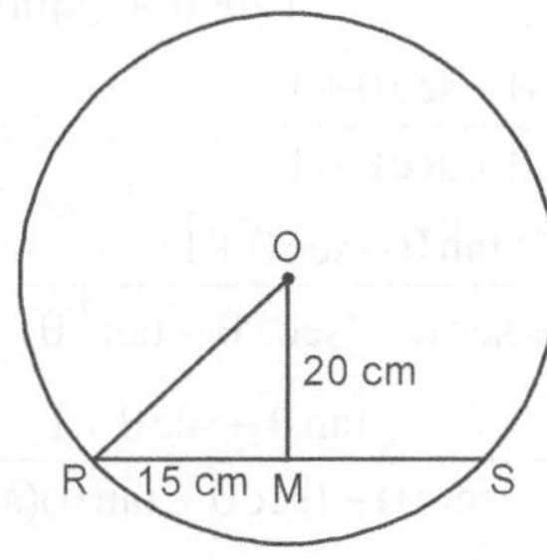

Let OM ⊥ RS

Then, OM = 20 cm

$\therefore$ RM = MS = 15 cm

Let OR = Radius

In ΔOMR,

$OR^2 = OM^2 + MR^2$

$\Rightarrow \quad OR^2 = (20)^2 + (15)^2$

$\Rightarrow \quad OR^2 = 400 + 225$

$\Rightarrow \quad OR^2 = 625$

$\Rightarrow \quad OR^2 = (25)^2$

$\Rightarrow \quad OR = 25$ cm

$\therefore$ The diameter of the circle $= 2r$

$= 2\,(OR) = 2 \times 25 = 50$ cm.

54. (C)

55. (B): $[a^3 - b^3 = (a - b)(a^2 + b^2 + ab)]$

Given, $\dfrac{(17)^3 - (7)^3}{(17^2 + 7^2 + k)} = 10$

$\Rightarrow \dfrac{(17-7)(17^2 + 7^2 + 17 \times 7)}{(17^2 + 7^2 + k)} = 10$

$\Rightarrow \dfrac{10(17^2 + 7^2 + 119)}{(17^2 + 7^2 + k)} = 10$

$\Rightarrow \dfrac{(17^2 - 7^2 + 119)}{(17^2 + 7^2 + k)} = 1$

$\Rightarrow 17^2 + 7^2 + 119 = 17^2 + 7^2 + k$

$\Rightarrow k = 119.$

56. (D): $4^2 - 3^2 + 6^2 - 5^2 + 8^2 - 7^2 + \ldots\ldots.\ 92^2 - 91^2$

$= 7 + 11 + 15 + \ldots + 183$

Here, $a = 7$, $d = 4$, th $= 183$

$\because$ th $= a + (n - 1)d$

$\therefore\ 183 = 7 + (n - 1) \times 4$

$\Rightarrow 4(n - 1) = 183 - 7 = 176$

$\Rightarrow n - 1 = 44$

$\Rightarrow n = 45$

Let $S_n = 7 + 11 + 15 + \ldots + 183$

then, $\quad S_n = \dfrac{n}{2}[2a + (n-1)d]$

$= \dfrac{45}{2}[2 \times 7 + (45-1) \times 4]$

$= \dfrac{45}{2} \times 2\,[7 + 44 \times 2]$

$= 45[7 + 88]$

$= 45 \times 95$

$= 4275.$

57. (A)

58. (B): From given bar-graph

$$A = F \times \frac{x}{100}$$

$$\Rightarrow \quad 200 = 100 \times \frac{x}{100}$$

$$\Rightarrow \quad x = 200\%$$

$\therefore$ Required per cent = 200%.

59. (A): Let cost price of an article is ₹ 100

Then, marked price = ₹ 120

Given, discount = 10%

$$\therefore \quad \text{Selling Price} = 120 \times \frac{100-10}{100}$$

$$= 120 \times \frac{90}{100}$$

$$= ₹\,108$$

$$\therefore \quad \text{Profit} = \text{SP} - \text{CP}$$

$$= 108 - 100$$

$$= ₹\,8$$

Profit percentage = 8%.

60. (C): Here, volume of 3 metallic cubes

$$\therefore \quad V_1 = (\text{side})^3 = (6)^3 = 216 \text{ cm}^3$$

$$V_2 = (8)^3 = 64 \times 8 = 512 \text{ cm}^3$$

$$V_3 = (10)^3 = 1000 \text{ cm}^3$$

$\therefore$ Volume of new cube = 216 + 512 + 1000

$\Rightarrow$ V = 1728 cm^3

$\Rightarrow$ V = 12 × 144 = 12 × 12 × 12

$\Rightarrow$ (side)^3 = (12)^3 cm^3

$\Rightarrow$ side = 12 cm

$\therefore$ Length of the side of the new cube = 12 cm.

61. (B): Let the average marks obtained by Y and Z is a

$$\Rightarrow \quad Y + Z = 2a \quad \text{...}(i)$$

Then the average marks obtained by X and Y

$$= a - 35$$

$$\Rightarrow \quad X + Y = 2(a - 35)$$

$$= 2a - 70 \quad \text{...}(ii)$$

$$\text{and} \quad Z = 85 \quad \text{...}(iii)$$

From (i) and (iii), Y = $2a$ – 85 ...(iv)

From (ii) and (iv),

$$X = 2a - 70 - 2a + 85$$

$$= 15$$

$\therefore$ The marks obtained by X is 15.

62. (B): Let cost price for P = ₹ x

Then, CP for Q = $x \times \frac{130}{100} = \frac{13}{10}x$

and CP for R = $\frac{13}{10}x \times \frac{120}{100} = \frac{13}{10} \times \frac{12}{10}x$

$\therefore$ The ratio of cost prices of P and R

$$= x : \frac{13}{10} \times \frac{12}{10}x = 1 : \frac{156}{100}$$

$$= 1 : \frac{39}{25} = 25 : 39.$$

63. (B): Here,

P = ₹ 12000, A = ₹ 13200, t = 2 years

$\therefore$ Simple Interest = A – P

$$= 13200 - 12000 = ₹\,1200$$

$$\because \text{ Rate} = \frac{\text{SI} \times 100}{\text{P} \times t} = \frac{1200 \times 100}{12000 \times 2} = 5\%$$

Given, the rate of interest was doubled

$$\therefore \text{ Simple Interest} = \frac{prt}{100}$$

$$= \frac{12000 \times 2 \times 5 \times 2}{100} = 2400$$

$$\therefore \quad \text{Amount} = \text{P} + \text{SI}$$

$$= 12000 + 2400 = ₹\,14400.$$

64. (D): $\dfrac{\tan\theta - \sec\theta + 1}{\tan\theta + \sec\theta - 1}$

$$= \frac{\tan\theta - \sec\theta + 1}{\tan\theta + \sec\theta - (\sec^2\theta - \tan^2\theta)}$$

$$= \frac{\tan\theta - \sec\theta + 1}{(\tan\theta + \sec\theta) - (\sec\theta - \tan\theta)(\sec\theta + \tan\theta)}$$

$$= \frac{\tan\theta - \sec\theta + 1}{(\tan\theta + \sec\theta)(1 - \sec\theta + \tan\theta)}$$

$$= \frac{1 - \sec\theta + \tan\theta}{(\tan\theta + \sec\theta)(1 - \sec\theta + \tan\theta)}$$

$= \dfrac{1}{\tan\theta + \sec\theta} = \dfrac{1}{\dfrac{\sin\theta}{\cos\theta} + \dfrac{1}{\cos\theta}}$

$= \dfrac{1}{\dfrac{\sin\theta + 1}{\cos\theta}} = \dfrac{\cos\theta}{(1+\sin\theta)}$

65. (D): Given, $A = \dfrac{18 \div 9 \times 4}{15 \div 3 \times 5} = \dfrac{2 \times 4}{5 \times 5} = \dfrac{8}{25}$ and

$B = \dfrac{18 \div 36 \times 3 + 5 \times 1 - 6}{18 \div 6 \times 20 - 3 \times 4 + 12}$,

$= \dfrac{18 \times \dfrac{1}{36} \times 3 + 5 \times 1 - 6}{18 \times \dfrac{1}{6} \times 20 - 3 \times 4 + 12} = \dfrac{\dfrac{3}{2} + 5 - 6}{60 - 12 + 12}$

$\Rightarrow B = \dfrac{\dfrac{3}{2} - 1}{60} = \dfrac{\dfrac{1}{2}}{60} = \dfrac{1}{120}$

$\Rightarrow B = \dfrac{1}{120}$

$\therefore \quad (A + B) = \dfrac{8}{25} + \dfrac{1}{120}$

$= \dfrac{192 + 5}{600} = \dfrac{197}{600}$

$\Rightarrow \quad (A + B) = \dfrac{197}{600}$

66. (C): Let Raman's income = ₹ 100

Then, expenditure = $100 \times \dfrac{50}{100}$ = ₹ 50

∴ Saving = 100 – 50 = ₹ 50

Again, increased income = $100 \times \dfrac{110}{100}$ = ₹ 110

and expenditure = $50 \times \dfrac{110}{100}$ = ₹ 55

∴ New saving = 110 – 55 = ₹ 55

Percentage increase in saving

$= \dfrac{55 - 50}{50} \times 100 = 5 \times 2 = 10\%.$

67. (A): Let two identical circles intersect each other at A and B such that both passes through the centre of the others. Its centres are O and O′.

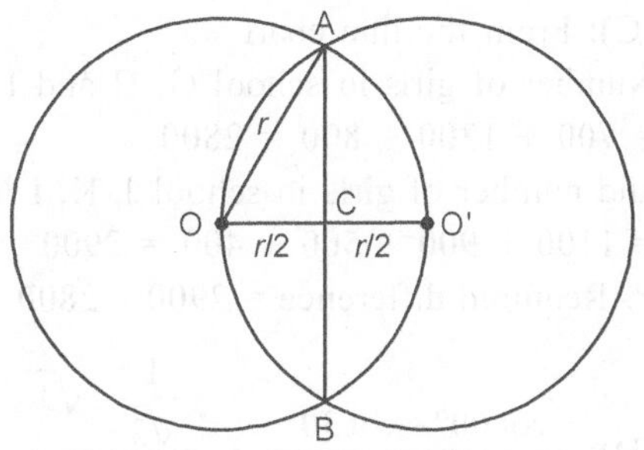

Then, common chord = AB = $16\sqrt{3}$ cm

$\Rightarrow$ AC = BC = $8\sqrt{3}$

OA = OO′ = r, OC = O′C = $\dfrac{r}{2}$

In ΔACO,

$$r^2 = \left(8\sqrt{3}\right)^2 + \left(\frac{r}{2}\right)^2$$

$\Rightarrow \quad r^2 - \dfrac{r^2}{4} = 64 \times 3$

$\Rightarrow \quad 3r^2 = 64 \times 3 \times 4$

$\Rightarrow \quad r^2 = 64 \times 4$

$\Rightarrow \quad r = 8 \times 2 = 16$

Hence, the radius of each circle = 16 cm.

68. (D): A's 1 days work = $\dfrac{1}{10}$

B's 1 days work = $\dfrac{1}{20}$

C's 1 days work = $\dfrac{1}{30}$

Ratio of work

$A : B : C = \dfrac{1}{10} : \dfrac{1}{20} : \dfrac{1}{30} = 6 : 3 : 2$

Given, total earning for the project = ₹ 1100

∴ Earning of A and C = $1100 \times \dfrac{6+2}{6+3+2}$

$= 1100 \times \dfrac{8}{11}$ = ₹ 800

and earning of B = $1100 \times \dfrac{3}{11}$ = ₹ 300

Hence, (A + C) – B = 800 – 300 = ₹ 500.

69. (C): From the line chart
Number of girls in school G, H and I
= 700 + 1300 + 800 = 2800
and number of girls in school J, K, L and M
= 1100 + 900 + 500 + 400 = 2900
∴ Required difference = 2900 – 2800 = 100.

70. (D): $\dfrac{\cot 60° - \cot 30°}{1+\cot 60°.\cot 30°} = \dfrac{\frac{1}{\sqrt{3}}-\sqrt{3}}{1+\frac{1}{\sqrt{3}}.\sqrt{3}}$

$= \dfrac{\frac{1-3}{\sqrt{3}}}{1+1}$

$= \dfrac{-2}{\sqrt{3}\times 2}$

$= \dfrac{-1}{\sqrt{3}}$

71. (D): From given pie-chart
The total number of girls in all these six school = 4000

∵ 100% = 360°

∴ $1\% = \dfrac{360°}{100} = \dfrac{18°}{5}$

∴ Value of central angle formed by sector F

$= 17\% = 17\times\dfrac{18°}{5} = 17 \times 3.6°$

= 61.2 degree.

72. (A) **73. (D)**

74. (C): Here, LCM of 6, 3, 6 and 4 = 12

(A) $(12)^{\frac{1}{6}} = (12)^{\frac{1}{6}\times 12} = (12)^2 = 144$

(B) $(11)^{\frac{1}{3}} = (11)^{\frac{1}{3}\times 12} = (11)^4 = 14641$

(C) $(125)^{\frac{1}{6}} = (125)^{\frac{1}{6}\times 12} = (125)^2 = 15625$

(D) $(5)^{\frac{1}{4}} = (5)^{\frac{1}{4}\times 12} = (5)^3 = 125$

∴ 15625 > 14641 > 144 > 125

$\Rightarrow (125)^{\frac{1}{6}} > (11)^{\frac{1}{3}} > (12)^{\frac{1}{6}} > (5)^{\frac{1}{4}}$

Hence, $(125)^{\frac{1}{6}}$ is largest among all.

75. (B): $a+\dfrac{1}{a} = 4$

$\Rightarrow \left(a+\dfrac{1}{a}\right)^2 = (4)^2$

$\Rightarrow a^2+\dfrac{1}{a^2}+2a\dfrac{1}{a} = 16$

$\Rightarrow a^2+\dfrac{1}{a^2} = 16 - 2$

$\Rightarrow a^2+\dfrac{1}{a^2} = 14$

Again, $\left(a^2+\dfrac{1}{a^2}\right)^2 = (14)^2$

$\Rightarrow a^4+\dfrac{1}{a^4}+2a^2.\dfrac{1}{a^2} = 196$

$\Rightarrow a^4+\dfrac{1}{a^4}+2 = 196$

$\Rightarrow a^4+\dfrac{1}{a^4} = 194.$

76. (D)	**77. (C)**	**78. (D)**
79. (B)	**80. (B)**	**81. (A)**
82. (B)	**83. (B)**	**84. (B)**
85. (A)	**86. (D)**	**87. (C)**
88. (B)	**89. (D)**	**90. (C)**
91. (A)	**92. (C)**	**93. (D)**
94. (C)	**95. (A)**	**96. (B)**
97. (D)	**98. (C)**	**99. (A)**
100. (D)		

Previous Paper (Solved)

SSC—Combined Higher Secondary Level–CHSL (10+2) TIER–1, Online Recruitment Exam–2021

(Exam held on 02-06-2022)

ENGLISH LANGUAGE

1. Parts of the given sentence have been given as options. One of them contains a grammatical error. Select the option that has the error.

When you have worked out this sum, you may went out to play.

A. When you have worked out
B. went out to play
C. this sum
D. you may

2. The following sentence has been split into four segments. Identify the segment that contains a grammatical error.

Going to the weekly market / in every Tuesday / is a ritual that has been followed / by generations in my family.

A. is a ritual that has been followed
B. by generations in my family
C. in every Tuesday
D. Going to the weekly market

3. Select the most appropriate ANTONYM of the given word.

Despair

A. Vile B. Hope
C. Annoy D. Definite

4. Select the INCORRECTLY spelt word.

A. Audience B. Comprehension
C. Competence D. Attendence

5. Select the most appropriate ANTONYM of the given word.

Wax

A. Wane B. Mourn
C. Error D. Insolent

6. Select the most appropriate option to substitute the underline segment in the given sentence.

It was apparent that the girl was <u>heading into</u> a serious disaster.

A. heading along B. heading for
C. heading down D. heading out

7. Select the INCORRECTLY spelt word.

A. kengaroo B. Vivacious
C. Ambiguous D. Itinerary

8. Select the option that can be used as a one-word substitute for the underlined group of words.

He requested the bank to give him more time as at present he was <u>unable to pay his debts</u>.

A. Destitute B. Meticulous
C. Reckless D. Bankrupt

9. Select the most appropriate meaning of the given idiom.

Dark horse

A. A person criticised
B. Loved person
C. An unexpected winner
D. A champion

10. Select the option that expresses the given sentence in passive voice. The people will make him the leader.

A. He had been made the leader by people.

B. He will be made the leader by the people.
C. He was made leader by the people.
D. People made him the leader.

11. Select the option that expresses the given sentence in passive voice.

I know him.

A. I am known to him.
B. He is known to myself.
C. He is known to me.
D. Let him be known to me.

12. Select the option that will improve the underlined part of the given sentence.

Mahatma Gandhi in undoubtedly one of the much popular authors of our times.

A. best B. total
C. most D. better

13. Select the most appropriate option that can substitute the underlined segment in the given sentence. If there is no need to substitute it, select 'No substitution required'. Sheela is trying for a job since last year.

A. was trying
B. have been trying
C. No substitution required
D. has been trying

14. In the following passage, a word has been deleted. Read the passage carefully and select the most appropriate option to fill in the blank.

Gifting is generally taken to be the easiest act to ________, if only you have the heart to part with something in your ________.

A. forsake, capacity
B. perform, possession
C. forgive, discretion
D. observe, control

15. Select the most appropriate option to fill in the blank.

He is a ______ in shining armour.

A. knit B. nite
C. night D. knight

16. Sentences of a paragraph are given below in jumbled order. Arrange the sentences in the correct order to form a meaningful and coherent paragraph.

(*a*) However, after studying the myths scientifically, only a simpleton would find them irrational or worthless.
(*b*) Moreover, it is wrong to analyse myths on the yardstick of their factual accuracy as they were designed to serve a greater, deeper purpose.
(*c*) Myths have always been regarded as a complex and intriguing aspect in human life
(*d*) In modern scientific world, they are essentially seen as something unscientific and meaningless.

A. (*d*), (*c*), (*a*), (*b*) B. (*d*), (*a*), (*c*), (*b*)
C. (*a*), (*c*), (*d*), (*b*) D. (*c*), (*d*), (*a*), (*b*)

17. Select the most appropriate meaning of the given idiom.

Be like chalk and cheese

A. Be absolutely lonely
B. Be absolutely rich
C. Be absolutely deceptive
D. Be absolutely different

18. Select the most appropriate ANTONYM of the word 'Lead' from the given sentence. All the class monitors were asked to follow the guide who was there to manage and control their visit to Yamuna Biodiversity Park.

A. Control B. Follow
C. Guide D. Manage

19. Select the most appropriate option that can substitute the underlined segment in the given sentence.

I had get back from Hyderabad last month.

A. got back from
B. had got back
C. get back from
D. had got back from

20. Select the most appropriate synonym of the given word.

Salubrious
A. Beneficial B. Vicarious
C. Insidious D. Septic

Directions (Qs. No. 21-25): *In the following passage, some words have been deleted. Read the passage carefully and select the most appropriate option to fill in each blank.*

While I was sitting there (1)_________ over my failure to keep from having to spend (2) glistering _________ summer months on the freaking Cote of Azur, Grandmere started (3)_________ me from the phone. She kept (4)_________ her fingers on the phone to catch my attention. I just sat there blinking at her until finally she put her hand over the receiver and (5)_________ (so that nobody listens), "Amelia! In my bedroom, there is something for you".

21. Select the most appropriate option to fill in blank number 1.
A. smirking B. sulking
C. grinning D. clapping

22. Select the most appropriate option to fill in blank number 2.
A. ours B. me
C. my D. mine

23. Select the most appropriate option to fill in blank number 3.
A. disconcerting B. beckoning
C. upsetting D. dismissing

24. Select the most appropriate option to fill in blank number 4.
A. piquing B. snapping
C. peering D. tapping

25. Select the most appropriate option to fill in blank number 5.
A. commended B. cheered
C. lauded D. hissed

GENERAL INTELLIGENCE

26. Study the given pattern carefully and select the number that can replace the question mark (?) in it.
First row- 5, 39, 8
Second row- 7, 36, 5
Third row- 11, ?, 9

(NOTE: Operations should be performed on the whole numbers, without breaking down the numbers into its constituent digits. E.g. 13 – Operations on 13 such as adding / deleting / multiplying etc. to 13 can be performed. Breaking down 13 into 1 and 3 and then performing mathematical operations on 1 and 3 is NOT allowed)
A. 60 B. 40
C. 50 D. 70

27. Select the option that is related to the fifth number in the same way as the second number is related to the first number and the fourth number is related to the third number.
6 : 96 : : 8 : 144 : : 5 : ?
A. 70 B. 90
C. 85 D. 75

28. Select the option that represents the correct order of the given words as they would appear in an English dictionary.
1. Catalyst
2. Carrot
3. Calcium
4. Calculate
5. Calendar
A. 4, 3, 5, 2, 1
B. 4, 5, 3, 2, 1
C. 3, 4, 5, 2, 1
D. 3, 2, 1, 4, 5

29. Three Statements are given followed by Three conclusions numbered I, II and III. Assuming the statements to be true, even if they seem to be at variance with commonly known facts, decide which of the conclusions logically follow(s) from the statements.

Statements:
All moons are suns.
No moon is a star.
Some stars are planets.
Conclusions:
I. Some suns are planets.
II. No sun is a star.
III. No planet is a moon.
A. Both conclusions I and II follow.
B. None of the conclusions follow.
C. Both conclusions I and III follow.
D. Only conclusion II follows.

30. The second number in the given number pairs is obtained by performing certain mathematical operation(s) on the first number. The same operation(s) are followed in all the number pairs except one. Find that odd number pair.
A. 43 : 84 B. 21 : 40
C. 15 : 210 D. 19 : 36

31. Select the correct combination of mathematical signs to replace the * signs and to balance the given equation.

16*6*69*81*3
A. –, +, ×, = B. ×, –, =, ÷
C. ÷, +, =, × D. +, =, ×, –

32. Which of the following letter-clusters will replace the question mark (?) in the given series to make it logically complete?

TVX, SUW, RTV, QSU, ?
A. TRP B. RPT
C. TPR D. PRT

33. Select the option that is related to the third term in the same way as the second term is related to the first term and the sixth term is related to the fifth term.

19 : 90 :: 25 : ? :: 13 : 60
A. 120 B. 100
C. 115 D. 110

34. Select the option that is related to the third word in the same way as the second word is related to the first word. (The words must be considered as meaningful English words and must NOT be related to each other based on the number of letters/number of consonants/vowels in the word)

Golf : Stick :: Cricket : ?
A. Bat B. Stadium
C. Ball D. Wicket

35. Select the correct combination of mathematical signs to replace the * signs and to balance the given equation.
127*13*3*129*41
A. +, =, +, – B. –, ×, =, –
C. ÷, –, =, – D. –, –, =, +

36. How many squares are there in the given figure?

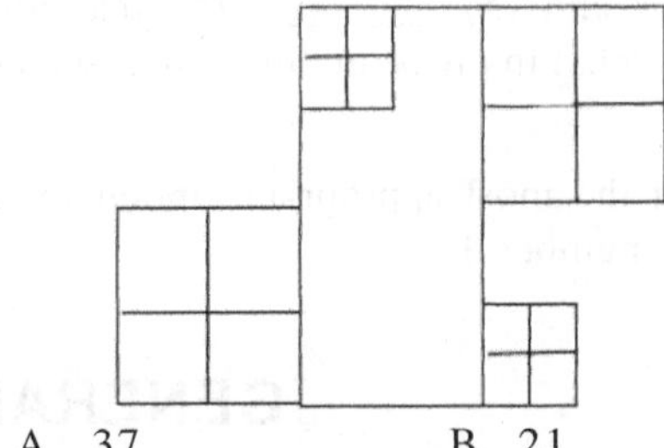

A. 37 B. 21
C. 36 D. 20

37. If A denotes '+', B denotes '×', C denotes '–' and D denotes '÷', then what will come in place of '?' in the following equation?

17 A (31 B 3) C (64 D 8) A 41 C (21 B 4) = ?
A. 69 B. 59
C. 61 D. 55

38. In a certain code language, 'MOTHER' is written as 'LNSGIV' and 'FATHER' is written as 'ZUSGIV'. How will 'WONDER' be written in that language?
A. DLWMIV B. DLMWIV
C. LDWMIV D. LDMWVI

39. Select the option that is embedded in the given figure as its part (rotation is NOT allowed).

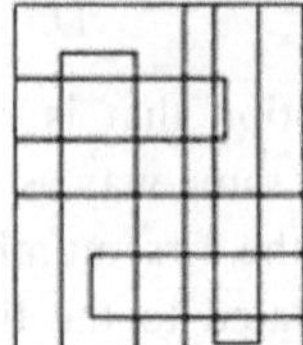

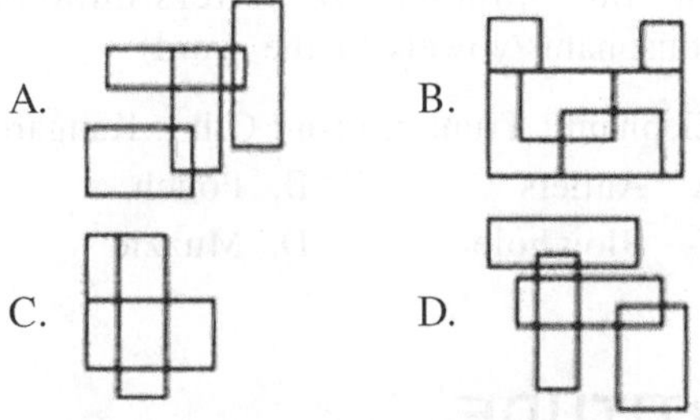

40. A paper is folded and cut as shown below. How will it appear when unfolded?

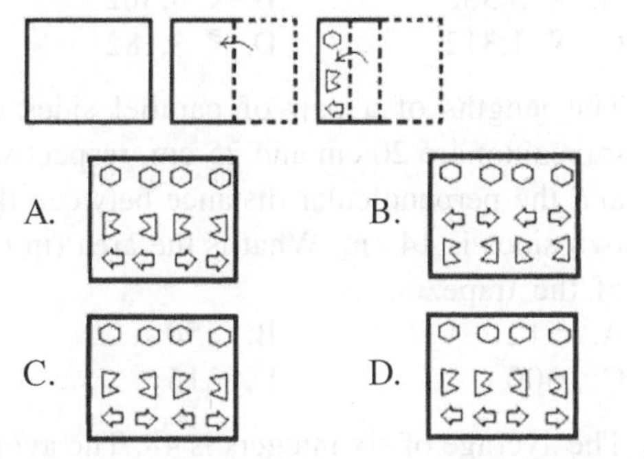

41. Select the correct mirror image of the given combination when the mirror is placed at MN as shown.

M

tyk472

N

A. ƧΓ4ʞʎɈ   B. Ƨ74ʞyt
C. ƧΓ4ʞyɈ   D. Ƨ74ʞyt

42. Select the correct mirror image of the given combination when the mirror is placed at 'PQ' as shown.

P

A7t9CK

Q

A. KƆ6ɈΓA   B. KƆeɈΓA
C. ʞƆeɈΓA   D. ʞƆ6Ɉ7A

43. Select the correct combination of mathematical signs to replace the * signs and to balance the given equation.

99*25*10*12*7

A. –, =, +, ×   B. +, =, +, ×
C. –, +, =, ×   D. –, =, +, +

44. If 31 December 2009 was Thursday, then what was the day of the week on 25 December 2010?

A. Monday   B. Sunday
C. Saturday   D. Tuesday

45. Select the correct combination of mathematical signs to sequentially replace the * signs and to balance the given equation.

16*4*8*10*2*43

A. ÷, ×, –, +, =   B. ÷, ×, +, –, =
C. ×, ÷, –, +, =   D. +, ×, –, ÷, =

46. In a certain code language, 'ACTOR' is written as '136812' and 'HEROINE' is written as '95128745'. How will 'HERO' be written in that language?

A. 95128   B. 95768
C. 95218   D. 95378

47. Which of the following numbers will replace the question mark (?) in the given series?

314, 285, 308, ?, 306, 293, 304

A. 277   B. 298
C. 287   D. 289

48. Which letter-cluster will replace the question mark (?) to complete the given series?

CIEO, JAAU, QSWA, XKSE,?

A. FCOI   B. ECOI
C. ECRI   D. FCRI

49. Two different positions of the same dice are shown, the six faces of which are marked from A to F. Select the letter that will be on the face opposite to the one showing 'D'.

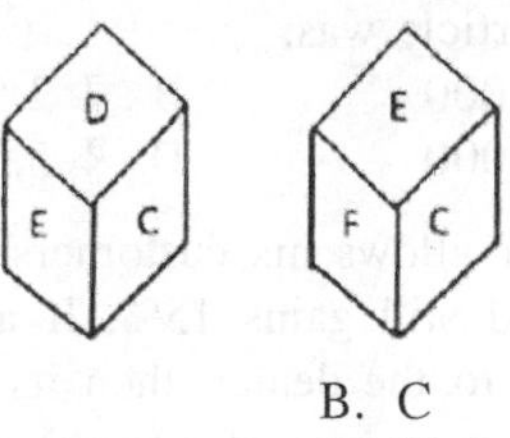

A. F   B. C
C. B   D. E

50. Select the option that is related to the fifth word in the same way as the second word is related to the first word and the fourth word is related to the third word. (The words must be considered as meaningful English words and must NOT be related to each other based on the number of letters/number of consonants/vowels in the word)

Elephant : Trunk :: Fish : Gill :: Kangaroo : ?

A. Antlers B. Pouch
C. Blowhole D. Muzzle

QUANTITATIVE APTITUDE

51. Ruksana travelled at 60 km/h while going from point A to point B, and returned via the same route at a different speed. If Ruksana's overall average speed during the two-way journey was 48 km/h, what was her speed while travelling from B to A?

A. 42 km/h B. 40 km/h
C. 45 km/h D. 36 km/h

52. What distance will be covered by a bus moving at 108 km/h in 40 seconds?

A. 1 km 600 m B. 1 km 400 m
C. 1 km 800 m D. 1 km 200 m

53. An arc on a circle that is 15 cm long subtends a 24° angle at the centre. What is the circumference of the circle?

A. 240 cm B. 220 cm
C. 236 cm D. 225 cm

54. The ratio of the radii of two right circular cylinders is 2 : 3. If their heights are in the ratio 5 : 3, find the ratio of their volumes.

A. 16 : 19 B. 3 : 4
C. 3 : 1 D. 20 : 27

55. An article is sold at a discount of 10% and an additional discount of 40% is allowed on cash payment. If Anita purchased an article by paying ₹ 2,700 in cash, the marked price of the article was:

A. ₹ 5,000 B. ₹ 2,500
C. ₹ 2,000 D. ₹ 5,500

56. A dealer allows his customers a discount of 15% and still gains 15%. If an article cost ₹ 2,500 to the dealer, then its marked price is (correct to nearest integer):

A. ₹ 3,382 B. ₹ 4,382
C. ₹ 1,312 D. ₹ 3,182

57. The lengths of a pair of parallel sides of a trapezium are 20 cm and 25 cm, respectively, and the perpendicular distance between these two sides is 14 cm. What is the area (in cm^2) of the trapezium?

A. 512 B. 250
C. 300 D. 315

58. The average of six integers is 48. The average of the first five integers is 70% of the sixth integer. The sixth integer is.

A. 64 B. 62
C. 68 D. 58

59. Two numbers X and Y are such that the sum of 18% of X and 8% of Y is one-third of the sum of 22% of X and 36% of Y. Find the ratio of X and Y.

A. 2 : 5 B. 3 : 11
C. 3 : 8 D. 8 : 3

60. Simplify the following expression.

$79 - [6 - \{4 - (8 \times (6 + 3))\}] \div 2$

A. 11.5 B. 2.5
C. 37 D. 42

61. Find θ, if $\cos\theta = -\frac{\sqrt{3}}{2}$.

A. $\frac{3\pi}{2}$ B. $\frac{5\pi}{6}$

C. $\frac{2\pi}{3}$ D. $\frac{4\pi}{3}$

62. What is the compound interest on ₹ 10,625 for 2 years at 8% interest per annum, if interest is compounded annually?

A. ₹ 1,768 B. ₹ 1,698
C. ₹ 1,625 D. ₹ 1,528

63. The smallest four-digit number which is divisible by 4, 8, 12 and 16 is:

A. 1010 B. 1008
C. 1006 D. 1012

64. If $\left(x - \frac{1}{x}\right) = 7.5$, what is the value of $\left(x^2 + \frac{1}{x^2}\right)$?

A. 54.25 B. 58.25
C. 60.25 D. 56.25

65. Which among the below option can be a square root of?

$(x^2 - 14x + 49)(x^2 + 6x + 9)$

A. $(x - 4)(x + 9)$ B. $(x - 1)(x + 17)$
C. $(x - 7)(x + 3)$ D. $(x - 3)(x + 8)$

66. If $(x^3 + y^3)^{2/3} = (x^2 + y^2)$, then the value of $\frac{x^2 + y^2}{xy}$ $x \neq 0, y \neq 0$, is:

A. $\frac{2}{3}$ B. $x^2 + y$
C. 1 D. $x + y^2$

67. Study the given graph and answer the following question.

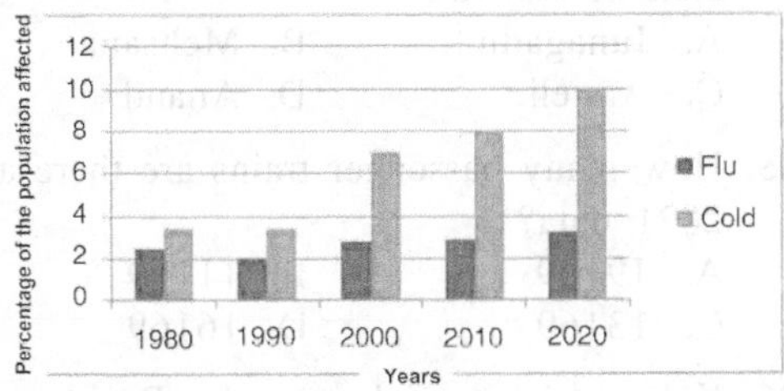

As per data available above in which of the given years was the percentage of the population affected by cold the minimum?

A. 1980 B. 1990
C. 2010 D. 2000

68. Study the given table and answer the question that follows.

Given that the total number of students is 100.

Subject	Marks out of 100				
	80 and above	60 and above	40 and above	20 and above	0 and above
A	9	31	81	92	100
B	4	20	67	81	100
C	7	26	74	87	100

The number of students who scored less than 80% marks in A is:

A. 73 B. 83
C. 91 D. 71

69. A man sold a radio set and gained one-eighth of its cost price. What is the profit per cent?

A. 20% B. 12.5%
C. 15.5% D. 18%

70. The table below gives the percentage of females and males in different professions, out of total 10000 people.

Profession	% of People	% of males	% of females
Teaching	20	50	50
Law	15	65	35
Medical	20	60	40
Engineering	24	55	45
Banking	21	52	48

On the basis of the information provided in the table, find the total number of males who are in the teaching profession.

A. 1000 B. 2000
C. 500 D. 1500

71. The radius of a hemispherical bowl is given as 7 cm. What is the capacity of the bowl? $\left(\pi = \frac{22}{7}\right)$

A. $718\frac{2}{3}$ cm^3 B. $812\frac{1}{3}$ cm^3
C. $618\frac{1}{3}$ cm^3 D. $518\frac{2}{3}$ cm^3

72. A pipe can fill a tank in 15 hours. Due to leakage in the bottom it is filled in 20 hours. If the tank is full, and the pipe is closed, how much time will the leak take to empty the entire tank?
A. 60 hrs B. 50 hrs
C. 40 hrs D. 30 hrs

73. Find the 4th proportional to 5, 10 and 12.
A. 8 B. 24
C. 48 D. 20

74. A man borrowed some money and returned it in two equal instalments of ₹ 3,025 each. If the rate of interest is 10% per annum, compound annually, find the sum borrowed.
A. ₹ 5,575 B. ₹ 6,250
C. ₹ 6,525 D. ₹ 5,250

75. In an election between two candidates, one of the candidates secured 35% of the votes cast and was defeated by the other candidate by 1296 votes. If there were no invalid votes, then the total number of votes polled was:
A. 4546 B. 4230
C. 4456 D. 4320

GENERAL AWARENESS

76. Which of the following instruments is played by P Mani Iyer?
A. Sarangi B. Violin
C. Mridangam D. Mandolin

77. Who among the following authors won the Kamaladevi Chattopadhyay NIF Book Prize in the year 2019?
A. Ornit Shani B. Jairam Ramesh
C. Milan Vaishnav D. Dinyar Patel

78. The election of the next Vice-President is to be held within _____ of the expiry of the term of office of the outgoing Vice-President.
A. 90 days B. 60 days
C. 120 days D. 75 days

79. In the Jayamma vs state of ______ case, in May 2021, the Supreme Court observed that dying declarations are admissible in evidence on the principle of necessity, as there is little hope of the maker surviving.
A. Andhra Pradesh B. Karnataka
C. Tamil Nadu D. Kerala

80. Which method of calculating the national income is also known as 'Industrial Origin Method'?
A. Expenditure Method
B. Income Method
C. Value Added Method
D. Monetary Measures Method

81. The famous folk musician Bhupen Hazarika belongs to which of the following states?
A. Assam B. Odisha
C. Madhya Pradesh D. Karnataka

82. Ustad Amjad Ali Khan, a renowned musician from India is known for playing which of the following instruments?
A. Sarod B. Jaltarang
C. Sarangi D. Veena

83. Which of the following dance forms is performed by Guru Vempati Chinna Satyam?
A. Manipuri B. Odissi
C. Bharatanatyam D. Kuchipudi

84. Modhera Dance Festival is an annual cultural phenomenon in the ______ district of the state of Gujarat.
A. Junagadh B. Mehsana
C. Amreli D. Anand

85. How many passenger trains are there as per 2021 data?
A. 19169 B. 11169
C. 13169 D. 16169

86. Kalamandalam Kshemavathy Pavithran was conferred the Padma Shri award for her contribution to which of the following dance forms?
A. Kuchipudi B. Bharatanatyam
C. Kathak D. Mohiniyattam

87. Which of the following novels is written by Kiran Desai?
A. The Ministry of Utmost Happiness
B. The Inheritance of Loss
C. Midnight's Children
D. The Golden House

88. C.V. Chandra Shekhar was conferred the Padma Bhushan for his contributions to which of the following forms of Dance?
A. Bharatanatyam B. Kathakali
C. Manipuri D. Kathak

89. In 1857, who was the first to experimentally demonstrate that the yeast responsible for making alcohol from sugar, and contaminating microorganisms found in normal air, could sour fermentation?
A. Alexander Fleming
B. Louis Pasteur
C. Fanny Hesse
D. Martinus Willem Beijerinck

90. Which of the following Carnatic instruments is performed by Rajna Swaminathan?
A. Violin B. Flute
C. Veena D. Mridangam

91. Who among the following sportspersons is one of the Arjuna Award 2021 winners?
A. Vikas Kumar B. Nishad Kumar
C. Bajrang Punia D. P.V. Sindhu

92. Which phylum of the plant kingdom consists of vascular plants, leaves (known as fronds), roots and sometimes true stems and entire trunks in tree ferns?
A. Angiosperm B. Pteridophyta
C. Bryophyta D. Gymnosperm

93. Who observed that in a mixture of non-reactive gases, the total gas pressure is equal to the sum of the partial pressures of the individual gases?
A. Antoine Lavoisier
B. John Dalton
C. Amedeo Avogadro
D. Robert Boyle

94. Which cycle shows the movement of water?
A. Carbon cycle B. Nitrogen cycle
C. Geological cycle D. Hydrological cycle

95. Which of the following pairs is NOT correctly matched?
A. Arun Jaitley cricket stadium – Bengaluru
B. Bharat Ratna Atal Bihari Vajpayee Cricket Stadium – Lucknow
C. Narendra Modi cricket stadium – Ahmedabad
D. Eden Garden – Kolkata

96. The autobiography 'My Experiments with Truth' was originally written in which language?
A. English B. Bengali
C. Gujarati D. Marathi

97. Who among the following secured one of the two silver medals for India at the Tokyo Olympics 2020?
A. Ravi Kumar Dahiya
B. Sushil Kumar
C. Bajrang Punia
D. KD Jadhav

98. Which chemical compound is composed of magnesium, sulphur and oxygen and is commonly used in detox bath to relax muscles and relieve pain in the shoulders, neck, back and scalp?
A. Epsom salt B. Potash alum
C. Rock salt D. Glauber's salt

99. The term 'dribble' is used in which of the following sports?
A. Basketball B. Baseball
C. Badminton D. Tennis

100. Which climate zone has an average temperature of over 64°F (18°C) throughout the year and more than 59 inches of rainfall each year?
A. Tropical zone
B. Temperate zone
C. Dry zone
D. Continental zone

ANSWERS

1. (B)	**2. (C)**	**3. (B)**
4. (D)	**5. (A)**	**6. (B)**
7. (A)	**8. (D)**	**9. (C)**
10. (B)	**11. (C)**	**12. (C)**
13. (D)	**14. (B)**	**15. (D)**
16. (D)	**17. (D)**	**18. (B)**
19. (A)	**20. (A)**	**21. (B)**
22. (C)	**23. (B)**	**24. (D)**
25. (D)		

26. (A): First row → 5, 39, 8

$\Rightarrow (5 + 8) \times 3 = 13 \times 3 = 39$

Second row → 7, 36, 5

$\Rightarrow (7 + 5) \times 3 = 12 \times 3 = 36$

Third row → 11, ?, 9

$\Rightarrow (11 + 9) \times 3 = 20 \times 3 = 60$

Hence, ? = Missing number = 60.

27. (D): $(6 + 10) \times 6 = 16 \times 6 = 96$

$(8 + 10) \times 8 = 18 \times 8 = 144$

and $(5 + 10) \times 5 = 15 \times 5 = 75$

Hence, 6 : 96 : : 8 : 144 : : 5 : $\boxed{75}$

Hence ? = Missing number = 75.

28. (C): Order of the given word

According to English dictionary

Calcium → Calculate → Calendar → Carrot → Catalyst.

29. (B): According to given statements

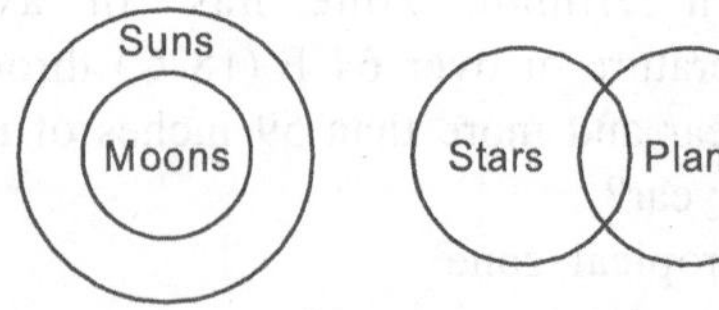

Conclusions: None of the conclusions follows.

30. (C): (A) 43 : 84 $\Rightarrow$ 84 – 43 = 41

(B) 21 : 40 $\Rightarrow$ 40 – 21 = 19

(C) 15 : 210 $\Rightarrow$ 210 – 15 = 195

(D) 19 : 36 $\Rightarrow$ 36 – 19 = 17

Hence, 41, 19 and 17 are prime numbers and 210 is non-price number

Hence, (C) 15 : 210 is odd number pair.

31. (B): 16*6*69*81*3

(A) –, ÷, × =

$\Rightarrow 16 - 6 \div 69 \times 81 = 3$

$\Rightarrow 16 - \frac{6}{69} \times 81 = 3$

$\Rightarrow 16 - \frac{2}{23} \times 81 = 3$

$\Rightarrow 16 - \frac{162}{23} = 3 \Rightarrow \frac{368}{23} = 3$

(Incorrect combination)

(B) ×, –, =, ÷

$\Rightarrow 16 \times 6 - 69 = 81 \div 3$

$\Rightarrow 96 - 69 = 27$

$\Rightarrow 27 = 27$ (correct combination)

(C) ÷, +, =, ×

$\Rightarrow 16 \div 6 + 69 = 81 \times 3$

$\Rightarrow \frac{8}{3} + 69 = 243$

$\Rightarrow \frac{8 + 207}{3} = 243$

$\Rightarrow \frac{215}{3} = 243$ (Incorrect combination)

(D) ÷, =, ×, –

$\Rightarrow 16 \div 6 = 69 \times 81 - 3$

$\Rightarrow \frac{8}{3} = 69 \times 81 - 3$

(Incorrect combination)

32. (D):

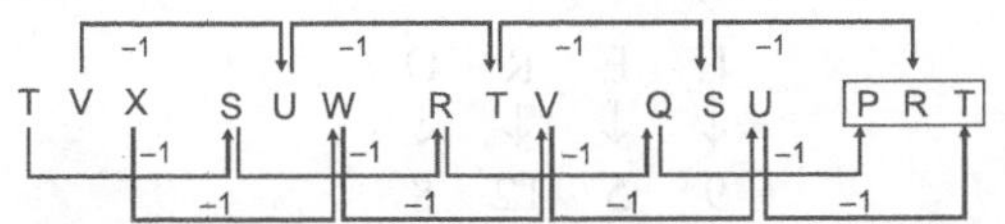

Hence, ? = The missing letter-clusters = PRT.

33. (A): 19 : 90

$\Rightarrow$ (19 – 4) × 6 = 15 × 6 = 90

25 : ?

$\Rightarrow$ (25 – 5) × 6 = 20 × 6 = 120

13 : 60

$\Rightarrow$ (13 – 3) × 6 = 10 × 6 = 60

Hence, 19 : 90 : : 25 : $\boxed{120}$: : 13 : 60

Hence, ? = the missing number = 120.

34. (A)

35. (B): 127*13*3*129*41

(A) +, =, ÷, –

$\Rightarrow$ 127 + 13 = 3 ÷ 129 – 41

$\Rightarrow$ $140 = \frac{1}{43} - 41$

(Incorrect combination)

(B) –, ×, =, –

$\Rightarrow$ 127 – 13 × 3 = 129 – 41

$\Rightarrow$ 127 – 39 = 88

$\Rightarrow$ 88 = 88

(Correct combination)

(C) ÷, –, =, –

$\Rightarrow$ 127 ÷ 13 – 3 = 129 – 41

$\Rightarrow$ $\frac{127}{13} - 3 = 88$

(Incorrect combination)

(D) –, –, =, +

$\Rightarrow$ 127 – 13 – 3 = 129 + 41

$\Rightarrow$ 127 – 26 = 170

$\Rightarrow$ 101 = 170

(Incorrect combination)

36. (D)

37. (B): Given, A = +, B = ×, C = –, D = ÷

17 A (31 B 3) C (64 D 8) A 41 C (21 B 4)

= 17 + (31 × 3) – (64 ÷ 8) + 41 – (21 × 4)

= 17 + 93 – 8 + 41 – 84

= 17 + 93 + 41 – (8 + 84)

= 151 – 92 = 59.

38. (C) **39. (C)** **40. (C)**

41. (B) **42. (C)**

43. (C): 99*25*10*12*7

(A) –, =, +, ×

$\Rightarrow$ 99 – 25 = 10 + 12 × 7

$\Rightarrow$ 74 = 10 + 84

$\Rightarrow$ 74 = 94

(Incorrect combination)

(B) +, =, +, ×

$\Rightarrow$ 99 + 25 = 10 + 12 × 7

$\Rightarrow$ 124 = 10 + 84

$\Rightarrow$ 124 = 94

(Incorrect combination)

(C) –, +, =, ×

$\Rightarrow$ 99 – 25 + 10 = 12 × 7

$\Rightarrow$ 99 + 10 – 25 = 84 $\Rightarrow$ 109 – 25 = 84

$\Rightarrow$ 84 = 84

(Correct combination)

(D) –, =, +, +

$\Rightarrow$ 99 – 25 = 10 + 12 + 7

$\Rightarrow$ 74 = 29

(Incorrect combination)

44. (C): Given, 31 December 2009 was Thursday

$\Rightarrow$ 25 December 2009 was Friday

$\because$ The year 2010 is an ordinary year

$\therefore$ It has 1 odd day

25 December 2009 was Friday

$\Rightarrow$ 25 December 2010 will be 1 day beyond Friday

Hence, It will be Saturday.

45. (D): 16*4*8*10*2*43

(A) ÷, ×, –, +, =

$\Rightarrow$ 16 ÷ 4 × 8 – 10 + 2 = 43

$\Rightarrow$ 4 × 8 – 10 + 2 = 43

$\Rightarrow$ 32 – 10 + 2 = 43

$\Rightarrow$ 32 – 8 = 43

$\Rightarrow$ 24 = 43

(Incorrect combination)

(B) ÷, ×, +, –, =

$\Rightarrow$ 16 ÷ 4 × 8 + 10 – 2 = 43

$\Rightarrow$ 4 × 8 + 10 – 2 = 43

$\Rightarrow$ 32 + 10 – 2 = 43

$\Rightarrow$ 42 – 2 = 43

$\Rightarrow$ 40 = 43

(Incorrect combination)

(C) ×, ÷, –, +, =

$\Rightarrow$ 16 × 4 ÷ 8 – 10 + 2 = 43

$\Rightarrow 16 \times 4 \times \frac{1}{8} - 10 + 2 = 43$

$\Rightarrow$ 8 – 10 + 2 = 43

$\Rightarrow$ 0 = 43

(Incorrect combination)

(D) +, ×, –, ÷, =

$\Rightarrow$ 16 + 4 × 8 – 10 ÷ 2 = 43

$\Rightarrow$ 16 + 4 × 8 – 5 = 43

$\Rightarrow$ 16 + 32 – 5 = 43

$\Rightarrow$ 48 – 5 = 43

$\Rightarrow$ 43 = 43

(Correct combination)

46. (A): Given,

A	C	T	O	R
↓	↓	↓	↓	↓
1	3	6	8	12

and

H	E	R	O	I	N	E
↓	↓	↓	↓	↓	↓	↓
9	5	12	8	7	4	5

Similarly,

H	E	R	O
↓	↓	↓	↓
9	5	12	8

Hence, HERO will be written as 95128.

47. (D):

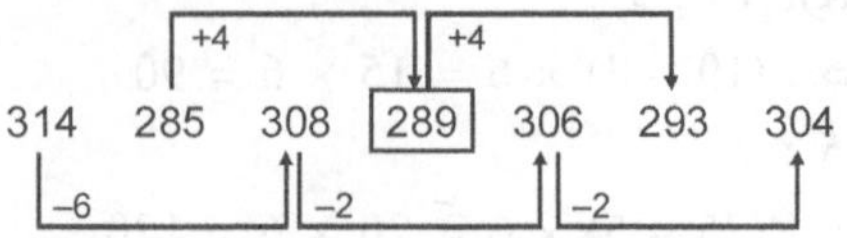

Hence, ? = The missing number.

48. (B):

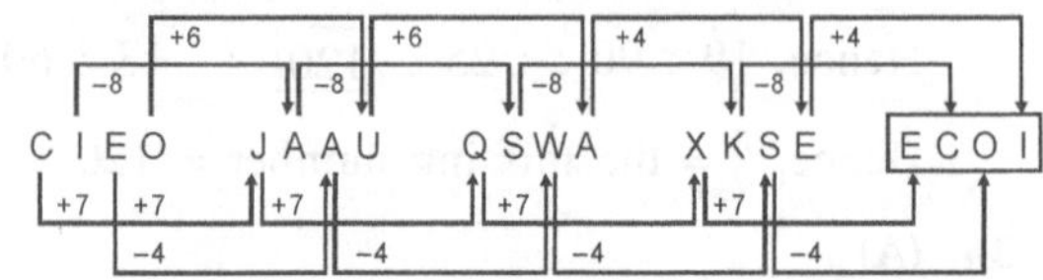

Hence, ? = The missing letter cluster = ECOI

49. (A): Here, E and C are common in both position of the dice.

$\therefore$ The face opposite to D = F.

50. (B)

51. (B): Average speed = $\frac{2xy}{x+y}$

$\Rightarrow 48 = \frac{2 \times 60 \times y}{60 + y}$

$\Rightarrow 48(60 + y) = 120y$

$\Rightarrow 48 \times 60 + 48y = 120y$

$\Rightarrow 48 \times 60 = 120y - 48y$

$\Rightarrow 48 \times 60 = 72y$

$\Rightarrow y = \frac{48 \times 60}{72} = \frac{48 \times 5}{6}$

$\Rightarrow = 8 \times 5 = 40$

$\Rightarrow y = 40$ km/h

Hence, Ruksana's speed was 40 km/h while travelling from B to A.

52. (D): Here, Speed = 108 km/h

$= 108 \times \frac{5}{18}$ m/s

$= 6 \times 5 = 30$ m/s

and time = 40 seconds

∴ Distane = Speed × time

$= 30 \times 40$ m = 1200 m

= 1000 m + 200 m

= 1 km 200 m.

53. (D): Given, An arc on a circle that is 15 cm long subtends at 24° angle at the centre.

∵ $24° = 15$ cm

∴ $1° = \frac{15}{24}$

⇒ $360° = \frac{15}{24} \times 360$

$= 15 \times 15 = 225$ cm

Hence, the required circumference of the circle = 225 cm.

54. (D): Let $r_1 = 2x$, $r_2 = 3x$ and $h_1 = 5y$, $h_2 = 3y$

Then, volume of two right circular cylinders

$V_1 = \pi r_1^2 h_1 = \pi(2x)^2 \times 5y$

and $V_2 = \pi r_2^2 h_2 = \pi(3x)^2 \times 3y$

Hence, the ratio of their volumes

$= V_1 : V_2$

$= \pi(2x)^2 \times 5y : \pi(3x)^2 \times 3y$

$= \pi \times 4x^2 \times 5y : \pi \times 9x^2 \times 3y$

$= 20 : 27.$

55. (A): Let the marked price of the article was ₹ x

Then, $x \times \frac{100-10}{100} \times \frac{100-40}{100}$ = ₹ 2700

⇒ $x \times \frac{90}{100} \times \frac{60}{100} = 2700$

⇒ $x \times \frac{9}{10} \times \frac{3}{5} = 2700$

⇒ $x \times \frac{27}{50} = 2700$

⇒ $x = \frac{2700 \times 50}{27}$

⇒ $x = 1000 \times 50 = 5000$

Hence, the required marked price = ₹ 5000.

56. (A): Let the marked price is ₹ x

Then, According to question

$x \times \frac{100-15}{100} = 2500 \times \frac{115}{100}$

⇒ $x \times \frac{85}{100} = 2500 \times \frac{23}{20}$

⇒ $x \times \frac{17}{20} = 2500 \times \frac{23}{20}$

⇒ $17x = 2500 \times 23$

⇒ $x = \frac{2500 \times 23}{17}$

⇒ $x = 2500 \times 1.3529$

= ₹ 3382.35 = ₹ 3382.

Hence, the required marked price

= ₹ 3382.

57. (D): The area of the trapezium

$= \frac{1}{2} \times$ (Sum of parallel side) × height

$= \frac{1}{2} \times (20 + 25) \times 14$ cm^2

$= 45 \times 7$ cm^2 = 315 cm^2.

58. (A): Let the sixth integer is x

Then, the average of first 5 integer

$= x \times \frac{70}{100} = \frac{7}{10}x$

⇒ Sum of first 5 integer = $\frac{7}{10}x \times 2 = \frac{7}{2}x$

and sum of 6 integer = 6×48

∴ $6 \times 48 - \frac{7}{2}x = x$

⇒ $x + \frac{7}{2}x = 6 \times 48$

⇒ $\frac{9}{2}x = 6 \times 48$

$$\Rightarrow \quad x = 6 \times 48 \times \frac{2}{9}$$
$$= 2 \times 16 \times 2 = 64$$

Hence, the sixth integer is 64.

59. (C): $x \times \frac{18}{100} + y \times \frac{8}{100} = \frac{1}{3}\left(x \times \frac{22}{100} + y \times \frac{36}{100}\right)$

$$\Rightarrow \quad \frac{18x}{100} + \frac{8y}{100} = \frac{1}{3}\left(\frac{22x}{100} + \frac{36y}{100}\right)$$
$$\Rightarrow \quad \frac{18x + 8y}{100} = \frac{1}{3}\left(\frac{22x + 36y}{100}\right)$$
$$\Rightarrow \quad 18x + 8y = \frac{1}{3}(22x + 36y)$$
$$\Rightarrow \quad 3(18x + 8y) = 22x + 36y$$
$$\Rightarrow \quad 54x + 24y = 22x + 36y$$
$$\Rightarrow \quad 54x - 22x = 36y - 24y$$
$$\Rightarrow \quad 32x = 12y$$
$$\Rightarrow \quad \frac{x}{y} = \frac{12}{32} = \frac{3}{8}$$
$$\Rightarrow \quad x : y = 3 : 8.$$

60. (D): $79 - [6 - \{4 - (8 \times (6 + 3))\}] \div 2$
$= 79 - [6 - \{4 - (8 \times 9)\}] \div 2$
$= 79 - [6 - \{4 - 72\}] \div 2$
$= 79 - [6 - \{-68\}] \div 2$
$= 79 - [6 + 68] \div 2$
$= 79 - [74] \div 2$
$= 79 - 37 = 42.$

61. (B): Given, $\cos\theta = \frac{-\sqrt{3}}{2}$

$$\Rightarrow \quad \cos\theta = -\cos\frac{\pi}{6}$$
$$\Rightarrow \quad \cos\theta = \cos\left(\pi - \frac{\pi}{6}\right)$$
$$\Rightarrow \quad \cos\theta = \cos\frac{5\pi}{6}$$

$[\cos(\pi - x) = -\cos x]$

$$\Rightarrow \quad \theta = \frac{5\pi}{6}.$$

62. (A): Given, P = ₹ 10,625, n = 2 years and r = 8% per annum

$\therefore$ Compound interest $= \text{P}\left(1 + \frac{r}{100}\right)^n - \text{P}$

$$= \text{P}\left[\left(1 + \frac{r}{100}\right)^n - 1\right]$$
$$= \text{P}\left[\left(1 + \frac{8}{100}\right)^2 - 1\right]$$
$$= \text{P}\left[\left(1 + \frac{2}{25}\right)^2 - 1\right]$$
$$= \text{P}\left[\left(\frac{27}{25}\right)^2 - 1\right]$$
$$= \text{P}\left[\frac{729}{625} - 1\right]$$
$$= 10625\left(\frac{104}{625}\right)$$
$$= 17 \times 104 = ₹\ 1768.$$

63. (B): Here,

LCM of 4, 8, 12 and 16 = 48

$\because$ Smallest 4-digit number = 1000

$$\therefore \quad \frac{1000}{48} = 20.8333$$

and $\quad 21 \times 48 = 1008$

Hence, the required smallest 4-digit number = 1008.

64. (B): Given,

$$\left(x - \frac{1}{x}\right) = 7.5$$
$$x^2 + \frac{1}{x^2} = \left(x - \frac{1}{x}\right)^2 + 2 \cdot x \cdot \frac{1}{x}$$
$$= (7.5)^2 + 2$$
$$= 56.25 + 2$$
$$= 58.25.$$

65. (C): $(x^2 - 14x + 49)(x^2 + 6x + 9)$

$= (x - 7)^2(x + 3)^2$

Square root of $(x^2 - 14x + 49)(x^2 + 6x + 9)$

$$= \sqrt{(x-7)^2(x+3)^2}$$

$$= (x - 7)(x + 3).$$

66. (A): Given,

$$\left(x^3 + y^3\right)^{2/3} = (x^2 + y^2)$$

$$\Rightarrow (x^3 + y^3)^2 = (x^2 + y^2)^3$$

$$\Rightarrow x^6 + y^6 + 2x^3y^3 = x^6 + 3x^4y^2 + 3x^2y^4 + y^6$$

$$\Rightarrow 2x^3y^3 = 3x^4y^2 + 3x^2y^4$$

$$\Rightarrow 2x^3y^3 = 3x^2y^2(x^2 + y^2)$$

$$\Rightarrow 2xy = 3(x^2 + y^2)$$

$$\Rightarrow \frac{x^2 + y^2}{xy} = \frac{2}{3}.$$

67. (B): From the given graph

The percentage of the population affected by cold

(A) 1980 $\Rightarrow$ 3.7%

(B) 1990 $\Rightarrow$ 3.6%

(C) 2010 $\Rightarrow$ 8%

(D) 2000 $\Rightarrow$ 10%

Hence, year 1990 was the % of the population affected by cold the minimum.

68. (C):

Subject	80 and above	60 and above	40 and above	20 and above	0 and above
A	9	31 – 9 = 22	81 – 31 = 50	92 – 81 = 11	100 – 92 = 8

$\therefore$ The number of students who scored less than 80% marks in A

$$= 22 + 50 + 11 + 8 = 91.$$

69. (B): Let the cost price of a radio = ₹ 100

then, profit = ₹$\frac{100}{8}$

$$\therefore \quad \text{Profit \%} = \frac{\text{Profit} \times 100}{\text{C.P.}}$$

$$= \frac{\frac{100}{8} \times 100}{100}$$

$$= \frac{100}{8} = 12.5\%.$$

70. (A): According to given information

The total number of people = 10000

$\therefore$ The total number of people who are in the teaching profession

$$= 10000 \times \frac{20}{100}$$

$$= 2000$$

Hence, the total number of males who are in the teaching profession

$$= 2000 \times \frac{50}{100}$$

$$= 1000.$$

71. (A): Given, The radius of a hemispherical bowl

$$= r = 7 \text{ cm}.$$

$\therefore$ Capacity (volume) of the bowl

$$= \frac{2}{3}\pi r^3$$

$$= \frac{2}{3} \times \frac{22}{7} \times (7)^3$$

$$= \frac{2}{3} \times 22 \times (7)^2$$

$$= \frac{44}{3} \times 49$$

$$= \frac{2156}{3} = 718\frac{2}{3}.$$

72. (A): Work done by the leak in 1 hour

$$= \frac{1}{15} - \frac{1}{20}$$

$$= \frac{4-3}{60} = \frac{1}{60}$$

Hence, Leak will empty the tank in 60 hours.

73. (B): Let the 4th proportional to 5, 10 and 12 be x

Then, $5 : 10 :: 12 : x$

$\Rightarrow \quad 5 \times x = 10 \times 12$

$\Rightarrow \quad x = \frac{10 \times 12}{5}$

$\Rightarrow \quad x = 2 \times 12$

$\Rightarrow \quad x = 24.$

74. (D): Principal

= (Present worth of ₹ 3025 due 1 year hence) + (Present worth of ₹ 3025 due 2 years hence)

$$= \frac{3025}{\left(1+\frac{10}{100}\right)} + \frac{3025}{\left(1+\frac{10}{100}\right)^2} = \frac{3025}{\frac{110}{100}} + \frac{3025}{\left(\frac{110}{100}\right)^2}$$

$$= 3025 \times \frac{10}{11} + 3025 \times \left(\frac{10}{11}\right)^2$$

$$= 3025 \times \frac{10}{11}\left(1+\frac{10}{11}\right)$$

$$= 275 \times 10 \times \frac{21}{11}$$

$= 25 \times 10 \times 21 = 250 \times 21 =$ ₹ 5250.

75. (D): Let the total number of votes polled was x.

Then, $x \times \frac{65}{100} - x \times \frac{35}{100} = 1296$

$\Rightarrow \quad x\left(\frac{65-35}{100}\right) = 1296$

$\Rightarrow \quad x\left(\frac{30}{100}\right) = 1296$

$\Rightarrow \quad x = \frac{1296 \times 10}{3}$

$\Rightarrow \quad x = 4320.$

76. (C)	**77. (A)**	**78. (B)**
79. (B)	**80. (C)**	**81. (A)**
82. (A)	**83. (D)**	**84. (B)**
85. (C)	**86. (D)**	**87. (B)**
88. (A)	**89. (B)**	**90. (D)**
91. (B)	**92. (B)**	**93. (B)**
94. (D)	**95. (A)**	**96. (C)**
97. (A)	**98. (A)**	**99. (A)**
100. (A)		

Previous Paper (Solved)

SSC—Combined Higher Secondary Level–CHSL (10+2) TIER–1, Online Recruitment Exam–2020

(Exam held on 04-08-2021)

ENGLISH LANGUAGE

1. Select the most appropriate option to substitute the underlined segment in the given sentence. If there is no need to substitute it, select 'No substitution'.

If he doesn't reach the station in time, he <u>would sure miss</u> the train.

A. would surely miss
B. No substitution
C. will sure missing
D. will surely miss

2. Select the most appropriate option to fill in the blank.

It is claimed that if you take a certain homeopathic medicine, it will ______ you against the coronavirus.

A. shelter B. immune
C. reinforce D. fortify

3. Select the most appropriate synonym of the given word.

WRY

A. straight B. frank
C. forthright D. crooked

4. In the given sentence, identify the segment which contains the grammatical error.

My mother generally read the local newspaper to keep abreast of the local news.

A. the local newspaper
B. of the local news
C. My mother generally read
D. to keep abreast

5. Select the most appropriate ANTONYM of the given word.

SUSTENANCE

A. refreshment B. livelihood
C. starvation D. nourishment

6. Select the INCORRECTLY spelt word.

A. superior B. superstition
C. superflous D. supreme

7. Select the option that will improve the underlined segment in the given sentence. In case no improvement is needed, select 'No improvement'

What a <u>palace</u> home!

A. pushy B. palatial
C. palatable D. No improvement

8. Select the most appropriate synonym of the given word.

MALIGNANT

A. vicious B. beneficial
C. loving D. healthy

9. Select the most appropriate meaning of the given idiom.

Under wraps

A. under estimate B. double layered
C. secretly D. underhand

10. Select the most appropriate ANTONYM of the given word.

DEVIOUS

A. Deceitful B. shrewd
C. straight D. calculating

11. Select the correct indirect form of the given sentence.

Anju said to Vijaya, "You can stay with us whenever you are in Delhi."

A. Anju told Vijaya that she could stay with them whenever she was in Delhi.
B. Anju told Vijaya that she could stay with them whenever you were in Delhi.
C. Anju told Vijaya that she can stay with us whenever she is in Delhi.
D. Anju told Vijaya that you can stay with us whenever you are in Delhi.

12. Select the option which means the same as the group of words given.

A government run by the wealthy people

A. oligarchy B. monarchy
C. plutocracy D. aristocracy

13. Select the correct passive form of the given sentence.

The Central Board of Secondary Education has launched a new helpline for students.

A. A new helpline for students is launched by the Central Board of Secondary Education.
B. A new helpline for students will be launched by the Central Board of Secondary Education.
C. A new helpline for students had been launched by the Central Board of Secondary Education.
D. A new helpline for students has been launched by the Central Board of Secondary Education.

14. Given below are four jumbled sentences. Out of the given options, pick the one that gives their correct order.

(*a*) He lived in a small house near the main road of a village.
(*b*) As both, he and his wife, worked hard, they made a small fortune.
(*c*) But one thing caused them great sorrow: they had no children.
(*d*) After he got married, he started a tailor's shop.

A. (*a*)(*b*)(*d*)(*c*) B. (*b*)(*d*)(*a*)(*c*)
C. (*a*)(*d*)(*b*)(*c*) D. (*b*)(*a*)(*c*)(*d*)

15. Select the most appropriate word to fill in the blank.

Debjyoti's short animation film ______ highlights the stark contrast between the rich and the poor in India.

A. poignantly B. strictly
C. carelessly D. sweetly

16. Select the most appropriate meaning of the given idiom.

On tenterhooks

A. Very sad B. Very tense
C. Very happy D. Very angry

17. Select the INCORRECTLY spelt word.

A. disappear B. until
C. twelth D. temperature

18. Examine the four jumbled sentences. Out of the given options, pick the one that gives their correct order.

(*a*) We gently put the fledgling back into the nest.
(*b*) One morning, we found one of the four fallen on the ground.
(*c*) The robin couple built a nest in our verandah and laid four eggs.
(*d*) Once they had hatched, they busily took turns feeding the four.

A. (*c*)(*d*)(*b*)(*a*) B. (*a*)(*c*)(*d*)(*b*)
C. (*b*)(*a*)(*d*)(*c*) D. (*d*)(*a*)(*b*)(*c*)

19. Select the word which means the same as the group of words given.

That which is incapable of being read or understood

A. Indelible B. Illegible
C. Illegal D. Intelligible

20. The following sentence has been split into four segments. Identify the segment which contains a grammatical error.

Deepu's mother / has repeated asked him / to lower the volume / of his mobile.

A. has repeated asked him
B. to lower the volume
C. of his mobile
D. Deepu's mother

Directions (Qs. No. 21-25): *In the following passage, some words have been deleted. Fill in the blanks with the help of the alternatives given. Select the most appropriate option for each blank.*

A year is hardly sufficient time for a Master to (1) ______ about a new school, leave alone absorb a distinct tradition like (2) ______. Most of the new appointees had not served in a residential school and (3) ______ time to learn. But the short tenure did not allow (4) ______. They could not develop understanding of the student and his (5) ______.

21. Select the most appropriate option for blank No. 1.
A. learnt B. learn
C. learns D. learning

22. Select the most appropriate option for blank No. 2.
A. ourselves B. himself
C. mine D. ours

23. Select the most appropriate option for blank No. 3.
A. needing B. need
C. needed D. needs

24. Select the most appropriate option for blank No. 4.
A. them B. those
C. these D. that

25. Select the most appropriate option for blank No. 5.
A. environmentalist B. environmental
C. environment D. environmentally

GENERAL INTELLIGENCE

26. Read the given statements and conclusions carefully. Assuming that the information given in the statements is true, even if it appears to be at variance with commonly known facts, decide which of the given conclusions logically follow(s) from the statements.

Statements : All computers are machines.
No television is a computer.
All televisions are instruments.

Conclusions:
I. Some instruments are machines.
II. Some machines are computers.
III. Some televisions are machines.

A. Only conclusion II follows.
B. Only conclusion I follows.
C. Only conclusions II and III follow.
D. None of the conclusions follow.

27. Select the combination of letters that when sequentially placed in the blanks of the given letter series will complete the series.

a_ _bcde_ _abbcd_ _aabb_ _ee
A. aeaebecd B. aeecdbea
C. abeaeecd D. abecdeae

28. Select the option in which the words share the same relationship as that shared by the given pair of words.
Ammeter : Electric current
A. Density : Lactometer
B. Pressure : Barometer
C. Hygrometer : Humidity
D. Polarimeter : Steps

29. 'Straw' is related to 'Nest' in the same way as 'Cotton' is related to '______'.
A. Textile industry B. Thread
C. Sewing D. Wool

30. Select the figure from among the given options that can replace the question mark (?) in the following series.

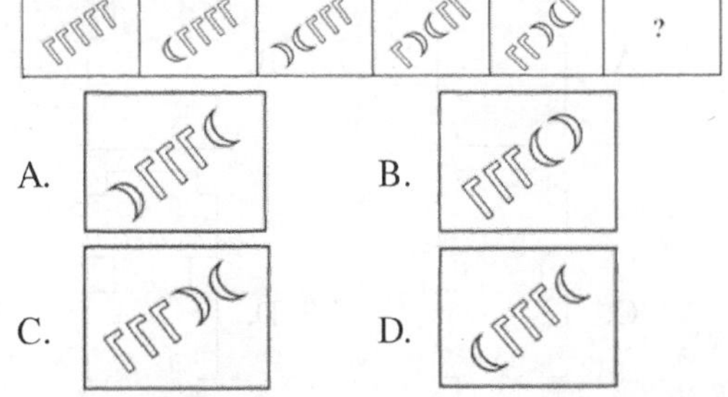

31. The sales boy of a washing machine store charges his customers 24% more than the cost price. If a customer paid ₹ 6,200 for a washing machine, then what was the cost price of the washing machine?

A. ₹ 5,500
B. ₹ 5,000
C. ₹ 6,200
D. ₹ 7,200

32. Study the given pattern carefully and select the number that can replace the question mark (?) in it.

28	16	27
44	16	15
84	?	24

A. 27 B. 30
C. 28 D. 29

33. Select the option that is related to the third number in the same way as the second number is related to the first number.

12 : 150 : : 14 : ?

A. 203 B. 502
C. 302 D. 205

34. The sequence of folding a piece of paper and the manner in which the folded paper has been cut is shown in the following figures. How would this paper look when unfolded?

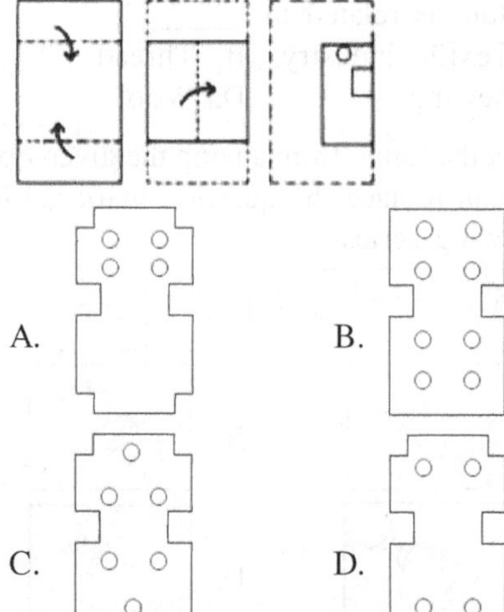

35. Select the number from among the given options that can replace the question mark (?) in the following series.

3, 5, 15, 41, ?, 173

A. 91 B. 112
C. 78 D. 106

36. Four letter-clusters have been given, out of which three are alike in some manner and one is different. Select the letter-cluster that is different.

A. NRJQ B. DHSZ
C. TXCJ D. GKPW

37. Select the option in which the given figure is embedded (rotation is NOT allowed).

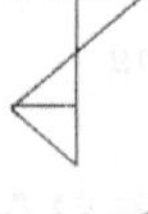

A. 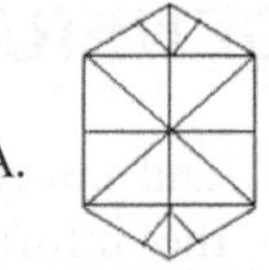

B. 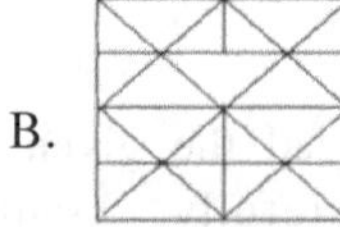

C. 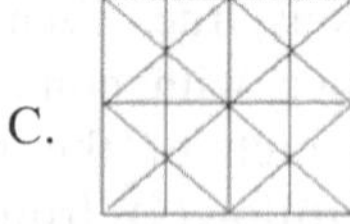

D. 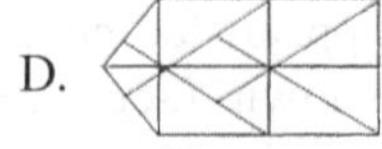

38. Find the number of triangles in the given figure.

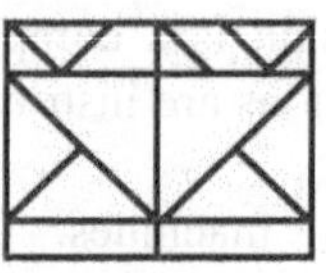

A. 15 B. 11
C. 14 D. 13

39. In a certain code language, FORWARD is written as CSZXQPE. How will NUMERAL be written in that language?

A. MZSDNTO B. KZQDLTL
C. KBQFLVM D. MUNELAR

40. Which two signs should be interchanged to make the following equation correct?

12 − 8 + 4 ÷ 2 × 8 = 4

A. − and × B. × and +
C. ÷ and − D. × and ÷

41. In a certain code language, HAMPER is coded as 17212322036 and INSULT is coded as 16286421340. How will SAFETY be coded in that language?

A. 621910550 B. 612195030
C. 629101350 D. 610195320

42. Select the option that is related to the third letter-cluster in the same way as the second letter-cluster is related to the first letter-cluster.

BYDW : UFSH : : CXFU : ?

A. TGQJ B. SHQJ
C. RIPK D. RIOL

43. Four words have been given, out of which three are alike in some manner and one is different. Select the word that is different.

A. Integrity B. Joviality
C. Honesty D. Truthfulness

44. A cube is made by folding the given sheet. In the cube so formed, how many dots lie opposite to the face having 4 dots?

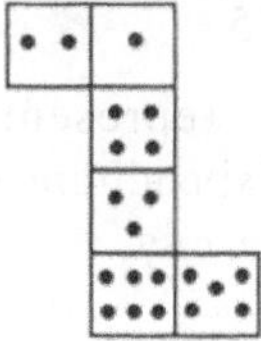

A. 2 B. 5
C. 6 D. 1

45. Select the Venn diagram that best represents the relationship between the following classes.

Women, Professors, Widows

A. 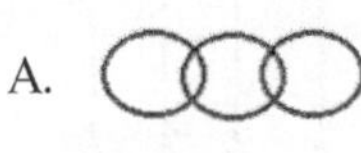 B. 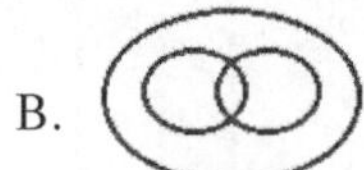

C.  D. 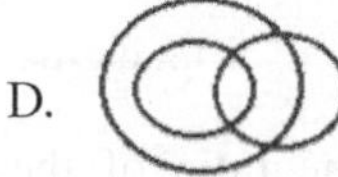

46. Snigda said that she met her mother's only brother's son's mother's father-in-law. Whom did she meet?

A. Father B. Uncle
C. Grandfather D. Brother

47. Four numbers have been given, out of which three are alike in some manner and one is different. Select the number that is different.

A. 6341 B. 6138
C. 5423 D. 1652

48. Select the option in which the numbers are related in the same way as are the numbers of the following set.

{9, 12, 18}

A. {7, 13, 27}
B. {21, 29, 44}
C. {5, 12, 24}
D. {13, 19, 31}

49. Select the correct option that indicates the arrangement of the given words in the order in which they appear in an English dictionary.

1. Multifocal
2. Movement
3. Multinomial
4. Moviemaker
5. Mutual fund

A. 4, 2, 3, 1, 5 B. 1, 5, 2, 3, 4
C. 4, 2, 1, 3, 5 D. 2, 4, 1, 3, 5

50. Select the correct mirror image of the given figure when the mirror is placed at the right side of the figure.

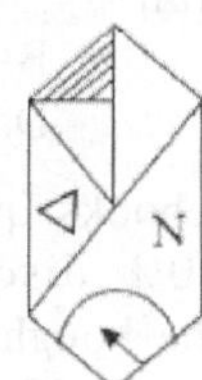

A. 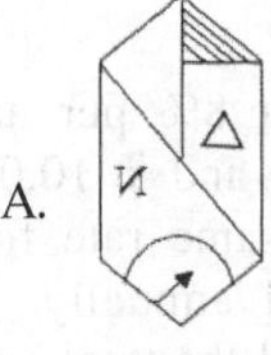 B. 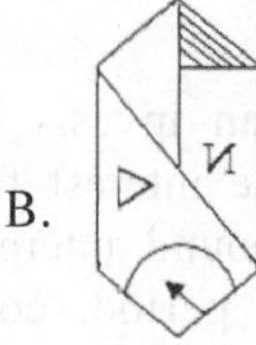

C. 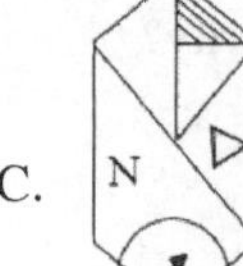 D. 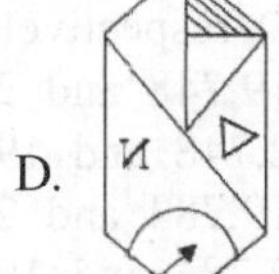

QUANTITATIVE APTITUDE

51. A solid metallic hemisphere of radius 6.3 cm is melted and recast into a right circular cylinder of radius 9 cm. What is the height (in cm, correct to one decimal place) of the cylinder?

A. 1.9 B. 2.7
C. 2.5 D. 2.1

52. If $\cos\theta = \frac{4x}{1+4x^2}$, then what is the value of $\sin\theta$?

A. $\frac{1+4x^2}{1-4x^2}$ B. $\frac{1+4x^2}{4x^2}$
C. $\frac{1-4x^2}{1+4x^2}$ D. $\frac{1-4x^2}{4x}$

53. In a triangle ABC, ∠BAC = 90° and AD is perpendicular to BC. If AD = 8.4 cm and BD = 4.8 cm, then the length of BC is:

A. 19.5 cm B. 15 cm
C. 18 cm D. 18.5 cm

54. Tap P can fill a cistern in 6 hours and tap Q can empty the full cistern in 10 hours. If both taps P and Q are kept open simultaneously, then in how many hours will the empty cistern be completely full?

A. 15 B. 18
C. 16 D. 12

55. One dozen notebooks quoted at ₹ 125 are available at 20% discount. How many notebooks can be bought for ₹ 75?

A. 10 B. 6
C. 9 D. 8

56. A man invests ₹ 7,000 at 8% per annum simple interest for 2 years and ₹ 10,000 at compound interest at the same rate for the same period, compounded annually. What will be the total interest and the total amount (in ₹) respectively, on maturity?

A. 19,748 and 2,874
B. 2,748 and 19,784
C. 19,784 and 2,784
D. 2,784 and 19,784

57. If (sin A – cos A) = 0, then what is the value of cot A?

A. $\frac{\pi}{6}$ B. 0
C. 1 D. $\frac{\pi}{4}$

58. A boat can travel with a speed of 19 km/h in still water. If the speed of the stream is 3 km/h, then what will be the total time (in hours) taken by the boat to go 88 km downstream and 24 km upstream?

A. 4.5 B. 5
C. 4 D. 5.5

59. A is 150% of B and B is 40% of C. If A + B + C = 20, then the value of 2B + 3C – 4A is equal to:

A. 16 B. 14
C. 20 D. 15

60. The following histogram represents the distribution of household expenditure (in ₹) of 200 manual workers in a city.

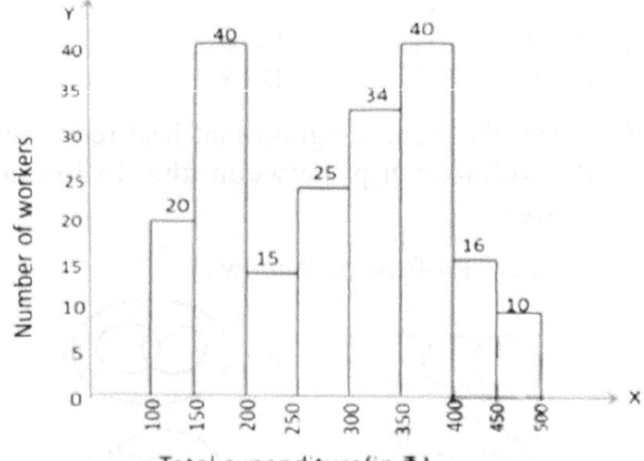

The ratio of the number of workers whose household expenditure is less than ₹ 200 to the number of workers whose household expenditure is ₹ 300 and above is:

A. 3 : 5 B. 2 : 5
C. 4 : 5 D. 3 : 4

61. Using algebraic identities, simplify the following expression.

$$\frac{(x^4+x^2+1)}{(x^2+x+1)}$$

A. $(x^2 - 2x + 1)$
B. $(x^2 + x + 1)$
C. $(x^2 + 2x + 1)$
D. $(x^2 - x + 1)$

62. Students of Primary, Middle, Secondary and Sr. Secondary classes collected donation for a Relief Fund as shown in the pie chart. If the donation collected from Middle classes was ₹ 6,750, then how much money was collected by the Primary classes?

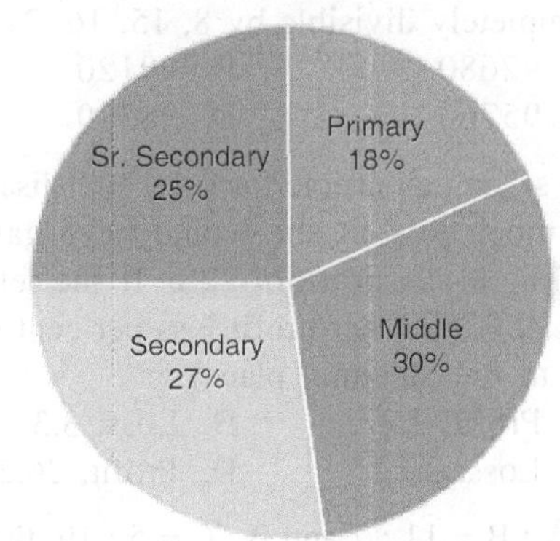

A. ₹ 4,050 B. ₹ 4,005
C. ₹ 4,500 D. ₹ 3,960

63. One-quarter of a circular pizza of diameter 28 cm was removed from the whole pizza. What is the perimeter (in cm) of the remaining pizza? (Take $\pi = \frac{22}{7}$)

A. 88 B. 94
C. 80 D. 66

64. The inner and outer radii of two concentric circles are 6.7 cm and 9.5 cm respectively. What is the difference between their circumferences (in cm)?

Take π = 22/7.

A. 20.5 B. 10.4
C. 6.5 D. 17.6

65. Study the given graph and answer the question that follows.

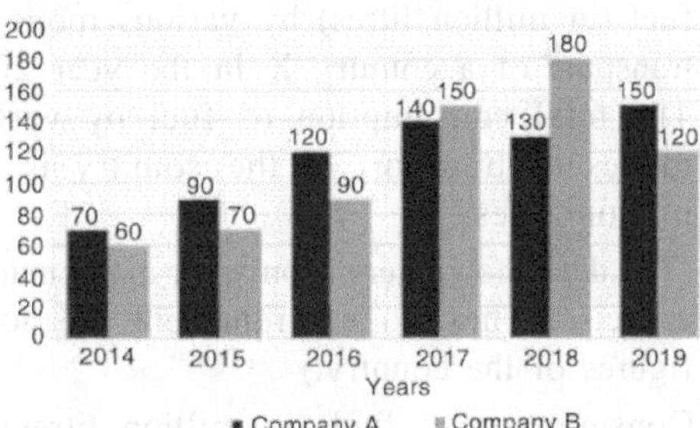

The average production of paper by company B in 2014, 2017 and 2018 was $13\frac{1}{3}\%$ less than the production of paper by company A in the year:

A. 2016 B. 2018
C. 2017 D. 2019

66. What is the perimeter (in cm) of an equilateral triangle whose height is 3.46 cm? Take $\sqrt{3} = 1.73$.

A. 10.4 B. 9
C. 6 D. 12

67. The value of $[\{(232 \div 29 \text{ of } 2) + 77 \times 10\} \div 18] - \frac{18 \times 8 \div 4 \text{ of } 3 - 4}{2 \times (8-6) + 1 - 2 \times 3 \div 4 \text{ of } \frac{1}{2}}$ is:

A. 39 B. 44
C. 33 D. 47

68. The string of a kite is 158 m long and it makes an angle of 30° with the horizontal. What is the height (in m) of the kite? Assume there is no slack in the string.

A. 100 B. 99
C. 79 D. 80

69. If $\left(x+\frac{1}{x}\right)^3 = 27$, then what is the value of $\left(x^2+\frac{1}{x^2}\right)$? Given that x is real.

A. 11 B. 25
C. 7 D. 9

70. Study the given pie-chart and answer the question that follows.

The pie-chart represents the consumption of fuel (in million litres) by various modes of transport of a country X in the year 2015. The total consumption of fuel by various modes of transport of the country is 800 million litres.

(The data shown here is only for mathematical exercise. They do not represent the actual figures of the country.)

Consumption of fuel (in million litres) by various modes of transport of a country X in the year 2015

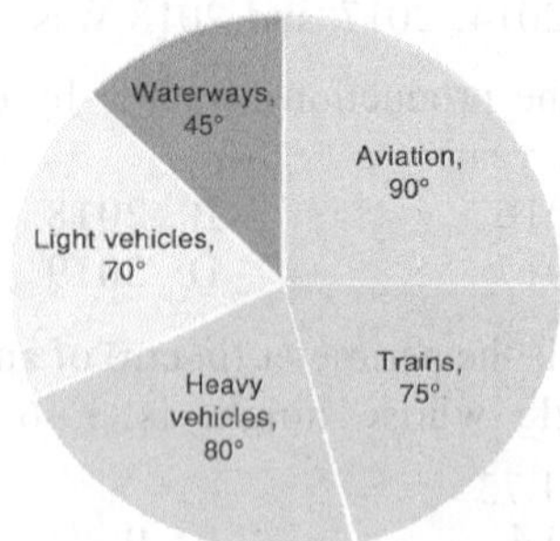

To obtain fuel, energy is required to run the machinery, which is to be produced by burning coal.

If 1 tonne of coal is burnt to produce 0.4 million litres of oil, then approximately what is the requirement of coal (in tonnes) for the Trains sector?

A. 417 B. 415
C. 418 D. 420

71. One-fifth of a journey is covered at a speed of 30 km/h, one-fourth of the journey at a speed of 25 km/h and the rest at 60 km/h. What is the average speed (in km/h, correct to one decimal place) for the whole journey?

A. 38.7 B. 30.6
C. 40.5 D. 25.4

72. If $a + b = p$, $ab = q$, then $(a^4 + b^4)$ is equal to:

A. $p^4 - 2p^2q^2 + q^2$ B. $p^4 - 4p^2q^2 + 2q^2$
C. $p^4 - 4p^2q + q^2$ D. $p^4 - 4p^2q + 2q^2$

73. What is the greatest five-digit number that is completely divisible by 8, 15, 16, 21 and 5?

A. 92680 B. 99120
C. 95760 D. 98320

74. By selling an article for ₹ 1,170, Elisa suffers as much loss as she would have gained by selling it at a profit of 22%. If she sells it for ₹ 1,450, then her profit loss per cent (correct up to one decimal place) is:

A. Profit, 3.3 B. Loss, 3.3
C. Loss, 26.2 D. Profit, 26.2

75. If A : B = 11 : 7 and B : C = 5 : 19, then what is A : B : C?

A. 55 : 35 : 133 B. 35 : 55 : 133
C. 35 : 133 : 55 D. 55 : 133 : 35

GENERAL AWARENESS

76. Who among the following is the first Indian pistol shooter to reach number one in world rankings by the International Shooting Sport Federation?

A. Heena Sidhu B. Kajal Saini
C. Tejaswini Sawant D. Suma Shirur

77. Who among the following has become the first woman umpire to officiate in a men's Test match in January 2021?

A. Danielle Wyatt B. Jess Jonassen
C. Suzie Bates D. Claire Polosak

78. Which part of soil has organic materials incorporated with the mineral matter, nutrients and water?

A. Horizon D B. Horizon C
C. Horizon A D. Horizon B

79. In which of the following states is Sabarimala Sree Dharma Sastha Temple located?

A. Karnataka
B. Telangana
C. Andhra Pradesh
D. Kerala

80. Identify the Indian state which was known as 'Pragjyotisha' during the epic period.
A. Assam B. Odisha
C. Kerala D. Bihar

81. What is the SI unit for measuring pressure?
A. Pascal B. Candela
C. Ampere D. Kelvin

82. Who among the following was appointed by AIFF (All India Football Federation) as its first Deputy General Secretary in January 2021?
A. Abhishek Yadav B. Praful Patel
C. Umesh Sinha D. Kushal Das

83. Kabartal Wetland was designated as a Ramsar site in 2020. In which of the following states is it located?
A. Haryana B. Bihar
C. Himachal Pradesh D. Punjab

84. ______ are gently sloping areas of the ocean basins.
A. Deep sea plains
B. Continental shelfs
C. Continental slopes
D. Oceanic deeps

85. Who among the following was appointed as the Chief Justice of the Andhra Pradesh High Court in January 2021?
A. Sharad Arvind Bobde
B. Hima Kohli
C. Rajan Datta
D. Arup Kumar Goswami

86. Who among the following Indian nationals got the 'Legion of Merit' Award 2020 from the US?
A. Dr Manmohan Singh
B. Narendra Modi
C. Dr K Sivan
D. General Bipin Rawat

87. Who among the following became the first Lokpal of India?
A. Dilip B Bhosale
B. Pradip Kumar Mohanty
C. Pinaki Chandra Ghose
D. Ajay Kumar Tripathi

88. In which of the following states did the Land Grabbing (Prohibition) Act, 2020 come into force in December 2020?
A. Punjab B. Maharashtra
C. Gujarat D. Madhya Pradesh

89. What happens to Indian exports when Indian rupee is devalued?
A. Export prices fluctuate
B. Exports become cheaper
C. Export prices remain stable
D. Exports become dearer

90. ______ is the process of turning on a computer and powering up the system.
A. Booting B. Loading
C. Saving D. Execution

91. What do you call a key on a computer keyboard that is used to move the pointer (cursor) around on the screen?
A. Navigation key B. Numeric key
C. Function key D. Control key

92. Vitamin B12 is generally NOT present in ______.
A. milk products B. plant foods
C. fish products D. poultry products

93. Who among the following is considered as the 'Father of Modern Atomic Theory'?
A. Robert Boyle B. John Dalton
C. Willard Gibbs D. Otto Hahn

94. ______ plains are formed due to the weathering of soluble rocks such as limestone and dolomite.
A. Glacial B. Karst
C. Deposition D. Desert

95. Which of the following state governments unveiled a Braille version of the Constitution of India in January 2021?
A. Haryana B. Andhra Pradesh
C. Punjab D. Maharashtra

96. In which of the following cities is the corporate centre of State Bank of India (SBI) situated?
A. Hyderabad B. Kolkata
C. Mumbai D. Bengaluru

97. In which of the following years was the Vijayanagar empire founded?
A. 1456 B. 1229
C. 1412 D. 1336

98. In which of the following years did Telangana become the 29th state of India after the reorganisation of the state of Andhra Pradesh?
A. 2014 B. 1994
C. 2010 D. 1998

99. 'Kati Bihu' in Assam is celebrated by lighting a lamp in front of a _____ tree/plant.
A. banyan B. tulsi
C. banana D. neem

100. Who among the following was awarded the Rabindranath Tagore Literary Award 2020?
A. Ashraf Patel B. Ranjitsingh Disale
C. Vidyut Mohan D. Raj Kamal Jha

ANSWERS

1	2	3	4	5	6	7	8	9	10
D	D	D	C	C	C	B	A	C	C
11	**12**	**13**	**14**	**15**	**16**	**17**	**18**	**19**	**20**
A	C	D	C	A	B	C	A	B	A
21	**22**	**23**	**24**	**25**	**26**	**27**	**28**	**29**	**30**
B	D	C	D	C	A	C	C	B	C
31	**32**	**33**	**34**	**35**	**36**	**37**	**38**	**39**	**40**
B	D	A	A	A	A	C	C	C	B
41	**42**	**43**	**44**	**45**	**46**	**47**	**48**	**49**	**50**
A	D	B	C	D	C	B	D	D	D
51	**52**	**53**	**54**	**55**	**56**	**57**	**58**	**59**	**60**
D	C	A	A	C	D	C	D	B	A
61	**62**	**63**	**64**	**65**	**66**	**67**	**68**	**69**	**70**
D	A	B	D	D	D	A	C	C	A
71	**72**	**73**	**74**	**75**	**76**	**77**	**78**	**79**	**80**
A	D	B	B	A	A	D	C	D	A
81	**82**	**83**	**84**	**85**	**86**	**87**	**88**	**89**	**90**
A	A	B	A	D	B	C	C	B	A
91	**92**	**93**	**94**	**95**	**96**	**97**	**98**	**99**	**100**
A	B	B	B	D	C	D	A	B	D

EXPLANATORY ANSWERS

26. According to given statements:

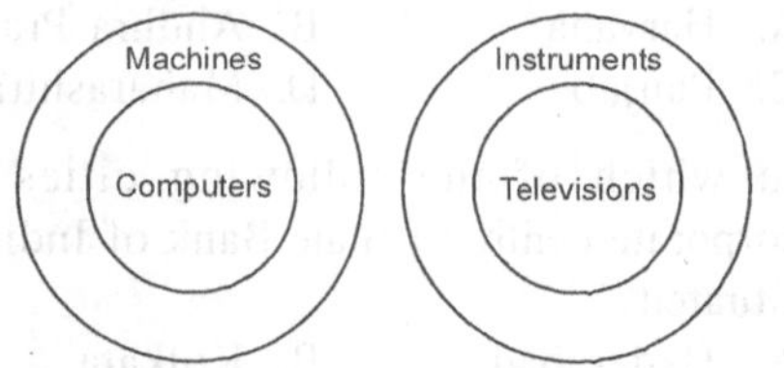

Conclusions: II. Some machines are computers.

27. A. a a e b c d e a e a b b c d b e a a b b c d e e

B. a a e b c d e e c a b b c d d b a a b b e a e e

C. a a b b c d e e a a b b c d e e a a b b c d e e

D. a a b b c d e e c a b b c d d e a a b b a e e e

Here, option (C) is correct, because section 'aabbcdee' is repeated in the series.

31. The cost price of the washing machine

$= ₹\ 6200 \times \frac{100}{100+24}$

$= ₹\ 6200 \times \frac{100}{124}$

$= 100 \times \frac{100}{2}$

$= 50 \times 100 = ₹\ 5000$

33. $12 \times 12 + \frac{12}{2} = 144 + 6 = 150$

and similarly,

$14 \times 14 + \frac{14}{2} = 196 + 7 = 203$

Hence, 12 : 150 : : 14 : 203.

35.

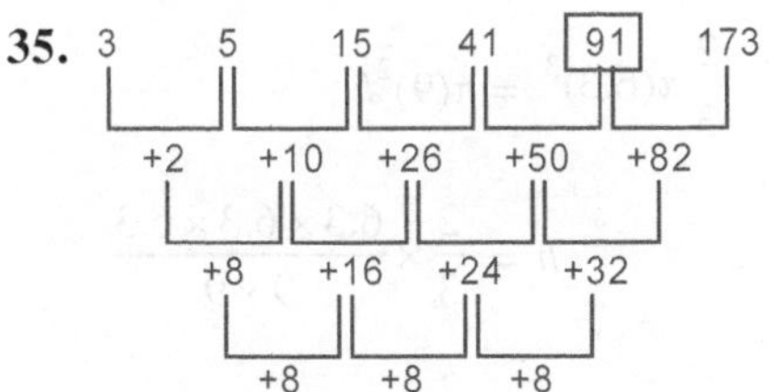

Hence, ? = the missing number = 91.

36. A. N R J Q (+4, –8, +7)

B. D H S Z (+4, +11, +7)

C. T X C J (+4, +5, +7)

D. G K P W (+4, +5, +7)

Hence, option (A) is different.

39. Given, F O R W A R D → C S Z X Q P E (–1, +1, –1, +1, –1, +1, –1)

Similarly, N U M E R A L → K B Q F L V M

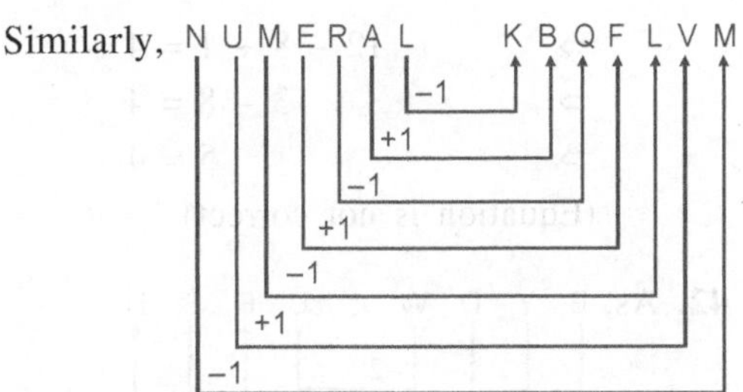

Hence, 'NUMERAL' will be written as KBQFLVM.

40. 12 – 8 + 4 ÷ 2 × 8 = 4

A. (– and ×)

∴ 12 × 8 + 4 ÷ 2 – 8 = 4

⇒ 12 × 8 + 2 – 8 = 4

⇒ 96 + 2 – 8 = 4

⇒ 98 – 8 = 4

⇒ 90 = 4

(Equation is not correct).

B. (× and +)

∴ 12 – 8 × 4 ÷ 2 + 8 = 4

⇒ 12 – 8 × 2 + 8 = 4

⇒ 12 – 16 + 8 = 4

⇒ 20 – 16 = 4

⇒ 4 = 4

(Equation is correct).

C. (÷ and –)

∴ 12 ÷ 8 + 4 – 2 × 8 = 4

⇒ $\frac{12}{8} + 4 - 2 \times 8 = 4$

⇒ $\frac{3}{2} + 4 - 16 = 4$

⇒ $\frac{3}{2} - 12 = 4$

⇒ $\frac{-21}{2} = 4$

(Equation is not correct).

D. (× and ÷)

∴ 12 – 8 + 4 × 2 ÷ 8 = 4

⇒ $12 - 8 + 4 \times \frac{1}{4} = 4$

$\Rightarrow \quad 12 - 8 + 1 = 4$

$\Rightarrow \quad 13 - 8 = 4$

$\Rightarrow \quad 5 = 4$

(Equation is not correct).

42. As,

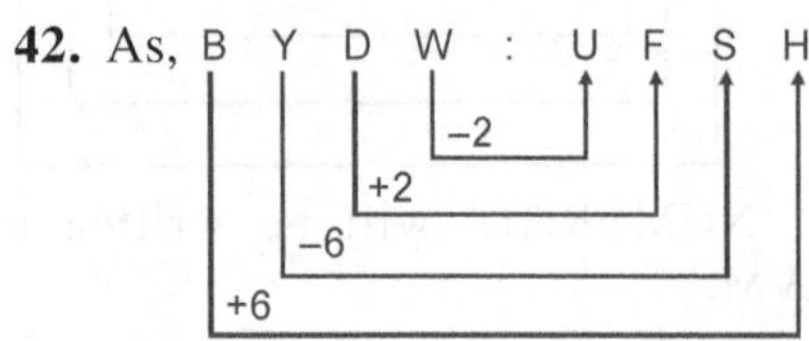

Similarly,

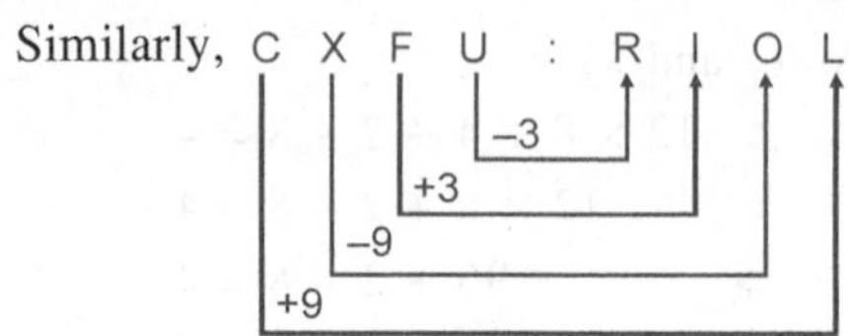

Hence, BYDW : UFSH : : CXFU : RIOL.

46.

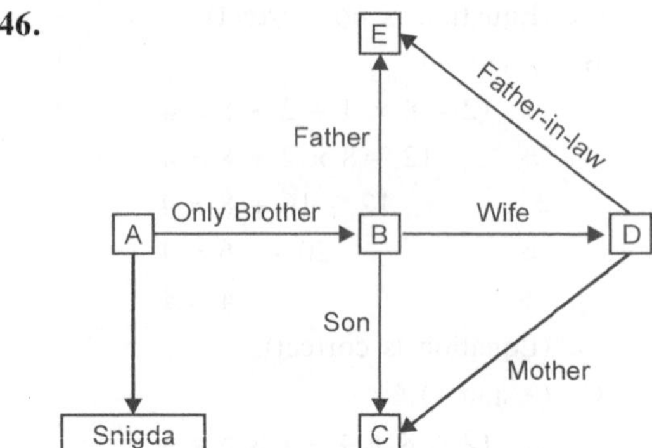

Hence, She met her grandfather.

47. A. 6341 $\Rightarrow$ $6 + 3 + 4 + 1 = 14$

B. 6138 $\Rightarrow$ $6 + 1 + 3 + 8 = 18$

C. 5423 $\Rightarrow$ $5 + 4 + 2 + 3 = 14$

D. 1652 $\Rightarrow$ $1 + 6 + 5 + 2 = 14$

Hence, option (B) is different.

48. 9 (+3) 12 (+6) 18

A. 7 (+6) 13 (+14) 27

B. 21 (+8) 29 (+15) 44

C. 5 (+7) 12 (+12) 24

D. 13 (+6) 19 (+12) 31

Hence, option (D) are related in the same way as the given set.

49. According to English dictionary
Movement → Moviemaker → Multifocal → Multinomial → Mutual fund.

51. Volume of hemispher

$$= \frac{2}{3}\pi r^3 = \frac{2}{3}\pi(6.3)^3 \text{ cm}^3$$

and the volume of right circular cylinder

$$= \pi r^2 h = \pi(9)^2 h \text{ cm}^3$$

$$\therefore \quad \frac{2}{3}\pi(6.3)^3 = \pi(9)^2 h$$

$$\Rightarrow \quad h = \frac{2}{3} \times \frac{6.3 \times 6.3 \times 6.3}{9 \times 9}$$

$$= \frac{2}{3} \times .7 \times .7 \times 6.3$$

$$= 2 \times .7 \times .7 \times 2.1$$

$$= 2.058 = 2.1 \text{ cm.}$$

52. Given, $\cos\theta = \dfrac{4x}{1+4x^2}$

$$\because \quad \sin^2\theta = 1 - \cos^2\theta$$

$$= 1 - \left(\frac{4x}{1+4x^2}\right)^2$$

$$= 1 - \frac{16x^2}{1+8x^2+16x^4}$$

$$= \frac{1+8x^2+16x^4-16x^2}{1+8x^2+16x^4}$$

$$= \frac{1-8x^2+16x^4}{1+8x^2+16x^4}$$

$\therefore \quad \sin^2\theta = \dfrac{(1-4x^2)^2}{(1+4x^2)^2}$

$\Rightarrow \quad \sin^2\theta = \left(\dfrac{1-4x^2}{1+4x^2}\right)^2$

$\Rightarrow \quad \sin\theta = \dfrac{1-4x^2}{1+4x^2}.$

54. Part filled in 1 hour by tap P $= \dfrac{1}{6}$

and part empted in 1 hour by tap Q $= \dfrac{1}{10}$

$\therefore$ The net part filled in 1 hour $= \dfrac{1}{6} - \dfrac{1}{10}$

$$= \frac{5-3}{30} = \frac{2}{30} = \frac{1}{15}$$

Hence, the empty cistern will be completely full in 15 hours.

55. The cost price of 1 dozen notebook

$$= ₹\ 125 \times \frac{80}{100}$$

$$= ₹\ 125 \times \frac{4}{5}$$

$$= 25 \times 4 = ₹\ 100$$

Hence, the number of notebooks can be bought for ₹ 75

$$= \frac{12}{100} \times 75 = \frac{3}{25} \times 75$$

$$= 3 \times 3 = 9.$$

56. Simple interest $= \dfrac{P \times r \times t}{100}$

$$= ₹\ \frac{7000 \times 8 \times 2}{100} = ₹\ 1120$$

$\therefore$ Amount = P + S.I.

= 7000 + 1120 = ₹ 8120

Compount Interest $= P\left[\left(1+\dfrac{r}{100}\right)^n - 1\right]$

$$= 10000\left[\left(1+\frac{8}{100}\right)^2 - 1\right]$$

$$= 10000\left[\left(1+\frac{2}{25}\right)^2 - 1\right]$$

$$= 10000\left[\left(\frac{27}{25}\right)^2 - 1\right]$$

$$= 10000\left[\frac{729}{625} - 1\right]$$

$$= 10000 \times \frac{104}{625}$$

$$= 16 \times 104 = 1664$$

Amount = P + C.I.

= 10000 + 1664 = ₹ 11664

Hence, the total interest

= ₹ 1120 + ₹ 1664 = ₹ 2784

and the total amount

= ₹ 8120 + ₹ 11664

= ₹ 19784.

57. Given, $\sin A - \cos A = 0$

$\Rightarrow \quad \sin A = \cos A$

$\Rightarrow \quad \dfrac{\cos A}{\sin A} = 1$

$\Rightarrow \quad \cot A = 1.$

58. Here, speed in downstream

= 19 + 3 = 22 km/hr

and speed in upstream = 19 − 3 = 16 km/hr

Total time will be taken by the boat to go 88 km downstream and 24 km upstream

$$= \frac{88}{22}\text{ hr} + \frac{24}{16}\text{ hr}$$

$$= \left(4+\frac{3}{2}\right)\text{ hr} = \frac{11}{2}\text{ hr}$$

= 5.5 hours.

59. Given, $A = B \times \frac{150}{100}$

$\Rightarrow \quad A = \frac{3}{2}B$

and $\quad B = C \times \frac{40}{100}$

$\Rightarrow \quad B = \frac{2}{5}C$

and $\quad A + B + C = 20 \quad \left[A = \frac{3}{2}B\right]$

$\Rightarrow \quad \frac{3}{2}B + B + C = 20$

$\Rightarrow \quad \frac{5}{2}B + C = 20 \quad \left[B = \frac{2}{5}C\right]$

$\Rightarrow \quad \frac{5}{2} \times \frac{2}{5}C + C = 20$

$\Rightarrow \quad C + C = 20$

$\Rightarrow \quad 2C = 20 \Rightarrow C = 10$

Now, $2B + 3C - 4A$

$$= 2 \times \frac{2}{5}C + 3C - 4 \times \frac{3}{2}B$$

$$= \frac{4}{5}C + 3C - 6B$$

$$= \frac{19}{5}C - 6 \times \frac{2}{5}C$$

$$= \frac{19}{5}C - \frac{12}{5}C$$

$$= \frac{19C - 12C}{5} = \frac{7}{5}C$$

$$= \frac{7}{5} \times 10 = 14.$$

60. From the given histogram

Required ratio

$= (20 + 40) : (34 + 40 + 16 + 10)$

$= 60 : 100 = 3 : 5.$

61.

$$x^2 + x + 1 \,\big)\, x^4 + x^2 + 1 \,\big(\, x^2 - x + 1$$

$$\begin{array}{r} x^4 + x^3 + x^2 \\ - \quad - \quad - \\ \hline -x^3 + 1 \\ -x^3 - x^2 - x \\ + \quad + \quad + \\ \hline x^2 + x + 1 \\ x^2 + x + 1 \\ - \quad - \quad - \\ \hline 0 \end{array}$$

$$\therefore \quad \frac{x^4 + x^2 + 1}{x^2 + x + 1} = \frac{(x^2 + x + 1)(x^2 - x + 1)}{(x^2 + x + 1)}$$

$$= x^2 - x + 1.$$

62. From the given Pie-chart

Let the total donation collected = ₹ x

Then, $\quad x \times \frac{30}{100} = 6750$

$\Rightarrow \quad x = \frac{67500}{3}$

Hence, donation collected by the primary classes

$$= \frac{67500}{3} \times \frac{18}{100}$$

$$= ₹\ 675 \times 6 = ₹\ 4050.$$

63. Given, diameter of a circular pizza = 28 cm

$\Rightarrow \quad 2r = 28$ cm

$\Rightarrow \quad r = 14$ cm

$\therefore$ Perimeter of a circular pizza = $2\pi r$

$$= 2 \times \frac{22}{7} \times 14$$

$$= 22 \times 4 = 88 \text{ cm}$$

$\because$ One-quarter of a circular pizza was removed from the whole pizza

$\therefore$ The perimeter of the remaining pizza

$$= 88 - \frac{88}{4} + 14 + 14$$

$$= 88 - 22 + 28$$

$$= 66 + 28 = 94.$$

64. Given, the inner and outer radii of two concentric circles are 6.7 cm and 9.5 cm

Hence, the difference between their circumference

$= 2\pi \times 9.5 \text{ cm} - 2\pi \times 6.7 \text{ cm}$

$= 2\pi(9.5 - 6.7) \text{ cm} = 2\pi \times 2.8 \text{ cm}$

$= 2 \times \frac{22}{7} \times 2.8 \text{ cm} = 2 \times 22 \times 0.4$

$= 0.8 \times 22 = 17.6 \text{ cm}$

66. Let the side of an equilateral triangle (ΔABC) is x cm

Given, height = 3.46 cm

$\therefore \quad h = AD = 3.46 \text{ cm}$

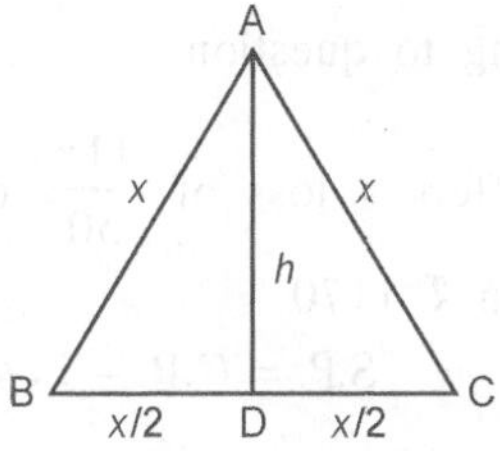

In ΔADC,

$$AD^2 + DC^2 = AC^2$$

$$\Rightarrow \quad h^2 + \left(\frac{x}{2}\right)^2 = x^2$$

$$\Rightarrow \quad h^2 = x^2 - \frac{x^2}{4}$$

$$\Rightarrow \quad h^2 = \frac{3}{4}x^2$$

$$\Rightarrow \quad x^2 = \frac{4h^2}{3}$$

$$\Rightarrow \quad x = \frac{2h}{\sqrt{3}} = \frac{2 \times 3.46}{1.73}$$

$$\Rightarrow \quad x = \frac{6.92}{1.73} \Rightarrow x = 4 \text{ cm}$$

Hence, the perimeter of an equilateral triangle

$= 3x$

$= 3 \times 4 = 12 \text{ cm.}$

67. $[\{(232 \div 29 \text{ of } 2) + 77 \times 10\} \div 18]$

$$- \frac{18 \times 8 \div 4 \text{ of } 3 - 4}{2 \times (8-6) + 1 - 2 \times 3 \div 4 \text{ of } \frac{1}{2}}$$

$$= \left[\{(232 \div 58) + 770\} \div 18\right] - \frac{18 \times 8 \div 12 - 4}{2 \times 2 + 1 - 2 \times 3 \div 2}$$

$$= \left[\{4 + 770\} \div 18\right] - \frac{18 \times 8 \times \frac{1}{12} - 4}{2 \times 2 + 1 - 3}$$

$$= \left[774 \div 18\right] - \frac{3 \times 8 \times \frac{1}{2} - 4}{4 + 1 - 3}$$

$$= 43 - \frac{12 - 4}{2} = 43 - \frac{8}{2}$$

$= 43 - 4 = 39.$

68. Let AC = string of a kite = 158 m

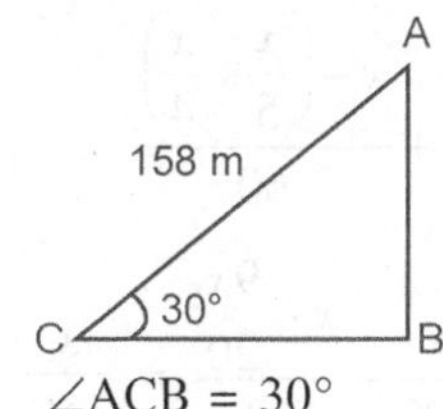

$\angle ACB = 30°$

AB = height of the kite

In ΔABC, $\sin 30° = \frac{AB}{AC}$

$$\Rightarrow \quad \frac{1}{2} = \frac{AB}{158}$$

$$\Rightarrow \quad AB = \frac{158}{2} = 79$$

$\Rightarrow \quad AB = 79 \text{ m.}$

69. Given, $\left(x + \frac{1}{x}\right)^3 = 27$

$$\Rightarrow \quad \left(x + \frac{1}{x}\right)^3 = (3)^3$$

$$\Rightarrow \quad \left(x + \frac{1}{x}\right) = 3$$

Squaring both sides, we get,

$$\left(x+\frac{1}{x}\right)^2 = 9$$

$$\Rightarrow \quad x^2+\frac{1}{x^2}+2.x.\frac{1}{x} = 9$$

$$\Rightarrow \quad x^2+\frac{1}{x^2}+2 = 9$$

$$\Rightarrow \quad x^2+\frac{1}{x^2} = 9 - 2$$

$$\Rightarrow \quad x^2+\frac{1}{x^2} = 7.$$

71. Let the distance of Journey = x km

$$\because \quad \text{Speed} = \frac{\text{Distance}}{\text{Time}}$$

$\therefore$ Total time in whole journey

$$= \frac{\frac{x}{5}}{30}+\frac{\frac{x}{4}}{25}+\frac{x-\left(\frac{x}{5}+\frac{x}{4}\right)}{60}$$

$$= \frac{x}{150}+\frac{x}{100}+\frac{x-\frac{9x}{20}}{60} = \frac{x}{150}+\frac{x}{100}+\frac{11x}{1200}$$

$$= \frac{8x+12x+11x}{1200} = \frac{31x}{1200} \text{ hours}$$

Hence, the average speed in the whole journey

$$= \frac{x}{\frac{31x}{1200}} = \frac{1200}{31} = 38.7 \text{ km/hr.}$$

72. Given, $a + b = p,\ ab = q$

$$\begin{aligned} a^4 + b^4 &= (a^2 + b^2)^2 - 2a^2b^2 \\ &= [(a + b)^2 - 2ab]^2 - 2a^2b^2 \\ &= (p^2 - 2q)^2 - 2q^2 \\ &= p^4 + 4q^2 - 4p^2q - 2q^2 \\ &= p^4 - 4p^2q + 2q^2. \end{aligned}$$

73. Here, the greatest 5-digit number = 99999

LCM of 8, 15, 16, 21 and 5 = 1680

$$\because \quad 99999 = 1680 \times 59 + 879$$
$$= 99120 + 879$$

Hence, 999120 is the greatest five digit number which is completely divisible by 8, 15, 16, 21 and 5.

74. Let C.P. of the article be ₹ x

Then, profit at the rate of 22%

$$= \frac{22}{100} \text{ of } x$$

$$= \frac{22x}{100} = \frac{11x}{50}$$

According to question,

Elisa suffers a loss of $\frac{11x}{50}$ on selling the article on ₹ 1170

Hence, S.P. = C.P. – Loss

$$\Rightarrow \quad 1170 = x - \frac{11x}{50}$$

$$\Rightarrow \quad 1170 = \frac{50x-11x}{50} = \frac{39x}{50}$$

$$\therefore \quad x = \frac{1170 \times 50}{39}$$

$$= 30 \times 50 = ₹\ 1500$$

Again, S.P. = ₹ 1450, C.P. = ₹ 1500

$\therefore$ Loss = C.P. – S.P.

= 1500 – 1450 = ₹ 50

$$\therefore \quad \text{Loss\%} = \frac{\text{Loss} \times 100}{\text{C.P.}}$$

$$= \frac{50 \times 100}{1500} = \frac{10}{3} = 3.3\%.$$

75. Given, A : B = 11 : 7 = 55 : 35

and B : C = 5 : 19 = 35 : 133

$\therefore$ A : B : C = 55 : 35 : 133.

Previous Paper (Solved)

SSC-Combined Higher Secondary Level–CHSL (10+2) Tier–1, Online Recruitment Exam–2019*

1. Select the most appropriate word to fill in the blank.

The police used tear gas to _____ the crowd.

A. disburse B. collect
C. attack D. disperse

2. Select the most appropriate meaning of the given idiom.

Take something with a pinch of salt

A. To take long to understand what is being said
B. To think of oneself as always right
C. To consider everyone a liar
D. To believe only part of something

3. Select the word that means the same as the given group of words.

A person weak and disabled by illness

A. Activist B. Invalid
C. Athlete D. Petitioner

4. Select the INCORRECTLY spelt word.

A. Preamble B. Pnemonia
C. Miscellaneous D. Deviation

Directions (Qs. No. 5-9): *In the following passage some words have been deleted. Fill in the blanks with the help of the alternatives given. Select the most appropriate option for each blank.*

All her life Ms. Foster had a great fear of missing a train, a plane, a boat or __(1)__ a theatre curtain. In other respects, she was not a __(2)__ nervous woman. But the mere thought of __(3)__ on occasions like these would throw her __(4)__ such a nervous state that a tiny muscle in the corner of her left eye would __(5)__ twitch. This would disappear once she had boarded the plane etc.

5. Select the most appropriate option for blank No. 1.

A. quite B. extremely
C. even D. hardly

6. Select the most appropriate option for blank No. 2.

A. usual B. general
C. particular D. particularly

7. Select the most appropriate option for blank No. 3.

A. be later B. being late
C. be late D. being later

8. Select the most appropriate option for blank No. 4.

A. into B. up
C. away D. in

9. Select the most appropriate option for blank No. 5.

A. begun over B. begun to
C. begin to D. begin over

10. Select the INCORRECTLY spelt word.

A. Conscentious B. Constraint
C. Resultant D. Expanse

11. In the sentence identify the segment which contains the grammatical error.

Subhash Gidwani is selling dolls, which are type of Madhya Pradesh's village culture, at the Annual Dastakar Bazaar, held in January every year in Delhi.

A. Subhash Gidwani is selling dolls
B. in the annual Dastakar Bazaar
C. held in January every year in Delhi
D. which are type of Madhya Pradesh's village culture

12. Given below are four jumbled sentences. Pick the option that gives their correct order.

* Exam held on 21-10-2020

(*a*) Finally, she takes the decision to go searching for livelihood in the nearby town.
(*b*) They are: Lakua and his wife, Nathuni.
(*c*) The latter, burdened with a paralytic husband and two children, battles to survive.
(*d*) The film 'Wayfarers' narrates the journey of a poor couple in Jharkhand.

A. *cdab* B. *dbac*
C. *dbca* D. *bacd*

13. Given below are four jumbled sentences. Pick the option that gives their correct order.

(*a*) The Emperor would view the comic acts from the jharokha, a special window of his palace.
(*b*) On the festival of Holi, the Emperor was entertained with mimicry, impersonation and play-acting.
(*c*) Bahadur Shah Jafar's life and times are described in a book called 'City of my heart.'
(*d*) Finally, the most talented of the performers would be generously awarded by the king.

A. *cbad* B. *cdba*
C. *adbc* D. *dacb*

14. Select the most appropriate option to substitute the underlined segment in the given sentence. If there is no need to substitute it, select 'No improvement'.

The Delhi Birla International School <u>alumnus occupy</u> leading positions in different areas of profession and service.

A. alumnus occupies
B. alumnus occupying
C. No improvement
D. alumni occupy

15. Select the correct indirect form of given sentence.

The foreigner said to the farmer, "Can you tell me the way to the nearest hotel?"

A. The foreigner told the farmer if he could tell him the way to the nearest hotel.
B. The foreigner suggested the farmer if he could tell him the way to the nearest hotel.
C. The foreigner exclaimed with the farmer if he could tell him the way to the nearest hotel.
D. The foreigner enquired of the farmer if he could tell him the way to the nearest hotel.

16. Select the most appropriate synonym of the given word.

CONGENIAL

A. Compatible B. Servile
C. Aloof D. Bombastic

17. Select the most appropriate ANTONYM of the given word.

PACIFIST

A. Orator B. Warmonger
C. Nihilist D. Peace-maker

18. Select the most appropriate meaning of the given idiom.

Full of sound and fury

A. A fiery and effective speaker
B. Someone who gets angry very quickly
C. Merely loud and angry words but ineffective
D. An angry and unruly mob

19. In the sentence identify the segment which contains the grammatical error.

You must make a choice immediately because there is few time left.

A. because there is
B. You must make
C. few time left
D. a choice immediately

20. Select the most appropriate word to fill in the blank.

Ritu is an ______ reader. I always find her with a book.

A. irritated B. erratic
C. avid D. inattentive

21. Select the most appropriate synonym of the given word.

PEDIGREE

A. Forbidden B. Illegitimate
C. Mongrel D. Lineage

22. Select the most appropriate option to substitute the underlined segment in the given sentence. If there is no need to substitute it, select 'No improvement'.

For the last two years Shweta has being diligently working with Rohingya refugees to create colourful table mats using their local weaving techniques.

A. have been B. has been
C. No improvement D. have being

23. Select the most appropriate ANTONYM of the given word.

PROLIFIC

A. Unproductive B. Rich
C. Abundant D. Several

24. Select the correct passive form of the given sentence.

Chhattisgarh organised the first ever 'All India Folk Dance Festival' in January 2020.

A. The first ever 'All India Folk Dance Festival' was organised by the Chhattisgarh State in January 2020.
B. The first ever 'All India Folk Dance Festival' was being organised by the Chhattisgarh State in January 2020.
C. The first ever 'All India Folk Dance Festival' will be organised by the Chhattisgarh State in January 2020.
D. The first ever 'All India Folk Dance Festival' had been organised by the Chhattisgarh State in January 2020.

25. Select the word that means the same as the given group of words.

Happening every two years

A. Centennial B. Biennial
C. Biannual D. Triennial

26. Four letter-cluster have been given, out of which three are alike in some manner and one is different. Select the odd letter-cluster.

A. BEYV B. MONL
C. NOPE D. HJSQ

27. The sequence of folding a paper and the manner in which the folded paper has been cut is shown in the following figures. How would this paper look when unfolded?

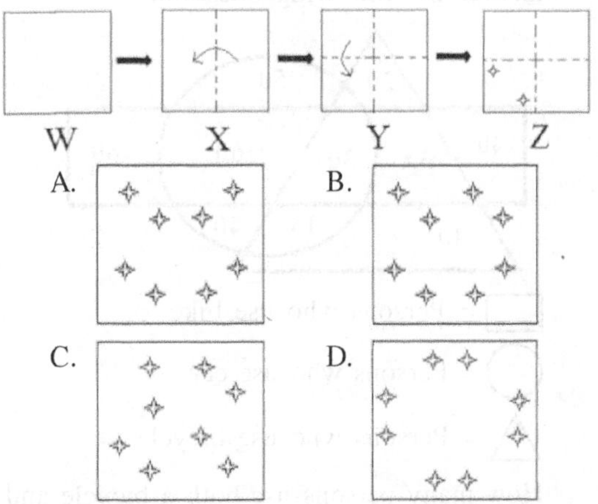

28. Select the number that can replace the question mark (?) in the following figure series.

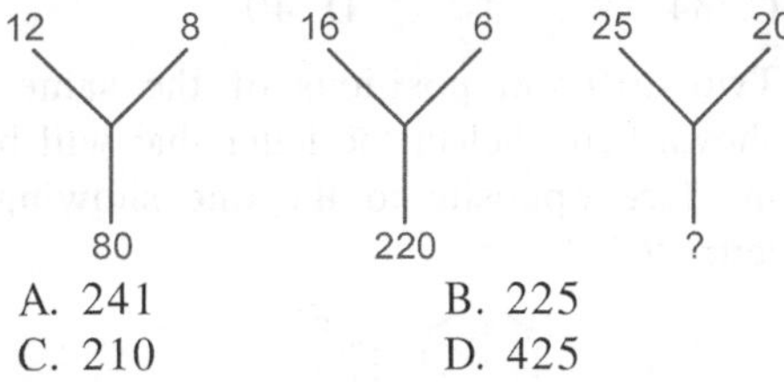

A. 241 B. 225
C. 210 D. 425

29. The rate of onion increased from ₹ 70 per kilogram to ₹ 120 per kilogram within a month. By what percentage (approximate) did the rate of onion increase?

A. 71.5% B. 80%
C. 65% D. 75.2%

30. Introducing a boy, I said, "His mother is the only daughter of my mother in law." How am I related to the boy?

A. Brother B. Father
C. Brother-in-law D. Nephew

31. How many triangles are there in the following figure?

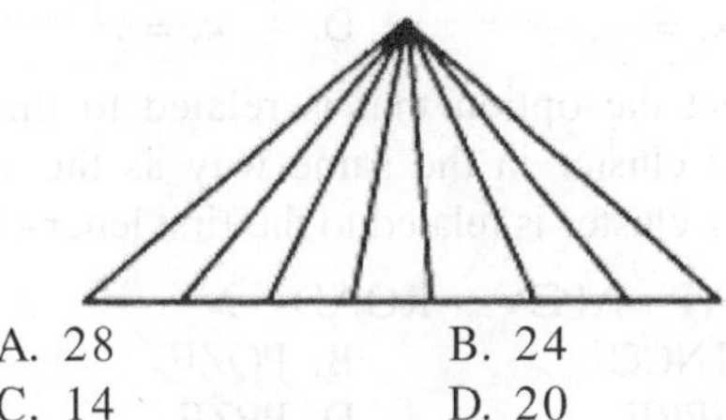

A. 28 B. 24
C. 14 D. 20

32. Study the given Venn diagram carefully and answer the following question.

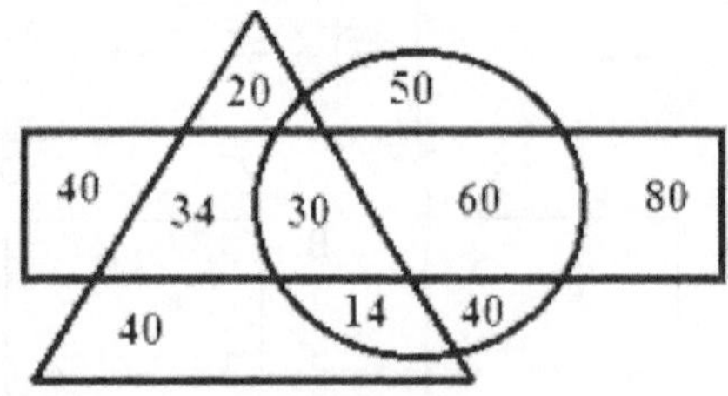

☐ = Persons who use bike

○ = Persons who use car

△ = Persons who use bicycle

How many persons use both a bicycle and a bike but not a car?

A. 14 B. 30

C. 34 D. 40

33. Two different positions of the same dice shown here. Select the letter that will be on the face opposite to the one showing the letter 'C'.

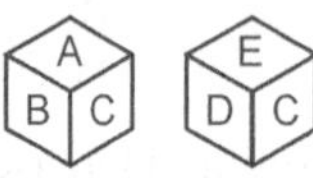

A. F B. A

C. E D. B

34. Four words have been given, out of which three are alike in some manner and one is different. Select the odd one.

A. Paris B. Istanbul

C. Maputo D. London

35. Select the correct combination of mathematical sign to replace 'A' sequentially and balance the following equation.

40 A 2 A 3 A 4 A 15

A. ÷, ×, =, × B. ×, ÷, +, =

C. ×, =, –, ÷ D. ÷, ×, = , –

36. Select the option that is related to the third letter-cluster in the same way as the second letter-cluster is related to the first letter-cluster.

COAT : APZV :: ROAD : ?

A. TNCC B. PQZF

C. SPBE D. PPZF

37. Four numbers have been given, out of which three are alike in some manner and one is different. Select the one that is different.

A. 729 B. 125

C. 216 D. 676

38. Select the Venn diagram best represents the relationship between the following classes.

Dirham, USD, Currency

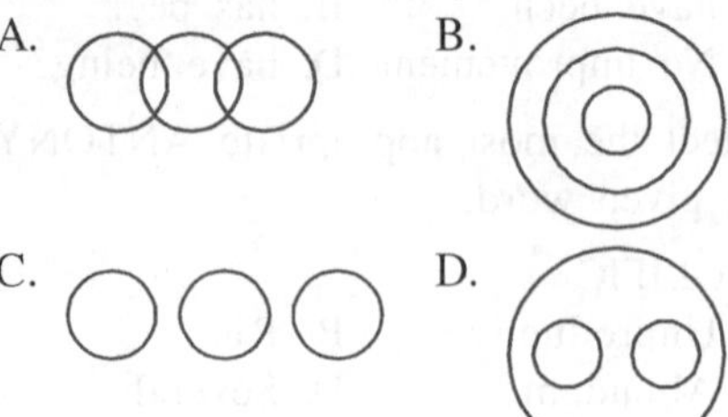

39. Read the given statements and conclusions carefully. Assuming that the information given in the statements is true, even if it appears to be at variance with commonly known facts, decide which of the given conclusions logically follows from the statements.

Statements:

1. All malls are kings.
2. No king is a heater.

Conclusions:

I. No mall is a heater.

II. All kings are malls.

A. Neither conclusion I nor II follows.

B. Only conclusion II follows.

C. Either conclusion I or II follows.

D. Only conclusion I follows.

40. In a certain code language, 'TELEVISION' is written as 'OPJTJWFMFU'. How will 'REMOTE' be written as in that language?

A. FUPNFS B. ETOMER

C. PUPFNS D. SFNPUF

41. Select the option in which the given figure is embedded.
(Rotation is not allowed)

A. B.

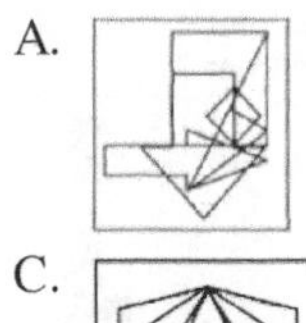

C. D.

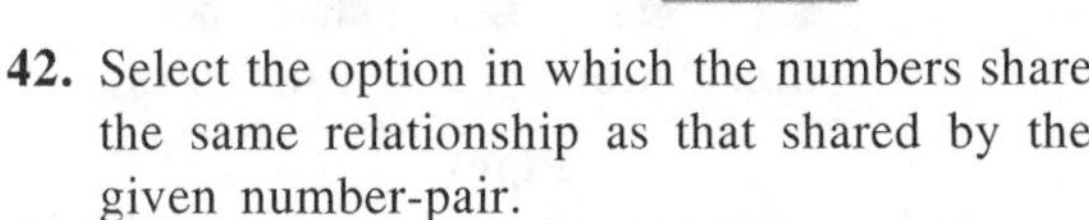

42. Select the option in which the numbers share the same relationship as that shared by the given number-pair.

4 : 25

A. 11 : 170 B. 6 : 49

C. 12 : 120 D. 6 : 36

43. Select the correct mirror image of the given figure.

A. B.

C. D.

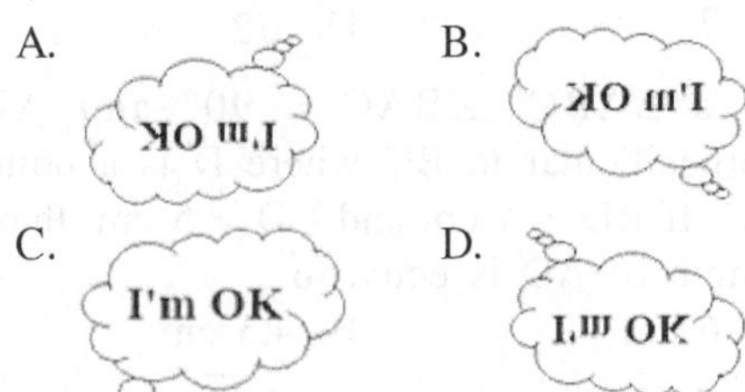

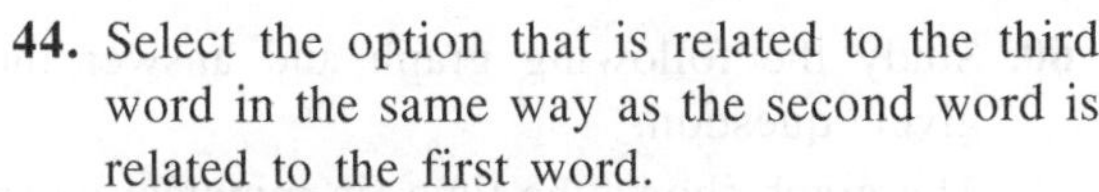

44. Select the option that is related to the third word in the same way as the second word is related to the first word.

Time : Second :: Length : ?

A. Meter B. Distance

C. Long D. Measuring Rule

45. 'TQUS' is related to 'UPVR' in the same way as 'FIRE' is related to ______.

A. GIRG B. GHSD

C. GIRF D. GHRD

46. In a certain code language 'TRAFFIC' is written as 'VTCHHKE'. How will 'POLICE' be written as in that language?

A. RMNGEC B. ONKHBD

C. RQNKEG D. RMJGEC

47. Select the number that can replace the question mark (?) in the following figure series.

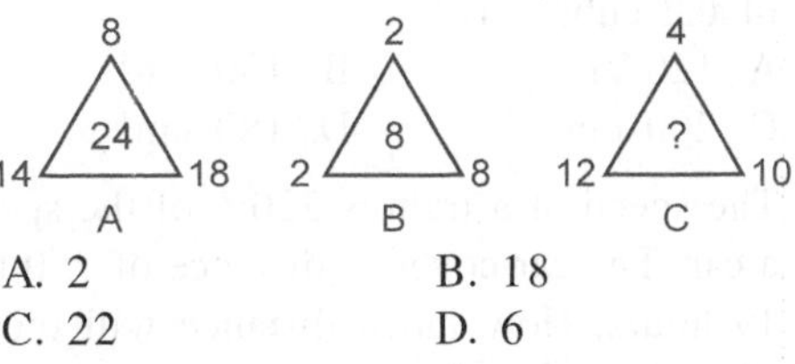

A. 2 B. 18

C. 22 D. 6

48. Select the combination of letters that when sequentially placed in the blanks of the given letter series will complete the series.

dabx_dab__d_b_xdab_x_

A. dxadadd B. xxxaxxd

C. xxcbxad D. axdaxxd

49. Select the number that can replace the question mark (?) in the following series.

6, 7, 16, 51, 208, ?

A. 2000 B. 2570

C. 1045 D. 1250

50. Arrange the given words in a logical and meaningful sequence.

1. Earth 2. Saturn
3. Jupiter 4. Mercury
5. Venus 6. Mars

A. 5, 4, 3, 2, 1, 6 B. 4, 5, 1, 6, 3, 2

C. 6, 3, 4, 1, 2, 5 D. 3, 1, 4, 2, 5, 6

51. If $\sqrt{x} = \sqrt{3} - \sqrt{5}$, then the value of $x^2 - 16x + 6$ is :

A. 0 B. 4

C. 2 D. –2

52. In a group of 150 people, $\frac{2}{5}$ are men, $\frac{1}{3}$ are women and the rest are children. The average age of the women is $\frac{4}{5}$ of the average age of the men. The average of the children is $\frac{1}{5}$ of the average age of the men. If the average age of the men is 50 years, then the average age of all the people in the group is :

A. 32 years B. 36 years

C. 35 years D. 28 years

53. The areas of three adjacent faces of a cuboid are 30 cm^2, 20 cm^2 and 24 cm^2. The volume of the cuboid is :

A. 120 cm^3 B. 150 cm^3
C. 200 cm^3 D. 180 cm^3

54. The speed of a train is 220% of the speed of a car. The car covers a distance of 950 km in 19 hours. How much distance will the train cover in $3\frac{1}{2}$ hours?

A. 385 km B. 380 km
C. 285 km D. 375 km

55. The side BC of a triangle ABC is extended to the point D. If $\angle ACD$ = 132° and $\angle B = \frac{4}{7}\angle A$, then the measure of $\angle A$ is equal to :

A. 60° B. 80°
C. 50° D. 84°

56. The pie-chart shows the percentage-wise distribution of the number of students in five different schools P, Q, R, S and T. The total number of students in all five schools together is 10,500.

Study the pie-chart and answer the question.

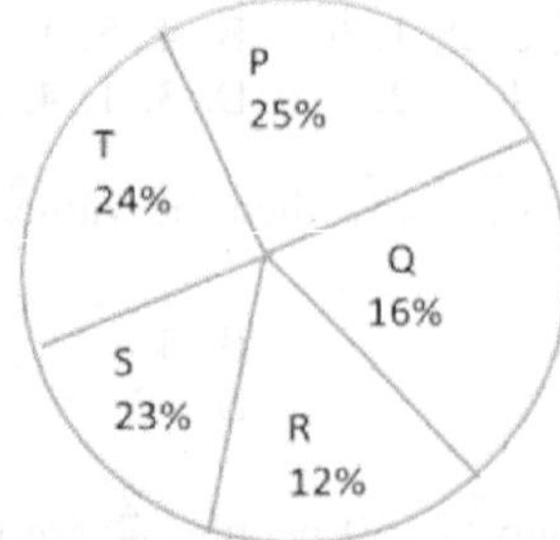

The number of students in school R is what per cent of the total number of students in schools Q and T together?

A. 30% B. 35%
C. 25% D. 40%

57. Study the following graph and answer the given question.

The graph shows the time (in minutes) taken by the pipes (A, B), (C, D), (E, F), (G, H) and (P, Q) to fill a tank.

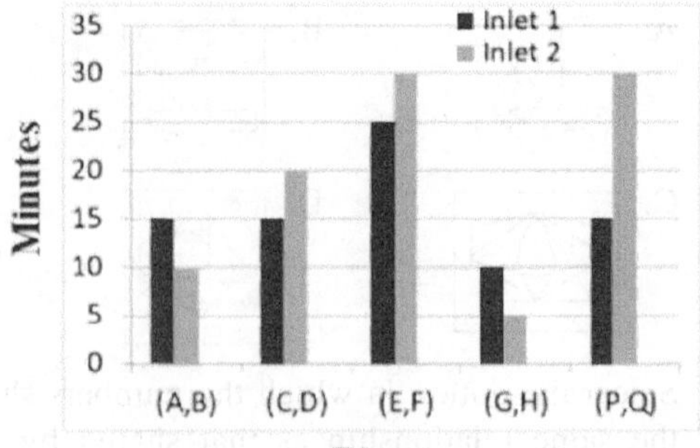

In how many minutes is an empty tank filled completely if pipe D fills it for half the time and then for the other half time, pipes C and D fill it together?

A. 15 minutes B. 18 minutes
C. 12 minutes D. 10 minutes

58. If $x = \frac{\sqrt{3}}{2}$, then the value of $\frac{\sqrt{1+x}+\sqrt{1-x}}{\sqrt{1+x}-\sqrt{1-x}}$ is equal to :

A. 3 B. $\sqrt{3}$
C. 2 D. $\sqrt{2}$

59. In a ΔABC, $\angle BAC$ = 90° and AD is perpendicular to BC where D is a point on BC. If BD = 4 cm and CD = 5 cm, then the length of AD is equal to :

A. 6 cm B. 4.5 cm
C. $2\sqrt{5}$ cm D. $5\sqrt{2}$ cm

60. Study the following graph and answer the given question.

The graph shows the time (in minutes) taken by the pipes (A, B), (C, D), (E, F), (G, H) and (P, Q) to fill a tank.

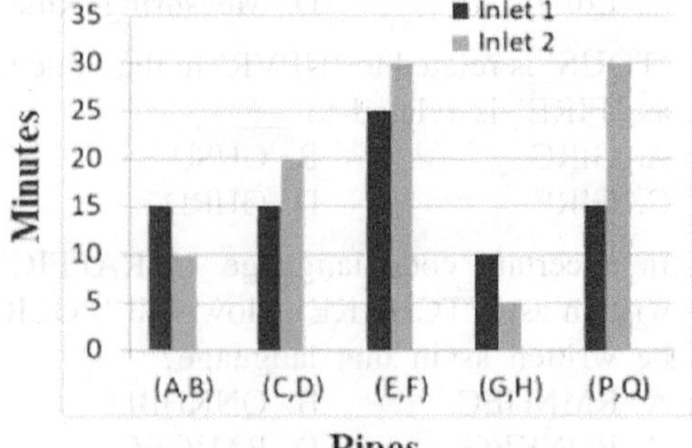

Two pipes P and Q are inlet pipes. If they are opened at alternate minutes and if pipe P is opened first, then in how many minutes will the tank be full?
A. 18 minutes
B. 20 minutes
C. 16 minutes
D. 30 minutes

61. The circles of same radius 13 cm intersect each other at A and B. If AB = 10 cm, then the distance between their centres is :
A. 18 cm
B. 12 cm
C. 24 cm
D. 26 cm

62. On selling 26 balls ₹ 1,350, there is a loss equal to the cost price of eight balls. The cost price of a ball is :
A. ₹ 70
B. ₹ 65
C. ₹ 60
D. ₹ 75

63. in the figure, a circle touches all the four sides of a quadrilateral ABCD whose sides AB = 6.5 cm, BC = 5.4 cm and CD = 5.3 cm. The length of AD is :

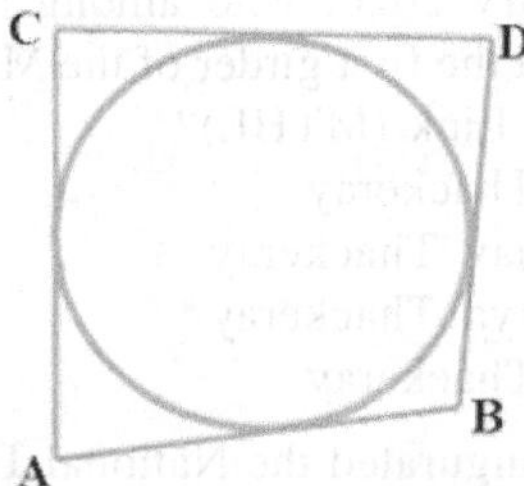

A. 4.6 cm B. 6.4 cm
C. 5.8 cm D. 6.2 cm

64. What is the third proportional to 16 and 24?
A. 36 B. 28
C. 34 D. 32

65. The pie-chart shows the percentage-wise distribution of the number of students in five different schools P, Q, R, S and T. The total number of students in all five schools together is 10,500.

Study the pie-chart and answer the question.

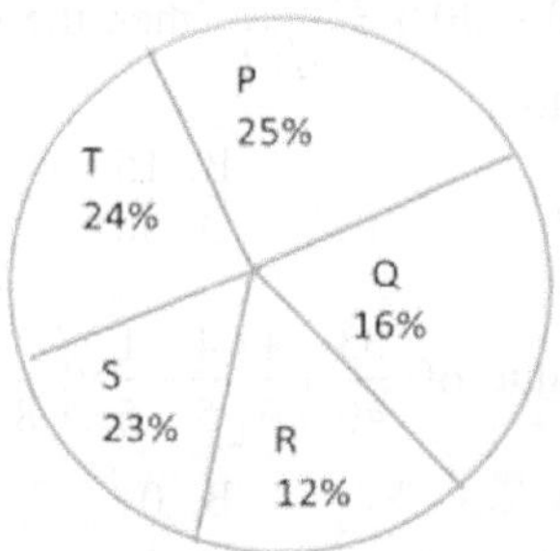

The difference between the central angles corresponding to schools T and R is :
A. 34.5° B. 44°
C. 43.2° D. 42.8°

66. If $a^3 + b^3 = 62$ and $a + b = 2$, then the value of ab is :
A. –9 B. 9
C. –6 D. 6

67. When a number is divided by 14, the remainder is 9. If the square of the same number is divided by 14, then the remainder will be :
A. 11 B. 9
C. 10 D. 8

68. If $\dfrac{\sec\theta + \tan\theta}{\sec\theta - \tan\theta} = 5$ and θ is an acute angle, then the value of $\dfrac{3\cos^2\theta + 1}{3\cos^2\theta - 1}$ is :
A. 3 B. 2
C. 1 D. 4

69. A sum at simple interest becomes two times is 8 years at a certain rate of interest p.a. The time in which the same sum will be 4 times at the same rate of interest at simple interest is :
A. 30 years B. 25 years
C. 24 years D. 20 years

70. If the price an eraser is reduced by 25%, a person can buy three more erasers for ₹ 2. How many erasers can be bought for ₹ 2 as the original price?
A. 8 B. 10
C. 12 D. 9

71. If $\sin(\theta + 30°) = \frac{3}{\sqrt{12}}$, then the value of θ is equal to :
A. 60° B. 15°
C. 45° D. 30°

72. The value of $\frac{33}{40} + \frac{1}{5}\left[\frac{4}{5} - \frac{1}{5} \times \left(\frac{7}{8} - \frac{5}{4}\right)\right]$ is :
A. 5 B. 0
C. 10 D. 1

73. The marked price of an article is 25° more than its cost price. If 10% discount is given on the marked price, then what is the profit percentage?
A. 12% B. 11.5%
C. 10% D. 12.5%

74. If $\sin(A - B) = \frac{1}{2}$ and $\cos(A + B) = \frac{1}{2}$, where $A > B > 0°$ and A + B is an acute angle, then the value of A is :
A. 45° B. 30°
C. 15° D. 60°

75. A is twice as good a workman as B and together they finish a piece of work in 22 days. In how many days will A alone finish the same work?
A. 11 days B. 44 days
C. 30 days D. 33 days

76. Which instrument is used to measure the level of humidity?
A. Fathometer B. Galvanometer
C. Hygrometer D. Hydrometer

77. The first barcode system was developed by:
A. Norman Joseph Woodland
B. John Mc Carthy
C. John Barger
D. David Bradley

78. Which of the following forms of martial arts is from Kerala?
A. Paika Akhada B. Gatka
C. Kalarippayattu D. Silambam

79. How many Vedangas are there in total?
A. Ten B. Six
C. Five D. Two

80. Which of the following characteristics of sound is measured in hertz (Hz)?
A. Frequency of the sound
B. Intensity of the sound
C. Wavelength of the sound
D. Loudness of the sound

81. In which year did NITI Aayog come into existence?
A. 2014 B. 2013
C. 2015 D. 2016

82. The term 'monsoon' is derived from a/an:
A. Italian word B. Latin word
C. Arabic word D. Greek word

83. In which year did the first Elected Parliament with two houses come into being in India?
A. 1952 B. 1953
C. 1954 D. 1955

84. Who is author of the book 'The Judgement: Inside Story of the Emergency in India'?
A. KM Munshi B. Indira Gandhi
C. Kuldip Nayar D. Jawaharlal Nehru

85. Who among the following is nicknamed the 'Baltimore Bullet'?
A. Tom Jager B. Ian Thorpe
C. Matt Biondi D. Michael Phelps

86. In January 2020, who among the following launched the first girder of the Mumbai Trans-Harbour Link (MTHL)?
A. Raj Thackeray
B. Uddhav Thackeray
C. Aaditya Thackeray
D. Bal Thackeray

87. Who Inaugurated the National Tribal Festival "Aadi Mahotsav" in New Delhi in November 2019?
A. Smriti Irani B. Amit Shah
C. N. Sitharaman D. Narendra Modi

88. Which country ranked first in the 2019 Human Development India Index?
A. Ireland B. Germany
C. Norway D. Switzerland

89. Who won the International Hockey Federation's (FIH) Player of the Year award in 2019?

A. Dhyan Chand B. Pargat Singh
C. Dilip Tirkey D. Manpreet Singh

90. The Hornbill Festival is celebrated in which state?
A. Assam B. Meghalaya
C. Nagaland D. Arunachal Pradesh

91. Telangana became the 29th state of India in which year?
A. 2015 B. 2014
C. 2016 D. 2017

92. Which of the following was invented by Walter Hunt?
A. Ship B. Safety pin
C. Scooter D. Safety lamp

93. Who among the following was a leader from Allahabad (now Prayagraj) in the revolt against the British in 1857?
A. Tatya Tope
B. Maulvi Liaquat Ali
C. Khan Bahadur Khan
D. Rani Laxmi Bai

94. The Bomdila Pass is located in which state?
A. Nagaland B. Arunachal Pradesh
C. Sikkim D. Himachal Pradesh

95. Trackball is which of the following devices?
A. Input device B. Touchpad
C. Output device D. Barcode reader

96. Which country is the 2019 ICC Cricket World Cup champion?
A. England B. Pakistan
C. India D. Australia

97. The Tropic of Cancer does NOT pass through which of the following Indian states?
A. Madhya Pradesh B. West Bengal
C. Andhra Pradesh D. Gujarat

98. Who among the following is one of the Deputy Operations Director of the Mars Orbiter Mission (MOM)?
A. Moumita Dutta
B. Nandini Harinath
C. Seetha Somasundaram
D. Minal Rohit

99. Which of the following is the second largest artificial lake in Asia?
A. Chilika Lake in Odisha
B. Chandubi Lake in Assam
C. Kolleru Lake in Andhra Pradesh
D. Dhebar Lake in Rajasthan

100. In October 2019, which of the following pairs of Indian cities was included by UNESCO in its network of 'Creative Cities' on the occasion of World Cities Day 2019?
A. Pune & Hyderabad
B. Jodhpur & Kolkata
C. Hyderabad & Mumbai
D. Delhi & Mumbai

ANSWERS

1	2	3	4	5	6	7	8	9	10
D	D	B	B	C	D	B	A	C	A
11	**12**	**13**	**14**	**15**	**16**	**17**	**18**	**19**	**20**
D	C	A	D	D	A	B	C	C	C
21	**22**	**23**	**24**	**25**	**26**	**27**	**28**	**29**	**30**
D	B	A	A	B	C	D	B	A	B
31	**32**	**33**	**34**	**35**	**36**	**37**	**38**	**39**	**40**
A	C	A	B	A	D	D	D	D	A
41	**42**	**43**	**44**	**45**	**46**	**47**	**48**	**49**	**50**
B	B	B	A	B	C	B	B	C	B
51	**52**	**53**	**54**	**55**	**56**	**57**	**58**	**59**	**60**
C	B	A	A	D	A	C	B	C	B

61	62	63	64	65	66	67	68	69	70
C	D	B	A	C	A	A	D	C	D
71	**72**	**73**	**74**	**75**	**76**	**77**	**78**	**79**	**80**
D	D	D	A	D	C	A	C	B	A
81	**82**	**83**	**84**	**85**	**86**	**87**	**88**	**89**	**90**
C	C	A	C	D	B	B	C	D	C
91	**92**	**93**	**94**	**95**	**96**	**97**	**98**	**99**	**100**
B	B	B	B	A	A	C	B	D	C

EXPLANATORY ANSWERS

26. 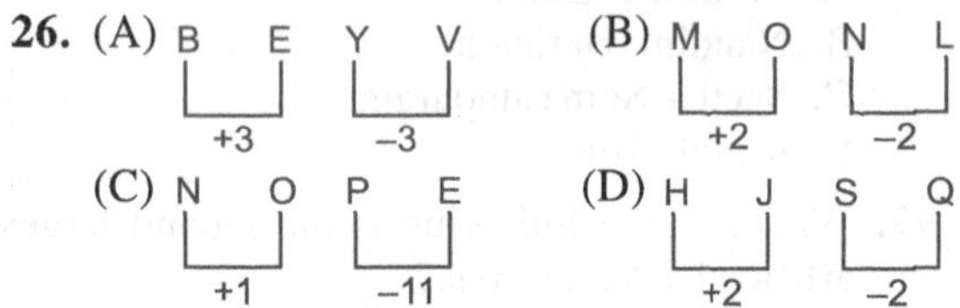

Hence Option (A), (B) and (D) are alike in some Manner and (C) is different.

28. 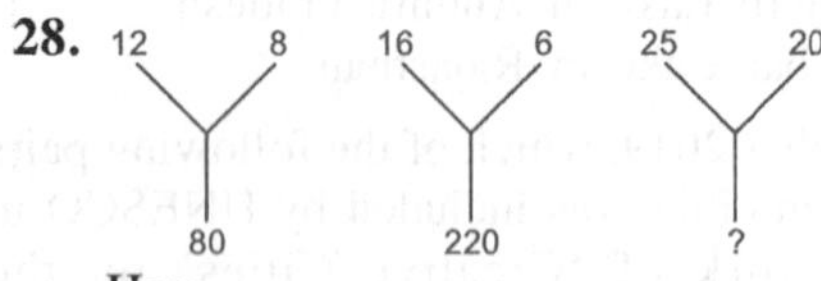

Here,

$(12 + 8) \times 4 = 20 \times 4 = 80$

$(16 + 6) \times 10 = 22 \times 10 = 220$

$(25 + 20) \times 5 = 45 \times 5 = 225$

29. Required rate of onion increasing %

$$= \frac{120-70}{70} \times 100\%$$

$$= \frac{50}{70} \times 100\% = \frac{500}{7}\%$$

$$= 71.4285\% = 71.5\%$$

30. 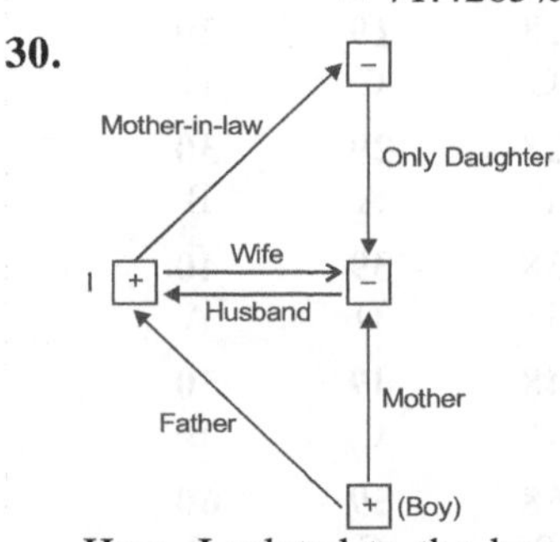

Here, I related to the boy as a father.

31. Here,

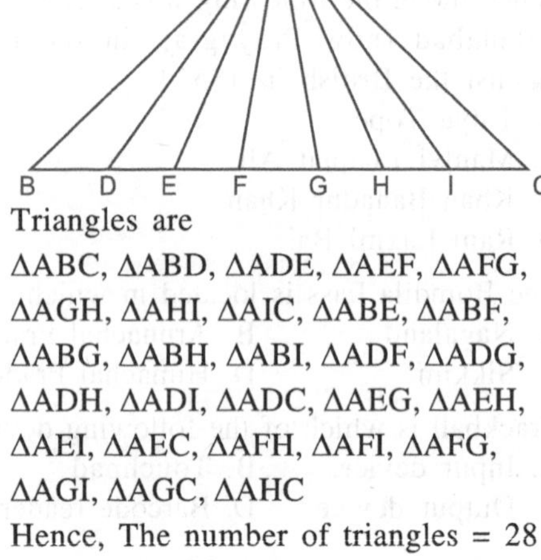

Triangles are

ΔABC, ΔABD, ΔADE, ΔAEF, ΔAFG, ΔAGH, ΔAHI, ΔAIC, ΔABE, ΔABF, ΔABG, ΔABH, ΔABI, ΔADF, ΔADG, ΔADH, ΔADI, ΔADC, ΔAEG, ΔAEH, ΔAEI, ΔAEC, ΔAFH, ΔAFI, ΔAFG, ΔAGI, ΔAGC, ΔAHC

Hence, The number of triangles = 28

33. Taking clockwise from letter C.

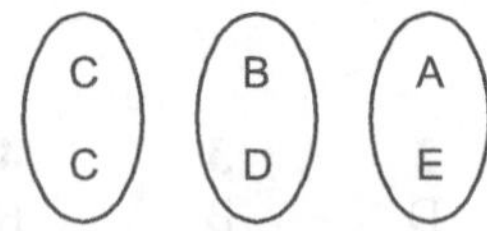

Here, opposite to the letter C = F,
Opposite to the letter B = D
and Opposite to the letter A = E

35. 40 A 2 A 3 A 4 A 15

After checking the options correct combination (A) ÷, ×, =, ×

$\therefore$ 40A2A3A4A15

$\Rightarrow 40 \div 2 \times 3 = 4 \times 15$

$\Rightarrow 20 \times 3 = 60$

$\Rightarrow 60 = 60$

36. 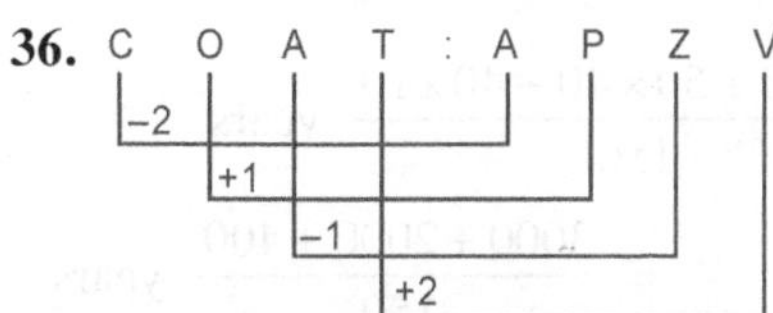

Similarly,

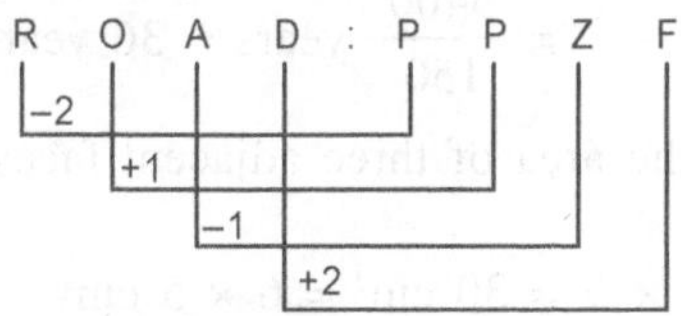

37. (A) $729 = 9^3$

(B) $125 = 5^3$

(C) $216 = 6^3$

(D) $676 = (26)^2$

39. Statements:

1. All malls are kings.
2. No king is a heater.

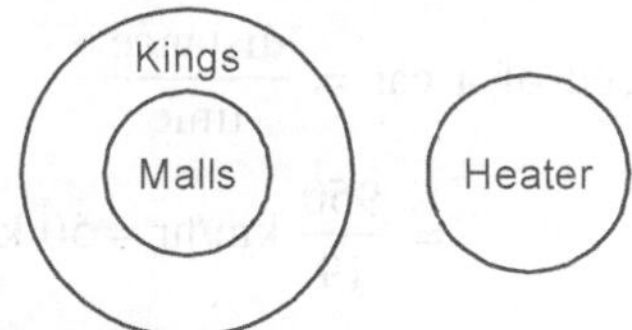

Conclusion:

I. No mall is a heater

Hence, only conclusion I follows.

40.

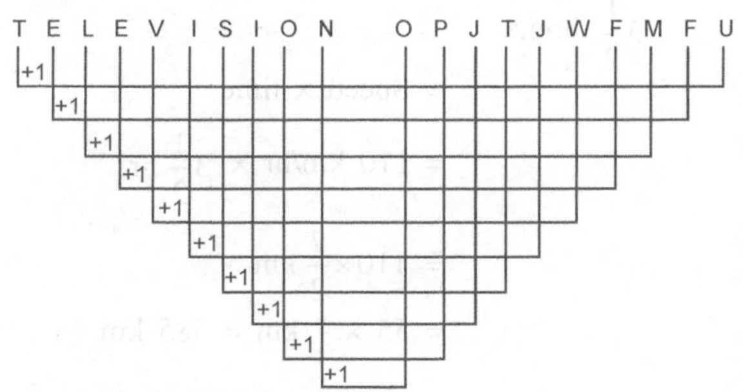

Similarly,

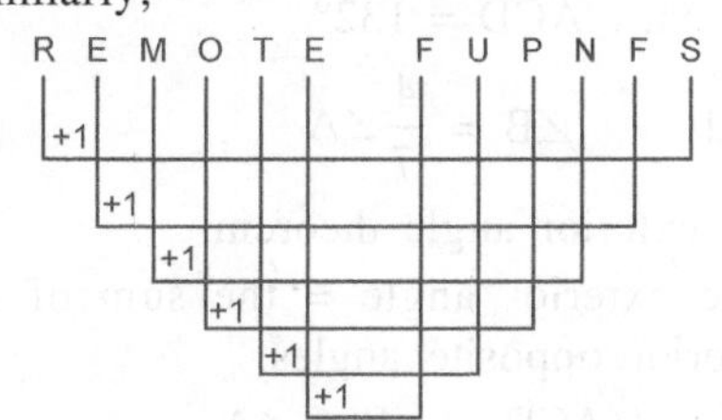

42. $4 : 25 \Rightarrow 4 : (4 + 1)^2$

$\because \quad (4 + 1)^2 = 5^2 = 25$

$6 : 49 \Rightarrow 6 : (6 + 1)^2$

$\Rightarrow \quad 6 : 7^2 = 6 : 49$

45. T Q U S U P V R

+1 –1 +1 –1

Similarly,

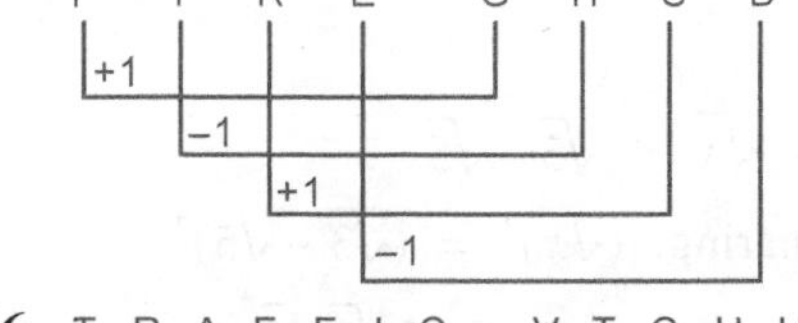

46. T R A F F I C V T C H H K E

+2 +2 +2 +2 +2 +2 +2

Similarly,

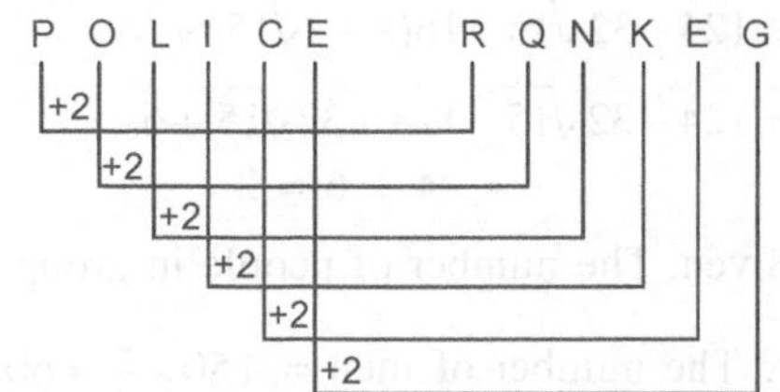

47.

Triangle A: top 8, centre 24, left 14, right 18
Triangle B: top 2, centre 8, left 2, right 8
Triangle C: top 4, centre ?, left 12, right 10

$\Rightarrow 14 + (18 - 8) \Rightarrow 14 + 10 = 24$

$\Rightarrow 2 + (8 - 2) \Rightarrow 2 + 6 = 8$

$\Rightarrow 12 + (10 - 4) \Rightarrow 12 + 6 = 18$

Hence, $\quad ? = 18$

48. dabx_dab_ _d_b_xdab_x_

after checking the options,

correct combination of letters (B) xxxaxxd

d a b x x d a b x x d a b x x d a b x x d

49. 6, 7, 16, 51, 208, ?

Here,

$6 \times 1 + 1 = 6 + 1 = 7,$

$7 \times 2 + 2 = 14 + 2 = 16,$

$16 \times 3 + 3 = 48 + 3 = 51,$

$51 \times 4 + 4 = 204 + 4 = 208$

and, $208 \times 5 + 5 = 1040 + 5 = 1045$

Hence, next number = ? = 1045

50. According to distance from Sun.

Sun: Mercury, Venus, Earth, Mars, Jupiter, Saturn

51. Given, $\sqrt{x} = \sqrt{3} - \sqrt{5}$

By squaring, $(\sqrt{x})^2 = (\sqrt{3} - \sqrt{5})^2$

$\Rightarrow \quad x = 3 + 5 - 2\sqrt{3}\sqrt{5}$

$\Rightarrow \quad x = 8 - 2\sqrt{15}$

$\Rightarrow \quad x^2 = (8 - 2\sqrt{15})^2$

$\Rightarrow \quad x^2 = 64 + 60 - 2 \times 8 \times 2\sqrt{15}$

$\Rightarrow \quad x^2 = 124 - 32\sqrt{15}$

Now, $x^2 - 16x + 6$

$= 124 - 32\sqrt{15} - 16(8 - 2\sqrt{15}) + 6$

$= 124 - 32\sqrt{15} - 128 + 32\sqrt{15} + 6$

$= -4 + 6 = 2$

52. Given, The number of people in group = 150

$\therefore$ The number of men $= 150 \times \frac{2}{5} = 60$

The number of women $= 150 \times \frac{1}{3} = 50$

and the number of children = 150 – (60 + 50)

= 150 – 110 = 40

Given, the average age of the men = 50 years

$\therefore$ The average age of the women

$= \frac{4}{5} \times 50 = 40$ years

and the average age of the children

$= \frac{1}{5} \times 50 = 10$ years

Hence, the average age of all the people in the group

$= \frac{60 \times 50 + 50 \times 40 + 40 \times 10}{150}$ years

$= \frac{3000 + 2000 + 400}{150}$ years

$= \frac{5400}{150}$ years = 36 years

53. Given, The area of three adjacent faces of a cuboid

$l \times b = 30 \text{ cm}^2 = 6 \times 5 \text{ cm}^2$

$b \times h = 20 \text{ cm}^2 = 5 \times 4 \text{ cm}^2$

and $\quad l \times h = 24 \text{ cm}^2 = 6 \times 4 \text{ cm}^2$

$\therefore$ Here, $l = 6$ cm, $b = 5$ cm and $h = 4$ cm

$\therefore$ The volume of the cuboid $= l \times b \times h$

$= 6 \times 5 \times 4 \text{ cm}^3 = 120 \text{ cm}^3$

54. Here, distance cover by car = 950 km

time = 19 hours

$\therefore$ Speed of a car $= \frac{\text{distance}}{\text{time}}$

$= \frac{950}{19}$ km/hr = 50 km/hr

$\therefore$ The speed of a train $= 50 \times \frac{220}{100}$ km/hr

= 110 km/hr

Hence, the distance will the train cover in $3\frac{1}{2}$ hours

= Speed × time

$= 110$ km/hr $\times 3\frac{1}{2}$ hr.

$= 110 \times \frac{7}{2}$ km

$= 55 \times 7$ km = 385 km

55. Given, $\angle ACD = 132°$

and $\quad \angle B = \frac{4}{7}\angle A$

By exterior angle theorem,

The exterior angle = the sum of the two interior opposite angles.

$\angle ACD = \angle B + \angle A$

$$\Rightarrow \quad 132° = \frac{4}{7}\angle A + \angle A$$

$$\Rightarrow \quad 132° = \frac{11}{7}\angle A$$

$$\Rightarrow \quad \angle A = 132° \times \frac{7}{11} = 12° \times 7 = 84°$$

Hence, $\angle A = 84°$

56. By given the pie-chart

The number of students in school R

$$= 10,500 \times \frac{12}{100}$$

$$= 105 \times 12 = 1260$$

and, the total number of students in school Q and T

$$= 10,500 \times \frac{16+24}{100}$$

$$= 10,500 \times \frac{40}{100}$$

$$= 105 \times 40 = 4200$$

Hence, the required per cent

$$= \frac{1260 \times 100}{4200}\%$$

$$= \frac{1260}{42}\% = 30\%$$

57. By given the graph

Let time is an empty tank filled completely $= x$ minute

$\because$ Pipe D's 1 minute's work $= \frac{1}{20}$

and Pipe (C + D)'s 1 minute's work $= \frac{1}{15} + \frac{1}{20}$

$$= \frac{4+3}{60} = \frac{7}{60}$$

According to question

$$\frac{x}{2}\left(\frac{1}{20}\right) + \frac{x}{2}\left(\frac{7}{60}\right) = 1$$

$$\Rightarrow x\left[\frac{1}{40} + \frac{7}{120}\right] = 1$$

$$\Rightarrow x\left[\frac{3+7}{120}\right] = 1$$

$$\Rightarrow x\left[\frac{10}{120}\right] = 1 \Rightarrow \left[\frac{1}{12}\right] = 1$$

$\Rightarrow \quad x = 12$ minutes

Hence, required minutes = 12 minutes

58. Given, $x = \frac{\sqrt{3}}{2}$

$$\therefore \frac{\sqrt{1+x}+\sqrt{1-x}}{\sqrt{1+x}-\sqrt{1-x}}$$

$$= \frac{\sqrt{1+x}+\sqrt{1-x}}{\sqrt{1+x}-\sqrt{1-x}} \times \frac{\sqrt{1+x}+\sqrt{1-x}}{\sqrt{1+x}-\sqrt{1-x}}$$

$$= \frac{(\sqrt{1+x}+\sqrt{1-x})^2}{(\sqrt{1+x})^2-(\sqrt{1-x})^2}$$

$$= \frac{1+x+1-x+2\sqrt{1+x}\cdot\sqrt{1-x}}{1+x-(1-x)}$$

$$= \frac{2+2\sqrt{1-x^2}}{1+x-1+x} = \frac{2(1+\sqrt{1-x^2})}{2x}$$

$$= \frac{1+\sqrt{1-x^2}}{x}, \qquad \left[\because x = \frac{\sqrt{3}}{2}\right]$$

$$= \frac{1+\sqrt{1-\left(\frac{\sqrt{3}}{2}\right)^2}}{\frac{\sqrt{3}}{2}} = \frac{1+\sqrt{1-\frac{3}{4}}}{\frac{\sqrt{3}}{2}}$$

$$= \frac{1+\sqrt{\frac{1}{4}}}{\frac{\sqrt{3}}{2}} = \frac{1+\frac{1}{2}}{\frac{\sqrt{3}}{2}} = \frac{\frac{3}{2}}{\frac{\sqrt{3}}{2}}$$

$$= \frac{3}{2} \times \frac{2}{\sqrt{3}} = \frac{3}{\sqrt{3}} = \sqrt{3}$$

59. Given in ΔABC, $\angle BAC = 90°$, $AD \perp BC$
$BD = 4$ cm and $CD = 5$ cm

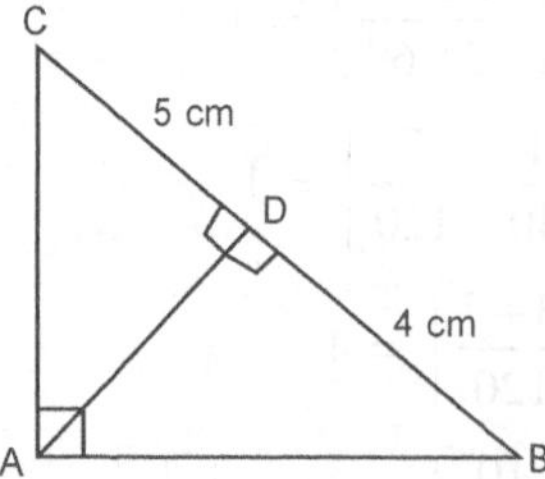

$\because$ ΔADC and ΔADB are similar triangle

$$\therefore \quad \frac{AD}{CD} = \frac{BD}{AD}$$

$\Rightarrow AD \times AD = BD \times CD$

$\Rightarrow \quad AD^2 = 4 \times 5$ cm

$\Rightarrow \quad AD^2 = 20$ cm

$\Rightarrow \quad AD = \sqrt{20}$ cm

$= \sqrt{4 \times 5}$ cm $= 2\sqrt{5}$ cm

Hence, the length of AD $= 2\sqrt{5}$ cm

60. Pipe P's 1 minute's work $= \frac{1}{15}$

and Pipe Q's 1 minute's work $= \frac{1}{30}$

(P + Q)'s 2 minute's work $= \frac{1}{15} + \frac{1}{30}$

$= \frac{2+1}{30} = \frac{3}{30} = \frac{1}{10}$

Similarly,

(P + Q)'s 20 minute's work $= 10 \times \frac{1}{10} = 1$

Hence, required time for full the tank
= 20 minutes

61. Given, The circle of same radius
$r = OA = O'A = 13$ cm
and $\quad AB = 10$ cm

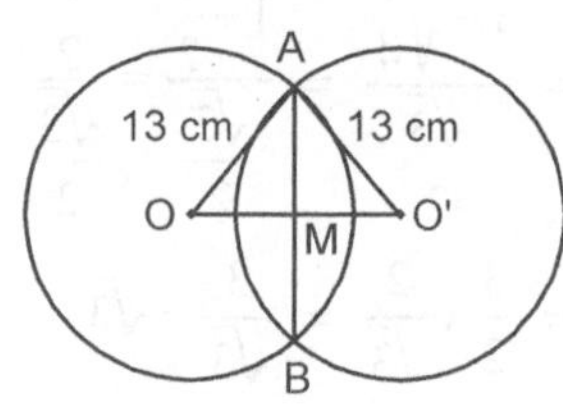

Let AB and OO′ bisect each other at M
then, $\quad AM = BM = 5$ cm

$\therefore$ ΔAMO and $\Delta AMO'$ are right angle triangle

$\therefore$ In ΔAMO

$OA^2 = AM^2 + OM^2$

$\Rightarrow \quad 13^2 = 5^2 + OM^2$

$\Rightarrow \quad OM^2 = 13^2 - 5^2 = 169 - 25 = 144$

$\Rightarrow \quad OM = 12^2$

$\Rightarrow \quad OM = 12$ cm

$\therefore \quad OO' = OM + MO'$

$= OM + OM = 2(OM)$

$= 2(12) = 24$ cm

Hence, the distance between their centres
$= OO' = 24$ cm

62. Let the cost price of a ball = ₹ x
Then, the cost price of 26 balls = ₹ $26x$

$\therefore \quad$ loss = the cost price of 8 balls

$\Rightarrow \quad$ loss $= 8x$

C.P. – S.P. = loss

$\Rightarrow 26x - 1350 = 8x$

$\Rightarrow 26x - 8x = 1350$

$\Rightarrow \quad 18x = 1350$

$\Rightarrow \quad x = \frac{1350}{18} = \frac{150}{2} = 75$

Hence, the cost price of a ball = ₹ x = ₹ 75

64. Let the third proportional $= x$
Then, $16 : 24 :: 24 : x$

$\Rightarrow \quad 16 \times x = 24 \times 24$

$\Rightarrow \quad x = \frac{24 \times 24}{16} = \frac{3 \times 24}{2} = 36$

Hence, $\quad x = 36$

65. By given the pie-chart

$100\% = 360°$

$1\% = \frac{360}{100}$

The dfifference between the central angles corresponding to schools T and R

$= (24 - 12)\% = 12\%$

$= 12 \times \frac{360}{100} = \frac{4320°}{100} = 43.20°$

66. Given, $a^3 + b^3 = 62$

and $a + b = 2$

$\therefore (a+b)^2 = 4$

$\Rightarrow a^2 + b^2 = 2ab = 4$

$\Rightarrow a^2 + b^2 = 4 - 2ab$

Now, $a^3 + b^3 = 62$

$\therefore (a+b)(a^2 - ab + b^2) = 62$

$\Rightarrow 2(a^2 + b^2 - ab) = 62$

$\Rightarrow 2(4 - 2ab - ab) = 62$

$\Rightarrow 4 - 3ab = 31$

$\Rightarrow 3ab = 4 - 31$

$\Rightarrow 3ab = -27$

$\Rightarrow ab = -9$

67. When a number is divided by 14, the remainder is 9.

Then, the number $= 14k + 9$, $k = 1$

$= 14 \times 1 + 9$

$= 14 + 9 = 23$

Square of $23 = (23)^2 = 529$

$\therefore \quad 529 = 14k + \text{Remainder}$

$= 14 \times 37 + 11$

Hence, the remainder will be 11.

68. Given, $\dfrac{\sec\theta + \tan\theta}{\sec\theta - \tan\theta} = 5$

$$\Rightarrow \frac{\dfrac{1}{\cos\theta} + \dfrac{\sin\theta}{\cos\theta}}{\dfrac{1}{\cos\theta} - \dfrac{\sin\theta}{\cos\theta}} = 5 \Rightarrow \frac{\dfrac{1+\sin\theta}{\cos\theta}}{\dfrac{1-\sin\theta}{\cos\theta}} = 5$$

$$\Rightarrow \frac{1+\sin\theta}{1-\sin\theta} = 5$$

$\Rightarrow 1 + \sin\theta = 5 - 5\sin\theta$

$\Rightarrow \sin\theta + 5\sin\theta = 5 - 1$

$\Rightarrow 6\sin\theta = 4 \Rightarrow \sin\theta = \dfrac{4}{6}$

$\Rightarrow \sin\theta = \dfrac{2}{3}$

$$\therefore \frac{3\cos^2\theta + 1}{3\cos^2\theta - 1} = \frac{3(1-\sin^2\theta)+1}{3(1-\sin^2\theta)-1}$$

$$= \frac{4 - 3\sin^2\theta}{2 - 3\sin^2\theta}$$

$$= \frac{4 - 3\times\left(\dfrac{2}{3}\right)^2}{2 - 3\times\left(\dfrac{2}{3}\right)^2}$$

$$= \frac{4 - 3\times\dfrac{4}{9}}{2 - 3\times\dfrac{4}{9}} = \frac{4 - \dfrac{4}{3}}{2 - \dfrac{4}{3}}$$

$$= \frac{\dfrac{12-4}{3}}{\dfrac{6-4}{3}} = \frac{\dfrac{8}{3}}{\dfrac{2}{3}} = \frac{8}{2} = 4$$

69. Let $p = x$, $t = 8$ years, $A = 2x$

Then, simple interest $= A - p = 2x - x = x$

$$\therefore \quad r = \frac{\text{S.I.}\times 100}{p\times t} = \frac{x\times 100}{x\times 8} = \frac{25}{2}\%$$

Again, $p = x$, $A = 4x$, $r = \dfrac{25}{2}\%$

$$t = \frac{\text{S.I.}\times 100}{p\times r}$$

$$= \frac{(A-p)\times 100}{x\times\dfrac{25}{2}} = \frac{(4x-x)\times 100}{x\times\dfrac{25}{2}}$$

$$= \frac{3x\times 100\times 2}{x\times 25} = 24 \text{ years}$$

Hence, required time = 24 years

71. Given, $\sin(\theta + 30°) = \dfrac{3}{\sqrt{12}}$

$\Rightarrow \sin(\theta + 30°) = \dfrac{3}{2\sqrt{3}} = \dfrac{\sqrt{3}}{2}$

$\Rightarrow \sin(\theta + 30°) = \sin 60°$

$\Rightarrow \theta + 30° = 60°$

$\Rightarrow \theta = 60° - 30°$

$\Rightarrow \theta = 30°$

72. $\dfrac{33}{40} + \dfrac{1}{5}\left[\dfrac{4}{5} - \dfrac{1}{5}\times\left(\dfrac{7}{8} - \dfrac{5}{4}\right)\right]$

$$= \frac{33}{40} + \frac{1}{5}\left[\frac{4}{5} - \frac{1}{5}\times\left(\frac{7-10}{8}\right)\right]$$

$$= \frac{33}{40} + \frac{1}{5}\left[\frac{4}{5} - \frac{1}{5} \times \frac{-3}{8}\right]$$

$$= \frac{33}{40} + \frac{1}{5}\left[\frac{4}{5} + \frac{3}{40}\right]$$

$$= \frac{33}{40} + \frac{1}{5}\left[\frac{32+3}{40}\right]$$

$$= \frac{33}{40} + \frac{1}{5} \times \frac{35}{40}$$

$$= \frac{33}{40} + \frac{7}{40}$$

$$= \frac{33+7}{40} = \frac{40}{40} = 1$$

73. Let the cost price of an article = ₹ 100

Then, the marked price = ₹ 125

Given, discount = 10% on the marked price

$\therefore$ Selling price = ₹ $125 \times \frac{100-10}{100}$

$= ₹\ 125 \times \frac{90}{100} = ₹\ \frac{5 \times 90}{4}$

$= ₹\ \frac{5 \times 45}{2} = ₹\ \frac{225}{2}$

= ₹ 112.50

Profit = S.P. – C.P.

= ₹ 112.50 – ₹ 100 = ₹ 12.50

Hence, profit percentage = 12.50%

74. Given, $\sin(A - B) = \frac{1}{2}$

$\Rightarrow \sin(A - B) = \sin 30°$

$\Rightarrow \quad A - B = 30°$ ...(*i*)

and $\cos(A + B) = \frac{1}{2} = \cos 60°$

$\Rightarrow \quad A + B = 60°$ ...(*ii*)

Adding (*i*) and (*ii*), we get

$2A = 90° \Rightarrow A = 45°$

Hence, the value of A is 45°.

75. Ratio of work efficiency of A and B

$\therefore \quad A : B = 2x : x$

Ratio of day(time) of A and B

$\therefore \quad A : B = x : 2x$

$\because$ (A + B)'s 1 day's work = $\frac{1}{22}$

$\therefore \quad \frac{1}{x} + \frac{1}{2x} = \frac{1}{22}$

$\Rightarrow \quad \frac{2+1}{2x} = \frac{1}{22}$

$\Rightarrow \quad \frac{3}{2x} = \frac{1}{22} \Rightarrow 2x = 3 \times 22$

$\Rightarrow \quad x = \frac{3 \times 22}{2} \Rightarrow x = 33$

Hence, A alone will finish the same work in x days = 33 days

Quantitative Aptitude

1 Simplification

Simplification is a mathematical operation by which a complex expression of numbers or fractions is converted into a simpler or less difficult form. It is erroneous to solve this type of questions on random basis and a very appropriate method is to apply BODMAS Rule for arriving at the solution of such problems. Each of the letters of the word 'BODMAS' when explained serially, has following implications:

1.	B	→	Bracket	[{ (‾) }]
2.	O	→	of	of
3.	D	→	Division	÷
4.	M	→	Multiplication	×
5.	A	→	Addition	+
6.	S	→	Subtraction	–

Therefore, for simplification, we should remove the brackets first. Thereafter operation for 'of', then for 'division', after that the operation for 'multiplication' and thereafter for 'addition' and at last operation for 'subtraction' should be carried out.

Important Notes

(a) In mathematical operations the word 'of' indicates multiplication.

(b) While removing brackets, first of all bar bracket '–' and after that small bracket '( )' is removed. Thereafter the curly bracket '{ }' and at last square bracket [ ] is removed.

EXAMPLES

Example 1. : Simplify the following expression:

$800 \div 8 \text{ of } 4 \times [40 - \{35 - (\overline{20-10} \div 2) + 6\}]$

Solution: For simplifying the given expression we will first remove bar bracket '–', then the small bracket '( )', thereafter the curly bracket '{ }' and at last the square bracket '[ ]'. 'BODMAS' Rule is applied to solve the expression.

$\therefore 800 \div 8 \text{ of } 4 \times [40 - \{35 - (\overline{20-10} \div 2) + 6\}]$

$= 800 \div 8 \text{ of } 4 \times [40 - \{35 - (10 \div 2) + 6\}]$

$= 800 \div 8 \text{ of } 4 \times [40 - \{35 - 5 + 6\}]$

$= 800 \div 8 \text{ of } 4 \times [40 - \{41 - 5\}]$

$= 800 \div 8 \text{ of } 4 \times [40 - 36] = 800 \div 8 \text{ of } 4 \times 4$

$= 800 \div 32 \times 4$

$= \frac{800}{32} \times 4 = 100$

Example 2: Simplyfy:

(a) $\frac{2.8 \times 2.8 - 1.2 \times 1.2}{2.8 - 1.2}$

(b) $(6.8)^2 + 6.8 \times 6.4 + (3.2)^2$

Solution:

(a) $\because \frac{2.8 \times 2.8 - 1.2 \times 1.2}{2.8 - 1.2} = \frac{(2.8)^2 - (1.2)^2}{2.8 - 1.2}$

$= \frac{(2.8+1.2)\,(2.8-1.2)}{2.8-1.2} = 2.8 + 1.2 = 4$

$[\because a^2 - b^2 = (a + b)(a - b)]$

(b) $\because (6.8)^2 + 6.8 \times 6.4 + (3.2)^2$

$= (6.8)^2 + 2 \times 3.2 \times 6.8 + (3.2)^2$

$= (6.8 + 3.2)^2 = (10)^2 = 100$

$[\because a^2 + 2ab + b^2 = (a + b)^2]$

Example 3: Simplify : $7680 \div 256 \div 64 \div 8$

Solution: $7680 \div 256 \div 64 \div 8 = \frac{7680}{256} \div 64 \div 8 =$

$30 \div 64 \div 8$

$= \frac{30}{64} \div 8 = \frac{15}{32} \div 8 = \frac{15}{32 \times 8} = \frac{15}{256}$

Example 4: Simplify:

$$b-\left[b-(a+b)-\left\{b-\left(b-\overline{a-b}\right)\right\}+2a\right]$$

Solution:

$$b-\left[b-(a+b)-\left\{b-\left(b-\overline{a-b}\right)\right\}+2a\right]$$

$$= b-\left[b-(a+b)-\{b-(b-a+b)\}+2a\right]$$

$$= b-\left[b-a-b-\{b-b+a-b\}+2a\right]$$

$$= b-\left[b-a-b-\{a-b\}+2a\right]$$

$$= b-\left[b-a-b-a+b+2a\right]$$

$$= b-b$$

$$= 0.$$

EXERCISE

1. If $75^2 - 65^2 = 2x$, then value of x is:

(a) 715 (b) 700
(c) 688 (d) 711
(e) None of these

2. What will be the value of $\dfrac{\frac{1}{3}\times 20\div 4}{\frac{1}{4}\times 25\div 5}$?

(a) $\frac{7}{3}$ (b) $\frac{2}{3}$
(c) $\frac{5}{3}$ (d) $\frac{10}{3}$
(e) $\frac{4}{3}$

3. Which of the following is the standard form of $\dfrac{(24\times 13)+(28\div 7)}{(24+13)-\left(\frac{14}{3}\text{ of }\frac{5}{8}\right)}$?

(a) $\frac{3792}{409}$ (b) $\frac{4792}{309}$
(c) $\frac{3792}{411}$ (d) $\frac{3092}{409}$
(e) None of these

4. What will be the value of $\dfrac{\left(\sqrt{6}+\frac{1}{\sqrt{6}}\right)^2}{\frac{1}{2}\text{ of }18+4}+\dfrac{2}{3}$?

(a) $\frac{101}{78}$ (b) $\frac{104}{71}$
(c) $\frac{101}{88}$ (d) $\frac{99}{57}$
(e) None of these

5. $\dfrac{(.08)^3+(.011)^3}{(.08)^2-.08\times .011+(.011)^2} = ?$

(a) .087 (b) 0.91
(c) .077 (d) .067
(e) 0.0091

6. What is the value of

$$22 \div \left[(28-13)\div\{(32-8)\div\left(5+\frac{1}{3}\right)\}\right]?$$

(a) 7.9 (b) 6.8
(c) 6.6 (d) 5.7
(e) None of these

7. What is the value of $\dfrac{(20^2-10^2)\div 5\times 3+10}{\frac{1}{3}\text{ of }27+10\div 2+1}$?

(a) $10\frac{2}{3}$ (b) $14\frac{1}{3}$
(c) 15 (d) $12\frac{2}{3}$
(e) None of these

8. What is the value of $11^2 - 6^2 \div 6 \times \frac{5}{2} + 2$ of 10?

(a) 126 (b) 108
(c) 110 (d) 125
(e) None of these

9. What is the value of $\frac{19}{17}$ of $\frac{28}{5}$ of $\left(\frac{17}{3} \div \frac{5}{3} \text{ of } 6\frac{1}{3}\right)$?

(a) $4\frac{9}{25}$ *(b)* $3\frac{8}{23}$

(c) $3\frac{9}{24}$ *(d)* $3\frac{8}{25}$

(e) $3\frac{9}{25}$

10. What is the value of $\left(17^{\frac{3}{2}} + 11^{3/2}\right)\left(17^{\frac{3}{2}} - 11^{3/2}\right)$?

(a) 3852 *(b)* 3582

(c) 3782 *(d)* 3258

(e) None of these

11. What is the value of $3 - [9 + \{14 - (6 - \overline{3 - 21})\}]$?

(a) 0 *(b)* 4

(c) 18 *(d)* 6

(e) None of these

12. $\dfrac{4\frac{1}{7} - 2\frac{1}{4}}{3\frac{1}{2} + 1\frac{1}{7}} \div \dfrac{1}{2 + \dfrac{1}{2 + \dfrac{1}{5 - \frac{1}{5}}}} = ?$

(a) 3 *(b)* $\frac{1}{8}$

(c) 8 *(d)* 1

(e) None of these

13. 25 – 5 [2 + 3 {2 – 2 (5 – 3) + 5} –10] ÷ 4 = ?

(a) 5 *(b)* 25

(c) 23.25 *(d)* 23.75

(e) None of these

14. $\dfrac{(6+6+6+6) \div 6}{4+4+4+4 \div 4} = ?$

(a) $3\frac{6}{13}$ *(b)* $\frac{4}{13}$

(c) $\frac{3}{2}$ *(d)* 1

(e) None of these

15. 18 – [5 – {6 + 2 (7 – 8 – 5)}] = ?

(a) 32 *(b)* 27

(c) 15 *(d)* 13

(e) None of these

16. A student was asked to solve the fraction $\dfrac{\frac{7}{3} + 1\frac{1}{2} \text{ of } \frac{5}{3}}{2 + 1\frac{2}{3}}$ and his answer was $\frac{1}{4}$.

By how much was his answer wrong?

(a) $\frac{23}{44}$ *(b)* $\frac{3}{44}$

(c) $1\frac{5}{44}$ *(d)* $\frac{23}{40}$

(e) None of these

17. 7 is added to a certain number, the sum is multiplied by 5 the product is divided by 9 and 3 is subtracted from the quotient. The remainder left is 12. Find the number.

(a) 60 *(b)* 40

(c) 30 *(d)* 20

(e) None of these

18. If $2 = x + \dfrac{1}{1 + \dfrac{1}{3 + \frac{1}{4}}}$, then the value of x is:

(a) $\frac{21}{17}$ *(b)* $\frac{18}{17}$

(c) $\frac{13}{17}$ *(d)* $\frac{12}{17}$

(e) None of these

19. The value of $\dfrac{2 + \dfrac{1}{3\frac{4}{5}}}{2 + \dfrac{1}{3 + \dfrac{1}{1 + \frac{1}{4}}}}$ is:

(a) $\frac{8}{7}$ *(b)* $\frac{3}{7}$

(c) $\frac{1}{7}$ (d) 1
(e) None of these

20. $\dfrac{1}{1+\dfrac{\frac{2}{3}}{1+\frac{2}{3}+\dfrac{\frac{8}{9}}{1-\frac{2}{3}}}}$ is equal to:

(a) $\frac{15}{13}$ (b) $\frac{13}{11}$
(c) $\frac{13}{15}$ (d) $\frac{11}{13}$
(e) None of these

21. $\frac{3}{4}\left(1+\frac{1}{3}\right)\left(1+\frac{2}{3}\right)\left(1-\frac{2}{5}\right)\left(1+\frac{6}{7}\right)\left(1-\frac{12}{13}\right)$ is simplified to:

(a) $\frac{1}{8}$ (b) $\frac{1}{7}$
(c) $\frac{1}{6}$ (d) $\frac{1}{5}$
(e) None of these

22. $\left(1+\frac{1}{2}\right)\left(1+\frac{1}{3}\right)\left(1+\frac{1}{4}\right)\ldots\left(1+\frac{1}{120}\right)$ is simplified to:

(a) 121 (b) 85.5
(c) 40.5 (d) 30
(e) None of these

23. $999\frac{995}{999}\times 999$ is simplified to:

(a) 999824 (b) 998999
(c) 999996 (d) 990809
(e) 998996

24. $\frac{3}{1^2.2^2}+\frac{5}{2^2.3^2}+\frac{7}{3^2.4^2}+\frac{9}{4^2.5^2}+\frac{11}{5^2.6^2}+\frac{13}{6^2.7^2}+\frac{15}{7^2.8^2}+\frac{17}{8^2.9^2}+\frac{19}{9^2.10^2}$ is simplified to:

(a) $\frac{101}{100}$ (b) 1
(c) $\frac{99}{100}$ (d) $\frac{1}{100}$
(e) None of these

25. $1+\frac{1}{4\times 3}+\frac{1}{4\times 3^2}+\frac{1}{4\times 3^3}$ is simplified to:

(a) $\frac{11}{18}$ (b) $\frac{121}{108}$
(c) $\frac{3}{2}$ (d) $\frac{31}{2}$
(e) None of these

26. $\frac{1}{1\cdot 2\cdot 3}+\frac{1}{2\cdot 3\cdot 4}+\frac{1}{3\cdot 4\cdot 5}+\frac{1}{4\cdot 5\cdot 6}$ is simplified to:

(a) $\frac{17}{30}$ (b) $\frac{13}{30}$
(c) $\frac{11}{30}$ (d) $\frac{7}{30}$
(e) None of these

27. $\dfrac{\left(\frac{3}{5}\right)^3-\left(\frac{2}{5}\right)^3}{\left(\frac{3}{5}\right)^2-\left(\frac{2}{5}\right)^2}$ is simplified to:

(a) 1 (b) $\frac{21}{25}$
(c) $\frac{25}{19}$ (d) $\frac{1}{5}$
(e) $\frac{19}{25}$

28. $\dfrac{(13)^3+7^3}{(13)^2+7^2-?}=20$

(a) 91 (b) 81
(c) 100 (d) 64
(e) None of these

29. $$\frac{\left(1+\frac{1}{1+\frac{1}{100}}\right)\left(1+\frac{1}{1+\frac{1}{100}}\right)-\left(1-\frac{1}{1+\frac{1}{100}}\right)\left(1-\frac{1}{1+\frac{1}{100}}\right)}{\left(1+\frac{1}{1+\frac{1}{100}}\right)+\left(1-\frac{1}{1+\frac{1}{100}}\right)}$$

is simplified to:

(a) $\frac{101}{200}$ (b) 101

(c) 200 (d) $\frac{200}{101}$

(e) None of these

30. $$\frac{\left(3\frac{2}{3}\right)^2-\left(2\frac{1}{2}\right)^2}{\left(4\frac{3}{4}\right)^2-\left(3\frac{1}{3}\right)^2}\div\frac{3\frac{2}{3}-2\frac{1}{2}}{4\frac{3}{4}-3\frac{1}{3}}$$ is simplified to:

(a) $\frac{97}{74}$ (b) $\frac{74}{97}$

(c) $\frac{37}{97}$ (d) $\frac{97}{37}$

(e) None of these

ANSWERS

1	2	3	4	5	6	7	8	9	10
(b)	(e)	(a)	(a)	(e)	(c)	(d)	(a)	(e)	(b)
11	**12**	**13**	**14**	**15**	**16**	**17**	**18**	**19**	**20**
(b)	(d)	(d)	(b)	(b)	(e)	(d)	(a)	(d)	(c)
21	**22**	**23**	**24**	**25**	**26**	**27**	**28**	**29**	**30**
(b)	(e)	(e)	(c)	(b)	(d)	(e)	(a)	(d)	(b)

SOME SELECTED EXPLANATORY ANSWERS

1. $\because \quad 75^2 - 65^2 = 2x$

$\Rightarrow (75 + 65)(75 - 65) = 2x$

$[\because a^2 - b^2 = (a+b)(a-b)]$

$\Rightarrow \quad 140 \times 10 = 2x$

$\Rightarrow \quad x = 70 \times 10 = 700$

$\therefore$ Value of x is 700.

2. $\because \dfrac{\frac{1}{3}\times 20 \div 4}{\frac{1}{4}\times 25 \div 5} = \dfrac{\frac{1}{3}\times 5}{\frac{1}{4}\times 5} = \dfrac{\frac{5}{3}}{\frac{5}{4}} = \dfrac{4}{3}.$

3. $\because \dfrac{(24\times 13)+(28\div 7)}{(24+13)-\left(\frac{14}{3}\text{ of }\frac{5}{8}\right)}$

$= \dfrac{312+4}{37-\frac{35}{12}} = \dfrac{316}{\frac{409}{12}} = \dfrac{3792}{409}.$

4. $\therefore \dfrac{\left(\sqrt{6}+\frac{1}{\sqrt{6}}\right)^2}{\frac{1}{2}\text{ of } 18 + 4} + \dfrac{2}{3}$

$= \dfrac{\left(\sqrt{6}\right)^2+\left(\frac{1}{\sqrt{6}}\right)^2+2.\sqrt{6}\frac{1}{\sqrt{6}}}{9+4}+\dfrac{2}{3}$

$= \dfrac{6+\frac{1}{6}+2}{13}+\dfrac{2}{3} = \dfrac{\frac{49}{6}}{13}+\dfrac{2}{3} = \dfrac{49}{78}+\dfrac{2}{3} = \dfrac{101}{78}.$

8. $11^2 - 6^2 \div 6 \times \frac{5}{2} + 2$ of 10

$= 11^2 - 6^2 \div 6 \times \frac{5}{2} + 20$

$= 11^2 - 6 \times \frac{5}{2} + 20$

$= 11^2 - 15 + 20 = 121 + 5 = 126.$

11. $3 - [9 + \{14 - (6 - \overline{3-21})\}]$
$= 3 - [9 + \{14 - (6 + 18\}]$
$= 3 - [9 + \{14 - 24\}]$
$= 3 - [9 - 10] = 3 + 1 = 4.$

13. $25 - 5\ [2 + 3\ \{2 - 2\ (5 - 3) + 5\} - 10] \div 4$
$= 25 - 5\ [2 + 3\ \{2 - 4 + 5\} - 10] \div 4$
$= 25 - 5\ [2 + 9 - 10] \div 4$
$= 25 - 5 \times 1 \times \frac{1}{4} = 25 - \frac{5}{4} = \frac{95}{4} = 23.75.$

15. $18 - [5 - \{6 + 2\ (7 - \overline{8-5})\}]$
$= 18 - [5 - \{6 + 2\ (7 - 3)\}]$
$= 18 - [5 - \{6 + 8\}]$
$= 18 - [5 - 14] = 18 + 9 = 27.$

16. $\dfrac{\frac{7}{3}+\frac{3}{2}\text{ of }\frac{5}{3}}{2+\frac{5}{3}} = \dfrac{\frac{7}{3}+\frac{5}{2}}{\frac{11}{3}} = \frac{29}{6} \times \frac{3}{11} = \frac{29}{22}$

Required difference

$= \frac{29}{22} - \frac{1}{4} = \frac{58-11}{44} = \frac{47}{44} = 1\frac{3}{44}.$

17. Let, $\dfrac{5\,(x+7)}{9} - 3 = 12$

$\Rightarrow \quad \dfrac{5\,(x+7)}{9} = 15$

$\Rightarrow \quad x + 7 = \dfrac{9 \times 15}{5} = 27$

$\therefore \quad x = 20.$

20. $\dfrac{1}{1+\dfrac{\frac{2}{3}}{1+\frac{2}{3}+\dfrac{8/9}{1-2/3}}} = \dfrac{1}{1+\dfrac{\frac{2}{3}}{1+\frac{2}{3}+\frac{8}{9}\times 3}}$

$= \dfrac{1}{1+\dfrac{\frac{2}{3}}{1+\frac{10}{3}}} = \dfrac{1}{1+\frac{2}{3}\times\frac{3}{13}} = \dfrac{1}{\frac{15}{13}} = \dfrac{13}{15}.$

21. $\frac{3}{4}\left(1+\frac{1}{3}\right)\left(1+\frac{2}{3}\right)\left(1-\frac{2}{5}\right)\left(1+\frac{6}{7}\right)\left(1-\frac{12}{13}\right)$

$= \frac{3}{4}\times\frac{4}{3}\times\frac{5}{3}\times\frac{3}{5}\times\frac{13}{7}\times\frac{1}{13} = \frac{1}{7}.$

22. $\left(1+\frac{1}{2}\right)\left(1+\frac{1}{3}\right)\left(1-\frac{1}{4}\right)\ldots\left(1+\frac{1}{120}\right)$

$= \frac{3}{2}\times\frac{4}{3}\times\frac{5}{4}\times\ldots\times\frac{121}{120} = \frac{121}{2} = 60.5.$

24. $\frac{3}{1^2.2^2}+\frac{5}{2^2.3^2}+\frac{7}{3^2.4^2}+\frac{9}{4^2.5^2}+\frac{11}{5^2.6^2}$

$+\frac{13}{6^2.7^2}+\frac{15}{7^2.8^2}+\frac{17}{8^2.9^2}+\frac{19}{9^2.10^2}$

$= 1-\frac{1}{4}+\frac{1}{4}-\frac{1}{9}+\frac{1}{9}-\frac{1}{16}+\frac{1}{16}-\frac{1}{25}+\frac{1}{25}$

$-\frac{1}{36}+\frac{1}{36}-\frac{1}{49}+\frac{1}{49}-\frac{1}{64}+\frac{1}{64}-\frac{1}{81}+$

$= 1-\frac{1}{100} = \frac{99}{100}.$

❑❑❑

2 L.C.M. & H.C.F.

L.C.M.

Multiple : A number is said to be multiple of other when it is exactly divisible by the other.

Common multiple : A common multiple of two or more numbers is a number which is exactly divisible by each of them. For example, for 2 and 3, common multiples are 6, 12, 18, 24 and so on.

Consider the two numbers 2 and 3

Multiple of 2 are 2, 4, 6, 8, 10, 12, ...

Multiple of 3 are 3, 6, 9, 12, 15, ...

$\therefore$ Common multiples are 6, 12, 18, ...

Least Common Multiple (L.C.M.) : L.C.M. of two or more given numbers is the least number which is exactly divisible by each of them. For example,

6 is a common multiple of 2 and 3

12 is also common multiple of 2 and 3

Methods to find out L.C.M.

L.C.M. of two or more given numbers is determined by following two methods:

1. By prime factorization method

2. By division method

1. **By prime factorization method :** Resolve the given numbers into their prime factors and then find the product of the highest power of all the factors that occur in the given numbers. This product will be the L.C.M.
2. **By division method :** This is the quicker method to find the prime factors and hence L.C.M.

   For determining L.C.M. of the numbers 40, 50, 60 and 80, following process of division is adopted:

2	40, 50, 60, 80
2	20, 25, 30, 40
2	10, 25, 15, 20
5	5, 25, 15, 10
	1, 5, 3, 2

Now required L.C.M.

$= 2 \times 2 \times 2 \times 5 \times 5 \times 3 \times 2 = 1200$

L.C.M. of decimal : First of all, we find out the L.C.M. of numbers without decimal and then, we see the number in which decimal is given in the minimum digit from right to left. We put the decimal in our result which is equal to that number of digits.

Example : Find the L.C.M. of 0.6, 9.6 and 0.36.

Sol : The given numbers are equivalent to 0.60, 9.60 and 0.36.

Now, we find out the L.C.M. of 60, 960 and 36, which is equal to 2880.

Hence, the required L.C.M. = 28.80.

L.C.M. of fraction : The L.C.M. of two or more fractions is the least fraction or integer which is exactly divisible by each of them.

If $\frac{a}{b}, \frac{c}{d}, \frac{e}{f}$ be the proper fractions, then their L.C.M. is given by

$$\frac{\text{L.C.M. of numerators } a, c, e}{\text{H.C.F. of denominators } b, d, f}$$

H.C.F.

Factor : One number is said to be a factor of other when it divides the other exactly. Hence, 5 and 7 are factors of 35.

Common factor : A common factor of two or more numbers is a number that divides each of them exactly. Hence, 5 is a common factor of 15, 25, 35 and 55.

Highest Common Factor (H.C.F.) : H.C.F. of two or more numbers is the largest number by which each given number is divisible without leaving any remainder.

An example : It is required to find the H.C.F. of 6 and 8. Factors of 6 are 1, 2, 3, 6 and Factors of 8 are 1, 2, 4, 8.

The common factors are 1, 2, but highest of these is 2. Hence, 2 is the H.C.F.

We can find H.C.F. by two methods:

1. By prime factorization method :

An example : Find the H.C.F. of 144, 336 and 2016.

Sol : $144 = 2 \times 2 \times 2 \times 2 \times 3 \times 3 = 2^4 \times 3^2$

$336 = 2 \times 2 \times 2 \times 2 \times 3 \times 7 = 2^4 \times 3 \times 7$

$2016 = 2 \times 2 \times 2 \times 2 \times 2 \times 7 \times 3 \times 3 = 2^5 \times 7 \times 3^2$

$\therefore$ H.C.F. of given numbers $= 2^4 \times 3 = 48$.

2. By division method

Divide the greater number by the smaller number, divide the divisor by the remainder, divide the remainder by the next remainder, and so on until no remainder is left. The last divisor is the required H.C.F.

H.C.F. of Decimals : First of all find the H.C.F. of the given numbers ignoring decimals and then put decimal at maximum digits from right to left.

An example : Find the H.C.F. of 0.0012, 1.6 and 2.8.

Sol : First we find the H.C.F. of 12, 16 and 28, which comes to 4.

So, H.C.F. of 0.0012, 1.6 and 2.8 will be 0.0004.

H.C.F. of Fractions :

If $\frac{a}{b}, \frac{c}{d}, \frac{e}{f}$, ... be the proper fraction, their H.C.F. is equal to $\frac{\text{H.C.F. of numerators}}{\text{L.C.M. of denominators}}$

EXAMPLES

Example 1 : Find the H.C.F. of 8, 9 and 16.

Solution: 8) 9 (1
8
1) 8 (8
8
×

$\therefore$ H.C.F. of 8 and 9 is 1.

Now, we will have to find out the H.C.F. of 1 and 16.

1) 16 (16
16
×

$\therefore$ H.C.F. of 1 and 16 is 1

Hence, the required H.C.F. of 8, 9 and 16 is 1.

Example 2 : Find the L.C.M. of 11, 33, 77 and 121.

Solution:

11	11, 33, 77, 121
	1, 3, 7, 11

Hence, required L.C.M. $= 11 \times 3 \times 7 \times 11 = 2541$

Example 3 : Determine the H.C.F. of $\frac{54}{9}, 3\frac{9}{17}$ and $\frac{36}{51}$.

Solution: $\frac{54}{9} = \frac{6}{1}, 3\frac{9}{17} = \frac{60}{17}$ and $\frac{36}{51} = \frac{12}{17}$

Now, H.C.F. of $\frac{6}{1}, \frac{60}{17}$ and $\frac{12}{17}$

$= \frac{\text{H.C.F. of 6, 60 and 12}}{\text{L.C.M. of 1, 17 and 17}}$

$\because$ H.C.F. of 6, 60 and 12 = 6

and L.C.M. of 1, 17 and 17 = 17

$\therefore$ Required H.C.F. $= \frac{6}{17}$

Example 4 : Find the L.C.M. of $4\frac{1}{2}$, 3 and $10\frac{1}{2}$.

Solution: $4\frac{1}{2} = \frac{9}{2}, 10\frac{1}{2} = \frac{21}{2}$

$\therefore$ L.C.M. of $\frac{9}{2}, \frac{3}{1}$ and $\frac{21}{2} = \frac{\text{L.C.M. of 9, 3 and 21}}{\text{H.C.F. of 2, 1 and 2}}$

$\because$ L.C.M. of 9, 3 and 21 = 63

and H.C.F. of 2, 1 and 2 = 1

Hence, required number $= \frac{63}{1} = 63$

EXERCISE

1. The L.C.M. of 6, 8, 10 and 12 is
(*a*) 120 (*b*) 60
(*c*) 240 (*d*) 130
(*e*) None of these

2. The H.C.F. of $\frac{5}{6}, \frac{6}{7}, \frac{7}{8}, \frac{8}{9}$ and $\frac{9}{10}$ is
(*a*) $\frac{1}{2420}$ (*b*) $\frac{1}{2520}$
(*c*) $\frac{1}{2660}$ (*d*) $\frac{1}{2540}$
(*e*) None of these

3. The L.C.M. of two numbers is 85 and their product is 1020. Their H.C.F. will be
(*a*) 16 (*b*) 27
(*c*) 12 (*d*) 22
(*e*) None of these

4. L.C.M. of 24, 28, 36 and 44 is a multiple of 24 and which of the following numbers?
(*a*) 441 (*b*) 368
(*c*) 337 (*d*) 197
(*e*) 231

5. H.C.F. of 420, 315 and 462 is
(*a*) 24 (*b*) 28
(*c*) 27 (*d*) 21
(*e*) None of these

6. The largest three-digit number, when divided by 6, 9 and 12 leaves 1 as remainder in each case, will be
(*a*) 887 (*b*) 987
(*c*) 973 (*d*) 730
(*e*) None of these

7. Two numbers are in the ratio of 8 : 15. If their H.C.F. is 4, the numbers are
(*a*) 32 and 60 (*b*) 16 and 30
(*c*) 80 and 150 (*d*) 64 and 120
(*e*) None of these

8. The largest number that will divide 226 and 272 leaving 1 and 2 as remainders respectively, is
(*a*) 36 (*b*) 45
(*c*) 55 (*d*) 59
(*e*) None of these

9. The product of two numbers is 2160 and their H.C.F. is 12. How many such pairs of numbers can be possibly formed?
(*a*) 3 (*b*) 1
(*c*) 5 (*d*) 2
(*e*) 2

10. The greatest number that will divide 33, 64 and 80 leaving 3, 4 and 5 as remainders respectively, is
(*a*) 10 (*b*) 20
(*c*) 15 (*d*) 22
(*e*) None of these

11. The greatest four-digit number completely divisible by 2, 3, 4 and 5 is
(*a*) 9960 (*b*) 9690
(*c*) 8990 (*d*) 9980
(*e*) None of these

12. Three bells ring respectively at an interval of 15 seconds, 20 seconds and 24 seconds. If they ring continuously for 12 minutes then how many times, during this period, will they ring together?
(*a*) 2 times (*b*) 6 times
(*c*) 5 times (*d*) 3 times
(*e*) None of these

13. The smallest number, on being successively divided by 5, 6, 8, 9 and 12 leaves 1 as remainder in each case and is completely divisible by 13, will be
(*a*) 4603 (*b*) 6305
(*c*) 4503 (*d*) 3601
(*e*) None of these

14. HCF of 4 × 27 × 3125, 8 × 9 × 25 × 7 and 16 × 81 × 5 × 11 × 49 is
(*a*) 1260 (*b*) 540
(*c*) 360 (*d*) 240
(*e*) 180

15. The LCM of $2^3 \times 3^2 \times 5 \times 11$, $2^4 \times 3^4 \times 5^2 \times 7$ and $2^5 \times 3^3 \times 5^3 \times 7^2 \times 11$ is :
(*a*) $2^5 \times 3^4 \times 5^3$
(*b*) $2^3 \times 3^2 \times 5$
(*c*) $2^5 \times 3^4 \times 5^3 \times 7^2 \times 11$

(*d*) $2^3 \times 3^2 \times 5 \times 7 \times 11$
(*e*) None of these

16. H.C.F. of 3240, 3600 and a third number is 36 and their L.C.M. is $2^4 \times 3^5 \times 5^2 \times 7^2$. The third number is

(*a*) $2^3 \times 3^5 \times 7^2$
(*b*) $2^5 \times 5^2 \times 7^2$
(*c*) $2^2 \times 5^3 \times 7^2$
(*d*) $2^2 \times 3^5 \times 7^2$
(*e*) None of these

ANSWERS

1	2	3	4	5	6	7	8	9	10
(*a*)	(*b*)	(*c*)	(*e*)	(*d*)	(*c*)	(*a*)	(*b*)	(*e*)	(*c*)
11	**12**	**13**	**14**	**15**	**16**				
(*a*)	(*b*)	(*d*)	(*e*)	(*c*)	(*d*)				

SOME SELECTED EXPLANATORY ANSWERS

1. $6 = 2 \times 3$; $8 = 2 \times 2 \times 2$
$10 = 2 \times 5$; $12 = 2 \times 2 \times 3$

It is clear that 2 occurs as prime factor maximum three times, 3 one time and 5 one time.

Hence, required L.C.M. $= 2 \times 2 \times 2 \times 3 \times 5 = 120$

2. H.C.F. of $\frac{5}{6}, \frac{6}{7}, \frac{7}{8}, \frac{8}{9}$ and $\frac{9}{10}$

$$= \frac{\text{H.C.F. of 5,6,7,8 and 9}}{\text{LCM of 6,7,8,9 and 10}}$$

Now H.C.F. of 5, 6, 7, 8 and 9 = 1

and L.C.M. of 6, 7, 8, 9 and 10 = 2520

$\therefore$ Required H.C.F. $= \frac{1}{2520}$

3. L.C.M. of two numbers × H.C.F. of the numbers = Product of the numbers

$\therefore \quad 85 \times \text{H.C.F.} = 1020$

$\therefore \quad \text{H.C.F.} = \frac{1020}{85} = 12$

9. Product of two numbers = their HCF × their LCM

$2160 = 12 \times \text{LCM}$

$\therefore \quad \text{LCM} = \frac{2160}{12} = 180$

Therefore such pairs of numbers in which product of numbers is 2160 and HCF is 12 will be only 2.

i.e., 12 × 180 and 36 × 60.

10. $33 - 3 = 30$, $64 - 4 = 60$ and $80 - 5 = 75$

Now, HCF of 30, 60 and 75:

$30 = 2 \times \underline{3 \times 5}$

$60 = 2 \times 2 \times \underline{3 \times 5}$

$75 = \underline{3 \times 5} \times 5$

$\because$ Common factor $= 3 \times 5 = 15$

$\therefore$ Required largest number = 15.

13. LCM of 5, 6, 8, 9 and 12 = 360. Hence, the smallest number which when divided by 5, 6, 8, 9 and 12 leaves 1 as remainder in each case will be 360 + 1 = 361. But 361 is not completely divisible by 13. Hence, on considering $360 \times 2 + 1$, $360 \times 3 + 1$,... , $360 \times n + 1$, we conclude that $360 \times 10 + 1 = 3601$ is the required number.

14. $4 \times 27 \times 3125 = 2^2 \times 3^3 \times 5^5$

$8 \times 9 \times 25 \times 7 = 2^3 \times 3^2 \times 5^2 \times 7$

$16 \times 81 \times 5 \times 11 \times 49 = 2^4 \times 3^4 \times 5 \times 7^2 \times 11$

$\therefore \quad \text{HCF} = 2^2 \times 3^2 \times 5 = 4 \times 9 \times 5 = 180$

15. $2^3 \times 3^2 \times 5 \times 11$; $\quad 2^4 \times 3^4 \times 5^2 \times 7$

and $\quad 2^5 \times 3^3 \times 5^3 \times 7^2 \times 11$

$\therefore \quad \text{LCM} = 2^5 \times 3^4 \times 5^3 \times 7^2 \times 11$

❑❑❑

3 Surds & Indices

SURDS

If x is a rational number and n is a positive integer, such that $x^{1/n} = \sqrt[n]{x}$ is irrational, since $\sqrt[n]{x}$ is called a surd of order n.

Laws of Surds:

(i) $\sqrt[n]{x} = x^{1/n}$ (ii) $\left(\sqrt[n]{x}\right)^m = \sqrt[n]{x^m}$

(iii) $\sqrt[m]{\sqrt[n]{x}} = \sqrt[mn]{x}$ (iv) $\left(\sqrt[n]{x}\right)^n = x$

(v) $\sqrt[n]{xy} = \sqrt[n]{x} \times \sqrt[n]{y}$ (vi) $\sqrt[n]{\frac{a}{b}} = \frac{\sqrt[n]{a}}{\sqrt[n]{b}}$

We know that $x \times x = x^2$, $x \times x \times x = x^3$, $x \times x \times x \times x = x^4$ ..., $x \times x \times x \times x \times x \times x$ ... n times $= x^n$.

In the given quantity x^n, x is called **base** and n is called **exponent** or **index** or **power**. We read x^n as x raised to the power n or, nth power of x.

Laws of Indices:

Law 1: *When m and n are natural numbers or positive integers and x is a non-zero real number, then* $x^m \times x^n = x^{m+n}$.

Law 2: *When m and n are natural numbers or positive integers and x is a non-zero real number, then* $x^m \div x^n = \frac{x^m}{x^n} = x^{m-n}$, *if* $m > n$ *and* $\frac{x^m}{x^n} = \frac{1}{x^{n-m}}$, *if* $n > m$.

Law 3: *When m and n are natural numbers or positive integers and x is a non-zero real number, then* $(x^m)^n = x^{mn}$.

Law 4: *When m and n are natural numbers or positive integers and x and y are non-zero real numbers, then* $(xy)^m = x^m \times y^m$.

ROOT

If 'x' is a positive real number, 'n' an integer and 'a' is a natural number such that $x^n = a$, then it means nth root of a is x. It is generally denoted as:

$$x^n = a \text{ or } x = \sqrt[n]{a} = a^{\frac{1}{n}}$$

Similarly, if x is a positive real number, 'p' an integer and 'q' is a natural number such that $x^{p/q} = a$ (where a is a non-zero real number) then it means that qth root of x is equal to pth root of 'a'.

$$i.e., x^{\frac{p}{q}} = a \Rightarrow \left(x^{\frac{1}{q}}\right)^p = a \Rightarrow x^{\frac{1}{q}} = a^{\frac{1}{p}} \Rightarrow$$

$$\sqrt[q]{x} = \sqrt[p]{a}$$

Important Note: *If x is any rational number other than zero, then* $x^0 = 1$

When the base is a non-zero real number and exponent is negative integer: Here, we shall find out the value of x^{-n} (where $x \neq 0$ and a positive integer).

From the first law of exponent,

$$x^{-n} \times x^n = x^{-n+n} = x^0$$

$$\Rightarrow \quad x^{-n} \times x^n = 1 \ (\because x^0 = 1)$$

Dividing both sides by x^n,

$$x^{-n} = \frac{1}{x^n},$$

Similarly, $x^n = \frac{1}{x^{-n}}$

Hence, x^{-n} means the reciprocal of x^n.

EXAMPLES

Example 1: Simplify the following using laws of exponents.

(a) $24\ a^7\ b^5\ c^2 \div 3a^5\ b^3\ c^4$

(b) $\frac{x^{-2}y^{-4}}{x^{-3}y^{-1}} \div \frac{y^{-2}}{x^{-1}}$

Solution:

(a) $24\ a^7\ b^5\ c^2 \div 3a^5\ b^3\ c^4$

$$= \frac{24a^7b^5c^2}{3a^5b^3c^4} = 8\left(\frac{a^7}{a^5}\right)\left(\frac{b^5}{b^3}\right)\left(\frac{c^2}{c^4}\right)$$

$$= 8\ a^{(7-5)}\ b^{(5-3)}\left(\frac{1}{c^{4-2}}\right) = \frac{8a^2b^2}{c^2}$$

(b) $\because \frac{x^{-2}y^{-4}}{x^{-3}y^{-1}} \div \frac{y^{-2}}{x^{-1}}$

$$= \frac{\frac{x^{-2}y^{-4}}{x^{-3}y^{-1}}}{\frac{y^{-2}}{x^{-1}}} = \frac{x^{-2}.y^{-4} \times x^{-1}}{x^{-3}.y^{-1} \times y^{-2}} = \frac{x^{-3}y^{-4}}{x^{-3}.y^{-3}}$$

$$= y^{-4+3} = y^{-1}$$

$$= \frac{1}{y}$$

Example 2: Evaluate the following:

$$\left[\left(\frac{2^{-1}}{3^{-4}}\right)^7 \div \left(\frac{3^{-5}}{2^{-2}}\right)^{-5}\right] 2^{-4}\ 3^{-2}$$

Solution :

$$\because \left(\frac{2^{-1}}{3^{-4}}\right)^7$$

$$= \frac{2^{-1 \times 7}}{3^{-4 \times 7}} = \frac{2^{-7}}{3^{-28}}$$

$$= \frac{3^{28}}{2^7} \text{ and } \left(\frac{3^{-5}}{2^{-2}}\right)^{-5} = \frac{3^{-5 \times -5}}{2^{-2 \times -5}} = \frac{3^{25}}{2^{10}}$$

$$\therefore \left[\left(\frac{2^{-1}}{3^{-4}}\right)^7 \div \left(\frac{3^{-5}}{2^{-2}}\right)^{-5}\right] 2^{-4}.3^{-2}$$

$$= \left(\frac{3^{28}}{2^7} \div \frac{3^{25}}{2^{10}}\right) 2^{-4}.3^{-2} = \frac{3^{28} \times 2^{10} \times 2^{-4} \times 3^{-2}}{2^7 \times 3^{25}}$$

$$= 3^{28-25-2} \times 2^{10-4-7} = 3^1 \times 2^{-1} = \frac{3}{2}$$

Example 3: If $5\sqrt{5} \times 5^3 \div 5^{-3/2} = 5^{a+2}$, what is the value of a?

Solution: $5\sqrt{5} \times 5^3 \div 5^{-3/2} = 5^{a+2}$

$$\Rightarrow \frac{5 \times 5^{\frac{1}{2}} \times 5^3}{5^{-3/2}} = 5^{a+2}$$

$$\Rightarrow 5^{1+\frac{1}{2}+3+3/2} = 5^{a+2}$$

$\Rightarrow 5^6 = 5^{a+2}$ $\qquad \Rightarrow 6 = a + 2$

$\Rightarrow \qquad a = 6 - 2 = 4$

EXERCISE

1. $(x^{2/3})^{-3/4}$ is equivalent to:

(a) $\frac{1}{x}$ (b) $\frac{1}{\sqrt{x}}$

(c) $\frac{1}{x^2}$ (d) $\frac{1}{x^{-2}}$

(e) None of these

2. The value of $\left(-\frac{1}{125}\right)^{-\frac{2}{3}}$ is:

(a) $\frac{1}{25}$ (b) 125

(c) 5 (d) $\frac{1}{5}$

(e) 25

3. The value of $27^3 \times 3^4 \div 3^{10}$ is equal to:
(a) 9 (b) 3
(c) 81 (d) $\frac{1}{27}$
(e) 27

4. The expression $\frac{(-1)^{132}}{5^{-1}+3^{-1}}$ is equivalent to:
(a) $\frac{16}{9}$ (b) $-\frac{15}{8}$
(c) $\frac{15}{8}$ (d) $\frac{17}{8}$
(e) None of these

5. $\sqrt{\frac{1}{\left(\frac{3}{4}\right)^{-2}}}+\sqrt[3]{\frac{27}{64}}$ is equivalent to:
(a) $\frac{2}{3}$ (b) $\frac{4}{5}$
(c) $\frac{13}{12}$ (d) $\frac{3}{2}$
(e) None of these

6. $\sqrt[3]{x^6} \div \sqrt[6]{x^{12}} \times x^{-3} \times \sqrt[3]{x^9}$ is equivalent to:
(a) $2x$ (b) 1
(c) $\frac{1}{3x^2}$ (d) $\frac{1}{x}$
(e) None of these

7. $\left[\left(2a^2\right)^3\right]^3 \left[\left(3a^3\right)^2\right]^2 \div \left[\left(6a^6\right)^2\right]^2$ is equivalent to:
(a) $36a^6$ (b) $32a^6$
(c) $32a^4$ (d) $34a^5$
(e) None of these

8. $\frac{\left[\left(3^{-2}\right)^{-5}\right]^{1/5}+\left[\left(4^{-3}\right)^{-6}\right]^{1/6}-1}{\left[\left(2^{-3}\right)^{-4}\right]^{1/4}}$ is equivalent to:
(a) 9 (b) 8
(c) 27 (d) $\frac{1}{3}$
(e) None of these

9. $\frac{3^{n+3}-3^{n+1}+3^n}{2\left(3^{n-1}\right)}+2^{-1}$ is equivalent to:
(a) 32 (b) 39
(c) 35 (d) 38
(e) None of these

10. $\left(\frac{x^a}{x^{-b}}\right)^{a^2-ab+b^2}\left(\frac{x^b}{x^{-c}}\right)^{b^2-bc+c^2}\left(\frac{x^c}{x^{-a}}\right)^{c^2-ca+a^2}$ is equivalent to:
(a) $x^{(a^2+b^2+c^2)}$ (b) $x^{2(a^3+b^3-c^3)}$
(c) $x^{2(a^3-b^3-c^3)}$ (d) $\frac{1}{x^{2(a^3+b^3+c^3)}}$
(e) None of these

11. The value of $\frac{(243)^{0.13}\times(243)^{0.07}}{(7)^{0.25}\times(49)^{0.075}\times(343)^{0.2}}$ is:
(a) $2\frac{2}{7}$ (b) $1\frac{3}{7}$
(c) $\frac{7}{3}$ (d) $3/7$
(e) None of these

12. $\left(\frac{x^b}{x^c}\right)^{(b+c-a)} \cdot \left(\frac{x^c}{x^a}\right)^{(c+a-b)} \left(\frac{x^a}{x^b}\right)^{(a+b-c)} = ?$
(a) x^{a+b+c} (b) $x^{ab+bc+ca}$ (c) 1
(d) x^{abc}
(e) None of these

13. $\frac{1}{1+x^{(b-a)}+x^{(c-a)}}+\frac{1}{1+x^{(a-b)}+x^{(c-b)}}+\frac{1}{1+x^{(b-c)}+x^{(a-c)}} = ?$
(a) x^{a+b+c} (b) x^{a-b-c}
(c) 1 (d) 0
(e) None of these

14. If m and n are whole numbers such that $m^n = 121$, then find the value of $(m-1)^{n+1}$.
(a) 1000 (b) 121
(c) 10 (d) 1
(e) None of these

15. If $10^{0.48} = x$, $10^{0.70} = y$ and $x^z = y^2$, then what is the approximate value of z?

(a) 3.7 (b) 1.73
(c) 1.88 (d) 1.45
(e) 2.9

16. Given that $2^x = 4^y = 8^z$ and $\left(\frac{1}{2x}+\frac{1}{4y}+\frac{1}{6z}\right) = \frac{24}{7}$, then find the value of z.

(a) $\frac{7}{64}$ (b) $\frac{7}{48}$
(c) $\frac{7}{32}$ (d) $\frac{7}{16}$
(e) None of these

ANSWERS

1	2	3	4	5	6	7	8	9	10
(b)	(e)	(e)	(c)	(d)	(b)	(b)	(a)	(d)	(e)
11	**12**	**13**	**14**	**15**	**16**				
(d)	(c)	(c)	(a)	(e)	(b)				

SOME SELECTED EXPLANATORY ANSWERS

1. $\left[x^{2/3}\right]^{-\frac{3}{4}} = x^{\frac{2}{3}\times\frac{-3}{4}} = x^{-\frac{1}{2}}$

$= \frac{1}{x^{\frac{1}{2}}} = \frac{1}{\sqrt{x}}$ $\left[\because \left(x^m\right)^n = x^{mn}\right]$

4. $\frac{(-1)^{132}}{5^{-1}+3^{-1}} = \frac{\left((-1)^2\right)^{66}}{5^{-1}+3^{-1}} = \frac{(1)^{66}}{5^{-1}+3^{-1}}$

$= \frac{1}{\frac{1}{5}+\frac{1}{3}} = \frac{1}{\frac{3+5}{15}} = \frac{1}{\frac{8}{15}} = \frac{15}{8}$

5. $\sqrt{\frac{1}{\left(\frac{3}{4}\right)^{-2}}} + \sqrt[3]{\frac{27}{64}} = \sqrt{\left(\frac{3}{4}\right)^2} + \sqrt[3]{\frac{3\times3\times3}{4\times4\times4}}$

$= \sqrt{\left(\frac{3}{4}\right)^2} + \sqrt[3]{\left(\frac{3}{4}\right)^3}$

$= \frac{3}{4}+\frac{3}{4} = \frac{6}{4} = \frac{3}{2}$

7. $[(2a^2)^3]^3\ [(3a^3)^2]^2 \div [(6a^6)^2]^2 = (8a^6)^3.\ (9a^6)^2$

$\div (36a^{12})^2 = \frac{(8)^3.a^{18}.(9)^2.a^{12}}{(36)^2.a^{24}} = 32a^6$

9. $\frac{3^{n+3}-3^{n+1}+3^n}{2\left(3^{n-1}\right)} + 2^{-1} = \frac{3^n\cdot3^3-3^n\cdot3+3^n}{2.3^n.3^{-1}} + 2^{-1}$

$= \frac{3^3-3+1}{2.3^{-1}} + 2^{-1} = \frac{3^4-3^2+3}{2} + \frac{1}{2}$

$= \frac{81-9+3}{2} + \frac{1}{2} = \frac{76}{2} = 38$

11. $\frac{(243)^{0.13}\times(243)^{0.07}}{(7)^{0.25}\times(49)^{0.075}\times(343)^{0.2}}$

$= \frac{\left(3^5\right)^{0.13}\times\left(3^5\right)^{0.07}}{(7)^{0.25}\times\left(7^2\right)^{0.075}\times\left(7^3\right)^{0.2}}$

$= \frac{(3)^{0.65}\times(3)^{0.35}}{(7)^{0.25}\times(7)^{0.15}\times(7)^{0.6}}$

$= \frac{(3)^{(0.65+0.35)}}{(7)^{(0.25+0.15+0.6)}} = \frac{3^1}{7^1} = \frac{3}{7}$

4 RATIO & PROPORTION

RATIO

In ratio we compare two quantities of the same kind and consider what multiple, part or parts one is of the other. In comparing 8 with 4, observe that it is 2 times 4. This comparison can be represented as 8 ÷ 4 or $\frac{8}{4}$.

Hence, *ratio is that relation between two numbers which is expressed by the fraction, the numerator is which is the measure of the first quantity and denominator is the measure of the second quantity.*

If the terms of a ratio be multiplied or divided by the same quantity the value of the ratio remains unaltered.

Thus, 3 : 4 is the same as 9 : 12 and 9 : 12 is the same as 3 : 4.

PROPORTION

The equality of two ratio is called proportion.

Consider the two ratios:

Ist ratio   2nd ratio

5 : 15   7 : 21

Since, 5 is one-third of 15 and 7 is one-third of 21, the two ratios are equal. The equality of two ratios is called proportion and the numbers 5, 15, and 7, 21 are said to be in **proportion.**

The proportion may be written as

5 : 15 : : 7 : 21 (5 is to 15 as 7 is to 21)

$\Rightarrow 5 : 15 = 7 : 21$

$$\Rightarrow \frac{5}{15} = \frac{7}{21}$$

The numbers 5, 15, 7 and 21 are called the terms. 5 is the first term, 15 the second, 7 the third, and 21 the fourth.

The first and fourth terms, *i.e.*, 5 and 21 are called extremes (end terms), and the second and the third terms, *i.e.*, 15 and 7 are called the **means** (middle terms), 21 is called the fourth proportional.

EXAMPLES

Example 1 : Find the third proportional to 5 and 15.

Solution: Suppose the third proportional to 5 and 15 is x.

$$5 : 15 :: 15 : x$$

But the product of the extremes is equal to the square of the mean.

$$\Rightarrow \quad 5 \times x = 15 \times 15$$

$$\Rightarrow \quad x = \frac{15 \times 15}{5} = 45$$

The required third proportional = 45

Example 2 : An amount is to be divided among A, B and C in the ratio of 3 : 5 : 6 respectively. If the difference between A and B's share is ₹ 600, what is C's share?

Solution: Trick : $\frac{A}{3} = \frac{B}{5} = \frac{C}{6}$

$$\Rightarrow \quad A = \frac{C}{2}, B = \frac{5C}{6}$$

$$B - A = 600$$

$$\Rightarrow \quad \frac{5C}{6} - \frac{C}{2} = 600 \Rightarrow C = ₹\ 1800$$

Example 3 : Sand and cement were mixed in the ratio 3 : 1 to make 100 tonnes. How much sand must be added to make the ratio 6 : 1?

Solution: The quantity of sand = $\frac{3 \times 100}{3+1}$

= 75 tonnes

and the quantity of cement = $\frac{1 \times 100}{3+1}$

= 25 tonnes

Suppose we add x tonnes of sand to make the ratio 6 : 1,

then $\frac{75 + x}{25} = \frac{6}{1}$

$\Rightarrow$ $75 + x = 150$

$\therefore$ $x = 150 - 75 = 75$ tonnes

EXERCISE

1. If A : B = 6 : 7 and B : C = 8 : 9, then A : B : C is:
   (a) 24 : 28 : 63 (b) 48 : 28 : 63
   (c) 48 : 56 : 63 (d) 24 : 56 : 63
   (e) None of these
2. The sum of two numbers is 20 and their difference is $2\frac{1}{2}$. What is the ratio of the numbers?
   (a) 11 : 7 (b) 9 : 11
   (c) 7 : 9 (d) 7 : 11
   (e) None of these
3. If 10% of x is the same as 20% of y, then $x : y$ is equal to :
   (a) 1 : 2 (b) 2 : 1
   (c) 5 : 1 (d) 10 : 1
   (e) None of these
4. One man adds 3 litres of water to 12 litres of milk and another 4 litres of water to 10 litres of milk. What is the ratio of the strenghts of the milk in the two mixtures?
   (a) 15 : 25 (b) 25 : 28
   (c) 28 : 25 (d) 15 : 28
   (e) None of these
5. ₹ 425 is divided among 4 men, 5 women and 6 boys such that the share of a man, a woman and a boy may be in the ratio of 9 : 8 : 4. What is the share of a woman?
   (a) ₹ 34 (b) ₹ 24
   (c) ₹ 44 (d) ₹ 37
   (e) None of these
6. A and B are two alloys of gold and copper prepared by mixing metals in proportions 7 : 2 and 7 : 11 respectively. If equal quantities of the alloys are melted to form a third alloy C, the proportion of gold and copper in C will be
   (a) 5 : 9 (b) 5 : 7
   (c) 7 : 5 (d) 9 : 5
   (e) None of these
7. The contents of two vessels containing water and milk are in the ratio 1 : 2 and 2 : 5 are mixed in the ratio 1 : 4. The resulting mixture will have water and milk in the ratio:
   (a) 21 : 54 (b) 31 : 74
   (c) 27 : 74 (d) 23 : 27
   (e) None of these
8. The monthly salary of A, B, C is in the proportion of 2 : 3 : 5. If C's monthly salary is ₹ 1200 more than that of A, then B's annual salary is:
   (a) ₹ 14400 (b) ₹ 24000
   (c) ₹ 12000 (d) ₹ 2000
   (e) ₹ 1200
9. The ratio between the ages of Kamla and Savitri is 6 : 5 and the sum of their ages is 44 years. The ratio of their ages after 8 years will be:
   (a) 5 : 6 (b) 7 : 8
   (c) 6 : 7 (d) 14 : 13
   (e) 8 : 7
10. Vinay got thrice as many marks in Maths as in English. The proportion of his marks in Maths and History is 4 : 3. If his total marks in Maths, English and History is 250 then, what is his marks in English?
    (a) 120 (b) 90
    (c) 40 (d) 80
    (e) None of these
11. A certain amount was divided between Kavita and Reena in the ratio 4 : 3. If Reena's share was ₹ 2400, the amount is:
    (a) ₹ 5600 (b) ₹ 3200
    (c) ₹ 9600 (d) ₹ 3800
    (e) None of these

12. A circle and a square have same area. Therefore, the ratio of the side of the square and the radius of the circle is :

(a) $\sqrt{\pi}:1$ *(b)* $1:\sqrt{\pi}$
(c) $1 : \pi$ *(d)* $\pi : 1$
(e) None of these

13. A, B and C can do a work in 20, 25 and 30 days respectively. They undertook to finish the work together for ₹ 2220, then the share of A exceeds that of B by:

(a) ₹ 120 *(b)* ₹ 180
(c) ₹ 300 *(d)* ₹ 600
(e) None of these

14. A bag contains 25 paise, 10 paise and 5 paise coins in the ratio 1 : 2 : 3. If their total value is ₹ 30, the number of 5 paise coin is:

(a) 50 *(b)* 100
(c) 135 *(d)* 200
(e) None of these

15. If ₹ 782 be divided into three parts, proportional to $\frac{1}{2}:\frac{2}{3}:\frac{3}{4}$; then the first part is:

(a) ₹ 204 *(b)* ₹ 196
(c) ₹ 190 *(d)* ₹ 182
(e) None of these

16. Two numbers are in the ratio 1 : 2. If 7 is added to both, their ratio changes to 3 : 5. The greater number is:

(a) 32 *(b)* 28
(c) 26 *(d)* 24
(e) None of these

17. A fraction which bears the same ratio to $\frac{1}{27}$ that $\frac{3}{11}$ does to $\frac{5}{9}$, is equal to:

(a) 55 *(b)* $\frac{3}{11}$
(c) $\frac{2}{11}$ *(d)* $\frac{1}{55}$
(e) None of these

18. If ₹ 510 be divided among A, B, C is such a way that A gets $\frac{2}{3}$ of what B gets and B gets $\frac{1}{4}$ of what C gets, then their shares are respectively:

(a) ₹ 150, ₹ 300, ₹ 60
(b) ₹ 120, ₹ 240, ₹ 150
(c) ₹ 60, ₹ 90, ₹ 360
(d) ₹ 120, ₹ 90, ₹ 300
(e) None of these

ANSWERS

1	2	3	4	5	6	7	8	9	10
(c)	(e)	(b)	(c)	(a)	(c)	(b)	(e)	(e)	(c)
11	**12**	**13**	**14**	**15**	**16**	**17**	**18**		
(a)	(a)	(b)	(e)	(a)	(b)	(d)	(c)		

SOME SELECTED EXPLANATORY ANSWERS

2.
$$\text{Ratio} = \frac{20 + \frac{5}{2}}{20 - \frac{5}{2}}$$

$$= \frac{22.5}{17.5} = \frac{225}{175} = \frac{9}{7}$$

$= 9 : 7.$

3. 10% of x = 20% of y

$$\Rightarrow \quad \frac{10}{100}x = \frac{20}{100}y$$

$$\therefore \quad \frac{x}{10} = \frac{y}{5} \quad \Rightarrow \frac{x}{y} = \frac{10}{5}$$

$$= \frac{2}{1} \Rightarrow x : y = 2 : 1.$$

4. Strength of milk in the first mixture

$$= \frac{12}{12+3} = \frac{12}{15}$$

Strength of milk in the second mixture

$$= \frac{10}{10+4} = \frac{10}{14}$$

$\therefore$ The ratio of their strengths

$$= \frac{12}{15} : \frac{10}{14}$$

$$= 12 \times 14 : 15 \times 10 = 28 : 25.$$

5. The ratio of shares of group of men, women and boys

$$= 9 \times 4 : 8 \times 5 : 4 \times 6 = 9 : 10 : 6$$

$\therefore$ Share of 5 women

$$= \frac{425}{9+10+6} \times 10 = ₹\ 170$$

$\therefore$ Share of 1 woman

$$= \frac{170}{5} = ₹\ 34.$$

6. $$\text{Gold in C} = \left(\frac{7}{9} + \frac{7}{18}\right) = \frac{21}{18} = \frac{7}{6}$$

$$\text{Copper in C} = \left(\frac{2}{9} + \frac{11}{18}\right) = \frac{15}{18} = \frac{5}{6}$$

$$\therefore \text{Gold : Copper} = \frac{7}{6} : \frac{5}{6} = 7 : 5.$$

8. Let the monthly salary of A, B, C be $2x$, $3x$ and $5x$

Then, $5x - 2x = 1200$

or, $3x = 1200$

$\therefore$ $x = 400$

B's monthly salary

$$= 3x = 3 \times 400 = ₹\ 1200.$$

9. Let their ages be $6x$ and $5x$ years.

$\therefore$ $6x + 5x = 44$

$\Rightarrow$ $11x = 44$

$\Rightarrow$ $x = 4$

So, their present ages are 24 years and 20 years

$\therefore$ Ratio of their ages after 8 years

$$= 32 : 28 = 8 : 7.$$

11. Let their shares be ₹ $4x$ and ₹ $3x$

Then, $3x = 2400 \Rightarrow x = ₹\ 800$

$\therefore$ Total amount $= 7x = 7 \times 800 = ₹\ 5600.$

12. Let the side of the square be x and the radius of the circle be y. Then,

$$x^2 = \pi y^2$$

$$\Rightarrow \frac{x^2}{y^2} = \pi \qquad \Rightarrow \frac{x}{y} = \sqrt{\pi}$$

$$\therefore \quad x : y = \sqrt{\pi} : 1$$

14. Ratio of their values

$$= \frac{1}{4} : \frac{2}{10} : \frac{3}{20} = 5 : 4 : 3$$

$\therefore$ Value of 5 paise coins

$$= ₹\left(30 \times \frac{3}{12}\right) = ₹\ 7.50$$

$\therefore$ Number of 5 paise coins

$$= \frac{750}{5} = 150.$$

15. $$\text{Here ratio} = \frac{1}{2} : \frac{2}{3} : \frac{3}{4} = 6 : 8 : 9$$

$$\text{Hence, Ist part} = \frac{6}{6+8+9} \times ₹\ 782$$

$$= \frac{6}{23} \times ₹\ 782 = ₹\ 204$$

17. Let the fraction be x

$$\text{Then,} \quad x : \frac{1}{27} = \frac{3}{11} : \frac{5}{9}$$

$$\Rightarrow \quad x \times 27 = \frac{3}{11} \times \frac{9}{5}$$

$$\therefore \quad x = \frac{3}{11} \times \frac{9}{5} \times \frac{1}{27} = \frac{1}{55}.$$

❑❑❑

5 AVERAGE

The average of any number of quantities of the same kind can be found by dividing their sum by their number. Thus,

$$\text{Average} = \frac{\text{Sum of quantities}}{\text{No. of quantities}}$$

$$\text{Sum of quantities} = \text{Their average} \times \text{Their number}$$

$$\text{Number of quantities} = \frac{\text{Sum of quantities}}{\text{Their average}}$$

When a body covers the same distance at two different speeds p km/hr and q km/hr, then its average speed for the whole journey is $\frac{2pq}{p+q}$ km/hr.

EXAMPLES

Example 1 : The average score of a cricketer for 10 matches is 38.9 runs. If the average for the first six matches is 42, find the average for the last 4 matches.

Solution: Total runs of the last four matches = 10 × 38.9 – 6 × 42 = 137

$$\therefore \quad \text{Average} = \frac{137}{4} = 34.25 \text{ run}$$

Example 2 : The average of 13 numbers is 52. The average of first seven of these numers is 48 and the average of the last seven numbers is 58. What is the seventh number?

Solution: Seventh number = (7 × 48 + 7 × 58) – 13 × 52 = 742 – 676 = 66

Example 3 : The average age of 8 persons increases by 2 years when a person comes in place of another person who is 24 years old. What is the age of the new person?

Solution: Age of new person = 8 × 2 + 24 = 16 + 24 = 40 years

Example 4 : The average age of 33 students and their teacher is 18 years. If the class teacher is 51 years old, what would be the average age of the students?

Solution: Average age of the students

$$= \frac{18 \times 34 - 51}{33} = \frac{612 - 51}{33} = 17 \text{ years}$$

Example 5 : The average salary of Prakash, Jayesh and Kailash is ₹ 1100. The average salary of Prakash and Kailash is ₹ 900. What is Jayesh's salary?

Solution: Total salary of Prakash, Jayesh and Kailash

= ₹ (1100 × 3) = ₹ 3300

Total salary of Prakash and Kailash

= ₹ (900 × 2) = ₹ 1800

∴ Salary of Jayesh = ₹ (3300 – 1800) = ₹ 1500

Example 6 : The average weight of 45 passengers on board of an aircraft is 50 kg. If the weight of 5 members of the crew is added, the average is reduced by half kilogram. What is the average weight of the crew members?

Solution: Total weight of 45 passengers

= 45 × 50 = 2250 kg

and the total weight of 45 passengers and the 5 crew = 50 × 49.5 = 2475 kg

∴ Total weight of 5 crews = 2475 – 2250

= 225 kg

$$\therefore \text{ Average weight of 5 crews} = \frac{225}{5} = 45 \text{ kg}$$

Example 7 : The average of Mukesh's marks in 7 subjects is 75. His average in 6 subjects excluding Science is 72. How many marks did he get in Science?

Solution: Marks in Science

$= 7 \times 75 - 6 \times 72 = 525 - 432 = 93$ marks

Example 8 : The average of 10 numbers is calculated as 15. It is discovered later on that while calculating the average one number, namely 36 was wrongly read is 26. Find the correct average.

Solution: Sum of numbers

$= (10 \times 15 - 26 + 36) = 160$

$\therefore$ Correct average $= \dfrac{160}{10} = 16$

Example 9. The average of 25 results is 18; that of first twelve is 14 and of last twelve is 17. Find the thirteenth result.

Solution: Thirteenth result

$= (25 \times 18 - 12 \times 14 + 12 \times 17) = 78$

EXERCISE

1. The average of first nine multiples of 3 is
   (*a*) 12.0 (*b*) 12.5
   (*c*) 15.0 (*d*) 18.5
   (*e*) None of these

2. The average of 13 numbers is 68, the average of first 7 numbers is 63 and the average of last 7 numbers is 70. What is the 7th number?
   (*a*) 43 (*b*) 45
   (*c*) 46 (*d*) 49
   (*e*) 47

3. Average age of 8 persons increased by 2 years, when two men whose ages are 20 and 24 years are replaced by two women. What is the average age of women?
   (*a*) 30 years (*b*) 31 years
   (*c*) 28 years (*d*) 33 years
   (*e*) None of these

4. A man had seven children. When their average age was 12 years, the child who was 6 years of age died. What was the average of the surviving children 5 years after the death of the child?
   (*a*) 15 years (*b*) 16 years
   (*c*) 17 years (*d*) 18 years
   (*e*) None of these

5. A batsman has a certain average of runs for 16 innings. In the 17th innings, he makes a score of 85 runs thereby increasing his average by 3. What is the average after the 17th inning?
   (*a*) 33 runs (*b*) 34 runs
   (*c*) 37 runs (*d*) 36 runs
   (*e*) None of these

6. The average of marks obtained by 120 candidates was 35. If the average of marks of passed candidates was 39 and that of failed candidates was 15, the number of candidates who passed the examination is
   (*a*) 100 (*b*) 110
   (*c*) 120 (*d*) 150
   (*e*) None of these

7. Out of three numbers, the first is twice the second and is half of the third. If the average of the three numbers is 56, the three numbers in order are
   (*a*) 48, 96, 24 (*b*) 48, 24, 96
   (*c*) 96, 24, 48 (*d*) 96, 48, 24
   (*e*) None of these

8. The average age of an adult class is 40 years. 12 new students with an average age of 32 years join the class, thereby decreasing the average by 4 years. The original strength of the class was
   (*a*) 10 (*b*) 11
   (*c*) 13 (*d*) 15
   (*e*) None of these

9. The average age of 24 students in a class is 10. If the teacher's age is included, the average increases by one. The age of the teacher is
   (*a*) 25 (*b*) 30
   (*c*) 35 (*d*) 40
   (*e*) None of these

10. If a, b, c, d, e are five consecutive odd numbers, their average is
    (*a*) $5(a + 4)$ (*b*) $\dfrac{abcde}{5}$
    (*c*) $5(a+b+c+d+e)$ (*d*) $(a + 4)$
    (*e*) None of these

11. The average of four positive integers is 72.5. The highest integer is 117 and the lowest integer is 15. The difference between the remaining two integers is 12. Which integer is higher of these two remaining integers?

(a) 85 (b) 84
(c) 73 (d) 70
(e) None of these

12. A student was asked to find the average of the numbers 3, 11, 7, 9, 15, 13, 8, 19, 17, 21, 14 and x. He found the average to be 12. What should be the number in place of x?

(a) 31 (b) 17
(c) 7 (d) 3
(e) None of these

13. If a, b, c, d, e are five consecutive numbers, their average is:

(a) $5(a + b + c + d + e)$ (b) $(a + 2)$
(c) $\frac{abcde}{5}$ (d) $5(a + 2)$
(e) None of these

14. The average of a, b, c is M and $ab + bc + ca = 0$, then the mean of a^2, b^2, c^2 is:

(a) $9M^2$ (b) $6M^2$
(c) $3M^2$ (d) M^2
(e) None of these

15. The average of five numbers is 27. If one number is excluded, the average becomes 25. The excluded number is

(a) 37 (b) 30
(c) 27 (d) 25
(e) None of these

ANSWERS

1	2	3	4	5	6	7	8	9	10
(c)	(e)	(a)	(d)	(c)	(a)	(b)	(e)	(c)	(d)
11	**12**	**13**	**14**	**15**					
(a)	(c)	(b)	(c)	(e)					

SOME SELECTED EXPLANATORY ANSWERS

1. Average

$$= \frac{3(1 + 2 + 3 + 4 + 5 + 6 + 7 + 8 + 9)}{9}$$

$$= \frac{135}{9} = 15.$$

6. Let the number of candidates who passed = x

$\Rightarrow 39 \times x + 15 \times (120 - x) = 120 \times 35$

$\Rightarrow \quad 24x = 4200 - 1800$

$\therefore \quad x = \frac{2400}{24} = 100.$

9. Age of the teacher = $(25 \times 11 - 24 \times 10)$ years = 35 years.

10. Average $= \frac{a + (a+2) + (a+4) + (a+6) + (a+8)}{5}$

$= (a + 4).$

11. Let the remaining two positive integers be x and $x + 12$

Now, $117 + x + 12 + x + 15 = 4 \times 72.5$

$\Rightarrow \quad 2x + 144 = 290$

$\Rightarrow \quad 2x = 146 \therefore x = 73$

Hence, required number = $x + 12$

$= 73 + 12 = 85.$

12. Here,

$$\frac{3+11+7+9+15+13+8+19+17+21+14+x}{12} = 12$$

$\Rightarrow 137 + x = 144 \therefore x = 7.$

13. Here, a, b, c, d and e are five consecutive numbers.

then, $b = a + 1$; $c = a + 2$; $d = a + 3$ and $e = a + 4$

Now, Their average

$$= \frac{a+b+c+d+e}{5} = \frac{a+a+1+a+2+a+3+a+4}{5}$$

$$= \frac{5a+10}{5} = \frac{5(a+2)}{5} = (a + 2).$$

❑❑❑

6 PERCENTAGE

The word 'per cent' or 'percentage' means 'for every one hundred'. In other words, it gives an indication of rate per hundred.

It is denoted by the symbol %.

For example, 5% means 5 out of one hundred or $\frac{5}{100}$.

Remember :

(i) For converting a per cent into a fraction, divide it by 100.

(ii) For converting a fraction into a per cent, multiply it by 100.

(iii) For converting a per cent into a decimal, shift the decimal point two places to the left.

(iv) For converting one given quantity (x) as a percentage of another given quantity (y), find $\frac{x}{y} \times 100$.

(v) There is no unit of percentage.

Important Facts:

For quickly solving the problems related to percentage, remember following rules:

(a) Of the given two numbers if the first is $x\%$ more than the second, then the second will be $\left(\frac{100 \times x}{100 + x}\right)\%$ less than the first.

(b) Of the given two numbers if the first is $x\%$ less than the second, then the second will be $\left(\frac{100 \times x}{100 - x}\right)\%$ more than the first.

(c) If two numbers are respectively $x\%$ and $y\%$ more than a third number, then the first number will be $\left(\frac{100 + x}{100 + y} \times 100\right)\%$ of the second.

(d) If two numbers are respectively $x\%$ and $y\%$ less than a third number, then the first number will be $\left(\frac{100 - x}{100 - y} \times 100\right)\%$ of the second.

EXAMPLES

Example 1: The population of a town is 45000. $\frac{11}{18}$th of them are males and the rest females, 40% of the females are married. Find the number of married males.

Solution: Number of males

$$= \frac{11}{18} \times 45000$$

$$= 27500$$

$\therefore$ No. of females $= 45000 - 27500$

$= 17500$

Thus, No. of married females

$= 40\%$ of $17500 = 7000$

$\Rightarrow$ The number of married males = 7000

Example 2: The population of a town is 40,000. If the population increases 20% every year, find the population after 3 years.

Solution: Population after 3 years

$$= 40000\left(1 + \frac{20}{100}\right)^3$$

$$= 40000 \times \frac{6}{5} \times \frac{6}{5} \times \frac{6}{5}$$

$$= 69120$$

Example 3 : In an examination 60% of the candidates passed in English, 55% in Mathematics and 25% failed in both subjects. Find the pass percentage.

Solution: Those failing in mathematics
$= 100 - 55 = 45\%$
Those failing in English
$= 100 - 60 = 40\%$
Failing in both = 25%
Failing in one or both the subjects
$= (45 + 40 - 25) = 60\%$
$\therefore$ Pass % = $100 - 60 = 40\%$

Example 4: Atul's marks in Science are 20 less than 60% of the total marks obtained by him in Science and Maths together. If his total marks are 250, what are his marks in Maths?

Solution: Marks obtained in Science = 60% of 250

$$- 20 = \frac{60}{100} \times 250 - 20 = 130$$

$\therefore$ Marks obtained in Maths = 250 – 130 = 120

EXERCISE

1. If x is 90% of y, then what per cent of x is y?
(a) 90 (b) 190
(c) 101.1 (d) 111.1
(e) None of these

2. The price of an article is cut by 10%. To restore it to the former value, the new price must be increased by :
(a) 10% (b) $9\frac{1}{11}\%$
(c) $10\frac{1}{9}\%$ (d) 11%
(e) $11\frac{1}{9}\%$

3. The income of a broker remains unchanged though the rate of commission is increased from 4% to 5%. The percentage of slump business is :
(a) 8% (b) 1%
(c) 12% (d) 80%
(e) 20%

4. 5% income of A is equal to 15% income of B and 10% income of B is equal to 20% income of C. If income of C is ₹ 2000, then total income of A, B and C is :
(a) ₹ 6000 (b) ₹ 18000 (c) ₹ 20000 (d) ₹ 14000
(e) None of these

5. A student who secures 20% marks in an examination fails by 30 marks. Another student who secures 32% gets 42 marks more than those required to pass. The percentage of marks required to pass is:
(a) 20 (b) 25
(c) 28 (d) 30
(e) None of these

6. In a college election, a candidate secured 62% of the votes and is elected by a majority of 144 votes. The total number of votes polled is:
(a) 600 (b) 800
(c) 925 (d) 1200
(e) None of these

7. The price of an article has been reduced by 25%. In order to restore the original price, the new price must be increased by :
(a) $33\frac{1}{3}\%$ (b) $11\frac{1}{9}\%$
(c) $9\frac{1}{11}\%$ (d) $66\frac{2}{3}\%$
(e) None of these

8. The price of cooking oil has increased by 25%. The percentage of reduction that a family should effect in the use of cooking oil so as not to increase the expenditure on this account is :
(a) 25% (b) 30%
(c) 20% (d) 15%
(e) None of these

9. In 40% of the people read newspaper X, 50% read newspaper Y, and 10% read both the papers. What percentage of the people read neither newspaper?
(a) 10% (b) 15%
(c) 18% (d) 25%
(e) 20%

10. The population of a town increases by 5% annually. If its population in 2008 was 138915, what it was in 2005?
(a) 110000 (b) 100000
(c) 120000 (d) 90000
(e) None of these

11. The population of a village is 4500. $\frac{5}{9}$th of them are males and rest females. If 40% of the males are married, then the percentage of married female is :

(a) 35 (b) 40
(c) 50 (d) 60
(e) None of these

12. A mixture of 40 litres of milk and water contains 10% water. How much water must be added to make water 20% in the new mixture?

(a) 10 litres (b) 7 litres
(c) 5 litres (d) 3 litres
(e) None of these

13. If $z = \frac{x^2}{y}$ and x, y both are increased in value by 10%, then the value of z is :

(a) unchanged
(b) increased by 10%
(c) increased by 11%
(d) increased by 20%
(e) None of these

14. If the price of a television set is increased by 25%, then by what percentage should the new price be reduced to bring the price back to original level?

(a) 15% (b) 18%
(c) 25% (d) 30%
(e) 20%

15. A candidate needs 35% marks to pass. If he gets 96 marks and fails by 16 marks, then the maximum marks are :

(a) 250 (b) 320
(c) 300 (d) 425
(e) None of these

ANSWERS

1	2	3	4	5	6	7	8	9	10
(d)	(e)	(e)	(b)	(b)	(a)	(a)	(c)	(e)	(c)
11	**12**	**13**	**14**	**15**					
(c)	(c)	(b)	(b)	(b)					

SOME SELECTED EXPLANATORY ANSWERS

1. $x = 90\%$ of y

$\Rightarrow \quad x = \frac{90}{100}y$

Required percentage $= \frac{y}{9y/10} = \frac{10}{9} \times 100$

$= 111.1\%$

2. Required percentage $= \frac{10}{100-10} \times 100$

$= \frac{10}{90} \times 100 = 11\frac{1}{9}\%$

8. Required reduction $= \left[\frac{r}{(100+r)} \times 100\right]$

$= \left(\frac{25}{125} \times 100\right)\% = 20\%$

9. Number of people read either one or both

$= 40 + 50 - 10 = 80\%$

Hence, number of people read neither newspaper $= 100 - 80 = 20\%$.

12. Water $= 10/100 \times 40 = 4$ litres

Let x litres of water be added,

Then, $x + 4 = \frac{20}{100}(40 + x)$

$\Rightarrow \quad 5x + 20 = 40 + x$

$\Rightarrow \quad 4x = 20$

$\therefore \quad x = 5$ litres.

14. Required reduction $= \frac{25}{100+25} \times 100 = 20\%$.

❑❑❑

7 Profit and Loss

A consumer who goes to the market and buys certain goods. The buyer is called a customer and the shopkeeper who sells the goods to him is called a retailer. The retailer purchases goods in turn in bulk from a wholesaler who keeps a large stock of goods and in this case, the retailer becomes the customer.

1. **Cost price (C.P.) :** Cost price is that price at which a particular article is bought. Profit and loss both are marked at cost price.
2. **Selling Price (S.P.) :** Selling price is that price at which a particular article is sold.
3. **Overheads :** The expenses incurred on transportation, maintenance, packaging, advertisements and the like are included as *Overhead.* These overheads and the profit when added to the cost price determine the selling price.
4. **Profit or Gain** : Whenever a person sells an article at price greater than the cost price he is said to have made a profit or gain.
   Profit or Gain = S.P. – C.P.
5. **Loss :** If S.P. is less than the C.P. there is loss.
   Loss = C.P – S.P

Some Basic Formulae :

(i) $\text{Gain \%} = \dfrac{\text{Gain} \times 100}{\text{C.P.}}$

(ii) $\text{Loss \%} = \dfrac{\text{Loss} \times 100}{\text{C.P.}}$

From these we can write direct expressions for S.P. and C.P.

(iii) $\text{S.P.} = \left(\dfrac{100 + \text{Gain\%}}{100}\right) \times \text{C.P.}$ in case of gain or profit

(iv) $\text{S.P.} = \left(\dfrac{100 - \text{Loss\%}}{100}\right) \times \text{C.P.}$ in case of loss

These can be rewritten as

$\text{C.P.} = \dfrac{100}{100 + \text{Gain\%}} \times \text{S.P.}$ in case of profit

$\text{C.P.} = \dfrac{100}{100 - \text{Loss\%}} \times \text{S.P.}$ in case of loss

(v) If the C.P. of x goods = S.P. of y goods, then

(a) $\text{Gain \%} = \dfrac{x - y}{y} \times 100$ [In case of $x > y$]

(b) $\text{Loss \%} = \dfrac{y - x}{y} \times 100$ [In case of $y > x$]

EXAMPLES

Example 1: A dishonest dealer professes to sell his goods at cost price, but he uses a weight of 950 gm for the kg. weight. Find his gain per cent.

Solution: $\text{Gain \%} = \dfrac{\text{Error}}{\text{True value} - \text{Error}} \times 100$

$= \dfrac{50}{950} \times 100 = 5.26\%$

Example 2: A man buys 5 apples for ₹ 3 and sold each for ₹ 2. What did he gain or loss?

Solution: C.P. of apples = ₹ 3 and S.P. of apples = ₹ 2 × 5 = ₹ 10

∴ Gain = ₹ 10 – ₹ 3 = ₹ 7

∴ $\text{Gain \%} = \dfrac{7}{3} \times 100 = 233\dfrac{1}{3}\%$

Example 3: I lose 20% by selling a watch for ₹ 64. What per cent shall I gain or loss by selling it for ₹ 100?

Solution: ₹ 64 = 80% of C.P.

∴ ₹ 100 = $\dfrac{80}{64} \times 100\%$ of C.P.

= 125% C.P.

Hence, Gain = 25%

Example 4: A radio dealer marks a radio with a price which is 20% more than the cost price and allows a discount of 10% on it. Find the gain per cent.

Solution: Let C.P. = ₹ 100 and Marked price

= ₹ 120

Since, S.P. = 90% of ₹ 120 = ₹ 108

(∵ Discount = 10%)

∴ Gain% = (108 – 100)% = 8%.

EXERCISE

1. Ashok bought 25 kg of rice at the rate of ₹ 6 per kg and 35 kg of rice at the rate of ₹ 7 per kg. He mixed the two and sold the mixture at the rate of Rs. 6.75 per kg. What was his gain or loss in the transaction?

(a) ₹ 16 gain *(b)* ₹ 16 loss
(c) ₹ 10 loss *(d)* ₹ 12 gain
(e) ₹ 10 gain

2. A horse and a cow were sold for ₹ 12000 each. The horse was sold at a loss of 20% and the cow at a gain of 20%. The entire transaction resulted in

(a) no loss no gain *(b)* loss of ₹ 1000
(c) gain of ₹ 1000 *(d)* loss of ₹ 2000
(e) None of these

3. Profit after selling a commodity for ₹ 425 is same as loss after selling it for ₹ 355. The cost of the commodity is :

(a) ₹ 285 *(b)* ₹ 390
(c) ₹ 295 *(d)* ₹ 400
(e) None of these

4. Ram bought 4 dozen apples at ₹ 12 per dozen and 2 dozen at ₹ 16 per dozen. He sold all of them to earn 20%. At what price per dozen did he sell the apples?

(a) ₹ 14.40 *(b)* ₹ 16.00
(c) ₹ 16.80 *(d)* ₹ 16.20
(e) None of these

5. Jimmy bought paper sheets for ₹ 7200 and spent ₹ 200 in transport. Paying ₹ 600 he had 330 boxes made, which he sold at ₹ 28 each. What is his profit percentage?

(a) 15.5 *(b)* 40
(c) 50 *(d)* 30
(e) None of these

6. A owns a house worth ₹ 10000. He sells it to B at a profit of 10% based on the worth of the house. B sells the house back to A at a loss of 10%. In this transaction A gets:

(a) no profit no loss
(b) profit of ₹ 1000
(c) profit of ₹ 1100
(d) profit of ₹ 1200
(e) None of these

7. At what price must Kantilal sell a mixture of 80 kg sugar at ₹ 6.75 per kg with 120 kg at ₹ 8 per kg to gain 20%?

(a) ₹ 7.50 per kg *(b)* ₹ 8.20 per kg
(c) ₹ 8.35 per kg *(d)* ₹ 9 per kg
(e) None of these

8. Subhash purchased a taperecorder at $\frac{9}{10}$ of its selling price and sold it at 8% more than its S.P. His gain is :

(a) 8% *(b)* 10%
(c) 18% *(d)* 20%
(e) None of these

9. A dealer marks his goods 20% above cost price. He then allows some discount on it and makes a profit of 8%. The rate of discount is:

(a) 12% *(b)* 10%
(c) 6% *(d)* 4%
(e) None of these

10. Tarun bought a T.V. with 20% discount on the labelled price. Had he bought it with 25% discount, he would have saved ₹ 500. At what price did he buy the T.V.?

(a) ₹ 5000 *(b)* ₹ 8000
(c) ₹ 9000 *(d)* ₹ 12000
(e) ₹ 10000

11. While selling a watch, a shopkeeper gives a discount of 5%. If he gives a discount of 7%, he earns ₹ 15 less as profit. The marked price of the watch is :

(a) ₹ 697.50 *(b)* ₹ 712.50
(c) ₹ 787.50 *(d)* ₹ 750.50
(e) None of these

12. Kabir buys an article with 25% discount on its marked price. He makes a profit of 10% by selling it at ₹ 660. The marked price is :

(a) ₹ 600 (b) ₹ 700
(c) ₹ 1000 (d) ₹ 885
(e) ₹ 800

13. A tradesman sells one kind of sugar at ₹ 3 per kg and loses 20 per cent and another kind of sugar at ₹ 5 per kg and gains 25 per cent. He mixes them together in equal proportion and sells the mixture at ₹ 6 per kg. What is his gain %?

(a) $53\frac{26}{31}\%$ (b) $51\frac{31}{26}\%$
(c) $54\frac{26}{31}\%$ (d) $55\frac{26}{31}\%$
(e) None of these

14. A fan is listed at ₹ 1400 and the discount offered is 10%. What additional discount must be given to bring the net selling price to ₹ 1200?

(a) $4\frac{16}{21}\%$ (b) 5%
(c) 6% (d) $16\frac{2}{3}\%$
(e) None of these

15. Samir purchased 150 quintals of wheat. One-fourth of the total quantity, he sold at a loss of 10%. At what gain per cent should he sell the remaining wheat to gain 10% on the whole transaction?

(a) $14\frac{1}{2}\%$ (b) $15\frac{2}{3}\%$
(c) $16\frac{2}{3}\%$ (d) $18\frac{2}{3}\%$
(e) None of these

16. If the cost price of 24 articles is equal to selling price of 21 articles, find the percentage gain or loss.

(a) 12.5 gain (b) 12.5% loss
(c) $14\frac{2}{7}\%$ gain (d) $14\frac{2}{7}\%$ loss
(e) None of these

17. The profit obtained after selling an article for ₹ 1,186 is the same as loss incurred after selling the same article for ₹ 1,098. Find the cost price of the article.

(a) ₹ 1100 (b) ₹ 1135
(c) ₹ 1142 (d) ₹ 1146
(e) None of these

18. A merchant professes to sell tea at the cost price but uses a false weight of 900 gm for a kilogram. His profit per cent in the transaction is:

(a) $9\frac{1}{11}\%$ (b) 10%
(c) $10\frac{2}{7}\%$ (d) 20%
(e) $11\frac{1}{9}\%$

19. The difference in selling a coat at profits of 4% and 6% is ₹ 12. The cost price of the coat is:

(a) ₹ 150 (b) ₹ 300
(c) ₹ 450 (d) ₹ 600
(e) None of these

20. A shopkeeper marks his goods at a price that would give him 20% profit and allows a discount of 10% in the sale on the marked price. What is his profit or loss per cent in the transaction?

(a) 8% profit (b) 12% profit
(c) 30% profit (d) 10% loss
(e) None of these

ANSWERS

1	2	3	4	5	6	7	8	9	10
(e)	(b)	(b)	(b)	(a)	(c)	(d)	(d)	(b)	(e)
11	**12**	**13**	**14**	**15**	**16**	**17**	**18**	**19**	**20**
(d)	(e)	(c)	(a)	(c)	(d)	(c)	(e)	(d)	(a)

SOME SELECTED EXPLANATORY ANSWERS

1. C.P. of 60 kg mixture

$= ₹ (25 \times 6 + 35 \times 7)$

$= ₹ 395$

S.P. of 60 kg mixtire

$= ₹ (60 \times 6.75) = ₹ 405$

$\therefore$ Gain $= ₹ (405 - 395) = ₹ 10$

3. Let C.P. $= ₹ x$

Then, $425 - x = x - 355$

$\Rightarrow 2x = 780$

$\therefore x = ₹ 390$

6. Final C.P. for A $= \frac{110}{100} \times \frac{90}{100} \times ₹ 10000$

$= ₹ 9900$

Hence, profit for A

$= \frac{10}{100} \times ₹ 10,000 + ₹ (10,000 - 9900)$

$= ₹ 1100.$

8. Let S.P. $= ₹ 100$;

C.P. for Subhash $= \frac{9}{10} \times 100$

$= ₹ 90$ and

S.P. $= ₹ 108$

Hence, gain % for Subhash

$= \frac{108 - 90}{90} \times 100$

$= 20\%.$

11. Let the marked price $= ₹ x$

Then, $\frac{7x}{100} - \frac{5x}{100} = 15$

$\Rightarrow \frac{x}{50} = 15 \quad \therefore x = ₹ 750.$

13. C.P. of both kinds of sugar of 1 kg each

$= \frac{100}{80} \times 3 + \frac{125}{100} \times 5 = \frac{15}{4} + 4$

$= ₹ \frac{31}{4}$

Hence, C.P. of 1 kg mixture

$= ₹ \frac{31}{8}$;

then, Gain $= 6 - \frac{31}{8} = ₹ \frac{17}{8}$

$\therefore$ Gain% $= \frac{17/8}{31/8} \times 100 = \frac{1700}{31} = 54\frac{26}{31}\%.$

14. Let second discount $= x\%$; then

$\frac{90}{100} \times \frac{(100 - x)}{100} \times 1400 = 1200$

$\Rightarrow (100 - x) = \frac{2000}{21}$

$\therefore x = 100 - \frac{2000}{21}$

$= \frac{100}{21} = 4\frac{16}{21}\%.$

18. Required pofit per cent

$= \frac{1000 - 900}{900} \times 100 = 11\frac{1}{9}\%.$

19. Here $2\% = 12$

$\therefore 100\% = \frac{12}{2} \times 100 = ₹ 600$

Hence, cost price of coat $= ₹ 600.$

❑❑❑

8 Simple & Compound Interest

INTEREST

Interest is the money paid for the use of money borrowed, *i.e.*, extra money paid for using other's money is called *interest.*

The sum borrowed is called the principal. The sum of interest and principal is called the *Amount.*

If the interest on a certain sum borrowed for a certain period is reckoned uniformly, then it is called simple interest, denoted by S.I.

Thus, if A = Amount, P = Principal,
I = Interest, T = Time (in year),
R = Rate per cent per annum, then

(*a*) $I = \frac{P \times R \times T}{100}$ (*b*) $P = \frac{100 \times I}{R \times T}$

(*c*) $T = \frac{100 \times I}{P \times R}$ (*d*) $R = \frac{100 \times I}{P \times T}$

(*e*) $P = \frac{100\,A}{100 + RT}$ (*f*) A = P + I.

COMPOUND INTEREST

In business transaction if interest as it becomes due is not paid to the lender but is added on to the principal, the money is said to be lent at *compound interest* and the total sum owed after a given time is called the amount at compound interest for that time.

After a certain period, the difference between the amount and the original principal is called the compound Interest (C.I.).

Some Important Formulae :

Let Principal = P
Time = n years
Rate = r% p.a.

then, the amount,

(*a*) when interest is compounded annually:

then, $\text{Amount} = P\left(1 + \frac{r}{100}\right)^n$

(*b*) when interest is compounded half yearly:

then, $\text{Amount} = P\left(1 + \frac{r/2}{100}\right)^{2n}$

(*c*) when interest is compounded quarterly :

then, $\text{Amount} = P\left(1 + \frac{r/4}{100}\right)^{4n}$

(*d*) when rates are r_1%, r_2% and r_3% for Ist, IInd and IIIrd year respectively;
then, Amount =

$$P\left(1 + \frac{r_1}{100}\right)\left(1 + \frac{r_2}{100}\right)\left(1 + \frac{r_3}{100}\right)$$

EXAMPLES

Example 1: If a certain sum of money at simple interest amounts to ₹ 2642 in 3 years and to ₹ 3235 in 4 years, what is the sum and rate of interest?

Solution: Here, P + 3I = 2642; P + 4I = 3235

Then, I = 3235 – 2642 = ₹ 593

Since, P = 2642 – 3 × 593
= ₹ 863

Hence, $R = \frac{593 \times 100}{863 \times 1} = 68.71\%$

Example 2: In what time does a sum of money become four times at the simple interest rate of 5% per annum?

Solution: Let principal = ₹ x; then amount = $4x$

Since, I = $4x - x$ = ₹ $3x$

Hence, $T = \frac{3x \times 100}{x \times 5} = 60$ years

Example 3: A sum was put at SI at a certain rate for 2 years. Had it been put at 3% higher rate, it would have fetched ₹ 300 more. Find the sum.

Solution: If R = 3%, T = 2 years;

then I = ₹ 300

Hence, $P = \frac{300 \times 100}{3 \times 2}$ = ₹ 5000

Example 4: Find the difference between the compound interest and the simple interest for the sum ₹ 2000 at 5% p.a. for 2 years.

Solution: Required difference

$$= 2000\left[\left(1+\frac{5}{100}\right)^2 - 1\right] - \frac{2000 \times 5 \times 2}{100}$$

$$= 2000 \times \frac{41}{400} - 200 = 205 - 200 = ₹\ 5$$

Example 5: If a sum of ₹ 13040 is to be paid back in two equal annual instalments at $3\frac{3}{4}\%$ per annum, what is the amount of each instalment?

Solution: Let each instalment be ₹ x; then,

$$\frac{x}{\left(1+\frac{15}{4 \times 100}\right)} + \frac{x}{\left(1+\frac{15}{4 \times 100}\right)} = 13040$$

$$\Rightarrow x.\frac{80}{83} + x.\left(\frac{80}{83}\right)^2 = 13040$$

$$\Rightarrow x.\frac{80}{83}\left(1+\frac{80}{83}\right) = 13040$$

$$\Rightarrow x\ .\frac{80}{83}.\frac{163}{83} = 13040$$

$$\therefore x = \frac{13040 \times 83 \times 83}{80 \times 163} = ₹\ 6889$$

Example 6: Find the compound interest on ₹ 1000 for 3 years at 5% p.a.

Solution:

$$\text{C.I.} = 1000\left[\left(1+\frac{5}{100}\right)^3 - 1\right] = 1000\left[\left(\frac{21}{20}\right)^3 - 1\right]$$

$$= 1000\left[\frac{9261 - 8000}{8000}\right]$$

$$= 1000 \times \frac{1261}{8000} = ₹\ 157.63$$

EXERCISE

1. If the simple interest on a certain sum of money at 6% per annum for 3 years is ₹ 90, the sum will be:

(a) ₹ 500 *(b)* ₹ 450
(c) ₹ 525 *(d)* ₹ 560
(e) None of these

2. If the simple interest on Re. 1 for 1 month is 1 paise, the rate per cent p.a. will be :

(a) 10% *(b)* 8%
(c) 12% *(d)* 6%
(e) None of these

3. A sum of money doubles itself in 20 years. In how many years will it triple itself at the same rate of simple interest?

(a) 30 years *(b)* 50 years
(c) 40 years *(d)* 45 years
(e) None of these

4. The simple interest on a certain sum of money is $\frac{25}{64}$ of the sum and the number of years equals the rate per cent p.a. The rate per cent p.a. will be :

(a) $7\frac{1}{2}\%$ *(b)* $5\frac{1}{4}\%$
(c) $6\frac{3}{4}\%$ *(d)* $6\frac{1}{4}\%$
(e) None of these

5. If the simple interest on a certain sum of money at 6% p.a. for 4½ years is ₹ 81, the sum will be:

(a) ₹ 325 *(b)* ₹ 225
(c) ₹ 300 *(d)* ₹ 340
(e) None of these

6. A sum of ₹ 1850 lent out for 5 years at 3% p.a. simple interest will amount to:

(a) ₹ 2227.75 *(b)* ₹ 2127.50
(c) ₹ 2137.50 *(d)* ₹ 2086.50
(e) None of these

7. A lent a sum of ₹ 1250 to B at a certain rate of interest for 3 years and a sum of ₹ 1500 to C at the same rate of interest for 2 years. If he was paid total ₹ 258.75 as interest in both cases, find the rate of interest at which money was lent by him.

(a) $4\frac{1}{6}\%$ *(b)* $6\frac{1}{4}\%$
(c) $2\frac{1}{7}\%$ *(d)* $3\frac{5}{6}\%$
(e) None of these

8. What annual instalment should be paid to clear the debt of ₹ 645 in 4 years at the rate of 5% p.a. simple interest?

(a) ₹ 160 *(b)* ₹ 185
(c) ₹ 180 *(d)* ₹ 190
(e) None of these

9. A borrowed ₹ 2500 at a certain rate of simple interest and ₹ 1500 at 3% higher rate of interest. If after 4 years the interest paid by him in both cases is ₹ 1140, the former rate of interest was :

(a) 5% *(b)* 8%
(c) 8½% *(d)* 5½%
(e) None of these

10. A and B borrowed an equal sum of money from a moneylender at the rate of 8% and 5½% p.a. respectively. If to clear the debt after 4 years, A paid Rs. 550 more than B, the total sum of money taken by them was :

(a) ₹ 12500 *(b)* ₹ 11000
(c) ₹ 11500 *(d)* ₹ 10500
(e) None of these

11. A sum of ₹ 2444 is divided among three parts in such a manner that simple interest on the three divided parts at 6% p.a. after 3, 4 and 5 years respectively remains equal. Such three parts will be:

(a) ₹ 780, ₹ 1040, ₹ 624
(b) ₹ 1040, ₹ 780, ₹ 624
(c) ₹ 624, ₹ 780, ₹ 1040
(d) ₹ 940, ₹ 880, ₹ 624
(e) None of these

12. If the sum of 8097 is divided among A, B and C in such a manner that amount received from these parts at 4% p.a. simple interest after 4, 5 and 6 years respectively remains equal, then A's part will exceed the B's part by :

(a) ₹ 85 *(b)* ₹ 87
(c) ₹ 75 *(d)* ₹ 63
(e) None of these

13. What will be the compound interest on ₹ 8000 for 3 years at 5% p.a.?

(a) ₹ 1361 *(b)* ₹ 1341
(c) ₹ 1260 *(d)* ₹ 1250
(e) ₹ 1261

14. What will be the amount if a sum of ₹ 2500 is invested for 1 year at 4% per annum compound interest, interest being compounded half-yearly?

(a) ₹ 2625 *(b)* ₹ 2601
(c) ₹ 2830 *(d)* ₹ 2901
(e) None of these

15. After how many years will ₹ 3375 become ₹ 4096 at $6\frac{2}{3}\%$ per annum compound interest?

(a) 4 years *(b)* 2 years
(c) 2½ years *(d)* 3 years
(e) None of these

16. A certain sum of money placed at compound interest amounts to ₹ 110 in 1 year and to ₹ 121 in 2 years. The rate of interest per annum is :

(a) 5% *(b)* 10%
(c) 8% *(d)* 4%
(e) None of these

17. The present population of a city is 80,000. If the rate of growth is 5% per year, find its population after 3 years.

(a) 88,100 *(b)* 95,600
(c) 92,610 *(d)* 84,600
(e) None of these

18. The difference between compound and simple interest on a certain sum of money for 2 years at 5% per annum is ₹ 21. Find the sum.

(a) ₹ 7200 *(b)* ₹ 8400
(c) ₹ 9200 *(d)* ₹ 8500
(e) None of these

19. In how many years will a sum of ₹ 19200 placed at 10% per annum compound interest yield an interest of ₹ 4032?
(a) 1½ years *(b)* 2½ years
(c) 2 years *(d)* 3 years
(e) None of these

20. A sum of money lent out at a certain rate of simple interest amounts to ₹ 6600 in 2 years and to ₹ 6900 in 3 years. What will be the compound interest on the same sum of money if lent out at the same rate for 2 years?
(a) ₹ 605
(b) ₹ 715
(c) ₹ 615
(d) ₹ 595
(e) None of these

21. A man deposits ₹ 1200 in a bank on the 1st day of each year. If the bank pays 5% per annum compound interest on deposited sum of money, what will be the amount to his credit on the 10th day of the second year?
(a) ₹ 2560 *(b)* ₹ 2210
(c) ₹ 2370 *(d)* ₹ 2860
(e) ₹ 2460

22. Two friends A and B jointly lent out ₹ 81,600 at 4% per annum compound interest, payable annually. 2 years after A gets the same amount as B gets after 3 years. The investment made by B was :
(a) ₹ 30,000 *(b)* ₹ 40,000 *(c)* ₹ 45,000 *(d)* ₹ 38,000
(e) None of these

ANSWERS

1	2	3	4	5	6	7	8	9	10
(a)	(c)	(c)	(d)	(c)	(b)	(d)	(c)	(e)	(b)
11	12	13	14	15	16	17	18	19	20
(b)	(e)	(e)	(b)	(d)	(b)	(c)	(b)	(c)	(c)
21	22								
(e)	(b)								

SOME SELECTED EXPLANATORY ANSWERS

1. $P = \frac{90 \times 100}{6 \times 3} = ₹\ 500.$

2. $\text{Rate} = \frac{1 \times 100}{100 \times \frac{1}{12}} = 12\%.$

5. $P = \frac{81 \times 100 \times 2}{6 \times 9}$

$= ₹\ 300.$

6. $I = \frac{1850 \times 3 \times 5}{100} = ₹\ 277.50.$

$\therefore$ Amount = ₹ 1850 + ₹ 277.50
= ₹ 2127.50

7. $\frac{1250 \times R \times 3}{100} + \frac{1500 \times R \times 2}{100} = 258.75.$

$\Rightarrow \quad 6750R = 25875$

$\therefore \quad R = \frac{25875}{6750} = \frac{23}{6} = 3\frac{5}{6}\%.$

8. Let annual instalment be ₹ x; then

$$x + \frac{x \times 3 \times 5}{100} + x + \frac{x \times 2 \times 5}{100} + x + \frac{x \times 1 + \times 5}{100} + x$$

$$= 645 + \frac{645 \times 4 \times 5}{100}$$

$$\Rightarrow \quad 4x + \frac{3x}{10} = 774$$

$$\Rightarrow \quad \frac{43x}{10} = 774$$

$$\therefore \quad x = \frac{774 \times 10}{43} = ₹\ 180.$$

9. Here, $\frac{2500 \times R \times 4}{100} + \frac{1500 \times (R+3) \times 4}{100}$

$$= 1140 \Rightarrow 160R = 960$$

$$\therefore \quad R = \frac{960}{160} = 6\%.$$

10. Here, $\frac{P \times 8 \times 4}{100} - \frac{P \times 11 \times 4}{100 \times 2} = 550$

$$\Rightarrow \quad \frac{8P}{25} - \frac{11P}{50} = 550 \qquad \Rightarrow \frac{P}{10} = 550$$

$$\therefore \quad P = 5500$$

Hence, total sum of money

$$= 2P = 2 \times 5500 = ₹\ 11000.$$

12. Let parts of A, B and C are ₹ a, ₹ b and ₹ c respectively; then,

$$a + \frac{a \times 4 \times 4}{100} = b + \frac{b \times 4 \times 5}{100} = c + \frac{c \times 4 \times 6}{100}$$

$$\Rightarrow \frac{29a}{25} = \frac{30b}{25} = \frac{31c}{25}$$

Hence, $a : b : c = 930 : 899 : 870$

Sum of proportionals

$$= 930 + 899 + 870 = 2699$$

$\therefore$ Out of 8097, A's part

$$= \frac{930}{2699} \times 8097 = ₹\ 2790;$$

$$\text{B's part} = \frac{899}{2699} \times 8097 = ₹\ 2697$$

Hence, it is clear that A's part exceeds B's part by ₹ 2790 – ₹ 2697 = ₹ 93.

13. $\therefore$

$$\text{C.I.} = 8000\left[\left(1+\frac{5}{100}\right)^3 - 1\right]$$

$$= 8000\left[\left(\frac{21}{20}\right)^3 - 1\right]$$

$$= \frac{8000 \times 1261}{8000} = ₹\ 1261.$$

14.

$$A = 2500\left(1+\frac{2}{100}\right)^2$$

$$= 2500\left(\frac{51}{50}\right)^2$$

$$= \frac{2500 \times 51 \times 51}{50 \times 50} = ₹\ 2601.$$

15. Here, $4096 = 3375\left(1+\frac{20}{3 \times 100}\right)^n$

$$\Rightarrow \quad \frac{4096}{3375} = \left(1+\frac{1}{15}\right)^n$$

$$\Rightarrow \quad \left(\frac{16}{15}\right)^3 = \left(\frac{16}{15}\right)^n$$

$$\therefore \quad n = 3 \text{ years.}$$

17. Population of the city after 3 years

$$= 80{,}000\left(1+\frac{5}{100}\right)^3$$

$$= 80{,}000 \times \frac{21}{20} \times \frac{21}{20} \times \frac{21}{20} = 92610.$$

19. Amount = ₹ 19200 + ₹ 4032 = ₹ 23232

Now, $23232 = 19200\left(1+\frac{10}{100}\right)^n$

$$\Rightarrow \quad \frac{23232}{19200} = \left(\frac{11}{10}\right)^n \Rightarrow \frac{121}{100} = \left(\frac{11}{10}\right)^n$$

$$\Rightarrow \quad \left(\frac{11}{10}\right)^2 = \left(\frac{11}{10}\right)^n$$

$$\therefore \quad n = 2 \text{ years.}$$

21. Required amount $= 1200\left(1+\frac{5}{100}\right) + 1200$

$$= 1200 \times \frac{21}{20} + 1200$$

$$= 1260 + 1200$$

$$= ₹\ 2460.$$

❑❑❑

9 Alligation or Mixture

Alligation deals with calculation of values or properties of a mixture. Alligation is the rule that enables us—

(1) to find the proportion in which the two or more ingredients at the given prices must be mixed to yield a mixture at the given price. This is termed as "Alligation Alternate".

(2) to calculate the average or mean value of a mixture when the prices of two or more ingredients which are to be mixed together and proportion in which they are to be mixed are given. This is termed as "Alligation Medial".

Rule of Alligation:

$$\frac{\text{Amount of Cheaper ingredient}}{\text{Amount of Dearer ingredient}} = \frac{\text{Cost price of Dearer} - \text{Mean Price}}{\text{Mean Price} - \text{Cost Price of Cheaper}}$$

Here cost price of unit quantity of the mixture is called the *Mean Price.*

The above rule may be represented schematically as under:

CP of unit quantity of cheaper ingredient (c) | CP of unit quantity of dearer ingredient (d)

Mean Price (m)

$(d - m)$ | $(m - c)$

(Cheaper quantity) : (Dearer quantity) = $(d - m) : (m - c)$

This relationship is very helpful in solving problems on mixture involving percentage values, rates, prices, speeds etc.

2. m gm of sugar solution has $x\%$ sugar in it. To increase the sugar content in the solution to $y\%$, quantity of sugar need to be added $= \frac{m(y-x)}{100-y}$

3. A vessel contains x litres of liquid A. y litres are withdrawn and replaced by liquid B. Next y litres of the mixture is withdrawn and again replaced by liquid B.
This operation is repeated n times.
$$\frac{\text{Quantity of liquid A left after } n\text{th operation}}{\text{Whole quantity of liquid A initially present}} = \left(\frac{x-y}{x}\right)^n \text{ or } \left(1-\frac{y}{x}\right)^n$$

EXAMPLES

Example 1: 12 litres of a mixture has wine and water in the ratio 2 : 3. How much water must be added to get wine to water ratio of 3 : 7 in the resultant mixture?

Solution: Fraction of water in the given mixture $= \frac{3}{5}$

For water to be added, fraction = 1

Fraction of water in the resultant mixture = $\frac{7}{10}$

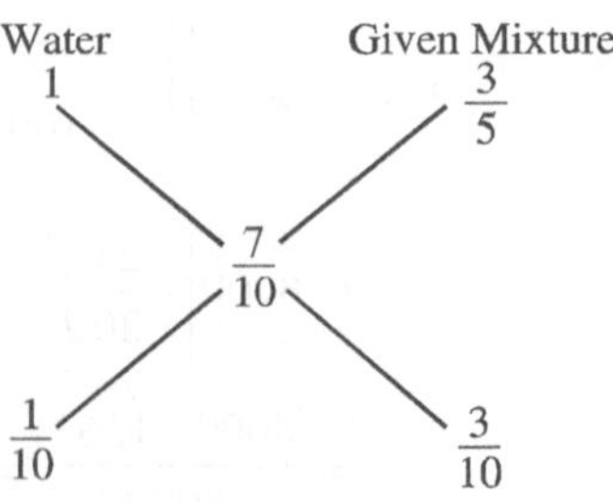

So, water must be added to the mixture in the ratio 1 : 3

Quantity of water to be added

$$= \frac{1}{3} \times 12 = 4 \text{ litres.}$$

Example 2: A person bought two tables for ₹ 2200. He sells one at 5% loss and the other at 6% profit and thus on the whole he neither gains nor loses. Find the cost price of each.

Solution:

CP of the table sold at 5% loss

$$= \frac{6}{6+5} \times 2200$$

= ₹ 1200

CP of the table sold at 6% profit

$$= \frac{5}{6+5} \times 2200$$

= ₹ 1000.

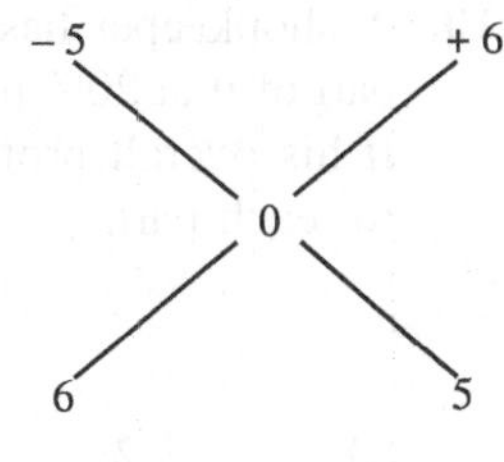

EXERCISE

1. In what proportion must tea at ₹ 62 per kg be mixed with tea at ₹ 72 per kg in order to obtain the mixture worth ₹ 65 per kg?
   (a) 4 : 6 (b) 7 : 3
   (c) 2 : 3 (d) 4 : 7
   (e) None of these
2. Find the quantity of rice @ ₹ 10 per kg. which should be mixed with 25 kgs of rice @ ₹ 8 per kg, so that on selling the mixture @ 15 per kg there is 80% profit.
   (a) 6 kgs (b) 7 kgs
   (c) 3 kgs (d) 5 kgs
   (e) None of these
3. A shopkeeper buys 26 kgs of milk @ ₹ 16 per kg. He also buys from another source an inferior quality of milk @ ₹ 10 per kg. How much quantity of the latter should he buy to mix it with the former so that he can sell the mixture @ ₹ 14 per kg without making any loss?
   (a) 13 kgs (b) 12 kgs
   (c) 14 kgs (d) 16 kgs
   (e) None of these
4. Two vessels A and B contain milk and water in the ratio 7 : 5 and 17 : 7 respectively. In what ratio mixtures from two vessels should be mixed to get a new mixture containing milk and water in the ratio 5 : 3?
   (a) 1 : 2 (b) 1 : 3
   (c) 2 : 3 (d) 3 : 2
   (e) None of these
5. Two vessels A and B contain mixture of milk and water in the ratio 4 : 1 and 9 : 11 respectively. They are mixed in the ratio of 3 : 2. Find the ratio of milk : water in the resulting mixture.
   (a) 34 : 16 (b) 33 : 17
   (c) 16 : 34 (d) 17 : 33
   (e) None of these
6. A person has two solutions of sugar with 30% and 50% concentration respectively. In what proportion should he mix two solutions to get 45% concentration in the resulting mixture?
   (a) 1 : 3 (b) 3 : 1
   (c) 2 : 3 (d) 3 : 2
   (e) None of these
7. 6 litres of milk and water mixture has 75% milk in it. How much milk should be added to the mixture to make it 90% pure?
   (a) 8 litres (b) 11 litres
   (c) 10 litres (d) 12 litres
   (e) None of these
8. In what ratio must water be added to spirit to gain 25% by selling it at cost price?
   (a) 1 : 4 (b) 4 : 1
   (c) 3 : 4 (d) 4 : 3
   (e) None of these
9. A shopkeeper has 50 kgs of rice. He sells a part of it at 20% profit and the rest at 40% profit. If he gains 25% on the whole, find the quantity of each part.
   (a) 12.5 kgs and 37.5 kgs
   (b) 37.5 kgs and 12.5 kgs
   (c) 23.5 kgs and 21.5 kgs
   (d) 21.5 kgs and 23.5 kgs
   (e) None of these

10. A shopkeeper has 100 kgs of tea. He sells a part of it at 20% profit and the rest at 5% loss. If his overall profit is 10%, find the quantity for each part.

(*a*) 20 kgs, 80 kg (*b*) 25 kgs, 75 kg
(*c*) 30 kgs, 70 kg (*d*) 60 kg, 40 kgs
(*e*) None of these

ANSWERS

1	2	3	4	5	6	7	8	9	10
(*b*)	(*d*)	(*a*)	(*e*)	(*b*)	(*a*)	(*e*)	(*a*)	(*b*)	(*d*)

SOME SELECTED EXPLANATORY ANSWERS

2. Cost price of the mixture

$$= 15 \times \frac{100}{180} = ₹\frac{25}{3} \text{ per kg}$$

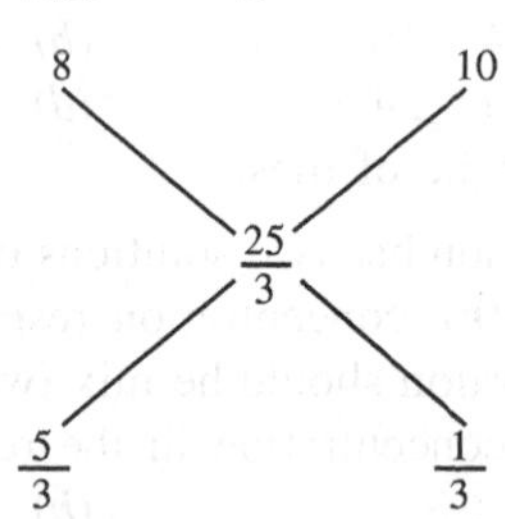

$$\frac{\text{Quantity of rice @ Rs. 8 per kg}}{\text{Quantity of rice @ Rs.10 per kg}} = \frac{5/3}{1/3} = \frac{5}{1}$$

Quantity of rice @ ₹ 10 per kg

$$= 25 \times \frac{1}{5} = 5 \text{ kgs.}$$

3.

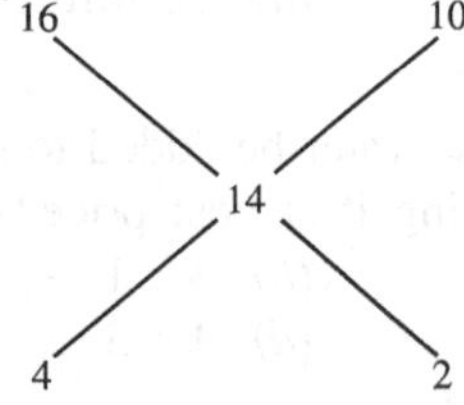

or 2 : 1

$$\frac{\text{Quantity of milk @ Rs.10 per kg}}{\text{Quantity of milk @ Rs. 16 per kg}} = \frac{1}{2}$$

So, quantity of milk @ ₹ 10 per kg.

$$= \frac{26}{2} = 13 \text{ kgs.}$$

5. Fraction is

A : $\frac{4}{5}$ $\frac{1}{5}$

B : $\frac{9}{20}$ $\frac{11}{20}$

$$(3A + 2B) = A \text{ and } B : \left(\frac{12}{5}+\frac{9}{10}\right) \left(\frac{3}{5}+\frac{11}{10}\right)$$

$$\frac{33}{10} \quad \frac{17}{10}$$

So, Ratio of milk : water in the resulting mixture = 33 : 17.

8. Let cost price of spirit be Re. 1 per litre.

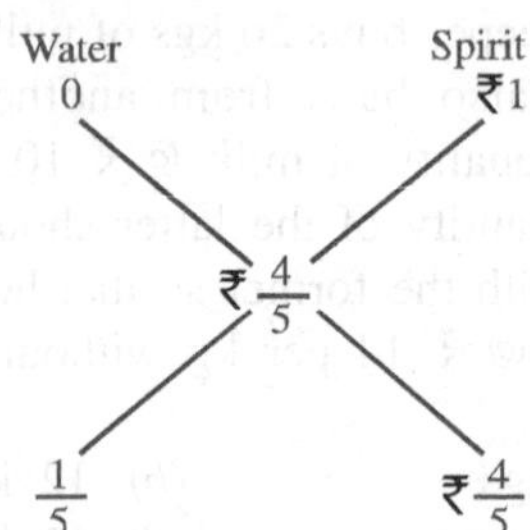

Then SP of mixture = ₹ 1 per litre

Gain = 25%

So, CP of mixture $= 1 \times \frac{100}{125} = ₹\frac{4}{5}$

We assume that CP of water is zero.

Using alligation rule on cost price,

Water should be mixed to spirit in the ratio

$\frac{1}{5} : \frac{4}{5}$ or 1 : 4.

❑❑❑

10 Time, Speed & Distance

Important Formulae:

1. Speed = Distance ÷ Time
2. Distance = Time × Speed
3. Time = Distance ÷ Speed
4. x km/hr $= \left(x \times \frac{5}{18}\right)$ m/sec
5. x metres/sec $= \left(x \times \frac{18}{5}\right)$ km/hr.
6. If the speed of a body is changed in the ratio $m : n$, then the ratio of the time taken changes in the ratio $n : m$.
7. When a man covers a certain distance with a speed of x km/h and another equal distance at the rate of y km/h, then for the whole journey, the average speed is given by

$$\text{Average speed} = \frac{2xy}{x+y} \text{ km/h.}$$

Important Facts:

1. The time taken by a train in passing a signal post or a telegraph pole or a man standing near a railway line $= \frac{\text{Length of the train}}{\text{Speed of the train}}$
2. The time taken by a train of length x passing a railway bridge or a platform or a tunnel or a train of length y at rest $= \frac{x+y}{\text{Speed}}$
3. (*a*) Time taken by faster train of length x and speed u to pass the slower train of length y and speed v in the same direction $= \frac{x+y}{u-v}$

   (*b*) Time taken by the trains in passing each other while moving in opposite direction $= \frac{x+y}{u+v}$
4. (*a*) Time taken by the train of length x and speed u to cross a man moving with speed v in same direction $= \frac{x}{u-v}$

   (*b*) Time taken by the train to cross a man moving in the opposite direction $= \frac{x}{u+v}$

When we simply say speed of a boat and swimmer, it usually means speed in still water. If the boat or the swimmer moves against the stream, then it is called *Upstream* and if it moves with the stream, it is called *Downstream.*

Hence, if x km per hour be the man's rate in still water, and y km per hour the rate of the current then

$x + y$ = man's rate with the current (called the downstream)

$x - y$ = man's rate against the current (called the upstream)

$x = \frac{1}{2}$ (downstream + upstream)

$y = \frac{1}{2}$ (downstream – upstream).

EXAMPLES

Example 1: A man covers a certain distance between his house and office on scooter. Having an average speed of 30 km/h, he is late by 10 min. However, with a speed of 40 km/h, he reaches his office 5 min. earlier. Find the distance between his house and office.

Solution: Let the distance between the house and the office be x km.

Difference of time

$= 5 - (-10) = 15 \text{ min} = \frac{1}{4}$ hr.

Here, $\frac{x}{30} - \frac{x}{40} = \frac{1}{4} \Rightarrow \frac{x}{120} = \frac{1}{4}$

$\therefore x = \frac{120}{4} = 30$ km.

Example 2: A car can complete a journey in 6 hours if it travels at 45 km/hr. At what speed (in km/hr) must it travel in order to complete the journey in 5 hours?

Solution: Distance covered by the car in 6 hours at 45 km/hr = 45 × 6 = 270 kms.

∴ In the second case speed of the car should be

$\frac{270}{5} = 54$ km/hr.

Example 3: A train 100 m long takes 9 seconds to cross a man walking at 5 km/h in the direction opposite to that of the train. Find the speed of the train.

Solution: Let the speed of the train be x km/h.

Relative speed = $(x + 5)$ km/h

$= \frac{5(x+5)}{18}$ m/sec

Now, $\frac{100}{\frac{5(x+5)}{18}} = 9 \Rightarrow x + 5 = \frac{20 \times 18}{9}$

∴ $x = 35$

Hence, speed of the train = 35 km/h.

Example 4: A platform is 131 metre long. If the speed of the train of 67 m long is 45 km/h, how long will it take to pass the platform?

Solution: Total distance = 131 + 67 = 198 m

and speed of the train = 45 km/h

$= 45 \times \frac{5}{18} = \frac{25}{2}$ m/s.

∴ Time taken to pass the platform

$= 198 \times \frac{2}{25} = 15.84$ sec.

Example 5: A boat can travel 35 km downstream in 5 hours. If it covers the same distance upstream in 7 hours, find the speed of the boat in still water.

Solution: Speed of the boat downstream

$= \frac{35}{5} = 7$ km/hr.

and speed of the boat upstream

$= \frac{35}{7} = 5$ km/hr.

Speed of the boat in still

water $= \frac{1}{2}$ (downstream + upstream)

$= \frac{1}{2}(7 + 5) = 6$ km/h

EXERCISE

1. A car moving at 48 km/hr completes a journey in 10 hours. By how much the speed of this car should be increased so as to do this journey in 8 hours?
   (a) 8 km/hr (b) 12 km/hr
   (c) 10 km/hr (d) 15 km/hr
   (e) None of these
2. Starting from a point at a speed of 4 km/hr a man reaches at a cerain place and returns back to the point from where he had started journey on bicycle at the speed of 16 km/hr. His average speed during the entire journey will be :
   (a) 6.4 km/h (b) 8.4 km/h
   (c) 5.4 km/h (d) 10 km/h
   (e) None of these
3. A motorist covers a certain distance at a average speed of 48 km/h in 45 minutes. What speed in km/h he must maintain to cover the same distance in 30 minutes?
   (a) 66 km/h (b) 79 km/h
   (c) 80 km/h (d) 72 km/h
   (e) None of these
4. Two points A and B are 150 km apart. A man completes his onward journey from A to B in 3 hours 20 minutes and return journey from B to A in 4 hours 10 minutes. His average speed during the entire journey will be less than his

average speed during the journey from A to B by :

(*a*) 5 km/h (*b*) 7.5 km/h
(*c*) 9 km/h (*d*) 3 km/h
(*e*) None of these

5. A policeman saw a thief at a distance of 200 m. The policeman and the thief started running at the same time. If the policeman runs at a speed of $4\frac{1}{6}$ m per second and the thief at a speed of $3\frac{1}{3}$ m per second, after what time the policeman will catch the thief?

(*a*) 12 min (*b*) 10 min
(*c*) 9 min (*d*) 4 min
(*e*) None of these

6. Kanchan walks from her home at 4 kms per hour and reaches her school 5 minutes late. If she walks at 5 kms per hour, she reaches the school 2½ minutes earlier. How far is the school from her home?

(*a*) 3.5 kms (*b*) 2.5 kms
(*c*) 2.75 kms (*d*) 3.2 kms
(*e*) None of these

7. A monkey wants to climb up a glazed pole. He climbs 12 metres in 1 minute and then he slips back 3 metres in the next minute. If the pole is 63 metre high, how long does he take to climb at the top of the pole?

(*a*) $11\frac{1}{4}$ min (*b*) $12\frac{1}{2}$ min
(*c*) $12\frac{3}{4}$ min (*d*) $14\frac{3}{4}$ min
(*e*) None of these

8. A and B start walking at the same time on a circular path with circumference 35 metre. If they walk in the same direction at 4 km/hr and 5 km/hr respectively, after what time will they meet together?

(*a*) 35 hours (*b*) 27 hours
(*c*) 24 hours (*d*) 40 hours
(*e*) None of these

9. A car covers four consecutive extensions of 3 km each at the speeds of 10 km/hr, 20 km/hr, 30 km/hr and 60 km/hr. Its average speed of journey is:

(*a*) 30 km/hr (*b*) 25 km/hr
(*c*) 20 km/hr (*d*) 10 km/hr
(*e*) None of these

10. A train is scheduled to cover the distance between two stations 70 km apart in an hour. If it travels the first 30 km at 60 km/hr can it complete the journey in time without exceeding a speed restriction of 80 km/hr?

(*a*) yes
(*b*) no
(*c*) can't be determined
(*d*) Data insufficient
(*e*) None of these

11. A train runs at 45 km per hour. How far does it go in 6 seconds?

(*a*) 72 m (*b*) 60 m
(*c*) 75 m (*d*) 70 m
(*e*) None of these

12. A motorist covers a distance of 39 km in 45 minutes, by moving at a speed of x km/hr for the first 15 minutes, then moving at double the speed for the next 20 minutes and then again moving at his original speed for the rest of journey. Then x is equal to :

(*a*) 31.2 (*b*) 42
(*c*) 40 (*d*) 52
(*e*) 36

13. If a train running at 72 km/hr crosses a coconut tree standing by the side of the track in 7 seconds, the length of the train is :

(*a*) 104 m (*b*) 140 m
(*c*) 504 m (*d*) 540 m
(*e*) None of these

14. Two trains are moving in the same direction at 45 km/hr and 25 km/hr. The faster train crosses a passenger travelling in the slower one in 18 seconds. The length of the faster train is :

(*a*) 100 m (*b*) 120 m
(*c*) 150 m (*d*) 180 m
(*e*) None of these

15. Two trains are moving at 50 km/hr and 70 km/hr in an opposite direction. Their lengths are 150 m and 100 m respectively. The time they will take to pass each other completely is :

(a) 3 seconds (b) $4\frac{1}{2}$ seconds

(c) 5 seconds (d) $7\frac{1}{2}$ seconds

(e) None of these

16. A train leaves Delhi at 9 A.M. at a speed of 30 km/hr. Another train leaves at 2 P.M. at a speed of 40 km/hr on the same day and in the same direction. How far from Delhi, will the two trains meet?

(a) 300 km (b) 400 km
(c) 600 km (d) 650 km
(e) None of these

17. Two trains are running in opposite direction with the speed of 62 km/hr and 40 km/hr respectively. If the length of one train is 250 metres and they cross each other in 18 seconds, what will be the length of the other train?

(a) 125 m (b) 250 m
(c) 260 m (d) 280 m
(e) None of these

18. The distance of earth from sun is 141,000,000 km and light travels from latter to former in 7 minutes and fifty seconds. Find the velocity of light per second.

(a) 30000 km (b) 3000 km
(c) 300000 km (d) 300 km
(e) None of these

19. If the speed of a boat in still water is 5 km/hr and its speed against the current is 2.5 km/hr, then what is its speed in the direction of the current?

(a) 7.5 km/hr (b) 12 km/hr
(c) 10 km/hr (d) 11.5 km/hr
(e) None of these

20. The speed of a motorboat in still water is 9 km/hr and the speed of the stream is 2.5 km/hr. Find the time taken by the motorboat to go 9.1 km against the stream.

(a) 1 hour 40 minutes
(b) 2 hours 24 minutes
(c) 3 hours 24 minutes
(d) 4 hours 24 minutes
(e) None of these

21. The boat goes 40 km upstream in 8 hours and 36 km downstream in 6 hours. Find the speed of the boat in still water.

(a) 5 km/hr (b) 6 km/hr
(c) 6.5 km/hr (d) 7 km/hr
(e) None of these

22. A boat goes 6 km upstream and back to the starting point in 2 hours. If the current of the stream runs at the rate of 4 km/hr, find the speed of the boat in still water.

(a) 6 km/hr (b) 8 km/hr
(c) 10 km/hr (d) 12 km/hr
(e) None of these

23. A man can swim 3 km/hr in still water. If the velocity of the stream be 2 km/hr, find the time taken by him to swim to a point 10 km upstream and back.

(a) 12 hours (b) 10 hours
(c) 8 hours (d) 6 hours
(e) None of these

24. A boat covers 24 km upstream and 36 km downstream in 6 hours, while it covers 36 km upstream and 24 km downstream in 6½ hours. Find the speed of the current.

(a) 3 km/hr (b) 4 km/hr
(c) 6 km/hr (d) 8 km/hr
(e) None of these

ANSWERS

1	2	3	4	5	6	7	8	9	10
(b)	(a)	(d)	(a)	(d)	(b)	(c)	(a)	(c)	(a)
11	**12**	**13**	**14**	**15**	**16**	**17**	**18**	**19**	**20**
(c)	(e)	(b)	(a)	(e)	(c)	(c)	(c)	(a)	(e)
21	**22**	**23**	**24**						
(e)	(b)	(a)	(e)						

SOME SELECTED EXPLANATORY ANSWERS

1. Let he has to increase his speed by x km/hr for given condition; then,

$$(48 + x) \times 8 = 48 \times 10$$
$$\Rightarrow \quad 48 + x = 60$$
$$\therefore \quad x = 12 \text{ km/hr}$$

2. Average speed during the entire journey

$$= \frac{2xy}{x+y} = \frac{2 \times 4 \times 16}{4+16}$$
$$= \frac{8 \times 16}{20} = 6.4 \text{ km/hr.}$$

3. Let required speed be x km/hr; then

$$x \times \frac{1}{2} = 48 \times \frac{3}{4}$$
$$\therefore \quad x = 48 \times \frac{3}{4} \times 2 = 72 \text{ km/hr.}$$

5. Suppose the policeman will catch the thief after t seconds

then, $\left(\frac{25}{6} - \frac{10}{3}\right)t = 200 \quad \Rightarrow \frac{5}{6}t = 200$

$$\therefore \quad t = \frac{200 \times 6}{5} = 240 \text{ sec} = 4 \text{ min.}$$

8. The two persons walk in the same direction

$\therefore$ Their relative speed = 5 – 4 = 1 km/hr

Distance covered in 1 round on the circular path = 35 km

$\therefore$ They will meet after $\frac{35}{1}$ = 35 hours.

10. Time taken in covering 30 km $= \frac{30}{60} = \frac{1}{2}$ hr

Remaining distance = 70 – 30 = 40 km

Hence, the train has to cover 40 km in $\frac{1}{2}$ hr

Hence, speed of the train = 40 × 2 = 80 km/hr

So, the train can complete the journey in time without exceeding a speed restriction of 80 km/hr.

11. Speed = 45 km/hr = $45 \times \frac{5}{18} = \frac{25}{2}$ m/s

Hence, distance covered $= \frac{25}{2} \times 6$ = 75 m.

13. Length of the train $= 72 \times \frac{5}{18} \times 7$ = 140 m.

14. The length of the faster train

$$= (45 - 25) \times \frac{5}{18} \times 18 = 20 \times 5 = 100 \text{ m.}$$

15. Required time

$$= \frac{(150+100)}{(50+70) \times \frac{5}{18}} = \frac{250 \times 18}{120 \times 5} = \frac{15}{2} = 7\frac{1}{2} \text{ sec.}$$

16. Let they will meet after t hours from starting the first train.

Then, $\quad t \times 30 = (t - 5)40$

$$\Rightarrow \quad 40t - 30t = 200$$
$$\Rightarrow \quad 10t = 200$$
$$\therefore \quad t = 20$$

Hence, required distance from Delhi

= 30 × 20 = 600 km.

18. Time = 7 min 50 sec. = 470 sec.

Velocity of light per second

$$= \frac{141{,}000{,}000}{470} = 300000 \text{ km.}$$

19. Let the speed of the boat downstream = x km/h.

Now, $\quad 5 = \frac{1}{2}(x + 2.5)$

$$\Rightarrow \quad x = 10 - 2.5 = 7.5 \text{ km/hr.}$$

21. Upstream speed $= \frac{40}{8}$ = 5 km/hr;

Downstream speed $= \frac{36}{6}$ = 6 km/hr

Hence, speed of the boat in still water

$$= \frac{1}{2}(6+5) = \frac{11}{2} = 5.5 \text{ km/hr.}$$

23. Downstream speed = (3 + 2) = 5 km/hr

Upstream speed = (3 – 2) = 1 km/hr

Required time $= \frac{10}{1} + \frac{10}{5}$ = 12 hrs.

❑❑❑

11 Time, Work & Wages

Important Facts:

1. If A can do a piece of work in n days, then work done by A in 1 day = $\frac{1}{n}$.
2. If work done by A in 1 day = $\frac{1}{n}$; then A can finish the whole work in n days.
3. If A is twice as good a workman as B then; Ratio of work done by A and B = 2 : 1.
   Ratio of times taken by A and B to finish a work = 1 : 2.

EXAMPLES

Example 1: A can do a piece of work in 6 days. B can do the same work in 3 days. How long would both of them take to do the same work?

Solution: Here, A's 1 day's work = $\frac{1}{6}$ and also B's 1 day's work = $\frac{1}{3}$

Hence, (A + B)'s 1 day's work = $\frac{1}{6}+\frac{1}{3}=\frac{1}{2}$

So, (A + B) could do the same work in 2 days.

Example 2: A, B and C working together can complete a piece of work in 24 days. C alone can complete this work in 48 days. A works twice as fast as B. How long would A take to finish the work working alone?

Solution: Here, (A + B + C)'s 1 day's work = $\frac{1}{24}$; C's 1 day's work = $\frac{1}{48}$

Ratio of work done of A and B = 2 : 1

Hence, ratio of their time taken = 1 : 2

Let A and B can finish the work x and $2x$ days respectively.

Now, $\frac{1}{x}+\frac{1}{2x}+\frac{1}{48}=\frac{1}{24} \Rightarrow \frac{3}{2x}=\frac{1}{48}$

$\therefore \quad x = 72$ days

Example 3: A contractor undertakes to complete a work in 20 days. He employs 18 labourers on this job but after 12 days he finds that only half of the work has been done. How many more labourer should he employ to complete the work within the scheduled period?

Solution: Here, remaining part of the work = $\frac{1}{2}$ and remaing number of days = 20 – 12 = 8 days

Hence, $8 \times x = 12 \times 18 \therefore x = \frac{12 \times 18}{8} = 27$

So, number of more labourers = 27 – 18 = 9

EXERCISE

1. 12 boys can do a piece of work in 16 days. In how many days can 6 boys do the same work?
   (a) 16 days (b) 32 days
   (c) 23 days (d) 24 days
   (e) None of these
2. A can do a piece of work in 8 days while B can do the same work in 16 days. If they start working together, how long would they take to complete half portion of this work?
   (a) $2\frac{2}{3}$ days (b) $3\frac{5}{7}$ days
   (c) $4\frac{1}{2}$ days (d) $3\frac{1}{2}$ days
   (e) None of these

3. A can do a piece of work in 4 days. B is 50% more efficient than A. How long would B alone take to finish this work?

(a) $3\frac{1}{3}$ days (b) $5\frac{1}{4}$ days

(c) $2\frac{2}{3}$ days (d) $1\frac{2}{3}$ days

(e) None of these

4. A and B working together complete a work in 35 days. If A takes 60 days to complete it, how long would B alone take to complete it?

(a) 64 days (b) 72 days

(c) 81 days (d) 84 days

(e) None of these

5. A few children working together can do a piece of work in 18 days. If the number of children employed on the work is made double, how long would they take to complete half of the work?

(a) $4\frac{1}{2}$ days (b) $2\frac{1}{3}$ days

(c) $8\frac{3}{4}$ days (d) $6\frac{1}{2}$ days

(e) None of these

6. 10 men or 18 boys can do a piece of work in 15 days. In how many days would 25 men and 15 boys complete the same work working together?

(a) $5\frac{1}{2}$ days (b) $4\frac{1}{2}$ days

(c) $6\frac{2}{3}$ days (d) $2\frac{1}{3}$ days

(e) None of these

7. Two persons A and B can complete a piece of work in 8 hours and 16 hours respectively. If they work at it alternately for an hour, A starting first, in how many hours will the work be finished?

(a) $9\frac{1}{3}$ hours (b) $10\frac{1}{2}$ hours

(c) $11\frac{1}{2}$ hours (d) $8\frac{1}{2}$ hours

(e) None of these

8. A cistern is filled by a tap in $3\frac{1}{2}$ hours. Due to a leak in the bottom of the cistern, it takes half an hour longer to fill the cistern. If the cistern is full, how long will it take the leak to empty it?

(a) 28 hours (b) 29 hours

(c) $31\frac{1}{3}$ hours (d) 38 hours

(e) None of these

9. A is twice as good a workman as B and thrice as good a workman as C. If C alone can do a piece of work in 24 days, how long would the three persons take to finish the work working together?

(a) $3\frac{3}{11}$ days (b) $4\frac{4}{7}$ days

(c) $4\frac{4}{11}$ days (d) $3\frac{4}{11}$ days

(e) None of these

10. Two pipes can fill a tank in 8 hours and 12 hours respectively whereas an escape pipe can empty it in 6 hours. If the three pipes are opened at 1 p.m., 2 p.m. and 3 p.m. respectively, at what time will the tank be filled?

(a) 7.00 a.m. (b) 8.00 a.m.

(c) 5.00 a.m. (d) 7.30 a.m.

(e) None of these

11. Working 7 hours daily 24 men can complete a piece of work in 27 days. In how many days would 14 men complete the same piece of work working 9 hours daily?

(a) 32 days (b) 31 days

(c) 36 days (d) 39 days

(e) None of these

12. Two men undertake to do a piece of work for ₹ 1400. First man alone can do this work in 7 days while the second man alone can do this work in 8 days. If they working together complete this work in 3 days with the help of a boy, how should money be divided?

(a) ₹ 600, ₹ 500, ₹ 300

(b) ₹ 600, ₹ 525, ₹ 275

(c) ₹ 600, ₹ 550, ₹ 250

(d) ₹ 500, ₹ 525, ₹ 375
(e) None of these

13. Amit takes twice as much time as Aryan and thrice as much as Ram to finish a piece of work. Together they finish the work in 1 day. What is the time taken by Amit to finish the work?
(a) 6 days (b) 5 days
(c) 3 days (d) 4 days
(e) None of these

14. A works twice as fast as B. If B can complete a piece of work independently in 12 days. Find in how many days A and B together can complete the work?
(a) 8 days (b) 6 days
(c) 4 days (d) 18 days
(e) None of these

15. The daily wages of a worker is ₹ 100. Five workers can do a work in 10 days. If you pay ₹ 20 more daily they agree to do 25% more work daily. If the proposal is accepted the total amount could be saved is:
(a) ₹ 500 (b) ₹ 300
(c) ₹ 250 (d) ₹ 200
(e) None of these

16. 12 men take 36 days to do a work while 12 women complete $\frac{3}{4}$th of the same work in 36 days. In how many days 10 men and 8 women together will complete the same work?
(a) 27 days (b) 12 days
(c) 6 days (d) 16 days
(e) Data inadequate

17. X and Y can do a work in 12 days, Y and Z in 15 days and Z and X can do the same work in 20 days. How long will they take to complete the work if all the three working together?
(a) 10 days (b) 9 days
(c) 8 days (d) $7\frac{1}{2}$ days
(e) None of these

18. A and B can do a piece of work in 30 days, while B and C can do the same work in 24 days and C and A in 20 days. They all work together for 10 days when B and C leave. How many days more will A take to finish the work?
(a) 36 days (b) 30 days
(c) 24 days (d) 18 days
(e) None of these

ANSWERS

1	2	3	4	5	6	7	8	9	10
(b)	(a)	(c)	(d)	(a)	(b)	(b)	(a)	(c)	(a)
11	**12**	**13**	**14**	**15**	**16**	**17**	**18**		
(c)	(b)	(a)	(c)	(d)	(a)	(a)	(d)		

SOME SELECTED EXPLANATORY ANSWERS

1. ∵ 12 boys can do a piece of work in 16 days.
∴ 1 boy will do the same piece of work in 16 × 12 days.
∴ 6 boys will do the same piece of work in $\frac{16 \times 12}{6}$ days = 32 days.

3. A's 1 day's work $= \frac{1}{4}$; Hence, B's 1 day's work $= \frac{150}{100} \times \frac{1}{4} = \frac{3}{8}$

So, B will do the whole work in $\frac{8}{3} = 2\frac{2}{3}$ days.

5. Let number of children be x;
Now x children can do the work in 18 days.
Hence, $2x$ children will do $\frac{1}{2}$ of the work in

$\frac{18 \times x}{2x \times 2} = \frac{9}{2}$ days

$= 4\frac{1}{2}$ days.

8. In 1 hour $\frac{2}{7}$ cistern is filled by the tap.

Hence, in $\frac{1}{2}$ hour $\frac{2}{14} = \frac{1}{7}$ cistern is filled by the tap.

So, $\frac{1}{7}$ cistern is emptied by the leakage in 4 hours.

So, 1 cistern will be emptied by the leakage in 28 hours.

9. Here, ratio of efficiency of A, B and C = 1 : $\frac{1}{2} : \frac{1}{3}$

So, ratio of their time taken to complete the work = 1 : 2 : 3

Now C completes the work in 24 days, so A and B will complete the work in 8 and 16 days respectively.

Hence, (A + B + C)'s 1 day's work

$$= \frac{1}{8} + \frac{1}{16} + \frac{1}{24} = \frac{11}{48}$$

Therefore, (A + B + C) will complete the work in $\frac{48}{11} = 4\frac{4}{11}$ days.

11. Working 7 hours a day 24 men can do the work in 27 days.

Hence, working 9 hours a day 14 men will do the work in $\frac{27 \times 24 \times 7}{9 \times 14} = 36$ days.

13. Let Amit, Aryan and Ram can finish the work in $x, \frac{x}{2}$ and $\frac{x}{3}$ days respectively, then

(Amit + Aryan + Ram)'s 1 day's work

$$= \frac{1}{x} + \frac{2}{x} + \frac{3}{x} = \frac{6}{x}$$

Now, $\frac{6}{x} = 1$ $\therefore x = 6$

Hence, Amit will finish the work in 6 days.

15. 25% more work daily means

10 days' work ≡ 8 days' work

Hence, saved amount

= ₹ 10 × 100 × 5 – ₹ 8 × 120 × 5

= ₹ 5000 – ₹ 4800 = ₹ 200

16. Ratio of work of a man and a woman = 1 : $\frac{3}{4}$ = 4 : 3

Ratio of their time taking = 3 : 4

Hence, 4 women ≡ 3 men

∴ 8 women ≡ 6 men

Now, 10 men + 8 women ≡ 10 men + 6 men = 16 men

Again, 12 men can complete the work in 36 days

Hence, 16 men will complete the work in $\frac{12 \times 36}{16} = 27$ days.

17. 2(X + Y + Z)'s 1 day's work

$$= \frac{1}{12} + \frac{1}{15} + \frac{1}{20} = \frac{12}{60} = \frac{1}{5}$$

Hence, (X + Y + Z)'s 1 day's work = $\frac{1}{10}$

Hence, they all together will complete the work in 10 days.

18. 2 (A + B + C)'s 1 day's work

$$= \frac{1}{30} + \frac{1}{24} + \frac{1}{20} = \frac{15}{120} = \frac{1}{8}$$

Hence, (A + B + C)'s 1 day's work = $\frac{1}{16}$

Now, A's 1 day's work = $\frac{1}{16} - \frac{1}{24} = \frac{1}{48}$

Again, (A + B + C)'s 10 days' work

$$= 10 \times \frac{1}{16} = \frac{5}{8}$$

Remaining part of work = $1 - \frac{5}{8} = \frac{3}{8}$, which will be done by A alone.

Hence, time taken by A to complete the remaining work = $\frac{3/8}{1/48} = \frac{3}{8} \times 48 = 18$ days.

❑❑❑

12 Partnership

When two or more than two persons agree to invest money to run a business jointly, this association or deal is called *partnership* and those who invest money are called *partners.* The total investment is called the *capital.*

Kind of Partners

There are two kinds of partners.

1. **Working or active partner :** When a partner devotes his time for the business in addition to invest his money, he is called a working partner. With mutual agreement, the active partners get some fixed percentage of profit as *working allowance.*
2. **Sleeping or non-active partner :** A partner who simply invests money, but does not attend to the business is called a sleeping partner.

Kind of Partnership :

(i) **Simple partnership :** If the capitals of several partners are invested for the same period, it is called a simple partnership.

(ii) **Compound or complex partnership :** If the capitals of the partners are invested for diffrent intervals of time, the partnership is called compound or complex.

EXAMPLES

Example 1: If A and B enter into a partnership, A contributes ₹ 7000 and B contributes ₹ 10000. If the profit at the end of the year amounts to ₹ 7310, what would be the share of B in the profit?

Solution: Ratio of their capitals= 7000 : 10000
= 7 : 10

Hence, share of B = $\frac{10}{17} \times 7310 =$ ₹ 4300

Example 2: Gulshan and Tarun invested ₹ 3900 and ₹ 4200 respectively in a business. If at the end of the year there was a profit of ₹ 2025 in the business, what will be the gain of Gulshan?

Solution: Ratio of the capitals of Gulshan and Tarun
= 3900 : 4200 = 13 : 14

Hence, Share of Gulshan in the profit

$= \frac{13}{27} \times 2025 =$ ₹ 975.

Example 3: A started a business with an investment of ₹ 80000. After 3 months, B also joined him with an investment of ₹ 50000. If at the end of the year total profit is ₹ 23,500, what profit will each of them get?

Solution: Ratio of Capitals of A and B
= (80000 × 12) : (50000 × 9) = 32 : 15

∴ A's profit = $\frac{32}{47} \times 23500 =$ ₹ 16000

B's profit = $\frac{15}{47} \times 23500 =$ ₹ 7500.

Example 4: Rajesh and Suresh invested ₹ 8000 and ₹ 1000 respectively in a business. After 6 months Naresh also joined them with an investment of ₹ 6000. If at the end of 3 years total profit is ₹ 9660, what profit will each of them get?

Solution: Ratio of their capitals
= (8000 × 36) : (1000 × 36) : (6000 × 30)
= 8 : 1 : 5

Share of Rajesh in the profit

$= \frac{8}{14} \times 9660 =$ ₹ 5520

Share of Suresh in the profit

$= \frac{1}{14} \times 9660 =$ ₹ 690

Share of Naresh in the profit

$= \frac{5}{14} \times 9660 =$ ₹ 3450

Example 5: A and B invested ₹ 2600 and ₹ 2800 respectively in a business. If at the end of 6 months, there was a profit of ₹ 1350 in the business, what will be the gain of A?

Solution: Ratio of their capitals

$= 2600 : 2800 = 13 : 14$

Share of A in the profit

$$= \frac{13}{27} \times 1350 = ₹\ 650.$$

Example 6: A and B start a business with the investment of ₹ 7500 and ₹ 6000 respectively. B is an active partner and therefore he gets 12½% of the profit separately for supervision of the trade. If total profit of the business is ₹ 2160, what will be the profit of B?

Solution: Separate profit of B for supervision of the

$$\text{trade} = \frac{25}{200} \times 2160 = ₹\ 270$$

Remaining profit = ₹ 2160 – ₹ 270

= ₹ 1890

Ratio of capitals of A and B

$= 7500 : 6000 = 5 : 4$

$$\text{B's share in the profit} = \frac{4}{9} \times 1890 = ₹\ 840$$

Hence, total profit of B = ₹ 840 + ₹ 270

= ₹ 1110.

Example 7: A, B and C together make a profit of ₹ 7200 in a business. If A invested ₹ 8000 in the business and A and C make profit of ₹ 1920 and Rs. 2880 respectively. What did B invest in the business?

Solution: Total profit in the business = ₹ 7200

B's profit = 7200 – (1920 + 2880)

= ₹ 2400

A's capital = ₹ 8000,

A's profit = ₹ 1920

$$\therefore \text{Capital invested by B} = \frac{8000}{1920} \times 2400 = ₹\ 10000$$

EXERCISE

1. A and B started a business with the investment of ₹ 80000 and ₹ 60000 respectively. At the end of the year total profit in the business will be divided between them in the ratio of :
   (a) 2 : 3 (b) 3 : 4
   (c) 2 : 1 (d) 4 : 3
   (e) None of these
2. A and B started a business in partnership with the investment of ₹ 4000 and ₹ 6000 respectively. If at the end of the year total profit is ₹ 2250, what will each of them get?
   (a) ₹ 900, ₹ 1350 (b) ₹ 800, ₹ 1450
   (c) ₹ 1000, ₹ 1250 (d) ₹ 1200, ₹ 1050
   (e) None of these
3. Sonu, Monu and Mohit together start a business with the investment of ₹ 1800, ₹ 1500 and ₹ 1600 respectively. If at the end of the year, Monu gains a profit of ₹ 900 the total profit in the business is :
   (a) ₹ 2880 (b) ₹ 2940
   (c) ₹ 3200 (d) ₹ 3240
   (e) None of these
4. Omdutt started a business with a capital of ₹ 8000. After six months, Sanjay joined him with investment of some capital. If at the end of the year each of them gets equal amount as profit, how much did Sanjay invest in the business?
   (a) ₹ 18000 (b) ₹ 17500
   (c) ₹ 16000 (d) ₹ 16500
   (e) None of these
5. A, B and C buy a farm for ₹ 100000. A contributes ₹ 40000 in it. They sell it, and from the profit B gets ₹ 2750 and C gets ₹ 1750. What would be the profit of A?
   (a) ₹ 2780 (b) ₹ 3000
   (c) ₹ 3280 (d) ₹ 2785
   (e) None of these
6. A and B jointly invest ₹ 2100 and ₹ 3100 respectively in a firm. A is an active partner and hence he gets 25% of the profit separately. If their business yields them total ₹ 1040 as profit, what will be the gain of each of them?
   (a) ₹ 415, ₹ 625 (b) ₹ 415, ₹ 575

(c) ₹ 515, ₹ 525 (d) ₹ 560, ₹ 480
(e) ₹ 575, ₹ 465

7. Two partners invested ₹ 12500 and ₹ 8500 respectively in a business and decided that 60% of the profit incurred from the business will be equally divided between them while remaining profit will be assumed as interest on their capitals. If one of the partners gets ₹ 300 more profit than the other, what is the total profit in the business?
(a) ₹ 3937.50 (b) ₹ 4940.50
(c) ₹ 3936.50 (d) ₹ 4156
(e) None of these

8. Neeraj and Birju are partners in a business. They divide between them the profit incurred in the business in such a proportion that $\frac{2}{5}$th portion of the profit gained by Neeraj is equal to $\frac{1}{3}$rd portion of the profit gained by Birju. If total profit in the business is ₹ 1210, find the profit earned by Birju.
(a) ₹ 780 (b) ₹ 660
(c) ₹ 680 (d) ₹ 590
(e) None of these

9. A, B and C together took under lease a pasture ground for ₹ 888. If in this pasture ground A put his 20 sheep out to graze for 2½ months, B put his 30 sheep out to graze for 4 months and C put his 36 sheep out to graze for 3½ months, find the lease amount paid by each of them.
(a) ₹ 205, ₹ 315, ₹ 378
(b) ₹ 228, ₹ 360, ₹ 378
(c) ₹ 170, ₹ 360, ₹ 358
(d) ₹ 228, ₹ 360, ₹ 300
(e) ₹ 150, ₹ 360, ₹ 378

10. A, B and C started a business with the investment of ₹ 5000, ₹ 6000 and ₹ 4000 respectively. A is an active partner and therefore he gets 30% of the profit separately. Rest of the profit is divided in the ratio of their capitals. If at the end of year, A's profit is ₹ 200 more than the sum of the profits made by B and C, find the profit made by each of them.
(a) ₹ 1620, ₹ 1242, ₹ 1178
(b) ₹ 1720, ₹ 1252, ₹ 1228
(c) ₹ 1510, ₹ 1187, ₹ 1133
(d) ₹ 1600, ₹ 840, ₹ 560
(e) None of these

ANSWERS

1	2	3	4	5	6	7	8	9	10
(d)	(a)	(b)	(c)	(b)	(e)	(a)	(b)	(e)	(d)

SOME SELECTED EXPLANATORY ANSWERS

2. Ratio of capitals of A and B

$= 4000 : 6000 = 2 : 3$

A's share in the profit

$= \frac{2}{5} \times 2250 =$ ₹ 900

B's share in the profit

$= \frac{3}{5} \times 2250 =$ ₹ 1350

3. Ratio of their capitals

$= 1800 : 1500 : 1600 = 18 : 15 : 16$

Sum of proportionals $= 18 + 15 + 16 = 49$

Monu's profit = ₹ 900

∴ Total profit in the business

$= \frac{900}{15} \times 49 =$ ₹ 2940

4. Investment by Omdutt for 1 month

= ₹ 8000 × 12 = ₹ 96000

Let Sanjay invested ₹ x for 6 months

∴ Capital of Sanjay for 1 month

= ₹ $x \times 6$ = ₹ $6x$

Now, $6x = 96000$

∴ $x =$ ₹ 16000

5. Here, ratio of capitals of A and (B + C)
= 40000 : 60000 = 2 : 3
Profit of (B + C) = 2750 + 1750 = ₹ 4500

Hence, A's profit = $\frac{4500}{3} \times 2$ = ₹ 3000

7. Ratio of their capitals = 12500 : 8500
= 25 : 17
Hence, sum of their ratios
= 25 + 17 = 42
and difference of ratios
= 25 − 17 = 8
Now total profit taken as interest
= $\frac{300}{8} \times 42$ = ₹ 1575
Hence, total profit in the business
= $\frac{100}{40} \times 1575$ = ₹ 3937.50

8. Let shares of Neeraj and Birju in profit are ₹ x and ₹ y respectively; then,

$\frac{2}{5}x = \frac{1}{3}y$

∴ $x : y = 5 : 6$

Hence, share of Birju
= $\frac{6}{11} \times 1210$ = ₹ 660

9. Ratio of their shares
= (20 × 5/2) : (30 × 4) : (36 × 7/2)
= 25 : 60 : 63

Sum of proportionals
= 25 + 60 + 63 = 148
Total lease amount
= ₹ 888
∴ Amount paid by A
= $\frac{25}{148} \times 888$ = ₹ 150
Amount paid by B
= $\frac{60}{148} \times 888$ = ₹ 360
Amount paid by C
= $\frac{63}{148} \times 888$ = ₹ 378

10. Ratio of capitals of A, B and C
= 5000 : 6000 : 4000 = 5 : 6 : 4
Let total profit in the business = ₹ x; then

$$\frac{30x}{100} + \frac{5}{15} \times \frac{70x}{100} - \frac{(6+4)}{15} \times \frac{70x}{100} = 200$$

$$\Rightarrow \frac{8x}{15} - \frac{7x}{15} = 200$$

∴ x = ₹ 3000

Hence, A's profit = $\frac{8 \times 3000}{15}$ = ₹ 1600;

B's profit = $\frac{6}{15} \times \frac{7 \times 3000}{10}$ = ₹ 840;

C's profit = $\frac{4}{15} \times \frac{7 \times 3000}{10}$ = ₹ 560.

❑❑❑

13 Problem Based on Age

IMPORTANT FACTS

1. The present age of the father is x times the age of his son. T years hence, the father's age become y times the age of his son. Then the present ages of the father and his son are:

   Present age of the son $= \frac{(y-1)T}{x-y}$ years and

   age of the father $= \frac{(y-1)T \times y}{x-y}$ years

2. T years ago, the father's age was x times that of his son and at present the father's age is y times the age of his son. Then their present ages are:

   Son's age $= \frac{T(x-1)}{x-y}$ years;

   Father's age $= \frac{T(x-1)}{x-y} \times y$ years.

EXAMPLES

Example 1: The sum of the ages of a son and father is 56 years. After 4 years, the age of the father will be three times that of the son. What is the age of the son?

Solution: Let ages of the son and father be x and $(56 - x)$ years respectively.

Then, $\frac{x+4}{56-x+4} = \frac{1}{3} \Rightarrow 3x + 12 = 60 - x$

$\Rightarrow 4x = 48 \qquad \therefore x = 12$

Hence, age of the son = 12 years.

Example 2: The age of Ram is 4 times the age of Shyam. If 5 years hence, Ram's age would be $1\frac{1}{2}$ times that of Shyam. What are their present ages?

Solution: Let the present age of Ram and Shyam be $4x$ and x years; then

$\frac{4x+5}{x+5} = \frac{3}{2} \Rightarrow 8x + 10 = 3x + 15$

$\Rightarrow 5x = 5 \qquad \therefore x = 1$

Hence, $4x = 4 \times 1 = 4$ years and $x = 1$ year

Example 3: The ratio of ages of the father and his son at present is 12 : 5. The difference of their age is 28 years. What will be the ratio of their ages after 8 years?

Solution: Let the present ages of father and his son be $12x$ and $5x$ years respectively; then

$12x - 5x = 28 \Rightarrow 7x = 28 \quad \therefore x = 4$

Now, $12x = 12 \times 4 = 48$ years and $5x = 5 \times 4 = 20$ years

After 8 years their age will be 48 + 8 = 56 years and 20 + 8 = 28 years

Hence, their ratio = 56 : 28 = 2 : 1

EXERCISE

1. The present ages of Sunil and Anil are 40 and 60 years respectively. How many years ago was the ratio of their ages 3 : 5?
   (a) 5 years (b) 10 years
   (c) 12 years (d) 15 years
   (e) None of these

2. The ratio of present ages of two brothers is 1 : 2 and 5 years ago the ratio was 1 : 3. What will be the ratio of their ages after 5 years?
   (a) 1 : 4 (b) 2 : 3
   (c) 3 : 5 (d) 5 : 6
   (e) None of these

3. The ratio of ages of A and B is 3 : 11. After 3 years the ratio becomes 1 : 3. What are the ages of A and B?
(*a*) 9 years, 33 years (*b*) 10 years, 40 years
(*c*) 9 years, 27 years (*d*) None of these
(*e*) None of these

4. Two years ago, the ratio of Ram's and Mohan's age was 3 : 2 and at present 7 : 5. What are their present ages?
(*a*) 14 years, 10 years (*b*) 15 years, 10 years
(*c*) 13 years, 9 years (*d*) None of these
(*e*) None of these

5. One year ago, the ratio of Yamini and Gamini's was 6 : 7 respectively. Four year hence, the ratio would become 7 : 8. Find the age of Gamini?
(*a*) 30 years (*b*) 32 years
(*c*) 36 years (*d*) 40 years
(*e*) None of these

6. The ratio of the present ages of Suresh and his daughter is 2 : 1. Six years hence, the ratio of their ages would be 23 : 13. Find the present age of Suresh?
(*a*) 35 years (*b*) 40 years
(*c*) 45 years (*d*) 50 years
(*e*) None of these

7. The ages of Surabhi and Neerja are in the ratio of 6 : 7 respectively. After 6 years the ratio of their ages will be 15 : 17. Find the age of Neerja.
(*a*) 24 years (*b*) 26 years
(*c*) 27 years (*d*) 32 years
(*e*) None of these

8. The present age of Deepak is 3 times the present age of his son. Five years hence, the ratio of their ages will be 34 : 13 respectively. The present age of Deepak is:
(*a*) 58 years (*b*) 60 years
(*c*) 63 years (*d*) 68 years
(*e*) None of these

9. A mother is 25 years older than her daughter. Five years ago, the age of the mother was 6 times the age of the daughter. What is the present age of mother?
(*a*) 25 years (*b*) 29 years
(*c*) 32 years (*d*) 35 years
(*e*) None of these

10. The mother is five times older than her son. After 4 years, the sum of their ages will be 44 years. What is the present age of the son?
(*a*) 5 years (*b*) 5½ years
(*c*) 7 years (*d*) 8 years
(*e*) None of these

11. The respective ratio of the ages of Shami, Nammi and Pammi is 3 : 4 : 5. The sum of their ages is 48 years. What will be the respective ratio of their ages 8 years hence?
(*a*) 4 : 5 : 6 (*b*) 5 : 6 : 7
(*c*) 5 : 7 : 8 (*d*) 6 : 7 : 8
(*e*) None of these

ANSWERS

1	2	3	4	5	6	7	8	9	10	11
(*b*)	(*c*)	(*a*)	(*a*)	(*c*)	(*b*)	(*e*)	(*c*)	(*d*)	(*e*)	(*b*)

SOME SELECTED EXPLANATORY ANSWERS

1. Let x years ago, the ratio of their ages was 3 : 5, then

$$\frac{40-x}{60-x} = \frac{3}{5}$$

$\Rightarrow$ $200 - 5x = 180 - 3x$

$\Rightarrow$ $2x = 20$ $\quad \therefore x = 10$ years

2. Let their present ages be x and $2x$ years; then

$$\frac{x-5}{2x-5} = \frac{1}{3}$$

$\Rightarrow$ $3x - 15 = 2x - 5 \quad \therefore x = 10$

Hence, their present ages 10 years and 20 years

Required ratio $= \dfrac{10+5}{20+5} = \dfrac{3}{5} = 3 : 5$

3. Let the ages of A and B be $3x$ and $11x$ years; then

$$\frac{3x+3}{11x+3} = \frac{1}{3}$$

$\Rightarrow$ $9x + 9 = 11x + 3$

$\Rightarrow$ $2x = 6 \quad \therefore x = 3$

Hence, their present age,

$3x = 3 \times 3 = 9$ years;

$11x = 11 \times 3 = 33$ years

4. Let the present ages of Ram and Mohan are $7x$ and $5x$ years; then

$$\frac{7x-2}{5x-2} = \frac{3}{2}$$

$\Rightarrow$ $14x - 4 = 15x - 6$

$\therefore$ $x = 2$

Hence, their present ages : $7 \times 2 = 14$ years and $5 \times 2 = 10$ years.

5. Let one year ago the ages of Yamini and Gamini were $6x$ and $7x$ years respectively; then

$$\frac{6x+5}{7x+5} = \frac{7}{8}$$

$\Rightarrow$ $48x + 40 = 49x + 35$

$\therefore$ $x = 5$

Hence, present ago of Gamini

$= 7x + 1 = 7 \times 5 + 1$

$= 36$ years.

6. Let the present ages of Suresh and his daughter be $2x$ and x years respectively; then

$$\frac{2x+6}{x+6} = \frac{23}{13}$$

$\Rightarrow$ $26x + 78 = 23x + 138$

$\Rightarrow$ $3x = 60 \quad \therefore x = 20$

Hence, present age of Suresh $= 2 \times 10$

$= 40$ years.

7. Let the present ages of Surabhi and Neerja are $6x$ and $7x$ years respectively; then,

$$\frac{6x+6}{7x+6} = \frac{15}{17}$$

$\Rightarrow$ $102x + 102 = 105x + 90$

$\Rightarrow$ $3x = 12$

$\therefore$ $x = 4$

Hence, present ages of Neerja

$= 7 \times 4 = 28$ years.

8. The present age of Deepak and his son be $3x$ and x years respectively; then

$$\frac{3x+5}{x+5} = \frac{34}{13}$$

$\Rightarrow$ $39x + 65 = 34x + 170$

$\Rightarrow$ $5x = 105$

$\therefore$ $x = 21$

Hence, present age of Deepak

$= 3x = 3 \times 21 = 63$

9. Let the present ages of mother and her daughter are $(x + 25)$ and x years respectively; then

$6(x - 5) = x + 25 - 5$

$\Rightarrow$ $6x - 30 = x + 20$

$\Rightarrow$ $5x = 50$

$\therefore$ $x = 10$

Hence, the age of the mother

$= 10 + 25 = 35$ years

10. Let the present ages of mother and her son be $5x$ and x years respectively; then

$5x + 4 + x + 4 = 44$

$\Rightarrow$ $6x = 36$

$\therefore$ $x = 6$ years.

11. Let the present ages of Shami, Nammi and Pammi are $3x$, $4x$ and $5x$ years respectively; then,

$3x + 4x + 5x = 48$

$\Rightarrow$ $12x = 48 \quad \therefore x = 4$

Hence, their present ages are 12, 16 and 20 years respectively.

So, required ratio

$= (12 + 8) : (16 + 8) : (20 + 8)$

$= 20 : 24 : 28 = 5 : 6 : 7.$

❑❑❑

14 MENSURATION

In this part of mensuration we often have to deal with the problem of finding the areas and perimeters of plane figures.

Triangle

1. Perimeter = 3 × side (Equilateral triangle)
2. Area $= \frac{1}{2} \times \text{base} \times \text{height}$, or

   Area $= \sqrt{s(s-a)(s-b)(s-c)}$

   where *a, b, c,* are the lengths of the sides of triangle and $s = \frac{a+b+c}{2}$

Right Angled Triangle : It is one whose one of the angles is right angle, *i.e.*, 90°.

1. $(\text{Hypotenuse})^2 = (\text{Perpendicular})^2 + (\text{Base})^2$
2. Area $= \frac{1}{2} \times \text{Base} \times \text{Perpendicular}$

Equilateral Triangle : All three sides are equal in length and all three angles are equal to 60°.

1. Area $= \frac{\sqrt{3}}{4} \times (\text{Side})^2$
2. Area $= \frac{(\text{Height})^2}{\sqrt{3}}$
3. Height $= \frac{\sqrt{3}}{2} \times \text{side}$
4. Perimeter = 3 × side

Isosceles Triangle : Two sides are equal in lengths.

1. Area $= \frac{b}{4}\sqrt{4a^2 - b^2}$

   where a = lengths of equal sides
   b = length of unequal side
2. In an isosceles right triangle,

   (a) Hypotenuse $= \sqrt{2} \times$ congruent side (a)

   (b) Area $= \frac{1}{2} \times a^2$

   (c) Perimeter $= \sqrt{2} \times a(\sqrt{2}+1)$

Rectangle

1. Area = length(l) × breadth(b)
2. Perimeter = $2(l + b)$
3. Diagonal $= \sqrt{l^2 + b^2}$

Square

1. Area = $(\text{Side})^2$
2. Perimeter = 4 × side
3. Diagonal $= \text{side} \times \sqrt{2}$

Parallelogram: In parallelogram opposite sides are parallel and equal. The two diagonals are not always equal but they bisect each other at the point of intersection.

Area = Base × Height.

Trapezium : It is a quadrilateral whose one pair of opposite sides is parallel. Other two opposite sides are oblique.

Area $= \frac{1}{2} \times \text{Height} \times (\text{Sum of parallel sides})$.

Here, height is the distance between the two parallel sides.

Rhombus : It is parallelogram whose all sides are equal and diagonals are bisect each other at right angle.

1. Area $= \frac{1}{2} \times \text{Product of diagonals}$
2. Side $= \sqrt{\left(\frac{d_1}{2}\right)^2 + \left(\frac{d_2}{2}\right)^2}$, where d_1 and d_2 are diagonals
3. Perimeter = 4 × side

Quadrilateral : Area $= \frac{1}{2} \times$ One diagonal × (Sum of perpendicular to it from the opposite vertices),

$= \frac{1}{2} \times d \times (a+b)$

Circle :

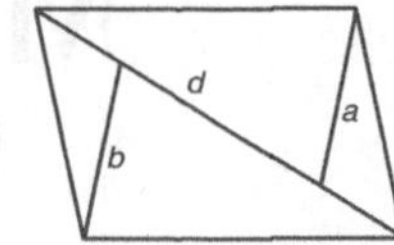

1. Diameter = 2 × Radius
2. Area = $\pi r^2 = \frac{\pi}{4}d^2$;

   where d = diameter = $\sqrt{\frac{4A}{\pi}}$

Polygon :

1. Interior angle + Exterior angle = 180°
2. Each interior angle = $\left(\frac{2n-4}{n}\right) \times 90°$

   where n = number of sides
3. Sum of Exterior angles = 360°
4. Perimeter = Number of sides × Length of side.
5. For an equilateral triangle of side 'a' (a) radius of inscribed circle $= \frac{a}{2\sqrt{3}}$ and side of the triangle = $2\sqrt{3}r$, (b) radius of circumcircle = $\frac{a}{\sqrt{3}}$
6. Area of regular polygon = $\frac{1}{2}$(No. of sides) (Radius of the inscribed circle)
7. Area of regular hexagon = $\frac{3\sqrt{3}}{2}(\text{side})^2$

   $= 2.598\ (\text{side})^2$
8. Area of a regular octagon

   $= 2\left(\sqrt{2}+1\right)(\text{side})^2 = 4.828\ (\text{side})^2$
9. Area of quadrilateral,

   $A = \sqrt{s(s-a)(s-b)(s-c)(s-d)}$

   where, $s = \frac{a+b+c+d}{2}$

Volume and Surface Area

In mensuration we often have to deal with the problem of finding the volume of solid figure.

Cuboid : A cuboid has six faces, each one a ractangle. It has 12 edges. For example, a rectangular brick.

Let Length = l, Breadth = b and Height = h, then,

1. Volume = (Length × Breadth × Height)
2. Whole Surface Area = $2(lb + bh + lh)$
3. Diagonal = $\sqrt{l^2 + b^2 + h^2}$
4. Area of 4 walls of a room = $2 \times h\ (l + b)$

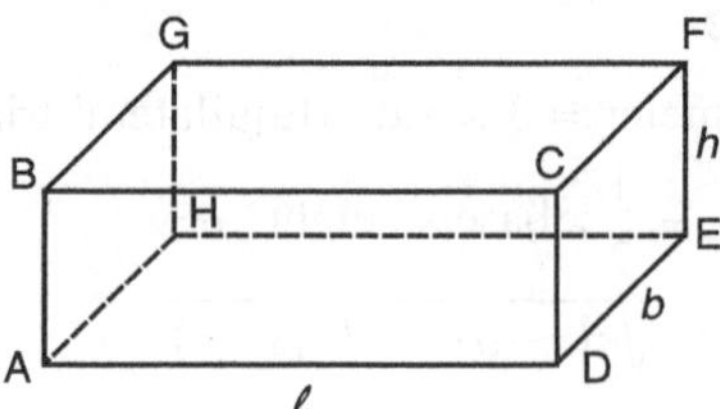

Cube : In a cube, Length = Breadth = Height

1. Volume = $(l)^3$
2. Length = $\sqrt[3]{\text{Volume}}$
3. Whole Surface Area = $6\ l^2$
4. Diagonal = $l \times \sqrt{3}$
5. Lateral Surface Area = $4\ l^2$

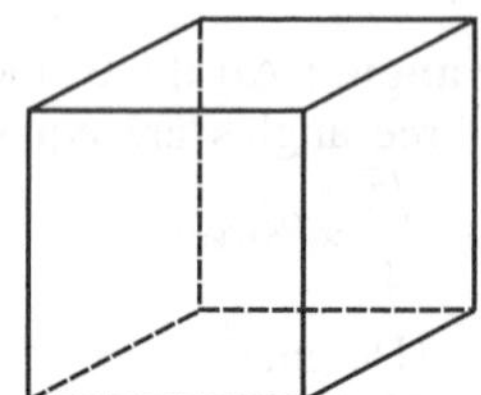

Cylinder :

1. Volume = $\pi r^2 h$
2. Curved Surface Area = $2\pi rh$
3. Total Surface Area = $2\pi r(r + h)$

   where r = radius, h = height

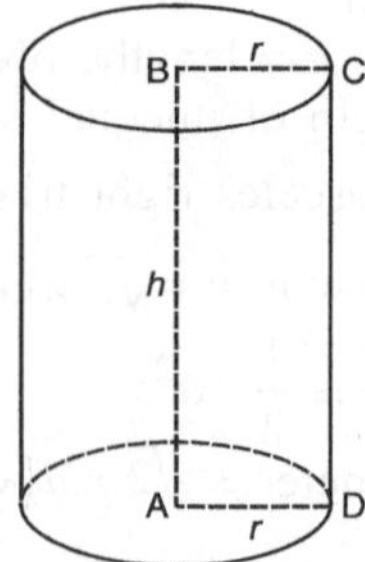

Spherical Cell :

1. Volume = $\frac{4}{3}\pi\left(R^3 - r^3\right)$
2. Total Surface Area = $4\pi(R^2 - r^2)$

where R = Outer radius

r = Inner radius

Sphere :

1. Volume $= \frac{4}{3}\pi r^3$
2. Surface Area = $4\pi r^2$

Semi-sphere :

1. Volume = $\frac{2}{3}\pi r^3$
2. Curved surface area = $2\pi r^2$
3. Total surface area = $3\pi r^2$

Cone :

1. Slant height (l) = $\sqrt{r^2 + h^2}$
2. Volume = $\frac{1}{3}\pi r^2 h$
3. Curved surface area = πrl
4. Total surface area = $\pi r (l + r)$
5. If the depth of the frustum of a cone be k and the radii of its ends are r_1 and r_2, then

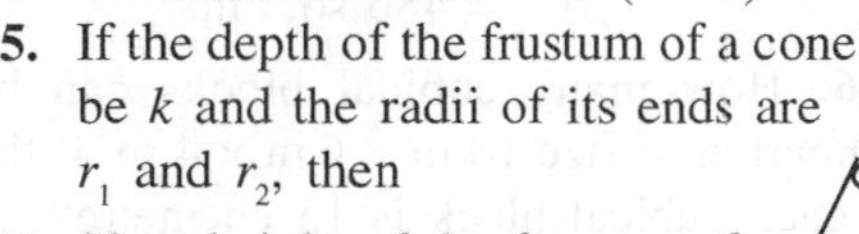

(i) Slant height of the frustum of a cone = $\sqrt{k^2 + (r_1 - r_2)^2}$

(ii) Curved surface of the frustum = $\pi(r_1 + r_2)\ l$.

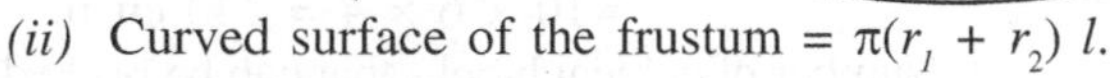

(iii) Volume = $\frac{\pi k}{3}\left(r_1^2 + r_1 r_2 + r_2^2\right)$

EXAMPLES

Example 1: Area of a rectangular field is 1600 sq. metre. If its length is four times its width, find the length of this rectangular field.

Solution: Suppose the length and the width of this field is $4x$ metres and x metres respectively.

$\therefore$ Area of the field = $4x \times x = 4x^2$ sq. metre

Since, $4x^2 = 1600 \Rightarrow x^2 = 400$

$\Rightarrow x = \sqrt{400} \Rightarrow x = 20$

$\therefore$ Length of the rectangular field

$= 4 \times 20 = 80$ m.

Example 2: Perimeter of the rectangular floor of a room is 100 m. If its length and breadth are in the ratio 3 : 2, find the area of this rectangular floor.

Solution: Suppose the length and the breadth of this rectangular floor are $3x$ metre and $2x$ metre respectively.

The perimeter of the floor = $2 \times (l + b)$

$= 2(3x + 2x)$

$= 2 \times 5x = 10x$ metre

Since $10x = 100 \therefore x = \frac{100}{10} = 10$

$\therefore$ Length of the floor = $3 \times 10 = 30$ m

And breadth of the floor = $2 \times 10 = 20$ m

$\therefore$ Area of the floor = $30 \times 20 = 600$ sq. m.

Example 3: The diagonal of a quadrilateral is 140 m and the offsets on it are 100 m and 30 m respectively. Find the area of this quadrilateral.

Solution: Area of the quadrilateral

$= \frac{1}{2} \times \text{diagonal} \times \text{sum of the offsets}$

$= \frac{1}{2} \times 140 \times (100 + 30)$

$= \frac{1}{2} \times 140 \times 130 = 9100$ sq. m.

Example 4: A circular path 3.5 m wide runs round outside a circular garden. If the circumference of the garden is 44 m, find the cost of levelling the path at 15 paise per sq. metre.

Solution: Circumference of the circular garden

$= 2\pi R = 44$ m

$\therefore$ Radius of the garden $= \frac{44}{2\pi} = \frac{44 \times 7}{2 \times 22} = 7$ m

Radius of the (garden + path)

$= 7 + 3.5 = 10.5$ m

$\therefore$ Area of the (garden + path) $= \frac{22}{7} \times (10.5)^2$

$= 346.5$ sq. m.

Area of the garden $= \frac{22}{7} \times 7 \times 7 = 154$ sq. m.

$\therefore$ Area of the path $= 346.5 - 154$

$= 192.5$ sq. m.

Hence, Cost of levelling the path at 15 paise per sq. metre = 192.5×0.15 = ₹ 28.88.

Example 5: Find the side and surface area of a cube whose volume is 729 cu cm.

Solution: Here, $(\text{side})^3 = 729$

$\Rightarrow$ $(\text{side})^3 = (9)^3$

$\Rightarrow$ side = 9 cm

Since, surface area $= 6 \times (9)^2 = 6 \times 81$
$= 486$ sq. cm.

Example 6: How many cubical blocks can be packed in a carton of size 10 m × 6 m × 4 m, if the volume of each cubical block is 15 cu metre?

Solution: Volume of the carton

$= l \times b \times h$

$= 10 \times 6 \times 4 = 240$ cu m

∴ Number of cubical blocks that can be packed in the carton $= \dfrac{240}{15} = 16$

Example 7: A 1100 cu cm iron cube is to be melted and recast into a iron rod in the form of a right circular cylinder. If diameter of the rod is kept 4 cm, what will be the length of this rod?

Solution: Suppose length of the rod = h cm

Radius of the rod $= \dfrac{4}{2} = 2$ cm

Here, Volume of the rod

= Volume of the iron cube

$\therefore \dfrac{22}{7} \times (2)^2 \times h = 1100$

$\Rightarrow h = \dfrac{1100 \times 7}{22 \times 4} = 87.5$ cm

∴ Rod will be 87.5 cm long.

Example 8: An open box is made of wood 3 cm thick. Its external length is 1.46 m, breadth is 1.16 m and height is 83 cm. Find the cost of painting the inner surface of the box at 50 paise per 100 cm^2.

Solution: Here, Internal length = 146 – 2 × 3 = 140 cm; Internal breadth = 116 – 2 × 3 = 110 cm and also, internal height = 83 – 3 = 80 cm

Since, Inner surface area of the open box
$= 140 \times 110 + 2 \times (140 + 110) \times 80$
$= 15400 + 40000$
$= 55400 \text{ cm}^2$

Required cost of painting

$= ₹\ \dfrac{50}{100} \times \dfrac{1}{100} \times 55400 = ₹\ 277$

Example 9: The diameter of a roller 120 cm long is 84 cm. If it takes 500 complete revolutions to level a playground, determine the cost of levelling at the rate of 30 paise per m^2.

Solution: Area of the playground

$= 500 \times \dfrac{22}{7} \times 42 \times 120$

$= 15840000 \text{ cm}^2 = 1584 \text{ m}^2$

Since, cost of levelling = Rs. $\dfrac{30}{100} \times 1584$
$= ₹\ 475.20$

Example 10: Some solid metallic circular cones, each with radius of the base 3 cm and height 4 cm, are melted to form a solid sphere of radius 6 cm. Find the number of right circular cones.

Solution: Let number of right circular cones be n; then,

$$n \times \frac{1}{3}\pi \times 3^2 \times 4 = \frac{4}{3}\pi \times 6^3$$

$$\therefore n = \frac{4 \times 6 \times 6 \times 6}{3 \times 3 \times 4} = 24$$

Example 11: If the ratio of volumes of two cones is 2 : 3 and ratio of radii of their bases is 1 : 2, then what will be the ratio of heights?

Solution: Here, $\dfrac{V_1}{V_2} = \dfrac{2}{3}$ and $\dfrac{r_1}{r_2} = \dfrac{1}{2}$; then

$$\frac{\frac{1}{3}\pi.(1)^2 \times h_1}{\frac{1}{3}\pi.(2)^2 \times h_2} = \frac{2}{3}$$

$$\therefore \frac{h_1}{h_2} = \frac{2}{3} \times \frac{4}{1} = \frac{8}{3}$$

Hence, required ratio = 8 : 3

EXERCISE

1. A field is in the form of a square whose perimeter is 580 m. Area of this field is
(a) 21025 sq. m. *(b)* 20225 sq. m.
(c) 30025 sq. m. *(d)* 19975 sq. m.
(e) None of these

2. Area of a circle is 154 sq. cm. Its circumference will be
(a) 37 cm *(b)* 48 cm

(c) 54 cm (d) 68 cm
(e) None of these

3. Perimeter of a rectangular field is 760 m and its length and breadth are in the ratio 11 : 8. Area of this rectangular field is
(a) 35200 sq. m. (b) 34700 sq. m.
(c) 35600 sq. m. (d) 45200 sq. m.
(e) None of these

4. If side of a square is reduced by 50%, its area will be reduced by
(a) 50% (b) 75%
(c) 80% (d) 60%
(e) None of these

5. If perimeter of a right angled triangle is six times its smallest side, then the three sides of this triangle are in the ratio of
(a) 13 : 5 : 12 (b) 12 : 13 : 5
(c) 12 : 5 : 13 (d) 13 : 5 : 10
(e) 13 : 12 : 5

6. If each side of a square is doubled, its area will become
(a) double (b) four times
(c) three times (d) eight times
(e) None of these

7. The difference between the areas of two squares is 225 sq. metres and each side of the bigger square is 25 metres. The side of the smaller square is
(a) 18 m (b) 21 m
(c) 20 m (d) 22 m
(e) None of these

8. If the circumference of a circle is equal to the perimeter of a square, then their areas are in the ratio of
(a) 14 : 11 (b) 7 : 8
(c) 14 : 13 (d) 13 : 11
(e) None of these

9. Three sides of a triangle are in the ratio of 17 : 15 : 8. If the perimeter of this triangle is 40 m, find its area
(a) 50 sq. m. (b) 49 sq. m.
(c) 60 sq. m. (d) 69 sq. m.
(e) None of these

10. If the length of a rectangle is increased by 20% and width is decreased by 15%, then its area
(a) decreases by 4% (b) increases by 2%
(c) decreases by 2% (d) increases by 3%
(e) None of these

11. Each side of a given square is 5 cm and assuming the two opposite sides of this square as diameters, two semicircles are drawn in the inside of the square. If these semicircles are cut out from the square, then the area of the remaining portion of the given square will be
(a) $(9 - 6.25\pi)$ sq. cm.
(b) $(24 - 6.25\pi)$ sq. cm.
(c) $(25 - 4.25\pi)$ sq. cm.
(d) $(36 - 6.25\pi)$ sq. cm.
(e) $(25 - 6.25\pi)$ sq. cm.

12. Two adjacent sides of a parallelogram are 40 m and 30 m respectively. If one diagonal of the parallelogram measures 50 m, find its area.
(a) 1100 sq. m. (b) 1300 sq. m.
(c) 1400 sq. m. (d) 1500 sq. m.
(e) None of these

13. Four sides of a trapezium are 50 cm, 17 cm, 25 cm and 12 cm respectively. If the first of the four sides is parallel to the third, find the area of this trapezium.
(a) 280 sq. cm. (b) 810 sq. cm.
(c) 270 sq. cm. (d) 225 sq. cm.
(e) None of these

14. A chord AB of a circle of radius 10 cm makes a right angle at the centre of the circle. The areas of the major and minor segments are:
(a) 220 cm^2; 30 cm^2
(b) 280 cm^2; 30 cm^2
(c) 285.5 cm^2; 28.5 cm^2
(d) 280.5 cm^2; 38.5 cm^2
(e) None of these

15. The parallel sides of a field which is in the shape of trapezium are 20 m and 41 m and the remaining two sides are 10 m and 17m. Find the cost of levelling the field at the rate of ₹ 30 per m^2.
(a) ₹ 7150 (b) ₹ 7220
(c) ₹ 7430 (d) ₹ 7350
(e) None of these

16. The difference between the length and breadth of a rectangle is 23 m. If its perimeter is 206m, then its area is:

(*a*) 1520 m^2 (*b*) 2420 m^2
(*c*) 2480 m^2 (*d*) 2520 m^2
(*e*) None of these

17. What will be the cost of building a fence around a circular field with area equal to 18,634 m^2; if the cost of building the fence per metre is ₹ 365?

(*a*) ₹ 1,76,660 (*b*) ₹ 1,86,680
(*c*) ₹ 2,10,660 (*d*) ₹ 2,76,660
(*e*) None of these

18. A solid in the form of a cuboid is 4 cm × 3 cm × 2 cm. Its volume will be

(*a*) 20 cu cm (*b*) 22 cu cm
(*c*) 28 cu cm (*d*) 24 cu cm
(*e*) None of these

19. Surface area of a cube is 1014 sq. cm. Its volume will be

(*a*) 2197 cu cm (*b*) 2297 cu cm
(*c*) 2179 cu cm (*d*) 2117 cu cm
(*e*) None of these

20. Two spheres have their surface areas in the ratio 9 : 16. Their volumes are in the ratio of

(*a*) 64 : 27 (*b*) 27 : 64
(*c*) 16 : 27 (*d*) 11 : 27
(*e*) None of these

21. Circumference of the base of a cylinder is 88 cm and height of the cylinder is 42 cm. Its volume is

(*a*) 25872 cu cm (*b*) 28572 cu cm
(*c*) 25870 cu cm (*d*) 22584 cu cm
(*e*) None of these

22. If a solid sphere of 3 cm radius is melted and recast into a right circular cone whose base radius is same as that of the sphere, the height of the cone will be

(*a*) 8 cm (*b*) 12 cm
(*c*) 6 cm (*d*) 5 cm
(*e*) None of these

23. Diameter of a roller is 2.4 m and it is 1.68 m long. If it takes 1000 complete revolutions once over to level a field, the area of the field is

(*a*) 12672 sq. m (*b*) 12671 sq. m
(*c*) 12762 sq. m (*d*) 11768 sq. m
(*e*) None of these

24. If each edge of a cube is increased by 10%, then by how much per cent will the surface area of this cube be increased?

(*a*) 21% (*b*) 18%
(*c*) 15% (*d*) 20%
(*e*) None of these

25. Height and base radius of a solid cylinder are 14 m and 4 m respectively. It is melted and recast into a solid cone of the same base radius as that of the cylinder, what will be the height of the cone?

(*a*) 21 m (*b*) 42 m
(*c*) 48 m (*d*) 54 m
(*e*) None of these

26. If the base radius of a cylinder is decreased by 25% and height is increased by 10%, then the curved surface area

(*a*) Decreases by 17.5%
(*b*) Increases by 16.5%
(*c*) Increases by 17.5%
(*d*) Decreases by 11.5%
(*e*) None of these

27. If the whole mass of a sphere can be tightly placed in a cube, then the volume of the cube and the volume of the sphere are in the ratio

(*a*) 7 : 12 (*b*) 22 : 21
(*c*) 21 : 11 (*d*) 20 : 7

28. A cone and a sphere have the same radius and the same volume. The ratio of the diameter of the sphere to the height of the cone is

(*a*) 1 : 3 (*b*) 3 : 2
(*c*) 2 : 1 (*d*) 2 : 3
(*e*) 1 : 2

29. A sphere of maximum volume is cut out from a hemisphere of radius *r*. Find the ratio of the volume of the hemisphere to that of the sphere.

(*a*) 2 : 1 (*b*) 3 : 1
(*c*) 3 : 2 (*d*) 4 : 1
(*e*) None of these

ANSWERS

1	2	3	4	5	6	7	8	9	10
(a)	(e)	(a)	(b)	(e)	(b)	(c)	(a)	(c)	(b)
11	**12**	**13**	**14**	**15**	**16**	**17**	**18**	**19**	**20**
(e)	(e)	(c)	(c)	(e)	(d)	(a)	(d)	(a)	(b)
21	**22**	**23**	**24**	**25**	**26**	**27**	**28**	**29**	
(a)	(b)	(a)	(a)	(b)	(a)	(c)	(e)	(d)	

SOME SELECTED EXPLANATORY ANSWERS

1. Here, $4 \times \text{side} = 580 \Rightarrow \text{side} = \frac{580}{4} = 145$ m

$\therefore$ Area $= (\text{side})^2 = (145)^2 = 21025$ sq. m.

2. Area of the circle $= \pi r^2 \Rightarrow \pi r^2 = 154$

$\Rightarrow r^2 = \frac{154 \times 7}{22} \Rightarrow r = 7$ cm

$\therefore$ Circumference of the circle $= 2\pi r$

$= 2 \times \frac{22}{7} \times 7 = 44$ cm.

3. Suppose length and breadth of the rectangular field are $11x$ m and $8x$ m.

$\therefore$ Perimeter of the field $= 2(11x + 8x) = 2 \times 19x = 38x$ m.

Now, $38x = 760$

$\Rightarrow x = \frac{760}{38} = 20$

$\therefore$ Length of the field $= 11 \times 20 = 220$ m

Breadth of the field $= 8 \times 20 = 160$ m

$\therefore$ Area of the field $= 220 \times 160 = 35200$ sq. m.

6. Area of the square $= x^2$ sq. m

Now, area of the new square $= (2x)^2 = 4x^2$ sq. m

Hence, it is clear that if side of a square is doubled, its area becomes four times.

7. Area of smaller square, $x^2 = 25^2 - 225 = 625 - 225 = 400$

$\Rightarrow x = \sqrt{400} = 20$ m

$\therefore$ Side of the smaller square = 20 m.

8. Here, $2\pi R = 4x \Rightarrow R = \frac{2x}{\pi}$

$\therefore$ Ratio between the areas of the circle and the square $= \pi R^2 : x^2$

$= \pi \times \left(\frac{2x}{p}\right)^2 : x^2 = \frac{4x^2}{\pi} : x^2 = 4 : \frac{22}{7} = 14 : 11$

11. Area of the remaining portion of the square

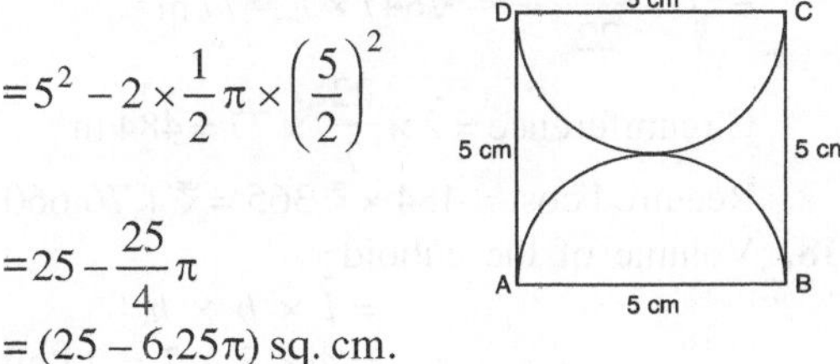

$= 5^2 - 2 \times \frac{1}{2} \pi \times \left(\frac{5}{2}\right)^2$

$= 25 - \frac{25}{4}\pi$

$= (25 - 6.25\pi)$ sq. cm.

12. Here, $50^2 = 40^2 + 30^2$

$\therefore$ Two triangles, *i.e.*, ΔABC and ΔADC are right angled triangle.

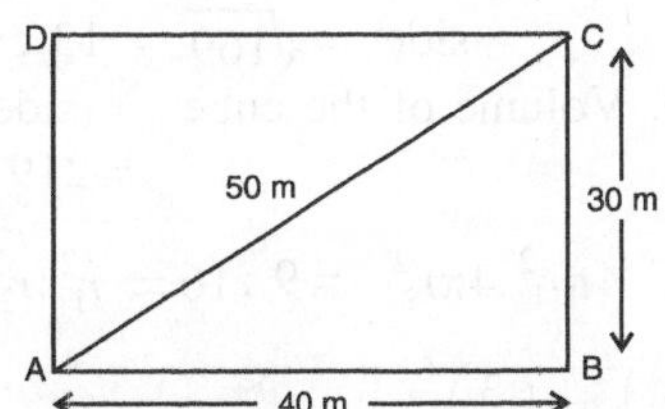

$\therefore$ Area of parallelogram ABCD $= 2 \times$ Area of Δ ABC $= 2 \times \frac{1}{2} \times 40 \times 30 = 1200$ sq.m.

14. Area of circle $= \frac{22}{7} \times (10)^2 = \frac{2200}{7}$ cm$^2 \approx 314$ cm^2

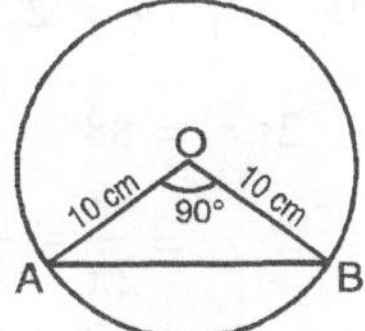

Area of minor segment

$$= \frac{90}{360} \times \frac{22}{7} \times 10^2 - \frac{1}{2} \times 10 \times 10$$

$$= \frac{550}{7} - 50$$

$$= \frac{200}{7} = 28.57 \approx 28.5 \text{ cm}^2$$

16. Here, $l - b = 23$ ...(i)
and also, $2(l + b) = 206 \quad \therefore l + b = 103$ ...(ii)

Hence, $l = \frac{1}{2}(103 + 23) = 63$ m;

$b = \frac{1}{2}(103 - 23) = 40$ m

Since, $A = 63 \times 40 = 2520 \text{ m}^2$

17. Radius of the circular field

$$= \sqrt{\frac{18634 \times 7}{22}} = \sqrt{847 \times 7} = 77 \text{ m}$$

Circumference $= 2 \times \frac{22}{7} \times 77 = 484 \text{ m}^2$

Required cost = 484 × ₹ 365 = ₹ 1,76,660

18. Volume of the cuboid

$= l \times b \times h$
$= 4 \times 3 \times 2 = 24$ cu. cm.

19. Here, $6 \times (\text{side})^2 = 1014$

$\Rightarrow (\text{side})^2 = \frac{1014}{6} = 169$

$\therefore$ side $= \sqrt{169} = 13$ cm

Hence, Volume of the cube $= (\text{side})^3 = (13)^3$
$= 2197$ cu cm.

20. Here, $4\pi r_1^2 : 4\pi r_2^2 = 9 : 16 \Rightarrow r_1^2 : r_2^2 = 9 : 16$

$$\Rightarrow \left(\frac{r_1}{r_2}\right)^2 = \left(\frac{3}{4}\right)^2 \qquad \Rightarrow r_1 : r_2 = 3 : 4$$

$$\Rightarrow \frac{r_1^3}{r_2^3} = \frac{27}{64} \qquad \Rightarrow r_1^3 : r_2^3 = 27 : 64.$$

Therefore, ratio of their volumes

$$= \frac{4}{3}\pi r_1^3 : \frac{4}{3}\pi r_2^3 = r_1^3 : r_2^3 = 27 : 64$$

21. Here, $2\pi r = 88$

$$\therefore \quad r = \frac{88}{2\pi} = \frac{88 \times 7}{2 \times 22} = 14 \text{ cm}$$

Since, volume of the cylinder

$$= \pi r^2 h = \frac{22}{7} \times (14)^2 \times 42$$
$$= 22 \times 2 \times 14 \times 42$$
$$= 25872 \text{ cu cm.}$$

23. Surface area of the roller $= 2\pi rh$

$$= 2 \times \frac{22}{7} \times 1.2 \times 1.68$$
$$= 12.672 \text{ sq. m}$$

In one complete revolution, the roller covers 12.672 sq. m.

$\therefore$ It will cover in 1000 revolutions
$= 12.672 \times 1000$
$= 12672$ sq. m

Hence, area of the field
$= 12672$ sq. m.

24. Percentage increase in the surface area of the cube

$$= \left(x + y + \frac{xy}{100}\right)\%$$

$$= \left(10 + 10 + \frac{10 \times 10}{100}\right)\%$$

$$= 21\%.$$

26. Change in the curved surface of the cylinder

$$= \left(-25 + 10 + \frac{-25 \times 10}{100}\right)\%$$

$$= (-15 - 2.5)\% = -17.5\%$$

$\therefore$ Curved surface of the cylinder will be decreased by 17.5%.

28. Here, $4/3\pi r^3 = \frac{1}{3}\pi r^2 h$

$\Rightarrow 4r = h$

$\Rightarrow 2d = h$

$\therefore \frac{d}{h} = \frac{1}{2}$

Hence, required ratio = 1 : 2

29. Required ratio $= \frac{\frac{2}{3}\pi r^3}{\frac{4}{3}\pi r^3} = \frac{8}{2} = \frac{4}{1} = 4:1$

❑❑❑

15 DATA INTERPRETATION (TABLE)

Data Interpretation is one of the easy sections of Bank PO Examination. It is an extension of Mathematical skills and accuracy. Data Interpretation is nothing but drawing conclusions and inferences from a comprehensive data presented numerically in tabular form by means of an illustration, viz., Graph, Pie chart etc. Sound knowledge of quantitative techniques is a prerequisite for good performance in this section. The thumb rule, as in the case of reading comprehension—read the passage rapidly but carefully and comprehend it at the same time—applies in this section too. However, unlike reading comprehension where one can afford to skip irrelevant portions of the passage, here even the minutest of details cannot be overlooked.

A good grasp of basic geometric as well as arithmetic formulae is must to score high in this section. Since such questions may require a fair amount of calculations, one should be able to multiply and divide quickly using short-cut methods. Familiarity with graphical representation of data like venn diagrams, graphs, pie diagrams, histogram, polygon etc. should be thorough. Once the data are grasped well, questions based on tables and graphs take little time.

In some Bank PO Exams data are presented in more than one table or graph. The aim is to test not only quantitative skills but also relative, comparative and analytical ability. The crux of the matter is to find a relationship between the two tables or graphs before attempting the questions.

EXERCISE

Directions (Qs. 1 to 5): *Study the following tables carefully and answer the questions given below:*

Number of Males and Females staying in various societies

Societies	Males	Females
A	250	350
B	400	150
C	300	275
D	280	300
E	180	250
F	325	300

Percentage of Children (Males and Females) in the societies

Societies	Children	Males	Females
A	25%	40%	60%
B	40%	75%	25%
C	16%	25%	75%
D	25%	80%	20%
E	40%	50%	50%
F	24%	46%	54%

1. What is the respective ratio of the number of the adult females to the total number of female children staying in all the societies together?

(*a*) 82 : 243
(*b*) 243 : 82
(*c*) 71 : 112
(*d*) 112 : 71
(*e*) None of these

2. What is the respective ratio of the total number of adult males in the societies A and B together to the total number of adult males in the societies E and F together?

(*a*) 14 : 17
(*b*) 17 : 14
(*c*) 75 : 79
(*d*) 79 : 75
(*e*) None of these

3. What is the difference between the number of male children in society B and the number of male children in society F?
(a) 14 (b) 26
(c) 84 (d) 96
(e) None of these

4. What is the total number of female children staying in all the societies together?
(a) 314 (b) 343
(c) 410 (d) 433
(e) None of these

5. What is the total number of members staying in all the societies together?
(a) 3000 (b) 3360
(c) 4100 (d) 4289
(e) None of these

Directions (Qs. 6 to 10): *Study the following table carefully and answer the questions given below:*

Quantity of Rice produced by Various states over the years (Quantity in Tonnes)

States ↓	YEARS					
	2003	**2004**	**2005**	**2006**	**2007**	**2008**
A	1500	1480	1620	1700	1540	1650
B	1250	1190	1400	1450	1320	1380
C	1160	1190	1310	1300	1340	1360
D	1520	1500	1480	1590	1630	1580
E	1440	1350	1430	1280	1380	1400
F	1600	1620	1510	1610	1580	1590

6. In which state has the production of rice increased continuously over the years?
(a) B (b) C
(c) D (d) A
(e) None of these

7. Which state produced the lowest quantity of rice over the years?
(a) A (b) C
(c) D (d) E
(e) None of these

8. Rice produced by State C in the year 2006 is approximately what per cent of the rice produced by State A in the same year?
(a) 69% (b) 72%
(c) 76% (d) 82%
(e) None of these

9. In which year was the production of rice the highest in all the states together?
(a) 2005 (b) 2006
(c) 2007 (d) 2008
(e) None of these

10. What is the respective ratio of the average quantity of rice produced by State D to the average quantity of rice produced by State F over the years?
(a) 69 : 79 (b) 138 : 155
(c) 276 : 317 (d) 310 : 317
(e) None of these

ANSWERS

1	2	3	4	5	6	7	8	9	10
(b)	(b)	(d)	(c)	(b)	(e)	(b)	(c)	(d)	(d)

SOME SELECTED EXPLANATORY ANSWERS

1. **In society A:**
Number of children

$$= \frac{25}{100} \times (250 + 350) = \frac{1}{4} \times 600 = 150$$

Number of male children $= \frac{40}{100} \times 150 = 60$

Number of female children $= 150 - 60 = 90$

In society B:

Number of children

$= \frac{40}{100} \times (400 + 150) = \frac{2}{5} \times 550 = 220$

Number of male children $= \frac{75}{100} \times 220 = 165$

Number of female children

$= 220 - 165 = 55$

In society C:

Number of children $= \frac{16}{100} \times (300 + 275)$

$= \frac{4}{25} \times 575 = 92$

Number of male children $= \frac{25}{100} \times 92 = 23$

Number of female children $= 92 - 23 = 69$

In society D:

Number of children $= \frac{25}{100} \times (280 + 300)$

$= \frac{1}{4} \times 580 = 145$

Number of male children $= \frac{80}{100} \times 145 = 116$

Number of female children

$= 145 - 116 = 29$

In society E:

Number of children

$= \frac{40}{100} \times (180 + 250) = \frac{2}{5} \times 430 = 172$

Number of male children $= \frac{50}{100} \times 172 = 86$

Number of female children $= 172 - 86 = 86$

In society F :

Number of children

$= \frac{24}{100} \times (325 + 300) = \frac{6}{25} \times 625 = 150$

Number of male children $= \frac{46}{100} \times 150 = 69$

Number of female children $= 150 - 69 = 81$

Hence, total number of female children $= 90 + 55 + 69 + 29 + 86 + 81 = 410$

Total number of adult females

$= (350 + 150 + 275 + 300 + 250 + 300) - 410$

$= 1625 - 410 = 1215$

Hence, required ratio $= 1215 : 410 = 243 : 82$

2. Total number of adult males in the society A and B $= (250 + 400) - (60 + 165)$

(As shown in solution : 1)

$= 650 - 225 = 425$

Total number of adult males in the society E and F $= (180 + 325) - (86 + 69)$

(As shown in solution : 1)

$= 505 - 155 = 350$

Hence, required ratio $= 425 : 350 = 17 : 14$

3. Male children in society B = 165

Male children in society F = 69

(As shown in solution : 1)

Hence, their difference $= 165 - 69 = 96$

4. Total number of female children = 410

(As shown in solution : 1)

5. Number of members

$= (250 + 350) + (400 + 150) + (300 + 275) + (280 + 300) + (180 + 250) + (325 + 300)$

$= 600 + 550 + 575 + 580 + 430 + 625$

$= 3360$

6. It is clear from the table that none of the state has the production of rice increased continuously over the years.

7. Production of rice by different states over the years:

A → 1500 + 1480 + 1620 + 1700 + 1540 + 1650 = 9490 tonnes

B → 1250 + 1190 + 1400 + 1450 + 1320 + 1380 = 7990 tonnes

C → 1160 + 1190 + 1310 + 1300 + 1340 + 1360 = 7660 tonnes

D → 1520 + 1500 + 1480 + 1590 + 1630 + 1580 = 9300 tonnes

E → 1440 + 1350 + 1430 + 1280 + 1380 + 1400 = 8280 tonnes

F → 1600 + 1620 + 1510 + 1610 + 1580 + 1590 = 9510 tonnes

Hence, the State C produced the lowest quantity of rice.

8. Required percentage $= \frac{1300}{1700} \times 100$

$= 76.47\% \approx 76\%$

9. Production of rice in different years by all states together:

2003 → 1500 + 1250 + 1160 + 1520 + 1440 + 1600 = 8470 tonnes

2004 → 1480 + 1190 + 1190 + 1500 + 1350 + 1620 = 8330 tonnes

2005 → 1620 + 1400 + 1310 + 1480 + 1430 + 1510 = 8750 tonnes

2006 → 1700 + 1450 + 1300 + 1590 + 1280 + 1610 = 8930 tonnes

2007 → 1540 + 1320 + 1340 + 1630 + 1380 + 1580 = 8790 tonnes

2008 → 1650 + 1380 + 1360 + 1580 + 1400 + 1590 = 8960 tonnes

Hence, in year 2008 the production of rice was the highest.

10. Average quantity of rice produced by State D

$= \frac{9300}{6} = 1550$ tonnes

(As shown in soluton : 7)

Average quantity of rice produced by State F

$= \frac{9510}{6} = 1585$ tonnes

(As shown in soluton : 7)

Hence, required ratio

$= 1550 : 1585$

$= 310 : 317$

❑❑❑

16 DATA INTERPRETATION (BAR GRAPHS AND PIE CHART)

BAR GRAPHS

A bar graph may be either horizontal or vertical. The important point to note about bar graphs is their bar length or height; the greater their length or height, the greater their value. Bar graphs usually present categorical and numeric variables grouped in class intervals. They consist of an axis and a series or labelled horizontal or vertical bars. The bars depict frequencies of different values of a variable or simply the different values or simply the different values themselves. The numbers on the *x*-axis of a bar graph or the *y*-axis of a column graph are called the scale.

PIE CHARTS

A pie chart is a way of summarising a set of categorical data or displaying the different values of a given variable (*e.g.*, percentage distribution). This type of chart is a circle divided into series of segments. Each segment represents a particular category.

EXERCISE

Directions : *Shown below is the multiple bar diagram depicting the changes in the student's strength of a college in four faculties from* 2000-01 *to* 2002-03. (*Scale* 1 *cm* = 100)

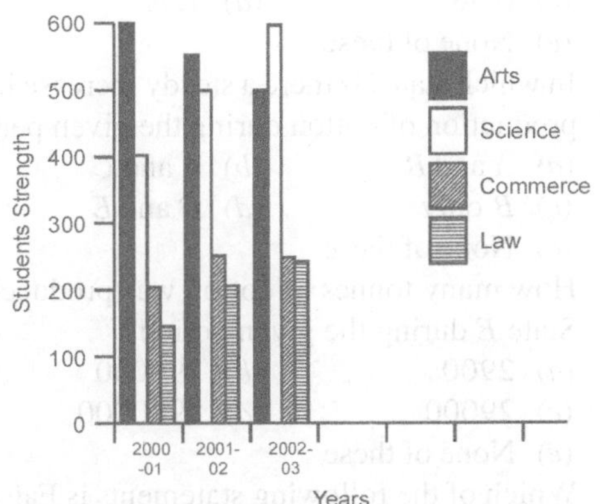

Study the above multiple bar chart and mark a tick against the correct answer in each of the following questions.

1. The percentage of students in science faculty in 2000-01 was :
   (*a*) 26.9 % (*b*) 27.8 %
   (*c*) 29.6 % (*d*) 30.2 %
   (*e*) None of the above
2. The percentage of students in law faculty in 2002-03 was :
   (*a*) 18.5 % (*b*) 15.6 %
   (*c*) 16.7 % (*d*) 14.8 %
   (*e*) None of the above
3. How many times the total strength was of the strength of commerce students in 2001-02?
   (*a*) 3 times (*b*) 4 times
   (*c*) 5 times (*d*) 6 times
   (*e*) None of the above
4. During which year the strength of arts faculty was minimum?
   (*a*) 2000-01 (*b*) 2001-02
   (*c*) 2002-03 (*d*) 2003-04
   (*e*) None of the above
5. How much per cent was the increase in science students in 2002-03 over 2000-01?
   (*a*) 50% (*b*) 150%
   (*c*) $66\frac{2}{3}$ % (*d*) 75%
   (*e*) None of the above
6. A regular decrease in students' strength was in the faculty of
   (*a*) Arts (*b*) Science
   (*c*) Commerce (*d*) Law
   (*e*) None of the above

ANSWERS

1	2	3	4	5	6
(*c*)	(*b*)	(*d*)	(*c*)	(*a*)	(*a*)

SOME SELECTED EXPLANATORY ANSWERS

1. Total number of students in 2000-01
= (600 + 400 + 200 + 150) = 1350
Number of science students in 2000-01 was 400.
Percentage of science students in 2000-01

$$= \left[\frac{400}{1350} \times 100\right] \% = 29.6\%$$

So, answer (*c*) is correct.

2. Total number of students in 2002-03
= (500 + 600 + 250 + 250)= 1600
Number of law students in 2002-03 is 250.
Percentage of law students in 2002-03

$$= \left[\frac{250}{1600} \times 100\right] \% = 15.6\ \%$$

So, answer (*b*) is correct.

3. Total strength in 2001-02
= (550 + 500 + 250 + 200) = 1500

$$\text{So, } \frac{\text{Total strength}}{\text{Strength of commerce students}} = \frac{1500}{250} = 6.$$

4. A slight look indicates that the strength in arts faculty in 2000-01, 2001-02 and 2002-03 was 600, 550 and 500 respectively. So, it was minimum in 2002-03.
So, answer (*c*) is correct.

5. Number of science students in 2000 - 01 was 400.
Number of science students in 2002 - 03 was 600.

$$\text{Percentage increase} = \left(\frac{200}{400} \times 100\right) \% = 50\%$$

Answer (*a*) is correct.

EXERCISE

Directions (Qs. 1 to 5) : *Examine the following graph carefully and answer the questions given below it.*

Production of Cotton bales of 100 kg. each in lacs in States during 2005-2006, 2006-2007, 2007-2008

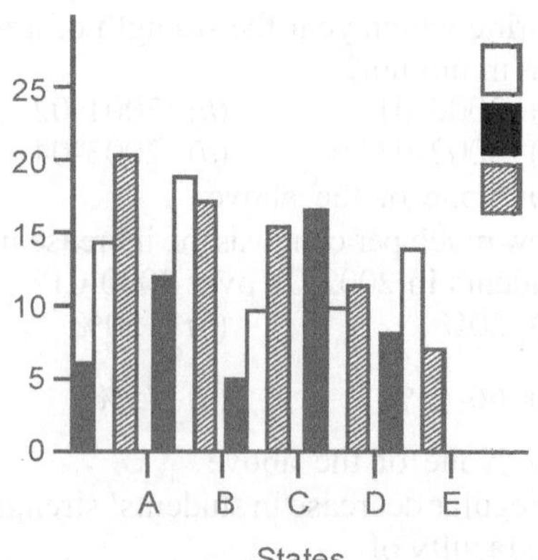

1. The production of State *D* in 2007-2008 is how many times its production in 2006-2007?

(*a*) 1.33 (*b*) 0.75
(*c*) 0.56 (*d*) 1.77
(*e*) None of these

2. In which states is there a steady increase in the production of cotton during the given period?

(*a*) *A* and *B* (*b*) *A* and *C*
(*c*) *B* only (*d*) *D* and *E*
(*e*) None of these

3. How many tonnes of cotton was produced by State *E* during the given period?

(*a*) 2900 (*b*) 290000
(*c*) 29000 (*d*) 2900000
(*e*) None of these

4. Which of the following statements is False?

(*a*) States *A* & *E* showed the same production in 2006-2007.
(*b*) There was no improvement in the production of cotton in State *B* during.
(*c*) State *A* has produced maximum cotton during the given period.
(*d*) Production of states *C* and *D* together is equal to that of State *B* during 2006-2007.
(*e*) None of these

Directions (Qs. 5 to 9): *Study the graph carefully to answer the questions that follow:*

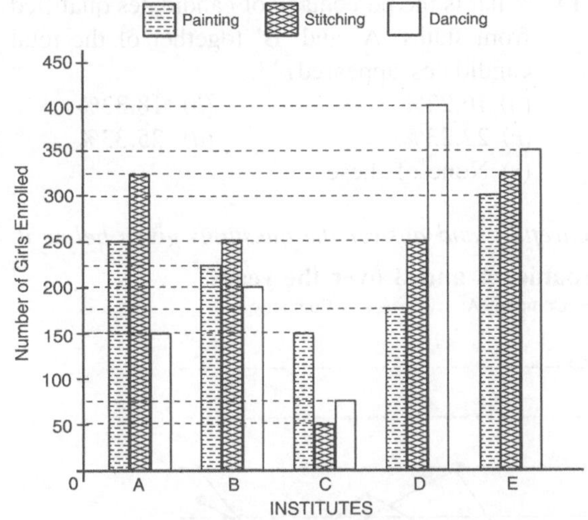

5. What is the respective ratio of total number of girls enrolled in Painting in the institutes A and C together to those enrolled in Stiching in the institutes D and E together?

(*a*) 5 : 4 (*b*) 5 : 7
(*c*) 9 : 8 (*d*) 16 : 23
(*e*) None of these

6. What is the respective ratio of total number of girls enrolled in Painting, Stiching and Dancing from all the Institutes together?

(*a*) 43 : 47 : 48 (*b*) 44 : 47 : 48
(*c*) 44 : 48 : 47 (*d*) 47 : 48 : 44
(*e*) None of these

7. What is the total number of girls enrolled in Painting from all the Institutes together?

(*a*) 1100 (*b*) 1150
(*c*) 1200 (*d*) 1275
(*e*) None of these

8. Number of girls enrolled in Stitching in Institute B forms approximately what per cent of the total number of girls enrolled in Stitching in the Institutes together?

(*a*) 21%
(*b*) 29%
(*c*) 33%
(*d*) 37%
(*e*) None of these

9. Number of girls enrolled in Dancing in Institute A forms what per cent of total number of girls enrolled in all the Hobby classes together in that Institute?

(*a*) 17.76% (*b*) 20.69%
(*c*) 31.23% (*d*) 33.97%
(*e*) None of these

Directions (Qs. 10 to 14): *Study the following graph and table carefully and answer the questions given below it:*

Distribution of Candidates appeared in a competitive examination from seven states Total Candidates appeared = 3 lakh

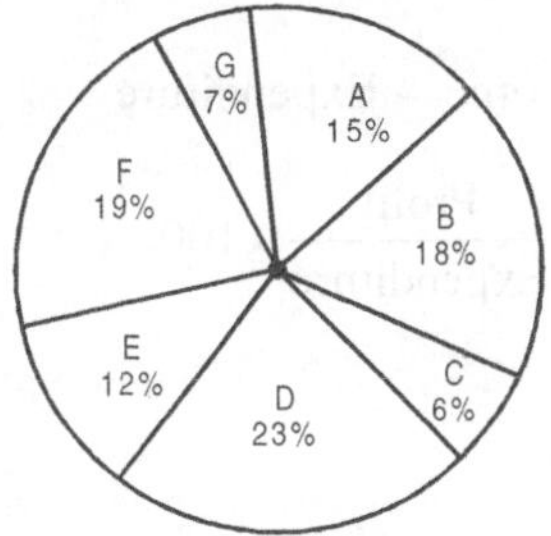

State-wise percentage and ratio of male and female qualified candidates

S		
A	49	4 : 5
B	61	6 : 4
C	54	7 : 8
D	45	3 : 2
E	65	7 : 6
F	57	11 : 8
G	48	9 : 11

10. What is the number of male candidates qualified from State 'G'?

(*a*) 4536 (*b*) 4568
(*c*) 5454 (*d*) 5544
(*e*) None of these

11. Which of the following pair of states have equal number of qualified male candidates?

(*a*) A and E (*b*) B and F
(*c*) C and E (*d*) C and G
(*e*) None of these

12. What is the total number of candidates qualified from states E and D together?
(a) 45540 (b) 54410
(c) 54450 (d) 54540
(e) None of these

13. What is the total number of female candidates qualified from states A and B together?
(a) 24526 (b) 25426
(c) 26426 (d) 26526
(e) None of these

14. What is the percentage of candidates qualified from states 'A' and 'B' together of the total candidates appeared?
(a) 16.23% (b) 18.33%
(c) 22.23% (d) 25.33%
(e) None of these

Directions (Qs. 15 to 19): *Study the following graph carefully and answer the questions given below it.*

Per cent profit earned by two Companies A and B over the years

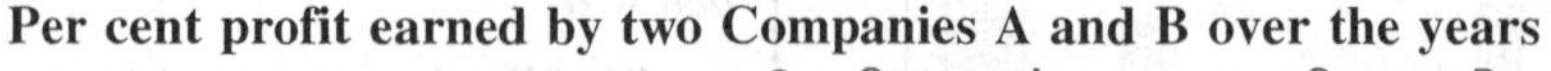

Profit = Income – Expenditure

$$\text{Profit\%} = \frac{\text{Profit}}{\text{Expenditure}} \times 100$$

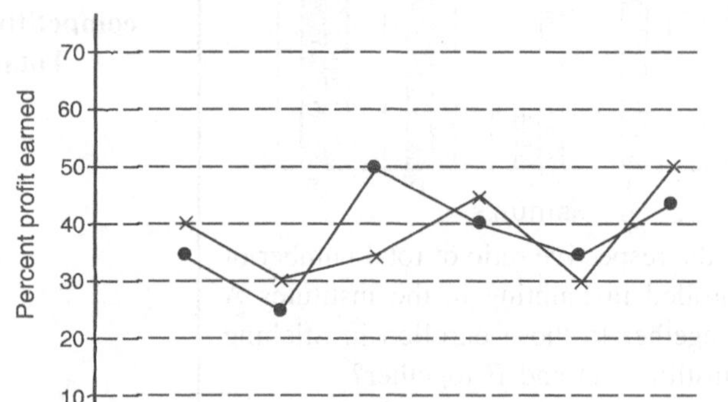

15. If the income of company A in 2005 was ₹ 1,42,500, what was its expenditure in that year?
(a) ₹ 95000 (b) ₹ 95500
(c) ₹ 99,500 (d) ₹ 1,05,000
(e) None of these

16. If the expenditure of Company 'A' in 2004 was ₹ 75 lakhs and income of Company A in 2004 was equal to its expenditure in 2005. What was the total income (in lakhs ₹) of the Company A in 2004 and 2005 together?
(a) 131.25 (b) 175
(c) 218.75 (d) 234.37
(e) None of these

17. Total expenditure of companies A & B together in 2008 was ₹ 13.5 lakhs. What was the total income of the two companies (in lakh Rs.) in that year?
(a) 19.75
(b) 20.25
(c) 19.575
(d) Cannot be determined
(e) None of these

18. Expenditure of company 'B' in 2006 was 90% of its expenditure in 2005. Income of Company 'B' in 2006 was what per cent of its income in 2005?
(a) $96\frac{2}{3}$ (b) $99\frac{1}{3}$
(c) 121.5 (d) 130.5
(e) None of these

19. Expenditure of company 'B' in years 2003 and 2004 were in the ratio of 5 : 7 respectively. What was the respective ratio of their incomes?
(a) 8 : 13 (b) 10 : 13
(c) 11 : 14 (d) 13 ; 14
(e) None of these

ANSWERS

1	2	3	4	5	6	7	8	9	10
(b)	(b)	(b)	(c)	(d)	(c)	(a)	(a)	(b)	(a)
11	**12**	**13**	**14**	**15**	**16**	**17**	**18**	**19**	
(d)	(c)	(b)	(b)	(a)	(d)	(d)	(a)	(b)	

SOME SELECTED EXPLANATORY ANSWERS

1. Suppose, it is x times

$$x = \frac{12}{9} = \frac{4}{3}$$

2. It is clear by graph.

3. 8 + 14 + 7 = 29 lakhs

$$\text{Its weight} = \frac{29 \times 100000}{1000} \times 100$$

4. State B = 48 lakh bales State A = 41 lakh bales

5. Total number of girls enrolled in Painting in the Institutes A and C

= 250 + 150 = 400

Total number of girls enrolled in Stitching in the Institutes D and E

= 250 + 325 = 575

Required ratio = 400 : 575 = 16 : 23

6. Total number of girls enrolled in Painting

= 250 + 225 + 150 + 175 + 300 = 1100

Total number of girls enrolled in Stitching

= 325 + 250 + 50 + 250 + 325 = 1200

Total number of girls enrolled in Dancing

= 150 + 200 + 75 + 400 + 350 = 1175

Hence, required ratio

= 1100 : 1200 : 1175 = 44 : 48 : 47

7. Total number of girls enrolled in Painting

= 250 + 225 + 150 + 175 + 300 = 1100

8. Number of girls enrolled in Stitching in Institute B = 250

Total number of girls enrolled in Stitching in all the Institutions

= 325 + 250 + 50 + 250 + 325 = 1200

Hence, required percentage

$$= \frac{250}{1200} \times 100 = 20.83 \approx 21\%$$

9. Number of girls enrolled in Dancing in Institute A = 150

Total number of girls enrolled in all the Hobby classes together in Institute A

= 250 + 325 + 150 = 725

Hence, required percentage

$$= \frac{150}{725} \times 100 = 20.69\%$$

10. Number of candidates qualified from State

$$G = \frac{48}{100} \times \frac{7}{100} \times 3,00,000 = 10080$$

Number of male candidates qualified from State

$$G = \frac{9}{9+11} \times 10080 = \frac{9}{20} \times 10080$$

= 4536

11. Qualified Male Candidates from different states:

$$A \rightarrow \frac{4}{9} \times \frac{49}{100} \times \frac{15}{100} \times 300000 = 9800$$

$$B \rightarrow \frac{6}{10} \times \frac{61}{100} \times \frac{18}{100} \times 300000 = 19764$$

$$C \rightarrow \frac{7}{15} \times \frac{54}{100} \times \frac{6}{100} \times 300000 = 4536$$

$$D \rightarrow \frac{3}{5} \times \frac{45}{100} \times \frac{23}{100} \times 300000 = 18630$$

$$E \rightarrow \times \frac{7}{13} \times \frac{65}{100} \times \frac{12}{100} \times 300000 = 12600$$

$$F \rightarrow \frac{11}{19} \times \frac{57}{100} \times \frac{19}{100} \times 300000 = 18810$$

$$G \rightarrow \frac{9}{20} \times \frac{48}{100} \times \frac{7}{100} \times 300000 = 4536$$

Hence, states C and G have equal number of qualified male candidates.

12. Required number of candidates

$$= \frac{65}{100} \times \frac{12}{100} \times 300000 + \frac{45}{100} \times \frac{23}{100} \times 300000$$

$= 23400 + 31050 = 54450$

13. Required number of female candidates

$$= \frac{5}{9} \times \frac{49}{100} \times \frac{15}{100} \times 300000 + \frac{4}{10} \times \frac{61}{100} \times \frac{18}{100} \times 300000$$

$= 12250 + 13176 = 25426$

14. Number of candidates qualified from states A and B together

$$= \frac{49}{100} \times \frac{15}{100} \times 300000 + \frac{61}{100} \times \frac{18}{100} \times 300000$$

$= 22050 + 32940 = 54990$

Required percentage $= \frac{54990}{300000} \times 100$

$= 18.33\%$

15. Let expenditure of Company A in 2005 = ₹ x; then

$$x + \frac{50}{100} \times x = 1{,}42{,}500 \quad \Rightarrow \frac{3x}{2} = 1{,}42{,}500$$

$$\therefore x = \frac{2 \times 1{,}42{,}500}{3} = ₹\ 95000$$

16. In 2004, expenditure of Company 'A' = ₹ 75 lakh

Since, income of the Company 'A' in 2004

$$= 75 + \frac{25}{100} \times 75 = ₹\ 93.75 \text{ lakhs}$$

Now, expenditure of the Company 'A' in 2005 = ₹ 93.75 lakhs

Since, income of the Company A in 2005

$$= 93.75 + \frac{50}{100} \times 93.75$$

= ₹ 140.62 lakhs

Hence, total income for both the years = 93.75 + 140.62 = ₹ 234.37 lakhs

17. Here total expenditure of both companies are given while their individual expenditures are needed to determine their incomes. So, the total income of the two companies cannot be determined by the given datas.

18. Let expenditure of Company B in 2005 = ₹ x; then

$$I_1 \text{ (Income)} = x + \frac{35}{100} x = ₹\ \frac{27x}{20}$$

Since, expenditure of Company B in 2006

$$= \frac{90}{100} \times ₹\ x = ₹ \frac{9x}{10}, \text{ then}$$

$$I_2 \text{ (Income)} = \frac{9x}{10} + \frac{45}{100} \times \frac{9x}{10}$$

$$= \frac{9x}{10} + \frac{81x}{200} = ₹ \frac{261x}{200}$$

Hence, required percentage

$$= \frac{261x/200}{27x/20} \times 100 = \frac{290}{3} = 96\frac{2}{3}\%$$

19. Let expenditures of Company B in 2003 and 2004 are ₹ $5x$ and ₹ $7x$ respectively; then their income in 2003, I_1

$$= 5x + \frac{40}{100} \times 5x = ₹\ 7x$$

Also their income in 2004,

$$I_2 = 7x + \frac{30}{100} \times 7x = ₹ \frac{91x}{10}$$

Hence, the required ratio $= 7x : \frac{91x}{10}$

$= 10 : 13.$

❑❑❑

17 PERMUTATION & COMBINATION

IMPORTANT RESULTS

(*i*) Number of permutations of n distinct things taken r at a time, $0 \le r \le n$

$= n(n-1)(n-2)\ldots(n-r+1)$

$= n!/(n-r)! = {}^nP_r$.

This is equivalent to filling r places by r objects taking from n distinct objects.

(*ii*) The number of permutations of n distinct objects taken all at a time $= n!$

(*iii*) The number of combinations of n objects taken r at a time, $0 \le r \le n = {}^nC_r$

$$= \frac{n!}{(n-r)!.r!}.$$

(*iv*) The number of permutations of n dissimilar things taken r at a time when each thing can be repeated any number of times $= n^r$.

(*v*) The number of combinations of n distinct objects taken r at a time when any object may be repeated any number of times

$=$ coefficient of x^r in $(1 + x + x^2 + \ldots + x^r)^n$

$=$ coefficient of x^r in $(1-x)^n = {}^{n+r-1}C_r$.

(*vi*) Number of combinations of n distinct things taken r at a time when p particular things always occur $= {}^{(n-p)}C_{(r-p)}$.

(*vii*) The number of permutations of n distinct things taken r at a time when p particular things always occur $= {}^{(n-p)}C_{(r-p)}.r!$.

(*viii*) Number of combinations of n distinct things taken r at a time when p particular things never occur $= {}^{(n-p)}C_r$.

(*ix*) Number of permutations (arrangements) of n distinct things taken r at a time when p particular things never occur $= {}^{(n-p)}C_r.r!$.

(*x*) Number of permutations of n things, taken all at a time when p_1 are alike of one kind, p_2 are alike of second kind, ..., p_r of them are alike of the rth kind $p_1 + p_2 + \ldots + p_r \le n$, and remaining things are all different $= n!/\{p_1!p_2! \ldots p_r!\}$.

(*xi*) If $3n$ things are to be divided into three equal groups, then the number of ways

$$= \frac{(3n)!}{n!.n!.n!.3!}.$$

(*xii*) If $3n$ things are to be divided equally between 3 persons (*i.e.*, division of $3n$ things into 3 equal groups with permutation of groups) then the number of ways

$$= \frac{(3n)!}{(n!)^3}.$$

(*xiii*) Greatest value of ${}^nC_r$

${}^nC_r$ is greatest when

$r = n/2$ if n is even

$r = (n-1)/2$ or $(n+1)/2$ if n is odd.

(*xiv*) ${}^nC_r = {}^nC_{n-r}$.

(*xv*) ${}^nC_r + {}^nC_{r+1} = {}^{n+1}C_{r+1}$.

(*xvi*) ${}^nC_r = {}^nC_s$

$\Rightarrow r = s$ or $r + s = n$.

(*xvii*) The number of circular permutations of n different things taken all at a time $= (n-1)!$

(*xviii*) The number of arrangements of n persons on a round table $= (n-1)!$.

(*xix*) The number of arrangements of n flowers to make a garland $= \frac{1}{2}(n-1)!$.

EXAMPLES

Example 1: In how many different ways can the letters of the word 'PRIDE' be arranged ?

Solution: Required number of arrangements

$= {}^5P_5 = 5! = 120$

Example 2: In how many different ways can the letters of the word 'PRAISE' be arranged ?

Solution: Required number of ways

$= {}^6P_6 = 6! = 720$

Example 3: On a shelf there are 4 books on Economics, 3 books on Management and 4 books on Statistics. In how many different ways can the books be arranged so that the books on Economics are kept together ?

Solution: Required number of different ways

$= {}^8P_8 \times {}^4P_4 = \underline{|8} \times \underline{|4}$

$= 40320 \times 24$

$= 967680$

Example 4: In how many different ways can the letters of the word 'PRETTY' be arranged?

Solution: Required ways $= \frac{\underline{|6}}{\underline{|2}} = 360$

Example 5: In how many different ways can the letters of the word 'PEANUT' be arranged ?

Solution: Required ways $= {}^6P_6 = \underline{|6}$

$= 6 \times 5 \times 4 \times 3 \times 2 \times 1 = 720.$

EXERCISE

1. How many seven digit numbers can be made from the number 3428651, using each digit only once?
   (a) 49 (b) 180
   (c) 5040 (d) 2520
   (e) None of these
2. How many words can be formed from the letters of the word 'DIRECTOR' so that the vowels are always together?
   (a) 2106 (b) 1206
   (c) 360 (d) 2160
   (e) None of these
3. In how many ways a committee of 5 members can be selected from 6 men and 5 ladies, consisting of 3 men and 2 ladies?
   (a) 120 (b) 220
   (c) 200 (d) 320
   (e) None of these
4. In how many ways can the letters of the word 'APPLE' be arranged?
   (a) 720
   (b) 120
   (c) 60
   (d) 180
   (e) None of these
5. How many words can be formed by using all the letters of the word. 'ALLAHABAD'?
   (a) 3780 (b) 1890
   (c) 7560 (d) 2520
   (e) None of these
6. How many words can be formed from the letters of the word 'SIGNATURE' so that the vowels always come together?
   (a) 720 (b) 1440
   (c) 2880 (d) 17280
   (e) None of these
7. In how many different ways can the letters of the word 'BANKING' be arranged so that the vowels always come together?
   (a) 120 (b) 240
   (c) 360 (d) 720
   (e) None of these
8. In how many ways can a group of 5 men and 2 women be made out of a total of 7 men and 3 women?
   (a) 63
   (b) 90
   (c) 126
   (d) 45
   (e) None of these

9. In a group of 6 boys and 4 girls, four children are to be selected. In how many different ways can they be selected such that at least one boy should be there?
(a) 159 *(b)* 194
(c) 205 *(d)* 209
(e) None of these

10. A box contains 2 white balls, 3 black balls and 4 red balls. In how many ways can 3 balls be drawn from the box, if at least one black ball is to be included in the draw?
(a) 32 *(b)* 48
(c) 64 *(d)* 96
(e) None of these

11. In how many ways can a team of 3 boys and 3 girls be selected from 5 boys and 4 girls?
(a) 14 *(b)* 40
(c) 18 *(d)* 140
(e) None of these

12. The number of ways of selecting 9 balls from 6 red, 5 white and 5 blue if each selection consists of 3 balls of each colour is :
(a) 1200 *(b)* 20000
(c) 2200 *(d)* 2000
(e) None of these

13. In how many ways can we select 4 red balls and 3 blue balls from 8 red balls and 9 blue balls?
(a) 8550 *(b)* 5850
(c) 5880 *(d)* 8580
(e) None of these

14. Find the number of diagonals of a decagon
(a) 45 *(b)* 35
(c) 55 *(d)* 25
(e) None of these

15. In how many ways can a student choose a programme of 5 courses if 9 courses are available and 2 specific courses are compulsary for every student?
(a) 53 *(b)* 14
(c) 35 *(d)* 28
(e) None of these

16. Seven different lecturers are to deliver lectures in seven periods of a class on a particular day. A, B and C are three of the lecturers. The number of ways in which a routine for the day can be made such that A delivers his lecture before B, and B before C, is
(a) 420 *(b)* 120
(c) 210 *(d)* 840
(e) None of these

17. The number of words that can be made by rearranging the letters of the word APURBA so that vowels and consonants alternate is
(a) 18 *(b)* 35
(c) 36 *(d)* 24
(e) None of these

18. The number of ways in which the letters of the word ARTICLE can be rearranged so that the even places are always occupied by consonants is
(a) 576 *(b)* ${}^4C_3 \times (4!)$
(c) $2(4!)$ *(d)* 288
(e) None of these

19. The number of ways in which a couple can sit around a table with 6 guests if the couple take consecutive seats is
(a) 1440 *(b)* 720
(c) 5040 *(d)* 2880
(e) None of these

20. The number of ways in which 20 different pearls of two colours can be set alternately on a necklace, there being 10 pearls of each colour, is
(a) $9! \times 10!$ *(b)* $5(9!)^2$
(c) $(9!)^2$ *(d)* $(18!)^2$
(e) None of these

21. There are 4 mangoes, 3 apples, 2 oranges and 1 each of 3 other varieties of fruits. The number of ways of selecting at least one fruit of each kind is
(a) 10! *(b)* 9!
(c) 4! *(d)* 5!
(e) None of these

22. The number of ways in which 6 different balls can be put in two boxes of different sizes so that no box remains empty is
(a) 62 *(b)* 64
(c) 36 *(d)* 60
(e) None of these

23. The number of arrangements of the letters of the word BHARAT taking 3 at a time is
(a) 72 *(b)* 120
(c) 14 *(d)* 48
(e) None of these

24. Find the number of different permutations of the letters of the word BANANA.
(a) 16 *(b)* 60
(c) 61 *(d)* 36
(e) None of these

25. A box contains two white balls, three black balls and four red balls. In how many ways can three balls be drawn from the box if at least one black ball is to be included in the draw?
(a) 16 *(b)* 32
(c) 64 *(d)* 128
(e) None of these

26. All the letters of the word EAMCET are arranged in possible ways. The number of such arrangement in which not two vowels are adjacent to each other is:
(a) 360 *(b)* 144
(c) 72 *(d)* 54
(e) None of these

27. The number of arrangements which can be made by using all the letters of the word LAUGH, if the vowels are adjacent, is:
(a) 10 *(b)* 24
(c) 48 *(d)* 120
(e) None of these

28. There are 10 lamps in a hall. Each one of them can be switched on independently. The number of ways in which the hall can be illuminated is:
(a) 10^2 *(b)* 1023
(c) 210 *(d)* 10!
(e) None of these

29. Everybody in a room shakes hands with everybody else. The total number of hand shakes is 66. The total number of persons in the room is:
(a) 11 *(b)* 12
(c) 8 *(d)* 14
(e) None of these

30. 20 persons are invited for a party. The number of ways in which they and the host can be seated at a circular table, if two particular persons be seated on either side of the host, is equal to:
(a) 18! . 2! *(b)* 18! . 3!
(c) 19! . 2! *(d)* 19! . 3!
(e) None of these

31. The number of ways in which 5 prizes be distributed among 4 boys, while each boy is capable of having any number of prizes is:
(a) 6^4 *(b)* 4^5
(c) $4! \cdot 2^4$ *(d)* 6 . (4!)
(e) None of these

32. In an examination there are three multiple choice questions and each question has 4 choices. Number of ways in which a student can fail to get all answers correct, is:
(a) 11 *(b)* 12
(c) 27 *(d)* 63
(e) None of these

33. 7 men and 7 women are to sit round a table so that there is a man on either side of a woman. The number of seating arrangement is:
(a) $(7!)^2$ *(b)* $(6!)^2$
(c) $6! \times 7!$ *(d)* 7!
(e) None of these

34. Three men have 4 coats, 5 waist coats and 6 caps. In how many ways can they wear them?
(a) 178200 *(b)* 172000
(c) 172800 *(d)* 1720800
(e) None of these

35. To fill 12 vacancies there are 25 candidates of which 5 are from scheduled castes. If 3 of the vacancies are reserved for scheduled caste candidates while the rest are open to all, find the number of ways in which the selection can be made.
(a) 4974200
(b) 4947200
(c) 4972400
(d) 4927400
(e) None of these

ANSWERS

1	2	3	4	5	6	7	8	9	10
(*c*)	(*d*)	(*c*)	(*c*)	(*c*)	(*d*)	(*d*)	(*a*)	(*d*)	(*c*)
11	**12**	**13**	**14**	**15**	**16**	**17**	**18**	**19**	**20**
(*b*)	(*d*)	(*c*)	(*b*)	(*c*)	(*d*)	(*c*)	(*a*)	(*a*)	(*b*)
21	**22**	**23**	**24**	**25**	**26**	**27**	**28**	**29**	**30**
(*c*)	(*a*)	(*a*)	(*b*)	(*c*)	(*c*)	(*c*)	(*b*)	(*b*)	(*a*)
31	**32**	**33**	**34**	**35**					
(*b*)	(*d*)	(*c*)	(*c*)	(*a*)					

SOME SELECTED EXPLANATORY ANSWERS

1. Required number of ways

$$= {}^7P_7 = \lfloor 7 = 5040$$

2. In the given word, we treat the vowels IEO as one letter.

Thus, we have DRCTR (IEO).

This group has 6 letters of which R occurs 2 times and others are different.

Number of ways arranging these letters

$$= \frac{6!}{2!} = 360.$$

Now 3 vowels can be arranged among themselves in 3! = 6 ways.

∴ Required number of ways

$$= (360 \times 6) = 2160.$$

3. (3 men out of 6) and (2 ladies out of 5) are to be chosen.

∴ Required number of ways

$$= ({}^6C_3 \times {}^5C_2)$$

$$= \left(\frac{6 \times 5 \times 4}{3 \times 2 \times 1} \times \frac{5 \times 4}{2 \times 1}\right) = 200.$$

4. The word 'APPLE' contains 5 letters, 1A, 2P, 1L and 1E.

∴ Required number of ways

$$= \frac{5!}{(1!)(2!)(1!)(1!)} = 60.$$

5. The word 'ALLAHABAD' contains 9 letters, namely 4A, 2L, 1H, 1B and 1D.

∴ Required number of words

$$= \frac{9!}{(4!)(2!)(1!)(1!)(1!)} = 7560.$$

6. The word 'SIGNATURE' contains 9 different letters.

When the vowels IAUE are taken together, they can be supposed to form an entity, treated as one letter.

Then, the letters to be arranged are SGNTR (IAUE).

These 6 letters can be arranged in

$${}^6P_6 = 6! = 720 \text{ ways.}$$

The vowels in the group (IAUE) can be arranged amongst themselves in

$${}^4P_4 = 4! = 24 \text{ ways.}$$

∴ Required number of words

$$= (720 \times 24) = 17280.$$

7. In the word 'BANKING', we treat the two vowels AI as one letter. Thus, we have BNKNG (AI).

This has 6 letters of which N occurs 2 times and the rest are different.

Number of ways of arranging these letters

$$= \frac{6!}{(2!)(1!)(1!)(1!)(1!)} = 360.$$

Now, 2 vowels AI can be arranged in

$2! = 2$ ways.

∴ Required number of ways

$= (360 \times 2) = 720.$

8. Required number of ways

$= ({}^7C_5 \times {}^3C_2)$

$= ({}^7C_2 \times {}^3C_1)$

$= \left(\frac{7 \times 6}{2 \times 1} \times 3\right) = 63.$

9. We may have (1 boy and 3 girls) or (2 boys and 2 girls) or (3 boys and 1 girl) or (4 boys).

∴ Required number of ways

$= ({}^6C_1 \times {}^4C_3) + ({}^6C_2 \times {}^4C_2) + ({}^6C_3 \times {}^4C_1) + ({}^6C_4)$

$= ({}^6C_1 \times {}^4C_1) + ({}^6C_2 \times {}^4C_2) + ({}^6C_3 \times {}^4C_1) + ({}^6C_2)$

$= (6 \times 4) + \left(\frac{6 \times 5}{2 \times 1} \times \frac{4 \times 3}{2 \times 1}\right) + \left(\frac{6 \times 5 \times 4}{3 \times 2 \times 1} \times 4\right) + \left(\frac{6 \times 5}{2 \times 1}\right)$

$= (24 + 90 + 80 + 15) = 209.$

10. We may have (1 black and 2 non-black) or (2 black and 1 non-black) or (3 black)

∴ Required number of ways

$= ({}^3C_1 \times {}^6C_2) + ({}^3C_2 \times {}^6C_1) + ({}^3C_3)$

$= \left(3 \times \frac{6 \times 5}{2 \times 1}\right) + \left(\frac{3 \times 2}{2 \times 1} \times 6\right) + 1$

$= (45 + 18 + 1) = 64.$

13. 4 red balls from 8 red balls can be selected in ${}^8C_4$ ways

3 blue balls from 9 balls can be selected in ${}^9C_3$ ways

∴ Total number of selection

$= {}^8C_4 \times {}^9C_3$

$= \frac{8 \times 7 \times 6 \times 5}{1 \times 2 \times 3 \times 4} \times \frac{9 \times 8 \times 7}{1 \times 2 \times 3}$

$= 70 \times 84 = 5880.$

14. A decagon has 10 vertices.

Join any two vertices in ${}^{10}C_2$ lines 10 lines will be sides.

∴ Number of diagonals

$= {}^{10}C_2 - 10$

$= \frac{10 \times 9}{1 \times 2} - 10$

$= 45 - 10 = 35$

16. As the order of A, B and C is not to change they are to be treated identical in arrangement. So, the required Number of ways

$= \frac{7!}{3!}.$

$= \frac{7 \times 6 \times 5 \times 4 \times 3 \times 2 \times 1}{3 \times 2 \times 1} = 840.$

18. The number of ways to fill the three even places by 4 consonants = ${}^4P_3$.

After filling the even places, remaining places can be filled in ${}^4P_4$ ways.

So, the required number of words

$= {}^4P_3 \times {}^4P_4$

$= 4! \times 4! = 24 \times 24 = 576.$

19. A couple and 6 guests can be arranged in $(7 - 1)!$ ways. But the two people forming the couple can be arranged among themselves in $2!$ ways.

∴ The required number of ways

$= 6! \times 2!$

$= 720 \times 2 = 1440.$

20. Ten pearls of one colour can be arranged in 1/2 $(10 - 1)!$ ways. The number of arrangements of 10 pearls of the other colour in 10 places between the pearls of the first colour = 10!.

∴ The required number of ways

$= \frac{1}{2} \times 9! \times 10!$

$= 5 \times 9! \times 9! = 5(9!)^2.$

22. Each ball can be put in 2 ways (either in one box or the other).

∴ 6 balls can be put in $2 \times 2 \times \ldots$ to six times, *i.e.,* 2^6 ways. But in two of the ways one box is empty. So, the required number of ways $= 2^6 - 2 = 62.$

24. BANANA
3A's, 2N's, B, i.e., 6 letters, 3 alike of one type and 2 of another type. Number of words taken all at a time is $\frac{6!}{3!\,2!} = \frac{6 \times 5 \times 4}{2} = 60$.

25. The required number of ways
$= {}^3C_1 \times {}^6C_2 + {}^3C_2 \times {}^6C_1 + {}^3C_3 = 64$.

26. First we place 3 consonant in 3! ways and then at four places (2 between them and 2 on sides) 3 vowels in which one vowels is repeated can be placed in ${}^4P_3/2!$ ways.
Hence, required number = $3!\ {}^4P_3/2! = 72$.

27. Considering two vowels together as a letter, there are 4 letters in all which can be arranged in 4! ways while 2 vowels can also be arranged in 2! ways.
$\therefore$ Total number of arrangements = $4!\,.\,2! = 48$.

28. Each bulb has two choices, either switched on or off.
$\therefore$ Required number = $2^{10} - 1 = 1023$
(Since in one way, when all switches are off, the hall will not be illuminated.)

29. Let there be n persons in a room.
$\therefore$ Total no. of shakehands

$$= {}^nC_2 = 66$$

$$\Rightarrow \quad \frac{1}{2}n(n-1) = 66$$

$$\Rightarrow \quad n^2 - n - 132 = 0$$

$$\Rightarrow \quad (n+11)(n-12) = 0$$

$$\Rightarrow \quad n = 12 \qquad (\because n \neq -11)$$

30. Host can sit on any seat. Two particular guests can sit on either sides of host in $2! = 2$ ways and remaining 18 guests in (18)! ways.
Hence, total ways = 2.(18)!.

31. Since every prize can be given by any of the four boys, so number of ways
$= 4 \times 4 \times 4 \times 4 \times 4 = 4^5$.

32. Each question can be answered in 4 ways and all questions can be answered correctly in only one way, so the required number of ways $= 4^3 - 1 = 63$.

33. First the seven women sit round the table in 6! ways and then seven men will sit in the spaces between every pair of two women in 7! ways.
$\therefore$ Required seating arrangements = $6! \times 7!$.

34. ${}^4P_3 \times {}^5P_3 \times {}^6P_3 = 172800$.

35. ${}^5C_3 \times {}^{22}C_9 = 4974200$.

❑❑❑

18 Probability

1. **Random Experiment:** If the result of an experiment is not certain and is any one of the several possible outcomes, the experiment is called a trial or a random experiment.

2. **Sample Space:** The set of all possible outcome of an experiment is called the sample space provided no two or more of these outcomes can occur simultaneously and exactly one of these outcomes must occur whenever the experiment is conducted.

3. **Events:** The outcomes of an experiment, *i.e.*, sample points of the sample space are usually known as simple events and any subset of the sample space 'S' is called an event.

   Thus throwing of a dice is an experiment, S = {1, 2, 3, 4, 5, 6} is the sample space, {1}, ... {6} are simple events and {1, 2}, etc., are events. The empty set ϕ is also an event as $\phi \subset S$ and it is called an impossible event. The sample space S is also a subset of S and so it is also an event. S represents the sure event, *i.e.*, certainty.

4. **Equally Likely Events:** A set of events is said to be equally likely if taking into consideration all the relevant factors there is no reason to expect one of them in preference to others.

   For example, when a fair coin is tossed, the occurrence of a tail or a head are equally likely.

5. **Exhaustive Events:** A set of events is said to be exhaustive if the performance of the experiment always results in the occurrence of atleast one of them.

   For example, if we throw a dice, then the events A_1 = {1, 2}, A_2 = {2, 3, 3} are not exhaustive as we can get 5 as outcome of the experiment which is not the member of any of the events A_1 and A_2. If we consider the events E_1 = {1, 2, 3} and E_2 = {2, 4, 5, 6}, then the set E_1, E_2, is exhaustive.

6. **Mutually Exclusive Events:** A set of events is said to be mutually exclusive if they have no point in common, *i.e.*, happening of one of them eliminates the happening of any of the remaining events. Thus E_1, E_2, E_3, ... are mutually exclusive iff $E_i \cap E_j = \phi$ for $i \neq E_1$ and E_2 are mutually exclusive.

7. **Complement of An Events:** The complement of an event A, denoted by $\overline{A}$, A' or A^c, is the set of all sample points of the space other than the sample points in A.

   e.g., In the experiment of throwing a fair dice, S = {1, 2, 3, 4, 5, 6}. If A = {1, 3, 5, 6}, then $\overline{A}$ = {2, 4}

   Note that $A \cap \overline{A} = S$.

8. **Classical Definition of Probability:** If there are n exhaustive mutually exclusive and equally likely outcomes of an experiment and m of them are favourable to an event A, the probability of the happening of A is defined as the ratio m/n.

   Thus, denoting the probability of the happening of an event A by p, we have $p = m/n$.

   Clearly p is a positive number not greater than unity, so that $0 \leq p \leq 1$.

   Since the number of cases in which the event A will not happen is $n - m$, the probability q that the event will not happen is given by $q = \frac{(n-m)}{n} = 1 - \frac{m}{n} = 1 - p$. $\therefore p + q = 1$

If probability of happening of an event A is 1, then A is certain event and if probability of happening of an event A is 0, then A is impossible event.

9. Odds in Favour and Odds against an Event: As a result of an experiment if *a* of the outcomes are favourable to an event E and *b* of the outcomes are against it, then we say that odds are *a* to *b* in favour of E or odds are *b* to *a* against E.

Thus, odds in favour of an event E

$$= \frac{\text{number of favourable cases}}{\text{number of unfavourable cases}}.$$

Similarly, odds against an event E

$$= \frac{\text{number of unfavourable cases}}{\text{number of favourable cases}}.$$

If odds in favour of an event are $a : b$ then the probability of the occurrence of that event is $\frac{a}{a+b}$ and the probability of the non-occurrence of that event is $\frac{b}{(a+b)}$.

Addition Theorem:

(*a*) If 'A' and 'B' are any two events in a sample space S, then

$$P(A \cup B) = P(A) + P(B) - P(A \cap B).$$

(*b*) If 'A' and 'B' are mutually exclusive then

$P(A \cap B) = 0$ so that

$$P(A \cup B) = P(A) + P(B).$$

(*c*) If A is any event in S, then $P(A') = 1 - P(A)$.

Total Probability Theorem:

The probability that one of several mutually exclusive events $A_1, A_2, ..., A_n$ will happen, is the sum of the probabilities of the separate events. In symbol,

$$P(A_1 + A_2 + ... + A_n) = P(A_1) + P(A_2) + ... + P(A_n).$$

Conditional Probability:

The probability of B under the assumption that A has occurred is called the conditional probability of B under the condition that the event A has taken place and is denoted by P(B/A). P(B/A) is read as "probability at the event B given A^B."

Conditional Probability Theorem:

If A and B are any two events in the sample space S, the conditional probability of B relative to A is given by

$$P(B/A) = \frac{P(B \cap A)}{P(A)}$$

$$= \frac{n(B \cap A)}{n(A)}$$

$$A \neq \phi.$$

Some Important Remarks about Coins, Dice and Playing Cards:

(*a*) **Coins:** A coin has a head side and a tail side. If an experiment consist of more than a coin, coins are considered to be distinct if not otherwise stated.

(*b*) **Dice:** A die (cubical) has six faces marked 1, 2, 3, 4, 5, 6. We may have tetrahedral (having four faces 1, 2, 3, 4) or pentagonal (having five faces 1, 2, 3, 4, 5) die. As in the case of dice, if we have more than one die, all dice are considered to be distinct if not otherwise stated.

(*c*) **Playing Cards:** A pack of playing cards usually contain 52 cards.

There are 4 suits (spade, heart, diamond and club) each having 13 cards. There are two colours — red (heart and diamond) and black (spade and club) each having 26 cards.

In thirteen cards of each suit, there are 3 face cards namely king, queen and jack, so there are in all 12 face cards (4 kings, 4 queens and 4 jacks).

Also there are 16 honours cards, 4 of each suit namely ace, king, queen and jack.

EXAMPLES

Example 1: A bag contains 7 Red balls, 4 Green balls and 5 Yellow balls. What is the probability that 3 balls drawn at random are either Green or Yellow?

Solution: Total ways $= {}^{16}C_3 = \dfrac{\underline{|16}}{\underline{|13}\ \underline{|3}}$

$= 560$

Favourable ways $= {}^4C_3 \times {}^5C_3$

$= \dfrac{\underline{|4}}{\underline{|3}\ \underline{|1}} \times \dfrac{\underline{|5}}{\underline{|3}\ \underline{|2}}$

$= 4 \times 10 = 40.$

$\therefore$ Reqd. Probability $= \dfrac{40}{560} = \dfrac{1}{14}.$

Example 2: A basket contains three Red and four Green balls. If four balls are drawn at random from the basket, what is the probability that two are Red and two are Green?

Solution: Reqd. Probability

$= \dfrac{{}^3C_2 \times {}^4C_2}{{}^7C_4} = \dfrac{3 \times 6}{35} = \dfrac{18}{35}.$

Example 3: A box contains 8 Red, 16 Blue, 4 Yellow and 12 Black bolls. Two balls are picked up randomly. What is the chance that both are Red?

Solution: Total results $= {}^{40}C_2 = \dfrac{40 \times 39}{2} = 780$

and favourable results $= {}^8C_2 = \dfrac{\underline{|8}}{\underline{|2}\ \underline{|6}} = \dfrac{8 \times 7}{2}$

$= 28.$

$\therefore$ Required probability $= \dfrac{28}{780} = \dfrac{7}{195}.$

Example 4: A bag contains 8 Red, 16 Blue, 12 Black and 4 Yellow marbles. One marbles is picked up randomly. What is the probability that it is not Blue?

Solution: Total results $= {}^{40}C_1 = 40$

Favourable results when it is Blue

$= {}^{16}C_1 = 16.$

$\therefore$ Favourable results when it is not Blue

$= 40 - 16 = 24$

$\therefore$ Reqd. probability $= \dfrac{24}{40} = 0.6.$

EXERCISE

Directions (Qs. 1 to 3) : *Study the information carefully to answer the questions that follow.*

A bucket contains 8 Red, 3 Blue and 5 Green marbles.

1. If 4 marbles are drawn at random, what is the probability that 2 are Red and 2 are Blue?

(a) $\dfrac{11}{16}$ *(b)* $\dfrac{3}{16}$

(c) $\dfrac{11}{72}$ *(d)* $\dfrac{3}{65}$

(e) None of these

2. If 2 marbles are drawn at random, what is the probability that both are Green?

(a) $\dfrac{1}{8}$ *(b)* $\dfrac{5}{16}$

(c) $\dfrac{2}{7}$ *(d)* 0

(e) None of these

3. If 3 marbles are drawn at random, what is the probability that none is Red?

(a) $\dfrac{3}{8}$ *(b)* $\dfrac{1}{16}$

(c) $\dfrac{1}{10}$ *(d)* 0

(e) None of these

Directions (Qs. 4 to 5) : *Study the information and answer the questions that follow.*

A basket contains 3 Red balls, 5 Blue balls and 2 Green balls.

4. If three balls are drawn at random, what is the probability that none is Blue?

(a) $\dfrac{1}{6}$ *(b)* $\dfrac{1}{12}$

(c) $\frac{1}{5}$ *(d)* $\frac{3}{10}$

(e) None of these

5. If four balls are drawn at random, what is the probability that at least one is Green?

(a) $\frac{2}{3}$ *(b)* $\frac{1}{2}$

(c) $\frac{1}{3}$ *(d)* $\frac{2}{5}$

(e) None of these

6. If two balls are drawn at random, what is the probability that both are Red?

(a) $\frac{1}{5}$ *(b)* $\frac{3}{10}$

(c) $\frac{3}{5}$ *(d)* $\frac{1}{15}$

(e) None of these

7. A dice is thrown once. Find the probability of getting a number greater than 3.

(a) $\frac{2}{3}$ *(b)* $\frac{1}{3}$

(c) $\frac{1}{2}$ *(d)* $\frac{3}{2}$

(e) None of these

8. A bag contains 5 Red balls, 8 White balls, 4 Green balls and 7 Black balls. If one ball is drawn at random, find the probability that it is Black.

(a) $\frac{7}{24}$ *(b)* $\frac{5}{24}$

(c) $\frac{5}{6}$ *(d)* $\frac{1}{4}$

(e) None of these

9. Find the probability that a number selected from the numbers 1 to 25 is not a prime number when each of the given number is equally to be selected.

(a) $\frac{9}{25}$ *(b)* $\frac{16}{25}$

(c) $\frac{21}{25}$ *(d)* $\frac{14}{25}$

(e) None of these

10. A bag contains 3 Red balls and 5 Black balls. A ball is drawn at random from the bag. What is the probability that the ball drawn is not Red?

(a) $\frac{3}{8}$ *(b)* $\frac{5}{8}$

(c) $\frac{1}{8}$ *(d)* $\frac{7}{8}$

(e) None of these

11. A die is thrown once. Find the probability of getting an odd number.

(a) $\frac{1}{2}$ *(b)* $\frac{3}{2}$

(c) $\frac{2}{3}$ *(d)* $\frac{1}{3}$

(e) None of these

12. A letter is chosen at random from the word REED the probability of choosing an E is –

(a) $\frac{3}{4}$ *(b)* $\frac{1}{2}$

(c) $\frac{1}{4}$ *(d)* $\frac{2}{3}$

(e) None of these

13. A card is drawn at random from a well-shuffled deck of playing cards. Find the probability that the card drawn is a card of spade or an ace.

(a) $\frac{11}{13}$ *(b)* $\frac{1}{26}$

(c) $\frac{4}{13}$ *(d)* $\frac{9}{13}$

(e) None of these

14. If a letter is chosen at random from the word TRIANGLE.
What is the probability that it a vowel?

(a) $\frac{3}{8}$ *(b)* $\frac{5}{8}$

(c) $\frac{1}{4}$ *(d)* $\frac{3}{4}$

(e) None of these

15. What is the chance that a leap year, selected at random, will contain 53 Sundays?

(a) $\frac{52}{365}$ (b) $\frac{52}{366}$

(c) $\frac{2}{7}$ (d) $\frac{5}{7}$

(e) None of these

16. In a book of 300 pages, if a page is opened at random; find the probability that the sum of the digits in its number is 10.

(a) $\frac{8}{15}$ (b) $\frac{9}{15}$

(c) $\frac{7}{75}$ (d) $\frac{14}{15}$

(e) None of these

17. A die is thrown once. Find the probability of getting an even number.

(a) $\frac{1}{3}$ (b) $\frac{1}{2}$

(c) $\frac{1}{4}$ (d) $\frac{1}{6}$

(e) None of these

18. Two friends were born in the year 2000. What is the probability that they have the same birthday?

(a) $\frac{1}{500}$ (b) $\frac{1}{730}$

(c) $\frac{1}{365}$ (d) $\frac{1}{366}$

(e) None of these

19. A number is chosen at random from among the first 30 natural numbers. The probability of the number chosen being prime is :

(a) $\frac{1}{3}$ (b) $\frac{3}{10}$

(c) $\frac{1}{30}$ (d) $\frac{11}{30}$

(e) None of these

20. The probability that a number selected at random from the set of numbers {1, 2, 3, 4, ..., 100} is a cube is :

(a) $\frac{1}{25}$ (b) $\frac{2}{25}$

(c) $\frac{3}{25}$ (d) $\frac{4}{25}$

(e) None of these

21. A single letter is selected at random from the word 'COLLEGE'. Find the probability of getting a vowel.

(a) $\frac{3}{7}$ (b) $\frac{4}{7}$

(c) $\frac{5}{7}$ (d) $\frac{2}{7}$

(e) None of these

22. A box contains 5 Red balls, 4 Green balls and 7 White balls. A ball is drawn at random from the box. Find the probability that the ball drawn is neither Red nor White.

(a) $\frac{2}{7}$ (b) $\frac{3}{4}$

(c) $\frac{1}{4}$ (d) $\frac{1}{2}$

(e) None of these

23. In a cricket match, a batsman hits boundary 8 times out of 40 balls he plays. Find the probability that he didn't hit boundary.

(a) 0.8 (b) 0.6

(c) 0.5 (d) 0.4

(e) None of these

24. Two coins are tossed simultaneously. The probability of getting atmost one head is :

(a) $\frac{1}{4}$ (b) $\frac{3}{4}$

(c) $\frac{1}{2}$ (d) $\frac{1}{4}$

(e) None of these

25. A bag contains 50 coins and each coin is marked from 51 to 100. One coin is picked at random. The probability that the number on the coin is not a prime number is :

(a) $\frac{1}{5}$ (b) $\frac{3}{5}$

(c) $\frac{2}{5}$ (d) $\frac{4}{5}$

(e) None of these

26. In a football match, a player makes 4 goals from 10 penalty kicks. The probability of converting a penalty kick into a goal by the player, is :

(a) $\frac{1}{4}$ (b) $\frac{1}{6}$

(c) $\frac{1}{3}$ (d) $\frac{2}{5}$

(e) None of these

27. Three unbiased coins are tossed. What is the probability of getting at least 2 heads?

(a) $\frac{1}{4}$ (b) $\frac{1}{2}$

(c) $\frac{1}{3}$ (d) $\frac{1}{8}$

(e) None of these

28. In a simultaneous throw of two dice, what is the probability of getting a total of 7?

(a) $\frac{1}{6}$ (b) $\frac{1}{4}$

(c) $\frac{2}{3}$ (d) $\frac{3}{4}$

(e) None of these

29. What is the probability of getting a sum 9 from two throws of a dice?

(a) $\frac{1}{6}$ (b) $\frac{1}{8}$

(c) $\frac{1}{9}$ (d) $\frac{1}{12}$

(e) None of these

30. Tickets numbered 1 to 20 are mixed up and then a ticket is drawn at random. What is the probability that the ticket drawn bears a number which is a multiple of 3?

(a) $\frac{3}{10}$ (b) $\frac{3}{20}$

(c) $\frac{2}{5}$ (d) $\frac{1}{2}$

(e) None of these

31. A card is drawn from a pack of 52 cards. The probability of getting a queen of club or a king of heart is :

(a) $\frac{1}{13}$ (b) $\frac{2}{13}$

(c) $\frac{1}{26}$ (d) $\frac{1}{52}$

(e) None of these

32. Two cards are drawn together from a pack of 52 cards. The probability that one is a spade and one is a heart, is :

(a) $\frac{3}{20}$ (b) $\frac{29}{34}$

(c) $\frac{47}{100}$ (d) $\frac{13}{102}$

(e) None of these

33. A bag contains 6 white and 4 red balls. Three balls are drawn at random. What is the probability that one ball is red and the other two are white?

(a) $\frac{1}{2}$ (b) $\frac{1}{12}$

(c) $\frac{3}{10}$ (d) $\frac{7}{12}$

(e) None of these

34. A box contains 20 electric bulbs, out of which 4 are defective. Two bulbs are chosen at random from this box. The probability that at least one of these is defective, is :

(a) $\frac{4}{19}$ (b) $\frac{7}{19}$

(c) $\frac{12}{19}$ (d) $\frac{21}{95}$

(e) None of these

35. Two dice are tossed. The probability that the total score is a prime number is :

(a) $\frac{1}{6}$ (b) $\frac{5}{12}$

(c) $\frac{1}{2}$ (d) $\frac{7}{9}$

(e) None of these

ANSWERS

1	2	3	4	5	6	7	8	9	10
(*d*)	(*a*)	(*a*)	(*b*)	(*c*)	(*d*)	(*c*)	(*a*)	(*b*)	(*b*)
11	**12**	**13**	**14**	**15**	**16**	**17**	**18**	**19**	**20**
(*a*)	(*b*)	(*c*)	(*a*)	(*c*)	(*c*)	(*b*)	(*d*)	(*a*)	(*a*)
21	**22**	**23**	**24**	**25**	**26**	**27**	**28**	**29**	**30**
(*a*)	(*c*)	(*a*)	(*b*)	(*d*)	(*d*)	(*b*)	(*a*)	(*c*)	(*a*)
31	**32**	**33**	**34**	**35**					
(*c*)	(*d*)	(*a*)	(*b*)	(*b*)					

SOME SELECTED EXPLANATORY ANSWERS

1. Total number of ways

$$= {}^{16}C_4 = \frac{\lfloor 16}{\lfloor 12 \lfloor 4} = 1820$$

And favourable number of ways

$$= {}^{8}C_2 \times {}^{3}C_2$$

$$= \frac{\lfloor 8}{\lfloor 6 \lfloor 2} \times \frac{\lfloor 3}{\lfloor 1 \lfloor 2} = 84$$

$$\therefore \text{ Reqd. probability} = \frac{84}{1820} = \frac{3}{65}.$$

2. Total number of ways

$$= {}^{16}C_2 = \frac{\lfloor 16}{\lfloor 14 \lfloor 2} = 120$$

And favourable number of ways

$$= {}^{5}C_2 = \frac{\lfloor 5}{\lfloor 3 \lfloor 2} = 10$$

$$\therefore \text{ Reqd. probability} = \frac{10}{120} = \frac{1}{12}.$$

3. Total number of ways

$$= {}^{16}C_3 = \frac{\lfloor 16}{\lfloor 13 \lfloor 3} = 560$$

Total number of ways when all the marbles are Red

$$= {}^{8}C_3 = \frac{\lfloor 8}{\lfloor 5 \lfloor 3} = 56$$

$\therefore$ Probability when all the three are Red

$$= \frac{56}{560} = \frac{1}{10}$$

$\therefore$ And probability when none is Red

$$= 1 - \frac{1}{10} = \frac{9}{10}.$$

4. Probability that none is blue

$$= \frac{{}^{5}C_3}{{}^{10}C_3} = \frac{10}{120} = \frac{1}{12}$$

5. Probability that none is green

$$= \frac{{}^{8}C_4}{{}^{10}C_4} = \frac{70}{210} = \frac{1}{3}$$

$\therefore$ Probability that at least one is green

$$= 1 - \frac{1}{3} = \frac{2}{3}$$

6. Probability that both are red

$$= \frac{{}^{3}C_2}{{}^{10}C_2} = \frac{3}{45} = \frac{1}{15}$$

7. Sample space S = {1, 2, 3, 4, 5, 6} ; $n(S) = 6$

Let A = "getting a number grater than 3" then

A = {4, 5, 6} ; $n(A) = 3$

$$P(A) = \frac{n(A)}{n(S)} = \frac{3}{6} = \frac{1}{2}.$$

9. We are given numbers from 1 to 25.

$n(S) = 25$.

Prime numbers from 1 to 25 are 2, 3, 5, 7, 11, 13, 17, 19, 23.

These are 9 prime numbers.

Let E denote the event 'Number drawn is not prime'.

$\therefore \quad n(\text{E}) = 25 - 9 = 16$

$$p(\text{E}) = \frac{n(\text{E})}{n(\text{S})} = \frac{16}{25}.$$

10. Total number of balls in the bag = 3 + 5 = 8

Let E denote the event 'ball drawn is red'.

$\therefore \quad n(\text{E}) = 3$ and $n(\text{S}) = 8$.

(*i*) $$p(\text{E}) = \frac{n(\text{E})}{n(\text{S})} = \frac{3}{8}$$

(*ii*) $$p(\text{not red}) = p(\bar{\text{E}})$$

$$= 1 - p(\text{E}) = 1 - \frac{3}{8} = \frac{5}{8}.$$

11. Sample S = {1, 2, 3, 4, 5, 6} ; $n(\text{S}) = 6$

Let F denote the event 'getting an odd number'.

$$\text{F} = \{1, 3, 5\}\ ;\ n(\text{S}) = 3$$

$$\therefore \quad \text{P(F)} = \frac{n(\text{F})}{n(\text{S})} = \frac{3}{6} = \frac{1}{2}.$$

12. The sample space is {R, E_1, E_2, D}

There are 2 ways to choose the letter E from the four letters

$$\therefore \quad \text{P(E)} = \frac{2}{4} = \frac{1}{2}.$$

13. There are 52 cards in a deck of 52 playing cards.

There are 13 spades and 4 aces in 52 playing cards. Out of 13 spades there is one ace.

∴ Favourable no ways for the card drawn to be spade or an ace = 13 spades + 3 aces = 16.

$$\therefore \text{ P(a card of spade or an ace)} = \frac{16}{52} = \frac{4}{13}.$$

14. Since there are 3 vowels out of a total of 8 letters, the probability of choosing a vowel is 3/8.

15. A Leap year has 366 days. In a leap year, here are 52 complete weeks (52 Sundays) and 2 days over these two days can be as follows. Sunday and Monday, Monday and Tuesday, Tuesday and Wednesday, Wednesday and Thursday, Thursday and Friday, Friday and Saturday, Saturday and Sunday.

Out of these 7 possibilities, only two (Saturday and Sunday; Sunday and Monday) are favourable for having 53 Sundays)

$$\text{Required chance} = \frac{2}{7}.$$

17. A die is thrown once. Its sample space is

S = {1, 2, 3, 4, 5, 6}, $n(\text{S}) = 6$

Let E : an even number,

then E = {2, 4, 6} Number of favourable cases = $n(\text{E}) = 3$

$$\therefore \quad \text{P(E)} = \frac{n(\text{E})}{n(\text{S})} = \frac{3}{6} = \frac{1}{2}.$$

18. Year 2000 is a leap year. There are 366 days in the year 2000. Total number of cases in which two friends can be born on the same day are 366.

Out of 366 days, number of favourable ways in which two friends have the same birthday = 1

$$\therefore \text{ Required probability} = \frac{1}{366}.$$

19. The prime numbers from first 30 natural numbers are 2, 3, 5, 7, 11, 13, 17, 19, 23, 29.

We find that there are 10 prime numbers from 1 to 30.

∴ Probability that the number chosen being prime is $= \frac{10}{30} = \frac{1}{3}.$

20. From the natural numbers 1 to 100 the four number 1, 8, 27 and 64 are cubes

$$\therefore \text{ Required Probability} = \frac{4}{100} = \frac{1}{25}.$$

23. Let A denote the event that the batsman did not hit a boundary.

We have, Total number of trials = 40

Number of trials in which the event A happened = 40 − 8 = 32

$\therefore \quad P(A) = \frac{32}{40} = \frac{4}{5} = 0.8.$

27. Here S = {HH, HT, TH, TT}.

Let E = Event of getting at least one head = {HT, TH, HH}.

$\therefore P(E) = \frac{n(E)}{n(S)} = \frac{4}{8} = \frac{1}{2}.$

28. We know that in a simultaneous throw of two dice,

$n(S) = 6 \times 6 = 36.$

Let E = Event of getting a total of 7 = {(1, 6), (2, 5), (3, 4), (4, 3), (5, 2), (6, 1)}.

$\therefore P(E) = \frac{n(E)}{n(S)} = \frac{6}{36} = \frac{1}{6}.$

29. In two throws of a die,

$n(S) = (6 \times 6) = 36.$

Let E = Event of getting a sum 9 = {(3, 6), (4, 5), (5, 4), (6, 3)}.

$\therefore P(E) = \frac{n(E)}{n(S)} = \frac{4}{36} = \frac{1}{9}.$

30. Here, S = {1, 2, 3, 4, ..., 19, 20}.

Let E = Event of getting a multiple of 3 = {3, 6, 9, 12, 15, 18}.

$\therefore P(E) = \frac{n(E)}{n(S)} = \frac{6}{20} = \frac{3}{10}.$

31. Here $n(S) = 52$.

Let E = Event of getting a queen of club or a king of heart.

Then, $n(E) = 2$.

$\therefore P(E) = \frac{n(E)}{n(S)} = \frac{2}{52} = \frac{1}{26}.$

32. Let S be the sample space. Then,

$$n(S) = {}^{52}C_2 = \frac{(52 \times 51)}{(2 \times 1)} = 1326.$$

Let E = Event of getting 1 spade and 1 heart.

$\therefore n(E) =$ Number of ways of choosing 1 spade out of 13 and 1 heart out of 13

$= ({}^{13}C_1 \times {}^{13}C_1) = (13 \times 13) = 169.$

$\therefore P(E) = \frac{n(E)}{n(S)} = \frac{169}{1326} = \frac{13}{102}.$

33. Let S be the sample space. Then,

$n(S) =$ Number of ways of drawing 3 balls out of 10

$$= {}^{10}C_3 = \frac{(10 \times 9 \times 8)}{(3 \times 2 \times 1)} = 120.$$

Let E = Event of drawing 1 red and 2 white balls

$\therefore n(E) =$ Number of ways of drawing 1 red ball out of 4 and 2 white balls out of 6

$$= ({}^4C_1 \times {}^6C_2) = \left(4 \times \frac{6 \times 5}{2 \times 1}\right) = 60.$$

$\therefore P(E) = \frac{n(E)}{n(S)} = \frac{60}{120} = \frac{1}{2}.$

34. P (None is defective)

$$= \frac{{}^{16}C_2}{{}^{20}C_2} = \left(\frac{16 \times 15}{2 \times 1} \times \frac{2 \times 1}{20 \times 19}\right) = \frac{12}{19}.$$

P (at least one is defective) $= \left(1 - \frac{12}{19}\right) = \frac{7}{19}.$

35. Clearly, $n(S) = (6 \times 6) = 36.$

Let E = Event that the sum is a prime number.

Then, E = {(1, 1), (1, 2), (1, 4), (1, 6), (2, 1), (2, 3), (2, 5), (3, 2), (3, 4), (4, 1), (4, 3), (5, 2), (5, 6), (6, 1), (6, 5)

$\therefore n(E) = 15$

$\therefore P(E) = \frac{n(E)}{n(S)} = \frac{15}{36} = \frac{5}{12}.$

❑❑❑

19 LOGARITHMS

Definition of Logarithms

If a is a positive real number ($\neq 1$) and $a^x = m$, then the exponent x is called the logarithm of the number m to the base a and is written as $\log_a m = x$

Similarly $10^2 = 100 \therefore \log_{10} 100 = 2$

Here 10 is the base and 2 is the logarithm of 100 or the logarithm of 100 to the base 10 is 2 and is read as log 100 to the base 10 is equal to 2.

Thus $2^3 = 8 \quad \therefore \quad \log_2 8 = 3$

$3^5 = 243 \quad \therefore \quad \log_3 243 = 5$

$4^4 = 256 \quad \therefore \quad \log_4 256 = 4$

$7^3 = 343 \quad \therefore \quad \log_7 343 = 3$

$5^4 = 625 \quad \therefore \quad \log_5 625 = 4$

$4^6 = 4096 \quad \therefore \quad \log_4 4096 = 6$

$2^{-2} = \frac{1}{4} \quad \therefore \quad \log_2 \frac{1}{4} = -2$

$\left(\sqrt{5}\right)^6 = 125 \quad \therefore \quad \log_{\sqrt{5}} 125 = 6$

Hence the logarithm of a number to a given positive real number base $\neq 1$ is index or the power to which the base must be raised in order to make it equal to the given number.

Common Logarithms

Any number except zero or unity, can be taken as the base of logarithms. But in practice all logarithms are calculated to the base 10. These are called 'Common Logarithms'. Usually the base 10 is not written but it is understood.

Thus log10 3296 is written as log 3296 with 10 omitted.

Some common logarithms are given below :

$10^1 = 10 \quad \therefore \quad \log 10 = 1$

$10^2 = 100 \quad \therefore \quad \log 100 = 2$

$10^3 = 1000 \quad \therefore \quad \log 1000 = 3$

$10^4 = 10000 \quad \therefore \quad \log 10000 = 4$

$10^5 = 100000 \quad \therefore \quad \log 100000 = 5$

However, all numbers are not integral powers of 10. For example, 593 can not expressed as power of 10. But 593 lies between 100 and 1000. So logarithm of 593 must be between 2 and 3.

EXERCISE

1. The characteristic of the logarithm of 0.00145 is:

(a) 1 (b) –2
(c) –3 (d) 0
(e) None of these

2. The characteristic of the logarithm of 0.00000531 is:

(a) 4 (b) –6
(c) –3 (d) –2
(e) None of these

3. If $\log_{10} 3 = 0.4771$, what is $\log_{10} 30^4$?

(a) 1.9084 (b) 4.771
(c) 5.9084 (d) 19.084
(e) None of these

4. The value of $\log_{1296} 6$ is:

(a) 4 (b) Between 5 and 6
(c) 0.25 (d) 216
(e) None of these

5. If $2 \log (a + b) = \log 9 + \log a + \log b$, then $a^2 + b^2$ is:

(a) 5 ab (b) 7 ab
(c) 9 ab (d) 11 ab
(e) None of these

6. The number of digits in 2^{64} is (given $\log_{10} 2 = 0.3010$)

(a) 20 (b) 25
(c) 30 (d) 33
(e) None of these

7. If log 27 = 1.431, then log 9 is equal to:
(a) 0.934 *(b)* 0.945
(c) 0.954 *(d)* 0.958
(e) None of these

8. If log x – 5 log 3 = –2, then x equals:
(a) 0.81 *(b)* 1.25
(c) 2.43 *(d)* 3.20
(e) None of these

9. If $\log_{10} m = b - \log_{10} n$, then m equals:
(a) bn *(b)* $10n - 10^b \cdot n$
(c) $b - 10^n$ *(d)* $\frac{10^b}{n}$
(e) None of these

10. If log 8 = 0.9031 and log 9 = 0.9542, then the value of log 6 is:
(a) 0.3010 *(b)* 0.4771
(c) 0.7781 *(d)* 1
(e) None of these

11. If log 2 = 0.3010 and log 3 = 0.4771, then the value of log (3240) is:
(a) 0.6020 *(b)* 2.9084
(c) 3.5104 *(d)* 4.5321
(e) None of these

12. The value of $\log_5\left(\frac{(125)(625)}{25}\right)$ is:
(a) 5 *(b)* 6
(c) 725 *(d)* 3135
(e) None of these

13. If $\log_{10} 2 = a$ and $\log_{10} 3 = b$, then $\log_5 12$ equals:
(a) $\frac{a+b}{1+a}$ *(b)* $\frac{2a+b}{1+a}$
(c) $\frac{a+2b}{1+a}$ *(d)* $\frac{2a+b}{1-a}$
(e) None of these

14. The value of $[\log_{10} (5 \log_{10} 100)]^2$ is:
(a) $\log_{10} 50$ *(b)* 10
(c) 2 *(d)* 1
(e) None of these

15. Given that log 8 = 0.9031 and log 9 = 0.9542, then the only logarithm that can not be found without the use of tables is:
(a) log 17 *(b)* $\log\left(\frac{5}{4}\right)$
(c) log (15) *(d)* log (600)

16. If log 2 = 0.3010 and log 3 = 0.4771, then the value of x that satisfies the equation $3^{x+3} = 135$ is approximately:
(a) 5.0 *(b)* 1.8
(c) 1.7 *(d)* 1.5
(e) None of these

17. $\log 8 \div \log \frac{1}{8}$ equals:
(a) 6 log 2 *(b)* log 2
(c) 1 *(d)* 1
(e) None of these

ANSWERS

1	2	3	4	5	6	7	8	9	10
(c)	(b)	(c)	(c)	(b)	(a)	(c)	(c)	(d)	(c)
11	**12**	**13**	**14**	**15**	**16**	**17**			
(c)	(a)	(d)	(d)	(a)	(d)	(d)			

❑❑❑

20 Linear and Quadratic Equation

REMEMBER

1. An equation of the form $ax^2 + bx + c = 0$, $a \neq 0$ in which the highest power of x is 2 and a, b, c are any three numbers free from x but $a \neq 0$ is called a *quadratic equation* or second *degree equation* in x.
2. A quadratic equation is satisfied by two values of x, *i.e.*, there are two roots of the quadratic equation.
3. The formula for solving a quadratic equation $ax^2 + bx + c = 0$ is:

$$x = \frac{-b \pm \sqrt{b^2 - 4ac}}{2a}$$

where $b^2 - 4ac$ is called *discriminant.*

(*i*) If $b^2 - 4ac > 0$, the two roots are real and different.

(*ii*) If $b^2 - 4ac = 0$, the two roots are real and equal.

(*iii*) If $b^2 - 4ac < 0$, the two roots are imaginary.

(*iv*) If $b^2 - 4ac$ is a perfect square and a, b, c are rational, the two roots are rational.

(*v*) If $b^2 - 4ac$ is not a perfect square and a, b, c, are rational, then the two roots are irrational.

4. *Linear Equations in two variables* : The equation of the form $ax + by + c = 0$, where a, b, c are real constants, is called a linear equation in two variables x and y. Two equations

$$a_1x_1 + b_1y_1 + c_1 = 0$$

and $\quad a_2x + b_2y + c_2 = 0$

which satisfy the same values of x and y are called linear simultaneous equations in two variables.

Important Rule:

(*i*) The solution is unique, if $\frac{a_1}{a_2} \neq \frac{b_1}{b_2}$.

(*ii*) The solutions are infinite, if $\frac{a_1}{a_2} = \frac{b_1}{b_2} = \frac{c_1}{c_2}$.

(*iii*) No solution, if $\frac{a_1}{a_2} = \frac{b_1}{b_2} \neq \frac{c_1}{c_2}$.

The equation $a_1x - b_1y = c$ and $a_2x^3 + b_2y^3 = c_2$ say are non-linear simultaneous equations in x and y.

EXAMPLES

Example 1: *Solve the equation:*

$$2(x - 3) = 9 + 3(x - 9)$$

Solution: $2(x - 3) = 9 + 3(x - 9)$

or $\quad 2 \times x - 2 \times 3 = 9 + 3 \times x - 3 \times 9$

or $\quad 2x - 6 = 9 + 3x - 27$

or $\quad 2x - 3x = 9 - 27 + 6$

or $\quad -x = -12$

$\therefore \quad x = 12$

Example 2: *Find two numbers whose sum is 64, and whose difference is 16.*

Solution: Let the smaller number be x.

Then another number $= 64 - x$

Difference, $(64 - x) - x = 16$

$\Rightarrow \quad 64 - 2x = 16$

$\Rightarrow \quad -2x = 16 - 64$

$= -48$

$\therefore \qquad x = \dfrac{-48}{-2} = 24$

$\therefore$ Second number = 64 – 24 = 40.

Example 3: *Solve:* $x^2 + (1 - p)x - p = 0$.

Solution: $x^2 + (1 - p)x - p = 0$

$\Rightarrow \quad x^2 + x - px - p = 0$

$\Rightarrow \quad x(x + 1) - p(x + 1) = 0$

$\Rightarrow \quad (x + 1)(x - p) = 0$

$\Rightarrow \quad x + 1 = 0$

or $\quad x - p = 0$

$\therefore \quad x = -1$

or $\quad x = p$

Thus, the two roots of the quardratic equation are –1 and p.

Example 4: *If the equations* $4x + 7y = 10$ *and* $10x + ky = 25$ *represent coincident lines, then find value of k.*

Solution: Since the two lines $y = -\dfrac{4}{7}x + \dfrac{10}{7}$, $y = -\dfrac{10}{k}x + \dfrac{25}{k}$ represent coincident lines.

$$-\frac{10}{k} = -\frac{4}{7}$$

$$\therefore \quad k = \frac{70}{4} = \frac{35}{2}$$

Example 5: *If the quadratic equation* $2x^2 + 3x + p = 0$ *has equal roots, then find the value of p.*

Solution: Since the given equation has equal roots,

$b^2 - 4ac = 0$

or $\quad 3^2 - 4.2.p = 0$

or $\quad 9 - 8p = 0$

$\therefore \quad p = \dfrac{9}{8}$

EXERCISE

1. The value of x in the equation $\dfrac{x+2}{x-1} = \dfrac{5}{2}$ is:

(a) 3 *(b)* 7
(c) 5 *(d)* 9
(e) None of these

2. 32 is divided into two parts such that if the larger is divided by the smaller, the quotient is 2 and the remainder is 5. The larger part is:

(a) 9 *(b)* 18
(c) 23 *(d)* 27
(e) None of these

3. If the sum of the roots of the equation $qx^2 + 2x + 3q = 0$ is equal to their product, then the value of q is:

(a) $-\dfrac{2}{3}$ *(b)* $\dfrac{3}{2}$
(c) 3 *(d)* – 6
(e) None of these

4. If $(x - 2)(x + 6) \geq 0$, then the solution set is:

(a) $\{x : x \geq 2\}$
(b) $\{x : x \leq 6\}$
(c) $\{x : x \leq -6\}$
(d) $\{x : x \geq 2 \text{ or } x \leq -6\}$
(e) None of these

5. If α, β are the roots of the quadratic equation $4x^2 - 4x + 1 = 0$, then $\alpha^3 + \beta^3$ is equal to:

(a) $\dfrac{1}{4}$ *(b)* $\dfrac{1}{8}$
(c) 16 *(d)* 32
(e) None of these

6. If the roots of the equation:

$$\lambda^2 + 8\lambda + \mu^2 + 6\mu = 0$$

are real, then μ lies between:

(a) –2 and 8 *(b)* –3 and 6
(c) –8 and 2 *(d)* –6 and 3
(e) None of these

7. The values of x satisfying the equation $5^{2x} - 5^{x+3} + 125 = 5^x$ are:

(a) 0 and 2 *(b)* –1 and 3
(c) 0 and –3 *(d)* 0 and 3
(e) None of these

8. Two students while solving a quadratic equation in x, one copied the constant term incorrectly and got the roots 3 and 2; while the other copies the constant term and coefficient of x^2 as –6 and 1 respectively. The correct roots are:

(a) 3, –2 *(b)* –3, 2

(c) –6, –1 (d) 6, –1
(e) None of these

9. For a given value of k, the product of roots of $x^2 - 2kx + 3k^2 - 4 = 0$ is 5. The roots may be characterised as:
(a) integral
(b) rational but not integral
(c) irrational
(d) imaginary
(e) None of these

10. If the roots of the equation $x^2 - 6x + 10 = 0$ are α and β, then $\alpha^2 + \beta^2$ is:
(a) –16 (b) 4
(c) 60 (d) 16
(e) None of these

11. Total salary of A and B is equal. If A gets 65% allowance of his basic salary and B gets 80% of his basic salary. If the basic salary of B is ₹ 1,100, then the basic salary of A is:
(a) ₹ 1,200 (b) ₹ 1,980
(c) ₹ 1,800 (d) ₹ 1,100
(e) None of these

12. The length of a field is twice its breadth. If the length is reduced by 5 metre and breadth is increased by 3 metre, the area remains as before. The length of the field is:
(a) 15 m (b) 30 m
(c) 12 cm (d) 25 m
(e) None of these

13. A student starts for a hostel 24 km away from his house on bicycle. If he increases his speed by 2 km per hour, he reaches 2 hours early. His speed in km/hour is:
(a) 8 (b) 6
(c) 4 (d) 3
(e) None of these

14. Ravi, after giving away 80% of his pocket money to Komal and 6% of the remaining to Kavita, has ₹ 47 left with him. The money with Ravi in the beginning was:
(a) ₹ 200 (b) ₹ 250
(c) ₹ 500 (d) ₹ 700
(e) None of these

15. The solution of the simultaneous linear equations $2x - 3y = 3$ and $4x - y = 11$ is:
(a) $x = 1, y = 1$ (b) $x = 3, y = 2$
(c) $x = 2, y = 3$ (d) $x = 3, y = 1$
(e) None of these

ANSWERS

1	2	3	4	5	6	7	8	9	10
(a)	(c)	(a)	(d)	(a)	(c)	(d)	(d)	(d)	(d)
11	**12**	**13**	**14**	**15**					
(a)	(b)	(c)	(b)	(d)					

SOME SELECTED EXPLANATORY ANSWERS

1.
$$\frac{x+2}{x-1} = \frac{5}{2}$$
$$2(x + 2) = 5(x - 1)$$
$$2x + 4 = 5x - 5$$
$$2x - 5x = -5 - 4$$
$$-3x = -9$$
$$x = \frac{-9}{-3} = 3$$

2. Let smaller number = x

$\therefore$ larger number = $32 - x$

According to the condition given,

larger number = 2 × smaller number + 5

$\Rightarrow (32 - x) = 2 \times x + 5$

$\Rightarrow 3x = 32 - 5 = 27$

$\therefore x = 9$

$\Rightarrow$ larger number = 32 – 9 = 23

3.
$$\alpha + \beta = \alpha\beta$$
or
$$\frac{-2}{q} = \frac{3q}{q} = 3$$
$$\Rightarrow q = \frac{-2}{3}$$

4. $(x-2)(x+6) \geq 0$

$\Rightarrow \quad (x-2) \geq 0$ and $(x+6) \geq 0$

$\Rightarrow \quad x \geq 2$ and $x \geq -6$

Also $(x-2)(x+6) \geq 0$

$\Rightarrow \quad (x-2) \leq 0$ and $(x+6) \leq 0$

$\Rightarrow \quad x \leq 2$ and $x \leq -6$

5. $\alpha + \beta = \frac{4}{4} = 1, \ \alpha\beta = \frac{1}{4}$

$\therefore \quad \alpha^3 + \alpha^3 = (\alpha+\beta)^3 - 3\alpha\beta(\alpha+\beta)$

$$= 1^3 - 3 \times \frac{1}{4} \times 1 = 1 - \frac{3}{4} = \frac{1}{4}$$

6. $\lambda^2 + 8\lambda + \mu^2 + 6\mu = 0$ (quadratic in λ)

Since roots are real,

$b^2 - 4ac \geq 0$

or $8^2 - 4(\mu^2 + 6\mu) \geq 0$

$\Rightarrow \quad \mu^2 + 6\mu - 16 \leq 0$

$\Rightarrow \quad (\mu + 8)(\mu - 2) \leq 0$

$\Rightarrow \quad \mu \geq -8$ and $\mu \leq 2$

or $\quad \mu \leq -8$ and $\mu \geq 2$

It means μ lies between -8 and 2.

7. $5^{2x} - 5^{x+3} + 125 = 5^x$

or $\quad 5^{2x} - 5^x(125 + 1) + 125 = 0$

or $\quad 5^x(5^x - 125) - 1(5^x - 125) = 0$

or $\quad (5^x - 1)(5^x - 125) = 0$

$\therefore \quad 5^x - 1 = 0$

or $\quad 5^x - 125 = 0$

or $\quad 5^x = 1 = 5^0$

$\therefore \quad x = 0$

or $\quad 5^x = 125 = 5^3$

$\therefore \quad x = 3$

8. Suppose the correct equation be

$$ax^2 + bx + c = 0$$

Taking c and the correct roots α and β, wrong roots as 3 and 2.

$\therefore \quad \alpha + \beta = 3 + 2 = 5 \quad$ ...(*i*)

Also $a = 1$ and $c = -6$,

$\alpha\beta = c/a = -6 \quad$ ...(*ii*)

Solving, we get the correct roots are 6 and –1.

9. By hypothesis,

$3k^2 - 4 = 5$

or $\quad 3k^2 = 9$

$\Rightarrow \quad k^2 = 3$

Disc. $= 4k^2 - 4(3k^2 - 4)$

$= -8 < 0$

Hence, roots are imaginary.

10. $x^2 - 6x + 10 = 0 \quad$ ...(1)

$\therefore \quad x - (\alpha + \beta)x + \alpha\beta = 0 \quad$ ...(2)

{$\because \alpha, \beta$ are the roots of (1)

Comparing (1) and (2),

$\alpha + \beta = 6$ and $\alpha\beta = 10$

$\therefore \quad \alpha^2 + \beta^2 = (\alpha+\beta)^2 - 2\alpha\beta$

$= 6^2 - 2 \times 10$

$= 36 - 20 = 16$

11. Let the basic salary of A = x

$\therefore$ A's total salary

$= x + 65\%$ of x

$$= x + x \times \frac{65}{100} = x + \frac{65x}{100} \quad \text{...(i)}$$

B's total salary

$= 1,100 + 80\%$ of $1,100$

$$= 1,100 + \frac{80 \times 1,100}{100}$$

$= 1,100 + 880 = 1,980 \quad$ ...(*ii*)

A's total salary = B's total salary (given)

$$\Rightarrow \quad x + \frac{65x}{100} = 1,980$$

$\Rightarrow \quad 100x + 65x = 1,980 \times 100$

$\Rightarrow \quad 165x = 1,980 \times 100$

$$\therefore \quad x = \frac{1,980 \times 100}{165}$$

$= ₹\ 1,200$

12. Let the breadth of the field = x metre

$\therefore$ length of the field = $2x$ metre

and area of the room = $2x \times x = 2x^2$ metre^2 ...(*i*)

New area = $(2x - 5)(x + 3) = 2x^2 + x - 15$ ...(*ii*)

Comparing (*i*) and (*ii*),

$$2x^2 = 2x^2 + x - 15$$

$\Rightarrow \quad x - 15 = 0$

$\therefore \quad x = 15$

Hence, length = 2 × 15 = 30 metre

13. Let the speed of the student be x km/hour

$\therefore$ Time taken to cover 24 km

$$= \frac{24}{x} \text{ hour} \quad ...(1)$$

When speed is $(x + 2)$ km/hour

Then time taken to cover 24 km

$$= \frac{24}{x+2} \text{ hours} \quad ...(2)$$

According to the condition given,

$$\frac{24}{x} - \frac{24}{x+2} = 2$$

$\Rightarrow 24(x + 2) - 24x = 2x(x + 2)$

$\Rightarrow 24x + 48 - 24x = 2x^2 + 4x$

$\Rightarrow \quad 2x^2 + 4x - 48 = 0$

$\Rightarrow \quad x^2 + 2x - 24 = 0$

$\Rightarrow \quad (x + 6)(x - 4) = 0$

$\therefore \quad x = -6$ or $x = 4$

neglecting negative value, the speed of the student is 4 km/hour.

14. Let the pocket money be x

$\therefore \quad 80\%$ of $x = \dfrac{80x}{100} = \dfrac{4x}{5}$

$$\text{Balance} = x - \frac{4x}{5} = \frac{x}{5}$$

Again 6% of $\dfrac{x}{5} = \dfrac{6}{100} \times \dfrac{x}{5} = \dfrac{3x}{250}$

The amount left with Ravi $= \dfrac{x}{5} - \dfrac{3x}{250} = 47$

$\Rightarrow \quad \dfrac{50x - 3x}{250} = 47 \Rightarrow \dfrac{47x}{250} = 47$

$\therefore \quad x = ₹\ 250$

15. $\quad 2x - 3y = 3 \quad ...(1)$

$\quad 4x - y = 11 \quad ...(2)$

Multiply equation (2) by (3), which gives

$\quad 12x - 3y = 33 \quad ...(3)$

Subtracting equation (1) from (3), we get

$\quad 10x = 30$

$\therefore \quad x = 3$

Substituting this value of x in (2), we have

$\quad 4 \times 3 - y = 11$

$\therefore \quad y = 12 - 11 = 1$

❑❑❑

21 Trigonometry

Trigonometery

1. In a right Δ the side between the reference angle and the right angle is treated as the **base**, the side opposite to the right angle as the **hypotenuse** and the remaining side is taken as the **perpendicular.**

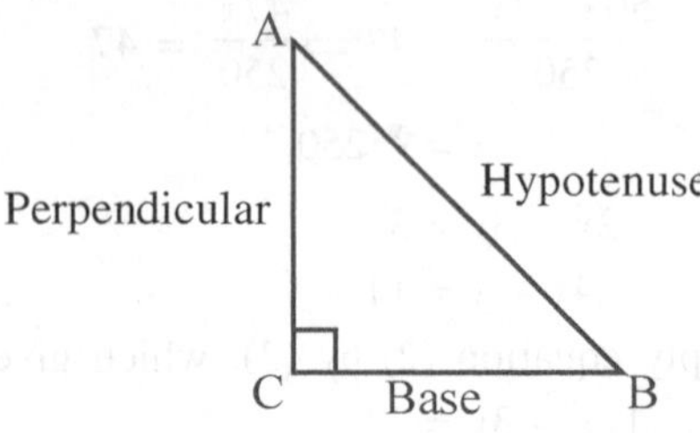

2. Trigonometric Ratios

Let **perpendicular** be **P, base** be **B** and **hypotenuse** be **H.** Then,

$$\sin\theta = \frac{P}{H} \qquad \frac{B}{P} = \cot\theta$$

$$\cos\theta = \frac{B}{H} \qquad \frac{H}{B} = \sec\theta$$

$$\tan\theta = \frac{P}{B} \qquad \frac{H}{P} = \operatorname{cosec}\theta$$

3. Reciprocals of Trigonometric Ratios

$$\sin\theta = \frac{1}{\operatorname{cosec}\theta} \qquad \frac{1}{\sin\theta} = \operatorname{cosec}\theta$$

$$\cos\theta = \frac{1}{\sec\theta} \qquad \frac{1}{\cos\theta} = \sec\theta$$

$$\tan\theta = \frac{1}{\cot\theta} \qquad \frac{1}{\tan\theta} = \cot\theta$$

$$\cot\theta = \frac{1}{\tan\theta} \qquad \frac{1}{\cot\theta} = \tan\theta$$

$$\sec\theta = \frac{1}{\cos\theta} \qquad \frac{1}{\sec\theta} = \cos\theta$$

$$\operatorname{cosec}\theta = \frac{1}{\sin\theta} \qquad \frac{1}{\operatorname{cosec}\theta} = \sin\theta$$

$$\frac{\sin\theta}{\cos\theta} = \tan\theta \qquad \frac{\cos\theta}{\sin\theta} = \cot\theta$$

4. Trigonometric Ratios of Complementary Angles

$$\sin\theta = \cos(90-\theta) \qquad \cos\theta = \sin(90-\theta)$$

$$\tan\theta = \cot(90-\theta) \qquad \cot\theta = \tan(90-\theta)$$

$$\sec\theta = \operatorname{cosec}(90-\theta) \qquad \operatorname{cosec}\theta = \sec(90-\theta)$$

$$\sin(90-\theta) = \cos\theta \qquad \cos(90-\theta) = \sin\theta$$

$$\tan(90-\theta) = \cot\theta \qquad \cot(90-\theta) = \tan\theta$$

$$\sec(90-\theta) = \operatorname{cosec}\theta \qquad \operatorname{cosec}(90-\theta) = \sec\theta$$

5. Trigonometric Identities

$$\sin^2\theta + \cos^2\theta = 1$$

$$\sin^2\theta = 1-\cos^2\theta = (1-\cos\theta)(1+\cos\theta)$$

$$(1-\cos\theta)(1+\cos\theta) = 1-\cos^2\theta = \sin^2\theta$$

$$\cos^2\theta = 1-\sin^2\theta = (1-\sin\theta)(1+\sin\theta)$$

$$(1-\sin\theta)(1+\sin\theta) = 1-\sin^2\theta = \cos^2\theta$$

$$1+\tan^2\theta = \sec^2\theta$$

$$\tan^2\theta = \sec^2 - 1 = (\sec\theta - 1)(\sec\theta + 1)$$

$$(\sec\theta - 1)(\sec\theta + 1) = \sec^2\theta - 1 = \tan^2\theta$$

$$1 = \sec^2\theta - \tan^2\theta = (\sec\theta - \tan\theta)(\sec\theta + \tan\theta)$$

$$(\sec\theta - \tan\theta)(\sec\theta + \tan\theta) = \sec^2\theta - \tan^2\theta = 1$$

$$1 + \cot^2\theta = \text{cosec}^2\theta$$

$$\cot^2\theta = \text{cosec}^2\theta - 1 = (\text{cosec}\,\theta - 1)(\text{cosec}\,\theta + 1)$$

$$(\text{cosec}\,\theta - 1)(\text{cosec}\,\theta + 1) = \text{cosec}^2\theta - 1 = \cot^2\theta$$

$$1 = \text{cosec}^2\theta - \cot^2\theta = (\text{cosec}\theta - \cot\theta)(\text{cosec}\theta + \cot\theta)$$

$$(\text{cosec}\theta - \cot\theta)(\text{cosec}\theta + \cot\theta) = \text{cosec}^2\theta - \cot^2\theta = 1$$

6. Trigonometric Values

	0°	30°	45°	60°	90°
$\sin\theta$	0	$\frac{1}{2}$	$\frac{1}{\sqrt{2}}$	$\frac{\sqrt{3}}{2}$	1
$\cos\theta$	1	$\frac{\sqrt{3}}{2}$	$\frac{1}{\sqrt{2}}$	$\frac{1}{2}$	0
$\tan\theta$	0	$\frac{1}{\sqrt{3}}$	1	$\sqrt{3}$	∞
$\cot\theta$	∞	$\sqrt{3}$	1	$\frac{1}{\sqrt{3}}$	0
$\sec\theta$	1	$\frac{2}{\sqrt{3}}$	$\sqrt{2}$	2	∞
$\text{cosec}\,\theta$	∞	2	$\sqrt{2}$	$\frac{2}{\sqrt{3}}$	1

Approximate Values

$\sqrt{2} = 1.414;$ $\sqrt{3} = 1.732;$

$\frac{1}{\sqrt{2}} = 0.707;$ $\frac{1}{\sqrt{3}} = 0.577;$

$\frac{\sqrt{3}}{2} = 0.866;$ $\frac{2}{\sqrt{3}} = 1.154$

7. Sum and Difference Formulae

$$\sin(A+B) = \sin A\cos B + \cos A\sin B$$

$$\sin(A-B) = \sin A\cos B - \cos A\sin B$$

$$\cos(A+B) = \cos A\cos B - \sin A\sin B$$

$$\cos(A-B) = \cos A\cos B + \sin A\sin B$$

$$\tan(A+B) = \frac{\tan A + \tan B}{1 - \tan A.\tan B}$$

$$\tan(A-B) = \frac{\tan A - \tan B}{1 + \tan A.\tan B}$$

8. Multiple and Submultiple Angles

$$\tan 2x = 2\sin x\cos x$$

$$\cos 2x = \cos^2 x - \sin^2 x = 2\cos^2 x - 1$$

$$= 1 - 2\sin^2 x$$

$$\sin 2x = \frac{2\tan x}{1 - \tan^2 x}$$

$$\sin 3x = 3\sin x - 4\sin^3 x$$

$$\cos 3x = 4\cos^3 x - 3\cos x$$

$$\tan 3x = \frac{3\tan x - \tan^3 x}{1 - 3\tan^2 x}$$

9. Trigonometric Ratios of Some Important Angles

$$\sin 15° = \frac{\sqrt{3}-1}{2\sqrt{2}} = \frac{\sqrt{6}-\sqrt{2}}{4} = \cos 75°$$

$$\cos 15° = \frac{\sqrt{3}+1}{2\sqrt{2}} = \frac{\sqrt{6}+\sqrt{2}}{4} = \sin 15°$$

$$\tan 15° = \frac{\sqrt{3}-1}{\sqrt{3}+1} = 2 - \sqrt{3} = \cot 75°$$

$$\cot 15° = \frac{\sqrt{3}+1}{\sqrt{3}-1} = 2 + \sqrt{3} = \tan 15°$$

HEIGHTS AND DISTANCES

(a) $a = c\cot\theta = b\cos\theta$

$b = c\,\text{cosec}\,\theta = a\sec\theta$

$c = b\sin\theta = a\tan\theta$

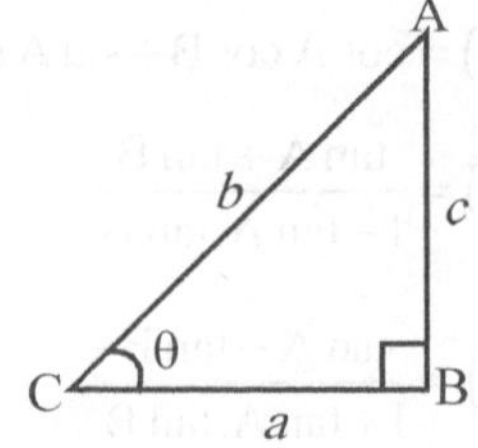

(b) $x = h(\cot\theta + \cot\alpha)$

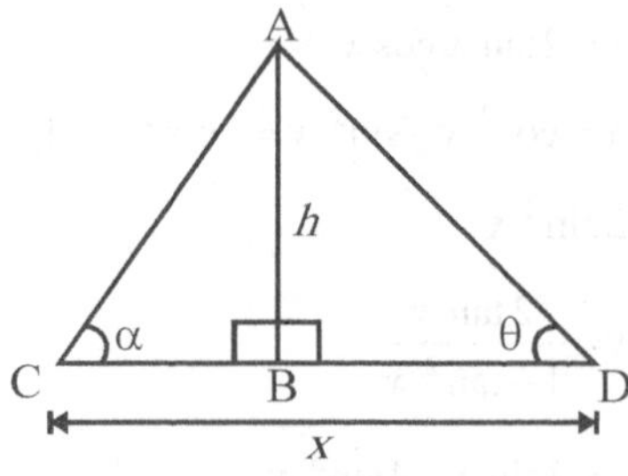

(c) $x = h(\cot\theta - \cot\alpha)$

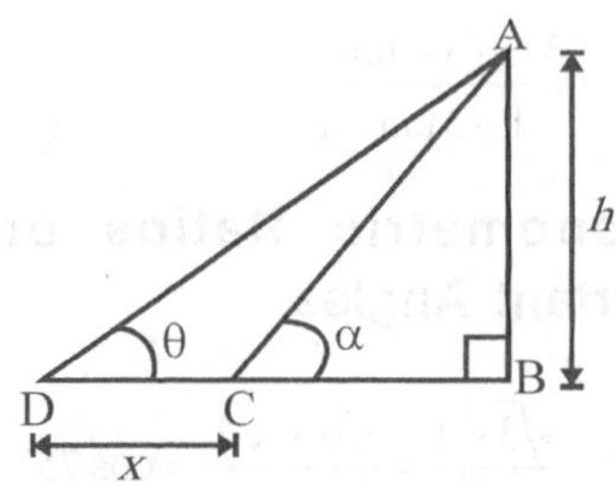

(d) $x = h(\cot\theta + \cot\alpha)$

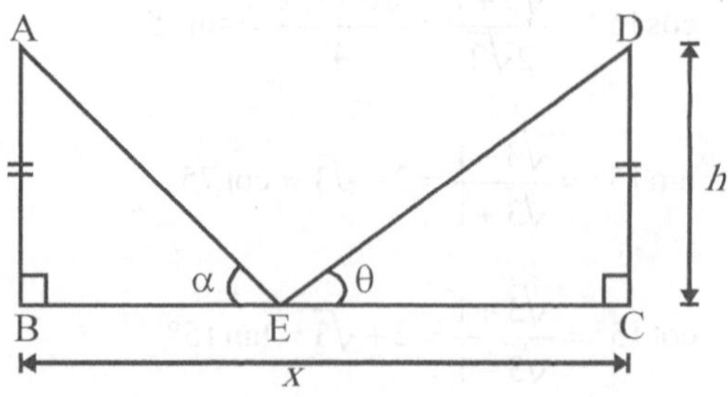

(e) 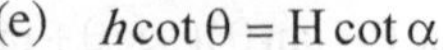 $h\cot\theta = \text{H}\cot\alpha$

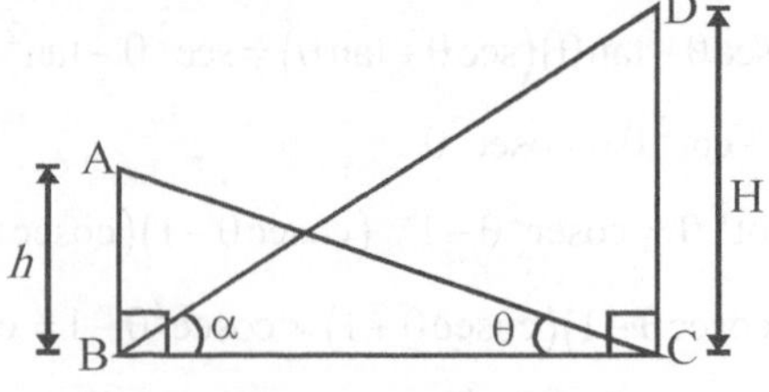

(f) $h = x(\tan\alpha - \tan\theta)$

$h\cot\alpha = \text{H}(\cot\theta - \cot\alpha)$

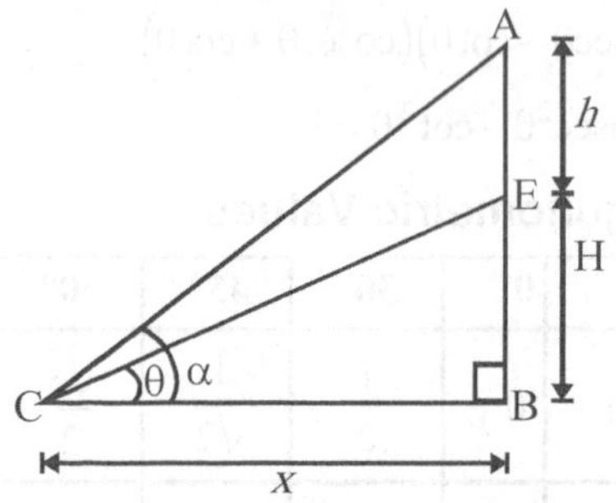

(g) $h\cot\theta = \text{H}(\cot\theta - \cot\alpha)$

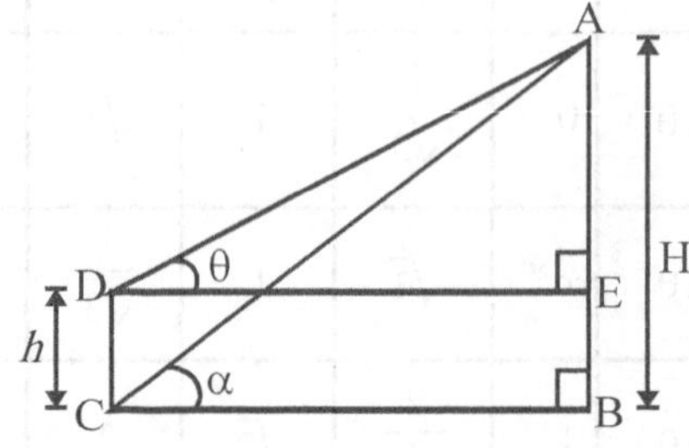

(h) $x = h\cot\alpha$

$h(\cot\alpha + \cot\theta) = \text{H}\cot\theta$

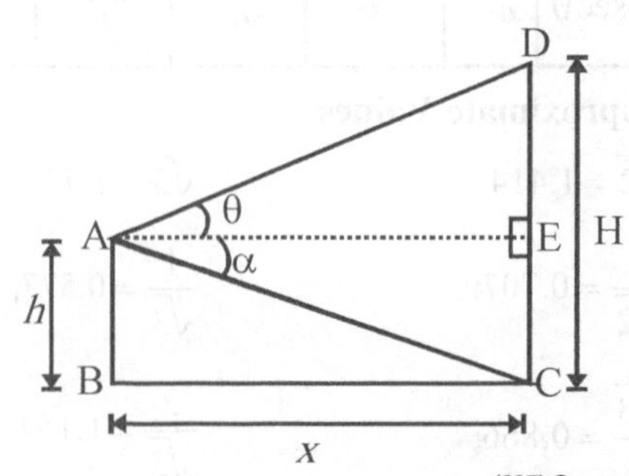

(i) $x = h(\cot\theta - \cot\alpha)$

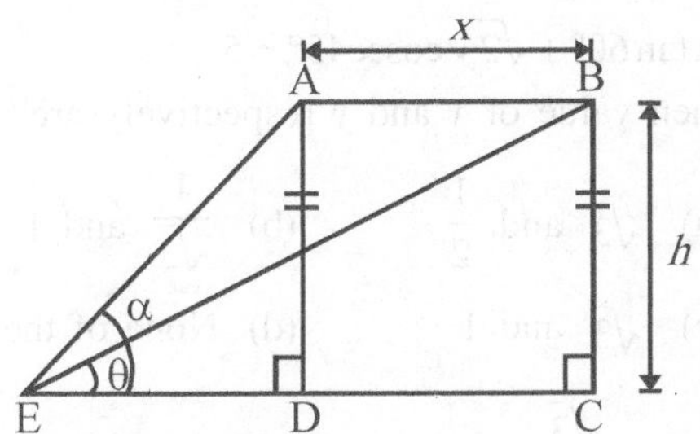

(j) $h = x\left(\dfrac{\tan\alpha + \tan\theta}{\tan\alpha - \tan\theta}\right)$

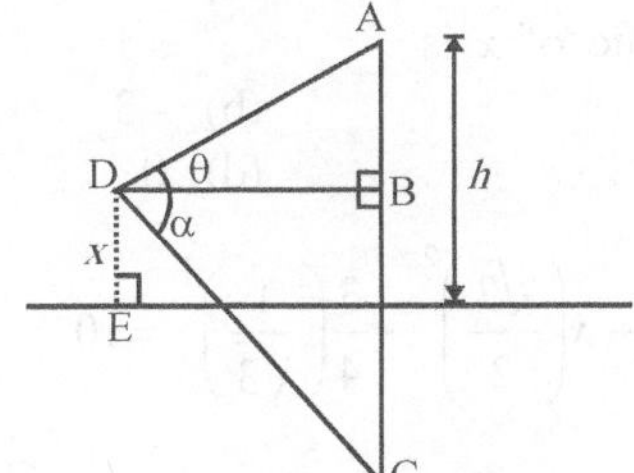

EXAMPLES

Example 1 :

If $\tan\theta = \dfrac{4}{5}$, then $\dfrac{1-\cos\theta}{1+\cos\theta} = ...$

(a) $\dfrac{1}{2}$ (b) $\dfrac{1}{8}$

(c) $\dfrac{1}{16}$ (d) $\dfrac{1}{4}$

Sol.

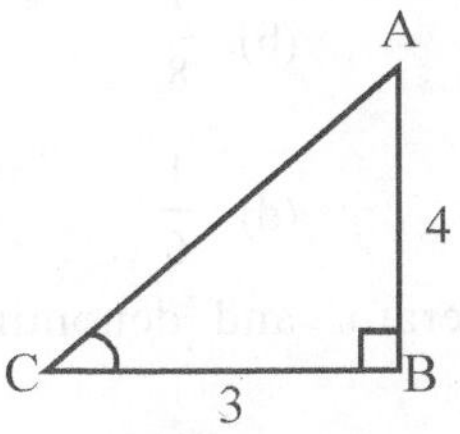

$\tan\theta = \dfrac{4}{3} \Rightarrow AB = 4, BC = 3$

$\Rightarrow AC^2 = 3^2 + 4^2 = 25$

$\Rightarrow AC = 5$

$\Rightarrow \cos\theta = \dfrac{3}{5}$

$$\frac{1-\cos\theta}{1+\cos\theta} = \frac{1-\frac{3}{5}}{1+\frac{3}{5}} = \frac{2}{8} = \frac{1}{4}$$

Hence, option (d) is correct.

Example 2 :

$3\sin^2 30° + 2\cos^2 45° - 5\tan^2 30° = ...$

(a) $\dfrac{1}{2}$ (b) $\dfrac{1}{12}$

(c) $\dfrac{1}{6}$ (d) $\dfrac{1}{3}$

Sol. L.H.S $= 3\times\left(\dfrac{1}{2}\right)^2 + 2\times\left(\dfrac{1}{\sqrt{2}}\right)^2 - 5\times\left(\dfrac{1}{\sqrt{3}}\right)^2$

$= 3\times\dfrac{1}{4} + 2\times\dfrac{1}{2} - 5\times\dfrac{1}{3} = \dfrac{1}{12}$

Hence, option (b) is correct.

Example 3 :

If $\sqrt{3}\cot\theta = 1,\ \ 0 \le \theta \le 90°$,
Then the value of $\cos^2\theta - \sin^2\theta$ is

(a) $\dfrac{1}{2}$ (b) $-\dfrac{1}{2}$

(c) $\dfrac{1}{\sqrt{2}}$ (d) 0

Sol. $\cot\theta = \dfrac{1}{\sqrt{3}} \Rightarrow \theta = 60°$

Then, $\cos^2 60° - \sin^2 60° = \left(\dfrac{1}{2}\right)^2 - \left(\dfrac{\sqrt{3}}{2}\right)^2$

$= \dfrac{1}{4} - \dfrac{3}{4} = -\dfrac{1}{2}$

Hence option (b) is correct.

Example 4 :

If $2\sec^2 60° + x\cos^2 30° - \frac{3}{4}\cot^2 60° = 10$, then the value of x is

(a) 3 (b) –3

(c) 2 (d) 0

Sol. $2(2)^2 + x\left(\frac{\sqrt{3}}{2}\right)^2 - \frac{3}{4}\left(\frac{1}{\sqrt{3}}\right)^2 = 10$

$\Rightarrow \ 8 + \frac{3}{4}x - \frac{1}{4} = 10$

$\Rightarrow \ \frac{3}{4}x = 10 - 8 + \frac{1}{4}$

$\Rightarrow \ x = \frac{9}{4} \times \frac{4}{3} = 3$

Hence, option (a) is correct.

Example 5 :

If $2\cos 3\theta = 1$ then $\theta =$ ....

(a) 20° (b) 40°

(c) 25° (d) None of these

Sol. $2.\cos 3\theta = 1 \Rightarrow \ \cos 3\theta = \frac{1}{2} = \cos 60°$

$\Rightarrow \ 3\theta = 60°$

$\Rightarrow \ \theta = 20°$

Hence, option (a) is correct.

Example 6 :

If $x^2 \tan^2 45° + 3\cos^2 60° - 7\sin^2 30° = 99$, then x = ...

(a) $\pm\frac{1}{2}$ (b) $\pm\sqrt{2}$

(c) ± 1 (d) ± 10

Sol. $x^2(1)^2 + 3\left(\frac{1}{2}\right)^2 - 7\times\left(\frac{1}{2}\right)^2 = 99$

$\Rightarrow \ x^2 + \frac{3}{4} - \frac{7}{4} = 99$

$\Rightarrow \ x^2 = 100$

$\Rightarrow \ x = \pm 10$

Hence, option (d) is correct.

Example 7 :

If $2x\sin 60° - 3y\tan 45° = 0$ and

$x\tan 60° + \sqrt{2}y\,\text{cosec}45° = 5$

then value of x and y respectively are

(a) $\sqrt{3}$ and $\frac{1}{2}$ (b) $\frac{1}{\sqrt{3}}$ and 1

(c) $\sqrt{3}$ and 1 (d) None of these

Sol. $\begin{cases} 2x.\frac{\sqrt{3}}{2} - 3y.1 = 0 \\ x.\sqrt{3} + \sqrt{2y}.\sqrt{2} = 5 \end{cases}$

$\Rightarrow \ \sqrt{3}x - 3y = 0$

$\sqrt{3}x + 2y = 5$

solving $x = \sqrt{3}, y = 1$

Hence, option (c) is correct.

Example 8 :

If $\tan\theta = \frac{2}{\sqrt{5}}$, then $\frac{\text{cosec}^2\theta - \sec^2\theta}{\text{cosec}^2\theta + \sec^2\theta} =$ ....

(a) $\frac{1}{9}$ (b) $\frac{1}{8}$

(c) $\frac{1}{7}$ (d) $\frac{1}{6}$

Sol. Dividing numerator and denominator by $\text{cosec}^2\theta$

We get $\frac{1 - \frac{\sec^2\theta}{\text{cosec}^2\theta}}{1 + \frac{\sec^2\theta}{\text{cosec}^2\theta}}$

However $\frac{\sec\theta}{\text{cosec}\theta} = \left(\frac{1}{\cos\theta}\right)\left(\frac{\sin\theta}{1}\right) = \tan\theta = \frac{2}{\sqrt{5}}$

The value of expression is

$\frac{1 - \frac{4}{5}}{1 + \frac{4}{5}} = \frac{1}{9}$

Hence, option (a) is correct.

Example 9 :

$(\sin A - \cos A)^2 + (\cos A - \sin A)^2 = ...$

(a) 2 (b) −2
(c) 1 (d) 0

Sol. $\sin^2 A + \cos^2 A - 2\sin A\cos A + \cos^2 A + \sin^2 A + 2\sin A\cos A$

$= 2\sin^2 A + 2\cos^2 A$

$= 2(\sin^2 A + \cos^2 A)$

$= 2$

Hence, option (a) is correct

Example 10 :

$\sqrt{1-\cos^2\theta} = \frac{\sqrt{3}}{2}$ and $0 \le \theta \le 90°$ then $\theta = ...$

(a) 60° (b) 30°
(c) 15° (d) 75°

Sol. $\sqrt{1-\cos^2\theta} = \sqrt{\sin^2\theta} = \sin\theta$

$\sin\theta = \frac{\sqrt{3}}{2} \Rightarrow \theta = 60°$

Hence option (a) is correct

Example 11 :

$\sin^6 A + \cos^6 A = ...$

(a) $1 + 3\sin^2 A\cos^2 A$

(b) $3\sin^2 A\cos^2 A - 1$

(c) $1 - 3\sin A\cos A$

(d) None of the above

Sol. $(\sin^2 A)^3 + (\cos^2 A)^3$

$= (\sin^2 A + \cos^2 A)^3 - 3\sin^2 A\cos^2 A\,(\sin^2 A + \cos^2 A)$

$= 1 - 3\sin^2 A\cos^2 A$

none of the option (a), (b) or (c) are correct. Hence option (d) is the correct answer.

Example 12 :

$\frac{\cot\theta + \mathrm{cosec}\theta - 1}{\cot\theta - \mathrm{cosec}\theta + 1} = ...$

(a) $\frac{1+\sin\theta}{\cos\theta}$ (b) $\frac{1-\sin\theta}{\cos\theta}$

(c) $\frac{1+\cos\theta}{\sin\theta}$ (d) $\frac{1-\cos\theta}{\sin\theta}$

Sol. Substitute 1 in the numerator only by $\mathrm{cosec}^2\theta - \cot^2\theta$

$\text{LHS} = \frac{\cot\theta + \mathrm{cosec}\theta - (\mathrm{cosec}^2\theta - \cos^2\theta)}{(\cot\theta - \mathrm{cosec}\theta + 1)}$

$= \frac{(\cot\theta - \mathrm{cosec}\theta + \cot\theta)(\mathrm{cosec}\theta - \cot\theta)}{(\cot\theta - \mathrm{cosec}\theta + 1)}$

$= \frac{(\cot\theta + \mathrm{cosec}\theta)(1 - \mathrm{cosec}\theta + \cot\theta)}{(1 - \mathrm{cosec}\theta + \cot\theta)}$

$= \cot\theta + \mathrm{cosec}\theta$

$= \frac{1+\cos\theta}{\sin\theta}$

Hence option (c) is correct.

Example 13 :

$\frac{1}{\sec A - \tan A} - \frac{1}{\cos A} = ...$

(a) $\frac{1}{\sec A} - \frac{1}{\sec A - \tan A}$

(b) $\frac{1}{\cos A} - \frac{1}{\sec A + \tan A}$

(c) $\frac{1}{\cos A} + \frac{1}{\sec A - \tan A}$

(d) None of the above

Sol. $\text{LHS} = \frac{1}{\sec A - \tan A} \times \frac{\sec A + \tan A}{\sec A + \tan A} - \frac{1}{\cos A}$

$= \frac{\sec A + \tan A}{\sec^2 A - \tan^2 A} - \frac{1}{\cos A}$

$= \sec A + \tan A - \sec A$

$= \tan A$

$= \sec A - \sec A + \tan A$

$= \sec A - (\sec A - \tan A)$

$= \sec A - \dfrac{(\sec A + \tan A)(\sec A + \tan A)}{\sec A + \tan A}$

$= \dfrac{1}{\cos A} - \dfrac{1}{\sec A + \tan A}$

Hence, option (b) is correct.

Example 14 :

$\cot 7°.\cot 23°.\cot 67°.\cot 83° =$ ....

(a) -1 (b) 1

(c) 0 (d) $\sqrt{3}$

Sol. $\cot 83° = \tan(90-83)° = \tan 7° = \dfrac{1}{\cot 7°}$

similarly $\cot 67° = \dfrac{1}{\cot 23°}$

$\Rightarrow$ LHS $= \cot 7°.\cot 23°.\dfrac{1}{\cot 23°}.\dfrac{1}{\cot 7°} = 1$

Hence, option (b) is correct

Example 15 :

Maximum and minimum value of $5\sin x + 3\cos x$ respectively are

(a) -8 and $+8$

(b) 2 and 8

(c) $-\sqrt{34}$ and $+\sqrt{34}$

(d) None of the above

Sol. A = 5, B = 3

maximum value $= \sqrt{A^2 + B^2} = \sqrt{5^2 + 3^2} = \sqrt{34}$

minimum value $= \sqrt{A^2 + B^2} = -\sqrt{34}$

Hence option (c) is correct.

Example 16 :

A vertical flagstaff is surmounted on the top of avertical tower. From a point on the ground the angle of elevation of the top and bottom of the flagstaff are 30° and 15° respectively. If the tower is 20 m high, the height of the flagstaff is

(a) 10.72 m

(b) 5.36 m

(c) 9.38 m

(d) None of the above

Sol.

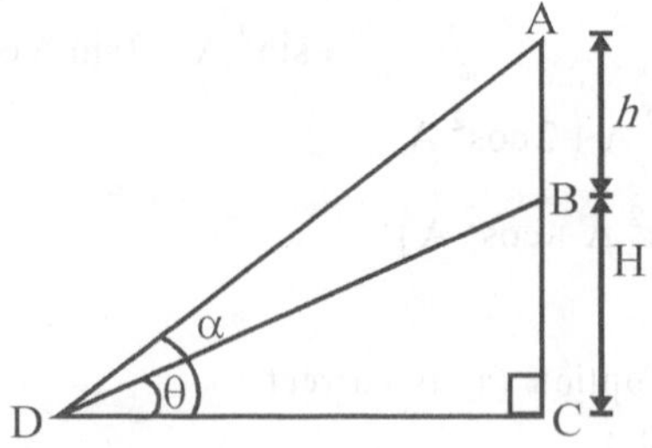

$\theta = 15°$, $\alpha = 30°$,

H = 20 m, h = ?

but $h = \dfrac{H(\cot\theta - \cot\alpha)}{\cot\theta}$

$\Rightarrow h = \dfrac{20(\cot 15° - \cot 30°)}{\cot 15°}$ m

$\Rightarrow h = \dfrac{20(2+\sqrt{3}-\sqrt{3})}{2+\sqrt{3}}$ m

$\Rightarrow h = \dfrac{40}{2+\sqrt{3}} \times \dfrac{2-\sqrt{3}}{2-\sqrt{3}}$ m

$\Rightarrow h = 40(2-\sqrt{3})$m

$\Rightarrow h \approx 40(2-1.732)$m

$\Rightarrow h \approx 10.72$m

Hence, option (a) is correct.

Example 17 :

An aircraft flying parallel to the ground is observed at an instant at an elevation of 30°. After 9 seconds the elevation changed to 60°. If the speed of the plane is 360 km/hr then the height at which it is flying is

(a) 450 m (b) $600\sqrt{3}$ m

(c) $900\sqrt{3}$ (d) $450\sqrt{3}$ m

Sol. Speed $= 360\dfrac{\text{km}}{\text{hr}} = 360\times\dfrac{5}{18}\text{ m/sec} = 100 \text{ m/sec}$

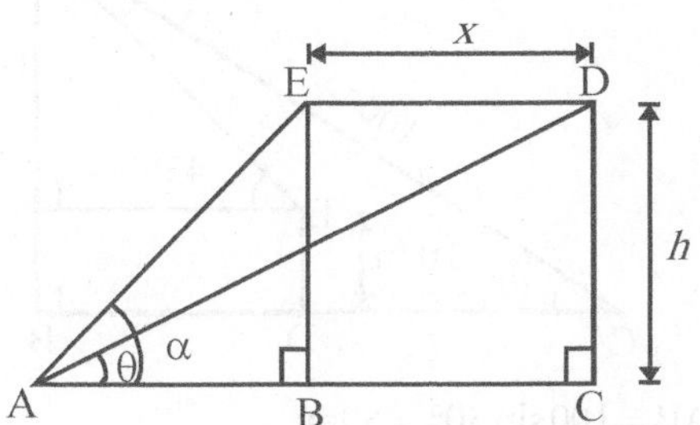

distance : $x = 100\times 9 \text{ m} = 900 \text{ m}$

$x = 900,\quad \theta = 30°,\quad \alpha = 60°,\quad h = ?$

but $h = \dfrac{x}{\cot\theta - \cot\alpha}$

$\Rightarrow\ h = \dfrac{900}{\cot 30° - \cot 60°}\text{m}$

$\Rightarrow\ h = \dfrac{900}{\left(\sqrt{3} - \dfrac{1}{\sqrt{3}}\right)}\text{m}$

$\Rightarrow\ h = 900\times\dfrac{\sqrt{3}}{2}\text{m}$

$\Rightarrow\ h = 450\sqrt{3}\text{ m}$

Hence option (d) is correct

Example 18 :

Two boats on either side of a light house observe the angles of elevation of the top to be 30° and 45° respectively. If the tower is 50m high and the boats and the light house are in same straight line, then the distance between the boats is

(a) 36.6 m (b) 366 m
(c) 236.6 m (d) 246.6 m

Sol.

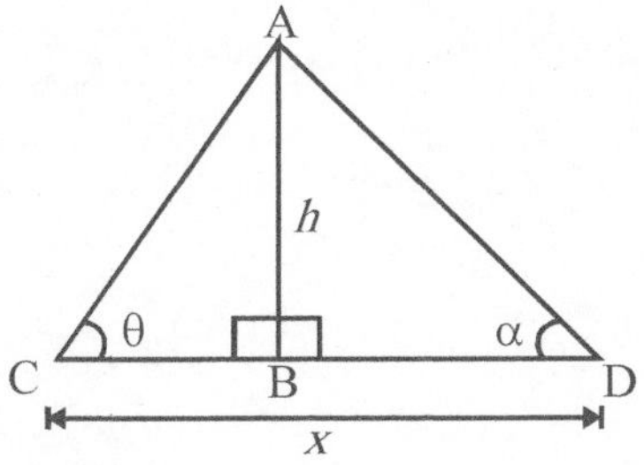

$\theta = 45°,\quad \alpha = 30°,\quad h = 50\text{m},\quad x = ?$

but $x = h(\cot\theta + \cot\alpha)$

$\Rightarrow\ x = 50(\cot 45° + \cot 30°)\text{m}$

$\Rightarrow\ x = 50\left(1+\sqrt{3}\right)\text{m}$

$\Rightarrow\ x \approx 50(1+1.732)\text{m}$

$\Rightarrow x \approx 236.6\text{m}$

Hence, option (c) is correct

Example 19 :

A tower in a city is 150 m high and a multistory hotel at the city centre is 20 m high. The angle of elevation of the top of the hotel is 5°, A building *h* meters high stands on the straight road connecting the tower and the hotel at a distance of 1.2 km from the tower. If the top of the hotel, top of the building and top of the tower are in a same straight line, then the distance of the tower from the hotel is

[use $\tan 5° = 0.0875, \tan 85° = 11.43$]

(a) 1386 m (b) 1486 m
(c) 1468 m (d) 1528 m

Sol.

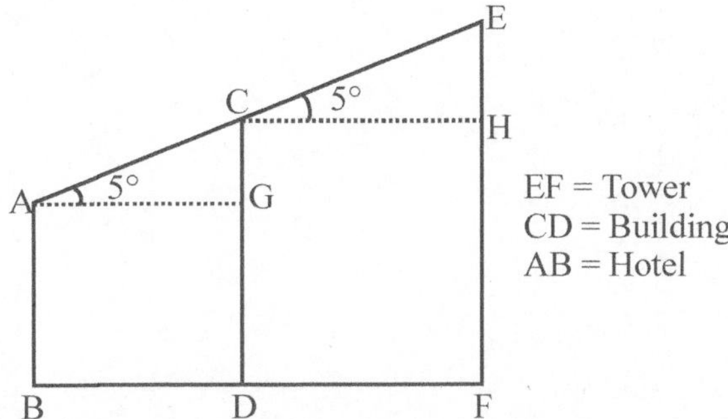

EF = 150 m; AB = 20 m; CD = *h*;
DF = 1.2 km = 1200 m; BF = ?
CH = DF = 1200 m
from Δ CHE, EH = 1200 tan 5°
$= 1200\times 0.0875 = 105$
CD = FH = 150 – 105 = 45 m
$GC = 45 - 20 = 25\text{m}$ [Note GD = AB]

From $\Delta AGC, AG = 25\cot 5°$

$= 25\tan 85° = 286$ m

Hence, $BF = 1200 + 286 = 1486$ m

Hence option (b) is correct

Example 20 :

A boy standing on ground on flying a kite with a 100 m long string. The string is inclined to the ground at an angle of 30°. Another boy is standing on the roof of a 10 m tall building and is flying a kite making an angle of elevation of 43° with the horizontal. If both the boys are on same side of the kites then the length of the string the second boy must have so that the two kites meet is ...... [Use cosec 43° = 1.466]

(a) 50.65 m (b) 58 m

(c) 58.64 m (d) None of the above

Sol.

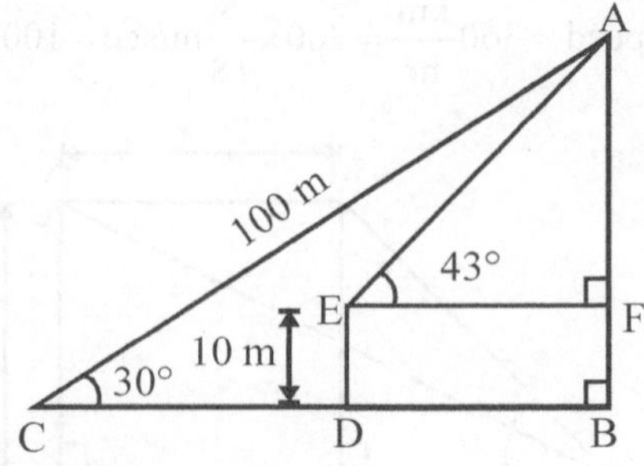

$AB = 100\sin 30° = 50$m;

$FB = DE = 10$m; $\Rightarrow AF = 40$m

$AE = AF\text{cosec}43°$

$AE = 40 \times 1.466$m

$AE = 58.64$ m

Hence, option (c) is correct.

❑❑❑

General Intelligence

LETTER SERIES

In letter series, the letters follow a definite order. The given series of letters can be in natural order or in reverse order or combination of both. The letters may be skipped or repeated or consecutive. The given series may be single or may even comprise of two different series merged at alternate positions. While attempting questions on letter series one should note the pattern of alphabet series.

Alphabets in natural series are :

A B C D E F G H I J K L M N O P Q R S T U V W X Y Z

A	E	J	O	T	Y
↓	↓	↓	↓	↓	↓
1st	5th	10th	15th	20th	25th

Alphabets in reverse series are :

Z Y X W V U T S R Q P O N M L K J I H G F E D C B A

Z	V	Q	L	G	B
↓	↓	↓	↓	↓	↓
1st	5th	10th	15th	20th	25th

Note : On reaching Z, the series restarts from A and on reaching A, it restarts from Z.

EXERCISE

Directions : *In each of the following series determine the order of the letters. Then from the given options select the one which will complete the given series.*

1. B Y C X D W E ?
(*a*) S (*b*) T
(*c*) U (*d*) V

2. B A F E J I P O ? U
(*a*) V (*b*) T
(*c*) S (*d*) Q

3. B A D C ? H G J I
(*a*) EF (*b*) FE
(*c*) FG (*d*) DF

4. ADG, XVT, BEH, WUS, ?
(*a*) VTR (*b*) CFI
(*c*) DFJ (*d*) STU

5. GMSY, IOUA, KQWC, ?
(*a*) MSYE (*b*) NSYE
(*c*) MTYE (*d*) MSYF

6. ADG, GJM, ?, SVY
(*a*) MPS (*b*) MQR
(*c*) MQS (*d*) SPM

7. XYZ, UVW, ?, OPQ
(*a*) RST (*b*) STU
(*c*) QRS (*d*) TUV

8. JOBS, KMEO, LKHK, ?, NGNC
(*a*) MJLH (*b*) LIKG
(*c*) MIKG (*d*) MNGM

9. AZ, GT, MN, ?, YB
(*a*) KF (*b*) TS
(*c*) RX (*d*) SH

10. BMY, DNW, FOU, ?
(*a*) HPT (*b*) HPS
(*c*) HQS (*d*) GPS

11. AZ, CX, EV, ?
(*a*) HU (*b*) GS
(*c*) GT (*d*) HT

12. DMP, FLN, HKL, JJJ, ?
(*a*) MIH (*b*) III
(*c*) LIH (*d*) MII

13. ECA, JHF, OMK, ?, YWU
(*a*) TRP (*b*) LNP
(*c*) QPN (*d*) RPT

14. ABP, CDQ, EFR, ?
(*a*) GHS (*b*) HGS
(*c*) GHR (*d*) GHT

15. BEH, KNQ, TWZ, ?
(*a*) IJL (*b*) BDF
(*c*) CFI (*d*) ADG

16. EJO, TYD, INS, XCH, ?
(*a*) MRW (*b*) NRV
(*c*) MRV (*d*) NRW

17. ABP, CDQ, EFR, ?
(*a*) GHS (*b*) GIS
(*c*) GGS (*d*) GJS

18. NRA, PRC, RRE, TRG, ?
(*a*) USI (*b*) VRI
(*c*) WRJ (*d*) TRI

19. FJKP, ILMQ, LNOR, OPQS, ?
(*a*) RQTV (*b*) RQSS
(*c*) RRST (*d*) RTTU

20. DQCP, EPEN, FOGL, GNIJ, ?
(*a*) HNLG (*b*) HLJG
(*c*) HOMI (*d*) HMKH

21. DFST, FSTD, STDF, ?
(*a*) TSFD (*b*) FDTS
(*c*) TDFS (*d*) SFDT

22. IXT, MAV, QDX, ?
(*a*) WGX (*b*) VHY
(*c*) UGZ (*d*) YHZ

23. QYK, ?, ISG, EPE
(*a*) NWJ (*b*) MVI
(*c*) NVI (*d*) MVJ

24. JMC, CLT, KND, ?, LOE, GPX
(*a*) ENV (*b*) DMX
(*c*) EOU (*d*) DRX

25. ZDV, XGS, VJP, ?
(*a*) SNM (*b*) TMM
(*c*) TNR (*d*) SNT

EXPLANATORY ANSWERS

1. (*d*) : There are two alternate series.

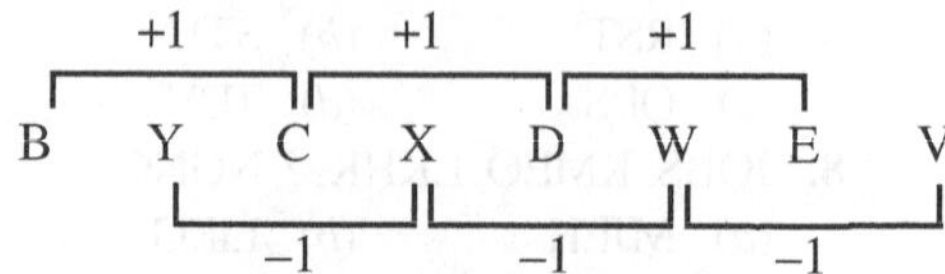

Series I : BCDE (natural order)
Series II : YXWV (reverse order)

2. (*a*) : Each vowel (AEIOU) is preceded by the letter that comes next to it in the natural alphabetical series.

B A F E J I P O V U

3. (*b*) : The letters in natural series are divided into sections of two letters each. The letters in each section are written backward.

<u>BA</u> <u>DC</u> <u>FE</u> <u>HG</u> <u>JI</u>

4. (*b*) : There are two alternate series.

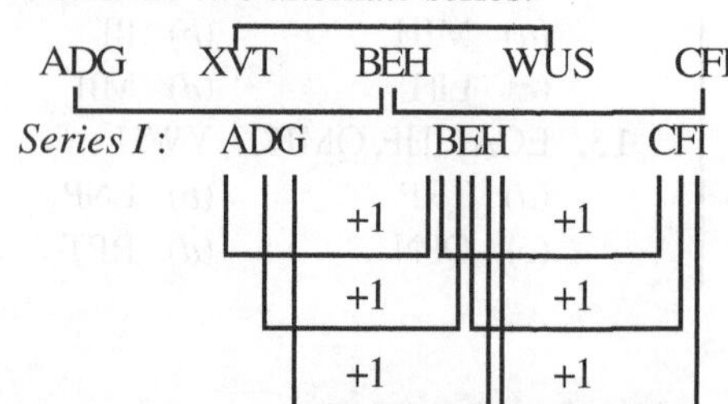

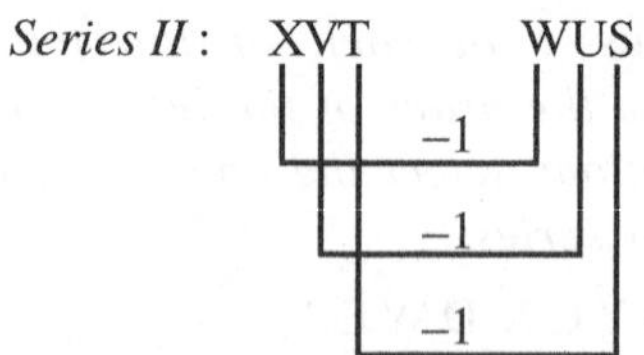

5. (*a*) : The series is formed by moving each letter two steps forward from one group to the next.

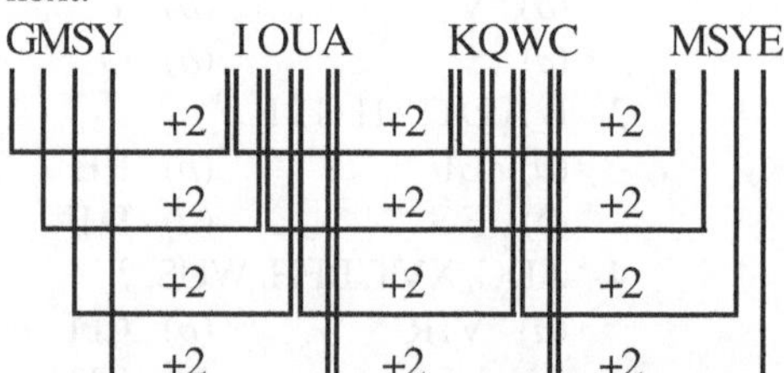

(The series restarts from A on reaching Z)

6. (*a*) : In each group of three letters the alphabet is in the succession of +3. The next group begins with the last alphabet of the previous group.

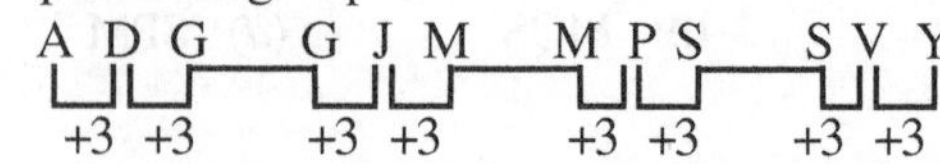

7. (*a*) : The alphabet from one group to the next are in recession of –3, *i.e.*,

XYZ UVW RST OPQ

–3 –3 –3
–3 –3 –3
–3 –3 –3

8. (*c*) : The alphabets in each group follow the pattern +1, –2, +3 and –4 respectively from one group to the next group.

9. (*d*) : The letters in one group correspond to the letters in the next group in the manner +6, –6 respectively, *i.e.*,

AZ GT MN SH YB

+6 +6 +6 +6
–6 –6 –6 –6

10. (*b*) : The letters in one group correspond to the letters in the next group in the manner +2, +1, -2 respectively, *i.e.*,

BMY DNW FOU HPS

+2 +2 +2
+1 +1 +1
–2 –2 –2

11. (*c*) : The letters in each group correspond to the letters in the next group in the manner +2, –2 respectively, *i.e.*,

AZ CX EV GT

+2 +2 +2
–2 –2 –2

12. (*c*) : The alphabets in each group correspond to the alphabets in the next group in the manner +2, –1, –2 respectively, *i.e.*,

DMP FLN HKL JJJ LIH

+2 +2 +2 +2
–1 –1 –1 –1
–2 –2 –2 –2

13. (*a*) : The alphabets in each group are moved five steps forward, *i.e.*,

ECA JHF OMK TRP YWU

+5 +5 +5 +5
+5 +5 +5 +5
+5 +5 +5 +5

14. (*a*) : The letters in one group correspond to the letters in the next group in the manner +2, +2, +1 respectively, *i.e.*,

ABP CDQ EFR GHS

+2 +2 +2
+2 +2 +2
+1 +1 +1

15. (*c*) : All the letters in each group are moved nine steps forward.

BEH KNQ TWZ CFI

+9 +9 +9
+9 +9 +9
+9 +9 +9

16. (*a*) : There are two alternate series :

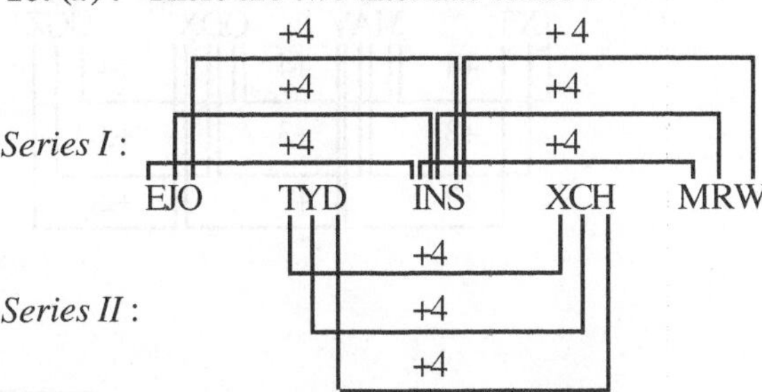

17. (*a*) : The letters in one group correspond to the letters in the next group in the manner +2, +2, +1 respectively, *i.e.*,

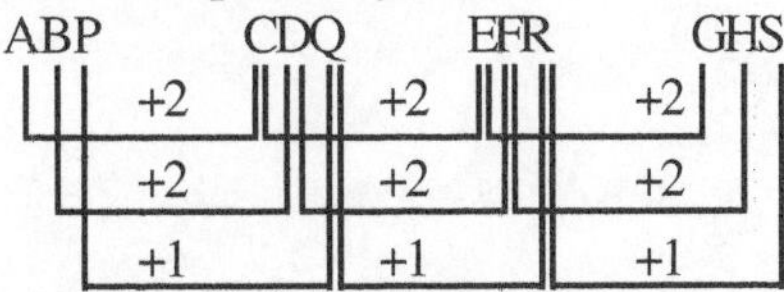

18. (*b*) : The first and third letters are moved two steps forwards while the middle letter remains unchanged, *i.e.*,

NRA PRC RRE TRG VRI

+2 +2 +2 +2
+2 +2 +2 +2

19. (*c*) : The four letters are moved 3, 2, 2, 1 steps forward respectively, *i.e.,*

FJKP ILMQ LNOR OPQS RRST

+3 +3 +3 +3
+2 +2 +2 +2
+2 +2 +2 +2
+1 +1 +1 +1

20. (*d*) : The letters in one group correspond to the letters in the next group in the manner, +1, –1, +2 –2 respectively, *i.e.,*

21. (*c*) : The first letter in each group is the last letter in the next group, *i.e.,*

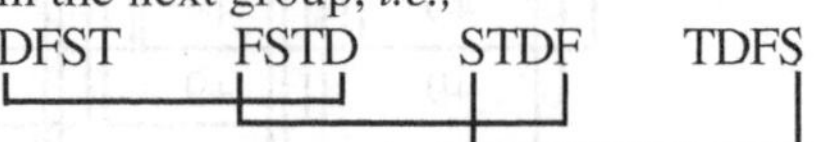

22. (*c*) : The three letters in each group are moved 4, 3 and 2 steps forward respectively, *i.e.,*

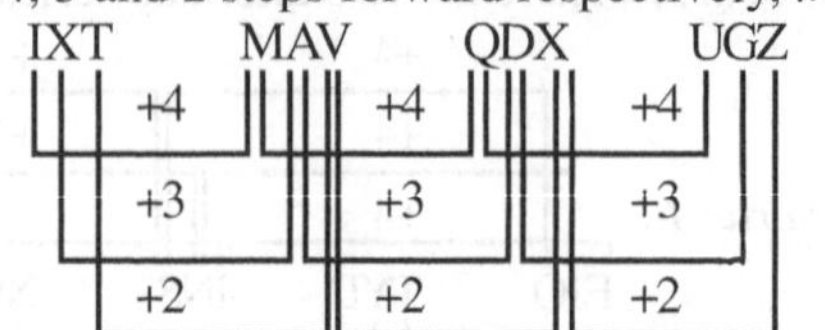

23. (*b*) : The three letters in each group are moved 4, 3 and 2 steps backward respectively, *i.e.,*

QYK MVI ISG EPE

–4 –4 –4
–3 –3 –3
–2 –2 –2

24. (*a*) : There are two alternate series :

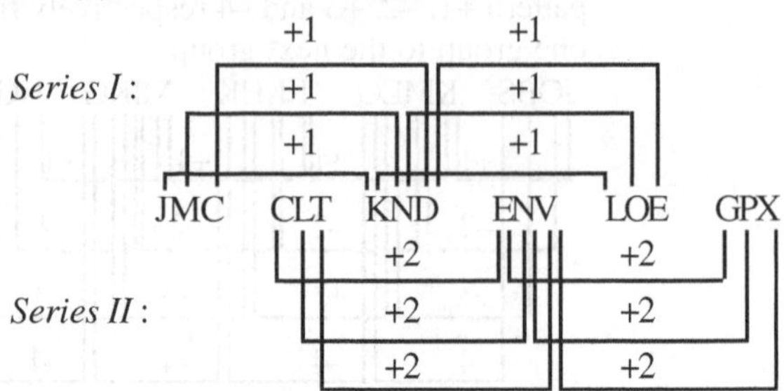

25. (*b*) : The letters in one group correspond to the letters in the next group in the manner –2, +3 –3 respectively, *i.e.,*

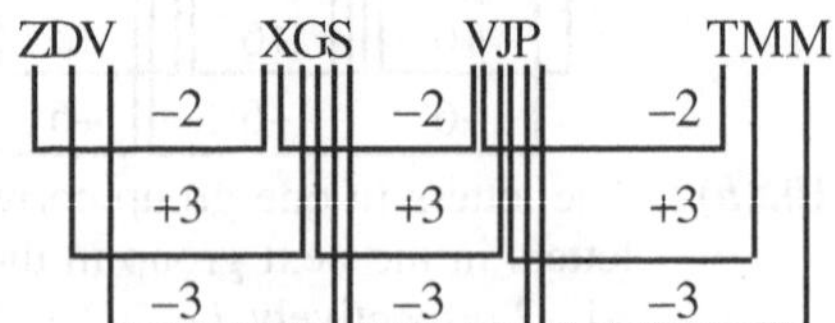

WRONG LETTER SERIES

In this type of series, the candidates are not required to find the letter or group of letters which will complete the given series but, they have to identify the letter or number which is wrong or misfit in the given series.

SOLVED EXAMPLE

1. Which of the following letters in the given series is wrong?

J M P T V Y

(*a*) J (*b*) P (*c*) T (*d*) Y

Ans. (*c*) : The letters in this series are moved three steps forward, *i.e.,*

J M P S V Y (+3 +3 +3 +3 +3)

Letter 'T' should have been 'S'.

EXERCISE

Directions : *Which letter(s) in each of the following series is wrong or is misfit in the series?*

1. AEHOU
(*a*) U (*b*) O
(*c*) H (*d*) E

2. CHMSWB
(*a*) C (*b*) S
(*c*) B (*d*) W

3. XSNICY
(*a*) Y (*b*) C
(*c*) S (*d*) I

4. ZAWBXC
(*a*) D (*b*) C
(*c*) X (*d*) W

5. MLONQPR
(*a*) R (*b*) O
(*c*) Q (*d*) L

6. DKRYFL
(*a*) L (*b*) D
(*c*) R (*d*) Y

7. LNQTWZCF
(*a*) C (*b*) Q
(*c*) L (*d*) F

8. XW, DC, CB, NM, PQ
(*a*) NM (*b*) CB
(*c*) PQ (*d*) XW

9. BEINSAI
(*a*) A (*b*) E
(*c*) S (*d*) I

10. ZTPKHF
(*a*) Z (*b*) P
(*c*) T (*d*) F

EXPLANATORY ANSWERS

1. (*c*) : The series is made with vowels only. AEIOU. I should be in place of H.

2. (*b*) : The letters in the series are moved five steps forward.

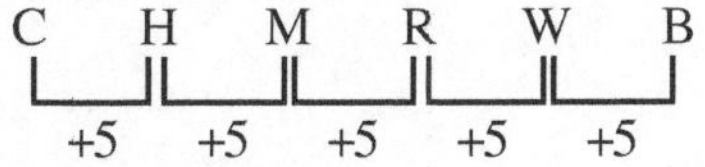

R should be in place of S
(The series restarts from A on reaching Z)

3. (*b*) : The pattern in the series is –5, *i.e.,*

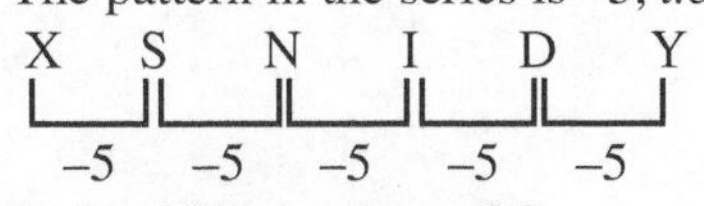

D should be in place of C.

4. (*d*) : There are two alternate series

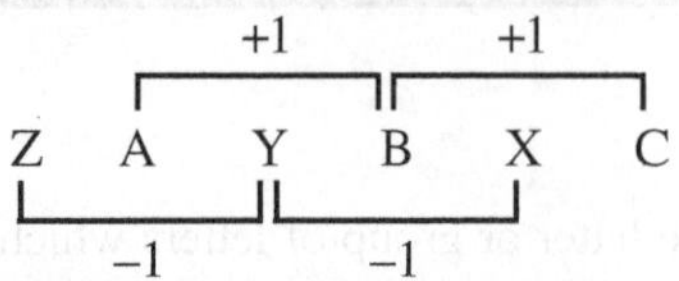

Series I : ZYX (reverse series)
Series II : ABC (natural series)
Y should be in place of W.

5. (*a*) : Two consecutive letters are written backwards.

ML ON QP SR

S should be in place of R.

6. (*a*) : The pattern in this series in moving the letters seven steps forward.

M should be in place of L.

7. (*c*) : The pattern in the series is +3

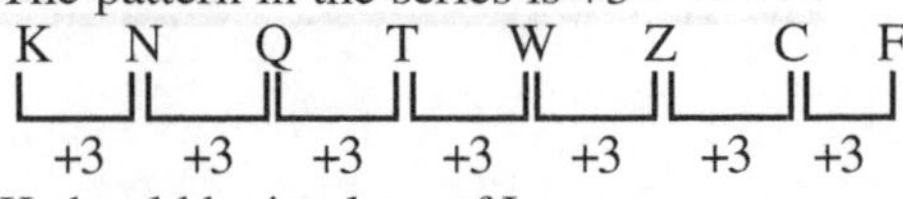

K should be in place of L.

8. (*c*) : The series is made with any two consecutive letters written backwards.

XW DC CB NM QP
← ← ← ← ←

Q should come before P in the series.

9. (*c*) : The difference between the letters is increased by one at each step.

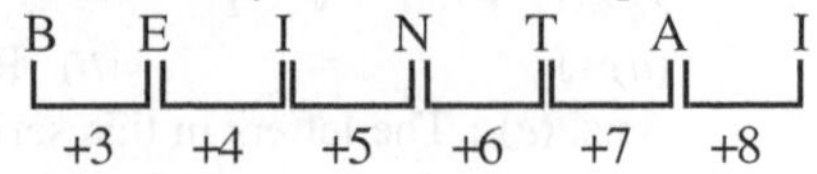

T should be in place of S.

10. (*b*) : The difference between the letters is decreased by one at each step.

O should be in place of P.

REPEAT SERIES

In this type of series, small letters of the alphabet are used to make a set of letters which are repeated. The candidate has to find the set of letters which will fit the blanks left in the given series in such a manner that one section of the series is further repeated in the same manner.

SOLVED EXAMPLE

1. Which of the following groups of letters will complete the given series?
ba-b-aab-a-b
(*a*) baab (*b*) abba (*c*) abaa (*d*) babb
Ans. (*b*) : The series is baab, baab, baab. Here the section 'baab' is repeated in the series.

Solving steps **:** The candidate has to look for clues to solve such series pattern. 'aab' in the Series indicates that 'b' in this series is preceded by two 'a' so, the first blank and the last blank will be filled by 'a'. Now the first set is formed, *i.e.,* 'baab' in the beginning. This set is repeated, so the second and third blanks will have 'b' filling them. Now, solve the exercise given below to know the different ways in which these series are formed.

EXERCISE

Directions : *Which of the following groups of letters will complete the given series?*

1. ab---b-bbaa-
(*a*) babba (*b*) abaab
(*c*) abbab (*d*) baaab

2. aa-ab--aaa-a
(*a*) baaa (*b*) abab
(*c*) aaab (*d*) aabb

3. -baa-aab-a-a
(*a*) baab (*b*) abab
(*c*) aaba (*d*) aabb

4. -a cca-ccca-acccc-aaa
(*a*) ccaa (*b*) acca
(*c*) caac (*d*) caaa

5. c-bbb--abbbb-abbb-
(*a*) abccb (*b*) bacbb
(*c*) aabcb (*d*) abacb

6. ac-cab-baca-aba-acac
(*a*) bcbb (*b*) aacb
(*c*) babb (*d*) acbc

7. --aba--ba-ab
(*a*) abbab (*b*) bbaba
(*c*) baabb (*d*) abbba

8. --babbba-a--
(*a*) bbaba (*b*) babbb
(*c*) baaab (*d*) ababb

9. k-mk-lmkkl-kk-mk
(*a*) lklm (*b*) lkmk
(*c*) lkmm (*d*) lkml

10. abc-d-bc-d-b-dd
(*a*) decdb (*b*) dadac
(*c*) cdabe (*d*) bacde

11. b-abbc-bbca-bcabb-ab
(*a*) acba (*b*) acaa
(*c*) cacc (*d*) cabc

12. aca-ac--a-ac
(*a*) babc (*b*) aaac
(*c*) cacc (*d*) caca

13. ba-cb-b-bab-?
(*a*) acbb (*b*) bcaa
(*c*) cabb (*d*) bacc

14. ab-aa-caab-aab-a
(*a*) bcbc (*b*) bbca
(*c*) cbcc (*d*) caba

15. -bbcaa-bcaa-bc-a-bca
(*a*) bacab (*b*) abbab
(*c*) abcba (*d*) bcaab

16. a-bccb-ca-cca-baab-c
(*a*) accab (*b*) abcaa
(*c*) bacaa (*d*) ababc

17. b-dabbcd-b-c-ab
(*a*) cabd (*b*) bcad
(*c*) dcba (*d*) acbd

18. a-ba-caacb-bc-
(*a*) acbb (*b*) cbab
(*c*) cbaa (*d*) cbba

19. c-baa-aca-cacab-acac-bca
(*a*) acbaa (*b*) cbaac
(*c*) bccab (*d*) bbcaa

20. -bcc-ac-aabb-ab-cc
(*a*) bacab (*b*) abaca
(*c*) aabca (*d*) bcaca

21. ab-ccca-bccc-bbcc-
(*a*) abbc (*b*) bbac
(*c*) bbca (*d*) cabc

22. -cbc-a-bcaac-ca
(*a*) aaba (*b*) caab
(*c*) bcab (*d*) aacb

23. ab-ba--ba-
(*a*) abba (*b*) baab
(*c*) baba (*d*) abab

24. yx-yx-yxz-xz-y-zyxz
(*a*) zzyx (*b*) xxzy
(*c*) yyzx (*d*) yzxz

25. xxxy-y-xxy-yxx-
(*a*) xyxy (*b*) yxyx
(*c*) yyxx (*d*) xxyy

EXPLANATORY ANSWERS

1. (*d*) : The series is abbaab, abbaab.
2. (*c*) : The series is aaaaba, aaaaba.
3. (*b*) : The series is aba, aba, aba, aba.
4. (*d*) : The series is c,a,cc,aa, ccc, aaa, cccc, aaaa.
5. (*a*) : The series is cabbbb, cabbbb, cabbbb.
6. (*b*) : The series is acac, abab, acac, abab, acac.
7. (*a*) : The series is ab, ab, ab, ab, ab, ab.
8. (*b*) : The series is bababb, bababb.
9. (*d*) : The series is klmk, klmk, klmk, klmk.
10. (*b*) : The series is abcdd, abcdd, abcdd.
11. (*d*) : The series is bcab, bcab, bcab, bcab, bcab.
12. (*c*) : The series is ac, ac, ac, ac, ac, ac.
13. (*d*) : The series is babc, babc, babc.
14. (*c*) : The series is abca, abca, abca, abca.
15. (*b*) : The series is abbca, abbca, abbca, abbca.
16. (*d*) : The series is aabcc, bbcaa, ccabb, aabcc.
17. (*a*) : The series is bcdab, bcdab, bcdab.
18. (*c*) : The series is acbabca, acbabca.
19. (*a*) : The series is cabaac, acabca, cabaac, acabca.
20. (*a*) : The series is bbccaa, ccaabb, aabbcc.
21. (*b*) : The series is abbccc abbccc.
22. (*d*) : The series is acbca acbca acbca.
23. (*d*) : The series is ab ab ab ab ab.
24. (*a*) : The series is yxz yxz yxz yxz yxz yxz.
25. (*b*) : The series is xxx yyy xxx yyy xxx.

NUMBER SERIES

In this type of series, the set of given numbers in a series are related to one another in a particular pattern or manner. The relationship between the numbers may be (i) consecutive odd/even numbers; (ii) consecutive prime numbers; (iii) squares/cubes of some numbers with/without variation of addition or subtraction of some number; (iv) sum/product/difference of preceding numbers; (v) addition/subtraction/multiplication/division by some number; and (vi) many more combinations of the relationships given above.

EXERCISE

Directions : *In the following questions, select the number(s) from the given options for completing the given series.*

1. 7776, 1296, 216, 36, 6, ?
(*a*) 6 (*b*) 0
(*c*) 3 (*d*) 1

2. 29282, 2662, 242, 22, ?
(*a*) 1 (*b*) 2
(*c*) 0 (*d*) 11

3. 1, 2, 2, 4, 16, ?, 65536
(*a*) 276 (*b*) 64
(*c*) 256 (*d*) 198

4. 3, 5, 9, 15, 23, ?, 45
(*a*) 37 (*b*) 35
(*c*) 31 (*d*) 33

5. 7, 21, 35, 49, 63, ?
(*a*) 70 (*b*) 77
(*c*) 81 (*d*) 108

6. 10, 14, 23, 39, 64, ?, 149
(*a*) 78 (*b*) 128
(*c*) 103 (*d*) 100

7. 6, 24, 29, 116, 121, ?, 489
(*a*) 468 (*b*) 484
(*c*) 243 (*d*) 363

8. 5, 50, 45, 450, 445, ?, 4445
(*a*) 4450 (*b*) 4600
(*c*) 4550 (*d*) 4500

9. 6.25, 9, 12.25, 16, 20.25, 25, 30.25?
(*a*) 36 (*b*) 32
(*c*) 28.25 (*d*) 40.25

10. 243, 5, 81, 15, 27, 45, 9, ?
(*a*) 5 (*b*) 15
(*c*) 135 (*d*) 27

11. 2, 7, 14, 23, ?, 47
(*a*) 31 (*b*) 38
(*c*) 28 (*d*) 34

12. 0, 1, 8, 27, 64, ?
(*a*) 125 (*b*) 128
(*c*) 256 (*d*) 121

13. 37, 47, 58, ?, 79, 95
(*a*) 71 (*b*) 69
(*c*) 68 (*d*) 67

14. 4, –8, 14, –22, 32, ?
(*a*) –44 (*b*) 42
(*c*) –42 (*d*) 44

15. 6, 7, 9, 11, 15, 15, 24, 19, ?
(*a*) 32 (*b*) 34
(*c*) 36 (*d*) 37

16. 2, 6, 12, 20, 30, ?
(*a*) 42 (*b*) 36
(*c*) 41 (*d*) 40

17. 1, 4, 5, 11, 9, 18, ?, 25
(*a*) 12 (*b*) 13
(*c*) 19 (*d*) 23

18. 27, 45, 9,15, 3, 5, ?
(*a*) 1 (*b*) 1/3
(*c*) 1/5 (*d*) 1/9

19. 3, 1/3, 14, 1/14, 25, 1/25, ?
(*a*) 1/36 (*b*) 34
(*c*) 35 (*d*) 36

20. 1/2, 3/4, 5/8, 7/16, ?
(*a*) 10/17 (*b*) 9/32
(*c*) 11/34 (*d*) 12/35

21. 4, 8, 7, 14, 12, 22, 19, ?, 28

(*a*) 12 (*b*) 24

(*c*) 28 (*d*) 32

22. 96, 90, 78, ?, 36, 6

(*a*) 60 (*b*) 72

(*c*) 48 (*d*) 54

23. 6, 3, 11, 8, 18, 15, 27, 24, ?, ?

(*a*) 36, 33 (*b*) 36, 35

(*c*) 38, 35 (*d*) 38, 34

24. 1, 6, 15, ?, 45, 66, 91

(*a*) 25 (*b*) 26

(*c*) 27 (*d*) 28

25. 1, 2, 5, 12, 27, 58, 121, ?

(*a*) 246 (*b*) 247

(*c*) 248 (*d*) 249

26. (2,1), (1,5), (5,7), (7,11), (11,13), ?

(*a*) (13, 15) (*b*) (13,17)

(*c*) (13, 19) (*d*) (15,16)

27. 2, 7, 4, 9, 6, 11, 8, 13, 10, 15, 12, ?

(*a*) 16 (*b*) 17

(*c*) 19 (*d*) 21

28. 1, 1, 3, 9, 6, 36, 10, 100, ?, 225

(*a*) 15 (*b*) 16

(*c*) 20 (*d*) 22

29. 2, 11, 7, 16, 12, ?, 17, 26

(*a*) 21 (*b*) 8

(*c*) 11 (*d*) 76

30. 54, 45, 38, 33, ?

(*a*) 32 (*b*) 31

(*c*) 30 (*d*) 29

EXPLANATORY ANSWERS

1. (*d*) : The numbers in this sequence are divided by 6 each time.

2. (*b*) : The numbers in the series are divided by 11 at each step.

3. (*c*) : The number in the series is product of all the numbers preceding it.

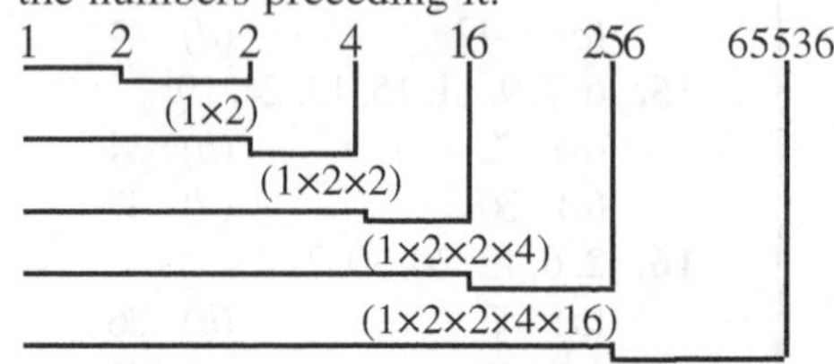

4. (*d*) : The difference between consecutive numbers increases by 2 at each step.

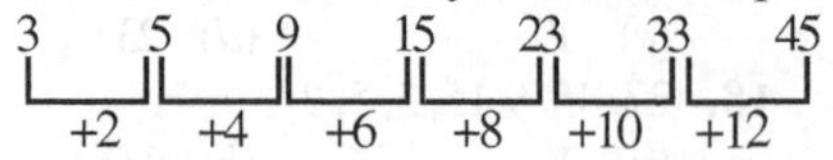

5. (*b*) : The series is multiplication of 7 by odd numbers starting from 3.

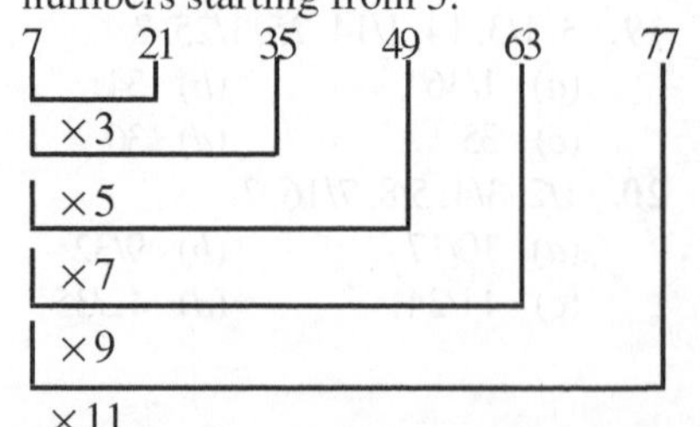

6. (*d*) : The number plus the square of numbers in natural order starting from 2 gives the next number in the series.

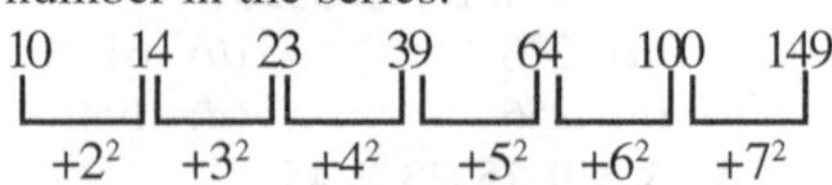

7. (*b*) : The sequence in the series is ×4, +5, which is repeated.

8. (*a*) : The sequence in the series is ×10, –5, which is repeated.

9. (*a*) : There are two alternate series :

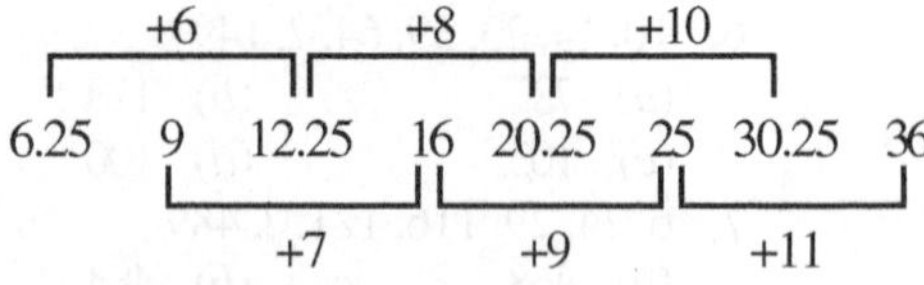

Series I : 6.25, 12.25, 20.25, 30.25 (sequence is +6, +8, +10)

Series II : 9, 16, 25, 36 (sequence is +7, +9, +11)

10. (*c*) : There are two alternate series :

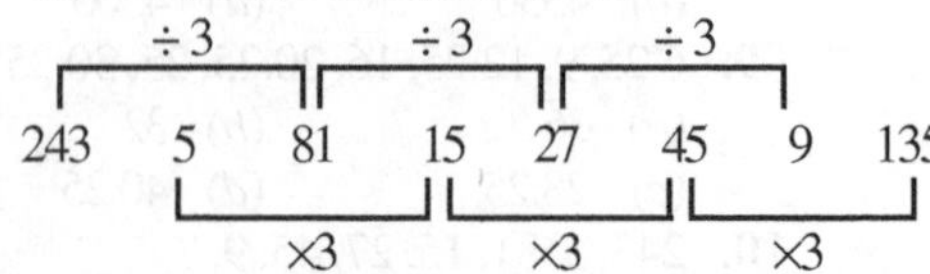

Series I : 243, 81, 27, 9 (division by 3)

Series II : 5, 15, 45, 135 (multiplication by 3)

11. (d) : The difference between two consecutive numbers is increasing by 2 starting from 5.

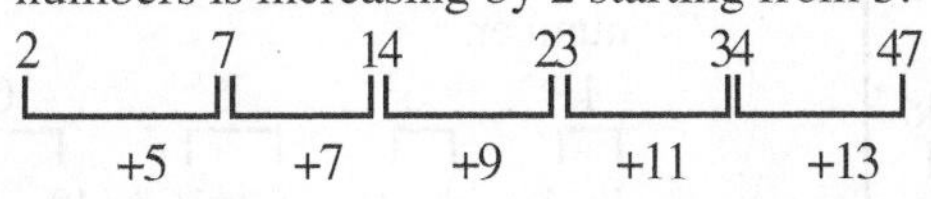

12. (a) : The numbers are cubes of numbers in natural order.

13. (a) : The sum of the digits of the number is added to the number to obtain the next number in the series.

37 47 58 71 79 95

+(3+7) +(4+7) +(5+8) +(7+1) +(7+9)

14. (a) : Alternate numbers are marked positive and negative, but the difference between their magnitude increases by 2 at each step.

4 – 8 14 – 22 32 – 44

4 6 8 10 12

15. (c) : There are two alternate series :

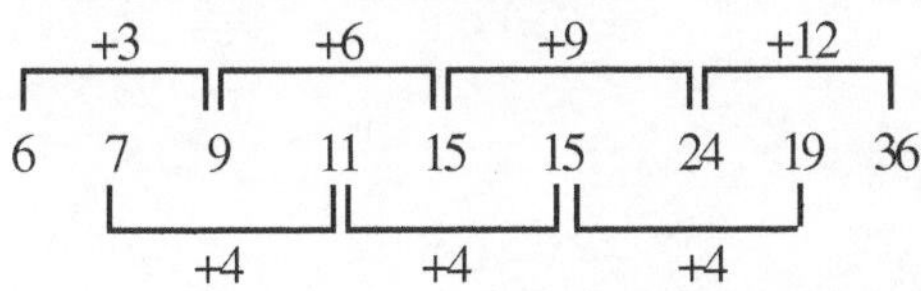

Series I : 6, 9, 15, 24, 36 (sequence is +3, +6, +9, +12)

Series II : 7, 11, 15, 19 (addition of 4 at each step)

16. (a) : The difference between the consecutive numbers in the series increases by 2 at each step.

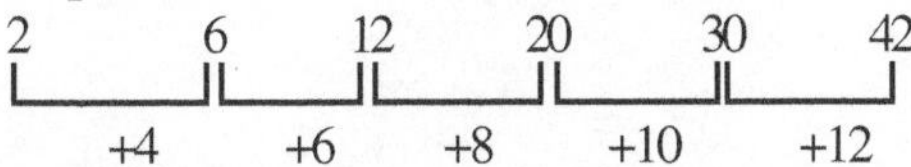

17. (b) : There are two alternate series :

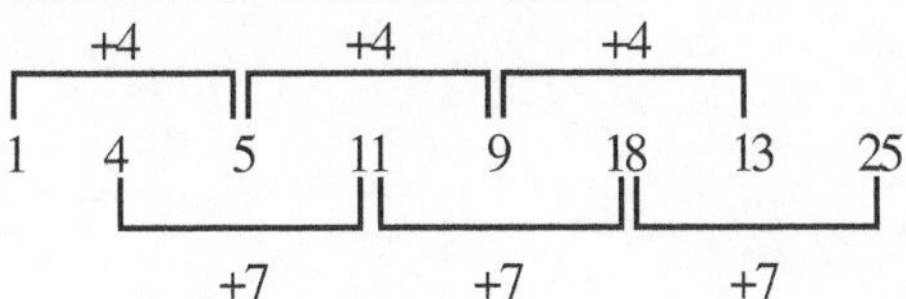

Series I : 1, 5, 9, 13 (addition of 4)

Series II : 4, 11, 18, 25 (addition of 7)

18. (a) : There are two alternate series :

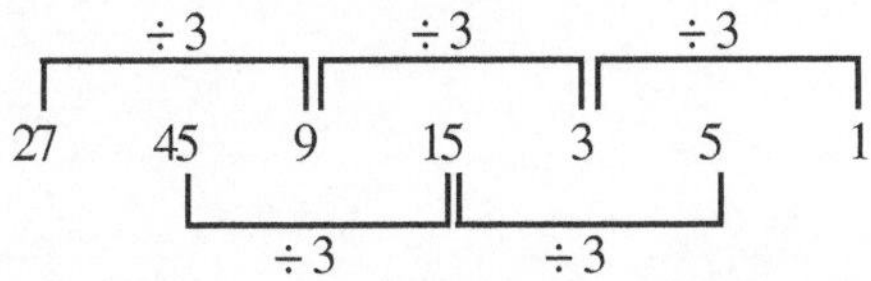

Series I : 27, 9, 3, 1 (division by 3)

Series II : 45, 15, 5 (division by 3)

19. (d) : Two consecutive numbers form a pair. The difference between the numbers placed at odd places increases by 11 and the second number is the fraction part of the number.

$3 \quad \frac{1}{3} \quad 14 \quad \frac{1}{14} \quad 25 \quad \frac{1}{25} \quad 36$

+11 +11 +11

20. (b) : In this fraction series the numbers on the top are increased by 2 and at the bottom, multiplied by 2.

21. (d) : There are two alternate series :

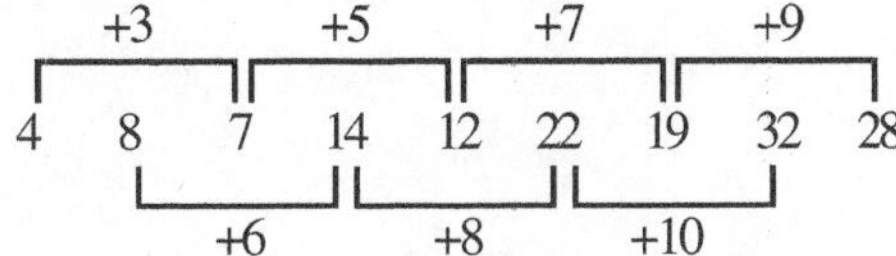

Series I : 4, 7, 12, 19, 28 (sequence is +3, +5, +7, +9)

Series II : 8, 14, 22, 32 (sequence is +6, +8, +10)

22. (a) : The series is formed by multiples of 6 in this manner :

$6 \times 16 = 96$

$6 \times 15 = 90 \qquad (16 - 1) = 15$

$6 \times 13 = 78 \qquad (15 - 2) = 13$

$6 \times 10 = 60 \qquad (13 - 3) = 10$

$6 \times 6 = 36 \qquad (10 - 4) = 6$

$6 \times 1 = 6 \qquad (6 - 5) = 1$

23. (c) : There are two alternate series :

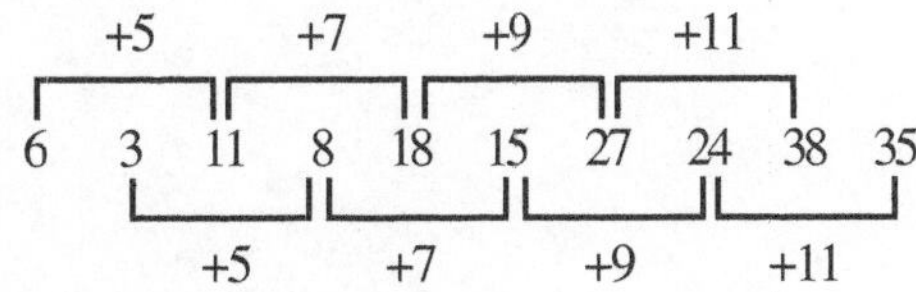

Series I : 6, 11, 18, 27, 38

Series II : 3, 8, 15, 24, 35

(Both series follow the pattern +5, +7, +9, +11)

24. (d) : The difference between the numbers in this series is increased by 4 at each step.

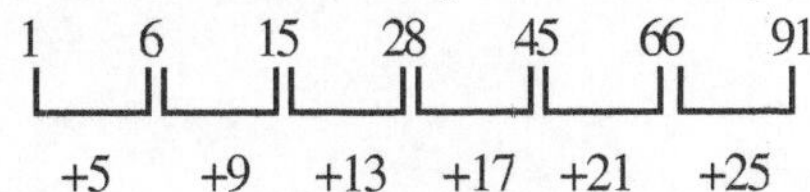

25. *(c)* : The sequence in this series is number into 2 plus the numbers in natural order starting from 0.

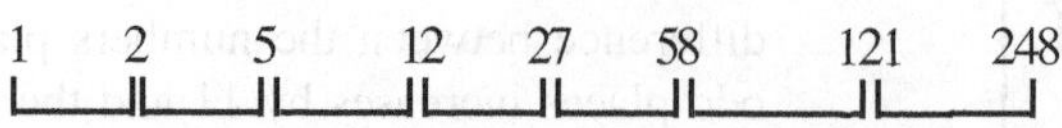

26. (b) : The second number in one section is the first number in the next section and the sequence of the second numbers in the sections is +4, +2 which is repeated.

27. *(b)* : The sequence followed in the series is +5, –3 which is repeated.

28. *(a)* : Two consecutive numbers form a pair. The difference between the first number increases in the manner +2, +3, +4, +5 and the second number is the square of the number.

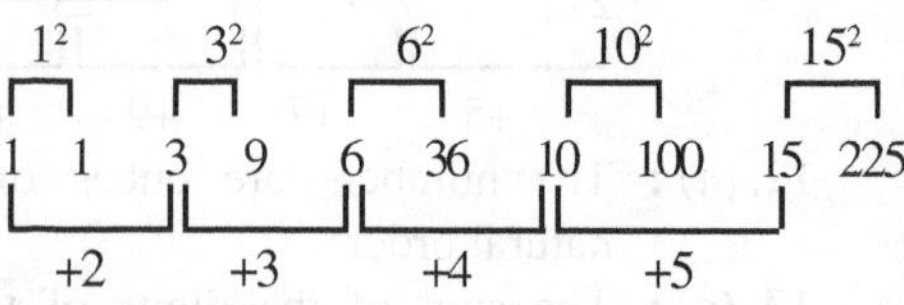

29. *(a)* : The sequence in the series is +9, – 4 which is repeated.

30. *(c)* : The difference between the numbers in the series is decreased by 2 at each step.

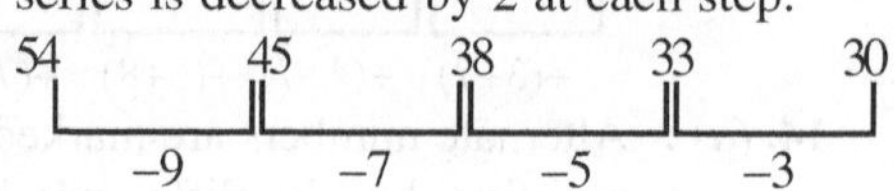

WRONG NUMBER SERIES

In this type of series, the given series may be complete but what needs to be identified is the number in the given completed series which is disturbing the sequential pattern of that series and does not fit in with the relationship shared between the other numbers.

EXERCISE

Directions : *In the given series find the number which is wrong.*

1. 5, 25, 120, 625, 3125, 15625
(*a*) 15625 (*b*) 625
(*c*) 120 (*d*) 5

2. 4, 8, 11, 22, 18, 36, 24, 50
(*a*) 8 (*b*) 22
(*c*) 36 (*d*) 24

3. 2, 4, 12, 24, 72, 142, 432
(*a*) 432 (*b*) 12
(*c*) 142 (*d*) 72

4. 2, 3, 4, 4, 6, 8, 9, 12, 16
(*a*) 3 (*b*) 9
(*c*) 6 (*d*) 12

5. 97, 91, 86, 83, 79, 77, 76, 76
(*a*) 86 (*b*) 76
(*c*) 91 (*d*) 83

6. 7, 11, 11, 9, 15, 7, 19, 5, 23, 1
(*a*) 5 (*b*) 7
(*c*) 1 (*d*) 9

7. 3, 7, 12, 28, 48, 118, 192, 448
(*a*) 12 (*b*) 118
(*c*) 28 (*d*) 7

8. 10, 100, 1100, 11000, 111000, 1210000
(*a*) 1210000 (*b*) 11000
(*c*) 100 (*d*) 111000

9. 24576, 6144, 1536, 386, 96, 24
(*a*) 386 (*b*) 6144
(*c*) 96 (*d*) 1536

10. 11, 13, 15, 17, 19, 23, 29, 31, 37
(*a*) 13 (*b*) 23
(*c*) 15 (*d*) 31

11. 36, 43, 49, 54, 60, 61, 63, 64
(*a*) 60 (*b*) 63
(*c*) 54 (*d*) 43

12. 3, 10, 41, 206, 1236, 8660
(*a*) 10 (*b*) 41
(*c*) 206 (*d*) 1236

13. 17, 25, 37, 50, 65, 82, 101
(*a*) 25 (*b*) 17
(*c*) 101 (*d*) 65

14. 12, 20, 38, 42, 56, 72
(*a*) 20 (*b*) 38
(*c*) 56 (*d*) 72

15. 5, 6, 11, 22, 42, 88, 176
(*a*) 5 (*b*) 42
(*c*) 176 (*d*) 11

16. 905, 180, 175, 35, 30, 6, 1
(*a*) 6 (*b*) 1
(*c*) 175 (*d*) 905

17. 5040, 840, 160, 42, 14, 7
(*a*) 7 (*b*) 160
(*c*) 14 (*d*) 840

18. 3, 32, 363, 3993, 43923
(*a*) 363 (*b*) 3
(*c*) 32 (*d*) 43923

19. 3, 18, 38, 78, 123, 178, 243
(*a*) 78 (*b*) 3
(*c*) 123 (*d*) 18

20. 0, 1, 2, 2, 4, 4, 6, 8, 8, 10
(*a*) 6 (*b*) 0
(*c*) 1 (*d*) 10

21. 5, 12, 16, 24, 27
(*a*) 12 (*b*) 16
(*c*) 24 (*d*) 27

22. 27, 36, 45, 60, 71, 99
(*a*) 27 (*b*) 45
(*c*) 60 (*d*) 71

23. 81, 64, 49, 35, 25, 16
(*a*) 64 (*b*) 35
(*c*) 25 (*d*) 16

24. 625, 125, 25, 5, 0
(*a*) 0 (*b*) 125
(*c*) 5 (*d*) 625

25. 25, 19, 17, 13, 11, 7
(*a*) 25 (*b*) 17
(*c*) 13 (*d*) 7

EXPLANATORY ANSWERS

1. (*c*) : The numbers in the series are multiplied by 5 to get the next number.

∴ 125 should be in place of 120.

2. (*d*) : Two numbers form a pair. The first number increases by 7 for the next pair and the second number is the double of first number.

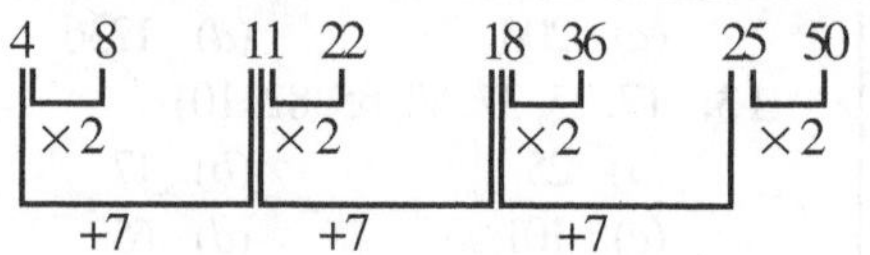

∴ 25 should be in place of 24.

3. (*c*) : There are two alternate series and in each series, the numbers are multiplied by 6 to get the next number.

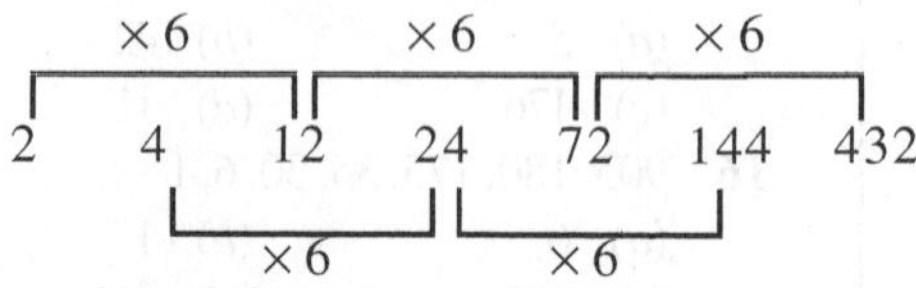

∴ 144 should be in place of 142.

4. (*b*) : There are three alternate series and in each series, the numbers are multiplied by 2 to get the next number.

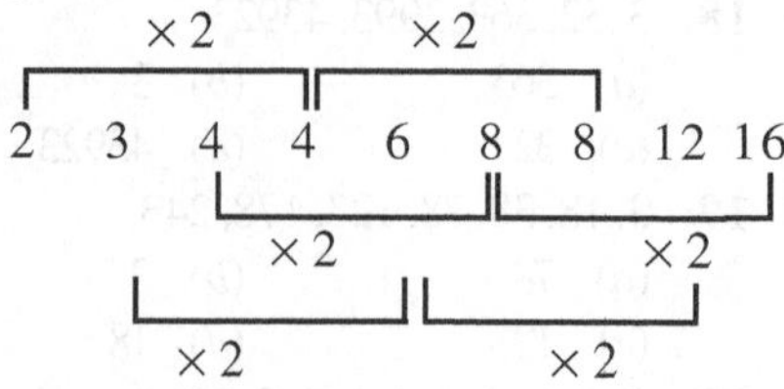

Series I : 2, 4, 8
Series II : 3, 6, 12
Series III : 4, 8, 16

∴ 8 should be in place of 9.

5. (*d*) : The difference between the consecutive numbers in the series decreases by 1 at each step.

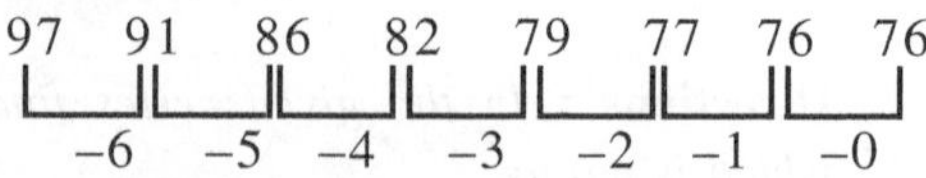

∴ 82 should be in place of 83.

6. (*c*) : There are two alternate series :

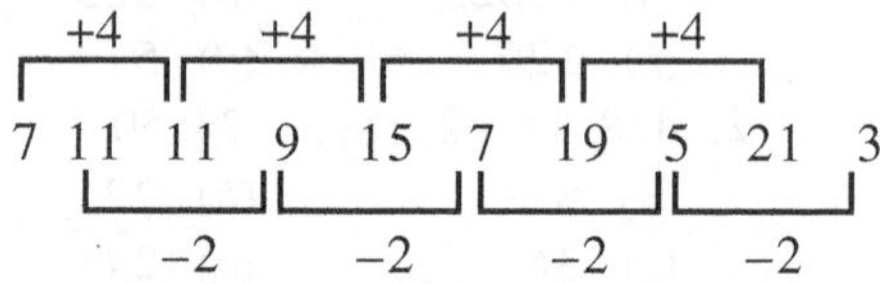

Series I : 7, 11, 15, 19, 23 (addition of 4)
Series II : 11, 9, 7, 5, 3 (subtraction of 2)

∴ 3 should be in place of 1.

7. (*b*) : There are two alternate series and in each series, the numbers are multiplied by 4 to get the next number.

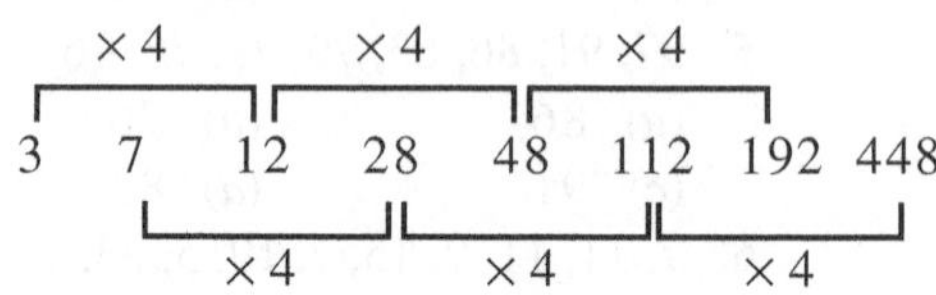

∴ 112 should be in place of 118.

8. (*d*) : The numbers in this series are multiplied by 10 and 11 alternately is, *i.e.,* × 10, × 11.

10 100 1100 11000 121000 1210000
× 10 × 11 × 10 × 11 × 10

∴ 121000 should be in place of 111000.

9. (*a*) : The numbers in this series are divided by 4 to get the next number.

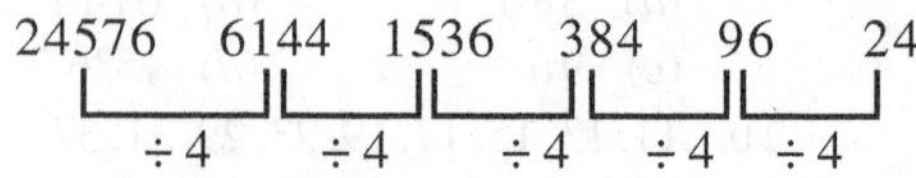

∴ 384 should be in place of 386.

10. (*c*) : The series comprises of prime numbers in increasing order. Only 15 is an exception.

11. (*a*) : The difference between two consecutive numbers is decreasing by 1 at each step.

36 43 49 54 58 61 63 64

+7 +6 +5 +4 +3 +2 +1

∴ 58 should be in place of 60.

12. (*d*) : The sequence followed in this series is :

$3 \times 3 + 1 = 10$

$10 \times 4 + 1 = 41$

$41 \times 5 + 1 = 206$

$206 \times 6 + 1 = 1237$; and

$1237 \times 7 + 1 = 8660$

∴ 1237 should be in place of 1236.

13. (*a*) : The numbers in the series are 1 plus the squares of numbers in natural order starting from 4.

17 26 37 50 65 82 101

↓ ↓ ↓ ↓ ↓ ↓ ↓

$4^2 + 1$ $5^2 + 1$ $6^2 + 1$ $7^2 + 1$ $8^2 + 1$ $9^2 + 1$ $10^2 + 1$

∴ 26 should be in place of 25.

14. (*b*) : The sequence followed in this series is :

$3 \times 4 = 12$

$4 \times 5 = 20$

$5 \times 6 = 30$

$6 \times 7 = 42$

$7 \times 8 = 56$

$8 \times 9 = 72$

∴ 30 should be in place of 38.

15. (*b*) : The numbers in the series are the sum of all the numbers preceding them.

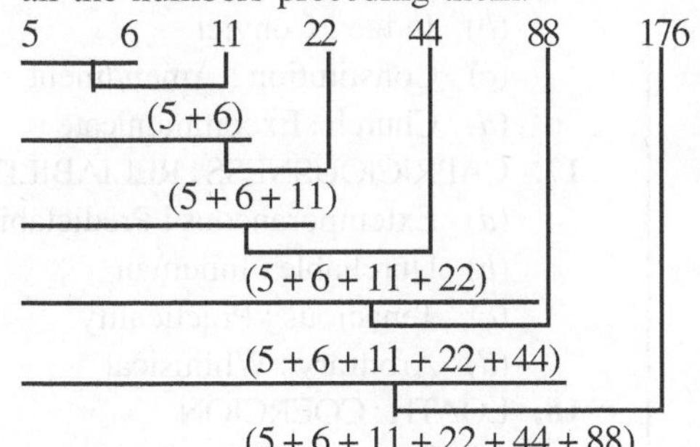

∴ 44 should be in place of 42.

16. (*d*) : The sequence followed in the series is ÷ 5, – 5 which is repeated.

900 180 175 35 30 6 1

÷5 –5 ÷5 –5 ÷5 –5

∴ 900 should be in place of 905.

17. (*b*) : The numbers in the series are divided by numbers in reverse order starting from 6 to get the next number.

5040 840 168 42 14 7

÷6 ÷5 ÷4 ÷3 ÷2

∴ 168 should be in place of 160.

18. (*c*) : The numbers in this series are multiplied by 11 to get the next number.

3 33 363 3993 43923

×11 ×11 ×11 ×11

∴ 33 should be in place of 32.

19. (*b*) : 3 is the only prime number in the series.

20. (*d*) : There are two alternate series :

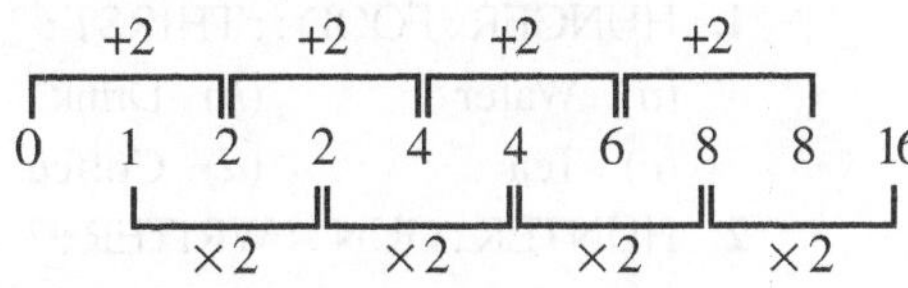

Series I : 0, 2, 4, 6, 8, (addition of 2)

Series II : 1, 2, 4, 8, 16 (multiplication by 2)

∴ 16 should be in place of 10.

21. (*c*) : The sequence in the series is +7, +4 which is repeated, *i.e.*,

5 12 16 23 27

+7 +4 +7 +4

∴ 23 should be in place of 24.

22. (*d*) : All other numbers are divisible by 3.

23. (*b*) : The sequence is the square of the number in decreasing order starting from 9, *i.e.*,

$9^2 = 9 \times 9 = 81$

$8^2 = 8 \times 8 = 64$

$7^2 = 7 \times 7 = 49$

$6^2 = 6 \times 6 = 36$

$5^2 = 5 \times 5 = 25$

$4^2 = 4 \times 4 = 16$

∴ 36 should be in place of 35.

24. (*a*) : The number in the series are divided by 5 to get the next number

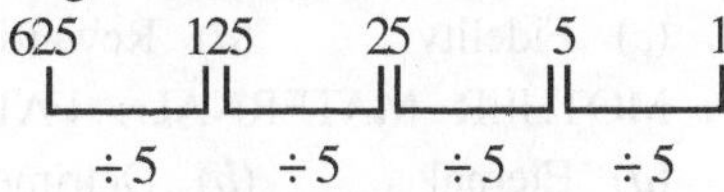

∴ 1 should be in place of 0 digit.

25. (*a*) : Other numbers are prime numbers.

WORD ANALOGY

In Analogy Tests, the relationship between two given words is established and then applied to the other words. The type of relationship may vary, so while attempting such questions the first step is to identify the type of relationship, which can be any one of the following.

EXERCISE

Directions : *In the questions given below one term is missing. Based on the relationship of the two given words find the missing term from the given options.*

1. HUNGER : FOOD : : THIRST : ?
(*a*) Water (*b*) Drink
(*c*) Tea (*d*) Coffee

2. HUNTER : GUN : : WRITER : ?
(*a*) Book (*b*) Pen
(*c*) Poem (*d*) Page

3. WOOL : SHEEP : : SILK : ?
(*a*) Saree (*b*) String
(*c*) Silkworm (*d*) Moth

4. FOOD : STOMACH : : FUEL : ?
(*a*) Engine (*b*) Automobile
(*c*) Rail (*d*) Aeroplane

5. WATER : SAND : : OCEAN : ?
(*a*) Island (*b*) River
(*c*) Desert (*d*) Waves

6. ADULT : BABY : : FLOWER : ?
(*a*) Seed (*b*) Bud
(*c*) Fruit (*d*) Butterfly

7. WRITER : READER : : PRODUCER : ?
(*a*) Creator (*b*) Contractor
(*c*) Creature (*d*) Consumer

8. ENTRANCE : EXIT : : LOYALTY : ?
(*a*) Treachery (*b*) Patriotism
(*c*) Fidelity (*d*) Reward

9. MOTHER : MATERNAL : : FATHER : ?
(*a*) Eternal (*b*) Detrimental
(*c*) Paternal (*d*) Formidable

10. PEARL : NECKLACE : : FLOWER : ?
(*a*) Plant (*b*) Garden
(*c*) Petal (*d*) Bouquet

11. ALPHABET : WORD : : WORD : ?
(*a*) Sound (*b*) Music
(*c*) Sentence (*d*) Dictionary

12. LIFE : DEATH : : HOPE : ?
(*a*) Cry (*b*) Pain
(*c*) Despair (*d*) Sad

13. GOOD : BAD : : VIRTUE : ?
(*a*) Blame (*b*) Sin
(*c*) Despair (*d*) Vice

14. BIRD : FLY : : SNAKE : ?
(*a*) Timid (*b*) Clatter
(*c*) Crawl (*d*) Hole

15. CAT : MOUSE : : BIRD : ?
(*a*) Cage (*b*) Trap
(*c*) Eagle (*d*) Worm

16. STATE : EXILE
(*a*) Police : Arrest
(*b*) Judge : Convict
(*c*) Constitution : Amendment
(*d*) Church : Excommunicate

17. CAPRICIOUSNESS : RELIABILITY
(*a*) Extemporaneous : Predictability
(*b*) Unreliable : Inhuman
(*c*) Tenacious : Practicality
(*d*) Arbitrary : Whimsical

18. LOATH : COERCION
(*a*) Detest : Caressing
(*b*) Irritate : Caressing
(*c*) Irate : Antagonism
(*d*) Reluctant : Persuasion

19. SCALES : FISH
(*a*) Lady : Dress (*b*) Tree : Leaves
(*c*) Bird : Feather (*d*) Skin : Man

20. TREE : SAPLING
(*a*) Hut : Mansion
(*b*) Giant : Dwarf
(*c*) Horse : Foal
(*d*) Ant : Elephant

21. CHALK : BLACKBOARD
(*a*) Door : Handle
(*b*) Table : Chair
(*c*) Ink : Paper
(*d*) Type : Paint

22. PRIMEVAL : MEDIEVAL
(*a*) Dinosaur : Dragon
(*b*) Gorilla : Soldier
(*c*) Evolution : Revelation
(*d*) Thorn : Rose

23. TRILOGY : NOVEL
(*a*) Rice : Husk
(*b*) Milk : Cream
(*c*) Fabric : Weaving
(*d*) Serial : Episode

24. PEDANT : ERUDITION
(*a*) Prude : Modesty
(*b*) Blunt : Politician
(*c*) Diplomats : Tactless
(*d*) Enemy : Friendly

25. FURY : IRE
(*a*) Convulsion : Spasm
(*b*) Amusement : Happiness
(*c*) Joke : Laugh
(*d*) Dispassion : Emotion

26. BaBy : TaTa : : LiLy : ?
(*a*) PooL (*b*) ROse
(*c*) HaNd (*d*) DoWN

27. BCDA : STUR : : KLMJ : ?
(*a*) VWXU (*b*) EFHG
(*c*) SRTU (*d*) QSRP

28. AEI : LPT : : CGK : ?
(*a*) OSV (*b*) RUY
(*c*) TXC (*d*) FJN

29. RUX : TRP : : BEH : ?
(*a*) SQN (*b*) QON
(*c*) QOM (*d*) QNL

30. CART : ART : : FOUR : ?
(*a*) RUN (*b*) TWO
(*c*) QUE (*d*) OUR

31. FIK : JGO : : DFR : ?
(*a*) BIO (*b*) HDV
(*c*) GCU (*d*) FLP

32. LJH : KKI : : CIA : ?
(*a*) BJB (*b*) DHB
(*c*) BJC (*d*) BBJ

33. ACE : HIL : : MOQ : ?
(*a*) SVW (*b*) TUX
(*c*) RTW (*d*) WUS

34. BCDE : WVUT : : QRST : ?
(*a*) EFHG (*b*) JIHG
(*c*) POML (*d*) GEDC

35. PNLJ : IGEC : : USQO : ?
(*a*) HJLN (*b*) LNJH
(*c*) NLJH (*d*) JHNL

36. DIMO : DMIO : : JUVR : ?
(*a*) JVRU (*b*) JRVU
(*c*) JVUR (*d*) JUVR

EXPLANATORY ANSWERS

1. (*a*) : Hunger is satiated by food, thirst by water.

2. (*b*) : Weapon of a hunter is a gun, weapon of a writer is a pen.

3. (*c*) : Wool is obtained from sheep, silk is obtained from silkworm.

4. (*a*) : Food is consumed in stomach, fuel is consumed in engine.

5. (*c*) : The related words are near opposites.

6. (*b*) : The youngone of an adult is a baby and that of a flower is a bud.

7. (*d*) : A writer aims to please the readers by his writings, a producer aims to please the consumers by his products.

8. (*a*) : The related words are opposites.

9. (*c*) : Relations on the mother's side are maternal and on the father's side paternal.

10. (d) : Many pearls make a necklace, many flowers make a bouquet.

11. (c) : More than one alphabet make a word, more than one word make a sentence.

12. (c) : The related words are opposites.

13. (d) : The related words are opposites.

14. (c) : Birds fly, snakes crawl.

15. (d) : Cat chases the mouse, bird chases the worm.

16. (d) : Punishment of leaving the State is exile, punishment of leaving the Church is excommunication.

17. (c) : The related words are antonyms.

18. (d) : Loathing is the result of constant coersion, reluctance is the result of constant persuasion.

19. (d) : Covering of the fish is scales, covering of man is skin.

20. (c) : Young tree is a sapling, young horse is a foal.

21. (c) : Chalk is used to write on blackboard, ink is used to write on paper.

22. (a) : The related words represent almost the same time period and answer option represents almost the same sized creatures.

23. (d) : Trilogy is section of a novel, episode is a section of a serial.

24. (a) : The related words are synonyms.

25. (b) : Fury causes ire, amusement causes happiness.

26. (c) : In each group the alternate letters are capitals.

27. (a) : In each group the first three letters are consecutive and they follow the fourth letter.

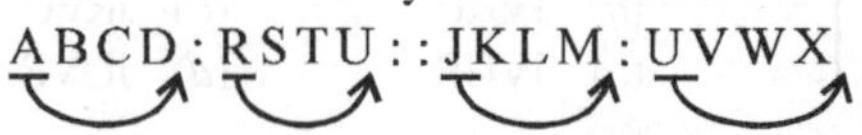

28. (d) : In each group the letters jump three letters between them, *i.e.,* they are moving to the fourth letter.

AEI : LPT :: CGK : FJN

+4 +4   +4 +4   +4 +4   +4 +4

29. (c) : The letters in first set are jumping two letters, *i.e.,* moving three steps forward and in the second they are jumping one letter, *i.e.* moving two steps backward.

RUX : TRP :: BEH : QOM

+3 +3   −2 −2   +3+3   −2 −2

30. (d) : The first set of letters drop the first letter to get the second set.

CART : ART :: FOUR : OUR

31. (b) : The three letters in first set are moved +4, −2, and +4 steps respectively.

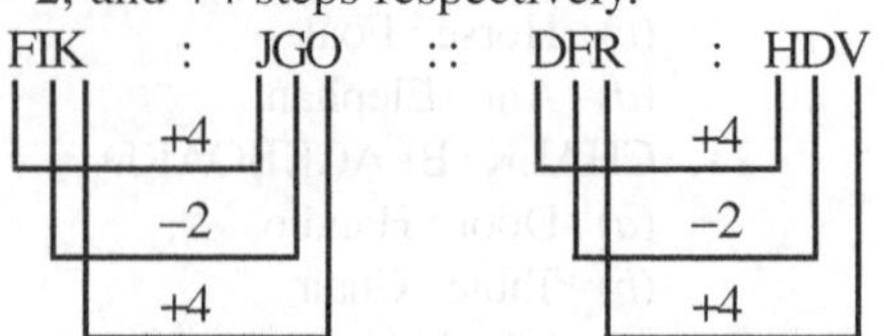

32. (a) : The letters in the first set are moved −1, +1 and +1 steps respectively.

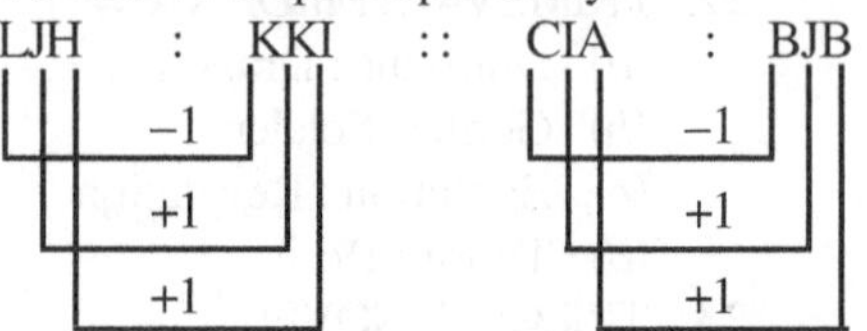

33. (b) : The three letters are moved +7, +6 and +7 steps forward respectively.

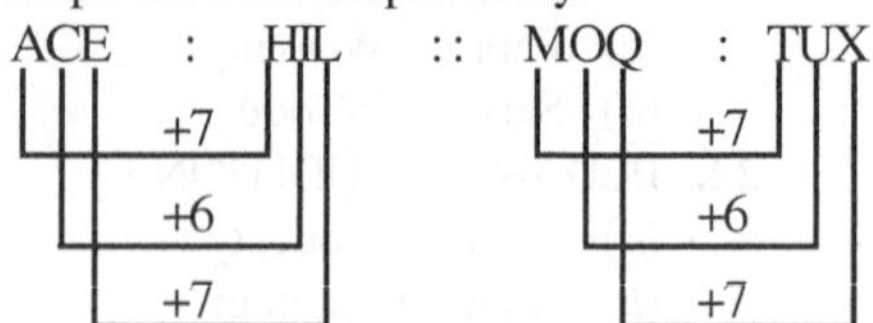

34. (b) : The consecutive letters in the first set are in natural order and in the second set, they are in reverse order.

BCDE : WVUT :: QRST : JIHG

35. (c) : The letters are moved seven steps backwards.

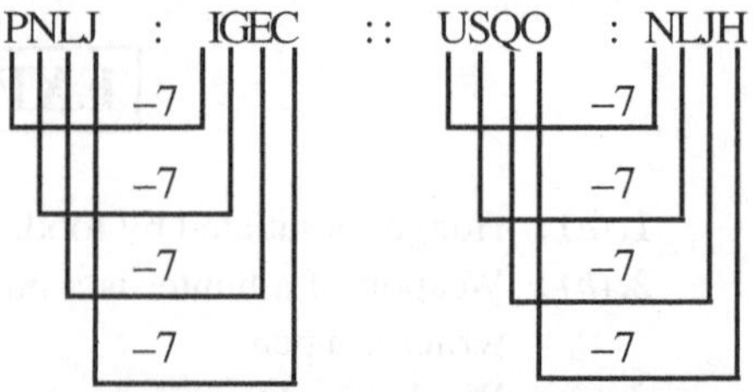

36. (c) : Only the middle letters are reversed to obtain the second set of letters.

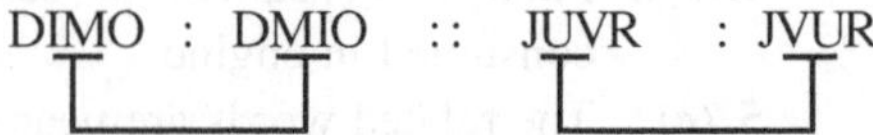

NUMBER ANALOGY

In number analogy also, the relationship between the given numbers is detected and then applied to the second part to find the missing numbers. This relationship between the numbers can be based on any of the following patterns : *(i)* numbers can be odd/even/prime numbers; *(ii)* numbers can be multiples of one number; *(iii)* numbers can be squares/cubes of different numbers; *(iv)* some numbers can be added to/ subtracted from/multiplied to/divided into the first number to get the second number; *(v)* the second number can be the sum/product/difference of the digits of first number; and *(vi)* combinations of any mathematical calculations given above can apply to the relationship between the two given numbers.

EXERCISE

Directions : *In the following questions, select the number from the given options which follows the same relationship as shared between the first two numbers.*

1. 1 : 11 : : 2 : ?
(*a*) 20 (*b*) 22
(*c*) 24 (*d*) 44

2. $\frac{1}{7} : \frac{1}{14} :: \frac{1}{9} : ?$
(*a*) $\frac{1}{88}$ (*b*) $\frac{1}{80}$
(*c*) $\frac{1}{81}$ (*d*) $\frac{1}{18}$

3. 0.16 : 0.0016 : : 1.02 : ?
(*a*) 10.20 (*b*) 0.102
(*c*) 0.0102 (*d*) 1.020

4. 663 : 884 : : 221 : ?
(*a*) 332 (*b*) 554
(*c*) 773 (*d*) 442

5. 16 : 0.16 : : ?
(*a*) 2 : 0.02 (*b*) 7 : 0.007
(*c*) 1.3 : 0.13 (*d*) 0.01 : 0.001

6. $3 : \frac{1}{3} :: ?$
(*a*) 6 : 12 (*b*) 5 : 2/15
(*c*) 8 : 1/8 (*d*) 9 : 27

7. 65 : 13 : : 180 : ?
(*a*) 93 (*b*) 36
(*c*) 133 (*d*) 102

8. 125 : 27 : : 343 : ?
(*a*) 729 (*b*) 64
(*c*) 216 (*d*) 512

9. 357 : 73 : : ?
(*a*) 429 : 94 (*b*) 201 : 21
(*c*) 138 : 38 (*d*) 93 : 39

10. 731 : 902 : : 655 : ?
(*a*) 646 (*b*) 800
(*c*) 793 (*d*) 556

11. 162 : 9 : : 310 : ?
(*a*) 33 (*b*) 27
(*c*) 16 (*d*) 4

12. 13 : 17 : : 15 : ?
(*a*) 19 (*b*) 11
(*c*) 21 (*d*) 16

13. 225 : 15 : : 256 : ?
(*a*) 26 (*b*) 16
(*c*) 20 (*d*) 28

14. 46 : 48 : : 54 : ?
(*a*) 59 (*b*) 40
(*c*) 67 (*d*) 62

15. 33 : 36 : : 21 : ?
(*a*) 9 (*b*) 18
(*c*) 25 (*d*) 32

16. 123 : 149 : : 201 : ?
(*a*) 202 (*b*) 404
(*c*) 401 (*d*) 227

17. 7 : 105 : : 5 : ?
(*a*) 97 (*b*) 83
(*c*) 75 (*d*) 61

18. 11 : 101 : : 73 : ?
(*a*) 153 (*b*) 330
(*c*) 543 (*d*) 703

19. 4 : 32 : : 8 : ?
(*a*) 34 (*b*) 68
(*c*) 92 (*d*) 128

20. 94 : 26 : : 62 : ?
(*a*) 16 (*b*) 22
(*c*) 39 (*d*) 48

EXPLANATORY ANSWERS

1. (*b*) : The first number is repeated to obtain the second number.

2. (*d*) : The first fraction is multiplied by half to obtain the second fraction.

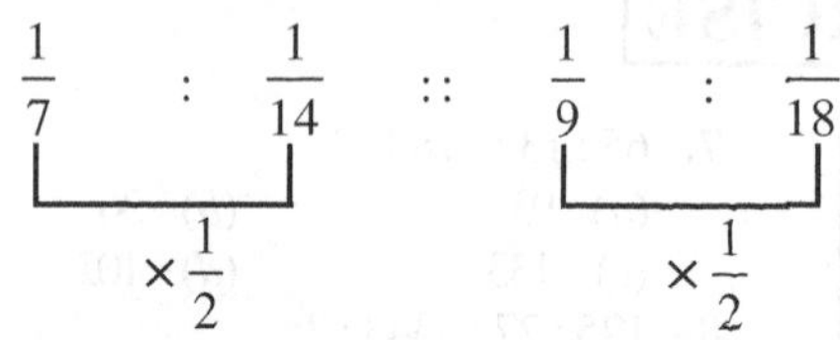

$\frac{1}{7} : \frac{1}{14} :: \frac{1}{9} : \frac{1}{18}$ ($\times\frac{1}{2}$, $\times\frac{1}{2}$)

3. (*c*) : The decimals are divided by 100.

0.16 : 0.0016 :: 1.02 : 0.0102 (÷ 100, ÷ 100)

4. (*d*) : The digits at tens and hundreds place is same but the digit at the units place is half the other identical digits.

66 3 : 88 4 :: 22 1 : 44 2

5. (*a*) : Of the two related numbers, the second number is the result of first number divided by 100.

16 : 0.16 :: 2 : 0.02 (÷ 100, ÷ 100)

6. (*c*) : Of the two related numbers, the second number is the part fraction of the first number, *i.e.* 3 is related to one-third $\left(\frac{1}{3}\right)$. Similarly, 8 will be related to one-eighth $\left(\frac{1}{8}\right)$.

7. (*b*) : The first number is divided by 5 to get the second number.

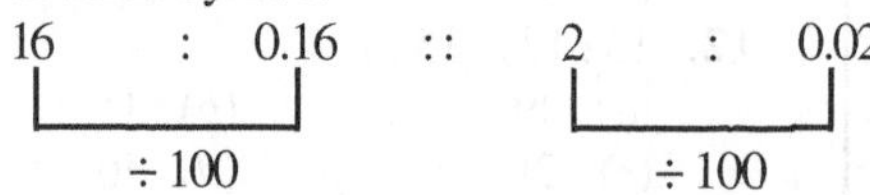

65 : 13 :: 180 : 36 (÷ 5, ÷ 5)

8. (*a*) : The numbers are cubes of different odd numbers.

125 : 27 :: 343 : 729
↓ ↓ ↓ ↓
5^3 3^3 7^3 9^3

9. (*a*) : The central digit of the first number is left out and the corner digits written in reverse order to get the second number.

357 : 73 :: 429 : 94

10. (*a*) : The sum of the digits of both the numbers is same.

$731 : 902 \rightarrow 7 + 3 + 1 = 9 + 0 + 2$ *i.e.* $11 = 11$

$655 : 646 \rightarrow 6 + 5 + 5 = 6 + 4 + 6$ *i.e.* $16 = 16$

11. (*d*) : The sum of the digits of the first number is the second number.

162 : 9 :: 310 : 4 (1 + 6 + 2, 3 + 1 + 0)

12. (*a*) : First number plus 4 gives the second number.

13 : 17 :: 15 : 19 (+4, +4)

13. (*b*) : The root of first number is the second number.

225 : 15 :: 256 : 16 ($\sqrt{225}$, $\sqrt{256}$)

14. (*b*) : The product of the digits of first number is multiplied by 2 to get the second number.

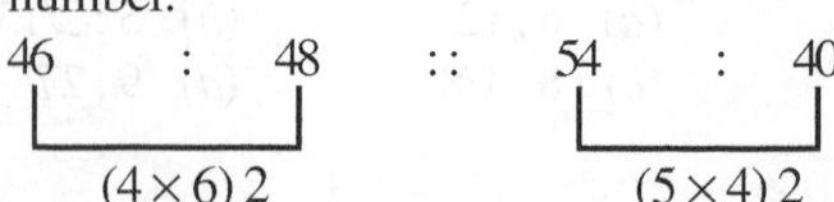

46 : 48 :: 54 : 40 ((4 × 6) 2, (5 × 4) 2)

15. (a) : The square of the sum of the digits of the first number is the second number.

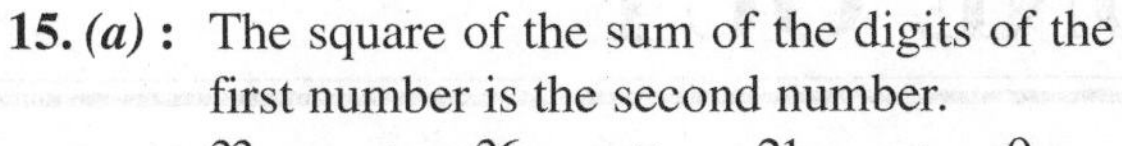

33 : 36 :: 21 : 9

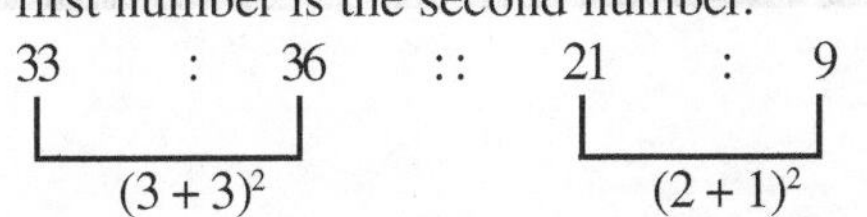

$(3+3)^2$ $(2+1)^2$

16. (c) : Each digit of the first number are squared to get the digits of the second number.

123 : 149 :: 201 : 401

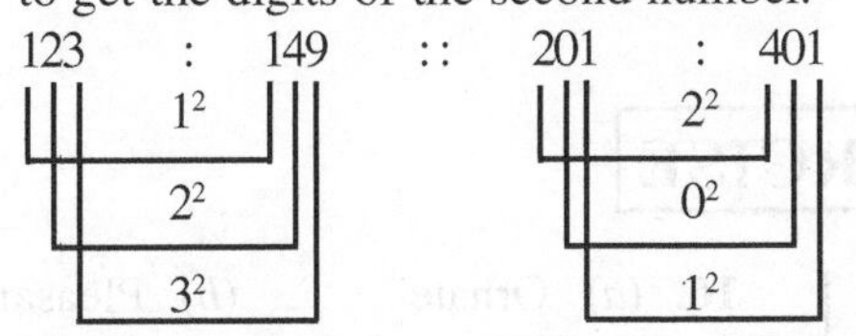

1^2, 2^2, 3^2 2^2, 0^2, 1^2

17. (c) : The first number is multiplied by 15 to get the second number.

7 : 105 :: 5 : 75

$\times 15$ $\times 15$

18. (d) : Zero is inserted in between the digits of the first number to get the second number.

11 : 1<u>0</u>1 :: 73 : 7<u>0</u>3

19. (d) : Double the first number multiplied by the number itself gives the second number.

4 : 32 :: 8 : 128

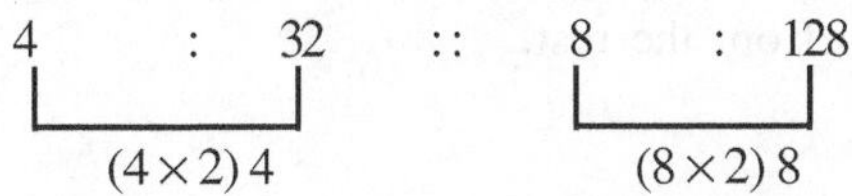

$(4\times 2)\,4$ $(8\times 2)\,8$

20. (a) : The sum of the digits of the first number multiplied by two gives the second number.

94 : 26 :: 62 : 16

$(9+4)\times 2$ $(6+2)\times 2$

ODD ONE OUT

In this type of classification, four words are given out of which three are almost same in matter or meaning and only one word is different from the common three. One has to find out the word which is different from the rest.

EXERCISE

Directions : *In each of the following questions, three words are alike in some manner. Spot the odd one out.*

1. (*a*) Green (*b*) Red (*c*) Colour (*d*) Orange

2. (*a*) Stable (*b*) Hole (*c*) Canoe (*d*) Sty

3. (*a*) Nose (*b*) Eyes (*c*) Skin (*d*) Teeth

4. (*a*) Venus (*b*) Moon (*c*) Pluto (*d*) Mars

5. (*a*) Happy (*b*) Gloomy (*c*) Lively (*d*) Cheerful

6. (*a*) Cone (*b*) Circle (*c*) Triangle (*d*) Rectangle

7. (*a*) Lead (*b*) Mercury (*c*) Copper (*d*) Iron

8. (*a*) Kite (*b*) Bird (*c*) Radar (*d*) Jet

9. (*a*) Knee (*b*) Shoulder (*c*) Ankle (*d*) Palm

10. (*a*) Deluge (*b*) Calamity (*c*) Catastrophe (*d*) War

11. (*a*) Cub (*b*) Chicken (*c*) Pig (*d*) Pup

12. (*a*) Rabbit (*b*) Crocodile (*c*) Earthworm (*d*) Snail

13. (*a*) Tree (*b*) Leaf (*c*) Bush (*d*) Herb

14. (*a*) Doctor (*b*) Teacher (*c*) Engineer (*d*) Diver

15. (*a*) Trot (*b*) Equestrian (*c*) Derby (*d*) Grunt

16. (*a*) Ornate (*b*) Pleasant (*c*) Decorate (*d*) Beautify

17. (*a*) Polo (*b*) Chess (*c*) Ludo (*d*) Squash

18. (*a*) Tutor (*b*) Principal (*c*) Pupil (*d*) Professor

19. (*a*) Pond (*b*) River (*c*) Stream (*d*) Brook

20. (*a*) Quotation (*b*) Duty (*c*) Tax (*d*) Octroi

21. (*a*) Root (*b*) Tree (*c*) Branch (*d*) Flower

22. (*a*) Mumbai (*b*) Chandigarh (*c*) Lucknow (*d*) Hyderabad

23. (*a*) Immortal (*b*) Eminence (*c*) Perpetual (*d*) Everlasting

24. (*a*) Spinach (*b*) Potato (*c*) Carrot (*d*) Ginger

25. (*a*) Van (*b*) Aeroplane (*c*) Helicopter (*d*) Transport

Directions : *Three of the following four in each question are alike in a certain way and so form a group. Select the group of letters that does not belong to that group.*

26. (*a*) ACE (*b*) LOR (*c*) GIK (*d*) VXZ

27. (*a*) TSR (*b*) LKJ (*c*) PQO (*d*) HGF

28. (*a*) EF LM (*b*) KJ SR (*c*) XW HG (*d*) ED YX

29. (*a*) JOPK (*b*) BOPC (*c*) QOPR (*d*) TOPS

30. (*a*) DfH (*b*) MoQ (*c*) UwY (*d*) lnO

31. (*a*) JKkL (*b*) OPpQ
(*c*) DEEf (*d*) VWwX

32. (*a*) BdfH (*b*) FHJL
(*c*) RTvX (*d*) uVwX

33. (*a*) DFHEG (*b*) TWXUV
(*c*) OQSPR (*d*) JLNKM

34. (*a*) FEUV (*b*) DCXW
(*c*) BAZY (*d*) HGTS

35. (*a*) UTSR (*b*) XYZW
(*c*) ONML (*d*) IHGF

Directions : *In each of the following questions, there are four options. Three numbers, in these options, are alike in certain manner. Only one number does not fit in. Choose the one which is different from the rest.*

36. (*a*) 1948 (*b*) 2401
(*c*) 966 (*d*) 1449

37. (*a*) 182 (*b*) 169
(*c*) 130 (*d*) 158

38. (*a*) 129 (*b*) 130
(*c*) 131 (*d*) 132

39. (*a*) 3215 (*b*) 9309
(*c*) 4721 (*d*) 2850

40. (*a*) 1776 (*b*) 2364
(*c*) 1976 (*d*) 3776

41. (*a*) 64 (*b*) 84
(*c*) 16 (*d*) 36

42. (*a*) 24 (*b*) 90
(*c*) 54 (*d*) 36

43. (*a*) 7658 (*b*) 1234
(*c*) 9876 (*d*) 6543

44. (*a*) 3 (*b*) 9
(*c*) 5 (*d*) 7

45. (*a*) 6450 (*b*) 1776
(*c*) 2392 (*d*) 3815

Directions : *In the following questions select the pair which is different from the other three.*

46. (*a*) Chair - Furniture
(*b*) Shirt - Garment
(*c*) Necklace - Jewellery
(*d*) Bogie - Engine

47. (*a*) Crayon - Paper
(*b*) Pencil - Lead
(*c*) Pen - Ink
(*d*) Brush - Paint

48. (*a*) War - Peace
(*b*) Real - Natural
(*c*) Premiere - First
(*d*) Wrath - Anger

49. (*a*) Finger - Thimble
(*b*) Head - Cap
(*c*) Waist - Tiara
(*d*) Foot - Shoe

50. (*a*) Day - Night
(*b*) Clever - Foolish
(*c*) Clear - Blurred
(*d*) Arrive - Come

Directions : *In the following questions, which of the following pair of letters is different from the other three?*

51. (*a*) FGH - HIJ (*b*) PQR - RST
(*c*) MNO - OPQ (*d*) CDE - DEF

52. (*a*) JuM - jUm (*b*) iLo - Ilo
(*c*) PSa - psA (*d*) ZeX - zEx

53. (*a*) NQT - JMP (*b*) CFI - RUX
(*c*) ADG - FGH (*d*) SVY - ORU

54. (*a*) DXD - XDX (*b*) KUK - UKU
(*c*) FHF - EHE (*d*) RSR - SRS

55. (*a*) AYT - BZU (*b*) FNG - EMF
(*c*) RWO - QVN (*d*) HJD - GIC

56. (*a*) POT - TOP (*b*) TAN - ANT
(*c*) BIN - NIB (*d*) DUB - BUD

57. (*a*) LT - HF (*b*) IN - VA
(*c*) ZE - XM (*d*) RB - SC

58. (*a*) MQU - CGK (*b*) BGL - TYD
(*c*) RWB - FKP (*d*) JOT - DIN

59. (*a*) JLN - KMO (*b*) GIK - HJL
(*c*) DFJ - EGI (*d*) OQS - PRT

60. (*a*) URS - UrS (*b*) JPL - JpL
(*c*) PQM - PqM (*d*) MoN - MON

Directions : *Which of the following pair of numbers is different from the other three pairs?*

61. (*a*) 28, 4 (*b*) 63, 7
(*c*) 56, 8 (*d*) 35, 5

62. (*a*) 3, 11 (*b*) 8, 16
(*c*) 5, 13 (*d*) 14, 24

63. (*a*) 13, 156 (*b*) 12, 144
(*c*) 15, 180 (*d*) 16, 176

64. (*a*) 32, 13 (*b*) 46, 20
(*c*) 51, 24 (*d*) 72, 45

65. (*a*) 5, 25 (*b*) 9, 81
(*c*) 4, 64 (*d*) 6, 36

66. (*a*) 91, 10 (*b*) 57, 12 (*c*) 69, 15 (*d*) 72, 13

67. (*a*) 20, 10 (*b*) 45, 27 (*c*) 15, 12 (*d*) 30, 18

68. (*a*) 7, 3 (*b*) 13, 9 (*c*) 11, 7 (*d*) 17, 8

69. (*a*) 10, 20 (*b*) 40, 50 (*c*) 30, 40 (*d*) 50, 60

70. (*a*) 16, 26 (*b*) 3, 4 (*c*) 26, 24 (*d*) 27, 25

EXPLANATORY ANSWERS

1. ***(c)*** **:** All others are types of colour.

2. ***(c)*** **:** Canoe is a boat. Others are resting places of birds/animals.

3. ***(d)*** **:** All others are sense organs.

4. ***(b)*** **:** All others are planets.

5. ***(b)*** **:** All others are expressions of joy.

6. ***(a)*** **:** All others are geometrical figures.

7. ***(b)*** **:** All others are solid metals.

8. ***(c)*** **:** All others are flying objects. Radar traces the objects in sky.

9. ***(d)*** **:** All others are joints in human body.

10. ***(d)*** **:** All others are nature-bound. Only war is man-made.

11. ***(c)*** **:** All others are young ones of animals.

12. ***(a)*** **:** All others are crawling animals.

13. ***(b)*** **:** All others are types of vegetation.

14. ***(d)*** **:** All others are professions, but only Diver's profession comprises of diving under water.

15. ***(d)*** **:** All other terms are related with activities of a horse.

16. ***(b)*** **:** All other words have the same meaning.

17. ***(a)*** **:** All others are indoor games.

18. ***(c)*** **:** All others are instructors. Pupil learns from the instructor.

19. ***(a)*** **:** All others are running forms of water.

20. ***(a)*** **:** All others are forms of taxes.

21. ***(a)*** **:** All others are parts of tree which are above the ground.

22. ***(b)*** **:** All are capitals but Chandigarh is the capital of two states.

23. ***(b)*** **:** All others have the same meaning.

24. ***(a)*** **:** All others are underground vegetables.

25. ***(d)*** **:** All others are means of transport.

26. ***(b)*** **:** The sequence in each group is +2. Only option B has sequence in +3, *i.e.*,

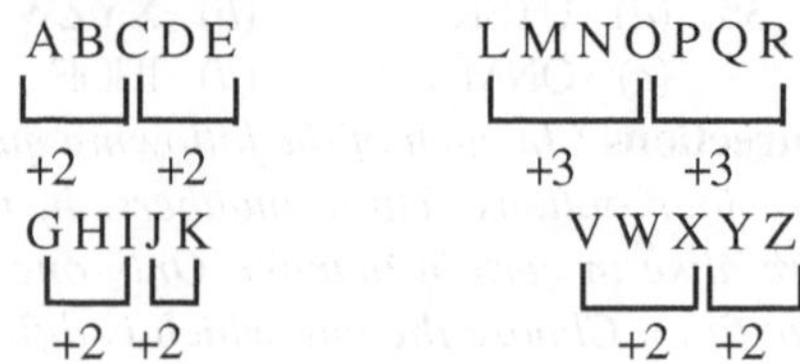

27. ***(c)*** **:** The sequence of alphabet in each group is in reverse order. Only option (*c*) has sequence in disturbed order.

28. ***(a)*** **:** Two consecutive alphabet in each group are in reverse sequence (–1), *i.e.*,

KJ SR ; XW HG ; ED YX
–1 –1 –1 –1 –1 –1

Only in option (*a*) the sequence is in natural order (+1), *i.e.*,

EF LM
+1 +1

29. ***(d)*** **:** In each group, letters 'OP' are common. The two corner alphabet are in natural order (+1); *i.e.*,

JOPK ; BOPC ; QOPR
+1 +1 +1

Only in option (*d*) they are in reverse order (–1); *i.e.*,

TOPS
–1

30. ***(d)*** **:** In other groups, only the alphabet in the centre is of lower case. In this option letter 'L' on the left is also in lower case.

31. ***(c)*** **:** In other groups, the third letter which is a repeat of the second alphabet is in lower case.

32. ***(d)*** **:** In each group, the sequence of the alphabet, irrespective of the case, is +2; *i.e.*,

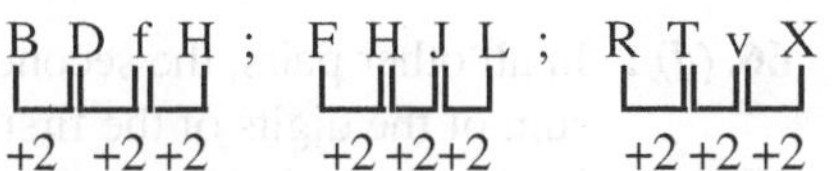

Only in option (*d*) the sequence is in natural order (+1), *i.e.*,

u V w X

+1 +1 +1

33. *(b)* : In each group; the alphabet at positions-first, fourth, second, fifth and third, form a natural sequence.
In option (*b*), the alphabet at positions first, fourth, fifth, second and third, form the natural sequence.

34. *(a)* : In each group, two alphabets in the corner and two alphabets in the centre correspond to their reverse order positioned alphabet.
i.e.,

natural order → A B C D E F G H I J K L M
reverse order → Z Y X W V U T S R Q P O N
natural order → N O P Q R S T U V W X Y Z
reverse order → M L K J I H G F E D C B A

As such—
D corresponds with W and
C corresponds with X.
B corresponds with Y and
A corresponds with Z.
H corresponds with S and
G corresponds with T.
Similarly,
F should correspond with U and
E should correspond with V;
i.e. letters 'UV' should be written as 'VU'

35. *(b)* : In each group, the alphabet are in reverse order.

36. *(a)* : Other numbers are divisible by 7.

37. *(d)* : Other numbers are multiples of 13.

38. *(c)* : 131 is a prime number.

39. *(b)* : In other numbers, no digit is repeated.

40. *(b)* : In other numbers, the last two digits are same.

41. *(b)* : All other numbers are perfect squares.

42. *(a)* : In other numbers, the sum of both the digits is 9.

43. *(a)* : In others, the digits are consecutive in natural or reverse series.

44. *(b)* : All others are prime numbers.

45. *(d)* : All other numbers are divisible by 2.

46. *(d)* : Bogie is a part of train which is a type of conveyance. Chair, Shirt and Necklace are types of furniture, garment and jewellery respectively.

47. *(a)* : The medium used for writing with pencil is lead, with pen it is ink and with brush, it is paint. With crayon it should be wax.

48. *(a)* : The pair of words are opposite. Other pairs are synonyms.

49. *(c)* : Tiara is worn on the head.

50. *(d)* : Other words are opposite to each other.

51. *(d)* : In all other groups, the letters are in natural series and the last letter of first part is the first letter of the second part.

52. *(b)* : In all other groups, only the vowel is in lower case in the first part and in second part the case is reversed.

53. *(c)* : In all other groups, the letters jump two letters in between them.

54. *(c)* : In all other groups, the single letter in first part is repeated in the second and vice versa.

55. *(a)* : In all other groups, the letters in the first part are one step forward than the corresponding letters in the second part.

56. *(b)* : In all other groups, the letters in the first part are written backwards in the second part.

57. *(d)* : All other groups have letters made by straight lines only.

58. *(a)* : In all other groups, the letters jump four letters in between then.

59. *(c)* : In all others groups, the letters jump one letter between them.

60. *(d)* : In all other groups, the second part is same as first except that the middle letter is changed to small letter.

61. ***(b)*** **:** In all other pairs 7 times the second number is the first number. In this option 9 times 7 is the first number.

62. ***(d)*** **:** In all other groups, the difference between the two numbers is 8.

63. ***(d)*** **:** In other groups 12 times, the first number is the second number. In this option 11 times the first number is the second number.

64. ***(a)*** **:** 13 is a prime number.

65. ***(c)*** **:** In all other pairs, the second number is a perfect square of the first.

66. ***(d)*** **:** In all other pairs, the second number is the sum of the digits of the first number.

67. ***(a)*** **:** In all other pairs, the numbers are divisible by 3.

68. ***(d)*** **:** In other groups, the difference between the numbers is 4.

69. ***(a)*** **:** In this option, the second number is double the first number. In other groups the difference between the two numbers is 10.

70. ***(a)*** **:** In other groups, the first digits of the two numbers are same (consider 3 and 4 as 03 and 04).

CODING AND DECODING

Coding is a secretive language which is used to change the representation of the actual term/word/value. This coded language can be framed by *(i)* moving the letters one or more steps forward or backward; *(ii)* substituting numbers for letters and vice–versa; *(iii)* writing the letters of the given word in reverse order in part or in whole; and *(iv)* replacing the letters in their natural series by the same positioned letters in their reverse series.

There is variety in ways of coding. Coding language is not only for words and numbers but also for hiding a group of words, statements or even sentences. This form of coding pattern may appear to be confusing but after solving only a few questions it is very easy to understand. Questions based on this coding pattern require no moving of steps or straining efforts of calculations, but only quick tallying or comparing ability. The codes can be letters or numbers.

EXERCISE

Directions : *In the following questions select the right option which indicates the correct code for the word or letter given in the question.*

1. If MUSK is coded as 146816, then ZERO will be coded as :

(*a*) 113811 (*b*) 122912
(*c*) 15915 (*d*) 2651815

2. If BAD is coded as 7, HIS as 9, LOW will be coded as :

(*a*) 50 (*b*) 8
(*c*) 23 (*d*) 5

3. In a certain code LIBERATE is written as 56403170, TRIBAL will be written in the same code as :

(*a*) 734615 (*b*) 736415
(*c*) 136475 (*d*) 034615

4. In certain military code, SYSTEM is written as SYSMET, and NEARER as AENRER, what will be the code for FRACTION?

(*a*) CRAFNOIT (*b*) FRCAITNO
(*c*) CARFNOIT (*d*) FRACNOIT

5. If CRUDE is written as BSTED, then MOIST will be coded as :

(*a*) NNJRU (*b*) LNHRS
(*c*) NPJTU (*d*) LPHTS

6. In a certain code ALPACA is written as ACAPLA. How will ANIMAL be written in that code?

(*a*) LAMINA (*b*) ALAMIN
(*c*) LAMNIA (*d*) AAMLIN

7. In a certain code FINGER is written as DGLECP. What will be the code for KIDNEY?

(*a*) IGBLCW (*b*) IGCLBW
(*c*) IBCGLE (*d*) IGBKCV

8. In a certain code QUESTION is written as NXBVQLLQ. How will REPLY be coded?

(*a*) YHMOV (*b*) OBMVI
(*c*) VHSOB (*d*) OHMOV

9. If in a certain code SKEW is coded as PNCY, then what will JXQV will stand for?

(*a*) MUTS (*b*) MUST
(*c*) MTSU (*d*) STUM

10. In a certain code LONDON is written as MPOEPO. What will IVOHSZ mean in the same code?

(*a*) HUNGRY (*b*) HUNDRY
(*c*) GRUNHY (*d*) HONDUS

11. In a certain code language 8514 is a code for HEAD, 3945 for RIDE and 057 for BEG. What will be the code for GRADE?

(*a*) 71345 (*b*) 73415
(*c*) 74135 (*d*) 73145

12. If MOTHERLAND is coded as 9501623748, how will DREAM be coded?
(*a*) 82697 (*b*) 86297
(*c*) 82769 (*d*) 82679

13. If OATH is coded in a certain language as TEYL, then how will WORD be coded?
(*a*) BWRH (*b*) HRWB
(*c*) BSWH (*d*) CSXI

14. If FINANCE is coded as GKQESIL, then how will BANK be coded in the same manner?
(*a*) CBOL (*b*) CDRP
(*c*) CCQO (*d*) CCPN

15. PLANNING is coded in a certain language as UFFHSCSA. How will AUTHORITY be coded in the same language?
(*a*) FOYBTLNND
(*b*) FYOTBNNLT
(*c*) FBOYTLNTN
(*d*) FBOYTNLTN

Directions : *In the following questions study the coded patterns and then select the right option from the given alternatives.*

16. In a certain language, (a) 'go ju mi' stands for 'plenty of money'; (b) pao ju go nei vu' for 'money creates lots of problems'; (c) 'kol vu nei' for 'problems create tension'; and (d) 'sol tun ju haw' for 'still money is needed'. Which of the following words stand for 'money'?
(*a*) nei (*b*) ju
(*c*) haw (*d*) go

17. In a certain language, (a) 'FOR' stands for 'old is gold'; (b) 'ROT' stands for 'gold is pure'; (c) 'ROM' stands for 'gold is costly'. How will 'pure old gold is costly' be written?
(*a*) TFROM (*b*) FOTRM
(*c*) FTORM (*d*) TOMRF

18. In a certain code '415' means 'milk is hot'; '18' means 'hot soup'; and '895' means 'soup is tasty'. What number will indicate the word 'tasty'?
(*a*) 9 (*b*) 8
(*c*) 5 (*d*) 4

19. In a certain code '643' means 'she is beautiful', '593' means 'he is handsome', and '567' means 'handsome meets beautiful'. What number will indicate the word 'meets'?
(*a*) 5 (*b*) 3
(*c*) 7 (*d*) 6

20. In a certain code language, (a) 'dugo hui mul zo' stands for 'work is very hard'; (b) 'hui dugo ba ki' for 'Bingo is very smart'; (c) 'nano mul dugo' for 'cake is hard', and (d) 'mul ki qu' for 'smart and hard'. Which of the following words stand for 'Bingo'?
(*a*) jalu (*b*) dugo
(*c*) ki (*d*) ba

Directions : *Read the given coded information and choose the correct answer from the given options.*

21. If 'water' is called 'blue', 'blue' is called 'red', 'red' is called 'white', 'white' is called 'sky', 'sky' is called 'rain', 'rain' is called 'green', 'green' is called 'air' and 'air' is called 'table', which of the following is the colour of milk?
(*a*) white (*b*) rain
(*c*) sky (*d*) green

22. If 'light' is called 'dark', 'dark' is called 'green', 'green' is called 'blue', 'blue' is called 'red', 'red' is called 'white' and 'white' is called 'yellow', what is the colour of blood?
(*a*) red (*b*) dark
(*c*) white (*d*) yellow

23. If 'sky' is called 'sea', 'sea' is called 'water', 'water' is called 'air', 'air' is called 'cloud' and 'cloud' is called 'river', then what do we drink when thirsty?
(*a*) sky (*b*) air
(*c*) water (*d*) sea

24. If 'yellow' means 'red', 'white' means 'green', 'red' means 'orange', 'blue' means 'white' and 'green' means 'blue', then the colour of sky is :
(*a*) white (*b*) green
(*c*) blue (*d*) yellow

25. If 'land' is called 'sky', 'sky' is called 'air', 'air' is called 'water', 'water' is called 'sand' and 'sand' is called 'solid', where do fishes swim?
(*a*) air (*b*) sky
(*c*) water (*d*) sand

EXPLANATORY ANSWERS

1. *(b)* **:** The coded number signifies the position of the alphabet in its reverse order of the alphabetical series (ZYXW...)

M U S K → MUSK
↓ ↓ ↓ ↓
14th 6th 8th 16th → 146816

Similarly,

Z E R O → ZERO
↓ ↓ ↓ ↓
1st 22nd 9th 12th → 122912

2. *(d)* **:** The coded number is the sum of number digits signifying the position of the alphabet in the natural order.

B A D
↓ ↓ ↓
2nd 1st 4th *i.e.,* 2 + 1 + 4 = 7

Similarly,

H I S
↓ ↓ ↓
8th 9th 19th *i.e.,* 8 + 9 + 19 = 36
further, 3 + 6 = 9

Also,

L O W
↓ ↓ ↓
12th 15th 23rd *i.e.,* 12 + 15 + 23 = 50
further, 5 + 0 = 0

3. *(b)* **:** The letters of the word TRIBAL are picked from LIBERATE. So will be the coded numbers.

L I B E R A T E → given word
5 6 4 0 3 1 7 0 → codes

Similarly,

T R I B A L → word to be coded
7 3 6 4 1 5 → answer codes

4. *(c)* **:** The word is divided into two equal parts and the letters of each part are written in reverse order.

SYS TEM SYS MET NEA RER AEN RER

Similarly,

FRAC TION CARF NOIT

5. *(d)* **:** The code is formed by moving the letters one step backwards and one step forward alternately.

CRUDE BSTED
−1
+1
−1
+1
−1

Similarly,

MOIST LPHTS
−1
+1
−1
+1
−1

6. *(a)* **:** The letters of the word are written backwards.

ALPACA ACAPLA

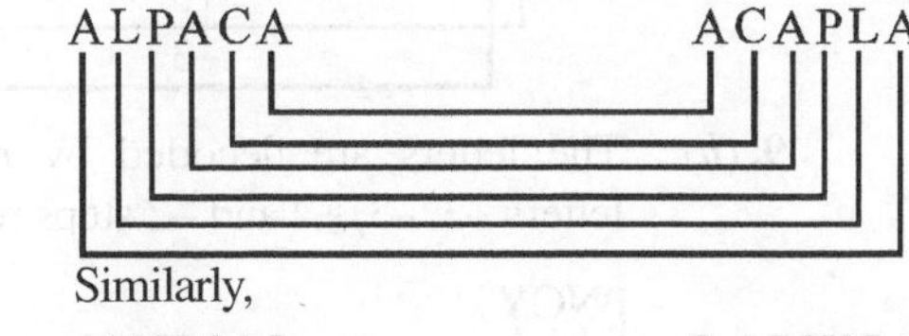

Similarly,

ANIMAL LAMINA

7. *(a)* **:** The word is coded by moving the letters two steps backwards.

FINGER DGLECP

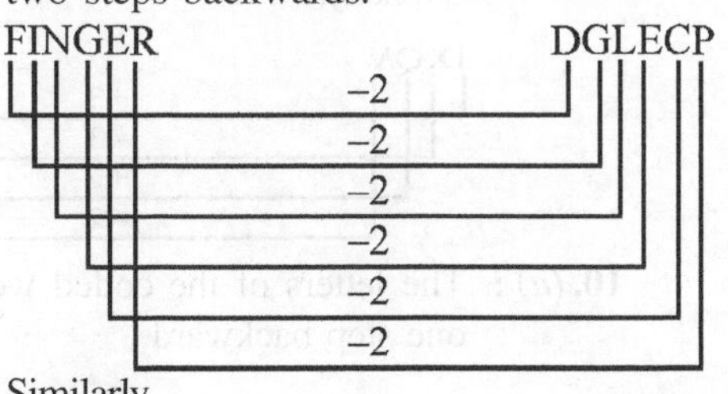

Similarly,

KIDNEY IGBLCW

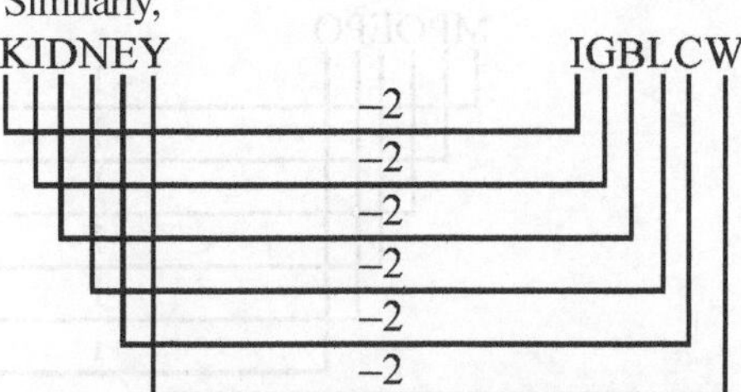

8. *(d)* **:** The letters of the word are coded by moving three steps backward and three steps forward alternately.

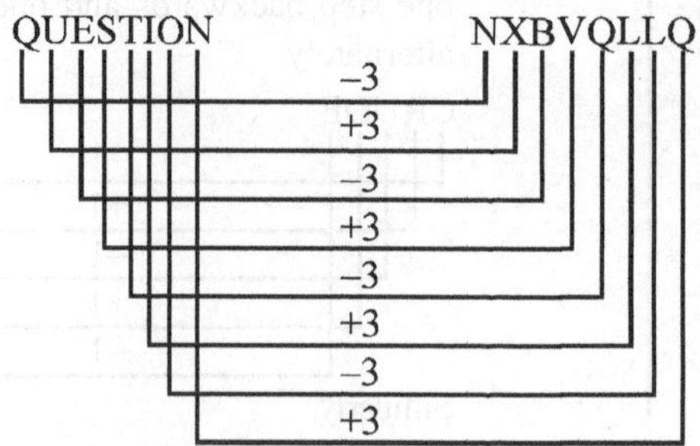

Similarly,

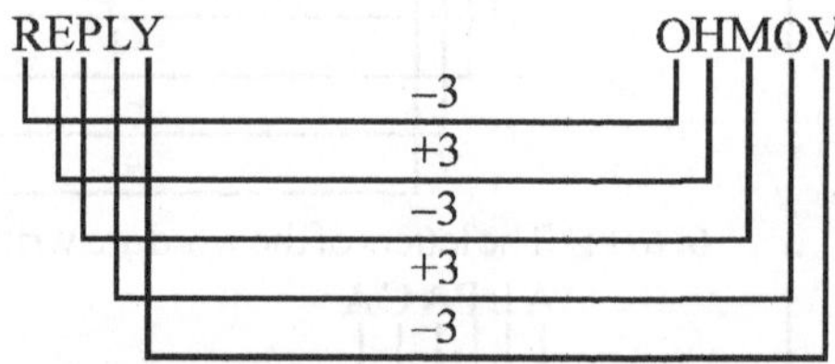

9. *(b)* **:** The letters are decoded by moving the letters +3, –3, +2 and –2 steps respectively.

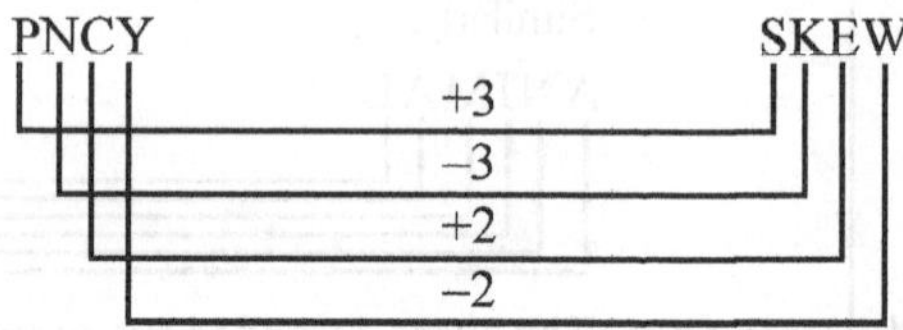

Similarly,

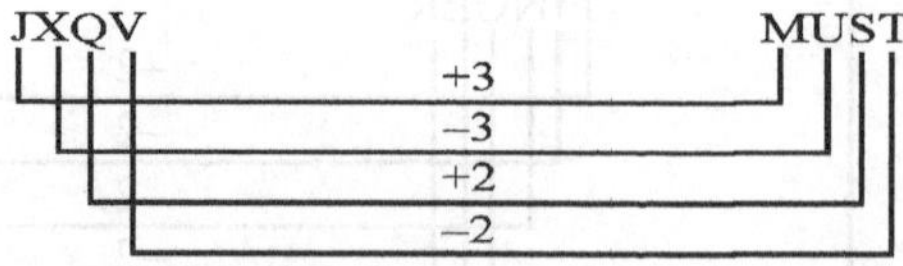

10. *(a)* **:** The letters of the coded word are moved one step backward.

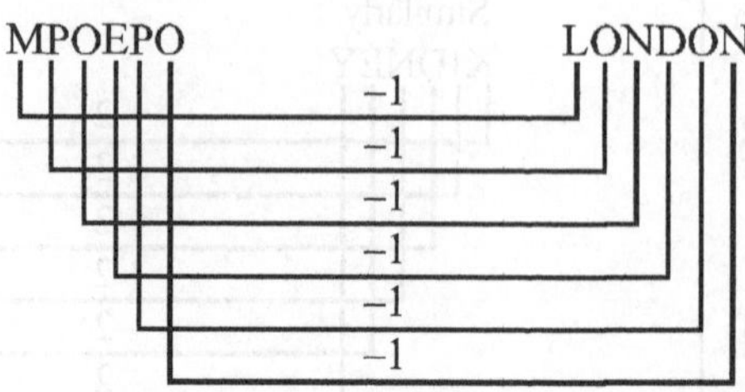

Similarly,

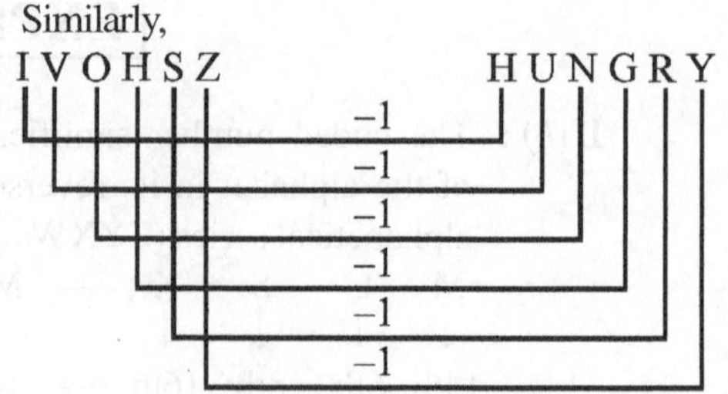

11. *(d)* **:** The word GRADE is framed by letters in the given words. So, in order to find the code for GRADE select the respective number codes.

H E A D   R I D E   B E G → letters
8 5 1 4   3 9 4 5   0 5 7 → codes

So,

G R A D E →letters
7 3 1 4 5 →answer codes

12. *(d)* **:** The letters of the word are coded by numbers. So to find the code for DREAM select the respective numbers.

M O T H E R L A N D → letters
9 5 0 1 6 2 3 7 4 8 → codes

So, D R E A M → letters
8 2 6 7 9 → answer codes

13. *(c)* **:** The letters are coded by moving five and four steps forward alternately.

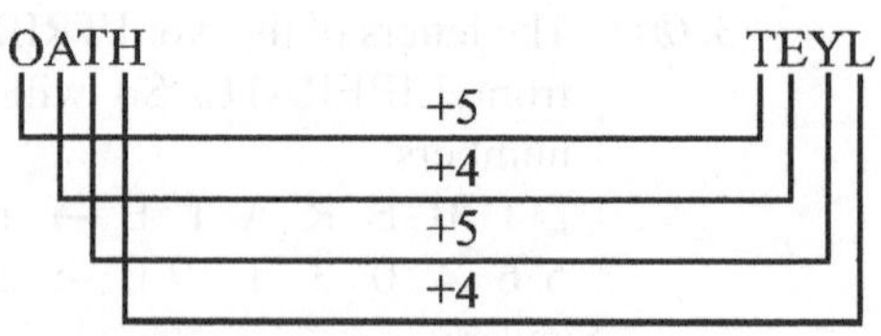

Similarly,

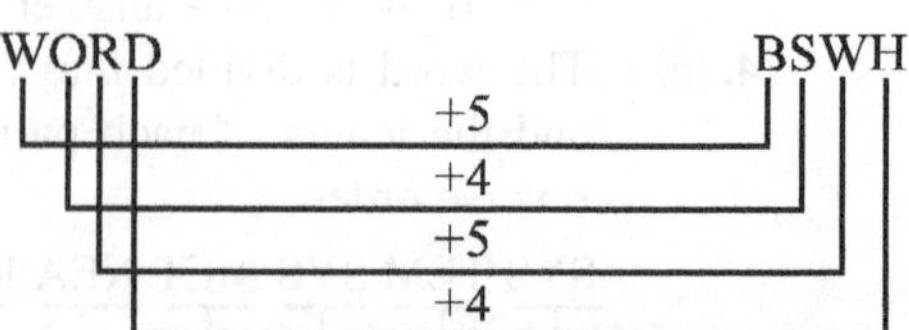

14. *(c)* **:** The letters of the word are coded by moving one step ahead and increasing the difference by one.

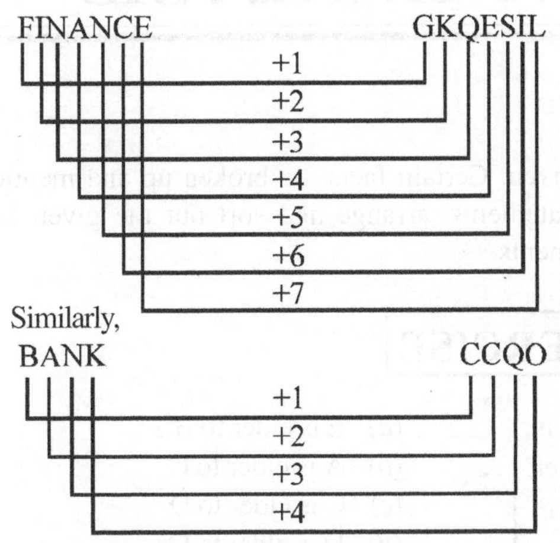

15. *(a)* **:** The letters of the word are coded by moving five steps forward and six steps backward alternately.

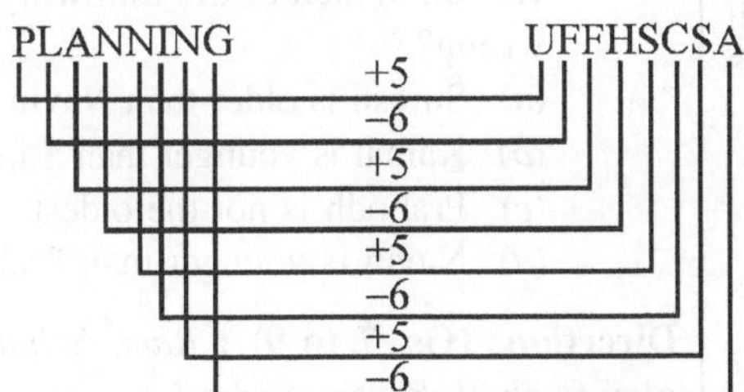

Similarly,

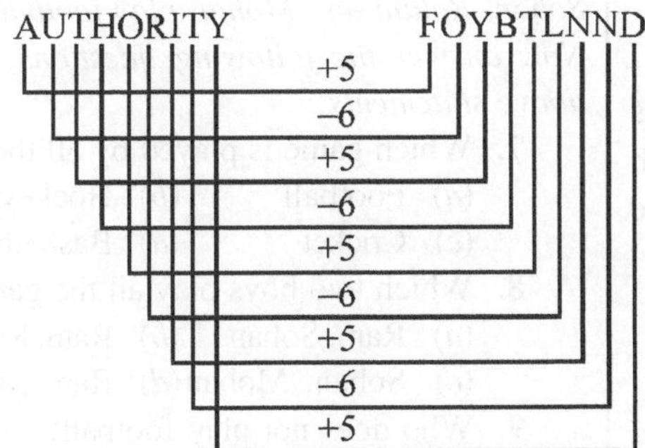

16. *(b)* **:**

Code	Sentence
1. go *ju* mi	plenty of *money*
2. pao *ju* go nei vu	*money* creates lots of problems
3. kol vu nei	problems create tension
4. sol tun *ju* haw	still *money* is needed

In 1st, 2nd and 4th codes and their sentences the word 'ju' is repeated and so is 'money'.

17. *(a)* **:**

Code	Sentence
1. FOR	old is gold
2. ROT	gold is pure
3. ROM	gold is costly

Therefore,

F	stands	for	old
O	stands	for	is
R	stands	for	gold
T	stands	for	pure
M	stands	for	costly

So, 'pure old gold is costly' will be written as 'TFROM'.

18. *(a)* **:**

Code	Sentence
1. 415	milk is hot
2. 18	hot soup
3. 895	soup is *tasty*

From 3rd code and its sentence neither number '9' is repeated nor the word 'tasty'.

19. *(c)* **:**

Code	Sentence
1. 643	she is beautiful
2. 593	he is handsome
3. 567	handsome *meets* beautiful

From 3rd code and its sentence, neither number '7' nor the word 'meets' is repeated.

20. *(d)* **:**

Code	Sentence
1. *dugo hui* mul zo	work *is very* hard
2. *hui dugo* **ba** *ki*	**Bingo** *is very smart*
3. nano mul *dugo*	cake is *hard*
4. mul *ki* qu	*smart* and hard

From 2nd code and its sentence, neither 'ba' nor 'Bingo' is repeated.
(Words repeated are in italics)

21. *(c)* **:** Colour of milk is 'white' and 'white' is called 'sky'.

22. *(c)* **:** Colour of blood is 'red' and 'red' is called 'white'.

23. *(b)* **:** We drink 'water' when we are thirsty and 'water' is called 'air'.

24. *(a)* **:** Colour of sky is 'blue' and 'blue' means 'white'.

25. *(d)* **:** Fishes swim in 'water' and 'water' is called 'sand'.

STATEMENT ANALYSIS

In these type of questions, a few statements are given. Certain facts are broken up and mentioned in these statements. What is required is to analyse the statements, arrange and sort out the given facts and then answer the questions related to the given statements.

EXERCISE

1. Among five friends, A is heavier than B; C is lighter than D; B is lighter than D but heavier than E. Who among them is the heaviest?
   (*a*) B (*b*) C
   (*c*) A (*d*) Can't say
2. Pune is bigger than Jhansi, Sitapur is bigger than Chittor. Raigarh is not as big as Jhansi, but is bigger than Sitapur. Chittor is not as big as Sitapur. Which is the smallest?
   (*a*) Jhansi (*b*) Pune
   (*c*) Chittor (*d*) Sitapur
3. Ajay works more than Ram. Alok works as much as Raju. Pankaj works less than Alok. Ram works more than Alok. Who works the most of all?
   (*a*) Ajay (*b*) Ram
   (*c*) Alok (*d*) Raju
4. Among five friends P, Q, R, S and T, who is the youngest? To arrive at the answer which of the following information given in the statements (A) and (B) is sufficient?
   (A) R is younger than P and T.
   (B) S is younger than Q.
   (*a*) Only A alone is sufficient
   (*b*) Either A or B is sufficient
   (*c*) Both A and B together are needed
   (*d*) Both A and B together are not sufficient
5. A is elder to B while C and D are elder to E who lies between A and B. If C be elder to B, which one of the following statements is necessarily true?
   (*a*) E is elder to B
   (*b*) A is elder to C
   (*c*) C is elder to D
   (*d*) D is elder to C
6. Suresh is as much older than Kamal as he is younger than Prabodh. Navin is as old as Kamal. Which of the following statements is wrong?
   (*a*) Suresh is older than Navin
   (*b*) Kamal is younger than Suresh
   (*c*) Prabodh is not the oldest
   (*d*) Navin is younger than Prabodh

Directions (Qs. 7 to 9) : *Ram, Sohan and Mohan play football, hockey and cricket. Ram, Ramesh and Mohan play hockey, cricket and basketball. Ram, Sohan, Rahim and Mohan play football and cricket. Now answer the following questions based on the above statements :*

7. Which game is played by all the boys?
   (*a*) Football (*b*) Hockey
   (*c*) Cricket (*d*) Basketball
8. Which two boys play all the games?
   (*a*) Ram, Sohan (*b*) Ram, Ramesh
   (*c*) Sohan, Mohan (*d*) Ram, Mohan
9. Who does not play football?
   (*a*) Ramesh (*b*) Sohan
   (*c*) Rahim (*d*) Mohan

Directions (Qs. 10 to 12) : *Read the following directions and answer the questions given below :*

There are five persons in a group. Out of these two are men. Only three persons know swimming, of which one is a man. There is a couple, of which the husband knows swimming. A is the younger sister of D and B is the husband of E. C is a swimming champion.

10. Who is the other man in the group?
(*a*) C (*b*) B
(*c*) A (*d*) D

11. The two women who know how to swim are:
(*a*) A and C (*b*) C and D
(*c*) D and E (*d*) A and E

12. The two persons who do not know how to swim are :
(*a*) B and D (*b*) D and E
(*c*) A and E (*d*) A and D

Directions (Qs. 13 to 15) : *Read the following statements and answer the questions given below :*

Rajat, Sushil and Nagesh play football, hockey and cricket. Rajat, Ramu and Nagesh play hockey, cricket and basketball. Rajat, Sushil, Mayank and Nagesh play football and cricket.

13. Which game is played by all the boys?
(*a*) Hockey (*b*) Basketball
(*c*) Football (*d*) Cricket

14. Who does not play football?
(*a*) Rajat (*b*) Nagesh
(*c*) Sushil (*d*) Ramu

15. Which of the following two boys play all the games?
(*a*) Nagesh, Rajat
(*b*) Mayank, Ramu
(*c*) Ramu, Nagesh
(*d*) Sushil, Mayank

Directions (Qs. 16 to 20) : *Read the following information and answer the questions given below:*

(*i*) P, Q, R, S, T and U are six members in a family in which there are two married couples.
(*ii*) T a teacher is married to the doctor who is mother of R and U.
(*iii*) Q the lawyer is married to P.
(*iv*) P has one son and one grandson.
(*v*) Of the two married ladies one is a housewife.
(*vi*) There is also one student and one male engineer in the family.

16. Who among the following is the housewife?
(*a*) Q (*b*) P
(*c*) S (*d*) T

17. Which of the following represents the group of females in the family?
(*a*) QTR (*b*) PSR
(*c*) PSU (*d*) Data inadequate

18. Which of the following is true about the granddaughter in the family?
(*a*) She is a student
(*b*) She is an engineer
(*c*) She is a lawyer
(*d*) Data Inadequate

19. How R is related to U?
(*a*) Brother
(*b*) Sister
(*c*) Brother or Sister
(*d*) Data inadequate

20. How is P related to R?
(*a*) Grandfather (*b*) Mother
(*c*) Sister (*d*) Grandmother

EXPLANATORY ANSWERS

1. (*d*) : The five friends in descending order of weight are : A/D, B/C, E or A/D, B, C/E. Either A or D is the heaviest.

2. (*c*) : The order of cities in descending order of size is : Pune, Jhansi, Raigarh, Sitapur, Chittor.

3. (*a*) : On the basis of doing work, the descending order will be : Ajay, Ram, Alok/Raju, Pankaj.

4. (*d*) : Statements are not inter-related.

5. (*a*) : The order in descending seniority will be : A/C/D, E, B.

6. (*c*) : On the basis of age the descending order will be : Prabodh, Suresh, Kamal/Navin.

Chart for Answers 7 to 9

Boy	*Games Played*
Ram	Football, Hocky, Cricket, Basketball
Sohan	Football, Hockey, Cricket
Mohan	Football, Hockey, Cricket, Basketball
Ramesh	Hockey, Cricket, Basketball
Rahim	Football, Cricket.

7. *(c)* **8.** *(d)* **9.** *(a)*

For Answers 10 to 12 the information chart will be :

A. Woman ((younger sister of D); knows swimming.

B. Man (husband of E); knows swimming

C. Woman; Swimming champion

D. Man (brother of A)

E. Woman (wife of B)

From the couple B & E, B (husband) knows swimming. C is a swimming champion. Three persons know how to swim of which only B is a man. So, the two women who know how to swim are C and A (the younger sister of D). There are two men in the group of five. One is B and the other will be D.

10. *(d)* **11.** *(a)* **12.** *(b)*

Chart for Answers 13 to 15

Boy	*Games Played*
Rajat	— Football, Hockey, Cricket, Basketball
Sushil	— Football, Hockey, Cricket, Basketball
Nagesh	— Football, Hockey, Cricket, Basketball
Ramu	— Hockey, Cricket, Basketball
Mayank	— Football, Cricket

13. *(d)* **14.** *(d)* **15.** *(a)*

Chart for Answers 16 to 20

P (female/housewife) — Q (male/lawyer) *Grandparents*

T (male/teacher) — S (female/doctor) *Parents*

R, U Children

(of R and U, one is a male engineer and one is a student)

16. *(b)* **:** One married lady S who is mother of R and U is a doctor. Q the lawyer is married to P. Of the two married ladies one is a house-wife. As Q is a lawyer the other married lady who is a housewife should be P.

17. *(d)* **:** Sex of R and U is not given.

18. *(a)* **:** P has one son T and one grandson either R or U one of whom is an engineer. So, the granddaughter is a student.

19. *(c)* **:** Sex of R and U is not given, but as both are children of S and one is a male engineer, the relationship between the two is of brother and sister.

20. *(d)*

PLACE ARRANGEMENT

Place arrangement generally refers to the positioning of persons or objects in a manner indicated by set of information given. One has to understand the order of placement and then attempt questions following the given information.

EXERCISE

Directions : *In the following questions, understand the arrangement pattern and then select the right answer from the given options :*

1. Five boys are sitting in a row. Raghu is not adjacent to Shyam or Amit. Ajay is not adjacent to Shyam. Raghu is adjacent to Mayank. If Mayank is at the middle in the row, then Ajay is adjacent to whom out of the following?
   (*a*) Amit (*b*) Raghu
   (*c*) Mayank (*d*) Shyam
2. Mini is to the right of Rajni but to the left of Ananta. Saya is to the right of Mini but to the left of Jaya. Who is on the extreme left if all the girls are facing North?
   (*a*) Jaya (*b*) Mini
   (*c*) Rajni (*d*) Saya
3. O, P, Q, R, S and T are standing on a bench according to their height. P is taller than O but shorter than S. Only S is taller than T. R is shorter than P but taller than Q. Who is the shortest?
   (*a*) O (*b*) Q
   (*c*) P (*d*) Cannot be said
4. Five personalities are living in a multistoried building. Mr. Effortless lives in a flat above Mr. Active, Mr. Charge lives in a flat below Mr. Diligent, Mr. Active lives in a flat above Mr. Diligent and Mr. Behaved lives in a flat below Mr. Charge. Who lives in the topmost flat?
   (*a*) Mr. Charge (*b*) Mr. Diligent
   (*c*) Mr. Effortless (*d*) Mr. Behaved
5. Six friends are sitting in a circle and playing cards. Kenny is to the left of Danny. Michael is in-between Bob and John. Roger is in between Kenny and Bob. Who is sitting to the right of Michael?
   (*a*) Danny (*b*) John
   (*c*) Kenny (*d*) Bob
6. Four girls A, B, C and D are sitting in a circle. B and C are facing each other. Which of the following is definitely true?
   (*a*) A is to the left of C
   (*b*) D is to the left of C
   (*c*) A and D are facing each other
   (*d*) A is not between B and C
7. Brijesh, Jayesh, Amar and Praveer are playing a game of cards. Amar is to the right of Jayesh who is to the right of Brijesh. Who is to the right of Amar?
   (*a*) Brijesh
   (*b*) Praveer
   (*c*) Brijesh or Praveer
   (*d*) Jayesh
8. In a pile of 10 books there are 3 of History, 3 of Hindi, 2 of Maths, and 2 of English. Taking from above there is an English book between a History and Maths book, a History book between a Maths and an English book, a Hindi book between an English and a Maths book, a Maths book between two Hindi books, and two Hindi books between a Maths and a History book. Book of which subject is at the sixth position from the top?
   (*a*) English (*b*) Hindi
   (*c*) History (*d*) Maths

9. Five persons A, B, C, D and E are sitting in a row facing you such that D is on the left of C and B is on the right of E. A is on the right of C and B is on the left of D. If E occupies a corner position, then who is sitting in the centre?
(*a*) A (*b*) B
(*c*) C (*d*) D

10. Six friends A, B, C, D, E and F are standing in a circle. B is between F and C; A is between E and D; F is to the left of D. Who is between A and F?
(*a*) C (*b*) B
(*c*) D (*d*) E

EXPLANATORY ANSWERS

1. (*b*) : The order of sitting is :
Amit, Shyam, Mayank, Ajay, Raghu
or
Ajay, Raghu, Mayank, Amit, Shyam

2. (*c*) : The order in which the girls are positioned is :
Rajni, Mini, Ananta, Saya, Jaya
or
Saya, Jaya, Ananta
or
Saya, Ananta, Jaya

3. (*d*) : In descending order of height, the standing positions are :

S		S
T		T
P	*or*	P
R		R
O		Q
Q		O

Either O or Q is the shortest. The informa-tion given is not enough to clarify the answer.

4. (*c*) : The personalities living in flats in multi-storied building are in order given below :
Mr. Effortless
Mr. Active
Mr. Diligent
Mr. Charge
Mr. Behaved

5. (*d*) : The order in which the friends are sitting is :

Danny
John Kenny
Michael Roger
Bob

6. (*c*) : The sitting positions are :

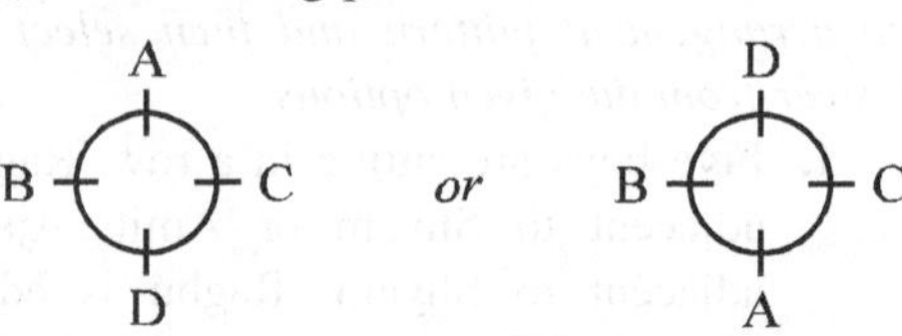

7. (*b*) : The order from left to light is :
Brijesh, Jayesh, Amar, Praveer

8. (*b*) : The pile of books is in the order :
1st — History
English
Maths
History
English
6th — Hindi
Maths
Hindi
Hind
10th — History

9. (*d*) : Sitting order while facing us is :
A, C, D, B, E

10. (*c*) : The pattern of standing is :

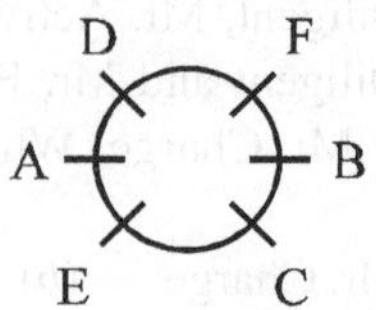

DIRECTION SENSE

In these type of tests, the directions in questions needs to be perceived. Such questions are based on the direction chart.

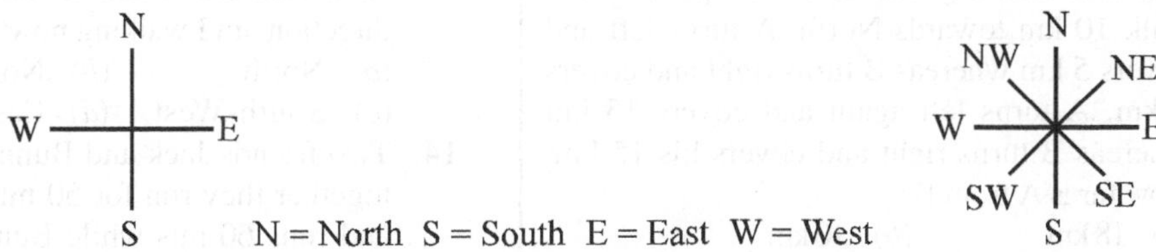

The sense of the different directions are guided by the left and right turns or angular turns.

EXERCISE

Directions : *In the following questions, select the right answer from the given options to depict the correct direction/distance.*

1. Kittu walks towards East and then towards South. After walking some distance he turns towards West and then turns to his left. In which direction is he walking now?

(*a*) North (*b*) South
(*c*) East (*d*) West

2. A person is driving towards West. What sequence of directions should he follow so that he is driving towards South?

(*a*) left, right, right
(*b*) right, right, left
(*c*) left, left, left
(*d*) right, right, right

3. Richa drives 8 km to the South, turns left and drives 5 km. Again, she turns left and drives 8 km. How far is she from her starting point?

(*a*) 3km (*b*) 5km
(*c*) 8km (*d*) 13km

4. Dingi runs 40 km towards North then turns right and runs 50 km. He turns right and runs 30 km, and once again turns right and runs 50 km. How far is he from his starting point?

(*a*) 90km (*b*) 50km
(*c*) 10km (*d*) 5km

5. If North is called North-West, North-West is called West, West is called South-West and so on. What will South-East be called?

(*a*) East (*b*) West
(*c*) North-East (*d*) South-East

6. A man travels 100 km towards South. From there he turns right and travels 100 km and again turns right to travel 50 km. Which direction is he in from his starting point?

(*a*) North (*b*) North-East
(*c*) East (*d*) South-West

7. A train runs 120 km in West direction, 30 km in South direction and then 80 km in east direction before reaching the station. In which direction is the station from the train's starting point?

(*a*) South-West (*b*) North-West
(*c*) South-East (*d*) South

8. Facing the West direction, Priya jogs for 20 m, turns left and goes further 40 m. She turns left again and jogs for 20 m. Then she turns right to go 20 m to reach the park. How far is the park from her starting point and in which direction?

(*a*) 20 m South (*b*) 40 m West
(*c*) 60 m South (*d*) 100 m East

9. If all the directions are rotated, *i.e.,* if North is changed to West and East to North and so on, then what will come in place of North-West?
(*a*) South-West (*b*) North-East
(*c*) East-North (*d*) East-West

10. A and B start together from one point. They walk 10 km towards North. A turns left and covers 5 km whereas B turns right and covers 3 km. A turns left again and covers 15 km whereas B turns right and covers his 15 km. How far is A from B?
(*a*) 18 km (*b*) 10 km
(*c*) 5 km (*d*) 8 km

11. Tarun is walking towards East. What direction he should not follow if he should walk towards North?
(*a*) right, right, left, right, right
(*b*) right, right, left, left, left
(*c*) right, right, right
(*d*) right, left, right, left

12. Sony and Moni start walking from a point. Sony walks in West direction and Moni in South direction. After covering 20 km, Soni turns left and walks 15 km. Moni walks 10 km, turns left and walks 5 km. Soni, then turns left again and walks 25 km, whereas Moni turns right and walks 5 km. How far are Sony and Moni from each other?
(*a*) 5 km
(*b*) They are back at the starting point
(*c*) They are at same place at the finishing point
(*d*) Data is insufficient

13. I was walking in South-East direction. After a while I turned 90° to the right and walked ahead. Later I turned 45° to the right. In which direction am I walking now?
(*a*) North (*b*) North-East
(*c*) South-West (*d*) East

14. Two friends Jack and Bunny start a race, and together they run for 50 mts. Jack turns right and runs 60 mts while Bunny turns left and runs 40 mts. Then Jack turns left and runs 50 mts while Bunny turns right and runs 50 mts. How far are the two friends now from each other?
(*a*) 60 mts (*b*) 100 mts
(*c*) 20 mts (*d*) 150 mts

15. A policeman left his police post and proceeded south 4 km, after hearing a loud sound from point A. On reaching the place he heard another sound and proceeded 4 km to his left to the point B, only to find that the sound was coming from left of B. From B he proceeded left to reach that place 4 km away. In which direction he has to go to reach his police post?
(*a*) North (*b*) South
(*c*) East (*d*) West

EXPLANATORY ANSWERS

1. (*b*) :

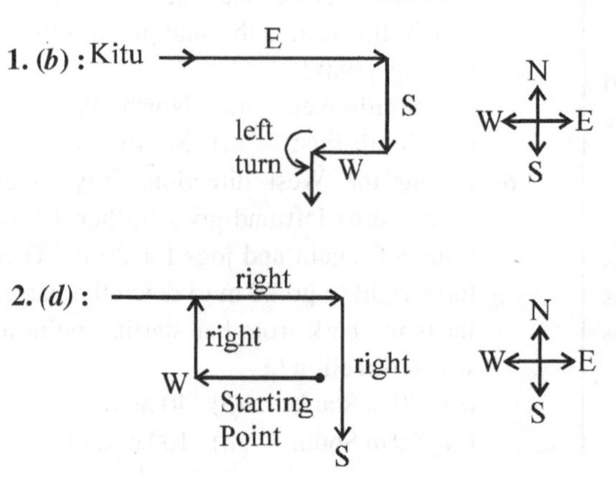

2. (*d*) :

3. (*b*) :

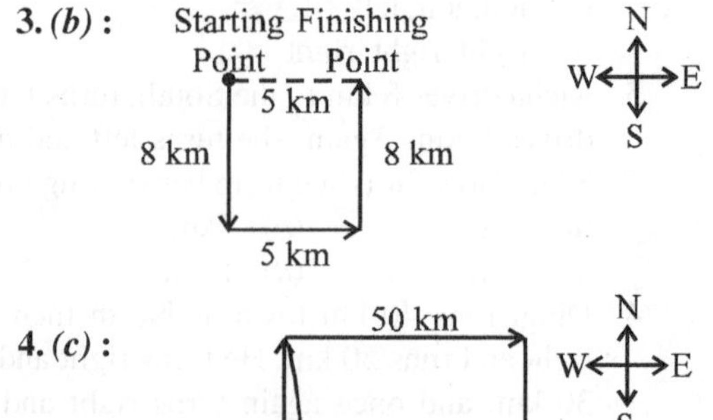

4. (*c*) :

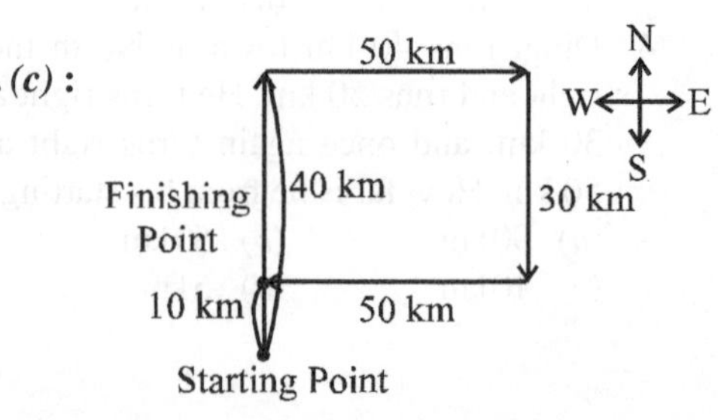

5. *(a)* :

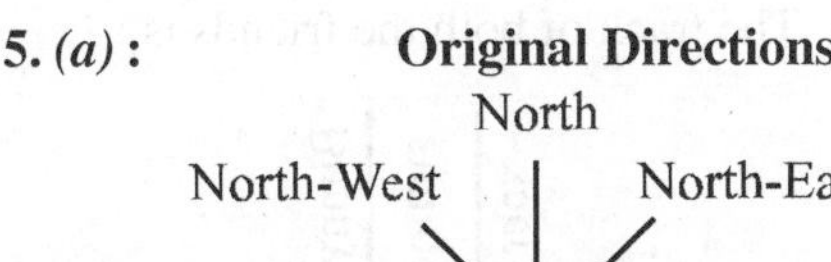

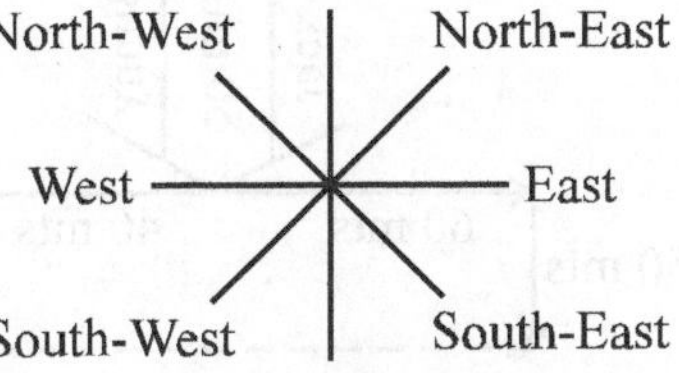

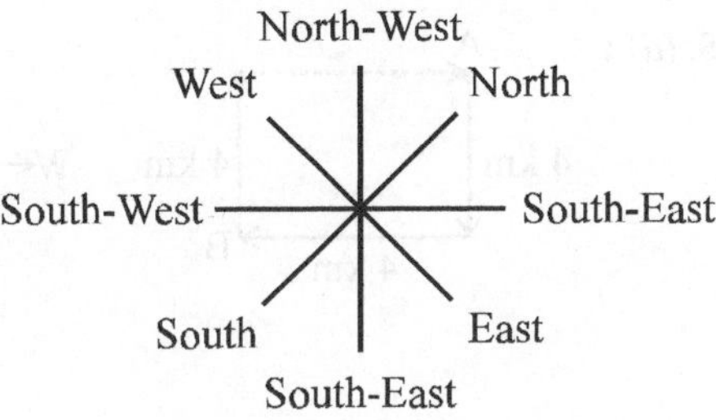

6. *(d)* :

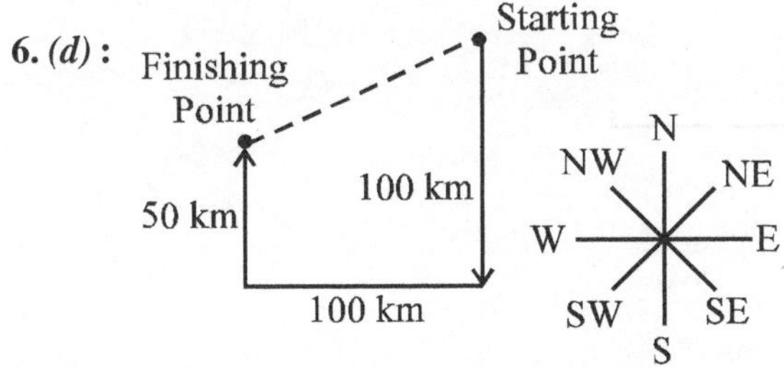

7. *(a)* :

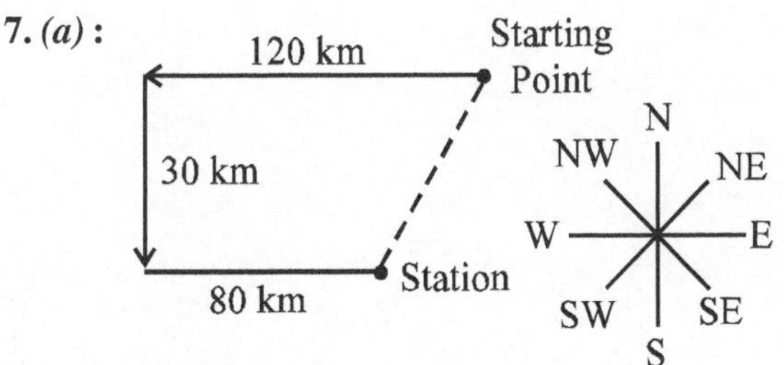

8. *(c)* : (40 + 20) = 60 metres South

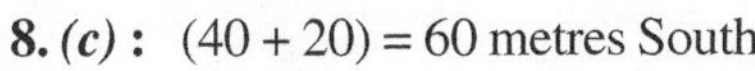

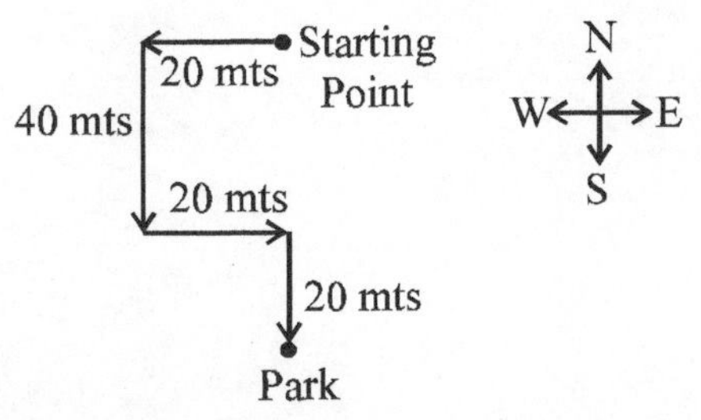

9. *(a)* :

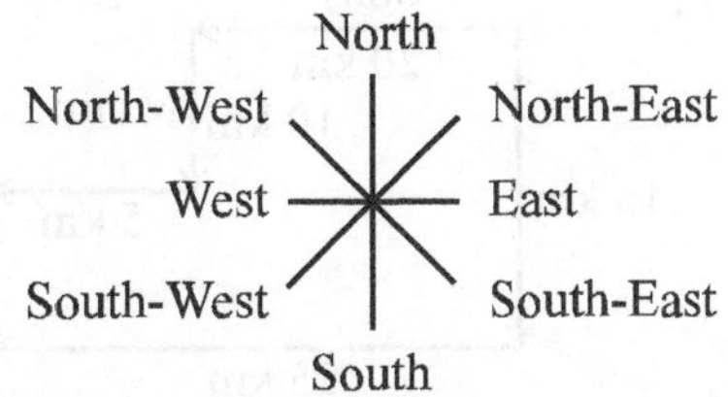

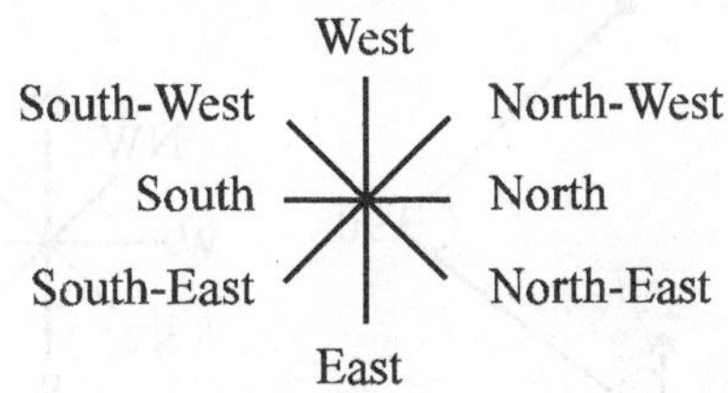

10. *(d)* :

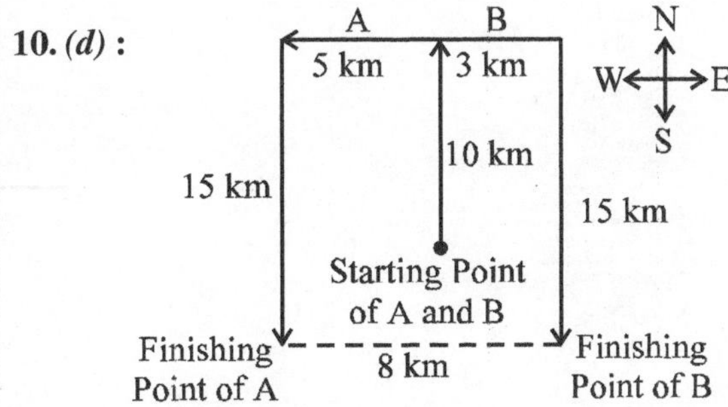

11. *(d)* :

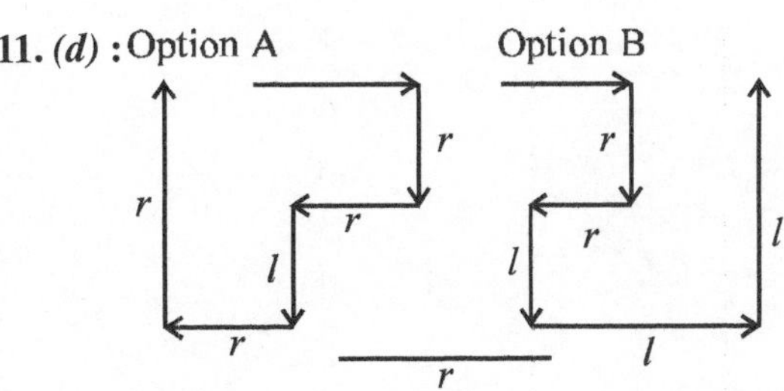

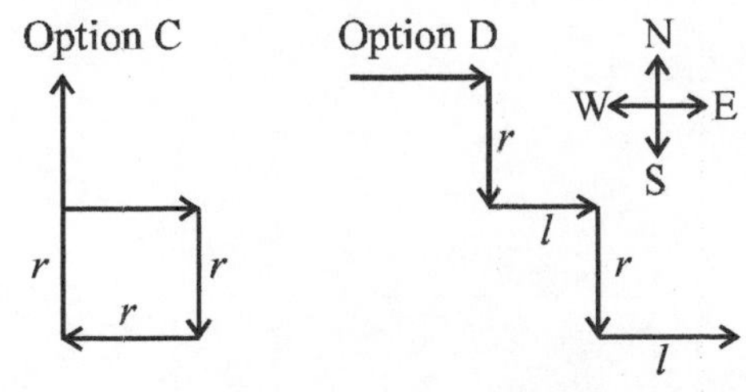

12. *(c)* :

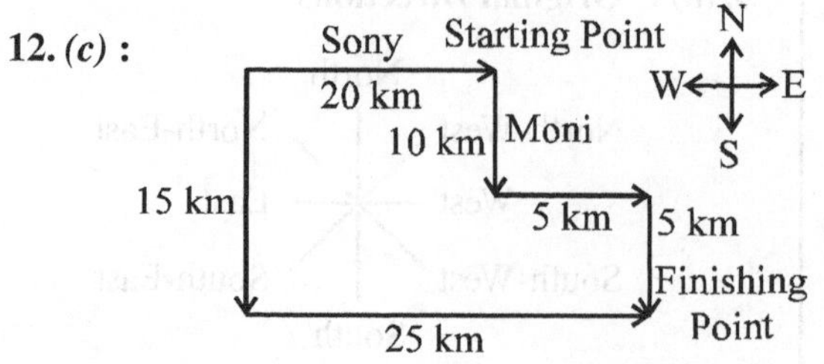

13. *(a)* : The direction of the movement is :

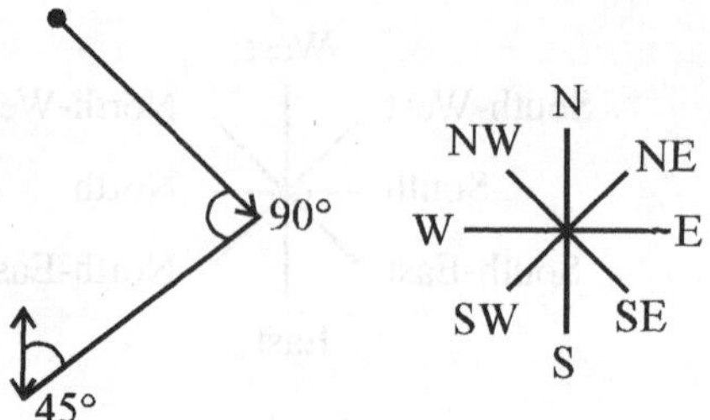

14. *(b)* : The track of both the friends is :

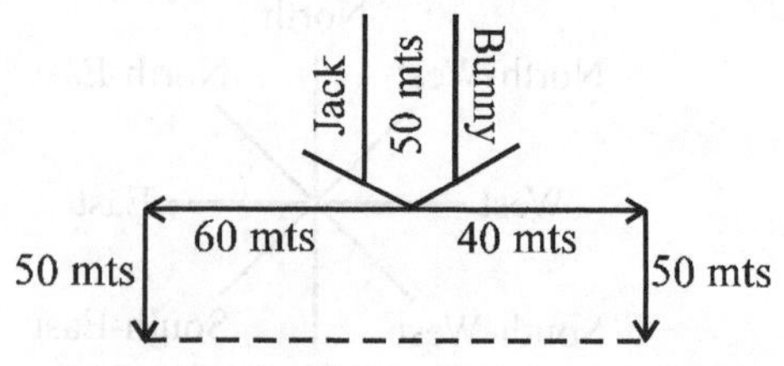

The two friends are 60 + 40 = 100 mts apart

15. *(d)* :

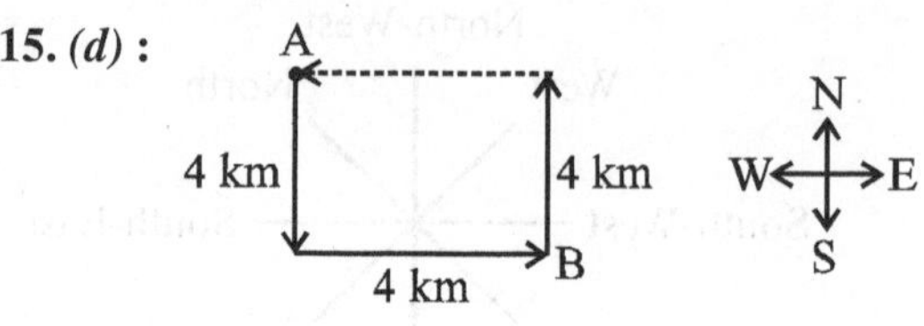

BLOOD RELATIONSHIPS

While attempting questions on blood relations, one should be clear of all the relation patterns that can exist between any two individuals. These type of questions are given mainly to test one's relationship ability.

Very well-known relations are :

Mother	Grandmother
Father	Grandfather
Son	Grandson
Daughter	Granddaughter
Brother	Brother-in-law
Sister	Sister-in-law
Niece	Father-in-law
Nephew	Mother-in-law
Uncle	Son-in-law
Aunt	Daughter-in-law
Husband	Cousin
Wife	

The patterns of some relationships which help in solving questions in these tests are :

Father's *or* Mother's Father	—	Grandfather (Paternal *or* Maternal)
Father's *or* Mother's Mother	—	Grandmother (Paternal *or* Maternal)
Father's *or* Mother's Son	—	Brother
Father's *or* Mother's Daughter	—	Sister
Father's Brother	—	Paternal Uncle
Father's Sister	—	Paternal Aunt
Mother's Brother	—	Maternal Uncle
Mother's Sister	—	Maternal Aunt
Uncle *or* Aunt's Son *or* Daughter	—	Cousin
Son's Wife	—	Daughter-in-law
Daughter's Husband	—	Son-in-law
Husband's *or* Wife's Brother	—	Brother-in-law
Husband's *or* Wife's Sister	—	Sister-in-law
Brother's Wife	—	Sister-in-law
Sister's Husband	—	Brother-in-law
Brother's Son	—	Nephew
Brother's Daughter	—	Niece

EXERCISE

Directions : *In each of the following questions keenly study the relationship mentioned between the persons, and then from the given options select the right relationship as the answer.*

1. A lady said, "The person standing there is my grandfather's only son's daughter". How is the lady related to the standing person?
(*a*) Sister
(*b*) Mother
(*c*) Aunt
(*d*) Cousin

2. Ajay is the brother of Vijay. Mili is the sister of Ajay. Sanjay is the brother of Rahul and Mehul is the daughter of Vijay. Who is Sanjay's Uncle?
(*a*) Rahul
(*b*) Ajay
(*c*) Mehul
(*d*) Data inadequate

3. A man introduced the boy coming with him as "He is son of the father of my wife's daughter". What relation did the boy bear to the man?
(*a*) Son-in-law
(*b*) Son
(*c*) Brother
(*d*) Father

4. If Amit's father is Billoo's father's only son and Billoo has neither a brother nor a daughter, what is the relationship between Amit and Billoo?
(*a*) Uncle — Nephew
(*b*) Father — Daughter
(*c*) Father — Son
(*d*) Cousins

5. Pointing to a woman in the photograph a man said, "She is the daughter of my grand-mother's only son. How is the woman related to the man?
(*a*) Mother (*b*) Daughter
(*c*) Sister-in-law (*d*) Sister

6. Pointing to a photograph, a woman said, "She is the only daughter of my mother's father." How is the woman related to the person in the photograph?
(*a*) Mother
(*b*) Grandmother
(*c*) Daughter
(*d*) Cannot be determined

7. Ram is the brother of Shyam and Mahesh is the father of Ram. Jagat is the brother of Priya and Priya is daughter of Shyam. Who is the uncle of Jagat ?
(*a*) Shyam
(*b*) Mahesh
(*c*) Ram
(*d*) Data insufficient

8. Introducing a man, a woman said, "His wife is the only daughter of my father". How is the man related to the woman?
(*a*) Husband
(*b*) Father
(*c*) Father-in-law
(*d*) Brother

9. If Maya is the only daughter of Richa's grandmother's brother, how is Maya's daughter related to Richa?
(*a*) Niece
(*b*) Cousin
(*c*) Aunt
(*d*) Mother

10. Pointing to a woman, a man said, "Her husband's mother is the wife of my father's only son". How is the man related to the woman?
(*a*) Son
(*b*) Brother-in-law
(*c*) Uncle
(*d*) Father-in-law

EXPLANATORY ANSWERS

1. (*a*) : Grandfather

Father
(only son)

Daughter ⟶ Lady
(standing person) (sister)

Lady's grandfather's son is lady's father and father's daughter will only be lady's sister.

2. (*d*) : 1. Mili ⟶ Ajay ⟶ Vijay
(sister) (brother) ↓
Mehul
2. Sanjay ⟶ Rahul (daughter)
(brother)

There are two sets of relationship. Information given is incomplete and no relation can be established between the two sets.

3. (*b*) : The relationship chart based on problem is :

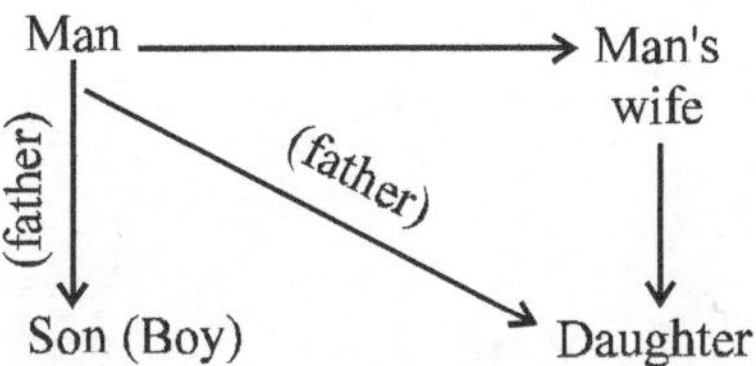

'Father of the man's wife's daughter' is the man himself and the boy in question is the man's son.

4. (*c*) : The relationship chart based on problem is :

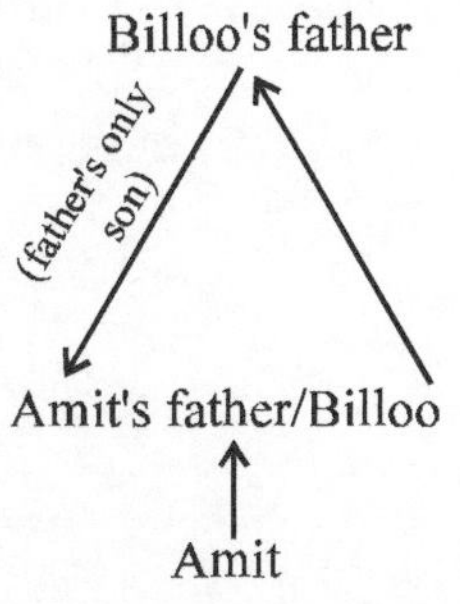

Amit's father is Billoo's father's only son means Billoo is the only son in question also, he is the father of Amit. It must be noted that Billoo has no brother which means he is single and also, when he has no daughter, Amit is his only son.

5. (*d*) : Man's Grandmother
↓
Grandmother's only son
A
↓
Man ⟵ (sister) Daughter

'My grandmother's only son' is the father of the man, and 'daughter of my grandmother's only son' is the sister of the man.

6. (*c*) : Woman's mother's father

↕

Person in photograph
(woman's mother/only daughter)
↑ (daughter)
Woman

'Only daughter of my mother's father' is the person in the photograph and she is also the mother of the woman. So, the woman is the daughter of the person in the photograph.

7. (*c*) :

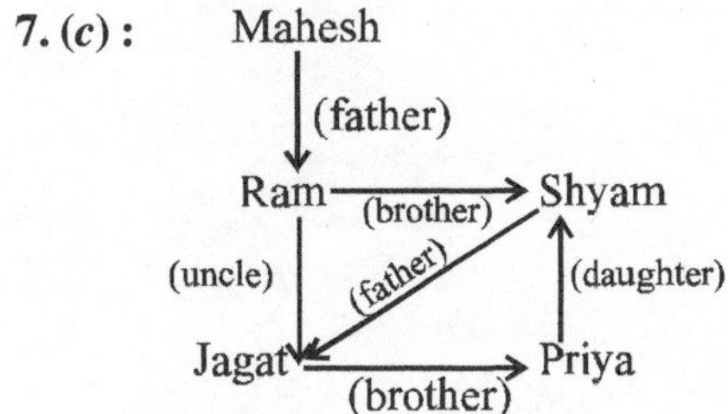

Jagat is brother of Priya and Priya is daughter of Shyam. So Shyam is also the father of Jagat. Ram is the brother of Shyam. So, Jagat's father's brother Ram is the uncle of Jagat.

8. (*a*) :

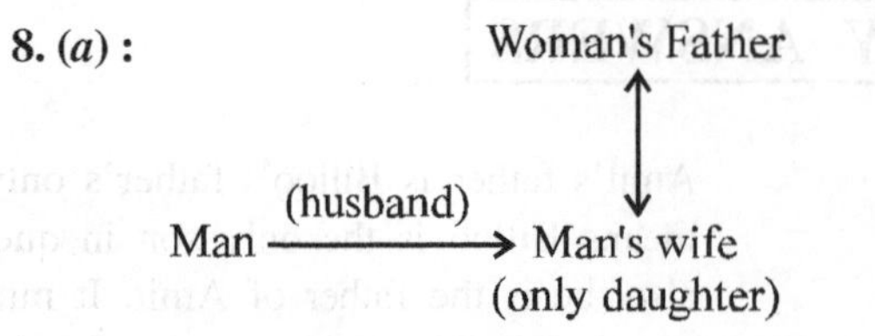

'Only daughter of my father' is the woman herself and the man is her husband.

9. (*b*) :

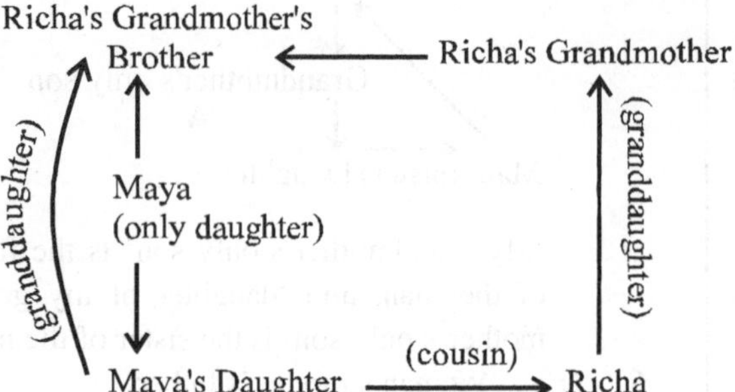

Both Maya's Daughter and Richa are granddaughters of a brother and a sister respectively. So Maya's daughter is the cousin of Richa.

10. (*d*) :

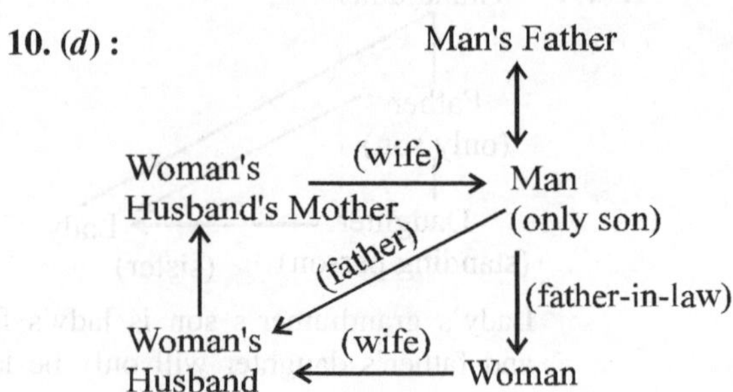

'My father's only son' is the man himself. 'Her husband's mother' is the wife of the man and so the man is the father of the woman's husband. As the woman is the wife of man's son, the man is the father-in-law of the woman.

ARRANGING IN ORDER

In these type of questions arrangement of given options is done on the basis of dictionary, size, rank, weight, natural sequence etc in ascending or descending order.

EXERCISE

1. Which one would be a meaningful order of the following?

1. Key 2. Door
3. Lock 4. Room
5. Switch on

(*a*) 5 1 2 4 3 (*b*) 4 2 1 5 3
(*c*) 1 3 2 4 5 (*d*) 1 2 3 5 4

2. If the following words are rearranged in the alphabetical order as in a dictionary, which will be the third word?

(*a*) Amphibian
(*b*) Amorphous
(*c*) Ambiguous
(*d*) Amphidextrous

3. In a telephone directory, which of the following names will appear in the middle?

(*a*) Randhir (*b*) Randesh
(*c*) Rama (*d*) Ramesh

4. Which one would be a meaningful order of the following?

1. Mother 2. Child
3. Milk 4. Cry
5. Smile

(*a*) 3 2 1 5 4 (*b*) 2 4 1 3 5
(*c*) 1 5 2 4 3 (*d*) 2 4 3 1 5

5. Which would be the proper order of the following?

1. Rainbow 2. Rain
3. Sun 4. Happy
5. Child

(*a*) 4 2 3 5 1 (*b*) 4 5 1 2 3
(*c*) 2 1 4 3 5 (*d*) 2 3 1 5 4

6. Which would be the proper order of the following? (in ascending order)

1. Trillion 2. Thousand
3. Billion 4. Hundred
5. Million

(*a*) 4 2 5 3 1 (*b*) 1 5 3 2 4
(*c*) 4 2 3 5 1 (*d*) 1 2 3 4 5

7. Which would be the proper order of the following?

1. Country 2. Furniture
3. Forest 4. Wood
5. Trees

(*a*) 4 3 2 1 5 (*b*) 2 4 1 5 3
(*c*) 1 3 5 4 2 (*d*) 1 2 3 4 5

8. If the following words are arranged in natural order, what will come in the last place in ascending order?

1. Captain 2. Brigadier
3. Major 4. Lieutenant-General
5. Lieutenant

(*a*) Lientenant-General
(*b*) Brigadier
(*c*) Captain
(*d*) Major

9. If these words are arranged according to dictionary then what word will come in the third place?

1. Originality 2. Originally
3. Originator 4. Original
5. Originate

(*a*) Originality (*b*) Originator
(*c*) Originate (*d*) Originally

10. What will be the natural order of the following?
1. Independence Day
2. Christmas
3. Diwali
4. Holi
5. Republic Day

(*a*) 5 4 1 3 2 (*b*) 5 1 4 3 2
(*c*) 4 1 5 3 2 (*d*) 2 3 4 1 5

11. If the following words are arranged in ascending order what word will be in the fourth place?
1. Air commodore
2. Wing Commander
3. Pilot Officer
4. Squadron Leader
5. Air Marshal

(*a*) Air Marshal
(*b*) Air Commodore
(*c*) Wing Commander
(*d*) Pilot Officer

12. What will be the natural order of the following words according to size?
1. Dog 2. Horse
3. Ant 4. Giraffe
5. Mouse

(*a*) 3 5 1 2 4 (*b*) 3 1 5 2 4
(*c*) 3 5 1 4 2 (*d*) 3 5 2 1 4

EXPLANATORY ANSWERS

1. (*c*) : With the Key you open a Lock, then open the Door to enter the Room and Switch on the light.

2. (*b*) : The dictionary order of the words is—Ambiguous, Ambivalent, **Amorphous,** Amphibian, Amphidextrous.

3. (*b*) : In telephone directory the order of names is—Ramesh, Rana, **Randesh,** Randhir, Renmurthi.

4. (*b*) : When a Child Cries the Mother gives him Milk and then he Smiles.

5. (*d*) : When it rains in the Sun a Rainbow is formed and the Child is Happy to see it.

6. (*a*) : The words are arranged in order of increasing amount.

7. (*c*) : The proper order of the words is—Country, Forest, Trees, Wood, Furniture. In a Country there are Forests comprising Trees the Wood of which are used to make Furniture.

8. (*a*) : The arrangement of ranks in ascending order is—Lieutenant, Captain, Major, Brigadier, **Lieutenant-General.**

9. (*d*) : The dictionary order of words is—Original, Originality, **Originally,** Originate, Originator.

10. (*a*) : The natural order of National Holidays in Calendar is—Republic Day (January), Holi (March), Independence Day (August), Diwali (October/November), Christmas (December).

11. (*b*) : The arrangement of ranks in ascending order is—Pilot Officer, Squadron Leader, Wing Commander, **Air Commodore,** Air Marshal.

12. (*a*) : The natural order of living beings according to increasing size is—Ant, Mouse, Dog, Horse, Giraffe.

CALENDAR, CLOCK & TIME

These are mathematical problem based on calculations of time by a clock or calendar and computations of speed or distances.

EXERCISE

1. If the day before yesterday was Thursday, when will Sunday be?
(*a*) Tomorrow (*b*) Day after tomorrow
(*c*) Today (*d*) Two days after today

2. Radha remembers that her father's birthday is after 16th but before 21st of March, while her brother Mangesh remembers that his father's birthday is before 22nd but after 19th of March. On which date is the birthday of their father?
(*a*) 19th (*b*) 20th
(*c*) 21st (*d*) Cannot be determined

3. A clock is so placed that at 12 noon its minute hand points towards north-east. In which direction does its hour hand point at 1.30 P.M.?
(*a*) East (*b*) West
(*c*) North (*d*) South

4. A couple married in 1980 had two children, one in 1982 and the other in 1984. Their combined ages will equal the years of the marriage in?
(*a*) 1986 (*b*) 1985
(*c*) 1987 (*d*) 1988

5. Manoj left home for the bus stop 15 minutes earlier than the usual time. It takes 10 minutes to reach the stop. He reached the stop at 8.40 a.m. What time does he usually leave home for the bus stop?
(*a*) 8.30 a.m. (*b*) 8.55 a.m.
(*c*) 8.45 p.m. (*d*) None of these

6. If the third day of a month is Monday, which of the following will be the fifth day from 21st of that month?
(*a*) Tuesday (*b*) Monday
(*c*) Wednesday (*d*) Thursday

7. Keshav runs a factory in three shifts of eight hours each with 210 employees. In each shift minimum of 80 employees are required to run the factory effectively. No employee can be allowed to work for more than 16 hours a day. At least how many employees will be required to work for 16 hours every day?
(*a*) 30 (*b*) 60
(*c*) Data inadequate (*d*) None of these

8. A clock shows the time as 3 : 30 p.m. If the minute hand gains 2 minutes every hour, how many minutes will the clock gain by 4 a.m.?
(*a*) 23 Minutes (*b*) 24 Minutes
(*c*) 25 Minutes (*d*) 26 Minutes

9. A train started from station 'A' and proceeded towards station 'B' at a speed of 48 km/hr. Forty-five minutes later another train started from station 'B' and proceeded towards station 'A' at 50 km/hr. If the distance between the two stations is 232 km, at what distance from station 'A' will the trains meet?
(*a*) 132 km (*b*) 144 km
(*c*) 108 km (*d*) 160 km

10. My uncle shall visit me after 64 days of my father's birthday. If my father's birthday falls on Tuesday, what shall be the day on my Uncle's visit?
(*a*) Wednesday (*b*) Sunday
(*c*) Tuesday (*d*) Monday

11. Arjun remembers that his mother's birthday is between fifteenth and twenty-first November. His sister remembers that their mother's birthday is between nineteenth and twenty-fifth November. If both of them remember correctly, on which day is their mother's birthday?
(*a*) Twentieth
(*b*) Twenty-first

(*c*) Twentieth or Twenty-first
(*d*) Twenty-second

12. If 3rd December 1999 is Sunday, what day is 3rd January 2000?
(*a*) Tuesday
(*b*) Wednesday
(*c*) Thursday
(*d*) Friday

13. Prabir starts for office every morning at 9.15 a.m. and reaches there at 9.55 a.m. On Wednesday he started five minutes later than the time he started on Friday. Three days out of five days in the week he started late, out of which Friday was one of the days. On how many days he started in time?
(*a*) Two (*b*) Three
(*c*) Four (*d*) One

EXPLANATORY ANSWERS

1. (*a*) : Thursday — Day-before-yesterday
Friday — Yesterday
Saturday — Today
Sunday — Tomorrow

2. (*b*) : Father's birthday

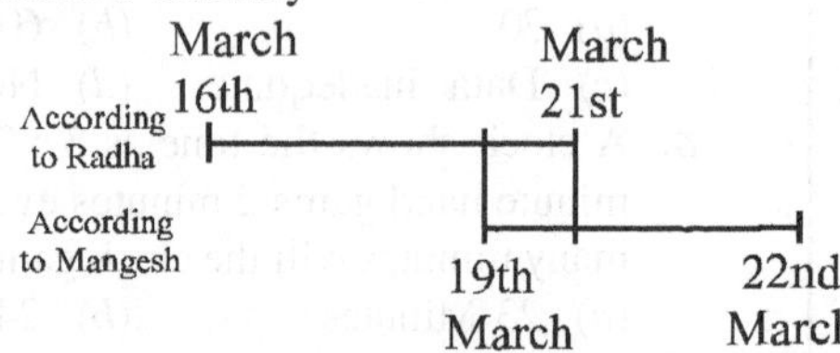

∴ Their father's birthday is on 20th March.

3. (*a*) :

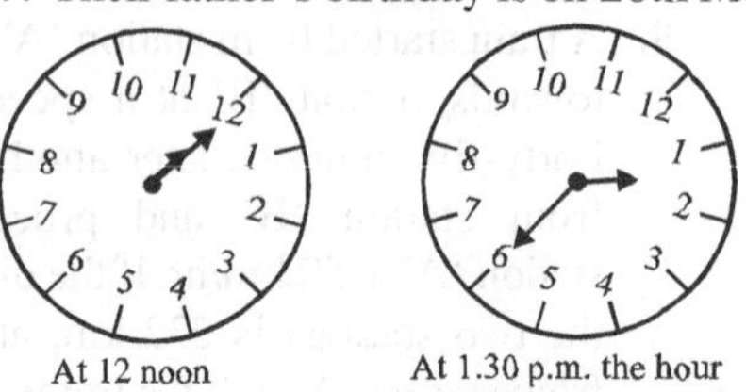

4. (*a*) : 1982 — 2 years later — 1st child
1984 — 4 years later — 2nd child
Total age of children — 2 years.
1985 — 5 years later — Total age of children : 4 years.
1986 — 6 years later — Total age of children : 6 years.

5. (*d*) : Manoj reached the bus stop at 8.40 a.m. He left his home at 8:40 – 10 minutes = 8:30 a.m. He left 15 minutes earlier than usual, so his actual time of leaving home is 8:30 am + 15 minutes = 8:45 a.m.

6. (*c*) : 3rd day of the month is Monday
5th day from 21st is 26th
26 – 3 = 23 days
23 days later, 23/7 leaves 2 days.
So, two days ahead of Monday will be Wednesday.

7. (*d*) : 80 employees are required for double shift.

8. (*c*) : Hours between 3:30 p.m. and 4 a.m. are — 12½ hours. Number of minutes gained will be 12½ × 2 = 25 minutes.

9. (*a*) : $\xleftarrow{\quad d \quad}|\xrightarrow{\quad 232-d \quad}$

i.e., $\dfrac{d}{48} = \dfrac{232-d}{50} + \dfrac{3}{4}$

$\dfrac{d}{48} = \dfrac{464-2d+75}{100}$

$100d = (539-2d)\,48$

$100d = 25872 - 96d$

$196d = 25872$

$d = 25872 \div 196 = 132$ km.

10. (*a*) : My father's birthday is on Tuesday.
64 ÷ 7 gives 1 as remainder
So, 63rd day will be Tuesday and one day ahead is the day when uncle shall visit *i.e.,* on Wednesday.

11. (*a*) : Mother's birthday

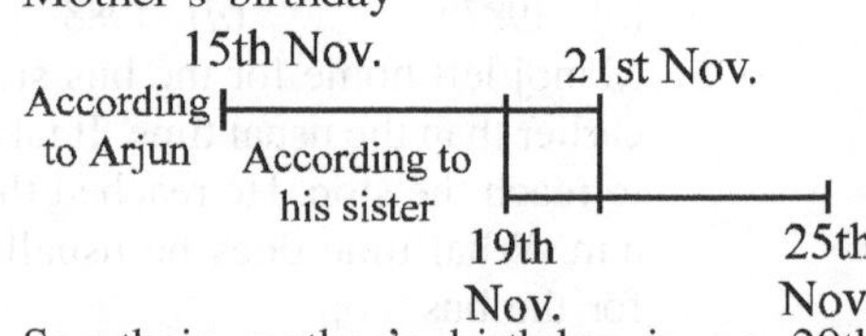

So, their mother's birthday is on 20th November.

12. (*b*) : 3rd December 1999 is Sunday. Number of days in-between 3rd December 1999 and 3rd January 2000 = 28 + 3 = 31 days 31 ÷ 7 gives 3 as remainder
So, 31st December 1999 will be Sunday and 3rd January 2000 will be 3 days ahad *i.e.* Wednesday.

13. (*a*) : Out of five days, he starts late on three days.

ROWS AND RANKS

These type of problems need easy calculations to find out the number of objects in a row, lane or queue or to find a person's rank in a class of certain number of students; or to find the total number of students.

EXERCISE

1. In a row of trees, one tree is fifth from either end of the row. How many trees are in the row?
   (*a*) 11 (*b*) 8
   (*c*) 10 (*d*) 9
2. Jaya ranks 5th in a class of 53. What is her rank from the bottom in the class?
   (*a*) 49th (*b*) 48th
   (*c*) 47th (*d*) 50th
3. Mohan ranks twenty-first in a class of sixty-five students. What will be his (Mohan's) rank if the lowest candidate is assigned rank 1?
   (*a*) 44th (*b*) 45th
   (*c*) 46th (*d*) Data inadequate
4. If Rahul finds that he is 12th from the right in a line of boys and 4th from the left, how many boys should be added to the line such that there are 28 boys in the line?
   (*a*) 12 (*b*) 14
   (*c*) 20 (*d*) 13
5. In a row of boys, Rajan is tenth from the right and Suraj is tenth from the left. When Rajan and Suraj interchange their positions, Suraj will be twenty-seventh from the left. Which of the following will be Rajan's position from the right?
   (*a*) Tenth
   (*b*) Twenty-sixth
   (*c*) Twenty-ninth
   (*d*) None of these
6. Mahesh and Suresh are ranked 11th and 12th respectively from the top in a class of 41 students. What will be their respective ranks from the bottom?
   (*a*) 32nd and 33rd
   (*b*) 29th and 30th
   (*c*) 30th and 31st
   (*d*) 31st and 30th
7. Uma ranked 8th from the top and 37th from bottom in a class. How many students are there in the class?
   (*a*) 47 (*b*) 46
   (*c*) 45 (*d*) None of these
8. In a queue, Sadiq is 14th from the front and Joseph is 17th from the end, while Jane is in between Sadiq and Joseph. If Sadiq be ahead of Joseph and there be 48 persons in the queue, how many persons are there between Sadiq and Jane?
   (*a*) 5 (*b*) 6
   (*c*) 7 (*d*) 8
9. Rohan ranked eleventh from the top and twenty-seventh from the bottom among the students who passed the annual examination in a class. If the number of students who failed in the examination was 12, how many students appeared for the examination?
   (*a*) 48
   (*b*) 49
   (*c*) 50
   (*d*) Cannot be determined
10. Some boys are sitting in a row. P is sitting fourteenth from the left and Q is seventh from the right. If there are four boys between P and Q, how many boys are there in the row?
   (*a*) 19 (*b*) 21
   (*c*) 25 (*d*) 23

EXPLANATORY ANSWERS

1. (*d*):

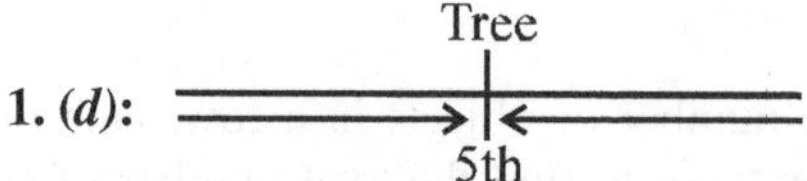

Total number of trees in the row are :
$(5 + 5) - 1 = 9$.

2. (*a*) :

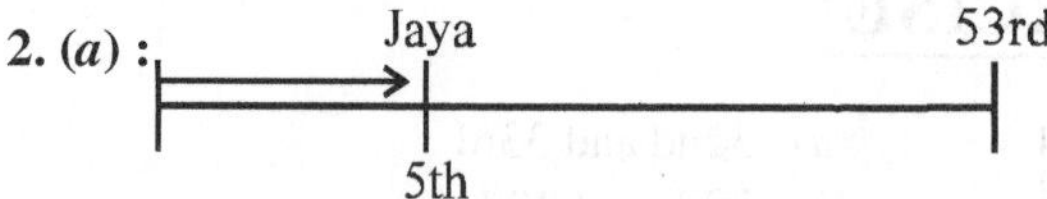

Jaya's rank from the bottom is :
$(53 - 5) + 1 = 49$th.

3. (*b*) :

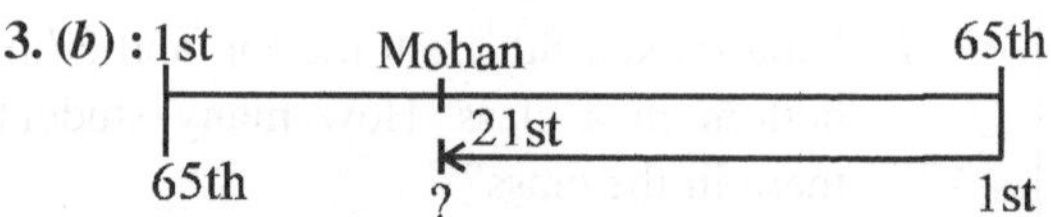

Note : Mohan's rank from the last or the question asked means the same.

Mohan's rank is $(65 - 21) + 1 = 45$th.

4. (*d*) :

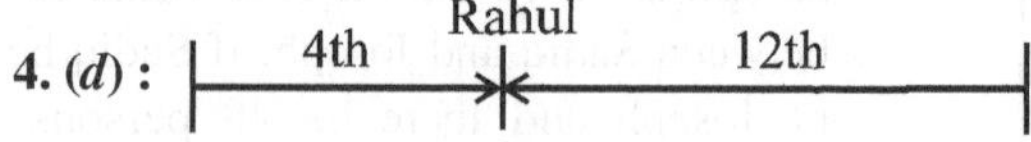

The number of boys in the line are :
$(4 + 12) - 1 = 15$

To make a line of 28 boys, $(28 - 15)$ *i.e.* 13 more boys are needed.

5. (*d*) :

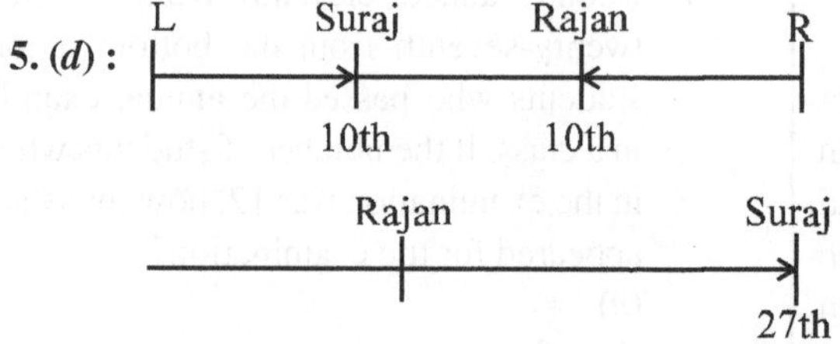

As the position of boys is equal from both ends, Rajan will also be 27th from the right after changing positions.

6. (*d*) :

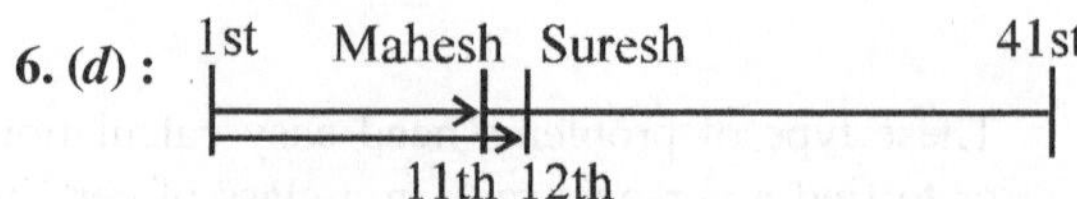

Mahesh's position from bottom is :
$(41 - 11) + 1 = 31$st

Suresh's position from bottom is :
$(41 - 12) + 1 = 30$th.

7. (*d*) : Uma — 8th, 37th

Total number of students in the class are :
$(8 + 37) - 1 = 44$.

8. (*c*) :

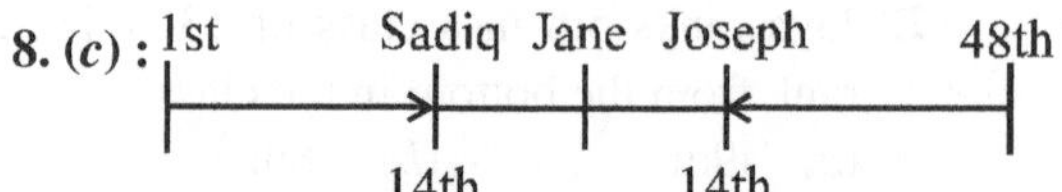

Sadiq's position from last is :
$(48 - 14) + 1 = 35$th

Number of persons between Sadiq and Joseph are $(35 - 17) - 1 = 17$

Jane is in-between Sadiq and Joseph *i.e.*, she's at 9th position from both the boys.

$\therefore$ there are 8 persons between Sadiq and Jane.

Note : $(8 + 8) - 1 = 17$.

9. (*b*) : Rohan — 11th, 27th

Number of students who passed the examination $(11 + 27) - 1 = 37$

Those who failed = 12

Total number of students who appeared in the examination = $37 + 12 = 49$.

10. (*c*) : P — 14th, 4, Q — 7th

The number of boys in the row are :
$(14 + 4 + 7) = 25$.

COMMON PROPERTY

In this type of test, the questions contain either numbers or words or letters which have a common property. From the given set of options the candidate has to select the one which bears the same property.

EXERCISE

1. Out of the given alternatives, choose the one that belongs to the given number group.
Given number group : (49, 25, 9)
(*a*) (39, 26, 13) (*b*) (36, 16, 4)
(*c*) (64, 27, 8) (*d*) (36, 25, 16)
2. Which one number is like the given number set : (363, 489, 579)?
(*a*) 281 (*b*) 382
(*c*) 471 (*d*) 562
3. Which set of numbers has the same property as the following numbers?
21, 38, 55
(*a*) 47, 64, 80 (*b*) 19, 36, 55
(*c*) 23, 40, 57 (*d*) 35, 62, 79
4. Which set of numbers is like the given number set : 1050, 210, 42?
(*a*) 75, 15, 3 (*b*) 60, 12, 2
(*c*) 125, 25, 6 (*d*) 95, 19, 3
5. Which set of numbers is like the given number set : 7, 77, 847?
(*a*) 9, 99, 989 (*b*) 1, 11, 131
(*c*) 6, 66, 726 (*d*) 8, 8, 948
6. Which of the following has the same property as RnTz, FnjK, BTbs, tfNL?
(*a*) FGhI (*b*) rRQd
(*c*) NOqB (*d*) GgTJ
7. Which set of numbers is like the given set : 53, 40, 27?
(*a*) 58, 27, 18 (*b*) 77, 63, 50
(*c*) 93, 80, 67 (*d*) 39, 26, 13
8. Which of the following words have same characteristics as Cap, Hat and Turban?
(*a*) Hair (*b*) Helmet
(*c*) Safety (*d*) Umbrella
9. Which set of letters is like the given set : WVU, EDC, LKJ?
(*a*) GHF (*b*) BAZ
(*c*) PON (*d*) WUT
10. Which number has the same property as the given numbers : 637, 399, 784?
(*a*) 161 (*b*) 535
(*c*) 493 (*d*) 257

EXPLANATORY ANSWERS

1. (*b*) : The numbers are squares of alternate numbers. $7^2 = 49$, $5^2 = 25$, $3^2 = 9$. Similarly, $6^2 = 36$, $4^2 = 16$, $2^2 = 4$.

2. (*c*) : The numbers are divisible by 3.

3. (*c*) : The difference between the numbers is 17, *i.e.*, 21 + 17 = 38; 38 + 17 = 55. Similarly, 23 + 17 = 40; 40 + 17 = 57.

4. (*a*) : The number divided by 5 is the next number, *i.e.*, 1050 ÷ 5 = 210; 210 ÷ 5 = 42. Similarly 75 ÷ 5 = 15; 15 ÷ 5 = 3.

5. (*c*) : The numbers are multiples of 11, *i.e.*, 7 × 11 = 77; 77 × 11 = 847. Similarly 6 × 11 = 66; 66 × 11 = 726.

6. (*b*) : Two letters are capital, two are small.

7. (*d*) : The difference between the numbers is 13 *i.e.* 53 – 13 = 40; 40 – 13 = 27. Similarly 39 – 13 = 26; 26 – 13 = 13.

8. (*b*) : All three are worn on the head and so is helmet.

9. (*c*) : The letters are in reverse consecutive order.

10. (*a*) : The numbers are divisible by 7.

PERMUTATIONS & COMBINATIONS

In these type of questions, the only factor essential is alertness. In every question, a word is given. By using the letters of this given word the options are formed. The candidates are required to find from the given options the word *(i)* which cannot be formed by using the letters of the given word or *(ii)* which can be formed by using the letters of the given word.

EXERCISE

Directions : *Find out the one word among the options which cannot be formed by using the letters of the word as given in each question.*

1. ROTATION
   (a) TORN (b) NOTE
   (c) TART (d) RAIN
2. PHILOSOPHY
   (a) SOIL (b) SHIP
   (c) SOLO (d) SPIN
3. SLAVATION
   (a) SNORT (b) LATVIA
   (c) SALIVA (d) AVAIL
4. ACADEMY
   (a) DEMY (b) MACE
   (c) DIRE (d) MADE
5. INCOGNITO
   (a) GOING (b) INACTION
   (c) IGNITION (d) TONGO
6. JUDICIARY
   (a) INJURY (b) CADDY
   (c) DICY (d) ACRID
7. DOCTRINE
   (a) CRUST (b) DOCTOR
   (c) TIRED (d) CREED
8. EDUCATED
   (a) DATE (b) CUTE
   (c) EAST (d) DUCT
9. INSUFFICIENT
   (a) ENTICE (b) SCENT
   (c) SUFFICE (d) THENCE
10. DECEMBER
    (a) REDEEM (b) DECREE
    (c) BRACED (d) MEMBER
11. FUGITIVE
    (a) EXIT (b) FIVE
    (c) GIVE (d) GIFT
12. CATASTROPHE
    (a) TASTE (b) CHEAP
    (c) POUCH (d) STARE
13. TORRENTIAL
    (a) TRAIL (b) MENTAL
    (c) LEARN (d) RETAIL
14. INFRASTRUCTURE
    (a) RAPTURE (b) INSECURE
    (c) CRAFTS (d) STRUCTURE
15. RECOMMEND
    (a) MEND (b) ROME
    (c) CANE (d) OMEN

Directions *: Find out the one word among the options which can be formed by using the letters of the word as given in each question.*

16. INVESTIGATE
    (a) INVERT (b) GLIDE
    (c) STING (d) ACTED
17. MAJORITY
    (a) MORE (b) JURY
    (c) READ (d) TRAY
18. WATERMELON
    (a) MAKER (b) WRITE
    (c) TOWER (d) NOVEL
19. PREDICTION
    (a) DESIRE (b) CREDIT
    (c) ACTION (d) PICKED
20. BARGAIN
    (a) GRAIN (b) BARGE
    (c) ANGRY (d) TRING

21. THERMOSTAT
(*a*) MOTHER (*b*) STAMEN
(*c*) THRUST (*d*) HOIST

22. LEARNED
(*a*) DREAM (*b*) CLEAR
(*c*) ELDER (*d*) DRAPE

23. ADVENTURE
(*a*) AWARE (*b*) EVENT
(*c*) TRUCE (*d*) DRIED

24. THANKSGIVING
(*a*) AVENGE (*b*) HAUNTS
(*c*) GRAINS (*d*) SAVING

25. NOCTURNAL
(*a*) CRUST (*b*) TRAIL
(*c*) CORAL (*d*) OCEAN

ANSWERS

1	2	3	4	5	6	7	8	9	10
(*b*)	(*d*)	(*a*)	(*c*)	(*b*)	(*a*)	(*a*)	(*c*)	(*d*)	(*c*)
11	**12**	**13**	**14**	**15**	**16**	**17**	**18**	**19**	**20**
(*a*)	(*c*)	(*b*)	(*a*)	(*c*)	(*c*)	(*d*)	(*c*)	(*b*)	(*a*)
21	**22**	**23**	**24**	**25**					
(*a*)	(*c*)	(*b*)	(*d*)	(*c*)					

SYMBOL SUBSTITUTION

Questions in these category are easy to attempt. Candidates must be quick in substituting symbols and calculations. The common pattern of questions asked are given below.

EXERCISE

1. If "+" means "–"; "–" means "×"; "×"means "÷" and "÷" means "+", then
$15 \times 5 \div 10 + 5 - 3 = ?$
(a) 9.5 (b) 0
(c) –2 (d) 24

2. If "+" means "×"; "–" means "÷"; "÷"means "+" and "×" means "–", then what will be the value of $20 \div 40 - 4 \times 5 + 6 = ?$
(a) 60 (b) 1.67
(c) 150 (d) 0

3. If × stands for addition, < for subtraction, + stands for division, > for multiplication, – stands for equal to, ÷ for greater than, and = stands for less than, state which of the following is true?
(a) $5 \times 3 < 7 \div 8 + 4 \times 1$
(b) $3 \times 4 > 2 - 9 + 3 < 3$
(c) $5 > 2 + 2 = 10 < 4 \times 8$
(d) $3 \times 2 < 4 \div 16 > 2 + 4$

4. If → stands for subract, ← stands for add, ↑↑ stands for multiply, ↓↓ stands for divide, ↔ for greater than, ⟷ stands for equal to, then which of the following alternatives is true?
(a) 4 ← 6 ↑↑ 2 ⟷ 3 → 12 ← 12
(b) 10 ↓↓ 5 ↑↑ 5 ⟷ 9 → 3 ← 4
(c) 15 ↑↑ 2 → 5 ⟷ 12 ↓↓ 4 ← 3
(d) 13 ↓↓ 13 ← 1 ↔ 20 → 5 ↑↑ 2

5. If Δ denotes =; + denotes >, – denotes <, □ denotes ≠, × denotes > and ÷ denotes < then a + b – c denotes
(a) b Δ c □ a
(b) b □ a ÷ c
(c) a ÷ b × c
(d) b – a + c

6. If '✱' denotes '×', 'Δ' denotes '÷', '□' denotes '–', '●' denotes '+', 'α' denotes '=' and 'β' denotes ≠, then which of the following euations is correct?
(a) 2 □ 10 ✱ 4 Δ 5 α 5 ● 12 Δ 6
(b) 27 Δ 9 ● 6 β 3 ✱ 6 □ 9
(c) 4 Δ 2 ✱ 0 α 7 Δ 1 ✱ 0
(d) 5 ● 6 Δ 3 □ 2 α 8 Δ 4 ✱ 3

7. If ↓ stands for '÷', ↑ stands for '×', → stands for '+' and ← stands for '–', then
25 ↓ 5 → 3 ↑ 6 ← 8 = ?
(a) 9 (b) 12
(c) 16 (d) 15

8. If the + and × signs of the following equations are interchanged, which will be the correct equation?
(a) $7 \times 5 + 3 = 20$
(b) $4 + 9 \times 1 = 42$
(c) $6 \times 5 + 8 = 46$
(d) $2 + 11 \times 4 = 28$

9. If '+' stands for multiplication, '×' stands for addition, '÷' stands for subtraction and '–' stands for division, then what will be the result of the following equation?
$7 \times 4 \div 10 \times 2 + 5 = ?$
(a) 7 (b) 0
(c) 11 (d) 15

10. If 'A' means '÷', 'B' means '+', 'C' means '×' and 'D' means '–', then
12 C 4 A 24 D 10 B 1 = ?
(a) $11\frac{1}{3}$ (b) 23
(c) –7 (d) $16\frac{4}{5}$

EXPLANATORY ANSWERS

1. (*c*) : $15 \div 5 + 10 - 5 \times 3$

$3 + 10 - 15 = -2$

2. (*d*) : $20 + 40 \div 4 - 5 \times 6$

$20 + 10 - 30 = 0$

3. (*c*) : (*a*) $5 + 3 - 7 > 8 \div 4 + 1$

$1 > 3$

(*b*) $3 + 4 \times 2 = 9 \div 3 - 3$

$11 = 0$

(*c*) $5 \times 2 \div 2 < 10 - 4 + 8$

$5 < 14$

(*d*) $3 + 2 - 4 > 16 \times 2 \div 4$

$1 > 8$

4. (*b*) : (*a*) $4 + 6 \times 2 = 3 - 12 + 12$

$16 = 3$

(*b*) $10 \div 5 \times 5 = 9 - 3 + 4$

$10 = 10$

(*c*) $15 \times 2 - 5 = 12 \div 4 + 3$

$25 = 6$

(*d*) $13 \div 13 + 1 > 20 - 5 \times 2$

$2 > 10$

5. (*d*) : What is given is $a > b < c$

The equations are :

(*a*) $b = c \neq a$ which is wrong

(*b*) $b \neq a < c$ which is wrong

(*c*) $a < b > c$ which is wrong

(*d*) $b < a > c$ which is correct

Therefore, (*d*) is the answer.

6. (*c*) : The solved equations will be :

(*a*) $2 - 10 \times 4 \div 5 = 5 + 12 \div 6$

$2 - 8 = 5 + 2$

$-6 = 7$ which is wrong

(*b*) $27 \div 9 + 6 \neq 3 \times 6 - 9$

$3 + 6 \neq 18 - 9$

$9 \neq 9$ which is wrong

(*c*) $4 \div 2 \times 0 = 7 \div 1 \times 0$

$2 \times 0 = 7 \times 0$

$0 = 0$ which is correct

(*d*) $5 + 6 \div 3 - 2 = 8 \div 4 \times 3$

$5 = 6$ which is wrong

7. (*d*) : $25 \div 5 + 3 \times 6 - 8$

$5 + 18 - 8 = 15$

8. (*c*) : After interchanging the signs the equations are :

(*a*) $7 + 5 \times 3 = 22$ which is wrong

(*b*) $4 \times 9 + 1 = 37$ which is wrong

(*c*) $6 + 5 \times 8 = 46$ which is correct

(*d*) $2 \times 11 + 4 = 26$ which is wrong

9. (*c*) : $7 + 4 - 10 + 2 \times 5$

$7 + 4 - 10 + 10 = 11$

10. (*c*) : $12 \times 4 \div 24 - 10 + 1$

$2 - 10 + 1 = -7$

MISSING NUMBERS

Playing with numbers and mathematical skills are needed to attempt these type of tests. The candidates have to work out the right combination of arithmetical symbols to arrive at the answer options which will take the place of the interrogation sign in the given questions.

EXERCISE

Directions : *In each question given below which one number can be placed at the sign of interrogation?*

1.

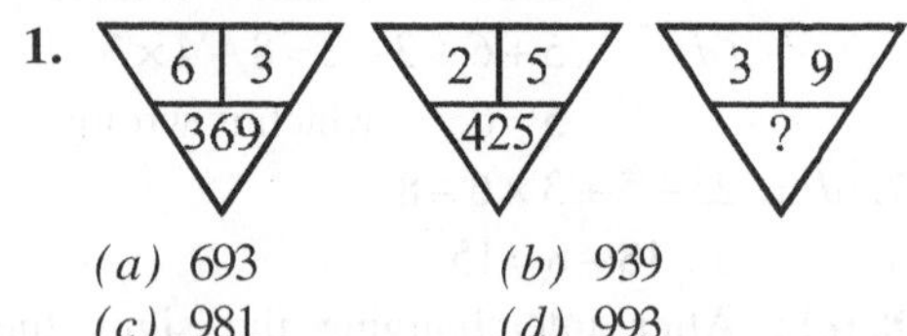

(*a*) 693 (*b*) 939
(*c*) 981 (*d*) 993

2.

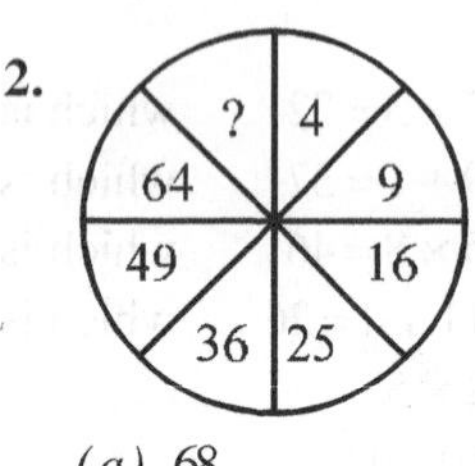

(*a*) 68 (*b*) 100
(*c*) 72 (*d*) 81

3.

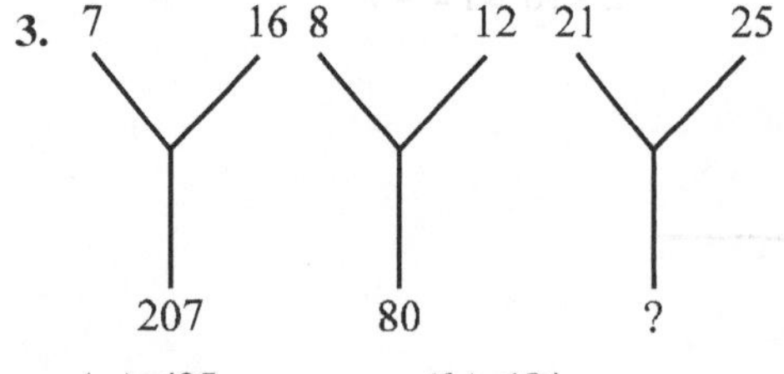

(*a*) 425 (*b*) 184
(*c*) 241 (*d*) 210

4.

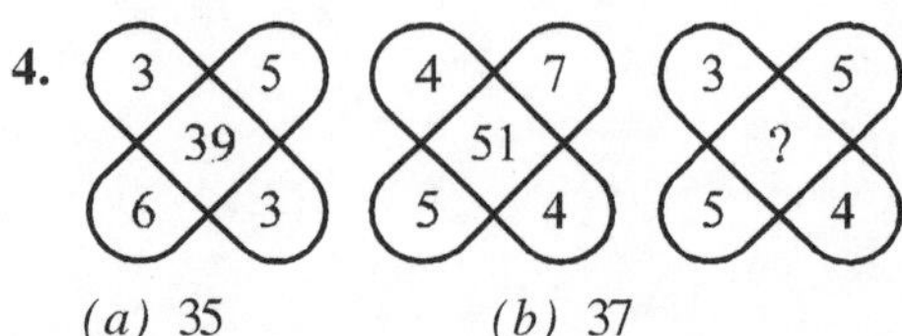

(*a*) 35 (*b*) 37
(*c*) 45 (*d*) 48

5.

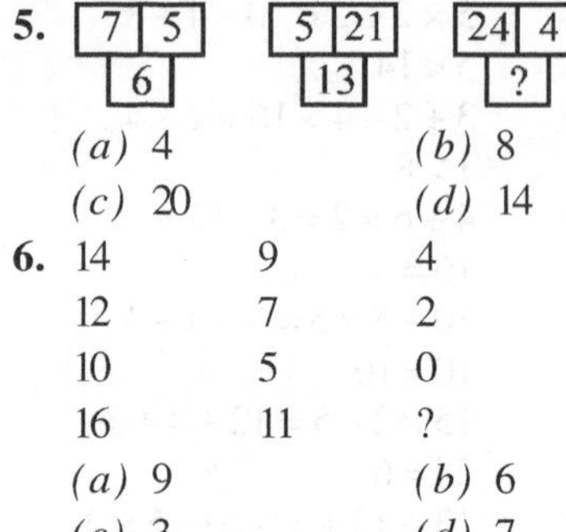

(*a*) 4 (*b*) 8
(*c*) 20 (*d*) 14

6.

14	9	4
12	7	2
10	5	0
16	11	?

(*a*) 9 (*b*) 6
(*c*) 3 (*d*) 7

7.

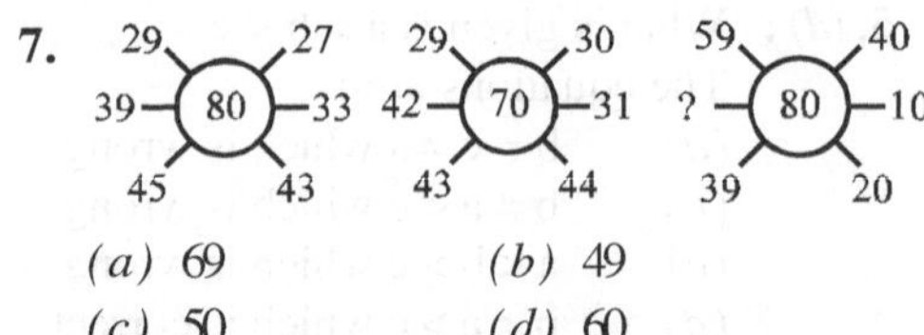

(*a*) 69 (*b*) 49
(*c*) 50 (*d*) 60

8.

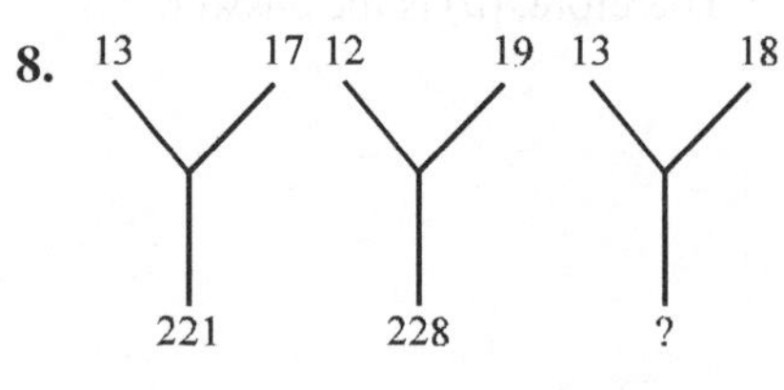

(*a*) 31 (*b*) 229
(*c*) 234 (*d*) 312

9.

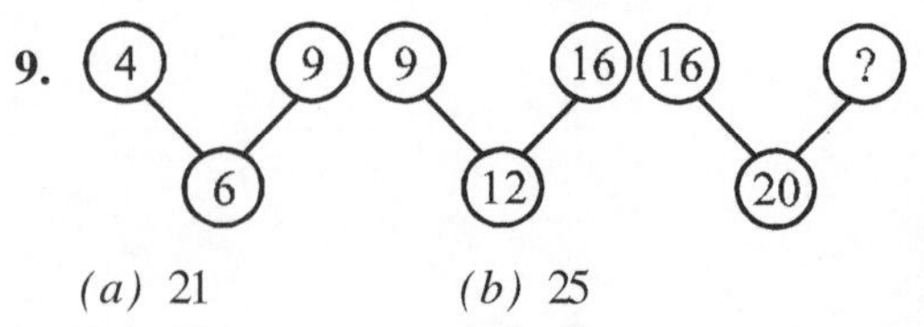

(*a*) 21 (*b*) 25
(*c*) 50 (*d*) 60

10.

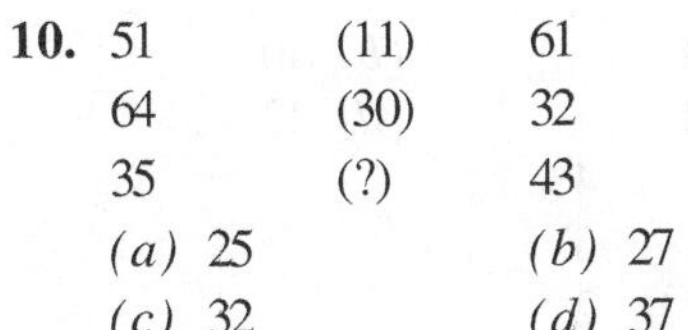

51	(11)	61
64	(30)	32
35	(?)	43

(*a*) 25 (*b*) 27
(*c*) 32 (*d*) 37

11.

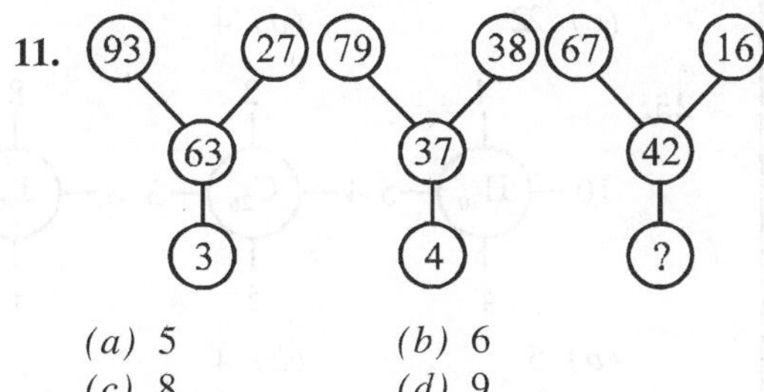

(*a*) 5 (*b*) 6
(*c*) 8 (*d*) 9

12.

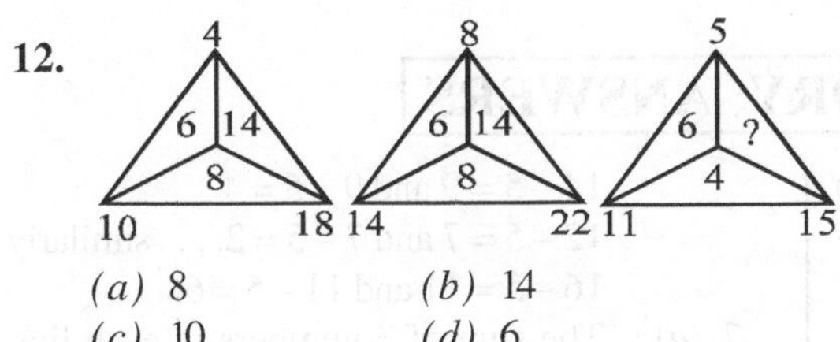

(*a*) 8 (*b*) 14
(*c*) 10 (*d*) 6

13.

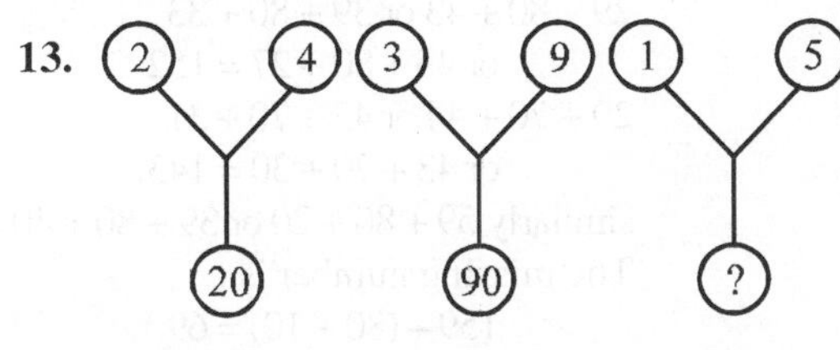

(*a*) 20 (*b*) 25
(*c*) 26 (*d*) 75

14.

27	22	50
13	12	26
9	2	?

(*a*) 12 (*b*) 39
(*c*) 18 (*d*) 24

15.

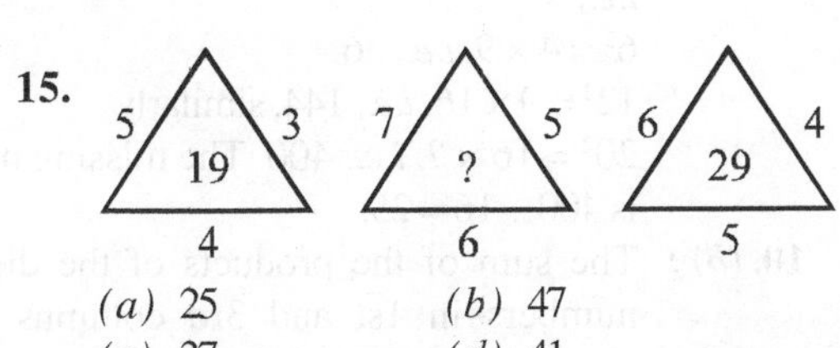

(*a*) 25 (*b*) 47
(*c*) 37 (*d*) 41

16.

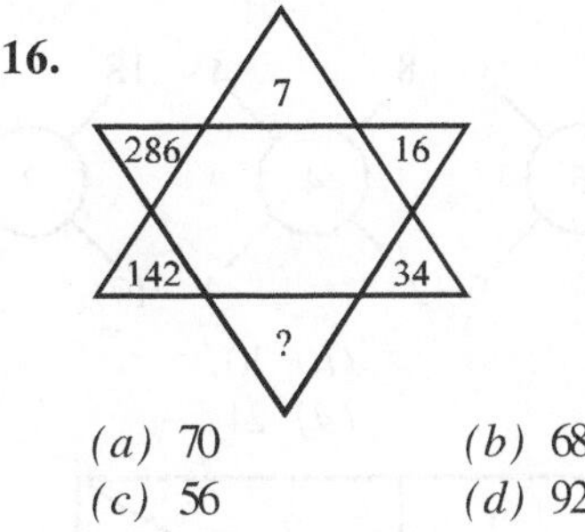

(*a*) 70 (*b*) 68
(*c*) 56 (*d*) 92

17.

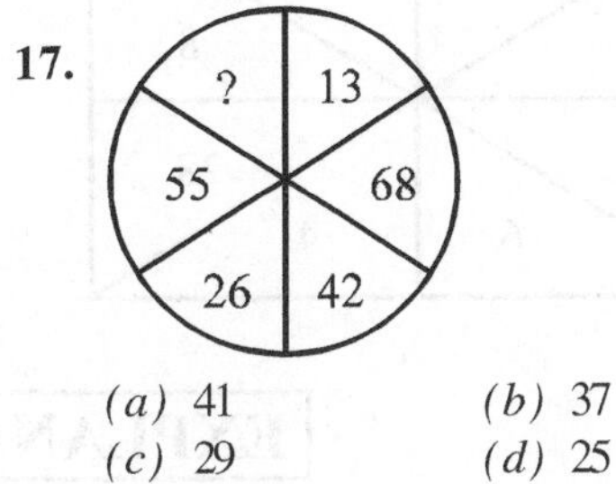

(*a*) 41 (*b*) 37
(*c*) 29 (*d*) 25

18.

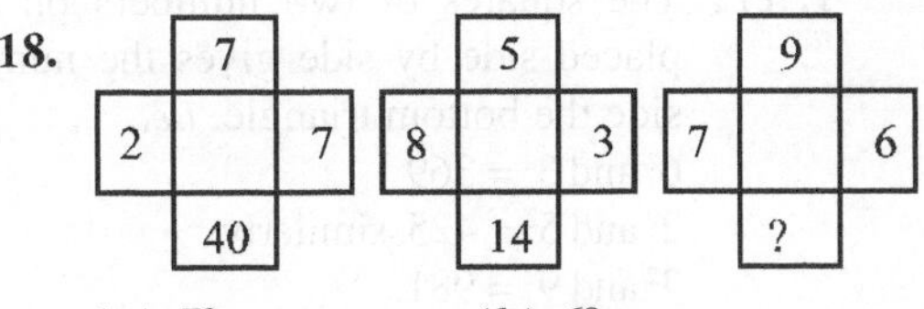

(*a*) 72 (*b*) 68
(*c*) 82 (*d*) 96

19.

42	(21)	22
78	(?)	84
162	(18)	99

(*a*) 12 (*b*) 13
(*c*) 60 (*d*) 72

20.

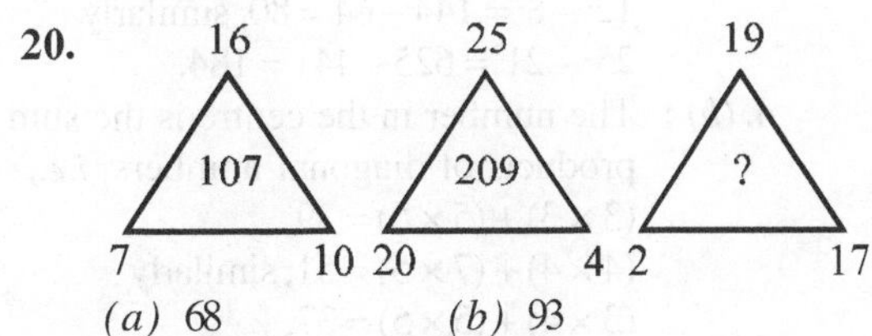

(*a*) 68 (*b*) 93
(*c*) 175 (*d*) 217

21.

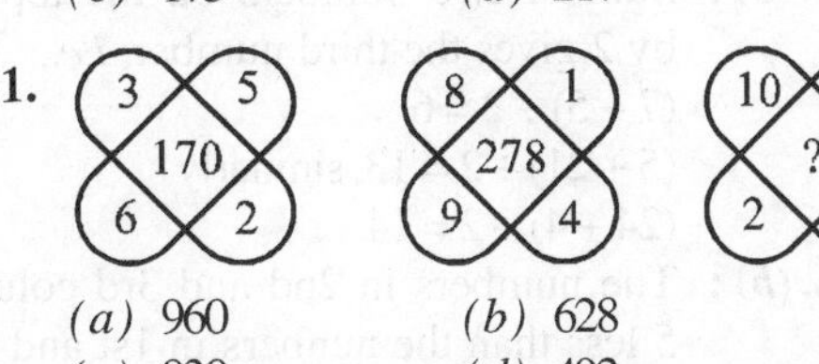

(*a*) 960 (*b*) 628
(*c*) 830 (*d*) 492

22.

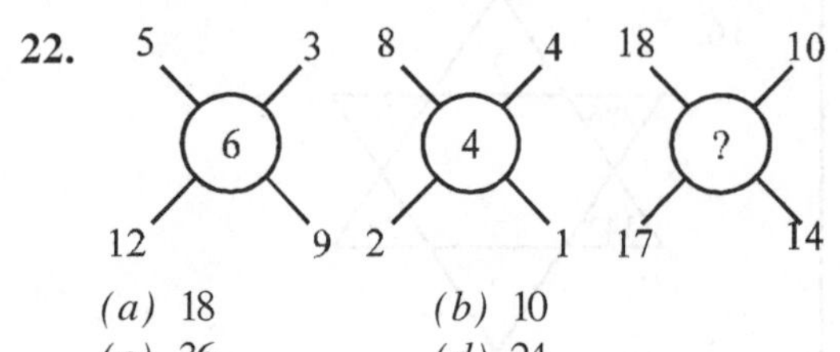

(a) 18 (b) 10
(c) 36 (d) 24

23.

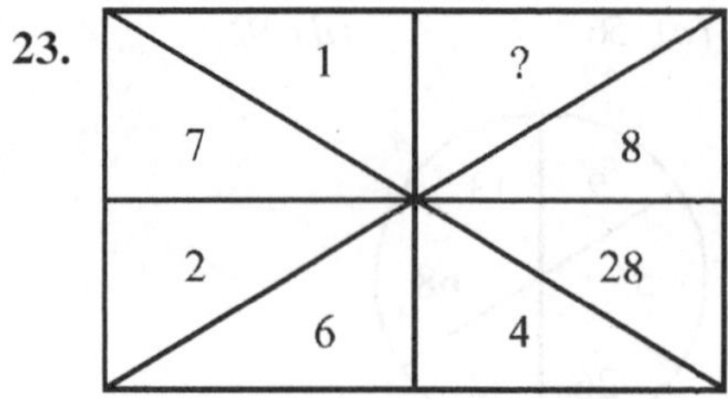

(a) 24 (b) 10
(c) 32 (d) 12

24. 6(40) 4
3(12) 3
7(?) 2

(a) 51 (b) 36
(c) 22 (d) 4

25.

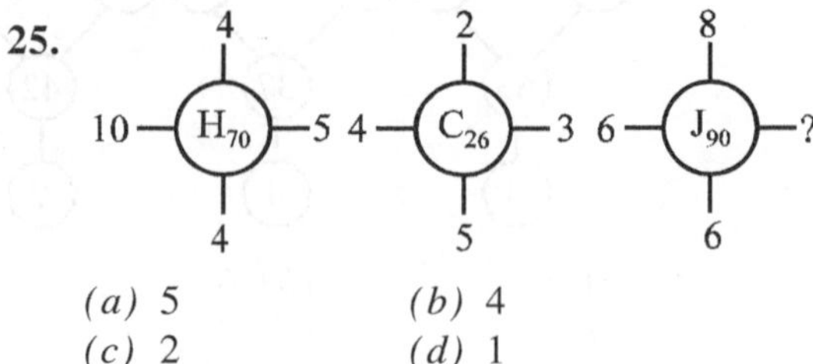

(a) 5 (b) 4
(c) 2 (d) 1

EXPLANATORY ANSWERS

1. *(c)* : The squares of two numbers on the top placed side by side gives the number inside the bottom triangle, *i.e.*,
6^2 and $3^2 = 369$
2^2 and $5^2 = 425$, similarly
3^2 and $9^2 = 981$.

2. *(d)* : Starting from number 4 the numbers are the squares of numbers in natural order *i.e.*, $2^2 = 4, 3^2 = 9, 4^2 = 16 \ldots\ldots 9^2 = 81$.

3. *(b)* : The number at the bottom is the difference of the squares of two numbers at the top, *i.e.*,
$16^2 - 7^2 = 256 - 49 = 207$
$12^2 - 8^2 = 144 - 64 = 80$, similarly
$25^2 - 21^2 = 625 - 441 = 184$.

4. *(b)* : The number in the centre is the sum of the products of diagonal numbers, *i.e.*,
$(3 \times 3) + (5 \times 6) = 39$
$(4 \times 4) + (7 \times 5) = 51$, similarly
$(3 \times 4) + (5 \times 5) = 37$.

5. *(d)* : Sum of two numbers on the top divided by 2 gives the third number, *i.e.*,
$(7 + 5) \div 2 = 6$
$(5 + 21) \div 2 = 13$, similarly
$(24 + 4) \div 2 = 14$.

6. *(b)* : The numbers in 2nd and 3rd columns are 5 less than the nunbers in 1st and 2nd columns respectively, *i.e.*,
$14 - 5 = 9$ and $9 - 5 = 4$
$12 - 5 = 7$ and $7 - 5 = 2$, . . . similarly
$16 - 5 = 11$ and $11 - 5 = 6$.

7. *(a)* : The sum of 3 numbers in each line in one figure is same, *i.e.*,
$29 + 80 + 43$ or $39 + 80 + 33$
or $45 + 80 + 27 = 152$
$29 + 70 + 44$ or $42 + 70 + 31$
or $43 + 70 + 30 = 143$,
similarly $59 + 80 + 20$ or $39 + 80 + 40 = 159$.
The missing number is :
$159 - (80 + 10) = 69$.

8. *(c)* : The number at the bottom is the product of two numbers at the top, *i.e.*,
$13 \times 17 = 221$
$12 \times 19 = 228$, similarly
$13 \times 18 = 234$.

9. *(b)* : Square of number at the bottom is equal to the product of two numbers at the top, *i.e.*,
$6^2 = 4 \times 9$, *i.e.*, 36
$12^2 = 9 \times 16$, *i.e.*, 144, similarly
$20^2 = 16 \times ?$, *i.e.*, 400. The missing number is $400 \div 16 = 25$.

10. *(b)* : The sum of the products of the digits of numbers in 1st and 3rd columns is the number in the 2nd column, *i.e.*,

$(5 \times 1) + (6 \times 1) = 11$
$(6 \times 4) + (3 \times 2) = 30$, similarly
$(3 \times 5) + (4 \times 3) = 27$.

11. *(d)* : The sum of numbers on right and centre subtracted from the number on the left gives the number at the bottom, *i.e.*,
$93 - (27 + 63) = 3$
$79 - (38 + 37) = 4$, similarly
$67 - (16 + 42) = 9$.

12. *(c)* : The number inside each triangle is the difference of the numbers at its base *i.e.*
$10 - 4 = 6$, $18 - 4 = 14$ and $18 - 10 = 8$
$14 - 8 = 6$, $22 - 8 = 14$ and $22 - 14 = 8$, similarly
$11 - 5 = 6$, $15 - 5 = 10$ and $15 - 11 = 4$.

13. *(c)* : The sum of squares of two numbers at the top gives the third number below, *i.e.*,
$2^2 + 4^2 = 20$
$3^2 + 9^2 = 90$, similarly
$1^2 + 5^2 = 26$.

14. *(a)* : The sum of numbers in 1st and 2nd column plus 1 is the number in the 3rd column, *i.e.*,
$27 + 22 + 1 = 50$
$13 + 12 + 1 = 26$, similarly
$9 + 2 + 1 = 12$.

15. *(d)* : The product of numbers on either side of the triangle plus the number at the base is the number inside the triangle, *i.e.*,
$(5 \times 3) + 4 = 19$
$(6 \times 4) + 5 = 29$, similarly
$(7 \times 5) + 6 = 41$.

16. *(a)* : Clockwise starting from number 7, the next number is obtained by doubling the number and adding 2, *i.e.*,
$(7 \times 2) + 2 = 16$
$(16 \times 2) + 2 = 34 \ldots$, similarly
$(34 \times 2) + 2 = 70$
$(70 \times 2) + 2 = 142$
$(142 \times 2) + 2 = 286$.

17. *(c)* : The difference between the numbers in opposite sectors is 13, *i.e.*,
$26 - 13 = 13$
$68 - 55 = 13$, similarly
The missing number is $42 - 13 = 29$
($42 + 13 = 55$ is not given as option).

18. *(b)* : The number at the bottom is obtained by subtracting the sum of two numbers in the centre grid line from the square of the number at the top, *i.e.*,
$7^2 - (2 + 7) = 40$
$5^2 - (8 + 3) = 14$, similarly
$9^2 - (7 + 6) = 68$.

19. *(b)* : The number inside the brackets is obtained by multiplying the number on the left by 2 and then dividing the product by the sum of digits of number on the right, *i.e.*,
$(42 \times 2) \div (2 + 2) = 21$
$(162 \times 2) \div (9 + 9) = 18$, similarly
$(78 \times 2) \div (8 + 4) = 13$.

20. *(a)* : Subtracting the sum of squares of two numbers at the base from the square of number at the apex gives the number inside the triangle, *i.e.*,
$16^2 - (7^2 + 10^2) = 107$
$25^2 - (20^2 + 4^2) = 209$, similarly
$19^2 - (2^2 + 17^2) = 68$.

21. *(c)* : The number in the centre is the product of all the 4 numbers minus 10, *i.e.*,
$(3 \times 5 \times 2 \times 6) - 10 = 170$
$(8 \times 1 \times 4 \times 9) - 10 = 278$, similarly
$(10 \times 6 \times 7 \times 2) - 10 = 830$.

22. *(d)* : The number inside the circle is the product of difference of two numbers above and difference of two numbers below, *i.e.*,
$(5 - 3)(12 - 9) = 6$
$(8 - 4)(2 - 1) = 4$, similarly
$(18 - 10)(17 - 14) = 24$.

23. *(a)* : Starting from number 1 anticlockwise the number in the diagonally opposite section is its multiplication by 4, *i.e.*,
$1 \times 4 = 4$, $7 \times 4 = 28$, $2 \times 4 = 8$, similarly
$6 \times 4 = 24$.

24. *(a)* : Square of the number on the left plus the number on the right is the number within brackets, *i.e.*,
$6^2 + 4 = 40$
$3^2 + 3 = 12$, similarly
$7^2 + 2 = 51$.

25. *(b)* : Letter H is 8th in order of alphabetical series. Taking the sum of numbers placed vertically outside the circle + 8; multiplying it by the number on the right; then subtracting from the product the number on the left, gives the number inside the circle, *i.e.*,

Step I $\rightarrow$ $4+8+4 = 16$

Step II $\rightarrow$ $16 \times 5 = 80$

Step III $\rightarrow$ $80-10 = 70$

Letter C is 3rd in order, so

Step I $\rightarrow$ $2+3+5 = 10$

Step II $\rightarrow$ $10 \times 3 = 30$

Step III $\rightarrow$ $30-4 = 26$

Similarly, J is 10th in order, so

Step I $\rightarrow$ $8+10+6 = 24$

Step II $\rightarrow$ $24 \times ?$

Step III $\rightarrow$ $(24 \times ?)-6 = 90$

Simplifying the above equation :

$24 \times ? = 90+6$, *i.e.*, 96

$? = 96 \div 24 = 4.$

MATRICES

In these type of questions, a set of numbers or letters are given in a figure which is divided into different cells. Some logic is applied to form a pattern in rows or columns. One of the cells is left empty. The candidates are required to analyse the logic and from the given options select one which will complete the given incomplete matrix.

EXERCISE

Directions (Qs. 1 to 5) : *In each question given below which one number when placed at the sign of interrogation shall complete the number matrix.*

1.

4	5	6
2	3	7
1	8	3
21	98	?

(*a*) 16 (*b*) 73
(*c*) 76 (*d*) 94

2.

3	6	8
5	8	4
4	7	?

(*a*) 9 (*b*) 8
(*c*) 7 (*d*) 6

3.

1	4	9	?
1	2	3	4
2	4	6	?

(*a*) 16 and 8 (*b*) 25 and 5
(*c*) 36 and 4 (*d*) 49 and 7

4.

7	16	9
5	21	16
9	?	4

(*a*) 29 (*b*) 21
(*c*) 13 (*d*) 42

5.

6	6	8
5	7	5
4	3	?
120	126	320

(*a*) 12 (*b*) 16
(*c*) 8 (*d*) 4

Directions (Qs. 6 to 10) : *In questions given below, a word is represented by only one set of numbers as given in any one of the alternatives. The sets of numbers given in the alternatives are represented by two classes of alphabets as in the 2 matrices given below. The columns and rows of matrix I are numbered from 0 to 4 and that of matrix II from 5 to 9. A letter from these matrices can be represented first by its row and next by column number. Identify the set for the word given in each question.*

6.

	0	1	2	3	4
0	E	A	T	S	H
1	A	H	T	A	S
2	E	H	A	S	T
3	H	E	A	T	S
4	S	H	T	A	E

	5	6	7	8	9
5	O	R	K	L	P
6	L	P	O	R	K
7	O	K	R	P	L
8	P	R	K	L	O
9	R	L	K	O	P

REAP

(*a*) 56, 00, 22, 59 (*b*) 68, 21, 22, 86
(*c*) 96, 00, 01, 99 (*d*) 86, 34, 24, 69

7.

	0	1	2	3	4
0	C	A	F	E	D
1	C	D	A	E	D
2	D	E	C	F	E
3	A	D	D	D	C
4	D	C	A	C	A

	5	6	7	8	9
5	T	R	R	S	M
6	S	T	M	R	S
7	R	S	P	T	P
8	P	S	T	R	T
9	P	M	P	M	S

FARM

(*a*) 02, 30, 85, 65 (*b*) 20, 31, 76, 68
(*c*) 23, 12, 68, 96 (*d*) 44, 43, 87, 57

8.

	0	1	2	3	4
0	C	H	H	N	N
1	I	N	C	B	B
2	N	E	C	H	I
3	I	C	N	E	I
4	B	B	E	C	I

	5	6	7	8	9
5	Y	P	S	P	K
6	K	T	S	R	R
7	K	Y	R	Y	Y
8	P	R	K	P	R
9	S	Y	S	T	S

PREY

(*a*) 82, 76, 34, 77 (*b*) 80, 70, 43, 12
(*c*) 94, 87, 43, 56 (*d*) 88, 77, 33, 79

9.

	0	1	2	3	4
0	D	K	A	E	C
1	C	D	K	A	E
2	K	C	E	A	D
3	K	C	D	E	A
4	E	D	A	K	C

	5	6	7	8	9
5	P	L	O	T	N
6	T	P	N	L	O
7	P	N	T	O	L
8	O	N	T	P	L
9	L	O	P	N	T

COLD

(*a*) 10, 85, 79, 24 (*b*) 31, 99, 77, 22
(*c*) 30, 66, 86, 43 (*d*) 44, 96, 95, 22

10.

	0	1	2	3	4
0	M	M	R	M	R
1	O	F	R	F	N
2	R	N	O	R	O
3	F	O	F	M	O
4	F	M	R	R	F

	5	6	7	8	9
5	T	G	J	T	G
6	P	J	G	G	U
7	U	T	P	T	J
8	U	T	T	J	P
9	G	U	G	T	P

TURF

(*a*) 57, 86, 44, 11

(*b*) 86, 75, 20, 32

(*c*) 77, 68, 41, 44

(*d*) 89, 97, 12, 30

EXPLANATORY ANSWERS

1. (*d*) : $4^2 + 2^2 + 1^2 = 21$, *i.e.*, $16 + 4 + 1 = 21$

$5^2 + 3^2 + 8^2 = 98$, *i.e.*, $25 + 9 + 64 = 98$

$6^2 + 7^2 + 3^2 = 36 + 49 + 9 = 94.$

2. (*d*) : Sum of numbers in each row is 17, *i.e.*,

$$3 + 6 + 8 = 17$$
$$5 + 8 + 4 = 17$$

So, $17 - (4 + 7) = 6.$

3. (*a*) : The root of number in first row is the number in the second row and this number multiplied by 2 is the number in the third row, *i.e.*,

$\sqrt{1} = 1$ and $1 \times 2 = 2$

$\sqrt{4} = 2$ and $2 \times 2 = 4$

$\sqrt{9} = 3$ and $3 \times 2 = 6$

So, square of 4, *i.e.*, 16 in the first row and 4×2, *i.e.*, 8 in the third row completes the matrix.

4. (*c*) :

$$7 + 9 = 16$$
$$5 + 16 = 21$$

$$9+4 = 13.$$

5. (c) :
$$6\times5\times4 = 120$$
$$6\times7\times3 = 126$$
So, 320 ÷ (8 × 5), *i.e.*, 8 in the third row completes the matrix.

6. (a) : R is represented by row 5, column 6
E by row 0, column 0
A by row 2, column 2
P by row 5, column 9.

7. (c) : F is represented by row 2, column 3
A by row 1, column 2
R by row 6, column 8
M by row 9, column 6.

8. (d) : P is represented by row 8, column 8
R by row 7, column 7
E by row 3, column 3
Y by row 7, column 9.

9. (a) : C is represented by row 1, column 0
O by row 8, column 5
L by row 7, column 9
D by row 2, column 4.

10. (b) : T is represented by row 8, column 6
U by row 7, column 5
R by row 2, column 0
F by row 3, column 2.

ALPHABET PROBLEMS

Alphabet problems are fun to attempt. They are based on alphabetical series in natural as well as reverse order.

Natural Order

A B C D E F G H I J K L M N O P Q R S T U V W X Y Z

Reverse Order

Z Y X W V U T S R Q P O N M L K J I H G F E D C B A

Note : The series starts from A on reaching Z and from Z on reaching A. Of these A E I O U are vowels and the rest are consonants.

EXERCISE

1. Which letter should be ninth letter to the left of ninth letter from the right if the first half of the alphabet is reversed?
(*a*) I (*b*) D
(*c*) F (*d*) E

2. Starting from the fifth letter from the left, if twelve letters are written in reverse order, then which letter will be the seventh to the left of the fourteenth letter from the right?
(*a*) N (*b*) H
(*c*) L (*d*) O

3. What letter will come in the centre of sixth letter from the right and thirteenth letter from the left?
(*a*) Q (*b*) R
(*c*) P (*d*) S

4. If in the word "DISTURBANCE", the first letter is interchanged with the last letter, the second letter is interchanged with the tenth letter and so on, which letter would come after the letter "T" in the newly formed word?
(*a*) I (*b*) U
(*c*) N (*d*) S

5. If it is possible to make a meaningful word with the third, the fifth, the seventh and the tenth letters of the word PROJECTION, which of the following is the third letter of that word? If no such word can be made, give 'X' as the answer. If more than one such word can be made, give 'M' as the answer.
(*a*) T (*b*) N
(*c*) O (*d*) M

6. A meaningful word is made if we take the first, fourth, fifth, seventh, tenth, eleventh and the twelfth letters of the word "FELICITATIONS". Which of the following will be the fifth letter of that word from the right end of that word?
(*a*) T (*b*) C
(*c*) N (*d*) I

7. On rearranging the jumbled spelling of the word SKARTINS, a language is obtained. What is the fifth letter from the right of the rearranged word?
(*a*) N (*b*) K
(*c*) R (*d*) S

8. If the 1st, 3rd, 5th, 7th, 10th and 13th letters of the word "ENTERTAINMENT" are used to make a meaningful word, then what two letters will come in the centre?
(*a*) AM (*b*) TT
(*c*) RE (*d*) NA

9. On rearranging the jumbled spelling of the word GRUBY a sport is obtained. What is the letter in the centre?
(*a*) R (*b*) B
(*c*) G (*d*) U

10. If the letters 'ERVSECI' can be rearranged to form a meaningful word what will be the fifth letter from the right?

(a) R *(b)* V
(c) E *(d)* None of these

11. From the word HASTEN how many independent meaningful English words can be made without changing the order of the letters and using each letter only once?

(a) 1 *(b)* 2
(c) 3 *(d)* 4

EXPLANATORY ANSWERS

1. *(d)* : MLKJIGHFEDCBANOPQRSTUVWXYZ

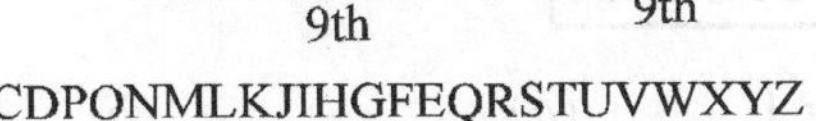

2. *(d)* : ABCDPONMLKJIHGFEQRSTUVWXYZ

7th 14th

3. *(a)* :

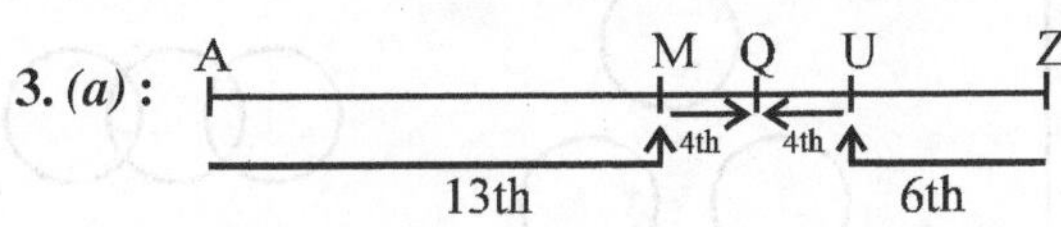

13th letter from left is 'M' and 6th letter from right is 'U'. The letter in the centre of 'M' and 'U' is 'Q'.

4. *(d)* : ECNABRUTSID

5. *(d)* : PROJECTION

The 3rd, 5th, 7th and 10th letters are OETN.

The words formed are TONE and NOTE.

6. *(b)* : FELICITATIONS

The 1st, 4th, 5th, 7th, 10th, 11th and 12th lettes are FICTION.

The word is FICTION and 5th letter from right is 'C'.

7. *(d)* : The word is SANSKRIT and 5th letter from right is 'S'.

8. *(b)* : ENTERTAINMENT

The 1st, 3rd, 5th 7th, 10th and 13th letters are ETRAMT.

The word formed is MATTER.

9. *(c)* : The sport is RUGBY. The letter in the centre is 'G'.

10. *(a)* : The word is SERVICE and fifth letter from right is 'R'.

11. *(b)* : The words formed are : HAS, TEN.

LOGICAL DIAGRAM

In these type of questions, a set of five different figures is given as options. Each figure represents a logical pattern of certain groups of related words wherein each word represents a class. One has to identify the most appropriate logical figure for the set of words given. Some of the relationships represented by these diagrams are given below. Understand the relationship patterns and then attempt the exercise following the explanation.

EXERCISE

Directions : *From the five logical Diagrams, select one which best illustrates the relationship among three given classes in the questions 1 to 10.*

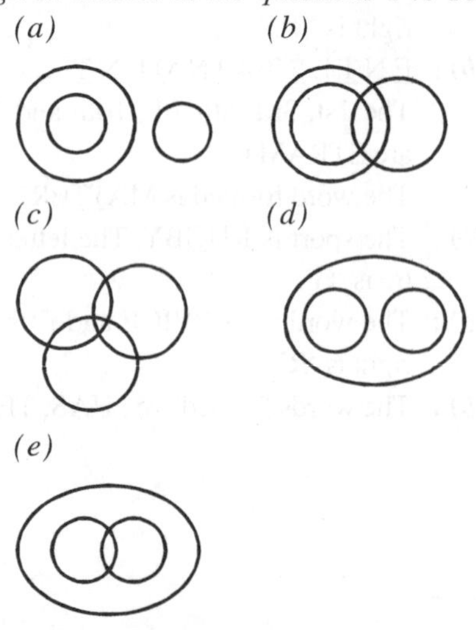

1. Birds, fruits, mangoes
2. Criminals, lawyers, bandits
3. Swimmers, bachelors, men
4. Smart, engineers, women
5. Vegetables, potatoes, brinjals
6. Grapes, sweet, fruit
7. Doctors, architects, humans
8. Scholars, people, Indians
9. Children, naughty, studious
10. Pens, pencils, stationery

Directions : *From the five logical diagrams select one which best illustrates the relationship among three given classes in questions 11 to 20.*

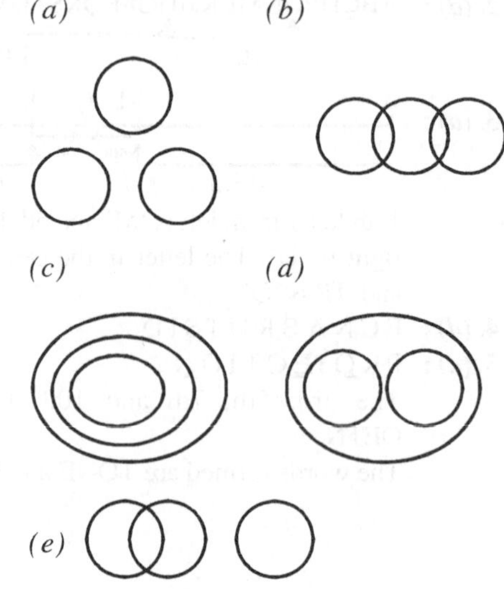

11. Ink, crayons, red
12. Canines, dogs, pups
13. Table, chair, stool
14. Ripe, mangoes, basket
15. Scholars, studious, illiterates
16. Cars, ships, means of conveyance
17. Age, number, thirteen
18. Country, state, continent
19. Father, parent, mother
20. Iron, metal, mercury

Directions : *From the five logical diagrams select one which best illustrates the relationship among three given classes in the questions 21 to 30.*

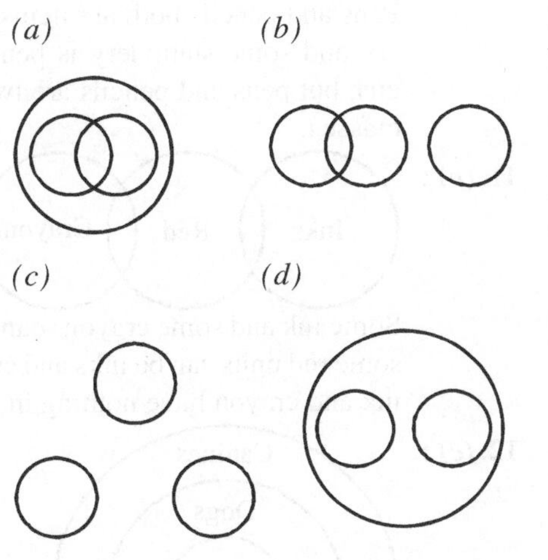

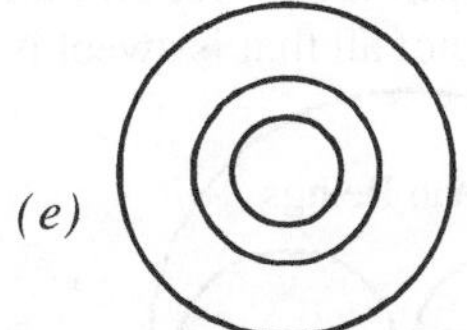

21. Lizards, Reptiles, Crocodiles
22. Whales, Tortoise, Fishes
23. Birds, Crows, Parrots
24. Sisters, Women, Mothers
25. Plants, Scientists, Men
26. Novels, Album, English
27. Sentences, Words, Paragraph
28. Beef, Mutton, Flesh
29. Principal, Student, Parent
30. Lily, Rose, Flower.

EXPLANATORY ANSWERS

1. *(a)* :

Fruits
Mangoes
Birds

All mangoes are fruits, but neither fruits, nor mangoes can be birds.

2. *(a)* :

Criminals
Bandits
Law-yers

All bandits are criminal, but neither criminals nor bandits can be lawyers.

3. *(b)* :

Men
Bache-lors
Swim-mers

All bachelors are men and some men and bachelors can be swimmers.

4. *(c)* :

Smart
Women
Engineers

Some women can be smart and some women can be engineers and vice–versa. Some engineers can be women and some engineers can be smart and vice–versa.

5. *(d)* :

Vegetables
Potatoes
Brinjals

Potatoes and brinjals are vegetables but they have nothing in common. Some vegetables are potatoes and some are brinjals.

6. *(b)* :

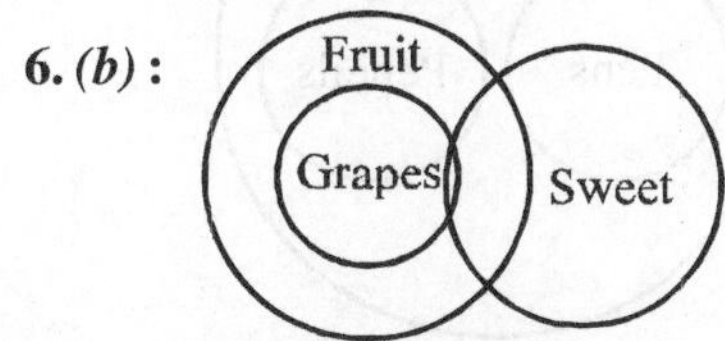

Some grapes are sweet and all grapes are fruit. But not all that is sweet is fruit.

7. *(d)* :

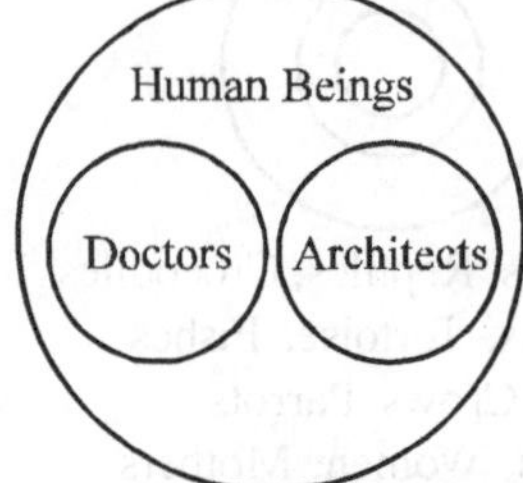

Doctors and architects are two separate classes, but all doctors and architects are humans and some humans are either doctors or architects.

8. *(e)* :

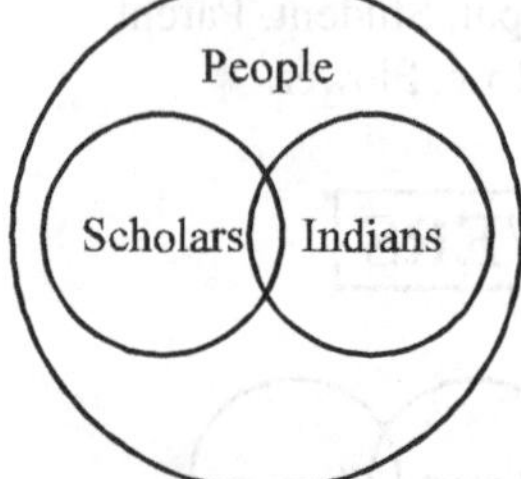

Some Indians can be scholars and some scholars can be Indians. All scholars and Indians are people.

9. *(c)* :

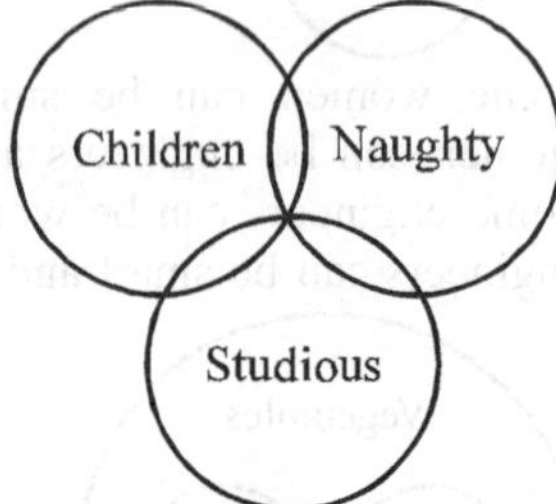

Some children can be naughty and some can be studious, some studious can be children and some naughty. Some naughty can be studious and some children.

10. *(d)* :

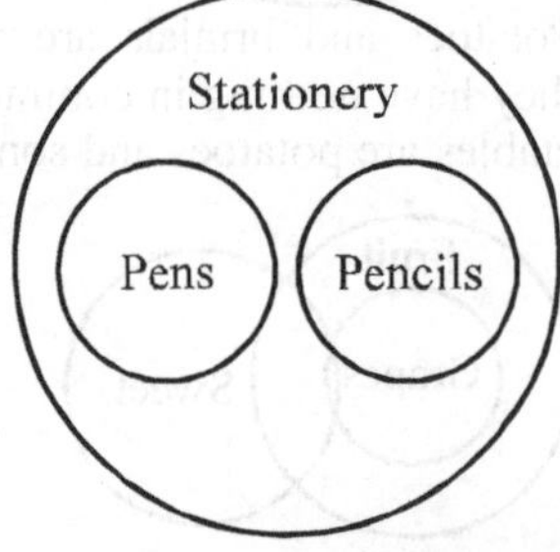

Pens and pencils both are items of stationery and some stationery is pens and pencils, but pens and pencils are two separate classes.

11. *(b)* :

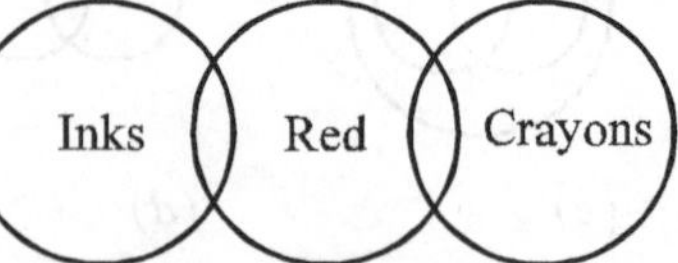

Some ink and some crayons can be red and some red units can be inks and crayons, but ink and crayon have nothing in common.

12. *(c)* :

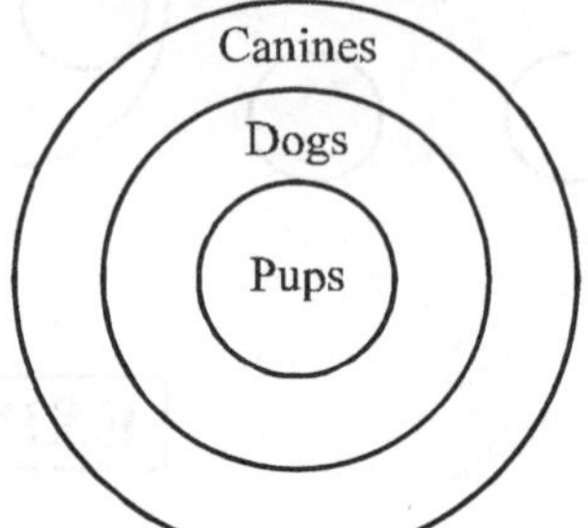

All pups are dogs and all dogs are canines. Some canines are dogs, of which some are pups.

13. *(a)* :

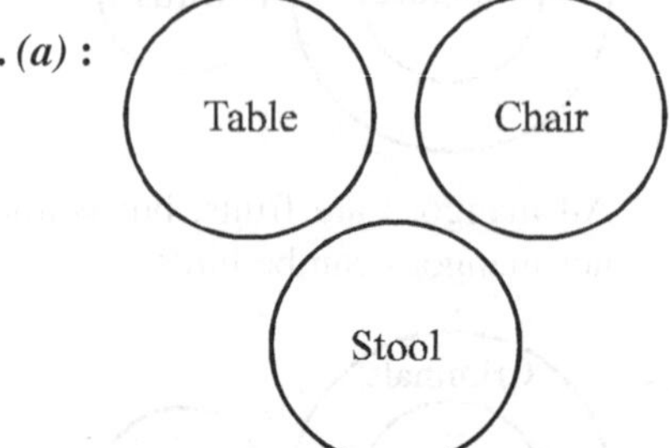

All three are different classes.

14. *(e)* :

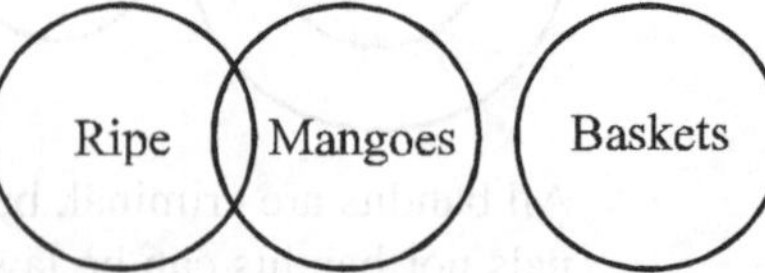

Some mangoes are ripe and some ripe units are mangoes, but neither ripe units nor mangoes can be baskets.

15. *(e)* :

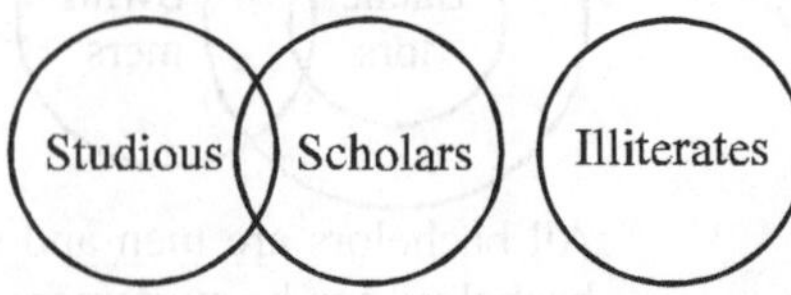

Some studious can be scholars and some scholars can be studious, but neither studious nor scholars can be illiterates.

16. *(d)* :

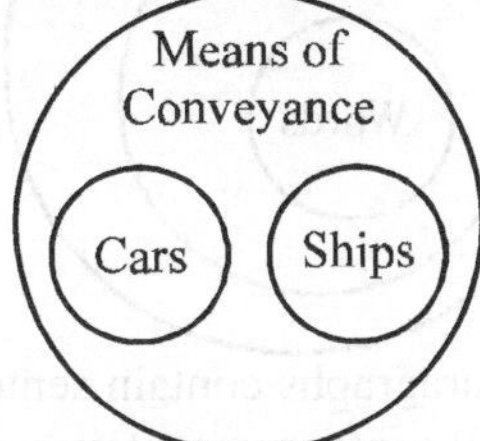

All cars and all ships are means of conveyance, but neither is contained in the other. Some means of conveyance are cars and some ships.

17. *(b)* :

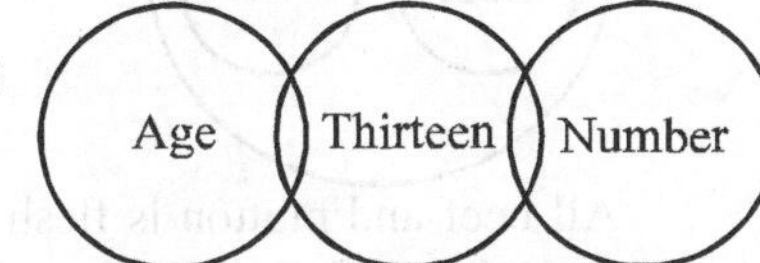

Some are aged thirteen and some numbers are thirteen. Some thirteen units are numbers and some ages. Age and number have nothing in common.

18. *(c)* :

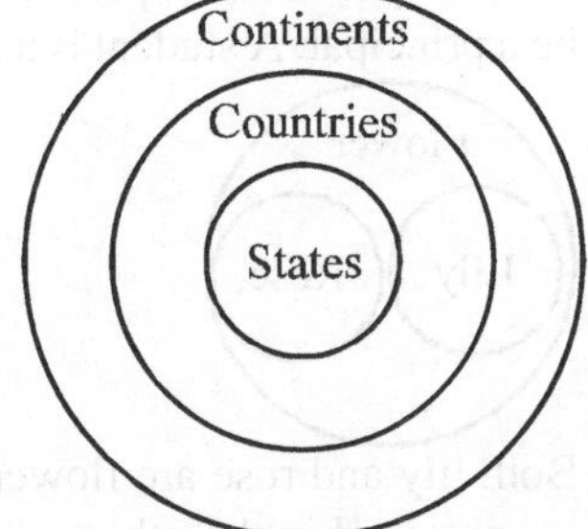

All continents contain countries within it and each country contains states within it.

19. *(d)* :

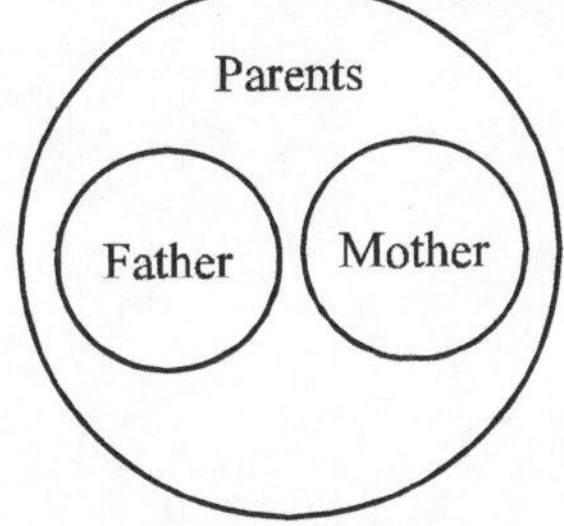

All fathers and mothers are parents, but they are two separate classes. Some of the parents are fathers and some are mothers.

20. *(d)* :

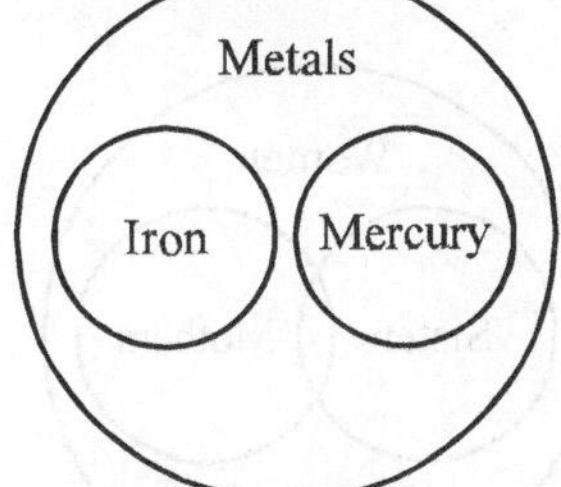

Iron and mercury are metals, but they have nothing in common. Some metals are iron and some mercury.

21. *(d)* :

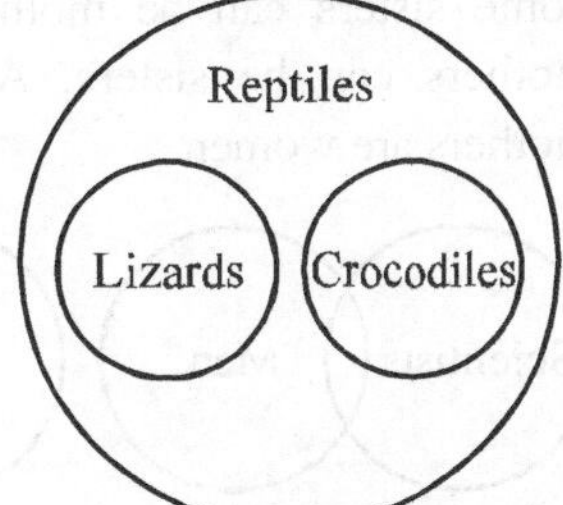

All lizards and crocodiles are reptiles, but neither is contained in the other. Some reptiles are lizards and some crocodiles.

22. *(c)* :

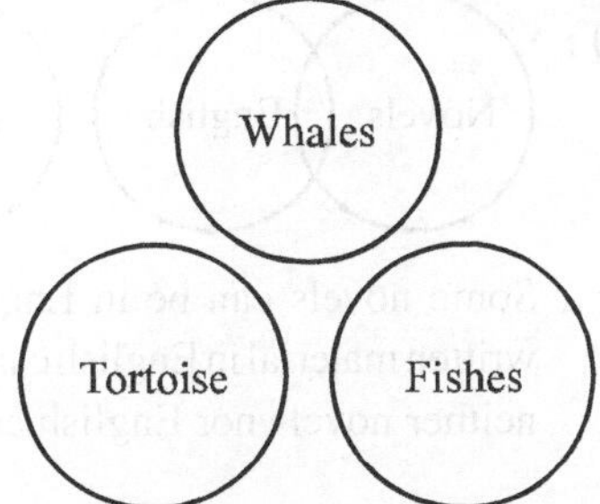

All three are different classes.

23. *(d)* :

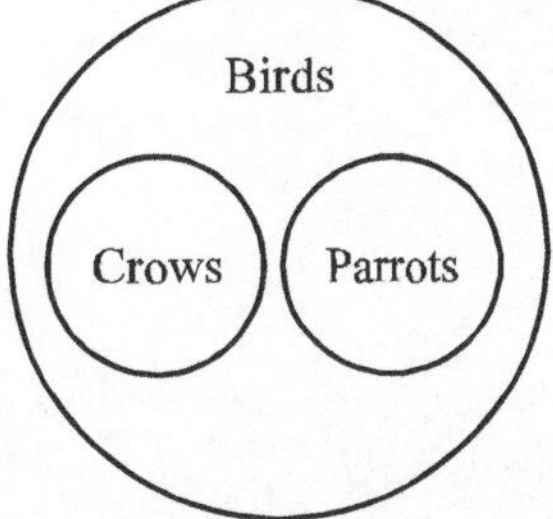

All crows and parrots are birds but neither is contained in the other. Some birds are crows and some parrots.

24. ***(a)*** **:**

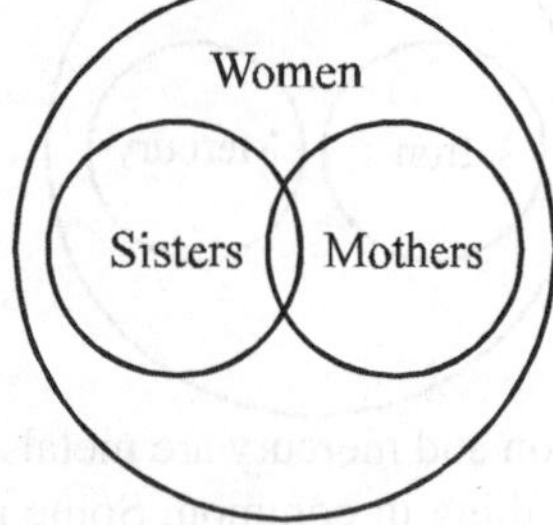

Some sisters can be mothers and some mothers can be sisters. All sisters and mothers are women.

25. ***(b)*** **:**

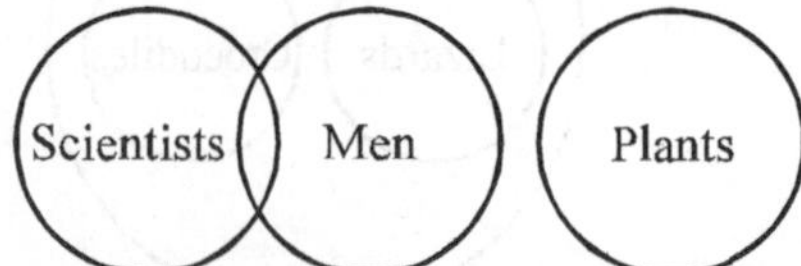

Some scientists can be men and some men can be scientists, but neither scientists nor men can be plants.

26. ***(b)*** **:**

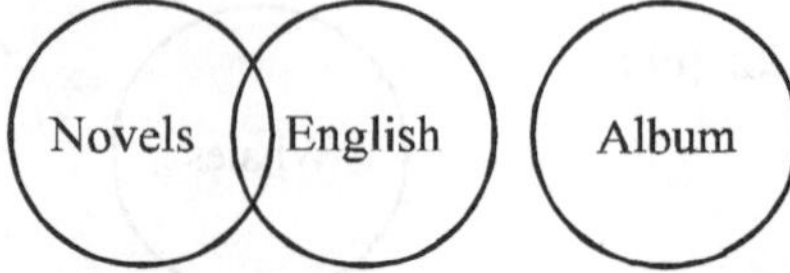

Some novels can be in English and some written material in English can be novels, but neither novels nor English can be album.

27. ***(e)*** **:**

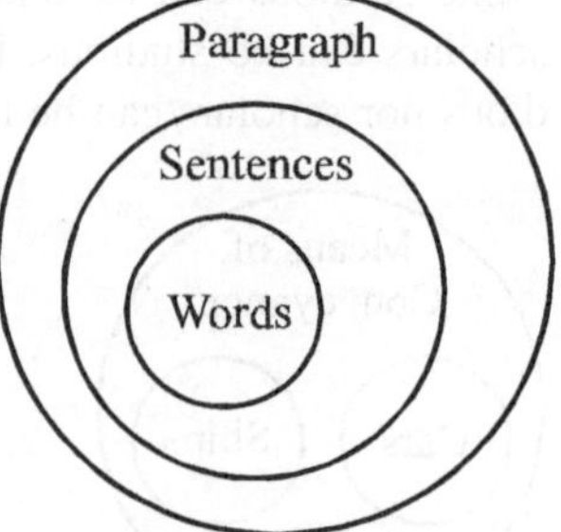

All paragraphs contain sentences within it and all sentences contain words within it.

28. ***(d)*** **:**

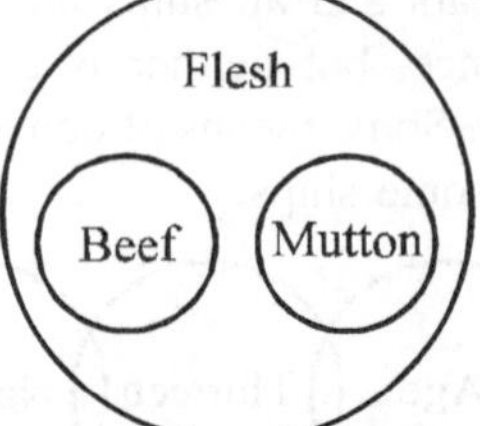

All beef and mutton is flesh of some animals. Some flesh is beef and some mutton.

29. ***(b)*** **:**

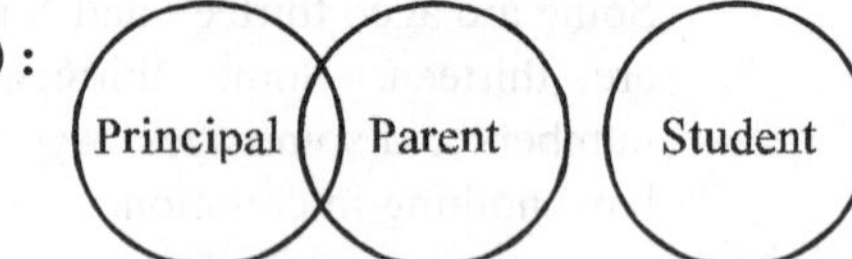

A Principal can be a parent and parent can be a principal. A student is a different class.

30. ***(d)*** **:**

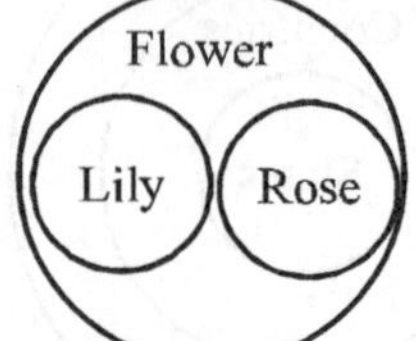

Both lily and rose are flowers. But neither is contained in the other.

SYLLOGISM

In this reasoning pattern, the two premises are followed by two conclusions drawn from them. Five options *(a)*, *(b)*, *(c)*, *(d)* and *(e)* are given as answers. Based on the two statements the candidate has to select the right option as answer.

EXERCISE

Directions : *In each question below are given two statements followed by two conclusions numbered I and II. You have to take the two given statements to be true even if they seem to be at variance from commonly known facts and then decide which of the given conclusions logically follows from the two given statements, disregarding commonly known facts. Read both the statements and—*

Give answer (a) if only conclusion I follows; give answer (b) if only conclusion II follows; give answer (c) if either I or II follows; give answer (d) if neither I nor II follows and give answer (e) if both I and II follows.

1. *Statements* *I* : All tomatoes are red.
II : All grapes are tomatoes.
Conclusions *I* : All grapes are red.
II : Some tomatoes are grapes.

2. *Statements* *I* : All painters are smilling.
II : Some authors are painters.
Conclusions *I* : All smiling authors are painters.
II : Some authors are smiling.

3. *Statements* *I* : All peons in this office are efficient.
II : Ramu is not efficient.
Conclusions *I* : Ramu is not peon in this office.
II : Ramu should be more efficient.

4. *Statements* *I* : All weavers are hard working.
II : No hard working men are foolish.
Conclusions *I* : No weavers are foolish.
II : Some foolish are weavers.

5. *Statements* *I* : All fishes are cars.
II : All cars are vegetables.
Conclusions *I* : Some vegetables are cars.
II : Some vegetables are fishes.

6. *Statements* *I* : Some dogs are pups.
II : All horses are pups.
Conclusions *I* : Some dogs are horses.
II : Some horses are dogs.

7. *Statements* *I* : All beautiful women are mothers.
II : All mothers are understanding.
Conclusions *I* : All beautiful women are understanding.
II : All mothers are beautiful women.

8. *Statements* *I* : Some toys are tables.
II : No table is black.
Conclusions *I* : Some toys are black.
II : Some toys are not black.

9. *Statements* *I* : All rivers are mountains.
II : Some rivers are deserts.
Conclusions *I* : Some mountains are deserts.
II : Some deserts are not mountains.

10. *Statements* *I* : All men are horses.
II : All horses are elephants.
Conclusions *I* : All men are elephants.
II : All elephants are men.

Directions : *In the following questions, select the set of conclusion which logically follows from the given statements.*

11. *Statements* *I:* All foxes are plates.
II: All plates are trees.
Conclusions I: All foxes are trees.
II: All trees are foxes.
III: Some trees are foxes.
IV: Some trees are plates.
(*a*) All conclusions are correct.
(*b*) Only conclusions I, III, and IV follow.
(*c*) Only conclusions II, III, and IV follow.
(*d*) Only conclusions I and IV follow.
(*e*) None of the above.

12. *Statements* *I:* Some cubes are squares.
II: All squares are circles.
Conclusions I: All cubes are circles.
II: Some circles are cubes.
III: Some circles are squares.
IV: All squares are cubes.
(*a*) Only conclusion I follows.
(*b*) Only conclusion I, II and III follow.
(*c*) All conclusions are correct.
(*d*) Only conclusions II and III follow.
(*e*) None of the above.

13. *Statements* *I:* All cups are goats.
II: All goats are tins.
Conclusions I: All goats are cups.
II: All tins are goats.
III: No cups are tins.
IV: No tins are cups.
(*a*) Only conclusions III and IV follow.
(*b*) Only conclusios I and II follow.
(*c*) Only conclusions I, II and III follow.
(*d*) All conclusions are correct.
(*e*) None of the above.

14. *Statements* *I:* All bombs are bags.
II: Some bags are jets.
Conclusions I: All bombs are jets.
II: All jets are bombs.
III: Some jets are bombs.
IV: Some bombs are jets.
(*a*) Only conclusion III follows.
(*b*) Only conclusions I and II follow.
(*c*) All conclusions are correct.
(*d*) Only conclusions III and IV follow.
(*e*) None of these.

15. *Statements* *I:* Some thorns are jackets.
II: Some jackets are boats.
Conclusions I: No thorns are boats.
II: All jackets are boats.
III: Some boats are thorns.
IV: No jackets are thorns.
(*a*) Either conclusion I or IV follows.
(*b*) Either conclusion I or II follows.
(*c*) Either conclusion I or III follows.
(*d*) No conclusion is correct.
(*e*) All conclusions are correct.

EXPLANATORY ANSWERS

1. *(e)* **:** When all tomatoes are red and all grapes are tomatoes, then all grapes are also red. When all grapes are tomatoes, then some tomatoes must be grapes. Therefore, both conclusions I and II are correct.

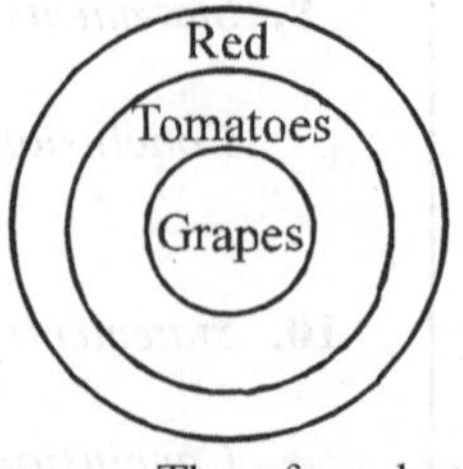

2. *(b)* **:** When all painters are smiling and some authors are painters, then some authors are smiling. Therefore, only conclusion II is correct.

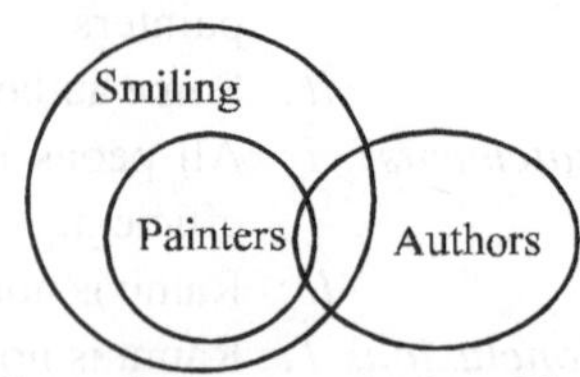

3. *(a)* **:** When all the peons of the office are efficient, then Ramu cannot be a peon in this office. Therefore, only conclusion I is correct.

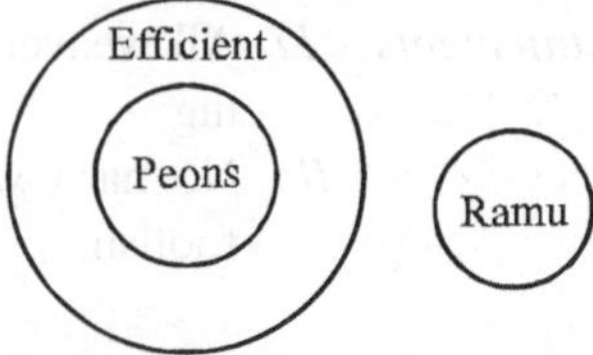

4. *(a)* **:** When all weavers are hardworking and no hardworking men are foolish, then no weavers are foolish. Therefore, only conclusion I is correct.

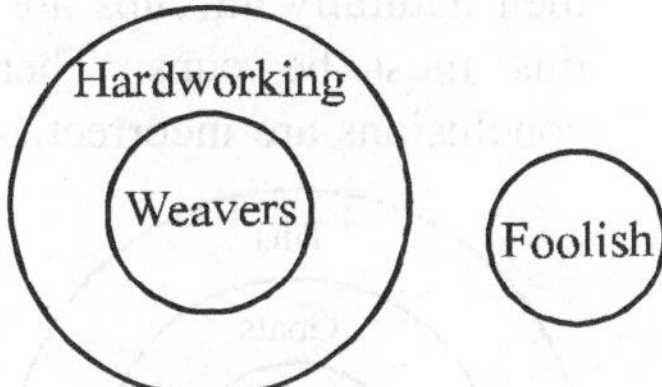

5. *(e)* **:** When all fishes are cars and all cars are vegetables, then all fishes will naturally be vegetables. This means that some vegetables are fishes. And when all cars are vegetables, then some vegetables will be cars naturally. Therefore, both the conclusions I and II are correct.

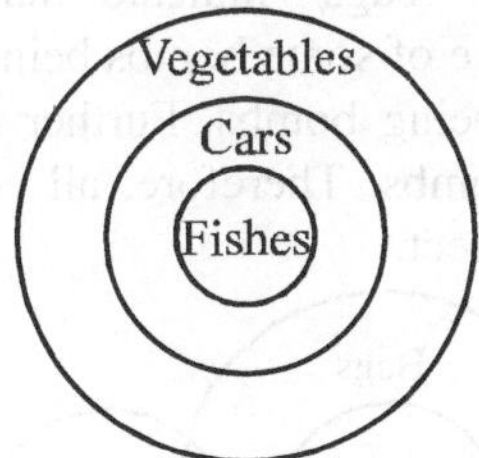

6. *(d)* **:** No relationship can be established between the two statements. Therefore, neither conclusion I nor conclusion II is correct.

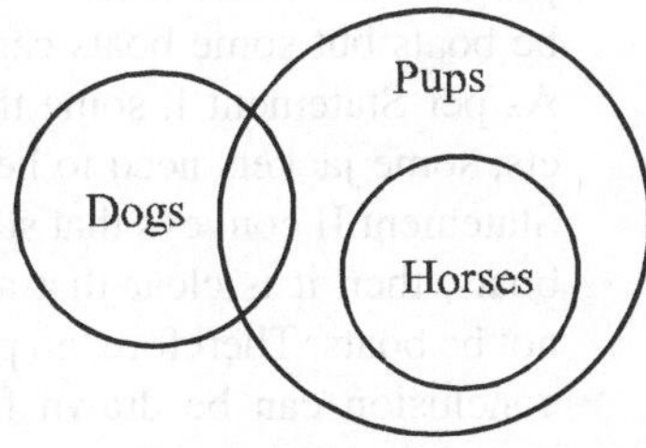

7. *(a)* **:** When all beautiful women are mothers and all mothers are understanding, then naturally all beautiful women are understanding. All mothers need not be beautiful women. Therefore, only conclusion I is correct.

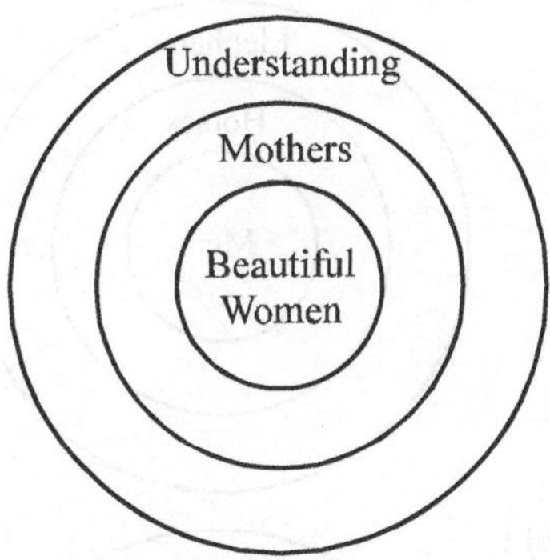

8. *(c)* **:** When some toys are tables and no table is black, then it is indicated that some toys can be black, as all toys are not tables. On the other hand, some toys may not be black. Therefore, there is a possibility that some toys may or may not be black. As such, either conclusion I or conclusion II can be correct.

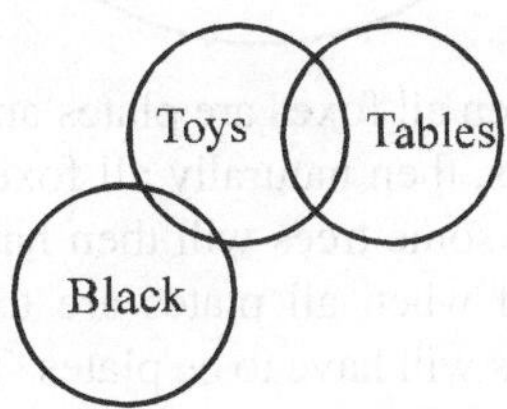

9. *(e)* **:** When all rivers are mountains and some rivers are deserts, then some deserts cannot be mountains and also, some mountains need not be deserts. Therefore, both conclusion I and conclusion II are correct.

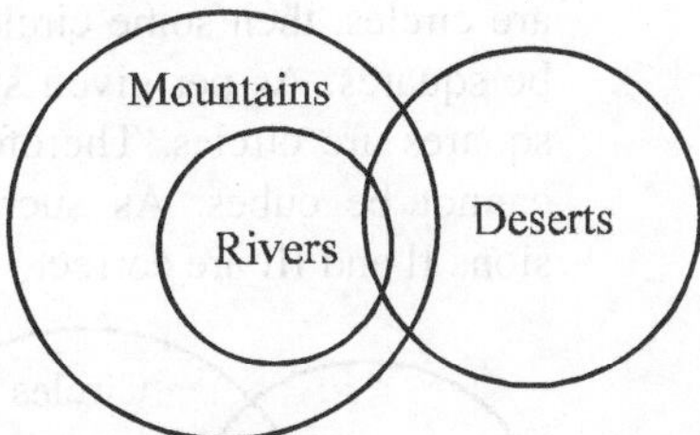

10. *(a)* **:** When all men are horses and all horses are elephants then, naturally all men are elephants, but all elephants need not be men. Therefore, only conclusion I is correct.

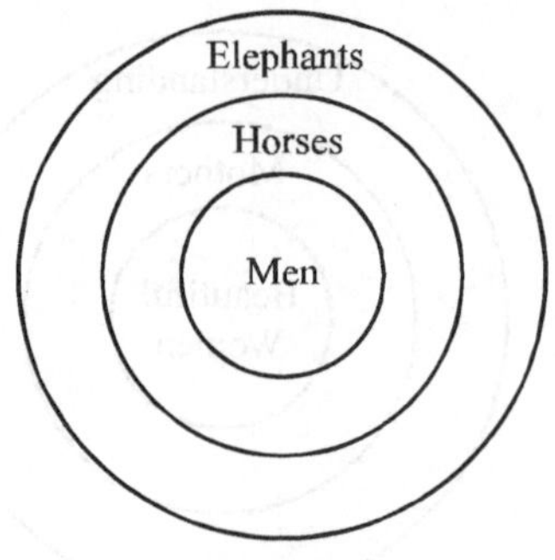

11. *(b)* :

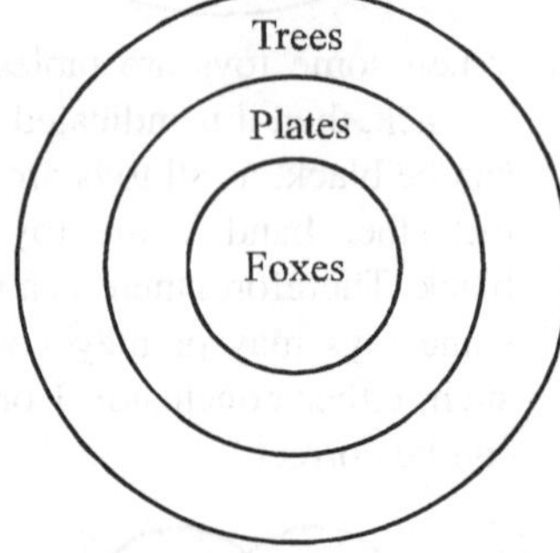

When all foxes are plates and all plates are trees, then naturally all foxes will be trees and some trees will then have to be foxes. And when all plates are trees then some trees will have to be plates. Therefore, only conclusions I, III and IV are correct.

12. *(d)* : When it is given that some cubes are squares and all squares are circles, then some cubes will naturally be circles, though all cubes cannot be circles. When some cubes are circles, then some circles will have to be cubes. And when all squares are circles, then some circles will have to be squares. As per given statement II, all squares are circles. Therefore all squares cannot be cubes. As such only conclusions II and III are correct.

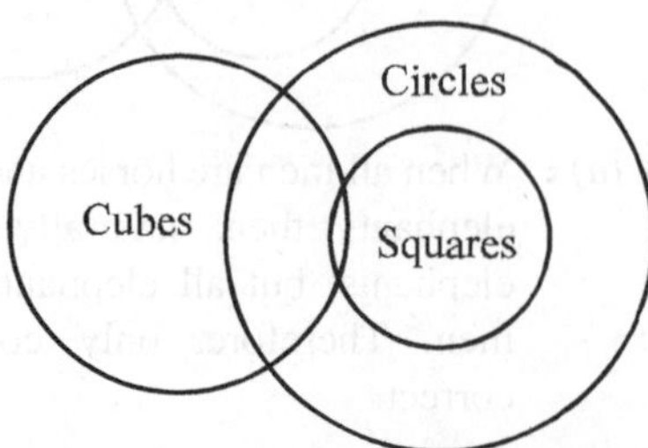

13. *(e)* : When all cups are goats, then only some goats can be cups. When all goats are tins, then only some tins can be goats. When all cups are goats and all goats are tins, then naturally all cups are tins and some tins must be cups. Therefore, all the conclusions are incorrect.

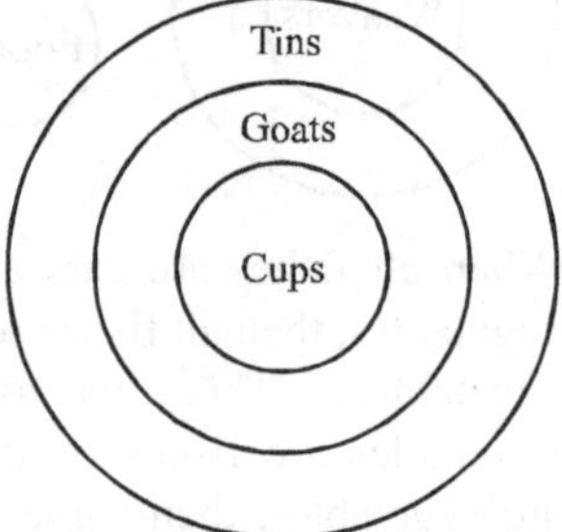

14. *(e)* : When all bombs are bags and some bags are jets then all bombs cannot be jets. 'Some bags' indicate that there is no chance of some bombs being jets, or some jets being bombs. Further all jets cannot be bombs. Therefore, all conclusions are incorrect.

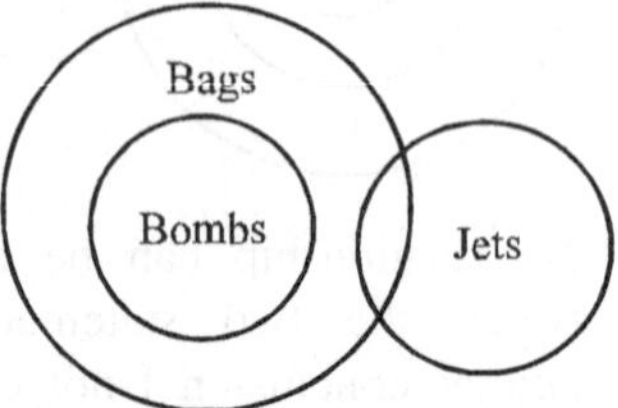

15. *(d)* : When some thorns are jackets and some jackets are boats, then some thorns may be boats but some boats cannot be thorns. As per Statement I, some thorns are jackets, some jackets need to be thorns. When Statement II conveys that some jackets are boats, then it is clear that all jackets cannot be boats. Therefore, no particular given conclusion can be drawn from the given statements.

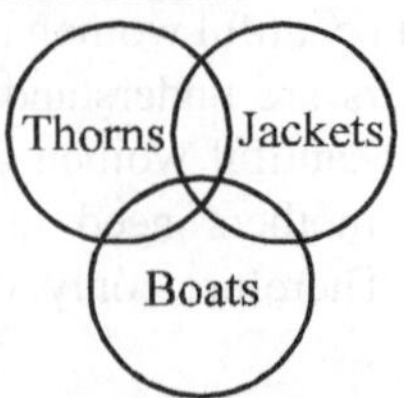

DRAWING CONCLUSIONS

In this reasoning pattern, a statement is given followed by two conclusions. The statement is to be taken as the fact. Then based on it one has to decide which of the conclusion(s) definitely follows or does not follow from the given statement.

EXERCISE

Directions : *In the following questions, each question has a statement followed by two conclusions. Taking the statement to be true, decide which of the given conclusions definitely follows from the given statement. Indicate your answer as (a) if only I follows; (b) if only II follows; (c) either I or II follows; (d) if neither I nor II follows; and (e) if both I and II follow.*

1. *Statement* : The Principal humiliated the teacher in the presence of students.

Conclusions I : The Principal did not like the teacher.

II : The teacher was not popular amongst his students.

2. *Statement* : Good health is dependent on right eating habits. Most of the people do not follow any rule regarding eating.

Conclusions I : Most of the people have poor health.

II : People are ignorant of proper eating habits.

3. *Statement* : Until our country achieves economic equality and political freedom, democracy would be meaningless.

Conclusions I : Political freedom and democracy go hand in hand.

II : Economic equality leads to real political freedom and democracy.

4. *Statement* : Black cloud follows thunder. Rains follow thunder.

Conclusions I : Thunder is the cause of rain.

II : Black cloud is the cause of thunder.

5. *Statement* : Practice is better than precept. Most doctors are heavy smokers.

Conclusions I : Most doctors cannot advise people not to smoke.

II : Doctors do not regard smoking as injurious.

6. *Statement* : Workers feel highly motivated when they get sense of involvement by participating in the management of companies.

Conclusions I : Workers should be motivated to produce more.

II : Workers should be allowed to participate in the management of companies.

7. *Statement* : Industrial revolution which first of all started in Europe has brought about modern age.

Conclusions I : Disparity between rich and poor results in revolution.

II : Revolution overhauls society.

8. *Statement* : America's defence secretary reiterated that they would continue to supply arms to Pakistan.

Conclusions I : Pakistan is incapable of manufacturing arms.

II : It would ensure peace in the region.

9. *Statement* : Poor people are more trustworthy as compared to the rich. They can do wonders if they are taken into confidence.

Conclusions I : Poor people are wonderful people.

II : By and large rich people are not trustworthy.

10. *Statement* : Government has spoiled many top ranking financial institutions by appointing bureaucrats as Directors of these institutions.

Conclusions I : Government should appoint Directors of the financial institutes taking into consideration the expertise of the person in the area of finance.

II : The Director of the financial institute should have expertise commensurate with the financial work carried out by the institute.

EXPLANATORY ANSWERS

1. ***(a)*** **:** Only conclusion I follows. Conclusion II is not confirmed by the given statement.

2. ***(a)*** **:** Conclusion I definitely follows. Conclusion II is not confirmed by the given statement.

3. ***(b)*** **:** Only conclusion II follows. Conclusion I cannot be drawn from the given statement.

4. ***(b)*** **:** Only conclusion II follows. Conclusion I is wrong as rains are the cause of thunder.

5. ***(e)*** **:** Both conclusion I and conclusion II follow from the statements as the doctors who are heavy smokers indicate that they do not regard smoking as injurious and thus, cannot advise people not to smoke.

6. ***(e)*** **:** Both conclusions I and II follow from the statement as involvement of workers boosts production and benefits the companies.

7. ***(b)*** **:** Only conclusion II follows. Conclusion I is not related the statement.

8. ***(d)*** **:** Neither conclusion I nor conclusion II follows. Both the conclusions are unrelated to the statement.

9. ***(b)*** **:** Only conclusion II follows. Conclusion I is not related to the statement.

10. ***(e)*** **:** Both conclusion I and conclusion II follow.

DRAWING ASSUMPTIONS

In this type of reasoning, a statement is given and assumptions are drawn from it. An assumption is something assumed, supposed and taken for granted. The implicity of the two assumptions is in question. The implication means the hidden meaning, something which is derived from and as such based upon the statement.

EXERCISE

Directions : *In each question below is given a statement followed by two assumptions numbered I and II. An assumption is something supposed or taken for granted. You have to consider the statement and the following assumptions and decide which of the assumptions is implicit in the statement. Give answer—*

(*a*) If assumption I is implicit.
(*b*) If assumption II is implicit.
(*c*) If either I or II is implicit.
(*d*) If neither I nor II is implicit.
(*e*) If both I and II are implicit.

1. *Statement* : Apart from the entertainment value of television, its educational value cannot be ignored.

Assumptions I : People take the television to be means of entertainment only.

II : The educational value of television is not realised properly.

2. *Statement* : Ten candidates who were on the waiting list could finally be admitted to the course.

Assumptions I : Wait-listed candidates get admission with difficulty.

II : A large number of candidates were on the waiting list.

3. *Statement* : In Mumbai, railway trains are indispensable for people in the suburbs to reach their places of work on time.

Assumptions I : Railway trains are the only mode of transport available in the suburbs of Mumbai.

II : Only railway trains run punctually.

4. *Statement* : The mangoes are too cheap to be good.

Assumptions I : When the mango crop is abundant, the prices go down.

II : The lower the selling price, the inferior is the quality of the commodity.

5. *Statement* : Of all the newspapers published in Delhi, 'The Time and Space' has the largest number of readers.

Assumptions I : Volume of readership of all the newspapers in Delhi is known.

II : No newspaper in Delhi other than 'The Time and Space' has large readership.

6. *Statement* : 'Smoking Prohibited'. A notice in a railway compartment.

Assumptions I : Some persons like to smoke in the compartment.

II : Some persons smoke in the compartment.

7. *Statement* : A friend in need is a friend indeed.

Assumptions I : Relatives are of no help in difficult circumstances.

II : Taking help from a friend is desirable.

8. *Statement* : When in Chennai, stay at Hotel 'X' for comfort and good service, because my best friend has recommended it.

Assumptions I : My best friend is trustworthy.

II : Comfort and good service cannot be expected from all hotels.

9. *Statement* : A friend in need is a friend indeed.

Assumptions I : A person needs help from others on certain occasions.

II : A friend is expected to help when needed.

10. *Statement* : 'Smoking Prohibited.' A notice in a railway compartment.

Assumptions I : Generally, people expect a notice.

II : Smoking is injurious to health.

Directions : *In each question below is given a statement followed by three assumptions number I, II and III. An assumption is something supposed or taken for granted. You have to consider the statement along with the assumptions and decide which of the assumptions is implicit in the statement. Then decide which of the alternatives is the correct answer.*

11. *Statement :*

"Use Riya Cold Cream for fair complexion"—an advertisement.

Assumptions :

I. People like to use cream for fair complexion.
II. People are easily fooled.
III. People respond to advertisements.

(a) Only I is implicit.
(b) Only II is implicit.
(c) Only I and III are implicit.
(d) Only I and II are implicit.
(e) All are implicit.

12. *Statement :*

"Slogans against smoking in office should be put on the notice board"—an employee in an office suggests.

Assumptions :

I. The employee felt that his suggestion will be considered.
II. People smoke in the office.
III. Some people will stop smoking after reading the slogans.

(a) Only I is implicit.
(b) Only I and II are implicit.
(c) Only II and III are implicit.
(d) None is implicit.
(e) All are implicit.

13. *Statement :*

"I want to present him a book on techniques of yoga on his birthday"—A tells B.

Assumptions :

I. A and B will be invited for the birthday celebrations.
II. The person to whom the book is to be presented, is not keeping good health.
III. Book is the best gift for birthdays.

(a) Only I and II are implicit.
(b) Only II and III are implicit.
(c) Only I and III are implicit.
(d) None is implicit.
(e) All are implicit.

14. *Statement :*

Keeping in view the financial constraint, the management institution has decided to charge at the time of providing employment in various organisations, a placement fee of Rs. 25000 from the organisation in which the student will be provided the employment.

Assumptions :

I. It will help in increasing the demand of the students belonging to the management institution.
II. The amount collected in this way will be purposeful.
III. It may be possible that the organisation providing employment may select less number of students in future.

(a) None follows.
(b) Only II and III follow.
(c) Only I follows.
(d) Only I and II follow.
(e) None of these.

15. *Statement :*
In order to reduce the gap between income and expenditure the company has decided to increase the price of its product from next month.

Assumptions :
I. The rate will remain more or less same after the increase.
II. The expenditure will more or less remain same in near future.
III. The rival companies will also increase the price of the similar product.
(a) All are implicit.
(b) Only II and III are implicit.
(c) Only I and II are implicit.
(d) Only III is implicit.
(e) None of these.

EXPLANATORY ANSWERS

1. *(e)* : Both assumptions I and II are implicit.

2. *(a)* : Assumption II is not implicit in the statement. Only assumption I is implicit.

3. *(d)* : Neither assumption I nor assumption II is implicit in the statement.

4. *(b)* : Assumption I is not implicit in the statement, because it states the principle of supply and prices. Only assumption II is implicit which states the principle of price-quality parity.

5. *(a)* : Assumption I is implicit in the statement because the largest readership may be established only if the volume of readership of all the newspapers is known.

6. *(b)* : Assumption II suggests that some persons smoke in the compartment. 'Smoking Prohibited' is the notice for those persons.

7. *(d)* : The statement highlights the criterion of a true friend.

8. *(e)* : Both assumptions I and II are implicit because *(i)* the advice is from a trustworthy best friend, and *(ii)* all hotels cannot provide comfort and good service.

9. *(b)* : Only assumption II is implicit because only a true friend helps in need.

10. *(d)* : None of the assumptions is implicit. The statement does not imply that people expect a notice or smoking is injurious to health.

11. *(c)* : The advertisement itself denotes that people like to use cream for fair complexion and they do respond to advertisements. Advertisements are for awareness of the product not for fooling people.

12. *(e)* : Suggestion for putting up the notice is made because some people must be smoking in office. Notice board is read by people in office and some may stop smoking after reading the slogans.

13. *(c)* : According to A presents are best gifts for birthdays and when A has bought the book he expects to be invited for the birthday celebration. Nothing is mentioned about health of the birthday person.

14. *(b)* : The amount collected will lessen the financial constraint and there is every possibility for selecting less number of students because of the fee charged.

15. *(e)* : The increased amount is not mentioned and nothing is said about the rival companies. As the rates are increased to meet the expenditure, the latter may remain same. Only assumption II is implicit.

COURSE OF ACTION

In these type of questions, a situation is presented and some courses of action are suggested in the context of that situation. The candidates are required to determine which course of action follows immediately from the given statement without letting their own perception influence the decision.

EXERCISE

Directions (Qs. 1 to 5) : *In each question below is given a statement followed by two courses of action numbered I and II. A course of action is a step or administrative decision to be taken for improvement, follow-up or further action in regard to the problems, policy, etc. on the basis of the information given in the statement. You have to assume everything in the statement to be true, then decide which of the given suggested courses of action logically follows for pursuing.*

Give answer (a) if only I follows; give answer (b) if only II follows; give answer (c) if either I or II follows; give answer (d) if neither I nor II follows and give answer (e) if both I and II follow.

1. *Statement :*
Although the Indian economy is still heavily dependent on agriculture, its share in global agricultural trade is less than the share of agricultural exports to total exports.
Courses of Action :
(*i*) Efforts should be made to increase our agricultural production.
(*ii*) The exports of non-agricultural commodities should be reduced.

2. *Statement :*
About 30 to 40 per cent of children who are enrolled, do not attend school on any given day.
Courses of Action :
(*i*) More schools should be started.
(*ii*) Reasons for this absenteeism should be found out.

3. *Statement :*
Certain mining industries in Gujarat may come to a standstill because of the notification issued by the Ministry of Environment and Forest banning mining operations and industries alike within 25 kms of National Park, the bird sanctuary and reserve forest areas.
Courses of Action :
(*i*) The Ministry should be asked to immediately withdraw the notification.
(*ii*) The Government should make efforts to shift the parks, sanctuaries and reserve forests to other non-mining areas.

4. *Statement :*
The Indian electronic component industry venturing into the West European markets faces tough competition from the Japanese.
Courses of Action :
(*i*) India should search for other international markets for its products.
(*ii*) India should improve the quality of the electronic components to compete with the Japanese in capturing these markets.

5. *Statement :*
Air export volumes have increased substantially over the past decade causing backlogs and difficulties for air cargo agents because of increased demand for space and service.
Courses of Action :
(*i*) Airlines and air cargo agents should jointly work out a solution to combat the problem.
(*ii*) The reasons for the increase in the volume of air export should be found out.

EXPLANATORY ANSWERS

1. (*d*) : India's share in global agricultural trade is less than the share of agricultural exports to total exports. Therefore, there is no necessity of increasing the agricultural production. Reducing the exports of non-agricultural commodity will not affect the share of agricultural exports. So, neither course of action follows.

2. (*d*) : About 30 to 40 per cent of enrolled children do not attend schools. Therefore, the decision to start more schools is pointless. The statement does not mention that a particular group of children do not attend schools. This means the percentage of absent children comprises of various children who are absent at different times. There cannot be specific reasons for this absenteeism. So, neither course of action follows.

3. (*d*) : The department cannot withdraw the notification because environment pollution must be checked around the game sanctuary and reserve forest areas. Further, it is coherent to shift the mining industries. So, neither course of action follows.

4. (*e*) : In the face of tough competition from the Japanese, India should either improve the quality of electronic components to capture the market or search for other international markets where Japanese have not captured the market. So, both the course of action follow.

5. (*a*) : The reasons for the increase in the volume of air exports according to the statement is, increase in demand for space and service. Therefore, the airlines and air cargo agents should jointly work out a solution to combat the problem. So, only course of action I follows.

VENN DIAGRAMS

In these type of questions, diagrammatic representation presents a logical illustration of particular class or statements based on which the questions are asked. A clear view of the diagram makes the concepts clear for attempting such questions.

EXERCISE

1. What is the number which is common to only two geometrical figures?

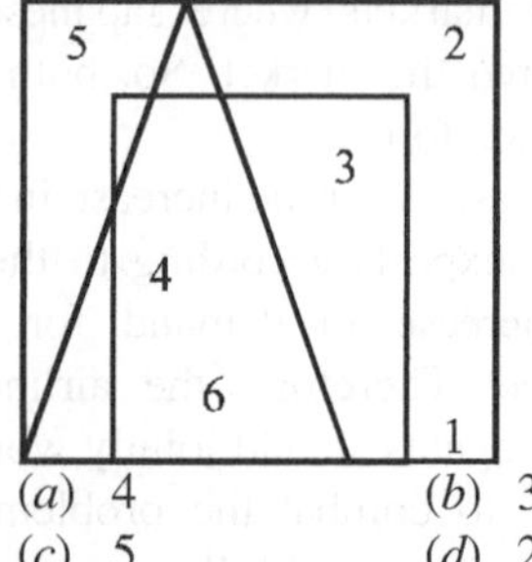

(*a*) 4 (*b*) 3
(*c*) 5 (*d*) 2

Directions (Qs. 2 and 3) : *In the following diagram, rectangle represents Hindi Announcers, circle represents English Announcers, square represents French Announcers, and triangle represents German Announcers.*

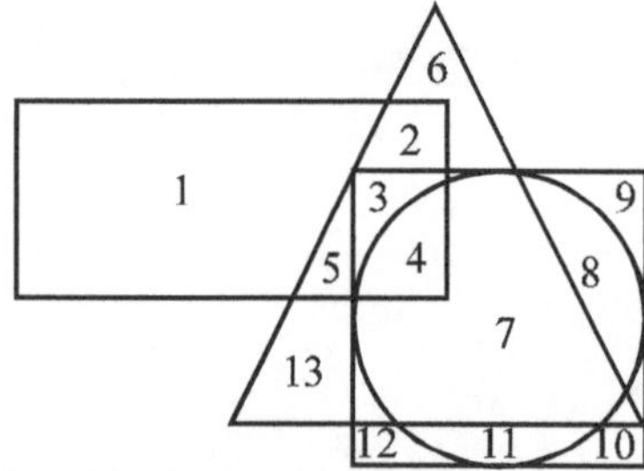

2. Which area represents those announcers who can present programmes in Hindi, French and German only?
(*a*) 1 (*b*) 2
(*c*) 3 (*d*) 4

3 Which area represents those announcers who can present programmes in French and English only?
(*a*) 7 (*b*) 9
(*c*) 11 (*d*) 13

Directions (Qs. 4 and 5) : *Study the diagram to answer these questions.*

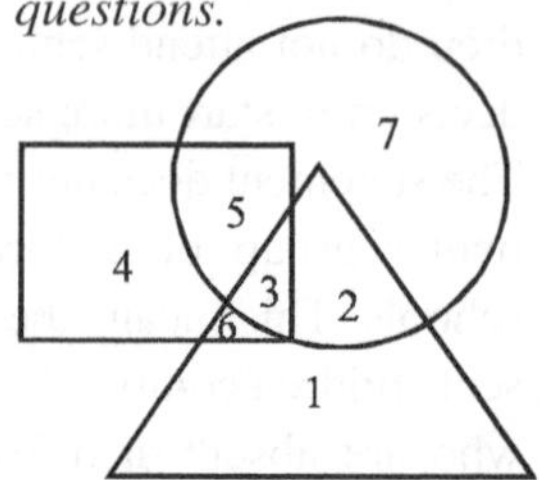

4. Which number is in all the geometrical figures?
(*a*) 5 (*b*) 6
(*c*) 2 (*d*) 3

5. Number 6 is in :
(*a*) Rectangle and triangle
(*b*) Circle and traingle
(*c*) Rectangle and circle
(*d*) Rectangle only

Directions (Qs. 6 to 9) : *In the following diagram*

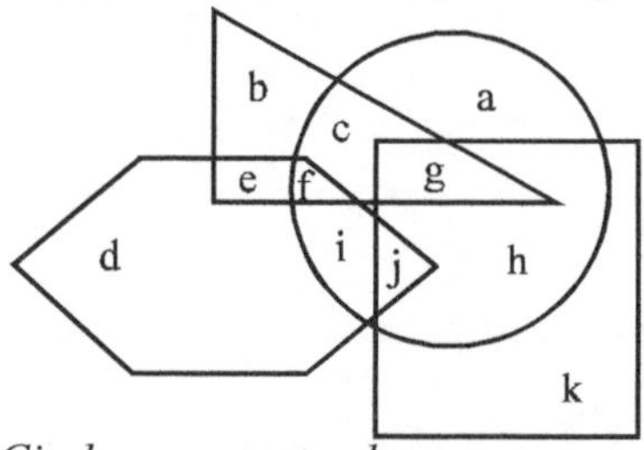

The Circle represents players
The Triangle represents outdoor games
The Hexagon represents indoor games and
The Square represents national level players
Study the diagram and answer the questions given below :

6. The letter in the section representing the players who play indoor games at national level is :
(*a*) f (*b*) i
(*c*) j (*d*) g

7. The letter representing the section of outdoor as well as indoor game players who do not play at the national level is :
(*a*) c (*b*) f
(*c*) e (*d*) i

8. The section representing national level players who do not play either outdoor or indoor games but still come under the category of players is :
(*a*) k (*b*) g
(*c*) c (*d*) h

9. Persons who play outdoor games but do not come under the category of players are represented in the section marked :
(*a*) b (*b*) c
(*c*) a (*d*) d

Directions (Qs. 10 to 13) : *Study the diagram given below.*

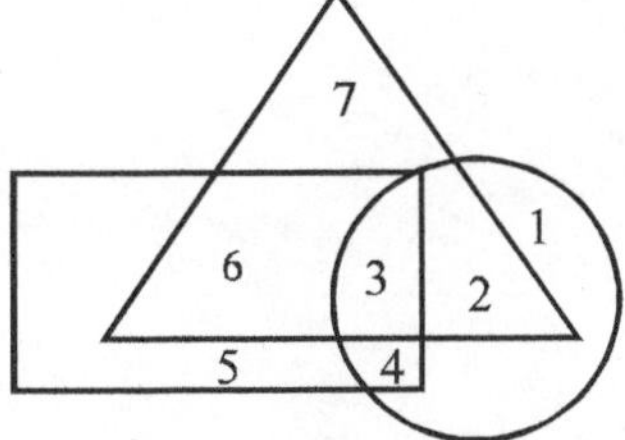

A college provides three different activities, students union represented by triangle, literary society represented by rectangle and social service league represented by circle.

10. Those who take part in both literary society and social service league but not in students union are represented by :
(*a*) 3 & 4 (*b*) 5 & 6
(*c*) 5 & 1 (*d*) 4

11. Those who take part in students union but not in social service league are represented by :
(*a*) 2 & 7 (*b*) 6 & 7
(*c*) 6 (*d*) 7

12. Those students who are members of literary society only and not of any other activity are represented by :
(*a*) 2 (*b*) 5
(*c*) 3 & 4 (*d*) 3

13. Those students who are members of all three groups are represented by :
(*a*) 2 (*b*) 3
(*c*) 4 (*d*) 6

EXPLANATORY ANSWERS

1. (*b*) :

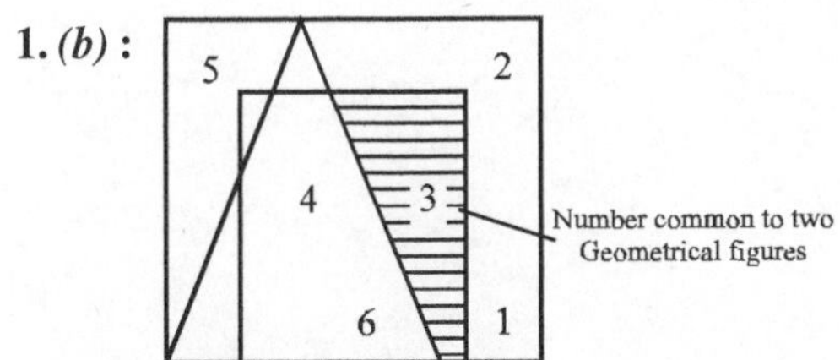

Note : Numbers 4 and 6 are common to all three geometrical figures.

2. (*c*), **3.** (*c*) :

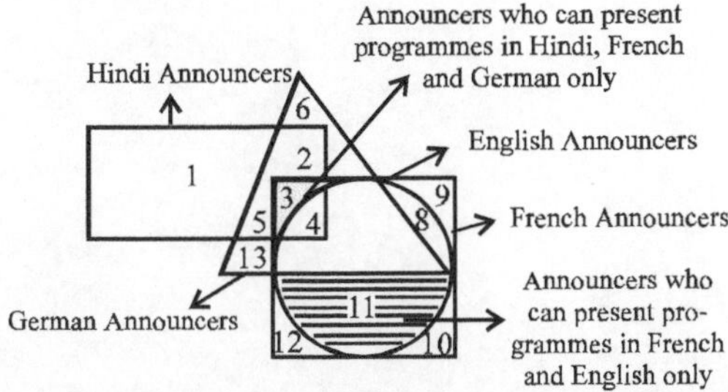

4. (*d*), **5.** (*a*) :

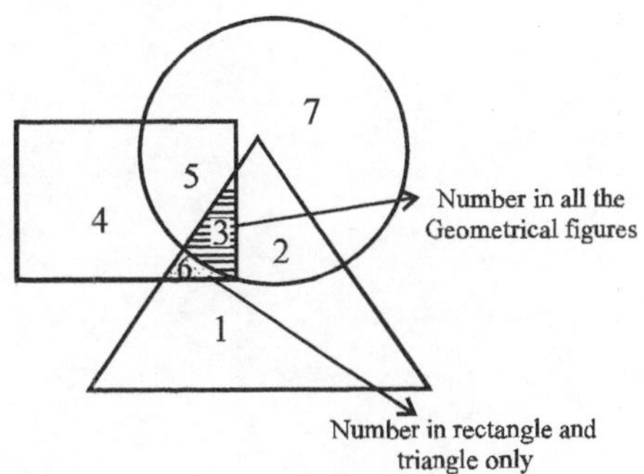

6. (*c*),
7. (*b*),
8. (*d*),
9. (*a*) :

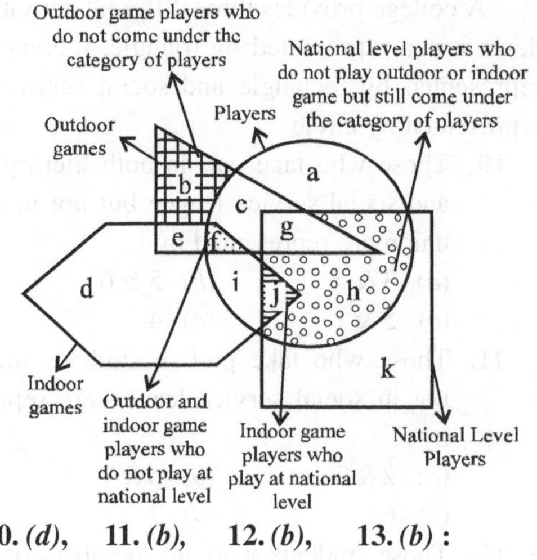

10. *(d)*, **11.** *(b)*, **12.** *(b)*, **13.** *(b)* :

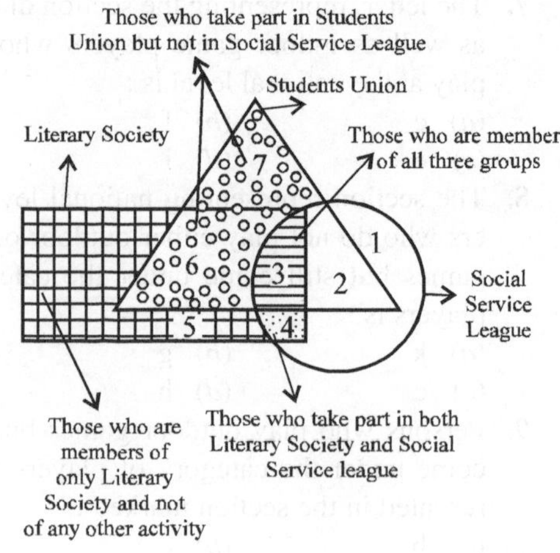

DIAGRAMMATIC PUZZLE

This test aims to judge your space visualisation, keen observation and analytical aptitude. In this test diagrams are given which may look puzzling. Questions are asked on the diagrams.

EXERCISE

1. How many squares are there in the figure given below?

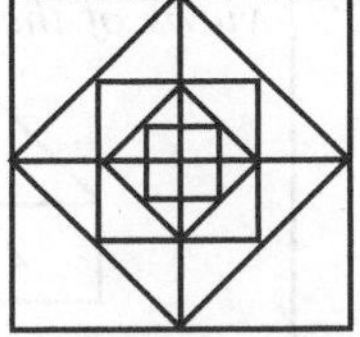

(*a*) 12
(*b*) 13
(*c*) 16
(*d*) 17

2. Find the number of squares in the following figure:

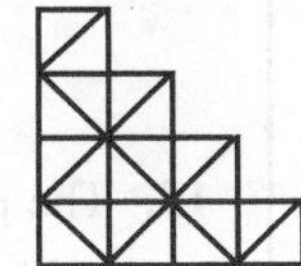

(*a*) 14
(*b*) 13
(*c*) 12
(*d*) 11

3. How many triangles are there in the figure given below?

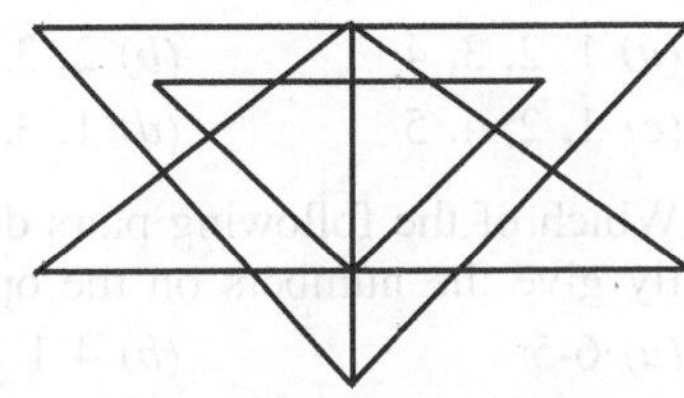

(*a*) 25 (*b*) 23
(*c*) 21 (*d*) 27

4.

```
                N
            I       K
        H       N       E
    T       I       K       R
        H       N       E
            I       K
                N
```

In how many different ways can the word THINKER be read from left to right in this diagram, each letter connecting to its neighbour along one of the marked lines.

(*a*) 16 (*b*) 12
(*c*) 8 (*d*) 20

5. Different designs can be made by placing a maximum of nine matchsticks. Which of the following designs cannot be made at all?

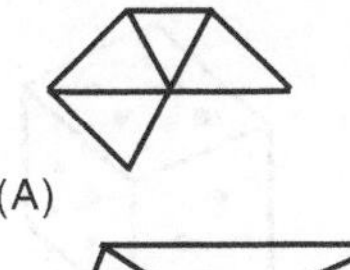
(A)

(B)

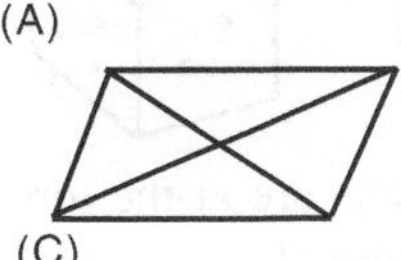
(C)

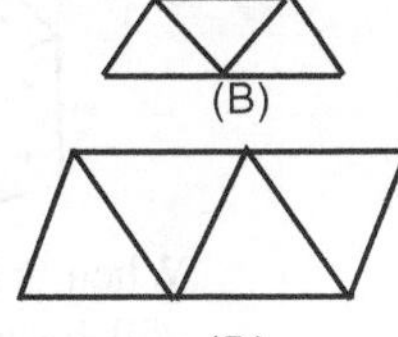
(D)

(*a*) A (*b*) B
(*c*) C (*d*) D

6. Two positions of a dice are shown below.

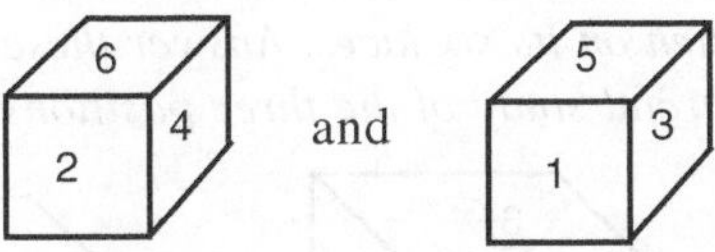

When 2 is at the bottom, what number will be at the top?

(*a*) 1 (*b*) 3
(*c*) 4 (*d*) 5

7. Six sides of a block are coloured Green, Blue, Red, Yellow, Orange and White in the following manner:

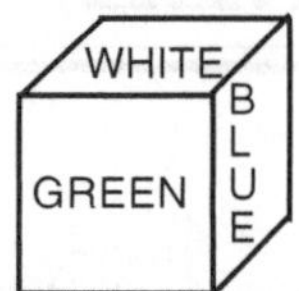

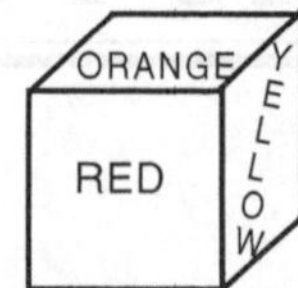

When Blue is on the top, which colour will be at the bottom?

(a) Orange (b) Red
(c) White (d) Yellow

8. Below are depicted the four different positions of a dice. Find the number of dots on the face opposite to the face with one dot.

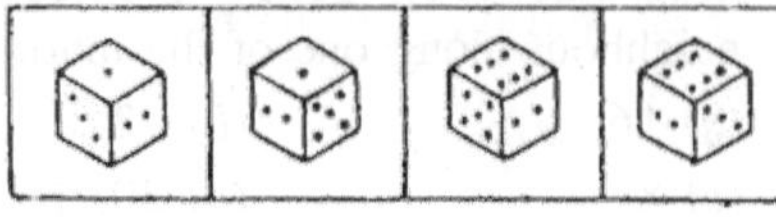

(a) 2 (b) 3
(c) 4 (d) 6

9. Two positions of a dice are shown below:

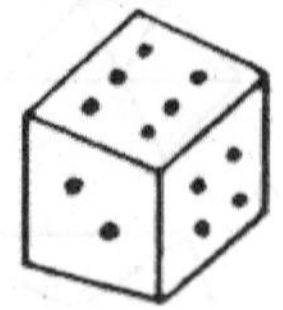

When 3 (three) dots are at the top, how many will be at the bottom?

(a) 1 (b) 2
(c) 4 (d) 5

Directions (Qs. 10 to 12): *Given below are three positions of the same cube having numbers 1 to 6 written on its six faces. Answer these questions after a careful study of the three positions of the cube.*

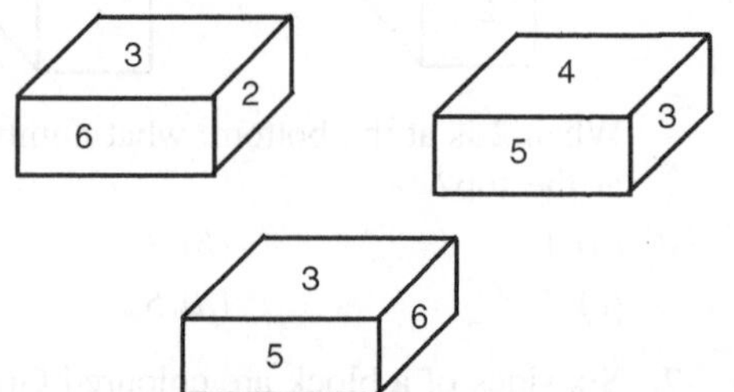

10. Which number occur's on the face opposite face 5?

(a) 5 (b) 3
(c) 2 (d) can't be determined

11. The face on the bottom in the first figure has the number:

(a) 5 (b) 1
(c) 4 (d) None of these

12. The number on the face opposite the face having number 6 is:

(a) 5 (b) 4
(c) 6 (d) 7

Directions (Qs. 13 to 15): *These questions are based on the following figures which depict three views of the same cube:*

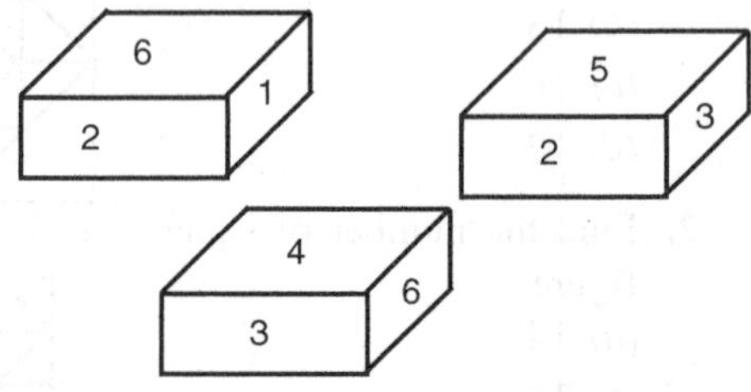

13. The number on the face opposite the face 1 is:

(a) 5 (b) 3
(c) 2 (d) 4

14. The numbers on the faces neighbouring the face marked 5 is:

(a) 1, 2, 3, 4 (b) 2, 3, 4, 6
(c) 1, 2, 4, 5 (d) 1, 3, 4, 6

15. Which of the following pairs does not correctly give the numbers on the opposite faces?

(a) 6-5 (b) 4-1
(c) 1-3 (d) 4-2

Directions (Qs. 16 to 18): *The figures given below show three positions of the same dice having 1, 2, 3, ...6 circles on its six faces. Answer these questions based on this dice.*

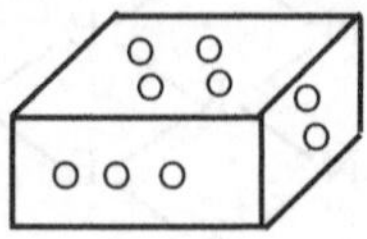
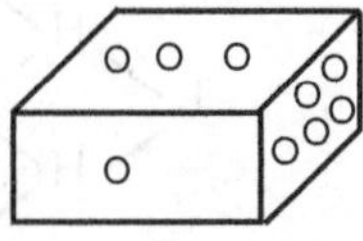
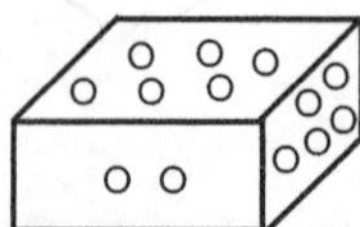

16. The number of circles on the face opposite to the one having three circles is:

(*a*) 6 (*b*) 5
(*c*) 7 (*d*) None of these

17. What is the number of circles on the face at the bottom of the first cube?

(*a*) 6 (*b*) 1
(*c*) 5 (*d*) None of these

18. How many circles will be there on the top face in the figure shown?

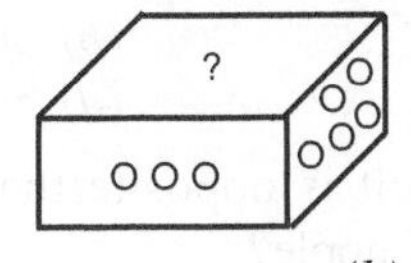

(*a*) 2 (*b*) 1
(*c*) 6 (*d*) 4

Directions (Qs. 19 and 20): *Study carefully the three views of the same cube shown below and then answer the questions.*

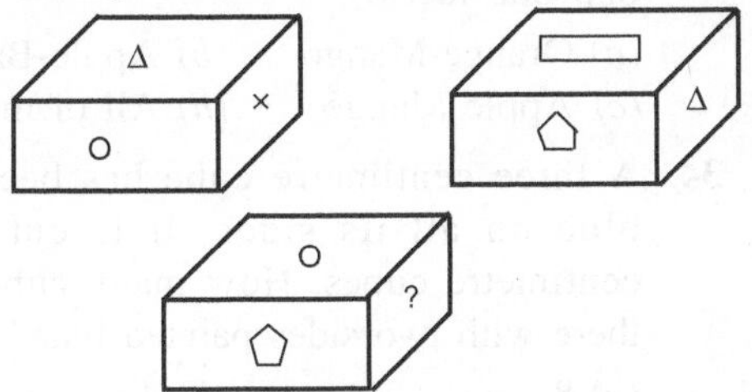

19. The figure on the face opposite the triangle is:

(*a*) pentagon
(*b*) circle
(*c*) question mark
(*d*) rectangle

20. Which of the following do not form correct pairs on opposite faces?

(*a*) circle-rectangle
(*b*) pentagon-cross
(*c*) rectangle-cross
(*d*) triangle-question mark

Directions (Qs. 21 and 22): *An electronics dealer selling colour TVs, VCRs and Computer (PCs) is offering Stereo Radio, Movable Trolley and Stainless Steel Rack free with these. The item which goes free with a particular item is written on the face opposite it on a cube. Two views of the cube are shown below:*

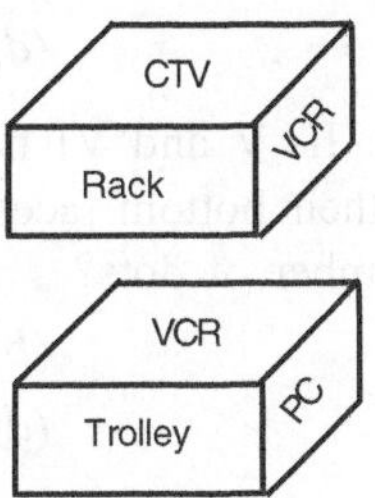

21. Stereo radio is being offered free with:

(*a*) Colour TV (*b*) Computer
(*c*) VCR (*d*) VCR or TV

22. The item offered free with the Computer is:

(*a*) Stainless Steel Rack
(*b*) Trolley
(*c*) Radio
(*d*) Radio or Trolley

Directions (Qs. 23 to 27): *In the following questions six dices with their top faces erased have been given. The opposite faces of the dices have dots which add up to thirteen. Work out the number of dots on the top faces, according to the question and spot your answer from amongst the given alternatives.*

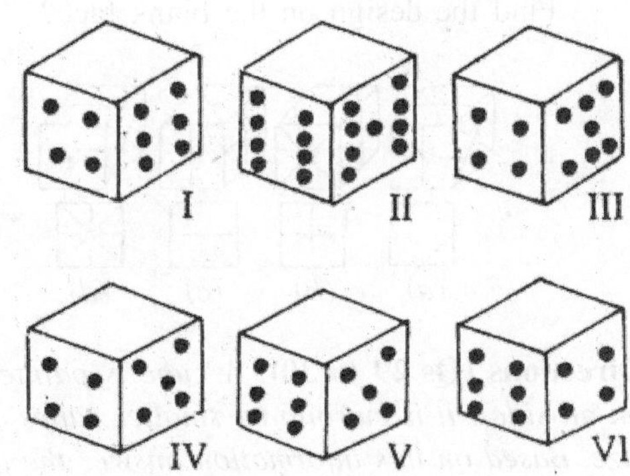

23. If the even numbered dices have odd number of dots at their top faces, what would be the total number of dots?

(*a*) 19 (*b*) 18
(*c*) 17 (*d*) 16

24. If dices, I, III and IV have odd number of dots at their top faces, what would be the total number of dots?

(*a*) 15 (*b*) 18

(*c*) 21 (*d*) 17

25. If dices, II, V and VI have even number of dots at their bottom faces, what would be the total number of dots?

(*a*) 18 (*b*) 20

(*c*) 16 (*d*) 24

26. If dices I, II and III have odd number of dots on their upper face and dices IV, V and VI have even number of dots on their bottom faces, then what would be the difference in the total number of top face dots between these two sets?

(*a*) 8 (*b*) 4

(*c*) 0 (*d*) 1

27. If the odd numbered dices have even number of dots at their bottom faces, what would be the total number of dots?

(*a*) 20 (*b*) 22

(*c*) 24 (*d*) 18

28. A cubical block with designs in its faces is presented as viewed from different directions. Find the design on the blank face?

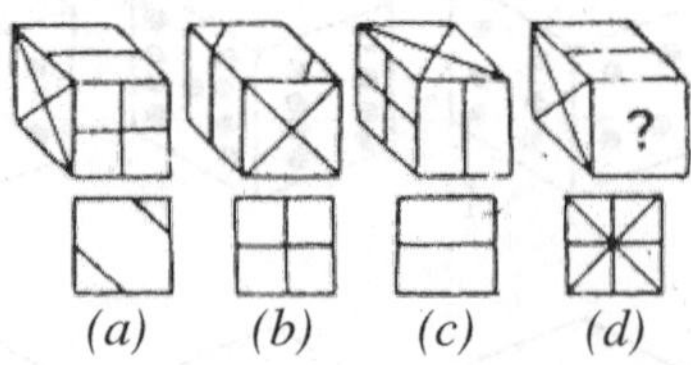

Directions (Qs 29 to 30): *A cube is painted white on all sides. It is cut into 64 smaller cubes of equal size. Based on this information answer the question given below.*

29. How many smaller cubes are painted on one side only?

(*a*) 4 (*b*) 8

(*c*) 16 (*d*) 24

30. How many smaller cubes are not painted at all?

(*a*) 8 (*b*) 6

(*c*) 4 (*d*) 1

Directions: *A toy cube has pictures of different fruits on its six faces. The top face has the picture of orange. Banana is adjacent to melon and orange. Apple is not at the bottom of the cube and melon is opposite the peach.*

31. The neighbouring faces of the sixth fruit mango, do not have the picture of:

(*a*) apple (*b*) orange

(*c*) peach (*d*) banana

32. Which fruit is opposite the face having the picture of apple?

(*a*) Banana (*b*) Peach

(*c*) Orange (*d*) Mango

33. Which one of the following does not represent the correct pair of fruits on the opposite faces?

(*a*) Orange-Mango (*b*) Apple-Banana

(*c*) Apple-Mango (*d*) All of the above

34. A three centimetre cube has been painted blue on all its sides. It is cut into one centimetre cubes. How many cubes will be there with two sides painted blue?

(*a*) 8 (*b*) 4

(*c*) 6 (*d*) 12

35. A cube is coloured with different colours on each side. Red is at the base and white at the top. The colours green, yellow, blue and purple respectively are painted on the four sides of the cube, in the clockwise direction. When the yellow side is changed as the base of the cube, which colour will be on the top?

(*a*) BLUE (*b*) GREEN

(*c*) PURPLE (*d*) RED

36. A four centimetre cube has been painted blue on all its sides. It is then cut into one cm cubes. How many cubes will be there with only one side painted?

(*a*) 24 (*b*) 16

(*c*) 8 (*d*) 32

EXPLANATORY ANSWERS

1. *(d)*
2. *(a)*
3. *(d)*
4. *(d)*
5. *(c)*
6. *(b)*
7. *(b)*
8. *(d)*
9. *(c)*

10. *(c)* 6, 2, 4, 5 are neighbouring faces of 3. 1 is opposite to 3. Also, 5 has neighbours 4, 3, 6 and 1. Hence 2 is opposite to 5.

11. *(b)* 3 and 1 form opposite pairs as shown in the above explanations.

12. *(b)*

13. *(b)* Neighbours of face 3 are faces marked 2, 5, 4 and 6. Therefore face 1 must be opposite to 3.

14. *(a)* 1, 2, 3, 4 are neighbours of 6. Therefore 6 and 5 must be on opposite faces. Hence neighbours of 5 are also 1, 2, 3 and 4.

15. *(b)*

16. *(a)* 2, 4, 1 and 5 circles are neighbouring faces of 3.

17. *(c)* 5 circles' face has neighbouring faces with 1, 3, 2 and 6 circles. Hence 4 and 5 circles faces form opposite pairs.

18. *(a)*

19. *(c)* The neighbouring faces of the face having a triangle on it have circle, cross mark, rectangle and pentagon marked on these as can be seen from Fig. (1) and (3). Therefore, the question mark must be opposite the triangle.

20. *(c)* Pentagon is opposite cross mark.

21. *(c)* Since neighbouring faces of VCR have CTV, Rack, Trolley and PC, it follows that Stereo radio is written opposite the VCR and hence is offered free with it.

22. *(a)* Considering the neighbouring of rack (Fig. 1), these are VCR, CTV, radio (which is opposite to VCR) and Trolley (Personal Computer) cannot be its neighbour, because then it goes free with CTV, (which is not true). Hence Rack must be free with a Personal Computer.

23. *(b)*
24. *(a)*
25. *(d)*
26. *(c)*
27. *(d)*
28. *(b)*
29. *(d)*
30. *(a)*

[**Notes to Qs. 29 and 30.** Of the 64 smaller cubes, 8 are painted on 3 sides, 24 are painted on 2 sides, 24 are painted on one side and 8 are not painted at all.]

31. *(b)* Because mango is on the face opposite to orange.

32. *(a)* Banana is on the face opposite to apple.

33. *(c)* Apple is not at the bottom, so it cannot be opposite to orange, which is at the top. Melon and peach are opposite each other, so none of these will be opposite to orange. Also, banana is one of its neighbours. So, the sixth fruit mango must be opposite to orange, and at the bottom.

34. *(d)*

35. *(c)* The sides are painted green, yellow, blue and purple respectively. So the colour opposite each will be the alternate one, *i.e.*, when yellow colour is at the base purple colour will be at the top.

36. *(a)* One side of the cube has four such cubes, therefore six sides of the cube will have 24 such cubes with only one side painted.

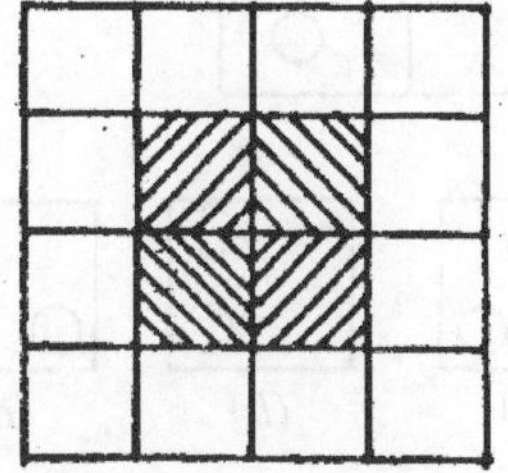

COMPLETING AN INCOMPLETE PATTERN

This test aims at judging the ability to comprehend correlations between geometric figures and diagrams and to perceive the structure of the design in its totality in order to select the appropriate part from amongst the answer figures for completion of each incomplete pattern.

In this test, a pattern/figure is given, a portion of which is left blank or incomplete. From the answer figures, you are required to select the figure which fits into the blank space in the incomplete figure.

EXERCISE

Directions (Qs. 1 to 18): *In each of the following questions a figure or a pattern or a design is given. A portion of that figure/pattern/design is blank or shown with a question mark. Below it are given four alternative figures. Choose a figure from the alternative figures which complete the given figure/pattern or design.*

1.

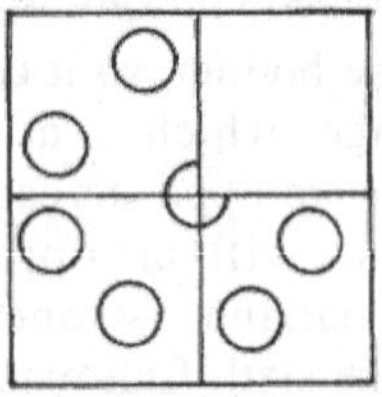

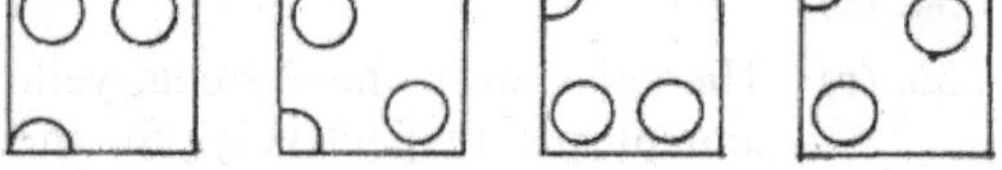

(a) (b) (c) (d)

2.

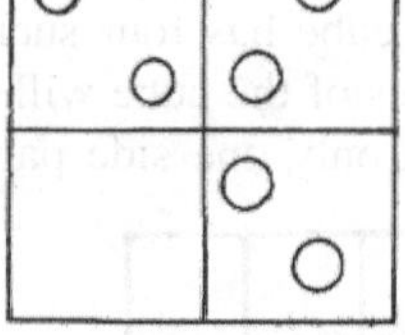

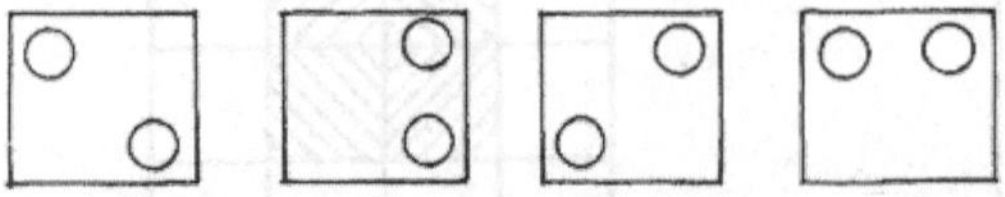

(a) (b) (c) (d)

3.

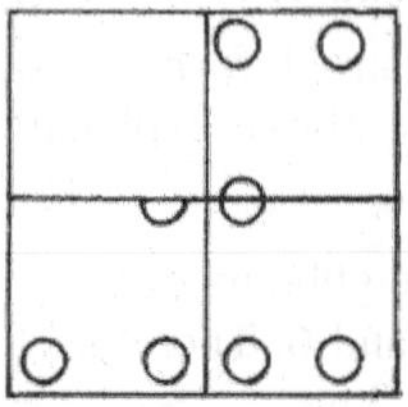

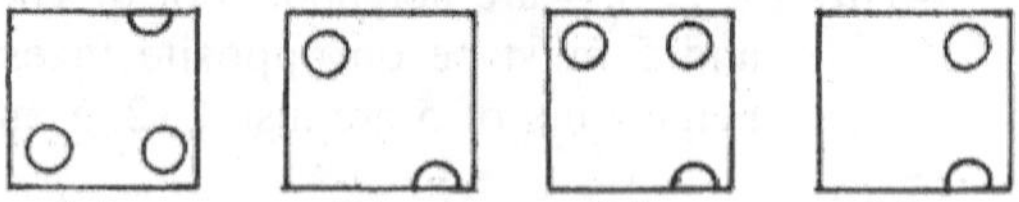

(a) (b) (c) (d)

4.

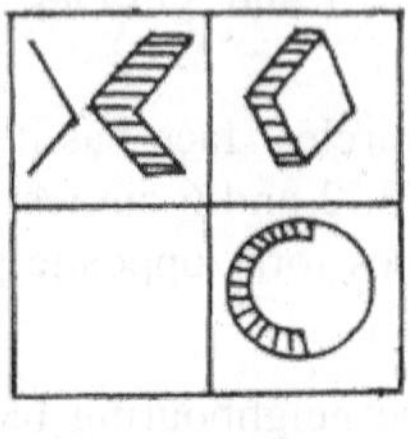

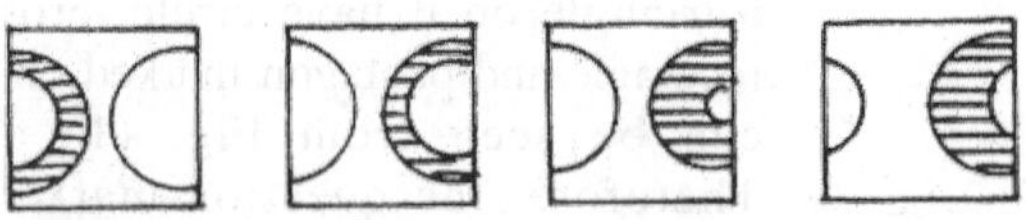

(a) (b) (c) (d)

5.

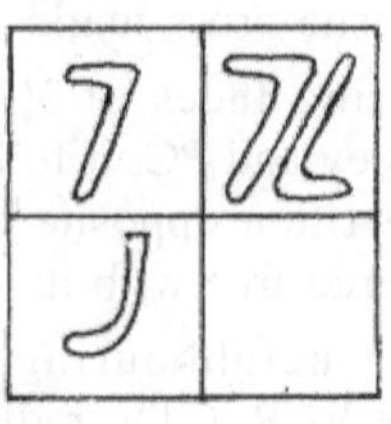

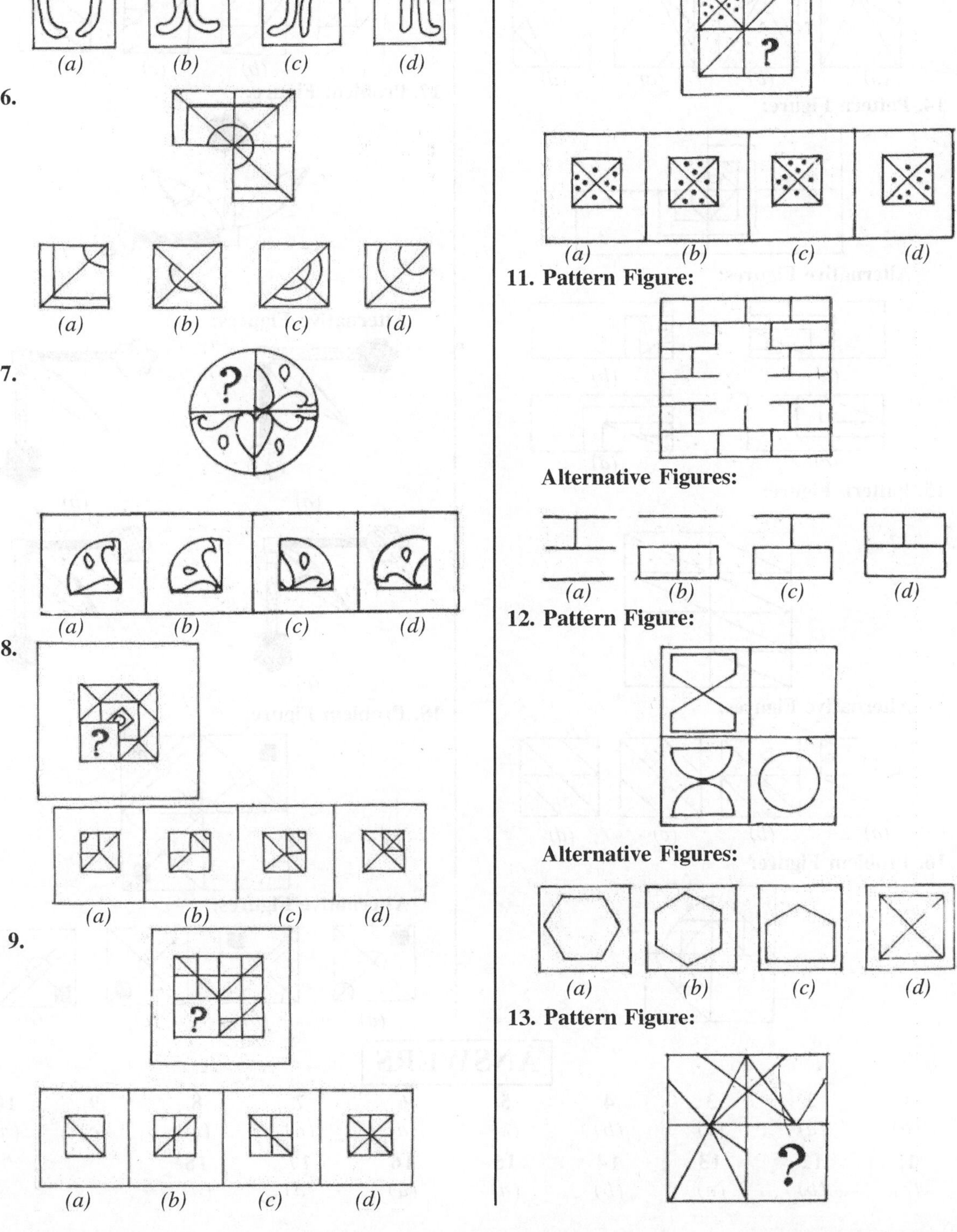

11. Pattern Figure:

Alternative Figures:

(a) (b) (c) (d)

12. Pattern Figure:

Alternative Figures:

(a) (b) (c) (d)

13. Pattern Figure:

?

Alternative Figures:

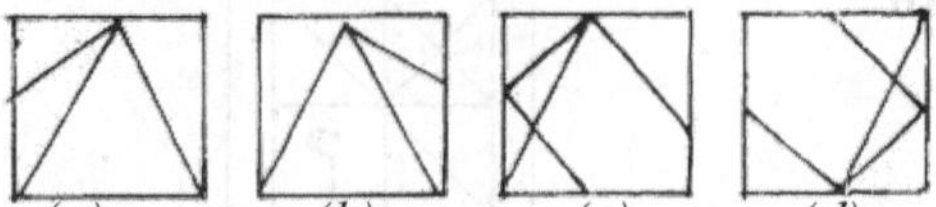

(a) (b) (c) (d)

14. Pattern Figure:

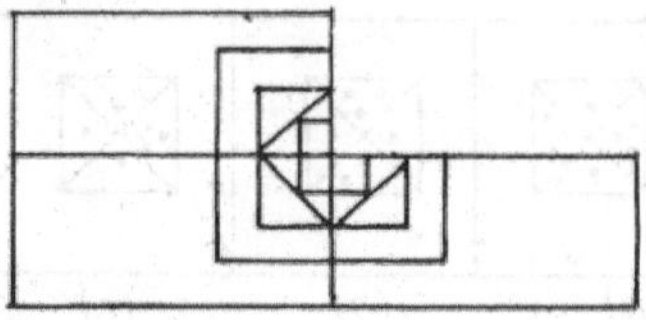

Alternative Figures:

(a) (b)

(c) (d)

15. Pattern Figure:

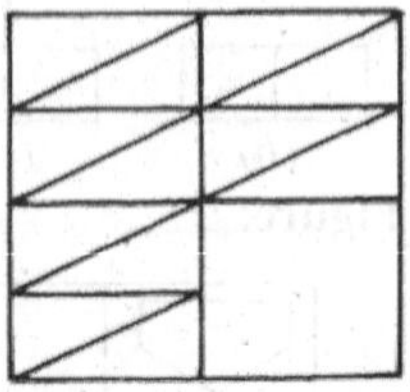

Alternative Figures:

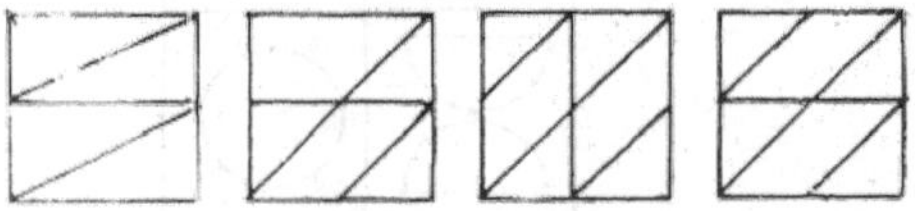

(a) (b) (c) (d)

16. Problem Figure:

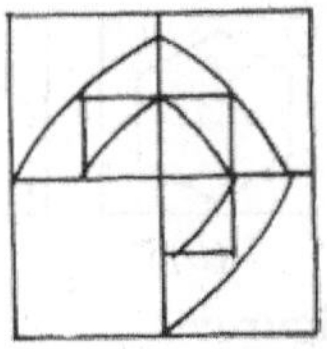

Alternative Figures:

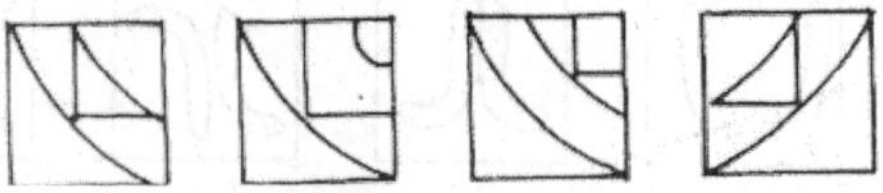

(a) (b) (c) (d)

17. Problem Figure:

Alternative Figures:

(a) (b)

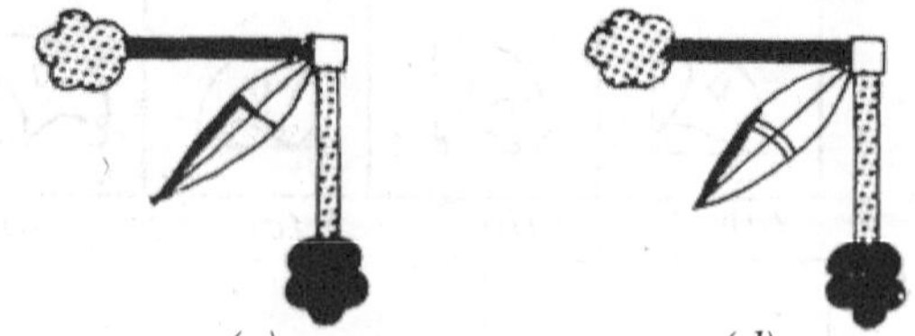

(c) (d)

18. Problem Figure:

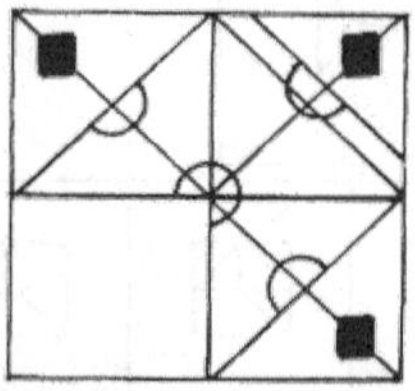

Alternative Figures:

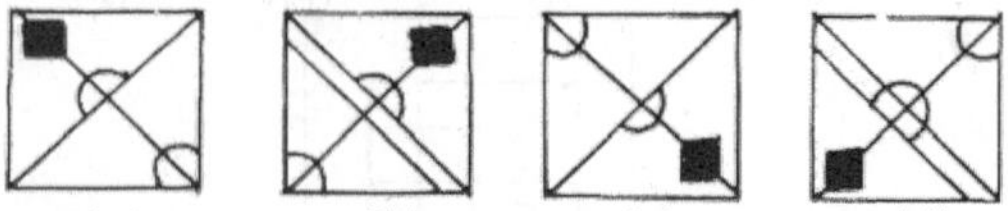

(a) (b) (c) (d)

ANSWERS

1	2	3	4	5	6	7	8	9	10
(b)	(c)	(c)	(b)	(c)	(a)	(d)	(c)	(c)	(a)
11	**12**	**13**	**14**	**15**	**16**	**17**	**18**		
(c)	(b)	(a)	(b)	(a)	(a)	(d)	(d)		

SPOTTING HIDDEN PATTERN

In this test, the problem figure comprises just one figure.

Below it are given four alternative figures. Of these four alternative figures, one figure is such that the problem figure is hidden into it. Candidates must observe very keenly the problem figure. They must then try to make a search of that (problem figure) among the alternative figures. It requires undiluted shape perception and sharp analytical capability to pin point the hiddern figure/design out of a large and jumbled figure.

EXERCISE

Directions: *In each of the following questions a figure is given at the top. Below it are given four figure alternatives. In each question, the figure given at the top is hidden in one of the four alternatives. Choose that alternatives.*

1. **Question Figure:**

Alternative Figures:

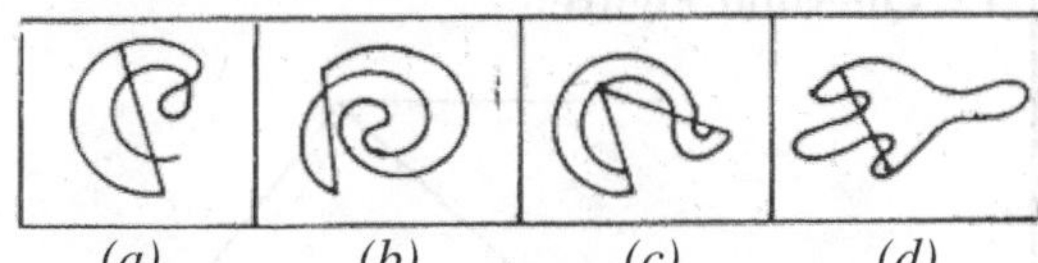

(a) (b) (c) (d)

2. **Question Figure:**

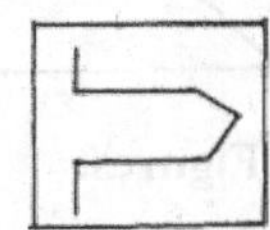

Alternative Figures:

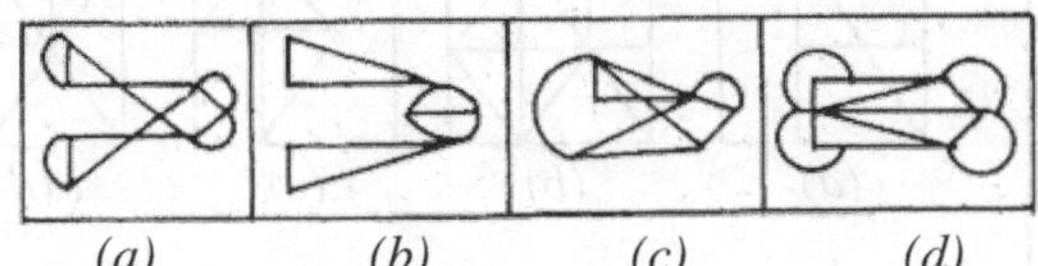

(a) (b) (c) (d)

3. **Question Figure:**

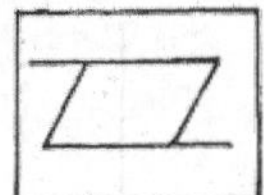

Alternative Figures:

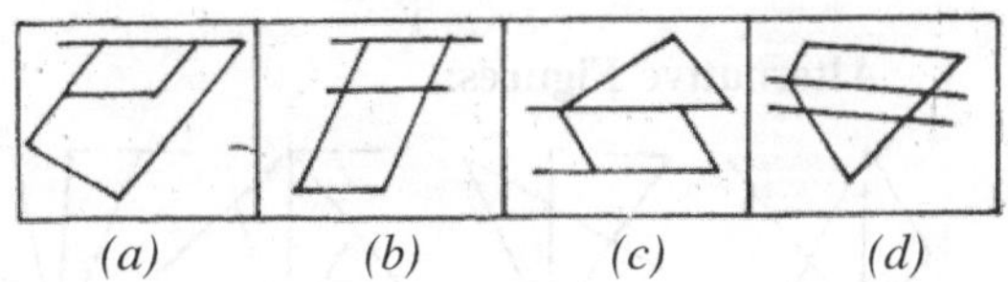

(a) (b) (c) (d)

4. **Question Figure:**

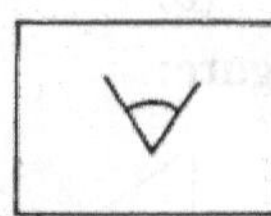

Alternative Figures:

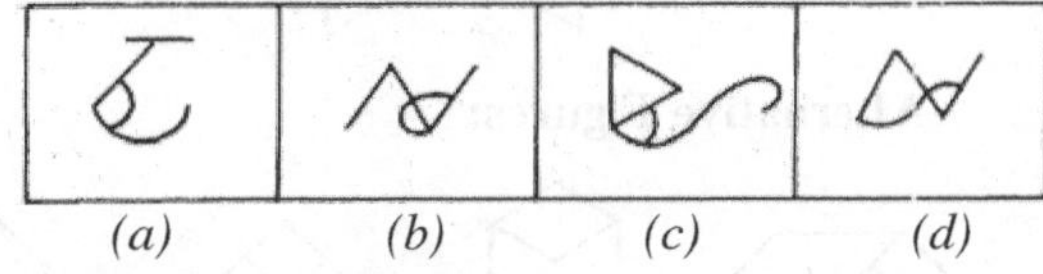

(a) (b) (c) (d)

5. **Question Figure:**

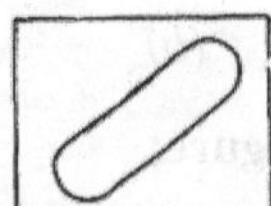

Alternative Figures:

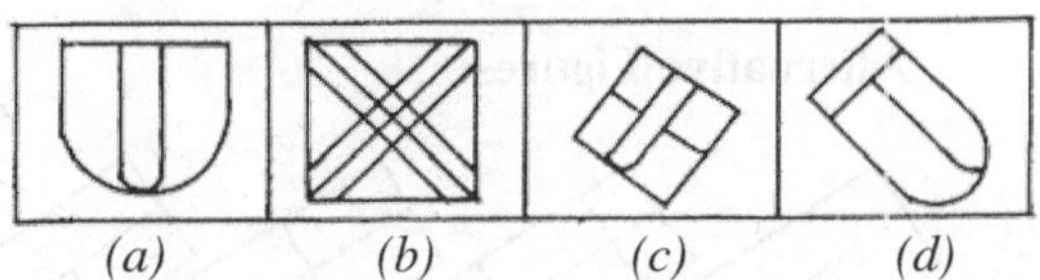

(a) (b) (c) (d)

6. **Question Figure:**

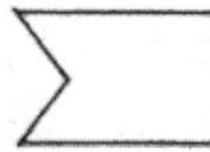

Alternative Figures:

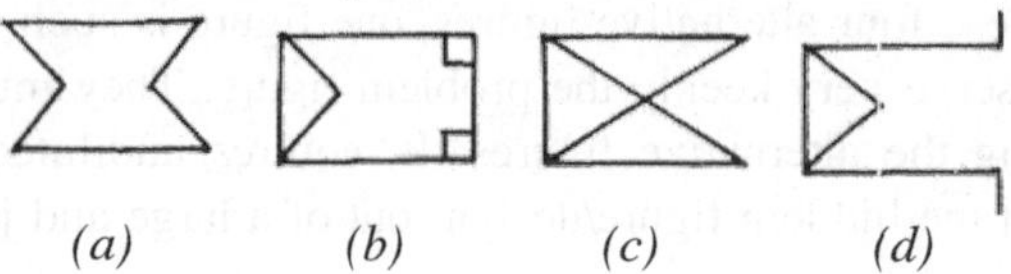

(a) (b) (c) (d)

7. **Question Figure:**

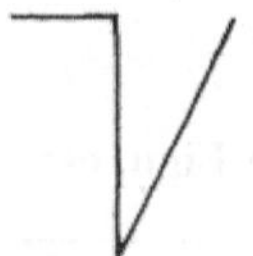

Alternative Figures:

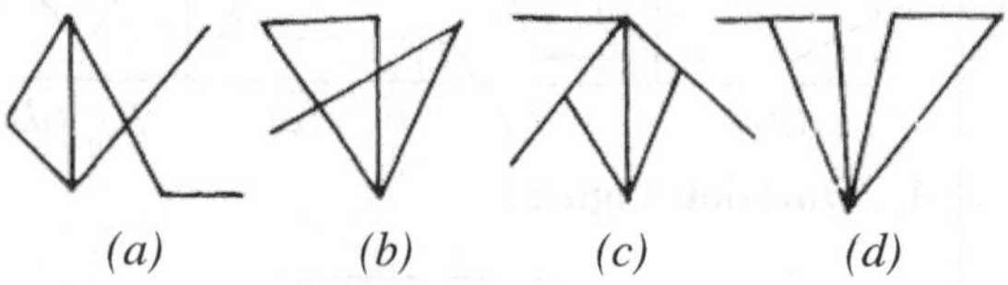

(a) (b) (c) (d)

8. **Question Figure:**

Alternative Figures:

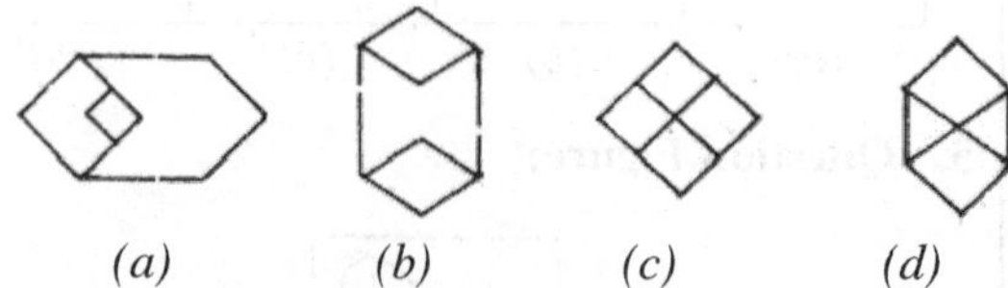

(a) (b) (c) (d)

9. **Question Figure:**

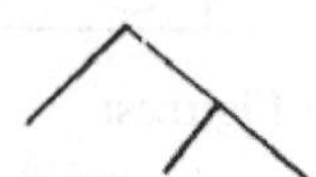

Alternative Figures:

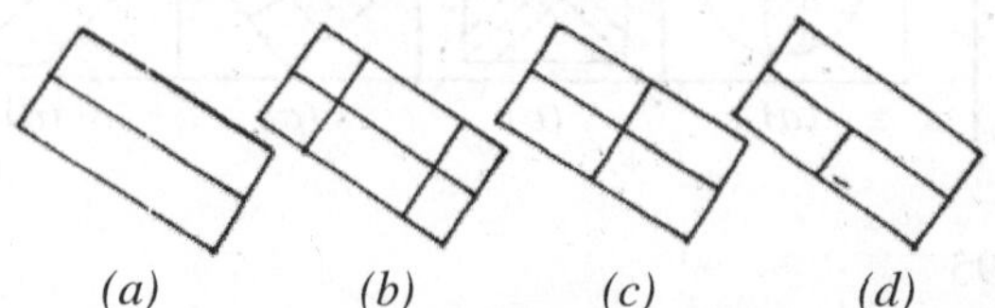

(a) (b) (c) (d)

10. **Question Figure:**

Alternative Figures:

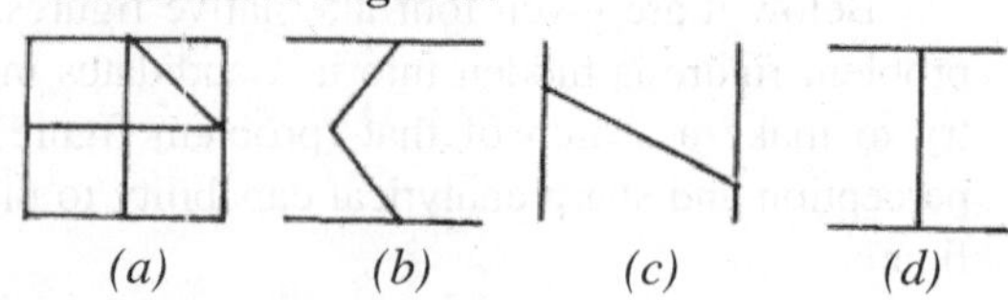

(a) (b) (c) (d)

11. **Question Figure:**

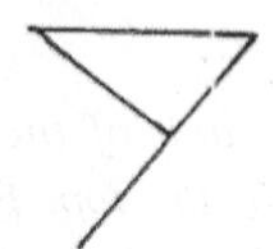

Alternative Figures:

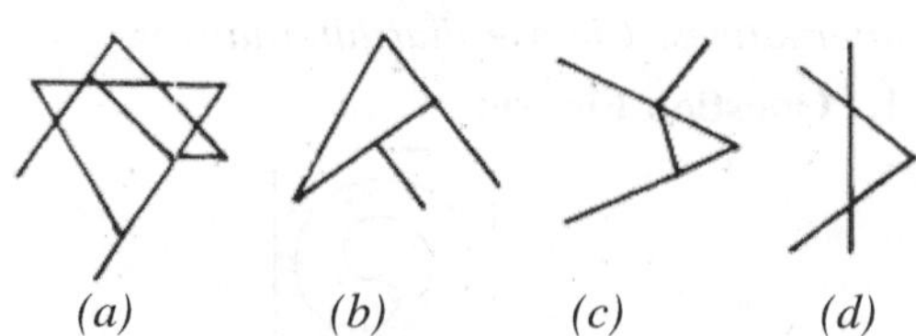

(a) (b) (c) (d)

12. **Question Figure:**

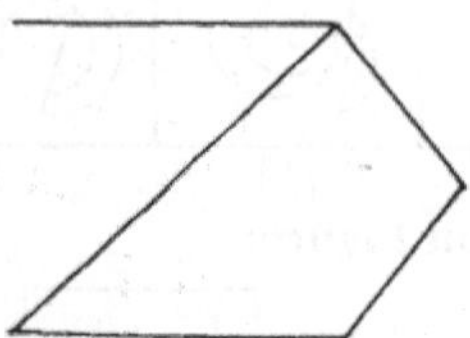

Alternative Figures:

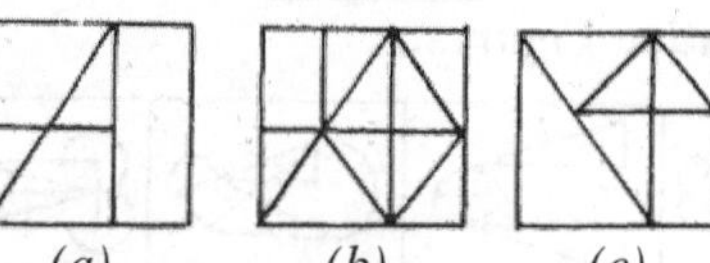

(a) (b) (c) (d)

13. **Question Figure:**

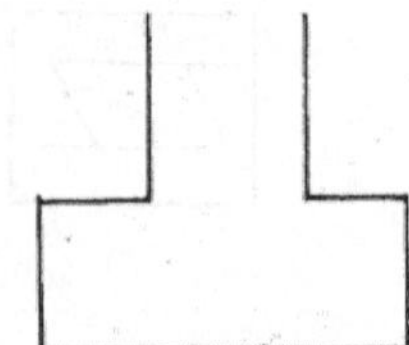

Alternative Figures:

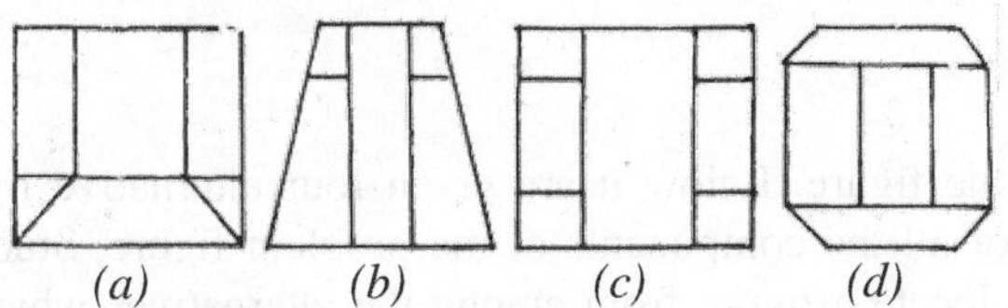

(a) (b) (c) (d)

14. Question Figure:

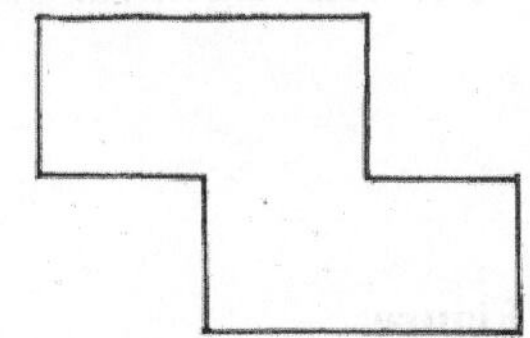

Alternative Figures:

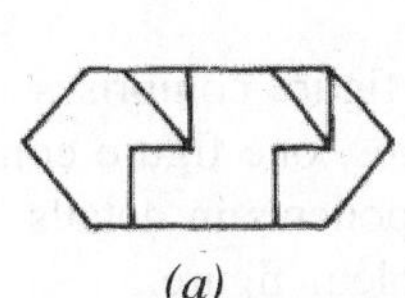

(a)

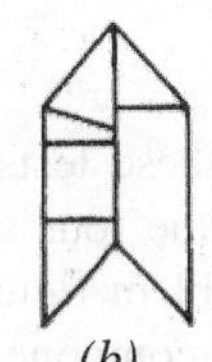

(b)

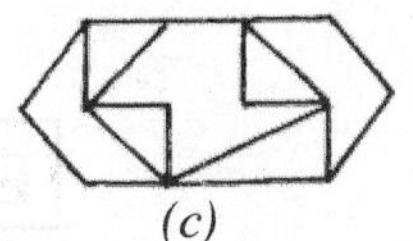

(c)

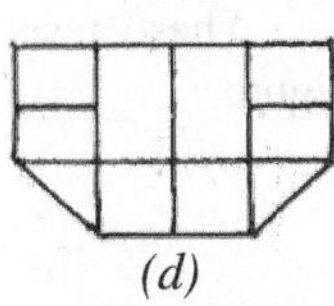

(d)

ANSWERS

1	2	3	4	5	6	7	8	9	10
(b)	(a)	(c)	(d)	(b)	(b)	(b)	(b)	(d)	(c)
11	**12**	**13**	**14**						
(b)	(b)	(a)	(c)						

COMPONENTS OF FIGURES

In these tests, the problem figure comprises only one figure. Below it are given four alternative figures. Of the four alternative figures, one figure consists of all the components of the problem figure. Study the problem figure and its components in details. Then locate a figure from among the alternatives which has the components of the problem figure.

These tests also include questions on parts-whole perception and rearrangement of parts of a given figure.

EXERCISE

TYPE - I

Directions (Qs. 1 to 13): *In these questions a figure is given. Its components are given in one of the four alternative figures given below. Choose the alternative figure which has the components of the given figure.*

1. Given Figure:

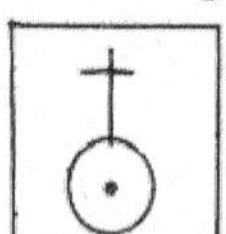

Alternative Figures:

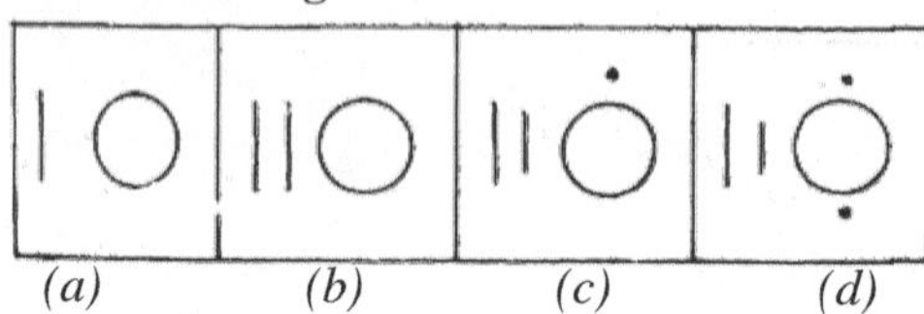

(a) (b) (c) (d)

2. Given Figure:

Alternative Figures:

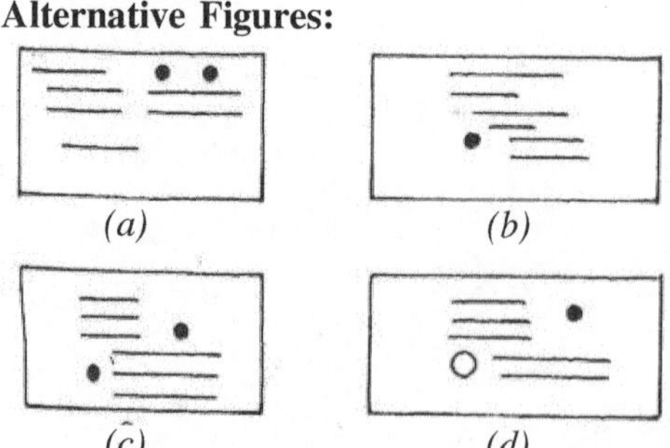

(a) (b) (c) (d)

3. Given Figure:

Alternative Figures:

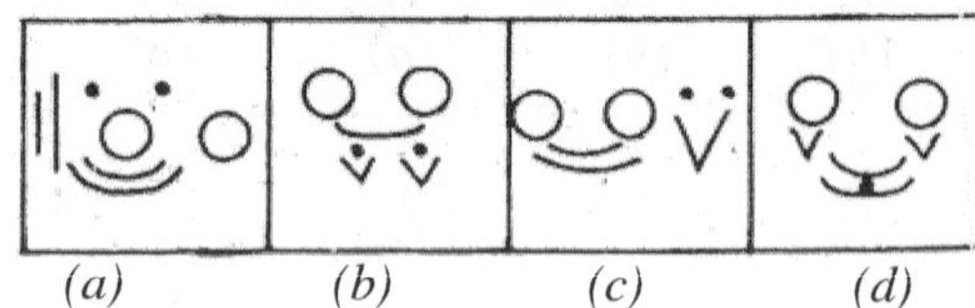

(a) (b) (c) (d)

4. Given Figure:

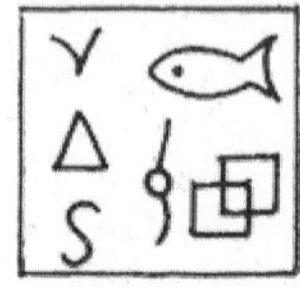

Alternative Figures:

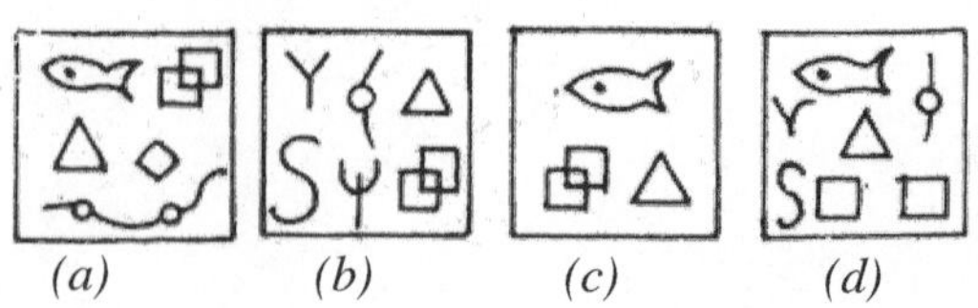

(a) (b) (c) (d)

5. Given Figure:

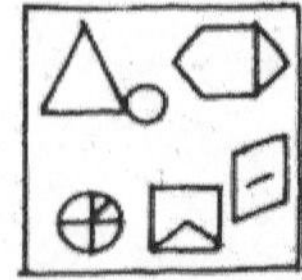

Alternative Figures:

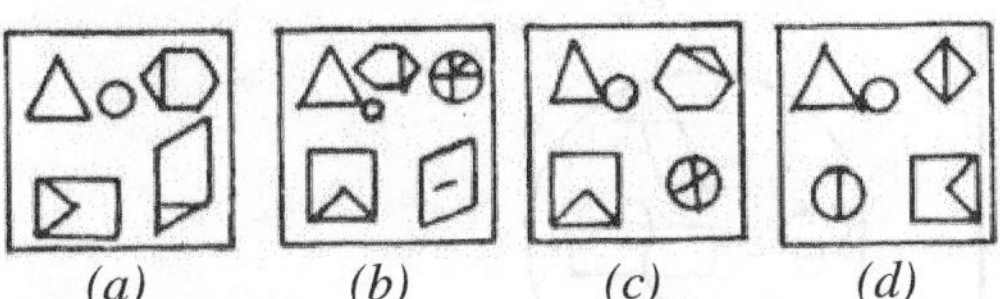

(a) (b) (c) (d)

6. Given Figure:

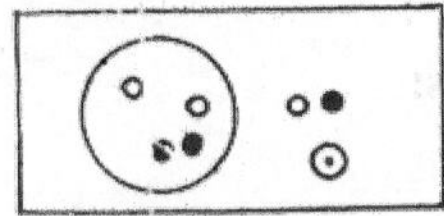

Alternative Figures:

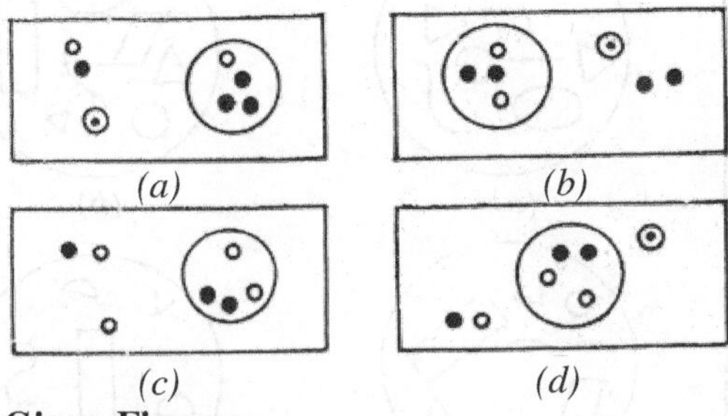

(a) (b) (c) (d)

7. Given Figure:

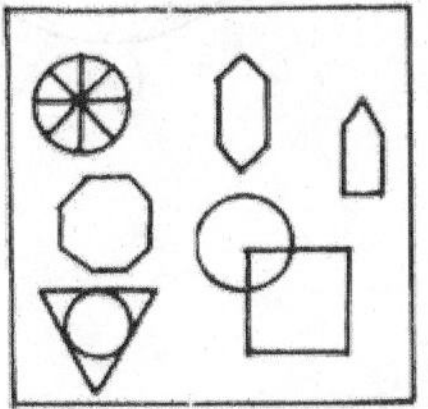

Alternative Figures:

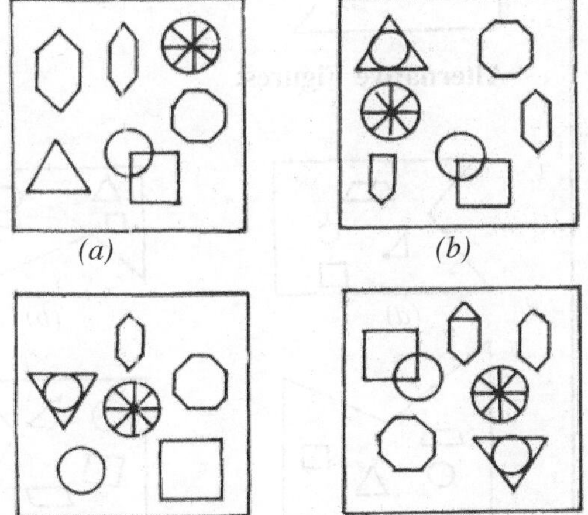

(a) (b) (c) (d)

8. Given Figure:

Alternative Figures:

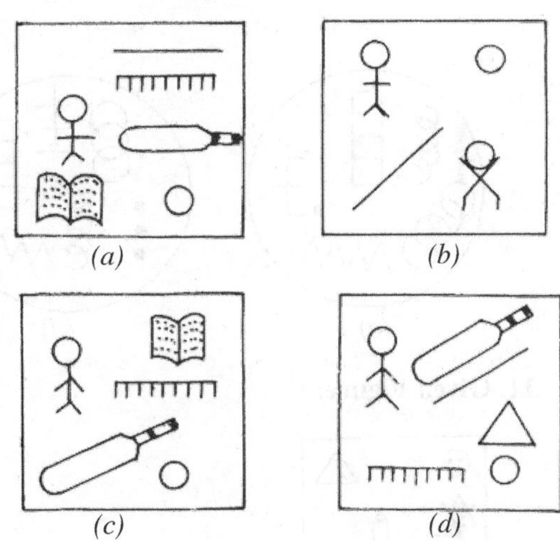

(a) (b) (c) (d)

9. Given Figure:

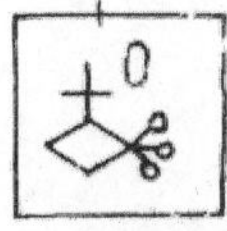

Alternative Figures:

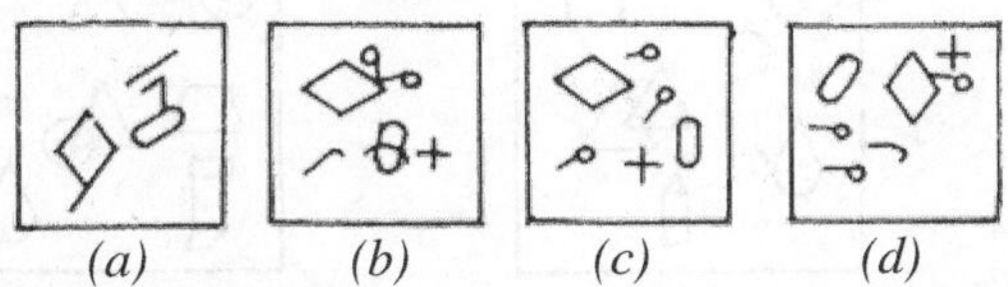

(a) (b) (c) (d)

10. Given Figure:

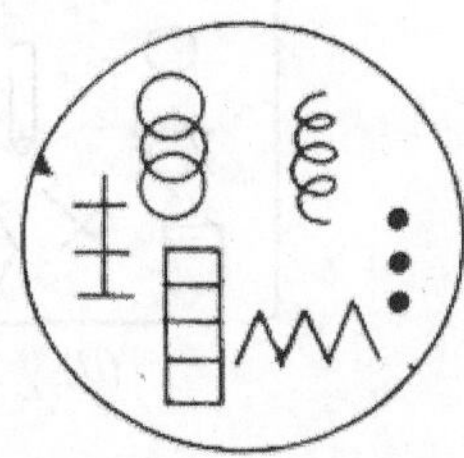

Alternative Figures:

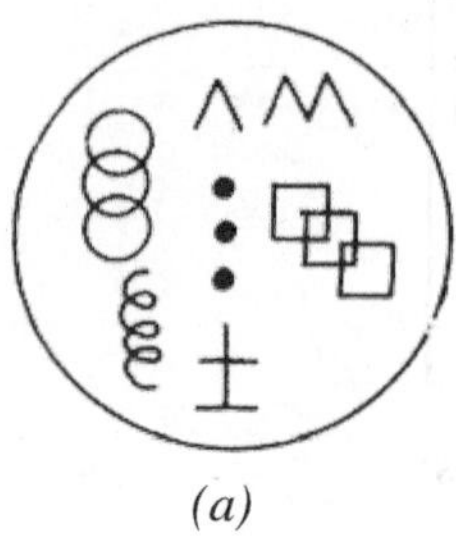

(a)

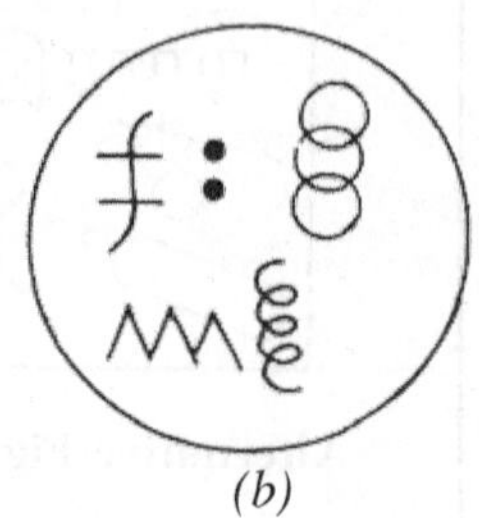

(b)

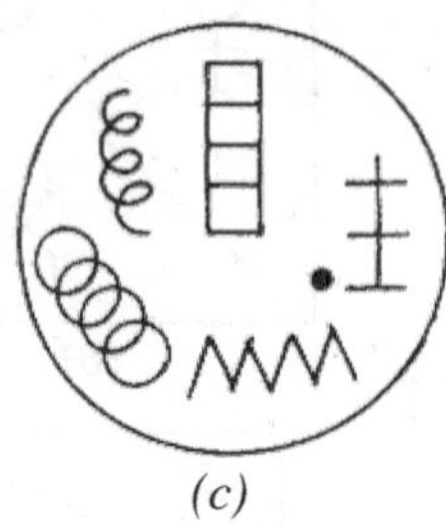

(c)

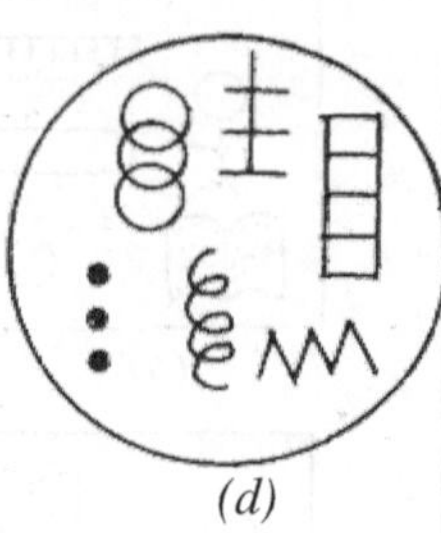

(d)

11. Given Figure:

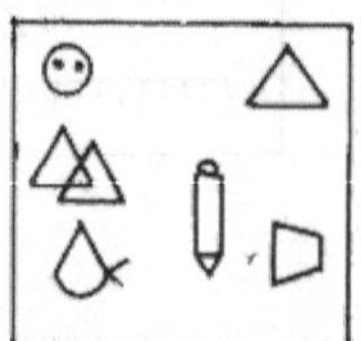

Alternative Figures:

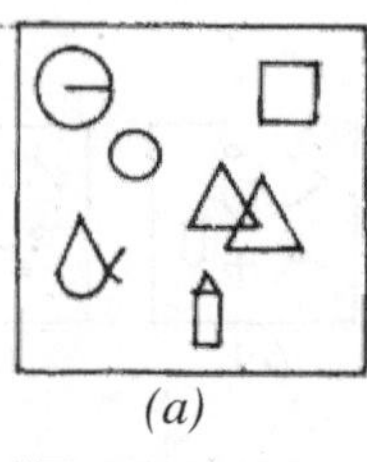

(a)

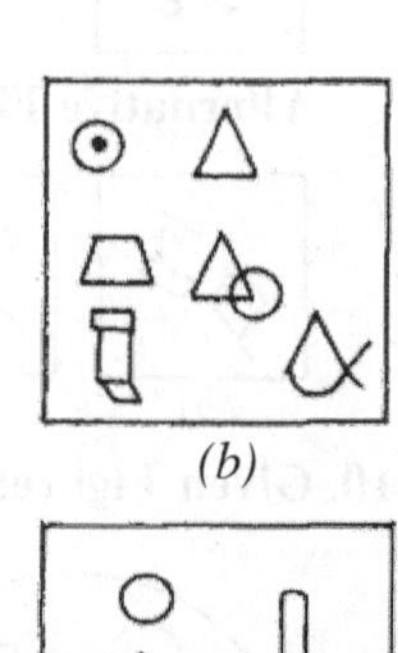

(b)

(c)

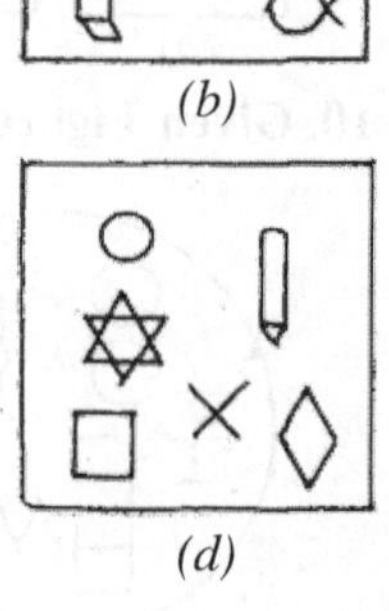

(d)

12. Given Figure:

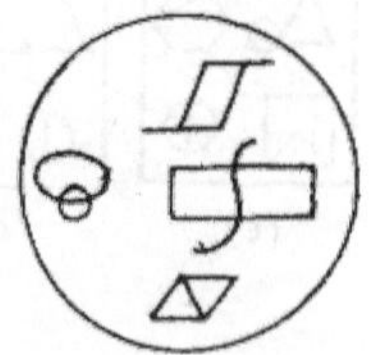

Alternative Figures:

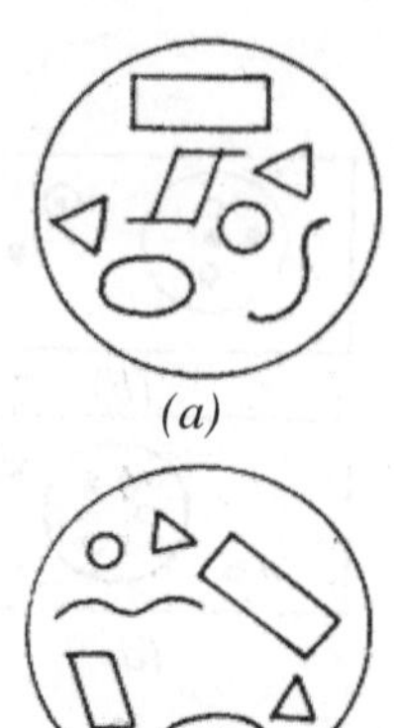

(a)

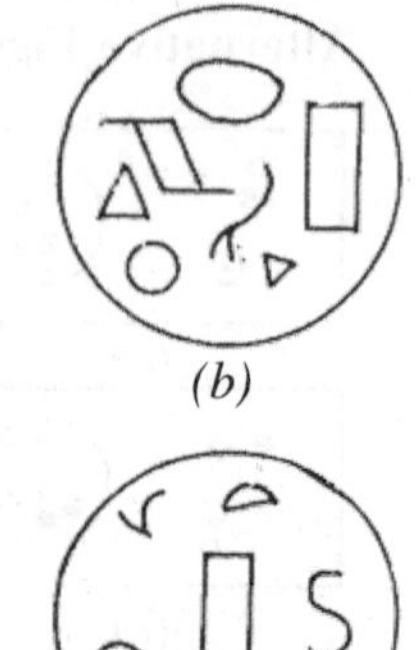

(b)

(c)

(d)

13. Given Figure:

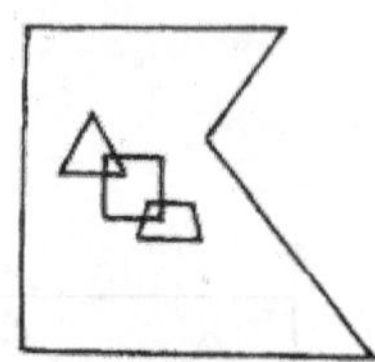

Alternative Figures:

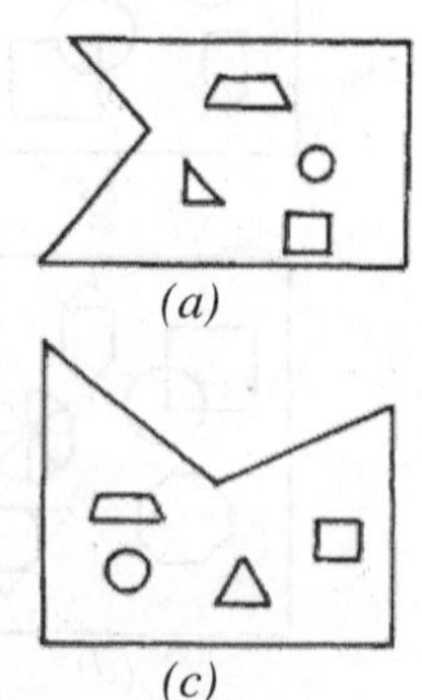

(a)

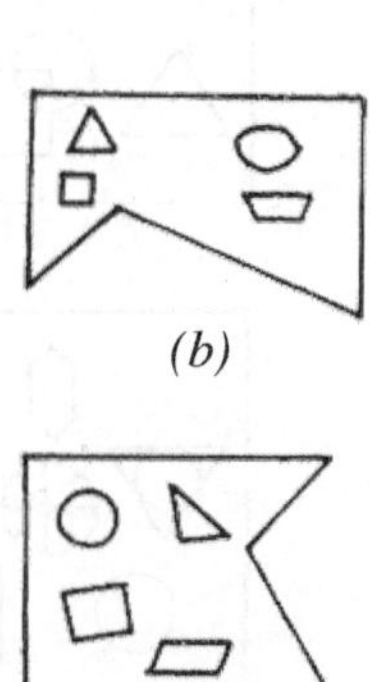

(b)

(c)

(d)

TYPE - II

Directions (Qs. 14 and 15): *In the following questions which of the alternatives will exactly make up the key figure?*

14. Key Figure:

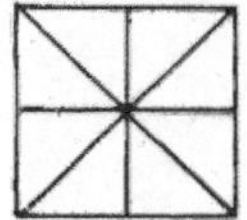

Alternative Figures:

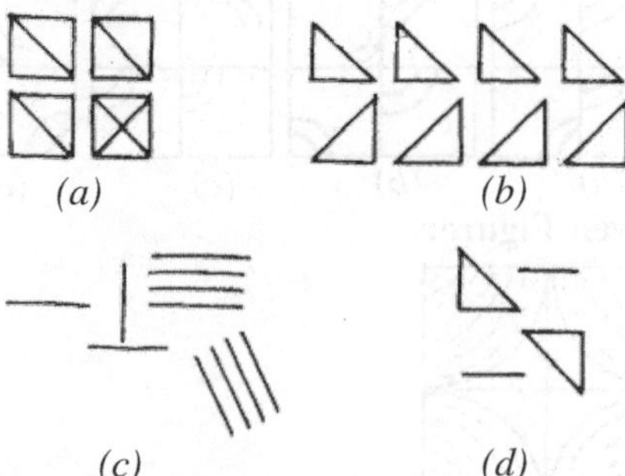

15. Key Figure:

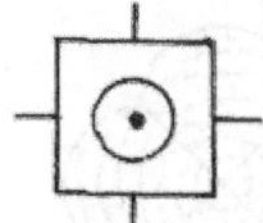

Alternative Figures:

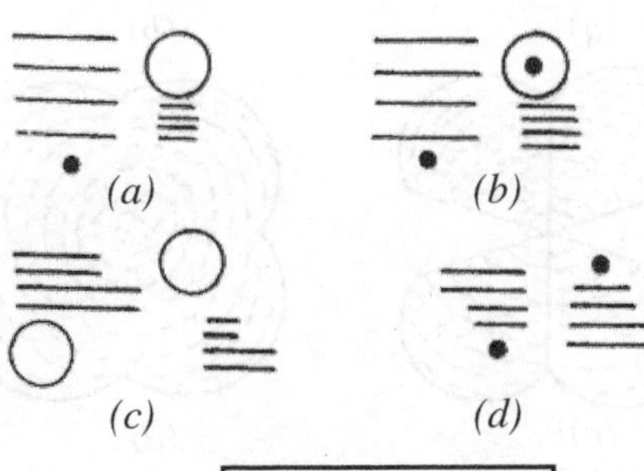

TYPE - III

Directions (Qs. 16 to 21): *In the Problem Figure you will find cut-out pieces of one of the response figures A, B, C or D given below. In each question identify the Response figure of which cut-out pieces are given in the problem figure.*

16. Problem Figure:

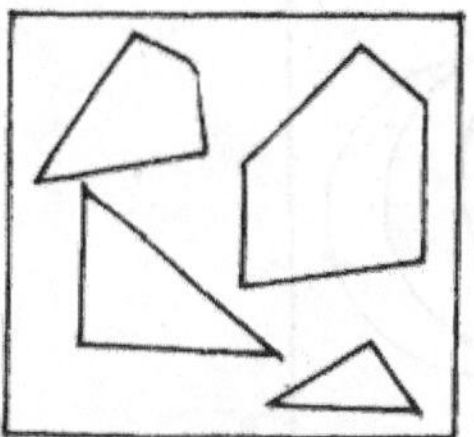

Answer Figures:

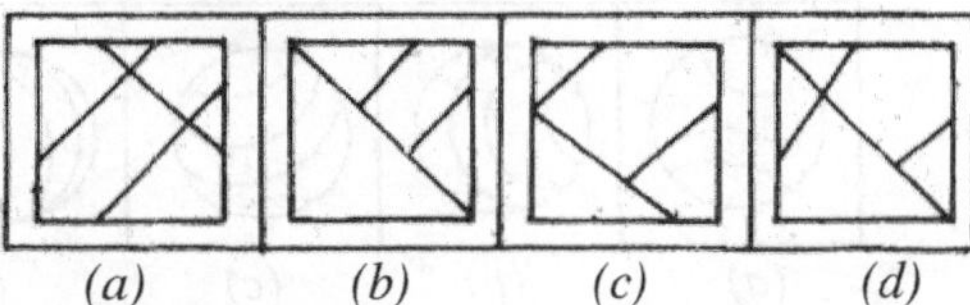

17. Problem Figure:

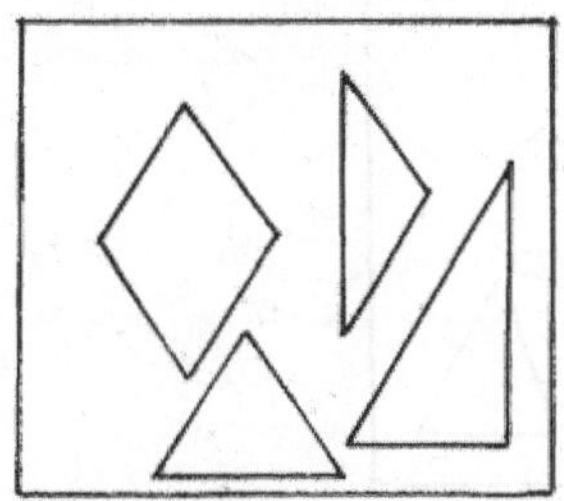

Answer Figures:

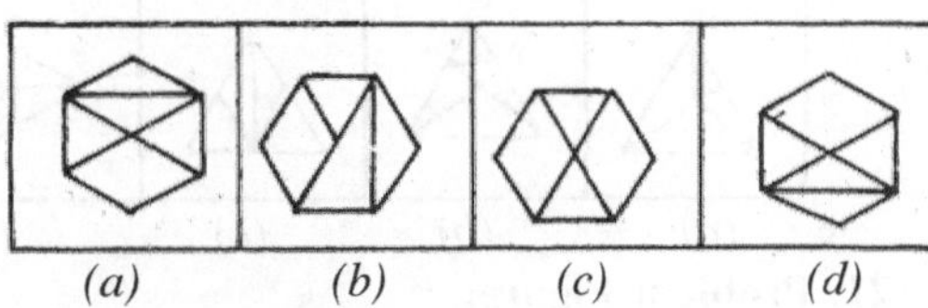

18. Problem Figure:

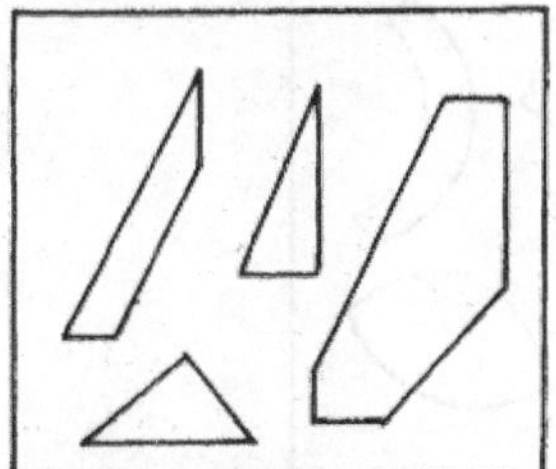

Answer Figures:

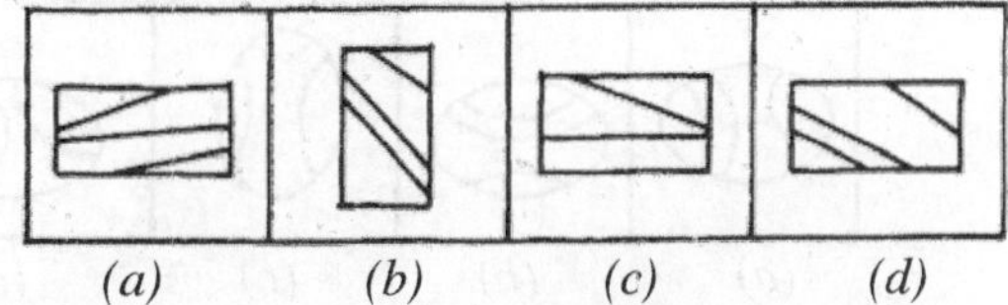

19. Problem Figure:

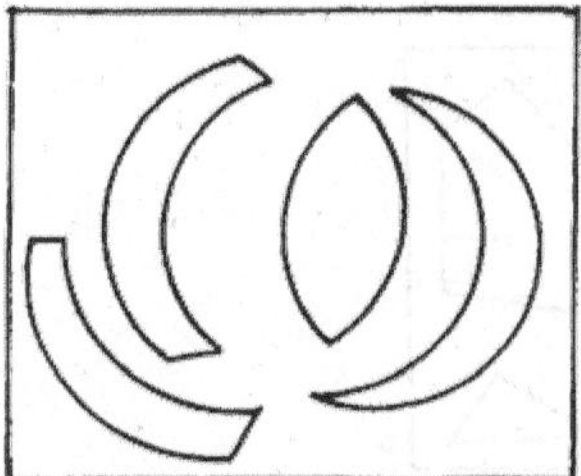

Answer Figures:

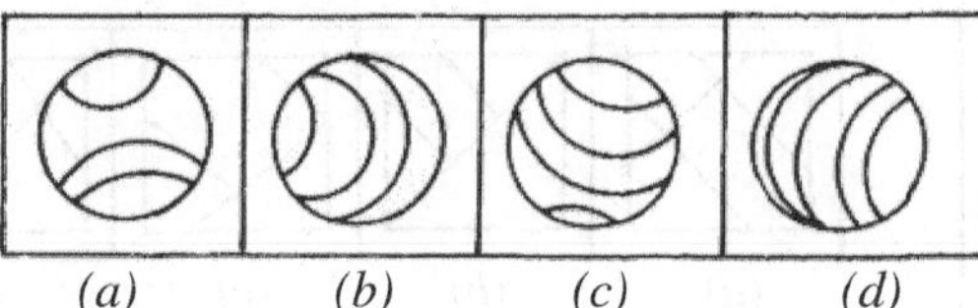

(a) (b) (c) (d)

20. Problem Figure:

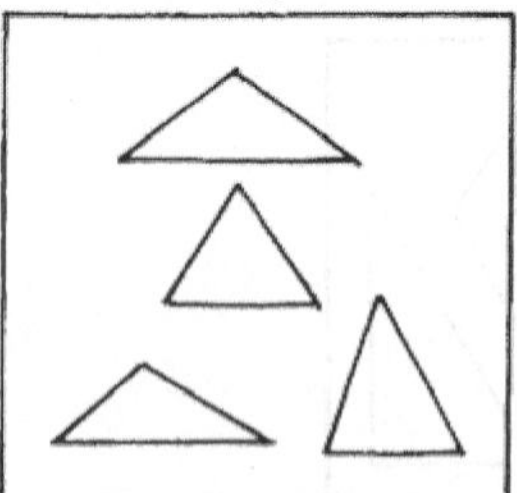

Answer Figures:

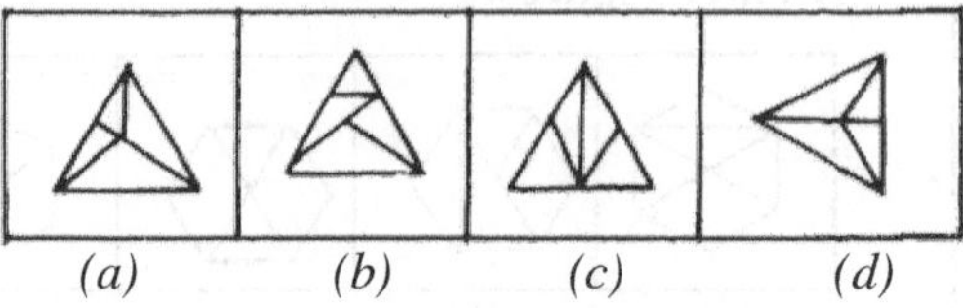

(a) (b) (c) (d)

21. Problem Figure:

Answer Figures:

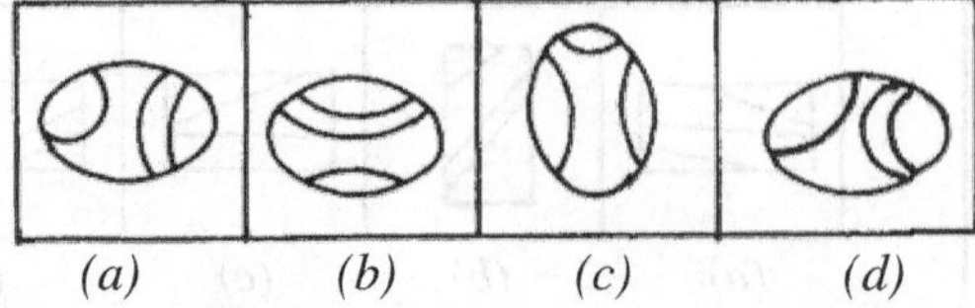

(a) (b) (c) (d)

TYPE - IV

Directions (Qs. 22 to 24): *In these questions, which figure is the rearrangement of the parts of the given figure.*

22. Given Figure:

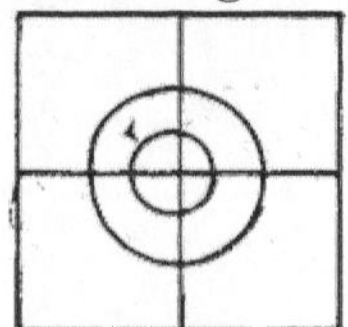

Answer Figures:

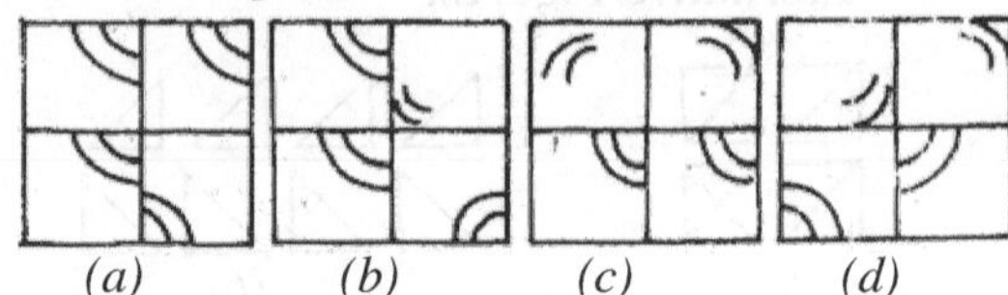

(a) (b) (c) (d)

23. Given Figure:

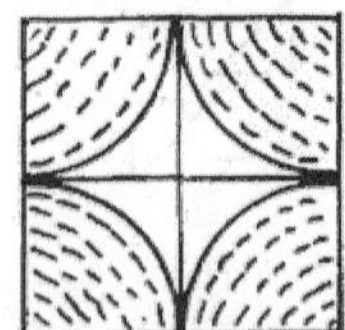

Answer Figures:

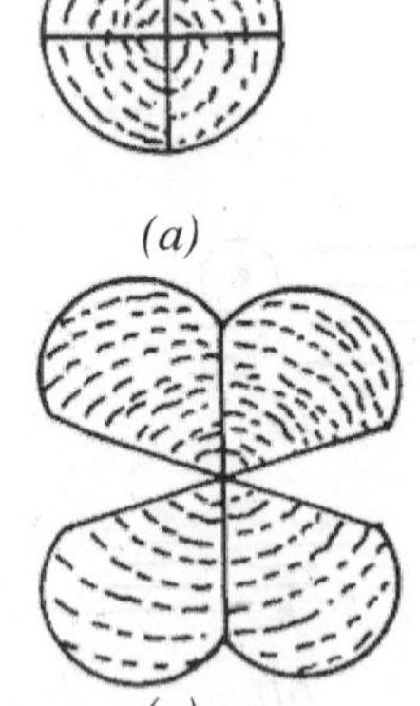

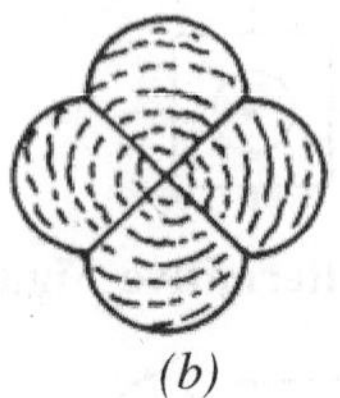

(a) (b)

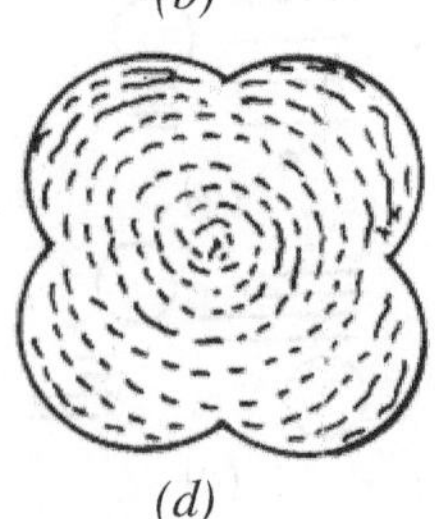

(c) (d)

24. Given Figure:

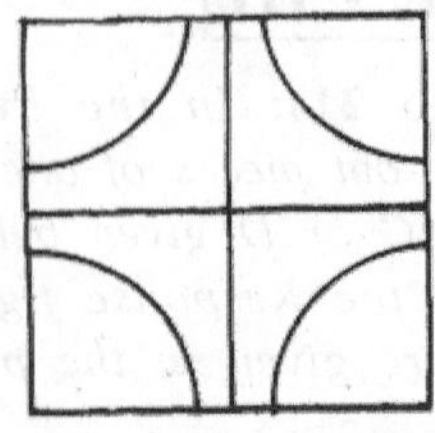

Answer Figures:

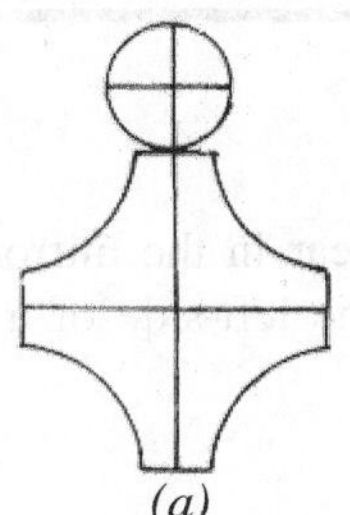
(a)

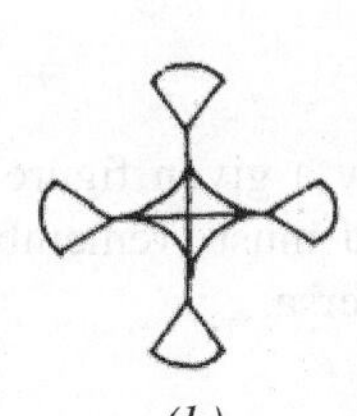
(b)

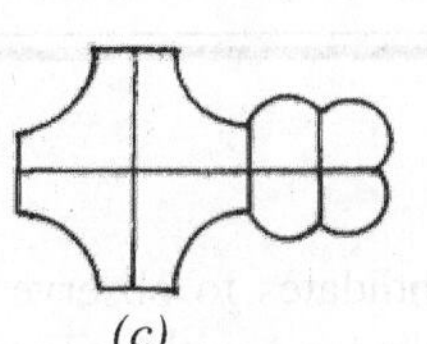
(c)

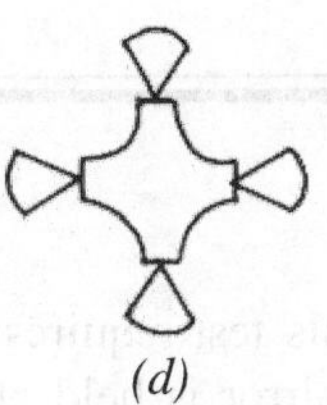
(d)

ANSWERS

1	2	3	4	5	6	7	8	9	10
(c)	(a)	(c)	(d)	(b)	(d)	(b)	(a)	(c)	(d)
11	**12**	**13**	**14**	**15**	**16**	**17**	**18**	**19**	**20**
(c)	(a)	(c)	(b)	(a)	(c)	(b)	(d)	(d)	(c)
21	**22**	**23**	**24**						
(d)	(a)	(a)	(a)						

LATERAL INVERSION

This test requires the candidates to observe carefully how a given figure will appear in the mirror, if the mairror is held at a particular position. For this test, you must remember that the left-side of a pattern appears to be on the right side in the mirror and vice-versa.

EXERCISE

Directions: *In the following questions, a figure is followed by four suggested mirror reflections of it. Assuming that the mirror is placed to the right of the figure, pick out the correct reflected figure.*

1. **Key Figure:**

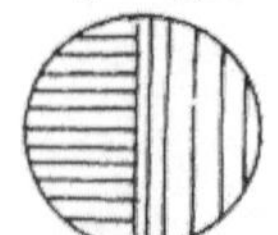

Answer Figures:

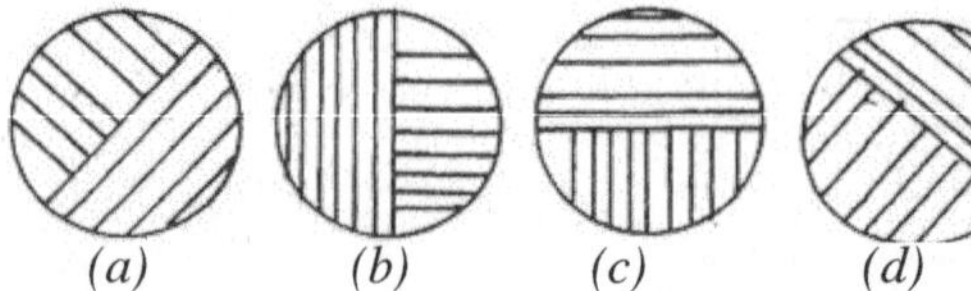

(a) (b) (c) (d)

2. **Key Figure:**

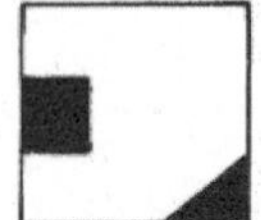

Answer Figures:

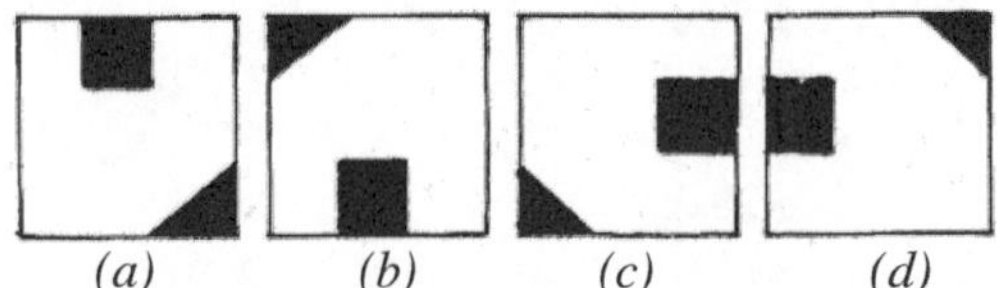

(a) (b) (c) (d)

3. **Key Figure:**

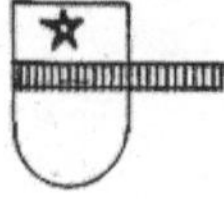

Answer Figures:

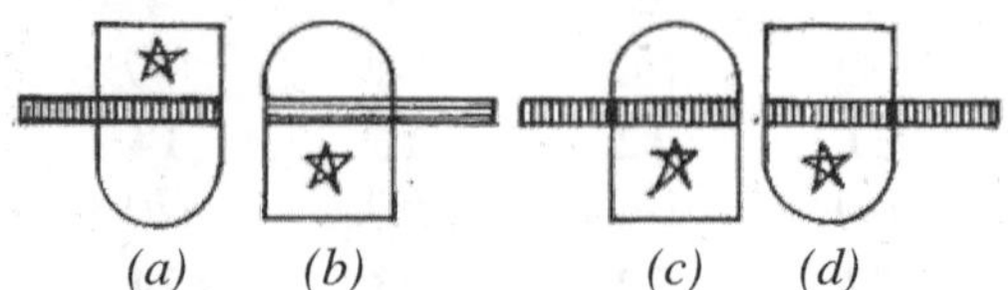

(a) (b) (c) (d)

4. **Key Figure:**

Answer Figures:

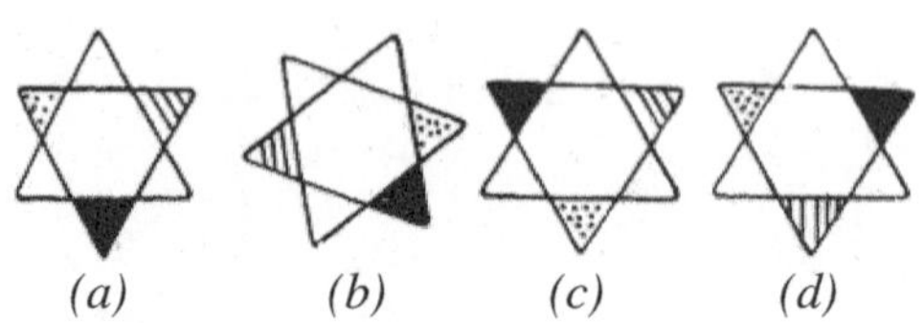

(a) (b) (c) (d)

5. **Key Figure:**

Answer Figures:

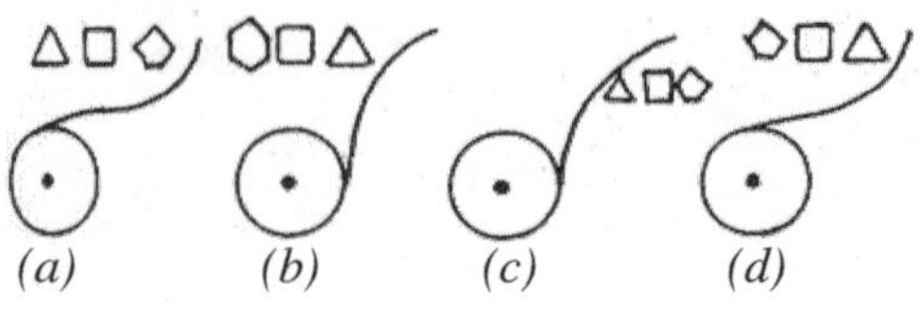

(a) (b) (c) (d)

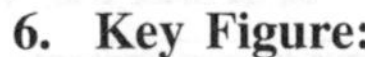

6. Key Figure:

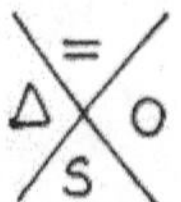

Answer Figures:

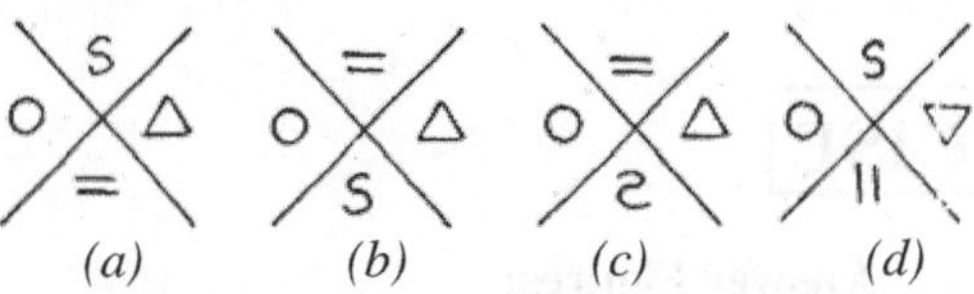

(a) (b) (c) (d)

7. Key Figure:

Answer Figures:

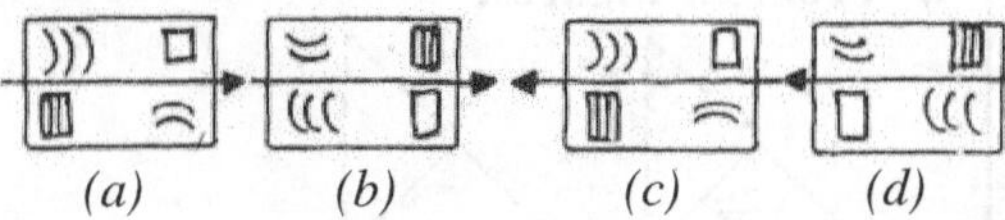

(a) (b) (c) (d)

Directions (Qs. 8 and 9): *In these questions, which of the Answer Figures is exactly the mirror image of the given figure when the mirror is held at AB?*

8. Given Figure:

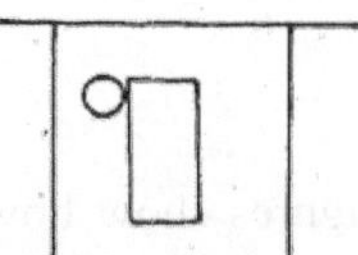

Answer Figures:

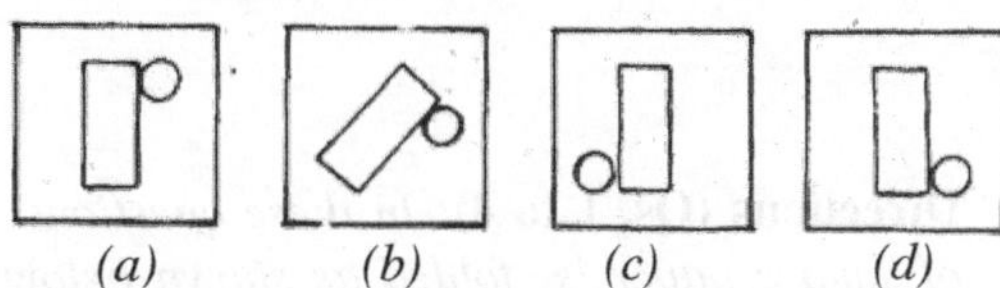

(a) (b) (c) (d)

9. Given Figure:

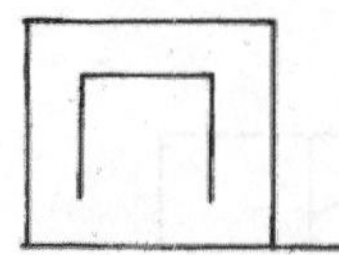

Answer Figures:

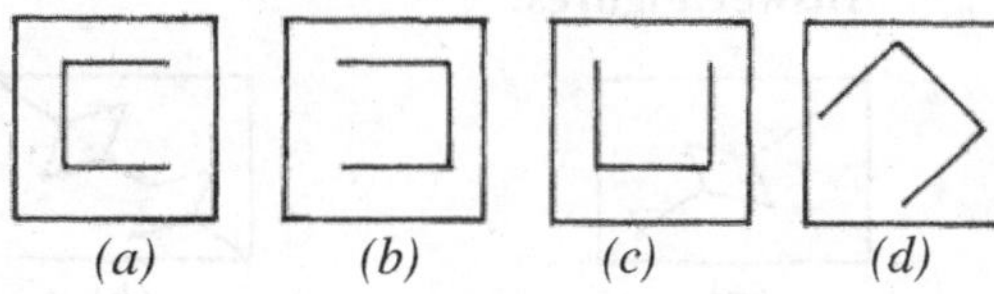

(a) (b) (c) (d)

ANSWERS

1	2	3	4	5	6	7	8	9
(b)	(c)	(a)	(c)	(d)	(c)	(d)	(c)	(c)

FOLDED OR UNFOLDED PATTERN

In this test, the problem figures show how a piece of paper or cardboard is folded and cut or punched. From the answer figures, you are required to choose the correct shape of the paper or cardboard when it is unfolded.

EXERCISE

Directions (Qs. 1 to 4): *In these questions, a piece of square paper is folded as shown below and a cut is made as marked. How would the paper look like when unfolded?*

1. Problem Figures:

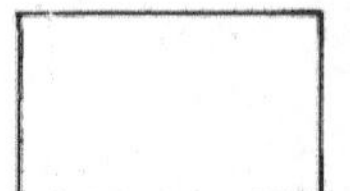
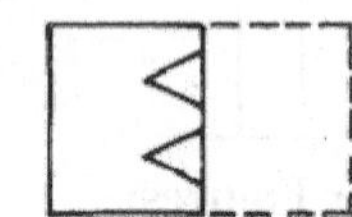

Answer Figures:

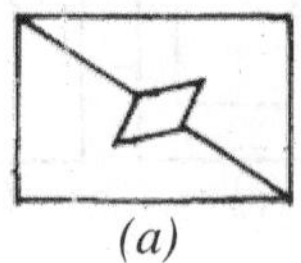
(a)

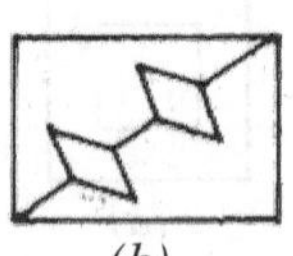
(b)

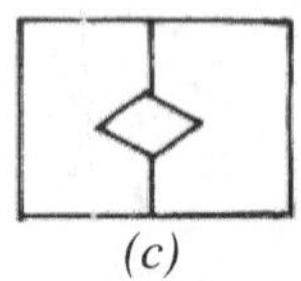
(c)

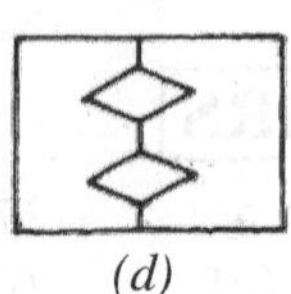
(d)

2. Problem Figures:

Answer Figures:

(a)

(b)

(c)

(d)

3. Problem Figure:

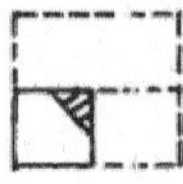

Answer Figures:

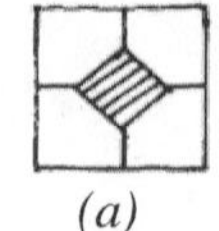
(a)

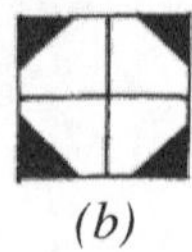
(b)

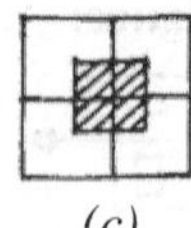
(c)

(d)

4. Problem Figures:

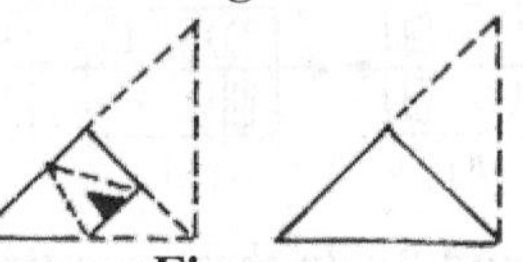

Answer Figures:

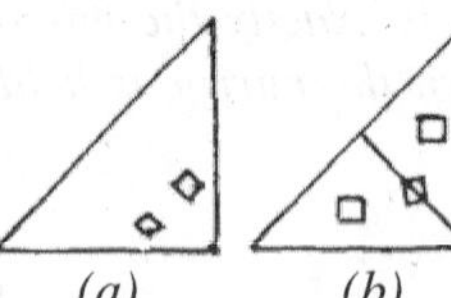
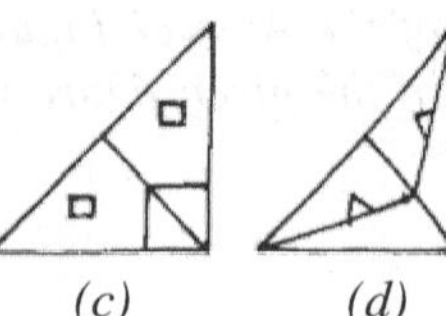

(a) (b) (c) (d)

Directions (Qs. 5 to 9): *As shown below, a paper is folded and then cut. How will the paper look like, when unfolded?*

5. Problem Figures:

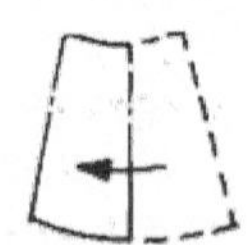

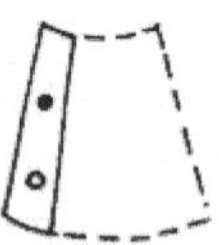

Answer Figures:

(a)

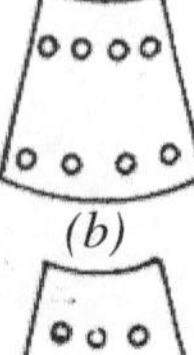
(b)

(c)

(d)

6. Problem Figures:

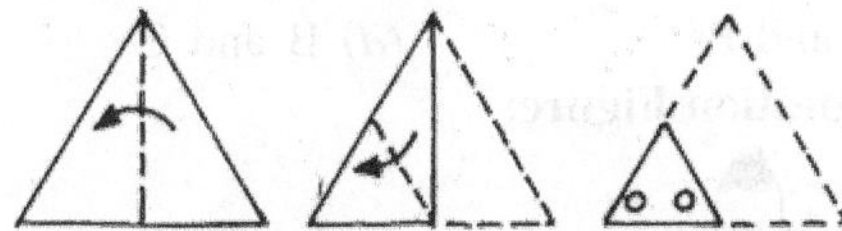

Answer Figures:

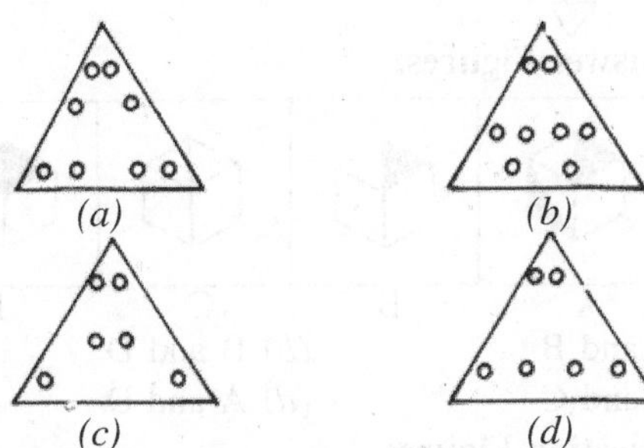

7. Problem Figures:

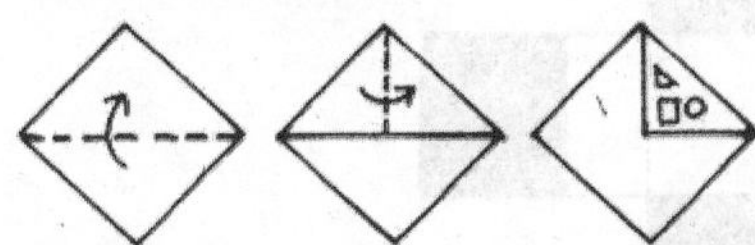

Answer Figures:

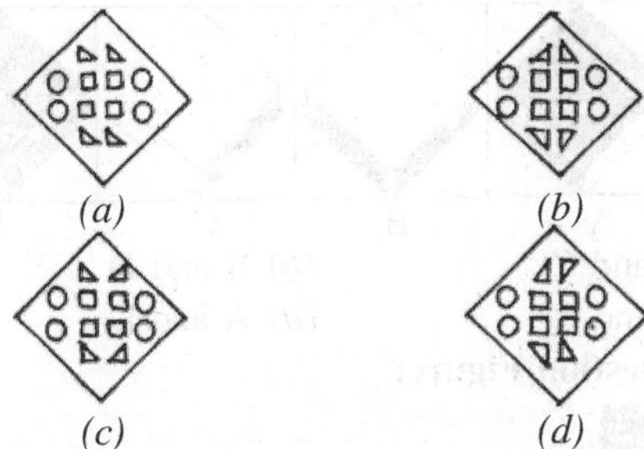

8. Problem Figures:

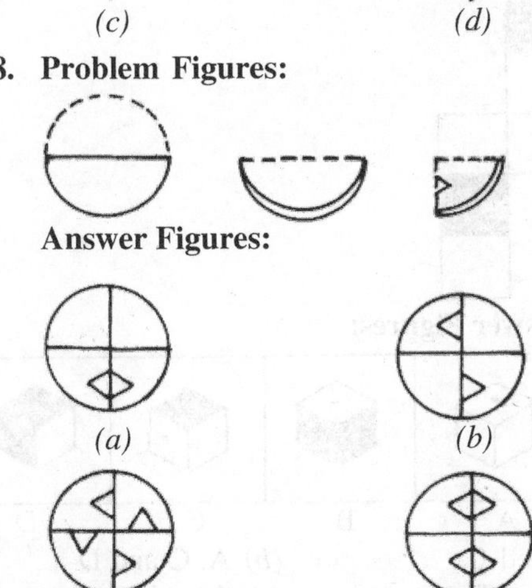

9. Problem Figures:

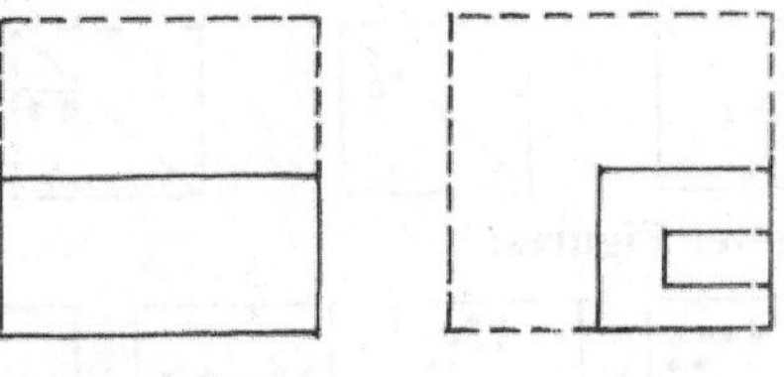

Answer Figures:

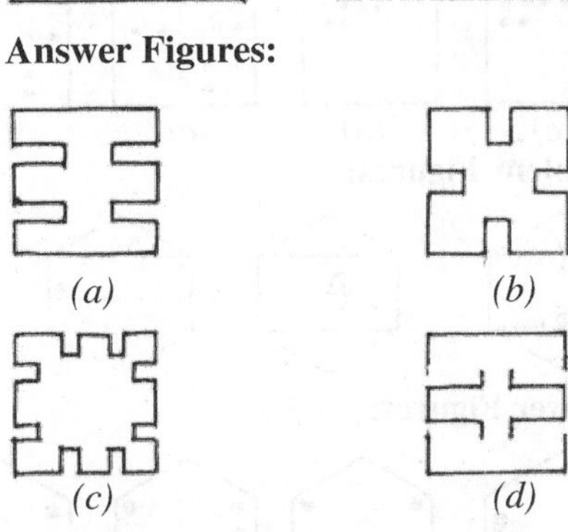

Directions (Qs. 10 to 14): *In these questions, a square/hexagonal sheet of paper has been folded and punched as shown by the top figures. You have to find out from amongst the four response figures how it will appear when opened?*

10. Problem Figures:

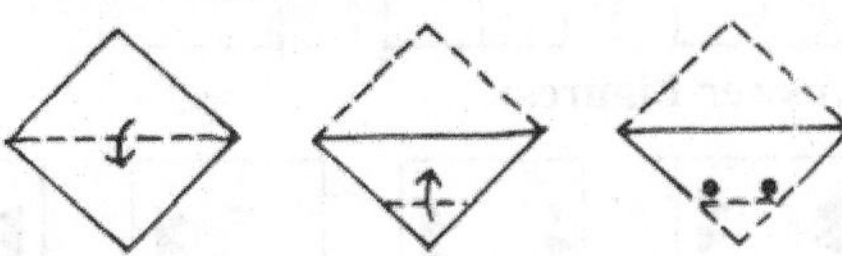

Answer Figures:

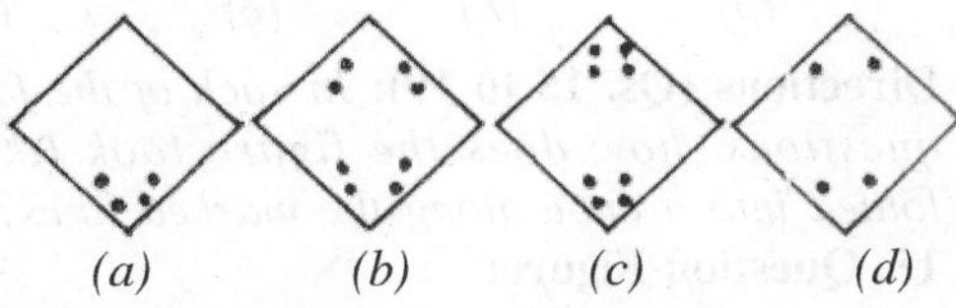

11. Problem Figures:

Answer Figures:

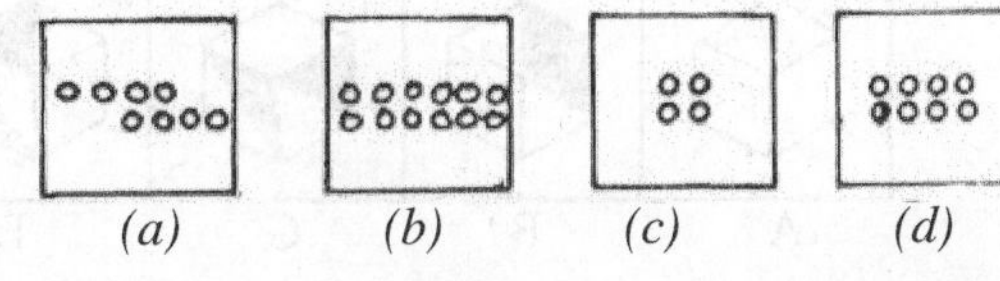

12. Problem Figures:

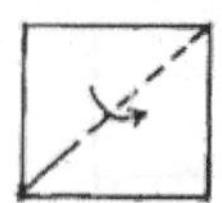 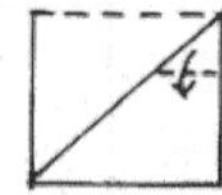 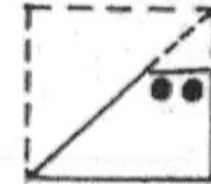

Answer Figures:

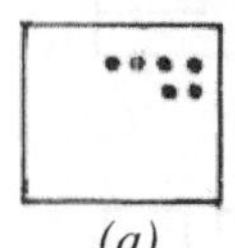 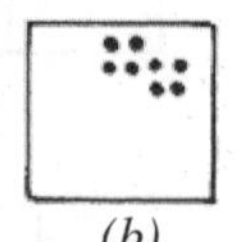 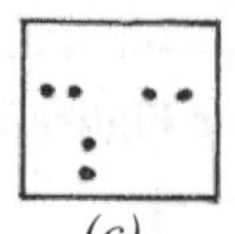 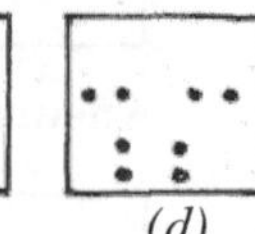

(a) (b) (c) (d)

13. Problem Figures:

  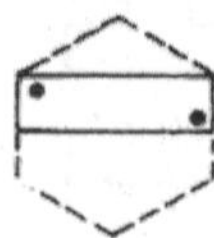

Answer Figures:

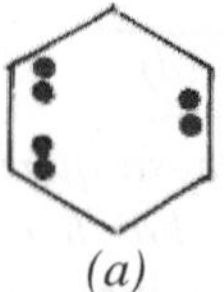 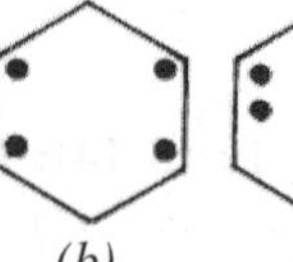 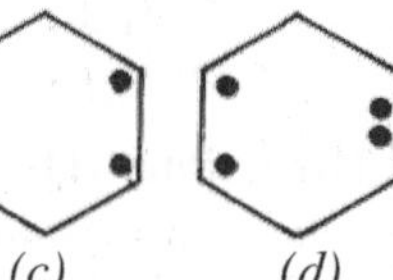

(a) (b) (c) (d)

14. Problem Figures:

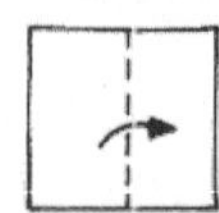 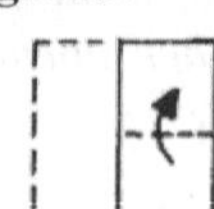 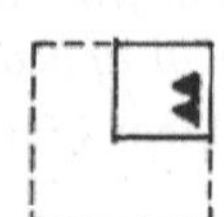

Answer Figures:

  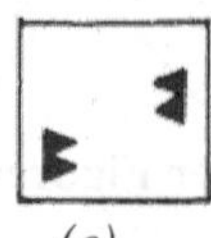 

(a) (b) (c) (d)

Directions (Qs. 15 to 19): *In each of the following questions, how does the figure look like when folded into a cube along the marked lines?*

15. Question Figure:

Answer Figures:

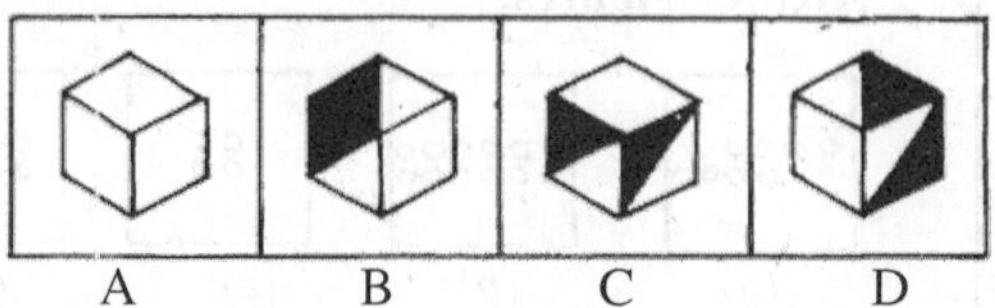

A B C D

(a) A and D (b) C and D
(c) A and B (d) B and C

16. Question Figure:

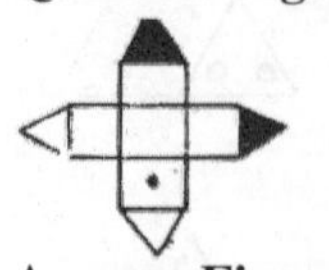

Answer Figures:

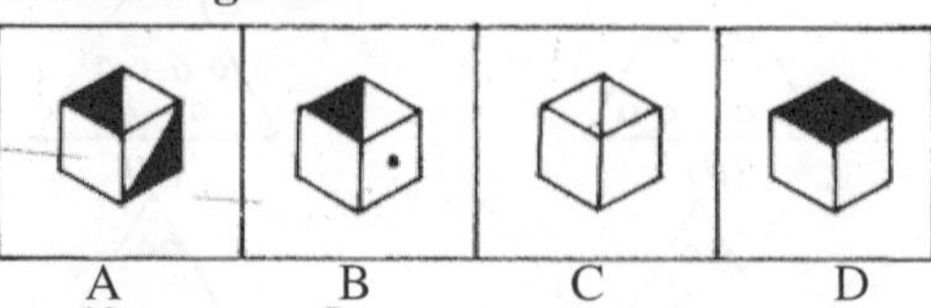

A B C D

(a) A and B (b) B and D
(c) B and C (d) A and D

17. Question Figure:

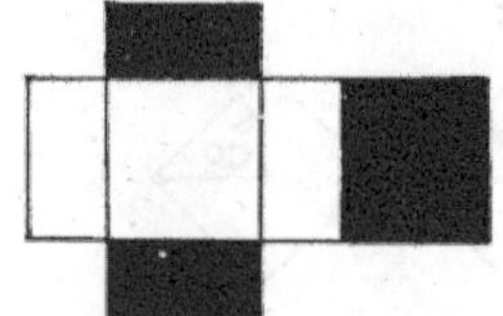

Answer Figures:

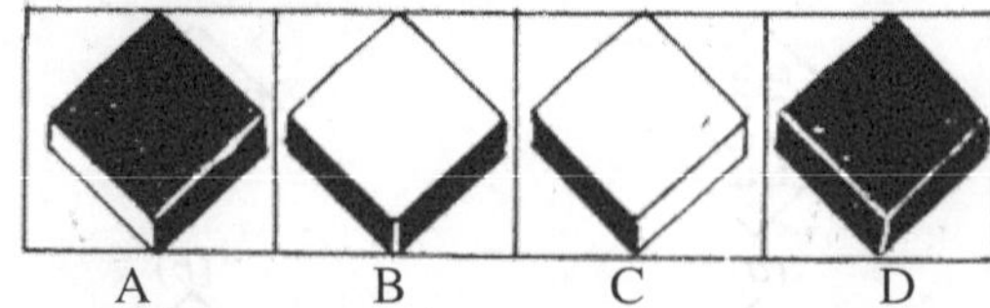

A B C D

(a) A and C (b) B and D
(c) B and C (d) A and D

18. Question Figure:

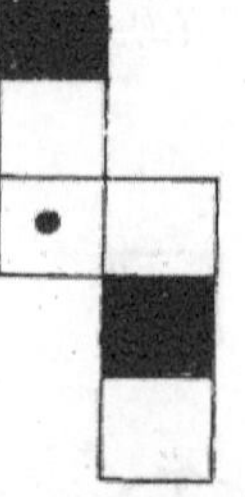

Answer Figures:

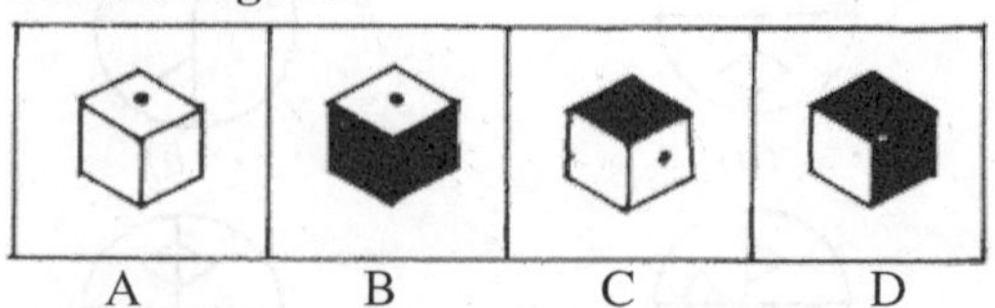

A B C D

(a) B and C (b) A, C and D
(c) B and D (d) A and D

19. Question Figure:

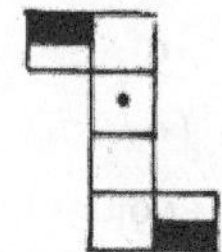

Answer Figures:

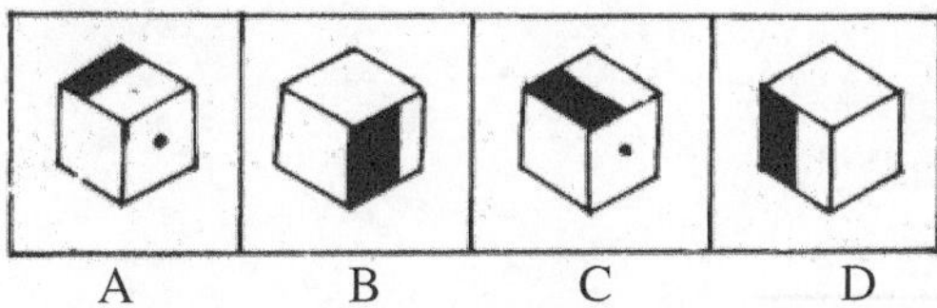

(*a*) A and B (*b*) B and C

(*c*) B and D (*d*) A, B, C and D

Directions (Qs. 20 to 24): *In the following questions, a square/hexagon transparent sheet with a pattern is given. You have to find out from amongst the four alternatives as to how the pattern appear when the sheet is folded at the dotted line.*

20. Transparent sheet:

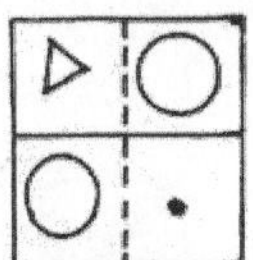

Response Figures:

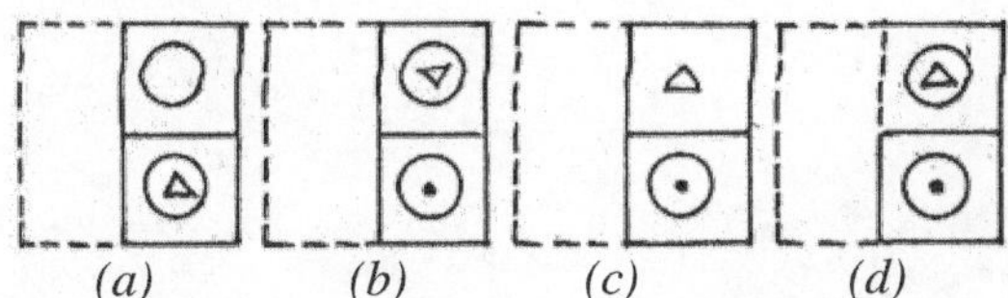

21. Transparent sheet:

Response Figures:

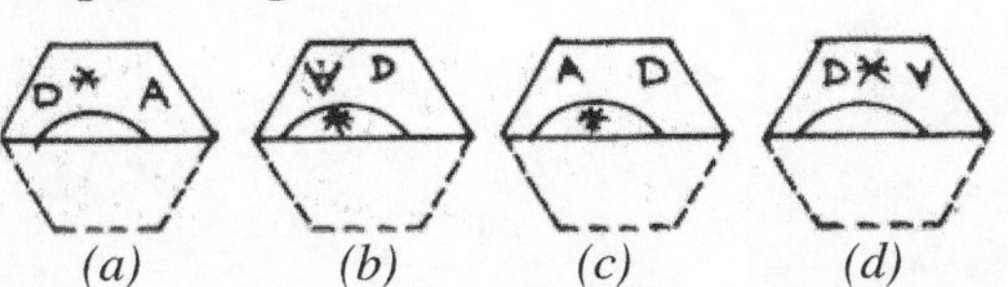

22. Transparent sheet:

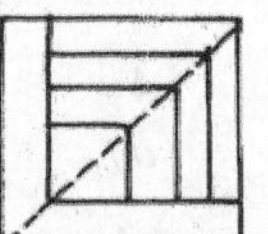

Response Figures:

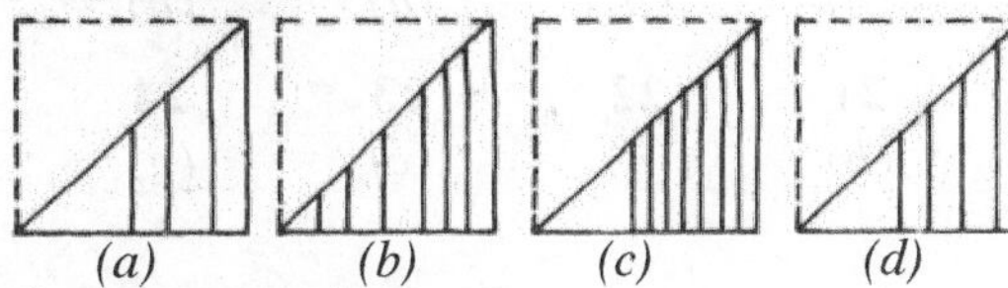

23. Transparent sheet:

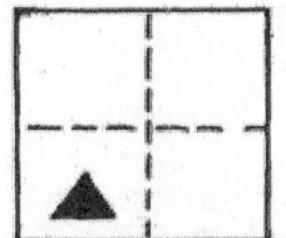

Response Figures:

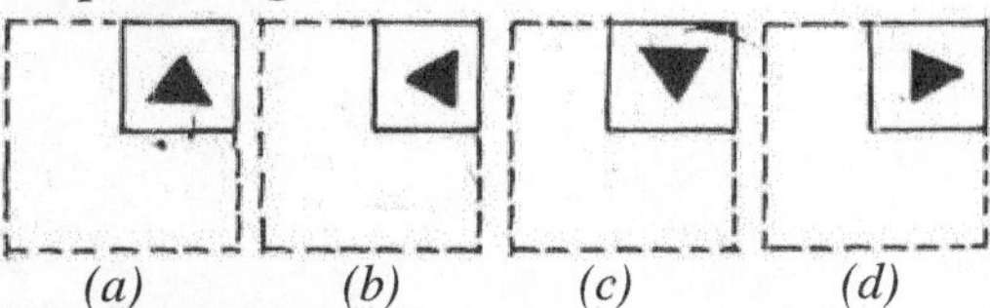

24. Transparent sheet:

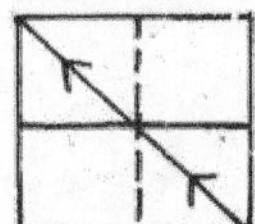

Response Figures:

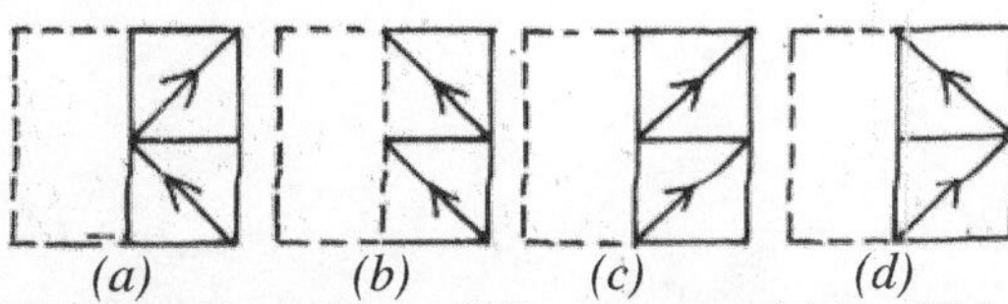

25. Find out the shape of the pattern which will be formed when the cardboard shown below is folded.

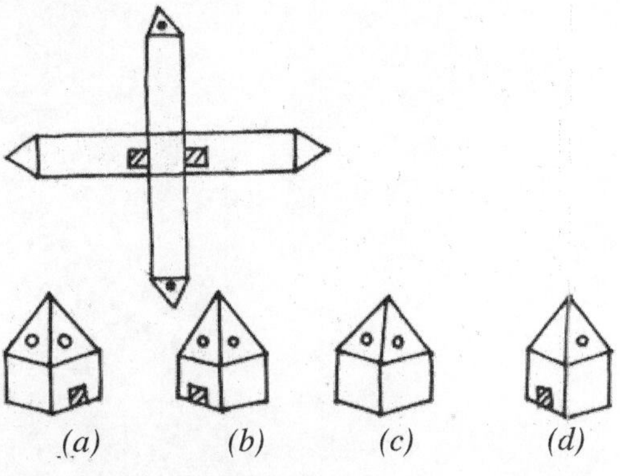

ANSWERS

1	2	3	4	5	6	7	8	9	10
(d)	*(d)*	*(a)*	*(a)*	*(b)*	*(a)*	*(b)*	*(d)*	*(a)*	*(c)*
11	**12**	**13**	**14**	**15**	**16**	**17**	**18**	**19**	**20**
(b)	*(b)*	*(a)*	*(b)*	*(a)*	*(c)*	*(a)*	*(b)*	*(d)*	*(b)*
21	**22**	**23**	**24**	**25**					
(b)	*(a)*	*(c)*	*(a)*	*(d)*					

YOUR SPACE

YOUR SPACE

English Language

1 Spelling Errors

The most common errors in English are of spellings of words. Even the most learned men are sometimes confused about the correct spellings of some words. One must keep and use a dictionary religiously. Never ignore and let pass a new word casually.

A number of question to test your knowledge of spellings are compiled here. Try to solve as many as you can.

Multiple Choice Questions

Directions: *Find the correctly spelt word out of the four options in each question.*

1. A. Accompalish B. Ackmplesh C. Acomplush D. Accomplish

2. A. Acommodation B. Acomodation C. Accomodation D. Accommodation

3. A. Astonished B. Astronished C. Astoneshed D. Asstonished

4. A. Benefeted B. Benefitted C. Benifited D. Benefited

5. A. Belligerent B. Beligirent C. Belligarant D. Belligerrent

6. A. Chancelery B. Chancellery C. Chancellary D. Chancelary

7. A. Discriminate B. Discremineta C. Discrimenate D. Discriminat

8. A. Damage B. Dammage C. Damaige D. Dammege

9. A. Efficiant B. Effecient C. Efficient D. Eficient

10. A. Extravagant B. Extreragent C. Extreregant D. Extravegent

11. A. Efflorascence B. Eflorescene C. Effllorescence D. Efflorescence

12. A. Equinimity B. Equanimmity C. Equannimity D. Equanimity

13. A. Farmament B. Farmement C. Fermament D. Fremament

14. A. Grieff B. Grief C. Grieef D. Grrief

15. A. Guarantee B. Garuntee C. Guaruntee D. Gaurantee

16. A. Hypocritical B. Hypocretical C. Hypocriticel D. Hypocirticel

17. A. Humurous B. Humorous C. Humoreus D. Humorrous

18. A. Itenerary B. Itinarery C. Itinarary D. Itinerary

19. A. Indipenseble B. Indispansible C. Indispensable D. Indipensable

20. A. Imprecticability B. Impracticebility
C. Impracticibility D. Impracticability

21. A. Incradulous B. Incredulous
C. Incridulous D. Incredalous

22. A. Juddicious B. Judiceous
C. Judicious D. Judiceus

23. A. Kleptomonia B. Kleptemonia
C. Kleptomania D. Klaptomania

24. A. Lackdaisical B. Lackadaisical
C. Lckadaisicle D. Lackadisical

25. A. Licentious B. Licontious
C. Licenttious D. Licientious

26. A. Meddicine B. Medicine
C. Medicene D. Medicinne

27. A. Meritricious B. Merefrecious
C. Meretricious D. Merritricious

28. A. Missunderstood B. Miesunderstood
C. Misunderstood D. Misunderstod

29. A. Occurad B. Occurred
C. Ocurred D. Occured

30. A. Osttentatious B. Ostentetious
C. Ostentatious D. Ostenttatious

31. A. Obnosious B. Obnoxeous
C. Obnoxious D. Obnoseous

32. A. Omenous B. Ominous
C. Ommineous D. Omineous

33. A. Pecification B. Pacification
C. Pecifacation D. Pecefication

34. A. Prograssive B. Progressive
C. Progresive D. Prograsive

35. A. Pasiveness B. Passiveness
C. Passeveniss D. Passivines

36. A. Polyendry B. Poliendry
C. Pollyendry D. Polyandry

37. A. Puerille B. Puerrile
C. Puerile D. Purrile

38. A. Pesanger B. Passenger
C. Pessenger D. Pasanger

39. A. Querrelsome B. Quarrelsame
C. Quarrelsome D. Querralsome

40. A. Rigourous B. Rigerous
C. Rigorous D. Regerous

41. A. Survellance B. Surveilance
C. Surveillance D. Survaillance

42. A. Schedule B. Schdule
C. Schedale D. Schedeule

43. A. Sepalchrle B. Sepalchral
C. Sepulchrle D. Sepulchral

44. A. Sympathetic B. Smypathetic
C. Sympothetic D. Sympethetic

45. A. Sincerely B. Sencerely
C. Sincerelly D. Sincerrely

46. A. Satellite B. Sattellite
C. Satelite D. Sattelite

47. A. Teracherous B. Treacherous
C. Treacheraus D. Treachereans

48. A. Uncivilized B. Uncevilized
C. Uncivillized D. Uncevelized

49. A. Vainglorious B. Vaniglorious
C. Vaniglerious D. Vaingloreus

50. A. Vulnarable B. Valnerable
C. Velnerable D. Vulnerable

ANSWERS

1	2	3	4	5	6	7	8	9	10
D	D	A	B	A	C	A	A	C	A
11	**12**	**13**	**14**	**15**	**16**	**17**	**18**	**19**	**20**
D	D	C	B	A	A	B	D	C	D
21	**22**	**23**	**24**	**25**	**26**	**27**	**28**	**29**	**30**
B	C	C	B	A	B	C	C	B	C
31	**32**	**33**	**34**	**35**	**36**	**37**	**38**	**39**	**40**
C	B	B	B	B	D	C	B	C	C
41	**42**	**43**	**44**	**45**	**46**	**47**	**48**	**49**	**50**
C	A	D	A	A	A	B	A	A	D

❑❑❑

2 Spotting Errors

The most common errors in English are of spellings, grammar and usage of words. By regular practice, the errors can be easily spotted and minimised.

Common Errors with Nouns and Noun-Phrases

Incorrect	Correct
1. I have bought new *furnitures.*	I have bought new *furniture.*
2. The wages of sin *are* death.	The wages of sin *is* death.
3. She told these *news* to her mother.	She told her mother this *news.*
4. He took *troubles* to do his work.	He took *trouble* (or pains) over his work.
5. The *cattles* were grazing.	The *cattle* were grazing.
6. He showered *many abuses* on me.	He showered *much abuse* on me.
7. I spent the holidays with my *family members.*	I spent the holidays with my *family.*
8. There is no *place* in this compartment.	There is no *room* in this compartment.
9. Write this new *poetry* in your *copy.*	Write this new *poem* in your *note-book.*
10. He took *insult* at this.	He took *offence* at this.
11. Put your *sign* here.	Put your *signatures* here.
12. She is my *cousin sister.*	She is my *cousin.*
13. *Sunil's* my *neighbour's* house was burgled.	*Sunil* my *neighbour's* house was burgled.
14. I lost a *ten-rupees* note.	I lost *a ten-rupee* note.
15. Road closed for *repair.*	Road closed for *repairs.*
16. His house is out of *repairs.*	His house is out of *repair.*
17. What is the *reason* of an earthquake?	What is the *cause* of an earthquake?
18. This building is made of *stones.*	This building is made of *stone.*
19. I disapprove of *these kinds* of games.	I disapprove of *this kind* of games.
20. Veena's and Sheela's father is ill.	Veena and Sheela's father is ill.
21. His *son-in-laws* are doctors.	His *sons-in-law* are doctors.
22. *Alms* is given to the *poor.*	*Alms* are given to the poor.
23. He always keeps his words.	He always keeps his *word.*
24. I carried the *luggages.*	I carried the *luggage.*
25. *Two-third* of the work is left.	*Two-thirds* of the work is left.

Common Errors with Pronouns

Incorrect	Correct
1. Both did not go.	Neither went.
2. We all did not go.	None of us went.
3. Each of these boys play.	Each of these boys plays.
4. Whoever does best he will get a prize.	Whoever does best will get a prize.
5. One should not waste his time.	A man should not waste his time.
6. I and she are sisters.	She and I are sisters.
7. He is wiser than me.	He is wiser than I.
8. Between you and I, Anil is not to be trusted.	Between you and me, Anil is not to be trusted.
9. Nobody was there but I.	Nobody was there but me.
10. Who is there ? It is me.	Who is there ? It is I.
11. Only he and me can use this card.	Only he and I can use this card.
12. Let you and I go now.	Let you and me go now.
13. Everyone got one's pay.	Everyone got his pay.
14. Everyone is frightened when they see a tiger.	Everyone is frightened when he sees a tiger.
15. These two friends are fond of one another.	These two friends are fond of each other.
16. I did not like him coming at that hour.	I did not like his coming at that hour.
17. Who do you think I met?	Whom do you think I met?
18. You should avail this opportunity.	You should avail yourself this opportunity.
19. When you have read these books, please return the same to me.	When you have read the books, please return them to me.
20. They that are humble need fear no fall.	Those that are humble need fear no fall.

Common Errors with Adjectives

Incorrect	Correct
1. These all oranges are good.	All these oranges are good.
2. He held the book in the both hands.	He held the book in both hands.
3. Both men have not come.	Neither man has come.
4. That man should do some or other work.	That man should do some work or other.
5. He is elder than I.	He is older than I.
6. Shakespeare is greater than any other poets.	Shakespeare is greater than any other poet.
7. He is a coward man.	He is a cowardly man.
8. Many villagers cannot write his own name.	Many villagers cannot write their own name.
9. Each of us loves our home.	Each of us loves his home.
10. Much efforts bring their reward.	Much effort brings its reward.
11. He found hundred rupees.	He found a hundred rupees.
12. He had leave of four days.	He had four days leave.

Incorrect	Correct
13. This is a worth seeing sight.	This is a sight worth seeing.
14. He will spend his future life here.	He will spend the rest of his life here.
15. There is a best teacher in that class.	There is a very good teacher in that class.
16. Of the two plans this is the best.	Of the two plans this is the better.
17. He is becoming strong every day.	He is becoming stronger every day.
18. He is worst than I.	He is worse than I.
19. Jaipur is hot than Delhi.	Jaipur is hotter than Delhi.
20. In our library the number of books is less.	In our library the number of books is small.

Common Errors with Verbs

Incorrect	Correct
1. He asked had we taken our luggage.	He asked if we had taken our luggage.
2. She asked what are you doing.	She asked what we were doing.
3. Rama asked to Anil why he is angry.	Rama asked Anil why he was angry.
4. He does not care for his money.	He does not take care of his money.
5. He does not care for his work.	He takes no care over his work.
6. No one cared for him after his mother died.	No one took care of him after his mother died.
7. He got angry before I said a word.	He got angry before I had said a word.
8. I met a man who was my tutor 20 years ago.	I met a man who had been my tutor twenty years ago.
9. I had been for walking yesterday.	I went for a walk yesterday.
10. If I shall do this I shall be wrong.	If I do this I shall be wrong.
11. I have left trekking.	I have given up trekking.
12. I came to know as to how he did this.	I learnt how he did this.
13. I came to know why he was sad.	I found out why he was sad.
14. He knows to swim.	He knows how to swim.
15. The criminal's head was cut.	The criminal's head was cut off.
16. I said to him to go.	I told him to go.
17. I told the teacher to excuse me.	I asked the teacher to excuse me.
18. He is troubling me.	He is giving me trouble.
19. I have got a hurt on my leg.	I have hurt my leg.
20. She gave a speech.	She made a speech.

Common Errors in Subject-Verb Agreement

Incorrect	Correct
1. The owners of this factory *is* very rich.	The owners of this factory *are* very rich.
2. The pleasures of nature that one can experience at Shimla *is* beyond description.	The pleasures of nature that one can experience at Shimla *are* beyond description.

Incorrect	Correct
3. There *is* no street lights in our colony.	There *are* no street lights in our colony.
4. He and I *am* entrusted with the job.	He and I *are* entrusted with the job.
5. Rice and curry *are* his favourite dish.	Rice and curry *is* his favourite dish.
6. The honour and glory of our country *are* at stake.	The honour and glory of our country *is* at stake.
7. Time and tide *waits* for none.	Time and tide *wait* for none.
8. All the passengers with the driver *was* killed.	All the passengers, with the driver, *were* killed.
9. The teacher, with her students, *were* going out.	The teacher, with her students, *was* going out.
10. I as well as they *am* tired.	I as well as they *are* tired.
11. Not only the soldiers but their captain also *were* captured.	Not only the soldiers but their captain also *was* captured.
12. Neither you nor I *were* selected.	Neither you nor I *was* selected.
13. Either of these two applicants *are* fit for the job but neither want to accept it.	Either of these two applicants *is* fit for the job but neither wants to accept it.
14. One of these students are sure to stand first.	One of these students *is* sure to stand first.
15. Everyone of these workers want a raise.	Everyone of these workers wants a raise.
16. None of these letters has been answered so far.	None of these letters *have* been answered so far.
17. None of the girls were present at the party.	None of the girls *was* present at the party.
18. Many a battle were fought on Indian soil.	Many a battle *was* fought on Indian soil.
19. A lot of work remain to be done.	A lot of work *remains* to be done.
20. The majority of these girls likes music.	The majority of these girls *like* music.

Common Errors in the Use of Modals/Auxiliary Verbs

Incorrect	Correct
1. When I shall see him I shall tell him this.	When I *see* him, I shall tell him this.
2. If I should do wrong, he would punish me.	If I *did* wrong, he would punish me.
3. Until he will have confessed his fault, he will be kept in prison.	Until he *has* confessed his fault, he will be kept in prison.
4. She will obey me.	She *shall* obey me.
5. You would work hard.	You *should* work hard.
6. You shall find him in the garden.	You *will* find him in the garden.
7. He must have died of exposure, but we cannot be certain.	He *might* have died of exposure, but we cannot be certain.
8. You might not show disrespect to your elders.	You *must* not show disrespect to your elders.
9. You may take exercise in order to maintain good health.	You *must* take exercise in order to maintain good health.
10. He must be a crook for all we know.	He *may* be a crook for all we know.

Common Errors in the Use of Adverbs

Incorrect	Correct
1. He is very much angry.	He is *very* angry.
2. She was very good enough to help me.	She was *good enough* to help me.
3. She runs much fast.	She runs *very* fast.
4. She runs very faster than Seema.	She runs *much* faster than Seema.
5. It is bitter cold today.	It is *bitterly* cold today.
6. He is a much learned man.	He is a very learned man.
7. She is thinking very hardly.	She is thinking very hard.
8. To tell in brief the film was boring.	*In short* the film was boring.
9. He told the story in details.	He told the story *in detail.*
10. I did it anyhow.	I *managed to do* it somehow.
11. Aeroplanes reach Europe soon.	Aeroplanes reach Europe quickly.
12. Before long there were dinosaurs on the earth.	*Long ago,* there were dinosaurs on the earth.
13. This book is too interesting.	This book is *very* interesting.
14. He lives miserly.	He lives in *a miserly* way.
15. Just I had gone when she came.	I had just gone when she came.
16. He sings good.	He sings *well.*
17. He sings good than I.	He sings *better* than I.
18. Really speaking it is cold.	*As a matter of fact* it is cold.
19. He is enough tall to reach the ceiling.	He is *tall enough* to reach the ceiling.
20. He went directly to his college.	He went *direct* to his college.

Common Errors in the Use of Conjunctions

Incorrect	Correct
1. As he is fat so he runs slowly.	As he is fat *he* runs slowly.
2. If he is fat then he will run slowly.	If he is fat, he will run slowly.
3. Though he is fat still he runs fast.	Though he is fat, *he runs* fast.
4. *As* I pulled the trigger at the sametime he shook my arm.	As I pulled the trigger, he shook my arm.
5. No sooner I had spoken than he left.	No sooner *had* I spoken than he left.
6. Not only he will go, but also he will stay there.	Not only *will he* go, but he *will also* stay there.
7. Neither he comes nor he writes.	Neither *does he* come nor *does he* write.
8. Scarcely he entered the room than the telephone rang.	Scarcely *had* he entered the room *when the* telephone rang.
9. Hardly she had left the house than it began to rain.	Hardly *had she* left the house *when* it began to rain.
10. He is the fastest runner and he comes last.	He is the fastest runner *but* he comes last.
11. She is as innocent as if she looks.	She is as innocent as she looks.
12. Until he does not try he must be punished.	He must be punished unless he tries.
13. I want to know as to why you are late.	I want to know why you are late.

	Incorrect	Correct
14.	I am fond of Chinese food as for example sweet and sour prawns.	I am fond of Chinese food, for example, sweet and sour prawns.
15.	He was angry therefore I ran away.	He was angry so I ran away.
16.	I was trying to work, at that time he was disturbing me.	While I was trying to work, he was disturbing me.
17.	Supposing if he is late, what will happen?	Supposing he is late (or if he is late) what will happen?
18.	He asked me that why I was late.	He asked me why I was late.
19.	Let us catch a taxi lest we should not get late.	Let us catch a taxi lest we should get late.
20.	She dresses herself like the teacher does.	She dresses herself as the teacher does.
21.	Wait while I come.	Wait *until* (or *till)* I come.
22.	Until, there is corruption in India, there can be little progress.	*As long* as there is corruption in India there can be little progress.
23.	I have never told a lie nor cheated anybody.	I have never told a lie *nor have I* cheated anybody.
24.	Both Mohan as well as Arun are responsible for this action.	Both Mohan *and* Arun are responsible for this action.
25.	Hindus and Muslims both are to blame for the riots.	*Both Hindus* and Muslims are to blame for the riots.

Common Errors in the Use of Prepositions

	Incorrect	Correct
1.	I will not listen him.	I will not listen *to* him.
2.	Copy this word by word.	Copy this word *for* word.
3.	He enquired from her where she lived.	He enquired *of* her where she lived.
4.	Sign here with ink.	Sign here *in* ink.
5.	Has she come in train or by foot?	Has she come *by* train or *on* foot?
6.	She said this at his face.	She said this *to* his face.
7.	Open the book on page one.	Open the book *at* page one.
8.	I was invited for lunch.	I was *invited to* lunch.
9.	I am ill since three months.	I have been *ill for* three months.
10.	This paper is inferior than that.	This paper is inferior *to* that.
11.	This resembles to that.	This *resembles* that.
12.	My brother is superior than you in strength.	My brother is superior *to* you in strength.
13.	He wrote me.	He wrote *to* me.
14.	I shall explain them this.	I shall explain this *to* them.
15.	Send this letter on my address.	Send this letter *to* my address.
16.	He suggested me this.	He suggested this *to* me.
17.	He goes *on his* work.	He goes *to his* work.
18.	He *reached to* Nagpur.	He *reached* Nagpur.
19.	He told *to me* to go.	He told *me* to go.
20.	The term begins *from* July 1st.	The term begins *on* July 1st.

Miscellaneous Errors

Incorrect	*Correct*
1. Many *homes* are lying vacant.	Many *houses* are lying vacant.
2. It is cool in the *shadow* of the tree.	It is cool in the *shade* of the tree.
3. She *keeps* good health.	She *enjoys* good health.
4. My leg is *paining*.	*I am feeling pain* in my leg.
5. *See* this word in the dictionary.	*Look up* this word in the dictionary.
6. The train will arrive *just now*.	The train will arrive *shortly*.
7. They are *pulling* on well.	They are *getting* on well.
8. The river has *over flown* its bank.	The river has *over flown* its banks.
9. He was appointed *on* the post.	He was appointed *to* the post.
10. Last but not *the least,* we have to discuss the problem of over population.	Last but not *least,* we have to discuss the problem of over population.
11. *Cities* after *cities* fell.	*City* after *city* fell.
12. What is the use Munir going there?	What is the use of Munir going there?
13. He *did many mischief*.	He *made much mischief*.
14. It is exact five *in* my watch.	It is exact five *by* my watch.
15. I will dine with them on *next Sunday*.	I will dine with them *Sunday next*.
16. Misfortunes when faced bravely and *manly* become less troublesome.	Misfortunes when faced bravely and *manfully* become less troublesome.
17. I am *laid down* with fever.	I am *laid up* with fever.
18. He is habituated to smoking.	He is *addicted* to smoking.
19. *According to my opinion* he is right.	*In my opinion* (or according *to me)* he is right.
20. Could you please *open* this knot?	Could you please *untie* this knot?

Multiple Choice Questions

Directions: *In this section, each sentence has three parts, indicated by (A), (B) and (C). Read each sentence to find out whether there is an error. If you find an error in any one of the parts (A, B, C), indicate your response by marking the letter related to that part. If a sentence has no error, indicate this by marking '(D)' which stands for "No error". Errors may belong to grammar, usage or idiom. Ignore errors of punctuation, if any.*

1. (A) Beware of/(B) a fair-weather friend/(C) who is neither a friend in need nor a friend indeed/ (D) No error.

2. (A) Copernicus proved/(B) that Earth/(C) moves round the Sun./(D) No error.

3. (A) Seldom we have been treated/(B) in such a rude manner/(C) by the police personnel./(D) No error.

4. (A) Some men are born great,/(B) some achieve greatness/(C) and some had greatness thrust on them./(D) No error.

5. (A) The property/(B) was divided/(C) among the two brothers./(D) No error.

6. (A) I am quite certain/(B) that the lady is not only greedy/(C) but miserly./(D) No error.

7. (A) The aircraft overloaded/(B) there was something wrong of the battery/(C) and the engine was making a queer noise/(D) No error.

8. (A) A thorough inquiry of the misappropriation of funds/(B) is now imperative/(C) to bring the guilty to book/(D) No error.

9. (A) The brilliant success in the examination/(B) as well as his record in sports/(C) deserves high praise/(D) No error.

10. (A) While travelling by a train/(B) on a cold winter night/(C) an argument rose between two passengers in our compartment/(D) No error.

11. (A) I cannot find/(B) where has he gone/(C) though I have tried may best/(D) No error.

12. (A) If I was/(B) the Prime Minister of India/(C) I would work wonders/(D) No error.

13. (A) Amit's severe bout of flu/(B) debilitated him so much/(C) that he was too tired to do for work for a week./(D) No error.

14. (A) This is the crux of the entire problem;/(B) everything centres on/(C) it being resolved./(D) No error.

15. (A) One of the major aims of the Air Force/(B) was the complete demolition of all means of transportation/(C) by the bombing of rail lines and terminals./(D) No error.

16. (A) His strong voice cut over/(B) the hum of conversation/(C) like a knife through butter./(D) No error.

17. (A) Even though they weren't expecting us/(B) they managed to knock up/(C) a marvellous meal./(D) No error.

18. (A) The celebrated singer was/(B) surrounded by the usual crowd/(C) of lackeys and hanger-ons./(D) No error.

19. (A) If it weren't/(B) for you,/(C) I wouldn't be alive today./(D) No error.

20. (A) He looked like a lion/(B) baulked from/(C) its prey./(D) No error.

21. (A) Widespread flooding/(B) is effecting/(C) large areas of the villages./(D) No error.

22. (A) She regards/(B) negotiating prices with customers/(C) as her special preserve./(D) No error.

23. (A) Often in political campaigns, a point is reached at which/(B) the candidates take out their gloves./(C) and start slugging with bare fists./(D) No error.

24. (A) If we really set to/(B) we can get the whole house/(C) cleaned in an afternoon./(D) No error.

25. (A) Pieces of rock plummeted/(B) down the mountainside/(C) in the ground below./(D) No error.

26. (A) Since the two parties each won/(B) the same number of seats,/(C) the minority party holds the balance of power./(D) No error.

27. (A) It's arrogant for you/(B) to assume you'll/(C)win every time./(D) No error.

28. (A) We've paid for our travel and accommodation,/(B) so we need only to take/(C) some pocket-money with us./(D) No error.

29. (A) There's no evidence to show/(B) that information technology secrets are more/(C) vulnerable in India than Britain or the US./(D) No error.

30. (A) It is shameful that hunting/(B) is still considered sport/(C) by some unscrupulous people in the civilized world./(D) No error.

31. (A) The Prime Minister's good looks won him/(B)the election but he has still to prove/(C) that he's not a just pretty face./(D) No error.

32. (A) The two books are the same/(B) except for the fact that this/(C) has an answer in the back./(D) No error.

33. (A) He estimated his income tax bill/(B) by extrapolation over figures/(C) submitted in previous years./(D) No error.

34. (A) The modern office block/(B) sticks out like a sore thumb/(C) among the old buildings in the area./(D) No error.

35. (A) I will try to put over/(B) some feelers to gauge/(C) people's reactions to our proposal./(D) No error.

36. (A) A major contribution of Mathura sculptors/(B)of that period were the creation and popularization/(C) of the Buddha's image in human form./(D) No error.

37. (A) Amit has been deceiving Mona/(B) for many years but she/(C) has not still tumbled to it./(D) No error.

38. (A) Mahavira was an advocate of nonviolence and vegetarianism,/(B) who revived and reorganized the Jain doctrine/(C) and established rules for their monastic order. (D) No error.

39. (A) Microwaves are the principle carriers/(B) of television, telephone and data transmissions/(C)between stations on earth and between the earth and satellites./(D) No error.

40. (A) An unit is an abstract idea,/(B) defined either by reference to/(C) a randomly chosen material standard or to a natural phenomenon./(D) No error.

41. (A) With the crisis deepening,/(B) the critics sense an opportunity/(C) about putting in place a more radical strategy./(D) No error.

42. (A) The salesman gave us/(B) a big spiel about why/(C) we should buy his product./(D) No error.

43. (A) I will need several weeks/(B) to invent the lie of the land before/(C) I can make any decision about the future of the business./(D) No error.

44. (A) You should be cautious/(B) and make a few discrete enquiries about/(C) the firm before you sign anything./(D) No error.

45. (A) Your husband doesn't/(B) believe that you are older/(C) than I./(D) No error.

46. (A) We are meeting today afternoon/(B) to discuss the matter/(C) and reach a compromise./(D) No error.

47. (A) Either Ram or/(B) you is responsible/(C) for this action./(D) No error.

48. (A) The student flatly denied/(B) that he had copied/(C) in the examination hall./(D) No error.

49. (A) By the time you arrive tomorrow/(B) I have finished/(C) my work./(D) No error.

50. (A) The speaker stressed repeatedly on/(B) the importance of improving/(C) the condition of the slums./(D) No error.

51. (A) The captain with the members of his team/(B) are returning/(C) after a fortnight./(D) No error.

52. (A) After returning from/(B) an all-India tour/(C) I had to describe about it/(D) No error.

53. (A) The teacher asked his students/(B) if they had gone through/(C) either of the three chapters included in the prescribed text./(D) No error.

54. (A) Although they are living in the country/(B) since they were married/(C) they are now moving to the town./(D) No error.

55. (A) Do you know/(B) how old were you/(C) when you came here?/(D) No error.

ANSWERS

1	2	3	4	5	6	7	8	9	10
D	B	A	C	C	C	B	A	D	C
11	**12**	**13**	**14**	**15**	**16**	**17**	**18**	**19**	**20**
B	A	C	C	B	A	A	C	C	C
21	**22**	**23**	**24**	**25**	**26**	**27**	**28**	**29**	**30**
C	A	A	A	C	A	A	B	D	B
31	**32**	**33**	**34**	**35**	**36**	**37**	**38**	**39**	**40**
C	C	C	D	A	B	C	C	A	A
41	**42**	**43**	**44**	**45**	**46**	**47**	**48**	**49**	**50**
C	D	D	D	C	A	B	D	B	A
51	**52**	**53**	**54**	**55**					
B	C	C	B	D					

❑❑❑

3 Articles

Definite and Indefinite Articles

(*i*) 'A' and 'an' are Indefinite Articles.

(*ii*) 'The' is Definite Article.

(*iii*) 'A' and 'an' modify a noun in a general way.

(*iv*) 'The' particularises it. *e.g.*,

Mohan has **a pen.**

The pen which you gave me was expensive.

Vowel and Consonant Sounds

(*i*) 'A' is used before words starting with the sound of a consonant.

(*ii*) 'An' is used before a vowel sound (vowels a, e, i, o, u) *e.g.*,

a book, a cat, a useful thing, a European girl, a university,

but an FDR, an MA, an honest boy, an hour, an owl, an egg, an umbrella, etc.

Use of Articles 'A' and 'An'

A cat mews. (*i.e.,* every cat)

The cat of my neighbour mews day and night. (*i.e.,* a particular cat)

He gave me **an** egg. (Here 'an' means 'one')

Use of Article 'The'

1. 'The' is used before names of rivers, mountains, seas, oceans:
   The Himalayas, the Ganga, the Yamuna, the Bay of Bengal, the Indian Ocean, the Nile, the English Channel, *etc.*
2. Names of newspapers and magazines:
   The Times of India, the Tribune, The Sun, *etc.*
3. Names of the famous and holy books:
   The Guru Granth Sahib, The Gita, The Ramayana, *etc.*
4. Names of creations of nature:
   the sun, the earth, the moon, the sky, *etc.*
5. While using Adjectives as Nouns:
   The poor should be helped by **the rich.**
6. Sometimes with the Comparative Degree:
   The more you think, **the more** you worry.
7. With the Superlative Degree:
   She is **the most intelligent** girl in our school.
8. Before the imaginary lines and directions:
   The Latitude, The Equator, the east, the west, etc.
9. Before the names of musical instruments:
   the violin, the piano, the flute, etc.
10. While using a Proper Noun as a Common Noun:
    Mohan is **the Sachin** of our team.

Omission of Article 'The'

1. Before some Nouns used to convey general sense, articles are not used but are used to particularise them:
   Man is mortal.
2. Before Proper Nouns:
   Rakesh is an intelligent boy.
3. With Abstract Noun:
   Childhood is the prime time of one's life.
   The childhood of Sohan was full of sorrow.
4. With Material Nouns:
   Milk is an essential food.
   The milk of the cow is sweet.

5. Usually no article is used before names of diseases:
   Cancer is a fatal disease.
   However, when we talk about a disease figuratively, we use an article before its name, *e.g.* Corruption is a cancer.
6. Names of games and language:
   I like football.
   I can speak Punjabi, Hindi and English.
7. Gold is a precious metal.

   NOTE: As you must have noted above, the definite article 'the' has been used where a noun is particularised.

Double Use of Article 'The'

Read the following sentences carefully to understand this :

1. The poet and novelist has been honoured.
   (The same person is the poet as well as novelist)
2. The poet and the novelist have been honoured.
   (The poet and the novelist are two different persons).
3. I have a black and white dog.
   (that is, one dog)
4. I have a black and a white dog.
   (that is, two dogs)

Multiple Choice Questions

Directions : *Fill in the blanks with suitable articles. Mark 'D' if no article required.*

1. Do you know .... boy in white?
A. a B. an
C. the D. No article

2. She is .... girl I am looking for.
A. a B. an
C. the D. No article

3. Have you read .... Mahabharat?
A. a B. an
C. the D. No article

4. ....rich are not always happy.
A. A B. An
C. The D. No article

5. Oranges are sold by .... dozen.
A. a B. an
C. the D. No article

6. Milk is sold by .... litre.
A. a B. an
C. the D. No article

7. .... Amazon is the longest river in the world.
A. A B. An
C. The D. No article

8. .... higher you climb, the colder it gets.
A. A B. An
C. The D. No article

9. She is .... untidy girl.
A. a B. an
C. the D. No article

10. I am .... M.A. is English.
A. a B. an
C. the D. No article

11. I have already spent .... few rupees I had.
A. a B. an
C. the D. No article

12. .... English are very hard-working.
A. A B. An
C. The D. No article

13. April is the fourth month of .... year.
A. a B. an
C. the D. No article

14. Rice is sold by .... kilogram
A. a B. an
C. the D. No article

15. She is .... best of the three girls.
A. a B. an
C. the D. No article

16. .... man in the car is a friend of mine.
A. A B. An
C. The D. No article

17. Brevity is .... soul of wit.
A. a B. an
C. the D. No article

18. .... thing of beauty is a joy for ever.
A. A B. An
C. The D. No article

19. .... little learning is a dangerous thing.
A. A B. An
C. The D. No article

20. .... best sauce for food is hunger.
A. A B. An
C. The D. No article

21. Birds of .... feather flock together.
A. a B. an
C. the D. No article

22. He makes .... living by begging.
A. a B. an
C. the D. No article

23. It is .... pity that he died so young.
A. a B. an
C. the D. No article

24. What .... nuisance it is?
A. a B. an
C. the D. No article

25. Delhi is .... London of India.
A. a B. an
C. the D. No article

26. Where is .... will, there is a way.
A. a B. an
C. the D. No article

27. Her father is .... physician and surgeon.
A. a B. an
C. the D. No article

28. This will benefit .... poor.
A. a B. an
C. the D. No article

29. ....bird in hand is better than two in a bush.
A. A B. An
C. The D. No article

30. As he is hard-working, he will win .... prize.
A. a B. an
C. the D. No article

31. .... water of this well is dirty.
A. A B. An
C. The D. No article

32. Only .... wearer knows where the shoe pinches.
A. a B. an
C. the D. No article

33. .... action will be taken against you.
A. A B. An
C. The D. No article

34. .... sun rises in the east.
A. A B. An
C. The D. No article

35. She was promoted to .... highest post.
A. a B. an
C. the D. No article

36. Did you see .... Taj Mahal?
A. a B. an
C. the D. No article

37. He is .... one-eyed man.
A. a B. an
C. the D. No article

38. This is .... useful book.
A. a B. an
C. the D. No article

39. Cloth is sold by .... metre.
A. a B. an
C. the D. No article

40. The sun sets in .... west.
A. a B. an
C. the D. No article

41. Amar bought......umbrella yesterday.
A. a B. an
C. the D. No article

42. Surinder is ...... honest boy.
A. a B. an
C. the D. No article

43. She wrote ...... book in French.
A. a B. an
C. the D. No article

44. ...... lion roars.
A. A B. An
C. The D. No article

45. ..... apple a day keeps the doctor away.
A. A B. An
C. The D. No article

46. John bought ...... car yesterday.
A. a B. an
C. the D. No article

47. His father is ..... engineer in the U.S.A.
A. a B. an
C. the D. No article

48. It is hard for ..... owl to fly during the day times.
A. a B. an
C. the D. No article

49. She had ..... rimmed hat.
A. a B. an
C. the D. No article

50. My uncle is ..... heart specialist.
A. a B. an
C. the D. No article

51. He looks as foolish as .... ass.
A. a B. an
C. the D. No article

52. Did you go to .... prison to visit him?
A. a B. an
C. the D. No article

53. I found .... one-rupee note in the market.
A. a B. an
C. the D. No article

54. It is a pleasure to meet such .... efficient man.
A. a B. an
C. the D. No article

55. The Sanyasi lived in a cave in .... Himalayas.
A. a B. an
C. the D. No article

56. There is .... union in our factory.
A. a B. an
C. the D. No article

57. He hit his wife on the head with .... umbrella.
A. a B. an
C. the D. No article

58. I caught him by .... collar.
A. a B. an
C. the D. No article

59. Child is .... father of man.
A. a B. an
C. the D. No article

60. He gazed at .... moon for two hours.
A. a B. an
C. the D. No article

ANSWERS

1	**2**	**3**	**4**	**5**	**6**	**7**	**8**	**9**	**10**
C	C	C	C	C	C	C	C	B	B
11	**12**	**13**	**14**	**15**	**16**	**17**	**18**	**19**	**20**
C	C	C	C	C	C	C	A	A	C
21	**22**	**23**	**24**	**25**	**26**	**27**	**28**	**29**	**30**
A	A	A	A	C	A	A	C	A	A
31	**32**	**33**	**34**	**35**	**36**	**37**	**38**	**39**	**40**
C	C	B	C	C	C	A	A	C	C
41	**42**	**43**	**44**	**45**	**46**	**47**	**48**	**49**	**50**
B	B	A	A	B	A	B	B	A	A
51	**52**	**53**	**54**	**55**	**56**	**57**	**58**	**59**	**60**
B	C	A	B	C	A	B	C	C	C

4 Prepositions

A Preposition is a word that comes before a Pronoun or a Noun and expresses the relationship between Noun or Pronoun and some part of the remaining sentence.

(*a*) He is busy **with** his work.
(*b*) The boy jumped **into** the river.
(*c*) The birds are chirping **in** the trees.

In these sentences the words **with**, **into** and **in** show the relationship between the verbs **busy, jumped** and **chirping** with the nouns **work, river** and **trees** respectively.

Position of the Preposition

A. A Preposition usually precedes its object.
(*i*) He laughs **at** the poor.
(*ii*) He is angry **with** you.
(*iii*) She agrees **with** me.

B. In the case of Relative Pronouns it comes after the subject.
(*i*) This is the boy whom I was looking **for**.
(*ii*) That is the pen whose mention I was making **of**.

C. In the following cases, the Preposition comes after its object.
(*i*) Where is the boy you were complaining **against**?
(*ii*) What things are there you are looking **for**?
(*iii*) Who is there, you are waiting **for**?

Omission of the Prepositon

In many cases when the sentences contain Nouns of Time or Place, the Prepositions **from, in** and **for** are often omitted.

(*i*) He walked many kilometres.
(*ii*) He came to see me last year.
(*iii*) As I could not find my puppy anywhere, I looked here and there.

Prepositions are small words that show the relationship between one word and another. Prepositions in the following sentences show the position of the paper in relation to the desk, the book, hand and the door.

The paper is **on** the desk.
The paper is **under** the book.
The paper is **in** his hand.
The paper is **by** the door.

Common Prepositions

about	at	by
in	onto	toward
above	before	concerning
inside	out	under
across	behind	despite
into	over	until
after	below	down
like	since	up
against	beneath	during
near	through	upon
along	beside	except
of	throughout	with
amid	between	for
off	till	within
among	beyond	from
on	to	without

Multiple Choice Questions

Directions: *Select the most appropriate preposition from the given alternatives to fill in the blanks and make the sentence meaningfully complete.*

1. Don't try to be an advocate ..... these criminals.
A. for B. with
C. across D. in

2. The audience admired him ..... his sweet voice.
A. to B. on
C. for D. at

3. I want to check your bag ..... fake currency notes.
A. to B. for
C. upon D. on

4. The dew drops clung .... the blades of grass.
A. for B. on
C. to D. in

5. The thief was chased ..... by the police.
A. on B. after
C. into D. at

6. Please carry this bag ..... my room.
A. on B. for
C. to D. in

7. A lorry bumped ..... a car.
A. on B. over
C. into D. to

8. They were begging ..... food.
A. for B. on
C. to D. after

9. She always boasts ..... her wealth.
A. of B. for
C. on D. after

10. She banged ..... the door violently.
A. for B. to
C. on D. down

11. I applied ..... the post of a clerk.
A. for B. on
C. in D. to

12. I applied ..... the Principal for the post of a teacher.
A. to B. on
C. with D. for

13. I begged ..... him not to divulge the secret.
A. for B. of
C. with D. to

14. You had better borrow a pen ..... Rakesh.
A. over B. into
C. from D. by

15. I baked a cake ..... the guests.
A. to B. for
C. on D. of

16. She is confident ..... (her) success.
A. with B. on
C. of D. for

17. The doctor will cure you ..... malaria.
A. of B. with
C. for D. from

18. This law is common ..... all.
A. to B. upon
C. over D. at

19. She was condemned ..... her bad hand writing.
A. on B. for
C. into D. of

20. In summer there will be a great demand ..... desert cooler.
A. on B. with
C. for D. of

21. We shall wait ..... you.
A. on B. for
C. towards D. after

22. Tom displayed his injury ..... all his friends.
A. for B. upon
C. to D. at

23. She distributed the sweets ..... the two brothers.
A. among B. between
C. for D. in

24. Please distribute these apples ..... all.
A. among B. to
C. for D. at

25. It rarely happened that he defended ..... an innocent person.
A. against B. for
C. upon D. at

26. The parents were disappointed ..... the performance of their son.
A. on B. with
C. at D. of

27. Common salt dissolves ..... water.
A. for B. in
C. with D. by

28. This medicare is free ..... sugar.
A. on B. to
C. from D. of

29. The manager granted leave ..... the clerk.
A. to B. on
C. into D. for

30. The air was heavy ..... aroma of perfumes.
A. on B. with
C. into D. from

31. She had a quick glance ..... the magazine.
A. at B. from
C. into D. to

32. The climate of Kashmir is favourable ..... me.
A. with B. in
C. to D. for

33. They hate you ..... your poverty.
A. for B. on
C. in D. of

34. He is eligible ..... this post.
A. for B. to
C. with D. at

35. The smoke was emerging ..... down the foot of the hill.
A. on B. to
C. from D. at

36. The criminal managed to escape ..... the prison.
A. upon B. from
C. with D. of

37. You should educate your friends ..... the benefits of living in villages.
A. on B. towards
C. upon D. in

38. She made a lot of efforts ..... win the match.
A. for B. to
C. upon D. at

39. The new inspector will enquire ..... the murder case.
A. on B. for
C. into D. at

40. The retired soldiers were exempted ..... all taxes.
A. from B. to
C. on D. of

41. She was adept ..... journalism.
A. at B. on
C. with D. in

42. She is afraid ..... snakes.
A. on B. to
C. of D. with

43. I agree ..... your proposal.
A. for B. on
C. to D. with

44. The children were amazed ..... so big a python.
A. at B. on
C. in D. with

45. She was anxious ..... the final match.
A. about B. on
C. with D. for

46. He apologized ..... his being late.
A. towards B. for
C. on D. as

47. The children were amused ..... his jokes.
A. for B. to
C. at D. on

48. She is angry ..... you.
A. to B. with
C. on D. for

49. She is angry ..... your teasing remark.
A. at B. in
C. for D. with

50. A big patch of land was allocated ..... the refugees.
A. to B. for
C. in D. upon

ANSWERS

1	2	3	4	5	6	7	8	9	10
A	C	B	C	B	C	C	A	A	C
11	**12**	**13**	**14**	**15**	**16**	**17**	**18**	**19**	**20**
A	A	B	C	B	C	A	A	B	C
21	**22**	**23**	**24**	**25**	**26**	**27**	**28**	**29**	**30**
B	C	B	A	A	C	B	C	A	B
31	**32**	**33**	**34**	**35**	**36**	**37**	**38**	**39**	**40**
A	C	A	A	C	B	A	B	C	A
41	**42**	**43**	**44**	**45**	**46**	**47**	**48**	**49**	**50**
A	C	C	A	A	B	C	B	A	A

❑❑❑

5 Synonyms & Antonyms

There are thousands of words in English language. No one can remember their meanings easily but with regular practice one can memorise most of them. A number of words with their Synonyms and Antonyms are compiled here. Try to learn as many as you can and answer the questions thereafter.

Words	*Synonyms*	*Antonyms*
Abandon	Cease, Forsake	Continue
Abhor	Hate, Loathe, Detest	Like, Love
Abiding	Enduring, Durable	Fleeting
Able	Proficient, Competent	Incompetent, Unfit
Ability	Skill, Power	Disability, Inability
Abortive	Fruitless, Futile	Fruitful, Successful
Abolish	Destroy, Undo	Restore, Revive
Abridge	Shorten, Curtail	Lengthen, Expand
Absolve	Forgive, Pardon, Excuse	Condemn
Accelerate	Hasten	Retard
Accord	Agreement, Harmony	Discord, Disagreement
Accumulate	Collect, Store, Amass	Distribute, Scatter
Adamant	Hard, Inflexible	Flexible
Adversity	Misfortune, Distress	Prosperity
Adept	Expert, Skilful	Inexpert, Unskillful
Aggravate	Heighten, Intensify	Quell, Suppress
Agile	Nimble	Clumsy, Undeft
Alert	Vigilant	Heedless
Allay	Calm, Soothe, Assuage	Arouse
Ameliorate	Improve, Advance, Amend	Worsen, Deteriorate
Ambiguous	Vague, Unclear	Clear
Amiable	Lovable, Agreeable	Disagreeable
Annihilate	Destroy	Create
Arduous	Hard, Strenuous	Easy

Words	*Synonyms*	*Antonyms*
Attacks	Assault	Defend
Audacity	Boldness	Cowardice
Auspicious	Favourable, Propitious, Lucky	Ominous, Inauspicious, Unlucky
Austere	Harsh, Severe, Rigorous	Easy-going
Authentic	True, Genuine	Spurious, False
Avarice	Greed	Generosity
Averse	Unwilling, Loath, Disinclined	Willing, Inclined
Aversion	Hostility, Hatred	Affinity, Liking
Base	Low, Mean, Ignoble	Noble, Exalted
Boisterous	Noisy, Stormy	Calm, Quiet
Brave	Courageous, Daring, Bold, Plucky	Cowardly, Dastardly, Timid
Brief	Short, Concise, Laconic	Lengthy, Diffuse
Bright	Vivid, Radiant	Dull, Dark
Brutal	Savage, Cruel	Humane, Kindly
Callous	Hard, Cruel, Indifferent	Soft, Tender, Concerned
Cautious	Careful, Wary	Rash, Reckless, Foolhardy
Censure (*n*)	Blame, Condemnation	Praise
Censure (*vb*)	Blame, Condemn	Praise, Commend
Circumscribed	Restricted, Confined, Limited	Unconfined, Unrestricted
Civil	Polite, Courteous, Gracious, Urbane	Rude, Uncivil, Impolite, Ungracious
Coerce	Compel, Force	Volunteer
Compassionate	Pitiful, Sympathetic, Merciful	Unsympathetic, Merciless, Cruel
Compress	Condense, Abbreviate	Expand, Lengthen
Conspicuous	Noticeable, Manifest	Inconspicuous
Constant	Steady, Steadfast, Uniform	Inconstant, Variable
Cordial	Friendly, Warm, Hearty	Cold, Unfriendly
Covert	Hidden, Secret	Overt, Open
Cruel	Savage, Ruthless, Vicious	Kind, Gentle, Benevolent
Cursory	Rapid, Superficial	Thorough, Exhaustive, Intensive
Credible	Believable, Probable, Plausible	Incredible, Unbelievable, Fantastic
Crafty	Cunning, Sly	Artless, Simple, Ingenuous
Costly	Expensive, Dear	Cheap, Inexpensive
Confidence	Trust, Reliance	Distrust, Doubt
Death	Decease, Demise	Existence, Life
Dearth	Scarcity, Lack, Want, Paucity, Shortage	Plenty, Abundance
Decay	Dissolution, Decline, Decomposition, Disintegration	Regeneration

Words	Synonyms	Antonyms
Deference	Respect, Reverence	Disrespect, Irreverence
Deficient	Lacking, Inadequate	Complete, Sufficient
Desolate	Lonely, Deserted	Crowded, Occupied
Destitute	Wanting, Needy	Rich, Affluent
Diligence	Industry, Perseverance	Idleness
Disgrace	Dishonour, Discredit	Honour, Credit
Dwindle	Decrease, Shrink	Grow, Increase
Earthly	Terrestrial, Mundane	Celestial, Heavenly, Unearthly
Eligible	Qualified, Suitable	Ineligible, Unsuitable
Emancipate	Liberate, Free	Enslave
Excited	Impassioned, Stimulated	Composed, Cool, Impassive
Extraordinary	Uncommon, Remarkable, Marvellous	Commonplace, Ordinary
Extravagant	Lavish, Prodigal, Wastrel, Spendthrift	Thrifty, Economical, Frugal
Fabricate	Construct, Make	Destroy
Fabulous	Fictitious, Mythical	Actual, Real
False	Untrue, Mendacious	True, Genuine
Famous	Well-known, Renowned	Obscure, Unknown
Fantastic	Fanciful, Imaginative, Visionary	Practical, Down to earth
Fearful	Nervous, Anxious, Afraid, Scared	Fearless, Dauntless
Felicity	Happiness	Sorrow
Gaiety	Joyousness, Hilarity	Mourning, Dullness
Garrulous	Talkative, Loquacious	Taciturn, Silent, Reserved
Generous	Liberal, Magnanimous	Stingy, Miserly
Gigantic	Huge, Colossal	Minute, Small
Graphic	Vivid, Pictorial, Meaningful	Vague
Guest	Visitor	Host
Guile	Fraud, Trickery	Artlessness, Ingenuousness
Gratitude	Gratefulness	Ingratitude, Ungratefulness
Gratuitous	Voluntary, Spontaneous, Unwarranted	Involuntary, Forced
Hamper	Hinder, Obstruct	Facilitate, Ease
Haughty	Arrogant, Proud	Humble, Modest
Hazardous	Dangerous, Perilous	Safe, Secure Protected
Headstrong	Obstinate, Stubborn	Weak-willed, Flexible

Words	*Synonyms*	*Antonyms*
Hope	Belief, Conviction, Expectation	Despair, Hopelessness
Improvident	Prodigal, Carelessness	Provident, Economical
Incessant	Unceasing, Continuous	Discontinuous
Indolent	Slothful, Lethargic	Active, Energetic
Joy	Delight, Pleasure	Sadness, Gloom
Jolly	Jovial, Merry	Gloomy, Sad
Judicious	Discreet, Prudent	Indiscreet, Injudicious
Knowledge	Enlightenment, Learning	Ignorance, Stupidity
Laborious	Industrious, Assiduous	Slothful, Lazy
Laxity	Slackness, Looseness	Firmness
Lenient	Mild, Forbearing	Strict, Stern
Lethal	Deadly, Fatal, Mortal	Life-giving, Vital, Vivifying
Liberal	Generous, Tolerant	Intolerant, Illiberal
Liberty	Freedom, Independence	Slavery, Bondage
Lively	Animated, Active	Dull, Listless
Loyal	Faithful, Devoted	Treacherous, Disloyal, Unfaithful
Lucky	Fortunate	Unlucky, Unfortunate
Lucrative	Profitable	Unprofitable
Magnanimous	Generous, Largehearted	Ungenerous, Stingy
Malady	Illness, Ailment	Health
Manifest	Noticeable, Obvious	Obscure, Puzzling
Meagre	Small	Plentiful, Large
Mean	Low, Abject	Noble, Exalted
Mendacious	False, Untruthful	Truthful
Misery	Sorrow, Distress	Happiness, Joy
Morbid	Sick, Diseased	Healthy
Mournful	Sorrowful, Sad	Joyful, Happy
Negligent	Careless, Heedless	Careful
Notorious	Infamous, Disreputable	Reputable
Obedient	Submissive, Compliant, Docile	Disobedient, Recalcitrant, Wayward
Obsolete	Antiquated, Out-of-Date	Current, Modern
Opportune	Timely, Seasonable	Inopportune
Opulence	Wealth, Riches	Penury, Poverty
Onerous	Heavy, Burdensome	Light, Easy
Palatable	Tasty, Delicious	Unpalatable
Pathetic	Touching	Joyous, Cheery
Persuade	Urge, Induce	Dissuade
Praise (*vb*)	Applaud, Eulogise	Condemn

Words	Synonyms	Antonyms
Praise (*n*)	Applause, Eulogy	Condemnation
Precarious	Risky, Uncertain	Safe, Certain
Pretence	Pretext, Excuse	Candour, Frankness
Propagate	Breed, Circulate	Terminate, Restrict
Quaint	Odd, Singular	Usual, Ordinary
Quell	Suppress, Subdue	Agitate, Arouse
Rare	Uncommon, Scarce	Common, Ordinary
Refined	Polished, Elegant	Crude, Coarse
Remote	Distant	Near, Close
Renown	Fame, Reputation	Infamy, Notoriety
Rigid	Stiff, Unyielding	Flexible, Yielding
Remorseful	Regretful, Repentant	Unrepentant
Rebellion	Revolt, Mutiny, Insurgency	Loyalty
Scared	Holy, Consecrated	Profane, Unholy
Sane	Sensible, Sound	Insane
Scold	Chide, Rebuke	Praise
Serious	Grave, Earnest	Frivolous
Shy	Bashful	Bold, Impudent
Simple	Plain, Artless	Complex, Cunning, Shrewd
Solitary	Single, Lonely, Secluded	Numerous, Multitude
Shallow	Superficial	Deep
Solace	Comfort, Relief	Discomfort, Grief
Spurious	Sham, False	Genuine, Authentic
Stagnant	Still, Motionless	Moving
Surplus	Excess	Deficit, Shortage
Tame	Gentle, Mild, Domesticated	Savage, Wild
Teacher	Instructor, Educator	Student, Pupil
Tedious	Wearisome, Monotonous	Agreeable, Lively
Temporal	Worldly, Secular	Spiritual
Temperate	Moderate	Immoderate, Intemperate
Tortuous	Winding, Circuitous	Straight, Direct
Tough	Hard, Strong	Tender, Soft, Flexible
Transient	Temporary, Fleeting	Lasting, Durable, Permanent
Trusworthy	Reliable	Unreliable, Untrustworthy
Tranquil	Calm	Agitated
Ugly	Unsightly, Repulsive	Beautiful, Attractive
Useful	Advantageous, Serviceable	Useless
Vehemence	Passion, Force	Apathy, Indifference

Words	Synonyms	Antonyms
Vindictive	Revengeful	Forgiving
Wholesome	Healthy	Unwholesome, Morbid, Unhealthy, Diseased
Wicked	Evil, Impious	Pious, Good
Wise	Sagacious, Erudite	Foolish, Stupid
Wrath	Anger, Fury, Rage	Love, Peace, Calm
Wreck	Ruin, Destroy	Create, Construct
Yield	Surrender, Submit	Resist, Revolt
Yielding	Submissive, Supple	Inflexible, Intractable
Yoke	Oppression, Bondage	Freedom
Zeal	Passion, Fervour	Apathy, Indifference
Zest	Relish, Enthusiasm	Distaste, Disrelish

Multiple Choice Questions

Directions (Qs. 1 to 50): *In the following questions choose the word which best expresses the MEANING of the given word.*

1. TEPID
   A. Hot B. Warm
   C. Cold D. Boiling
2. MAYHEM
   A. Jubilation B. Havoc
   C. Excitement D. Defeat
3. TIMID
   A. Fast B. Slow
   C. Medium D. Shy
4. CANTANKEROUS
   A. Quarrelsome B. Rash
   C. Disrespectful D. Noisy
5. PRECARIOUS
   A. Cautious B. Critical
   C. Perilous D. Brittle
6. TACITURNITY
   A. Dumbness B. Changeableness
   C. Hesitation D. Reserve
7. INEBRIATE
   A. Dreamy B. Stupefied
   C. Unsteady D. Drunken
8. HARBINGER
   A. Massenger B. Steward
   C. Forerunner D. Pilot
9. INTIMIDATE
   A. To hint B. Frighten
   C. Bluff D. Harass
10. IRONIC
    A. Inflexible
    B. Bitter
    C. Good-natured
    D. Disguisedly sarcastic
11. STRINGENT
    A. Tense B. Stringy
    C. Strict D. Causing to shrink
12. ECSTATIC
    A. Animated B. Bewildered
    C. Enraptured D. Willful
13. COMMENSURATE
    A. Measurable B. Proportionate
    C. Beginning D. Appropriate
14. DESTITUTION
    A. Humility B. Moderation
    C. Poverty D. Beggary

15. ASCEND
A. Leap B. Grow
C. Deviate D. Mount

16. UNCOUTH
A. Ungraceful B. Rough
C. Slovenly D. Dirty

17. LYNCH
A. Hang B. Madden
C. Killed D. Shoot

18. LAUD
A. Lord B. Eulogy
C. Praise D. Extolled

19. CORRESPONDENCE
A. Agreements B. Contracts
C. Documents D. Letters

20. VENUE
A. Place B. Agenda
C. Time D. Duration

21. STERILE
A. Barren B. Arid
C. Childless D. Dry

22. SYNOPSIS
A. Index B. Mixture
C. Summary D. Puzzle

23. GERMANE
A. Responsible B. Logical
C. Possible D. Relevant

24. PONDER
A. Think B. Evaluate
C. Anticipate D. Increase

25. CANNY
A. Obstinate B. Handsome
C. Clever D. Stout

26. ABUNDANT
A. Ripe B. Cheap
C. Plenty D. Absent

27. CONSEQUENCES
A. Results B. Conclusions
C. Difficulties D. Applications

28. SHIVER
A. Shake B. Rock
C. Tremble D. Move

29. DILIGENT
A. Progressive B. Brilliant
C. Inventive D. Hard-working

30. DISTANT
A. Far B. Removed
C. Reserved D. Separate

31. FORAY
A. Excursion B. Contest
C. Ranger D. Intuition

32. FRUGALITY
A. Foolishness B. Extremity
C. Enthusiasm D. Economy

33. GARNISH
A. Paint B. Garner
C. Adorn D. Abuse

34. VIGOUR
A. Strength B. Boldness
C. Warmth D. Enthusiasm

35. CANDID
A. Apparent B. Explicit
C. Frank D. Bright

36. BRIEF
A. Limited B. Small
C. Little D. Short

37. GARRULITY
A. Credulity B. Senility
C. Loquaciousness D. Speciousness

38. FURORE
A. Excitement B. Worry
C. Flux D. Anteroom

39. NEUTRAL
A. Unbiased B. Non-aligned
C. Undecided D. Indifferent

40. LAMENT
A. Complain B. Comment
C. Condone D. Console

41. ADVERSITY
A. Failure B. Helplessness
C. Misfortune D. Crisis

42. TURN UP
A. Land up B. Show up
C. Crop up D. Come up

43. DEIFY
A. Flatter B. Challenge
C. Worship D. Face

44. ERROR
A. Misadventure B. Misgiving
C. Ambiguity D. Blunder

45. SHALLOW
A. Artificial B. Superficial
C. Foolish D. Worthless

46. MASSACRE
A. Murder B. Stab
C. Assassinate D. Slaughter

47. COMBAT
A. Conflict B. Quarrel
C. Feud D. Fight

48. VORACIOUS
A. Wild B. Hungry
C. Angry D. Quick

49. IMPROMPTU
A. Offhand B. Unimportant
C. Unreal D. Effective

50. RABBLE
A. Mob B. Noise
C. Roar D. Rubbish

Directions (Qs. 51 to 100): *In the following questions choose the word which is the exact OPPOSITE of the given words.*

51. STRINGENT
A. General B. Vehement
C. Lenient D. Magnanimous

52. FLIMSY
A. Frail B. Filthy
C. Firm D. Flippant

53. BUSY
A. Occupied B. Engrossed
C. Relaxed D. Engaged

54. ADAPTABLE
A. Adoptable B. Flexible
C. Yielding D. Rigid

55. LOVE
A. Villainy B. Hatred
C. Compulsion D. Force

56. BALANCE
A. Disbalance B. Misbalance
C. Debalance D. Imbalance

57. RELINQUISH
A. Abdicate B. Renounce
C. Possess D. Deny

58. MOUNTAIN
A. Plain B. Plateau
C. Precipice D. Valley

59. FICKLE
A. Courageous B. Sincere
C. Steadfast D. Humble

60. PERENNIAL
A. Frequent B. Regular
C. Lasting D. Rare

61. RARELY
A. Hardly B. Definitely
C. Frequently D. Periodically

62. STARTLED
A. Amused B. Relaxed
C. Endless D. Astonished

63. ADHERENT
A. Detractor B. Enemy
C. Alien D. Rival

64. QUIESCENT
A. Indifferent B. Troublesome
C. Weak D. Unconcerned

65. CONDENSE
A. Expand B. Distribute
C. Interpret D. Lengthen

66. BENIGN
A. Malevolent B. Soft
C. Friendly D. Unwise

67. OBSCURE
A. Implicit B. Obnoxious
C. Explicit D. Pedantic

68. HYPOCRITICAL
A. Gentle B. Sincere
C. Amiable D. Dependable

69. EVASIVE
A. Free B. Honest
C. Liberal D. Frank

70. INDUSTRIOUS
A. Indifferent B. Indolent
C. Casual D. Passive

71. EXTRICATE
A. Manifest B. Palpable
C. Release D. Entangle

72. LUCID
A. Glory B. Noisy
C. Obscure D. Distinct

73. INSIPID
A. Tasty B. Stupid
C. Discreet D. Feast

74. OBEYING
A. Ordering B. Following
C. Refusing D. Contradicting

75. VICTORIOUS
A. Defeated B. Annexed
C. Destroyed D. Vanquished

76. COMMISSIONED
A. Started B. Closed
C. Finished D. Terminated

77. VANITY
A. Pride B. Humility
C. Conceit D. Ostentious

78. ZENITH
A. Acme B. Top
C. Nadir D. Pinnacle

79. TANGIBLE
A. Ethereal B. Concrete
C. Actual D. Solid

80. REPRESS
A. Inhibit B. Liberate
C. Curb D. Quell

81. EPILOGUE
A. Dialogue B. Prelude
C. Post script D. Epigram

82. FRAUDULENT
A. Candid B. Direct
C. Forthright D. Genuine

83. LOQUACIOUS
A. Reticent B. Talkative
C. Garrulous D. Verbose

84. NIGGARDLY
A. Frugal B. Thrifty
C. Stingy D. Generous

85. PERTINENT
A. Irrational B. Irregular
C. Insistent D. Irrelevant

86. FAINT-HEARTED
A. Warm-hearted B. Full-blooded
C. Hot-blooded D. Stout-hearted

87. VIOLENT
A. Humble B. Harmless
C. Gentle D. Tame

88. STATIONARY
A. Active B. Mobile
C. Rapid D. Busy

89. HONORARY
A. Dishonourable B. Reputed
C. Paid D. Official

90. COMMON
A. Rare B. Small
C. Petty D. Poor

91. REPEL
A. Attend B. Concentrate
C. Continue D. Attract

92. ARTIFICIAL
A. Red B. Natural
C. Truthful D. Solid

93. CAPACIOUS
A. Limited B. Caring
C. Foolish D. Changeable

94. PROVOCATION
A. Vocation B. Pacification
C. Peace D. Destruction

95. METICULOUS
A. Mutual B. Shaggy
C. Meretricious D. Slovenly

96. ABLE
A. Disable B. Inable
C. Unable D. Enable

97. COMFORT
A. Uncomfort B. Miscomfort
C. Discomfort D. None of these

98. GAIN
A. Loose B. Fall
C. Lost D. Lose

99. SYNTHETIC
A. Affable B. Natural
C. Plastic D. Cosmetic

100. ACQUITTED
A. Freed B. Burdened
C. Convicted D. Entrusted

ANSWERS

1	2	3	4	5	6	7	8	9	10
B	B	D	A	B	D	D	C	B	D
11	**12**	**13**	**14**	**15**	**16**	**17**	**18**	**19**	**20**
C	C	B	C	D	A	C	C	D	A
21	**22**	**23**	**24**	**25**	**26**	**27**	**28**	**29**	**30**
A	C	D	A	C	C	A	C	D	A
31	**32**	**33**	**34**	**35**	**36**	**37**	**38**	**39**	**40**
A	D	C	A	C	D	C	A	A	A
41	**42**	**43**	**44**	**45**	**46**	**47**	**48**	**49**	**50**
C	B	C	D	B	D	D	B	A	A
51	**52**	**53**	**54**	**55**	**56**	**57**	**58**	**59**	**60**
C	C	C	D	B	D	C	D	C	D
61	**62**	**63**	**64**	**65**	**66**	**67**	**68**	**69**	**70**
D	B	B	A	C	A	C	B	B	B
71	**72**	**73**	**74**	**75**	**76**	**77**	**78**	**79**	**80**
D	C	A	A	A	D	B	C	A	B
81	**82**	**83**	**84**	**85**	**86**	**87**	**88**	**89**	**90**
B	D	B	D	D	D	C	B	C	A
91	**92**	**93**	**94**	**95**	**96**	**97**	**98**	**99**	**100**
D	B	A	B	D	C	C	D	B	C

❑❑❑

6 One Word Substitutions

There are many words in English language which can be perfectly used for a number of words. These words help in expressing ideas in a short and correct manner for the right occasion. Such words not only enhance the vocabulary but also enable you to economise in the use of words to a great extent. Try to learn as many as you can.

Denoting Numbers

- A collection of poems *anthology*
- A number of merchant ships protected by warships (in war-time) *convoy*
- A number of stars grouped together *constellation*
- A number of hired applauders, *i.e.* persons paid to clap *claque*
- A number of people at church *congregation*
- A number of people gathered together for some common purpose *gathering, assembly, society*
- A group of people who get together to work for some cause of common interest *coterie*
- A number of workmen, prisoners, thieves *gang*
- A number of sheep *flock*
- A number of geese *gaggle*
- A number of leopards *leap*
- A number of lions, monkeys *pride, troop*
- A number of herrings, mackerel *shoal*
- A number of fish taken in a net *catch, haul*
- A number of whales, porpoises *school, gam*
- A number of oxen or horses (two or more) harnessed together *team*
- A number of ships, cars, buses *fleet*

Denoting Places

- A place where bees are kept *apiary*
- A place where birds are kept *aviary*
- A place where fishes are kept *aquarium*
- A dwelling-place of an animal underground *burrow*
- A squirrel's home *drey*
- A nest of a bird of prey *eyrie, aerie*

- ❑ A place where spirituous liquors are produced *distillery*
- ❑ A place where clothes are washed and ironed *laundry*
- ❑ A place where Government records are kept *archives*
- ❑ A place where treasures of art, curiosities, etc. are preserved or exhibited *museum*
- ❑ A place where fruit trees are grown *orchard*

Pertaining to the Literary Sphere

- ❑ A work whose writer is unknown *anonymous*
- ❑ A record of one's life written by oneself *autobiography*
- ❑ The history of the life of a person *biography*
- ❑ The heading or short description of a newspaper article, chapter of a book etc. *caption*
- ❑ A humorous play, having a happy ending *comedy*
- ❑ A list of books in a library *catalogue, bibliography*
- ❑ A book in which the events of each day are recorded *diary*
- ❑ A books containing the words of a language with their definitions, in alphabetical order *dictionary*
- ❑ A book of names and addresses *directory*
- ❑ A short speech by a player at the end of a play *epilogue*
- ❑ A brief summary of a book *epitome*
- ❑ A book containing information on all branches of knowledge *encyclopedia*
- ❑ To remove the offensive portions of a book *expurgate*
- ❑ A speech delivered without earlier preparation *extempore*
- ❑ A noisy or vehement speech intended to excite passions *harangue*
- ❑ A written account, usually in book form of the interesting and memorable experiences of one's life *memoirs*
- ❑ A note to help the memory *memorandum*
- ❑ A declaration of plans and promises put forward by a candidate for election, political party or a sovereign *manifesto*
- ❑ A short speech by a player at the beginning of a play *prologue*
- ❑ Literary theft, or passing off an author's original work as one's own *plagiarism*
- ❑ Speaking aloud to oneself *soliloquy*
- ❑ A play with a sad or tragic end *tragedy*

Pertaining to Religion

- ❑ One who believes that man can have no knowledge of God but only of natural phenomena *agnostic*
- ❑ One who renounces his religious vows or forsakes his religious principles *apostate*
- ❑ One who does not believe in existence of God *atheist*
- ❑ One intolerantly devoted to a particular creed *bigot*
- ❑ To utter profane language against God or anything holy *blaspheme*
- ❑ A breaker of church images *iconoclast*
- ❑ Worship of images or idols *idiolatory*

- ❑ One who believes in God *theist*
- ❑ One who believes in only one God *monotheist*
- ❑ One who believes in many Gods *polytheist*

Pertaining to Government

- ❑ To give up a throne or other office of dignity *abdicate*
- ❑ Absence of government *anarchy*
- ❑ Government by Sovereign of uncontrolled authority *autocracy, despotism*
- ❑ Government by departments of states *bureaucracy*
- ❑ Government of the people, for the people and by the people *democracy*
- ❑ Government by the nobility *aristocracy*
- ❑ The right of self-government *autonomy*
- ❑ Government by a few *oligarchy*
- ❑ Government by the wealthy *plutocracy*
- ❑ Government by divine guidance *theocracy*
- ❑ To decide a political question by the direct vote of the whole electorate *referendum*
- ❑ Sweeping governmental change *revolution*
- ❑ The science of government *politics*

Pertaining to Professions

- ❑ One who attends to the diseases of the eye *oculist*
- ❑ One who tests eyesight and sells spectacles *optician*
- ❑ One who attends to the teeth *dentist*
- ❑ One skilled in the care of hands and feet *chiropodist*
- ❑ A physician who assists women at child-birth *obstetrician*
- ❑ One who drives a motorcar *chauffeur*
- ❑ One who makes or sells candles *chandler*
- ❑ One who preserves the skins of animals and mounts them so as to resemble the living animals *taxidermist*
- ❑ One who compiles a dictionary *lexicographer*
- ❑ One who writes books *author*
- ❑ One skilled in the treatment of diseases of animals *veterinarian*
- ❑ A tradesman who manages funerals *undertaker*
- ❑ One who draws up contracts and lends money on interest *scrivener*
- ❑ One who lends money and keeps goods as security *pawnbroker*
- ❑ A teacher who travels from place to place to give instruction. *peripatetic*
- ❑ One who travels from place to place selling miscellaneous articles *hawker, pedlar*
- ❑ One who collects postage stamps *philatelist*
- ❑ One who lends money at exorbitant interest *usurer*
- ❑ One who takes care of a building *janitor*
- ❑ One who sells sweets and pastries *confectioner*
- ❑ One who works in a coalmine *collier*
- ❑ One who flies an aeroplane *pilot, aviator*

- ❑ One who studies rocks and soils — *geologist*
- ❑ One who shoes horses — *farrier*
- ❑ A professional rider in horses races — *jockey*
- ❑ One who deals in silks, cotton, woollen, and linen goods — *mercer*
- ❑ One who deals in wines — *vintner*
- ❑ One who deals in fish — *fishmonger*
- ❑ One who deals in iron and hardware — *ironmonger*
- ❑ One who sells fruits, vegetables, etc. from a barrow — *costermonger*
- ❑ One who sets type in a printing office — *compositor*

Pertaining to Medicine

- ❑ A substance which destroys or weakens germs — *antiseptic*
- ❑ Any medicine which produces insensibility — *anaesthetic*
- ❑ A medicine to counteract poison — *antidote*
- ❑ Want or poorness of blood — *anaemia*
- ❑ A medicine which alleviates pain — *anodyne*
- ❑ To cut off a person's body a part which is infected — *amputate*
- ❑ One who is recovering from illness — *convalescent*
- ❑ To be able to tell the nature of disease by its symptoms — *diagnose*
- ❑ A disease affecting many persons at the same place and time — *epidemic*
- ❑ A disease confined to a particular district or place — *endemic*
- ❑ To disinfect by smoke — *fumigate*
- ❑ Free or exempt from infection — *immune*
- ❑ A person who is sick — *invalid*
- ❑ A cure for all diseases — *panacea*
- ❑ A disease widely epidemic — *pandemic*
- ❑ Confinement to one place to avoid spread of infection — *quarantine*

Pertaining to Characteristics and Actions

- ❑ One who devotes his life to the welfare and interests of other people — *altruist*
- ❑ One who can use both hands with equal ease — *ambidexterous*
- ❑ One who fishes with a rod — *angler*
- ❑ One who kills secretly or by surprise — *assassin*
- ❑ A person who collects things belonging to ancient times — *antiquary*
- ❑ One who is always finding faults — *censorious*
- ❑ One living at the same time as another — *contemporary*
- ❑ One who sneers at the aims and beliefs of his fellowmen — *cynic*
- ❑ One who delights in speaking about oneself — *egotist*
- ❑ One who exalts his own opinion — *egoist*
- ❑ One who dies for a noble cause — *martyr*
- ❑ One who retires from society to live a solitary life — *recluse, hermit*
- ❑ One who maliciously sets fire to buildings — *incendiary*

- One who is banished from his home or his country — *exile*
- One who takes refuge in a foreign country — *refugee, alien*
- One who runs away from justice or the law — *fugitive*
- One who walks in his sleep — *somnambulist*
- One who looks on the bright side of things — *optimist*
- One who looks on the dark side of things — *pessimist*
- A hater of mankind — *misanthropist*
- One who knows everything — *omniscient*
- One who is all powerful — *omnipotent*
- One who is present everywhere — *omnipresent*
- One who devotes his service or wealth for the love of mankind — *philanthropist*
- One new to anything — *novice, tyro, neophyte*
- One who engages in any pursuit for the love of it, and not for gain — *amateur*
- One who journeys to a holy place — *pilgrim*
- A leader of the people who can sway his followers by his oratory — *demagogue*
- One who has special skill in judging art, music, tastes, etc. — *connoisseur*
- One whose reasoning is clever yet false — *sophist*
- One who makes a display of his learning — *pedant*
- One who is indifferent to pain or pleasure — *stoic*
- One who loves his country and serves it devotedly — *patriot*
- One devoted to the pleasures of eating and drinking — *epicure*
- One who poses to be what he is not — *hypocrite, impostor*
- One who foretells events — *prophet*
- One who pretends to know a great deal about everything — *mountebank, charlatan, quack*
- One versed in many languages — *linguist*
- One who cannot pay one's debts — *insolvent*
- One who takes over after another in office or employment — *successor*
- One who has been before another in office or employment — *predecessor*
- One who is opposed to intellectual progress — *obscurant*
- One who abstains from alcoholic drinks — *teetotaller*
- One who hides away on a ship to obtain a free passage — *stowaway*
- One who spends very little — *miser*
- One who spends too much — *spendthrift*

Pertaining to War

- An unprovoked attack by an enemy — *aggression*
- Shells, bombs, military stores — *ammunition*
- A place where naval or military weapons are made or stored — *ordnance*
- An agreement between belligerents to stop fighting — *armistice*
- A general pardon of offenders — *amnesty*
- To reduce to nothing — *annihilate*
- Nations carrying on warfare — *belligerents*

- To surround a place with the intention of capturing *besiege*
- To camp in the open air without tents or covering *bivouac*
- To seize for military use *commandeer*
- A person who is forced by law to become a soldier *conscript*
- An order prohibiting ships to leave the ports *embargo*
- A number of firearms being discharged continuously *fusillade*
- To make an examination or preliminary survey of enemy territory for military objectives *reconnoitre*

Pertaining to Marriage and Children

- One who marries a second wife or husband while the legal spouse is alive *bigamist*
- One vowed to a single or unmarried life *celibate*
- One engaged to be married *fiancé, fiancee*
- A child whose parents are dead *orphan*
- A hater of marriage *misogamist*
- One who has more than two wives at a time *polygamist*

Pertaining to Death

- Dead and decaying flesh (esp. of animals) *carrion*
- A monument set up for persons who are buried elsewhere *cenotaph*
- To preserve a dead body from putrefaction *embalm*
- Words inscribed on a tomb *epitaph*
- An examination of dead body *postmortem, autopsy*
- An account in the newspaper of the funeral of one deceased *obituary*
- The property left to someone by a will *legacy*
- Occurring after death *posthumous*
- The act of killing a human being *homicide*
- Murder of a new born child *infanticide*
- Murder of a brother *fratricide*
- Murder of a sister *sororicide*
- Murder of a mother *matricide*
- Murder of a father *patricide*
- Murder of a parent *parricide*
- Murder of a king *regicide*

Pertaining to Sciences and Arts

- The study of all heavenly bodies and the earth in relation to them *astronomy*
- The science of land management *agronomics*
- The study of mankind *anthropology*
- The study of physical life or living matter *biology*
- The study of plants *botany*
- The art of beautiful handwriting *calligraphy*

- ❑ The science which deals with the varieties of human race *ethnology*
- ❑ The study of the origin and history of words *etymology*
- ❑ The study of coins *numismatics*
- ❑ The study of human face *physiognomy*
- ❑ The art of making fireworks *pyrotechnics*
- ❑ The study of birds *ornithology*
- ❑ The study of languages *philology*
- ❑ At home equally on land or in water *amphibious*
- ❑ The inside of a nut *kernel*
- ❑ The central or innermost part of fruit *core*
- ❑ The animals of a certain region *fauna*
- ❑ The plants and vegetation of a certain region *flora*
- ❑ Absence of rain for a long time *drought*
- ❑ To supply land with water by artificial means *irrigate*
- ❑ One who studies plant and animal life *naturalist*
- ❑ A cud-chewing animal, *e.g.* the cow *ruminant*
- ❑ A gnawing animal, *e.g.* the rat *rodent*
- ❑ A four-footed animal *quadruped*
- ❑ Animals which carry their young in a pouch, *e.g.* kangaroo *marsupials*
- ❑ Soil composed largely of decayed vegetable matter *humus*
- ❑ A preparation for killing insects *insecticide*
- ❑ A plant or animal growing on another *parasite*
- ❑ Living for many years *perennial*

Miscellaneous

- ❑ Loud enough to be heard *audible*
- ❑ Not distinct enough to be heard *inaudible*
- ❑ Fit for food *edible*
- ❑ Unfit for human consumption *inedible*
- ❑ Fit to be chosen or selected *eligible*
- ❑ Not having the qualities for being chosen *ineligible*
- ❑ Writing that is easy to read *legible*
- ❑ Writing that is difficult to decipher *illegible*
- ❑ Able to read *literate*
- ❑ Unable to read *illiterate*
- ❑ Born of married parents *legitimate*
- ❑ Born of unmarried parents *illegitimate*
- ❑ To send back a person to his own country *repatriate*
- ❑ To banish from one's country *expatriate*
- ❑ To move from one country to another *migrate*
- ❑ One who leaves his country to settle in another *emigrant*
- ❑ One who comes into a foreign country to settle there *immigrant*

- ❑ Incapable of being redeemed from evil, *i.e.* beyond correction — *incorrigible*
- ❑ That which cannot be rubbed out or blotted out — *ineffaceable, indelible*
- ❑ That which cannot be conquered — *invincible*
- ❑ Incapable of making errors — *infallible*
- ❑ That which cannot be avoided or prevented — *inevitable*
- ❑ Incapable of being burnt — *incombustible*
- ❑ That which easily catches fire — *inflammable, flammable*
- ❑ That which cannot be seen — *invisible*
- ❑ Living for ever — *immortal*
- ❑ Increase the gravity of an offence — *aggravate*
- ❑ Ordinary or commonplace remark — *platitude*
- ❑ That which cannot be satisfied — *insatiable*
- ❑ That which cannot be repaired — *irreparable*
- ❑ That which cannot be imitated — *inimitable*
- ❑ Persons (or efforts) that cannot be wearied — *indefatigable*
- ❑ One who eats too much — *glutton*
- ❑ To destroy completely — *annihilate*
- ❑ A statement open to more than one interpretation — *ambiguous*
- ❑ A round about way of speaking — *circumlocution*
- ❑ Cautious observation of events, etc. — *circumspection*
- ❑ That which cannot be hurt — *invulnerable*

Multiple Choice Questions

Directions: *Below are given some statements each of which is capable of being expressed by one word only. Each statement is followed by four such words of which only one is correct. Out of the given alternatives A, B, C and D choose the correct word which very closely fits each definition.*

1. A set of papers giving information about a person or event:
   A. editorial B. agenda
   C. dossier D. clippings
2. List and explanations of technical, difficult, etc. terms:
   A. preface B. glossary
   C. bibliography D. appendix
3. One who pays too much care to his clothes and personal appearance:
   A. conscious B. dandy
   C. cynosure D. leer
4. A child born after death of father:
   A. effeminate B. immature
   C. fatherless D. posthumous
5. A person who is hard to please:
   A. insensible B. hypocrite
   C. egoist D. fastidious
6. Complete failure in something attempted:
   A. fiasco B. vain
   C. falsies D. flop
7. A word which can be interpreted in any way:
   A. confusing B. misnomer
   C. ambiguous D. precise
8. A group of persons united by common interests:
   A. society B. class
   C. clique D. coterie

9. A person who is inexperienced and easily deceived:
A. fool B. immature
C. blackhorn D. greenhorn

10. Instruction by question and answer:
A. interrogatory B. catechism
C. bulletin D. alibi

11. Record of events by someone with first hand knowledge:
A. novice B. report
C. memoir D. itinerary

12. A mode of talk familiar to a particular group or profession:
A. jargon B. colloquial
C. slang D. abuses

13. Person who is crazy:
A. lackadaisical B. tarter
C. scrupulous D. loony

14. A person who readily believes others:
A. hasty B. immature
C. credulous D. credible

15. One who eats human flesh:
A. beast B. cannibal
C. maneater D. carnivorous

16. Intentional destruction of racial groups:
A. genocide B. homicide
C. fratricide D. communal riot

17. One with weakness of mind caused by old age:
A. dastard B. dotard
C. fop D. philanderer

18. Study of insects:
A. zoology B. philology
C. entomology D. etymology

19. A critical judge of any art particularly fine arts:
A. connoisseur B. veteran
C. philistine D. dilettante

20. One who introduces items of an entertainment:
A. consort B. compere
C. director D. introducer

21. A combination of business firms:
A. enterprise B. franchise
C. cartel D. autonomous

22. Freeing of suppressed emotions:
A. catastrophe B. catharsis
C. epilogue D. chagrin

23. One who believes in the power of fate:
A. optimist B. pessimist
C. fearful D. fatalist

24. The murder of brother:
A. genocide B. homicide
C. salvage D. fratricide

25. Additional to proper payment:
A. premium B. overtime
C. ex-gratia D. fringe

26. A person or thing used to tempt somebody into a position of danger:
A. decoy B. provocateur
C. jinx D. scapegoat

27. Custom of having more than one husband at the same time:
A. polygamy B. polyandry
C. bigamy D. sexagenary

28. A person of refined taste in food and drink:
A. emeritus B. epicure
C. glutton D. gourmand

29. A tombstone inscription:
A. epithet B. encomium
C. epistle D. epitaph

30. An office which has no work but high salary:
A. fortuitous B. gratuitous
C. sinecure D. ceremonial

31. One who is indifferent to pains and pleasure of life:
A. stoic B. metaphysical
C. pessimist D. sceptic

32. List of names of persons showing duties to be performed by each in turn:
A. notice B. bulletin
C. roster D. agenda

33. Long angry speech of criticism or accusation:
A. track record B. tirade
C. taut D. outburst

34. One who is in favour of never drinking alcoholic drinks:
A. idealist B. uxorious
C. teetotaller D. unalcoholic

35. Trying to win favour by flattery and charm:
A. smarmy B. shrewish
C. toady D. loquacious

36. A decision on which one cannot go back:
A. incorrigible B. irrevocable
C. rigid D. invulnerable

37. The science that studies the varieties of human race:
A. phrenology B. physiology
C. sociology D. ethnology

38. A person who hates women:
A. philogynist B. philatelist
C. misogamist D. misogynist

39. A group of people in a particular grade in an organisation:
A. colleague B. staff
C. echelon D. commission

40. Honourably discharged from service:
A. emeritus B. latitudinarian
C. infallible D. meritorious

41. One who does not believe in the existence of God:
A. atheist B. altruist
C. agnostic D. flippant

42. The large money paid for an early retirement:
A. goldmine B. golden handshake
C. gratuity D. lion's share

43. A hater of learning and knowledge:
A. misologist B. misogynist
C. philologist D. philanthropist

44. One who lives and acts for the welfare of others:
A. misanthrope B. credulous
C. altruist D. gregarious

45. Mental weariness for want of occupation:
A. desperate B. depression
C. fatigue D. ennui

46. That which makes it difficult to recognise the presence in real of somebody or something:
A. cover B. mask
C. make-up D. camouflage

47. To bear a hand in one's new business:
A. partnership B. interfere
C. assist D. join

48. One who renounces the world and practices self-discipline in order to attain salvation:
A. devotee B. ascetic
C. theist D. parsimonious

49. A place where gambling is practiced:
A. hotel B. motel
C. casino D. stadium

50. A sad song is a:
A. dirge B. elegy
C. ditty D. knell

ANSWERS

1	2	3	4	5	6	7	8	9	10
C	B	B	D	D	A	C	C	D	B
11	**12**	**13**	**14**	**15**	**16**	**17**	**18**	**19**	**20**
C	A	D	C	B	A	B	C	A	B
21	**22**	**23**	**24**	**25**	**26**	**27**	**28**	**29**	**30**
C	B	D	D	D	A	B	B	D	C
31	**32**	**33**	**34**	**35**	**36**	**37**	**38**	**39**	**40**
A	C	B	C	A	B	D	D	C	A
41	**42**	**43**	**44**	**45**	**46**	**47**	**48**	**49**	**50**
A	B	A	C	D	D	C	B	C	A

❑❑❑

Idioms and Phrases

- An idiom is a group of words established by usage as having a meaning different from the individual words.
- A phrase is a small group of words standing together as an idiomatic expression.

  Learn and practise as may as you can.

Idioms and Idiomatic Phrases

- **ABC** (basic principles)
  She does not know the ABC of photography.
- **At one's beck and call** (ready to obey)
  He had a dozen men at his beck and call.
- **At sixes and sevens** (in disorder)
  The drawing room articles were lying at sixes and sevens on the floor.
- **A wet blanket** (a discouraging person)
  Don't allow Rakesh to accompany you to the hunting trip because he is a wet blanket.
- **A big gun** (an important person)
  Mr Smith is a big gun in our city.
- **At a stone's throw** (at a short distance from)
  My school is at a stone's throw from my house.
- **A man of word** (a person who keeps his promise)
  Mr Sharma is a man of word.
- **A man of a few words** (a remarkable person)
  Gandhiji was a man of a few words.
- **At arm's length** (to keep away)
  We should always keep bad boys at arm's length
- **A bolt from the blue** (a sudden and unexpected event)
  The news of my friend's death came to me like a bolt from the blue.
- **A man of letters** (a scholar)
  Radha Krishnan was a man of letters.
- **A hard nut to crack.** (a puzzling problem)
  To get a win over American basket ball team is a hard nut to crack for India.
- **A yeoman's service** (service which is beneficial to the human beings)
  He did yeoman's service through his life.
- **A snake in the grass** (a hidden foe)
  Beware of him because he seems to be a snake in the grass.
- **Acid test** (hard test)
  The election will be an acid test for the ruling party.
- **A wolf in sheep's clothing** (a hypocrite)
  You should not keep company with him because he is a wolf in sheep's clothing.
- **At the eleventh hour** (at the last moment)
  The war was about to start but fortunately at the eleventh hour a messenger came to the PM with a message of peace.
- **A great card** (an important person)
  Mr Sood is a great card in the ministry of finance.
- **A fool of the first water** (one completely foolish)
  Being a fool of the first water he could not solve even the simplest sum.
- **A bone of contention** (to be the cause of quarrel)
  Kashmir is the bone of contention between India and Pakistan.
- **A green hand** (not very much experienced)
  We shall pay a little to a green hand.
- **All in all** (completely)
  Rajesh is all in all in this office.
- **A bed of roses** (a comfort)
  Life is not a bed of roses.

- **An apple of discord** (to be the cause of)
  Kashmir is an apple of discord between India and Pakistan.
- **A white elephant** (of no use)
  This sort of glib talker always proves a white elephant in the end.
- **A red letter day** (An important day)
  15th August is a red letter day for the Indians.
- **By hook or by crook** (by any means fair or foul)
- **Black sheep** (a traitor)
  Later on Mr XYZ proved a black sheep.
- **By dint of** (by means of)
  By dint of hard work, she earned a lot of money.
- **Break ones back** (to work hard to get something)
  He broke his back to earn his livelihood.
- **Break the back of** (accomplish the hardest part of a certain job)
  There is nothing to be worried about as we've already broken the back of the problem.
- **Beat about the bush** (to go on talking on some worthless topic)
  Stop this beating about the bush, come to the main task.
- **Beyond one's means** (beyond one's budget)
  He is living beyond his means, therefore, he is sure to get ruined.
- **Cut loose** (Keep away)
  India should cut loose from bad politics.
- **Chips of the same block** (having the same taste)
  They are the chips of the same block.
- **Cut-throat competition** (a stiff competition)
  There is a cut-throat competition among the publishers in the market.
- **Come what may** (no matter what happens)
  I'll do it come what may.
- **Drop someone a line** (send a letter, etc.)
  Please drop me a line of your well-being.
- **Dull the edge of** (reduce the intensity of)
  Take this pill and it will dull the edge of pain.
- **From hand to mouth** (without any saving)
  The poor factory worker is living from hand to mouth.
- **Fair and square** (clean)
  One must be fair and square in one's dealing.
- **Hard of hearing** (somewhat deaf)
  She is a bit hard of hearing.
- **In the good books of** (be good in one's mind)
  Jack is in the good books of his teachers.
- **In black and white** (in written)
  Don't give him anything in black and white.
- **In cold blood** (mercilessly)
  The old woman was murdered in cold blood.
- **In a crack** (all of a sudden or rapidly)
  The thief left the place in a crack.
- **In full swing** (in full force)
  The studies of the students are going on in full swing.
- **In the twinkling of an eye** (quickly)
  The monkey ate up grams in the twinkling of an eye.
- **Keep the ball rolling** (to maintain the progress of some activity)
  After the death of his father he had to take the charge of his office to keep the ball rolling.
- **Neck and neck** (even)
  There is a neck and neck fight between the two boxers.
- **Once in a blue moon** (seldom)
  She visits her brother once in a blue moon.
- **Slow and steady** (slowly but continually)
  Slow and steady wins the race.
- **To cut a sorry figure** (present oneself in a bad way)
  She cut a sorry figure on the stage.
- **To give a red carpet reception** (to give a warm welcome)
  The PM was given a red carpet reception in America.
- **To dance one's tune** (to follow someone submissively)
  He always dances to his brother's tune.
- **To turn a deaf ear to** (to disregard)
  She turned a deaf ear to her parents' advice.

✦ **To call a spade a spade** (to speak the truth)
Gandhiji always called a spade a spade.

✦ **To bring to book** (to scold)
The naughty boy was brought to book by the teacher.

✦ **To cut short** (to reduce)
Smoking will cut short your life.
He wants to get money by hook or by crook.

✦ **To grease the palm of** (to bribe)
Rohit greased the palm of the clerk and got the file moved.

✦ **Through thick and thin.** (under all circumstances)
We'll stand by you through thick and thin.

✦ **To die by inches** (to die a painful death)
The old man died by inches.

✦ **To eat one's words** (to retract one's statement)
You'll have to eat your words because you have spoken without thinking.

✦ **To burn the midnight oil** (to work hard)
You'll have to burn the midnight oil if you want to get good marks.

✦ **To poke one's nose into** (to meddle with)
It is bad to poke your nose into others' affair.

✦ **To fall flat** (to have no effect)
His father's advice fell flat on him.

✦ **To make a clean breast of** (to confess)
He made a clean breast of his involvement in the bomb blast.

✦ **To get the better of** (overcome)
Anger got the better of him.

✦ **To break somebody's back** (to give too much work to him to do)
She broke his back by giving him so much hard work to do.

✦ **Throw cold water on** (to discourage)
She tried to throw cold water on his plan but he was well-determined.

✦ **The long and short of** (in brief)
The long and short of his lecture is that we should live like brothers.

✦ **To burn one's fingers** (to get oneself in trouble)
You have burnt your fingers by speaking against him.

✦ **To turn over a new leaf** (to change the course of life)
He has turned over a new leaf in his life.

✦ **To have one's own axe to grind** (to have vested interest)
He has his own axe to grind in this matter.

✦ **To take to one's heels** (to run away)
The thief took to his heels as soon as he saw the policeman.

✦ **To move heaven and earth** (to make too much effort)
The young man moved heaven and earth to find a job.

✦ **To be caught red handed** (to be caught at the time of committing a crime)
The clerk was caught red handed when he was accepting bribe from Mr ABC.

✦ **To receive with open arms** (to give a warm welcome)
The new president of the club was received with open arms by the members.

✦ **To be born with a silver spoon in one's mouth** (to be born in a rich family)
Mr. J. L. Nehru was born with a silver spoon in his mouth.

✦ **To come to light** (to be known)
A new disease has recently come to light.

✦ **To be the apple of one's eye** (be very dear)
He is the apple of his parent's eye.

✦ **To make fun of** (laugh at)
The children made fun of the waiter in the hotel.

✦ **To let the cat out of the bag** (to divulge secret)
It was Sohan who let the cat out of the bag by telling the real matter.

✦ **To open a new chapter** (to start some habit, etc.
By drinking, you've opened a new chapter in your life.

✦ **To make the flesh creep** (to terrify)
The story made my flesh creep.

✦ **To lose ground** (to retreat)
After fighting for some time the Pakistani army began to lose ground.

✦ **To bring to book** (to punish)
The student was brought to book by the teacher.

✦ **To show a clean pair of heels** (to run away)
The thief showed a clean pair of heels as soon as he saw the policeman approaching.

✦ **To gain ground** (to be established)
He gained ground in India in a few years.

✦ **To get wind of** (to get information)
I got wind of his secret plans.

✦ **Under a cloud** (be in trouble or in a state of disgrace or suspicion)
His company seemed to be under a cloud as it had no funds to pay the wages to the workers.

Verbal Phrases

✦ **Act upon** (to follow)
I acted upon my father's advice.

✦ **Act upto** (to perform within limits)
He acted upto his conscience.

✦ **Act beyond** (to perform crossing limits)
We should not act beyond our capacity.

✦ **Act for** (to perform in place of someone else)
The vice principal acted for the principal.

✦ **Back up** (to make a queue)
The vehicles began to back up.

✦ **Back down** (withdraw claim in the presence of opposition)
The leader backed down from his previous statement.

✦ **Back off** (draw back some plan or action)
They backed off from building a flyover.

✦ **Back out** (withdraw from a promise, etc.)
The government backed out of its promise.

✦ **Break down** (stop working) My car broke down on the highway.

✦ **Break into** (enter in certain premises by breaking the door, etc.)
Last night a thief broke into my neighbour's.

✦ **Break off** (stop all of a sudden)
She broke off and began to think over about her/his hand.

✦ **Break out** (spread)
Cholera has broken out in the town.

✦ **Break out of** (escape from)
A prisoner broke out of the prison last night.

✦ **Break up** (disperse)
The cloud of fog began to break up as the sun rose.

✦ **Break something up** (Cause something to break into small pieces)
She broke up the chocolate to distribute it among the girls.

✦ **Break with** (Cut off connection after quarrelling with someone)
He has broken with his brother.

✦ **Call on** (pay a visit to somebody)
I'll call on Mohan's today.

✦ **Call out** (to start)
The workers have called out a strike.

✦ **Call off** (to stop the strike etc.)
The workers have called off the strike.

✦ **Call at** (to visit someone's house)
I called at his house yesterday.

✦ **Call in** (send for)
Please call in the doctor.

✦ **Carry on** (continue)
Please carry on your work.

✦ **Carry something out** (perform a task)
Our company is carrying out a big deal with a foreign company.

✦ **Carry something over** (postpone)
The fancy dress competition had to be carried over till Monday)

✦ **Carry someone off** (kill somebody)
Cancer carried her off on the day of her 20th birthday.

✦ **Come of age** (get established)
As our company has come of age, so, there is no problem in selling our goods.

✦ **Come of** (belong to)
She comes of a royal family.

✦ **Come over** (surmount)
We at last came over all our problems.

- **Come off** (to take place)
The marriage of my brother comes off in the next month.
- **Come round** (agree)
At last he came round to my views.
- **Come under** (fall in the category of)
All these animals come under the same species.
- **Come down with** (suffer from)
She came down with whopping cough.
- **Come from** (be the nature of)
She came from London.
- **Come about** (happen)
The explosion came about when the worker struck the match to light a cigarette.
- **Cut off** (die)
The princess was cut off in the prime of her life.
- **Cut down** (reduce)
The prices of consumer goods should be cut down.
- **Cut someone out** (exclude someone)
His father cut him out of his will.
- **Fall in**
She fell in love with the prince.
- **Fall down** (fail)
The deal fell down for lack of transparency.
- **Fall out** (quarrel)
She fell out with his elder brother.
- **Fall through** (fail)
The project fell through for lack of funds.
- **Get away** (escape)
She got away with her life.
- **Get by** (to accomplish something with great difficulty)
She is not rich. She has just enough to get by.
- **Get on** (perform)
How are you getting on with your studies?
- **Get out** (become known)
The news got out that the PM was paying a visit to Russia.
- **Get over** (overcome)
At last I got over all obstacles.
- **Get up** (rise)
When do you get up in the morning?
- **Give up** (stop)
He gave up smoking.
- **Give out** (emit)
Garlic gives out a pungent smell.
- **Give in** (collapse)
The bridge gave in under the heavy load.
- **Give away** (distribute)
The Principal gave away the prizes.
- **Give out** (announce)
It was given out that the President of India would visit the place soon.
- **Go off** (explode)
The gun went off suddenly.
- **Go on** (continue)
She went on about how she flew the aeroplane.
- **Go through** (examine)
I'll go through this book later on.
- **Go up** (be built)
The construction of the house is going up.
- **Grind on** (continue for a long time in a tedious way)
The discussion over political issues ground on.
- **Grind something out** (produce something a tedious way)
She will grind some more short stories.
- **Look out** (be careful)
Look out! there is a snake.
- **Look down upon** (hate)
We should not look down upon the poor.
- **Look at** (watch)
Look at the blackboard.
- **Look after** (take care of)
We ought to look after our old parents.
- **Look into** (investigate)
The new police inspector will look into the matter.
- **Look up** (rise)
The prices of consumer goods are looking up.

✦ **Look back** (think of the past)
It made her feel disolate when she looked back on things of the past.

✦ **Make up** (to fulfil)
I'll make up my deficiency in Mathematics.

✦ **Make out** (understand)
I could not make out what she said.

✦ **Make up one' mind** (to resolve)
I have made up my mind to settle in the USA.

✦ **Make off** (leave hurriedly)
She made off without informing anybody.

✦ **Make something over** (transfer)
She should make her property over to her sons.

✦ **Make over** (hand over)
He made over the charge of the file to Mr Robert.

✦ **Pull back** (retreat)
The government has pulled back from its previous policy.

✦ **Pull something down** (demolish)
The authorities concerned pulled down a few building which were illegally built on government land.

✦ **Pull out** (pluck)
The child pulled out a few petals of the flower.

✦ **Pull through** (recover)
The patient will pull through.

✦ **Push on** (continue a journey)
It was getting darker but we pushed on.

✦ **Push at** (exert force)
He pushed at the bell, but it did not ring.

✦ **Push for** (demand persistently)
The workers have been pushing for the installation of new machines for five years.

✦ **Put out** (extinguish)
She put out the light.

✦ **Put on** (wear)
He put on an overcoat.

✦ **Put off** (postpone)
The plan had to be put off.

✦ **Put by** (spare something for future)
We must put by some money for future.

✦ **Put up with** (stay)
Your aunt is out of town for a couple of days, you may put up with us till she comes.

✦ **Put something down** (record something)
She put a new idea down on the paper.

✦ **Take after** (resemble)
He takes after his father.

✦ **Take off** (remove)
He took off his shoes.

✦ **Take something out** (obtain)
You may take out some money from Rohit if you want to purchase this car.

✦ **Take to** (fall into the habit of)
He took to gambling.

✦ **Turn something down** (reject something)
The judge turned down his appeal.

✦ **Turn on** (attack)
The thief turned on him with a knife.

Multiple Choice Questions

Directions: *Some idioms/phrases are given below with their probable meanings. Select the options with their correct meanings.*

1. Carry out
A. To take from one place to another
B. To continue
C. To obey
D. To make efforts

2. In the same boat
A. A worn out choice
B. Indifferent
C. In identical circumstances
D. Carry off

3. In one's good book
A. A costly book
B. A priceless treasure

C. In one's favour
D. An enchanting beauty

4. Keep a straight face
A. To do make up
B. To change clothes
C. Assume responsibility
D. To remain serious

5. To be above board
A. To have a good height
B. To be honest in any business deal
C. To have no debts
D. To try to be beautiful

6. On the face of it
A. To agree
B. From an action
C. More than enough
D. Apparently

7. Let the bygones be bygones
A. In one's favour
B. To pretend
C. To forget the past
D. Other choice

8. To split hairs
A. Major distinctions
B. Hair with two ends
C. To make minute distinction
D. Without distinction

9. Bread and butter
A. Both bread and butter
B. Something essential
C. Livelihood
D. Relevant things

10. To bell the cat
A. To catch a cat and tie a bell round its neck
B. To make an effort
C. To be quick
D. To face a risk

11. Hard and fast
A. Strict
B. Solid
C. Fast moving
D. Some hard surface

12. Part and parcel
A. The part of a parcel
B. An essential part
C. A missing parcel
D. Some part of a machine sent by parcel

13. Null and void
A. Something invalid
B. Something that can be avoided
C. Something that can be nullified
D. Something evil

14. To make clean breast of
A. To gain prominence
B. To praise oneself
C. To confess without reserve
D. To destroy before it blooms

15. Trump card
A. A powerful means of achieving an object
B. Resourcefulness
C. The best gamble to attain success
D. None of these

16. Tall talk
A. A discussion continued for a long time
B. A high sounding talk
C. A meaningful talk
D. A useless talk

17. Small talk
A. Gossip
B. A discussion carried on for a long time
C. A brief discussion
D. None of these

18. Throw out of gear
A. To replace
B. Hinder, disturb
C. To decide
D. Take up tune

19. To and fro
A. Back and forth
B. Puzzled
C. Amazed
D. Reprove

20. To bell the cat
A. To do an easy job
B. To be indifferent to
C. To undertake a difficult job
D. To clarify

21. To be under cloud
A. Puzzle
B. Enjoy the favour
C. Talk thoughtlessly
D. To be under suspicion

22. A labour of love
A. A tragic end
B. A funny thing
C. Not fruitful
D. Work done without payment

23. Follow suit
A. Follow an example B. Wear a new dress
C. Irrelevant D. A gay person

24. Foul play
A. Bad intentions
B. A play not well acted
C. A play not liked by the audience
D. None of these

25. To pick holes
A. To find some reason to quarrel
B. To destroy something
C. To criticise someone
D. To cut some part of an item

26. To smell a rat
A. To see signs of plague epidemic
B. To get bad smell of a dead rat
C. To suspect foul dealings
D. To be in a bad mood

27. To put a spoke in one's wheel
A. To encourage
B. Act without restraint
C. Risk something
D. To obstruct one's progress

28. To pull one's leg
A. To give up B. Take care of
C. To befool D. To know

29. To play with fire
A. Grasp the truth
B. To handle something dangerous
C. To ridicule
D. To flee away

30. To reckon with
A. Take up time
B. Make an inventory
C. To deal with
D. Submit to punishment

31. To run short
A. Talk until one is tired at
B. Apply to oneself
C. To get rid of
D. To have or be too little

32. A man of letters
A. A postman B. A learned man
C. A hypocrite D. An ignorant man

33. A maiden speech
A. A speech made in the parliament
B. A speech made before unmarried girls
C. A speech made by a political leader
D. A speech made for the first time

34. Order of the day
A. An order passed on a particular day
B. A current law
C. Something common or general
D. None of these

35. To end in smoke
A. To make completely understand
B. To ruin oneself
C. To excite great applause
D. None of these

36. To give vent to
A. To allow to flow forth
B. To prove a failure
C. To amass wealth
D. To evade

37. To eat humble pie
A. To apologise or confess
B. To order
C. To flatter
D. To get rid of

38. A black sheep
A. An unlucky person
B. A negro
C. An ugly person
D. None of these

39. To catch a tartar
A. To trap wanted criminal with great difficulty
B. To catch a dangerous person
C. To meet with disaster
D. To deal with a person who is more than one's watch

40. Sit on fence
A. To remain neutral
B. To show contempt
C. To enjoy the surroundings
D. To become fond of

41. Pay off old scores
A. To repay the debt
B. To have revenge
C. To invite
D. Secretly

42. Turn turtle

A. To cheat
B. To be lopsided
C. To frustrate
D. To dance to the tune

43. Wash one's hands of

A. To refuse B. To assist
C. To abuse D. To refuse to be

44. Under duress

A. Under compulsion
B. Willing
C. To elicit information
D. To demand

45. To turn the tables

A. To ruin someone
B. To turn the situation to one's own side
C. To reverse the situation
D. To move from one point to another

46. On the cards

A. Possibly B. Probably
C. Openly D. Likely

47. To leave someone in the lurch

A. To come to compromise with someone
B. Constant source of annoyance to someone
C. To put someone at ease
D. To desert someone in his difficulties

48. To play second fiddle

A. To be happy, cheerful and healthy
B. To reduce importance of one's senior
C. To support the role and view of another person
D. To do back seat driving

49. To yearn for

A. To weep for
B. To remember
C. To admire
D. To long for intensely

50. Call off

A. To finish B. To withdraw
C. To postpone D. To cry

ANSWERS

1	2	3	4	5	6	7	8	9	10
C	C	C	D	B	D	C	C	C	D
11	**12**	**13**	**14**	**15**	**16**	**17**	**18**	**19**	**20**
A	B	A	C	C	B	A	B	A	C
21	**22**	**23**	**24**	**25**	**26**	**27**	**28**	**29**	**30**
D	D	A	A	C	C	D	C	B	C
31	**32**	**33**	**34**	**35**	**36**	**37**	**38**	**39**	**40**
D	B	D	C	D	A	A	D	B	A
41	**42**	**43**	**44**	**45**	**46**	**47**	**48**	**49**	**50**
B	B	D	A	C	D	D	C	D	B

❑❑❑

8 Narration

Direct and Indirect Narration/Speech

The exact words spoken by the speaker are known as Direct Speech.

The words spoken by somebody and expressed by someone else with some modification are known as Indirect Speech.

(*a*) Ram says to me, "You do not help me."

(*b*) Ram tells me that I do not help him.

The sentence (*a*) shows the words spoken by Ram. So, it is a sentence of Direct Speech.

The sentence (*b*) shows the words spoken by Ram and expressed by someone else with certain modification. So, it is a sentence of Indirect Speech.

The following points should be noted while changing Direct Speech into Indirect speech:

1. The verb outside the inverted commas is called the Reporting Verb.
2. The verb or sentence inside the inverted commas is called the Reported Speech.
3. If the Reporting verb is in the Present or Future Tense, there is no change in the tense in the Reported Speech.
4. If the Reporting Verb is in the Past Tense, the Tense in the Reported Speech is changed.
5. The Reporting verb may be in any Tense, in it the Pronouns are changed as under:
   (*i*) First Person according to Subject
   (*ii*) Second Person according to Object
   (*iii*) Third Person, No change.
6. If the Reporting verb is in the Past Tense the Adverb will change as under in the Indirect Speech.

Direct	***Indirect***
now	then
here	there
after	before
today	that day
yesterday	the previous day
these	those
tomorrow	the next day
last week	the previous week
this	that

7. Adjectives/Determiners are changed as under:

Direct	***Indirect***
this	that
these	those

Rules for Change of Tense

Reporting Verb	Reporting Speech	Change of Tense
Present Tense	Any Tense	No change
Future Tense	Any Tense	No change
Past Tense	Present/Future Tense	Change into corresponding Past Tense
Past Tense	Past Indefinite Tense	Change into Past Perfect Tense
Past Tense	Past Continuous Tense	Change into Past Perfect Continuous Tense
Past Tense	Past Perfect/Perfect Continuous Tense	No change
Past Tense	Universal Truth	No change
Past Tense	Proverb	No change

Transformation of Speech Based on Special Rules

1. Rule Related to Interrogative Sentence

- If the answer of an interrogative sentence is possible in yes-no manner.

  Illustration.

  Dhoni said to Sachin, "Will you help me?"

  Dhoni asked Sachin whether he would help him.

  (**Note :** The answer of R.S. is possible in yes-no manner)

  Rule of Transformation from Direct to Indirect speech

  Step I : Change R.V. into ask.

  Step II : In place of comma use 'if/whether'.

  Step III: Change interrogative sentence into assertive sentence.

- If the answer of an interrogative sentence is not possible in yes-no manner.

  Illustration:

  Sachin said to Dhoni, "What do you want?"

  Sachin asked Dhoni what he wanted.

  (**Note :** Only in Step II, you have to avoid comma and inverted comma and rest will be same as mentioned above).

2. Rule related to Imperative Sentence

- Imperative sentence is a sentence which shows Order/Advice/Request

  Illustration:

  My teacher said to me, "Go there".

  My teacher ordered me to go there.

  Rule of Transformation from Direct to Indirect Speech

  Step I : Change R.V. as per meaning/sense of R.S. into order/request/advise.

  Step II : In place of comma, use 'to'.

  Step III: Rest portion will be same.

3. Rule related to Optative Sentence

- Optative sentence is a sentence which expresses the feeling of bless/curse/pray/wish.

  Illustration:

  Mother said to me, "May you live long!"

  Mother blessed me that I might live long.

  Rule of Transformation from Direct to Indirect Speech

  Step I : Change R.V. as per meaning/sense of R.S. into bless/curse/pray/wish.

  Step II : In place of comma, use 'that'.

  Step III: Change optative sentence into assertive sentence.

4. Rule related to Exclamatory Sentence

- Exclamatory sentence is a sentence which takes note of exclamatory (!) mark in that sentence showing inner feeling.

  Illustration:

  She said, "Alas! I am ruined".

  She exclaimed with sorrow that she was ruined.

  Rule of Transformation from Direct to Indirect Speech

  Step I : Change R.V. as per meaning/sense of R.S. into exclaim/exclaims/exclaimed/will or shall exclaim + joy/sorrow/anger/surprise/applause/contempt.

  Step II : Change comma into that.

  Step III: Change note of exclamation (!) into full stop (.)

  Step IV : Change exclamatory sentence into assertive sentence.

Universal, Historical truth, etc.

If the Reported Speech expresses a Universal or Historical or Habitual truth, its Tense will not change.

1. The teacher said to the students, "The sun rises in the east."

   The teacher told the students that the sun rises in the east.

2. My father said to me, "The First Battle of Panipat was fought in 1526."

   My father told me that the First Battle of Panipat was fought in 1526.

Multiple Choice Questions

Directions (Qs. 1 to 13): *Select the correct Indirect Speech for the following sentences:*

1. I said to him, "I shall help you."
A. I told him that I can help him.
B. I told him that I would help him.
C. I told him that I will help him.
D. I told him that I shall be helping him.

2. My Teacher said to me, "The earth revolves round the sun."
A. My teacher told me that the earth revolves round the sun.
B. My teacher told me that the earth revolve round the sun.
C. My teacher told me that the earth had been revolving round the sun.
D. My teacher told me that the earth has been revolving round the sun.

3. I said to my friend, "My father daily goes for a walk."
A. I told my friend that my father daily goes for a walk.
B. I told my friend that my father daily went for a walk.
C. I told my friend that my father has to go for a walk.
D. I told my friend that my father had gone for a walk.

4. He said to me, "May God bless you!"
A. He requested that God can bless me.
B. He prayed that God can bless me.
C. He prayed that God might bless me.
D. He prayed that God will bless me.

5. The patient said, "Thank you, doctor."
A. The patient thanked the doctor.
B. The patient requested the doctor with thanks.
C. The patient told the doctor thanks.
D. The patient suggested the doctor thanks.

6. Satish said, "No, I shall not talk to him."
A. Satish told that he should not talk to him.
B. Satish suggested that he would not have talked to him.
C. Satish exclaimed with sorrow that he would not talk with him.
D. Satish refused to talk to him.

7. The child said, "What a lovely place!"
A. The child exclaimed with sorrow that it was a lovely place.
B. The child thought that the place was lovely.
C. The child exclaimed with joy that the place was very lovely.
D. The child suggested that the place was lovely.

8. He said, "What a fool I have been!"
A. He told himself with sorrow that he was a fool.
B. He confessed with regret that he had been a great fool.
C. He said himself a fool.
D. He suggested that he could be a fool.

9. He said, "Alas! I am ruined."
A. He told me that he had been ruined.
B. He exclaimed with joy that he had been ruined.
C. He exclaimed with sorrow that he was ruined.
D. He told me that he should not be ruined.

10. The accused said, "I am not guilty."
A. The accused exclaimed with sorrow that I am not guilty.
B. The accused exclaimed with joy that he was not guilty.
C. The accused stated that he was not guilty.
D. The accused told me that he has not been guilty.

11. My teacher said, "The earth is round".
A. My teacher said that the earth was round.
B. My teacher says that the earth is round.
C. My teacher said that the earth is round.
D. My teacher ordered that the earth is round.

12. He said, "What a place it is!"
- A. He said that it was a very fine place.
- B. He said that is a very fine place.
- C. He said that the place is fine.
- D. He exclaimed with joy/surprise that it was a very fine place.

13. Ria said, "Shall I thread the needle?"
- A. Ria asked if she should thread the needle.
- B. Ria asked if she shall thread the needle.
- C. Ria ordered if she should thread the needle.
- D. Ria says that if she would thread the needle.

Directions (Qs. 14 to 33): *Pick out the correct alternative that completes the incomplete sentence which is changed into Indirect Narration.*

14. She said to me, "I shall see you as soon as I get time."
She told me:
- A. that she will see me as soon as she will get time.
- B. that she would see me as soon as she would get time.
- C. she would see me whenever she got time.
- D. that she would see me whenever she gets time.

15. My secretary said to me, "Your plane will leave if you do not go at once."
My secretary told me that:
- A. her plane would leave if she did not go at that time.
- B. her plane would leave if I do not go at once.
- C. my plane would leave if I did not go at that very time.
- D. my plane will leave if I did not go at that time.

16. My mother said to me, "Don't quarrel among yourselves".
My mother:
- A. forbade me to quarrel among ourselves.
- B. asked me not to quarrel among ourselves.
- C. asked me that not to quarrel among ourselves.
- D. asked me to quarrel not among ourselves.

17. Her father said to her mother, "Excuse the daughter."
Her father:
- A. requested her mother to excuse the daughter.
- B. asked her mother to excuse the daughter.
- C. asked her mother to have excused the daughter.
- D. asked her mother to have been excused.

18. He said to his friend, "Wait here till father comes."
He requested his friend:
- A. to wait here till father had come.
- B. that to wait there till his friend came.
- C. to wait there till father came.
- D. to wait here until his friend came.

19. She said to her maid, "Run and catch the thief."
She ordered her maid:
- A. ran and catch the thief.
- B. that to run and to catch the thief.
- C. ran and caught the thief.
- D. to run and catch the thief.

20. Anita said to Sunita, "What are you doing?"
Anita asked Sunita:
- A. what she will be doing.
- B. that what she is doing.
- C. that what she was doing.
- D. what she was doing.

21. She said to me, "Are you meeting me today?"
She enquired of me:
- A. whether I am meeting her that day.
- B. whether I was meeting her today.
- C. whether I was meeting her that day.
- D. I was meeting her that day.

22. Nitish said to me, "When did you buy this pen?"
Nitish asked me:
- A. when I was to buy that pen.
- B. when I would buy that pen.
- C. when I had bought that pen.
- D. when I was buying that pen.

23. She said to me, "Are you going to market?"
She enquired of me:
A. I am going to market.
B. I was going to market.
C. if I was going to market.
D. if I had been going to the market.

24. Damini said, "Why did not you change your clothes?"
Damini asked me:
A. why I had not changed my clothes.
B. why I did not change my clothes.
C. why I would not change my clothes.
D. why I have not been changing my clothes.

25. Umesh said to me, "Have you read that novel?"
Umesh asked me:
A. if he was reading that novel.
B. if he had read that novel.
C. if I had read that novel.
D. if I was reading that novel.

26. She said to me, "I shall forgive you."
She told me:
A. that she will forgive me.
B. that she was going to forgive me.
C. that she will not forgive me.
D. that she would forgive me.

27. I said to her, "It was very hot last night."
I told her:
A. that it had been very hot the previous night.
B. that it was very hot the previous night.
C. that it has been very hot the last night.
D. that it had been very hot this night.

28. She said to me, "I thank you for the help you have given."
She:
A. told me that she thanked me for the help I had given.
B. thanked me for the help I have given.
C. thanked to me for the help I have given.
D. thanked me for the help I had given.

29. Mohini said to me, "Trust in God."
Mohini advised me:
A. that I should trust in God.
B. should trust in God.
C. trusted in God.
D. to trust in God.

30. I said to him, "Let us go to school."
I told him:
A. we would go to school.
B. we shall go to school.
C. that we would go to school.
D. that we should go to school.

31. Rajni said, "May God bless you?"
Rajni:
A. exclaimed with wish that God might bless me.
B. expressed a wish that God might bless me.
C. asked God to bless me.
D. shouted with joy to bless me.

32. My mother said me, "Do not have so many friends."
My mother forbade me:
A. to have so many friends.
B. not to have so many friends.
C. to have been so many friends.
D. to possess so many friends.

33. Ram said, "Pay attention to me."
Ram asked:
A. pay attention to him.
B. paid attention to him.
C. having paid attention to him.
D. to pay attention to him.

Directions (Qs. 34 to 50): *In questions below, the sentences have been given in Direct/Indirect Speech. Out of the four alternatives suggested select the one which best expresses the given sentence in Indirect/Direct Speech.*

34. She said that her brother was getting married
A. She said, "Her brother is getting married."
B. She told, "My brother is getting married"
C. She said, "My brother is getting married".
D. She said, "My brother was married".

35. "Please don't go away", she said.
A. She said to please her and not go away.
B. She told me to go away.
C. She begged me not to go away.
D. She begged that I not go away.

36. "If you don't keep quiet I shall shoot you", he said to her in a calm voice.
A. He warned her to shoot if she didn't keep quiet calmly.
B. He said calmly that I shall shoot you if you don't be quiet.
C. He warned her calmly that he would shoot her if she didn't keep quiet.
D. Calmly he warned her that be quiet or else he will have to shoot her.

37. I told him that he was not working hard.
A. I said to him, "You are not working hard."
B. I told him, "You are not working hard."
C. I said, "You are not working hard."
D. I said to him, "He is not working hard."

38. She said that she would finish the work the next day.
A. She said, "I will finish the work the next day."
B. She said, "I will finish the work tomorrow."
C. She said, "You will finish the work tomorrow."
D. She said, "I finished the work."

39. She said to him, "Why don't you go today?"
A. She asked him why he did not go that day.
B. She said to him that why he don't go today.
C. She asked him not to go today.
D. She asked him why he did not go today.

40. "Are you alone, my son?" asked a soft voice close behind me.
A. A soft voice asked that what I was doing there alone.
B. A soft voice said to me are you alone son.
C. A soft voice from my back asked if I was alone.
D. A soft voice behind me asked if I was alone.

41. My cousin said, "My room-mate had snored throughout the night."
A. My cousin said that her room-mate snored throughout the night.
B. My cousin told me that her room-mate snored throughout the night.
C. My cousin complained to me that her room-mate is snoring throughout the night.
D. My cousin felt that her room-mate may be snoring throughout the night.

42. He asked Rama if he needed his help then.
A. He said to Rama, "Do you need my help?"
B. He told Rama, "Tell me if you need help."
C. He asked Rama, "Do I need your help?"
D. He said to Rama, "Do you need my help now?"

43. Nita ordered her servant to bring her a cup of tea.
A. Nita told her servant, "Bring a cup of tea."
B. Nita said, "Bring me a cup of tea."
C. Nita said to her servant, "Bring me a cup of tea."
D. Nita said to her servant, "Bring her that cup of tea."

44. He exclaimed with joy that India had won the Sahara Cup.
A. He said, "India has won the Sahara Cup."
B. He said, "India won the Sahara Cup."
C. He said, "How! India will win the Sahara Cup."
D. He said, "Hurrah! India has won the Sahara Cup."

45. The boy said, "Who dare call you a thief?"
A. The boy enquired who dared call him a thief.
B. The boy asked who called him a thief.
C. The boy told that who dared call him a thief.
D. The boy wondered who dared call a thief.

46. The little girl said to her mother, "Did the sun rise in the East?
A. The little girl said to her mother that the sun rose in the East.
B. The little girl asked her mother if the sun rose in the East.
C. The little girl said to her mother if the sun rises in the East.
D. The little girl asked her mother if the sun is in the East.

47. Dhruv said that he was sick and tired of working for that Company.

A. Dhruv said, "I am sick and tired of working for this Company."

B. Dhruv said, "He was tired of that Company."

C. Dhruv said to me, "I am sick and tired of working for this Company."

D. Dhruv said, "I will be tired of working for that Company."

48. He said to his father, "Please increase my pocket-money."

A. He told his father, please increase the pocket-money.

B. He pleaded his father to please increase my pocket-money.

C. He requested his father to increase his pocket-money.

D. He asked his father increase his pocket-money.

49. She said to her friend, "I know where is everyone."

A. She told that she knew where was everyone.

B. She told her friend that she knew where was everyone.

C. She told her friend she knew where is everyone

D. She told her friend that she knows where was everyone.

50. His father ordered him to go to his room and study.

A. His father said, "Go to your room and study."

B. His father said to him, "Go and study in your room."

C. His father shouted, "Go right now to your study room."

D. His father said firmly, "Go and study in your room."

ANSWERS

1	2	3	4	5	6	7	8	9	10
B	A	A	C	A	D	C	B	C	C
11	**12**	**13**	**14**	**15**	**16**	**17**	**18**	**19**	**20**
C	D	A	B	C	A	B	C	D	D
21	**22**	**23**	**24**	**25**	**26**	**27**	**28**	**29**	**30**
C	C	C	A	C	D	A	A	A	D
31	**32**	**33**	**34**	**35**	**36**	**37**	**38**	**39**	**40**
B	A	D	C	C	C	A	B	A	D
41	**42**	**43**	**44**	**45**	**46**	**47**	**48**	**49**	**50**
A	D	C	B	A	B	A	C	B	A

❑❑❑

9 Voice

A sentence in active voice focuses on the person or thing doing the action. A sentence in passive voice focuses on the person or thing affected by the action.

e.g.,

The idol was built. (Active voice)
Someone built the idol. (Passive voice)

Transformation of Voice

- Voice and Tense are closely associated with each other.
- Tense plays an important role while transforming the voice.

On the basis of following points, voice can be transformed from active to passive voice.

The Present Indefinite Tense

Active voice: Subject + V_1 + Object
Passive voice: Subject + is, am, are + V_3 + by + Object

1. **Active voice:** He sings sweet songs.
   Passive voice: Sweet songs are sung by him.
2. **Active voice:** She does not cause any hindrance in my work.
   Passive voice: No hindrance in my work is caused by her.
3. **Active voice:** Do they love their country?
   Passive voice: Is their country loved by them?

The Present Continuous Tense

Active voice: Subject + is/am/are + V_1 + ing + Object.
Passive voice: Subject + is/am/are + being + V_3 + by + Object.

1. **Active voice:** She is cooking food.
   Passive voice: Food is being cooked by her.
2. **Active voice:** Rita is not knitting a sweater.
   Passive voice: A sweater is not being knitted by Rita.
3. **Active voice:** Is Meena baking a cake?
   Passive voice: Is a cake being baked by Meena?

The Present Perfect Tense

Active voice: Subject + has/have + V_3 + Object.
Passive voice: Subject + has/have + been + V_3 + by + Object.

1. **Active voice:** I have written an essay.
   Passive voice: An essay has been written by me.
2. **Active voice:** They have not whitewashed the fence.
   Passive voice: The fence has not been whitewashed by them.
3. **Active voice:** Have you cut the cake?
   Passive voice: Has the cake been cut by you?

The Past Indefinite Tense

Active voice: Subject + V_2 + Object
Passive voice: Subject + was/were + V_3 + by + Object

1. **Active voice:** He composed a new song.
   Passive voice: A new song was composed by him.
2. **Active voice:** He did not operate the computer.
   Passive voice: The computer was not operated by him.
3. **Active voice:** Did she catch a fish?
   Passive voice: Was a fish caught by her?

The Past Continuous Tense

Active voice: Subject + was/were + V_1 + ing + Object

Passive voice: Subject + was/were + being + V_3 + by + Object

1. **Active voice:** The farmers were ploughing the fields.
   Passive voice: The fields were being ploughed by the farmers.
2. **Active voice:** He was not administering the new drug to the patient.
   Passive voice: The new drug was not being administered to the patient by him.
3. **Active voice:** Was she sewing a dress?
   Passive voice: Was a dress being sewn by her?

The Past Perfect Tense

Active voice: Subject + had + V_3 + Object.

Passive voice: Subject + had + been + V_3 + by + Object

1. **Active voice:** He had issued me an import licence.
   Passive voice: I had been issued an import licence.
2. **Active voice:** We had not visited the Taj.
   Passive voice: The Taj had not been visited by us.
3. **Active voice:** Who had taught you English?
   Passive voice: By whom had you been taught English?

The Future Indefinite Tense

Active voice: Subject + will/shall + V_1 + Object.

Passive voice: Subject + will/shall + be + V_3 + by + Object.

1. **Active voice:** He will remove the dust from the shelf.
   Passive voice: The dust from the shelf will be removed by him.
2. **Active voice:** He will not open the main gate.
   Passive voice: The main gate will not be opened by him.
3. **Active voice:** Will you help us?
   Passive voice: Shall we be helped by you?

The Future Perfect Tense

Active voice: Subject + will/shall + have + V_3 + Object.

Passive voice: Subject + will/shall + have + been + V_3 + by + Object.

1. **Active voice:** They will have sold their house by then.
   Passive voice: Their house will have been sold by them by then.
2. **Active voice:** He will not have informed the police about it.
   Passive voice: The police will not have been informed about it by him.
3. **Active voice:** Will they have accepted the deal?
   Passive voice: Will the deal have been accepted by them?

Imperative Sentences

1. **Active voice:** Open the window.
   Passive voice: You are ordered to open the window.

   Or

   Let the window be opened.
2. **Active voice:** Please/kindly open the window.
   Passive voice: You are requested to open the window.
3. **Active voice:** Never make a noise.
   Passive voice: A noise should never be made.

Infinitives

1. **Active voice:** It is time to open the shop.
   Passive voice: It is time for the shop to be opened.
2. **Active voice:** He begged the officer to forgive him.
   Passive voice: He begged the officer to be forgiven.
3. **Active voice:** He has to break the door.
   Passive voice: The door has to be broken by him.

Prepositional Verb

1. **Active voice:** She laughed at the beggar.
   Passive voice: The beggar was laughed at by her.
2. **Active voice:** He listened to the news.
   Passive voice: The news was listened to by him.
3. **Active voice:** They called in the doctor.
   Passive voice: The doctor was called in by them.

Double Object

1. **Active voice:** He gave me a pen.
   Passive voice: A pen was given to me by him.
   Or
   I was given a pen by him.
2. **Active voice:** She told us a story.
   Passive voice: A story was told (to) us by her.
   Or
   We were told a story by her.

Use of Preposition other than 'by'

1. **Active voice:** The jug contains juice.
   Passive voice: Juice is contained in the jug.
2. **Active voice:** The audience thronged the hall.
   Passive voice: The hall was thronged with the audience.
3. **Active voice:** I know her.
   Passive voice: She is known to me.

Quasi Passive Verbs

1. **Active voice:** Quinine tastes bitter.
   Passive voice: Quinine is bitter when tasted.
   Or
   Quinine is bitter when it is tasted.
2. **Active voice:** Sugar is sweet (to taste).
   Passive voice: Sugar is sweet when tasted.
   Or
   Sugar is sweet when it is tasted.

Implied Sentences

1. **Active voice:** The driver drove the bus.
   Passive voice: The bus was driven.
2. **Active voice:** Someone read the news.
   Passive voice: The news was read.
3. **Active voice:** They say work is worship.
   Passive voice: It is said that work is worship.

Multiple Choice Questions

Directions (Qs. 1 to 20): *In the following questions, a sentence has been given in Active/Passive Voice. Out of the four alternatives suggested, select the one that Best Expresses the same sentence in Passive/Active Voice.*

1. Circumstances will oblige me to go.
   A. I will oblige the circumstances and go.
   B. I shall be obliged to go by the circumstances.
   C. Under the circumstances, I should go.
   D. I shall be obliged by the circumstances to go.
2. We waste much time on trifles.
   A. Much time was wasted on trifles.
   B. Much time will be wasted on trifles.
   C. Much time is wasted by us on trifles.
   D. Much time is wasted on trifles.
3. Mohan gave the beggar an old shirt.
   A. An old shirt was given to Mohan by the beggar.
   B. An old shirt was given to the beggar by Mohan
   C. The begger was gave an old shirt by Mohan.
   D. An old shirt was gave to the beggar by Mohan.
4. They have made him a king.
   A. A king has been made by him.
   B. He was made a king by them.
   C. They have been made kings by him.
   D. He has been made a king by them.

5. Who taught you English?
A. By whom English was taught to you?
B. By whom you were taught English?
C. By whom was English taught to you?
D. By whom are you taught English?

6. Was he knocking at the door?
A. Was the door being knocked at by him?
B. Was the door being knocked by him?
C. Was the door knocked by him?
D. Was the door knocking at him?

7. What was Rani doing?
A. What was done by Rani?
B. What was Rani being done?
C. What was being done by Rani?
D. What was being doing Rani?

8. Why were you wasting your time?
A. Why was your time being wasted?
B. Why was your time being wasted by you?
C. Why was your time wasted by you?
D. Why was your time wasted?

9. She has laid out a small garden.
A. A small garden has been laid by her.
B. A small garden has laid her.
C. A small garden being laid by her.
D. A small garden has been laid out by her.

10. She had already solved all the sums.
A. All the sums had already been solved by her.
B. All the sums have already been solved by her.
C. All the sums have been solved by her.
D. All the sums are solved by her.

11. He will have posted the letter.
A. The letter has been posted by him.
B. The letter will be posted by him.
C. The letter will have been posted by him.
D. The letter is posted by him.

12. They will have sold all the books by 4 P.M.
A. All the books will be sold by 4 P.M.
B. All the books will have been sold by 4 P.M.
C. All the books were being sold by 4 P.M.
D. All the books must be sold by 4 P.M.

13. Do you speak English?
A. Is English spoken by you?
B. Does English spoken by you?
C. Is English being spoken by you?
D. Does English being spoken by you?

14. Had they seen me before?
A. Had myself been seen by them before?
B. Had me being seen by them before?
C. Had I been seen by them before?
D. Had I being seen by them before?

15. May I take this pen?
A. May this pen will be taken by me?
B. May this pen shall be taken by me?
C. May this pen should be taken by me?
D. May this pen be taken by me?

16. Can we send it by air?
A. Can this be sent by air?
B. Can it be sent by air?
C. Can it go by air?
D. Can it be send by air?

17. Who wrote this book?
A. By whom was this book written?
B. By whom is this book written?
C. By whom was this book being written?
D. By whom is this book being written?

18. What did you buy?
A. What is bought by you?
B. What is being bought by you?
C. What was bought by you?
D. What was being bought by you?

19. Whom do you want?
A. Who is wanted by you?
B. Who is being wanted by you?
C. You are wanted by whom?
D. You are being wanted by whom?

20. When will you raise this question?
A. When this question will be raised by you?
B. When will this question be raised by you?
C. When this question is being raised by you?
D. When is this question being raised by you?

Directions (Qs. 21 to 35): *In each of the following questions, a sentence is given in Active Voice. Below it are given four alternatives suggesting the Passive Voice form of the above sentence. Choose the correct alternative.*

21. Who did this?
A. This was done by whom?
B. By whom was this done?
C. Who has done this?
D. By whom this was done?

22. One should keep ones promises.
A. Promises should be kept.
B. Ones promises should be kept by one.
C. Promises must be kept.
D. Ones promises one should keep.

23. Give the order.
A. Order given.
B. Order be given.
C. Let the order be given.
D. Order may be given by you.

24. You will have to do it.
A. It will be done by you.
B. It will have to be done by you.
C. It has to be done by you.
D. It would have to be done by you.

25. Keep to the left.
A. You are ordered to keep to the left.
B. You ought to keep to the left.
C. You are advised to keep to the left.
D. You must keep to the left.

26. They will arrange a party.
A. A party will have to be arranged by them.
B. A party they will have to arrange.
C. A party will be arranged by them.
D. A party by them will be arranged.

27. Someone has picked my pocket.
A. My pocket is picked.
B. My pocket has picked.
C. My pocket has been picked.
D. My pocket was picked.

28. He kept me waiting.
A. I kept waiting for him.
B. I kept waiting by him.
C. I was waiting for him.
D. I was kept waiting by him.

29. Why do you tell a lie?
A. Why is a lie told by you?
B. Why is told a lie by you?
C. Why is told by you a lie?
D. Why has a lie been told by you?

30. I have written a letter.
A. A letter is written by me.
B. A letter has been written by me.
C. A letter was written by me.
D. A letter had been written by me.

31. They will have helped you.
A. You will have helped by them.
B. You will have been helped by them.
C. You will be helped by them.
D. You will be helped by them.

32. Open the door.
A. Door may be opened.
B. Let the door be open.
C. Let the door be opened.
D. Door be opened.

33. I am reading a book.
A. A book is read by me.
B. A book is being read by me.
C. A book has been read by me.
D. A book in been read by me.

34. Why did your brother write such a letter?
A. Why your brother wrote such a letter?
B. Why was by brother written such a letter?
C. Why was such a letter written by your brother?
D. Why was written such a letter by your brother?

35. Did you run a great risk?
A. Was a great risk run by you?
B. Was run a great risk by you?
C. Was by you run a great risk?
D. Had you run a great risk?

Directions (Qs. 36 to 45): *In each of the following questions, a sentence is given in Passive Voice. Below it are given four alternatives suggesting the Active Voice form of the above sentence. Choose the correct alternative.*

36. He was made king.
  A. He became king.
  B. They made him king.
  C. They had made him king.
  D. He has been made king.

37. Good news is expected by us.
  A. We are expecting good news.
  B. We have been expecting good news.
  C. We had expected good news.
  D. We expect good news.

38. The child must be looked after.
  A. The child you must look after.
  B. You must look after the child.
  C. You must look the child after.
  D. You may look after the child.

39. What is wanted by you?
  A. What you want?
  B. What did you want?
  C. What do you want?
  D. What you do want?

40. Your father is known to me.
  A. I am known to your father.
  B. I know your father.
  C. I have known your father.
  D. I knew your father.

41. She may be told the story by you.
  A. The story may be told by you to her.
  B. You may tell the story to her.
  C. You may tell her the story.
  D. You may tell to her the story.

42. Duty ought to be done.
  A. Let duty be done.
  B. One ought to do one's duty.
  C. One should do his duty.
  D. Do you duty.

43. Is English spoken by you?
  A. Did you speak English?
  B. Do you speak English?
  C. Have you spoken English?
  D. Do you know how to speak English?

44. Gold coins are contained in this box.
  A. This box contains gold coins.
  B. This box has contained gold coins.
  C. This box is containing gold coins.
  D. This box has gold coins.

45. Character is revealed by manners.
  A. Manners revealed character.
  B. Manners reveal character.
  C. Manners have revealed character.
  D. Manners do reveal character.

ANSWERS

1	2	3	4	5	6	7	8	9	10
D	C	B	D	C	A	C	B	D	A
11	**12**	**13**	**14**	**15**	**16**	**17**	**18**	**19**	**20**
C	B	A	C	D	B	A	C	A	B
21	**22**	**23**	**24**	**25**	**26**	**27**	**28**	**29**	**30**
B	A	C	B	C	C	C	D	A	B
31	**32**	**33**	**34**	**35**	**36**	**37**	**38**	**39**	**40**
B	C	B	C	A	B	D	B	C	B
41	**42**	**43**	**44**	**45**					
C	B	B	A	B					

❑❑❑

10 Sentence Completion

Filling the blanks is such an exercise that starts with the primary schools and continues at the highest level of competitive examinations. One must practise it regularly to score well.

Multiple Choice Questions

Directions: *Pick out the most effective word(s) from the given words to fill in the blanks and make the sentence meaningfully complete.*

1. One requires great .... to teach and handle little children who are restless.
A. patience B. attitude
C. determination D. knowledge

2. The researchers will .... some of the causes of increasing poverty in the state.
A. fund B. investigate
C. promote D. circulate

3. I usually perform .... when nobody is watching me.
A. alone B. good
C. better D. hard

4. It was .... to everyone that the minister had been drinking.
A. observed B. known
C. discovered D. realised

5. I would rather stay indoors .... the rain stops.
A. so B. waiting
C. until D. usually

6. The process should be completed as far as possible within a week, ... which the matter should be brought to notice of the officer concerned.
A. following B. failing
C. realizing D. referring

7. The officers are ..... to regular transfers.
A. free B. open
C. subject D. available

8. All letters received from Government should ..... be acknowledged.
A. suddenly
B. obviously
C. immediately
D. occasionally

9. Mumbai office ..... a meeting of senior officials to discuss the high incidence of frauds.
A. attended B. convened
C. reported D. registered

10. The note should be ..... to all the concerned departments for their consideration.
A. regulated B. requested
C. carried D. forwarded

11. Your present statement does not .... what you said last week.
A. accord to B. accord in
C. accord with D. accord for

12. I had a vague .... that the lady originally belonged to Scotland.
A. notion B. expression
C. imagination D. theory

13. The prisoner showed no .... for his crimes.
A. hatred B. obstinacy
C. remorse D. anger

14. It is inconceivable that in many schools children are subjected to physical .... in the name of discipline.
A. violation B. exercise
C. violence D. security

15. We have not yet fully realised the .... consequences of the war.
A. happy B. pleasing
C. grim D. exciting

16. Happiness consists in being .... what we have.
A. contented to B. contented with
C. contented for D. contented in

17. His rude behaviour is a .... his organization.
A. disgrace for
B. disgrace on
C. disgrace upon
D. disgrace to

18. No child is .... understanding. One has to wait and provide proper guidance.
A. dull to B. dull in
C. dull of D. dull for

19. I am fully .... the problems facing the industry.
A. alive with B. alive to
C. alive for D. alive on

20. The Romans were .... science.
A. bad in B. bad to
C. bad for D. bad at

21. Although I was .... of his plans, I encouraged him, because there was no one else who was willing to help.
A. sceptical B. remorseful
C. fearful D. excited

22. You have no business to .... pain on a weak and poor person.
A. inflict B. put
C. direct D. force

23. Her uncle died in a car accident. He was quite rich. She suddenly .... all her uncle's money.
A. succeeded B. caught
C. gave D. inherited

24. There was a major accident. The plane crashed. The pilot .... did not see the tower.
A. likely B. probably
C. scarcely D. hurriedly

25. The car we were travelling in .... a mile from home.
A. broke off B. broke down
C. broke into D. broke up

26. What are you .... in the kitchen cupboard?
A. looking in B. looking on
C. looking to D. looking for

27. I did not see the point of .... waiting for them, so I went home.
A. hanging around B. hang on
C. hang together D. hanging up

28. He lost confidence and .... of the deal at the last minute.
A. backed out B. backed on
C. backed down D. backed onto

29. To the dismay of all the students, the class monitor was ..... berated by the principal at a school assembly.
A. critically B. ignominiously
C. prudently D. fortuitously

30. All attempts to revive the fishing industry were ..... failure.
A. foredoomed to B. heading at
C. predicted for D. estimated to

31. There are ..... parked outside than yesterday.
A. fewer cars
B. few cars
C. less cars
D. a small number of cars

32. The minister had to ..... some awkward questions from reporters.

A. fend B. fend at
C. fend out D. fend off

33. The ..... of evidence was on the side of the plaintiff since all but one of the witnesses testified that his story was correct.

A. propensity B. force
C. preponderance D. brunt

34. Attention to detail is ..... of a fine craftsman.

A. hallmark B. stamp
C. seal of authority D. authenticity

35. Behaving in a .... and serious way, even in a .... situation, makes people respect you.

A. calm, difficult
B. steady, angry
C. flamboyant, tricky
D. cool astounding

36. Along with a sharp rise in ...., a recession would eventually result in more men, women, and children living in ....

A. crime, apathy
B. fatalities, poor
C. deaths, slums
D. unemployment, poverty

37. The government has .... to provide financial aid to the ones .... by severe floods in the city.

A. desired, troubled B. promised, havoc
C. failed, affected D. wanted, struck

38. An airplane with .... passengers on board made an unscheduled .... as the airport to which it was heading was covered with thick fog.

A. imitable, slip B. faulty, stop
C. variety, halt D. numerous, landing

39. Deemed universities .... huge fees, but have not been successful in providing .... education to our students.

A. collect, maintaining
B. pay, better
C. ask, good
D. charge, quality

40. If the banks desire to .... profit, they should get rid of .... measures.

A. lose, concentrate
B. increase, populist
C. earn, unhealthy
D. maximise, traditional

41. Leadership defines what the future should look like and ...... people with that vision.

A. aligns B. develops
C. trains D. encourages

42. We upset ourselves by responding in an ...... manner to someone else's actions.

A. unabashed B. irrational
C. arduous D. arguable

43. All the people involved in that issue feel a great ...... to his suggestion.

A. contradiction B. adherence
C. indifference D. repugnance

44. These elections will be remembered as much for its anti-incumbency mood as for its ...... mandate.

A. invincible B. rational
C. unprecedented D. deliberate

45. How do you expect us to stay in such a ...... building even if it can be hired on a nominal rent?

A. scruffy B. disperate
C. fragmented D. robust

46. ...... efforts from all concerned are required to raise the social and economic conditions of our countrymen.

A. Perpetual B. Dynamic
C. Massive D. Exploring

47. Many companies see technology as a ...... for a whole host of business problems.

A. consideration B. preference
C. linking D. panacea

48. Known as devout and serious person, she also has ...... sense of humour.

A. better B. plentiful
C. quick D. good

49. The matter would have become serious if ...... action had not been taken.
A. hasty B. fast
C. timely D. unusual

50. The ...... with which he is able to yield the paint brush is really remarkable.
A. ease B. practice
C. majesty D. sweep

51. You must ensure the correctness of the information before ....
A. drawing B. enabling
C. learning D. jumping

52. The rocket .... the target and did not cause any casualty.
A. sensed B. reached
C. missed D. exploded

53. It is desirable to take .... in any business if you want to make profit.
A. advice B. risk
C. loan D. recourse

54. They wasted all the money on purchase of some .... items.
A. excellent B. important
C. significant D. trivial

55. When he found the wallet his face glowed but soon it faded as the wallet was ....
A. empty B. vacant
C. recovered D. stolen

56. He has served the country by .... many significant positions.
A. appointing
B. creating
C. developing
D. holding

57. The frequent errors are a result of the student's ....
A. talent B. smartness
C. carelessness D. perception

58. The robbers eventually .... in breaking into the house.
A. succeeded B. decided
C. caught D. trained

59. I finally .... her to stay another day.
A. advised B. persuaded
C. suggested D. called

60. Most of the people who .... the book exhibition were teachers.
A. witnessed B. presented
C. conducted D. attended

ANSWERS

1	2	3	4	5	6	7	8	9	10
A	B	C	A	C	B	C	C	B	D
11	12	13	14	15	16	17	18	19	20
C	A	C	C	C	B	D	B	B	D
21	22	23	24	25	26	27	28	29	30
B	C	C	B	C	C	D	A	B	A
31	32	33	34	35	36	37	38	39	40
A	D	D	A	A	D	C	D	C	B
41	42	43	44	45	46	47	48	49	50
A	A	D	C	A	A	D	D	C	A
51	52	53	54	55	56	57	58	59	60
A	C	B	D	A	D	C	A	B	D

❑❑❑

11 Sentence Improvement

One may use the same words in many ways but the best way is only one that makes the perfect usage of the words and conveys the proper meaning of the expression. Try it yourself in the following questions.

Multiple Choice Questions

Directions: *In these questions, a part of the sentence is bold. Below are given alternatives to the bold part at A, B and C which may improve the sentence. Choose the correct alternative. In case no improvement is needed, your answer is 'D'.*

1. Discreet salience **is extremely important** to create that 'irresistible-yet-unattainable' image for brands that want to take India seriously

A. was extremely important
B. is mainly important
C. was important extremely
D. No Improvement

2. This, over a designer outfit that he wanted for a friend's party and **that his sensitive** parents refused him.

A. which his sensitive
B. which his insensitive
C. that his insensitive
D. No Improvement

3. Goa was full of non-Goa property hunters **rushing about buying up the place** like tomorrow was an expired lease.

A. rushing in buying up the place
B. rushed about buying up the place
C. rushing about to buy up the place
D. No Improvement

4. Property hunting is a **tired and hungry** making business.

A. is a tiresome and hungry
B. is a tiring and hungry
C. is a tiring and waste
D. No Improvement

5. Cultural differences aside, **till luxury need speaks** in a manner that befits.

A. luxury still needs to speak
B. luxury still need to speak
C. luxury till need to speak
D. No Improvement

6. Indian food—the culinary avatar of the subcontinent's social history presented on a platter—**is without doubt the best food** in the world.

A. is undoubtedly the greatest food
B. is without doubt greatest food
C. is best food without doubt
D. No Improvement

7. It must retain the language of poetry. **It needed to create** stories, and not statements.
A. It needed creating
B. It needs creating
C. It needs to create
D. No Improvement

8. This year, Asia-Pacific has become the first region **to reach aggregate profiting** in biotech.
A. to reach aggregated profitability
B. to reach aggregate profitability
C. to reach aggregate of profit
D. No Improvement

9. India is deviating to embrace the West. If Western luxury brands deviate a little, **albeit selectively**, they will find rich Indian arms open far and wide.
A. though selectively
B. however selectively
C. albeit selectedly
D. No Improvement

10. China and India continued to attract attention and deals, motivated by the desire to increase access to these **largest and growing** drug markets and by the need to lower the costs of drug development.
A. larger and growing
B. large and growing
C. larger and grown
D. No Improvement

11. Luxury brands are **still above of the** clover curve here, with their elite (small) audiences.
A. still ahead of the
B. still in the
C. still far of the
D. No Improvement

12. Agencies **hence needed to be** sure of returns before investing, say admen.
A. hence needs to be
B. so needs to be
C. hence need to be
D. No Improvement

13. India is still a nascent market and that's the spirit everyone's **looking at it**.
A. looking for it B. looking in it
C. looking with it D. No Improvement

14. Questioning the state's move to allow women to serve liquor but not dance in bars **of the ground that** dancing aroused physical lust.
A. on the grounds that
B. of the grounds that
C. over the grounds that
D. No Improvement

15. For England the positives from their crushing series lose come in the shape of James Anderson and Kevin Pietersen, **both of which** have made significant strides up the rankings.
A. both of which B. both of whom
C. both of who D. No Improvement

16. International campaigns can work well for luxury here, **but context cannot be** ignored.
A. so context cannot be
B. but context cannot
C. but context couldn't
D. No Improvement

17. For one, the Indian luxury context, **while evolved rapidly**, still has its own meaning, and its own implications.
A. while evolved rapid
B. which evolving rapidly
C. while evolving rapidly
D. No Improvement

18. But too much of availability can compromise a luxury brand or **made it lose** its lustre.
A. make her lose B. make him lose
C. make it lose D. No Improvement

19. Still, it's under-the-upper **layers themselves who** are aspiring for slivers of luxury.
A. layers themselves which
B. layer itself who
C. layers themself which
D. No Improvement

20. It is like saying Hindi movies, with skimpily dressed dancers, would **effect public** order.
A. effect your B. affect public
C. affected public D. No Improvement

21. The court held that a few women being involved in prostitution was no **justice to deny other** bar girls the right to livelihood.
A. justification to declare other
B. justification to deny other
C. justice to let other
D. No Improvement

22. All-rounder cricketer has also made some progress **over the** player rankings.
A. above the B. at the
C. up the D. No Improvement

23. Former minister on Sunday **joined hands** with a suspended Lok Sabha member to float a new political outfit.
A. folded hands
B. walked hand in hand
C. shaked hands
D. No Improvement

24. Pakistan's former ministers will meet in London on Monday **to ask** a strategy to return home from exile.
A. to chalk out
B. to negotiate
C. to create
D. No Improvement

25. It's a family potboiler, medical thriller and political drama **all in one**–except that it's all too real and all too grim.
A. all 3 in one
B. all coupled into one
C. all rolled into one
D. No Improvement

26. India's efforts to get international support for its civil nuclear energy programme got **a go ahead on** Sunday as Germany indicated it would not come in the way of the India-US nuclear deal.
A. a life in B. a boost on
C. a boost at D. No Improvement

27. Is it time for old bungalows to **bite the dust**?
A. go down B. get down
C. come down D. No Improvement

28. The bungalows was an outward manifestation of a certain **way in life**, and with that era gone.
A. way for life B. way of life
C. way at life D. No Improvement

29. The builder Mittals will reportedly **raise their money**-raking high-rise behind it.
A. highten their money
B. rise their money
C. raise there money
D. No Improvement

30. The impatient present has usually demolished **more of the** past before we wake up to the irretrievable loss.
A. much of B. much of their
C. much of the D. No Improvement

31. Preservation is a romantic notion; demolition **quiet** more practical reasons.
A. has many, B. had many,
C. have many, D. No Improvement

32. You must get back to your **charming self** and impress the audience with your social skills.
A. own self B. main self
C. own uniqueness D. No Improvement

33. Stay focused on your goals and don't **get disturbed by** non-materialistic possessions.
A. get involved by
B. get betrayed by
C. get distracted by
D. No Improvement

34. You may appear more optimistic than your detractors **may want it to be**.
A. want you to be
B. wish yourself to be
C. seek you be
D. No Improvement

35. There are a number of mineral springs in the Czech territory, which **has been used** for medicinal purposes since the early 15th century.
A. have been used B. had been used
C. has being used D. No Improvement

36. The picturesque mountains **offers** excellent bungee jumping spots.
A. shows B. provides
C. offer D. No Improvement

37. Begin your **meal with** traditional faves like potato soup, beef soup with liver dumplings or dill soup made from sour milk.
A. meals with B. meal in
C. meals of D. No Improvement

38. You can also **go to the** National Museum building and the famous Prague State Opera.
A. went to B. visit the
C. saw D. No Improvement

39. If they close the Gulf for a **length of time** to shipping, then certainly we could look at $150, probably higher.
A. larger amount of time
B. larger duration of time
C. larger amount of hours
D. No Improvement

40. **More of them** are owned by the state and even the privately-owned ones are open to the public.
A. Most of which B. Most of them
C. Most of all D. No Improvement

41. Constructed in the ninth century by the Prince Booivoj, the castle has transformed **oneself** from a wooden fortress surrounded by earthen bulwarks to the imposing form it has today.
A. himself B. herself
C. itself D. No Improvement

42. Apart from frequent art exhibitions, **their are also** permanent collections devoted to archaeology, anthropology, mineralogy, natural history and numismatics.
A. there is also B. there are also
C. their are also D. No Improvement

43. You can visit the Czech Museum of Fine Arts, **at a** permanent exhibition on Czech Kubism.
A. with a
B. for a
C. in a
D. No Improvement

44. Tensions **above** Iran come at a time of strong demand for energy.
A. under B. inside
C. over D. No Improvement

45. Because its shores line the narrow Straits of Hormuz, Iran **could quickly hit** both military and commercial shipping.
A. will quickly hit
B. shall quickly hit
C. will be quick hitting
D. No Improvement

46. For most people who exercise **at the** morning, there is no getting around the question: Eat and run? Or run and eat later?
A. in the
B. in
C. at the time of
D. No Improvement

47. Are ad agencies even attempting to peer into the keyhole of this indulgence sanctum to garner consumer insights **ahead of** the curve?
A. above
B. over
C. within
D. No Improvement

48. Too many people rush into the world of credit and don't stop to think about how **their actions could affect their** credit score and ability to qualify for credit in the future.
A. their actions may affect their
B. their actions might affect their
C. their actions will affect their
D. No Improvement

49. According to the report, **number of deal with** vaccines were energized by concerns around avian flu, SARS, and biodefence products, while looming patent expirations led to more deals in generics.
A. number of deals in
B. number of deal in
C. number of deals with
D. No Improvement

50. This is how the Bombay High Court responded to the state government's purported **moral stand which** dance bars were causing grave harm to society.
A. moral stand in
B. moral stand at
C. moral stand that D. No Improvement

51. If you have a high credit limit, use **at least a** third of it.
A. atleast a
B. at last a
C. utmost a
D. No Improvement

52. Fitness experts will say that **first eating provides** fuel for a proper workout.
A. eating in the beginning provides
B. first eat provides
C. eating first provides
D. No Improvement

53. One study that examined the claim directly in 1995 found that a group of people did **burned much calories from fat on days** when they exercised on an empty stomach than on days when they had a small breakfast first.
A. burn more calories from fat on days
B. burn more calorie from fat on days
C. burnt more calories from fat on days
D. No Improvement

54. Carefree children spent their afternoons **to run about barefoot**, their clothes dusty, and telltale twigs of the neighbour's mango tree in their hair.
A. running barefoot in the sun
B. run about barefoot in the sun
C. running about barefoot in the sun
D. No Improvement

55. A year ago, a 13-year-old girl attempted suicide because her mother **refuses to pay his** mobile bills.
A. refuses to pay her
B. refused to pay her
C. refused to pay his
D. No Improvement

ANSWERS

1	2	3	4	5	6	7	8	9	10
D	C	D	B	A	D	C	C	D	B
11	**12**	**13**	**14**	**15**	**16**	**17**	**18**	**19**	**20**
C	C	D	A	C	D	C	C	C	C
21	**22**	**23**	**24**	**25**	**26**	**27**	**28**	**29**	**30**
B	C	C	A	C	B	D	B	D	C
31	**32**	**33**	**34**	**35**	**36**	**37**	**38**	**39**	**40**
A	D	C	A	D	C	A	B	D	B
41	**42**	**43**	**44**	**45**	**46**	**47**	**48**	**49**	**50**
C	B	A	C	D	A	D	C	A	C
51	**52**	**53**	**54**	**55**					
C	C	A	C	B					

❑❑❑

12 Reordering Words & Sentences

Different words form a sentence and convey their meaning only when arranged in a proper order. A Paragraph is formed from sentences, it will convey its true meaning and purpose only when the sentences are arranged in a proper manner. Try and practise it in this exercise.

Multiple Choice Questions

Directions (Qs. 1 to 20): *In the following questions, some parts of the sentence have been jumbled up. You are required to rearrange these parts which are labelled P, Q, R and S to produce the correct sentence. Choose the option with proper sequence.*

1. We are doing
P : to the people
Q : to give relief
R : all we can
S : but more funds are needed
The correct sequence should be
A. P Q R S B. R Q P S
C. Q P R S D. S P Q R

2. The man
P : when he was
Q : in the office last evening
R : could not finish
S : all his work
The correct sequence should be
A. P Q R S B. Q R S P
C. R Q P S D. R S P Q

3. The people decided
P : they were going
Q : how much
R : to spend
S : on the construction of the school building
The correct sequence should be
A. Q P R S B. P Q R S
C. P R Q S D. S Q P R

4. The man said that
P : those workers
Q : would be given a raise
R : who did not go on
S : strike last month
The correct sequence should be
A. P Q R S B. P R S Q
C. Q P R S D. R S P Q

5. I think
P : the members
Q : are basically in agreement
R : of the group
S : on the following points
The correct sequence should be
A. R Q P S B. S Q R P
C. P R Q S D. P Q S R

6. While it was true that
P : I had
Q : to invest in industry
R : some lands and houses
S : I did not have ready cash

The correct sequence should be
A. P Q R S B. P R S Q
C. S Q P R D. Q P R S

7. P : But for your help
Q : to finish this work
R : it would not have been possible
S : in time
The correct sequence should be
A. P R Q S B. S P Q R
C. R P Q S D. P Q R S

8. The boy
P : in the competition
Q : who was wearing spectacles
R : won many prizes
S : held in our college
The correct sequence should be
A. P Q R S B. R P S Q
C. Q R P S D. Q P S R

9. About 200 years ago,
P : in the south of India
Q : an old king
R : ruled over a kingdom
S : called Rajavarman
The correct sequence should be
A. Q S R P B. P Q R S
C. Q P S R D. Q S P R

10. P : his land
Q : a wooden plough
R : the Indian peasant still uses
S : to cultivate
The correct sequence should be
A. R Q P S B. Q P S R
C. S R Q P D. R Q S P

11. He was a man,
P : even if he had to starve
Q : who would not beg
R : borrow or steal
S : from anyone
The correct sequence should be
A. P Q R S B. P R Q S
C. Q R S P D. Q P R S

12. P : in the progress of
Q : universities play a crucial role
R : our civilization
S : in the present age
The correct sequence should be
A. S Q P R B. Q R S P
C. Q R P S D. S Q R P

13. P : far out into the sea
Q : for the next two weeks there were further explosions
R : which hurled
S : ashes and debris
The correct sequence should be
A. Q R P S B. R S P Q
C. Q R S P D. S R P Q

14. William Shakespeare,
P : in his lifetime
Q : the great English dramatist
R : wrote thirty-five plays
S : and several poems
The correct sequence should be
A. P Q R S B. R S P Q
C. Q S R P D. Q R S P

15. Whenever I am,
P : with an old friend of mine
Q : in New Delhi
R : to have dinner
S : I always try
The correct sequence should be
A. S Q P R B. Q S R P
C. R P S Q D. P R Q S

16. P : I don't know
Q : must have thought
R : what people sitting next to me
S : but I came away
The correct sequence should be
A. R S Q P B. R Q S P
C. P Q R S D. P R Q S

17. P : in estimating the size of the earth
Q : but they were hampered by the lack of instruments of precision
R : ancient astronomers
S : used methods which were theoretically valid
The correct sequence should be
A. R P Q S B. P R Q S
C. R S Q P D. R P S Q

18. P : It is a pity that
Q : by offering a handsome dowry
R : a number of parents think that
S : they will be able to ensure the happiness of their daughters

The correct sequence should be
A. S Q R P B. P R S Q
C. P S R Q D. P R Q S

19. The common man
P : in nurturing
Q : a more active role
R : communal harmony
S : should play

The correct sequence should be
A. P R S Q B. S Q P R
C. S Q R P D. P R Q S

20. The doctor
P : able to find out
Q : what has caused
R : the food poisoning
S : has not been

The correct sequence should be
A. S P R Q B. P R Q S
C. P R S Q D. S P Q R

Directions (Qs. 21 to 40): *A number of sentences are given below which when properly sequenced form a coherent paragraph. Each sentence is labelled as abcdef...... Choose the most logical order of sentences from among the given choices to construct a coherent paragraph:*

21. (a) Parts of northern region were pounded by heavy rains today,
(b) Vehicular traffic came to a near halt.
(c) As mid and high altitude areas of Himachal Pradesh were in grip of severe cold wave with snow lashing the tribal areas and mid ranges receiving showers.
(d) As the sky remained heavily overcast with dark clouds reducing the visibility considerably.
(e) A large number of tourists were forced to buy heavy woollens and stay indoors due to inclement weather.

A. ecabd B. adecb
C. edabc D. acbde

22. (a) The idea is that students should be able to find employment for themselves after the course.
(b) The Central Board of Secondary Education is planning a revamp of its vocational courses.
(c) For this it is necessary to tie up with the industry as well as mobilise schools for their support.
(d) While others will be made less academic and more in tune with the needs of the industry.
(e) A number of courses have been identified as 'deadwood' and will be done away with.

A. bedac B. abcde
C. acebd D. baced

23. (a) Clearly, age is not a deterrent in one's choice of learning.
(b) Perhaps, it was because of her childhood desire.
(c) When Rachna came to Delhi eight years back, she had not anticipated a career in the field of art.
(d) She has been successful in the various exhibitions that she has been part of in terms of business.
(e) She had got into expressing her thoughts with the help of a brush and colours only because her daughter refused to get initiated into it.
(f) She feels that her use of colour appeals to people.

A. aedcbf B. cdefba
C. cebadf D. acdebf

24. (a) The rehabilitation record has been dismal.
(b) It has been two years years since the earthquake rudely rattled the people of Gujarat.
(c) And since then, life has been a constant struggle.
(d) The quake set Gujarat's clock back by 10 years.
(e) Things changed forever.

A. bedca B. bcade
C. dbace D. edcba

25. (a) In fact, success in exams depended on rote learning from old notes.
(b) when he was studying civil engineering in a college in Gujarat.
(c) He was detained for lack of attendance.
(d) Lectures were soporific, classes rarely worth attending and 80 per cent attendance compulsory.
(e) The college became a trap he hated.
(f) His is a plight many engineers across India would identify with.
(g) He found the going tough.
A. abcdgef B. bgdacef
C. fabcdge D. abcdefg

26. (a) In a country that has close to 600 recognised engineering colleges, there are only seven IITs.
(b) Barring a few exeptions, the academic atmosphere in these is moribund.
(c) The very best students usually get there.
(d) many waste themselves in frustration.
(e) Most of those who get into engineering are good students.
(f) but about 1.25 lakh others and up in the remaining colleges.
A. aecfbd B. abecdf
C. abcdef D. acfbed

27. (a) Whatever the job market, common wisdom says that IIT graduates will find jobs where others have failed.
(b) The IIT brand name is a ticket to success.
(c) When recruiters go headhunting, the IITs are still top of their list.
(d) Its possessor is understood to have an excellent academic record and the will to succeed.
(e) In the job market, that counts.
A. bdeac B. abcde
C. abdce D. dbace

28. (a) It will pave the way ....
(b) signalling a new beginning in strategic ties......
(c) for a tangible Indian economic presence in Iran and Central Asia.
(d) Iran has offered India valuable road linkages to central Asia ......
(e) aimed at promoting peace and economic cooperation in the region.
A. dbeac B. debca
C. acebd D. abced

29. (a) A good college is essential for a successful career and admissions are based on marks.
(b) The marks-based system followed by all the boards in the country recognises only a small percentage of students as successful.
(c) The marks one scores in the crucial board exams dictate the path his life takes.
(d) Anyone scoring below a certain percentage is automatically branded a 'failure'.
(d) So if you cannot make it into the best college, your career is over even before it has started.
A. abcde B. bcdea
C. bdcae D. abdec

30. (a) The project has already started on an experimental basis in the west district.
(b) A website is soon going to be launched where application forms can be downloaded and submitted.
(c) Standing in a queue at a government office to submit application form will be a thing of the past.
(d) A unique code will be alloted while submitting the form which will help in finding the status of the application.
A. abcd B. dabc
C. cbda D. badc

31. (a) To curb bio-terrorism is a difficult task.
(b) To check these attacks and lessen their impact, we need an impartial team of sincere, strong and dedicated men.
(c) The media can play a strong role in stopping this unnecessary spread of panic.
(d) Since bio-terrorism is not visible or easily detectable, it can be used often.
(e) Men who honour the lives of their fellow countrymen before their own.

A. abcde B. dabce
C. adbec D. acbed

32. (a) He was dying.
(b) No one was ready to touch him as even shifting him from one place to another would lead to profuse bleeding.
(c) He was a five-day old infant, premature and bleeding profusely.
(d) Even if injected one small needle, blood would ooze out and continue to flow for an hour at a stretch.
(e) This small being had haematoma, a thick blood clot in his brain.
A. edbca B. cabde
C. eacdb D. cedba

33. (a) The day I don't treat a patient, I feel ....
(b) I have enough to eat, I crave for blessings now.
(c) But if a financially weak patient gives me only ₹ 50, I don't mind.
(d) Each month I do three to four operations free of cost.
(e) I have lost something in life.
(f) My consultation fee is ₹ 300.
A. fcdeab B. dfcbae
C. fcabde D. bdfcea

34. (a) When he was rushed to the nearby Primary Health Centre after his fall, the doctor referred him to a hospital.
(b) This worsened his injury.
(c) Had a little precaution been exercised after the accident, Tarun would have continued with his gymnastic classes.
(d) He was paralysed from waist downwards when he fell from the vaulting horse while doing gymnastics.
(e) However, the doctor forgot to tell Tarun's parents to take him on a stretcher as he had suffered spinal injuries.
(f) Tarun is wheelchair bound for two years.
A. fdeabc B. abcdef
C. fdcaeb D. fdbcae

35. (a) As the temperature rises, staying hydrated can become a greater challenge for people exercising both indoors and out.
(b) Several things can influence this process, including age, gender, physical conditioning. humidity and a lack of sufficient fluids.
(c) In hot weather, individuals can lose as much as two quarts of sweat per hour.
(d) As we age, we have a lower perceived level of thirst in response to fluid loss and early stages of dehydration.
(e) If not replenished, this can lead to dehydration, heat exhaustion and even heatstroke.
A. abcde B. dbcae
C. cbdea D. acebd

36. (a) The leopard was discovered in the servant quarters of a farmhouse.
(b) The injuries appeared to have been caused by the paws of the leopard, and were not teeth wounds.
(c) It took the wild life officials, Delhi Police and Delhi zoo vets eight hours to capture the leopard that had wandered into a factory in south Delhi.
(d) The leopard then jumped into the factory where the workers managed to lock it in a small generator room before calling in the police.
(e) Before its capture, the leopard attacked two women and a man in the farmhouse.
A. aebdc B. bdaec
C. eadbc D. adbec

37. (a) Police suspect a carpenter working at John's house as he has not reported for work since the day the boy went missing.
(b) John did not return home in the afternoon.
(c) John's mother had herself put the boy on the vehicle in the morning.
(d) John smiled at him and was last seen walking up to him.
(e) His parents called the school and were told John had not been to school at all and had been marked absent.
(f) He was about to enter the school when someone called out his name.

A. cfdbea B. debfca
C. bfdaec D. abcdef

38. (a) However, the mayhem over the last few months is deeply shocking.
(b) Yet I do not agree with the prophets of doom who see nothing but disaster ahead.
(c) When I came back to my motherland India after a stay in Switzerland, I felt I was trading a hotbed of intense religious and political violence for peace and quiet.
(d) I think our nation is searching for an identity.
(e) And a new vision of the future will emerge from this.

A. abcde B. cabde
C. cebad D. bedca

39. (a) An integrated and combined approach was required to reveal the mystery of the brain —its structure, composition and function.
(b) Since the early 80's, scientists were clear that the brain would be the final frontier to conquer.
(c) The initiative was flagged off and came to be known as the Human Brain Project.
(d) But that wasn't easy because understanding the brain involved completely integrating information from the level of the gene to the level of behaviour.
(e) To fulfill this requirement a group of American scientists from various disciplines decided to work together.

A. acbed B. bdaec
C. abdec D. badec

40. (a) A product is something that is made in a factory, a brand is something that is bought by a consumer.
(b) The trick therefore, lies in the brand positioning.
(c) For a consumer, the satisfaction of becoming associated with a name that is the 'best' and the 'leader' is far more important and at times makes him ignore the price factor.
(d) Brands come and go.
(e) Still there are those who manage to stay and develop an affinity with consumers.

A. aebcd B. debac
C. decab D. aecdb

ANSWERS

1	2	3	4	5	6	7	8	9	10
B	D	A	B	C	C	A	C	A	D
11	**12**	**13**	**14**	**15**	**16**	**17**	**18**	**19**	**20**
C	A	C	D	B	D	C	B	B	D
21	**22**	**23**	**24**	**25**	**26**	**27**	**28**	**29**	**30**
D	A	C	A	B	D	A	A	C	C
31	**32**	**33**	**34**	**35**	**36**	**37**	**38**	**39**	**40**
C	D	B	C	D	A	A	B	B	B

❑❑❑

13 Comprehension Passages

PASSAGES

Directions: *Read the following passages and answer the questions given below each.*

PASSAGE-1

In the Roman times, defected enemies were generally put to death as criminals for having offended the emperor of Rome. In the middle ages, however, the practice of ransoming of returning prisoners in exchange for money became common. Though some saw this custom as a step towards a most humane society, the primary reasons behind it were economic rather than humanitarian.

In those times, rulers had only a limited ability to raise taxes. They could neither force their subject to fight nor pay them to do so. The promise of material compensation in the form of goods and ransom was therefore the only way of inducing combatants to participate in a war. In the middle ages, the predominant incentive for the individual soldiers was the expectation of spoils. Although collecting ransom clearly brought financial gain, keeping a prisoner and arranging for his exchange had its cost. Consequently, procedures were devised to reduce transaction costs.

One such device was a rule asserting that the prisoner had to assess his own value. This compelled the prisoner to establish a value *without too much distortion;* indicating too low a value would increase, the captive's chances of being killed, while indicating too high a value would either ruin him financially or create a prohibitively expensive ransom that would also result in death.

1. It can be inferred from the passage that a medieval soldier

A. was less likely to kill captured members of opposing armies than was a soldier of the Roman Empire

B. was similar to a 20th century terrorist in that he operated on a basically independent level and was motivated solely by economic incentives

C. had few economic options and chose to fight because it was the only way to earn an adequate living

D. was motivated to spare prisoners' lives by humanitarian rather than economic ideals

2. Which of the following best describes the change in policy from executing prisoners in Roman times to ransoming prisoners in the middle ages?

A. The emperors of Rome demanded more respect than did medieval rulers and thus Roman subjects went to greater lengths to defend their nation

B. It was a reflection of the lesser degree of direct control medieval ruler had over subjects

C. It became a show of strength and honour warrior of the middles ages to be able to capture and return their enemies

D. Medieval soldiers were not as hum-anitarian as their ransoming practices might have indicated

3. The primary purpose of the passage is to
   A. discuss the economic basis of the medieval practice of exchanging prisoners for ransom
   B. examine the history of the treatment of prisoner of war
   C. emphasize the importance of a warrior's code of honour during the middle ages
   D. explore a way of reducing the cost of ransom
4. The author uses the phrase *"without too much distortion"* in order to
   A. indicate that prisoners would fairly assess their worth
   B. emphasize the important role medieval prisoners played in determining whether they should be ransomed
   C. explain how prisoners often paid more than an appropriate ransom in order to increase their chances for survival
   D. suggest that captors and captives often had understanding relationships

PASSAGE-2

The world dismisses curiosity by calling it idle or mere idle curiosity—even though curious persons are seldom idle. Parents do their best to extinguish curiosity in their children because it makes life difficult to be faced everyday with a string of unanswerable questions about what makes fire hot or why grass grows. Children whose curiosity survives parental discipline are invited to join our university. With the university, they go on asking their questions and trying to find the answers. In the eyes of a scholar, that is what a university is for. Some of the questions which the scholars ask, seem to the world to be scarcely worth asking, let alone answering. They asked questions too minute specialised for you and me to understand without years of explanation. If the world inquires of one of them why he wants to know the answer to a particular question he may say especially if he is a scientist, that the answer will in some obscure way make possible a new machine or weapon or gadget. He talks that way because he knows that the world understands and respects utility.

But to you who are now part of the university, he will say that he wants to know the answer simply because he does not know it, the way the mountain climber wants to climb a mountain, simply because it is there. Similarly a historian asked by an outsider why he studies history may come out with the argument that he has learnt to repeat on such occasions, something about knowledge of the past making it possible to understand the present and mould the future. But if you really want to know why a historian studies the past, the answer is much simpler, something happened and he would like to know what. All this does not mean that the answers which scholars find to their questions have no consequences. They may have enormous consequences but these seldom form the reason for asking the questions or pursuing the answers. It is true that scholars can be put to work answering questions for the sake of the consequences as thousands are working, now, for example, in search of a cure for cancer. But this is not the primary function of the scholars. For the consequences are usually subordinate to the satisfaction of curiosity.

1. According to the passage, the children make life difficult for their parents
   A. by their ceaseless curiosity
   B. by unceasing bombardment of questions
   C. by asking irrelevant questions
   D. by posing profound questions
2. The common people consider some of the questions that the scholars ask unimportant
   A. as they are too lazy and idle
   B. as they are too modest
   C. as it's beyond their comprehension
   D. as it is considered a waste of time
3. A historian really studies the past
   A. to comprehend the present and to reconstruct the future
   B. to explain the present and plan the future
   C. to understand the present and make fortune
   D. to understand the present and mould the future

4. Children whose curiosity survives parental discipline means
   A. children retaining their curiosity in spite of being discouraged by their parents
   B. children pursuing their mental curiosity
   C. children's curiosity subdued due to parents' intervention
   D. children being disciplined by their parents
5. According to the passage, parents do their best to discourage curiosity in their children
   A. because they have no time
   B. because they have no patience to answer them
   C. because they feel that their children ask stupid questions continuously
   D. because they are unable to answer all their questions

PASSAGE-3

The factor of geographical distribution is equally, possibly even more, significant that English is spoken as first or native language in at least four continents of the world, Russian in two, Chinese and the Indian languages in one. English is without question the closest approach to a world language today. It goes without saying that no two persons ever have an identical command of their common language. Certainly, they have not precisely the same vocabulary. There are at least minor differences in pronunciation, indeed the same individual will not pronounce his vowels and consonants in absolutely identical fashion everytime he utters them. Everyone possesses, in addition, certain individual traits of grammatical form and syntactical order, constituting that peculiar and personal quality of language which we term as style. All of this is implicit in the well-known phrase, 'Style is the man.' No men are identical, no two styles are the same. If this be true of but two persons, the potential of differences resident in a language spoken by more than 200 million truly staggers imagination.

1. The author argues that English is the closest approach to a world language because
   A. there are more native speakers of English than of any other language
   B. English has less number of mutually unintelligible dialects
   C. the geographical distribution of English covers a much greater area
   D. other languages are much too complex to be world languages
2. The fact that the same individual will not pronounce his vowels and consonants identically everytime shows that
   A. literary style varies from person to person
   B. mutual intelligibility is a myth
   C. vocabulary varies from individual to individual
   D. no two persons speak the same language exactly the same way
3. It is evident from the passage that style is
   A. a strange type of language
   B. a language where one does not have to be particular about correctness and grammar
   C. language used in a particular way by an individual
   D. a question of grammatical and syntactic correctness
4. According to some authorities
   A. more people speak Chinese dialect than English
   B. more people speak English as an auxiliary language than as a first language
   C. more people speak English in the UK than in England
   D. about one-fourth of the world's population speaks English
5. The overall implication of the passage is that
   A. to suppose that 230 million people speak English as a native language would certainly be an underestimate
   B. the 55 million inhabitants of the British Isles speak like the 30 million inhabitants of the dominions and colonies
   C. a little less than half the native English speakers in the world live in the US

D. about one-tenth of the total English-speaking world population lives in British dominions and colonies

PASSAGE-4

What is the future which awaits our children? The underlying assumption of the question, that Indian children have a common future, is itself dubious. It can legitimately be asked whether a student who is well-fed, attending a boarding school in the salubrious climate of the hills and learning to use computers has any future in common with a malnourished child who goes to a school with no blackboards, if indeed he does go to school. The latter may have no worthwhile future at all. And it might be worthwhile to analyse the significance of this marginalisation of more than 75 per cent of the children of this country.

The failure to provide an infrastructure for primary education in the villages of India more than 40 years after independence is in sharp contrast with the sophisticated institutions, for technical institutes of higher education are funded by the government, which essentially means that the money to support them comes from taxes. And, since indirect taxation forms a substantial part of the taxes collected by the government, the financial burden is borne by all the people. L.K. Jha put it graphically when he observed that 25 paise of every rupee spent on educating an IIT student comes from the pockets of men and women whose children may never enter a proper classroom.

1. The author is trying to highlight which of the following?
   A. Faulty system of direct taxes
   B. The greatness of L.K. Jha
   C. Need of sophisticated education for rural poor
   D. Need to have common future for Indian children

2. Which of the following pairs have been termed as 'sharp contrast' by the author?
   (*i*) Infrastructure for technical education
   (*ii*) Lack of infrastructure for rural primary schools
   (*iii*) 25 paise of every rupee earned by Government is spent on education
   (*iv*) The financial burden of higher technical education is borne by all people
   (*v*) 75% of children have limited opportunities
   A. (*ii*) and (*iv*) B. (*ii*) and (*iii*)
   C. (*iii*) and (*iv*) D. (*i*) and (*ii*)

3. Which of the following statements is not true?
   (*i*) The author welcomes Govt.'s initiative on primary education
   (*ii*) 75% of the children have a bright future
   (*iii*) 25% cost of educating a technocrat comes from poor people
   A. Only (*i*) B. Only (*ii*)
   C. Only (*iii*) D. Only (*i*) and (*ii*)

4. According to the author, who among the following does not have a hopeful and prosperous future?
   (*i*) All students from technical institutes
   (*ii*) All students financially supported by the Government
   A. Only (*i*) B. Only (*ii*)
   C. Both (*i*) and (*ii*) D. Neither (*i*) nor (*ii*)

5. What seems to be the likely answer of the author to the question posed by him in the first sentence of the passage?
   (*i*) There is no common future for the Indian children
   (*ii*) The future is worthwhile for majority of Indian children
   (*iii*) The majority may never enter a proper classroom
   A. Only (*i*) B. Only (*ii*)
   C. Only (*iii*) D. Both (*i*) and (*ii*)

6. What seems to be the purpose of the author in writing this passage?
   A. Setting goals for children of upper middle class
   B. Questioning the legitimacy of public schools
   C. Highlighting lack of infrastructural facilities for primary education
   D. Focusing on inequality in educational opportunities

PASSAGE-5

Cyber crime is the branded stigma defacing the culture and magnanimity of computer technology. It is upkeeping the flag with indomitable triumph against developing computer technology worldwide.

Modern age is striding with marching steps of technology revolution beating the past decade of ancestral belief with ultimate care. Computer invention has unfolded the mystery of quick access with the objective of minimum manpower and cutting the time consumption parameters.

As each coin has dual face of its portrait, likewise computer technology is sick of creeping virus. Synthetic man-made dilemma of site hackers activation is causing setback to the expanding anchor of revolutionary device with great loss of time, economy and data profile as suffered by consumers. A recent report from Internet security firm Websense estimates that 85.6 per cent of all the unwanted e-mails contained links to spam sites. The company's data suggests that the number of malicious sites grew 233 per cent in the last six months and saw 671 per cent growth in the number of malicious sites during the last year. In June alone, the total number of e-mails detected as containing viruses increased by 600 per cent compared to May.

Chat rooms, blogs and message-boards where the users post comments have been identified as the top targets of hackers and spammers due to the high traffic these attract. According to Websense, 95 per cent of user-generated comments to blogs, chat rooms and message-boards during the first half of the year were malicious.

It is advisable not to click on spurious links and stay away from keying in passwords at unknown sites as they are most likely to be spammed. Hackers can steal your passwords and log in to your account and access critical information like account numbers and contact details among other things.

1. The above passage is:
   A. an advisory for the computer users.
   B. an advisory for the Internet users.
   C. a warning against possible threat to the Internet users.
   D. related to chat rooms, blogs and message boards.
2. People who use chat rooms and blogs,
   A. are safe and have no threats from spam.
   B. are more prone to malicious e-mails.
   C. create virus and hack the accounts of others.
   D. are unsafe.
3. According to the writer, it is not safe to:
   A. log on to spurious links.
   B. access one's own account frequently.
   C. have essential information stored in a computer.
   D. include data-stealing code.
4. Hackers and spammers, according to the writer, are:
   A. a new threat to the Internet users and the economy.
   B. only pranksters and not serious threat to the system.
   C. trained, professional technocrats who are an asset.
   D. not expert professionals.
5. Which word in the passage is synonym of *weblog*?
   A. blog B. password
   C. site D. e-mail
6. Which agency has assessed the data record with spam sites?
   A. Microsoft
   B. Internet security from Google
   C. Websense
   D. Spammers
7. Which month dominates the e-mails detection data record?
   A. May B. June
   C. Last six months D. Last year

PASSAGE-6

Progress in life depends a good deal on crossing one threshold after another. Some time ago, a man watched his little nephew try to write his name. It was hard work, very hard work. The little boy had arrived at an effort threshold. Today he writes his name with comparative ease. No new threshold confronts him. This is the way with all of us. As soon as we cross one threshold, as soon as we conquer one difficulty, a new difficulty appears, or should appear. Some people make the mistake of steering clear of thresholds. Anything that requires genuine thinking and use of energy, they avoid. They prefer to stay in a rut where thresholds are not met. Probably, they have been at their job a number of years. Things are easy for them. They make no effort to seek out new obstacles to overcome. Real progress stops under such circumstances.

Some middle-aged and elderly people greatly enrich their lives by continuing to cross thresholds. One man went into an entirely new business when he was past middle life and made success of it, De Morgan didn't start to write novels until he was past sixty. Psychologists have discovered that man can continue to learn throughout his life. And it is undoubtedly better to try and fail than not to try at all. There one can be placed in the category of the Swiss mountaineer of whom it was said, *"He died climbing"*. When a new difficulty arises to obstruct your path, do not complain. Accept the challenge. Determine to cross this threshold as you have crossed numerous other thresholds in your past. In the words of a poet, do not rest but strive *to pass from dream to grander dream.*

1. What obstructs real progress in life?
A. Remaining at one and the same post
B. Avoiding the thinking and energy
C. Shunning every work
D. Stopping education

2. What does progress in life depend upon?
A. Good habits
B. Hardwork
C. Overcoming one difficulty after another
D. Spirit of service and cooperation

3. What does *'He died climbing'* signify?
A. He died when he was climbing the hill
B. He died before getting at the top
C. He strove hard till the last moment of life
D. He climbed the hill and then died

4. What does *'to pass from dream to grander dream'* mean?
A. Always having greater and greater aspiration in life
B. Seeing one good dream and then greater aspiration in life
C. Making plan after plan
D. Seeing one dream after the other

5. What did the man entering a new business past middle life do of his business?
A. He miserably failed in it
B. He achieved partial success
C. He dropped the business after some time
D. He achieved good success in it

6. How can you accomplish the most difficult tasks?
A. By mobilizing all possible resources
B. By avoiding all obstacles
C. By sticking to hardwork
D. By doing it bit by bit and persisting in the effort

7. What does De Morgan's life teach?
A. That it is futile to learn many things
B. That one is never old in case he has vigour
C. That it is never too late to learn
D. That creative writing can be made even late in life

8. How do middle-aged and elderly people add brilliance to their lives?
A. By overcoming difficulty one after another
B. By getting sycophants to surround them
C. By making fine speeches
D. By acquiring resourcefulness

9. What should we do when a new difficulty obstructs our path?
A. Run away from it
B. Be bold and face it
C. Manoeuvre to get it removed
D. Enlist other people's help to get it over

10. When did De Morgan start to write novels?
A. When he was sixty years old
B. When he was below sixty
C. When he studied psychology
D. None of these

PASSAGE-7

It is *heartening* to know that if one had not had any heart attack earlier and he stops smoking, his chances of having a heart attack *drop* to that of a non-smoker in about six months' time. Stopping of smoking is also the single most effective means of secondary prevention (recurrence of a heart attack) in heart patients.

Smoking leads to pain and stiffness in the legs while walking. No amount of drugs can help. The only remedy is to give up smoking. If women smoke during pregnancy, there is an increased risk of death of the baby in the womb or soon after birth. Even where the baby survives, there is likelihood of delayed physical and intellectual development of the baby till it reaches 11 years of age.

Still worse the fact about smoking is that passive smoking is equally dangerous. Passive smokers are those who do not smoke but being in the company of smokers have to inhale smoke exhaled by the smokers They are equally prone to heart diseases, lung cancer and bronchitis, for no fault of theirs. It is seen that the incidence of these diseases is greater among women whose husbands are *heavy* smokers As such, every non-smoker has a fundamental right to safeguard himself against the danger of passive smoking. "Your smoking is injurious to my health and I have a right to stop you from smoking" could be the slogan against passive smoking. It is a great threat to the health of the individual, the family and the society. In fact one has to choose between health and smoking including passive smoking. *One cannot have both.*

Another matter of *grave concern* about smoking is the long time interval between the start of smoking habit and the manifestation of deadly diseases like cancer, chronic bronchitis and heart attack. People are generally not aware of the link between smoking and the misery they have to undergo years later and younger people often fall victim to this menacing habit under the wrong impression that they are *immune* to its disastrous effects, not realising that they are *heading* towards catastrophe. The prolonged incubation period of many tobacco-related diseases has prevented recognition of the size of the threat and the *grim* picture of chronic and life-threatening diseases.

1. What is "passive smoking"?
A. Giving up the habit of smoking abruptly
B. Exhaling smoke by a non-smoker
C. Unintended intake of smoke exhaled by smokers
D. Smoking cigarettes which are harmless in nature

2. The effects of passive smoking are more and more prominently observed among
A. the children
B. the smokers
C. the wives of smokers
D. the non-smokers

3. Which of the following is a heartening thing, according to the author?
A. People who have had a heart attack stop smoking
B. It takes only six months for any person to quit smoking
C. The smoker carries the risk of heart attack for six months
D. None of these

4. Which of the following statements is/are false in the context of the passage?
(*i*) Passive smokers are not free from risk of heart diseases
(*ii*) Intake of certain medicines helps recover pain and stiffness in legs caused by smoking
(*iii*) Younger people are immune to the disastrous effects if their regular smoking is under control

A. (*i*) and (*ii*) only B. (*ii*) and (*iii*) only
C. (*ii*) only D. (*iii*) only

5. Which of the following is not mentioned in the passage as a likely result of smoking by women during pregnancy?
A. Death of baby before birth
B. Death of baby after birth
C. Survival of baby with some abnormality
D. Abnormal delay in the childbirth

6. Which of the following is considered by the author as a matter of "grave concern"?
   A. Inordinate delay in appearance of symptoms of hazards of smoking
   B. Long time required for giving up the habit of smoking
   C. Manifestation of deadly diseases like cancer, bronchitis, etc.
   D. Lack of awareness of people regarding the hazards of smoking
7. The youth feel that they are immune to the hazardous effects of smoking because
   A. these effects of smoking are not visible within a short time span
   B. they do not realise that they are heading towards disaster
   C. they feel a great thrill in acquiring the habit of smoking
   D. the link between smoking and its disastrous effects cannot be established
8. Which factor prevents people from realising the extent of threat of smoking hazards?
   A. Their lack of awareness of civic responsibilities
   B. Their firm belief that they are not immune to these hazards
   C. The less disastrous effects of tobacco-related diseases
   D. None of these
9. The last sentence of the third para *"One cannot have both"* means
   A. active smoking and passive smoking
   B. smoking and risk of heart diseases
   C. threat to the individual and also to the family
   D. None of these

Directions (Qs. 10 to 12): *Choose the word which is most nearly the **SAME** in meaning as the word given in bold capitals as used in the passage.*

10. HEADING

A. crowning B. marching
C. adorning D. title

11. HEAVY

A. excessive B. bulky
C. large D. thick

12. DROP

A. roll B. escape
C. remove D. reduce

Directions (Qs. 13 to 15): *Choose the word which is most nearly the **OPPOSITE** in meaning of the word given in bold capitals as used in the passage.*

13. GRIM

A. dim B. dark
C. presentable D. pleasant

14. IMMUNE

A. free B. vulnerable
C. powerful D. weak

15. HEARTENING

A. cheerful B. miserable
C. frightening D. dangerous

PASSAGE-8

The happy man is the man who lives objectively, who has free affections and wide interests, who secures his happiness through these interests and affections and through the fact that they, in turn, make him an object of interest and affection to many others. To be the recipient of affection is a potent cause of happiness, but the man who demands affection is not the man upon whom it is *bestowed.* The man who receives affection is, speaking broadly, the man who gives it. But it is useless to attempt to give it as a calculation, in the way in which one might lend money at interest, for a calculated affection is not genuine and is not felt to be so by the recipient.

What then can a man do who is unhappy because he is encased in self? So long as he continues to think about the causes of his unhappiness, he continues to be self-centred and therefore does not get outside the vicious circle, if he is to get outside it, it must be genuine interests, not by simulated interests adopted merely as a medicine. Although this difficulty is real, there is nevertheless much that he can do if he has rightly diagnosed his trouble. If, for example, his trouble is due to a sense of sin, conscious or unconscious, he can first persuade his conscious mind that he has no reason to feel sinful and then proceed, to plant his rational conviction in his unconscious mind, concerning himself meanwhile with some more or less neutral activity. If he succeeds in *dispelling* the sense of sin, it is possible that genuine objective interests will arise spontaneously. If his trouble is self-pity, he can deal with it in the same manner after first persuading himself that there is nothing extraordinarily unfortunate in his circumstances.

If fear is his trouble, let him practise exercises designed to give courage. Courage has been recognised from time immemorial as an important virtue, and a great part of training of boys and young men has been devoted to producing a type of character capable of fearlessness in battle. But moral courage and intellectual courage have been much less studied, they also, however, have their technique. Admit to yourself everyday at least one painful truth, you will find this quite useful. Teach yourself to feel that life still be worth living even if you were not, as of course you are, immeasurably superior to all your friends in virtue and in intelligence. Exercises of this sort prolonged through several years will at last enable you to admit facts *without flinching* and will, in so doing, free you from the empire of fear over a very large field.

1. Who according to the passage is the happy man?
   A. who is encased in self
   B. who has free affection and wide interests
   C. who is free from worldly passions
   D. who has externally centre passions

2. According to the passage, calculated affection
   A. appears to be false and fabricated
   B. makes other pen-on to love you
   C. turns into permanent affection over a period of time
   D. leads to self-pity

3. Which of the following virtues, according to the passage, has been recognised for long as an important virtue?
   A. Patriotism   B. Sacrifice
   C. Courage   D. Self-consciousness

4. Which of the following, according to the passage, has not been studied much?
   A. Feeling of guilt and self-pity
   B. The state of mind of an unhappy man
   C. How to get absorbed in other interests
   D. Moral and intellectual courage

5. If a man is suffering from a sense of sin
   A. he should invite opinion of others
   B. he should admit his sin at once
   C. he should consciously realize that he has no reason to feel sinful
   D. he should develop a fearless character

6. What happens to a man who demands affection?
   A. His feelings are reciprocated by others
   B. He tends to take a calculated risk
   C. He becomes a victim of a viscious circle
   D. None of these

7. What should a man do who is suffering from the feeling of self-pity?
   A. He should control his passions and emotions
   B. He should persuade himself that everything is alright in his circumstances
   C. He should seek affection from others
   D. He should develop a feeling of fearlessness

8. How to get out of the viscious circle mentioned in the passage?
   A. By practicing skills of concentration
   B. By inculcating the habits of self-absorption
   C. Being true to others and one's internal circumstances
   D. None of these

9. Which of the following statements is not *true* in the context of the passage?
   A. Happy man has wide interests
   B. Courage has been recognized as an important virtue
   C. Unhappy man is encased in self

D. Issue of intellectual courage has been extensively studied

10. Which of the following words is ***SIMILAR*** in meaning of the word **'bestowed'** as used in the passage?
A. Conferred B. Accommodated
C. Trusted D. Withdrawn

11. Which of the following statements is *true* in the context of the passage?
A. All passions stem from unhappiness
B. The happy man lives in subjectively
C. Any virtue has a dark side also
D. One feels happy if one receives affection

12. Which of the following words is ***SIMILAR*** in meaning to the word **'flinching'** as used in the passage?
A. Wincing B. Convincing
C. Explaining D. Debating

13. What happens when you think about cause of your unhappiness?
A. You try to introspect and look critically at yourself
B. You realize that the life can be lived in different ways
C. You try to practice exercise designed to give courage
D. You remain a self-centred person

14. What according to the passage is the real cause of happiness?
A. Material rewards and incentives received
B. Critical analysis of the happy state of mind
C. Affection received from others
D. Calculated risks taken

15. Which of the following words is ***OPPOSITE*** in meaning of the word **'dispelling'** as used in the passage?
A. Giving B. Accumulating
C. Projecting D. Scattering

PASSAGE-9

Education, particularly higher education, is the obvious but crucially important instrument for nation building. As Confucious has said:

"If you are thinking of one year, plant rice. If you are thinking of a decade, plant trees. If you are thinking of a century, educate the people."

When we set about the task of higher education, we should be absolutely clear in our perception of the goals of education in the specific context of our nation's development. No *doubt,* one of the important aims of education would be to create the required range and nature of trained manpower assessed to be needed by different sectors of national growth. The entire educational apparatus must be geared progressively to fulfill the requirements of different phases of our growth in every sector—primary, secondary and *tertiary.* The aim must be to ensure that our country does not experience either *paucity,* or a *surfeit* of trained manpower in any specific segment of our economy. The requirements of our country, as a free, democratic, secular, socialist, nation, *aspiring* for rapid development, *entail* a specific recipe for our educational institutions. Today's educational institutions must therefore be developed accordingly and must regulate themselves to give the country the precise nature and quantum of trained manpower as projected by the requirements of our planned economy.

1. The author has quoted thoughts of Confucious to stress
A. importance of planting trees for human beings
B. the worthless efforts in planting rice
C. the benefits of investing in education
D. the need for assessing manpower requirement

2. Which statement cannot be made on the basis of the passage?
A. Higher education should keep in view the requirements of national economy
B. Higher education has not been employed for nation building
C. All levels of education have a role to play in nation's growth
D. In our country we need to have a specially planned educational system

3. The writer believes that
A. there are no problems related to higher education
B. investment in education is of long-range
C. higher education should be used to assess manpower needs
D. aims of higher education in India are absolutely clear

4. The author's expectations from higher education, are essentially
A. unrealistic B. confusing
C. critical D. vague

5. The writer indicates that
A. higher education did not play any role in national growth
B. primary education did not play any role in national growth
C. our nation experiences paucity of trained manpower in many sectors
D. today's higher education has no precise goals to achieve

6. Author has used the word 'apparatus' to indicate the
A. scientific nature of education
B. complicated organization demanded by education
C. readily visible benefits of education
D. entire equipment of education to perform particular function

7. Which of the following has not been conveyed by the passage?
A. Education at any level can contribute in nation building
B. Manpower needs in many areas can be fulfilled through higher education
C. Rapid development of our nation is possible through higher education
D. Present higher education does not ensure surfeit of trained manpower

8. This passage is likely to be addressed to
A. politicians only
B. scientists only
C. students only
D. cannot be said

9. Choose a suitable title to the passage:
A. Manpower Planning in India
B. Importance of Higher Education
C. Demands of Higher Education
D. Role of Higher Education in India

Directions (Qs.10 to 12): *Choose the word which is most nearly the* ***SAME*** *in meaning as the word given in bold capitals as used in the passage.*

10. DOUBT
A. suspicion B. certain
C. definite D. sure

11. TERTIARY
A. last B. important
C. third D. terminal

12. ASPIRING
A. inquiring B. awaiting
C. involving D. striving

Directions (Qs.13 to 15): *Choose the word which is most* ***OPPOSITE*** *in meaning as the word given in bold capitals as used in the passage.*

13. PAUCITY
A. moderate B. enormity
C. mediocrity D. littleness

14. SURFEIT
A. abundance B. redundancy
C. repletion D. lack

15. ENTAIL
A. entitled B. ensure
C. dismiss D. retain

PASSAGE-10

Books are a great treasurehouse of knowledge. They are the living examples of man's *march* on the path to higher and higher civilisation. The great men who died long ago, live in their books. We feel their very personality and existence when we read their books. We feel as if they were conversing with us.

Books not only store civilization but also carry it forward. All coming generations get the light of knowledge from the books written by their ancestors and try to improve upon that knowledge. Civilization cannot make much *headway* in a country where there are not many *great* books. We get through books the latest knowledge in the fields of arts, science, commerce, etc. This knowledge is helpful to us and *enables* us to achieve success in the field of our choice.

Books are never failing friends. They never *desert* us, not even when all fair-weather friends have deserted us. They dispel the dark clouds of gloom from our minds and increase our happiness if we are already happy. Through the ages, the scriptures and other great books have provided immeasurable *solace* to the wounded and strife-torn humanity.

There may be books prescribed for some course or profession, but then there are books for general study. The books of literature—poetry, drama, novel, short stories, etc., are generally highly thrilling and inspiring if they are written by a good author. There may be tragic, comical or humorous books. The question is that of an individual's choice.

To be a lover of books, though not to be bookworm, is a sign of good luck. A voracious reader gets much *more pleasure* from reading books than a miser gets in hoarding money. The knowledge embedded in books is valueless; so is pleasure obtained from reading them. A good book absorbs the whole spirit of man; the reader's pleasure is indescribable.

1. Which of the following, according to the passage, is not true about books?
   A. They are source of inspiration
   B. They are source of knowledge
   C. They are source of happiness
   D. They are means of livelihood

2. How do the books help in progress of civilization?
   A. Based on the earlier books new knowledge is obtained
   B. The books provide solution to many problems
   C. The books inspire the scientists
   D. Not mentioned in the passage

3. How do the books make people more happy?
   A. They help the reader to overcome the shadows of uncertainty
   B. They help bring in joy by amusing the reader through their content
   C. They help the reader to understand the darker side of life
   D. Not mentioned in the passage

4. Which of the following is the author's view about the knowledge and pleasure derived from books?
   (*i*) We get more of knowledge and less of pleasure
   (*ii*) We get more of pleasure and less of knowledge
   (*iii*) We get knowledge and pleasure in equal measure
   A. only (*i*) B. only (*ii*)
   C. either (*i*) or (*ii*) D. only (*iii*)

5. The high quality of books produced by a country indicates:
   A. it has a high rate of literacy
   B. it has a progressive civilization
   C. it is not an industrialised nation
   D. it has learned ancestors

6. Why are the books, according to the passage, called never-failing friends?
   A. Books do not betray individuals
   B. Books are inanimate
   C. Books always give companionship to the reader
   D. Books are available in the market anytime unlike others

7. How do the books help in bringing peace in the minds of people?
   A. Books provide information about the past civilization
   B. Books help people learn to take correct steps with the help of the recorded information
   C. Books act as a window to the minds of the great men
   D. Not mentioned in the passage

8. Which of the following has been described as a sign of good luck?
   A. Being a miser
   B. Having lot of money
   C. Advancing the culture
   D. A passion for books

Directions (Qs. 9 to 12): *Choose the word which is most nearly the **SAME** in meaning as the word given in bold capitals as used in the passage.*

9. SOLACE
A. peace B. tranquillity
C. calmness D. console

10. ENABLES
A. helps B. succeeds
C. promotes D. stops

11. HEADWAY
A. higher B. forge
C. movement D. improve

12. MARCH
A. move B. progress
C. pass D. register

Directions (Qs. 13 to 15): *Choose the word which is most **OPPOSITE** in meaning of the word given in bold capitals as used in the passage.*

13. GREAT
A. small B. thin
C. short D. ordinary

14. PLEASURE
A. displeasure B. pain
C. happiness D. hardship

15. DESERT
A. waterhole B. bitter
C. accompany D. propel

PASSAGE-1

1	2	3	4
A	B	A	A

PASSAGE-2

1	2	3	4	5
A	C	D	A	D

PASSAGE-3

1	2	3	4	5
A	D	C	D	A

PASSAGE-4

1	2	3	4	5	6
D	A	D	A	A	D

PASSAGE-5

1	2	3	4	5	6	7
A	D	A	A	A	C	B

PASSAGE-6

1	2	3	4	5
A	C	C	A	D
6	7	8	9	10
D	B	A	B	D

PASSAGE-7

1	2	3	4	5
C	C	D	B	D
6	7	8	9	10
A	A	D	D	B
11	12	13	14	15
A	D	D	B	C

PASSAGE-8

1	2	3	4	5
B	A	C	D	C
6	7	8	9	10
D	B	D	D	A
11	12	13	14	15
D	D	D	C	B

PASSAGE-9

1	2	3	4	5
D	D	C	D	D
6	7	8	9	10
D	A	D	B	A
11	12	13	14	15
C	D	B	D	C

PASSAGE-10

1	2	3	4	5
D	A	D	D	B
6	7	8	9	10
A	D	D	D	A
11	12	13	14	15
D	B	D	B	C

❑❑❑

14 Cloze Test

A cloze test is a procedure in which a person is asked to supply words that have been removed from a passage as a test of his ability to comprehend text. Practise it regularly to score well.

PASSAGES

Directions: *In each of the following passages some numbered blank spaces are given. For each numbered blank space four answer choices are given. Pick out the one which is the most appropriate for that blank space, keeping the trend of the passage in mind.*

Passage-1

Mankind's most ....(1).... treasure of thoughts is carefully preserved in the golden casket of books. The ....(2).... of books is as vast as the universe, for there is no corner of it which they have left ....(3).... . There is no ....(4).... of books on any topic, be it as simple as the composition of sodium nitrate or as ....(5).... as the mechanism of a spacecraft rocketing towards Mars. The ....(6).... of books is not only most easily available but is enlightened, dependable and lifelong. In times of distress they make us stoically ....(7).... of the object that causes uneasiness and we learn to ....(8).... with the sting of adversity.

Questions

1. A. costly B. important C. valuable D. vast

2. A. area B. scope C. storage D. kingdom

3. A. unexplored B. unseen C. untouched D. unapproached

4. A. lack B. dearth C. shortage D. insufficiency

5. A. extricate B. intricate C. intrinsic D. internecine

6. A. company B. assistance C. friendship D. companionship

7. A. defiant B. defendant C. defensible D. delusive

8. A. adapt B. adopt C. exist D. co-exist

Passage-2

Though the government has tried to ....(1).... Naxalism with all its might, much more needs to be done to totally root out the ....(2).... of Naxalism. The roots of Naxalism ....(3).... economic backwardness and social exploitation of the peasants and the weaker classes. Thus, the best way to ....(4).... Naxalism is to bring the naxals ....(5).... the mainstream. ....(6).... policies and schemes should be implemented effectively ....(7).... the Naxals economically stable. They should be ....(8).... to participate in democratic processes. The government has to ....(9).... the social upliftment of the Naxals. Use of force in ....(10).... Naxalism will yield little success.

Questions

1. A. crush B. handle C. tackle D. suppress
2. A. menace B. whole C. gamut D. stems
3. A. lies in B. are in C. abound in D. exist in
4. A. crash B. crush C. break D. defy
5. A. in B. on C. into D. within
6. A. Current B. Latest C. Occurring D. Existing
7. A. so that B. so as to make C. such that D. to make
8. A. insisted B. brought C. encouraged D. forced
9. A. assure B. insure C. guarantee D. ensure
10. A. countering B. defying C. banishing D. desecrating

Passage-3

We are living in very exciting ....(1).... . The ....(2).... change is dizzying and the impact this progress is having on our present and — more importantly — on our future is difficult to ....(3).... in its ...(4).... . This is the age of ....(5).... micro-processors, sophisticated software, new hardware technology and high bandwidth, high-speed networks. The PC gave us a new way to work, play and ....(6).... . In fact, it brought ....(7).... our desktops computing power, which until a few years ....(8).... had only been available to corporates. With the ....(9).... of the internet, the PC ....(10).... us the most convenient and flexible way to head on to the Net.

Questions

1. A. periods B. days C. phase D. times
2. A. phase B. pace C. sphere D. drastic
3. A. guess B. forecast C. comprehend D. approximate
4. A. whole B. entirety C. fruition D. fullness
5. A. strong B. changing C. powerful D. sonorous
6. A. convey B. communicate C. entertain D. enjoy
7. A. onto B. to C. on D. at
8. A. back B. earlier C. behind D. before
9. A. addendum B. adherence C. afoot D. advent
10. A. allowed B. privileged C. brought D. offered

Passage-4

What is required today in our country is ....(1).... of a new political culture based on full respect for human liberty, on pluralism and on a better social deal for all. The major ....(2).... facing us today is to carry out democratic transformation in all the ....(3)...., social, cultural, economic and political. The events of the 20th century ....(4).... one thing absolutely clear that human ....(5)...., everywhere, specially in countries whose political structures were ....(6).... to reflect the revolutionary aspirations of the people ....(7).... not only under stress and strain but are ....(8).... vast upheavals because of the ....(9).... of democracy. At the same time it has also to be understood that democracy cannot be ....(10).... into a static mould.

Questions

1. A. growing B. developing C. creating D. creation
2. A. development B. crisis C. challenge D. drawback
3. A. corners B. context C. realm D. spheres
4. A. have made B. has made C. had made D. made

5. A. travails B. traverse
C. traps D. transverse

6. A. supposed B. meant
C. caused D. forced

7. A. were B. was
C. are D. have been

8. A. developing B. evolving
C. experiencing D. faced with

9. A. denial B. rebuff
C. rebuttal D. absence

10. A. shaped B. flex
C. frozen D. caused

Passage-5

For centuries, women not only in India but all over the world ....(1).... treated as ....(2).... secondary position to men. ....(3).... human history men ....(4).... far greater power then women to name, classify, and order the worlds in which they both live. ....(5).... studies in various parts of the world point out to a wide ....(6).... in male and female roles ....(7).... cultures and demonstrate the possibility of change in these sex-determined roles. The 20th century in particular ....(8).... the cause of gender justice by internationalizing struggles for equality ....(9).... women and other oppressed people. Women's struggles against their ....(10).... were intertwined in ....(11).... degrees with ideologies and movements based on the values of freedom, self-determination, equality, democracy and justice.

Questions

1. A. has been B. have been
C. had been D. were

2. A. occupying B. taking
C. possessing D. serving

3. A. All through B. Throughout
C. Since D. From

4. A. have B. had
C. have had D. enjoy

5. A. Sociological B. Anthropological
C. General D. Practical

6. A. concord B. repulsion
C. disagreement D. variation

7. A. among B. across
C. between D. of

8. A. developed B. evolved
C. promoted D. entertained

9. A. for B. to
C. among D. by

10. A. subsidiary B. subsequent
C. subservience D. subordination

11. A. various B. varying
C changing D. differing

Passage-6

Visualisation is a strong ....(1).... to memory. Those persons who ......(2)..... a powerful memory cannot do so without taking the help of visualisation. Such persons have developed the skills to ....(3).... visualisation even in such ....(4).... tasks as remembering names and numbers. These persons have the names and numbers ....(5).... in their brain even after hearing those names and figures only once. On the other hand those who take the help of revising to memorise ....(6).... to forget it once they have ....(7).... the practice of revising ....(8).... the ones who have applied visualisation to memorise. Psychologists ....(9).... in visualisation a powerful tool for personality development. The more you visualise, the more you are ....(10).... your attitude and behaviour to the blue prints of your vision and ....(11).... more you are inching towards success.

Questions

1. A. way B. path
C. aid D. symptom

2. A. command B. master
C. rule D. enjoy

3. A. use B. apply
C. put D. place

4. A. trivial B. difficult
C. mundane D. unscrupulous

5. A. impress B. imprinted
C. impinge D. store

6. A. bent B. incline
C. prone d. tend

7. A. dropped B. left
C. gave up D. given up

8. A. unlike B. opposite
C. contrary D. not like

9. A. found B. have found
C. sees D. finds

10. A. shaping B. moulding
C. making D. attuning

11. A. actually B. factually
C. subsequently D. consequently

Passage-7

The development of an area depends on the resources ....(1).... in the area, the needs and ....(2).... of the people living there and the technological skill ....(3).... by them. Humans play an important and decisive role in the ....(4).... of development of an area. We choose the ....(5).... of resources which could be developed to our ....(6).... . The natural ....(7).... available in an area ....(8).... value as a resource only when people find a use for them. There are ....(9).... where large potential resources are available, but they ....(10).... developed for economic reasons. Lack of capital for investments, roads and railway lines, and other ....(11).... facilities may stand in the way of resource development.

Questions

1. A. present B. prevalent
C. available D. exist

2. A. inspirations B. aspirations
C. ambitions D. curiosity

3. A. handled B. practised
C. availed D. possessed

4. A. system B. design
C. pattern D. style

5. A. class B. group
C. variety D. types

6. A. good B. advantage
C. approach D. favour

7. A. secrets B. phenomenon
C. products D. endowments

8. A. get B. acquire
C. possess D. takes

9. A. instances B. events
C. circumstances D. happenings

10. A. have not yet been
B. haven't been
C. are not yet
D. yet have not been

11. A. common B. general
C. infrastructural D. structural

Passage-8

The Naxal problem in India is basically socio-economic in ....(1).... . The main reasons ....(2).... the Naxal movement in India are the ....(3).... of peasants and their weak social and economic position. ....(4).... of the peasants are landless labourers whose lands have been ....(5).... occupied by the landlords. Moreover, the landlords give ....(6).... wages to the peasants. Their ....(7).... suffering at the hands of the landlords thus encourage many peasants to take law ....(8).... their own hands. Due to their poor economic condition the peasants easily ....(9).... the trap of the naxal leaders who have their ....(10).... interests. Illiteracy, unemployment, police excesses, corruption and ....(11).... administration further ....(12).... this complex problem.

Questions

1. A. form B. shape
C. behaviour D. nature

2. A. for B. of
C. in D. behind

3. A. complaisance B. exploitation
C. domination D. exculpation

4. A. Many B. Much
C. Most D. All

5. A. imperiously B. imperatively
C. forcefully D. forcibly

6. A. improper B. small
C. inadequate D. insufficient

7. A. long B. brutal
C. pathetic D. great

8. A. in B. into
C. on D. by

9. A. fall into B. fell in C. fell in D. fell into

9. A. fall into B. fall in
C. fell in D. fell into

10. A. selfish B. vested
C. vicious D. vindictive

11. A. failed B. improper
C. inefficient D. bureaucratic

12. A. heighten B. deepen
C. add D. worsen

Passage-9

No doubt various ....(1).... and Acts are there to eliminate the ....(2).... practice of child labour. But the ....(3).... is that, these are not being implemented in both letter and spirit, for which the ....(4).... of the problem remains as it was. Therefore a judicious, pragmatic, integrated and time-bound ....(5).... supplemented by ....(6).... follow-up action is essential to ....(7).... the problem that ....(8).... deep root in our Society. It is true that child labour can't be ....(9)... with a magic wand. If we ....(10).... time-bound goals and follow, of course, with the ....(11).... assistance of ILO and UNICEF, it is possible to eliminate the problem of child labour. With strong political will power and people's backing nothing is ....(12).... . Rather ....(13).... the bud we should let it blossom and spread its fragrance all around. ....(14).... lies the progress and prosperity of the society.

Questions

1. A. means B. methods
C. source D. provisions

2. A. unjust B. inhuman
C. mal D. illegal

3. A. anxiety B. abrasion
C. tragedy D. conclusion

4. A. magnitude B. depth
C. gravity D. soaring

5. A. approach B. analysis
C. survey D. scheme

6. A. continuous B. thorough
C. throughout D. regular

7. A. outroot B. uproot
C. downroot D. grassroot

8. A. have B. has
C. had D. has taken

9. A. wipe out B. wipe off
C. wipe up D. wiped

10. A. keep B. put
C. put up D. set

11. A. ongoing B. continuing
C. unending D. frequent

12. A. insurmountable B. intangible
C. inscrutable D. incorrigible

13. A. killing B. hurting
C. destroying D. nipping

14. A. Here B. There
C. Therein D. Herein

Passage-10

Every action we perform ....(1).... a result. And, naturally, we lay claim ....(2).... the results or fruits ....(3).... from that action in the ....(4).... that it is we who perform the action. This is .....(5).... ignorance because ....(6).... is it the Lord who ....(7).... the result of any action, it is by His will ....(8).... that even the action is accomplished. The will of the Lord ....(9).... whether we cooperate with His will or strive ....(10).... . If God wills that an action takes place, he arranges for the ....(11).... for it to happen. It is ....(12).... experience that sometimes despite our best efforts we ....(13).... achieve the results we desire, and at other times the seemingly most ....(14).... situations mysteriously get ....(15).... . ....(16).... way man chooses to act, both the act and the outcome of the cost are dependent ....(17).... on the will of the Lord.

Questions

1. A. produce B. produces
C. causes D. undergoes

2. A. on B. at
C. to D. for

3. A. occurring B. obtaining
C. deriving D. falling

4. A. belief B. hope
C. fantasy D. folly

5. A. sheen B. keen
C. sheer D. sheathe

6. A. alone B. only that
C. not only D. for only

7. A. declares B. decides
C. ordains D. ornate

8. A. completely B. entirely
C. only D. alone

9. A. prevails always
B. prevails everywhere
C. is prevalent
D. always prevails

10. A. alone B. always
C. constantly D. independently

11. A. wherewithal B. whereabouts
C. whatsoever D. wherefore

12. A. usual B. general
C. universal D. common

13. A. does not B. may not
C. do not D. might not

14. A. intractable B. intangible
C. internecine D. intricate

15. A. subsided B. resolved
C. solved D. converted

16. A. Whatever B. All the
C. All those D. Whichever

17. A. mainly B. actually
C. entirely D. generally

ANSWERS

PASSAGE-1

1	2	3	4	5	6
C	D	A	B	B	D
7	**8**				
A	D				

PASSAGE-2

1	2	3	4	5	6
C	A	A	B	C	D
7	**8**	**9**	**10**		
B	C	D	A		

PASSAGE-3

1	2	3	4	5	6
D	B	C	B	C	B
7	**8**	**9**	**10**		
A	D	D	D		

PASSAGE-4

1	2	3	4	5	6
D	C	D	A	A	B
7	**8**	**9**	**10**		
C	C	A	C		

PASSAGE-5

1	2	3	4	5	6
B	A	B	C	B	D
7	**8**	**9**	**10**	**11**	
B	C	D	D	B	

PASSAGE-6

1	2	3	4	5	6
C	A	B	C	B	D
7	**8**	**9**	**10**	**11**	
A	A	B	D	D	

PASSAGE-7

1	2	3	4	5	6
C	B	D	C	D	B
7	**8**	**9**	**10**	**11**	
D	B	A	A	C	

PASSAGE-8

1	2	3	4	5	6
D	A	B	C	D	C
7	**8**	**9**	**10**	**11**	**12**
A	B	A	B	C	D

PASSAGE-9

1	2	3	4	5	6
D	B	C	A	A	D
7	**8**	**9**	**10**	**11**	**12**
B	D	B	D	B	A
13	**14**				
D	C				

PASSAGE-10

1	2	3	4	5	6
B	C	B	A	C	C
7	**8**	**9**	**10**	**11**	**12**
C	D	D	D	A	D
13	**14**	**15**	**16**	**17**	
C	A	B	D	C	

❑❑❑

General Awareness

INDIAN HISTORY

ANCIENT INDIA

INDUS VALLEY CIVILISATION
(2500-1750 BC)

- The earliest excavations in the Indus valley were done at Harappa in the West Punjab and Mohenjodaro in Sindh. Both places are now in Pakistan.

Important Sites

- The most important sites are Kot Diji in Sindh, Kalibangan in Rajasthan, Ropar in the Punjab, Banawali in Haryana, Lothal, Surkotada and Dhaulavira, all the three in Gujarat.
- Mohenjodaro is the largest of all the Indus cities and it is estimated to have spread over an area of 200 hectares.

Indus Valley Civilisation : An Objective Study

Major Sites	*Excavators*	*Year*	*River*	*Location*	*Important Findings*
1. Harappa	D.R. Sahni	1921	Ravi	West Punjab (Pakistan)	Granaries, Virgin Goddess, Cemetery, Stone symbol of Lingam and Yoni
2. Mohenjodaro	R.D. Banerjee	1922	Indus	Sindh (Pakistan)	Great Bath, Great Granary, Assembly Hall, Proto-Shiva, Brick Kilns, Mesopotamian seals
3. Chanhudaro	N.G. Mazumdar	1931	Indus	Sindh (Pakistan)	Bronze toy cart, Ink-pot, Lipstick, City without a citadel
4. Kalibangan	B.B. Lal & B.K. Thapar	1953	Ghaggar	Ganganagar (Rajasthan)	Decorated bricks, ploughed field surface, Firealtars
5. Lothal	S.R. Rao	1957	Bhogwa	Ahmedabad (Gujarat)	Dockyard, Rice husk, Fire altars, Double burial
6. Banawali	R.S. Bist	1973	Ghaggar	Hissar (Haryana)	Toy plough, Gridiron pattern of Town planning.
7. Dholavira	R.S. Bist	1990	Luni	Kutchh (Gujarat)	A Large well & a bath, A stadium
8. Surkotada	J. Joshi	1964	—	Gujarat	Bones of Horse, Pot burials

Salient Features of the Harappan Culture

- The Harappan Civilization was primarily Urban.
- Mohenjodaro and Harappa were the planned cities.
- The large-scale use of burnt bricks in almost all kinds of constructions are the important characteristics of the Harappan culture.
- Another remarkable feature was the underground drainage system connecting all houses to the street drains which were covered by stone slabs or bricks.
- The most important public place of Mohenjodaro is the Great Bath measuring 39 feet length, 23 feet breadth and 8 feet depth.

- Agriculture was the most important occupation. In the fertile soils, farmers cultivated two crops a year. They were the first who had grown paddy.
- Wheat and barley were the main crops grown besides sesame, mustard and cotton.
- Animals like sheep, goats and buffalo were domesticated. The use of horse is not yet firmly established.
- Bronze and copper vessels are the outstanding examples of the Harappan metal craft.
- A large number of seals numbering more than 2000 have been discovered.

Social Life

- Jewelleries such as bangles, bracelets, fillets, girdles, anklets, ear-rings and finger rings were worn by women. These ornaments were made of gold, silver, copper, bronze and semi precious stones.
- Fishing was a regular occupation while hunting and bull fighting were other pastimes.
- Manufacture of terracotta (burnt clay) was a major industry of the people.
- Figures of animals such as sacred bull and dove were discovered. The figures of Mother Goddesses were used for religious purposes.
- Most of the inscriptions were engraved on seals. It is interesting to note that the Indus script has not yet been deciphered.
- The Pipal tree was used as a religious symbol.
- The origin of the '*Swastika*' symbol can be traced to the Harrapan Civilization.
- The chief male deity was Pasupati, (proto-Siva) represented in seals as sitting in a yogic posture with three faces and two horns.

THE VEDIC PERIOD

RIG VEDIC AGE (1500 - 1000 B.C.)

- The Early Vedic period is known from the *Rig Veda*.
- The *Rig Veda* refers to Saptasindhu or the land of seven rivers. This includes the five rivers of the Punjab, namely, Jhelum, Chenab, Ravi, Beas and Sutlej along with the Indus and Saraswati.
- Historians view that the Aryans came from Central Asia. They entered India through the Khyber pass between 2000 B.C. and 1500 B.C. They first settled in seven places in the Punjab region which they called Sapta Sindhu. Slowly, they moved towards the Gangetic Valley.
- The Aryan Civilisation was a rural civilisation.

Vedic Literature

- The word 'Veda' is derived from the root 'vid', which means to know and signifies 'superior knowledge'.
- The Vedic literature consists of the four Vedas – Rig, Yajur, Sama and Atharva.
- The *Rig Veda* is the earliest of the four Vedas divided into 10 mandalas and it consists of 1028 hymns. The hymns were sung by *Hotri* in praise of various gods.
- The *Yajur Veda* consists of various details of rules to be observed at the time of sacrifice. Its hymns were recited by *Adharvayus*.
- The *Sama Veda* is set to tune for the purpose of chanting during sacrifice. It is called the book of chants and the origins of Indian music are traced in it. Its hymns were recited by *Udgatri*.
- The *Atharva Veda* contains details of rituals.
- Besides the Vedas, there are other sacred works like the Brahmanas, the Aranyakas, the Upanishads, and the epics Ramayana and Mahabharata.

Political Organisation

- During this period, the kingdom was tribal in character. Each tribe formed a separate kingdom.
- The basic unit of political organisation was *kula* or family.
- The highest political unit was called *jana* or tribe.
- There were several tribal kingdoms during the Rig Vedic period such as Bharatas, Matsyas, Yadus and Purus. The head of the kingdom was called as *rajan* or king.
- There were two popular bodies called the *Sabha* and *Samiti*. The former seems to have been a

council of elders and the latter, a general assembly of the entire people.

Social Life

- Family was the basis of the society.
- The head of the family was known as *grihapathi*.

Economic Condition

- The Rig Vedic Aryans were pastoral people and their main occupation was cattle rearing. Their wealth was estimated in terms of their cattle.
- Carpentry was another important profession.

RELIGION

- The important Rig Vedic gods were Prithvi (Earth), Agni (Fire), Vayu (Wind), Varuna (Rain) and Indra (Thunder).
- Indra was the most popular among them during the early Vedic period.
- There were also female gods like Aditi and Ushas. There were no temples and no idol worship during the early Vedic period.

Rigvedic Rivers

River	Name in Rigveda
Indus	Sindhu
Jhelum	Vitasta
Chenab	Asikni
Ravi	Parushini
Beas	Vipasa
Sutlej	Sutudri
Gomati	Gomal
Saraswati	Sarasvati
Ghaggar	Prishadavati

LATER VEDIC PERIOD (1000–600 B.C.)

- This age is also called as the Epic Age because the two great epics the Ramayana and Mahabharata were written during this period.
- The Sama, Yajur, Atharva Vedas, Brahmanas, Aranyakas, Upanishads and the two epics are the sources of information for this period.

Political Organisation

- Larger kingdoms were formed during the later Vedic period.
- The king performed various rituals and sacrifices to strengthen his position. They include Rajasuya (consecration ceremony), Asvamedha (horse sacrifice) and Vajpeya (chariot race).
- Kingship became hereditary.
- Kings assumed titles like Ekrat, Samrat and Sarvabhauma.

Economic Condition

- Iron was used extensively in this period and this enabled the people to clear forests and to bring more land under cultivation. Agriculture became the chief occupation.
- Taxes like Bali, Sulk and Bhaga were collected from the people.
- Wealth was calculated in terms of cows.

Social Life

- The four divisions of society (Brahmins, Kshatriyas, Vaisyas and Sudras) or the Varna system was thoroughly established during the Later Vedic period.
- The Ashrama system was formed to attain 4 purusharthas. They were *Dharma*, *Artha*, *Kama* and *Moksha*.

Religion

- Gods of the Early Vedic period like Indra and Agni lost their importance. Prajapathi (the creator), Vishnu (the protector) and Rudra (the destroyer) became prominent during the Later Vedic period.

JAINISM AND BUDDHISM

JAINISM

- Jainism originated in the 6th century B.C. It rejected Vedic religion and avoided its rituals.
- Founded by Rishabha Deva. Rishabha Deva was succeeded by 23 Thirthankaras (prophets). Mahavira was the 24th Thirthankara.

Vardhamana Mahavira (540-468 B.C.)

- Vardhamana was born in a village called Kundagrama near Vaishali in Bihar.
- His father was *Siddhartha*. He was the head of a famous Kshatriya clan.

- His mother was *Trisala*. She was a princess of the Lichchhavi clan. She was the sister of the ruler of Vaishali.
- Vardhamana was married to *Yasoda,* a princess. They had a daughter.
- At the age of 30, he left his home and family. He became an ascetic (monk). He wandered from place-to-place in search of truth for 12 years.
- In the 13th year of his penance, he attained the highest spiritual knowledge called Kevalya or Jnana. Thereafter, he was called Mahavira and Jina. His followers were called Jains and his religion Jainism.
- He died at the age of 72 in 468 B.C. at a place called Pavapuri near modern Rajgir in Bihar.

Teachings of Jainism

- The three principles of Jainism, also known as Triratnas (three gems), are:
  1. right faith.
  2. right knowledge.
  3. right conduct.
- Mahavira preached his disciples to follow the five principles. They are:
  1. Ahimsa—not to injure any living beings
  2. Satya—to speak the truth
  3. Asteya—not to steal
  4. Tyag—not to own property
  5. Brahmacharia—to lead a virtuous life.

Spread of Jainism

- Mahavira preached his religion in Prakrit language which was the language of the masses.
- Chandragupta Maurya, Kharavela of Kalinga and the royal dynasties of south India such as the Gangas, the Kadambas, the Chalukyas and the Rashtrakutas patronised Jainism.
- Jainism was divided into two sects after Vallabhi Council, namely *Svetambaras* (wearing white dresses) under Sthulbhadra and *Digambaras* (naked) under Bhadrabahu.
- The first Jain Council was convened at Pataliputra by Sthulabahu, the leader of the *Digambaras*, in the beginning of the 3rd century B.C.
- The second Jain Council was held at Vallabhi in 5th century A.D. The final compilation of Jain literature called *Twelve Angas* was completed in this council.

BUDDHISM

Gautama Buddha (563-483 B.C.)

- Buddha's original name was *Siddhartha.*
- Siddhartha was born in the Lumbini Garden near Kapilavastu in Nepal. His father was Suddhodana. He was a Sakya chief of Kapilavastu. His mother, Mayadevi, died when Siddhartha was only seven days old. He was brought up by his step mother Mahaprajapati Gauthami.
- At the age of sixteen Siddhartha, married Yasodhara and gave birth to a son, Rahul.
- The sight of an old man, a diseased man, a corpse and an ascetic turned him away from worldly life. He left home at the age of twenty-nine in search of Truth.
- He wandered for seven years and at last, he sat under a bodhi tree at Bodh Gaya in Bihar and did intense penance, after which he got Enlightenment (Nirvana) at the age of thirty-five. Since then, he became known as the Buddha or 'the Enlightened One'.
- Buddha delivered his first sermon at Sarnath near Banaras (now Varanasi).
- He died at the age of 80 in 483 B.C. at Kushinagar in Uttar Pradesh.

Teachings of Buddha

- The Four Noble Truths of Buddha are:
  1. The world is full of suffering.
  2. The cause of suffering is desire.
  3. If desires are get rid off, suffering can be removed.
  4. This can be done by following the Eightfold Path.
- The Eightfold Path consists of:
  1. Right Thought.
  2. Right Belief.
  3. Right Speech.

4. Right Action.
5. Right Living.
6. Right Efforts.
7. Right Knowledge.
8. Right Meditation.

Buddhist Literature

- In Pali language.
- Buddhist scriptures in Pali are commonly referred to as *Tripitakas, i.e.*, 'Three Baskets'.
- ***Vinaya Pitaka:*** Rules of discipline in Buddhist monasteries.
- ***Sutta Pitaka:*** Largest, contains collection of Buddha's sermons.
- ***Abidhamma Pitaka:*** Explanation of the philosophical principles of the Buddhist religion.

Main Buddhist Councils

Buddhist Council	Time	Place	Chairman	Patron
First	483 BC	Rajagriha	Mahakashyapa	Ajatasatru
Second	383 BC	Vaishali	Sabakamuni	Kalashoka
Third	250 BC	Patliputra	Moggaliputta Tissa	Ashoka
Fourth	AD 72	Kundalvana	Vasumitra, Ashwaghosa	Kanishka

The Mahajanapadas

Mahajanapadas	Capital
1. Kashi	Varanasi
2. Kosala	Shravasti
3. Anga	Champanagri
4. Magadh	Girivraj or Rajgriha
5. Vajji	Vaishali
6. Malla	Kushinagar and Pavapuri
7. Chedi	Shuktimati
8. Vatsa	Kaushambi
9. Kuru	Hastinapur, Indraprastha and Isukara
10. Panchal	Ahichhatra and Kampilya
11. Matsya	Viratnagar
12. Surasen	Mathura
13. Asmaka	Paudanya
14. Avanti	Ujjaini
15. Gandhara	Taxila
16. Kamboj	Rajpur (Hatak)

DYNASTIES OF ANCIENT INDIA

HARYANKA DYNASTY

- Bimbisara was the founder of Haryanka Dynasty.
- He was a contemporary of both Vardhamana Mahavira and Gautama Buddha.
- During his rule, Darius I, the Achaemenian emperor, conquered the Indus Valley area.
- Ajatasatru imprisoned his father Bimbisara.
- The first Buddhist Council was convened by Ajatasatru at Rajgir.
- The immediate successor of Ajatasatru was Udayin.
- Udayin laid the foundation of the new capital at Pataliputra situated at the confluence of the two rivers, the Ganges and the Sone.
- Shishunaga was the founder of Shishunaga dynasty.
- After Shishunaga, the mighty empire began to collapse. His successor was Kakavarman or Kalasoka. During his reign, the second Buddhist Council was held at Vaishali.
- Kalasoka was killed by the founder of the Nanda dynasty.

NANDAS

- The fame of Magadha scaled new heights under the Nanda dynasty.
- Mahapadmananda was the founder of Nanda rule in Magadha.
- The last Nanda ruler was Dhana Nanda. Alexander invaded India during his rule.

MAURYAN EMPIRE

CHANDRAGUPTA MAURYA (322–298 B.C.)

- Chandragupta Maurya was the founder of the Mauryan Empire. He overthrew Nanda dynasty with the help of Chanakya.
- Chandragupta defeated Seleukos Nikator, the Greek general of Alexander, in a battle in 305 B.C.
- Seleukos sent Megasthenes as Greek Ambassador to the Court of Chandragupta. Megasthenes wrote *Indica*.
- Chandragupta was a follower of Jainism.
- He came to Sravana Belgola, near Mysore with a Jain monk called Bhadrabahu. The hill in which he lived until his death is called Chandragiri.
- Chanakya served as prime minister during the reigns of Chandragupta and Bindusara.

BINDUSARA (298–273 B.C.)

- Chandragupta Maurya was succeeded by his son Bindusara.
- Bindusara was called by the Greeks as "*Amitraghatha*" meaning, slayer of enemies.

ASHOKA (273–232 B.C.)

- Ashoka was the most famous ruler of the Mauryan dynasty.
- The most important event of Ashoka's reign was his victorious war with Kalinga in 261 B.C.
- Ashoka convened the Third Buddhist Council at Pataliputra around 250 B.C. in order to strengthen the *Sangha*. It was presided over by Moggaliputta Tissa.
- Ashoka's edicts and inscriptions were deciphered by James Prinsep in 1837.
- The last Mauryan king, Brahadratha was killed by his minister Pushyamitra Sunga. It put an end to the Mauryan Empire.

SUNGAS

- The founder of the Sunga dynasty was *Pushyamitra Sunga*, who was the commander-in-chief under the Mauryas.
- He ascended the throne of Magadha in 185 B.C.
- Pushyamitra was a staunch follower of Brahmanism. He performed two asvamedha sacrifices.
- After the death of Pushyamitra, his son Agnimitra became the ruler.
- Agnimitra was a great conqueror. He was also the hero of the play *Malavikagnimitram* written by Kalidasa.

KANVA

- The last Sunga ruler was Devabhuti, who was murdered by his minister Vasudeva Kanva, the founder of the *Kanva dynasty*.
- The Kanva dynasty ruled for 45 years. After the fall of the Kanvas, the history of Magadha was a blank until the establishment of the Gupta dynasty.

SATAVAHANAS

- The founder of the Satavahana dynasty was Simuka.
- The greatest ruler of the Satavahana dynasty was *Gautamiputra Satakarni.*
- The greatest port of the Satavahanas was Kalyani on the west Deccan. Gandakasela and Ganjam on the east coast were the other important seaports.
- The fine painting at Amaravathi and Nagarjunakonda caves belong to this period.

SANGAM AGE
(300 B.C. TO A.D. 300)

- The Sangam Age constitutes an important chapter in the history of South India.
- According to Tamil legends, there existed three Sangams (Academy of Tamil poets) in ancient Tamil Nadu popularly called Muchchangam. These Sangams flourished under the royal patronage of the Pandyas.
- *The first Sangam,* held at then Madurai, chaired by Agastya.
- *The second Sangam* was held at Kapadapuram, chaired by Tolkappiyar.
- *The third Sangam* at Madurai was founded by Mudathirumaran.

Political History

- The Tamil country was ruled by three dynasties namely the Chera, Chola and Pandyas during the Sangam Age.

CHERAS

- The Cheras ruled over parts of modern Kerala. Their capital was Vanji and their important seaports were Tondi and Musiris.
- The greatest Chera King was *Senguttuvan*.

CHOLAS

- The Chola kingdom of the Sangam period extended from modern Tiruchi district to southern Andhra Pradesh.
- Their capital was first located at Uraiyur and then shifted to Puhar. Kaveripattinam served as their port.

GUPTA PERIOD

- The Gupta period is considered as the *Golden Age* in the history of India because this period witnessed all round developments in Religion, Literature, Science, Art and Architecture.

CHANDRAGUPTA I (320-334 A.D.)

- In the beginning of the 4th Century A.D., Sri Gupta established a small Kingdom at Pataliputra. He is considered as the founder of the Gupta dynasty.
- The first notable ruler of the Gupta dynasty was Chandragupta I. He assumed the title *Maharajadhiraja*. The Meherauli Iron Pillar inscription mentions his extensive conquests.
- Chandragupta I is considered to be the founder of the Gupta era which starts with his accession in A.D. 320.

SAMUDRAGUPTA (335-380 A.D.)

- Samudragupta was the greatest of the rulers of the Gupta dynasty. The Allahabad Pillar inscription provides a detailed account of his reign.
- Because of his military achievements, Samudragupta was hailed as '*Indian Napoleon*'.

CHANDRAGUPTA II (380-414 A.D.)

- Samudragupta was succeeded by his son Chandragupta II Vikramaditya.
- The greatest of the military achievements of Chandragupta II was his war against the Saka *satraps* of western India.
- The famous Chinese pilgrim, Fahien visited India (A.D. 399 - A.D. 414) during the reign of Chandragupta II.

SUCCESSORS OF CHANDRAGUPTA II

- Kumaragupta (415-455) was the son and successor of Chandragupta II. His reign was marked by general peace and prosperity.
- Kumaragupta was the founder of the Nalanda University.
- Kumaragupta was followed by *Skandagupta* who ruled from A.D. 456 to A.D. 468.
- After Skandagupta's death, many of his successors like Purugupta, Narasimhagupta, Buddhagupta and Baladitya could not save the Gupta empire from the Huns. Ultimately, the Gupta power totally disappeared due to the Hun invasions and later by the rise of Yasodharman in Malwa.

PUSHYABHUTI DYNASTY (600 - 647 A.D.)

- The greatest king was *Harshavardhana*, son of Prabhakar Vardhana of Thaneshwar. He shifted the capital to *Kannauj*.
- *Hieun Tsang* visited during his reign.
- He established a large monastery at Nalanda. Banabhata adorned his court, wrote Harshacharita and Kadambari. Harsha himself wrote three plays–Priyadarshika, Ratnawali and Nagananda.

PALLAVAS

- The Pallavas established their kingdom in Tondaimandalam by Simhavishnu with its capital at Kanchipuram.
- Other great Pallava rulers were Mahendravarman I, Narasimhavarman I, and Narasimhavarman II.
- The *Kailasanatha temple* at Kanchipuram is the greatest architectural masterpiece of the Pallava art.

CHALUKYAS (543-755 A.D.)

- Pulakesin I was the founder of the Chalukya dynasty. He established a small kingdom with Vatapi or Badami as its capital.
- The structural temples of the Chalukyas exist at Aihole, Badami and Pattadakal (Virupaksha temple). Cave temple architecture was also famous under the Chalukyas. Their cave temples are found in Ajanta, Ellora and Nasik.

RASHTRAKUTAS (755-975 A.D.)

- The art and architecture of the Rashtrakutas were found at Ellora and Elephanta.

CHOLAS

- Cholas became prominent in the ninth century and established an empire comprising the major portion of South India. Their capital was Tanjore.
- The founder of the Chola kingdom was Vijayalaya.
- Rajaraja Chola built the famous Brihadeeswara temple at Tanjore.
- *Dancing Figure of Shiva* (Nataraja) belong to Chola period.

MEDIEVAL INDIA

ARAB CONQUEST OF SIND

- In 712 A.D., Muhammad bin Quasim invaded Sind. Quasim defeated Dahir, the ruler of Sind and killed him in a well-contested battle.

Mahmud of Ghazni

- In 1024, Mahmud marched from Multan across Rajaputana, defeated the Solanki King Bhimadeva I, plundered Anhilwada and sacked the famous temple of Somanatha. This was his last campaign in India. Mahmud died in 1030 A.D.
- Mahmud patronized art and literature. *Firdausi* was the poet-laureate in the court of Mahmud.

Muhammad Ghori

- Prithviraj Chauhan defeated Ghori in the first battle of Tarain near Delhi in 1191 A.D.
- In the Second Battle of Tarain in 1192, Muhammad Ghori thoroughly routed the army of Prithiviraj, who was captured and killed.
- After his brilliant victory over Prithviraj at Tarain, Muhammad Ghori returned to Ghazni leaving behind his favourite general Qutb-ud-din Aibak to make further conquests in India.

SULTANATE PERIOD

SLAVE DYNASTY (1206-1290)

- The Slave dynasty was also called Mamluk dynasty. Mamluk was the Quranic term for slave.

Qutb-ud-din Aibak

- Qutb-ud-din Aibak was a slave of Muhammad Ghori, who made him the Governor of his Indian possessions.
- After the death of Ghori in 1206, Aibak declared his independence. He assumed the title Sultan and made Lahore his capital.
- Muslim writers call Aibak Lakh Baksh or giver of lakhs because he gave liberal donations to them.
- He built the famous Quwat-Ul-Islam mosque at Delhi. He began the construction of the famous Qutb Minar at Delhi but did not live long to complete it. It was later completed by Iltutmish.

Iltutmish (1210-1236 A.D.)

- Iltutmish belonged to the Ilbari tribe and hence his dynasty was named as Ilbari dynasty.
- He shifted his capital from Lahore to Delhi.
- He organised the *Iqta system* and introduced reforms in civil administration and army.

Raziya (1236-1240 A.D.)

- She appointed an Abyssinian slave Yakuth as Master of the Royal Horses.
- In 1240, Altunia, the governor of Bhatinda revolted against her. She went in personally to

suppress the revolt but Altunia killed Yakuth and took Raziya prisoner.

- Bahram Shah, son of Iltutmish killed her.

Balban (1266-1286 A.D.)

- Balban introduced rigorous court discipline and new customs such as prostration and kissing the Sultan's feet to prove his superiority over the nobles.
- He also introduced the Persian festival of *Nauroz* to impress the nobles and people with his wealth and power.
- He established a separate military department - *diwan-i-arz* – and reorganized the army.

KHILJI DYNASTY (1290-1320 A.D.)

- The founder of the Khilji dynasty was Jalaluddin Khilji.
- Ala-ud-din Khilji was the greatest ruler of the Khilji Dynasty.
- He was the first Muslim ruler to extend his empire right upto Rameshwaram in the South.
- The Sultan had built a new city called Siri near Delhi.
- Amir Khusrau the great Persian poet, patronised by Balban, continued to live in Ala-ud-din Khilji's court also.
- He introduced the system of *dagh* (branding of horses) and prepared *huliya* (descriptive list of soldiers).
- Ala-ud-din Khilji maintained a large permanent standing army and paid them in cash from the royal treasury.

TUGHLAQ DYNASTY

- Ghiyas-ud-din Tughlaq was the founder of the Tughlaq dynasty.
- To have the capital at the centre of the empire and safe from the Mongol raids, Tughlaq chose Devagiri as his new capital in A.D. 1327. The Sultan renamed the new capital Daulatabad.
- In 1329-30, Muhammad-bin-Tughlaq introduced a token currency.
- Firoz Shah Tughlaq became Sultan after the death of Muhammad-bin-Tughlaq in A.D. 1351.
- He was the first Sultan to impose irrigation tax.
- He had built new towns of Firozabad, Jaunpur, Hissar and Firozpur.
- Timur—Mongol leader of Central Asia, ordered general massacre in Delhi (AD 1398) at the time of Nasiruddin Mahmud (later Tughlaq king).

SAYYID DYNASTY

- Before his departure from India, Timur appointed Khizr Khan as governor of Multan. He captured Delhi and founded the Sayyid dynasty in 1414.
- Mubarak Shah, Mohammed Shah and Alam Shah were some of the other important noteworthy rulers of Sayyid Dynasty.

LODHI DYNASTY

- The Lodhis were Afghans.
- Bahlol Lodhi was the first Afghan ruler while his predecessors were all Turks. He died in 1489 and was succeeded by his son, Sikandar Lodhi.
- In 1504, Sikandar Lodhi founded the city of Agra and transferred his capital from Delhi to Agra.
- Babar marched against Delhi and defeated and killed Ibrahim Lodhi in the first battle of Panipat (1526).

BAHMANI AND VIJAYANAGAR KINGDOMS

- The break up of the Delhi Sultanate provided an opportunity for the rise of a number of kingdoms in the Deccan.
- After the decline of the Tughlaqs, there arose two important kingdoms in the Deccan. They were the Bahmani and Vijayanagar kingdoms.

VIJAYANAGAR EMPIRE

- The Vijayanagar Kingdom was set up in A.D. 1336. Its aim was to check the spread of Muslim power and protect Hindu Dharma in South India.
- Four dynasties – Sangama, Saluva, Tuluva and Aravidu – ruled Vijayanagar from A.D. 1336 to 1672.

- Vijayanagar was founded in 1336 by Harihara and Bukka of the Sangama dynasty.
- The Moroccan traveller, Ibn Batuta, Venetian traveller Nicolo de Conti, Persian traveller Abdur Razzak and the Portuguese traveller Domingo Paes were among them who left valuable accounts on the socio-economic conditions of the Vijayanagar Empire.
- The Hampi ruins and other monuments of Vijayanagar provide information on the cultural contributions of the Vijayanagar rulers.

KRISHNA DEVA RAYA (1509-1530)

- The Tuluva dynasty was founded by Vira Narasimha.
- The greatest of the Vijayanagar rulers, Krishna Deva Raya belonged to the Tuluva dynasty.
- Krishna Deva Raya himself authored a Telugu work, *Amukthamalyadha* and Sanskrit works, *Jambavati Kalyanam* and *Ushaparinayam*.
- He built the famous *Vittalaswamy* and *Hazara Ramaswamy* temples at Vijayanagar.
- Krishna Deva Raya renovated Virupaksha temple in A.D. 1510.
- After his death the enemies of Vijayanagar joined together and defeated the Vijayanagar ruler in the battle of Talaikota.

BAHMANI KINGDOM

- The founder of the Bahmani kingdom was Alauddin Bahman Shah also known as Hasan Gangu in 1347. Its capital was Gulbarga.
- Ahmad Wali Shah shifted the capital from Gulbarga to Bidar.
- *Gol Gumbaj* was built by *Muhammad Adil Shah*; it is famous for the so called '*Whispering Gallery*'.
- *Quli Qutub Shah* built the famous *Golcunda Fort*.

MUGHAL EMPIRE
(1526-1707 AD)

BABAR (1526-1530 AD)

- Babar was the founder of the Mughal Empire in India.
- On 21st April, 1526 the first Battle of Panipat took place between Babar and Ibrahim Lodhi, who was killed in the battle.
- Babar was the first one to use guns or artillery in a battle on the Indian soil.
- Babar defeated Rana Sanga of Mewar in the battle of Kanwah in A.D. 1527.
- Babar was a soldier-scholar and wrote his own autobiography called Babar Nama in Turkish language.

HUMAYUN (1530-1556 AD)

- Sher Shah defeated Humayun at Chausa in A.D. 1539 and again at Kannauj in A.D. 1540.
- After losing his kingdom, Humayun became an exile for the next fifteen years.
- In 1555, Humayun defeated the Afghans and recovered the Mughal throne. After six months, he died in 1556 due to his fall from the staircase of his library.
- *Gulbadan Begum*, Humayun's half-sister wrote *Humayun-nama.*

SHER SHAH SURI

- The founder of the Sur dynasty was Sher Shah, whose original name was Farid.
- Sher Shah became the ruler of Delhi in 1540.
- Sher Shah organized a brilliant administrative system. The central government consisted of several departments.
- He built a new city on the banks of the river Yamuna near Delhi. Now the old fort called Purana Quila and its mosque is alone surviving.
- He built a Mausoleum at Sasaram, which is considered as one of the master pieces of Indian architecture.

AKBAR (1556-1605 AD)

- When Akbar ascended the throne in A.D. 1556 he was only 14 years old. His guardian Bairam Khan served him as a faithful minister and tutor.
- Bairam Khan, along with Akbar met Hemu in the second Battle of Panipat in 1556. Hemu was initially successful, but lost his consciousness after an arrow hit him. Akbar killed him.

- Battle of Haldighati, was fought between Rana Pratap of Mewar and Mughal army led by Man Singh. Some hisorian say that this battle was indecisive but some say that Rana Pratap was defeated.
- Akbar abolished the pilgrim tax and in 1562, he abolished Jaziya.
- Akbar evolved a new faith called Din-i-Illahi or Divine Faith.

JAHANGIR (1605-1627 AD)

- When Akbar died, Prince Salim succeeded with the title Jahangir (Conqueror of World) in 1605.
- Jahangir's eldest son, Khusrau, rebelled against him. He was arrested and put into prison. *Guru Arjun Dev, the fifth Sikh Guru* was executed by Jahangir.
- In 1611, Jahangir married Mehrunnisa who was known as Nurjahan (Light of World).
- Jahangir died in A.D. 1627.

SHAHJAHAN (1628-1658 AD)

- The reign of Shahjahan is generally considered as the *Golden Age* of the Mughal period.
- Shahjahan is called as the *Prince of Builders*. He had built the Jama Masjid and Red Fort in Delhi and Taj Mahal in Agra.
- Fine arts like painting, music and literature reached high level of development during Shahjahan's time.

AURANGAZEB (1658-1707 AD)

- Aurangazeb was the last great Mughal ruler. He ascended the throne after killing his three brothers Dara, Shuja and Murad in a fratricidal war.
- Aurangazeb defeated Sikandar Shah of Bijapur and annexed his kingdom.
- Aurangazeb was against the Sikhs and he executed the ninth Sikh Guru Tegh Bahadur.
- He was called *Darvesh* or a *Zinda Pir*. He forbade *Sati*. Conquered Bijapur (AD 1686) and Golconda (AD 1687) and reimposed Jaziya and Pilgrim tax in AD 1679.
- He built *Biwi ka Makbara* on the tomb of his queen *Rabaud-Durani* at Aurangabad; *Moti Masjid* within Red Fort, Delhi; and the Jami or Badshahi Mosque at Lahore.
- Aurangazeb died in A.D. 1707.

LATER MUGHALS / FALL OF THE MUGHALS

Bahadur Shah (1707-1712)

- Assumed the title of *Shah Alam I.*

Jahandar Shah (1712-1713)

- First puppet Mughal emperor. He abolished *jaziya.*

Farrukhsiyar (1713-1719)

Mohammad Shah (1719-1748)

- Nadir Shah (*of Iran*) defeated him in the Battle of Karnal (1739) and took away *Peacock throne* and *Kohinoor diamond.*

Ahmad Shah (1748-1754)

Alamgir II (1754-1759),

Shah Alam II (1759-1806)

Akbar II (1806-1837)

- He gave Ram Mohan Roy the title '*Raja*'. He sent Raja Ram Mohan Roy to London to seek a raise in his allowance.

Bahadur Shah II (1837-1857)

- He was confined by the British to the Red Fort. During the revolt of 1857, he was proclaimed the Emperor by the rebels. He was deported to Rangoon after that.

Literature of Mughal Period

Author	Work
Babar	Tuzuk-i-Babari
Abul Fazal	Ain-i-Akbari, Akbarnamah
Jahangir	Tuzuk-i-Jahangiri
Hamid	Padshahnama
Darashikoh	Majm-ul-Bahrain
Mirza Md Qasim	Alamgirnama

THE MARATHAS

SHIVAJI (1627-1680 AD)

- Shivaji was born at Shivner in 1627. His father was Shahji Bhonsle and mother Jija Bai.

- His religious teacher was Samarth Ramdas and guardian was Dadaji Kondadev.
- In 1674, Shivaji crowned himself at Raigarh and assumed the title Chatrapathi.
- *Ashtapradhan* (eight ministers) helped in administration. These were Peshwas, Sar-i-Naubat (Military), Mazumdar or Amatya (Accounts); Waqenavis (Intelligence); Surnavis (Correspondence); *Dabir* or *Sumanta* (Ceremonies); *Nyayadhish* (Justice); and *Panditrao* (Charity).
- Successors of Shivaji were Shambhaji, Rajaram and *Shahu* (fought at Battle of Khed in AD 1708).

THE PESHWAS

- Balaji Vishwanath was the first Peshwa. He began his career as a small revenue official and became Peshwa in 1713.
- Baji Rao I was the eldest son of Balaji Vishwanath. He was considered as the "greatest exponent of guerilla tactics after Shivaji".
- It was during reign of Balaji Baji Rao (Nanasaheb) when the Marathas lost the Third Battle of Panipat.
- Baji Rao II (last Peshwa) was the first Maratha to have fled from the British attacks instead of fighting with them. Baji Rao II surrendered to Sir John Malcom.

THE SIKH

- Guru Nanak Dev was the founder of Sikhism, the religion that draws its elements from both Hinduism and Islam.
- Name of the ten Sikh Gurus and their works are given below:
  1. **Guru Nanak Dev (1469-1539AD):** The founder of Sikhism.
  2. **Guru Angad Dev (1504-1552AD):** Developed Gurmukhi.
  3. **Guru Amar Das (1479-1574AD):** Struggled against Sati system and Purdah system.
  4. **Guru Ram Das (1534-1581AD):** Founded Amritsar, the holy city of Sikhism.
  5. **Guru Arjun Dev (1563-1606AD):** He built the *Swarn Mandir* (Golden Temple).
  6. **Guru Hargobind (1595-1644 AD):** Established Akal Takht.
  7. **Guru Har Rai (1630-1661 AD)**
  8. **Guru Har Krishan (1656-1664 AD)**
  9. **Guru Tegh Bahadur (1621-1675 AD)**
  10. **Guru Gobind Singh (1666-1708 AD):** Founded the Khalsa and Sikh baptism, composed many poems, and nominated the Sikh sacred text as the final and enduring Guru.

MODERN INDIA

THE ADVENT OF THE EUROPEANS

THE PORTUGUESE

- Vasco-da-Gama, a Portuguese explorer, sailed through the route of Cape of Good Hope and reached near Calicut on 20th May 1498 A.D. during the reign of King Zamorin (Hindu King of Calicut).
- Vasco-da-Gama founded a factory at Cannanore on his second visit to India in 1501. In due course, Calicut, Cochin and Cannanore became the Portuguese trading centres.
- Francisco Almeida came to India in 1505. He was the first Governor of Portuguese possessions in India.
- The real founder of Portuguese power in India was *Alfonso de Albuquerque*. He captured Goa from the rulers of Bijapur in 1510. It was made their headquarters.

THE DUTCH

- The United East India Company of the Netherlands founded a factory at Masulipatnam in 1605. They built their first fort on the main land of India at Pulicut in 1609, near Madras (Chennai). They captured Nagapattinam from the Portuguese.
- They made Agra, Surat, Masulipatnam and Chinsura in Bengal as their trading centres.

THE DANES

- The Danish East India Company was established in 1616 in Denmark.
- They came to South India and founded a factory at Tranquebar (Tharangambadi) in 1620. They also made settlements at Serampore near Calcutta (Kolkata).

THE ENGLISH

- The English East India Company was formed in 1599 under a charter granted by Queen Elizabeth in 1600.
- The East India Company sent Sir William Hawkins to the court of the Mughal Emperor Jahangir in 1609 to obtain permission to erect a factory at Surat.
- In 1615, Sir Thomas Roe, another British merchant, came to Jahangir's court. He stayed for three years and succeeded in getting permission to set up their trading centres at Agra, Surat, Ahmedabad and Broach.
- In 1690, the British got permission from Aurangazeb to build a factory on the site of Calcutta. In 1696 a fort was built at that place. It was called Fort William.

THE FRENCH

- The French East India Company was established in 1664 under the inspiring and energetic leadership of Colbert, the economic adviser of the French King Louis XIV.
- In 1667, the first French factory was established at Surat by Francis Caron who was nominated as Director-General.
- French were defeated by English in the *Battle of Wandiwash* (1760).

EAST INDIA COMPANY

- After the Battle of Plassey in 1757 and the Battle of Buxar in 1764, the East India Company became a political power.
- India was under the East India Company's rule till 1858 when it came under the direct administration of the British Crown.
- Robert Clive was the first Governor of Fort William under the Company's rule.

GOVERNOR-GENERALS OF BENGAL

Warren Hastings (1772-85 AD)

- In 1772, the Company appointed Warren Hastings as the Governor of Fort William.
- The Dual System introduced by Robert Clive was abolished by Warren Hastings.
- Warren Hastings was known for his expansionist policy. His administration witnessed the Rohilla War, the First Anglo-Maratha War and the Second Anglo-Mysore War.
- Pitt's India Act (1784) was passed.

Lord Cornwallis (1786-93 AD)

- Cornwallis inaugurated the policy of making appointments mainly on the basis of merit thereby laying the foundation of the Indian Civil Service.
- Lord Cornwallis introduced Permanent Revenue Settlement.
- Tipu Sultan signed the Treaty of Srirangapatnam in 1792 with the British.

Sir John Shore (1793-98 AD)

- Played an important role in the introduction of Permanent Settlement.
- *Battle of Kharda* between the Nizams and the Marathas (1795).

Wellesley (1798-1805)

- Wellesley came to India with a determination to launch a forward policy that he adopted to achieve his object is known as the 'Subsidiary Alliance'.
- The Fourth Anglo-Mysore War started in 1799. The war was short and decisive. Tipu fought till his capital Srirangapatnam was captured and he himself was shot dead.
- Peshwa Baji Rao II signed the *Treaty* of *Bassein* with the British in 1802. It was a subsidiary treaty and the Peshwa was recognized as the head of the Maratha kingdom.
- The Treaty of Deogaon(1803) was signed between Bhonsle and Wellesley.

Lord Minto (1807-1813)

- Lord Minto concluded the Treaty of Amritsar with Ranjit Singh of Punjab in 1809.
- The Charter Act of 1813 was passed during this period.

Lord Hastings (1813-1823)

- Anglo Nepal War (1814-1816) and Treaty of Sugauli (1816).
- Third Maratha War (1817-18), dissolution of Maratha confederacy and creation of Bombay Presidency.
- He encouraged the freedom of the Press and abolished the censorship introduced in 1799.

GOVERNOR-GENERALS OF INDIA

Lord William Bentinck (1828-1835)

- Charter Act of 1833 was passed and he was made the first Governor-General of India. Before him, the designation was Governor-General of Bengal.
- The social reforms of William Bentinck made his name immortal in the history of British India. These include the abolition of *Sati*, the suppression of Thugs and the prevention of female infanticide.
- The Government Resolution in 1835 made English the official and literary language of India.

Lord Metcalfe (1835-36 AD)

- Known as liberator of press in India.

Lord Auckland (1836-42 AD)

- First Afghan War (1838-42), a disaster for the English.

Lord Ellenborough (1842-44 AD)

- Brought an end to Afghan war. War with Gwalior (1843), *Annexation of Sind* by Charles Napier (1843).

Lord Hardinge (1844-48 AD)

- First Anglo-Sikh War (1845-46) and Treaty of Lahore (1846). Gave preference to English educated persons in employment.

Lord Dalhousie (1848-1856)

- The Doctrine of Lapse was applied by Dalhousie.
- The first railway line connecting Bombay with Thane was opened in 1853.

VICEROYS OF INDIA

Lord Canning (1856-62 AD)

- Lord Canning became the first Viceroy of India in 1858.
- Revolt of 1857, Mutiny took place. Indian Penal Code 1860 was passed.

Lord Elgin (1862 AD)

- Wahabi Movement.

Lord John Lawrence (1864-69 AD)

- Established the *High Courts* at Calcutta, Bombay and Madras in 1865.
- Telegraphic communication was opened with Europe. Created the Indian Forest Department.

Lord Northbrooke (1872-76 AD)

- Kuka Rebellion in Punjab, Famine in Bihar.

Lord Lytton (1876-80)

- In 1878, the Vernacular Press Act was passed. This Act empowered a Magistrate to secure an undertaking from the editor, publisher and printer of a vernacular newspaper that nothing would be published against the English Government. This Act crushed the freedom of the Indian press.
- In 1878, the Arms Act was passed. This Act prevented the Indians to keep arms without appropriate license.
- Lord Lytton also held a Darbar at Delhi in 1877 in which Queen Victoria was declared as the Empress of India. This extravagant Darbar cost millions of ruppes.
- In 1878, the Statutory Civil Service was established exclusively for Indians.

Lord Ripon (1880-84 AD)

- Lord Ripon repealed the Vernacular Press Act and earned much popularity among Indians.

- Ripon appointed a Commission in 1882 under the chairmanship of Sir William Hunter.
- The Commission came to be known as the Hunter Commission. The Commission recommended for the expansion and improvement of the elementary education of the masses.
- Ripon was founder of local self-government in modern India.

Lord Dufferin (1884-88 AD)

- *Third Burmese War* (1885-86 AD). Establishment of the Indian National Congress in 1885.

Lord Lansdowne (1888-94 AD)

- Factory Act of 1891 granted weekly holiday and stipulated working hours for women and children.

Lord Elgin II (1894-99 AD)

- Southern uprisings of 1899. Great famine of 1896-1897 and Lyall Commission on famine was established.

Lord Curzon (1899-1905 AD)

- Curzon instituted in 1902, a Universities Commission to go into the entire question of university education in the country.
- On the basis of the findings and recommendations of the Commission, Curzon brought in the Indian Universities Act of 1904, which brought all the universities in India under the control of the government.

Lord Minto (1905-10 AD)

- Swadeshi Movement (1905-08); foundation of Muslim League (1906); Surat Session and split in the Congress (1907). Morley-Minto Reforms (1909).

Lord Hardinge (1910-16 AD)

- Capital shifted from Calcutta to Delhi (1911); Delhi Durbar; Partition of Bengal was cancelled. The Hindu Mahasabha was founded in 1915 by Pandit Madan Mohan Malaviya.

Lord Chelmsford (1916-21 AD)

- Gandhi returned to India (1915) and founded the Sabarmati Ashram (1916), Champaran Satyagraha, Satyagraha at Ahmedabad (1981), Kheda Satyagraha (1918).
- Rowlatt Act (March, 1919) and the Jallianwala Bagh Massacre (13th April, 1919).
- Khilafat Committee was formed and Khilafat Movement started (1919-20).
- Non-Cooperation Movement started (1920-22).

Lord Reading (1921-26)

- Moplah Rebellion (1921) took place. *Kakori Train* Robbery on 1st August, 1925. *Communal Riots* of 1923-25 in Multan, Amritsar, Delhi etc.

Lord Irwin (1926-31 AD)

- Lahore Session of Congress and *Poorna Swaraj* Declaration (1929).
- Simon Commission visited India in 1927.
- Dandi March (12th March, 1930). Civil Disobedience Movement (1930).
- First Round Table Conference was held in England in 1930. Gandhi-Irwin Pact.

Lord Willingdon (1931-36 AD)

- *Second Round Table Conference* in London in 1931 and *third* in 1932.

Lord Linlithgow (1936-43 AD)

- Congress Ministries resignation celebrated as '*Deliverance Day*' by the Muslim League (1939), the Lahore Resolution (23rd March, 1940) of the Muslim League demanding separate state for the Muslims. (It was at this session that Jinnah propounded his Two-Nation Theory). Outbreak of World War II in 1939. Cripps Mission in 1942. Quit India Movement (8th August, 1942).

Lord Wavell (1943-47 AD)

- Cabinet Mission Plan (16th May, 1946).
- First meeting of the Constituent Assembly was held on 9th December, 1946.
- Arranged the Shimla Conference on 25th June, 1945 with Indian National Congress and Muslim League but failed.

Lord Mountbatten (March to Aug, 1947)

- Last viceroy of British India and the first Governor-General of free India.
- Partition of India decided by the 3rd June Plan or Mountbatten Plan.

NATIONAL MOVEMENT
(1885-1947)

INDIAN NATIONAL CONGRESS (1885)

- Allan Octavian Hume, a retired civil servant in the British Government took the initiative to form an all-India organization. Thus, the Indian National Congress was founded and its first session was held at Bombay in 1885. W.C. Banerjee was its first president. It was attended by 72 delegates from all over India.
- The second session was held in Calcutta in 1886 and the third in Madras in 1887.
- Between 1885 and 1905, the Congress leaders were moderates. The Moderates had faith in the British justice and goodwill. They were called moderates because they adopted peaceful and constitutional means to achieve their demands.
- In 1905, Gopal Krishna Gokhale founded the Servants of India Society to train Indians to dedicate their lives to the cause of the country.

Partition of Bengal (1905)

- By Lord Curzon on 16th October, 1905 through a royal proclamation, reducing the old province of Bengal in size by creating East Bengal and Assam out of the rest of Bengal.
- The partition of Bengal in 1905 provided a spark for the rise of extremism in the Indian National Movement.
- Curzon's real motives behind this partition were:
  - ❒ To break the growing strength of Bengali nationalism since Bengal was the base of Indian nationalism.
  - ❒ To divide the Hindus and Muslims in Bengal.
  - ❒ To show the enormous power of the British Government in doing whatever it liked.

Swadeshi Movement (1905)

- The Swadeshi Movement involved programmes like the boycott of government service, courts, schools and colleges and of foreign goods. It was both a political and economic movement.
- Lal, Bal, Pal and Aurobindo Ghosh played an important role.

Muslim League (1906)

- In December 1906, Muslim delegates from all over India met at Dacca for the Muslim Educational Conference.
- Taking advantage of this occasion, Nawab Salimullah of Dacca proposed the setting up of an organisation to look after the Muslim interests. The proposal was accepted.
- The All-India Muslim League was finally set up on December 30, 1906.

Minto Morley Reforms (1909)

- Minto, the Viceroy and Morley, the Secretary of State for India jointly proposed reforms to the Indian Councils. An Act, called the Indian Councils Act or the Minto-Morley Reforms Act was passed in 1909.
- A separate communal electorate was introduced for the Muslims.

The Lucknow Pact (1916)

- During the 1916 Congress session at Lucknow two major events occurred. The divided Congress became united. An understanding for joint action against the British was reached between the Congress and the Muslim League and it was called the Lucknow Pact.
- The signing of the Lucknow Pact by the Congress and the Muslim League in 1916 marked an important step in the Hindu-Muslim unity.

The Home Rule Movement (1916)

- Two Home Rule Leagues were established, one by B.G. Tilak at Poona in April 1916 and the other by Mrs. Annie Besant at Madras in September 1916.
- While Tilak's Movement concentrated on

Maharashtra, Annie Besant's Movement covered the rest of the country.

August Declaration

- On 20 August, 1917, Montague, the Secretary of State in England, promised the gradual development of self-governing institutions in India.
- This August Declaration led to the end of the Home Rule Movement.

Rowlatt Act (1919)

- In 1917, a committee was set up under the presidentship of Sir Sydney Rowlatt to look into the militant Nationalist activities. On the basis of its report the Rowlatt Act was passed in March 1919 by the Central Legislative Council. As per this Act, any person could be arrested on the basis of suspicion. No appeal or petition could be filed against such arrests.
- This Act was called the Black Act and it was widely opposed. An all-India hartal was organized on 6 April, 1919.

Jallianwala Bagh Massacre (13 April, 1919)

- On 13th April, the Baisakhi day (harvest festival), a public meeting was organized at the Jallianwala Bagh (garden). Gen. Dyer marched in and without any warning opened fire on the crowd. The firing continued for about 10 to 15 minutes and it stopped only after the ammunition exhausted.
- According to official report 379 people were killed and 1137 wounded in the incident. There was a nationwide protest against this massacre and Rabindranath Tagore renounced his knighthood as a protest.

Khilafat Movement (1920)

- The chief cause of the Khilafat Movement was the defeat of Turkey in the First World War.
- The Muslims in India were upset over the British attitude against Turkey and launched the Khilafat Movement.
- Ali brothers, *Mohd Ali* and *Shaukat Ali* started this movement. It was jointly led by the Khilafat leaders and the Congress.

Non-Co-operation Movement (1920-22)

- Mahatma Gandhi announced his plan to begin Non-Cooperation with the government as a sequel to the Rowlatt Act, Jallianwala Bagh massacre and the Khilafat Movement. It was approved by the Indian National Congress at the Nagpur session in December, 1920.
- The Congress observed the Non-Co-operation movement in 1920. The main aim of this movement was to attain Swaraj through non-violent and peaceful means.
- The whole movement was abruptly called off on 11th February, 1922 by Gandhi following the Chauri-Chaura incident in the Gorakhpur district of U.P. Many top leaders of the country were stunned at this sudden suspension of the Non-Co-operation Movement.
- On 5th February an angry mob set fire to the police station at *Chauri-Chaura* and twenty two police men were burnt to death.

Swaraj Party

- Leaders like Motilal Nehru and Chittranjan Das formed a separate group within the Congress known as the Swaraj Party on 1 January, 1923.
- The Swarajists wanted to contest the council elections and wreck the government from within.

Simon Commission (1927)

- The Act of 1919 included a provision for its review after a lapse of ten years. However, the review commission under the chairmanship of Sir John Simon was appointed by the British Government two years earlier of its schedule in 1927.
- Indian leaders opposed the commission, as there were no Indians in it, they cried *Simon Go Back*.
- The government used brutal repression and at Lahore, *Lala Lajpat Rai* was severely beaten in lathi-charge.

Nehru Report (1928)

- The Secretary of State, Lord Birkenhead, challenged the Indians to produce a Constitution that would be acceptable to all. The challenge was accepted by the Congress, which convened an all party meeting on 28 February, 1928.

- A committee consisting of eight was constituted to draw up a blueprint for the future Constitution of India. It was headed by Motilal Nehru. The Report published by this Committee came to be known as the Nehru Report.

Lahore Session (1929)

- On Dec. 19, 1929, under the Presidentship of J.L. Nehru, the INC, as its Lahore session, declared Poorna Swaraj (Complete Independence) as its ultimate goal.
- On Dec. 31, 1929, the newly adopted tricolour flag was unfurled and Jan. 26, 1930 was fixed as the First Independence Day, which was to be celebrated every year.

Dandi March (1930)

- On 12th March, 1930, Gandhi began his famous March to Dandi with his chosen 79 followers to break the salt laws. He reached the coast of Dandi on 5 April, 1930 after marching a distance of 200 miles and on 6 April formally launched the Civil Disobedience Movement by breaking the salt laws.

Civil Disobedience Movement

- Countrywide mass participation by women.
- The Garhwal soldiers refused to fire on the people at Peshawar.

Round Table Conference

- The first Round Table Conference was held in November 1930 at London and it was boycotted by the Congress.
- On 8th March, 1931 the Gandhi-Irwin Pact was signed. As per this pact, Mahatma Gandhi agreed to suspend the Civil-Disobedience Movement and participate in the Second-Round Table Conference.
- In September 1931, the Second Round Table Conference was held at London. Mahatma Gandhi participated in the Conference but returned to India disappointed.
- In January 1932, the Civil-Disobedience Movement was resumed.

Poona Pact (1932)

- The idea of separate electorate for the depressed classes was abandoned, but seats reserved for them in the provincial legislature were increased.
- Thus, Poona Pact agreed upon a joint electorate for upper and lower castes.

Demand for Pakistan

- *Chaudhary Rehmat Ali* gave the term *Pakistan* in 1933.
- In March 1940, the Muslim League demanded the creation of Pakistan.

Cripps Mission (1942)

- The British Government in its effort to secure Indian co-operation in the Second World War sent Sir Stafford Cripps to India on 23 March, 1942. This is known as Cripps Mission.
- The main recommendations of Cripps was the promise of Dominion Status to India.
- Congress rejected it. Gandhi called Cripp's proposals as a "Post-dated Cheque".

Quit India Movement (1942-1944)

- The All India Congress Committee met at Bombay on 8th August, 1942 and passed the famous Quit India Resolution. On the same day, Gandhi gave his call of 'do or die'.
- On 8th and 9th August, 1942, the government arrested all the prominent leaders of the Congress. Mahatma Gandhi was kept in prison at Poona. Pandit Jawaharlal Nehru, Abul Kalam Azad, and other leaders were imprisoned in the Ahamednagar Fort.
- Quit India Movement was the final attempt for country's freedom.

Indian National Army (INA)

- On July 2, 1943, Subhash Chandra Bose reached Singapore and gave the rousing war cry of *'Dilli Chalo'*. He was made the President of Indian Independence League and soon became the supreme commander of the Indian National Army. He gave the country the slogan of *Jai Hind.*

- INA had three fighting brigades named after Gandhi, Azad and Nehru. Rani of Jhansi Brigade was an exclusive women force. INA headquarters were at Rangoon and Singapore.

Cabinet Mission (1946)

- The Cabinet Mission put forward a plan for solution of the constitutional problem. A proposal was envisaged for setting up an Interim Government, which would remain in office till a new government was elected on the basis of the new Constitution framed by the Constituent Assembly.
- Elections were held in July 1946 for the formation of a Constituent Assembly.
- Muslim league observed the *Direct Action Day* on 16 August, 1946.
- An Interim Government was formed under the leadership of Jawaharlal Nehru on 2 September, 1946.

Mountbatten Plan (1947)

- On 20 February 1947, Prime Minister Atlee announced in the House of Commons the definite intention of the British Government to transfer power to responsible Indian hands by a date not later than June 1948.
- Lord Mountbatten armed with vast powers became India's Viceroy on 24 March, 1947. The partition of India and the creation of Pakistan appeared inevitable to him.
- After extensive consultation Lord Mountbatten put forth the plan of partition of India on 3 June, 1947. The Congress and the Muslim League ultimately approved the Mountbatten Plan.

Indian Independence Act, 1947

- The salient features of this Act was the partition of the country into India and Pakistan would come into effect from 15 August, 1947.
- On 15th August, 1947 India, and on the 14th August Pakistan came into existence as two independent states.
- Lord Mountbatten was made the first Governor General of Independent India, whereas Mohammad Ali Jinnah became the first Governor General of Pakistan.
- C. Rajagopalachari became the first and last Indian Governor-General of India. When India became a Republic on 26 January, 1950 Dr. Rajendra Prasad became the first President of our country.

Socio-Religious Movements and Organisation

Name of the Organisation	Founder	Year	Place
Atmiya Sabha	Ram Mohan Roy	1815	Calcutta
Brahmo Samaj	Ram Mohan Roy	1828	Calcutta
Dharma Sabha	Radhakanta Dev	1829	Calcutta
Tattvabodhini Sabha	Debendranath Tagore	1839	Calcutta
Nirankaris	Dayal Das, Darbara Singh, Rattan Chand etc.	1840	Punjab
Manav Dharma Sabha	Durgaram Manchharam	1844	Surat
Paramhansa Mandli	Dadoba Pandurung	1849	Bombay
Namdharis	Ram Singh	1857	Punjab
Radha Swami Satsang	Tulsi Ram	1861	Agra
Brahmo Samaj of India	Keshab Chandra Sen	1866	Calcutta
Dar-ul-Ulum	Maulana Hussain Ahmed	1866	Deoband
Prarthna Samaj	Atmaram Pandurung	1867	Bombay
Arya Samaj	Swami Dayanand Saraswati	1875	Bombay
Theosophical Society	Madam H.P. Blavatsky and Col. H.S. Olcott	1875	New York (USA)
Sadharan Brahmo Samaj	Anand Mohan Bose	1878	Calcutta

Deccan Education Society	G.G. Agarkar	1884	Pune (Poona)
Muhammadan Educational Conference	Syed Ahmad Khan	1886	Aligarh
Indian National Conference	M.G. Ranade	1887	Bombay
Deva Samaj	Shivnarayan Agnihotri	1887	Lahore
Nadwah-ul-Ulama	Maulana Shibli Numani	1894	Lucknow
Ramakrishna Mission	Swami Vivekananda	1897	Belur
Servents of Indian Society	Gopal Krishna Gokhale	1905	Bombay
Poona Seva Sadan	Mrs. Ramabai Ranade and G.K. Devadhar	1909	Pune (Poona)
Social Service League	N.M. Joshi	1911	Bombay
Seva Samiti	H.N. Kunzru	1914	Allahabad

Newspapers and Journals

- *Bengal Gazette* (1780) (India's first newspaper)—James Augustus Hikky
- *Kesari*—B.G. Tilak
- *Maratha*—B.G. Tilak
- *Sudharak*—G.K. Gokhale
- *Amrit Bazar Patrika*—Shishir Kumar Ghosh and Motilal Ghosh
- *Yugantar*—Bhupendranath Datta and Birender Kumar Ghosh
- *Bombay Chronicle*—Firoze Shah Mehta
- *New India (Daily)*—Annie Besant

Books and Authors

- *Causes of the Indian Mutiny*—Sir Syed Ahmed Khan
- *Ghulam Giri*—Jyotiba Phule
- *Anandmath*—Bankim Chand Chatterjee
- *Satyarth Prakash*—Swami Dayanand
- *Unhappy India*—Lala Lajpat Rai
- *India Divided*—Dr. Rajendra Prasad
- *The Discovery of India*—J.L. Nehru
- *Neel Darpan*—Dinbandhu Mitra
- *Hind Swaraj*—M.K. Gandhi
- *What Congress and Gandhi have done to the untouchables*—Dr. B.R. Ambedkar

Important Sayings

- *'Back to Vedas'*—Dayanand Saraswati
- *'Dilli Chalo!'*—Subhash Chandra Bose's battle cry of *Azad Hind Fauj*
- *'Do or Die'*—Mahatma Gandhi (while launching Quit India movement in 1942)
- *'Give me blood and I will give you freedom'*—Subhash Chandra Bose (in his address to soldiers of *Azad Hind Fauj)*
- *'My ultimate aim is to wipe every tear from every eye'*—Jawaharlal Nehru
- *'Swaraj is my birthright and I will have it'*—Bal Gangadhar Tilak
- *'Inqualab Zindabad'*—Bhagat Singh
- *'Jai Jawan, Jai Kisan'*—Lal Bahadur Shastri
- *'Sarfaroshi ki tamanna Ab Hamare Dil mein Hai'*—Ram Prasad Bismill
- *'Saare Jahan Se Achcha,* Hindustan Hamara'—Dr. Mohammed Iqbal
- *'Hindi, Hindu, Hindustan'*—Bhartendu Harishchandra
- *'Vande Mataram'*—Bankim Chandra Chatterjee

❐ ❐ ❐

GEOGRAPHY

WORLD GEOGRAPHY

THE UNIVERSE

- Existing matter and energy are together known as **Universe.**

GALAXY

- A galaxy is a huge system of billions of stars and clouds of dust and gases.
- Our solar system is a part of *Milky Way* galaxy.
- There are millions of galaxies that make the Universe.

STARS

- Stars account for 98 per cent of the matter in a galaxy. The stars nearest to the earth are *Proxima Centauri, Alpha Centauri, Barnard's Star, Sirius* and so on. Of these, *Sirius* is the brightest.

LIGHT YEAR

- Light year is the distance travelled by light in one year at a speed of 2,99,792.5 km. per second.

SOLAR SYSTEM

- The Sun, eight planets, satellites and some other celestial bodies known as asteroids and meteoroids form the solar system.

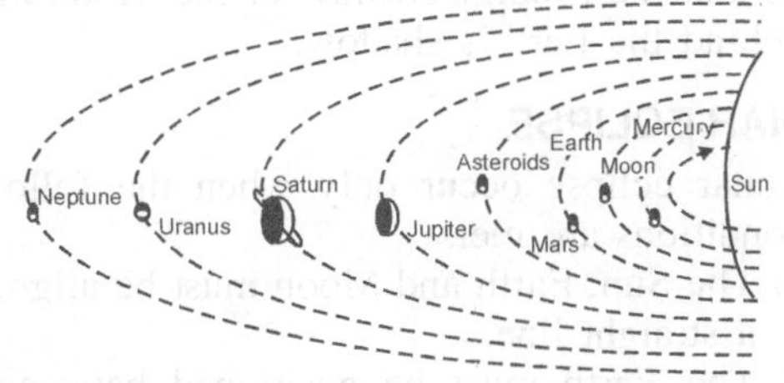

SUN

- The Sun is in the centre of the solar system.
- The Sun is a mixture of gases. It consists of 92% hydrogen, 7.8% helium and 0.2% other gases.
- The Sun is about 150 million km away from the earth.
- The sun is an ultimate source of energy for life on Earth.
- Sunlight takes 8 min 16.6 sec to reach earth.

Facts about Sun

Diameter	—1.392 × 10^6 km
Volume	—1.304 × 106 times the volume of earth
Temperature	—6000°C at surface and 15 million degree C at the centre
Relative density	—1.4
Gravitational Pull	—28 times the gravitational pull of the earth

Facts about Planets

Closest to Sun	*Mercury*
Farthest from Sun	*Neptune*
Heaviest	*Jupiter*
Hottest	*Venus*
Inner	*Mercury, Venus, Earth, Mars*
Largest	*Jupiter*
Smallest	*Mercury*
Moons, None	*Mercury, Venus*
Moon; Largest	*Ganymede (Jupiter), larger than Mercury*
Nearest to Earth	*Venus*
Orbits; Order	*Mercury (closest to Sun), Venus, Earth, Mars, Jupiter, Saturn, Uranus, Neptune.*
Rings/largest number	*Saturn*
Spin; Backwards	*Venus (East to West)*

COMETS

- It has a head and a tail. Its tail originates only when it gets closer to the sun. The tail can be 20-30 million km long. It always point away from the sun because of the force exerted by solar wind and radiation on the cometory material.

THE EARTH

- The earth is the third nearest planet to the Sun.
- From the outer space, the earth appears blue because its two-thirds surface is covered by water. It is, therefore, called a blue planet.
- It is the densest of all planets.
- Rotation is the movement of the earth on its axis. Due to this rotation, day and night occur.
- The earth takes about 23 hours 56 minutes and 4 seconds to complete one rotation around its axis.
- Earth takes 365¼ days (one year) to revolve around the sun.

THE EARTH: FACTS AND FIGURES

- *Mass of Earth*—5.972 × 10^{21} tonnes
- *Density of Earth*—5.517 times that of water
- *Volume of Earth*—1.083 × 10^{11} cubic km
- *Equatorial circumference*—4.007 × 104 km
- *Polar Diameter*—12,714 km
- *Equatorial Diameter*—12756 km
- *Polar or Meridional circumference*—4.0 × 10^4 km
- *Estimated Age*—At least 4600 million years
- *Land Surface*—148,951,000 sq km
- *Water Surface*—361,150,000 sq km (71 per cent of total area)
- *Highest Point of the land surface*—Mt. Everest (8,848 metres)
- *Lowest point of the land surface*—Shores of the Dead Sea (396 metres below the sea level)
- *Greatest Ocean depth*—Mariana Trench, East of Philippines (11,033 metres below the sea level)

THE MOON

- Earth has only one satellite, that is, the moon.
- Its diameter is only one-quarter that of the earth. It is about 3,84,400 km away from us.
- The moon moves around the earth in about 27 days. It takes exactly the same time to complete one spin. As a result, only one side of the moon (only 59% of its surface) is visible to us on the earth.
- Moonlight takes 1.3 sec. to reach earth.

LATITUDE

- Imaginary lines drawn parallel to the equator. Measured as an angle whose apex is at the centre of the earth.
- The equator represents 0° latitude, while the North Pole is 90°N and the South Pole 90°S.
- 23½°N represents Tropic of Cancer while 23½°S represents Tropic of Capricorn.

LONGITUDE

- It is the angular distance measured from the centre of the earth. On the globe the lines of longitude are drawn as a series of semicircles that extend from the North Pole to the South Pole through the equator. They are also called meridians.
- The distance between any two meridians is not equal. At the equator, 1 degree = 111 km. At 30°N or S, it is 96.5 km. It goes on decreasing this way until it is zero at the poles.

INTERNATIONAL DATE LINE

- It is the 180° meridian running over the Pacific Ocean, deviating at Aleutian Islands, Fiji, Samoa and Gilbert Islands.
- Travellers crossing the Date Line from west to east repeat a day and travellers crossing it from east to west lose a day.

INDIAN STANDARD TIME (IST)

- Indian Standard Time is calculated on the basis of 82.5°E longitude which passes through Uttar Pradesh, Madhya Pradesh, Odisha, Chattisgarh and Andhra Pradesh.

ECLIPSES

- Sun is the only source of light for both the Earth and Moon. Eclipses occur when the light thus received is either blocked by the earth or by the Moon.
- Eclipses occur when either the Earth moves behind the Moon's shadow or the Moon moves behind the Earth's shadow.

LUNAR ECLIPSE

- Lunar eclipse occur only when the following conditions are met.
  1. The Sun, Earth and Moon must be aligned in a straight line.
  2. The Earth must be positioned between the Sun and the Moon.
  3. The Moon must be in its full phase (Full Moon).

SOLAR ECLIPSE

- Solar eclipses occur only when the following conditions are met.
  1. The Sun, Earth and Moon must be aligned in a straight line.

2. The Moon must be positioned between the Sun and the Earth.
3. Must be a New Moon day.

ROCKS

- Rocks are composed of many minerals such as silica, aluminium, iron and magnesium. The nature of the rock is determined by the presence of its minerals.
- Rocks can be classified into three types:
  1. ***Igneous rocks*** are formed by magma that reaches the earth's surface along deep cracks and at volcanic vents. e.g., Mica, Granite etc.
  2. ***Sedimentary rocks*** are formed by the accumulation and cementation of mud, silt, or sand derived from weathered igneous rock fragments. e.g., Gravel, Peat, Gypsum etc.
  3. ***Metamorphic rocks*** are igneous or sedimentary rocks that have been altered by heat and/or pressure, either because they have been buried and folded deep in the crust, or because they have come into contact with molten igneous rock, e.g., Gneiss, Marble, Quartzite etc.

VOLCANOES

Sudden eruption of hot magma (molten rock), gases, ash and other material from inside the Earth to its surface.

- ***Active*** which erupts frequently, e.g., Mauna Loa (Hawaii), Etna (Sicily), Vesuvius (Italy), Stromboli (Mediterranean Sea).
- ***Dormant*** Not erupted for quite sometime, e.g., Fujiyama (Japan), Krakatoa (Indonesia), Barren Island (Andamans).
- ***Extinct*** Not erupted for several centuries, e.g., Arthur's Seat, Edinburgh, Scotland.

EARTHQUAKES

- Earthquakes are a form of wave energy that is transferred through bedrock. It is transmitted from the point of the earthquake focus, as spherical seismic waves. They travel in all directions outward.
- The intensity of earthquake waves is recorded by *Seismograph*.

LANDFORMS

- There are three major landforms: mountains, plateaus and plains.

MOUNTAINS

- A mountain can be defined as an area of land that rises abruptly from the surrounding region.
- There are three types of mountains- *Fold Mountains, Block Mountains* and the ***Volcanic Mountains***.
- Himalayas, Alps, Andes, Rockies, Atlas, etc are examples of Fold Mountains.
- The Aravali range in India is one of the oldest **fold mountain** systems in the world.
- The Rhine valley and the Vosges mountain in Europe are examples of such mountain systems.
- Volcanic mountains are formed due to volcanic activity.
- Mt. Kilimanjaro in Africa and Mt. Fujiyama in Japan are examples of such mountains.

Major Mountain Ranges of the World

Range	Location	Highest Peak (m)	Length (km)
Andes	South America	6,960	7,200
Himalayas-Karakoram-Hindukush	South Central Asia	8,848	4,800
Rockies	North America	4,401	4,800
Great Dividing Range	East Australia	2,228	3,600
Western Ghat	Western India	2,637	1,610
Caucasus	Europe	5,642	1,200
Alaska	USA	6,194	1,130
Alps	Europe	4,808	1,050
Apennines	Europe	2,912	—
Ural	Asia	1,895	—
Atlas	North West Africa	—	1,930

PLATEAUS

- A plateau is an elevated flat land. It is a flat-topped table land standing above the surrounding area.

Principal Mountain Peaks of the World

Mountains	Height in Metres
1. Mount Everest	8,848
2. K-2 (Godwin Austen)	8,611
3. Kanchenjunga	8,597
4. Lhotse	8,511
5. Makalu I	8,481
6. Dhaulagiri I	8,167
7. Mansalu I	8,156
8. Chollyo	8,153
9. Nanga Parbat	8,124
10. Annapurna I	8,091
11. Gasherbrum I	8,068
12. Broad Peak I	8,047
13. Gasherbrum II	8,034
14. Shisha Pangma (Gosainthan)	8,014
15. Gasherbrum III	7,952

PLAINS

- A relatively low-lying and flat land surface with least difference between its highest and lowest points is called a Plain.

OCEANS

- Oceans of the world is classified into four groups: the Pacific, the Atlantic, the Arctic and the Indian.
- The Pacific is the largest ocean, being twice the size of the Atlantic. It covers about a third of the Earth's surface, and contains more than half the water on the planet.

Oceans of the World

Names	Area (Sq. Km.)	Greatest Depth
Pacific	166,240000	Mariana Trench
Atlantic	86,560000	Puerto Rico Trench
Indian	73430000	Java Trench
Arctic	13230000	—

Major Rivers of the World

River	Origin	Falls in	Length (Km.)
Nile	Victoria lake	Mediterranean Sea	6,650
Amazon	Andes (Peru)	Atlantic Ocean	6,428
Yangtze	Tibetan Kiang Plateau	China Sea	6,300
Mississippi Missouri	Itaska lake (USA)	Gulf of Mexico (USA)	6,275
Yenisei	Tannu-Ola Mts.	Arctic Ocean	5,539
Hoang Ho	Kunlun Mts.	Gulf of Chibli	5,464
Ob	Altai Mts., Russia	Gulf of Ob	5,410
Congo	Lualaba & Luapula rivers	Atlantic Ocean	4,700
Amur	Northeast China	Sea of Okhotsk	4,444
Lena	Baikal Mts	Laptev Sea	4,400
Mekong	Tibetan Highlands	South China Sea	4,350
Mackenzie	Great Slave Lake	Beaufort Sea	4,241
Niger	Guinea	Gulf of Guinea	4,200

Major Gulfs of the World

Names	Area (Sq. Km.)	Names	Areas (Sq. Km.)
Gulf of Mexico	15,44,000	Gulf of St. Lawrence	2,37,000
Gulf of Hudson	12,33,000	Gulf of California	1,62,000
Arabian Gulf	2,38,000	English Channel	89,900

Important Straits of the World

Straits	Water Bodies joined	Area
Bab-al-Mandeb	Red Sea & Arabian Sea	Arabia & Africa
Bering	Arctic Ocean & Bering Sea	Alaska & Asia
Bosphorus	Black Sea & Marmara Sea	Turkey
Dover	North Sea & Atlantic Ocean	England & Europe
Florida	Gulf of Mexico & Atlantic Ocean	Florida & Bahamas Islands
Gibralter	Mediterranean Sea & Atlantic Ocean	Spain & Africa
Malacca	Java Sea & Bay of Bengal	India & Indonesia
Palk	Bay of Bengal & Indian Ocean	India & Sri Lanka
Magellan	South Pacific & South Atlantic Ocean	Chile
Sunda	Java Sea & Indian Ocean	Indonesia

Important Lakes of the World

Lake	Location	Area (Sq. Km.)
Caspian	Russia and CIS	371000
Superior	Canada and USA	82414
Victoria	Tanzania (Africa)	69485
Huron	Canada and USA	59596
Michigan	USA	58016
Tanganyika	Africa	32892
Baikal	Russia (CIS)	31502
Great Bear	Canada	31080
Malawi	Malawi (Tanzania)	30044
Great Slave	Canada	28438

Highest Waterfalls of the World

Name(s) (Foreign)	Location
Angel (Salto Angel)	Canaima Nat'l Park, Venezuela
Tugela	Natal Nat'l Park, South Africa
Utigord (Utigordsfoss)	Norway
Monge (Mongefoss)	Marstein, Norway
Gocta Cataracts	Chachapoyas, Peru
Mutarazi (Mtarazi)	Nyanga Nat'l Park, Zimbabwe
Yosemite	Yosemite Nat'l Park, California, U.S.
Espelands (Espelandsfoss)	Hardanger Fjord, Norway
Lower Mar Valley (Ostra Mardolafoss)	Eikesdal, Norway
Tyssestrengene	Odda, Norway

Important Cities on River Banks (World)

City	Country	River
Adelaide	Australia	Torrens
Amsterdam	Netherlands	Amsel
Alexandria	Egypt	Nile
Ankara	Turkey	Kazil
Bangkok	Thailand	Chao Praya
Basra	Iraq	Eupharates and Tigris
Baghdad	Iraq	Tigris
Berlin	Germany	Spree
Bonn	Germany	Rhine
Budapest	Hungary	Danube
Bristol	UK	Avon
Buenos Aires	Argentina	Laplata
Chittagong	Bangladesh	Majyani
Canton	China	Si-Kiang
Cairo	Egypt	Nile
Chung King	China	Yang-tse-kiang
Cologne	Germany	Rhine
Dandzing	Germany	Vistula
Dresden	Germany	Elbe
Dublin	Ireland	Liffy
Hamburg	Germany	Elbe
Kabul	Afghanistan	Kabul
Karachi	Pakistan	Indus
Khortoum	Sudan	Confluence of Blue & White Nile
Lahore	Pakistan	Ravi
Leningrad	Russia	Neva

City	Country	River
Lisbon	Portugal	Tagus
Liverpool	England	Messey
London	England	Thames
Moscow	Russia	Moskva
Montreal	Canada	St. Lawrence
Nanking	China	Yang-tse-kiang
New Orleans	U.S.A.	Missisipi
New York	U.S.A.	Hudson
Ottawa	Canada	Ottawa
Paris	France	Seine
Philadelphia	U.S.A	Delaware
Perth	Australia	Swan
Prague	Czech Republic	Vitava
Quebec	Canada	St. Lawrence
Rome	Italy	Tiber
Rotterdam	The Netherlands	New Moss
Stalingrad	Russia	Volga
Shanghai	China	Yang-tse-kiang
Sidney	Australia	Darling
Saint Louis	U.S.A	Mississippi
Tokyo	Japan	Arakava
Vienna	Austria	Danube
Warsaw	Poland	Vistula
Washington D.C.	U.S.A.	Potomac
Yangoon	Myanmar	Irawaddy

World's Geographical Surnames

City of Sky-scrapers—New York
City of Seven Hills—Rome
City of Dreaming Spires—Oxford
City of Golden Gate—San Francisco
City of Magnificent Buildings—Washington D.C.
City of Eternal Springs—Quito (S. America)
China's Sorrow—Hwang Ho
Cockpit of Europe—Belgium
Dark Continent—Africa
Emerald Isle—Ireland
Eternal City—Rome
Empire City—New York
Forbidden City—Lhasa (Tibet)
Garden City—Chicago
Gate of Tears—Strait of Bab-el-Mandeb
Gift of the Nile—Egypt
Granite City—Aberdeen (Scotland)
Hermit Kingdom—Korea
Herring Pond—Atlantic Ocean
Holy Land—Jerusalem
Island Continent—Australia
Islands of Cloves—Zanzibar
Isle of Pearls—Bahrein (Persian Gulf)
Key to the Mediterranean—Gibralter
Land of Cakes—Scotland
Land of Golden Fleece—Australia
Land of Maple Leaf—Canada
Land of Morning Calm—Korea
Land of Midnight Sun—Norway
Land of the Thousand Lakes—Finland
Land of the Thunderbolt—Bhutan
Land of White Elephant—Thailand
Land of Thousand Elephants—Laos
Land of Rising Sun—Japan
Loneliest Island—Tristan De Gunha (Mid-Atlantic)
Manchester of Japan—Osaka
Pillars of Hercules—Strait of Gibraltar
Pearl of the Antilles—Cuba
Playground of Europe—Switzerland
Quaker City—Philadelphia
Queen of the Adriatic—Venice
Roof of the World—The Pamirs, Central Asia
Sugar bowl of the world—Cuba
Venice of the North—Stockholm
Windy City—Chicago
Whiteman's grave—Guinea Coast of Africa
Yellow River—Huang Ho (China)
Sickman of Europe—Turkiye

Important Boundaries

Durand Line	Pakistan & Afghanistan
MacMohan Line	India & China
Radcliff Line	India & Pakistan
Maginot Line	France & Germany
Oder Niesse Line	Germany & Poland
Hindenberg Line	Poland & Germany (at the time of First World War)
38th Parallel	North & South Korea
49th Parallel	USA & Canada

Continents: Some Facts

Continent	Biggest Counrty	Highest Peak	Longest River
Asia	China	Mt. Everest (8848 m)	Yangtze Kiang
Africa	Algeria	Mt. Kilimanjaro (5895 m)	Nile
North America	Canada	Mt. Mckinley (6194 m)	Mississippi Missouri
South America	Brazil	Mt. Acancagua (6960 m)	Amazon
Europe	Russia	Mt. Elbrus (5642 m)	Ob
Australia	Australia	Mt. Coscuisco (2228 m)	Darling
Antarctica	—	Vinson Massif (5140 m)	—

INDIAN GEOGRAPHY

AREA AND LOCATION

- India is in the southern parts of the Asian continent. In the west of India lies the Arabian Peninsula while in the east lies the Indo-China Peninsula.
- India extends between 8°4' N and 37°6' N latitudes and between 68°7' E and 97°2' E longitudes.
- India, has a total geographic area of 32,87,263 sq. km. This is only 2.42 % of the total geographic area of the world but holds 17 per cent of the world's population.
- The 23½°N, which is the Tropic of Cancer, runs across the country.
- India has a length of 3214 km from north to south and 2933 km from east to west. It has a land frontier of 15200 km.
- The total length of the coastline of the mainland, Lakshadweep Islands and Andaman and Nicobar Islands is 7,516.6 km.
- India ranks seventh among the countries of the world, in terms of the geographical extent.
- India is bordered on three sides by water and on one by land, it is also a peninsula.
- India shares its common border with Afghanistan and Pakistan in the north-west, China and Bhutan in the north, and Bangladesh in the east. In the south, Sri Lanka is separated from India by a strait, known as the Palk Strait.
- 82°30' E longitude is considered as the Indian Standard Meridian. The local time of this longitude is taken as the Indian Standard Time (IST). This is 5½ hours ahead of the Greenwich Mean Time.

THE INDIAN STATES ON INTERNATIONAL BOUNDARIES ARE:

- ***Bordering Pakistan:*** Jammu and Kashmir, Punjab, Rajasthan, Gujarat.
- ***Bordering China:*** Ladakh, Himachal Pradesh, Uttarakhand, Sikkim, Arunachal Pradesh.
- ***Bordering Nepal:*** Bihar, Uttarakhand, UP, Sikkim, West Bengal.
- ***Bordering Bangladesh:*** West Bengal, Mizoram, Meghalaya, Tripura, Assam.
- ***Bordering Bhutan:*** West Bengal, Sikkim, Arunachal Pradesh, Assam.
- ***Bordering Myanmar:*** Arunachal Pradesh, Nagaland, Manipur, Mizoram.
- ***Bordering Afghanistan:*** Jammu and Kashmir (Pakistan-occupied area).

Important Passes

Jammu and Kashmir	Burzi-La
Himachal Pradesh	Bara La, Cha-La, Shipki-La
Uttarakhand	Niti-La, Lipu-Lekh-La
Sikkim	Jelep-La, Nathu-La
Arunachal Pradesh	Bomdi-La
Ladakh	Joji-La

Heighest Mountain Peaks of India

Peaks	Elevation• (in mts.)
Godwin Austin (K2)	8611*
Kanchenjunga	8598
Nanga Parvat	8126
Gasherbrum	8068*
Broad Peak	8047*
Dastegil	7885*
Masherbrum (East)	7821
Nanda Devi	7817
Masherbrum (West)	7806*
Rakoposhi	7788*
Kamet	7756
Saser Kangdi	7672

• *Above mean sea level in metres.*

* *Situated in Pak occupied Kashmir (PoK).*

Towns at River Banks

Town	River
Agra	Yamuna
Prayagraj	Confluence of the Ganges and the Yamuna
Ayodhya	Saryu
Badrinath	The Ganges
Kolkata	Hooghly
Cuttuck	Mahanadi
Delhi	Yamuna
Dibrugarh	Brahmaputra
Ferozepur	Satluj
Guwahati	Brahmaputra
Hardwar	The Ganges
Hyderabad	Musi
Jabalpur	Narmada
Kanpur	The Ganges
Kota	Chambal
Kurnool	Tungbhadra
Lucknow	Gomti
Ludhiana	Sutlej
Nasik	Godavari
Pandharpur	Bhima
Patna	The Ganges
Sambalpur	Mahanadi
Srinagar	Jhelum
Srirangapattam	Cauveri
Surat	Tapti
Varanasi	The Ganges
Vijaywada	Krishna

Important Waterfalls of India

Waterfall	Hgt (Mt.)	River	State
Kunchikal	455	Varahi	Karnataka
Dudhsagar	310	Mandvi	Goa
Jog/Gersoppa	260	Sharavati	Karnataka
Rakim Kund	168	Gaighat	Bihar
Chachai	127	Bihad	Madhya Pradesh
Kevti	98	Mahanadi	Madhya Pradesh
Sivasamudram	90	Cauveri	Karnataka

Important Lakes of India

Name of lake	State/UT
Pulicat Lake	Tamil Nadu & Andhra Pradesh Border
Sambhar Lake	Rajasthan
Tso Moriri Lake	Jammu & Kashmir
Vembanad Lake	Kerala
Wular & Dal Lakes	Jammu and Kashmir
Chilka Lake	Odisha
Kolleru Lake	Andhra Pradesh
Loktak Lake	Manipur
Lonar Lake	Maharashtra
Pangong Lake	Ladakh

Rivers of India

Name	Originates From	Falls Into
Yamuna	Yamunotri	Ganga
Chambal	Singar Chouri Peak, Vindhyan escarpment	Yamuna
Ghaghara	Matsatung Glacier	Ganga

Name	Originates From	Falls Into
Kosi	Near Gosain Dham Peak	Ganga
Sabarmati	Aravalis	Gulf of Khambat
Krishna	Western Ghats	Bay of Bengal
Godavari	Nasik district in Maharashtra	Bay of Bengal
Caveri	Brahmagir Range of Western Ghats	Bay of Bengal
Tungabharda	Western Ghats	Krishna
Ganges	Combines Sources	Bay of Bengal
Sutlej	Mansarovar Rakas lakes	Chenab
Indus	Near Mansarovar Lake	Arabian Sea
Ravi	Kullu Hills near Rohtang Pass	Chenab
Beas	Near Rohtang Pass	Sutlej
Jhelum	Verinag in Kashmir	Chenab
Son	Amarkantak	Ganga
Brahmaputra	Near Mansarovar Lake	Bay of Bengal
Narmada	Amarkantak	Gulf of Khambat
Tapti	Betul District in Madhya Pradesh	Gulf of Khambat
Mahanadi	Raipur District in Chhattisgarh	Bay of Bengal
Luni	Aravallis	Rann of Kuchchh
Ghaggar	Himalayas	Near Fatehabad
Betwa	Vindhyanchal	Yamuna

Geographical Surnames

Bengal's Sorrow	Damodar River
City of Palaces	Kolkata
Gateway of India	Mumbai
Pink City	Jaipur
Paris of India	Jaipur
Manchester of India	Ahmedabad
Kashmir of South	Kerala
Son of Sea	Lakshadweep
Queen of Mountains	Mussourie
Iron City	Jamshedpur
Hollywood of India	Mumbai
Scotland of East	Meghalaya
City of Nababs	Lucknow
City of Temples & Ghats	Varanasi
Land of Five Rivers	Punjab
City of Golden Temple	Amritsar
Garden of India	Bangaluru
Spice Garden of India	Kerala
City of Lakes	Srinagar
Twin City	Hyderabad-Secunderabad
City of Seven Islands	Mumbai
Diamond Harbour	Kolkata
Switzerland of India	Kashmir
Rice Bowl	Chhattisgarh
Fruit Bowl	Himachal Pradesh
Ganga of South	Cauvery
Pitsburg of India	Jamshedpur
City of Bridges	Srinagar
Residence of God	Prayagraj
A Cross-road (Quadrivial) of National Highways	Kanpur
Heart of India	Delhi
Black River	Sharda
City of Festivals	Madurai
Queen of Deccan	Pune
Sorrow of Bihar	Kosi River

Some Major Irrigational and Multipurpose Projects

S.No.	Name of Project	Related State	River
1.	Bargi Project	Madhya Pradesh	Bargi
2.	Beas	Joint Venture of Haryana, Punjab and Rajasthan	Beas
3.	Bhadra	Karnakata	Bhadra
4.	Bhakra Nangal	Haryana, Punjab and Rajasthan	Sutluj
5.	Bhima I	Maharashtra	Pawana
6.	Bhima II	Maharashtra	Krishna
7.	Chambal	Joint Project of M.P. and Rajasthan	Chambal
8.	Damodar Valley Project	West Bengal and Bihar	Damodar
9.	Dulhasti Power Project	Jammu and Kashmir	Chenab
10.	Farakka	West Bengal	Hooghly
11.	Gandak	Bihar and U.P.	Gandak
12.	Ghataprabha	Karnataka	Ghataprabha
13.	Hasdeo Bango Project	Madhya Pradesh, Chhattisgarh	Hasdeo
14.	Hirakud	Odisha	Mahanadi
15.	Jayakwadi	Maharashtra	Godavari
16.	Kakrapara	Gujarat	Tapti
17.	Kangsbati	West Bengal	Kangsbati and Kumari
18.	Karjan	Gujarat	Karjan
19.	Kosi	Bihar	Kosi
20.	Koyana	Maharashtra	Koyana
21.	Krishna Project	Maharashtra	Krishna
22.	Kukadi	Maharashtra	Kukadi
23.	Left Bank Ghagra Canal	Uttar Pradesh	Ghagra
24.	Madhya Ganga Canal	Uttar Pradesh	Ganga
25.	Mahanadi Delta Scheme	Odisha	(The irrigation scheme will utilise releases from Hirakund Reservoir)
26.	Mahi	Gujarat	Mahi
27.	Malaprabha	Karnataka	Malaprabha
28.	Mayurakshi	West Bengal	Mayurakshi
29.	Nagarjunasagar	Andhra Pradesh	Krishna
30.	Panam	Gujarat	Panam
31.	Parambikulam Aliyar	Tamil Nadu and Kerala	Perimbikulam
32.	Pochampad	Andhra Pradesh	Godavari
33.	Pong Dam	Punjab	Beas
34.	Ramganga	Uttarakhand	Ramganga
35.	Ranjit Sagar Dam (Thein Dam)	Punjab	Ravi
36.	Rihand	Uttar Pradesh	Rihand
37.	Sabarmati	Gujarat	Sabarmati

S.No.	Name of Project	Related State	River
38.	Sharda Sahayak	U.P.	Ghagra
39.	Sone High Level Canal	Bihar	Sone
40.	Tawa	Madhya Pradesh	Tawa
41.	Tehri Dam	Uttarakhand	Bhagirathi
42.	Tungabhadra	Andhra Pradesh and Karnataka	Tungabhadra
43.	Ukai	Gujarat	Tapti
44.	Upper Krishna	Karnataka	Krishna
45.	Upper Penganga	Maharashtra	Penganga
46.	Uri Power Project	Jammu and Kashmir	Jhelum

Major Indian Crops

Crops	Temp(°c)	Water(cm)	States where Produced
Wheat	15°-25°	60-90	Uttar Pradesh, Madhya Pradesh, Punjab, Haryana
Rice	24°-26°	80-200	West Bengal, Telangana, Uttar Pradesh, Punjab, Andhra Pradesh, Bihar
Maize	18°-21°	50-60	Karnataka, Bihar, Madhya Pradesh, Maharashtra, Uttar Pradesh
Jowar	20°-35°	40-60	Maharashtra, Madhya Pradesh, Karnataka
Soyabean	25°-27°	50-120	Madhya Pradesh, Maharashtra, Rajasthan
Cotton	20°-30°	80-150	Gujarat, Maharashtra, Telangana, Karnataka, Madhya Pradesh
Tobacco	20°-25°	75-80	Andhra Pradesh, Madhya Pradesh, Gujarat, Karnataka, Maharashtra, Uttar Pradesh
Tea	24°-30°	100-200	Assam, West Bengal, Kerala, Tamil Nadu, Uttar Pradesh
Ground Nut	15°-25°	60-130	Gujarat, Rajasthan, Maharashtra
Pulses	20°-35°	40-60	Madhya Pradesh, Maharashtra, Rajasthan

Mineral Wealth at a Glance (Metallic Minerals)

Mineral	Chief Producers
Bauxite	Odisha, Gujarat, Jharkhand
Chromite	Odisha, Karnataka
Coal	Jharkhand, Odisha
Copper	Rajasthan, Madhya Pradesh
Diaspore	Uttar Pradesh, Madhya Pradesh
Gold	Karnataka
Iron	Odisha, Karnataka, Goa
Lead	Rajasthan, Andhra Pradesh
Lignite	Tamil Nadu, Jammu & Kashmir
Manganese	Odisha, Karnataka
Natural Gas	Gujarat, Assam
Petroleum	Gujarat, Assam, Andhra Pradesh
Silver	Rajasthan, Jharkhand, Gujarat
Tungsten	Rajasthan
Zinc	Rajasthan, Maharashtra

Zones and Headquarters of Indian Railways

S.No.	Zone	Headquarters
1.	Central	Mumbai
2.	Eastern	Kolkata
3.	Northern	New Delhi
4.	North-Eastern	Gorakhpur
5.	North-East Frontier	Maligaon, Guwahati
6.	Southern	Chennai
7.	South-Central	Secunderabad
8.	South-Eastern	Kolkata
9.	Western	Mumbai
10.	East Coast	Bhubaneswar
11.	East Central	Hajipur
12.	North Central	Prayagraj
13.	North Western	Jaipur
14.	South Western	Hubballi (Hubli)
15.	West Central	Jabalpur
16.	South East Central	Bilaspur
17.	Metro Railway	Kolkata
18.	South Coast Railway	Vishakhapatnam (Proposed)

Major National Highways

NH	Connects
NH 44	Srinagar to Kanyakumari
NH 27	Porbandar to Silchar
NH 48	Delhi to Chennai
NH 52	Sangrur to Ankola
NH 30	Sitarganj to Ibrahimpatnam
NH 6	Jorabat to Seling
NH 53	Hazira to Paradip
NH 16	East Coast (West Bengal) to Chennai
NH 66	Panvel to Kanyakumari
NH 19	Delhi to Kolkata

Major Ports of Country

1. Syama Prasad Mookerjee (Kolkata)
2. Mumbai
3. J.L. Nehru Port (Nhava Sheva)
4. V.O. Chidambarnar (Tuticorin)
5. Chennai
6. Mormugao
7. New Mangalore
8. Paradeep
9. Deendayal (Kandla)
10. Vishakhapatnam
11. Cochin
12. Kamarajar (Ennore).

Major International Airports in India

International Airports	City
Indira Gandhi International Airport	Delhi
Anna International Airport	Chennai
Sri Guru Ram Das Jee International Airport	Amritsar
Rajiv Gandhi International Airport	Hyderabad
Calicut International Airport	Kozhikode
Chhatrapati Shivaji International Airport	Mumbai
Kempegowda International Airport	Bengaluru
Dabolim International Airport in Vasco di Gama City	Goa
Netaji Subash Chandra Bose International Airport	Kolkata
Trivendrum International Airport	Thiruvananthapuram
Lokpriya Gopinath Bordoloi International Airport	Guwahati
Sardar Vallabhbhai Patel International Airport	Ahmedabad

❑ ❑ ❑

INDIAN POLITY

INDIAN CONSTITUTION

- Demand for a Constituent Assembly composed of the people of India officially asserted by the Congress for the first time in 1935.
- The election for Indian Constitution Assembly held in 1946 according to the *Cabinet Mission Plan*.
- The first session of the Assembly was held in New Delhi on December 9, 1946. *Sachidanand Sinha* was elected provisional chairman of the session.
- On December 11, 1946, Dr. Rajendra Prasad was elected as the Permanent Chairman of the Constituent Assembly.
- The Constitution was framed by the Constituent Assembly of India, set-up in December 1946, in accordance with the Cabinet Mission Plan, under the Chairmanship of Sachidanand Sinha, initially.
- The total membership of Constituent Assembly after partition was 299, among them 70 were representatives from the Indian states and others from British India.
- The Chairman of the Drafting Committee was **Dr. BR Ambedkar**, also called the Father of the Constitution.
- The Constituent Assembly took 2 years, 11 months and 18 days to complete the Constitution.
- The Constitution, adopted on 8th November, 1949, contained 395 Articles and Schedules.
- The Constitution was delayed till 26th January because, in 1929, on this day Indian National Congress demanded Poorna Swaraj in Lahore Session under JL Nehru.
- Indian Constitution is a comprehensive document and it is the lengthiest written Constitution in the World.

THE PREAMBLE

- ***The Preamble of the Constitution:*** "We the people of India, having solemnly resolved to Constitute India into a Sovereign, Socialist, Secular Democratic Republic and to secure to all its citizen:

  Justice, Social, economic and political;

  Liberty of thought, expression, belief, faith and worship;

  Equality of status and of opportunity; and to promote among them all;

  Fraternity assuring the dignity of the individual and the unity and integrity of the nation;

  In our Constituent Assembly, this twenty-sixth day of November, 1949, do hereby adopt, enact and give to ourselves this constitution."

Foreign Sources of Indian Constitution

Foreign Sources	*Subject*
Britain	Parliamentary system, collective responsibilities of Cabinet
America	Fundamental right, Independent Judiciary, Judicial review
Canada	Division of powers
Ireland	Directive principles
Germany	Emergency provisions
Russia	Fundamental duties
Australia	Concurrent list

IMPORTANT ARTICLES

PART - I

UNION AND ITS TERRITORIES (ARTICLE 1 - 4)

- The Constitution says, "India, that is Bharat, shall be a Union of States".

- Parliament has the power to create any State, reduce it, change the name of boundaries of any State.

PART - II

CITIZENSHIP (ARTICLE 5 - 11)

- The Constitution provides for a single Citizenship.
- ***Indian Citizenship can be acquire:***
  1. by birth
  2. by descent
  3. by registration
  4. by naturalisation
  5. by incorporation of territory
- ***Indian Citizenship can be lost by:***
  1. renunciation;
  2. termination — it takes place if a citizen of India voluntary acquires the citizenship of another country; and
  3. deprivation — if the Government terminates the citizenship.

PART - III

FUNDAMENTAL RIGHTS (ARTICLE 12 - 35)

- Following fundamental rights are enjoyed by every Indian citizen, irrespective of caste, colour, creed and sex:
  1. ***Right to Equality:*** No special privileges, no distinction on grounds of religion, caste, creed and sex.
  2. ***Right to Freedom:*** The right to freedom of expression and speech, the right to choose one's own profession, the right to reside in any part of the Indian Union.
  3. ***Right to Freedom to Religion:*** Except when it is in the interest of public order, morality, health or other conditions, everybody has the right to profess, practice and propagate his religion freely.
  4. ***Cultural and Educational Rights:*** The Constitution provides that every community can run its own institutions to preserve its own culture and language.
  5. ***Right against Exploitation:*** Traffic in human beings and forced labour and the employment of children under 14 years in factories or mines, are punishable offences.
  6. ***Rights to Constitutional Remedies:*** When a citizen finds that any of his fundamental rights has been encroached upon, he can move the Supreme Court, which has been empowered to safeguard the fundamental rights of a citizen (Article 32).

PART - IV

DIRECTIVE PRINCIPLES OF STATE POLICY (ARTICLE 36 - 51)

- Directive principles are not enforceable through courts. Main aim of Directive principles is to provide social and economic base of a genuine democracy.

Some Important Directive Principles:

- Provisions for adequate means of livelihood for all citizens (Art. 39).
- Right to work (Art. 41).
- Right to human condition of work and maternity relief (Art. 42).
- Right to a living wage and condition of work ensuring decent standard of life of worker (Art. 43).
- Common Civil Code (Art. 44).
- Prohibit consumption of liquor (Art. 47).
- Prevent slaughter of useful cattle (Art. 48).
- Organise Panchayati Raj (Art. 40).
- Separate the judiciary from the executive (Art. 50).
- Protect and maintain places of historic monuments (Art. 49).
- International peace (Art. 51).

PART - IV A

FUNDAMENTAL DUTIES (ARTICLE 51A)

- The fundamental duties for the Indian citizens have been incorporated in the Constitution through the Constitution (42nd) Amendment Act, 1976. These duties are:
  1. to abide by the Constitution and respect its ideals and institutions, the National Flag and the National Anthem;

2. to cherish and follow the noble deeds which inspired our national struggle for freedom;
3. to uphold and protect the sovereignty, unity and integrity of India;
4. to defend the country and render national service when called upon to do so;
5. to promote harmony and the spirit of common brotherhood amongst all the people transcending religious, regional or sectional diversities and to renounce practices derogatory to the dignity of women;
6. to value and preserve the rich heritage of our composite culture;
7. to protect and improve natural environment including forests, lakes, rivers and wildlife, and to have compassion for living creatures;
8. to develop the scientific temper, humanism and the spirit of inquiry and reform;
9. to safeguard public property and to abjure violence;
10. to strive towards excellence in all spheres of individual and collective activity so that the nation constantly rises to higher levels of endeavour and achievement.
11. who is parent or guardian to provide opportunities for education to his child or, as the case may be, ward between age of six and fourteen years.

PART - V

UNION (ARTICLE 52 - 151)

The President

- The President is the Constitutional head of the Republic of India. He is more or less the titular head of the executive.
- He is the constitutional head but not the real executive. The real power is vested in the hands of the Council of Ministers.
- President is the first citizen of India.
- ***Qualifications:*** (i) Indian citizen, (ii) age not less than 35 years, (iii) should have qualification for election to Lok Sabha, (iv) should not hold any office of profit, (v) should not be a Member of Parliament or State Legislature.
- ***Election:*** Indirectly elected through Electoral College consisting of elected members of both the Houses of the Parliament and elected members of the Legislative Assemblies of the States.
- According to the 70th Amendment Act, 1992, the expression 'States' include the National Capital Territory of Delhi and the Union Territory of Puducherry. Members of the Legislative Councils have no right to vote in the Presidential election.
- ***Powers:*** He makes appointments to all the constitutional posts.
- He can address either House of Parliament and dissolve Lok Sabha.
- All Bills passed by Parliament must receive his assent to become an Act.
- He issues ordinances when Parliament is not in session. No Money Bill can be introduced in Lok Sabha without his recommendation.
- He appoints 12 members of special repute in the Rajya Sabha.
- He has the power of *Pardon* to a criminal in special cases.
- The President holds the office for a period of five years. He is eligible for re-election.
- He is also entitled to rent free official residence called Rashtrapati Bhawan.

Vice-President

- ***Article 63*** of the Constitution stipulates a Vice-President for India.
- The Vice-President acts as the ex-officio Chairman of the Council of States (Rajya Sabha).
- He is elected by an electoral college consisting of the members of both Houses of Parliament in accordance with the system of proportional represen-tation by means of the single trans-ferable vote. He must be a citizen of India, not less than 35 years of age, and should be eligible for election as a member of the Council of States.

- Disputes in connection with election of a president or a vice-president are to be a dealt with in accordance with Article-71. Such disputes shall be decided by the Supreme Court.

Council of Ministers

- The Constitution of India provides for a parliament system of government under which the President is only Constitutional ruler and the real power is exercised by the Council of Ministers, headed by the Prime Minister.
- Council of Ministers is composed of all Union Ministers—the Prime Minister, Cabinet Ministers and Ministers of State.
- The Council of Ministers is Collectively responsible to the Lok Sabha.
- The Prime Minister is a link between the President and the Council of Ministers.

Prime Minister

- The Prime Minister is the leader of the majority party in the Parliament.
- He is appointed by the President. Other Ministers are appointed by the president on his advice.
- The Prime Minister is the head of the Government and the head of the Council of Ministers.
- Jawaharlal Nehru was the first Prime Minister and the longest serving so far.

Union Legislature

- The Legislature of the Union, which is called 'Parliament' consists of the President and the two Houses of Parliament known as the Council of states (Rajya Sabha) and the House of the People (Lok Sabha).

RAJYA SABHA

- The Rajya Sabha is the Upper House of the Parliament and it is constituted of representatives from the States or the Constituent units of the Indian Union.
- It is a permanent body, one third of its members retiring after every two years.
- Its maximum strength is 250. Out of these, twelve members are nominated by the President from well-known personalities in the realm of Science, Art, Literature and Social Service. Rest of 238 representatives of the States and Union Territories are elected.
- Currently, the strength of the Rajya Sabha is 245.

LOK SABHA

- The Lok Sabha whose life is five years, is the Lower House of Parliament and comprises of members directly elected by the people.
- The House of the people (Lok Sabha) at present consists of 543 members directly elected from the states and Union Territories. (By the 104th amendment of the constitution the reservation for two members of Anglo Indian Community nominated by President have been abolished).
- The House of the People shall continue for five years (unless sooner dissolved) from the date of its meeting and no longer and the expiry of the said period of 5 years shall operate as dissolution of the House.

Parliamentary Committees

- There are several Parliamentary Committees to assist the Parliament in its deliberations.
- These are appointed or elected by the respective Houses of Lok Sabha and Rajya Sabha on a motion made or are nominated by their presiding officers.
- Among the Standing Committees, three are financial Committees:
  - (*i*) Public Account Committee;
  - (*ii*) Estimate Committee;
  - (*iii*) Public undertaking Committee.

Speaker of Lok Sabha

- Speaker is elected by the Lok Sabha from among its members.
- The Speaker will have the final power to maintain order within the House of the People and to interpret its rules of procedure.
- A Deputy-Speaker is also elected to officiate in absence of the Speaker.
- *G.V. Mavlankar* was the first Speaker of the Lok Sabha (1952-1956).

Supreme Court

- The Constitution provides for the Supreme Court, which consists of Chief Justice and 33 judges. They are appointed by the President of India.

QUALIFICATION AND TENURE

- Eligibility conditions for a judge of the Supreme Court are that he must be : (i) a citizen of India; (ii) a judge of a high court for a minimum period of 5 years; or (iii) an advocate of a high court for at least ten years or a distinguished jurist.
- Judges hold office till the age of 65.
- They can resign earlier or can be removed by the President on the recommendation of the two Houses of the Parliament by 2/3rd majority of the members present and voting.

Powers

- *Original jurisdiction:* Cases involving Government of India and the states or cases involving the enforcement of Fundamental Rights fall under original jurisdiction.
- *Appellate Jurisdiction:* In cases which are brought to it in the form of appeals against the judgement of the lower courts—It hears appeals in civil and criminal cases.
- *Advisory functions:* the Supreme Court advises the President on the constitutionality of a particular legal matter. However, its advice is not binding on the President.

Other Powers:

1. it is a court of record and can punish for contempt of itself;
2. it can make rules for regulating the practice and procedure of courts with the approval of the President; and
3. it can recommend to the President the removal of chairman and members of the UPSC. Supreme Court enjoys the power of judicial review (right of the court which declares as unconstitutional, the laws passed by the legislature and orders issued by executive) though it is not specifically mentioned in the Constitution.

- The first Chief Justice of India was H.J. Kania (1950-51).

COMPTROLLER AND AUDITOR GENERAL (CAG) (ARTICLE 148-151)

- The Comptroller and Auditor General of India is guardian of the public purse.
- It is his duty to see that not a *paisa* is spent out of consolidated fund of India or of a state without the authority of the appropriate legislature.
- He is appointed by President of India.
- A person with long administrative experience and knowledge of accounts is appointed.
- Holds office for 6 yrs or till 65 yrs of age.
- The President can remove him only on the recommendation of the 2 houses of Parliament (as in case of judge of Supreme Court).
- The CAG submits its reports to the President (in case of accounts relating to the Union Government) or to the State Governors (for State Government Accounts).
- The first CAG of India was *V Narahari Rao* (1948-1954).
- The CAG is not eligible for further office under the Union or State Governments. The expenses of the office of the CAG is charged to the Consolidated Fund of India.

ATTORNEY GENERAL OF INDIA

- The Attorney General of India is the first law officer of the Government of India.
- Though he is not a member of cabinet he has the right to speak in the House of Parliament, but he has no right to vote.
- The Attorney General of India shall be appointed by the President and shall hold office during his pleasure.
- His duty shall be to give advice on such legal matter from time-to-time as may be referred to him by the President.
- To be appointed as Attorney General, a candidate must be qualified to be appointed as a Judge of the Supreme Court.
- The Attorney General can participate in proceedings of the Parliament without the Right to Vote (Article 88).
- The first Attorney General of Independent India was MC Setalvad (1950-1963).

PART - VI

THE STATES (ARTICLE 152 - 237)

THE GOVERNOR

- The Governor is appointed by the President and holds office during the pleasure of the President.
- Apart from the power to appoint the council of ministers, if the governor finds that the government of state cannot be carried on in accordance with the provisions of the constitution (Art. 356), he may send his report to the President who may assume to himself the functions of the government of the state. (This is popularly known as 'President's Rule').
- Article 161 gives the Governor the power to grant pardons, reprieves, remission of punishment to persons convicted under the state law.
- Article 171 states that the States where Legislative Councils exists, the Governor can nominate some members from amongst those distinguished in literature, science, arts, cooperative movement and social service.

STATES LEGISLATURE (ARTICLE 168 - 212)

- The state legislature consists of Governor and legislative assembly.
- In some state like *Bihar, Maharashtra, Andhra Pradesh, Karnataka, Uttar Pradesh and Telangana* have a legislative council.
- The membership of the council should not be more than *one-third* of the legislative assembly but not less than 40.
- The legislative assembly of each state shall be composed of members chosen by direct election on the basis of adult suffrage and the number of members shall not be more than 500 or less than 60.
- The assembly of Sikkim, Goa, Puducherry and Mizoram have less than 60 members.

HIGH COURTS (ARTICLE 214-232)

- The High Court stands at the apex of the State Judiciary.
- As per the Constitution, there shall be a High Court in each State. But there may be a common High Court for two or more States and Union Territory, if it is provided by a law of the Parliament. For example, the Chennai High Court has its Jurisdiction over the State of Tamil Nadu and the Union Territory of Puducherry.
- The State Government has no control over it.
- There are 25 High Courts in India.
- The Calcutta High Court, established in 1862, is the oldest High Court in India.

THE PANCHAYATS (ARTICLE 243-243 O)

- Panchayati Raj was introduced in India with a view to associate the people with administration at grass-root level.
- It is a three-tier system as recommended by Balwant Rai Mehta Committee.
- Introduced by the 73rd Amendment Act, 1992 which envisaged a three tier system of local governance.

  These are:

  1. Gram Panchayat at the village level
  2. Panchayat Samiti at the block level
  3. Zila Parishad at the district level.

Jurisdiction and Seat of High Courts

Name	Year	Territorial Jurisdiction	Seat
Allahabad	1866	Uttar Pradesh	Prayagraj (Bench at Lucknow)
Bombay	1862	Maharashtra, Goa, Dadar and Nagar Haveli and Daman and Diu	Mumbai (Benches at Nagpur, Panaji and Sambhaji Nagar)
Calcutta	1862	West Bengal and Andaman & Nicobar	Kolkata (Circuit Benches at Sri Vijaya Puram and Jalpaiguri)
Chhattisgarh	2000	Chhattisgarh	Bilaspur

Name	Year	Territorial Jurisdiction	Seat
Delhi	1966	Delhi	Delhi
Gauhati	1948	Assam, Nagaland, Mizoram and Arunachal Pradesh	Guwahati (Benches at Kohima, Aizawl and Itanagar)
Gujarat	1960	Gujarat	Ahmedabad
Himachal Pradesh	1971	Himachal Pradesh	Shimla
Jammu & Kashmir and Ladakh	1928	Jammu & Kashmir, Ladakh	Srinagar and Jammu
Jharkhand	2000	Jharkhand	Ranchi
Karnataka	1884	Karnataka	Bengaluru (Circuit Benches at Dharwar and Gulbarga)
Kerala	1958	Kerala & Lakshadweep	Kochi (Ernakulam)
Madhya Pradesh	1956	Madhya Pradesh	Jabalpur (Benches at Gwalior and Indore)
Madras	1862	Tamil Nadu & Puducherry	Chennai (Bench at Madurai)
Orissa	1948	Odisha	Cuttack
Patna	1916	Bihar	Patna
Punjab and Haryana	1966	Punjab, Haryana and Chandigarh	Chandigarh
Rajasthan	1949	Rajasthan	Jodhpur (Bench at Jaipur)
Sikkim	1975	Sikkim	Gangtok
Uttarakhand	2000	Uttarakhand	Nainital
Tripura	2013	Tripura	Agartala
Meghalaya	2013	Meghalaya	Shillong
Manipur	2013	Manipur	Imphal
Telangana	2019	Telangana	Hyderabad
Andhra Pradesh	2019	Andhra Pradesh	Amravati

THE MUNICIPALITIES (ARTICLE 243 P-243 ZG)

- Big cities have municipal corporations headed by the elected Mayor.
- For small towns there are elected boards or councils, in turn, elect their Presidents.
- Introduced by the 74th Amendment Act, 1993 which envisages three types of urban local bodies, namely, municipality (nagar palika), city council (nagar panchayat).
- Municipal governance in India was first introduced in Madras in 1688.

PART - XIII

(ARTICLE 301 - 307)

- In this part from Article 301-307 trade, commerce and intercourse within the territory of India are given.

PART - XIV

(ARTICLE 308 - 323)

- In this part services under the union and the states are given.
- ***Article 312:** All India Services* and ***Article 315:*** Public Service Commissions for the Union and for the States.
- The first Public Service Commission was set up in 1926, on the recommendations of the Lee Commission.

UNION PUBLIC SERVICE COMMISSION (UPSC)

- This Commission is responsible for:
  1. recruitment to all civil services and posts, under the Union Government by written examinations, interviews and promotions, and
  2. advising the Government on all matters relating to methods of recruitment, principles to be followed in making promotions and transfers. Its Chairman is appointed by the President.

STAFF SELECTION COMMISSION (SSC)

- The Union Government has constituted a Staff Selection Commission for recruitment to non-technical Class III posts in the central government and in subordinate offices.

- The Administrative Reforms Commission had recommended the setting up of such a Commission.
- The Commission has also been entrusted with the responsibility of making recruitment to Group 'B' services like Assistants' and Stenographers Grade 'C'.
- The Commission has a chairman and two members.

ELECTIONS (ARTICLE 324-329)

- The Constitution provides for an independent election commission to ensure free and fair election to the Parliament, the State legislature and the offices of President and Vice-President.
- Consists of Chief Election Commissioner +2 Election Commissioners. They all enjoy equal powers.
- The Chief Election Commissioner and other Election Commissioners are appointed by the President.
- Election Commissioners are appointed for a term of 5 yrs.
- They are not eligible for re-appointment. Also, they cannot hold any office of profit after their retirement.
- The Election Commission was established on 25th January, 1950 under Article 324 of the Constitution.
- The first Chief Election Commissioner was *Sukumar Sen.*

Functions

- Preparation of electoral rolls and keeping voters list updated.
- Recognition of various political parties and allotment of election symbols.

NITI AAYOG

- The Indian government has replaced Planing Commission with a new institution named **NITI Aayog (National Institution for Transforming India).**
- The Niti Aayog will comprise the following:
  1. Prime Minister of India as the Chairperson.
  2. Governing Council comprising the Chief Ministers of all the States and Lt. Governors of Territories.
  3. Regional Councils will be formed to address specific issues and contingencies impacting more than one state or a region. These will be formed for a specified tenure. The Regional Councils will be convened by the Prime Minister and will comprise of the Chief Ministers of States and Lt. Governors of Territories in the region. These will be chaired by the Chairperson of the NITI Aayog or his nominee.
  4. Experts, specialists and practitioners with relevant domain knowledge as special invitees nominated by the Prime Minister.
- The full-time organizational framework will comprise of, in addition to the Prime Minister as the Chairperson:
  1. Vice-Chairperson : To be appointed by the Prime Minister.
  2. Members : Full-time. : 3
  3. Part-time members : Maximum of 2 from leading universities research organizations and other relevant institutions in an ex-officio capacity. Part time members will be on a rotational basis.
  4. Ex Officio members : Maximum of 4 members of the Council of Ministers to be nominated by the Prime Minister.
  5. Chief Executive Officer : To be appointed by the Prime Minister for a fixed tenure, in the rank of Secretary to the Government of India.
  6. Secretariat as deemed necessary.

FINANCE COMMISSION

- The constitution of the Finance Commission is laid down in Art. 280.
- The chairman must be a person having experience in public affairs; and the other four members also having wide experience in financial matters.

- It consists of Chairman and 4 other members.
- It shall be the duty of the Finance Commission to advice the President on matters such as the distribution between the Union and States of the net proceeds of taxes that is required to be shared.
- The Finance Commission is not a permanent body. It is dissolved after it has submitted its recommendations.

Important Amendments to the Constitution

First Amendment, 1951	:	Added Ninth Schedule.
Twenty-second Amendment, 1969	:	Formation of Meghalaya within the state of Assam was facilitated.
Twenty-sixth Amendment, 1971	:	The privy and privileges of the former rulers of Indian States were abolished.
Thirty-first Amendment, 1973	:	The upper limit of representation of states was raised from 500 to 525. The upper limit for representation of the UTs was reduced from 25 to 20.
Thirty-sixth Amendment, 1975	:	Sikkim was made a full-fledged state of Indian Union and it was included in the First Schedule.
Thirty-eight Amendment, 1975	:	This act led to the amendment of Article 123, Article 213 and Article 352 which stated that the satisfaction of President or of Governor contained in these Articles would be called in question in any court of law.
Forty-second Amendment, 1976	:	This amendment was done in accordance with the recommendations of Swaran Singh Committee and included a number of amendments.
Forty-third Amendment, 1977	:	It provided for the restoration of the Jurisdiction of the Supreme Court and High Courts, curtailed by the enactment of the Constitution (Forty-Second Amendment) Act, 1976.
Forty-fourth Amendment, 1978	:	The right to property was deleted as Fundamental Right and was made a legal right.
Fifty-third Amendment, 1986	:	The Act grants statehood to the Union Territory of Mizoram, thus making it the 23rd State of the Indian Unions.
Fifty-sixth Amendment, 1987	:	The UT of Goa converted into Goa state through this amendment whereas Daman and Diu were organised under a new UT.
Seventy-third Amendment, 1992	:	It is concerning Panchayati Raj.
Seventy-fourth Amendment, 1992	:	It is regarding Municipal Boards and Corporations.
Eighty-ninth Amendment, 2003	:	It provides for constitution of a separate National Commission for Scheduled Tribes. (Earlier, there was a combined National Commission for both SC/STs).
Ninety-first Amendment, 2003	:	It is regarding restricting the total number of Ministers including Prime Minister/Chief Minister in Lok Sabha and State Legislatures to 15% of the total number of the Union or State Legislatures.
Ninety-sixth Amendment, 2011	:	Amendment of 8th Schedule, it replaces 'Orissa' with 'Odisha'.
Ninety-eight Amendment, 2013	:	(Insert Article 371 J) To empower the Governor of Karnataka to take steps to develop Hydrabad Karnataka Region.

Ninety-ninth Amendment, 2015	:	The amendment is in toto quashed by Supreme Court on 16 October, 2015.
One hundredth and first Amendment, 2016	:	The act amends the Constitution to introduce "The Goods and Services Tax (GST)."
One hundredth and Third Amendment, 2019	:	The Act providing 10 per cent reservation in government jobs and educational institutions to Economically Weaker Sections (EWS) of General Category, came into effect on January 14, 2019.
One hundredth and Fourth Amendment, 2019	:	This Act ceased the reservation of seats for Anglo-Indians in the Lok Sabha and Legislative assemblies and extended reservations for SCs and STs for up to ten years.
One hundredth and Sixth Amendment, 2023	:	This Act provides 33% reservation for women in Lok Sabha and State Legislative Assemblies.

NATIONAL SYMBOLS

STATE EMBLEM

- State Emblem of India is an adaptation from the Sarnath Lion Capital of Ashoka. It was adopted by the Government of India on January 26, 1950. In the adapted form, only three lions are visible, the fourth being hidden from the view.
- The wheel (Dharma Chakra) appears in relief in the centre of the abacus with a bull on the right and a horse on the left.
- The bell-shaped lotus has been omitted. The words ''Satyameva Jayate'' meaning "Truth alone triumphs'' are inscribed below the Emblem in Devanagari script.

NATIONAL FLAG

- The National Flag of India is a horizontal tricolour of deep saffron (Kesari), white and dark green in equal proportion.
- In the centre of the white band there is a wheel in navy blue colour. It has 24 spokes.
- The ratio of the length and the breadth of the flag is 3 : 2. Its design was adopted by the Constituent Assembly of India on July 22, 1947.

NATIONAL ANTHEM

- Rabindranath Tagore's song 'Jana-gana-mana' was adopted by the Constituent Assembly as the National Anthem of India on January 24, 1950.

Jana-gana-mana-adhinayaka jaya he,
Bharata-bhagya-vidhata
Punjab-Sindh-Gujarat-Maratha-
Dravida-Utkala-Banga
Vindhya-Himachala-Yamuna-Ganga
Uchhala-jaladhi-taranga.
Tava subha name jage,
Tava subha asisa mange,
Gahe tava jaya gatha,
Jana-gana-mangala-dayak,
jaya he Bharata bhagya vidhata,
Jaya he, jaya he, jaya he,
Jaya jaya jaya, jaya he.

NATIONAL SONG

- Bankim Chandra Chatterji's 'Vande Mataram' which was a source of inspiration to the people in their struggle for freedom, has been adopted as National Song. It has an equal status with the National Anthem.

Vande Mataram
Sujalam, suphalam, malayaja-shitalam,
Shasya shyamalam, Mataram
Shubhrajyotsna, pulkita yaminim,
Phulla kusumita drumadalashobhinim,
Subhasinim sumadhura—bhashinim,
Sukhadam, Varadam, Mataram.

- **National Bird and Animal of India:** Peacock and Tiger.
- **National Aquatic Animal:** Dolphin
- **National Flower:** Lotus
- **National Calendar:** It was adopted on March 22, 1957. It has 365 days in the year and the first month of the year is Chaitra.

❒ ❒ ❒

GENERAL SCIENCE

PHYSICS

PHYSICAL QUANTITIES

- Physical quantities may be divided in two classes: 1. Scalar Quantities 2. Vector Quantities
- A scalar quantity is one which has only magnitude.
- A vector quantity has both magnitude and direction.
- Force, Velocity, Momentum, Acceleration are examples of vector quantities.
- Mass, length, time, volume, speed, energy, work are examples of scalar quantities.

UNITS

- All measurements in physics require standard units.
- In 1960, the General Conference of Weights and Measures recommended that a metric system of measurements called the International System of Units, abbreviated as SI units, be used.

Some Important Units

S.No.	Units	Quantity
1.	Metre	Length
2.	Kilogram	Mass
3.	Second	Time
4.	Ampere	Electric Current
5.	Candela	Luminous Intensity
6.	Newton	Force
7.	Joule	Workdone
8.	Watt	Power
9.	Coulomb	Electric Charge
10.	Volt	Potential Difference
11.	Ohm	Electrical Resistance
12.	Farad	Capacitance
13.	Henry	Inductance
14.	Lumen	Luminous Flux

- Very small distances are measured in micro-meters or (microns) (μm), angstroms (Å), nanometers (nm) and femtometres (fm).

MOTION

- When a body changes its position with respect to something else as time goes on, we say the body is in motion.
- There are two types of motion—translational (linear) and rotational (spin).
- The motion of a car on a road is translational whereas the motion of a top, spinning on its axis is rotational.

SPEED

- It is a scalar form of velocity and is defined as the distance travelled in one second.
- Speed = $\frac{\text{distance travelled}}{\text{time required}}$
- SI unit of speed is m/s.

VELOCITY

- The distance covered by an object in a specified direction in unit time interval is called velocity.
- The SI unit of velocity is m/s.
- Velocity is a vector quantity.

ACCELERATION

- The velocity of a body changes due to change in its speed or direction or both. The rate of change of the velocity of a body is called its acceleration.
- Acceleration = $\frac{\text{change in velocity}}{\text{time taken}}$

FORCE AND MOTION

GRAVITATIONAL FORCE

- It is the force of attraction between two masses.
- It is gravitational force that holds the moon in its orbit round the earth and the earth in its orbit round the sun.
- *Newton's Law of Universal Gravitation* states that every particle in the universe attracts every other particle with a force that is directly proportional to the product of their masses and inversely proportional to the square of the distance between them.
- The value of G is 6.67×10^{-11} SI units.

CENTRIPETAL FORCE

- The force acting towards the centre on a particle executing uniform circular motion is called centripetal force and is given by

$$F = \frac{mv^2}{r}$$

where, m = Mass of the object
v = Speed
r = Radius of the Circular Path

- In case of the moon, gravitational force between the earth and the moon acts as the centripetal force.
- Centripetal force always acts on the particle performing circular motion.

CENTRIFUGAL FORCE

- The pseudo force that balances the centripetal force in uniform circular motion is called centrifugal force.
- Centrifugal force is directed away from the centre along the radius.
- The centrifugal force is zero exactly at the poles and maximum at the equator.

WEIGHT

- The weight of a body is the force with which the earth attracts the body towards its centre.
- The mass of a body is a constant quantity whereas its weight varies slightly from place-to-place on the earth.
- The weight of a body is maximum at the poles and minimum at the equator. This variation in weight is due to:

  1. the shape of the earth.
  2. the rotation of the earth about its axis.
- The weight of an object is less at high elevations than at sea level.
- At the centre of the earth, the weight of a body would be zero.
- On the surface of the moon the value of the acceleration due to gravity is nearly one-sixth of that on earth and, therefore, an object on the moon would weigh only one-sixth its weight on the earth. The mass of an object on the moon would be the same as on earth.
- The weight of a body would be more if the earth stopped rotating. Conversely, if the speed of rotation were higher, the weight would be less.
- A person weighs more in a lift, which is accelerating upward.
- An astronaut feels weightless in a spaceship because he is not pushing against anything.

FRICTION

- Friction is the force which opposes the relative motion of two surfaces in contact.
- It is friction between the ground and the soles of our shoes that makes walking possible and it is lack of friction that makes our feet slip on highly polished surfaces.
- Friction in machines wastes energy and also causes wear and tear. This friction is reduced by using (1) lubricants, and (2) ball bearings.

NEWTON'S LAWS OF MOTION

First Law

- Every object continues in its state of rest or of uniform motion in a straight line if no net force acts upon it. It is also known as *law of inertia.*
- **Examples:** 1. An unwary passenger in a fast-moving bus falls forward when it stops suddenly. This happens because the feet of the passenger come to rest suddenly whereas his upper part of body continues to be in motion. 2. A person

getting down from a moving bus has to run some distance, in the direction of the bus, before stopping. If he does not run he is bound to fall because his feet come to rest whereas his body continues to be in motion.

Momentum

- The momentum of a body is defined as the product of its mass and velocity.

Second Law

- This law states that "the rate of change of momentum of a body is proportional to the applied force and takes place in the direction of the force."
- If we express force (F) in Newtons, mass (m) in kilograms and acceleration (a) in metres per second squared, we can write the second law as; $F = ma$.
- In travelling the same distance, a car consumes more fuel on a crowded road than on a free road. This happens because the car has to stop and start quite often on a crowded road. The repeated acceleration requires a force (second law), which ultimately comes from the fuel. On a free road the car runs at almost uniform speed requiring fewer accelerations and hence less fuel consumption.

Third Law

- This law states that "to every action there is an equal and opposite reaction."
- When a bullet is fired from a gun, equal and opposite forces are exerted on the bullet and the gun.
- The engine in a jet aeroplane works on the same principle as a rocket but there is a difference in the method of obtaining the high velocity as jet.

IMPULSE

- If a force acts on a body for a very short time, then the product of force and time is called the impulse.

  Impulse= Change in momentum

  = Force × Time

Application of Impulse

1. A cricket player draws his hand back while catching.
2. A person jumping on hard cement floor receives more injuries than a person jumping on muddy or sandy floor.

WORK, POWER AND ENERGY

WORK

- Whenever a force acting on a body displaces it, work is said to be done.

  Work = Force × Distance moved in the direction of force.
- Work is a scalar quantity and its SI unit is Joule (J).

POWER

- Power is defined as the rate of doing work.

$$\text{Power} = \frac{\text{Work done}}{\text{Time taken}}$$

- The SI unit of power is Watt (W) and is also measured in horse power.

  1 HP = 746 W

ENERGY

- Energy is defined as the capacity to do work.

Kinetic Energy

- The energy possessed by an object due to its motion is called kinetic energy and is described by the expression

$$KE = \frac{1}{2}mv^2$$; where, m = mass of the object

v = speed

Potential Energy

- Potential energy is the energy possessed by the body by virtue of its position, configuration or any condition of stress or strain.
- There are many examples of potential energy. A stone held at some height above the ground has potential energy. Water in an elevated reservoir possesses potential energy.

Transformation of Energy

S.No.	Equipment	Transformation
1.	Dynamo	Mechanical energy into electrical energy
2.	Microphone	Sound energy into electrical energy
3.	Loud Speaker	Electrical energy into sound energy
4.	Electric Bulb	Electrical energy into light and heat energy
5.	Battery	Chemical energy into electrical energy
6.	Electrical Motor	Electrical energy into mechanical energy

CENTRE OF GRAVITY

- The centre of gravity of a body is the point where the whole weight of the body can be considered to act.
- Racing cars are build low and with wide wheel bases to reduce the risk of overturning at sharp bends.
- While crossing a river in a boat, passengers are not allowed to stand. This keeps the CG of the system (boat and passengers) low and ensures stability.

ARTIFICIAL SATELLITES

- In the case of a satellite, the centripetal force is provided by the gravitational pull of the earth.
- If the speed of a satellite is more than 11.2 km/s or 25,000 miles/hour, the satellite would escape the earth entirely and would never come back. This is called escape velocity.
- The existence of gaseous atmosphere on the earth is due to the high value of its escape velocity.

Geostationary Satellites

- Geostationary satellites are stationary with respect to an observer on the earth. Their time period is 24-hour. There height above the surface of earth is 36,000 km. They are always in equatorial plane and their orbits are circular. They are also called parking orbits.

DENSITY AND RELATIVE DENSITY

DENSITY

- The mass per unit volume of a substance is called its density.

$$\text{Density} = \frac{\text{Mass}}{\text{Volume}}$$

- The SI unit of density is kilogram per metre cubed (kg/m^3).
- The relative density of a substance is the ratio of the density of the substance to the density of water.
- Relative density has no unit.

PRESSURE

- Pressure is defined as force acting per unit area.

$$\text{Pressure} = \frac{\text{Force}}{\text{Area}}$$

- The SI unit of pressure is newton per metre squared or pascal.
- Broad wooden sleepers are placed below the rails to reduce the pressure exerted by the weight of a train.
- The pressure of water increases with depth, therefore bottom of a dam is made much thicken than the top.
- The pressure exerted on an enclosed liquid at one place is transmitted equally throughout the liquid. This is called Pascal's Principle.
- Hydraulic presses, hydraulic brakes, hydraulic door closers, etc. are applications of the Pascal's Principle.
- At high attitudes where atmosphere pressure is less nose bleeding may occur due to the greater pressure of blood.
- In an aircraft flying at high altitude, normal atmospheric pressure is maintained by the use of air pumps. If this were not done, the crew and passengers would experience difficulty in breathing and consequently face dangers.
- Atmospheric pressure is measured with an instrument called the *Barometer*.

ARCHIMEDE'S PRINCIPLE

- This principle states that when a body is wholly or partially immersed in a fluid, it experiences an upthrust (upward force) equal to the weight of the fluid displaced.
- An iron nail sinks in water whereas a ship made of iron and steel floats. This is due to the fact that a ship is hollow and contains air and, therefore, its density is less than that of water.
- The density of sea water is more than that of river water, due to this a ship sinks less in sea water. It is for this reason that a ship rises a little when it enters a sea from a river.
- It is because of the higher density of sea water that it is easier to swim in the sea.
- A balloon filled with a light gas, such as hydrogen, rises because the average density of the balloon and the gas is less than that of air. The balloon cannot rise indefinitely because the density of the air decreases with increasing altitude. At a certain height, where the density of air is equal to the average density of the balloon, it ceases to rise and drifts sideways with the wind.
- When an ice block floats in water the water level will remain the same when all the ice melts into water.
- A *hydrometer* is an instrument used for measuring the relative density of liquids.
- A special type of a hydrometer called *Lactometer* is used for testing milk by measuring its density.

SURFACE TENSION

- Surface tension is that property of liquids owing to which they tend to acquire minimum surface area.
- Surface tension is caused by molecular attractions.
- When a paint brush is dipped in water all its hair spread out but when it is taken out it is covered with a thin film of water which contracts due to surface tension and pulls the hair together.
- Liquid drops, such as raindrops, oildrops, drops of molten metals, dewdrops etc. are all spherical because their surface tend to contract in order to have minimum surface area. For a given volume, a sphere has the minimum surface area.
- Soaps and detergents lower the surface tension of water. This increases the wetting power of water or its ability to detach dirt particles from clothes and untensils.
- The force of attraction between unlike molecules is called **adhesion** and that between like molecules **cohesion.**
- The melted wax of a candle is drawn up into the wick by capillary action. Oil rises up a lamp wick for the same reason.
- If one end of a sugar cube is dipped into tea, the entire cube is quickly wet on account of capillary action.

VISCOSITY

- The force which opposes the relative motion between different layers of liquid or gases is called viscous force.
- Viscosity is the property of liquids and gases both.

BERNOULLI'S THEOREM

- According to Bernoulli's theorem, in case of streamline flow of incompressible and non-viscous fluid (ideal fluid) through a tube, total energy (sum of pressure energy, potential energy and kinetic energy) per unit volume of fluid is same at all points.

  1. When a bowler spins a ball, it changes its direction (swings) in the air due to unequal pressure acting on it.

HEAT

- Heat is that form of energy which flows from one body to other body due to difference in temperature between the bodies. The amount of heat contained in a body depends upon the mass of the body.

TEMPERATURE

- The temperature of a body is the quantity that tells how hot or cold it is with respect to some standard body.

MEASUREMENT OF TEMPERATURE

- Temperature is measured by a thermometer.
- A thermometer may be graduated in following scales—
  1. The upper and lower points of centigrade scale are 100°C and 0°C.
  2. The upper and lower points of Fahrenheit scale are 212°F and 32°F.
  3. The upper and lower points of Reaumur scale are 80°R and 0°R.
  4. The upper and lower points of Kelvin scale are 373K and 273K.
  5. The upper and lower points of Rankine scale are 672° Ra and 460° Ra.
- At –40 degrees both celsius and Fahrenheit scales will show identical readings.
- Water cannot be used in a thermometer becaues it freezes at 0°C and also because of its irregular expansion.

THERMAL EXPANSION

- Solids, liquids and gases generally expand when heated and contract when cooled.
- Gaps have to be left in railway tracks to make allowance for expansion, otherwise the rails will buckle. Allowance is made for the expansion of long steel bridges. One end of such bridge is fixed while the other rests on rollers.
- Telephone wires sag more in summer than in winter due to thermal expansion.

EXPANSION OF WATER

- Water has its minimum volume and maximum density at 4°C.

TRANSMISSION OF HEAT

- There are three ways of heat transmission: 1. Conduction; 2. Convection; 3. Radiation.

Conduction

- In this process, heat is transferred from one place to other place by the successive vibration of the particles of the medium without bodily movement of the particles of the medium.
- Conduction takes place mainly in solids.
- Air is a very bad conductor of heat. The good insulating properties of wool, cotton, etc. are mainly due to the air spaces they contain.

Convection

- In this process, heat is transferred by the actual movement of particles of the medium from one place to other place.
- In liquids and gases heat is transmitted by convection.

Radiation

- In this mode of heat transmission heat is transferred from one place to another without effecting the intervening medium.

HEAT CAPACITY

- The heat capacity of a body is defined as the heat required to raise the temperature of the body by 1K. Its SI unit is J/K.

SPECIFIC HEAT CAPACITY

- The specific heat capacity of a substance is the heat required to raise the temperature of a unit mass of the substance by 1K.
- Its SI unit is J/kg K.
- It is because of its high specific heat capacity that water is used as a cooling liquid in car engine.

LATENT HEAT

- It is defined as the amount of heat absorbed or given out by a body during the change of state.
- Each gram of ice that melts absorbs 336 J of heat.

EVAPORATION

- Water can change into the vapour state either by boiling or by evaporation at lower temperatures.
- When sweat evaporates from the skin it draws much heat from the body and produces a cooling sensation.
- In summer, water is stored in pitchers for cooling. Water oozes out of the pores of the pitchers and cools on evaporation.

- The rate of evaporation increases with increase in temperature.

REFRIGERATOR

- In a refrigerator, cooling is produced by the evaporation of a volatile liquid, freon, inside a copper coil (evaporator), which surrounds the freezer.
- The cooling unit (freezer) in a refrigerator is fitted near the top to cool the whole of the interior.

RELATIVE HUMIDITY

- Relative humidity is defined as the ratio of the mass of water vapour in a given volume of air to the mass required for saturating the same volume of air at the same temperature.
- Relative humidity is measured with an instrument called the hygrometer.

PRESSURE COOKER

- The boiling point of a liquid depends on external pressure.
- When the atmospheric pressure is 76 cm of mercury, water boils at 100°C. But when the pressure is increased, the boiling point of water is raised.
- In a pressure cooker, water boils at temperatures higher than 100°C due to increased pressure. The increased boiling temperature allows water to hold more heat which cooks food faster.
- At higher altitudes, atmospheric pressure is reduced. This lowers the boiling point of water and food takes much longer to cook.

WAVE MOTION

- Wave motion may be defined as the transfer of energy without the net transfer of matter.
- If the particles of the medium vibrate perpendicular to the direction of propagation of wave, the wave is called transverse wave.
- Light waves are transverse waves.
- If the particles of the medium vibrate in the direction of propagation of wave, the wave is called longitudinal wave.
- Sound waves are longitudinal waves.

ELECTROMAGNETIC WAVE

- Electromagnetic waves include an enormous range of frequencies—from radio waves with frequencies less than 10^5 Hz to gamma rays having frequencies greater than 10^{20} Hz.
- All electromagnetic wave have the same speed (3×10^8 m/s) in vacuum. The relation $v = n\lambda$ holds good for all electromagnetic waves.

RADIO AND TELEVISION TRANSMISSION

- Radio waves sent out by radio stations are reflected by the ionosphere and can be received anywhere on the earth.
- At night the radio reception improves because the layers of the ionosphere are not exposed to sunlight and are more settled.
- Radar (Radio detection and ranging) employs high frequency radio waves for detecting objects like ships and aeroplanes.
- In microwave oven, when the waves fall on the food, these are absorbed by water, fats, sugars and certain other molecules whose consequent vibrations produce heat. Since heating occurs inside the food, without warming the surrounding air, the cooking time is greatly reduced.
- In microwave oven, food cannot be cooked in metal vessels because the metal blocks out the microwaves.

LIGHT

- Light is a form of energy which is propagated as electromagnetic waves.
- Light is a transverse wave.
- Speed of light in vacuum is 3×10^8 m/s.
- Light takes 8 minute 16.6 second to reach from sun to earth.

REFLECTION

- When light is incident upon a surface, part of it is reflected. But certain surfaces like mirrors and polished metals reflect almost all the light incident upon them.
- The law of reflection states that the angle of incidence is equal to the angle of reflection.

- To see full image in a plane mirror, a person requires a mirror of at least half of his height.

INCLINED MIRROR (NO. OF IMAGES)

- When an object is placed between two inclined mirrors, several images of the object are formed.

CURVED MIRRORS

- There are two types of curved spherical mirrors—1. Concave Mirror, 2. Convex Mirror.
- Concave mirror can concentrate the sun's radiation falling on it at one point, it can be used as a burning glass.
- Concave mirrors are also used in solar cookers.
- Large concave mirrors are used in reflecting telescopes for observing and photographing distant stars and other heavenly bodies.
- Concave mirror is also used as a shaving or make-up mirror.
- Small concave mirrors are used by dentists for examining teeth.
- Concave parabolic mirrors are used in searchlight and headlamps of cars.
- Convex mirrors are also used as rear view mirrors in vehicles.

REFRACTION

- When a ray of light passes from one medium to other it suffers a change in direction at the boundary of separation of two media. This phenomenon is called refraction.
- When a ray passes from one medium to another optically denser medium, e.g., from air to water or glass, it bends towards the normal. Conversely, a ray passing from water or glass into air is bent away from the normal.
- Rivers appear shallow, coin in a beaker filled with water appears raised, due to refraction.
- Another effect of refraction is the apparent upward bending of the immersed portion of a stick when dipped in water.
- It is due to refraction, produced by the earth's atmosphere, that the sun is visible for several minutes after it has set below the horizon. Thus, atmospheric refraction tends to lengthen the day.
- When the sun (or moon) is near the horizon, it appears elliptical, i.e., with the vertical diameter less than the horizontal diameter. This happens because rays from the lower edge of the sun are bent more than those from the upper edge (Atmospheric Refraction).
- One of the most interesting effects of atmospheric refraction and Mirage is a combined effect of atmospheric refraction and total internal reflection.

DISPERSION

- White light consists of seven colours—violet, indigo, blue, green, yellow, orange and red. These colours are called the spectrum of the white light.
- Violet has the minimum wavelength (or maximum frequency) and red the maximum wavelength (or minimum frequency).
- Due to different speeds, the colours are refracted through different angles and therefore, when a narrow beam of white light passes through a glass prism, it is split up into its constituent colours. This separation of light into colours is called dispersion.

COLOUR OF OBJECTS

- We see objects because of the light they reflect.
- When a rose is viewed in white light, its petals appear red and the leaves appear green, because the petals reflect the red part of the white light and leaves reflect the green part. The remaining colours are absorbed. When the same rose is viewed in green light, the petals will appear black and the leaves green. In blue or yellow light both the petals and leaves will appear black.
- Red, blue and green are primary colours.

LENSES

- There are mainly two types of lenses:
  1. Convex or Converging Lens
  2. Concave or Diverging Lens
- Converging or convex lens is used as a magnifying glass.
- Power of a lens is its capacity to deviate a ray.

Power of a lens is measured as the reciprocal of the focal length.

$$P = \frac{1}{f}$$

- SI unit of power of lens is dioptre (D).
- The power of a converging lens is positive and that of a diverging lens is negative.
- For all positions of the object, the images formed by diverging (concave) lens are virtual, erect and diminished.

EYE

- The light entering the eye is focused by the eye-lens to form an image on the retina.
- In front of the eye, lens is the coloured part of eye, called the iris, which automatically adjusts the size of the pupil to the intensity of light falling on it.
- In bright light the iris automatically shuts tighter, reducing the amount of light entering the pupil. This protects the retina from getting damaged.
- When a person enters a dark room after being in bright light, he is not able to see clearly for a while because the iris is unable to dilate the pupil immediately.
- Least distance of distinct vision is 25 cm.

DEFECTS OF VISION

- A person suffering from long sight (hyper-metropia) can clearly see objects at infinity but cannot see near objects clearly. This defect is caused by the eyeball being too short and can be corrected by wearing converging lenses.
- In the case of a person suffering from short sight (myopia), the eye ball is too long and distant objects are focused in front of the retina. This defect can be corrected by wearing diverging lenses.
- *Astigmatism:* Curvature of cornea becomes irregular and image is not clear. Cylindrical lens is used.

SCATTERING OF LIGHT

- When light falls on atoms and molecules, it is scattered in all directions.
- Scattering of light is maximum for violet colour and minimum for red colour.
- Blue colour of sky is due to scattering of light.
- In the evening, the sun is lower in the sky and its light has to traverse a longer path through the atmosphere to reach an observer. Thus, at sunset, blue, green and other colours having been scattered only red and some orange light reach us and the sun appears a deep orange-red.
- In outerspace, *i.e.,* beyond the atmosphere, there is nothing to scatter the sunlight and therefore the sky appears dark and stars are visible even in the presence of the sun.

INTERFERENCE OF LIGHT

- The superposition of two (or more) waves of the same kind that pass the same point in space at the same time is called interference.
- Beautiful colours seen in soap bubbles and oil films on water are produced due to the interference of white light reflected by these surfaces.
- LASER (Light Amplification by Stimulated Emission of Radiation) is an optical device which produces an intense beam of coherent monochromatic light.
- Examples of Interference of Light: Holography, Laser.

DIFFRACTION OF LIGHT

- When a beam of light passes through a narrow slit or an aperture, it spreads out to a certain extent into the region of geometrical shadow. This is an example of diffraction, *i.e.,* of the failure of light to travel in a straight line.

SOUND

- Sound waves are longitudinal and cannot travel in vacuum. The transmission of sound requires a medium : air, liquid or solid.
- The longitudinal mechanical waves which lie in the frequency range 20 Hz to 20,000 Hz are called audible or sound waves. These waves are sensitive to human ear.

- The longitudinal mechanical waves having frequencies less than 20 Hz are called Infrasonic. These waves are produced by sources of bigger size such as earthquakes, volcanic eruptions, ocean waves etc.
- The longitudinal waves having frequencies greater than 20,000 Hz are called ultrasonic waves. Human ear cannot detect these waves. But some animals such as cats, dogs, bats can detect these waves.

PITCH

- The pitch (shrillness of a sound) depends on its frequency.
- A sound of higher frequency has a higher pitch.
- The pitch of a woman's voice is higher than that of a man.

LOUDNESS

- The relative loudness of a sound is measured in decibels (db).
- All stringed instruments, such as the violin, sitar, guitar, etc. have sound boxes attached to increase the loudness.

SPEED OF SOUND

- The presence of water vapour in the air increases the speed of sound.
- Sound travels faster through warm air than through cold air. The speed of sound is higher on a hot day than on a cold day.
- Thunder is heard much after the flash of lightning is seen because of the wide difference in the speeds of light and sound.

REFLECTION OF SOUND

- When a sound wave is reflected by a distant obstacle, such as a wall or a cliff, an echo is heard.
- To hear echo, the minimum distance between the observer and reflector should be 17 m.
- Exploration of underwater gas and oil is done by detecting the echoes of shock waves produced by explosions on the water surface.
- Bats emit ultrasonic waves of frequencies up to 80,000 Hz and use the reflection of these waves (echoes) to determine the presence and distance of objects on their way and from them respectively.

DOPPLER EFFECT

- The Doppler effect is the change in frequency of a wave (sound or light) due to the motion of the source or observer.
- It is due to the Doppler effect that the whistle of a train appears shriller when it approaches a listener than when it moves away from him.

ELECTRICITY

- Electricity produced by friction between two dissimilar objects is known as static electricity. Depending on the nature of the objects, one acquires a positive charge and the other an equal negative charge. For example, if a glass rod is rubbed with silk, the rod acquires positive charge and the silk an equal negative charge.
- *Lightning* is a gigantic electric discharge occurring between two charged clouds or between a charged cloud and the earth.

CONDUCTOR

- Conductors are those materials which allow electricity (charge) to pass through themselves.
- Metals conduct electricity because they have a large number of conduction or free electrons.

INSULATORS

- Insulators are those materials which do not allow electricity to flow through themselves. Insulators have no free electrons.

SUPER CONDUCTORS

- The resistance of metals to flow of electricity reduces with decreasing temperature. At temperatures near absolute zero, metals have almost zero resistance and became super conductors.

SEMI-CONDUCTORS

- Certain materials, such as silicon and germanium, have electrical resistivity intermediate between those of conductors and insulators. These materials are termed as semi-conductors.

- Semi-conductors are good insulators in their pure crystalline form but their conductivity increases when small amounts of impurities are added to them.

ELECTRIC CURRENT

- Electric current is simply the flow of electric charge. In solid conductors the flow of electrons and in fluids the flow of ions as well as electrons constitute the current.
- SI units of electric current is Ampere (A).

ELECTRICAL RESISTANCE

- When electric current flows through a conductor, e.g., a metallic wire, it offers some obstruction to the current. This obstruction offered by the wire is called its electrical resistance.
- SI unit of Resistance is ohm.

OHM'S LAW

- If physical conditions like temperature, intensity of light etc. remains unchanged then electric current flowing through a conductor is directly proportional to the potential difference across its ends.

ELECTRIC MOTOR

- In an electric motor, electrical energy is converted into mechanical energy.
- Electric fans, mixers, washing machines, etc. work on electric motors.

INVERTER

- An inverter is a device which converts DC to AC. The inverters used in homes and offices are specially designed to:
  1. Convert DC from a battery to AC, and
  2. Charge the battery.

FUSE

- Electric fuse is a protective device used in series with an electric appliance to save it from being damaged due to high current.
- A fuse is a short piece of wire made of a tin-lead alloy, which has a low melting point.
- Fuses are always connected in the live wire in series.

COST OF ELECTRICITY

- The consumption of electrical energy in a house is measured in the unit kWh.
- Kilowatt hour is equal to the energy consumed in the circuit at the rate of 1 kilowatt for 1 hour.

MAGNETISM

- A magnet attracts and holds pieces of iron but does not attract pieces of copper.
- Iron, cobalt, nickel and certain alloys are strongly magnetic whereas copper, wood, glass, etc. are non-magnetic.
- Our earth behaves as a powerful magnet whose south pole is near the geographical north pole and whose north pole is near the geographical south pole.

ATOMIC & NUCLEAR PHYSICS

- Atom consists of three fundamental particles electron, proton and neutron. All the protons and neutrons are present in the central core of atom called nucleus. Electrons revolve around the nucleus.
- The total number of protons in the nucleus is called atomic number (Z).
- The total number of proton and neutrons in the nucleus is called mass number (A).
- Ernest Rutherford, discovered nucleus by the scattering of α-particles from gold foil.

RADIOACTIVITY

- Henry Bacquerel (1896) observed that a photographic plate blackened, when placed near double sulphate of potassium and uranium. He further observed that uranium emitted special kind of rays. They were called Becqueral rays.
- Pierre and Marie Curie observed that the radiation from pitchblende was four times stronger than uranium. In 1898, they finally discovered two new substances—Polonium and Radium. These newly discovered substances were called radioactive substances and this property of these substances was named radioactivity.
- No radioactive substance emits both α and β particles simultaneously.

X-RAYS

- X-rays are electromagnetic radiations having wavelength from a fraction of an Angestrom to about 100Å. They were discovered by Rontgen during his studies on the electrical discharge phenomena in gases—he found that an unknown radiation was produced when electrons collided with the walls of the tubes.

ATOMIC ENERGY

- India today ranks sixth in the atomic energy programmes. It has developed the required know-how and expertise to manufacture nuclear weapons, but it believes in the peaceful uses of atomic power. The Atomic Energy Commission was set-up in the country in 1948 under the Chairmanship of Dr. H. J. Bhabha.
- ***Bhabha Atomic Research Centre (BARC):*** The Bhabha Atomic Research Centre at Trombay near Mumbai (Maharashtra) has four research reactors: (*i*) APSARA—It is the first atomic reactor in Asia; (*ii*) CIRUS—It is a joint Indo-Canadian project; (*iii*) PURNIMA II—a zero energy fast reactor, and (*iv*) DHRUVA—a high power completely indigenous nuclear research reactor with most advanced laboratories in the world. Another fast breeder reactor KAMINI at Kalpakkam has been constructed. Today India is the seventh country in the world and the first developing nation to have mastered the fast breeder reactor technology.
- **Nuclear Power:** Under Nuclear Power Corporation of India Limited (NPCIL) there are seven nuclear power stations in operation in six States: (*i*) Tarapur—Maharashtra, (*ii*) Rawatbhata—Rajasthan, (*iii*) Kalpakkam—Tamil Nadu, (*iv*) Narora—U.P., (*v*) Kakrapara—Gujarat, (*vi*) Kaiga—Karnataka and (*vii*) Kudankulam—Tamil Nadu.
- **Heavy Water:** Heavy water is one of the essential input for Pressurised Heavy Water Reactors (PHWRs) used both as a coolant and moderator. The first heavy water plant was set-up in 1962 in Nangal. Subsequently 7 more plants have been set-up at (*i*) Baroda, (*ii*) Tuticorin, (*iii*) Kota, (*iv*) Talcher, (*v*) Thal, (*vi*) Hazira and (*vii*) Manuguru.
- **Research and Development Centres:** Four research centres namely (*i*) Bhabha Atomic Research Centre, Trombay (Maharashtra), (*ii*) Indira Gandhi Centre for Atomic Research, Kalpakkam (Tamil Nadu), (*iii*) Centre for Advanced Technology, Indore (Madhya Pradesh), (*iv*) Variable Energy Cyclotron Centre at Kolkata (West Bengal) are focal points of research and development work in nuclear energy and related discipline.
- **India's Nuclear Explosions:** On May 18, 1974 India conducted her first underground nuclear explosion at Pokhran (Rajasthan) in the Thar desert, 20 km. away from Jaisalmer, at a depth of more than 100 metres. The successful explosion made India the sixth nuclear nation in the world.
- India conducted 5 nuclear explosion tests at Pokhran in two phases on May 11 and May 13, 1998 and became a nuclear power state.

IMPORTANT INVENTIONS

Name of Invention	*Inventor*	*Nationality*	*Year*
Aeroplane	Orville & Wilbur Wright	U.S.A.	1903
Ball-Point Pen	John J. Loud	U.S.A.	1888
Barometer	Evangelista Torricelli	Italy	1644
Bicycle	Kirkpatrick Macmillan	Britain	1839-40
Bifocal Lens	Benjamin Franklin	U.S.A.	1780
Car (Petrol)	Karl Benz	Germany	1888
Celluloid	Alexander Parkes	Britain	1861
Cinema	Nicolas & Jean Lumiere	France	1895

Name of Invention	*Inventor*	*Nationality*	*Year*
Clock (mechanical)	I-Hsing & Liang Ling-Tsan	China	1725
Diesel Engine	Rudolf Diesel	Germany	1895
Dynamo	Hypolite Pixii	France	1832
Electric Lamp	Thomas Alva Edison	U.S.A.	1879
Electric Motor (DC)	Zenobe Gramme	Belgium	1873
Electric Motor (AC)	Nikola Tesla	U.S.A.	1888
Electro-magnet	William Sturgeon	Britain	1824
Electronic Computer	Dr. Alan M. Turing	Britain	1943
Film (moving outlines)	Louis Prince	France	1885
Film (musical sound)	Dr. Le de Forest	U.S.A.	1923
Fountain Pen	Lewis E. Waterman	U.S.A.	1884
Gramophone	Thomas Alva Edison	U.S.A.	1878
Helicopter	Etienne Oehmichen	France	1924
Jet Engine	Sir Frank Whittle	Britain	1937
Laser	Charles H. Townes	U.S.A.	1960
Lift (Mechanical)	Elisha G. Otis	U.S.A.	1852
Locomotive	Richard Trevithick	Britain	1804
Machine Gun	James Puckle	Britain	1718
Microphone	Alexander Graham Bell	U.S.A.	1876
Microscope	Z. Janssen	Netherlands	1590
Motor Cycle	G. Daimler	Germany	1885
Photography (on film)	John Carbutt	U.S.A.	1888
Printing Press	Johann Gutenberg	Germany	c.1455
Razor (safety)	King C. Gillette	U.S.A.	1895
Refrigerator	James Harrison & Alexander Catlin	U.S.A.	1850
Safety Pin	Walter Hunt	U.S.A.	1849
Sewing machine	Barthelemy Thimmonnier	France	1829
Ship (steam)	J.C. Perier	France	1775
Ship (turbine)	Hon. Sir C. Parsons	Britain	1894
Skyscraper	W. Le Baron Jenny	U.S.A.	1882
Slide Rule	William Oughtred	Britain	1621
Steam Engine (condenser)	James Watt	Britain	1765
Steel Production	Henry Bessemer	Britain	1855
Steel (stainless)	Harry Brearley	Britain	1913
Submarine	David Bushnell	U.S.A.	1776
Tank	Sir Ernest Swinton	Britain	1914
Telegraph	M. Lammond	France	1787
Telegraph Code	Samuel F.B. Morse	U.S.A.	1837
Telephone (perfected)	Alexander Graham Bell	U.S.A.	1876
Television (mechanical)	John Logie Baird	Britain	1926
Television (electronic)	P.T. Farnsworth	U.S.A.	1927
Thermometer	Galileo Galilei	Italy	1593
Transformer	Michael Faraday	Britain	1831
Transistor	Bardeen, Shockley & Brattain	U.S.A.	1948
Washing Machine (elec.)	Hurley Machine Co.	U.S.A.	1907
Zip-Fastener	W.L. Judson	U.S.A.	1891

Important Discoveries

Discovery	Discoverer	Nationality	Year
Aluminium	Hans Christian Oerstedt	Denmark	1827
Atomic number	Henry Moseley	England	1913
Atomic structure of matter	John Dalton	England	1803
Chlorine	C.W. Scheele	Sweden	1774
Electromagnetic induction	Michael Faraday	England	1831
Electromagnetic waves	Heinrich Hertz	Germany	1886
Electromagnetism	Hans Christian Oersted	Denmark	1920
Electron	Sir Joseph Thomson	England	1897
General theory of relativity	Albert Einstein	Switzerland	1915
Hydrogen	Henry Cavendish	England	1766
Law of electric conduction	Georg Ohm	Germany	1827
Law of electromagnetism	Andre Ampere	France	1826
Law of falling bodies	Galileo	Italy	1590
Laws of gravitation & motion	Isaac Newton	England	1687
Laws of planetary motion	Johannes Kepler	Germany	1609-10
Magnesium	Sir Humphry Davy	England	1808
Neptune (Planet)	Johann Galle	Germany	1846
Neutron	James Chadwick	England	1932
Nickel	Axel Cronstedt	Sweden	1751
Nitrogen	Daniel Rutherford	England	1772
Oxygen	Joseph Priestly, C.W. Scheele	England, Sweden	1772
Ozone	Christian Schonbein	Germany	1839
Pluto	Clyde Tombaugh	U.S.A	1930
Plutonium	G.T. Seaborg	U.S.A	1940
Proton	Ernest Rutherford	England	1919
Quantum Theory	Max Planck	Germany	1900
Radioactivity	Antoine Bacquerel	France	1896
Radium	Pierre & Marie Curie	France	1898
Silicon	Jons Berzelius	Sweden	1824
Special theory of relativity	Albert Einstein	Switzerland	1905
Sun as centre of solar system	Copernicus	Poland	1543
Uranium	Martin Klaproth	Germany	1789
Uranus (Planet)	William Herschel	England	1781
X-rays	Wilhelm Roentgen	Germany	1895

Scientific Instruments

Name of Instrument	*Used for*
Altimeter	measuring altitude
Ammeter	measuring strength of an electric current
Anemometer	measuring the velocity of wind
Audiometer	measuring level of hearing
Barometer	measuring atmospheric pressure
Callipers	measuring the internal and external diameters of tubes
Calorimeter	measuring quantity of heat
Compass	finding out direction
Dynamo	converting mechanical energy into electrical energy
Galvanometer	detecting and determining the strength of small electric currents
Hydrometer	measuring specific gravity of a liquid
Hygrometer	measuring the humidity in the atmosphere
Lactometer	measuring the purity of milk
Manometer	measuring the gaseous pressure
Micrometer	measuring minute distances, angles, etc.
Microscope	seeing magnified view of very small objects
Photometer	measuring intensity of light from distant stars
Pyrometer	measuring high temperatures
Radar	detecting and finding the presence and location of moving objects like aircraft, missile, etc.
Radiometer	measuring the emission of radiant energy
Rain Gauge	measuring the amount of rainfall
Seismograph	measuring and recording the intensity and origin of earthquake shocks
Sextant	measuring altitude and angular distances between two objects or heavenly bodies
Spectrometer	measuring the refractive indices
Spherometer	measuring the curvature of spherical objects/surface
Sphygmomanometer	measuring blood pressure
Stethoscope	ascertaining the condition of heart and lungs by listening to their function
Stroboscope	viewing objects that are moving rapidly with a periodic motion as if they were at rest
Tachometer	measuring the rate of revolution or angular speed of a revolving shaft
Telescope	viewing magnified images of distant objects
Thermocouple	measuring the temperature inside furnaces and jet engines
Thermometer	measuring human body temperature
Thermostat	regulating constant temperature
Ultrasonoscope	measuring utrasonic sounds
Viscometer	measuring the viscosity of a fluid
Voltmeter	measuring potential difference between two points.

CHEMISTRY

ELEMENTS

- An element may be defined as a substance which is made by same type of atoms and it can neither be broken into, nor built from two or more simpler substances by any known physical or chemical methods, e.g., copper, silver, hydrogen, carbon, oxygen, nitrogen, gold, iron etc.

COMPOUNDS

- A compound may be defined as a substance which contains two or more elements combined in some fixed proportion by weight and which can be decomposed into two or more elements by any suitable method.
- The properties of a compound are entirely different from those of the elements from which it is made.
- Some common examples of compounds are water, sugar, salt, aspirin, chloroform, alcohol and ether.

MIXTURES

- A material containing two or more elements or compounds in any proportion is a mixture.
- The components of a mixture can be separated by physical means like filtration, sublimation and distillation.

ATOMIC STRUCTURE

ATOM

- Atom is the smallest part of the element that takes part in a chemical reaction. Atom of an element can not be changed into that of another element by a chemical or physical means. It does not exist in free state.

MOLECULE

- A molecule is the smallest part of an element or compound that is capable of existing independently.

ATOMIC WEIGHT (OR ATOMIC MASS)

- The atomic mass of an element is the number of times its atom is heavier than 1/12th of the mass of carbon (C^{12}) atom.
- The unit used to measure atomic mass is called atomic mass unit, *i.e.,* amu.

ELECTRON

- The electron is a fundamental particle of an atom which carries a unit negative charge. It was discovered by J.J. Thomson in 1897.

PROTON

- It is a fundamental particle of an atom carrying a unit positive charge. It was discovered by Rutherford and Goldstein in 1886.

NEUTRON

- It is a fundamental particle of an atom carrying no charge. It was discovered by Chadwick in 1932.

ISOTOPES

- The atoms of the same element having different mass numbers are called isotopes.

ISOBARS

- Elements having the same atomic mass but differ in atomic number are called isobars.

ISOTONES

- Elements having the same number of neutrons are called isotones.

OXIDATION AND REDUCTION

- Oxidation is a process in which a substance adds on oxygen or loses hydrogen. In modern terms, oxidation is the process in which a substance loses electrons.
- Reduction is a process in which a substance adds on hydrogen or loses oxygen. In modern terms, reduction is the process in which a substance gains electrons.
- Oxidation and reduction always occur simultaneously. If one substance is oxidised, another is reduced. The reaction in which this oxidation-reduction process occurs is called a redox reaction.

- Oxidising agents are substances which bring about the oxidation of other substances, e.g., Potassium Permanganate, Potassium Dichromate, Nitric Acid, Hydrogen Peroxide, etc.
- Reducing agents are substances which bring about the reduction of other substances, e.g., hydrogen sulphide, hydrogen, carbon, sulphur dioxide, etc.

ACIDS, BASES AND SALTS

ACID

- An acid is any compound that can react with a base to form a salt, the hydrogen of the acid being replaced by positive metallic ion. According to modern theory, an acid is a compound which yields hydrogen ions (protons) to a base in a chemical reaction. In a water solution, an acid tastes sour, turns blue litmus red and produces free hydrogen ions.

Acid	Sources
Citric Acid	Lemons or Oranges (Citrus Fruits)
Lactic acid	Sour milk
Tartaric acid	Grapes
Acetic acid	Vinegar
Maleic acid	Apples
Oxalic acid	Tomato
Formic acid	Red ants

BASES

- Such compounds which gives salt and water with acid known as bases. Bitter in taste, turns red litmus paper into blue, contains replaceable hydroxyl group.
- Some important bases are sodium hydroxide, potassium hydroxide, sodium carbonate and ammonium hydroxide.
- All alkalies are bases but all bases are not alkalies because all bases are not soluble in water.

SALTS

- Salts are ionic compounds containing a positive ion (cation) and a negative ion (anion).
- When an acid reacts with a base, a salt and water are formed. This reaction is called neutralization since the acid and base neutralize each other's effect.

ELECTROLYSIS

- The process of decomposition of an electrolyte by the passage of an electric current through its molten state or its aqueous solution is called electrolysis.
- Device through which electric current is passed known as electrodes.

METALLURGY

- Metals occur in nature, in the native (in free state) as well as in the combined state.
- Naturally occurring materials containing metals are called minerals.
- A mineral from which a given metal is obtained economically is called an ore.
- The process of extraction of a metal in a pure state on a large scale from its ore by Physical and Chemical means is called metallurgy.
- The rocky and siliceous matter that associated with the ore is known as gangue.
- Substance that is added to ore to remove the gangue is known as flux.
- The process of removal of gangue from the ore is known as concentration.
- Calcination is the heating of the ore in the absence of air. This method is employed for obtaining the metal oxides from carbonates and hydroxides.
- Roasting is the heating of the ore in the presence of air. On roasting, part of the ore is oxidised to form an oxide. This oxide is then reduced to the metal.
- The industrial reduction process for obtaining metal from the treated ore is called smelting.

AMALGUM

- An alloy in which one of the component metals is mercury is known as amalgum.

IRON AND STEEL

- Iron is extracted from its ores by the blast furnace process.

- Iron obtained from blast furnace is called pig iron or cast iron containing about 5% carbon.
- Pure iron is called wrought iron which does not contain carbon more than 0.2%, or any other impurities or constituents.
- Steel contains 0.25% – 2% carbon and varying amounts of other elements.

CARBON AND ITS COMPOUNDS

ALLOTROPY

- Such substances which having the same chemical properties, but differ in physical properties, known as allotropes and this property is called allotropy.

DIAMOND

- Diamond is the purest form of carbon.
- It is non-conductor of heat and electricity.
- It is the hardest natural substance.
- It burns in air at 900°C and gives out CO_2.

GRAPHITE (BLACK LEAD)

- It is good conductor of heat and electricity.
- Graphite is used in making lead pencils.
- Graphite is also used as electrodes, lubricant, moderators, electrotyping and carbon arc.

AMORPHOUS FORMS OF CARBON

1. Wood Charcoal – Obtained from wood
2. Sugar Charcoal – Obtained from cane sugar
3. Bone or Animal Charcoal – Obtained from animal bones
4. Coke Charcoal – Obtained from coal

CARBON MONOXIDE (CO)

- Carbon monoxide is an active poison and is very dangerous as it is a colourless and odourless gas and can not, therefore, be easily detected.
- The extremely poisonous nature of carbon monoxide is a result of its combining with the haemoglobin of the blood to form carboxyhaemoglobin, which is not decompassed by any of the processes in the body.

HYDROCARBONS

- Compounds of carbon and hydrogen are called hydrocarbon.
- A natural source of hydrocarbon is petroleum obtained from sedimentary rocks.
- Compounds having the same molecular formula but differ in properties due to different structural formula known as isomers and this property is called isomerism.

SATURATED HYDROCARBONS (ALKANES)

- Containing single covalent bonds only.
- Such compounds are, in general, called alkanes for instance, Methane, Ethane, Propane, Butane.

UNSATURATED HYDROCARBONS

- Containing multiple bonds.
- Compounds with double bonds are called alkenes, e.g. ethylene, propyene etc. and triple bond containing compounds are called alkynes, e.g. acetylene, propyne etc.
- Benzene is an unsaturated cyclic hydrocarbon with the structure.
- Compounds derived from benzene are called aromatic compounds.

FUELS

Solid Fuels

- These contain carbon and, during combustion, form mainly carbon dioxide and carbon monoxide with a large amount of heat.
- Examples of solid fuels are wood, coal, coke and paraffin wax.

Liquid Fuels

- These are basically mixtures of several hydrocarbons. During combustion, they form carbon dioxide and water.
- Liquid fuels are obtained as different fractions during the distillation of petroleum.
- Examples of liquid fuels are kerosene oil, petrol, diesel oil and alcohol.

Gaseous Fuels

- Gaseous fuels do not leave ash on burning and have high content of heat.
- The main gaseous fuels are liquefied petroleum gas (LPG, mainly a mixture of propane and

butane and used in homes for cooking, water gas ($CO + H_2$), producer gas ($CO + N_2$), coal gas (mixture of hydrogen, methane, ethylene, carbon monoxide, nitrogen, oxygen and carbon dioxide) and natural gas (mixture of methane, ethane, propane and butane with traces of higher hydrocarbons obtained from oil well, above petroleum).

PETROLEUM AND NATURAL GAS

- Natural gas contains about 80% methane and 10% ethane, the remaining 10% being a mixture of higher gaseous hydrocarbons.
- Compressed Natural Gas (CNG) is natural gas filled in cylinders under high pressure.
- The quality of petrol for use in car engines is denoted by their anti-knock properties.
- To increase octane number, tetra ethyl lead (TEL) is added to petrol.

HEAVY WATER

- Chemically heavy water is deuterium oxide.
- Heavy water is used in nuclear reactors as a moderator because it slows the fast moving neutrons.

Hard and Soft Water

- Water which produces lather with soap solution readily is called soft water.
- Water which does not produce lather with soap solution readily is called hard water.
- The hardness of water is due to presence of the bicarbonates, chlorides and sulphates of calcium and magnesium.
- Temporary hardness of water is due to the presence of bicarbonates of calcium and magnesium.
- Permanent hardness of water is due to presence of sulphates, chlorides, nitrates of calcium and magnesium.

GLASS

- Ordinary glass is solid mixture of silica, sodium silicate and calcium silicate.
- Soft glass is a soda-lime silicate glass. It melts at low temperature. It is used in manufacturing of bottles, test tubes etc.
- Hard glass is potash lime silicate and melts at high temperature in comparison to soft glass and is used in manufacturing of flask etc.
- Flint glass is a lead potash silicate and is used in manufacturing of prism, lens and optical instruments.
- Pyrex glass is a mixture of sodium aluminium borosilicates. It is used in manufacturing of high quality equipments in laboratory because it does not melt at very high temperature.
- Safety glass is prepared by placing a layer of transparent plastic glass between two layers of glass by means of a suitable adhesive. It is used in making wind screen of automobiles, aeroplanes, trains etc.

CEMENT

- The approximate composition of Portland cement is:
  1. Calcium Oxide → 62%
  2. Silica → 22%
  3. Alumina → 7.5%
  4. Magnesia → 2.5%
  5. Ferric Oxide → 2.5%
- A small amount of gypsum is added to slow down the setting of cement.
- Cement containing excess amount of lime cracks during setting while cement containing less amount of lime is weak in strength.
- Cement containing no iron is white but hard to burn.

POLYMERS AND PLASTICS

- A polymer is a large molecule, built up from many hundreds of thousands of small unit called monomeric units or monomers.
- The process of formation of polymers from monomers is called polymerization.
- Plastics are cross-linked polymers and very tough.
- Some examples of plastics are — Celluloid, Bakelite and Vinyl Plastics.

RUBBER

- Natural and Synthetic rubbers are examples of polymers.
- Natural rubber is isomer of isoprene.

- When the natural rubber is heated along with sulphur called vulcanisation. The resulting rubber is elastic, hard and strong.
- Synthetic rubbers are made by polymerisation of chloroprene, styrene and butadiene mixtures and isobutylene.

SOAPS

- The soaps are sodium salts of higher fatty acids. They are useful only in soft water as they form an insoluble precipitate in hard water. This precipitate consists of salts of calcium and magnesium of higher fatty acids. No lather or emulsion is formed and washing is not possible.

Some Importants Alloys

Alloys	*Composition*
Brass	Cu, Zn
Bronze	Cu, Sn
Gun metal	Cu, Sn, Zn
Bel metal	Cu, Sn
German silver	Cu, Zn, Ni
Dutch metal	Cu, Zn
Aluminium	Al, Cu
Nichrome	Ni, Fe, Cr, Mn
Chromium steel	Cr, C, Fe

Chemical Formulae, Commercial Name of Chemical Compounds

Commercial Name	Chemical Compounds	Chemical formulae
Common salt	Sodium chloride	$NaCl$
Baking soda	Sodium bicarbonate	$NaHCO_3$
Washing soda	Sodium carbonate	$Na_2CO_3 . 10H_2O$
Caustic soda	Sodium hydroxide	$NaOH$
Chilli salt peter	Sodium nitrate	$NaNO_3$
Soda ash	Sodium carbonate	Na_2CO_3
Hypo	Sodium thiosulphate	$Na_2S_2O_3 . 5H_2O$

BIOLOGY

BRANCHES OF BIOLOGY

(*a*) **Anthropology:** Deals with the scientific study of man and the mankind.

(*b*) **Agronomy:** Deals with the management of farms and science of crop production.

(*c*) **Apiculture:** Deals with the process of bee keeping for commercial purposes.

(*d*) **Entomology:** Deals with the structure, habits and classification of insects.

(*e*) **Eugenics:** Deals with improving the human race.

(*f*) **Pathology:** Deals with the nature of disease, their causes, symptoms, effects, their cure and control.

(*g*) **Physiotherapy:** Deals with the treatment of diseases, body weakness or defects with the help of massage and exercise etc.

(*h*) **Sericulture:** Deals with the production of raw silk from silkworm.

(*i*) **Pharmacology:** Deals with the knowledge and manufacture of drugs.

(*j*) **Occupational therapy:** Deals with treating the physically handicapped or injured persons through exercise etc.

(*k*) **Psychology:** Deals with the study of human mind, its behaviour and mental qualities.

(*l*) **DNA finger printing:** Technique to help identify a person on the basis of genes.

ANIMALS/PLANTS

- The organisms that closely resemble one another

are placed in one group, the groups which have similarities are combined together into larger groups, and these into still larger ones. The most inclusive category is kingdom. Other major categories, in descending order are: phylum, class, order, family, genus, and species. Man belongs to Animal kingdom, chordata division or phylum, Mammalia class, Primates order, Hominidae family, Homo genus and Sapiens species.

CELL THEORY

- Cell is the basic unit of structure of all living organisms. According to the cell theory, all organism are composed of cells and cell products and growth and development results from the division and differentiation of cells.
- Cells membrane surrounds all living cells.
- Nucleus is the most important cell organelle which controls and coordinates all cell activities and also concerned with the transmission of heredity characters.
- Mitochondria, ribosomes, lysosomes and dictyosomes are present in plant and animal cells.
- Only plant cells have cell wall, chloroplast and vacuole.
- Viruses constitute a difficulty since in many ways they are intermediate between living and dead matter.
- The cell is said to be made up of a substance called Protoplasm which has two main constituents cytoplasm and nucleus, and is bounded by a cell membrane on outside.
- Cells take up the raw materials for metabolism through the cell membrane from extracellular fluid surrounding them.
- Cytoplasm inside is responsible for maintaining the internal distribution of organelles and also for free cell movements.
- Mitochondria inside provides energy for reactions inside the cell. Ribosomes are responsible for the synthesis of proteins.
- The Endoplasmic Reticulum helps in addition of other sugar units to proteins and their transportation to other parts of the cell.

FOOD

- It is a nutritive substance taken by an organism for growth, work, repair and maintaining life processes. It provides energy to do work and maintain body heat, provides materials for the growth of the body, makes necessary materials for reproduction and provides materials for the repair of damaged cells and tissues of our body.
- **Carbohydrates:** For a normal person, 400 to 500 gms of carbohydrates are required daily but for sportspersons, growing children and nursing mothers, it is on higher side.
- **Proteins:** They are complex organic compounds made up of carbon, hydrogen, oxygen and nitrogen. The building blocks of Protein are Amino acids and there are large number of amino acids.
- Proteins are essential for the growth of children and teenagers, and for maintenance and making good the wear and tear of the body tissues in adults.
- An adult needs about 1 gm of protein per kg of body weight.
- **Fats:** They are esters of long chain fatty acids and an alcohol called glycerol. Fats also contain atoms of carbon, hydrogen and oxygen.
- The main function of fats in the body is to provide a steady source of energy and for this purpose, they are deposited within the body.
- One gm of fat gives 37 kilojoules of energy which is more than double of that given by carbohydrates.
- Fats, the richest source of energy to our body, can be stored in the body for subsequent use. Fats, soluble in organic solvents and insoluble in water, also supply fat-soluble vitamins to our body.
- **Minerals:** Some of the important minerals needed by our body are — iron, iodine, calcium, phosphorus, sodium, potassium, zinc, copper, magnesium, chloride, fluoride and sulphur.
- We get most of the minerals in combined form from plant sources. Deficiency of these minerals causes many diseases.
- **Energy Requirements:** The energy requirement of a body varies according to age, sex, lifestyle, occupation, climate and special situations like pregnancy and lactation.

Age	Energy requirements
5 years	6000 kJ per day
11 years	9000 kJ per day
18 years	11000 kJ per day
Adult (normal work)	9600 kJ per day
Adult (heavy work)	12000 kJ per day
Adult (very heavy work)	16000 kJ per day

- **Vitamins:** They act as catalysts in certain chemical reactions of metabolism in our body.
- They don't provide energy to our body nor form body tissues.
- More than 15 types of vitamins are known and only 2 vitamins — D and K can be formed in our body.

Vitamin	Necessity	Source
Vitamin A	For maintaining healthy eyesight, normal skin and hair	Cod liver oil, fish, eggs, milk, carrot, leafy vegetables.
Vitamin B_1	For growth, carbohydrate metabolism, functioning of heart, nerves and muscles.	Milk, soya-food, meat, whole cereals, green vegetables.
Vitamin C	For keeping teeth, gums and joints healthy, for increasing resistance of body to infection	Citrus fruits, guava, tomatoes.
Vitamin D	For normal growth of bones and teeth	Milk, eggs, butter, cod liver oil, sun light.
Vitamin E	For normal reproduction, functioning of muscles and protection of liver	Green leafy vegetables, milk, butter, tomato.
Vitamin K	For normal clotting of blood and normal functioning of liver	Green leafy vegetables, soyabean, tomato.

- **Roughage:** Though it does not provide any energy to the body, yet keeps the digestive system in order, by helping in retaining water in the body and preserving constitution.
- The main source of roughage are salads, cabbage, corn cob, porridge, vegetables and fruits with stems.

DISEASES

COMMUNICABLE DISEASES

- They are the diseases which can be transmitted from reservoirs of infection or infected person to the healthy but susceptible persons.
- The disease causing agent or the pathogen can be transmitted directly or indirectly.

DEFICIENCY DISEASES

- These occur due to deficiency of some nutrients in the diet or some hormone due to hypo activity or damage to endocrine glands.

Diet Deficiency	Disease
Protein	Kwashiorkor
Protein-energy malnutrition	Marasmus
Vitamin A	Night-blindness, Xerophthalmia
Vitamin B_1	Beri-Beri
Vitamin B_2	Cheilosis
Vitamin B_5	Pellagra
Vitamin C	Scurvy
Vitamin D	Rickets (in children), (in adult) Osteomalacia
Vitamin K	Hypothrombinemia
Iron	Anaemia
Iodine	Goitre
Fluoride	Dental caries
Calcium and phosphorus	Affects formation of bones and teeth

Hormone Deficiency	Disease
Insulin	Diabetes
Thyroxine	Cretinism (child), Goitre
STH	Dwarfism, Gigantism

ALLERGIC DISEASE

- In these diseases, body becomes hypersensitive to some foreign agents, allergens, which cause inflammation when come in contact with the body or enter inside the body.

- Foreign agents can be dust, pollens, certain-foods, serum, certain drugs or fabrics.
- The unfavourable response of the body to allergens is called allergic reaction. Asthma and hay fever are allergic diseases.

BACTERIAL DISEASES

- Bacteria are minute organisms which are known to cause a number of diseases:

Disease	Incubation period	Spread through
Tuberculosis	2-10 weeks	Air-borne,droplet infection
Diptheria	2-6 days	Air-borne droplet infection
Cholera	6 hours to 2-3 days	Contaminated food and water. House flies are the vectors
Leprosy	Upto 5 years	Prolonged and intimate contact
Whopping cough	7-14 days	Droplet infection
Tetanus	3-21 days	Entry of cysts through any wound made by sharp object, dog bite or fall on the road
Typhoid	1-3 weeks	Directed and Contact
Plague	2-6 days	Rats and bed-bugs transmit the germs
Pneumonia	1-3 days	Air-borne

VIRAL DISEASES

Disease	Incubation period	Spread through
Chicken-pox	12-20 days	Direct contact with infected persons or infected objects
Smallpox	12 days	Droplet infection
Poliomyalitis	7-14 days	Direct and oral
Measles	10 days	Droplet infection
Mumps	12-26 days	Droplet infection
Rabies	1-3 months	Bite of rabied animal like dogs, monkeys, cats
Influenza	24-28 hours	Air-borne

DISEASES CAUSED BY PROTOZOA

- Amoebiasis (Amoebic dysentery), Malaria, Kala-azar, Trypanosomiasis and Giardiasis are main diseases caused by Protozoans.
- Malaria is a parasitic infection.

SYSTEM OF HUMAN BODY

DIGESTIVE SYSTEM

- The digestive system consists of alimentary canal and digestive glands. Alimentary canal is about 8-10 meters long tube of varying diameter. Food is taken in through mouth.
- The tongue helps in ingestion, chewing, tasting and swallowing of food and mixing of food and saliva.
- Salivary glands secret saliva which helps in digestion of starch. Gastric glands present in the mucosa of the stomach, provide acidic medium for the food digestion.
- Liver, the largest sized, reddish brown gland of body, secrets bile. Liver is present in the right upper part of the abdomen. The bile secreted by the liver is stored in gall bladder. It helps in the emulsification and digestion of fats.
- Pancreas is the second largest gland in human body and secretes pancreatic juices. Intestine also secret juices.

RESPIRATORY SYSTEM

- Oxygen is needed for the oxidation and expelling of carbon dioxide is necessary to avoid its-accumulation. This process of exchange of gases between the environment and the body, is called respiration.
- In some unicellular organisms like aerobic bacteria, amoeba, hydra, etc. there is direct exchange of gases between the carbon dioxide of the body and oxygen of water.
- There is no blood for transport of gases. However, in larger and complex form of animals, specialised respiratory organs are developed.
- Amphibians respire through skin, fishes through gills and mammals, birds and reptiles through lungs.
- A normal adult inspires or expires about 500 ml of gas with each breath and about 72 breathes per minutes.

CIRCULATORY SYSTEM

- Main components of the circulatory system are heart, blood vessels and blood.

- Heart is a thick, muscular, contractile and automatic pumping organ. In birds and mammals, heart is divided into four chambers.
- Arteries are thick walled blood vessels which always carry the blood away from the heart to various body parts.
- Veins are thin walled blood vessels which always carry the blood from various parts generally to the heart.
- In an adult healthy person, the normal rate of heart beat at rest is about 70-72 times per minute.

BLOOD

- It is red, opaque, somewhat sticky and viscous fluid in the body of animals.
- It is slightly alkaline (pH = 7.4), heavier than water (sp gr = 1.05) and five times more viscous than distilled water.
- Blood forms 6 to 10% of the body weight.
- An adult, on average, has about 6.8 litres of blood.
- Blood contains plasma and blood corpuscles with the former occupying 55-60% of the volume.
- Plasma transports food components, metabolic wastes and hormones; keeps constant level of pH of blood, maintains body temperature and helps in blood clotting.
- Erythrocytes or red blood corpuscles (RBCs), leukocytes or white blood corpuscles (WBCs) and blood platelets are other parts of the blood.
- Due to the presence of iron containing pigment haemoglobin, RBCs are red in colour. The RBCs are crucial for ex-change of oxygen and carbon dioxide. WBCs are nucleated and non-pigmented cells. They are larger in size than RBCs but far less in number (1 : 600).
- WBCs play an important role in immune system of the body. Blood platelets cause the coagulation of blood and clot formation to prevent excessive bleeding.
- Human blood is divided into four main Groups— A, B, AB and O.
- The plasma of Group A blood contains an anti-B factor and vice-versa, so that people of Groups A and B cannot accept each other's blood.
- Group AB contains neither anti-A nor anti-B factor and people with this group can receive transfusions from both but can give to neither.
- Group O contains both anti-A and anti-B and can receive blood only from Group O but can donate blood to all Groups. Group O is called universal donor because they can donate to all the Groups.
- Group AB is called universal acceptor because they can accept blood from all Groups.

SKELETON SYSTEM

- The frame or the hard structure of the human body is composed from the bones and the organs of making such frame are called skeleton system.

Bones

- Bone is the hardest tissue of the body and form the largest section of the body weight.
- Bones contain organic as well as inorganic matters. With advancing age, the inorganic matter's share increases, causing the bones to become more brittle.
- Long bones such as humerus and femur are hollow while small bones are solid.

EXCRETORY SYSTEM

- In men, excretory system is formed of one pair of kidneys, one pair of ureters, a urinary bladder and a urethra. Kidney is about 10 cm long, bean shaped, dark-red and slightly flattened structure.
- Sweet glands, oil glands, lungs and liver also act as additional excretory organ.
- In case of kidney failure, a man can treated by hemodialysis or transplantation of a kidney from a donor's body.

NERVOUS SYSTEM

- The system which controls and coordinates the body functions, retains memory and receives and sends signals, is called the nervous system.
- The nervous system comprises brain, spinal cord, nerves and nerve fibres.
- Human brain weighs about 1200 to 1400 gm. Main parts of the brain are cerebrum, cerebellum and medulla oblongata.

- Cerebrum controls voluntary function and is site of intelligence, will power, emotions, etc.
- Cerebellum controls involuntary functions like heart beat, respiration, etc.
- Spinal cord is about 45 cm long and about 35 gm in weight. It conducts impulses to and from the brain and controls reflex actions of the body.
- Various cranial (arising from ending into brain) and spinal nerves (arising from spinal cord) control smell, vision, movements of body parts, taste and hearing.

REPRODUCTION SYSTEM

- In this type of reproduction, there is formation and fusion of sex cells, called gametes.
- Organism develops from the zygote through embryo formation.
- It generally involves two parents — male and female.
- The offsprings are different from the parent as variations appear due to new combinations of genes. So, it plays an important role in evolution.
- All higher plants and animals reproduce sexually.

CHROMOSOMES

- Plants and animals have fixed number of chromosomes per cell.
- Genes are located on chromosomes and are responsible for transfer of characteristics from one cell to the next either in the same organism or from parents to offspring.
- Man has 23 pairs of chromosomes, of which one pair is sex chromosomes.
- Males child inherits X chromosomes from the female parent and Y from the male parent.
- Female child receives a X chromosome each from either of its parents.
- Mendel was the first scientist to explain transmission of units from reproductive cells of the parents to the off-springs.

CLONING

- It is the process of producing genetically identical copies of a biological material, starting from a single cell. The original genes are transplanted and thus one can produce organisms of known and desirable characteristics.

GENETIC ENGINEERING

- It is the method of artificial synthesis of new genes and their subsequent transplantation or methods of correcting the defective genes.
- It has helped in producing plants and animals with specific characters.
- So, crippling hereditary diseases can also be cured like hemophilia etc.

DNA FINGERPRINTING

- It consists of examining repetitive DNA in the genome for variations in the length of restriction fragments.
- Every individual has his own pattern, so that fingerprinting can match blood to a particular person, and patterns are inherited from parent to child, allowing the method to identify relationships between individuals.

IN-VITRO FERTILIZATION

- When a sperm and an egg are made to fertilize outside a living body (usually a test tube), it is called in-vitro fertilization.
- This process has been used to impregnate several females who could not do so through natural means.

Diseases and the Parts of Body they Affect

AIDS—Immune system of body	*Gout*—Joints of bone
Arthritis—Inflammation of joints	*Jaundice*—Liver
Asthma—Lungs	*Meningitis*—Brain or spinal cord
Cataract—Eyes	*Pleurisy*—Pleura (inflammation of)
Conjunctivitis—Eyes	*Polio*—motor neurons
Diabetes—Pancreas	*Pneumonia*—Lungs
Diphtheria—Throat	*Pyorrhoea*—Sockets of teeth
Glaucoma—Eyes	*Tuberculosis*—Lungs
Eczema—Skin	*Typhoid*—Intestine
Goitre—Front of the neck (due to enlargement of thyroid gland)	*Malaria*—Spleen
	Leukaemia—Blood
	Rickets—Bones

SPACE RESEARCH

First in Space

✶ First creator of rules regarding space research	Isaac Newton
✶ First artificial satellite launched in space	Sputnik-1 (1957)
✶ First living being sent in space	Louika (a dog)
✶ Firstever manned spacecraft	Vostok-I
✶ First man in space	Yuri Gagarin U.S.S.R. (1961)
✶ First woman in space	Valentina Tereshkova U.S.S.R. (June 1963)
✶ First man who moved in space out of the spacecraft	Alexi Livonov U.S.S.R. (June 1965)
✶ First person to land on moon	Neil Armstrong, America (21st July, 1969)
✶ First fourwheeled carriage without human being on moon	Leunokhev-I U.S.S.R. (1970)
✶ First space lab in orbit	Skylab (America, 1973)
✶ First space shuttle	Columbia (America, 1981)
✶ First Indian (man) in space	Squadron leader—Rakesh Sharma (13th April, 1984)
✶ First Indian (Woman) in space	Kalpana Chawla (19th Nov., 1997)
✶ First American woman in space	Sailyride (1983)
✶ First spacecraft on Mars	Pathfinder (6 July, 1997)
✶ First woman who lead spacecraft	Allin Collis (America)
✶ First spacecraft without man	Shenzoo, China (20th Nov. 1999)

Indian Space Programme : At a Glance

Satellite	*Date*	*Type*	*Launch Vehicle*	*Result*
Aryabhatta	19-04-75	Scientific	Cosmos	successful
Bhaskara I	07-06-79	Geosurvey	Cosmos	successful
Rohini	10-08-79	Geosurvey	S.L.V.3	unsuccessful
Rohini D-1	18-07-80	Geosurvey	S.L.V.3	successful
Rohini	31-05-81	Scientific	S.L.V.3	successful
Apple	19-06-81	Communication	Ariane	successful
Bhaskara II	20-11-81	Geosurvey	Cosonos	successful
INSAT-1A	10-04-82	Multipurpose	Delta	unsuccessful
Rohini	17-04-83	Scientific	S.L.V.3	successful
INSAT-1B	30-08-83	Multipurpose	Space Shuttle	successful
SROSS I	24-03-87	Technical	ASLV-D1	unsuccessful
IRS-1A	17-03-88	Remote sensing	Vostok	successful
SROSS II	17-07-88	Technical	ASLV-D2	unsuccessful
INSAT-1C	21-07-88	Multipurpose	Ariane-4	unsuccessful
INSAT-1D	12-06-90	Multipurpose	Delta	successful
IRS-1B	29-08-91	Remote sensing	Vostok	successful
INSAT-2A	10-07-92	Multipurpose	Ariane	successful
INSAT-1D	12-06-90	Multipurpose	Delta	successful
IRS-1B	29-08-91	Remote sensing	Vostok	successful
INSAT-2A	10-07-92	Multipurpose	Ariane	successful
IRS-ID	29-09-97	Remote sensing	PSLV	successful
INSAT-3B	22-03-2000	Multipurpose	Ariane	successful

Satellite	Date	Type	Launch Vehicle	Result
G-SAT-1	18-04-2001	Multipurpose	GSLV-D	successful
INSAT-3E	28-09-2003	Communication	Ariane-5	successful
Cartosat-1 & hamsat	05-05-2005	Maping and Communication	PSLV-C6	successful
Chandrayaan-I	22-10-2008	Maping and Scientific	PSLV-C11	successful
CARTOSAT-2B	12-07-2010	Communication	PSLV-C15	successful
GSAT-12	15-07-2011	Communication	PSLV-C17	successful
RISAT-1	26-04-2012	Remote Sensing	PSLV-C19	successful
GSAT-7	30-08-2013	Defence	Ariane-5	successful
MOM	5-11-2013	Mapping	PSLV-C25	successful
IRNSS-1B	04-04-2014	Mapping and Scientific	PSLV-C24	successful
GSAT-16	07-12-2014	Communication	Ariane-5	successful
IRNSS-1D	28-03-2015	Mapping and Scientific	PSLV-C27	successful
IRNSS-1E	20-01-2016	Mapping and Scientific	PSLV-C31	successful
Cartosat-2 & others	22-06-2016	Mapping and Scientific	PSLV-C34	successful
Scatsat-1 & others	26-09-2016	Multipurpose	PSLV-C35	successful
RESOURCESAT-2A	07-12-2016	Remote Sensing	PSLV-C36	successful
CARTOSAT-2 & 103 others	15-02-2017	Multipurpose	PSLV-C37	successful
GSAT-17	29-06-2017	Earth observation Satellite	Ariane-5 ECA	successful
Cartosat-2F & others	12-01-2018	Multipurpose	PSLV-C40	successful
GSAT-6A	29-03-2018	Communication	GSLV-F08	successful
GSAT-7A	19-12-2018	Military Satellite	GSLV-MK-II-F11	successful
Cartosat-3	27-11-2019	Earth Imagine Satellite	PSLV-C47	successful
GSAT-30	17-01-2020	Communication	Ariane-5	successful
EOS-01	07-11-2020	Earth Observation	PSLV-C49	successful
CMS-01/GSAT-12R	17-12-2020	Communication	PSLV-XLC50	successful
Amejonia and 19 others	28-02-2021	Communication	PSLV-C51	successful
EOS-04	14-02-2022	Earth Observation	PSLV-C52	successful
GSAT-24"	23-06-2022	Communication	Ariane-5	successful
DS-E0 and others	30-06-2022	Mapping	PSLV-C53	successful
Oceansat-3 and 8 others	26-11-2022	Earth observation Satellite	PSLV-C54	successful
EOS-07	10-02-2023	Earth observation Satellite	SSLV-02	successful
TeLEOS-2 and LUMILITE-4	22-04-2023	Communication	PSLV-C55	successful
Chandrayaan-3	14-07-2023	Lunar observation	LVM-3	successful
DS-SAR and 6 others	30-07-2023	Earth observation	PSLV-C56	successful
Aditya-L1	02-09-2023	Solar Mission	PSLV-C57	successful
XPoSat	01-01-2024	Earth observation	PSLV-C58	successful
INSAT-3DS	17-02-2024	Meteorological	GSLV-F14	successful
EOS-08	16-08-2024	Earth observation	SSLV-D3	successful
Proba-3	05-12-2024	Earth Observation	PSLV-C59	successful
NVS-02	29-01-2025	Navigation	GSLV-F15	successful
NISAR	30-07-2025	Earth Observation	GSLV-F16	successful
CMS-03	02-11-2025	Communication	LVM3-M5	successful

COMPUTER

- The computer is the system of that electronic device through which various informations are processed on the basis of a definite set of instructions called program and mathematical (numerical) and non-mathematical both types of informations are processed.
- The first mechanical computer was composed or fabricated by Blaise Pascal in 1642 and it is called Pascalene.
- But in 1833, Charles Babbage first time conceived an automatic calculator or computer.
- Charles Babbage is called the father of modern computer.
- Herman made an electronic tabulating machine based on punch cards which operates automatically.
- In 1937, first mechanical computer Mark-I was fabricated by Howard Akeen.
- The most outstanding contribution in the development of modern computer goes to John Wan Newmaan who brought the 2nd revolution in the area of computer in 1951.
- He discovered EDVAC (Electronic Discrete Variable Automatic Computer) and utilised the stored program and the binary number system in the computer.

FUNCTIONS OF COMPUTER

- 1. Collection and composition (input) of datas;
  2. Storage of datas.
  3. Processing of datas.
  4. Retrieval or output of the proccessed informations and datas.

UNITS OF COMPUTER

1. Input unit.
2. Central processing unit–CPU.
3. External Memory unit.
4. Output unit.

- The CPU of the computer is called brain of the computer and sometimes CPU is also called Micro Processor of the computer.
- The data is entered through the input unit in the computer and through the central processing unit with the help of External Memory Unit datas are arranged and processed.
- Ultimately by the output unit these datas or informations are issued or released.

PARTS OF COMPUTER

- **Monitor :** The monitor of the computer is like a television in which the picture appears in the form of doted points on the screen and these are called pixels.
- **Hard Disc and Floppy Disc :** The Hard Disc is the permanent disc in the computers while the Floppy Disc is the disc utilised when datas or informations are to be transferred from one computer to another.
- **Mouse :** The mouse of the computer is like the remote control of TV through which computer is directly regulated or controlled without utilising the key-board.
- **Printer :** The printer is a device which prints any documents or processed informations of the computer.

SOME HIGH LEVEL LANGUAGES

1. **FORTRAN :** This language was developed for solving the mathematical formulae very quickly and conveniently.
2. **COBOL :** This language was developed for the commerical purposes. For the processing of this language a group of sentences is selected called paragraph and all paragraphs composed are called a section, while all sections composed are called a division.
3. **BASIC :** In basic a definite part of the prescribed instruction is only inserted in the computer.
4. **ALGOL :** This was basically fabricated and designed for the complex algebraic calculations.
5. **PASCAL :** It is an amplified and modified form of ALGOL.

6. **COMAL :** This computer language is used for the students of secondary level.
7. **LOGO :** This language is used for children and kids for drawing Graphic line diagrams.
8. **PROLOG :** This language is developed in 1973 in France and is used for Artificial Intelligence which is capable and equivalent to the logical program.
9. **FORTH :** This language was invented by Charles Mure which is frequently used in all types of the works in the computer.

COMPUTER VIRUS

- The computer virus is an electronic code which is used to abolish or erradicate the inclusive informations or programs of the computer.
- Some important computer viruses are Micheleanjalo, Dork Avangor, kilo, filip, Macmug, Scores, Casecade, Jeruslem, Date crime, Coloumbs crime, Internet virus, Pachcom, Pach EXE, COM-EXE, Marizuana, C-brain, bloody, Chenge Mungu and Desi etc.

COMPUTER NETWORKING

- There are two types of networkings which are usually occur—Local Area Networking (LAN) and Wide Area Networking (WAN).

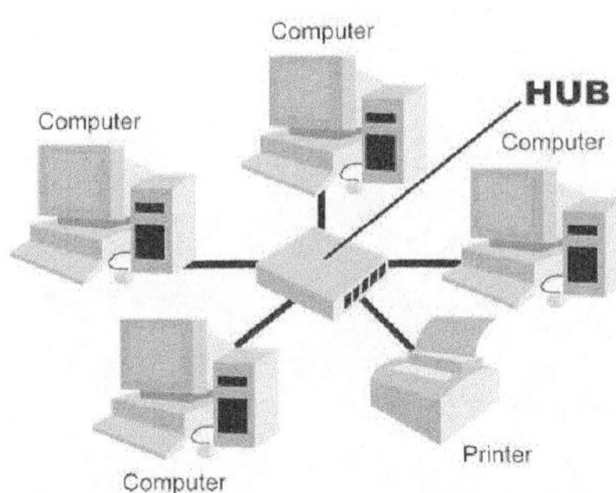

- By LAN all the computers of the same buildings are connected like the computers of university premises, computers of offices etc.
- By WAN all the comptuers of a large area are connected like the computers of all the offices of a city or town etc.
- In India a very large computer network namely INDONET has been installing through which all the main towns and cities has to be interlinked.

COMPUTER TERMINOLOGY

- **Bit :** The bit is a unit of measurement of the electronic data. One bit is either 0 or 1 but not both. On composing 8 bits, 1 byte is formed.
- **Bug :** The Bug is the error in the computer program or system and its eradication is called Debug.
- **Byte :** Total eight bits compose a byte. Thus 8 bits = 1 byte.
- **CD-ROM :** A CD like of music CD in which data can be stored substantially called CD-ROM. In a CD with comparison to floppy extremely more datas can be stored but one problem in it is that one time recorded data can not be deleted or modified.
- **Chip :** It is a thin slice on which by a special mechanism a circuit is designed which is normally made from Silicon.
- **Memory System :** The place where computer data and program are temporarily kept is called Memory system. Usually memory is implied from RAM.
- **Modem :** The device which converts digital signals into analogue signals and vice-versa is called Modem.
- **RAM :** It is Random Access Memory (a place) where datas to be processed are kept temporarily and it is unstable memory.
- **ROM :** It is Read Only Memory and it is stable or Non-valatile memory which doesn't ended after power off.
- **Scanner :** It is a device through which graphic image is transformed to digital image and the scanners are of usually two types one desktop and another hand operating.

PROGRAMING

- Computers perform phenomenal feats of calculation, but they do not do so in a complicated way.

- They actually carry out very simple operations, such as addition and subtraction.
- They achieve their fantastic computing power by carrying out these operations at incredible speed.
- The programme, or set of instructions for operating the computer, is therefore written as a sequence of very simple steps.

Several computer languages have been developed for different applications, including BASIC, COBOL, FORTRAN and PASCAL. Writing programmes is very skilled and time-consuming work.

- But for most typical computer applications ready-written programmes are available, called "packages".

❒ ❒ ❒

GENERAL KNOWLEDGE

FIRST IN THE WORLD

✶ First Chinese visitor to India	*Fahien*
✶ First foreign invader of India	*Alexander, the Great (Greek)*
✶ First person to climb Mt. Everest	*Tenzing Norgay (India) and Edmund Hillary (New Zealand) (1953)*
✶ First atom bomb dropped at	*Hiroshima (Japan)*
✶ First man in the space	*Yuri Gagarin (former USSR)*
✶ First woman in the space	*Valentina Tereshkova (former USSR)*
✶ First person to walk in the space	*Alexei Leonov (former USSR)*
✶ First person to land on the moon	*Neil Armstrong (USA)*
✶ First and the only woman to have climbed Mt. Everest twice	*Santosh Yadav (Indian; May, 1992; May, 1993)*
✶ First person on Mt. Everest without oxygen	*Phu Dorjee (Indian; May 9, 1984)*
✶ First person to climb Mt. Everest twice	*Nawang Gombu*
✶ First President of the USA	*George Washington*
✶ First woman Prime Minister	*Sirimavo Bandaranaike (Sri Lanka)*
✶ First person to swim across English Channel	*Mathew Webb*
✶ First woman to swim across English Channel	*Gertrude Caroline Ederle*
✶ First woman to climb Mt. Everest	*Junko Tabei (Japan)*
✶ First woman to climb Mt. Everest alone and without oxygen supplies	*Alison Hargreaves (Britain: May 13, 1995)*
✶ First Aeroplane to fly around the world without refuelling	*Voyager (Dec. 1986)*
✶ First test-tube Baby	*Louise Brown (UK; 1978)*
✶ First all-talking Film	*Jaz Singer (1927)*
✶ First Secretary-General of the UN	*Trygve Lie (Norway: 1946-53)*
✶ First woman President of the UN General Assembly	*Vijayalakshmi Pandit (India: 1953)*
✶ First woman to reach North Pole	*Ann Bancroft (1986)*
✶ First person to reach North Pole	*Robert Peary*
✶ First person to reach South Pole	*Amundsen (1911)*
✶ First woman to command Spacecraft in Space	*Ellin Collins*

SUPERLATIVES (WORLD)
(The Largest, Biggest, Smallest, Longest, Highest)

Airport	*Largest*	King Fahd International Airport, Dammam (Saudi Arabia)
Animal,	*Tallest*	Giraffe (Average height 6.09 m)
	Largest and Heaviest	Blue Whale (190 tonnes)
	Longest recorded	Boot lace Worm (55 m)
	Fastest	Cheetah (Approximately 100 km/hr)
Bay,	*With max. shore line*	Hudson Bay (Canada: 12268 km)
	With maximum area	Bay of Bengal (India: 217 million hc)
Building,	*Tallest*	Burj Khalifa (Dubai, 818 meter)
Canal,	*Big ship (longest)*	Suez Canal (160 km)
	Busiest	Kiel Canal (North Sea)
Canyon/Gorge,	*Deepest*	Hells Canyon, Snake River (Idaho : 7900 ft)
	Largest	Grand Canyon (Colarado River; USA; 446 km)
Church,	*Largest*	Basilica of St. Peter (Vatican City Rome– Area 23000 sq.m.)
City,	*Largest in Area*	Jiuquan Gansu, China (Area 1,67,996 Sq km)
Continent,	*biggest*	Asia (30,928,605 km^2)
	Smallest	Australia Mainland (Area 8,426,635 km^2)
Country,	*Largest in Population*	China (over 138.5 crore)
	Largest in Area	Russia (17,075,000 sq. km)
	With largest electorate	India (over 90 crores)
	Smallest independent	State of Vatican City (109 acre)
Delta,	*Largest*	Sundarban's Ganga-Brahmaputra delta (1,05,000 sq. km)
Desert,	*Largest*	Sahara (N. Africa; maximum length 5,150 km EW; maximum width 3,200 km NS)
Dome,	*Largest*	Singapore National Stadium (310 m)
Epic,	*Longest*	Mahabharata
Fish,	*Largest fresh water*	Plabeuk (China, Laos and Thailand)
	Most abundant	Bristle mouth
	Most venomous	Stone Fish (Indo-Pacific Waters)
Film,	*Most Oscars*	Ben Hur (11 Oscars–1959); Titanic (11 Oscars–1998); The Lord of Rings : The Return of the King (11 Oscars—2003).
Fountain,	*Tallest*	King Fahd's Fountain (Jeddah, Saudi Arabia)

Fruit,	*Most nutritive*	Avocado (Vitamins A, C, E and Proteins; Central and South America)
	Least nutritive	Cucumber
Gulf,	*Largest*	Gulf of Mexico (1,544,000 sq. km)
Island,	*Biggest*	Greenland (Kalaatdlit Nunaat–2,175,000 sq km)
Lake,	*Largest*	Caspian Sea (Azerbaijan, Russia, Iran border: 37.18 lakh km^2)
	Deepest	Baikal (Siberia)
	Largest (fresh water)	Superior Lake (USA–Canada border: 82,350 km^2)
Library,	*Biggest*	United States Library of Congress (Washington D.C. founded in 1800, contains 101 million items)
	Biggest non-statutory	New York Public Library
Mountain,	*Highest peak*	Mt. Everest (8848 m; Nepal)
	Highest range	Himalayas, Asia (upto 4200 m)
	Greatest mountain range	Himalaya-Karakoram (96 out of 109 peaks over 7315 m are here)
Museum,	*Largest*	American Museum of Natural History, New York
Ocean,	*Largest and Deepest*	The Pacific (Area: 166,240,000 km^2; Depth: 10,924 m)
Peninsula,	*Largest*	Arabia (3.25 million sq. km)
Places,	*Coldest (annual mean)*	Polus Nedostupnosti (Antarctica –58°C)
	Driest (annual mean)	Desierto de Atacame (near Calama; Chile; rainfall nil)
	Hottest (annual mean)	Dallol (Ethiopia; 34.4°C mean temperature)
	Rainiest (annual mean)	Mowsyrnam near Cherapunji (Meghalaya; India; 11873 mm)
	Windiest	The Commonwealth Bay (Gales reach 320 km/ph)
Planet,	*Biggest*	Jupiter (equatorial diameter 142984 km)
	Brightest, hottest and nearest to Earth	Venus
	Nearest to Sun	Mercury
Plateau,	*Highest*	Tibetan Plateau (Central Asia: 4900 m)
Platform,	*Longest (rail)*	Shree Siddharoodha Swamiji Railway Station Hubballi, Karnataka, India (1507 m. long)
Railway Line,	*Longest*	Trans-Siberian Railway (Moscow-Nakhodka: 9438 km)
Railway Station,	*Largest*	Grand Central Terminal (New York City; 19 hc)

Religion,	*Oldest*	Hinduism
Religion,	*Largest*	Christianity
Rivers,	*Longest*	(i) Nile (6650 km) (ii) Amazon (6437 km)
Road,	*Longest*	Pan American Highway (from Alaska-Brasila: 24140 km)
Sea,	*Largest*	Philippine Sea (5,695,000 sq. km)
Star,	*Brightest*	Sirius A (also called Dog Star)
Swimming	*Longest*	English Channel
Telescope,	*Largest (radio)*	Five Hundred meter Apertune Spherical Telescope (FAST), China.
Temple,	*Largest*	Angkor Wat (Cambodia: 402 acres)
Tunnel,	*Longest (railway)*	Gotthard Base Rail Tunnel (Switzerland; 57.1 km)
	Largest (road)	Laerdal, Norway (24.51 km)
Volcano	*Greatest concentration in*	Indonesia
	Highest (extinct)	Cerro Aconcagua (6960 m; Andes)
	Highest (dormant)	Volcan Llullaillaco (6723 m; Argentina-Chile)
	Highest (active)	Ojos del Salado (Chile-Argentina)
Waterfall,	*Highest*	Salto-Angel (in Venezuela on a branch of river Carrao, depth 807 m.)
	Largest	Khone Falls (Laos; width 10.8 km)

CAPITAL & CURRENCIES

Country	*Capital*	*Currency*
∗ Afghanistan	Kabul	Afghani
∗ Albania	Tirana	Lek
∗ Algeria	Algiers	Dinar
∗ Angola	Luanda	New Kwanza
∗ Argentina	Buenos Aires	Peso
∗ Armenia	Yeravan	Dram
∗ Australia	Canberra	Dollar
∗ Austria	Vienna	Euro
∗ Azerbaijan	Baku	Manat
∗ Bahrain	Manama	Dinar
∗ Bangladesh	Dhaka	Taka
∗ Barbados	Bridgetown	Dollar
∗ Belarus	Minsk	Ruble
∗ Belgium	Brussels	Euro
∗ Benin	Porto Novo	Franc
∗ Bhutan	Thimphu	Ngultrum[1]
∗ Bolivia	La paz	Dollar
∗ Botswana	Gaborone	Pula
∗ Brazil	Brasilia	Real
∗ Bosnia Herzegovina	Sarajevo	Dinar
∗ Bulgaria	Sofia	Lev

Country	Capital	Currency
✶ Cambodia	Phnom-Penh	Riel
✶ Canada	Ottawa	Dollar
✶ Chile	Santiago	Peso
✶ China	Beijing	Yuan
✶ Colombia	Bogota	Peso
✶ Congo Republic	Brazzaville	Franc CFA
✶ Croatia	Zagreb	Kuna
✶ Cuba	Havana	Peso
✶ Cyprus	Nicosia	Euro
✶ Czech Republic	Prague	Koruna
✶ Denmark	Copenhagen	Krone
✶ Ecuador	Quito	Sucre
✶ Egypt	Cairo	Pound
✶ Estonia	Tallinn	Euro
✶ Ethiopia	Addis Ababa	Birr
✶ Fiji	Suva	Dollar
✶ Finland	Helsinki	Euro
✶ France	Paris	Euro
✶ Georgia	Tbilisi	Lari
✶ Germany	Berlin	Euro
✶ Ghana	Accra	Cedi
✶ Greece	Athens	Euro
✶ Guatemala	Guatemala City	Quetzal
✶ Guyana	George Town	Dollar
✶ Hungary	Budapest	Forint
✶ Iceland	Reykjavik	Krona
✶ India	New Delhi	Rupee
✶ Indonesia	Jakarta	Rupiah
✶ Iran	Teheran	Rial
✶ Iraq	Baghdad	Dinar
✶ Ireland	Dublin	Euro
✶ Israel	Jerusalem	Shekel
✶ Italy	Rome	Euro
✶ Jamaica	Kingston	Dollar
✶ Japan	Tokyo	Yen
✶ Jordan	Amman	Dinar
✶ Kazakhstan	Akmola	Tenge

Country	Capital	Currency
✶ Kenya	Nairobi	Shilling
✶ Korea (S)	Seoul	Won
✶ Korea (N)	Pyongyang	Won
✶ Kyrgyzstan	Bishkek	Som
✶ Kuwait	Kuwait City	Dinar
✶ Laos	Vientiane	Kip
✶ Latvia	Riga	Euro
✶ Lebanon	Beirut	Pound
✶ Liberia	Monrovia	Dollar
✶ Libya	Tripoli	Dinar
✶ Lithuania	Vilnius	Litas
✶ Luxembourg	Luxembourg	Euro
✶ Macedonia	Skopje	Dinar
✶ Malawi	Lilongwe	Kwacha
✶ Malaysia	Kuala Lumpur	Ringgit
✶ Maldives	Male	Rufiyaa
✶ Mali	Bamako	Franc
✶ Mauritius	Port Louis	Rupee
✶ Mexico	Mexico City	Peso
✶ Moldavia	Chisinau	Leu
✶ Mongolia	Ulan Bator	Tugrik
✶ Morocco	Rabat	Dirham
✶ Mozambique	Maputo	Metical
✶ Myanmar	Nay Pyi Taw	Kyat
✶ Namibia	Winohoek	Dollar
✶ Nepal	Kathmandu	Rupee
✶ Netherlands	Amsterdam	Euro
✶ New Zealand	Wellington	Dollar
✶ Nigeria	Abuja	Naira
✶ Norway	Oslo	Krone
✶ Oman	Muscat	Rial
✶ Pakistan	Islamabad	Rupee
✶ Panama	Panama City	Balboa
✶ Peru	Lima	New Sole
✶ Philippines	Manila	Peso
✶ Poland	Warsaw	Zloty
✶ Portugal	Lisbon	Euro
✶ Qatar	Doha	Riyal
✶ Romania	Bucharest	Leu
✶ Russia	Moscow	Ruble

Country	Capital	Currency
✶ Saudi Arabia	Riyadh	Rial
✶ Senegal	Dakar	Franc
✶ Slovakia	Bratislava	Euro
✶ Spain	Madrid	Euro
✶ Sri Lanka	Colombo	Rupee
✶ Sudan	Khartoum	Dinar
✶ Suriname	Paramaribo	Guilder
✶ Sweden	Stockholm	Krona
✶ Switzerland	Berne	Swiss Francs
✶ Syria	Damascus	Pound
✶ South Africa	Capetown (Legislative) Pretoria *(Administrative)*	Rand
✶ Tadzhikistan	Dushanbe	Ruble
✶ Taiwan	Taipei	Dollar
✶ Tanzania	Dodoma	Shilling

Country	Capital	Currency
✶ Thailand	Bangkok	Baht
✶ Tunisia	Tunis	Dinar
✶ Turkiye	Ankara	Lira
✶ Turkmania	Ashikabad	Manat
✶ Uganda	Kampala	Shilling
✶ Ukraine	Kiev	Hyrvnia
✶ United Arab Emirates	Abu Dhabi	Dirham
✶ U.K.	London	Pound Sterling
✶ U.S.A.	Washington	Dollar
✶ Uruguay	Montevideo	Peso
✶ Uzbekistan	Tashkent	Som
✶ Venezuela	Caracas	Bolivar
✶ Vietnam	Hanoi	Dong
✶ Yemen	Sana'a	Rial
✶ Zimbabwe	Harare	Dollar
✶ Congo (Democratic Republic)	Kinshasa	Franc
✶ Zambia	Lusaka	Kwacha

GEOGRAPHICAL EXPLORATIONS/DISCOVERIES

Place	Explorer/Discoverer	Nationality	Year
America	Christopher Columbus	Italy	1492
Hawaii Islands (Sandwich Islands)	Captain James Cook	England	1778
Newfoundland	John Cabot	England	1497
New Zealand	Abel Janszoon Tasman	Holland	1642
North Pole	Robert Peary	USA	1909
Sea Route to India (via Cape of Good Hope)	Vasco da Gama	Portugal	1498
South Pole	Roald Amundsen	Norway	1911

NATIONAL MONUMENTS OF SOME FAMOUS COUNTRIES

Monument	Country	Monument	Country
Great Wall of China	China	Pyramid (Giza)	Egypt
Taj Mahal (Agra)	India	Kinder Disk	Denmark
Emperial Palace (Tokyo)	Japan	Leaning Tower of Pisa	Italy
Opera House (Sydney)	Australia	Statue of Liberty (New York)	USA
Eiffel Tower (Paris)	France	Kremlin (Moscow)	Russia

INTELLIGENCE AGENCIES OF SOME PROMINENT COUNTRIES

Country	Intelligence Agency
∗ India	*Research & Analysis Wing (RAW), Intelligence Bureau (I.B.), Central Bureau of Investigation (C.B.I.)*
∗ Pakistan	*Inter Service Intelligence (I.S.I.)*
∗ U.S.A.	*Central Intelligence Agency (CIA), Federal Bureau of Investigation (FBI)*
∗ Britain	*Military Intelligence (M.I.)-5 and 6, Special Branch, Ultra, Joint Intelligence Organisation*
∗ Israel	*Mosad*
∗ Egypt	*Mukhabarat*
∗ Japan	*Nicho*
∗ Russia	*K.G.B. (Komitel Gosudarstvennoy Bezopasnosty) (Committee for State Security)*
∗ Canada	*Security Intelligence Service (SIS)*
∗ S. Africa	*Bureau of State Security (BSS)*
∗ Iran	*Sabak*
∗ Iraq	*Al-Mukhabarat*
∗ Australia	*Australian Security and Intelligence Organisation (ASIO)*
∗ France	*S.D.E.C.E.*
∗ Spain	*C.E.S.I.D.*

MAJOR LANGUAGES OF THE WORLD AND THEIR SPEAKERS

Listing the languages spoken by approximately 1% of humankind (those spoken by more than 60,000,000 people), this table enumerates speakers of each tongue as a primary language.

Language	Speakers (millions)
∗ Chinese	1,322
∗ Spanish	471
∗ English	369
∗ Arabic	349
∗ Hindi	342
∗ Portuguese	232
∗ Bengali	228
∗ Russian	153
∗ Japanese	126
∗ Lahnda	99
∗ Punjabi (Western)	93
∗ Javanese	84
∗ Marathi	83
∗ Telugu	82
∗ Turkish	82
∗ Malay	81
∗ French	79
∗ Korean	77
∗ Tamil	77
∗ German	76
∗ Vietnamese	76
∗ Urdu	69
∗ Italian	64
∗ Persian	65

Source : The World Almanac 2022

IMPORTANT NEWS AGENCIES OF THE WORLD

Agency	Country
PTI, UNI, UNIVARTA	India
Antara	Indonesia
Tanjug	Serbia
Associated Press (AP)	America
Reuters, NAFEN	United Kingdom
Angence France Press (AFP)	France
TASS	Russia

NAME OF PARLIAMENTS OF SOME COUNTRIES

Country	Name of Parliament	Country	Name of Parliament
Afghanistan	Shora	Norway	Storting
Argentina	National Congress	Poland	Sejm
Australia	Federal Parliament	Russia	Federal Assembly (Council of the Federation and State Duma
Austria	National Assembly	South Africa	National Assembly and Senate
Bangladesh	Jatiya Sansad	Spain	Cortes Generales
India	Lok Sabha and Rajya Sabha	Sweden	Riksdag
Bhutan	Tshogdu (National Assembly)	Switzerland	Federal Assembly (Nationalrat and Standerat)
Britain	House of Commons and House of Lords	North Korea	Supreme People's Assembly
Canada	House of Commons and Senate	South Korea	National Assembly
China	National People Congress	U.S.A.	Congress (Senate and House of Representatives)
Denmark	Folketing	Ethiopia	Federal Council and House of Representatives
Iran	Majlis (Islamic Consultative Assembly)	Iceland	Alpingi
Israel	Knesset	Bulgaria	National Assembly
Japan	Diet	Cuba	National Assembly of People's Power
Myanmar	Pyithu Hluttaw (People's Assembly)		
Nepal	Rashtriya Panchayat		
The Netherlands	States-General		

LARGEST AND SMALLEST COUNTRIES (Top 5)

Largest Country (Area-wise)	Largest Country (Population-wise)	Smallest Country (Area-wise)	Smallest Country (Population-wise)
Russia	China	Vatican City	Vatican City
Canada	India	Monaco	Tuvalu
China	USA	Nauru	Nauru
United States	Indonesia	Tuvalu	Palau
Brazil	Brazil	San Marino	San Marino

MAJOR RELIGIONS OF THE WORLD

Religion	Member	Percentage	Religion	Member	Percentage
Christianity	2.5 billion	32.2%	Buddhism	545 million	6.9%
Islam	1.9 billion	24.7%	Sikhism	27 million	0.27%
Hinduism	1.0 billion	13.5%	Jews	14 million	0.14%

NATIONAL EMBLEMS OF IMPORTANT COUNTRIES

Country	National Emblem	Country	National Emblem
America	Golden Rod	Australia	Kangaroo
Ireland	Shamrock	Italy	White Lily
Israel	Candelabrum	Iran	Rose
Canada	White Lily	Great Britain	Rose
Chile	Candor and Huemul	Germany	Corn Flower
Japan	Chrysanthemum	Zimbabwe	Zimbabwe Bird
Denmark	Beach	Turkey	Crescent and Star
The Netherlands	Lion	New Zealand	Kiwi, Fern Southern Cross
Norway	Lion	Nepal	Kukri
Pakistan	Crescent	Poland	Eagle
France	Lily	Belgium	Lion
Bangladesh	Water Lily	Mongolia	The Soyombo
Russia	Double headed eagle	Lebanon	Cedar Tree
Sudan	Secretary Bird	Syria	Eagle
India	Lioned Capital		

FIRST IN INDIA

- ∗ The first Indian to get the Nobel Prize for Literature — *Rabindra Nath Tagore*
- ∗ The first Indian to get the Nobel Prize for Physics — *C.V. Raman*
- ∗ The first Indian to get the Nobel Prize for Peace — *Mother Teresa*
- ∗ The first Indian to get the Nobel Prize for Economics — *Amartya Sen*
- ∗ The first Indian to get Special Oscar award (1992) — *Satyajit Ray*
- ∗ The first and the last Indian Governor-General of free India — *C. Rajagopalachari*
- ∗ The first woman to become the Governor of a State — *Smt. Sarojini Naidu*
- ∗ The first Indian Commenders-in-Chief — *General K.M. Cariappa*
- ∗ The first ever woman to become the Chief Minister of a State — *Smt. Sucheta Kripalani*
- ∗ The first Indian woman President of UN General Assembly — *Smt. Vijaylakshmi Pandit*
- ∗ The first Indian to become the President of International Court of Justice — *Dr. Nagendra Singh*
- ∗ The first Indian woman to swim across the English Channel — *Ms. Aarti Saha*
- ∗ The first Indian girl to become Miss Universe — *Miss Sushmita Sen*
- ∗ The first Indian girl to become Miss World — *Rita Faria*
- ∗ The first Indian to swim across the English Channel — *Mihir Sen*
- ∗ The first Field Marshal — *S.H.F.J. Manekshaw*
- ∗ The first Indian recipient of Victoria Cross — *Khudadad Khan*
- ∗ The first Indian to conquer Mt. Everest — *Sherpa Tenzing (May 29, 1953)*
- ∗ The first Indian Cosmonaut (man) — *Rakesh Sharma (April 3, 1984)*

* The first Indian Cosmonaut (woman) — *Kalpana Chawla (Nov. 19, 1997)*
* The first woman to climb Mt. Everest — *Miss Bachendri Pal (May 23, 1984)*
* The first ICS — *Satyendranath Tagore*
* The first to address the UN General Assembly in Hindi — *Atal Bihari Vajpayee*
* The first Newspaper — *Bengal Gazette (Jan 27, 1780)*
* The first Postage Stamp issued — *In 1852*
* The first Telegraph line laid — *In 1851 (Calcutta-Diamond Harbour)*
* The first Railways run — *April 16, 1853 (Bombay-Thane)*
* The first Electric Train run — *1925 (Bombay-Kurla)*
* The first Atomic Power Station — *Tarapore (Maharashtra)*
* The first passenger-cum-cargo ship made in India — *Harshavardhan*
* The first Satellite — *Aryabhatta (1975)*
* The first President of the Indian National Congress — *W.C. Banerjee*
* The first President of Indian Republic — *Dr. Rajendra Prasad*
* The first woman judge of the Supreme Court — *Ms Fatima Bibi*
* The first to climb Everest without oxygen — *Phu Dorjee (1987)*
* The first film (movie) — *Raja Harishchandra*
* The first film (talkie) — *Alam Ara*
* The first Metro Railway — *Calcutta Metro Railway*
* The first Test-tube baby, scientifically documented — *Born on August 6, 1986 at K.E.M. Hospital, Bombay*
* The first TV Centre — *At Delhi*
* The first Indian to get an Oscar — *Bhanu Athaiya*
* The first woman pilot in IAF — *Ms Harita Kaur Deol*
* The first woman to get Olympic Medal — *Karnam Malleswari*
* The first woman Foreign Secretary — *Chokila Iyer*

SUPERLATIVES (INDIA)

Highest, Biggest, Largest and Longest in India

* Award for Gallantry, highest — *Param Vir Chakra*
* Award, highest civilian — *Bharat Ratna*
* Bank, with largest number of branches — *State Bank of India*
* Road Bridge, Longest — *Bhupen Hazarika Bridge, Assam (9.15 km)*
* Road and Rail Bridge, Longest — *Bogibeel Bridge, Brahmaputra River, Assam*
* Cattle Fair, Largest — *Sonepur (Bihar)*
* City, Most Populous — *Mumbai metropolis*
* Corridor, Longest — *Rameshwaram Temple corridor (4,000 ft.)*
* Desert, Largest — *Thar (Rajasthan)*
* Dam, Longest — *Hirakud Dam (Odisha)*
* Delta, Largest — *Sunderban's Delta*

∗ Dome, Largest	*Gol Gumbaj (Bijapur)*
∗ Dam, Highest	*Tehri Dam (260 m)*
∗ Gateway, Highest	*Buland Darwaja at Fatehpur Sikri (176 ft.)*
∗ Fresh Water Lake, Largest	*Wular Lake (Kashmir)*
∗ Literacy, Highest	*Kerala (94%)*
∗ Museum, Largest	*Indian Museum (Kolkata)*
∗ Mosque, Biggest	*Jama Masjid (Delhi)*
∗ Peak, Highest**	*K-2 (Pak-Occupied Kashmir)*
∗ Railway Platform, Longest	*Shree Siddharoodha Swamiji Railway Station Hubballi, Karnataka (1507 m. long)*
∗ Railway Bridge, longest	*Vembanad Bridge, Kerala (4.6 km)*
∗ River, Longest***	*The Ganges (2525 Km)*
∗ Rainfall, Highest (annual mean)	*Mowsynram near Cherrapunji (1178 cm)*
∗ Road Longest	*NH-44 (3,745 km)*
∗ State, with maximum forest cover	*Madhya Pradesh*
∗ State, with maximum density of population	*Bihar*
∗ Telescope, Largest in Asia	*Vainu Bappu Telescope (at Kavalur: Chennai) 2.34m*
∗ Tunnel, Longest (Road)	*Dr. Shyama Prasad Mukherjee Tunnel (9.28 kms, J & K)*
∗ Tunnel, Longest (Railway)	*T-50 Tunnel, Khari-Sumber section (12.77 kms) Jammu & Kashmir.*
∗ Tallest Minaret	*Qutub Minar (Delhi 72.5 m.)*
∗ Waterfall, Highest	*Kunchikal Waterfall (Karnataka: 455 m.)*
∗ Zoo, Largest	*Arignar Anna Zoological Park, Chennai, Tamil Nadu*

** *Highest peak in the world is Mount Everest, which is in Nepal. K-2 is the second highest peak in the world. It is 8,611 metres high.*

*** *Indus and Brahmaputra (each 2900 km). Both of them, however, cover a long distance outside India.*

TABLE OF PRECEDENCE

1. President
2. Vice-President
3. Prime Minister
4. Governors of States within their respective states
5. Former Presidents

5A. Deputy Prime Minister

6. Chief Justice of India, Speaker of Lok Sabha
7. Cabinet Ministers of the Union, Chief Ministers of States within their respective States
   Deputy Chairman NITI Aayog, former Prime Ministers
   Leaders of opposition in Rajya Sabha and Lok Sabha

7A. Holders of the Bharat Ratna Decoration

8. Ambassadors Extraordinary and Plenipotentiary and High Commissioners of Commonwealth Countries accredited to India, Chief Ministers of States outside their respective States
9. Judges of the Supreme Court
10. Deputy Chairman Rajya Sabha, Deputy Chief Minister of States, Deputy Speaker Lok Sabha, Members of the NITI Aayog, Minister of State of the Union and Other Minister in the Ministry of Defence.

BOOKS AND AUTHORS

FOREIGN

Book	Author
✶ As You Like It	*William Shakespeare*
✶ A Tale of Two Cities	*Charles Dickens*
✶ Ben Hur	*Lewis Wallace*
✶ Das Kapital	*Karl Marx*
✶ David Copperfield	*Charles Dickens*
✶ Hamlet	*William Shakespeare*
✶ Iliad	*Homer*
✶ Inferno	*A. Dante*
✶ In Memoriam	*Lord Tennyson*
✶ Ivanhoe	*Walter Scott*
✶ Julius Caesar	*William Shakespeare*
✶ Lady Chatterley's Lover	*D.H. Lawrence*
✶ Lajja	*Taslima Nasreen*
✶ Les Miserable	*Victor Hugo*
✶ Leviathan	*Thomas Hobbes*
✶ Lolita	*V. Nobokov*
✶ Lycidas	*John Milton*
✶ Mein Kampf	*Adolf Hitler*
✶ Moor's Last Sigh	*Salman Rushdie*
✶ Mother	*Maxim Gorky*
✶ Mother India	*Katherine Mayo*
✶ Nana	*Emile Zola*
✶ Odyssey	*Homer*
✶ Origin of Species	*Charles Darwin*
✶ Othello	*William Shakespeare*
✶ Paradise Lost	*John Milton*
✶ Paradise Regained	*John Milton*
✶ Path to Power	*Margaret Thatcher*
✶ Pickwick Papers	*Charles Dickens*
✶ Razor's Edge	*Somerset Maugham*
✶ Republic	*Plato*
✶ The Tempest	*William Shakespeare*
✶ Time Machine	*H.G. Wells*
✶ Tom Sawyer	*Mark Twain*
✶ Treasure Island	*R.L. Stevenson*
✶ Twelfth Night	*William Shakespeare*
✶ Unto This Last	*John Ruskin*
✶ Utopia	*Thomas More*
✶ Wealth of Nations	*Adam Smith*
✶ Wonder that was India	*A.L. Basham*

INDIAN

Book	Author
✶ Ain-i-Akbari	*Abul Fazal*
✶ Anand Math	*Bankim Chandra Chatterjee*
✶ Arthashastra	*Kautilya*
✶ A Suitable Boy	*Vikram Seth*
✶ Bhagwat Gita	*Ved Vyas*
✶ Chidambara	*Sumitranandan Pant*
✶ Devdas	*Sarat Chandra Chatterjee*
✶ Discovery of India	*Jawaharlal Nehru*
✶ Ganadevata	*Tarashankar Bandopadhyaya*
✶ Geet Govind	*Jaya Dev*
✶ Geetanjali	*R. N. Tagore*
✶ Glimpses of World History	*Jawaharlal Nehru*
✶ Godaan	*Prem Chand*
✶ Gul-e-Nagma	*Firaq Gorakhpuri*
✶ Harsh Charita	*Bana Bhatta*
✶ India Divided	*Dr. Rajendra Prasad*
✶ Justice of Peace ke Aansu	Janardan Prasad Singh
✶ The Judgement	*Kuldip Nayyar*
✶ Kadambari	*Bana Bhatta*
✶ Kagaz Te Kanwas	*Amrita Pritam*
✶ Kamayani	*Jai Shankar Prasad*
✶ Kitni Nawon Mein Kitni Bar	*S. H. Vatsyayan*
✶ Kumar Sambhav	*Kalidas*
✶ Mahabharata	*Ved Vyas*
✶ Malgudi Days	*R.K. Narayan*
✶ Meghdoot	*Kalidas*
✶ Mritunjaya	*B.K. Bhattacharya*
✶ Mudrarakshasa	*Vishakhadatta*
✶ Prison Diary	*Jaya Prakash Narayan*
✶ Raghuvansha	*Kalidas*
✶ Rajtarangini	*Kalhana*
✶ Ramayana	*Balmiki*
✶ Ramcharit Manas	*Tulsidas*
✶ Rukh Te Rishi	*Harbhajan Singh*
✶ Satyarth Prakash	*Swami Dayanand*
✶ Sur Sagar	*Surdas*
✶ The Guide	*R.K. Narayan*

IMPORTANT DATES AND DAYS OF THE YEAR

✶ **JANUARY**

5-11 Road Safety Week
12 National Youth Day
15 Army Day
15-21 Pin Code Week
23 National Day of Patriotism
26 Republic Day
30 Martyr's Day

✶ **FEBRUARY**

1-14 Oil Conservation Fortnight
14 Valentine's Day

✶ **MARCH**

4 National Safety Day
8 International Women's Day
15 Consumers' Day
16 Immunisation Day
21 World Forest Day
22 World Day for Water
24 World Meteorological Day
1-7 Preservation of Blindness Week

✶ **APRIL**

7 World Health Day
7-13 Handloom Week
14-20 Fire Service Week
18 World Heritage Day
22 World Earth Day

✶ **MAY**

1 May Day
5 National Labour Day
8 World Red Cross Day
11 National Technology Day
15 International Day of the Family
17 World Telecommunication Day
24 Commonwealth Day
31 World No-Tobacco Day

✶ **JUNE**

5 World Environment Day
21 World Yoga Day
26 International Day against Drug Abuse and Illicit Trafficking

✶ **JULY**

11 World Population Day

✶ **AUGUST**

1-7 World Breast feeding Week
10 Sanskrit Divas
15 Independence Day
20 Sadbhavana Divas

✶ **SEPTEMBER**

1-7 National Nutrition Week
5 Teachers' Day
8 International Literary Day
14 Hindi Diwas
23 World Deaf Day
27 World Tourism Day

✶ **OCTOBER**

2 Gandhi Jayanti
International Day of Non Violence
Anti-Leprosy Day
4 World Animal Day
6 World Habitat Day *(Ist Monday)*
8 Indian Air Force Day
14 World Standard Day
15 International Day of Rural Women
16 World Food Day
24 United Nations Day
27 Infantry Day
28 World Thrift Day
31 Anti-Terrorism Day

✶ **NOVEMBER**

2 All Saints Day
14 Children's Day
15-21 National Cooperative Week
19-25 Quami Ekta Week
20 Child Rights Day
26 Constitution Day

✶ **DECEMBER**

1 World AIDS Day
3 World Day for the Disabled
4 Naval Day
7 Flag Day
8 SMRC Day
10 Human Rights Day
14 National Energy Conservation Day

INDIAN DEFENCE

- The Supreme Command of the Armed Forces is vested in the hands of the President of the Country.
- The responsibility for national defence, however, rests with the Cabinet. All important questions having a bearing on defence are decided by the Cabinet Committee on Political Affairs, which is presided over by the Prime Minister.
- The Defence Minister is responsible to Parliament for all matters concerning the Defence Services.
- All the administrative and operational control of Armed Forces are exercised by the Ministry of Defence. The three services—Army, Navy and Air Force function through their respective service head-quarters headed by the chief of Staff. The post of Chief of Defence Staff (CDS) was created in 2019.

Indian Army Commands

Command	*HQ Location*
Eastern Command	Kolkata
Western Command	Chandigarh
Northern Command	Udhampur
Southern Command	Pune
Central Command	Lucknow
Training Command	Shimla
South-Western Command	Jaipur

Indian Air Force Commands

Command	*HQ Location*
Western Air Command	New Delhi
Sout-Western Air Command	Gandhinagar
Central Air Command	Allahabad
Eastern Air Command	Shillong
Southern Air Command	Thiruvananthapuram
Training Command	Bengaluru

Indian Navy Commands

Command	*HQ Location*
Eastern Naval Command	Vishakhapatnam
Western Naval Command	Mumbai
Southern Naval Command	Cochin

Commissioned Ranks in Defence Services

Army	*Navy*	*Air Force*
General	Admiral	Air Chief Marshal
Lieutenant-General	Vice-Admiral	Air Marshal
Major-General	Rear-Admiral	Air Vice-Marshal
Brigadier	Commodor	Air Commodor
Colonel	Captain	Group Captain
Lieutenant-Colonel	Commander	Wing Commander
Major	Lt.Commander	Squadron Leader
Captain	Lieutenant	Flight Lieutenant
Lieutenant	Sub-Lieutenant	Flying Officer

Internal Security Organisations of India

S. No.	*Name of Organisation*	*Year of Creation*	*Headquarters*
1.	Assam Rifles (A.R.)	1835	Shillong
2.	Central Reserve Police Force (CRPF)	1939	New Delhi
3.	Territorial Army	1948	In different States
4.	Indo-Tibetan Border Police	1962	New Delhi
5.	Home Guard	1962	In different States

S. No.	Name of Organisation	Year of Creation	Headquarters
6.	Coast Guard	1978	New Delhi
7.	Border Security Force (B.S.F.)	1965	New Delhi
8.	Central Industrial Security Force (CISF)	1969	New Delhi
9.	National Security Guard	1984	New Delhi
10.	Police	—	In different States

Army Institutes

1.	Sainik Schools upto +2 Level	33 places in India
2.	Rashtriya Indian Military College (prepare for entrance to N.D.A.)	Dehradun
3.	National Defence Academy (three services)	Khadakwasla, Pune
4.	Indian Military Academy (Army)	Dehradun
5.	Officers Training Academy (3 services) Short Courses	Chennai
6.	National Defence College	New Delhi
7.	The College of Combat	Mhow
8.	The College of Military Engineering	Kirkee
9.	Military College of Telecommunication Engineering	Mhow
10.	The Armoured Corps Centre and School	Ahmed Nagar
11.	The School Artillery	Deolali
12.	The Infantry School	Mhow and Belgaum
13.	College of Material Management	Jabalpur

Air Force Institutions

✶ Air Force Academy	Hyderabad
✶ Flying Instructors School	Tambaram, Chennai
✶ Air Force Administrative College	Coimbatore
✶ Helicopter Training School	Hakimpet
✶ The College of Air Warfare	Secunderabad
✶ Air Force Technical College	Jalahalli

UNITED NATIONS (UN)

- The United Nations (UN) is an association of states which have pledged themselves to maintain international peace and security and cooperate in solving international political, economic, social cultural and humanitarian problems towards achieving this end.
- Trygve Lie of Norway (1946-52) was the first Secretary-General of the UN.
- ***Origin:*** UN Charter was signed by 50 members on June 26, 1945. Poland signed the charter later to become one of the original 51 member-states. It officially came into existence on October 24, 1945.
- ***UN Charter:*** The Charter is the Constitution of the UN and contains its aims and objectives and rules and regulations for its functioning.
- ***Aims and Objectives:*** They are security, welfare and human rights.
- ***Headquarters:*** New York.
- ***Flag:*** The flag is light blue in colour, and emblazoned in white, in its centre is the UN symbol—a polar map of world embraced by twin olive branches open at the top.
- ***Official Languages:*** The official languages of the UN are: English, French, Chinese, Russian, Arabic and Spanish. However, working languages are English and French only.

- ***Present Membership:*** At present 193 countries are members of the UN. South Sudan is the latest entrant to this world organisation.
- ***Main Organs of the UN:*** There are six main organs:
  1. General Assembly
  2. Security Council
  3. Economic and Social Council
  4. Trusteeship Council
  5. International Court of Justice, and
  6. Secretariat.

1. *General Assembly:* It consists of representative of all members of the UN. Each member country has only one vote. It meets once a year and passes UN Budget. It is the main place for discussions and policy making in the UN.
2. *Security Council:* It is the Executive body of the UN and is mainly responsible for maintaining international peace and security. It has 15 members, 5 of which (USA, UK, France, Russia and China) are permanent members. The 10 non-permanent members are elected by General Assembly for two-year term and are not eligible for immediate re-election.
3. *Economic and Social Council:* It has 54 members elected by General Assembly.
4. *Trusteeship Council:* It looks after interest of the people in areas not yet independent and leads them towards self-government.
5. *International Court of Justice:* It has 15 judges, no two of whom may be nationals of the same state. They are elected by General Assembly and Security Council for a term of 9 years. The Court elects its President and Vice-President for a 3-year term.
6. *Secretariat:* It is the Secretariat of the UN and is headed by the Secretary General.

Some Important UN Agencies

UN Agencies	Headquarters	Year of Establishment
∗ United Nations (U.N.)	New York	1945
∗ International Monetary Fund (I.M.F.)	Washington D.C.	1945
∗ World Health Organisation (W.H.O.)	Geneva	1948
∗ Food & Agricultural Organisation (FAO)	Rome	1945
∗ International Labour Organisation (ILO)	Geneva	1919
∗ UNESCO	Paris	1946
∗ Universal Postal Union (UPU)	Berne	1874
∗ UNIDO	Vienna	1966
∗ International Atomic Energy Agency (IAEA)	Vienna	1957
∗ United Nations Development Programme (UNDP)	New York	1965
∗ UNICEF	New York	1946
∗ International Maritime Organisation (IMO)	London	1958
∗ World Meteorological Organisation (WMO)	Geneva	1950
∗ International Telecommunication Union (ITU)	Geneva	1865
∗ World Trade Organisation (WTO)	Geneva	1995
∗ International Development Association (IDA)	Washington D.C.	1960
∗ World Intellectual Property Organisation (WIPO)	Geneva	1967

Famous International Organisations

International Organisations	Headquarters	Year of Establishment
∗ International Court of Justice	The Hague	1946
∗ International Civil Aviation Organisation (ICAO)	Montreal	1947
∗ International Finance Corporation (IFC)	Washington D.C	1956
∗ Arab League	Cairo	1945
∗ Commonwealth of Nations	London	1949
∗ International Bank for Reconstruction and Development (IBRD)	Washington D.C.	1945
∗ Organisation of Islamic Cooperation (OIC)	Jeddah (Saudi Arabia)	1969
∗ Red Cross	Geneva	1863
∗ Interpol	Lyons	1923
∗ Asian Development Bank (ADB)	Manila	1966
∗ North Atlantic Treaty Organisation (NATO)	Brussels	1949
∗ Association of South East Asian Nations (ASEAN)	Jakarta	1967
∗ South Asian Association for Regional Cooperation (SAARC)	Kathmandu	1985
∗ Asia-Pacific Economic Cooperation (APEC)	Singapore	1989
∗ Organisation for Economic Cooperation and Development (OECD)	Paris	1961
∗ Organisation of Petroleum Exporting Countries (OPEC)	Vienna	1960
∗ Commonwealth of Independent States (CIS)	Minsk	1991
∗ International Olympic Committee (IOC)	Lausanne (Switzerland)	1894
∗ European Union (EU)	Brussels	Changed form of EEC Established in 1958
∗ Amnesty International (AI)	London	1961
∗ Shanghai Cooperation Organisation (SCO)	Beijing	2001
∗ BRICS Development Bank	Shanghai	2014

AWARDS AND HONOURS

NATIONAL AWARDS

BHARAT RATNA

- Bharat Ratna is India's highest Civilian Award. It was first awarded in 1954.
- The actual award is designed in the shape of a *peepal* leaf with Bharat Ratna inscribed in Devanagri script in the Sun Figure.
- This is India's highest civilian award. It is given for exceptional work on art, literature, science and recognition of public service of the highest order.
- The emblem, the Sun and the rim are of platinum.
- The inscriptions are in burnished bronze.
- Government servants are not eligible for it.

REPUBLIC DAY AWARDS

Padma Awards

They fall in line after the Bharat Ratna. They are also discontinued in 1977 along with the Bharat Ratna and award was started again in 1980.

There are three Padma Awards:

- ***Padma Vibhushan:*** This award is given for exceptional and distinguished service in any field, including service rendered by Govt. servants.
- ***Padma Bhushan:*** This award is given for distinguished service of a high order in any field, including service rendered by Govt. servants.
- ***Padma Shri:*** This award is given for distinguished service in any field, including service rendered by Government servants.

Gallantry Awards

- ***Param Vir Chakra:*** The highest award for bravery or some daring and pre-eminent act of valour or self-sacrifice in the presence of the enemy, whether on land, at sea or in the air.
- ***Mahavir Chakra:*** It is the second highest decoration and is awarded for acts of conspicuous gallantry in the presence of the enemy, whether on land, at sea or in the air.
- ***Vir Chakra:*** It is the third in order of awards given for acts of gallantry in the presence of enemy, whether on land, at sea or in the air.
- ***Ashok Chakra:*** This medal is awarded for the most conspicuous bravery or some daring or pre-eminent act of valour or self-sacrifice on land, at sea or in the air but not in the presence of enemy.
- ***Vishishta Sewa Medal:*** It is awarded to personnel of all the three Services in class I, II and III in recognition of distinguished service of the "most exceptional" and "exceptional" and a "high" order respectively. Prefixes Parma and Ati are added before first two categories of medals respectively.
- ***Jeewan Raksha Padak:*** Awarded for meritorious acts or a series of acts of a human nature displayed in saving life from drowning, fire and rescue operations in mines etc.

OTHER NATIONAL AWARDS

SAHITYA AKADEMI AWARDS

- These prizes are awarded annually to the authors of the most outstanding books of literary merit published in each of the 22 languages which are specified in the Eighth Schedule of the Constitution.
- There are also two awards for Rajasthani and English. The award, in form of a casket containing an inscribed copper plate and a cheque of ₹ 1 lakh is given to the author or his/her heir.

DADA SAHEB PHALKE AWARD

- The award carries a cash prize of ₹ 15 lakh, a Shawl and Swarna Kamal.
- Mrs Devika Rani Roerich was the first person to receive Dadasaheb Phalke Award in 1969.

BHARATIYA JNANPITH AWARD

- Instituted in 22nd May, 1961, carries a cash prize of ₹ 21 lakh, a citation and a bronze replica of Vagdevi (Saraswati).
- Instituted by a literary organisation in India.

SARASWATI SAMMAN

- Given for outstanding literary works, value ₹ 15 lakh.

VYAS SAMMAN

- This is awarded by KK Birla Foundation for outstanding Hindi Literary work by an Indian citizen that was published in the past decade. This carries a cash prize of ₹ 4.0 lakh.

BHARTENDU HARISHCHANDRA AWARDS

- The Bhartendu Harishchandra Awards were instituted in 1983, by the Ministry of Information and Broadcasting for original Hindi writing on any subject in mass communications like journalism, publication, advertising, broadcasting films, etc.

KALIDAS SAMMAN

- Instituted by the Madhya Pradesh Government, the award is of the value of ₹ 2 lakh.

KABIR SAMMAN

- The award is conferred annually on a person of literature of very high order on the basis of his or her superb creativity and consistent commitment to the most recent and latest trends of literary creation in any of the Indian languages. The award carries ₹ 3 lakh and a letter of citation.

INTERNATIONAL AWARDS

NOBEL PRIZES

- These Prizes were instituted in 1901 by a Swedish scientist, Dr. Alfred Nobel; the discoverer of Dynamite.
- Six prizes are awarded annually for (i) Chemistry, (ii) Physics, (iii) Medicine, (iv) Literature, (v) Peace and (vi) Economics —started since 1969.
- **Indians Honoured with Nobel Prize:** So far, following Indians have been honoured with these prizès. Their names are (i) Rabindra Nath Tagore for Literature, for his book 'Gitanjali', in 1913, (ii) Dr. C.V. Raman for Physics in 1930, for his discovery of 'Raman Effect', (iii) Mother Teresa for Peace in 1979, (iv) Prof. Amartya Sen in 1998 for Economics and (v) Kailash Satyarthi for Peace in 2014.

  In addition, four non-resident Indians have also been awarded the Nobel Prize. They are: (i) Hargobind Khurana for Medicine in 1968, (ii) Subramanian Chandrasekhar for Physics in 1983, (iii) Venkatraman Ramkrishnan for Chemistry in 2009, (iv) Abhijit Vinayak Banerjee for Economics in 2019.

GANDHI PEACE PRIZE

- The government instituted this ₹ 1 crore prize on the lines of the Nobel Peace Prize in 1995.
- It is the highest Civilian International award by the Govt. of India.

RAMON MAGSAYSAY AWARD

- The Ramon Magsaysay Award, named after a Philippines President, who died in an air crash in 1957, is given annually to Asian nationals or institutions who have made worthy contributions to public service, community leadership, journalism, literature and the creative arts and international understanding. It carries a gold medal, a certificate and US$ 50,000. It is awarded on August 31, every year. The Ramon Magsaysay Award is Asia's highest honor and is widely regarded as the region's equivalent of the Nobel Prize. It celebrates the memory and leadership example of the third Philippline president after whom the award is named, and is given every year to individuals or organizations in Asia who manifest the same selfless service and transformative influence that ruled the life of the late and beloved Filipino leader.

INDIRA GANDHI PRIZE FOR PEACE, DISARMAMENT AND DEVELOPMENT

- The award was instituted in the memory of Mrs. Indira Gandhi to foster creative cooperation among nations of the world.

MISS WORLD

- This competition was established in 1951 by the 'Miss World Incorporation'. The Winner of this competition gets cash as prize and she is selected on her physical and intellectual genius.

MISS UNIVERSE

- This competition was established in year 1952 by 'Miss Universe Incorporation'. The winner of this competition gets cash as prize. The most beautiful girl is selected in this competition on the basis of her beauty and multifarious genius.

Highest Honours of Some Countries

Country	Highest Honour
India	Bharat Ratna
Pakistan	Nishan-e-Pakistan
Kuwait	Mubarak-Al-kabir Medal
Saudi Arabia	Shah Abdul Aziz Medal
Argentina	The Order of Sona Martin
Nicaragua	Augusto-Caesar Sandino Order
Vietnam	The Order of the Golden Star
Hungary	The Order of Banner
Britain	Member of British Empire, Victoria Cross
Japan	Order of Moulovenice Sun
Denmark	Order of Diana Brog
France	Legend of Honour
America	Presidential Medal of Freedom
Germany	Pore Lee Merit Iron Cross
The Netherlands	Netherlands Lion

SPORTS

OLYMPICS

- First of all these games were held by the Greeks in 776 B.C. on Mount Olympus in honour of the Greek God Zeus. In this way, the history of Olympic Games is about twenty eight hundred years old. These games continued to be held every four years until 394 A.D. when these games were stopped by a royal order of the emperor of Rome.
- The modern Olympic Games which started in Athens in 1896, are the result of the devotion and dedication of a French educator Baron Pierre de Coubertin and the first Olympic meet in the modern series was held in 1896 in Athens, the Capital of Greece. Since then, they are being held every four years except for breaks during world wars.
- The Olympic flag is white in colour with five coloured rings, each ring symbolic of a continent. Summer as well as Winter Olympics are held in the same year.
- The official Olympic Motto is *Citius, Altius, Swifter, Higher, Stronger*. The Head Office of International Olympic Committee (IOC) is at Lausanne (Switzerland).

COMMONWEALTH GAMES

- The Commonwealth Games are held every four years, in the year in which Asian Games are held. All the Commonwealth Countries (former colonies of Britain) can take part in it.
- The first Commonwealth Games were held in 1930 at Hamilton (Canada). There are currently 54 members of the Commonwealth of Nations, and 71 teams participated in the games.

ASIAN GAMES

- After the Second World War, most of the Asian Countries gained independence. On the lines of Olympic Games, Asian Games were planned every four years. India hosted the first Asian Games in 1951.

WORLD CUP CRICKET

- The first Cricket World Cup was organised in England in 1975. A separate women's Cricket World Cup has been held every 4 years since 1973.

HOCKEY WORLD CUP

- The first Hockey World Cup was organised in Barcelona (Spain) in 1971. Women's Hockey World Cup has been held since 1974.

FOOTBALL WORLD CUP

- The Football World Cup is organised by FIFA (Federation of International Football Association). The World Cup is called 'Jules Rimet Cup' named after the name of FIFA President Jules Rimet. The first Football World Cup was organised in Uruguay in 1930.
- In 1942 and 1946, the Football World Cup was not played due to World War II.

SPORTS TERMS

- ✶ ***Badminton:*** Mixed doubles; Deuce; Drop; Smash; Let; Foot work; Setting.
- ✶ ***Base Ball:*** Pitcher; Put out, Strike; Home; Bunt.
- ✶ ***Billiards:*** Cue; Jigger; Pot; Break; In Baulk; In Off; Cannons.
- ✶ ***Boxing:*** Upper cut; Round; Punch; Bout; Knock down; Hitting below the belt; Ring.
- ✶ ***Bridge:*** Finesse; Dummy; Revoke; Grand Slam; Little Slam; No Trump; Rubber.
- ✶ ***Chess:*** Bishop, Gambit; Checkmate; Stalemate.
- ✶ ***Cricket:*** L.B.W. (leg before wicket); Creases, Popping-creases; Stumped; Bye; Leg-Bye; Googly; Hattrick; Maiden over; Drive; Bowling; Duck; Follow-on; No ball; Leg Break; Silly point; Cover point; Hit-wicket; Late-cut; Slip; Off-spinner; In-swing.
- ✶ ***Football:*** Off Side; Block; Drop-kick; Penalty-kick (or goal kick); Corner-kick; Free-kick; Dribble; Thrown-in; Foul.
- ✶ ***Golf:*** Boggy; Foursome; Stymic; Tee; Put; Hole; Niblic; Caddie; Links; The green; Bunker.
- ✶ ***Hockey:*** Carried; Short Corner; Bully; Sticks; Off side; Roll in; Striking Circle; Under-cutting; Dribble.
- ✶ ***Horse racing:*** Jockey; Punter.
- ✶ ***Polo:*** Bunker; Chukker; Mallet.
- ✶ ***Tennis:*** Back hand drive; Volley; Smash; Half-volley; Deuce; Service; Let; Grand Slam.

ALL THE HEROES

Sportsman	Game
Anand Amritraj	Tennis
Arati Saha	Swimming
Ashok Malik	Golf
Althea Gibson	Tennis
Ashe Arthur	Tennis
Mohd. Azharuddin	Cricket
A.K. Ghosh	Chess
Anju Dua	Gymnastics
Balbir Singh	Hockey
Bannerji, P.K.	Football
Bedi, B.S.	Cricket
Bapu Nadkarni	Cricket
Benaud, Richie	Cricket
Ben Johnson	Athletics
Bobby Fischer	Chess
Boris Becker	Tennis
Bharat Ram	Golf
Chetan Baboor	Table Tennis
Borde, Chandu	Cricket
Budding, Ingo	Tennis
Bungert, Williams	Tennis
Chandrashekhar	Cricket
Chandgi Ram	Wrestling
Charanjit Singh	Hockey
Carl Lewis	Athletics
Chuni Goswami	Football
Clandius	Hockey
Clive Loyd	Cricket
Connoly	Tennis
Chris Evert	Tennis
Dhyan Chand	Hockey
Dara Singh	Wrestling
Dinesh Khanna	Badminton
Diwan, G.	Table Tennis
Dolly Zazir	Swimming
Durrani, Salim	Cricket
Das, Susan	Tennis
Don Bradman	Cricket
Emerson, Roy	Tennis
Erlend Kops	Badminton
Elena Shushunova	Gymnastics
Flash Gordon	Wrestling
Florence Griffith Joyner	Athletics
Gurang Mehta	Chess
Goolagong, Even	Tennis
Ghose, A.L.	Golf
Hamida Bano	Wrestling
Haneef	Cricket
Harbans Singh	Wrestling
Harnek Singh	Hockey
Hasan Sardar	Hockey
Hazare, V.	Cricket
Henry Cotton	Golf
Hutton, Len	Cricket
Imran Khan	Cricket
Ivan Lendle	Tennis
Jaideep Mukherjee	Tennis
Jasjit Singh	Tennis
Jarnail Singh	Football
Jayant Vohra	Table Tennis
kapil Dev	Cricket
Maradona	Football
Martina Navratilova	Tennis
Mike Tyson	Boxing
Mohammed Ali Clay	Boxing
Mohammed Shahid	Hockey
Narendra Hirwani	Cricket
Nawab Pataudi	Cricket
Rod Lever	Tennis
RS Gentle	Hockey
Sachin Tendulkar	Cricket
Seth, T. N.	Badminton
Shirley Fry	Tennis
Shonny Liston	Boxing
Shiny Abraham	Athletics
Steffi Graf	Tennis
Sunil Gavaskar	Cricket
Udham Singh	Hockey
Umrigar, Poly	Cricket
Urmila Thapar	Tennis
Usha P.T.	Athletics
Vijay Amrithraj	Tennis
Vivian Richard	Cricket
Wasim Akram	Cricket
Wilson Jones	Billiards
Woong Pong	Badminton
Worrel, Frank	Cricket
Zafar Iqbal	Hockey

IMPORTANT CUPS & TROPHIES

International

✶ *American Cup* : Yacht Racing
✶ *Ashes* : Cricket
✶ *Davis Cup* : Lawn Tennis
✶ *Derby* : Horse Race
✶ *Grand National* : Horse Streple Chase Race
✶ *Jules Rimet Trophy* : World Soccer Cup
✶ *King's Cup* : Air Races
✶ *Merdeka Cup* : Football
✶ *Swaythling Cup* : Table Tennis (Men)
✶ *Ryder Cup* : Golf
✶ *Thomas Cup* : Badminton
✶ *U. Thant Cup* : Tennis
✶ *Walker Cup* : Golf
✶ *Wightman Cup* : Lawn Tennis
✶ *Rothman's Trophy* : Cricket
✶ *European Champions Cup* : Football
✶ *Edgbaston Cup* : Lawn Tennis
✶ *Grand Prix* : Lawn Tennis

National

✶ *Agha Khan Cup* : Hockey
✶ *Beighton Cup* : Hockey
✶ *Bombay Gold Cup* : Hockey
✶ *C.K. Naydu Trophy* : Cricket
✶ *Deodhar Trophy* : Cricket
✶ *Duleep Trophy* : Cricket
✶ *Durand Cup* : Football
✶ *Dhyan Chand Trophy* : Hockey
✶ *Dr. B.C. Roy Trophy* : Football (Junior)
✶ *Ezra Cup* : Polo
✶ *Guru Nanak Cup* : Hockey
✶ *Holkar Trophy* : Bridge
✶ *Irani Trophy* : Cricket
✶ *Murugappa Gold Cup* : Hockey
✶ *Nehru Trophy* : Hockey
✶ *Nixan Gold Cup* : Football
✶ *Rani Jhansi Trophy* : Cricket
✶ *Ranji Trophy* : Cricket
✶ *Rangaswami Cup* : Hockey
✶ *Ramanujan Trophy* : Table Tennis
✶ *Rene Frank Trophy* : Hockey
✶ *Rohinton Baria Trophy* : Cricket
✶ *Rovers Cup* : Football
✶ *Santosh Trophy* : Football
✶ *Subroto Cup* : Football

Stadiums & Places Associated with Sports

Name of Stadium	*Sports*	*Place*
Arun Jaitley Stadium	Cricket	Delhi
Jawaharlal Nehru Stadium	Athletics	Delhi
Shivajee Stadium	Hockey	Delhi
Ambedkar Stadium	Football	Delhi
Brabourne Stadium	Cricket	Mumbai
Wankhede Stadium	Cricket	Mumbai
National Stadium	Hockey etc.	Mumbai
Eden Garden	Cricket	Kolkata
Green Park Stadium	Cricket	Kanpur
Keenan Stadium	Cricket	Jamshedpur
Barabati Stadium	Cricket	Cuttack
Lords, Oval, Leeds	Cricket	Britain
Hedingle Manchester	Cricket	Britain
Black Heath	Rugby Football	London
Henley	Boat race	England
Wembley Stadium	Football	London
Narendra Modi Stadium	Cricket	Ahmedabad
White City	Dog-race	England
Aintree	Horse-race	England
Tentbridge	Cricket	England
Patnee Martlake	Boat-race	England
Tibankham	Rugby Football	England
Sandy Lodge	Golf	Scotland
Brooklyn	Baseball	New York
Melbourne	Cricket	Australia

Name of Playing Compound of Different Games

Name of Compound	Related Sports
Court	Lawn Tennis, Badminton, Netball, Hand ball, Volleyball, Squash, Kho-Kho, Kabaddi
Diamond	Baseball
Ring	Boxing, Skating, Wrestling, Circus, Riding display
Course	Golf
Board	Table Tennis
Pool	Swimming
Mat	Judo, Karate II
Arena	Horse Riding
Vellodrum	Cycling
Field	Polo, Football, Hockey
Track	Athletics
Pitch	Cricket, Rugby
Rink	Ice Hockey

❐ ❐ ❐

Multiple Choice Questions

1. Match List-I with List-II and select the correct answer from the codes given below the lists:

List-I

(*a*) Napoleon Bonaparte
(*b*) Jean Jacques Rousseau
(*c*) Croce
(*d*) Madame Roland

List-II

1. 'A history is contemporary history'
2. 'Liberty what crimes are committed in thy name'
3. 'Man is born free but everywhere he is in chains.'
4. 'I am the Child of Revolution'

Codes :

	(*a*)	(*b*)	(*c*)	(*d*)
A.	1	2	3	4
B.	4	3	1	2
C.	3	4	2	1
D.	3	4	1	2

2. Abraham Lincon was elected the President of United States in:
A. 1862 B. 1860
C. 1875 D. 1855

3. Who was known as the 'Prince of Humanists'?
A. Francisco Petrarch B. Dante
C. Boccacio D. Erasmus

4. D-Day is the day when:
A. Germany declared war on Britain
B. US dropped the atom bomb on Hiroshima.
C. Allied Troops landed in Normandy
D. Germany surrendered to the allies

5. Whose teachings inspired the French Revolution?
A. Locke
B. Rousseau
C. Hegel
D. Plato

6. At a time when empires in Europe were crumbling before the might of Napoleon which one of the following Governor-Generals kept the British flag flying high in India?
A. Warren Hastings B. Lord Cornwallis
C. Lord Wellesley D. Lord Hastings

7. Which one of the following statements regarding Fascism in Italy is *not* true?
A. The Fascists came to power as a result of popular uprising
B. In 1926, all political parties except Mussolini's party were banned
C. The Fascists suppressed the Socialist movement
D. The Fascists were hostile to the Communists

8. The fall of Czar Nicholas-II is known as:
A. Bloody Sunday
B. Bolshevik Revolution
C. February Revolution
D. October Revolution

9. Industrial Revolution took place first in:
A. France B. Germany
C. United Kingdom D. Japan

10. The British Prime Minister at the outbreak of World War II was :
A. Churchill B. Baldwin
C. Attlee D. Chemberlain

11. The 'Great Depression' (1929) economic crisis was met by adopting the policy of
A. Stimulus B. Marshall Plan
C. New Deal D. Open Door

12. The slogan "No taxation without representation" was raised during the:
A. American War of Independence
B. Russian Revolution
C. French Revolution
D. Indian Freedom struggle

13. In the nineteenth century the people of Europe started moving from the villages to the cities due to the impact of :
A. Epidemics
B. War
C. Industrialisation
D. Population explosion in villages

14. The important cause of the Civil War in America was:
A. Abolition of slavery
B. Quest for freedom
C. Industrialisation
D. Rebellion by the native Americans

15. Industrial Revolution could not have come about without:
A. Merchant capitalism
B. The Enclosure Movement
C. The services of the proletariat class
D. An agricultural revolution

16. Consider the following statements :
The French Revolution came about mainly due to the :
1. Extreme poverty of the people
2. Impact of the works of great writers
3. Cruelty of the rulers
4. Impact of impulsive reaction
Which of the above statements are correct?
A. 1, 2 and 4 B. 2 and 3
C. 1, 3 and 4 D. 1, 2, 3 and 4

17. Asia's oldest and largest Buddhist monastery is situated in :
A. Tawang (Arunachal Pardesh)
B. Lhasa (Tibet)
C. Trincomallee (Sri Lanka)
D. Ulan Bator (Mongolia)

18. Who was the main architect of the Russian Revolution?
A. Karl Marx B. Lenin
C. Stalin D. Tolstoy

19. V.I. Lenin is associated with :
A. Russian Revolution of 1917
B. Chinese Revolution of 1949
C. German Revolution
D. French Revolution of 1789

20. Which one of the following statements is *not* correct?
A. Voltaire believed in Natural Religion
B. Rousseau wrote *Social Contract*
C. Montesquieu authored *The Spirit of Laws*
D. Necker believed in 'General Will'

21. 6th April, 1930 is well known in the history of India because this date is associated with..........
A. Dandi March by Mahatma Gandhi
B. Quit India Movement
C. Partition of Bengal
D. Partition of India

22. Which ruler enforced the system of 'Price Control' in India?
A. Mohammad Tughlak
B. Razia Begum
C. Alauddin Khilji
D. Sher Shah Suri

23. The concept of 'Din-e-Elahi' was founded by which king?
A. Dara Shikoh B. Akbar
C. Sher Shah Suri D. Shahjahan

24. Who are supposed to be the earliest inhabitants of India? Where did they come from?
A. Aryans from Central Asia
B. Dravidians from Mediterranean
C. Negroids from Africa
D. Bhils and the Santhals from West Asia

25. The one chief characteristic of temple architecture of the Gupta Age was :
A. Absence of dome
B. Huge size
C. Beautiful carvings
D. absence of a covered courtyard for the gathering of worshippers

26. The Rigveda consists of :
A. 1000 hymns B. 2028 hymns
C. 1028 hymns D. 1038 hymns

27. The central point in Ashoka's dharma was :
A. royalty to kings
B. peace and non-violence
C. respect to elders
D. religious tolerance

28. The social evil which was conspicuously absent during ancient India was :
A. *Sati*-System B. *Devadasi*-System
C. Polygamy D. *Purdah*-System

29. Which, among the following, can be accepted as a novelty introduced by Mughal emperors to their buildings?
A. Domes B. Minarets
C. Arches D. Attached gardens

30. The first ruler of India who defeated Muhammud of Ghur was :
A. Mularaja II of Gujarat
B. Prithviraja Chauhan of Delhi
C. Jayachand of Kannauj
D. Parmaldeva of Bundelkhand

31. What important event happened in India in 1911?
A. Bengal was partitioned
B. Non-Cooperation movement was launched
C. India's capital was shifted from Calcutta to Delhi
D. Mahatma Gandhi presided over the Congress session

32. The first phase of the Congress Party (1885-1905) was characterized by its efforts to secure:
A. limited independence
B. complete freedom
C. Indianization of services
D. constitutional reforms

33. The Muslim League demanded a separate homeland for the Indian Muslims openly for the first time at its annual session held in Lahore in the year :
A. 1931 A.D. B. 1936 A.D.
C. 1940 A.D. D. 1941 A.D.

34. Under whose governorship did the East India Company secure the Diwani Rights in Bengal, Bihar and Odisha from Emperor Shah Alam?
A. Lord Cornwallis
B. Lord William Bentinck
C. Lord Clive
D. Lord Wellesley

35. The Simon Commission was generally boycotted by the Indian political parties. What was the reason for this general non-cooperation?
A. the Commission aimed at dividing the people
B. it was an 'all white' Commission
C. it came after the Jallianwala Bagh carnage
D. it was an eye wash

36. Aligarh Muslim University was founded by :
A. Dr. Saifuddin Kitchlu
B. Mohammad Ali Jinnah
C. Sir Syed Ahmed Khan
D. Maulana Mohammad Ali

37. Ibn Batutah was an African traveller visiting India during the time of :
A. Alivardi Khan
B. Ala-ud-din Khalji
C. Iltutmish
D. Mohammad-bin-Tughlaq

38. The battle of Wandiawash was fought in :
A. 1726 B. 1760
C. 1818 D. 1857

39. The abolition of *Sati* by government regulation was at the time of :
A. Warren Hastings B. Lord Wellesley
C. Lord Bentinck D. Lord Ahmerst

40. Pick out the wrong combination :
A. Dilwara Temple : Mt. Abu
B. Pashupati Temple : Kathmandu
C. Padmanabh Temple : Bangalore
D. Minakshi Temple : Madurai

41. Match the following:
(a) Chanhudaro *(b)* Kalibangan
(c) Lothal *(d)* Surkotada
1. Alleged discovery of the skeleton of horse.
2. Bead making.
3. Traces of a dock and ship on seal.
4. Evidence of ploughing the fields.

The Correct code is :

	(a)	*(b)*	*(c)*	*(d)*
A.	2	4	3	1
B.	2	1	3	4
C.	1	2	3	4
D.	2	1	4	3

42. Match the Harappan settlements with the banks of rivers on which they were located :

(*a*) Harappa	1. Ravi
(*b*) Mohenjodaro	2. Indus
(*c*) Ropar	3. Sutlej
(*d*) Kalibangan	4. Ghaggar
(*e*) Lothal	5. Bhogava

Codes :

	(*a*)	(*b*)	(*c*)	(*d*)	(*e*)
A.	1	2	3	4	5
B.	1	2	3	5	4
C.	2	1	3	5	4
D.	2	1	4	3	5

43. The Goddess 'Kannagi' whose many temples were erected during the 'Sangam Age' was the goddess of :

A. Chastity B. Love
C. Prowess D. Wisdom

44. The Jain goal of life is to attain deliverance from the fetters of mudane existence, the way to which lies through three jewels. Which one of the following was not included among the 'three jewels' of Jainism?

A. Right faith B. Right action
C. Right knowledge D. Right conduct

45. The most striking feature of the Ashokan pillar is polish. Name the Ashokan pillar which is considered to be the most graceful of all Ashokan pillars.

A. Sarnath
B. Rampurva
C. Laurya-Nandangarh
D. Rummindei

46. Which are the correct statements?

1. The land grants, started in Satavahana period, paved the way for feudal developments in India.
2. Silk and spices were the Chief Indian export articles of Indo-Roman trade.
3. The Guptas issued the largest number of gold coins in ancient India.
4. The first memorial of a 'SATI' dated 510 A.D. is found at Eran in Madhya Pradesh.

A. 1 and 2 B. 1, 3, and 4
C. 1 and 4 D. 1, 2, 3 and 4

47. Who among the following patronised the 'Gandhara' (Indo-Greek style) School of Art?

A. Ashoka, the Great
B. Harsha Vardhana
C. Kanishka
D. Chandragupta Vikramaditya

48. The Sultanate of Delhi had five ruling dynasties. The dynasty having longest and shortest period were :

A. Ilbari and Khalji
B. Tughlaq and Khalji
C. Tughlaq and Sayyid
D. Ilbari and Lodis

49. Which one of the following events took place at the last during reign of Muhammad-bin-Tughlaq?

A. Introduction of token currency
B. Increase of land-revenue in Doab
C. Transfer of Capital from Delhi to Devagiri.
D. Conquest of Khurasan and Iraq

50. The most learned medieval Muslim ruler who was well versed in various branches of learning including astronomy, mathematics and medicine was :

A. Jalaluddin Khilji
B. Sikander Lodi
C. Ghiyasuddin Tughlaq
D. Muhammad-bin-Tughlaq

51. The 'Sufis' had 12 silsilas. They propounded the idea of Union with God through:

A. Love B. Rituals
C. Fasts D. Prayers

52. Match the following:

(*a*) Peshwa	1. Foreign affairs
(*b*) Panditrao	2. Audit and accounts
(*c*) Amatya	3. Providing grants to scholars
(*d*) Sumant	4. General supervision
	5. Military affairs

Select the correct code :

	(*a*)	(*b*)	(*c*)	(*d*)
A.	2	3	4	5
B.	4	1	2	3
C.	4	3	2	1
D.	3	1	4	2

53. The Regulating Act of 1773 can be regarded as the first measure to :
A. assert the right of British Parliament to legislate for India
B. separate the legislature from the executive
C. separate the judiciary from the executive
D. centralise law-making

54. What was the exact constitutional status of the Indian Republic on 26th January, 1950?
A. A Democratic Republic
B. A Sovereign, Democratic Republic
C. A Sovereign, Secular, Democratic Republic
D. A Sovereign, Socialist, Secular, Democratic Republic

55. When the British obtained the grant of Diwani of Bengal, Bihar and Odisha they acquired the right to :
A. maintain law and order in these territories
B. administer civil justice and collect revenue in these territories
C. collect revenue and establish revenue administration in these territories
D. militarily defend these territories

56. Which of the following were responsible for the growth of nationalism in India during the British rule?
1. Economic exploitation of India.
2. Impact of western education.
3. Role of the Press.
Select the correct answer using the codes given below :
Codes:
A. 1, 2 and 3 B. 1 and 2
C. 2 and 3 D. 1 and 3

57. Which one of the following nationalist leaders has been described as being radical in politics but conservative on social issues?
A. G.K. Gokhale
B. B.G. Tilak
C. Lala Lajpat Rai
D. Madan Mohan Malviya

58. Provincial Autonomy in British India was envisaged by the :
A. Act of 1909 B. Act of 1919
C. Act of 1935 D. Act of 1947

59. Dyarchy means :
A. double government
B. a government in which the centre is very powerful
C. a government based on division of power between centre and provinces
D. None of the above

60. The Indian National Congress observed 'Independence Day' for the first time on 26th January in :
A. 1920 B. 1925
C. 1930 D. 1947

61. ....is situated near the banks of Sabarmati River
A. Bhavnagar B. Aurangabad
C. Ahmedabad D. Rajkot

62. Sericulture is:
A. science of the various kinds of serum
B. artificial rearing of fish
C. art of silkworm breeding
D. study of various cultures of a community

63. The most abundant constituents of earth's crust are:
A. Igneous rocks
B. Sedimentary rocks
C. Metamorphic rocks
D. Granite

64. Indian Standard Time is based on:
A. 80°E longitude B. 82½°E longitude
C. 110°E longitude D. 25°E longitude

65. Tides in the oceans are caused by :
A. Gravitational pull of the moon on the earth's surface including sea water
B. Gravitational pull of the sun on the earth's surface only and not on the sea water
C. Gravitational pull of the moon and the sun on the earth's surface including the sea water
D. None of these

66. Nagarjunasagar Project is situated on the river:
A. Tungabhadra
B. Cauvery
C. Krishna
D. Godavari

67. The difference between the Indian Standard Time and the Greenwich Mean Time is:
A. – 3½ hours B. + 3½ hours
C. – 5½ hours D. + 5½ hours

68. Which of the following dams is not on Narmada river?
A. Indira-Sagar Project
B. Maheshwar Hydel Power Project
C. Jobat Project
D. Koyna Power Project

69. Which of the following statements is **not true** about the availability of water on the earth, the crisis for which is going to increase in the years to come?
A. About 97.5 per cent of the total volume of water available on the earth is salty
B. 80 per cent of the water available to us for use comes in bursts as monsoons
C. About 2.5 per cent of the total water available on the earth is polluted water and cannot be used for human activities
D. Possibility is that some big glaciers will melt in the coming ten-fifteen years and sea level will rise by 3-4 metres all over the earth

70. Which of the following is **not** a cash crop?
A. Jute B. Paddy
C. Cashewnut D. Sugarcane

71. Through which States does Cauvery River flow?
A. Gujarat, M.P., Tamil Nadu
B. Karnataka, Kerala, Tamil Nadu
C. Karnataka, Kerala, Andhra Pradesh
D. M.P., Maharashtra, Tamil Nadu

72. Indian Standard Time is the local time of 82½°E which passes through :
A. Guntur B. Delhi
C. Allahabad D. Kolkata

73. The 17th parallel defines the boundary between:
A. North and South Korea
B. USA and Canada
C. North and South Vietnam
D. China and Russia

74. During the period of south-west monsoon, Tamil Nadu remains dry because:
A. the winds do not reach this area
B. there are no mountains in this area
C. it lies in the rain shadow area
D. the temperature is too high to let the winds cool down

75. Which country does top in producing cocoa?
A. Cote d'Ivoire B. Brazil
C. Ghana D. Nigeria

76. The biggest reserves of thorium are in :
A. India B. China
C. The Soviet Union D. U.S.A.

77. The Girnar Hills are situated in which of the following states?
A. Gujarat B. Karnataka
C. Madhya Pradesh D. Maharashtra

78. During December 22nd the sun is vertically over:
A. Tropic of Cancer
B. Tropic of Capricorn
C. The Equator
D. None of the above

79. Photosphere is described as the :
A. Lower layer of atmosphere
B. Visible surface of the sun from which radiation emanates
C. Wavelength of solar spectrum
D. None of the above

80. Broadly, there are three layers of the earth of the crust, the mantle and the core. The crust forms what percentage of the volume of the earth?
A. 0.5% B. 2.5%
C. 7.5% D. 12.5%

81. The grassland of Argentina is known as :
A. Pampas B. Campos
C. Savanna D. None of the above

82. Different seasons are formed because :
A. Sun is moving around the earth
B. of revolution of the earth around the Sun on its orbit
C. of rotation of the earth around its axis
D. All of the above

83. Eskers and Drumlins are features formed by:
A. underground water
B. running water
C. the action of wind
D. glacial action

84. Match List-I and List-II and select the correct answer using the codes given below the Lists :

List-I *(Rivers)*	**List-II** *(Towns)*
(*a*) Ghaghara	1. Lucknow
(*b*) Brahmaputra	2. Hoshangabad
(*c*) Narmada	3. Ahmedabad
(*d*) Sabarmati	4. Guwahati
	5. Ayodhya

	(*a*)	(*b*)	(*c*)	(*d*)
A.	4	5	1	2
B.	5	4	2	3
C.	5	4	3	1
D.	3	5	2	1

85. Which of the statements as regards the consequences of the movement of the earth is not correct?
A. Revolution of the earth is the cause of the change of seasons.
B. Rotation of the earth is the cause of days and nights.
C. Rotation of the earth causes variation in the duration of days and nights.
D. Rotation of the earth effects the movement of winds and ocean currents.

86. The world is divided into :
A. 12 time zones
B. 20 time zones
C. 24 time zones
D. 36 time zones

87. The 'Kiel' canal links the :
A. Pacific and Atlantic Oceans
B. Mediterranean Sea and Red Sea
C. Mediterranean Sea and Black Sea
D. North Sea and Baltic Sea

88. Match the following :

List-I	**List-II**
(*a*) Himadri	1. Outer Himalayas
(*b*) Shivalik	2. Inner Himalayas
(*c*) Himanchal	3. Middle Himalayas
(*d*) Sahyadri	4. Western Ghats

Codes:

	(*a*)	(*b*)	(*c*)	(*d*)
A.	1	2	3	4
B.	4	2	3	1
C.	2	1	3	4
D.	1	2	3	4

89. The term 'Regur' refers to:
A. Laterite soils
B. Black Cotton soils
C. Red Soils
D. Deltaic Alluvial Soils

90. Location of sugar industry in India is shifting from north to south because of:
A. cheap labour
B. expanding regional market
C. cheap and abundant supply of power
D. high yield and high sugar content in sugarcane

91. Consider the following statements :
1. Ozone is found mostly in the Stratosphere.
2. Ozone layer lies 55-75 km above the surface of the earth.
3. Ozone absorbs ultraviolet radiation from the Sun.
4. Ozone layer has no significance for life on the earth.

Which of the above statements are correct?
A. 1 and 3 B. 2 and 4
C. 2 and 3 D. 1 and 4

92. Match List-I with List-II and select the correct answer using the codes given below the Lists :

List-I *(Crops)*	**List-II** *(Producer)*
(*a*) Banana	1. Brazil
(*b*) Cocoa	2. Cote d'Ivoire
(*c*) Coffee	3. India
(*d*) Tea	4. China

Codes :

	(*a*)	(*b*)	(*c*)	(*d*)
A.	2	3	1	4
B.	3	2	1	4
C.	3	2	4	1
D.	2	3	4	1

93. Darjeeling and Dharamsala would be the right places to visit if one wanted to get a clear view respectively of :
A. Kanchanjunga and Dhauladhar ranges
B. Nandadevi and Dhauladhar ranges
C. Kanchanjunga and Nandadevi ranges
D. Nandadevi and Nanga Parvat

94. Atmosphere exists because:
A. The Gravitational force of the Earth
B. Revolution of the Earth
C. Rotation of the Earth
D. Weight of the gases of atmosphere

95. Victoria lake is located in the continent:
A. Africa
B. Asia
C. North America
D. South America

96. The famous Lagoon Lake of India is :
A. Dal Lake B. Chilka Lake
C. Pulicat Lake D. Mansarover

97. Where are most of the earth's active volcanoes concentrated?
A. Indian Ocean B. Pacific Ocean
C. Aral Sea D. Atlantic Ocean

98. Through which of the following states does the river Chambal flow?
A. U.P., M.P., Rajasthan
B. M.P., Gujarat, U.P.
C. Rajasthan, M.P., Bihar
D. Gujarat, M.P., U.P.

99. Which country is called the sugar bowl of the world?
A. Cuba B. India
C. Argentina D. USA

100. The area covered by forest in India as per ISFR-2023 is:
A. 46% B. 33%
C. 21.76% D. 25.50%

101. A closed economy is the one which :
A. does not permit emigration or immigration
B. permits emigration but no immigration
C. engages in no foreign trade
D. engages in no foreign and domestic trade or transit

102. In a developed economy the major share of employment originates in the :
A. primary sector B. tertiary sector
C. secondary sector D. any of the above

103. The Economic and Social Commission for Asia and Pacific (ESCAP) is located at :
A. Bangkok B. Kuala Lumpur
C. Manila D. Singapore

104. Commercial vehicles are not produced by which of the following companies in India?
A. TELCO B. Ashok Leyland
C. DCM Daewoo D. Birla Yamaha

105. In India, the Public Sector is most dominant in:
A. transport
B. steel production
C. commercial banking
D. organised term-lending financial institutions

106. The main argument advanced in favour of small scale and cottage industries in India is that:
A. cost of production is low
B. they require small capital investment
C. they advance the goal of equitable distribution of wealth
D. they generate a large volume of employment

107. The most serious economic problems of India are:
A. Poverty and unemployment
B. Stagnation, not poverty
C. Unemployment, not poverty
D. Underdevelopment, not poverty

108. Which of the following is not one of the three central problems of an economy?
A. What to produce
B. How to produce
C. When to produce
D. For whom to produce

109. Gender Responsive Budgeting has been adopted in India in the year:
A. 2017 B. 2004
C. 2014 D. 2005

110. In which of the following industries in India are the maximum number of workers employed?
A. Sugar B. Jute
C. Textiles D. Iron and Steel

111. Terrace Cultivation is practiced mostly:
A. in urban areas
B. on slopes of mountains
C. on tops of hills
D. in undulating tracts

112. Which of the following is a Selective Credit Control method?
A. Bank Rate
B. RBI directives
C. Cash Reserve Ratio
D. Open market operations

113. Which of the following taxes is not shared by the Central Government with the States?
A. Union excise duties
B. Customs duty
C. Income tax
D. Estate duty

114. ICICI is the name of a:
A. Financial Institution
B. Chemical Industry
C. Cotton Industry
D. Chamber of Commerce and Industry

115. Structural Unemployment arises due to
A. Deflationary conditions
B. Heavy industry bias
C. Shortage of raw material
D. Inadequate productive capacity

116. Which of the following is the largest single source of the government's earning from tax revenue?
A. Excise duties
B. Customs duties
C. Corporation tax
D. Income tax

117. The largest public sector bank in India is:
A. Central Bank of India
B. Punjab National Bank
C. State Bank of India
D. Indian Overseas Bank

118. Which of the following statements best explains the term contraband goods?
A. Goods produced only for exports
B. Goods produced in joint sector only
C. Goods for the trading of which licence is not required
D. Goods that are forbidden, from export, import or even possession, by law

119. Price in the market is fixed by:
A. Stock exchange rates
B. The demand and supply ruling in the market at a particular time
C. The Finance Minister
D. None of the above

120. Devaluation of currency helps to promote:
A. National Income
B. Savings
C. Imports at lower cost
D. Exports

121. Balanced economic growth can be achieved only if:
A. All the sectors of economy grow at the same rate
B. Population growth is arrested
C. All the inter dependent sectors grow in harmony
D. Basic and heavy industries are assigned highest priority

122. Which one of the following contributes most to the National Income in India?
A. Service Sector
B. Industrial Sector
C. Foreign Trade Sector
D. Agricultural Sector

123. IMF is the result of:
A. Brettonwood conference
B. Rome conference
C. Geneva conference
D. Hawana conference

124. Index 'Residex' is associated with:
A. Share Prices
B. Land Prices
C. Mutual Funds Prices
D. None of the above

125. The term 'devaluation' means:
A. Reducing the value of a currency in terms of another currency
B. Increasing the value of a currency
C. Revising the value of a currency
D. None of the above

126. Per capita net availability of pulses has shown a tendency of:
A. Increase over time
B. Decrease over time
C. Constant over time
D. First increase then decrease

127. National Income is the same as:
A. Net national product at market price
B. Net domestic product at market price
C. Net national product at factor cost
D. Net domestic product at factor cost

128. Which one of the following is not an example of indirect tax?
A. Sales tax B. Excise duty
C. Customs duty D. Expenditure tax

129. The major aim of devaluation is to:
A. encourage imports
B. encourage exports
C. encourage both exports and imports
D. discourage both exports and imports

130. Structural unemployment arises due to:
A. deflationary conditions
B. heavy industry bias
C. shortage of raw materials
D. inadequate productive capacity

131. When was the Family Planning Programme officially started in India?
A. 1950 B. 1952
C. 1956 D. 1962

132. When was the Reserve Bank of India nationalised?
A. 1947 B. 1949
C. 1950 D. 1951

133. Which of the following is *not* a feature of the Indian economy?
A. High rate of population growth
B. Disguised unemployment
C. Lowest rate of adult literacy
D. High rate of exports

134. The 'Relative Deprivation' approach for measuring poverty has been adopted by:
A. developing countries
B. developed countries
C. under-developed countries
D. None of the above

135. One of the main factors that led to rapid expansion of Indian exports is:
A. Imposition of import duties
B. Liberalisation of the economy
C. Recession in other countries
D. Diversification of exports

136. Sustainable economic development means an increase in the rate of growth of real:
A. total and per capita product
B. total and per capita product and level of literacy rate
C. total and per capita product and life expectancy at birth
D. total and per capita product, taking into account the cost of degradation of the quality of environment in this process

137. Functional unemployment occurs when:
A. unemployed have no qualification for job
B. people frequently change their job
C. people were thrown out from job due to recession
D. None of these

138. Which among the following does **not** have a 'free trade zone'?
A. Kandla B. Mumbai
C. Visakhapatnam D. Thiruvanantpuram

139. Sun Belt of USA is important for which one of the following industries?
A. Cotton textile
B. Petrochemicals
C. Hi-tech electronics
D. Food Processing

140. Commercial banking system in India is
A. unit banking B. branch banking
C. mixed banking D. None of the above

141. Who gives recognition to political parties in India?
A. Parliament

B. President
C. Supreme Court
D. Election Commission

142. The Quorum of the Legislative Council is :
A. one-fourth of its total membership
B. one-third of its membership
C. one-tenth of its membership
D. 25

143. The Indian Constitution is:
A. federal
B. unitary
C. a happy mixture of the federal and unitary
D. federal in normal times and unitary in times of emergency

144. Universal adult franchise implies a right to vote to all:
A. adult residents of the State
B. adult male citizens of the State
C. residents of the State
D. adult citizens of the State

145. When a resolution prefering a charge against the President has been passed by a specified majority in the House, it is sent to the other House for investigation. If, as a result of such an investigation, a resolution is passed through a specified majority by the other House, declaring that the charge has been sustained, the President shall leave his office. The specified special majority must not be less than :
A. two-third of the members present and voting
B. one-third of the members present and voting
C. three-fourth of the members present and voting and two-third of the total membership
D. two-third of the total membership

146. Which one of the following judicial powers of the President of India has been *wrongly* listed?
A. he appoints the Chief Justice and other judges of the Supreme Court
B. he can remove the judges of the Supreme Court on grounds of misconduct
C. he can consult the Supreme Court on any question of law or fact which is of public importance
D. he can grant pardon, reprieves and respites to persons punished under Union Law

147. The Vice-president of India can be removed from his office before the expiry of his term if :
A. the Rajya Sabha passes a resolution by a majority of its members and the Lok Sabha agrees with the resolution
B. if the Supreme Court of India recommends his removal
C. the President so desires
D. None of the above

148. 'Sengol', installed in the new Parliament building of India, was seen as a symbol of the path of service, duty and nation in which Empire of the past?
A. Gupta Empire B. Shunga Empire
C. Pandyan Empire D. Chola Empire

149. Which of the following statements is constitutionally not true about the passing of the Union Budgets and Finance Bill in India?
1. Under the law, Finance Bill should be adopted by both the Houses of the Parliament within 45 days of its introduction.
2. If the Finance Bill is not adopted within specified period, the government loses its authority to levy the taxes proposed in the budgets.
3. In the absence of full budget, a vote-on-account gives the power to the government to spend.
4. Government cannot raise revenues without a proper approval of the Finance Bill
A. Only 2 B. Only 3
C. Only 4 D. Only 1, 2 and 3

150. Normally, on whose advice the President's Rule is imposed in a State?
A. Chief Minister
B. Legislative Assembly
C. Governor
D. Chief Justice of High Court

151. Which Article of the Indian Constitution deals with Amendment procedure?
A. Article 368 B. Article 358
C. Article 367 D. All of these

152. Government is the agency through which the will of :
A. the state is expressed
B. the people is expressed
C. the head of the state is expressed
D. the majority is expressed

153. In a unitary system of government :
A. The centre is all powerful
B. The centre is weaker than the states
C. The centre and states stand at par
D. The states and centre are supreme in their respective spheres

154. In Cabinet System of Government the real executive authority rests with :
A. The Council of Ministers
B. The Prime Minister
C. The Constitution
D. The Parliament

155. The Head of the State under a parliamentary government:
A. is an elected representative
B. is a hereditary person
C. is a nominated person
D. may be any one of the above

156. In the event of a ministerial proposal being defeated on the floor of the legislature, under the parliamentary system :
A. the government waits for a general no-confidence motion
B. the minister concerned is taken to task by the Prime Minister
C. the minister is forced to resign
D. the whole Council of Ministers resign

157. The "due process of law" is an essential characteristic of the judicial system of:
A. UK B. France
C. USA D. India

158. Under the Constitution it is :
A. obligatory for the President to accept the advice of the Council of Ministers but is not obliged to follow it
B. obligatory for the President to accept the advice of the Council of Ministers
C. not obligatory for the President to seek or accept the advice of the Council of Ministers
D. obligatory for the President to seek the advice of the Council of Ministers if his own party is in power

159. Which one of the following statements is correct?
A. the Presiding Officer of Rajya Sabha is elected every year
B. the Presiding Officer of Rajya Sabha is elected for a term of two years at a time
C. the Presiding Officer of Rajya Sabha is elected for a term of six years
D. the Vice-President of India is the ex-officio Presiding Officer of Rajya Sabha

160. The introduction of "no confidence" motion in the Lok Sabha requires the support of at least:
A. 50 members B. 70 members
C. 60 members D. 80 members

161. The High Court comes under :
A. State List B. Union List
C. Concurrent List D. None of the above

162. Which one of the following has been wrongly listed as a Fundamental Duty of the Indian citizens?
A. to develop scientific temper, humanism and spirit of inquiry and reform
B. to work for raising the prestige of the country in the international sphere
C. to protect and improve the natural environment
D. to strive towards excellence in all spheres of individual and collective activity

163. Which one of the following is not a Fundamental Duty as outlined in Article 51A of the Constitution?
A. to abide by the Constitution and respect its ideals
B. to defend the country and render national service when called upon to do so

C. to work for the moral upliftment of the weaker sections of society
D. to preserve the rich heritage

164. The main characteristics of the Directive Principles of State Policy given in the Indian Constitution are :
A. not enforceable by any court
B. fundamental in the governance of the country
C. 'Like instruments, instructions, political manifesto and a code of moral precepts which have to guide governors of the country'
D. no law can be passed, which is opposed to these principles

165. Of the following which are true?
A. In a State, the Legislative Council is dominant with regard to non-financial bills and the Legislative Assembly with regard to financial (money) bills
B. Vidhan Parishad can virtually block legisla-tion even if the same is passed by the Vidhan Sabha
C. In case of a tie between the two Houses, the Governor is duty-bound to call a joint session of the two Houses to have the issue settled on a majority verdict
D. If a Bill is twice approved by the Vidhan Sabha, it becomes law even if rejected by the Vidhan Parishad

166. Which one of the following types of emergency can be declared by the President?
A. Emergency due to threat of war and external aggresion
B. Emergency due to break-down of constitu-tional machinery in a State
C. Financial emergency on account of threat to the financial credit of India
D. all the three emergencies

167. The chairman of which of the following parliamentary committees is invariably from the members of ruling party?
A. Committee on public undertakings
B. Public accounts committee
C. Estimates committee
D. Committee on delegated legislation

168. Which of the following is not a formally prescribed device available to the members of parliament?
A. Question hour
B. Zero hour
C. Half-an-hour discussion
D. Short duration discussion

169. Which of the following is not a tool of executive control over public administration?
A. Power of appointment and removal
B. Line agencies
C. Appeal to public opinion
D. Civil services code

170. If the Speaker of the State Legislative Assembly decides to resign, he should submit his resignation to the:
A. Judges of the High Court
B. Deputy Speaker
C. Chief Minister
D. Finance Minister

171. The Constitution of India provides for the nomination of two members of Lok Sabha by the President to represent:
A. the Parsis
B. men of eminence
C. the business community
D. the Anglo-Indian community

172. India is a Federal State because of:
A. dual judiciary
B. dual citizenship prevalent here
C. share of power between the Centre and the States
D. rigid Constitution

173. Residuary Subjects are those subjects which are:
A. contained in the State list
B. contained in the Union list
C. contained in the Concurrent list
D. not covered by any of the three lists

174. Which of the following writs can be issued, by the Supreme Court, to enforce Fundamental Rights?
A. Writ of Habeas Corpus
B. Writ of Mandamus
C. Writ of Quo Warranto
D. All of these

175. When the offices of both the President and the Vice-President of India are vacant, who will discharge their functions?
A. Prime Minister
B. Home Minister
C. Chief Justice of India
D. The Speaker

176. The Supreme Court tenders advice to the President of India on a matter of law or fact:
A. on its own
B. only when such advice is sought
C. only if the matter relates to some basic issue
D. only if the issue poses a threat to the unity and integrity of the country

177. Six months shall **not** intervene between two sessions of the Indian Parliament because :
A. it is the customary practice
B. it is the British convention followed in India
C. it is an obligation under the Constitution of India
D. None of the above

178. The States of the Indian Union can be recognised or their boundaries altered by:
A. the Union Parliament by a simple majority in the ordinary process of legislation
B. two-thirds majority of both the Houses of Parliament
C. two-thirds majority of both the Houses of Parliament and the consent of the legislatures of concerned States
D. an executive order of the Union government with the consent of the concerned State governments

179. The Basic Feature theory of the Constitution of India was propounded by the Supreme Court in the case of :
A. Minerva Mills Vs. Union of India
B. Golaknath Vs. State of Punjab
C. Maneka Gandhi Vs. Union of India
D. Keshavananda Vs. State of Kerala

180. Which one of the following writs is issued by a court in case of illegal detention of a person?
A. Habeas corpus B. Mandamus
C. Certiorari D. Quo-warranto

181. Name the instrument with the help of which a sailor in a submarine can see the objects on the surface of the sea.
A. Telescope B. Periscope
C. Gycroscope D. Stereoscope

182. 'HEMOPHILLIA' is the disease of ....
A. liver B. blood
C. brain D. bones

183. Vitamin A is abundantly found in ....
A. Brinjal B. Tomato
C. Carrot D. Cabbage

184. .... is not soluble in water.
A. Vitamin A B. Vitamin B
C. Vitamin C D. None of these

185. The blood vessels with the smallest diameter are called ....
A. capillaries B. arterioles
C. venules D. lymphatics

186. Out of the following .... has the greatest elasticity.
A. steel B. rubber
C. aluminium D. annealed copper

187. Cooking gas is a mixture of which of the following two gases?
A. Carbon Dioxide and Oxygen
B. Butane and Propane
C. Carbon Monoxide and Carbon Dioxide
D. Methane and Ethylene

188. The substance most commonly used as a food preservative is:
A. sodium carbonate B. tartaric acid
C. acetic acid D. benzoic acid

189. Normally, the substances that fight against diseases in human systems are known as:
A. dioxyribonucleic acids
B. carbohydrates
C. enzymes
D. antibodies

190. The SI unit of temperature is ....
A. Kelvin B. Celsius
C. Fahrenheit D. None of the above

191. One of the common fungal diseases of man is :
A. plague B. ringworm
C. cholera D. typhoid

192. A clear sky is blue because:
A. red light is scattered more than blue
B. ultraviolet light has been absorbed
C. blue light is scattered more than red
D. blue light has been absorbed

193. Jenner introduced the method of making people immune to :
A. small pox B. rabies
C. cholera D. polio

194. The largest cell in the human body is :
A. Nerve cell B. Live cell
C. Muscle cell D. Kidney cell

195. What is the device that steps up or steps down the voltage?
A. Dynamo B. Conductor
C. Inductor D. Transformer

196. The protein deficiency disease is known as :
A. Kwashiorker B. Cirrhosis
C. Eczema D. Clycoses

197. Iron deficiency causes :
A. rickets B. anaemia
C. cirrhosis D. goitre

198. Blood group of an individual is controlled by :
A. Haemoglobin B. Shape of RBC
C. Shape of WBC D. Genes

199. In a normal man the amount of blood pumped out by the heart per minute is about :
A. 1 litre B. 3 litres
C. 4 litres D. 5 litres

200. Red/green colour blindness in man is known as :
A. Protanopia
B. Deutetanopia
C. Both A and B above
D. Marfan's syndrome

201. The blue colour of the water in the sea is due to :
A. Reflection of the blue light by the impurities in sea water
B. Reflection of the blue sky by sea water and scattering of blue light by water molecules
C. Absorption of other colours by water molecules
D. None of the above

202. The image formed on the retina of the eye is:
A. upright and real
B. larger than the object
C. small and inverted
D. enlarged and real

203. Unit of loudness of sound is:
A. bel B. decibel
C. phon D. none of these

204. Oil rises up the wick in a lamp :
A. because oil is volatile
B. due to the capillary action phenomenon
C. due to the surface tension phenomenon
D. because oil is very light

205. The 'stones' formed in human kidney consist mostly of :
A. calcium oxalate
B. sodium acetate
C. magnesium sulphate
D. calcium

206. We hear the sound later, while the light is seen earlier:
A. because light's speed is more than that of sound
B. because lights travel in a straight direction while sound in a zigzag direction
C. because sound's frequency is lower than light
D. All of the above

207. Which part of an eye is transplanted?
A. Cornea
B. Retina
C. Iris
D. Sciera

208. The Universal donor group of blood is:
A. O B. A
C. B D. AB

209. The green colour of the leaf is due to :
A. Presence of Chloroplast
B. Presence of Chromium
C. Presence of Nicoplast
D. Presence of excess of oxygen

210. Voice of a child is more shrill than that of an elderly person because:
A. the pitch of the child's voice is higher than that of the person
B. the pitch is lower
C. the child is more energetic
D. None of the above

211. Camel uses its hump for :
A. storing water
B. storing fat
C. for balancing the body
D. temperature regulation

212. A man standing in a free falling lift releases a ball from his hand. The ball would be :
A. moving down
B. moving up
C. stationary
D. moving up and down

213. To change the quality of sound produced by an instrument we need to vary the:
A. pitch
B. loudness
C. amplitude
D. number of overtonnes

214. The disease caused by Asbestos is:
A. Emphysema B. Paralysis
C. Diarrhoea D. Dysentery

215. Sweetness of a sound depends upon its
A. wavelength
B. frequency
C. amplitude
D. periodicity and regularity

216. Bats can fly in the dark because :
A. they have a better vision in the dark
B. the pupils of their eyes are very big
C. they are guided by ultrasonic waves produced by them
D. any bird can do so

217. Blood is formed in the human adult by the :
A. heart B. spleen
C. kidney D. bone marrow

218. Pencil 'lead' is made up of:
A. graphite B. charcoal
C. lead oxide D. lampblack

219. The deficiency of which one of the following vitamins leads to bleeding of gums and loosening of teeth?
A. Vitamin D B. Vitamin C
C. Vitamin B D. Vitamin A

220. How much blood does a normal person have in his body?
A. 8 litres B. 4 to 5 litres
C. 10 litres D. 2 litres

221. Match List-I with List-II and select the correct answer using the codes given below the Lists :

List-I	List-II
(*a*) Visakhadatta	1. Mrichhakatika
(*b*) Shudraka	2. Ritusamhara
(*c*) Kalidasa	3. Kamasutra
(*d*) Vatsyayana	4. Devichandraguptam

Codes :

	(*a*)	(*b*)	(*c*)	(*d*)
A.	1	4	2	3
B.	4	1	3	2
C.	1	4	3	2
D.	4	1	2	3

222. In which one of the following langauges is the *Dalit* writing more conspicuous?
A. Punjabi B. Assamese
C. Marathi D. Odiya

223. The first writer to use Urdu as the medium of poetic expression was:
A. Amir Khusrau
B. Mirza Ghalib
C. Bahadur Shah Zafar
D. Faiz

224. The religious text of the Zoroastrians is named as:
A. Torah B. The Analects
C. Tripatika D. Zend Avesta

225. Name the music duo which composed music for Raj Kapoor's film 'Bobby'?
A. Laxmikant Pyarelal B. Shankar Jaikishen
C. Kalyanji Anandji D. Nadeem Shravan

226. Raja Harishchandra, an early Indian film, was produced by :
A. D.G. Phalke B. Ashok Kumar
C. Ardeshir Irani D. None of the above

227. All films are certified by .... before they are publicly exhibited.
A. Films Division
B. National Film Development Corporation (NFDC)
C. Directorate of Advertising and Visual Publicity (DAVP)
D. Central Board of Film Certificate (CBFC)

228. Who among the following was the director of the film 'Taal'?
A. Gulzar B. Shekhar Kapoor
C. Satish Shah D. Subhash Ghai

229. Who amongst the following actresses has played the leading role in the film Elizabeth?
A. Gwyneth Paltrow B. Cate Blanchett
C. Simi Garewal D. Kim Basinger

230. The film 'Train to Pakistan' is based on the novel of the same name, written by:
A. Bhishma Sahani
B. Khushwant Singh
C. Amrita Pritam
D. Khwaja Ahmed Abbas

231. Which of the following is a folk dance form of Jharkhand?
A. Pali B. Jhumar
C. Nati D. Chhau

232. The first feature film (talkie) to be produced in India was:
A. Hatimtai B. Alam Ara
C. Pundalik D. Raja Harishchandra

233. Who directed the film "Bombay"?
A. Shyam Benegal B. Meera Nair
C. Shekhar Kapoor D. Mani Ratnam

234. Late Iftekhar Ahmad was famous in which of the following fields?
A. Acting B. Singing
C. Music D. Literature

235. Who among the following is the director of the film 'Kaho Na Pyar Hai'?
A. Subhash Ghai
B. Shekhar Kapoor
C. Ramesh Sippy
D. Rakesh Roshan

236. The character played by Jim Carrey in the movie *Man on Moon* is based on:
A. Andy Kaufman B. Edwin Aldrin
C. John Glenn D. Neil Armstrong

237. A popular Hindi film-based on the famous Sanskrit play *Mrichhakatika*, was titled:
A. Meghadoot B. Amrapali
C. Utsav D. Shakuntala

238. Who composed the song 'Zara Yad Karo Kurbani'?
A. Javed Akhtar
B. Pradeep
C. Nusrat Fateh Ali Khan
D. Raghupati Sahay 'Firaq'

239. Who was the producer of the serial 'Mahabharat'?
A. Shyam Benegal B. B.R. Chopra
C. Ramanand Sagar D. Mani Ratnam

240. Which of the following is a folk dance of Rajasthan?
A. Garba B. Dandya
C. Jhumar D. Kathak

241. 'The Colonel' is the nickname of which Indian Test Cricketer?
A. Colonel C.K. Naidu
B. Rahul Dravid
C. Mohinder Amarnath
D. Dilip Vengsarkar

242. The term 'Grandmaster' is used in which of these games?
A. Judo B. Chess
C. Bridge D. Karate

243. The term "Derby" is related with which of the following?
A. Polo B. Swimming
C. Racing D. Horse Racing

244. With which game is Geet Sethi associated?
A. Basketball B. Chess
C. Snooker D. Tennis

245. Beighton Cup is related with which of the following?
A. Hockey B. Polo
C. Cricket D. Soccer

246. Match List-I with List-II and select the correct answer using the codes given below the Lists :

List-I	**List-II**
(a) Basketball	1. Lob
(b) Bridge	2. Revoke
(c) Golf	3. Pivot
(d) Tennis	4. Bunker

Codes :

	(a)	*(b)*	*(c)*	*(d)*
A.	2	3	1	4
B.	2	3	4	1
C.	3	2	1	4
D.	3	2	4	1

247. The head office of the International Cricket Council (ICC) is situated in :
A. Zimbabwe B. Australia
C. South Africa D. UAE

248. Match the following :

List-I	**List-II**
(a) Deodhar Trophy	1. Volleyball
(b) Durand Cup	2. Football
(c) Davis Cup	3. Cricket
	4. Tennis

Codes:

	(a)	*(b)*	*(c)*
A.	3	2	4
B.	3	1	4
C.	2	3	1
D.	1	2	4

249. Which of the following is called 'Grand Slam'?
A. Winning the highest number of medals in the Olympic games
B. Winning the men's singles title in Wimbledon Championship
C. Winning the Wimbledon Singles title successively for two years
D. Winning all the four championships Australian, French, Wimblendon and US

250. With which game is the term 'butterfly stroke' associated?
A. Swimming B. Cricket
C. Gliding D. Skiing

251. Who is the first Indian to win the 'International Grand Master' title in Chess?
A. Anupama Abhayankar
B. Bhagyashree Sathe Thipsay
C. Vishwanathan Anand
D. D.V. Prasad

252. The XXII Commonwealth Games were held in 2022 in:
A. Kuala Lumpur B. Bangkok
C. Victoria D. Birmingham

253. The term 'Tee' is associated with which of the following sports?
A. Golf B. Table Tennis
C. Polo D. Judo

254. The famous woman Tennis player who was stabbed during a match, is
A. Steffi Graf B. Monica Seles
C. Mary Pierce D. Martina Navratilova

255. The term 'Baseline' is related to which of the following?
A. Golf B. Hockey
C. Badminton D. Polo

256. In which Indian State did the game of Polo originate?
A. Manipur B. Rajasthan
C. Gujarat D. West Bengal

257. Narendra Modi Stadium is located at:
A. Hyderabad B. Chennai
C. Ahmedabad D. Prayagraj

258. Rafael Nadal is the well-known player associated with:
A. Hockey B. Cricket
C. Tennis D. Chess

259. Neeraj Chopra is the well-known player associated with :
A. Javelin Throw B. Golf
C. Table Tennis D. Chess

260. Eden Garden, a famous Cricket stadium, is located in :
A. Kanpur B. Kolkata
C. Jamshedpur D. Pune

261. Maharaja Ranjit Singh Trophy is associated with :
A. Golf B. Hockey
C. Soccer D. Tennis

262. Harmanpreet Kaur is a distinguished player in which of the following games?
A. Swimming B. Weightlifting
C. Cricket D. Archery

263. Cricket was an Olympic event at which of the following Olympics?
A. London, 1908 B. Amsterdam, 1928
C. Paris, 1900 D. Melbourne, 1956

264. WISPA competitions are associated with :
A. Squash B. Yatching
C. Boxing D. Billiards

265. Ryder Cup is the famous trophy of :
A. Golf B. Chess
C. Boxing D. Polo

266. Davis Cup is associated with the sport of :
A. Cricket B. Football
C. Tennis D. Hockey

267. 'Volley', 'Chop' and 'Drive Spine' are the term associated with :
A. Lawn Tennis B. Badminton
C. Table Tennis D. Golf

268. Lal Bahadur Shastri Stadium is located at :
A. Hyderabad B. Chennai
C. Ahmedabad D. Varanasi

269. The first winner of Major Dhyan Chand Khel Ratna Award was :
A. Geet Sethi
B. Sachin Tendulkar
C. Viswanathan Anand
D. Karnam Malleswari

270. The winner of 2023 ICC Men's Cricket World Cup is:
A. Australia B. Sri Lanka
C. Bangladesh D. England

271. The first team event introduced in 1900 at Paris Olympics was :
A. Hockey B. Football
C. Cricket D. Baseball

272. Which of the following international tennis tournaments is held on grass court?
A. US Open B. French Open
C. Wimbledon D. Australian Open

273. Which cricketer is nicknamed as the pied piper of Punjab?
A. Yuvraj Singh
B. Harbhajan Singh
C. Mohinder Amarnath
D. Navjot Singh Sidhu

274. 'Merdeka Cup' is associated with ....
A. Golf B. Football
C. Squash D. Hockey

275. The first time athletes marched into the stadium behind their nation's flag in Olympics:
A. at St. Louis 1904 B. at London 1908
C. at Antwerp 1920 D. at Paris 1924

276. The "Dronacharya Award" is associated with:
A. Eminent Surgeons B. Famous Sports Person
C. Sport Coaches D. Expert Engineers

277. Which cricketer is nicknamed as 'Jumbo'?
A. Venkatesh Prasad B. Anil Kumble
C. Glenn McGrath D. Shane Warne

278. The first time the Olympic Games were organised by a private company at:
A. Montreal, 1976 B. Los Angeles, 1984
C. Atlanta, 1996 D. Rome, 1960

279. In which Asian Games Cricket was played first?
A. Guangzhou, 2010 B. Doha, 2006
C. Busan, 2002 D. Seoul, 1986

280. The term 'Penalty cick' is used in :
A. Hockey B. Football
C. Baseball D. Golf

281. Which of the following countries is not a member of North Atlantic Treaty Organisation (NATO)?
A. Norway B. United Germany
C. Portugal D. Australia

282. Khmer Rouge is a dictatorial party of :
A. Cambodia B. Indonesia
C. Malaysia D. Thailand

283. Which country is not a member of SAARC?
A. Russia B. Bangladesh
C. Nepal D. Pakistan

284. The headquarters of WTO is located at :
A. Geneva B. Paris
C. The Hague D. Washington

285. The main function of the World Trade Organisation (WTO) is:
A. enforcing of Uruguay Round Agreements
B. facilitating multi-lateral trade relations of member countries and reviewing trade policies
C. administering trade dispute settlement procedures
D. None of the above

286. The Secretary-General of the UNO is appointed by the:
A. General Assembly
B. Security Council
C. Trusteeship Council
D. World Bank

287. The United Nations officially came into existence in 1945 on :
A. November 24 B. October 14
C. October 24 D. November 14

288. Which one of the following is true of the International Court of Justice?
A. The Judges of the Court are appointed according to the discretion of the Secretary General
B. No two Judges may belong to the same country
C. The Court consists of 20 Judges
D. The statute of the International Court of Justice is not an integral part of the UN Charter

289. Which of the following was not among the six founding countries of the European Community?
A. Belgium B. France
C. Germany D. UK

290. The smallest country in South America is:
A. Ecuador B. Guyana
C. Surinam D. Uruguay

291. In which year "Human Rights Resolution" was adopted by the U.N.?
A. 1945 B. 1946
C. 1947 D. 1948

292. Where is the headquarters of INTERPOL located?
A. Berlin B. California
C. Lyons D. Montreal

293. Parliament of which of the following countries is known as Great People's Khural?
A. Malaysia B. Mongolia
C. Thailand D. Indonesia

294. Numbers of major organs of United Nations are:
A. 3 B. 4
C. 5 D. 6

295. When is the UN Day celebrated?
A. October 24 B. January 24
C. June 24 D. September 24

296. Which one of the following organ of United Nations is known as the 'Policeman of the World'?
A. Security Council
B. International Court of Justice
C. The Secretariat
D. General Assembly

297. The members of the NAFTA include:
A. USA, Canada and Mexico
B. USA, Canada, Mexico and UK
C. USA, UK, Russia and Mexico
D. USA, Canada and Brazil

298. The sits of International Court of Justice is located at :
A. Vienna B. Paris
C. Hague D. New York

299. Which of the following is known as the Constitution of the UN?
A. UN Charter
B. UN Assembly
C. UN Security Council
D. UN Secretariat

300. The Headquarters of the Amnesty International is located at :
A. New York
B. London
C. Geneva
D. Addis-Ababa

301. Who is the author of the book 'PRISON DIARY'?
A. Bal Gangadhar Tilak
B. Rajendra Prasad
C. Jai Prakash Narayan
D. Jawahar Lal Nehru

302. Who is the author of 'Satanic Verses'?
A. Lewis Carrol B. Salman Rushdie
C. Parry Mason D. Mulk Raj Anand

303. Who wrote 'Gitanjali'?
A. Kalidas
B. Gopal Das 'Neeraj'
C. Rabindra Nath Tagore
D. Jawahar Lal Nehru

304. Who, among the following, scholars flourishing during the Gupta Age, was the author of *Dasakumara-Charita?*
A. Asanga B. Dignaga
C. Dandina D. Bhattin

305. The author of *Gitagovinda* was:
A. Halayudha B. Jayadeva
C. Kalhana D. Jona-raja

306. "Ingenious Pain" is a book/novel written by:
A. Andrew Miller B. Santa Monica
C. Ben Johnson D. Bill Gates

307. Who amongst the following is the author of the famous book "An Equal Music"?
A. Salman Rushdie B. Shasthivrata
C. Vikram Seth D. Kamla Markandeya

308. The famous Moorti Devi Award is given for excellence in which of the following fields?
A. Medicine
B. Science & Technology
C. Social Service
D. Literature

309. Who has written "Devdas"?
A. Tarasankar Bandyopadhyay
B. Bankim Chandra Chattopadhyay
C. Rabindranath Tagore
D. Sarat Chandra Chattopadhyay

310. "Ain-i-Akbari" is written by:
A. Todar Mal B. Abul Fazal
C. Sheikh Saadi D. Mirza Ghalib

311. "Alice in Wonderland" is written by :
A. Lewis Carrol B. Chester Bowles
C. Charles Dickens D. Jonathan Swift

312. "Mrichchhakatikam" is written by :
A. Vishakhadatta B. Vatsyayana
C. Sudraka D. Bana Bhatt

313. "My Experiments with Truth" is written by :
A. Jawaharlal Nehru
B. M.K. Gandhi
C. Abul Kalam Azad
D. Rajendra Prasad

314. Who wrote the book "India Wins Freedom"?
A. Maulana Abul Kalam Azad
B. Mahatma Gandhi
C. Sir Mohammad Iqbal
D. Abdul Gaffar Khan

315. Match List-I with List-II and select the correct answer using the codes given below the Lists :

List-I	List-II
(*a*) *Emma*	1. Graham Greene
(*b*) *Mother India*	2. E.M. Forster
(*c*) *Human Factor*	3. Jane Austen
(*d*) *Passage to India*	4. Katherine Mayo

Codes :

	(*a*)	(*b*)	(*c*)	(*d*)
A.	2	1	4	3
B.	3	4	1	2
C.	3	1	2	4
D.	4	2	1	3

316. 'Poverty and Un British Rule in India' is written by:
A. R.C. Dutt B. J.L. Nehru
C. D.B. Naoroji D. S.N. Sen

317. Name the author of the book *A Passage to England.*
A. E.M. Forster
B. Nirad C. Choudhuri
C. Vikram Seth
D. Eric Segal

318. The author of the book 'The Struggle in My Life' is:
A. Mandela B. J.L. Nehru
C. Tilak D. Gokhale

319. Which one among the following State capitals is closest to the Equator?
A. Panaji
B. Bhubaneswar
C. Hyderabad
D. Mumbai

320. Which of the following books is not written by Salman Rushdie?
A. The Satanic Verses
B. Shame
C. Naked Face
D. Midnight's Children

321. The different schools of modern socialism derive their strength primarily from the writings of ....?
A. Joseph Stalin B. Leo Tolstoy
C. Mao Tse-tung D. Karl Marx

322. Baba Amte was famous as a ....
A. Painter B. Singer
C. Politician D. Social Worker

323. Central Government says that .... was received well by citizens as 'imandari ka utsav'.
A. Demonetization
B. Goods and Services Tax
C. E-NAM
D. All of the above

324. Mr. Yehudi Menuhin, was a famous:
A. Sitarist B. Cartoonist
C. Journalist D. Violinist

325. Sundarlal Bahuguna, a famous environmentalist, was associated with :
A. Chipko Movement
B. Narmada Bachao Andolan
C. Satyagraha Movement
D. Anti-corruption Movement

326. Mother Teressa's native place was :
A. Albania B. France
C. Greece D. Italy

327. The live polio vaccine which can be taken by mouth was developed by :
A. Albert Sabin B. Edward Jenner
C. Jonas Salk D. Selman Waksman

328. Which of the following language is used for webpage development?
A. FORTRAN
B. C or C++
C. BASIC
D. HTML

329. The "Last Supper" is a famous renaissance painting. It was a masterpiece of :
A. Michael Angelo B. Leonardo da Vinci
C. Titian D. Raphael

330. Dhyanchand is associated with which sports?
A. Badminton B. Hockey
C. Tennis D. Football

331. 'Man is born free, yet every where he is in chains'. This was said by:
A. Voltaire B. John Stuart Mill
C. Rousseau D. Karl Marx

332. Who among the following was a prominent social reformer?
A. Baba Gurmukh Singh
B. Raja Mahendra Pratap
C. Bipin Chandra Pal
D. Jotiba Govind Phule

333. Whose real name was Gadadhar Chhattopadhyaya?
A. Swami Vivekanand
B. Ram Krishna Paramhansa
C. Dayanand Saraswai
D. Raja Ram Mohan Rai

334. Who was known as "Man of Destiny"?
A. Napoleon B. Nehru
C. Hitler D. Mussolini

335. Who discovered that mosquito served as a carrier of malaria?
A. Jonas Salk B. Ronald Ross
C. Louis Pasteur D. Robert Koch

336. Who was the first woman Governor of an Indian State?
A. Sushila Nayar B. Sucheta Kripalani
C. Sarojini Naidu D. Sulochana Modi

337. Who among the following founded the Bhartiya Jana Sangh?
A. Deen Dayal Upadhyaya

B. Veer Savarkar
C. Dr. Ram Manohar Lohia
D. Dr. Shyama Prasad Mukherjee

338. Who among the following President of India held his office for two successive terms?
A. V.V. Giri
B. Dr. Rajendra Prasad
C. Dr. S. Radhakrishnan
D. None of these

339. Ustad Amjad Ali Khan is an exponent of:
A. Flute B. Sitar
C. Sarod D. Tabla

340. Who is the first non-Indian to receive the Bharat Ratna?
A. Martin Luther King
B. Zubin Mehta
C. Mother Teressa
D. Khan Abdul Ghaffar Khan

ANSWERS

1	2	3	4	5	6	7	8	9	10
B	C	D	C	B	C	A	C	C	D
11	**12**	**13**	**14**	**15**	**16**	**17**	**18**	**19**	**20**
C	A	C	A	A	D	A	B	A	D
21	**22**	**23**	**24**	**25**	**26**	**27**	**28**	**29**	**30**
A	C	B	C	D	C	B	D	D	B
31	**32**	**33**	**34**	**35**	**36**	**37**	**38**	**39**	**40**
C	D	C	C	B	C	D	B	C	C
41	**42**	**43**	**44**	**45**	**46**	**47**	**48**	**49**	**50**
A	A	A	B	C	D	C	B	B	D
51	**52**	**53**	**54**	**55**	**56**	**57**	**58**	**59**	**60**
A	C	A	B	B	A	B	C	A	C
61	**62**	**63**	**64**	**65**	**66**	**67**	**68**	**69**	**70**
C	C	B	B	C	C	D	D	D	B
71	**72**	**73**	**74**	**75**	**76**	**77**	**78**	**79**	**80**
B	C	C	C	A	A	A	B	B	A
81	**82**	**83**	**84**	**85**	**86**	**87**	**88**	**89**	**90**
A	B	D	B	C	C	D	C	B	D
91	**92**	**93**	**94**	**95**	**96**	**97**	**98**	**99**	**100**
A	B	A	A	A	B	B	A	A	C
101	**102**	**103**	**104**	**105**	**106**	**107**	**108**	**109**	**110**
C	B	A	D	D	D	A	C	D	C
111	**112**	**113**	**114**	**115**	**116**	**117**	**118**	**119**	**120**
B	B	B	A	D	C	C	D	B	D
121	**122**	**123**	**124**	**125**	**126**	**127**	**128**	**129**	**130**
C	A	A	B	A	D	C	D	B	D
131	**132**	**133**	**134**	**135**	**136**	**137**	**138**	**139**	**140**
B	B	D	A	B	D	B	D	D	C
141	**142**	**143**	**144**	**145**	**146**	**147**	**148**	**149**	**150**
D	C	D	D	D	B	A	D	C	C

151	152	153	154	155	156	157	158	159	160
A	B	A	A	A	D	C	B	D	A
161	**162**	**163**	**164**	**165**	**166**	**167**	**168**	**169**	**170**
B	B	C	B	D	D	C	B	B	B
171	**172**	**173**	**174**	**175**	**176**	**177**	**178**	**179**	**180**
D	C	D	D	C	B	C	A	D	A
181	**182**	**183**	**184**	**185**	**186**	**187**	**188**	**189**	**190**
B	B	C	A	A	A	B	D	D	A
191	**192**	**193**	**194**	**195**	**196**	**197**	**198**	**199**	**200**
B	C	A	A	D	A	B	D	D	A
201	**202**	**203**	**204**	**205**	**206**	**207**	**208**	**209**	**210**
B	B	B	B	A	A	A	A	A	A
211	**212**	**213**	**214**	**215**	**216**	**217**	**218**	**219**	**220**
B	A	A	A	D	C	D	A	B	B
221	**222**	**223**	**224**	**225**	**226**	**227**	**228**	**229**	**230**
D	C	A	D	A	A	D	D	B	B
231	**232**	**233**	**234**	**235**	**236**	**237**	**238**	**239**	**240**
D	B	D	A	D	D	C	B	B	C
241	**242**	**243**	**244**	**245**	**246**	**247**	**248**	**249**	**250**
D	B	D	C	A	D	D	A	D	A
251	**252**	**253**	**254**	**255**	**256**	**257**	**258**	**259**	**260**
C	D	A	B	C	A	C	C	A	B
261	**262**	**263**	**264**	**265**	**266**	**267**	**268**	**269**	**270**
B	C	C	A	A	C	C	A	C	A
271	**272**	**273**	**274**	**275**	**276**	**277**	**278**	**279**	**280**
B	C	A	B	A	C	B	B	A	B
281	**282**	**283**	**284**	**285**	**286**	**287**	**288**	**289**	**290**
D	A	A	A	B	A	C	B	D	C
291	**292**	**293**	**294**	**295**	**296**	**297**	**298**	**299**	**300**
D	C	B	D	A	A	A	C	A	B
301	**302**	**303**	**304**	**305**	**306**	**307**	**308**	**309**	**310**
C	B	C	C	B	A	C	D	D	B
311	**312**	**313**	**314**	**315**	**316**	**317**	**318**	**319**	**320**
A	C	B	A	B	C	B	A	A	C
321	**322**	**323**	**324**	**325**	**326**	**327**	**328**	**329**	**330**
D	D	A	D	A	A	C	D	B	B
331	**332**	**333**	**334**	**335**	**336**	**337**	**338**	**339**	**340**
C	D	B	A	B	C	D	B	C	D

❐ ❐ ❐